FAMILY LAW

FIFTH EDITION

FAMILY LAW

FIFTH EDITION

WILLIAM P. STATSKY

WEST
THOMSON LEARNING™

Australia Canada Mexico Singapore Spain United Kingdom United States

WEST LEGAL STUDIES

Family Law, Fifth Edition
by William P. Statsky

Business Unit Director:
Susan L. Simpfenderfer

Executive Editor:
Marlene McHugh Pratt

Senior Acquisitions Editor:
Joan M. Gill

Developmental Editor:
Rhonda Dearborn

Editorial Assistant:
Lisa Flatley

Executive Production Manager:
Wendy A. Troeger

Production Manager:
Carolyn Miller

Executive Marketing Manager:
Donna J. Lewis

Channel Manager:
Nigar Hale

Cover Image:
Family Ties, 1999; Diana Ong
(b. 1940/Chinese-American)
Computer Graphics;
Diana Ong/SuperStock

Printed in the United States
5 XXX 05

For more information contact Delmar,
3 Columbia Circle, PO Box 15015,
Albany, NY 12212-5015.

Or find us on the World Wide Web at
www.thomsonlearning.com or www.westlegalstudies.com

Library of Congress Cataloging-in-Publication Data

Statsky, William P.
Family law/William P. Statsky.—5th ed.
p. cm.
"West Legal Studies series."
Includes index.
ISBN 0-7668-3358-5
1. Domestic relations—United States. I. Title.

KF505 .S83 2001
346.7301′5—dc21 2001045555

NOTICE TO THE READER

Publisher does not warrant or guarantee any of the products described herein or perform any independent analysis in connection with any of the product information contained herein. Publisher does not assume, and expressly disclaims, any obligation to obtain and include information other than that provided to it by the manufacturer.

The reader is notified that this text is an educational tool, not a practice book. Since the law is in constant change, no rule or statement of law in this book should be relied upon for any service to any client. The reader should always refer to standard legal sources for the current rule or law. If legal advice or other expert assistance is required, the services of the appropriate professional should be sought.

The Publisher makes no representation or warranties of any kind, including but not limited to, the warranties of fitness for particular purpose or merchantability, nor are any such representations implied with respect to the material set forth herein, and the publisher takes no responsibility with respect to such material. The publisher shall not be liable for any special, consequential, or exemplary damages resulting, in whole or part, from the reader's use of, or reliance upon, this material.

For my own domestic relations: Pat, Jess, Gabe, Joe, Brenda, Rich, Clara, Bob, Matthew, Stan, Randy, Pani, Ann, Ann, Ann, et al.

BY THE SAME AUTHOR

Case Analysis and Fundamentals of Legal Writing, 4th ed. St. Paul: West Group, 1995 (with J. Wernet)

Essentials of Paralegalism, 3d ed. St. Paul: West Group, 1997

Essentials of Torts, 2d ed. St. Paul: West Group, 2001

Family Law: The Essentials. St. Paul: West Group, 1997.

Inmate Involvement in Prison Legal Services: Roles and Training Options for the Inmate as Paralegal. American Bar Association, Commission on Correctional Facilities and Services, 1974.

Introduction to Paralegalism: Perspectives, Problems and Skills, 6th ed. St. Paul: West Group, 2002

Legal Desk Reference. St. Paul: West Group, 1990 (with B. Hussey, M. Diamond, & R. Nakamura)

The Legal Paraprofessional as Advocate and Assistant: Roles, Training Concepts and Materials. Center on Social Welfare Policy and Law, 1971 (with P. Lang)

Legal Research and Writing: Some Starting Points, 5th ed. St. Paul: West Group, 1999

Legal Thesaurus/Dictionary: A Resource for the Writer and Computer Researcher. St. Paul: West Group, 1985

Legislative Analysis and Drafting, 2d ed. St. Paul: West Group, 1984

Paralegal Employment: Facts and Strategies for the 1990s, 2d ed. St. Paul: West Group, 1993

Paralegal Ethics and Regulation, 2d ed. St. Paul: West Group, 1993

Rights of the Imprisoned: Cases, Materials and Directions. Indianapolis: Bobbs-Merrill Company, 1974 (with R. Singer)

Torts: Personal Injury Litigation, 4th ed. St. Paul: West Group, 2001

What Have Paralegals Done? A Dictionary of Functions. National Paralegal Institute, 1973

BRIEF CONTENTS

CONTENTS

TABLE OF CASES

TABLE OF FIGURES

Chapter 10

Chapter 11

Chapter 12

Chapter 13

Chapter 14

Chapter 15

Chapter 16

Chapter 17

A NOTE TO THE STUDENT: THE MEANING OF "YOUR STATE"

Throughout many of the assignments in this book, you will see the phrase "your state" (e.g., the state code of your state). The objective of many of these assignments is to help you relate the law outlined in the chapters of this book to the specific law of a particular state: "your state." The phrase "your state" can have several meanings:

- The state where you intend to use your skills—where you hope to be employed.
- The state where you are studying (which may be different from the state where you will be employed).
- The state where you are now working (which may be different from the state where you hope to be employed).

Ask your instructor which meaning of "state" to use. If the choice is yours and you know the state where you will be employed, select this state as the focus of the assignments in this book.

PREFACE

Say it isn't true. A recent *New York Times* story reported that a well-known divorce attorney was giving out pens to prospective clients that said, "Sue Someone You Love." This is not the image the legal profession wishes to project to the public. Yet newspapers, magazines, and talk shows do seem to give the impression that our society is in a litigation frenzy: "Son Sues to Divorce His Mother," "Wife Demands Half of Husband's Medical Practice in Divorce Settlement," "Surrogate Mother Refuses to Turn Over Baby," "Live-in Lover Seeks Palimony."

Our goal in this book is to sort through the headlines to find an accurate picture of the state of family law today and the role of the attorney-paralegal team within it. We are living in an era of great change in the practice of family law. The primary focus of the family law practitioner is no longer adultery and who gets the house. No-fault divorce has made marriage relatively easy to dissolve. The women's movement has helped bring about major shifts in determining what property can be split after a divorce and how to split it. The country has declared war on the "deadbeat" parent who fails to pay child support. Major new enforcement mechanisms have been designed to find these parents and make them pay. To the surprise of many, courts have come to the aid of unmarried fathers seeking to undo the adoption of their children. Science and technology have unleashed new concepts of motherhood and parentage. The law has not been able to keep pace with the scientific revolution taking place in the test tube and in the womb.

In short, there is a lot to talk about! It's a fascinating time to study family law.

CHAPTER FORMAT

Each chapter includes features designed to assist students in understanding the material:

- A chapter outline at the beginning of each chapter provides a preview of the major topics discussed in the chapter.
- Tables are used extensively to clarify concepts and present detailed information in an organized chart form.
- Assignments that ask students to apply concepts to particular fact situations are included in each chapter. These assignments cover critical skills such as analysis, investigation, interviewing, and drafting.
- A chapter summary at the end of each chapter provides a concise review of the main concepts discussed.
- Selected terms are defined in the margin next to the text to which the terms are relevant.
- Key terms are printed in boldface type the first time they appear in the chapter. A list of key terms also appears at the end of each chapter to help students review important terminology introduced in that chapter.
- Ethics questions and Internet resources are found at the end of most chapters.

CHANGES TO THE FIFTH EDITION

- Major new material has been added on civil unions (the equivalent of same-sex marriage), domestic partnership, domestic violence, covenant marriage, premarital agreements, adoption by gays and lesbians, confidentiality of adoption records, grandparent rights, sperm bank scandals, the legal status of frozen embryos, and "reality TV" family law (i.e., the legitimacy of a "marriage" ceremony performed before an audience of millions).
- Several important family law developments have been based on the cases of well-known individuals: actors Woody Allen and Mia Farrow (child custody and allegations of sexual abuse) and baseball player Barry Bonds (premarital agreements).
- New computer material has been added on child custody and visitation scheduling and on child-support worksheets on the Internet.
- The number of chapters has been reduced from 21 to 17 through a consolidation of material. For example, the first three chapters of the fourth edition have been combined into one chapter (chapter 1).
- Two features have been added to the end of almost every chapter: an "Ethics in Practice" hypothetical and an "On the Net" resource that lists Internet sites relevant to the material in the chapter.
- Margin comments have been added to documents such as sample family law agreements.
- The general instructions for the assignments have been moved from chapter 1 to appendix A.
- Internet resources on family law (Family Law Online) have been added to the section on finding family law in chapter 1.
- A new introduction has been added to chapter 1 on five of the major themes of family law in the twenty-first century.
- Job descriptions and paralegal roles have been added to chapter 1, and expanded coverage of paralegal roles has been provided in other chapters.
- The chapter on legal interviewing (chapter 3) has been expanded to provide a more comprehensive focus on compiling a family history in contested or complex cases.
- New developments on the enforceability of premarital agreements have been added to chapter 4. The chapter also includes a comprehensive checklist on the enforceability of premarital agreements.
- Chapter 5, on marriage formation, adds new material on marriage alternatives such as civil unions and domestic partnerships.
- Chapter 6 includes a discussion of the legal implications of the TV sensation "Who Wants to Marry a Multimillionaire?"
- The chapters on divorce grounds and procedure have been combined; the resulting revised chapter (chapter 7) now appears before the chapters on child custody and support. It includes coverage of dissolution procedures for Vermont civil unions, bifurcated divorces, and the domestic relations exception in federal courts.
- The role of domestic violence in child-custody decisions has been added to chapter 8.
- Chapter 8 also includes a major decision of the United States Supreme Court on grandparent visitation over the objection of a fit custodial parent.
- The most recent custody jurisdiction statute (the Uniform Child Custody Jurisdiction and Enforcement Act) is covered in chapter 8.

- The most important development in the field of child support has been the enactment of the Uniform Interstate Family Support Act, covered in chapter 10.
- New child-support enforcement methods covered in chapter 10 include new hire reporting, passport denial, and financial institution data matching ("freeze and seize")
- The tax chapter (chapter 11) includes an expanded discussion of innocent spouse relief.
- The material in chapter 12 on domestic violence has been expanded to include a client sensitivity checklist and a paralegal's firsthand account of working with women who have been abused.
- Reporting requirements in cases of suspected child abuse and neglect have been added to chapter 14.
- Coverage of adoption by gays and lesbians has been expanded in chapter 15. Chapter 15 also includes recent developments in the confidentiality of adoption records in light of efforts by adopted children to locate their biological parents.
- Chapter 16 includes recent developments in the law governing the disposal of frozen embryos when divorcing spouses disagree about what to do with them.
- Chapter 17 includes a discussion of whether an award of tort damages to one spouse can be divided upon divorce as part of a property division.

SUPPLEMENTS

- The **Instructor's Manual Test Bank** contains competencies, answers to selected assignments, and teaching suggestions.
- **Computerized Test Bank.** The Test Bank in the Instructor's Manual is also available in a computerized format on CD-ROM. The platforms supported include Windows 3.1, Windows 95, Windows NT, and Macintosh. Features include:
  - Multiple methods of question selection
  - Multiple outputs—that is, print, ASCII, RTF
  - Graphic support (black and white)
  - Random questioning output
  - Special character support
- **State-Specific Supplements** are available for California, Florida, New York, and Texas as online resources. These supplements are keyed to each chapter in the text and point out state-specific information when it differs from the text's discussion. These supplements are available online at www.westlegalstudies.com as downloadable electronic supplements. Go to the home page and click on "Resources" or "Book Links."
- **Online Resources** can be accessed at www.westlegalstudies.com where you will find a Web page dedicated to this book with valuable information such as hot links and sample materials to download, as well as other West Legal Studies products.
- **WESTLAW®,** West's online computerized legal-research system, offers "hands-on" experience with a system extensively used in law offices. Qualified adopters can receive ten free hours of WESTLAW®. WESTLAW® can be assessed with Macintosh and IBM PCs and compatibles. A modem is required.
- **Strategies and Tips for Paralegal Educators,** a pamphlet by Anita Tebbe of Johnson County Community College, provides teaching strate-

gies specifically designed for paralegal educators. A copy of this pamphlet is available to each adopter. Quantities for distribution to adjunct instructors are available for purchase at a minimal price. A coupon in the pamphlet provides ordering information.

- **Survival Guide for Paralegal Students,** a pamphlet by Kathleen Mercer Reed and Bradene Moore, covers practical and basic information to help students make the most of their paralegal courses. Topics covered include choosing courses of study and note-taking skills.
- **West's Paralegal Video Library** offers the following videos at no charge to qualified adopters:
  - *The Drama of the Law II* (paralegal issues video)
    ISBN 0-314-07088-5
  - *I Never Said I Was a Lawyer* (paralegal ethics video)
    ISBN 0-314-08049-X
  - *Arguments to the United States Supreme Court*
    ISBN 0-314-07070-2

ACKNOWLEDGMENTS

A word of thanks to the reviewers who made valuable suggestions:

- Patricia Adongo
  University of La Verne
- Sarah Barthalamu
  Valdosta State
- Sally Bisson
  College of St. Mary
- Jeane Dibble
  Southern Illinois University
- Yvonne Ekern
  West Valley College
- Gerald Haigh
  Glenville State College
- Regina Judge
  Montclair State University
- Deborah Kukowski
  Moorehead State University
- Barbara Ricker
  Andover College
- Julia O. Tryk
  Cuyahoga Community College

CHAPTER 1

INTRODUCTION TO FAMILY LAW AND PRACTICE

CHAPTER OUTLINE

FAMILY LAW IN THE TWENTY-FIRST CENTURY

family law
The body of law that defines relationships, rights, and duties in the formation, existence, and dissolution of marriage and other family units.

Family law consists of legal principles that define relationships, rights, and duties within family units such as those formed by marriage. We will spend a good deal of time studying the rules of family law that have been part of our history for many years, but we must recognize that this area of the law is still growing. The world of our grandparents was dramatically different from today's world as we begin the twenty-first century. Among our vast population, the concept of a family is diverse and is shifting. Today, for example, more than 25 percent of all children under the age of eighteen live with only one parent. Furthermore, when two adults are at home, they are not always mother and father. The "two-mommy" or "two-daddy" household is no longer an isolated family unit that the law can ignore. We live in a society that sometimes appears to be in a state of perpetual change. Courts and legislatures have not always been able to fit traditional family law principles into the realities of modern life. New principles have had to be created. One of our central themes will be how family law has evolved in response to the shifting boundary lines of how people choose to live together.

Five important developments in family law are a product of this turmoil. They have shaped our recent history and will continue to play major roles in the twenty-first century. Here is an overview of these developments, which we will be studying throughout the chapters of this book along with the traditional principles of family law.

Equality of the Sexes: The Struggle Continues

There was a time in our history when a wife could not make her own will or bring a lawsuit in her own name. Without the consent of her husband, there was relatively little that she could do. Two centuries ago, the greatest scholar of the day, Blackstone, declared that "the very being or legal existence of a woman was suspended during the marriage, or at least was incorporated and consolidated into that of her husband."[1] Indeed, in the eyes of the law, the husband and wife were one person, and that person was the husband. Carried to its logical extreme, this theory meant that a husband could not be convicted of raping his wife, as this would amount to a conviction for raping himself!

Much progress has been made in abandoning this theory of the law based on male dominance. "The laws relating to marriage have undergone many changes during the last century, largely toward the goal of equalizing the status of husbands and wives."[2] It is important to keep in mind, however, that reforms in the law do not always translate into reforms in human behavior. No matter how many laws we pass to prevent domestic violence, for example, the safety of women in intimate relationships continues to be a serious problem. Thirty percent of murders against women are committed by their husbands and boyfriends. Other examples of the continuing imbalance in the male-female relationship can be cited. Recently, a court was asked to interpret a marital agreement between Mr. and Mrs. Spires that contained the following provisions:

Mrs. Spires:

- may not withdraw any money from the bank without Mr. Spires's express permission
- may not "attempt to influence the status/intensity" of any relationship that Mr. Spires may have "with other individuals outside of the marriage unless the husband verbally requests input from the wife"
- may not "dispute" Mr. Spires in public "on any matter"
- must "conduct herself in accordance with all scriptures in the Holy Bible applicable to marital relationships germane to wives and in accordance with the husband's specific requests"
- must maintain a sexual relationship that "remains spontaneous and solely with the husband"
- must "carry out requests of the husband in strict accordance, i.e., timeliness, sequence, scheduling, etc."
- may not receive any loan or gift without first obtaining Mr. Spires's permission.[3]

The date the parties entered this agreement was 1991, not 1791 or 1891. Although the court eventually declared the agreement to be unenforceable, the fact that such a case had to be litigated in the 1990s suggests that not everyone in society accepts the legal principle of equality between the sexes. Fortunately, most do accept it. Nevertheless, anyone engaged in the practice of family law must be prepared to find serious discrepancies between the laws on the books and how people in fact conduct their lives. These discrepancies will continue to generate considerable business for family law practices.

Federalization of Family Law

The vast majority of family law is created and enforced by the states. As Chief Justice Rehnquist has said, domestic relations "has been left to the states from time immemorial."[4] Congress, federal courts, and federal administrative agencies have historically played relatively minor roles in family law. When

---

[1]Quoted in *Warren v. State,* 255 Ga. 151, 154, 336 S.E.2d 221, 223 (1985).
[2]*Baker v. State,* 744 A.2d 864, 883 (Vt. 1999).
[3]*Spires v. Spires,* 743 A.2d 186 (D.C. 1999).
[4]*Santosky v. Kramer,* 455 U.S. 745, 769, 102 S. Ct. 1388, 1403, 71 L. Ed. 2d 599, 617 (1982) (dissent).

parties want a divorce, for example, they go to a state court, not to a federal court.

Although state law continues to dominate the field, federal law is becoming increasingly important. Major changes in the state law of paternity, for example, have been due to interpretations of the federal Constitution by the United States Supreme Court. Competent legal representation in a divorce settlement must include advice on how federal tax laws affect alimony and property division. The same is true for the impact of our federal bankruptcy laws. Interstate child-custody disputes are now substantially regulated by federal statutes such as the Parental Kidnaping Prevention Act. Perhaps the most dramatic inroad of federal law has been in the area of child support. Congress has passed laws that have led to national standards in the enforcement of child support. Though it is an overstatement to say that family law is now totally federalized, it is clear that the role of federal law in family law is significant and is increasing. Not everyone is happy with this trend, as we will see.

The Contract Dimension of Family Law

Marriage is a status in the sense that it is a legal entity that imposes certain rights and obligations, often in spite of what both spouses agree to do. For example, once parties are married, they cannot agree on their own to dissolve their marriage so that each can marry someone else. Spouses cannot divorce themselves. They need a court order of divorce. Nor can they agree that either or both can have additional spouses. A basic requirement of the law is one spouse at a time.

Many of these requirements remain central to the institution of marriage. However, one of the modern trends in family law is to allow parties to enter enforceable contracts that help define their rights and obligations to each other. When we study premarital agreements, for example, we will see a greater willingness of the courts to allow the parties to define important components of the marriage they are about to enter, particularly in the area of finances. To an increasing degree, marriage is viewed as an economic partnership that is subject to mutual modification, rather than as an eternal union of love benevolently presided over by the husband. There are still limits on what parties can do by contract. Spouses cannot, for example, enter an agreement that would be detrimental to the welfare of their children. Courts will carefully scrutinize such agreements to ensure that they are in the best interests of the child. It is sometimes said that in every marriage there is a third party—the state—that imposes rights and obligations on the spouses. This is still true, although we have begun to see more flexibility in what the parties are allowed to do by contract. This trend is even greater in family units created as alternatives to marriage, as we will see when we study contract cohabitation and domestic partnership.

Science and Law

Scientific breakthroughs have created startling challenges for family law. Nowhere is this more evident than in the new science of motherhood. New ways to create babies have given us the reality of multiple mothers of the same child (e.g., a birth mother and a genetic mother). This has forced legislatures and courts to redefine traditional areas of the law. The wonders of science are by no means over. We can expect to see new scientific breakthroughs, necessitating further rethinking of traditional family law.

Emerging Recognition of Gay Rights

For years, homosexuals have been unsuccessful in asserting that they are entitled to the same family law rights as heterosexuals. To a significant extent, this argument is still unsuccessful today. Recent developments, however, suggest that the tide may be turning. Many states, for example, now say that adoption applications by gays will be treated the same as those by heterosexuals. Adoption in such states will not be denied solely on the basis of sexual orientation. Dramatic developments in Hawaii and Vermont almost led to the legalization of same-sex marriages. Vermont came the closest by creating the "civil union." This is a new relationship that has the same state rights and duties as an opposite-sex marriage. Although there has been major opposition to the assertion of any gay rights in family law, there is a noticeable trend in favor of equal application of family law to heterosexuals and homosexuals.

As family law moves into the twenty-first century, these are some of the major themes that will continue to demand the attention of courts, legislatures, and family law practitioners.

THE SCOPE OF FAMILY LAW

To work in an office where family law is practiced, you need compassion, flexibility, skill, and, above all, an ability to handle a wide diversity of problems. While some cases are straightforward and "simple," many are not. A veteran attorney observed that a family law practice requires everyone "to become an expert in many fields of law and not just one."[5]

Assume that you are a paralegal working for Karen Smith, an attorney in your state. One of the clients of the office is Susan Miller, who lives out of state. The attorney receives the following e-mail message from Ms. Miller:

> *2/7/99*
>
> *Karen Smith:*
>
> *I am leaving the state in a week to come live with my mother. She will help me move everything so that we can start a new life. I must see you as soon as I arrive. Yesterday my husband called from his business. He threatened me and the children. I will bring the twins with me. I don't know where my oldest boy is. He is probably with his father getting into more trouble.*
>
> *Susan Miller*

The checklist below lists many of the questions that are potentially relevant to the case of Susan Miller. As a paralegal, you might be asked to conduct preliminary interviews and field investigation on some of the questions. Others may require legal research in the law library or online. (Later in the chapter we cover paralegal roles in family law in greater detail.) Many of the technical terms in this list will be defined in subsequent chapters. Our goal here is simply to demonstrate that the scope of the law covered in a family law practice can be very broad.

Criminal Law

- Has Mr. Miller committed a crime? What kind of threats did he make? Did he assault his wife and children?
- Has he failed to support his family? If so, is the nonsupport serious enough to warrant state or federal criminal action against him?
- Even if he has committed a crime, would it be wise for Ms. Miller to ask the district attorney to investigate and prosecute the case?

---

[5]John Greenya, *Family Affairs: Seven Experts in Family Law Discuss Their Experiences . . .*, 9 Washington Lawyer 23, 31 (Nov./Dec. 1994).

- Is there any danger of further criminal acts by her husband? If so, what can be done, if anything, to prevent them? Can she obtain a restraining order to keep him away?
- Is Ms. Miller subject to any penalties for taking the children out of state?

Divorce/Separation/Annulment Law

- What does Ms. Miller want?
- Does she know what her husband wants to do?
- Does she have grounds for a divorce?
- Does she have grounds for an annulment? (Were the Millers validly married?)
- Does she have grounds for a judicial (legal) separation?
- Does Mr. Miller have grounds for a divorce, annulment, or judicial separation against his wife?

Law of Custody

- Does Ms. Miller want sole physical and legal custody of all three children? (Is she the natural mother of all three? Is he their natural father? Are there any paternity problems?) Will Mr. Miller want custody? What is the lifestyle of the parent or parents seeking custody? Is joint custody an option?
- If she does not want a divorce, annulment, or judicial separation, how can she obtain custody of the children?
- Does she want anyone else to be given temporary or permanent custody of any of the children (e.g., a relative)? Will such a person make a claim for custody *against* Ms. Miller?
- If she wants custody, has she jeopardized her chances of being awarded custody by taking the children out of state?

Support Law

- Is Mr. Miller adequately supporting his wife? Is she supporting him?
- Is he adequately supporting the three children? Do they have any special medical or school needs? If so, are these needs being met?
- Are the children now covered under Mr. Miller's health insurance policy? Is Ms. Miller covered? Is there a danger that the policy will be changed?
- Can Ms. Miller obtain a court order forcing Mr. Miller to support them while she is deciding whether she wants to terminate the marital relationship?
- If she files for divorce, annulment, or judicial separation, can she obtain a temporary support order while the case is in progress?
- If she files for divorce, annulment, or judicial separation and loses, can she still obtain a support order against him?
- Does Mr. Miller have assets (personal property or real property) against which a support order can be enforced? Is there a danger he might try to hide or transfer these assets?
- If he cannot be relied upon for support and she cannot work, does she qualify for public assistance such as Temporary Assistance to Needy Families (TANF)?
- Would she be entitled to more support in the state she is coming from or in this state?
- Is Mr. Miller supporting any other children, such as from a previous marriage? If so, how would this affect his duty to support the three he had with Ms. Miller?

Contract/Agency Law

- While she is living apart from her husband, can she enter into contracts with merchants for the purchase of food, clothing, furniture, medical care, prescriptions, transportation, and other necessaries and make *him* pay for them? Can she use his credit?
- Has she already entered into such contracts?
- Can he obligate her on any of his current or future debts?
- Has she ever worked for him or otherwise acted as his agent?
- Has he ever worked for her or otherwise acted as her agent?
- Have the children (particularly the oldest child) entered into any contracts under their own names? If so, who is liable for such contracts? Can they be canceled or disaffirmed?

Real and Personal Property Law

- Do either or both of them own any real property (e.g., land)? If so, how is the real property owned? How is title held? Individually? As tenants by the entirety? Who provided the funds for the purchase?
- What rights does she have in his property?
- What rights does he have in her property?
- What is his income? Can his wages be garnished?
- Does Mr. or Ms. Miller have a pension plan from prior or present employment? Can one spouse (or ex-spouse) obtain rights in the pension plan of the other spouse (or ex-spouse)?
- What other personal property exists—cars, bank accounts, stocks, bonds, furniture? Who owns this property?

Corporate Law/Business Law

- What kind of business does Mr. Miller have? Is it a corporation? A partnership? A sole proprietorship? If the parties separate and obtain a divorce, will Ms. Miller be entitled to a share of the business as part of the division of marital property?
- What are the assets and liabilities of the business?
- Is there a danger that Mr. Miller or his business might go into bankruptcy? If so, how would this affect her rights to support and to a share of the marital property? How would it affect his duty of child support?

Tort Law

- Has he committed any torts against her (e.g., assault, fraud, conversion)?
- Has she committed any torts against him?
- Can one spouse sue another in tort?
- Have the children (particularly the oldest) damaged any property or committed any torts for which the parents might be liable?

Civil Procedure/Conflict of Law

- If a court action is brought (e.g., for divorce, custody, separate maintenance), what court would have jurisdiction? A court in this state? A court in the state where he resides?
- How can service of process be made?
- If she sues and obtains a judgment in this state, can it be enforced in another state?

Evidence Law

- What factual claims will Ms. Miller be making, e.g., that Mr. Miller has hidden money or other assets that could be used to support the family?
- What testimonial evidence (oral statements of witnesses) exists to support her claims?
- How much of this evidence is admissible in court?

- How much of the admissible evidence is likely to be believed by a judge or jury?
- What documentary evidence should be pursued (e.g., marriage and birth certificates, records of purchases)?
- Whose depositions should be taken, if any?
- What claims will Mr. Miller make against Ms. Miller? What evidence is he likely to use to support these claims? What objections can be made to this evidence?

Juvenile Law

- Can a dependency or child neglect petition be brought against Mr. Miller? Against Ms. Miller?
- Why is she upset about her eldest son? Has he committed any "acts of delinquency"?
- Is he a Person in Need of Supervision (PINS) or a Child in Need of Supervision (CHINS)?
- If he has damaged anyone else's property, can a parent be financially responsible for the damage?

Tax Law

- Have Mr. Miller and his wife filed joint tax returns in the past?
- Are any refunds due (or money owed) on past returns?
- In a property settlement following a divorce or separation, what would be the most advantageous settlement for Ms. Miller from a tax perspective?
- What arrangement might Mr. Miller seek in order to obtain the best tax posture? What is negotiable? What will he be willing to give up to obtain his tax objectives? Will he, for example, cooperate in allowing her to have sole physical and legal custody of the children in exchange for her cooperation in ensuring that his alimony payments are deductible?

Estate Law

- Do they both have their own wills? If so, who are the beneficiaries? If there is no divorce, can he leave Ms. Miller out of his will entirely?
- Who receives their property if they die without a will while they are separated or after a divorce?
- Are there any life insurance policies on Mr. Miller's life, with Ms. Miller or the children as beneficiaries? If so, is he allowed to change these beneficiaries?

Professional Responsibility/Ethics

- Is Mr. Miller represented by counsel? If so, can we contact Mr. Miller directly, or must all communications to him be made through his attorney? If he is not yet represented, are there limitations on what we can and cannot say to him?
- If Ms. Miller can find her eldest son, can she simply take him away from her husband when the latter is not around? Would this be illegal? What is the ethical obligation of an attorney whose client is about to do something illegal?

Miscellaneous

- Can Mr. Miller be forced to pay legal fees that Ms. Miller will incur in her disputes with him?
- Can she be forced to pay his legal fees?

The purpose of this book is to examine these questions that could arise in a case such as *Miller v. Miller.* More specifically, the purpose is to equip you with the skills needed to be able to raise and to help answer such questions that could arise in your state.

PARALEGAL ROLES IN FAMILY LAW

First we will take a more specific look at the possible range of paralegal responsibilities in a family law practice. Keep in mind, however, that no two paralegals will have identical job descriptions. According to veteran paralegal, Yasmin Spiegel, "Your skills and interests, as well as the degree of trust and communication between you and your boss, will determine the tasks that you will be assigned."[6] Nevertheless, it is possible to identify some of the commonly performed tasks of many paralegals. Here are two job descriptions written by different bar associations. Following their lists of tasks, we will read more from Yasmin Spiegel as she provides a flesh-and-bones perspective of life in the trenches. Although her focus is on California, her observations are pertinent to the life of a family law paralegal in any state.

Attorney's Guide to Practicing with Legal Assistants XIII (35)–(37)

(State Bar of Texas, 1986). Reprinted with permission.

General Responsibilities

Assist attorney through all phases of divorce and custody proceedings, including drafting pleadings, investigating financial affairs of the parties, assisting in discovery and at trial, and maintaining close relationship with client, all as illustrated by the following examples.

All job functions must be performed under the *direct supervision of a lawyer.* The words "draft," "drafting," and "prepare" mean a preliminary writing to be approved by the attorney.

Specific Duties

Initial Client Interview (After attorney has talked with client)

1. Establish rapport with client and gather facts pertaining to preparation of initial pleadings.
2. Have client sign . . . forms necessary for initial discovery, such as authorizations for medical records, income tax returns, employment records, etc.
3. Instruct client how to prepare the financial information statement and other forms to aid in discovery of the parties' assets and liabilities.
4. Prepare memorandum to the file.

Initial Pleadings

1. Draft pleadings.
2. After attorney approval, arrange for client's signature if applicable, see that pleadings are filed, get hearing set if necessary, and arrange for service if necessary.
3. Put hearing date on calendar and notify client of the date.

Preparation for Temporary Hearing and Post-Hearing Procedure

1. Arrange for client to meet with attorney for briefing as to what to expect at the hearing and to discuss the client's financial information statement.
2. Draft temporary orders for attorney approval.
3. Transmit temporary orders to opposing counsel for approval, and upon receipt of executed orders, return to attorney for review and filing.
4. Keep in close contact with client to ensure compliance with temporary orders.
5. Set up child support payment account for client if he/she receives an award of child support.

Discovery

1. Monitor deadlines set by the court, such as filing of sworn inventory and appraisement, production of tax returns and other documents, appraisals, etc.
2. Work with client in obtaining all information necessary to prepare an inventory and appraisement, submit to attorney for approval, obtain client's signature, file with the court, and submit copy to opposing counsel.
3. Review inventory received from opposing counsel, compare with client's inventory, and prepare a memorandum for attorney evaluating both.

[6] Yasmin Spiegel, *Family Law for Paralegals,* 6 The Journal 7 (Sacramento Association of Legal Assistants, June 1986).

4. If separate property (as opposed to marital property) is involved, work with client on tracing.
5. Draft written interrogatories and requests for admissions.
6. Assist client in answering interrogatories and requests for admissions; then submit proposed answers to attorney.
7. Schedule, attend with attorney, and index depositions.
8. Act as intermediary between the attorney and accountants, appraisers, private investigators, and other agents.

Trial and Post-Trial

1. Prepare trial notebook.
2. Organize and index necessary exhibits.
3. Prepare, file, and follow up on service of subpoenas.
4. Schedule and notify witnesses as instructed by attorney.
5. Attend trial with attorney.
6. Draft final decree.
7. Follow up on entry of decree or order, and draft all necessary closing documents, such as deeds, title transfers, stock transfers, etc.

Duties . . . of the Family Law Legal Assistant

(Colorado Bar Association Legal Assistant Committee, 1986). Reprinted with permission.

Family law legal assistants may perform all or part of the following tasks:

A. *Screen Prospective Clients by Telephone Interviews*

B. *Commencement of Action*

1. Initial interview with client to obtain information for pleadings.
2. Prepare initial pleadings, including petition, summons and waiver of service, affidavit as to children, and response.
3. Draft correspondence with clients, courts, and other attorneys.
4. Arrange for service of process.

C. *Temporary Orders*

1. Prepare motions for temporary orders or temporary injunctions.
2. Notice and set hearings.
3. Assist in settlement negotiations.
4. Draft stipulations for temporary orders after negotiations.

D. *Financial Affidavits*

1. Work with clients in gathering and compiling financial information.
2. Analyze income and expense information provided by client.
3. Work with accountants, financial advisers, brokers, and other financial experts retained by client.
4. Retain appraisers for real estate, business and personal property.
5. Prepare financial affidavits.

E. *Discovery*

1. Prepare discovery requests.
2. Assist clients in gathering documents and data to respond to discovery requests.
3. Prepare responses to discovery requests.
4. Organize, index, and summarize discovered materials.

F. *Settlement Negotiations*

1. Assist attorney in analysis of proposed settlements.
2. Research legal questions and assist in drafting briefs and memoranda.
3. Assist in drafting separation agreements.

G. *Hearings*

1. Notice and set final orders hearing.
2. Research legal questions and assist in drafting briefs and memoranda.
3. Assist in preparation of trial exhibits and trial notebook.
4. Arrange for expert witnesses and assist in preparing witnesses and clients for trial.
5. Attend hearings.
6. Prepare final decree.

H. *Post Decree*

1. Prepare documents for transfers of assets.
2. Arrange for filing and recording of transfer documents.
3. Review bills for tax-deductible fees and prepare opinion letters to client.
4. Draft pleadings for withdrawal from case.

I. *Special Projects*

1. Develop forms for gathering information from client.
2. Maintain files on the following: separation-agreement provisions, current case law, resource materials for clients, and experts in various fields (e.g., custody, evaluation, business appraisals, etc.).

Family Law for Paralegals

by Yasmin Spiegel

6 The Journal 7 (Sacramento Association of Legal Assistants, June 1986). Reprinted with permission.

The role of a legal assistant in a family law practice is exciting and varied. Whereas all areas of law can be interesting, the opportunities for client contact, full involvement and case responsibility in family law make it a truly satisfying area of specialty. Family law affords tremendous scope for helping people in a very basic change in their lives. With the divorce rate at roughly 50 percent, there are few families who haven't been touched in some way by the problems and trauma of a court action. Our job as legal assistants can be to smooth the way through this difficult time for the client, making the experience kinder, easier to understand, more efficient, and hopefully, less expensive. Divorce is not the only area covered in family law. Adoption, grandparent visitation issues, and emancipation of minors also come under this topic. . . .

The teamwork between attorney and legal assistant is crucial to the success of a paralegal working in the family law area. Your skills and interests, as well as the degree of trust and communication between you and your boss, will determine the tasks that you will be assigned. If there is good communication and rapport between you as team members, the clients will come to rely on both of you in handling the case, and your participation will be invaluable.

In my office the attorney conducts the initial interview with the client. This is primarily done to establish the attorney/client bond, which is crucial to the successful processing of the case. Any general questions which the client has about the dissolution process, as well as discussing strategy, fees and expectations are all done at this stage. If there is an immediate need for temporary orders, such as restraining orders or temporary custody or support, the attorney will begin the information gathering process by taking detailed notes of the client's situation. The initial interview is usually concluded by inviting me into the office to be introduced as the "paralegal who will be assisting me with your case." This gives me the authority to contact the client on behalf of the attorney to gather more detailed information, and to answer the client's questions as to general procedure. I find that the clients are, for the most part, pleased to know that a paralegal will be working on their case. I am usually more accessible than the attorney to answer their questions, or to convey information, and they are billed at a lower rate for my time.

It is usually my responsibility to draft the opening documents. These include the summons, petition, and the income and expense forms. With the recent adoption of . . . income and expense forms, this job has become quite critical. The . . . forms are complicated and in some instances intimidating, and clients often need a lot of assistance in filling them out. I find that often our women clients don't understand that the forms are meant to demonstrate "need" for support. They spend all their time trying to make their income on the form come out even with their expenses, and that is usually impossible. It is often my job to tell them that if they don't show the court any evidence of the need for support, the judge won't order any. I am also responsible for drafting mediation counseling stipulations, property declarations and even orders to show cause and motions for pendente lite relief. I rely on notes from the attorney, as well as my own interviews with the client to obtain facts necessary to create the pleadings. The attorney then reviews the documents for accuracy and obtains the signature of the client. When the documents are filed, I see that the papers are served on the client's spouse and keep the client informed of subsequent developments.

Discovery plays an important role in family law. Over the years my office has developed a set of family law interrogatories on our computer, which can be modified and used to flush out the details of . . . community, quasi-community, and separate property. Any real property or pension plans must be appraised for their value as community property, and this is also the responsibility of the legal assistant. Building a strong working relationship with the various legal support personnel, such as appraisers, actuaries, deposition reporters, mediation and rehabilitation counselors, process servers, and photocopy services is essential. These people trust and respect my role as professional and as a representative of my office, and often go out of their way to assist us in emergencies because of the relationship which we have built over the years.

Preparing and arranging the service of deposition notices is another important part of family law practice which falls within the scope of the paralegal's responsibility. After the transcript of the deposition has come back from the reporter, it is my job to index and summarize it for the attorney's use in trial preparation. Comparing the bank account dates, numbers, balances and other descriptions of property with the opposing party's previous descriptions is an important part of establishing the full extent of a community or separate property interest and achieving an equal division.

Child custody and visitation is often the most traumatic aspect of a family law case. Parents who are separating are often terrified of what the effect will be on their children, and are frequently afraid that dividing their households will result in loss of closeness and opportunities for quality parenting time. Fortunately, . . . courts lean heavily in favor of joint custody whenever feasible. Mediation counseling programs have been set up . . . to assist parents in working out arrangements for custody and visitation with the assistance of trained facilitators. The agreements they work out are then presented as stipulations to the court. Wherever possible, a judge will not hear a motion for custody or visitation until the parties have been to mediation. This is practical and beneficial, since the mediation session is often the first time that the parties have been able to sit down and actually *listen* to each other since their problems began. It also provides a beginning for the future cooperation that they will have to achieve to be separated parents with children in common. It is my job as legal assistant to prepare the mediation counseling stipulation, to see that it is signed by all parties and attorneys, to make sure that it is filed with the court, and then arrange contact between the mediator and the parties.

If the parties are unable to settle their disputes (and we try very hard to settle every family law case without the necessity of a trial) then I draft a trial brief setting out the facts, the history of the case, the contested and uncontested issues, our proposal for an equal division of property, and a memorandum setting forth the applicable law. Updated income and expense and property declarations must be filed along with the trial brief, and any appraisals or actuarial analyses of pension funds must also be updated as of the time of trial.

Before the day of the trial, I contact the client to make sure that he or she is psychologically prepared to go, and make arrangements with the client for last minute prepping by the attorney. I organize the file to make all exhibits and necessary documents fingertip-accessible to the attorney trying the case, and I subpoena any witnesses who may be needed. It is very hard to get a firm court date because of case congestion, and the client must be assisted in dealing with the resulting anxiety and inconvenience. If the case does go to trial, I often go along to help my boss keep organized with respect to the documents, take notes as to areas of inquiry to be explored, run emergency errands, and keep the witnesses organized.

When the judgment is prepared, either by stipulation in the form of a marital settlement agreement, or by reducing a decision by the trial court to judgment form, I often draft the first document for review by the attorney and client. Keeping track of dates, such as deadlines for appeal, and eligibility for final judgment is also my responsibility. Preparing transfer deeds and noticing pension plans of the divorced spouse's interest are some of the wrap-up details.

As the family law case progresses, a paralegal becomes intimately familiar with the client's life and affairs. You are in a unique position to offer comfort and guidance to people in deep transition. While the legal professional's role should never be confused with that of a therapist or psychiatrist, your positive attitude and sensitivity to the client's situation can make a big difference in how they experience the adjustment to what amounts to an entirely new life. Over the past six years in a practice which is predominantly devoted to family law, I have watched hundreds of clients pass through this difficult change in their lives, heal their wounds, and create more successful and satisfying lifestyles. This is a very rewarding part of my job.

While I have had to skip over many areas of a legal assistant's responsibilities in the area of family law, I have tried to give you a sense of some of the duties that a paralegal may have. Your particular tasks will be assigned by the attorney. Short of giving the client legal advice and appearing as their representative in court, there is tremendous scope for the utilization of paralegals in a family law practice.

THE SKILLS ASSIGNMENTS IN THE BOOK

To help you develop the ability to perform many of the tasks mentioned in these job descriptions, eleven categories of skills assignments are presented in chapters of this book. Your instructor will decide which of these assignments you will be doing. The categories are as follows:

1. *Legal analysis assignment*

   In this assignment, you are given a set of facts and asked to apply one or more of the legal principles discussed in the text to those facts. Another legal analysis assignment asks you to apply the **holding** of a court opinion to a new set of facts. A holding is the court's answer to one of the legal issues it has been asked to resolve in the opinion.

holding
The court's answer to a legal issue, given in an opinion.

2. *State code assignment*

   A great deal of family law is found in your state statutory code. In the state code assignment, you will be asked to determine what your state code says about a particular topic.

common law
Judge-made law in the absence of statutory or other controlling law.

3. *Court opinion assignment*
   Two of the major categories of court opinions are those that interpret statutes and those that create and interpret **common law.** The common law is judge-made law in the absence of statutory or other controlling law. If a problem exists for which there is no governing statute, a court may have the authority to create common law to solve that problem. In the court opinion assignment, you will be asked to find both kinds of court opinions written by state courts in your state on a family law issue.
4. *Complaint drafting assignment*
   Draft a complaint acceptable in your state on a specific family law controversy.
5. *Agreement drafting assignment*
   Agreements are often used in a family law practice by parties who wish to define an aspect of their relationship or to avoid litigation. In this assignment, you will be asked to draft such agreements.
6. *Checklist formulation assignment*
   Examine a statute or common law principle and design a checklist of questions that an interviewer would ask (or that an investigator would pursue) to help determine whether that statute or common law principle applies.
7. *Investigation strategy assignment*
   Formulate a plan for gathering new facts or for substantiating facts that you already have on a family law problem.
8. *Interview assignment*
   Role-play an interviewer who will conduct a legal interview on a hypothetical (i.e., assumed) set of facts in a family law case.
9. *Interrogatory assignment*
   Draft a set of **interrogatories,** which are questions sent to an opposing party in litigation to help your side prepare for trial.
10. *Flowchart assignment*
    Present a step-by-step outline of a particular legal procedure in your state.
11. *Systems assignment*
    Interview someone who now works in a family law office, to determine what system(s) the office uses to accomplish some aspect of client service.

interrogatories
A written set of factual questions sent by one party to another before the trial begins. (One of the discovery devices.)

The general instructions for most of these assignments are found in Appendix A of the book. Within each assignment, you will find specific instructions. In addition, you may be referred to Appendix A where you will find general instructions for that category of assignment.

ASSESSING YOUR OWN BIASES

Working in family law is not for the faint of heart. "One of the worst kept secrets in legal practice is the toll that domestic relations work can take on a lawyer's staff, resources, and psyche."[7] Case stories of clients are often emotionally draining. The client's world may be falling apart in a volcano of pain, anger, and confusion.

Inevitably, you will have personal feelings about a case. A client's objective or personality might give you a sense of discomfort or unease. The question is

[7]Jennifer J. Rose, *The Ten Commandments of Family Law . . .*, 39 Practical Lawyer 85 (Jan. 1993).

whether the personal feelings will become the basis of a **bias,** which is a predisposition to think and to act in a certain way. How would you answer the following question: "Am I objective enough that I can assist a person even though I have a personal distaste for what that person wants to do or what that person has done?" Many of us would quickly answer "yes" to this question. We all like to feel that we are levelheaded and not susceptible to letting our prejudices interfere with the job we are asked to accomplish. Most of us, however, have difficulty ignoring our personal likes and dislikes.

bias
An inclination or tendency to think and to act in a certain way. A danger of prejudgment.

ASSIGNMENT 1.1

In the following cases, to what extent might an individual be hampered in delivering legal services because of personal reactions toward the client? Identify potential bias.

a. Mr. Smith, the client of your office, is being sued by his estranged wife for custody of their two small children. Mr. and Mrs. Smith live separately, but Mr. Smith has had custody of the children during most of their lives while Mrs. Smith has been in the hospital. Mrs. Smith has charged that Mr. Smith often yells at the children, leaves them with neighbors and day care centers for most of the day, and is an alcoholic. Your investigation reveals that Mrs. Smith will probably be able to prove all these allegations in court.
b. Mrs. Jones is being sued by Mr. Jones for divorce on the ground of adultery. Mrs. Jones is the client of your office. Thus far your investigation has revealed that there is considerable doubt over whether Mrs. Jones did in fact commit adultery. During a recent conversation with Mrs. Jones, however, she tells you that she is a prostitute.
c. Jane Anderson is seeking an abortion. She is not married. The father of the child wants to prevent her from having the abortion. Jane comes to your office for legal help. She wants to know what her rights are. You belong to a church that believes abortion is murder. You are assigned to work on the case.
d. Paul and Victor are a gay couple who want to adopt Sammy, a six-month-old baby whose parents recently died in an automobile accident. Sammy's maternal grandmother is not able to adopt him because of her age and health. She opposes the adoption by Paul and Victor because of their lifestyle. Paul and Victor are clients of your office in their petition for adoption. You agree with the grandmother's position, but have been assigned to work on the case.
e. Tom Donaldson is a client of your office. His former wife claims that he has failed to pay court-ordered alimony payments and that the payments should be increased substantially because of her needs and his recently improved financial status. Your job is to help Tom collect a large volume of records concerning his past alimony payments and his present financial worth. You are the only person in the office who is available to do this record gathering. It is clear, however, that Tom does not like you. On a number of occasions, he has indirectly questioned your ability.

Having analyzed the fact situations in Assignment 1.1, do you still feel the same about your assessment of your own **objectivity?** Clearly, we cannot simply wish our personal feelings away or pretend that they do not exist. Nor are there any absolute rules or techniques that apply to every situation you will be asked to handle. Nor are the following admonitions very helpful: "Be objective," "be dispassionate," "don't get personally involved," "control your feelings." Such admonitions are too general, and when viewed in the abstract, they may appear not to be needed, because we want to believe that we are always objective, dispassionate, detached, and in control.

objectivity
The state of being dispassionate; the absence of a bias.

We must recognize that there are facts and circumstances that arouse our emotions and tempt us to impose our own value judgments. Perhaps if we know where we are vulnerable, we will be in a better position to prevent our reactions from interfering with our work. It is not desirable for you to be totally dispassionate and removed. A paralegal who is cold, unfeeling, and incapable of empathy is not much better than a paralegal who self-righteously scolds a client. It is clearly not improper for a paralegal to express sympathy, surprise, and perhaps even shock at what unfolds from the client's life story. If these feelings are genuine and if they would be normal reactions to the situation at a given moment, then they should be expressed. The problem is *how to draw the line* between expressing these feelings and reacting so judgmentally that you interfere with your ability to communicate with the client now and in the future. Again, there are no absolute guidelines. As you gain experience in the art of dealing with people, you will develop styles and techniques that will enable you to avoid going over that line. The starting point in this development is to recognize how easy it is to go over the line.

Some paralegals apply what is called the "stomach test." If your gut tells you that your personal feelings about the case are so intense that you may not be able to do a quality job for the client, you need to take action.[8] Talk with your supervisor. You may have some misunderstandings about the case that your supervisor can clear up. You may be able to limit your role in the case or be reassigned to other cases. Without breaching client confidentiality, contact your local paralegal association to try to talk with other paralegals who have handled similar situations. They may be able to give you some guidance.

Attorneys often take unpopular cases involving clients who have said or done things that run the gamut from being politically incorrect to being socially reprehensible. As professionals, attorneys are committed to the principle that *everyone* is entitled to representation. Paralegals should have this same commitment. But attorneys and paralegals are human beings. No one can treat every case identically. In the final analysis, you need to ask yourself whether your bias is so strong that it might interfere with your ability to give the needs of the client 100 percent of your energy and skill. If so, you have an obligation not to work on the case.

conflict of interest
Divided loyalty that actually or potentially places a person at a disadvantage even though he or she is owed undivided loyalty.

Ethical concerns also dictate this result. As we will see in chapter 2, attorneys have an ethical obligation to avoid a **conflict of interest.** Such a conflict exists when an attorney has divided loyalties. An obvious example is an attorney who represents both parties in a legal dispute they have with each other. A less obvious example is an attorney whose personal feelings could interfere with his or her obligation to give a client vigorous representation. The attorney's personal feelings should not be in conflict with a client's legitimate need for undiluted advocacy. Is the attorney going to be loyal to his or her personal feelings and values, or to the client's cause? Clients should not be subjected to such conflicts of loyalties. When a conflict of this kind exists, the attorney has an ethical obligation not to take the case. The same obligation applies to paralegals. There should be no interference with anyone's inclination to give the client a total commitment.

ASSIGNMENT 1.2

a. Think about your past and present contacts with people who have irritated you the most. Make a specific list of what bothered you about these people. Suppose that you are working in a law office where a client did one of the things on your list. Could you handle such a case?

b. In the relationship among husband, wife, and child, many things can be done that would be wrong (i.e., illegal, immoral, improper) according to your personal system of values. Make a list of the ten things that could be done by

[8] Shari Caudron, *Crisis of Conscience,* 12 Legal Assistant Today 73, 75 (Sept./Oct. 1994).

husband, wife, or child to another family member (e.g., husband to wife, child to parent) that would be most offensive to your sense of values. Assume that a client in the office where you work has done one of these ten things and is being challenged in court by someone because of it. Your office is defending the client against this challenge. What difficulties do you see for yourself in being able to assist this client?

"MY SISTER'S DIVORCE"

Most people are fascinated by family law and almost always have a question or two that they would love to ask someone. Once your relatives, friends, neighbors, and acquaintances find out that you work in a family law office, you will probably become a target of inquiries. Inevitably, while talking to someone in a social gathering, you will find yourself being asked about child support rights or about "my sister's divorce." Be careful. If you answer a legal question about the facts of a particular person's case, you are giving legal advice and may be engaging in the unauthorized practice of law. It makes no difference whether you answer the question correctly or incorrectly. Nor is it relevant that your advice is free. Nonattorneys cannot give legal advice on matters that ultimately require resolution by a court. There are some areas, such as social security, where you do not have to be an attorney to answer legal questions. This is rarely true in family law.

It may be awkward for you to decline to answer legal questions, especially when they cover topics on which you may be more knowledgeable than some attorneys. People you know may not appreciate being told that they should consult an attorney for legal questions they ask you. Yet this is the proper response. Do not risk misleading someone and being charged with the unauthorized practice of law. There are many self-help books and Internet sites that provide information about the law. If you are aware of some good ones, there is nothing wrong with referring the questioner to them. This is quite different from telling someone what laws might apply to particular facts. Of course, you can also suggest that the person contact your law office for legal assistance. We will return to these themes when we discuss ethical issues in a family law practice in chapter 2.

VIOLENCE IN A FAMILY LAW PRACTICE

Unfortunately, violence must be one of the concerns of a family law practice. In chapter 10 (on child support), for example, we will see that special measures must be taken to protect a mother from violence once she asserts a claim for child support against a father. In chapter 12 (on the legal rights of women), we will examine other dimensions of domestic violence.

Violence can also be directed at family law offices. At a recent legal conference, the speaker asked a group of about 120 experienced family law attorneys if anyone in the room had experienced violent actions or threats in their practice. Almost all the attorneys in the room raised their hand. One woman told the group, "Just yesterday, I [learned that] my client and I were in grave danger."[9] Many attorneys are upgrading their office security systems; some acknowledge that when interviewing a new client, they consciously assess whether taking the case might pose personal risks to anyone in the office.

---

[9]A.P. Roth, *Dangerous Divorces,* California Lawyer 23, 24 (Feb. 1994).

Family Court personnel are also concerned. Violence has erupted in the corridors of some courthouses and occasionally in the courtroom itself. "In 1992, a San Jose man fighting for custody of his three children shot and wounded three deputies."[10] At a retirement party for family law court commissioner Abe Gorenfeld, he pointed to the "bullet hole still visible in the ceiling outside his fifth-floor courtroom where a woman fired her pistol at her soon-to-be ex-husband and missed."[11] Many courthouses now have elaborate security systems at the entrances. Some courts, however, have been slow to add such security. One court did not do so until a bailiff discovered a gun in the lunch box of an estranged husband sitting in a courtroom.

Of course, violence is not an everyday occurrence in family law offices and courthouses. Out-of-control, angry, frustrated citizens exist throughout our society. However, we all should be aware of the reality that volatile emotions often exist within families undergoing disintegration. Individuals who perceive themselves as victims are sometimes capable of lashing out against anyone involved in what they irrationally feel is an unresponsive legal system. Caution is the order of the day.

FINDING FAMILY LAW

Introduction

Law books and online legal resources are important tools for an attorney. The same should be true of the paralegal. Because there is so much law, and because a good deal of it is constantly changing, no one—including an experienced judge—can be expected to know all the family law of a particular state. In a child-support case, for example, the question is not so much, "What is the law of child support?" as it is "What is the law of child support *today*?" Understanding general principles is helpful as a starting point, but more is usually needed in the actual practice of law. And the ticket of admission to current law is the law library.

In this section, we will cover some of the fundamentals of the law library from the viewpoint of the family law practitioner. The section is not intended as a substitute for a full course in legal research, nor does it assume that you have already had such a course. Rather, we highlight some of the basics so as to reinforce what you may have learned elsewhere, or to give you a headstart on what you will be learning for the first time elsewhere.

primary authority
Any law that a court could rely on in reaching its conclusion.

secondary authority
Any nonlaw that a court could rely on in reaching its conclusion.

Two major categories of legal materials are relevant to a family law practice: those containing **primary authority** and those containing **secondary authority.** A court will want to know what primary authority is available to resolve a legal dispute in a family law case—or in any kind of case. Primary authority is any law that a court could rely on in reaching its conclusion (e.g., a statute, court opinion, court rule, constitutional provision, administrative regulation, or ordinance). Secondary authority is any nonlaw that a court could rely on in reaching its conclusion (e.g., a legal encyclopedia, legal treatise, or law review article). The main value of secondary authority is that it helps you locate and interpret primary authority.

Important Publications for Family Law Practitioners

Among the most important legal materials to which a family law practitioner should have access are the state statutory code, court rules, court opinions, practice manual, and legal newspaper. All are available in a traditional law library in book or paper format. Codes, rules, and opinions are also available online, for a fee, through commercial databases such as WESTLAW, Lexis-

---

[10]Roth, *Dangerous Divorces,* at 24.
[11]Deborah Belgum, *82-Year-Old Jurist Bows Out. . . ,* Los Angeles Times, Jan. 6, 1997, at B1.

Nexis, and Loislaw. All three may also be available on the Internet at no cost, although they are not always as comprehensive, current, and reliable as the commercial databases. Here is a closer look at the materials in book or paper format (later in the chapter, we will examine legal materials online):

Your State Statutory Code The statutes of the legislature govern many aspects of family law. They will probably be found in three or four volumes of the **statutory code** for your state. (See Appendix A for more about using statutory codes.)

statutory code
A collection of statutes written by the legislature, organized by subject matter.

Court Rules **Court rules** (also called rules of court) govern the mechanics of litigation before a particular court. They cover many of the procedural aspects of divorces, annulments, adoptions, etc. The rules often contain standard forms that are either required or recommended.

court rules
Rules of procedure that govern the mechanics of litigation before a particular court.

State Court Opinions and Digests A **court opinion** is a written explanation of the court's resolution of a legal issue. These opinions are printed in full in volumes called **reporters.** There are usually several sets of reporters containing the opinions of your state courts, particularly the highest state court. There may be an official reporter published by the state itself. In addition, there is a regional reporter published by a private company (West Group) containing the opinions of the highest state courts (and some lower courts) of a cluster of states in the same region of the country. You need to find out what region your state is in so that you can find your regional reporter.

court opinion
The written explanation by a court of why it reached a certain conclusion or holding.

reporters
The volumes that contain the full text of court opinions.

Almost every state has a **digest,** a set of volumes that contains small paragraph summaries of the court opinions of that state. Most of the regional reporters also have regional digests that give summaries of the opinions in their respective regional reporter. The largest digest covering every state is the *American Digest System.* You need to have access to your individual state digest, or to your regional digest (if one exists for your region), or to the *American Digest System.*

digest
Book or set of books containing small paragraph summaries of court opinions.

Practice Manual Many states have a **practice manual** covering a variety of topics such as Family Law, Probate Law, Corporate Law, etc. In addition to summaries of the law, the manuals usually contain practical information, e.g., standard forms, checklists.

practice manual
A practical treatise often containing standard forms along with checklists, summaries of the law, etc.

Legal Newspapers The **legal newspaper** gives current cases, docket calendars for local courts, news on what the legislature and bar association are doing, etc.

legal newspaper
A newspaper (published daily, weekly, etc.) devoted to legal news.

SAMPLE PROBLEM

Let us assume that you work in a law office whose client signed a surrogate motherhood contract. She agreed to be artificially inseminated with the semen of a man who is not her husband and, upon birth, to allow the child to be adopted by this man and his wife. Problems have arisen in this arrangement. Your supervisor asks you to do some legal research on the legality of surrogacy contracts. Later, in chapter 16, we will study such contracts in greater detail. For now our goal is simply to give you an overview of some of the law books you might consult when researching a family law case such as this.

Starting with Primary Authority

One possible starting point would be to go directly to law books containing or indexing primary authority.

EXAMPLE OF A STATUTORY CODE VOLUME

STATUTES To find out if there are any statutes on surrogacy, check the index of your state statutory code. It might lead you to such statutes. See Exhibit 1.1 for an example. For a summary of techniques to use when trying to find statutory law, see Appendix A.

Exhibit 1.1 Example of a family law statute: *Michigan Compiled Laws Annotated*, §§ 772.851 and 772.855 (1993)

772.851. Short title

This act shall be known and may be cited as the "surrogate parenting act".
P.A. 1988, No. 199, § 1, Eff. Sept. 1, 1988.

722.855. Contracts; void and unenforceable

A surrogate parentage contract is void and unenforceable as contrary to public policy.
P.A. 1988, No. 199, § 5, Eff. Sept. 1, 1988.

COURT OPINIONS Exhibit 1.2 gives an example of a page from a regional reporter volume containing *Doe v. Attorney General*, a court opinion on the legality of surrogate motherhood contracts. One of the major ways to find such opinions is through the digests, which, as indicated, are volumes of small paragraph summaries of court opinions. Another way is to use computer databases such as those found on WESTLAW, Lexis-Nexis, Loislaw, and the Internet. In Exhibit 1.3 you will find the beginning of a WESTLAW page containing *Doe v. Attorney General*, the same case we looked at in a reporter volume in Exhibit 1.2. For a summary of techniques to use when trying to find court opinions, see Appendix A.

Starting with Secondary Authority

Another option is to start with secondary authority. This approach is often valuable when you are doing research in an area of the law that is new to you. Secondary authority will not only give you leads to primary authority, but will also often give you background information about the law. This background can be tremendously helpful in providing basic terminology and general understanding. Here are some of the main secondary authorities:

legal encyclopedia
A multivolume set of books that summarizes almost every major legal topic.

LEGAL ENCYCLOPEDIAS A **legal encyclopedia** is a multivolume set of books that summarizes almost every major legal topic. The two most important national legal encyclopedias are:

- *American Jurisprudence, 2d* (West Group) *(Am. Jur. 2d)*
- *Corpus Juris Secundum* (West Group) *(C.J.S.)*

Exhibit 1.4 contains a page from a volume of *American Jurisprudence, 2d* on surrogate motherhood. Exhibit 1.5 contains a page from a volume of *Corpus Juris Secundum* on the same topic. In addition to these national encyclopedias, some states have their own encyclopedia covering the law of one state, e.g., *Florida Jurisprudence, 2d; Michigan Law and Practice.*

legal treatise
A book written by a private individual (or by a public official writing as a private citizen) that provides an overview, summary, or commentary on a legal topic.

LEGAL TREATISES A **legal treatise** is a book written by a private individual (or a public official writing as a private citizen) that provides an overview, summary, or commentary on a legal topic. Exhibit 1.6 contains a page from a widely used legal treatise on family law, Homer H. Clark, *The Law of Domestic Relations in the United States* (2d ed. 1987). If the legal treatise contains very practical material such as litigation techniques and standard forms, it is often also called a formbook or a practice manual.

Exhibit 1.2 Sample page from a regional reporter volume containing a family law court opinion: *Doe v. Attorney General,* 487 N.W.2d 484 (Mich. Ct. App. 1992)

DOE v. ATTORNEY GENERAL Mich. **484**

Cite as 487 N.W.2d 484 (Mich.App. 1992)

Caption (parties, their litigation status, docket number, dates, etc.)

194 Mich.App. 432

Jane DOE, John Doe, Rena Roe, Richard Roe, Carol Coe, Carl Coe, Paula Poe, and Nancy Noe, Plaintiffs-Appellants,

v.

ATTORNEY GENERAL, Defendant-Appellee.

Docket No. 113775.

Court of Appeals of Michigan.

Submitted March 20, 1990, at Detroit.

Decided June 1, 1992, at 9:10 a.m.

Released for Publication August 28, 1992.

Syllabus (summary of the entire opinion)

Infertile couples and prospective surrogate mothers brought action for declaratory judgment against state Attorney General regarding constitutionality of Surrogate Parenting Act. The Circuit Court, Wayne County, John H. Gillis, Jr., J., granted summary disposition for the Attorney General, and plaintiffs appealed. The Court of Appeals, Holbrook, P.J., held that: (1) case or controversy existed concerning constitutionality of statute, giving court jurisdiction for declaratory judgment; (2) state had compelling interests sufficient to warrant governmental intrusion into protected area of privacy in matter of procreation; and (3) surrogate parentage contract involving voluntary relinquishment after conception of female's parental rights to child, is void and unenforceable.

Affirmed in part and reversed in part.

Murphy, J., concurred and filed opinion.

Headnote (summary of a portion of the opinion) At the top, you find Key Topic and Number "Declaratory Judgment 124." You can take this key topic and number to any West digest to try to find additional cases. →

1. Declaratory Judgment ⚿ 124

"Case or controversy" existed, for purposes of declaratory judgment, despite agreement as to interpretation of statute, where attorney for infertile couples and prospective surrogate mothers later informed trial court that he misunderstood agreement with state concerning constitutionality of interpretation of Surrogate Parenting Act. M.C.L.A. §722.851 et seq.; U.S.C.A. Const. Amends. 5, 14; MCR 2.605(A).

2. Constitutional Law ⚿ 82(10), 274(5) ← Headnote (summary of a portion of the opinion) At the top, you find Key Topic and Numbers "Constitutional Law 82(10)" and "274(5)". You can take them to any West digest to try to find additional cases.

Due process clauses of State and Federal Constitutions, together with penumbral rights emanating from specific guarantees of the Bill of Rights, protect individual decisions in matters of childbearing from unjustified intrusion by the state. U.S.C.A. Const. Amends. 5, 14.

American Civil Liberties Union Fund of Michigan by Robert A. Sedler, Elizabeth L. Gleicher and Paul J. Denenfeld, Detroit, for plaintiffs-appellants.

Frank J. Kelley, Atty. Gen., Gay Secor Hardy, Sol. Gen., and A. Michael Leffler and Vincent J. Leone, Asst. Attys. Gen., for defendant-appellee.

Attorneys who litigated the case

Before HOLBROOK, P.J., and MURPHY and JANSEN, JJ.

HOLBROOK, Presiding Judge. ← Name of judge who wrote the opinion

In this action for a declaratory interpretation of the Surrogate Parenting Act, M.C.L. § 722.851 *et seq.;* M.S.A. § 25.-248(151) *et seq.,* plaintiffs appeal as of right from an order of the Wayne Circuit Court granting defendant's motion for summary disposition for failure to state a claim. We affirm in part and reverse in part.

The body of the opinion begins.

Plaintiffs are infertile couples and prospective surrogate mothers. In their suit, filed on August 4, 1988, plaintiffs assert that if the Surrogate Parenting Act were interpreted as being an outright ban on surrogacy contracts for pay, the statute would deny them their constitutionally protected privacy rights and would offend the Due Process and Equal Protection Clauses of the state and federal constitutions. . . .

EXAMPLE OF A REGIONAL REPORTER VOLUME

Exhibit 1.3 Sample screen from WESTLAW containing a family law court opinion: *Doe v. Attorney General*, 487 N.W.2d 484 (Mich. Ct. App. 1992)

START*START*START*START*START*START*START*START*START*START*START*START*START*START*START*START*START*
Copr. (C) West 1995 No claim to orig. U.S. govt. works
(Cite as: 194 Mich.App. 432, 487 N.W.2d 484)

Jane DOE, John Doe, Rena Roe, Richard Roe, Carol Coe, Carl Coe, Paula Poe, and Nancy Noe, Plaintiffs-Appellants,
v.
ATTORNEY GENERAL, Defendant-Appellee.
Docket No. 113775.
Court of Appeals of Michigan.
Submitted March 20, 1990, at Detroit.
Decided June 1, 1992, at 9:10 a.m.
Released for Publication August 28, 1992.

Infertile couples and prospective surrogate mothers brought action for declaratory judgment against state Attorney General regarding constitutionality of Surrogate Parenting Act. The Circuit Court, Wayne County, John H. Gillis, Jr., J., granted summary disposition for the Attorney General, and plaintiffs appealed. The Court of Appeals, Holbrook, P.J., held that: (1) case or controversy existed concerning constitutionality of statute, giving court jurisdiction for declaratory judgment; (2) state had compelling interests sufficient to warrant governmental intrusion into protected area of privacy in matter of procreation; and (3) surrogate parentage contract involving voluntary relinquishment after conception of female's parental rights to child, is void and unenforceable.

Affirmed in part and reversed in part.

Murphy, J., concurred and filed opinion. . . .

EXAMPLE OF AN *AM. JUR. 2D* VOLUME

Exhibit 1.4 Example of a discussion of a family law topic from a volume of *American Jurisprudence, 2d:* 59 Am. Jur. 2d § 3 (1987)

59 Am Jur 2d PARENT AND CHILD § 4

§ 3. —"Surrogate mother"

The surrogate mother arrangement is an arrangement between a surrogate mother and a husband and wife, whereby the surrogate mother agrees to be artificially inseminated with the husband's semen, bear a child, and relinquish all rights regarding that child to the husband and wife. They agree to pay the costs of the surrogate mother's pregnancy and to accept the child at birth. In addition, they may agree to pay the surrogate mother a fee in excess of the costs of bearing a child.[22] The legality and enforceability of a surrogate mother arrangement is questionable.[23]

legal periodical
An ongoing publication (e.g., published quarterly) that contains articles, studies, reports, or other information on legal topics.

annotation
A set of notes or commentaries on something. The most widely used annotations are those printed in *American Law Reports*.

LEGAL PERIODICALS A **legal periodical** is an ongoing publication (e.g., published quarterly) that contains articles, studies, reports, or other information on legal topics. Many legal periodicals are published by law schools, such as the one in Exhibit 1.7 from the *Marquette Law Review.*

ANNOTATIONS An **annotation** is a set of notes or commentaries on something. The most widely used annotations are those printed in:

- *American Law Reports* (A.L.R.)
- *American Law Reports, Second Series (A.L.R.2d)*
- *American Law Reports, Third Series (A.L.R.3d)*
- *American Law Reports, Fourth Series (A.L.R.4th)*
- *American Law Reports, Fifth Series (A.L.R.5th)*
- *American Law Reports, Federal Series (A.L.R. Fed)*

All six sets are sometimes referred to collectively as *American Law Reports* or *ALRs.* Exhibit 1.8 contains an example of an annotation on surrogacy from *A.L.R.4th.*

Exhibit 1.5 Example of a discussion of a family law topic from a volume of *Corpus Juris Secundum:* 2 C.J.S. § 25 (1972, Supp. 1994)

2 C.J.S. **ADOPTION OF PERSONS §§ 24-25**

§ 25. In General

While an adoption relationship cannot ordinarily be created by private contract, contracts for the adoption of persons are usually not considered as opposed to public policy and in some circumstances such a contract may be treated as an adoption and enforced with consequences equivalent to a formal adoption. . . .

While surrogate parenting agreements in which the surrogate mother receives payment for bearing and surrendering the baby to the natural father and his wife for adoption have been prohibited,[29.5] such surrogate parenting agreements which compensate the surrogate mother have been given legal effect.[29.10]

A contractual provision in a surrogate parenting agreement purporting to terminate the parental rights of the surrogate mother does not conform to statutory prerequisites for termination and is invalid and unenforceable.[29.15]

EXAMPLE OF A *C.J.S.* VOLUME

EXAMPLE OF A LEGAL TREATISE

Exhibit 1.6 Example of a page from a legal treatise on family law: Homer H. Clark, *The Law of Domestic Relations in the United States* § 21.9, pp. 669–670 (2d ed. 1987)

§ 21.9 Adoption—The Surrogate Mother Contract

If the soundness of the solutions to legal problems varied directly with the number of words devoted to the problems and with the number of persons engaged in producing the words, we would need to have no fears about being able to cope with the difficulties created by surrogate mother contracts.[1] The legal and nonlegal output on the subject has been enormous[2] and will doubtless continue at the same rate until some other fascinating and unanswerable question appears. Unfortunately, however, the ability to solve legal problems probably varies inversely with the number of words expended. Generally acceptable methods of dealing with these contracts therefore do not seem likely to be devised.

EXAMPLE OF A LEGAL PERIODICAL

Exhibit 1.7 Example of a page from a legal periodical article on family law: 76 *Marquette Law Review* 675 (1993)

SURROGATE GESTATOR: A NEW AND HONORABLE PROFESSION

JOHN DWIGHT INGRAM

I. INTRODUCTION

In recent decades, sex without reproduction has become common and widely accepted, and more recently medical science has made it increasingly possible to have reproduction without sex. The former is much more enjoyable than the latter for most of us and, while it does entail some moral and legal issues, is a great deal less complex than the latter.[1] A major cause of the complexity of the issues associated with noncoital reproduction is that, while "science [tends to] look . . . forward to anticipate new and unforeseen possibilities, the law looks backward, drawing its support from precedent."[2] Our society seems to first develop and perfect medical and scientific techniques, and only later consult experts in ethics and law to determine if we *should* be doing that which in fact we already *are* doing. Meanwhile, we try to resolve disputes arising from new reproductive technologies by using "old legal codes of paternity, maternity, baby-selling, adoption, and contracts."[3]

EXAMPLE OF AN *A.L.R.4TH* VOLUME

Exhibit 1.8 Example of a page from an annotation on family law: 77 *A.L.R.4th 70* (1990)

ANNOTATION

VALIDITY AND CONSTRUCTION OF SURROGATE PARENTING AGREEMENT

by

Danny R. Veilleux, J.D.

I. Preliminary Matters

§ 1. Introduction

[a] Scope

This annotation collects and analyzes the reported cases in which the courts have construed or considered the validity of a surrogate parenting agreement. For the purposes of this annotation, the "surrogate parenting" or "surrogacy" agreement refers to a contract in which the natural or "surrogate" mother, for a fee, agrees to conceive a child through artificial insemination with the sperm of the natural father, to bear and deliver the child to the natural father, and to terminate all of her parental rights subsequent to the child's birth. Although the parties to a surrogacy agreement generally anticipate the eventual adoption of the child by the natural father's wife, this annotation will discuss all surrogacy agreements, regardless of whether they contain any provisions concerning such adoption. Moreover, the surrogate mother's husband, or the natural father's wife, assuming either parent is married, may be a party to the surrogacy agreements included within the scope of this annotation.

MARTINDALE-HUBBELL The *Martindale-Hubbell Law Directory* contains a listing of the names and addresses of many of the practicing attorneys in the country. It also has a unit called the Martindale-Hubbell Law Digest. It contains brief summaries of the law of every state. Exhibit 1.9 contains an example of a page from the summary for New York on surrogacy parenting.

WORDS AND PHRASES *Words and Phrases* is a multivolume legal dictionary published by West Group. Most of its definitions come from court opinions. Exhibit 1.10 presents an excerpt from the "S" volume of the dictionary, where the phrase "surrogate parentage contract" is defined. Note that the case defining this phrase is the same case we examined earlier in Exhibits 1.2 and 1.3, *Doe v. Attorney General.* One of the common features of different secondary authorities is that they often refer you to the same laws.

EXAMPLE OF A *MARTINDALE-HUBBELL LAW DIGEST* VOLUME

Exhibit 1.9 Example of a family law topic discussed in the "Martindale-Hubbell Law Digest" volume of the *Martindale-Hubbell Law Directory*

MARTINDALE-HUBBELL LAW DIGEST

Surrogate parenting contracts void. (D. R. L. §124). Payments or receipts of payments of compensation in connection with surrogate parenting prohibited. (D. R. L. §123).

Effect of Adoption.—Adopted child after Mar. 1, 1964 does not retain right to inherit from natural family upon making of order of adoption but will inherit from his adoptive parents and their kindred. All inheritance rights by adopted child from his natural parents is terminated, except where natural parent remarries and consents to adoption of child in which case, adopted child only inherits through natural parent who has remarried and consented to adoption and not from other natural parent. Where adoptive parent is married to natural parent, or is natural grandparent or descendant of natural grandparent, adopted child can inherit through natural grandparents or descendants of natural grandparents dying after Aug. 31, 1987. Adopted and natural children have all rights of fraternal relationship, including inheritance from each other. Rights of inheritance of adoptive child extends to distributees of such child. (D. R. L. §117).

Wills of persons dying after Mar. 1, 1964 or inter vivos instruments theretofore executed which are subject to being revoked or amended shall be affected by this law, otherwise provisions of this section in effect prior to that date shall be applicable. (D. R. L. §117).

Setting Aside Adoption.—See supra, subhead Order.

Exhibit 1.10 Example of a page from *Words and Phrases* (1994) on which a family law term is defined

SURROGATE PARENTAGE CONTRACT

"Surrogate parenting contract," which is void and unenforceable under Surrogate Parenting Act, consists of (1) conception, through either natural or artificial insemination, of, or surrogate gestation by female and (2) voluntary relinquishment of her parental rights to the child; but contract that does not contain both such elements is not void or unenforceable under the Act even when entered into for compensation. Doe v. Attorney General, 487 N.W.2d 484, 488, 194 Mich.App. 432.

SURROGATE TEST

Supplier of blood bank cannot be held liable for transmission of AIDS virus on the basis of having failed to employ a "surrogate test" for identifying donors who were at a high risk for transmitting AIDS (acquired immune deficiency syndrome), even though recipient asserted that blood supplier should have used the test for hepatitis B core antibody. Doe v. American Red Cross Blood Services, S.C. Region, D.S.C., 125 F.R.D. 637, 640.

EXAMPLE OF A *WORDS AND PHRASES* VOLUME

ASSIGNMENT 1.3

a. What is the name of the statutory code containing the statutes of your legislature? If more than one exists, list each one.

b. In this code, find any statute on divorce. Quote and cite the first line from this statute.

c. Find the court rules of any court in your state that can hear family law cases. Select any court rule on any family law topic. Quote and cite the first sentence of this rule.

d. What is the name of the regional reporter that contains the court opinions of the highest state court in your state?

e. How many West digests contain small paragraph summaries of the opinions of your state courts? Name each one.

f. Go to the "Descriptive Word Index" of any digest covering your state courts. List any three key topics and numbers on divorce.

g. Go to one of the three key topics and numbers in the main volumes of your digest. Under that key topic and number, find one case written within the last ten years by a state court of your state. What is the citation of this case? What key topics and numbers did you find it digested under?

h. Go to the reporter volume that contains the case you identified in question (g). What is the name of the court that wrote this opinion? Quote and cite the first line of the opinion.

i. What is the name of the legal newspaper most practitioners rely on in your state? In a recent issue of this newspaper, find any reference to a family law topic or case. Quote from and cite the reference.

j. Go to *American Jurisprudence, 2d.* Use the index volumes to find any topic on divorce. What topic did you select? Find that topic in the main volumes of *Am. Jur. 2d.* Quote and cite the first line of that topic in the encyclopedia.

k. In the footnotes for the topic you selected in *Am. Jur. 2d,* find a citation to an opinion written by a state court of your state. (Be sure to check the pocket part for the volume you are using.) If you cannot find such an opinion, pick another divorce topic until you can. What is the citation of the opinion?

l. Go to *Corpus Juris Secundum.* Use the index volumes to find any topic on divorce. What topic did you select? Find that topic in the main volumes of *C.J.S.* Quote and cite the first line of that topic in the encyclopedia.

continued

m. In the footnotes for the topic you selected in *C.J.S.*, find a citation to a court opinion written by a state court of your state. (Be sure to check the pocket part for the volume you are using.) If you cannot find such an opinion, pick another divorce topic until you can. What is the citation of the opinion?

n. Use the card or computer catalog to find any legal treatise that covers the law of your state alone. Go to the index in that treatise to find a discussion of any family law topic of your state. Quote and cite the first sentence of this discussion. If the legal treatise you selected does not cover the family law of your state, pick another treatise.

o. Find a legal periodical article that meets the following criteria: it covers a family law topic, and the name of your state appears in the title of the article. Quote and cite the first sentence of this article. (To find such an article, use whatever legal periodical index system is available in your library, e.g., *LegalTrac, Legal Resource Index, Index to Legal Periodicals.*)

p. Go to the *Index to Annotations.* Use it to find any annotation on any family law topic in *A.L.R., A.L.R.2d, A.L.R.3d, A.L.R.4th, A.L.R.5th,* or *A.L.R. Fed.* Go to this annotation. Find a reference in the annotation to any court opinion written by a court of your state. What is the citation of the annotation? What is the citation of the court opinion you found in the annotation? If the annotation you select does not cite an opinion from your state, pick another annotation from the *Index to Annotations.*

q. Go to the "Martindale-Hubbell Law Digest" volume of *Martindale-Hubbell Law Directory.* Find the summary for your state. Find a discussion of any family law topic. Quote and cite the first sentence of this discussion.

r. Go to the legal dictionary, *Words and Phrases.* Look up the definition of one of the following words: *adultery, antenuptial, domicile, joint custody,* or *alimony.* Find a definition written by a state court of your state. What word did you select? What is the definition? What is the citation of the opinion from which this definition is taken?

Family Law Online

online
Connected to a host computer system or information service, often through a telephone line.

It is now possible to obtain a great deal of **online** information that is relevant to a family law practice. In addition to research into court opinions, statutes, and other primary authorities, a law firm often must do factual research. An example of factual research is to try to uncover personal and business assets that an estranged spouse may be trying to hide.

Internet
A self-governing network of networks to which millions of computer users around the world have access.

World Wide Web
A tool that allows a computer user to navigate locations on the Internet that are often linked by hypertext.

Three major commercial online databases, for which the firm pays a subscription fee, are WESTLAW, Lexis-Nexis, and Loislaw. In addition, you can obtain a great deal of information on the **Internet** through the **World Wide Web.** Most of it is free once you have the basic connection to the Internet. Greater caution is needed, however, when using information found on the Internet. Unlike the commercial database services, the Internet is not regulated or monitored. Consequently, you cannot have the same assurance as to the accuracy of materials obtained from Internet sites that you can for those obtained from the commercial services or, indeed, from traditional bound volumes. Nevertheless, the vast resources of the Internet are useful as starting points. Exhibit 1.11 presents the home pages of four sites of particular interest to a family law office.

Here is a list of additional relevant Internet addresses. Most of these sites consist of comprehensive links to other sites that will lead you to:

- family laws of particular states,
- practicing family law attorneys, and
- resources on the emotional dimension of many family law legal problems

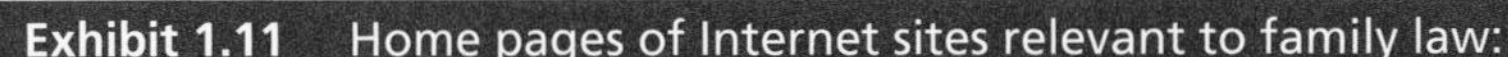

Exhibit 1.11 Home pages of Internet sites relevant to family law:

a. Findlaw: Family Law Links
http://www.findlaw.com/01topics/15family/index.html
(Screen reproduced courtesy of FindLaw.)

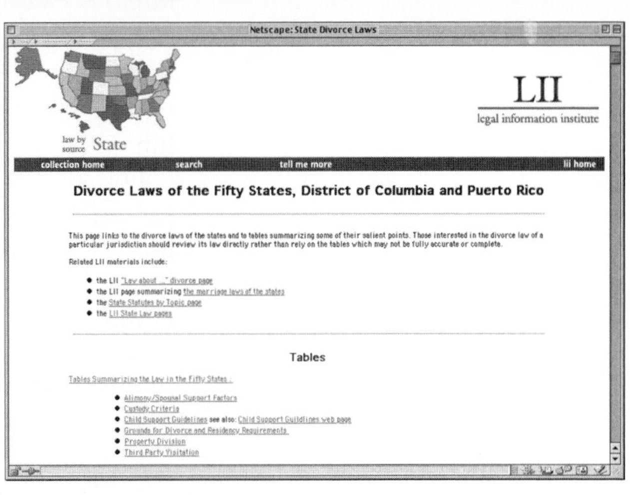

b. Cornell Legal Information Institute (Divorce)
http://www.law.cornell.edu/topics/Table_Divorce.htm
(Screen reproduced courtesy of Legal Information Institute, Cornell Law School.)

c. Federal Office of Child Support Enforcement
http://www.acf.dhhs.gov/programs/cse
(Screen reproduced courtesy of Federal Office of Child Support Enforcement.)

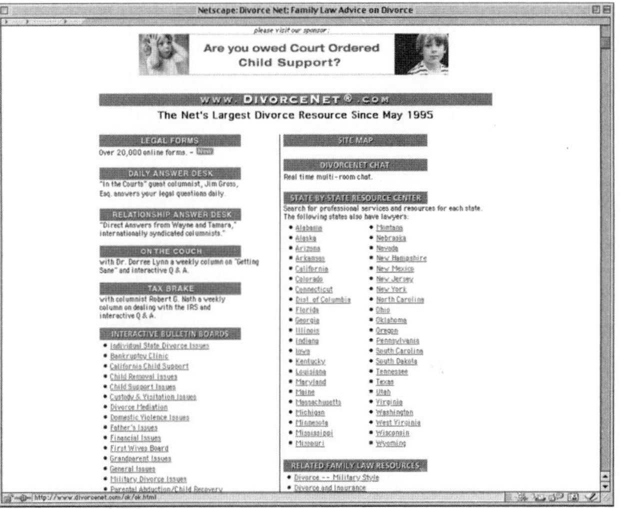

d. DivorceNet.com
http://www.divorcenet.com/index.html
(Screen reproduced courtesy of LawTek Media Group, LLC.)

At the end of each chapter in this book, you will find a list of Internet sites that are specifically related to the subject matter of particular chapters.

Finally, here are some additional sites that will provide extensive links (except where indicated in brackets):

About Divorce Support: Legalities
http://divorcesupport.about.com/cs/legalities/index.htm

American Bar Association: Family Law Quarterly
http://www.abanet.org/family/familylaw/home.html
[abstracts of scholarly articles on family law; links to good tables on state law]

CataLaw: Family and Juvenile Law
http://www.catalaw.com/topics/Family.shtml

Cornell Legal Information Institute (Divorce)
http://www.law.cornell.edu/topics/Table_Divorce.htm

Divorce Law Information
http://www.divorcelawinfo.com
[online advice]

Divorce Magazine
http://www.divorcemagazine.com
[magazine on emotional and legal issues involving divorce]

DivorceNet
http://www.divorcenet.com
[resource for finding family law attorneys in every state; interactive bulletin boards on divorce issues]

Electronic Reference Desk (Emory): Family Law
http://www.law.emory.edu/LAW/refdesk/subject/family.html

Find Forms: Legal Forms Search Engine
http://www.findforms.com
[covers approved forms for many states in family law and other areas of the law]

FindLaw: Family Law
http://www.findlaw.com/01topics/15family/index.html

Galaxy: Family Law Links
http://www.galaxy.com/galaxy/Government/Law/Family-Law.html

Georgetown Law Library: Family Law Links
http://www.ll.georgetown.edu/lr/rs/family.html

Hieros Gamos: Family Law
http://www.hg.org/family.html

Jurist: Law Guides: Family Law
http://jurist.law.pitt.edu/sg_fam.htm
[law professors teaching family law; family law resources]

LLRX (Law Library Resource Exchange): International Family Law
http://www.llrx.com/features/int_fam.htm

Megalaw: Family Law Links
http://www.megalaw.com/index.php3?content=research/TopicIndex/topfamily.html

My Counsel
http://www.mycounsel.com/content/familylaw

SplitUp
http://www.split-up.com
[emotional and legal issues of divorce]

United States Census Bureau
http://www.census.gov
[statistics on marriages, divorces, etc.]

ASSIGNMENT 1.4

a. Is your state statutory code on the Internet? If so, give its address (uniform resource locator or URL) and quote from any statute on this site that covers divorce.

b. Try to find the Internet address of the Web site of any law firm in your state that handles family law cases. If you cannot find one, select a neighboring state.

c. What adoption resources specifically geared to your state are on the Internet? Select any three, give their addresses, and describe their services.
d. Go to the main site for your state government and your county government. On these sites, how many state or county government agencies can you find that have authority over some aspect of child support? Pick any three, give their addresses, and describe their function. Be sure to include the major statewide agency responsible for child support.

SUMMARY

Family law defines relationships, rights, and duties in the formation, duration, and dissolution of marriage and other family units. Some of the major trends in the development of family law are the equality of the sexes, the federalization of family law, the increase in the role of contracts, the need for new laws to respond to scientific advances in childbearing, and the expansion of the family law rights of gays and lesbians. Someone working in a family law practice may encounter legal problems in a wide variety of areas in addition to basic family law. These other areas include criminal law, contract law, corporate and business law, real estate and property law, tort law, civil procedure law, evidence law, juvenile law, tax law, and estate law. Paralegals in family law perform many functions such as interviewing clients, drafting temporary orders and other court pleadings, preparing financial statements, preparing clients and witnesses for hearings and trials, maintaining the files, and assisting in discovery and trial. Because the cases handled in a family law practice can be emotionally charged, the need for professionalism and objectivity is clear, particularly if the office is representing a client who has done something that clashes with a worker's personal values. Do not give legal advice to friends and relatives who are seeking answers to legal questions concerning the facts of their specific legal problems. Violence is a concern in family law. Perhaps more than in any other area of law practice, there is a potential for violence among family members, and sometimes between defendant and opposing counsel.

Because family law is constantly changing, anyone working in this area must know how to keep current. The main resource for doing so is primary sources in traditional law books and online. The six most important legal publications for the family law practitioner are the state statutory code, court rules, court opinions, digests, practice manuals, and legal newspapers. There are two main ways to begin your research task. First, go directly to the primary sources, such as the statutory code (through their indexes), and the reporter volumes (through digests). You can also access these sources through computer databases such as WESTLAW, Lexis-Nexis, and Loislaw. Second, you could start with some of the main secondary sources, such as legal encyclopedias, legal treatises, legal periodicals, and annotations in the A.L.R. series. A great deal of information relevant to a family law practice is available online from commercial, fee-based services and from free sites on the Internet through the World Wide Web.

KEY CHAPTER TERMINOLOGY

family law
holding
common law
interrogatories
bias
objectivity
conflict of interest
primary authority
secondary authority
statutory code
court rules
court opinion
reporters
digest
practice manual
legal newspaper
legal encyclopedia
legal treatise
legal periodical
annotation
online
Internet
World Wide Web

ETHICS AND MALPRACTICE IN FAMILY LAW

CHAPTER OUTLINE

ETHICS

Introduction

ethics
Standards or rules of behavior to which members of an occupation, profession, or other organization are expected to conform.

An **ethics** study in one state revealed that 25 percent of all grievances filed against attorneys involved family law cases.[1] This was almost double the percentage for every other area of practice. An uncomfortably large number of family law clients eventually turn on their own attorney with a charge of unethical conduct. "Emotions tend to run high among the clients of divorce lawyers and it's not unusual for clients to 'blame' their lawyers for their misery, deservedly or not."[2] Needless to say, everyone working in a family law practice must be scrupulous about ethical matters. A family law paralegal cannot know too much about ethics.

sanctions
Penalties or punishments of some kind.

There are two main kinds of ethics: those that could lead to **sanctions** when violated and those that are not enforced by sanctions. All attorneys are subject to ethical rules that are backed by sanctions. These rules are called canons of ethics, codes of ethics, or rules of professional responsibility. They are issued and enforced by the courts, usually through the state bar association. The sanctions that courts can impose on attorneys for unethical conduct include a reprimand, suspension, or disbarment.

What happens when *paralegals* violate the canons of ethics? They could face immediate dismissal, but because they cannot be full members of the bar, they cannot be reprimanded, suspended, or "disbarred" by the courts for unethical behavior. Attorneys, however, can be sanctioned for a paralegal's failure to comply

[1] *Report: Lawyer Discipline,* Washington State Bar News 37 (Aug. 1993).

[2] *All Lawyers May Have It Bad with the Public, But Family Lawyers. . . ,* 11 Compleat Lawyer 6 (Winter 1994). (Source: New York Times, Sept. 5, 1993).

with the ethical duties described in this chapter. This is one of the reasons it is critically important that attorneys properly supervise their paralegals, as we will see. Some paralegal associations have written their own code of paralegal ethics. To a large extent, these codes are based on the ethical rules governing attorneys. The paralegal codes, however, are not backed by meaningful sanctions. If an association determines that a paralegal has violated its ethical code, it might remove the paralegal from the association or revoke any certification earned from the association, but this would not affect his or her right to practice as a paralegal.

ASSIGNMENT 2.1

a. Give the full citation to the ethical rules that govern the conduct of attorneys in your state.
b. What is the name of the bar association committee in your state that has jurisdiction over the ethical standards of attorneys? What disciplinary powers does this committee have over attorneys?
c. If an attorney is dissatisfied with the ruling of this committee concerning his or her ethical conduct, to what court can the attorney appeal? (To find answers to these questions, check your state statutory code and your state constitution. See General Instructions for the State Code Assignment in Appendix A. In addition, you may want to contact your state bar association. Ask it to send you any descriptive literature available on the system for disciplining attorneys.)
d. Draft a flowchart of all the procedural steps that must be taken to discipline an attorney for unethical conduct. (See General Instructions for the Flowchart Assignment in Appendix A.)

The American Bar Association (ABA) is a voluntary national bar association; attorneys are not required to be members. Although the ABA publishes ethical rules, it does not discipline attorneys for unethical conduct. Such conduct is regulated by the state court and the state bar association. The role of the ABA is to *propose* ethical rules for consideration by the various states. A state is free to adopt, modify, or reject the ethical rules recommended by the ABA. In view of the prestige of the ABA, many states have adopted its proposals with little change. The most recent proposals of the ABA are found within the very influential *Model Rules of Professional Conduct.* The following overview is based on these rules.

Ethical issues for the family law practitioner arise in the following major areas:

- Competence
- Fees
- Confidentiality of information
- Conflict of interest
- Safekeeping of property
- Withdrawal
- False statements/failure to disclose
- Misconduct
- Communication with the other side
- Nonattorney assistants
- Solicitation
- Advertising
- Unauthorized practice of law

Competence

Attorneys have an ethical obligation to represent their clients competently (Rule 1.1). A classic example of an incompetent family law attorney is one who accepts more cases than his or her office can handle. As a consequence, court dates and other filing deadlines are missed, documents are lost, and the attorney fails to determine what law governs each case. Such an attorney is practicing law "from the hip"—unethically.

competent
Using the knowledge, skill, thoroughness, and preparation reasonably needed to represent a particular client.

uncontested
Not disputed; not challenged.

Attorneys must be **competent.** The amount of knowledge and skill they need depends on the complexity of the case. A great deal may be needed when representing a wife in a divorce case where the issue is the present value of the husband's partially vested pension or his partnership interest in a foreign business. Relatively less is required for a garden-variety, **uncontested** divorce case in which the parties have no children and no assets.

How do ethical attorneys become competent? They draw on the general principles of analysis learned in law school. They take the time needed to *prepare* themselves. They spend time in the law library. They talk with their colleagues. In some instances, they formally associate themselves with more experienced attorneys in the area. An attorney who fails to take these steps is acting unethically if his or her knowledge and skill are not what is deemed reasonably necessary to represent a particular client.

Victory is not the measure of competence. Competent attorneys can lose cases. There is nothing unethical about losing a case if the attorney used the knowledge and skill reasonably needed to represent the client who lost. Some clients, however, have unreasonable expectations about the outcome of their case. Consequently, everyone in the law firm, particularly attorneys and paralegals, must avoid saying anything that could be interpreted as guaranteeing a particular result. For example, compare the following statements:

> "The court will grant you full custody."
>
> "While we can never predict what a court will do, we have good arguments that the court should grant you full custody."

The first statement can be interpreted as a warranty that the client is certain to be given full custody. If this result does not occur, the attorney might lose a breach-of-contract or breach-of-warranty suit brought by the client. In such a suit, the attorney cannot raise the defense that he or she competently represented the client in the custody dispute. A guarantee, once established, is measured by the result promised, not by whether reasonable knowledge and skill were used.

Fees

Attorney fees must be reasonable (Rule 1.5). There is no absolute rule on when a fee is excessive and therefore unreasonable. A number of factors must be considered: the amount of time and labor involved, the complexity of the matter, the experience and reputation of the attorney, the customary fee in the locality for the same kind of case, etc. The basis or rate of the fee should be communicated to the client before or soon after the attorney starts to work on the case. This is often done in the contract of employment called the **retainer.** (Two other meanings of *retainer* are the money paid by a client to ensure that an attorney will be available to work for the client and the deposit against future fees and costs of representation.)

retainer
(1) The contract of employment between attorney and client. (2) A fee to ensure an attorney's availability. (3) A deposit against future fees and costs.

fixed fee
A fee that is paid regardless of the outcome of the case.

contingent fee
A fee that is dependent on the outcome of the case.

There are two main kinds of fees: fixed or contingent. A **fixed fee** is one that is paid regardless of who wins the case. It may be a flat sum, an hourly rate, or a combination. A **contingent fee** is dependent on the outcome of the case, e.g., an attorney receives 30 percent of a jury award in a negligence case, but nothing if the client loses the case.

In most states, contingent fees in family law cases are unethical if they are directly tied to obtaining a divorce or to the amount of alimony, support, or property settlement. A main argument against contingent fees in such cases is that the attorney might be so anxious to obtain the divorce or a certain amount from the other side that he or she will interfere with possibilities of reconciliation between the parties—because the contingent fee is not paid if the parties get back together. When a benefit to one person conflicts or might conflict with a benefit to another person, a conflict of interest exists. An example is an attorney who has a contingent fee contract with a family law client on an alimony or child-support issue. The benefit to the attorney (receiving a fee only if the divorce goes through) conflicts with a benefit to the client (keeping alive the possibility of reconciliation). We discuss conflicts of interest in greater detail later in this chapter.

Suppose, however, that the parties are already divorced and the dispute is about unpaid alimony or child support—**arrearages.** Some states allow attorneys to charge a contingent fee in such cases. Because the marriage has already been dissolved, there is little likelihood that the attorney's personal interest in collecting this kind of contingent fee will hinder a reconciliation.

arrearages
Money overdue and unpaid.

ASSIGNMENT 2.2

Dan and Elaine were divorced in 1999. The divorce decree ordered Dan to pay $350 a month in child support for their daughter, which he has faithfully paid. A year later, Elaine goes to an attorney to seek help in obtaining an increase in child support to $500 a month. Is there any policy reason against the attorney taking this case for a fee of 20 percent of everything a court orders Dan to pay above $350 a month? (See General Instructions for the Legal Analysis Assignment in Appendix A.)

Finally, we examine the problem of **fee splitting.** This can occur in different situations. First, two lawyers from different firms might split a fee. For example:

fee splitting
(1) One bill to a client covering the fee of two or more attorneys not in the same firm. (2) Giving a nonattorney part of the fee of a particular client.

> *Ed Jones, Esq., and Mary Smith, Esq., both work on behalf of a client seeking a divorce. The client receives one bill for the work of both attorneys even though they work for different law firms.*

The attorneys are splitting or dividing the fee between them. This arrangement is proper under certain conditions, e.g., the total fee is reasonable, the client is told about and does not object to the participation of all the attorneys involved.

Second, an attorney might give part of a fee to a nonattorney. For example:

> *Bob Davis, Esq., has a large divorce practice. He has an arrangement with Alice Grover, an independent paralegal, under which Davis will pay Grover 40 percent of the fees he collects from every client she refers to him.*

This kind of fee splitting between an attorney and nonattorney involving a particular client is unethical even if the total amount of the fee is reasonable and the client consents to the split.

Confidentiality of Information

Attorneys must not disclose "information relating to representation of a client" unless the client consents to the disclosure or unless the attorney is reasonable in believing that the disclosure is needed to stop the client from committing a crime that is likely to lead to "imminent death or substantial bodily harm" (Rule 1.6). The confidentiality rule applies to *all* information relating to the representation of a client, whatever its source. The prohibition is not limited to so-called secrets or matters explicitly communicated in confidence. Here are some examples of unethical breaches of confidentiality:

- At home, a paralegal tells her husband that J. K. Thompson is one of the new divorce clients in the office where the paralegal works.

- In an elevator crowded with strangers, a paralegal tells her supervisor that the adoption notice in the Smith case came in today's mail.
- In an attorney's office, a client file is left open on the desk, where child-custody documents are visible to and glanced at by an electrician who is in the office repairing a light fixture.

The confidentiality rule is designed to encourage clients to discuss their cases fully and frankly with the law office they have hired, including embarrassing or legally damaging information. Arguably, clients would be reluctant to tell the office everything if they had to worry about whether an attorney, paralegal, or anyone else in the office might reveal the information to others.

In some situations, however, it is proper for an attorney to breach confidentiality. For example:

An attorney represents a husband in a bitter divorce case against his wife. During a meeting at the law firm, the husband shows the attorney a gun and says he is going to use it to kill his wife later the same day.

Can the attorney tell the police what the husband said? Yes. It is not unethical for an attorney to reveal information about a client if the attorney reasonably believes the disclosure is necessary to prevent the client from committing a criminal act that could lead to someone's imminent death or substantial bodily harm.

Conflict of Interest

conflict of interest
Divided loyalty that actually or potentially places a person at a disadvantage even though he or she is owed undivided loyalty.

Attorneys must avoid a conflict of interest with their clients (Rule 1.7). As we said earlier, a **conflict of interest** exists when a benefit to one person conflicts or might conflict with a benefit to another person. More precisely, it consists of divided loyalty that actually or potentially places a person at a disadvantage even though this person is owed undivided loyalty. Assume, for example, that a salesman does part-time work selling the same kind of products of two competing companies. The salesman has a conflict of interest. How can he serve two masters with the same loyalty? How does he divide his customers between the two companies? There is an obvious danger that he will favor one over the other. The fact that he may try to be fair in his treatment of both companies does not eliminate the conflict of interest. The potential exists for one of the companies to be disadvantaged. It may be that the two companies are aware of the problem and are not worried. This does not mean that there is no conflict of interest; it simply means that the affected parties are willing to take the risks involved in the conflict. As we shall see, consent is often a valid defense to a conflict-of-interest charge. Consent, however, does not mean that there was no conflict of interest.

In a family law practice, a number of conflict-of-interest issues can arise:

- Multiple representation
- Former client/present adversary
- Law firm disqualification
- Business transactions with a client
- Gifts from a client
- Loaning money to a client
- Sex with a client
- Bias

Multiple Representation

Bob and Patricia Fannan are separated, and they both want a divorce. They are contesting who should have sole custody of the children and how the marital property should be divided. Mary Franklin, Esq., is an attorney that Jim and Mary know and trust. They decide to ask Franklin to represent both of them in the divorce.

In this case, Franklin has a conflict of interest due to **multiple representation.** How can she give her undivided loyalty to both sides? On the custody question, for example, how can Franklin vigorously argue that Bob should have sole custody, and at the same time vigorously argue that Patricia should have sole custody? A client is entitled to the *independent professional judgment* of an attorney, particularly in a case where the parties are disputing or contesting a factual or legal issue. How can Franklin act independently for two different people who are at odds with each other? Franklin's commitment to be fair and objective in giving her advice to the parties will not solve the difficulty. Her role as attorney is to be a *partisan advocate* for the client. It is impossible for Franklin to play this role for two clients engaged in such a dispute. A clear conflict of interest exists. In every state, it would be unethical for Franklin to represent both Bob and Patricia in this case even though both parties consent to the multiple representation. Representing more than one side in a contested case is the most important example of an instance in which consent is *not* a defense to a conflict-of-interest charge against an attorney.

multiple representation
Representing more than one side in a legal matter or controversy. Also called *joint representation* and *common representation.*

Suppose, however, that the divorce case involved different facts:

> *Jim and Mary Smith are separated, and they both want a divorce. They have been married only a few months. There are no children and no marital assets to divide. George Davidson, Esq., is an attorney that Jim and Mary know and trust. They decide to ask Davidson to represent both of them in the divorce.*

Can Davidson ethically represent both sides here? Some states *will* allow him to do so, on the theory that there is not much of a conflict between the parties; hence, the potential for harm in multiple representation is almost nonexistent. Other states, however, disagree. They frown on multiple representation even in so-called friendly divorces of this kind.

The ABA *Model Rules of Professional Conduct* do not impose an absolute ban on multiple representation, although they certainly discourage it.

> It is unethical for an attorney to represent one client (client A) if doing so would be "directly adverse" to the interests of another client (client B) unless two conditions are met:
> (a) the attorney is reasonable in believing that client B would not be adversely affected by the attorney's representation of client A, and
> (b) both clients agree (consent) to allow the multiple representation after the risks are explained to them (Rule 1.7).

In the Smith divorce, both conditions can probably be met. Jim and Mary Smith are going through an uncontested divorce (called an "even dissolution" in some states). Their divorce will be little more than a paper procedure, as there is no real dispute between the parties. Hence Davidson *would* be reasonable in believing that his representation of Jim would not adversely affect Mary, and vice versa. Davidson can represent both sides so long as Jim and Mary consent to the multiple representation after Davidson clearly explains to both of them whatever risks might be involved in doing so.

Nevertheless, attorneys are urged to avoid multiple representation even when ethically proper. The divorce may have been "friendly" when granted, but years later, one of the ex-spouses may attack the attorney for having had a conflict of interest. When reminded that both parties consented to the multiple representation, the ex-spouse will inevitably respond by saying, "I didn't understand what I was being asked to consent to."

The coming of no-fault divorce (discussed in chapter 7) has in part been due to a desire to take some of the animosity out of the divorce process. A full **adversary** confrontation is not needed in every case, particularly when there is no custody dispute and few assets to divide. Hence there are pressures on the bar associations and the courts to relax the conflict-of-interest rules in divorce

adversary
(1) Involving a dispute between opposing sides who argue their case before a neutral official such as a judge. (2) An opponent.

cases in which the actual disputes between the parties are minimal or nonexistent. The legal profession is sensitive to the criticism that a too-strict application of the rules in such cases simply results in more business for more attorneys. Nevertheless, the cautious attorney remains understandably reluctant to take chances.

Former Client/Present Adversary

Jessica Winters, Esq., represented Gregory Noonan in his divorce action against his former wife, Eileen Noonan. In this action, Eileen received custody and alimony. Five years later, Eileen wants to reopen the case in order to obtain more alimony. Winters no longer represents Gregory, who now has a different attorney. Eileen hires Winters in her action for increased alimony.

A former client is now an adversary. Winters once represented Gregory; she now represents a party who is suing Gregory. Without the consent of the former client (Gregory), it is unethical for Winters to "switch sides" and represent Eileen against him. Consent is needed whenever the second case is the same as the first one, or when the two are substantially related. It is not necessary that the two cases involve the same set of parties. Without Gregory's consent, it would be equally unethical for Winters to represent one of his children who later sues the father for support to force him to pay college expenses. Such an action would be substantially related to the original divorce action.

Why is this so? If the cases are the same or are substantially related, the likelihood is strong that the attorney will use information learned in the first case to the detriment of the former client in the second case. Winters undoubtedly found out a good deal about Gregory when she represented him in the divorce case. She might now be able to use this information *against* him in Eileen's attempt to increase her alimony or in the child's attempt to force him to pay college expenses.

Winters had a duty of loyalty when she represented Gregory. This duty does not end once the attorney's fees are paid. The duty continues if the same case arises again or if a substantially related case arises later—even if the attorney no longer represents the client. A conflict of interest would exist if Winters subsequently acquires a new client who goes against Gregory in the same case or in a substantially related case. Her new duty of loyalty to the second client would clash with her *continuing* duty to the former client in such a case.

Suppose, however, that the second case against a former client is totally unrelated to the first. The attorney still has an ethical obligation to refrain from using any information relating to the representation in the first case to the disadvantage of the former client in the second case. There is no ban on taking the case, but if the office has any information relating to the first case, that information cannot be used against the former client in the second case.

Law Firm Disqualification

Two years ago, John Farrell, Esq., represented the father in a custody dispute with the child's maternal grandparent. The father won the case, but the grandmother was awarded limited visitation rights. The grandmother now wants to sue the father for failure to abide by the visitation order. She asks John Farrell to represent her. (The father is now using a different law firm.) John declines because of a conflict of interest, but he sends her to his law partner down the corridor.

If an attorney is disqualified from representing a client because of a conflict of interest, every attorney in the *same law firm* is also disqualified unless the client being protected by this rule consents to the representation. In the Farrell example, the *father* would have to consent to the representation of the grandmother by the partner or, indeed, by John Farrell himself. The disqualification of the partner and the entire law firm is called an **imputed disqualification.** It occurs when an attorney causes another attorney or law firm to be disqualified. In effect, John Farrell's knowledge about the father is imputed (i.e., attributed) to the partner and everyone else in the firm.

imputed disqualification
A loss of qualification that is forced upon or attributed to someone or something else.

A paralegal can also cause the imputed disqualification of a law firm. This situation most commonly arises when the paralegal switches jobs. For example:

> *Claire Anderson is a paralegal at the firm of Lawrence Burton, Esq. Her sole assignment is to work on the Vickers divorce case. The firm represents Sam Vickers. One of Anderson's tasks is to make an inventory of all the assets of Sam Vickers. His wife, Karen Vickers, is represented by Edward Walsh, Esq. Before this case comes to trial, Anderson quits her job with Burton and becomes a paralegal with Walsh, who immediately assigns her to the Vickers case. When Burton finds out that Anderson has performed substantial work on the Vickers case, he makes a motion in court to disqualify Walsh from continuing to represent Karen Vickers.*

This motion will probably be granted. A conflict of interest exists that will cause the imputed disqualification of Edward Walsh from any further involvement in the Vickers case. Claire Anderson once worked as a paralegal on behalf of Sam Vickers and acquired information about him in the process. She is now in a position to use this knowledge against him. Her knowledge is imputed to her new employer, Edward Walsh, who is therefore now disqualified and must withdraw from the case. Karen Vickers must find someone else to represent her.

Suppose, however, that Claire Anderson had *not* done any substantial paralegal work on the Vickers case before she arrived at the new firm. Is her new employer still disqualified? In many states, the answer is *no,* if the new employer places a **Chinese wall** around the paralegal. This involves isolating the **tainted** paralegal from the case through specific steps such as ordering the paralegal to say nothing about the case and have no involvement with it, instructing all other employees in the firm to refrain from discussing the case with the paralegal, and physically storing the file on the case in a section of the office away from the paralegal. If a paralegal with a conflict of interest is effectively screened from the case in this manner, most states will not impose an imputed disqualification on the paralegal's new employer.

Chinese wall
Steps taken in an office to prevent a tainted employee from having any contact with a particular case in order to avoid the disqualification of the office from the case.

tainted
Having a conflict of interest in a case.

CASE

Ethics Opinion: RPC 176[3]

July 21, 1994
Ethics Committee of the North Carolina State Bar
19 North Carolina State Bar Newsletter 16 (1994); 1994 Westlaw 899356

Background: *In most states, attorneys can submit ethical questions to the ethics committee of their state bar association. Names of specific clients are not mentioned. The question or inquiry is presented in a generic form to preserve the confidentiality of the clients involved.*

Inquiry

Attorney A had two full-time staff members: a receptionist/secretary and a paralegal/secretary ("Paralegal"). Paralegal's normal duties included working on personal injury actions and real estate matters. On occasion, Paralegal helped with domestic actions. While Paralegal was employed by Attorney A, Attorney A represented Client A in a domestic matter. Paralegal denies working on the case on a regular basis while she was employed by Attorney A. Paralegal also denies having any knowledge of the specific facts of the case. Attorney A contends that Paralegal was substantially involved in assisting in the representation of Client A and was privy to confidential information

[3]Reprinted with the permission of the N.C. State Bar.

continued

CASE

Ethics Opinion: RPC 176—*Continued*

regarding Client A. It is clear that Paralegal had some exposure to the case while employed by Attorney A.

After the employment of Paralegal was terminated by Attorney A, Paralegal went to work for Attorney B in another law firm. Attorney B represents Client B in same domestic action in which Attorney A represents Client A.

Attorney A has requested that Attorney B withdraw from the representation of Client B because of Paralegal's prior involvement in the action. Should Attorney B withdraw from the representation of Client B?

Opinion

No, Attorney B may continue to represent Client B in the case and may continue to employ Paralegal. . . . However, Attorney B must take extreme care to ensure that Paralegal is totally screened from participation in the case even if Paralegal's involvement in the case while employed by Attorney A was negligible. See RPC 74. This requirement is consistent with a lawyer's duty, pursuant to Rule 3.3(B), to make reasonable efforts to ensure that the conduct of a nonlawyer over whom the lawyer has direct supervisory authority is compatible with the professional obligations of the lawyer including the obligation to avoid conflicts of interest and to preserve the confidentiality of client information.

ASSIGNMENT 2.3

a. Opinion RPC 176 says that "extreme care" must be used to ensure that the tainted paralegal is "totally screened" from the family law ("domestic") case. Make a list of the steps Attorney B can take to accomplish this.

b. Assume that the paralegal makes a mistake and discloses something relatively unimportant about the case to Attorney B. For example, the paralegal tells Attorney B that the client in the case was once late for an appointment at the law office of Attorney A. Do you think the North Carolina Ethics Committee would conclude that Opinion RPC 176 had been violated?

Business Transactions with a Client

Paul Kelly, Esq., is Ed Johnson's attorney in a divorce case. Johnson owns a cleaning business for which Kelly does some of the legal work. Johnson offers to allow Kelly to buy a 30 percent interest in the business. Kelly would continue as Johnson's attorney.

Assume that the business runs into difficulties and Johnson considers bankruptcy. He goes to Kelly for advice on bankruptcy law. Kelly has dual concerns: to give Johnson competent legal advice, and to protect his own 30 percent interest in the business. Bankruptcy may be good for Johnson, but disastrous for Kelly's investment, or vice versa. How can he give Johnson independent professional advice when the advice may go against Kelly's own interest?

This is not to say, however, that it is always unethical for an attorney to enter a business transaction with a client. If certain strict conditions are met, it can be proper. The rule is as follows:

> A business transaction with a client is allowed if three conditions are met: (a) the terms of the transaction are "fair and reasonable" and are clearly explained to the client in writing,
>
> (b) the client has an opportunity to consult with another attorney on the advisability of entering the transaction, and
>
> (c) The client gives his or her written consent to entering the transaction (Rule 1.8).

In our example, Johnson must be given the chance to consult with an attorney other than Kelly on the prospect of letting Kelly buy a 30 percent interest in the business; Kelly would have to give Johnson a clear, written explanation of their business relationship; and the relationship must be fair and reasonable to Johnson.

Gifts from a Client

> *William Stanton, Esq., has been the family attorney of the Tarkinton family for years. At Christmas, Mrs. Tarkinton gave Stanton a television set and told Stanton to change her will so that Stanton's daughter would receive funds to cover her college education.*

Generally, attorneys are allowed to accept a gift from a client. If, however, a document must be prepared to carry out the gift, it is unethical for the attorney to prepare that document. A conflict of interest would exist. In our example, it would probably be in Mrs. Tarkinton's interest to have the will written so that she could retain maximum flexibility on how much she would pay for the college education and so that she could change her mind if she wanted to. Yet it would be in Stanton's interest to try to write the will so that it would be difficult for her to back out of her commitment.

Thus, an attorney cannot prepare a document such as a will, a trust fund instrument, a contract, etc., that results in any substantial gift from a client to the attorney, or to the attorney's children, spouse, parents, brothers, or sisters. If a client wants to make such a gift, another attorney must prepare the document. There is, however, one exception. If the client is *related* to the person receiving the gift, the attorney can prepare the document.

There does not appear to be any ethical problem in taking the gift of the television set. No documents are involved.

Loaning Money to a Client

> *Henry Harris, Esq., is Barbara Atkinson's attorney in a divorce action against her husband. While the case is pending, Harris agrees to lend Atkinson living expenses and court filing fees.*

It can be a conflict of interest for an attorney to give financial assistance to a client in connection with current or planned litigation. A loan covering litigation expenses, however, is an exception to this rule. In our example, the main difficulty is the loan to cover the client's living expenses. Suppose that the husband makes an offer to settle the case with Barbara. There is a danger that Harris's advice will be colored by the fact that he has a financial interest in Barbara—he wants to have his loan for living expenses repaid. The offer to settle from the husband may not be enough to cover the loan. Should he advise Barbara to accept the offer? It may be in Barbara's interest to accept the offer, but not in the attorney's own interest. Such divided loyalty is the essence of a conflict of interest.

As indicated, a major exception concerns the expenses of litigation, such as filing fees and other court costs. It is not unethical for an attorney to lend the client money to cover such expenses.

Sex with a Client

One of the more dramatic examples of a conflict of interest is the attorney who develops a romantic relationship with a current client, particularly a sexual relationship. Family law clients often come to attorneys when the clients are most vulnerable. Under such circumstances, it is unconscionable for the attorney to take advantage of this vulnerability. An attorney with a physical or emotional interest in a client will be looking for ways to increase that interest and to inspire a reciprocal interest from the client. Needless to say, this may not be what the client needs, but the attorney's own need could well cloud his or her ability to put the client's welfare first. The only way to maintain professional independence is for attorneys—as well as their paralegals and other employees—to avoid these kinds of relationships with current clients. When the cases are over, however, and they cease being clients, such relationships are less likely to constitute a conflict of interest.

Surprisingly, however, only a few states specifically mention this subject in their code of ethics. Those that do are hesitant to impose prohibitions. The Florida code, for example, provides that sexual conduct is prohibited only if it can be shown that the conduct "exploits the lawyer-client relationship" (Rule 4-8.4). In California, a member of the bar shall not:

> (B) (1) Require or demand sexual relations with a client incident to or as a condition of any professional representation; or
>
> (2) Employ coercion, intimidation, or undue influence in entering into sexual relations with a client; or
>
> (3) Continue representation of a client with whom the member has sexual relations if such sexual relations cause the member to perform legal services incompetently . . . .
>
> (C) Paragraph (B) shall not apply to . . . ongoing consensual sexual relationships which predate the initiation of the lawyer-client relationship [Rule 3-120].

Bias

On how bias in an attorney or paralegal can be a conflict of interest, see "Assessing Your Own Biases" in chapter 1.

Safekeeping of Property

An attorney shall hold client property separate from the attorney's own property (Rule 1.15). Every law office has an account that is used to pay items such as salaries, rent, and other office expenses. Client funds must not be placed in this account; client funds *must* be kept in separate accounts (Rule 1.15.) The **commingling of funds** is unethical no matter how accurate the records are on who owns the amounts in the account. In a commingled account, the danger is simply too great that client funds will be used for non-client purposes. This is extremely important for paralegals to know, as they are often placed in charge of bookkeeping records in a law firm. Their supervising attorney may tell them that "it's OK to put everything in a single account." Doing something unethical, however, is never OK.

commingling of funds
Mixing general law-firm funds with client funds in a single account. More broadly, combining one's own funds with the funds of persons to whom a fiduciary duty is owed.

Withdrawal

Attorneys are not required to take every case. Furthermore, once attorneys begin a case, they are not obligated to stay with a client until the case is over. If, however, the attorney has been appointed or assigned to the case by a judge, or if the case has already begun in court, the permission of the court must usually be obtained before withdrawal is ethical.

There are circumstances in which an attorney must not accept a case or must withdraw from a case:

- The representation of the client would violate the law, e.g., the attorney is asked for advice on how to defraud the Internal Revenue Service on an alimony deduction.
- The representation of the client would violate ethical rules, e.g., the attorney discovers he or she has a conflict of interest with the client that cannot be cured by consent.
- The client fires the attorney.
- The attorney's physical or mental condition has deteriorated (e.g., alcohol problems, depression due to grief) to the point where the attorney's ability to represent the client has been materially impaired (Rule 1.16).

An attorney has the option of withdrawing if the client insists on an objective that the attorney considers "repugnant" (e.g., the client wants to pursue custody litigation solely to harass the other parent) or "imprudent" (e.g., the client insists that a motion be refiled that the attorney feels is an obvious waste of time and is likely to incur the anger of the court).

False Statements/Failure to Disclose

An attorney must not knowingly (1) make false statements of "material fact or law" to a court or other tribunal; (2) fail to tell a court or other tribunal about a "material fact" that is needed to avoid providing assistance to the client to commit fraud or a crime; (3) fail to tell a court or other tribunal about legal authority that the attorney knows is "directly adverse" to the attorney's client; or (4) offer evidence the attorney knows is false (Rule 3.3(a)). One of the reasons the legal profession is held in low esteem by the general public is the perception that attorneys do not always comply with Rule 3.3(a).

The implications of subsection 3 of the rule are particularly startling.

Karen Singer and Bill Carew are attorneys opposing each other in a bitter divorce case involving a large sum of money. Singer is smarter than Carew. Singer knows about a very damaging but obscure case that goes against her client. Because of sloppy research, Carew does not know about it. Singer never mentions the case and it never comes up during the litigation.

Singer may pay a price for her silence. She is subject to sanctions for a violation of her ethical obligation of disclosure under Rule 3.3(a)(3).

Misconduct

An attorney shall not commit a criminal act that reflects adversely on the fitness of the attorney. Nor shall an attorney engage in any conduct involving dishonesty, fraud, or misrepresentation (Rule 8.4). Conduct of an attorney that constitutes a crime (e.g., stealing a client's property) can lead to criminal prosecution by the state and to ethical discipline by the bar association. If the state decides not to prosecute, discipline for ethical misconduct under Rule 8.4 is still possible if the bar association (and the supervising court) determines that what the attorney did involved dishonesty, fraud, or misrepresentation.

Communication with the Other Side

If attorney A knows that an opposing party is represented by attorney B, then attorney A cannot communicate with that party about the case unless attorney B consents to the communication (Rule 4.2). If an attorney knows that an opposing party is not represented, that attorney must not give this party the impression that the attorney is uninvolved in the case (Rule 4.3). The great fear is that an attorney will take advantage of the other side.

Dan and Theresa Kline have just separated and are thinking about a divorce. Each claims the marital home. Theresa hires Thomas Darby, Esq., to represent her. Darby calls Dan to ask if Dan is interested in settling the case.

It is unethical for Darby to contact Dan about the case if Darby knows that Dan has his own attorney. (The same would be true of efforts to contact Dan made by paralegals or other employees of Darby.) The communication must be with Dan's attorney. Only the latter can give Darby permission to communicate with Dan. If Dan does not have an attorney, Darby can talk with Dan, but he must not allow Dan to be misled about Darby's role. Dan must be made to understand that Darby works for the other side. It would be unethical for Darby to suggest that he is **disinterested.** The only advice Darby can ethically give Dan in such a situation is to obtain his own attorney.

disinterested
Impartial; having no desire or interest in either side winning.

Nonattorney Assistants

Attorneys act unethically if they do not properly supervise nonattorneys working in the office. Such supervision must include "appropriate instruction" on the ethical rules governing an attorney's conduct (Rule 5.3).

> *Thomas Monroe, Esq., has a busy family law practice consisting of himself and a part-time secretary. He decides to hire Alex Ogden, a paralegal who recently graduated from a paralegal program. Ogden did not take a family law course in school and has never worked in this area of the law. Monroe gives him the files of all current divorce cases and asks him to "read through them to get an idea of the kind of cases we handle in this office." Since Ogden arrived, Monroe has spent a great deal of time in court. Ogden is often alone in the office. During these times, divorce clients call with questions about their cases. Ogden takes these calls and answers the questions as best he can based on whatever information he finds in the files and on his general understanding of family law. Here are examples of questions he has answered: "When is the date of my next hearing?" "Have you received the appraisal from my husband's lawyer?" "Can I sue my ex-husband for the slanderous things he has been saying about me to our daughter?"*

legal advice
Telling a specific person how the law applies to the facts of that person's legal problem or concern.

Monroe is unethically failing to supervise his paralegal. Indeed, there seems to be almost no supervision at all. An attorney cannot hire a paralegal and then disappear. Employees must be given needed on-the-job training and supervision. One of the dangers of having unsupervised employees is that they might give clients **legal advice.** This would be unethical even if the advice were correct. The first two examples of questions Ogden answered (on the date of a hearing and the receipt of an appraisal) do not call for legal advice. They are simply factual questions that do not require the application of law to the facts of a particular client's legal problem. The opposite is true of the last example. Ogden would be providing legal advice if he tells a client whether her husband can be sued for slander.

Solicitation

An attorney must not telephone or meet with someone with whom the attorney has no family or prior professional connection if a purpose of the contact is to seek to be retained for a monetary fee (Rule 7.3).

> *Frank Ellis, Esq., stands outside the office of a marriage counselor and gives a business card to any depressed, angry, or otherwise distraught husband or wife coming out of the office after a therapy session. The card says that Ellis is an attorney specializing in divorce cases.*

Ellis's way of looking for prospective divorce clients is pejoratively referred to as "ambulance chasing." There is no indication that Ellis is related to any of the people coming out of the therapy sessions, nor that he has any prior professional relationship with them, e.g., as former clients. Ellis appears to have one goal: finding a source of fees. His conduct is therefore unethical under Rule 7.3. This kind of solicitation would also be improper for the attorney's paralegals or other employees whom he sends out to try to "drum up business." The goal of the rule is to avoid exerting undue influence on a stranger in need. Citizens should not be pressured into using the legal system or into using a particular attorney at a time when they may be vulnerable to such pressure.

A different result would follow if Ellis engaged in proper *advertising,* a topic to which we now turn.

Advertising

An attorney must not engage in false or misleading advertising in the newspaper, on television, or in other media (Rule 7.2). At one time, almost all forms of advertising by attorneys were disallowed. In 1977, however, the United States Supreme Court stunned the legal profession by holding that truthful advertising cannot be completely prohibited.[4] The First Amendment protects such advertising. Furthermore, truthful and nonmisleading advertising to the general public does not pose the same danger of undue pressure on specific persons from attorneys primarily interested in money.

The Supreme Court opinion has had a dramatic impact on the legal profession. Prior to the opinion, traditional attorneys considered most forms of advertising to be highly offensive to the dignity of the profession. Many still do. Although the 1977 opinion forced the profession to change, the scope of this change is still the subject of debate, because the Supreme Court did not prohibit all regulation of attorney advertising. Consequently, states differ on what regulations should be imposed.

Unauthorized Practice of Law

An attorney must not help a nonattorney engage in the unauthorized practice of law. Lay people can represent themselves. Thus, an attorney who gives assistance to such people in their endeavor is not engaging in the unauthorized practice of law. Suppose, however, that an attorney assists a nonattorney in helping *others* with their legal problems:

> *Sam Grondon is a nonattorney who sells Do-It-Yourself Divorce Kits. A kit contains all the forms for a divorce in the state, plus written instructions on how to use the forms. Paulene Unger, Esq., writes the kits and obtains a royalty from Sam on every sale. She never talks to any buyers of the kits. Most customers make their purchase by mail without talking to Sam. A few customers go to Sam's house to buy the kits. Occasionally, Sam will answer questions to help these buyers decide which forms they need to file and how to fill them out.*

Has Paulene assisted a nonattorney in the unauthorized practice of law? Yes, but only with respect to the customers who come to Sam's home and receive in-person instruction on selecting and filling out the forms. Such activity is the unauthorized practice of law, and an attorney must not assist someone to engage in it. It is proper for a nonattorney to sell (and, indeed, to write) how-to-do-it texts and to give written instructions on using the material in the texts—so long as the instructions are not directed at a particular person. Giving generalized legal instructions to the public at large is not the practice of law. Kits on divorcing yourself, suing your landlord, incorporating, etc., are illegal only when personal legal advice is provided along with the kits—as when Sam helped particular buyers select and fill out the forms. An attorney acts unethically to the extent that he or she is associated with a nonattorney engaged in such activity.

Earlier we said that paralegals should not give legal advice. If an attorney-employer allows such advice to be given by paralegals in the office, the attorney is allowing, and therefore is assisting, nonattorneys (the paralegals) to engage in the unauthorized practice of law.

---

[4]*Bates v. State Bar of Ariz.*, 433 U.S. 350 (1977).

ASSIGNMENT 2.4

Smith is an attorney who works at the firm of Johnson & Johnson. He represents Ralph Grant, who is seeking a divorce against his wife, Alice Grant. In their first meeting, Smith learns that Ralph is an experienced carpenter who is out of work and has very little money. Smith's fee is $150 an hour. Ralph has no money and has been having trouble finding work, so Smith tells Ralph that he will not have to pay the fee if the court does not grant him the divorce. One day while Smith is working on another case involving Helen Oberlin, he learns that Helen is looking for a carpenter. Smith recommends Ralph to Helen, and she hires him for a small job.

Six months pass. The divorce case is dropped when the Grants reconcile. In the meantime, Helen Oberlin is very dissatisfied with Ralph's carpentry work for her; she claims he did not do the work he contracted to do. She wants to know what she can do about it. She tries to call Smith at Johnson & Johnson, but is told that Smith does not work there anymore. Another lawyer at the firm, Georgia Quinton, Esq., helps Helen.

Have any ethical violations occurred in this situation? See the General Instructions for the Legal-Analysis Assignment in Appendix A.

OTHER WRONGDOING

In addition to disciplinary actions by the bar association and state court for unethical conduct, a number of other sanctions are possible. Those listed here are separate from the discipline imposed on attorneys for unethical conduct, but often the same conduct that leads to one of the following sanctions is also the basis for a disciplinary action for unethical conduct. The phrase *legal malpractice* usually refers to the last item on the list, negligence.[5]

- Contempt of court
- Criminal action
- Malicious prosecution
- Abuse of process
- Defamation
- Negligence

Contempt of Court

An attorney can be cited for contempt of court for conduct such as insulting a judge in open court or flagrantly disobeying a court order. The punishment for such conduct can be a fine or imprisonment.

Criminal Conduct

An attorney, like any citizen, can be convicted of a crime. Stealing a client's funds, for example, can lead to a larceny or embezzlement conviction. Obstruction of justice and certain kinds of income tax evasion are also crimes.

Malicious Prosecution

Malicious prosecution is a tort brought against someone for maliciously instituting legal proceedings. Here is an example of how an attorney could become a defendant in a malicious prosecution action:

After a bitter divorce proceeding, Diana is awarded custody of the only child of the marriage. George, her ex-husband, asks his attorney to institute proceedings against Diana to remove custody of the child from her because

---

[5]See also W. Statsky. *Torts: Personal Injury Litigation* (4th ed. 2001).

she is a prostitute. It is clear to the attorney, however, that Diana is not a prostitute and that George wants to bring the action solely to "get even" with her. Nevertheless, the attorney agrees to go ahead. The strategy they decide to take is to file a criminal neglect case against Diana because of the prostitution. They ask a court to take the child away from her. George is the complaining witness against Diana in the criminal neglect proceeding.

The prosecutor loses the criminal case; Diana is acquitted of criminal neglect.

Diana now brings a malicious prosecution civil suit against both *George and his attorney. She will win if she can establish the elements of the tort of malicious prosecution. The proceedings must have ended in her favor. That happened here when Diana was acquitted of the criminal charge. The tort also requires proof of malice, which means that the primary purpose in bringing the case was improper. That was so because George and his attorney did not bring the case against Diana in the good faith belief that it could be won; they both knew that the criminal charge had no foundation.*

Abuse of Process

Suppose an attorney advises a client to institute an otherwise valid criminal action against an individual solely for the purpose of pressuring that individual to settle a pending divorce action on favorable terms. The attorney and the person initiating the criminal action may both be liable for the separate tort called *abuse of process.* They both misused the criminal court process: forcing someone to settle a divorce suit is not one of the purposes of the criminal law.

Defamation

In the course of heated litigation, it would not be uncommon for an attorney to defame one of the parties, a nonparty witness, or the other attorney. If, however, the defamation occurs in connection with a court proceeding, the defaming attorney enjoys the defense of absolute privilege.

Negligence

negligence
Unreasonable conduct that causes injury or damage to someone to whom the actor owes a duty of reasonable care.

One in every seventeen attorneys will be sued for **negligence** during his or her career. In a negligence suit against an attorney, the standard of care against which the attorney's conduct will be measured is the *reasonable person,* with the qualification that because the attorney holds him or herself out as a person with special skills, the standard of care will be a reasonable person possessing such skills. The attorney will not be liable simply because he or she made a mistake or lost a case. Unless the attorney specifically guarantees a result, the standard of care will be reasonableness, not warranty. Expressed in greater detail, the standard is as follows:

> An attorney who acts in good faith and in an honest belief that his advice and acts are well founded and in the best interest of his client is not answerable for a mere error of judgment or for a mistake in a point of law which has not been settled by the court of last resort in his State and on which reasonable doubt may be entertained by well-informed lawyers.
>
> Conversely, he is answerable in damages for any loss to his client which proximately results from a want of that degree of knowledge and skill ordinarily possessed by others of his profession similarly situated, or from the omission to use reasonable care and diligence, or from the failure to exercise in good faith his best judgment in attending to the litigation committed to his care.[6]

---

[6]*Hodges v. Carter,* 239 N.C. 517, 519–20, 80 S.E.2d 144, 145–46 (1954).

A distinction should be made between:

- A mistake that could have been made by any attorney in good standing using the skill and knowledge normally possessed by attorneys, and
- A mistake that would not have been made by an attorney in good standing using the skill and knowledge normally possessed by attorneys.

Only the latter category of mistake is considered unreasonable and hence will lead to liability for negligence. The test is not whether the *average* attorney would have made the mistake. The focus is on the attorney *in good standing* using the knowledge and skills *ordinarily* or *normally* found in attorneys.

It is important to keep in mind that the attorney is the *agent* of the client. While the attorney is representing the client (within the scope of the attorney's "employment"), the client is bound by what the attorney does. This includes both successes and mistakes. Therefore, if the attorney makes a mistake and the client loses the case as a result, the client's recourse is to sue the attorney and try to establish that an unreasonable mistake was made that would not have been made by an attorney in good standing using the skill and knowledge normally possessed by attorneys.[7]

When family law attorneys are charged with legal malpractice, the most frequent error alleged by the client is the failure to obtain the client's consent to an action taken on the client's behalf. Other common errors include failure to follow a client's instructions, failure to know the law, inadequate investigation, and insufficient supervision of staff.[8] The problem is serious. "Claims against family law practitioners account for the fourth highest percentage of all malpractice claims against lawyers."[9]

Avoiding Malpractice: Practice Guide[10]

With the dramatic increase in the number of malpractice claims that are being asserted against lawyers, the need for methods of reducing a lawyer's potential exposure to liability is obvious. There are a variety of practices lawyers can institute to improve their chances of avoiding malpractice:

- Decline representation of prospective clients whose legal matter, expectation about the legal system, or personality gives a strong impression of trouble.
- Use a system to screen prospective clients' cases for actual and potential conflicts of interest.
- If a prospective client's business is declined, put that decision in writing and send a nonengagement letter to the would-be client. [The letter should explicitly state that the lawyer is not accepting the case and that the individual should seek other counsel.]
- Establish what services the client wants and shape the client's expectations to encourage an understanding of what the lawyer and legal system can and cannot accomplish, and how long it may take to resolve the matter.
- Do not make promises or guarantees of results unless they can be fulfilled.

[7]Depending upon the kind of mistake the attorney made, some courts might permit the client to "undo" the error by correcting it, e.g., permit a client to file a document even though the client's attorney had negligently allowed the deadline for filing to pass. It is rare, however, that the courts will be this accommodating. A client will have to live with the mistakes of his or her attorney and seek relief solely by suing the attorney for negligence. See R. Mallen & V. Levit, *Legal Malpractice* 45ff (1977).

[8]American Bar Association, National Legal Malpractice Center, *Predominant Errors in Family Law,* in *History of Statistical Analysis* (1985).

[9]Lauren O'Brien & Mark S. Kannett, *Common Areas of the Family Law Malpractice Exposure,* 14 Fair$hare 7 (no. 4, Apr. 1994).

[10]Reprinted with permission from *ABA/BNA's Lawyers' Manual on Professional Conduct,* pp. 301:1001. Copyright © 1989 by the American Bar Association/The Bureau of National Affairs, Inc.

- Always use a written representation agreement that sets out both the objects of the retainer and the details of the fee arrangement.
- Maintain rapport with the client and keep him or her informed of all the significant occurrences in the case.
- Bill the client regularly and detail the services rendered.
- Research both the facts and law of the client's case before commencing legal action on his or her behalf.
- Have an effective time and docket control system.
- Refer cases to, or associate with, more experienced counsel when necessary, but check the other lawyer's qualifications first to assure his or her good standing and expertise.
- Do not withhold legal services on the sole basis that the client has not paid your fee. [If you must withdraw from a case, do so properly. If the case has already begun in court, you may need the court's permission to withdraw.]
- Stay out of business deals with clients.
- Think twice before suing a client to recover payment of your fee.
- Be aware of situations in which liability to nonclient third parties could arise.

PARALEGALS

Our concern is twofold: when is a paralegal liable for his or her wrongdoing, and when is the employing attorney liable for the wrongdoing of the paralegal? The governing principle of employer liability is **respondeat superior.** Assume that George Rothwell is a paralegal working for Helen Farrell, Esq. In the course of George's job, he does some negligent work that harms a client. Helen Farrell, Esq., is liable to the client for this negligence even if she did nothing wrong or negligently herself. She is **vicariously liable** because she stands in the place of someone else who actually committed the wrong.

respondeat superior
Doctrine stating that an employer is responsible for the conduct of employees while they are acting within the scope of employment.

vicariously liable
Being liable or incurring liability because of what someone else has done or failed to do.

It is important to keep in mind, however, that employees are *also* responsible for their own torts. The client in this example could elect to bring a direct action against the paralegal, George Rothwell, for negligence.

Respondeat superior is simply a basis upon which liability can be imposed on the employer in the event that the client decides not to sue the employee directly or decides to sue both the employer and the employee. Of course, the client cannot obtain double damages by suing the master (employer) and the servant (employee). There can be only one recovery. The choice is usually to pursue the **deep pocket.** Most often, of course, this is the employer.

deep pocket
The person who probably has sufficient resources to pay damages if a judgment is awarded by a court.

When a paralegal makes a serious mistake leading to a malpractice claim against the law firm by a client, a frequent allegation is that the attorney failed to supervise the paralegal adequately. Too often busy family law attorneys overrely on their paralegals. According to one malpractice specialist, overdelegation without supervision can be a serious problem, "[e]specially in the domestic relations area, where paralegals are extensively utilized. . . . I have seen attorneys allow their paralegals to do all of the client's work except for court appearances. There are situations where the client never once met or talked to an attorney."[11] The potential for malpractice claims in such offices is high.

---

[11]Stacey Hunt, *Attorney Supervision of Paralegals,* Recap 10 (California Alliance of Paralegal Associations, Fall 1998).

CASE

In Re Eloy F. Martinez

107 N.M. 171, 754 P.2d 842 (1988)
Supreme Court of New Mexico

Background: *John Felix is the paralegal of Eloy F. Martinez, Esq., a New Mexico attorney. The paralegal committed a number of improprieties, e.g., he failed to inform clients that he was not an attorney and he gave legal advice to a client. A grievance was filed against Martinez before the disciplinary board governing attorneys in the state. The board found that Martinez acted unethically in the way he ran his practice. He now appeals to the Supreme Court of New Mexico. (The portion of the opinion reprinted below pertains to the family law case on which the paralegal worked.)*

Decision on Appeal: *The conclusion of the Disciplinary Board is affirmed.*

Opinion of Court:

PER CURIAM . . .

Martinez employed the services of [a] legal assistant named John Felix, who is not a licensed attorney. Felix maintained his own office separate from the offices of Martinez. . . . In early February 1987, Martinez accepted a $1000 retainer from Nina Martinez (no relation to him) to obtain for her a divorce and a restraining order against her husband. She told [Martinez] that the matter was of some urgency. Martinez never filed a divorce petition or sought a restraining order, although his legal assistant Felix represented to Nina Martinez that this had been done. In early April, Nina Martinez became the respondent in a divorce action filed by her husband and was forced to leave the family home with her children. Martinez filed a brief response to the petition on behalf of his client, but took no steps to preserve for her any share of the community assets, which were subsequently disposed of by her husband.

Nina Martinez wrote to Martinez in mid-May discharging him as her attorney and requesting a refund. When Martinez did not respond to her letter, she retained the services of another attorney who also wrote to Martinez requesting the file, an accounting, and a refund of any unused portion of the fee advanced to him by Nina Martinez. Martinez signed and returned a Substitution of Attorney, but otherwise ignored the attorney's requests.

In this instance, Martinez violated SCRA 1986, 16-103[1] by his lack of diligence in representing a client. His failure to provide his client with an accounting of her money and an appropriate refund as requested or to produce any records to even indicate the money had been placed in trust and appropriate records maintained violated SCRA 1986, 16-115(A) and (B).[2] A fee of $1000 constitutes a clearly excessive fee under the facts presented and is violative of SCRA 1986, 16-105(A).[3] The failure of Martinez to protect his client's interests upon withdrawal by promptly forwarding the file to her new attorney and refunding any fee that was advanced but not earned, violated SCRA 1986, 16-116(D).[4] . . . [T]he misconduct of a legal assistant is imputed to an attorney under SCRA 1986, 16-503(C).[5] Martinez thus bears

---

[1]RULE 16-103. A lawyer shall act with reasonable diligence and promptness in representing a client.

[2]RULE 16-115. Safekeeping property.

A. Holding another's property separately. A lawyer shall hold property of clients or third persons that is in a lawyer's possession in connection with a representation separate from the lawyer's own property. Funds shall be kept in a separate account. . . . Complete records of such account funds and other property shall be kept by the lawyer . . . and shall be preserved for a period of five (5) years after termination of the representation of the client in the matter or the termination of the fiduciary or trust relationship.

B. Notification of receipt of funds or property. Upon receiving funds or other property in which a client or third person has an interest, a lawyer shall promptly notify the client or third person.. . .

[3]RULE 16-105. Fees. A. Determination of reasonableness. A lawyer's fee shall be reasonable. The factors to be considered in determining the reasonableness of a fee include the following:

(1) the time and labor required, the novelty and difficulty of the questions involved, and the skill requisite to perform the legal service properly; . . . .

[4]RULE 16-116. Declining or terminating representation. . . .

D. Orderly termination. Upon termination of representation, a lawyer shall take steps to the extent reasonably practicable to protect a client's interests, such as giving reasonable notice to the client, allowing time for employment of other counsel, surrendering papers and property to which the client is entitled and refunding any advance payment of fee that has not been earned. The lawyer may retain papers relating to the client to the extent permitted by law, or the Rules of Professional Conduct.

[5]RULE 16-503. With respect to a nonlawyer employed or retained by or associated with a lawyer: . . .

C. a lawyer shall be responsible for conduct of such a person that would be a violation of the Rules of Professional Conduct if engaged in by a lawyer if:

(1) the lawyer orders or, with the knowledge of the specific conduct, ratifies the conduct involved; or

(2) the lawyer is a partner in the law firm in which the person is employed, or has direct supervisory authority over the person, and knows of the conduct at a time when its consequences can be avoided or mitigated but fails to take reasonable remedial action.

responsibility for the misrepresentations of Felix to Nina Martinez about the status of her divorce and has again violated SCRA 1986, 16-804(C).[6] The entire course of conduct by Martinez in this instance was prejudicial to the administration of justice. . . .

IT IS THEREFORE ORDERED that Eloy F. Martinez be and hereby is suspended indefinitely from the practice of law . . . effective May 9, 1988. His reinstatement will not be automatic, but shall occur only after a reinstatement proceeding . . . where Martinez will have the burden of demonstrating by clear and convincing evidence that he has the requisite moral qualifications and is once again fit to resume the practice of law. . . .

IT IS FURTHER ORDERED that the Clerk of the Supreme Court strike the name of Eloy F. Martinez from the roll of those persons permitted to practice law in New Mexico and that this Opinion be published in the State Bar of New Mexico News and Views and in the New Mexico Reports. . . .

[6]RULE 16-804. It is professional misconduct for a lawyer to: . . . C. engage in conduct involving dishonesty, fraud, deceit or misrepresentation; . . .

ASSIGNMENT 2.5

What specific conduct of the paralegal was unethical? Make a list of what Martinez should have done when he hired the paralegal to have avoided such conduct.

SUMMARY

Two of the worst things that can happen to an attorney are (1) to be disciplined by the bar association for unethical conduct; (2) to be sued in court by a client for malpractice.

Ethical rules govern the conduct of attorneys. The violation of these rules can lead to the ultimate sanction of disbarment. There are, however, no ethical rules governing paralegals that are backed by comparable sanctions. Yet attorneys can be sanctioned for what paralegals do in the law office. An attorney has an ethical obligation to give proper supervision to paralegals.

There are thirteen major categories of ethical violations. It is unethical for an attorney to fail to have the knowledge and skill that are reasonably necessary to represent a particular client; to charge an unreasonable fee, or to charge most forms of contingent fees in a family law case; to reveal information relating to the representation of a client; to represent a client to whom the attorney cannot give undivided loyalty; to commingle general law firm funds with client funds in the same account; to withdraw from a case improperly; to make false statements to a tribunal or to fail to disclose certain information to the tribunal; to communicate with the other side without the permission of the latter's attorney; to fail to inform paralegals and other employees of the attorney's ethical responsibilities; to solicit prospective clients improperly; to advertise in a false or misleading manner; and to assist a nonattorney to engage in the unauthorized practice of law.

Closely related to (and often overlapping) these ethical violations are other kinds of wrongdoing by attorneys. For example, a lawyer can be sued for malicious prosecution and, most importantly, negligence. In addition, the attorney is liable, under the doctrine of respondeat superior, for similar wrongdoing committed by a paralegal within the office. The paralegal is also individually liable for such wrongdoing. The client can sue the paralegal, the supervising lawyer, or both until the client's damages have been paid.

KEY CHAPTER TERMINOLOGY

ethics
sanctions
competent
uncontested
retainer
fixed fee
contingent fee
arrearages
fee splitting
conflict of interest
multiple representation
adversary
imputed disqualification
Chinese wall
tainted
commingling of funds
disinterested
legal advice
negligence
respondeat superior
vicariously liable
deep pocket

ETHICS IN PRACTICE

You are a paralegal working at the law office of David Smith, Esq. Your first assignment is to draft a divorce petition for the case of *Harris v. Harris,* which is to be heard the next day. Your office represents Elaine Harris in her divorce action against her husband, Paul Harris. You never took family law in school. After Smith gives you this assignment, he leaves for the day and asks you to bring the petition to him in court tomorrow. You do the best you can. On your way to court, you see a woman crying on the steps of the court. As you pass by, you give her one of Smith's business cards and tell her that she may want to contact Smith if she has any family legal problems. Inside the building, you see a man standing alone next to a phone booth. He looks like the photo of Paul Harris that is in the file. You ask him if he is Paul Harris, and he says that he is. You tell him that you represent his wife and you ask him if he is going to contest the divorce. After he tells you that his wife is lying about his assets, you walk away. What ethical problems do you see?

ON THE NET: MORE ON ETHICS IN A FAMILY LAW PRACTICE

LegalEthics.com (ethics rules and opinions of your state)
http://www.legalethics.com/ethics.law

Association of Professional Responsibility Lawyers (ethics rules and opinions of your state)
http://www.aprl.net/statetop.html

Advertising and Solicitation (link to your state's rule)
http://www.abanet.org/adrules

Family Law Articles (Couch & Couch) (click Ethics)
http://adams.patriot.net/~crouch/fln/ixlyrw.html

CHAPTER 3

COMPILING A FAMILY HISTORY

CHAPTER OUTLINE

INTRODUCTION

Many family law clients go through life-changing events such as a divorce. Competent representation of such clients can require an enormous amount of fact gathering. Often the office must compile the equivalent of a life history of the client and the client's family. This history can have social, psychological, spiritual, and financial dimensions—each of which can require numerous detailed facts to be understood comprehensively and used strategically. Often there are no simple answers to questions such as:

- Who should have custody of the kids?
- What kind of financial support is needed and available?

In this chapter we introduce some of the essential factual building blocks of a life history that can be relevant to such questions. To compile this history, legal interviewing is perhaps the major technique used by attorneys and paralegals. Investigation is another.

Some attorneys will ask a new client to fill out a lengthy questionnaire on his or her married life. The client might be asked to write a detailed narrative or autobiography that describes major events of the marriage, wrongs or improprieties committed by both spouses, strengths and weaknesses of each as a marital partner and as a parent, changes in each spouse's standard of living before and during the marriage, contributions each spouse made to the raising of the children, circumstances of separations, etc. If the client has the stamina and ability to write such a document, it can be very helpful.

Not all law offices will ask for all this life history at one time. There may be an extended interview early in the case and then a series of involved follow-up interviews on different aspects of the case as it unfolds. In some offices, however, the compilation of a comprehensive life history begins as soon as it is clear that the case:

contested
Disputed; challenged.

- will be **contested**
- will raise complex issues
- will involve relatively large sums of money.

Before we begin our introduction to comprehensive fact gathering, we will briefly examine several critical documents that are often prepared during a law firm's early contact with a prospective client. We will also explore some of the sensitive dimensions of legal interviewing in a family law practice.

EARLY CONSIDERATIONS

letter of nonengagement
A letter sent by an attorney to a prospective client explicitly stating that the attorney will not be representing this person.

meritorious
Having a reasonable basis to believe that a person's claim or defense will succeed.

retainer
The contract of employment between attorney and client.

letter of authorization
A letter that tells the recipient that the office represents the client and that the client consents to the release of any information about the client to the office.

When an attorney first meets with a prospective client, one of the first concerns is whether to accept the case. If the decision is not to accept the case, the office should send out a **letter of nonengagement** to avoid or refute a later claim by the prospective client who says he or she thought the office was going to provide representation. A client may be rejected for a number of reasons, such as the attorney's belief that the prospective client does not have a **meritorious** case, the presence of a conflict of interest (see chapter 2), the likelihood that the office would not be able to collect its fees and costs of representation, etc. If the decision is to accept the case, the attorney explains the scope of the representation, the fees, and the costs involved. If the client agrees, the arrangement is formalized in the **retainer** (see Exhibit 3.1). The client is also asked to sign a **letter of authorization,** which will help the office obtain needed facts about the client from outside organizations. The example in Exhibit 3.2 presents a general letter of authorization that can be used with many different kinds of organizations. An alternative is to have the client sign more than one letter of authorization that will be addressed to individual organizations such as the Internal Revenue Service (for tax records), an accounting firm once used by the client's business (for financial records), a doctor or hospital (for health records), etc.

WHAT DOES THE CLIENT WANT?

A number of assumptions can be made about many clients with family law problems:

- Clients are not sure what they want, in spite of what they say.
- Clients keep changing their minds about what they want.
- Clients are not aware of their legal and nonlegal options.
- The family law problem involves other legal problems about which the client is unaware and about which even you may be unaware at the outset.

Suppose that a client walks into the office and tells the attorney, "I want a divorce." The following observations *might* be possible about the client:

1. The client has an incorrect understanding of what a divorce is.
2. The client says she wants a divorce because she thinks this is the only legal remedy available to solve her problem.

Exhibit 3.1 Example of a retainer in a family law case. Reprinted with permission of Honohan, Epley, Haymond, Braddock & Brenneman (Iowa City, Iowa).

ATTORNEY-CLIENT CONTRACT

DISSOLUTION OF MARRIAGE

IT IS AGREED between ______________________________ as Client, and Honohan, Epley, Haymond, Braddock & Brenneman, Attorney, as follows:

1. EMPLOYMENT. Client employs Attorney to represent Client in connection with an action involving a dissolution of the marriage of the client.

Attorneys agree to represent the client in this matter and to pursue the matter on client's behalf with reasonable diligence, to inform the client as to the progress of the matter and make such recommendations as may be needed. Attorney agrees to report all settlement offers promptly to client. If it is necessary, attorneys shall represent the client in trial or on appeal. Attorneys agree to keep confidential all client matters unless authorized by client to release information as requested by attorney. Client understands and agrees that the attorney may release confidential information to other attorneys in the firm and to law clerks and paralegals employed by the firm. Client understands that during the handling of the matters involved in the dissolution of marriage that attorney may be required pursuant to Court order or rule to release information material to the dissolution of marriage and client authorizes the attorney to disclose such information as is required under order of Court or pursuant to Court rules.

• The retainer alerts the client that paralegals and law clerks (usually students still in law school) may be working on the case.

As a part of said employment, the firm of Honohan, Epley, Haymond, Braddock & Brenneman is hereby authorized to investigate all matters involving the dissolution of marriage on client's behalf and to represent client in negotiations with attorneys and representatives of client's spouse and to appear on behalf of client in the District Court and to file appropriate pleadings in the matter of client's dissolution of marriage.

It is understood that the client makes all final determinations as to the type of action to be taken in the matter and the attorney will advise the client of the action needed to be taken. This final determination includes the right of the client to dismiss the dissolution of marriage action. It is understood that the decision of the client is limited to the decisions as to types of actions to be taken and dismissal and settlement offers. The attorney shall make all decisions regarding the procedures to be taken and the handling of the matter.

Client agrees that this employment is between the client and the firm of Honohan, Epley, Haymond, Braddock & Brenneman and includes all attorneys in the firm, including partners and associates and that different attorneys may work on client's matter. Honohan, Epley, Haymond, Braddock & Brenneman employs paralegals and law clerks to assist them in their practice and may use said paralegals and law clerks to assist in the conduct of client's dissolution of marriage under the supervision of an attorney and client agrees to the use of paralegals and law clerks. Paralegals or law clerks may contact the client to obtain information or to report to the client on behalf of the attorneys. Client agrees to cooperate with the paralegals and law clerks.

2. HOURLY RATE. Client shall pay a fee per hour for attorney work and a fee per hour for the work of law clerks and paralegals in the performance of this contract. Said hourly rates being set by the firm of Honohan, Epley, Haymond, Braddock & Brenneman from time to time. Client understands that the hourly rates for various tasks performed in the office vary by the individual who performs the task and the task undertaken and has had the current hourly rate schedule explained to client. Client further understands that from time to time these rates change and agrees to pay the future rates. Attorney agrees to send client a bill approximately every thirty (30) days, which shall specify the work done since the previous bill and the fee due. All fees shall be due and payable at the time of billing. Attorney agrees to accept and client agrees to pay $ ____________ per (week, month) to be applied toward attorney fees. Any unused portion of such installments shall be refunded to client when the case is completed. Unpaid bills will draw interest at a rate of ______ % per annum.

• Billing information: client will pay attorney, paralegal, and law clerk fees as well as all specific categories of expenses listed.

Notwithstanding attorney's agreement to accept an installment payment in lieu of payment in full each month, client agrees to pay his or her outstanding account in full by one month prior to a trial date or one week prior to taking a default judgment unless a different arrangement is made in writing. Client agrees also to pay money in addition to the monthly fees from time to time as requested by attorney to avoid accumulating an outstanding account with attorney in excess of $500.

3. ADVANCE FEE. Client shall advance a fee of $ ____________ to be applied toward attorney fees as incurred prior to the commencement of work by the attorneys. Any unused portion of the retainer shall be refunded to client.

4. EXPENSES. Client shall pay for long distance telephone calls, travel expenses, photocopies, photographs, securing records or documents, hospital records, medical reports, medical examination, court costs, depositions, expert witness fees, and all other expenses incurred on behalf of client. Client shall advance the sum of $ ____________ for filing fees and service fees before the Petition shall be filed, and shall advance additional expense money from time to time as requested by attorney to pay anticipated expenses. Any unpaid expense may be billed periodically by attorney and shall be paid by client upon receipt of the bill.

Client and Attorney agree that no deposition will be taken or expert witness employed without prior agreement by client, except for depositions taken by the other side. Client further agrees that if he or she has agreed to a deposition or the hiring of an expert, that he or she shall pay $ ____________ (per week,

continued

Exhibit 3.1 Example of a retainer in a family law case. Reprinted with permission of Honohan, Epley, Haymond, Braddock & Brenneman (Iowa City, Iowa).—*Continued*

month) as an advance against expenses for depositions and expert witnesses if requested by attorney. Client agrees to pay other expenses determined reasonable and necessary by attorney. Any unused expense money advanced to attorney by client shall be refunded to client or credited to any unpaid balance of attorney fees.

5. WITHDRAWAL. Non-payment of expenses, fees, or installment payment as agreed upon herein shall be a basis for attorney's withdrawal from representation of client. Attorney shall give client reasonable notice before withdrawing so that client may have adequate time to find other counsel. In the event that any rule of Court in which this matter is filed requires Court approval prior to withdrawal, the attorney will obtain such approval prior to withdrawal.

6. RESPONSIBILITY FOR PAYMENT. Client accepts the responsibility of making the above payments. Attorney cannot accept payments from opposing clients. If the opposing party agrees or is ordered to pay all attorney fees, these payments must be made through the Clerk of Court and will be credited to client's account upon receipt. However, if the opposing party fails to make payments for attorney fees the primary obligation for payment is with client.

7. TOTAL FEES. Client understands that attorney makes no representation as to the total attorney fees and costs for the prosecution of this case. Client understands and agrees that fees and costs depend upon the circumstances of the case. An estimate has been given to client initially but both parties understand this to be an estimate only and not the expected cost of the prosecution of the case.

Client further understands that the client may elect at any time to drop the prosecution of the case or to change attorney. These elections are personal to the client and solely the client's choice. In the event that the client terminates the employment of Honohan, Epley, Haymond, Braddock & Brenneman the client shall be liable for the fees accrued to date and shall pay said fees upon termination.

8. PLACE OF PAYMENT. All sums due herein shall be paid at attorney's office at the address stated below.

9. NO GUARANTEE. Attorney makes no guarantee as to the outcome of the case.

10. ADDITIONAL TERMS. Any additional terms agreed to between the parties shall be set out in an exhibit attached to this agreement and by this reference incorporated into this agreement. If there is no exhibit, this agreement shall constitute the entire agreement and the client understands that no representations not set out in this agreement are a part hereof.

11. BINDING AGREEMENT. Client acknowledges that client has read this agreement and understands the provisions of this agreement and that this agreement is binding upon the parties and client agrees to abide by the terms of this agreement.

Dated this ________ day of ____________________, 20 ____.

____________________________ (Client)

HONOHAN, EPLEY, HAYMOND, BRADDOCK
& BRENNEMAN
330 E. Court St.
P.O. Box 3010
Iowa City, Iowa 52244

By: ____________________

dom/domcont3

• *In some cases (e.g., when an attorney has already filed a notice of appearance in court), the permission of the court is needed before the attorney can withdraw from representing a client.*

3. If the client knew that other remedies existed (e.g., annulment, judicial separation, a support order), she would consider these options.
4. What really troubles the client is that her husband beats the kids; a divorce is the only way she thinks she can stop it.
5. The client does not want a divorce. She is being pressured by her husband to institute divorce proceedings. He has threatened her with violence if she refuses.
6. The client consciously or unconsciously wants and needs an opportunity to tell someone how badly the world is treating her, and if given this opportunity, she may not want to terminate the marriage.
7. If the client knew that marriage or family counseling was available in the community, she would consider using it before taking the drastic step of going to a law office for a divorce.

If any of these observations is correct, think of how damaging it would be for someone in the law office to take out the standard divorce forms and quickly fill them out immediately after the client says, "I want a divorce." This response would not be appropriate without first probing beneath the statement to determine what in fact is on the client's mind. Some clients who speak only

Exhibit 3.2 Example of a general letter of authorization. Reprinted with permission of Honohan, Epley, Haymond, Braddock & Brenneman (Iowa City, Iowa).

HONOHAN, EPLEY, HAYMOND, BRADDOCK & BRENNEMAN
330 E. Court St.
P.O. Box 3010
Iowa City, Iowa 52244

_____________ _____, 20 ______

To Whom It May Concern:

______________________ is a client of this office. The client requests that you cooperate in revealing to our office any and all facts pertaining to the client. We will be contacting you to make specific requests for information in this regard. The client's authorization and waiver of confidentiality is printed below.

Sincerely,

____
Attorney for

____

Authorization

Honohan, Epley, Haymond, Braddock & Brenneman is my legal counsel. I authorize you to release any information pertaining to me that is requested by Honohan, Epley, Haymond, Braddock & Brenneman or by anyone designated in writing by this law firm. I hereby waive confidentiality as to such information. You are further authorized to discuss any aspect of this information with this law firm or its agents.

______________________ _____________ _____, 20 ______
(signature of client)

dom/authoriz.form

of divorces and separation agreements are receptive to and even anxious for reconciliation. The danger exists that the client might be steered in the direction of a divorce because no other options are presented to her, because no one takes the time to help her express the ideas, intentions, and desires that are lurking beneath the seemingly clear statement, "I want a divorce."

This is not to say that you must be prepared to psychoanalyze every client or that you must always distrust what the client initially tells you. It is rather a recognition of the fact that *most people are confused about the law and make requests based upon misinformation as to what courses of action are available to solve problems.* Common sense tells us to avoid taking all statements at face value. People under emotional distress, particularly in situations of family conflict, need to be treated with sensitivity. We should not expect them to be able to express their intentions with clarity all the time in view of the emotions involved and the sometimes complicated nature of the law.

ASSIGNMENT 3.1

For each of the following statements made by a client, what areas do you think would be reasonable to probe to determine if the statement is an accurate reflection of what the client wants? What misunderstandings do you think the client might have? What further questions would you want to ask to be sure that you have identified what the client wants?

a. "I want to commit my husband to a mental institution."
b. "I can't control my teenage son anymore. I want him placed in a juvenile home."
c. "I want to put my baby daughter up for adoption."

INTERVIEWING GUIDELINES

Additional sensitivity concerns are outlined in some of the following guidelines for conducting a client interview:

1. Set aside an adequate amount of time to conduct the interview. You do not want to be rushed. Try to avoid taking calls during the interview.
2. Dress conservatively and professionally.
3. Clear away open files and papers of other clients. You do not want to violate their confidentiality by allowing a stranger to see anything in their files. Confidentiality is another reason to avoid taking calls during the interview. A client in the office should not be able to hear you discuss the cases of other clients on the phone.
4. Make sure the client is comfortable. Offer coffee or water. Have a supply of tissues available.
5. At the beginning of the interview, give the client your business card that states your name, title, address, and phone number.
6. Make sure the client knows you are not an attorney. It is usually not enough to tell the client that you are a "paralegal" or a "legal assistant." In addition to stating your title, use the word "nonattorney" or the phrase "I am not an attorney," so that there will be no misunderstanding. You can also say that you will be working closely with the attorney handling the case.
7. Prepare the client for what will happen during the interview. Explain that you may need to meet with the client more than once. Let the client know you will be taking detailed notes to obtain and record an accurate picture of the case.
8. Maintain eye contact as much as possible even though you are taking notes.
9. Use great sensitivity in obtaining facts from the client. You are about to learn a large number of highly personal facts about the client's life. Think of how you would feel if you were revealing such facts about yourself to a stranger. Think of how you would want this other person to react to what you are revealing. At such a vulnerable time, clients need understanding and compassion. (For a discussion of the sensitivity required when interviewing a woman who has been a victim of domestic violence, see the end of chapter 12.)
10. Listen carefully. The best way to build rapport with a client is to demonstrate that you are listening to everything the client has been saying. A useful technique is to repeat back a portion of what the client has told you. Not only does this tend to assure the client that you have been listening, but it also often triggers the client's memory to provide more detail or explanation. Another technique is to refer back to something the client said as the basis of a new question (e.g., "Earlier you said that you rarely used the vacation home. Could you tell me more about the vacation home?").
11. Encourage the client to do most of the talking. If you receive a one-or two-word answer, ask the client to explain the answer in greater detail.
12. Encourage the client to express his or her feelings whenever this might be helpful in obtaining underlying facts (e.g., "How did you feel when your husband told you that your daughter wanted to live with him?").
13. Take your notes in the language of the client. Use quotation marks as often as possible (e.g., client said she is "certain the father is unable to raise the children on his own"). Avoid extensive paraphrasing in which you restate what the client said in your own words.

14. Never talk down to or criticize a client.
15. Avoid disparaging comments about the opposing attorney or about the client's spouse.
16. Do not give legal advice. If the client asks you a legal question, say that you are not permitted to give legal advice but that you would be glad to bring the question to the attorney's attention. This may not always be easy to do, particularly when you feel that you know the answer and when your good relationship with the client makes it awkward to pull back. The reality, however, is that when you answer a legal question by giving legal advice, you are probably engaging in the unauthorized practice of law. (See chapter 2.)
17. Clients will often ask you what their chances of success are. The only appropriate answer you can give is that the office will do the best it can. Never give a client any reason to believe you think the client will win.
18. Let the client know how to reach you if he or she thinks of other relevant information after the interview is over.
19. Make mental notes on the client's personality. Here is how one attorney described this aspect of the interview: "Assess the client's personality" and whether the office "can work with this person. Watch for red flags or danger signals, including the client who is emotionally distraught or vengeful; is inconsistent with the story or avoids answering questions; has unrealistic objectives; suggests use of improper influence or other unethical or illegal conduct; rambles, wanders off the subject, or constantly interrupts you;" tells the office "how to run the case; has already discharged or filed disciplinary complaints against other lawyers; has a personality disorder; or is flirtatious."[1] In your report or memorandum to your supervisor on the interview, be sure to include your observations and assessments relevant to concerns such as these.

FAMILY HISTORY CHECKLIST

Not everything asked for in the checklist in Exhibit 3.3 will be pertinent to every case.[2] If a married couple has no children, for example, there is no point in pursing questions on child rearing. With these obvious exceptions, however, the inclination of the cautious office is to be comprehensive. How does the office decide what facts to pursue? The standard should not be whether a set of facts will definitely be relevant to the case, but whether an area of inquiry is reasonably likely *to lead to* relevant facts and to uncover as-yet unknown legal issues. Initially, it may not appear relevant, for example, to ask a client about where her husband's former wife worked. Yet this inquiry may prove to be quite valuable if it leads to information about current business assets of the husband that the client never knew about. Relevant facts have a way of materializing from seemingly irrelevant lines of inquiry. Sometimes you do not know what you are looking for until you find it.

---

[1]*The Initial Interview,* 12 Family Advocate 6 (Winter 1990).

[2]Some of the checklist questions are based on Form 4, *Affidavit* [on financial resources], Supreme Court of the United States; *A History for Your Attorney,* 15 Family Advocate 12 (Summer 1992); *What Your Lawyer Needs to Know,* 15 Family Advocate 28 (Summer 1992); L. Brown, *A Family Legal Information Check List,* 3 Practical Lawyer 60 (no. 6, Oct. 1957); L. Barrett, *The Initial Interview with a Divorce Client,* 23 Practical Lawyer 75 (no. 4, June 1977); L. Brown, *Manual for Periodic Checkup* (1983); Allan Chay & Judith Smith, *Legal Interviewing in Practice* (1996).

Exhibit 3.3 Checklist for compiling a family history

CLIENT'S NAME:
STREET ADDRESS:
E-MAIL ADDRESSES:
PHONE NUMBER, RESIDENCE:
PHONE NUMBER, BUSINESS:
FAX NUMBER:
OFFICE FILE NUMBER:

Table of Contents

I. DOCUMENTS THE CLIENT SHOULD BE ASKED TO BRING TO THE LAW OFFICE, IF AVAILABLE

- Premarital agreement.
- Any documents you were given prior to signing the premarital agreement.
- Marriage license.
- Prior divorce or annulment decree with this or other spouses.
- Powers of attorney the client and spouse gave each other.
- Other written agreements between client and spouse entered prior to and during the marriage, e.g., custody agreements.
- Recent tax returns (last three years).
- Tax assessments or bills.
- Deeds of property the client or spouse received as a gift prior to the marriage.
- Deeds of property the client or spouse received as a gift during the marriage.
- Deeds of property the client or spouse purchased during the marriage.
- Several recent pay stubs of client and spouse.
- Business records such as copies of articles of incorporation and partnership agreements, if either or both of the parties operated a business during the marriage.
- Net worth statements (financial statements) of client, spouse, or business of either.
- Recent bank statements for all personal and business accounts of client and spouse.
- Recent securities statements, e.g., mutual funds.
- Recent statement from pension fund.
- Copies of loan or refinancing applications made by client or spouse.
- Copies of recent major bills, e.g., mortgage payment, tuition bill, hospital bill.
- Credit reports on client, spouse, or business.
- Wills and codicils to wills.
- Trust agreements.
- Medical records of client.
- Police records if relevant to domestic violence committed during the marriage.
- Separation agreement the parties have signed or drafts of such an agreement the parties have considered.
- Birth certificates of children.
- Court documents in which the client, the spouse, or both were parties.

- *If the client does not have any of these documents, ask the client if he or she thinks they exist and, if so, where they might be obtained.*

- Client's résumé.
- Spouse's résumé.

II. CONFLICT-OF-INTEREST INFORMATION

- Client's maiden name (if a woman).
- Other names used by client.
- Has this office ever represented the client before?
- Has this office ever represented any relatives of the client?
- Has this office ever represented any business associates of the client?
- Names of other attorneys the client has contacted about this case.
- Names of attorneys who have represented the client on any other matter in the past.
- Spouse's full name.
- Other names used by spouse.
- Has this office ever represented the spouse before?
- Has this office ever represented any relatives of the spouse?
- Has this office ever represented any business associates of the spouse?
- Names of other attorneys who have represented the spouse on any matter in the past.

• Before a law office accepts a client, it must do a conflict-of-interest check to determine whether the office can ethically represent the client. (See chapter 2.)

III. EMERGENCY CONCERNS

- If court proceedings have already been initiated by the client or spouse, are there any future court dates on which the client is required to make an appearance or to file any pleadings?
- Does the client think there is a danger the spouse will remove the children out of state? (Protective order needed?)
- Is the spouse abusing the client or the children? (Protective order needed?)
- Is the other spouse aware that the client is seeking legal services? If not, is there a danger of a hostile reaction when this becomes known?
- Does the client think there is a danger the spouse will give away marital assets? (Protective order needed?)
- Does the client think there is a danger the spouse will conceal marital assets? (Protective order needed?)
- While waiting for a court date on the divorce case, do client and children have immediate support needs? (Motion for support pending the outcome of the case? Application for public assistance?)
- Is the client suffering emotional trauma? (Provide recommended list of psychologists, other counselors, or support agencies.)
- Did the parties have joint credit cards or joint charge cards? (Cancel as soon as possible? Should client apply for credit in own name? Open own accounts?)
- Did the client cosign or guarantee a loan secured by the spouse? (Contact the lender to cancel client's backing of any future indebtedness incurred by spouse?)
- Is the client or spouse currently pregnant? Due date? Are prenatal concerns being met?

IV. BACKGROUND

- How did the client select this law office? Referral?
- How long has the client lived at current address?
- How many consecutive months has the client been a resident of this county?
- Address of the most recent three prior residences of the client and the dates at each residence.
- Client's date of birth.
- Client's place of birth.
- Client's race.
- Client's social security number.
- Client's present occupation(s) and length of time in this field.
- Prior occupations of the client.
- Highest grade of school or college completed. Date(s) completed.
- Client's religious affiliation and extent of involvement.

• Length of residence may be important to establish the court's in rem jurisdiction (through domicile) and to establish venue. (See chapter 7.)

- Is the spouse represented by counsel? If so, when was that counsel retained? Who is paying for his or her services? What is the attorney's name, address, phone number, e-mail address, and fax number?
- Spouse's current residence street address, e-mail address(es), phone number(s), and fax number.
- Is there a different mailing address?
- How long has the spouse lived at this address?
- How many consecutive months has the spouse been a resident of this county?
- Address of the most recent three prior residences of the spouse and the dates at each residence.
- Spouse's date of birth.
- Spouse's place of birth.
- Spouse's race.
- Spouse's social security number.
- Spouse's present occupation(s) and length of time in this field.
- Business address of the spouse, phone number(s), e-mail address(es), fax number.

• If the spouse is represented by an attorney, all contacts with the spouse must be through that attorney. (See chapter 2.)

continued

Exhibit 3.3 Checklist for compiling a family history—*Continued*

- Prior occupations of the spouse.
- Highest grade of school or college completed. Date(s) completed.
- Spouse's religious affiliation and extent of involvement.

V. MARITAL FACTS

- Date of current marriage.
- Place where marriage ceremony occurred.
- Date on marriage license.
- Blood tests or other formalities that were required to obtain the license.
- Name and address of person who performed marriage ceremony.
- Date on marriage certificate.
- Names and addresses of witnesses to the marriage ceremony.
- Facts that would lead others to believe the parties were married, e.g., whether they used the same last name, whether they introduced each other to others as "my husband" and "my wife."
- At the time of the marriage, did either have a prior marriage that was not ended by divorce or death?
- How old were the client and spouse when they married?
- Are they related to each other by blood (e.g., cousins) or by marriage (e.g., in-laws)?
- Were both able to perform all marital functions upon marriage?
- Did both go through the marriage ceremony with the full and free intention to become husband and wife?
- When the parties went through the marriage ceremony, did either lie about or misrepresent anything so important that the victim would not have agreed to marry if he or she had known the truth, e.g., whether the party wanted to have children?
- For each child born to the marriage, state his or her full name, date of birth, place of birth, current address, prior addresses, length of time child has spent at current address and at each prior address, adults with whom the child has lived since birth, past sources of support, and current sources of support.
- For each child to whom the client or the spouse was an adoptive parent, guardian, or stepparent, state the child's full name, date of birth, place of birth, current address, prior addresses, length of time child has spent at current address and at each prior address, adults with whom the child has lived since birth, past sources of support, and current sources of support. Also state the circumstances of how the child came into the family.
- If client was ever married before, state the name of each former spouse, his or her current address (if still alive), the date, place, and circumstances of each marriage, how each marriage was terminated, the names of all children born or adopted in this marriage, and how these children are (or were) supported.
- If the spouse of the client was ever married before, state the name of each former spouse, his or her current address (if still alive), the date, place, and circumstances of each marriage, how each marriage was terminated, the names of all children born or adopted in this marriage, and how these children are (or were) supported.
- State known sources of support (employment, family business) of former spouses of client's spouse.
- State all outstanding debts or obligations owed to or by former spouses, e.g., alimony, child support, property division. Was a court order used?

• Whether others believed the parties to be married could be relevant to whether a common law marriage was formed (in states that allow such a marriage) if there was no marriage ceremony. (See chapter 5.)

• These questions are relevant to whether grounds for an annulment (e.g., nonage or fraud) might exist. (See chapter 6.)

VI. DETERIORATION OF MARRIAGE

- Does the client want the divorce? Why or why not?
- Does the spouse want the divorce? Why or why not?
- When did the marriage start to deteriorate? State the circumstances.
- Length of time the parties have had marital difficulties.
- Are the parties now separated?
- If so, state the date the separation began, who initiated it, the reason the client thinks the separation occurred, the reason the spouse thinks the separation occurred, where each party and the children have lived since the separation, and how each party and the children have been supported since the separation.
- Have the parties ever separated in the past?
- If so, for each separation, state the dates involved, who initiated the separation, the reason the client thinks the separation occurred, the reason the spouse thinks the separation occurred, where each party and the children lived during the separation, how each party and the children were supported during the separation, and the circumstances of the end of the separation leading to a resumption of the marital relationship.
- Does the client think there is a realistic chance of reconciliation? Why or why not?
- Does the spouse think there is a realistic chance of reconciliation? Why or why not?
- Have the parties ever attempted marital counseling? If so, who initiated each effort and to what extent was the effort successful? Who was the counselor? How was he or she paid?
- Does either party now want to try marital counseling? Why or why not?

• Note that questions about who caused the breakdown of the marriage are generally not relevant in the era of no-fault divorce. (See chapter 7.)

VII. PRIOR CONTRACTS

- Do the parties have a premarital agreement?
- Date it was signed.
- Names and addresses of the attorneys, if any, who represented either party during the negotiation and drafting of the premarital agreement.
- Other individuals consulted, e.g., accountant, financial planner, business associate, friend or relative.
- Location of the original agreement.
- Describe the nature of the disclosure the spouse gave the client concerning the spouse's financial assets and worth before the client signed the agreement.
- Describe the nature of the disclosure the client gave the spouse concerning the client's financial assets and worth before the spouse signed the agreement.
- What rights did each side waive in the agreement, e.g., dower and curtesy?
- Describe the provisions in the agreement for the client and for the spouse in the event of a divorce.
- Describe the provisions in the agreement for the client and for the spouse upon the death of either during the marriage.
- Have the parties discussed or entered a separation agreement?
- Date it was signed.
- Were the parties already separated when it was signed?
- Names and addresses of the attorneys, if any, who represented either party during the negotiation and drafting of the separation agreement.
- Location of the original agreement.
- Summarize the major provisions in the agreement on support, custody, and property division.
- Have the client and spouse entered employment agreements with each other at a place of business? Have they entered such agreements with a business owned by either?
- Summarize the major provisions in the agreement.
- Has the client or spouse ever lent the other money?
- If so, describe the major terms of the agreement, e.g., interest charged. What is the present status of the loan? What amounts have been repaid?
- Where are these loan documents kept?
- Names and addresses of the attorneys, if any, who represented either party during the negotiation and drafting of the loan agreement.
- Has a relative of the client ever lent the spouse any money? Describe the circumstances and present status of the loan.
- Has a relative of the spouse ever lent the client any money? Describe the circumstances and present status of the loan.

• The validity of a premarital agreement may depend, in part, on whether the parties had independent counsel and fully disclosed each other's assets and liabilities prior to signing the agreement. (See chapter 4.)

• If the client had a different attorney during the preparation of the separation agreement, the law office must make sure the prior attorney-client relationship has terminated. There should be no substantive contact with a person who is already represented by counsel. (See chapter 2.)

VIII. ITEMIZED EXPENSES (where relevant, state whether the expense is for client only or for children only; use monthly figures where appropriate; to obtain a monthly figure for an expense that is incurred less frequently than monthly, add the total spent for that item for the year and divide by 12)

- Mortgage (state whether mortgage payments include taxes and insurance).
- Rent.
- Real property taxes.
- Homeowner association fees.
- Utilities: gas/oil.
- Utilities: electric.
- Utilities: water and sewer.
- Water softener.
- Telephones.
- Internet service provider.
- Maintenance of house.
- Maintenance of swimming pool.
- Gardener.
- Groceries.
- Restaurants.
- Clothes: purchase.
- Clothes: maintenance (tailor, laundry, etc.).
- Shoes.
- Maid.
- Baby-sitter.
- Day care center.
- School expenses: tuition.
- School expenses: books and supplies.
- School expenses: tutoring.
- School expenses: transportation.
- School expenses: after-school programs.
- School expenses: miscellaneous.

continued

Exhibit 3.3 Checklist for compiling a family history—*Continued*

- Lessons: music, dance, sports, theater, etc.
- Equipment maintenance: music, sports, etc.
- Summer camp.
- Visitation expenses when child visits noncustodial parent (transportation, phone calls, meals, etc.).
- Car: payments.
- Car: gas.
- Car: maintenance.
- Car: registration.
- Car: tolls.
- Car: automobile club dues.
- Insurance premium: house.
- Insurance premium: car.
- Insurance premium: life.
- Insurance premium: dental.
- Insurance premium: health.
- Insurance premium: disability.
- Uninsured costs for medical doctors, dentists, orthodontists, homeopathic/holistic practitioners, prescription and nonprescription drugs, glasses and eye care, etc.
- Hairdresser.
- Haircuts.
- Toiletries and cosmetics.
- Pets: veterinarian.
- Pets: food and supplies.
- Entertainment.
- Cable TV access.
- Vacation.
- Film and camera supplies.
- Contribution: church/synagogue.
- Contribution: other charity.
- Newspaper/magazine subscriptions.
- Allowances for child.
- Membership: country club.
- Other membership, e.g., YMCA/YWCA.
- Cost of gifts (birthdays, holidays, etc.).
- Payments to IRA or other retirement fund.
- Accountant/tax preparer fees.
- Court-ordered payments of child support or alimony from a prior marriage.
- Miscellaneous expenses.

IX. HEALTH INFORMATION

- Physical and emotional health history of client (condition before marriage, during marriage, since separation, major problems, names and addresses of treating physicians or counselors, dates of hospitalizations or other major treatments, diagnosis for future, etc.).
- Physical and emotional health history of spouse (condition before marriage, during marriage, since separation, major problems, names and addresses of treating physicians or counselors, dates of hospitalizations or other major treatments, diagnosis for future, etc.).
- Physical and emotional health history of each child (condition while parents were together, since separation, major problems, names and addresses of treating physicians or counselors, dates of hospitalizations or other major treatments, diagnosis for future, etc.).

• *The health of a party can be relevant to many issues (e.g., future medical expenses, need for alimony, ability to care for a child, capacity to understand agreements signed before and during the marriage). (See chapters 4, 6, 8, and 9.)*

X. WILLS AND TRUSTS

- Kinds of wills in existence (client's separate will? spouse's separate will? joint will?). Address the following topics for each will.
- Date signed/executed.
- Name and address of attorney who prepared the will.
- Names and addresses of witnesses.
- Location of original.
- Name and address of initial executor; name and address of alternate/successor executor.
- Guardian for minor children.
- Primary beneficiaries (who receives what).
- Remainder beneficiaries.
- Codicils or amendments (reasons for changes, dates executed, summary of changes).
- Names and addresses of witnesses.
- Kinds of trusts in existence (testamentary trust? inter vivos trust? other?). Address the following topics for each trust.
- Date signed/executed.

- Name and address of attorney who prepared the trust.
- Names and addresses of witnesses.
- Location of original.
- Name and address of initial trustee; name and address of alternate/successor trustee.
- Description of assets/property to go in the trust.
- Lifetime beneficiaries.
- Remainder beneficiaries.
- Amendments (reasons for changes, dates executed, summary of changes).

XI. REARING AND CUSTODY OF CHILDREN

- Names of natural (birth) children, adopted children, and stepchildren. Address the following topics for each child.
- Location of birth certificate.
- Names and addresses of natural parents (does birth certificate accurately state this information?).
- Reasons client wants custody.
- Reasons spouse wants custody.
- Client's feelings about joint custody.
- Spouse's feelings about joint custody.
- Strengths and weaknesses of client as a parent.
- Strengths and weaknesses of spouse as a parent.
- Career responsibilities and goals of client and how they affect availability of client to care for the child.
- Career responsibilities and goals of spouse and how they affect availability of spouse to care for the child.
- Does either client or spouse expect to move in the future? If so, why, and how will the move affect visitation opportunities of the other parent?
- Relatives of client in the area who are available to help client with child care.
- Relatives of spouse in the area who are available to help spouse with child care.
- Child's relationship with other children in the home.
- Court actions, e.g., paternity petition, child support, guardianship, adoption, juvenile delinquency (include dates; names and addresses of courts and agencies involved, attorneys, and parties; reasons court action was initiated; name of person who initiated proceeding; outcome/decision of court; major events since, etc.).
- Police involvement, e.g., misconduct by child, abuse of child by others (include dates, names and addresses of enforcement agencies involved; reasons police became involved; name of person who called police; action taken by police; major events since, etc.).
- Religious activities of child: describe role of each parent.
- Major school functions: describe role of each parent.
- Homework: describe role of each parent.
- After-school activities at home, at friend's house, at playground: describe role of each parent.
- Sports: describe role of each parent.
- Medical and dental appointments: describe role of each parent.
- Birthdays: describe role of each parent.
- Vacations: describe role of each parent.
- Discipline at home: describe role of each parent.
- Other major events in child's life: describe role of each parent.
- Attitude of child toward each parent. Where would child like to live (if old enough to express a preference)?
- Client's efforts to encourage child to have positive attitude about spouse.
- Spouse's efforts to encourage child to have positive attitude about client.
- Child's awareness of client's sexual relationships with others since separation from the spouse. Impact on the child.
- Child's awareness of spouse's sexual relationships with others since separation from the client. Impact on the child.
- Third parties who might be witnesses to the home environment, e.g., neighbors, relatives, teachers, day care providers, clergy, counselors, friends.

XII. BUSINESSES

- Ownership (solely owned by client? solely owned by spouse? jointly owned?). Address the following topics for each business.
- Name of business. Description of its products or services.
- Legal category of business (partnership? corporation? limited liability company? sole proprietorship?).
- Address of headquarters and all major branches or entities.
- Names and addresses of accountants or others responsible for compiling and storing financial records of the business.

continued

Exhibit 3.3 Checklist for compiling a family history—*Continued*

- Date the business was created or entered.
- Source of funds used to start the business.
- Source of funds used to develop the business.
- Distribution of profits.
- Location of accounts in which profits were deposited. Ownership of these accounts.
- Most recent financial statement for the business and who prepared it. Where is statement located?
- Nature and extent of business debt, losses, or liabilities.
- Location of business tax returns for prior years and names of persons who prepared them.
- Partnership: kind (limited, general, etc.).
- Partnership: profit and loss history.
- Partnership: percentage interest of client and of spouse.
- Partnership: names of other partners.
- Partnership: provisions for sale of a partner's interest.
- Partnership: provisions for termination.
- Corporation: kind (public, closely held, etc.).
- Corporation: state of incorporation.
- Corporation: names and addresses of incorporators.
- Corporation: total issued shares. Kinds of shares.
- Corporation: profit and loss history.
- Corporation: number and kind of shares owned by client or spouse.
- Corporation: names of officers of corporation.
- Corporation: names of officers and of members of board of directors.
- Corporation: provisions for sale of stock.
- Corporation: provisions for dissolution.
- Limited liability company: profit and loss history.
- Limited liability company: percentage owned by client and spouse.
- Limited liability company: other owners or principals and their roles.
- Sole proprietorship: profit and loss history.

XIII. EMPLOYMENT HISTORY (answer separately for client and for spouse)

- Name and address of employer. Address the following topics for the current employer and for each prior employer.
- Dates employed.
- Title and responsibilities.
- Name of supervisor.
- Compensation history. Methods of payment (periodic salary? commission? deferred compensation? dividends?).
- Deductions from salary.
- Bonus availability. Other incentive plans. History.
- Cost of living adjustments.
- Benefits: pension (defined-benefit plan? defined-contribution plan?).
- Benefits: deferred savings plan, profit sharing plan, stock options.
- Benefits: life insurance.
- Benefits: health insurance (amount of cash surrender value?).
- Benefits: dental insurance.
- Benefits: disability insurance.
- Benefits: vacation.
- Benefits: sick leave.
- Benefits: severance pay.
- Benefits: union.
- Benefits: perks (payment of membership fees at clubs or professional associations, company car, company yacht, recreational facilities, entertainment allowance, sports tickets).

XIV. CONTRIBUTIONS TO CAREER ENHANCEMENT

- During the marriage, did the client or spouse enhance his or her career, such as by obtaining education or training?
- How did one spouse contribute to the enhancement of the other's career during the marriage? Took a job to support the family? Used personal funds to help pay for the other's education? Agreed to assume all child-raising and household chores while the other pursued education?
- Did one spouse postpone his or her own career enhancement during the marriage so that the other's career could be enhanced?
- Before the parties were married, did either contribute to the career enhancement of the other?

XV. REAL PROPERTY

- Ownership (solely owned by client? solely owned by spouse? jointly owned?). Address the following topics for each.
- Legal category (joint tenancy? tenancy by the entirety? tenancy in common? fee simple? landlord-tenant interest? other?).

- *Although the law office should determine who has legal title to all property, the distribution*

- Nature of the property (residence? vacation? time-share? business? rental property? vacant land?).
- Location/address.
- Persons currently using/benefiting from property.
- Original cost. Date of purchase.
- Name and address of seller.
- Source of funds used to purchase.
- Amount owed on the property. Name and address of creditor/mortgagee.
- Source of funds used to pay ongoing debt.
- Current fair market value of property (written appraisal available?).
- If acquired by gift, name and address of the donor. Circumstances of the gift.
- Improvements made to property. Dates and sources of funds used.
- Sources of funds used to pay insurance covering the property.
- Sources of funds used to pay taxes on the property.

XVI. STOCKS, BONDS, OTHER ACCOUNTS, SAFE DEPOSIT BOXES (Address the following topics for each separately owned item.)

- Stocks: names of corporations.
- Stocks: name of owner as shown on stock certificate.
- Stocks: number of shares.
- Stocks: certificate numbers.
- Stocks: dates acquired.
- Stocks: cost of shares.
- Stocks: source of funds used to purchase.
- Bonds: name of corporation or obligor.
- Bonds: name of owner as shown on bond certificate.
- Bonds: dates acquired.
- Bonds: bond numbers.
- Bonds: face amount at maturity. Maturity date.
- Bonds: interest rate.
- Bonds: coupons attached.
- Bonds: cost of bond.
- Bonds: source of funds used to purchase.
- Mutual funds: kinds, source of funds to purchase.
- Certificates of deposit (kinds, name of owners, amounts, banks or institutions issuing, dates opened and renewed, maturity dates, interest earned, penalties, source of funds used to open).
- Money market accounts (kinds, name of owners, amounts, banks or institutions issuing, dates opened and renewed, maturity dates, interest earned, penalties, source of funds used to open).
- IRA accounts (kinds, amounts, name of owners, banks or institutions issuing, dates opened and renewed, maturity dates, interest earned, penalties, source of funds used to open).
- 401K account (kinds, amounts, name of owners, banks or institutions issuing, dates opened and renewed, features, interest earned, penalties, source of funds used to open).
- Keogh plan (kinds, amounts, name of owners, banks or institutions issuing, dates opened and renewed, features, interest earned, penalties, source of funds used to open).
- Checking accounts (kinds, amounts, name of owners, dates opened, banks or institutions issuing, features, interest earned, penalties, source of funds used to open).
- Savings accounts (kinds, amounts, name of owners, dates opened, banks or institutions issuing, features, interest earned, penalties, source of funds used to open).
- Christmas club accounts (kinds, amounts, name of owners, dates opened, banks or institutions issuing, features, interest earned, penalties, source of funds used to open).
- Safe deposit box (banks or institutions holding, dates opened, number of box, persons authorized to enter, contents).

XVII. OTHER PERSONAL PROPERTY (Address the following topics for each item of personal property with a value over $100.)

- Ownership (solely owned by client? solely owned by spouse? jointly owned?).
- Nature of the property, e.g., furniture, jewelry, precious metals, antiques, art, china, furs, cars, boats, sporting equipment, coin collection, stamp collection, planes, pets, other.
- Location/address.
- Persons currently using/benefiting from property.
- Original cost. Date of purchase.
- Name and address of seller.
- Source of funds used to purchase.
- Amount owed on the property. Name and address of creditor/mortgage.
- Source of funds used to pay ongoing debt.
- Current fair market value of property (written appraisal available?).

of property upon divorce is usually not totally dependent on the identity of the title holder. What will be key is whether the property is considered marital property (as opposed to separate property), regardless of who holds title. (See chapter 8.)

continued

Exhibit 3.3 Checklist for compiling a family history—*Continued*

- If acquired by gift, name and address of the donor. Circumstances of gift.
- Improvements made to property. Dates and sources of funds used.
- Sources of funds to pay insurance covering the property.

XVIII. INSURANCE

- Life insurance: name and address of insurance company, policy number, beneficiaries (state whether beneficiaries can be changed), face amount, amount of premium, source of funds used to pay
premiums, date premiums are due, assignability of policy, loans against policy, other benefits.
- Health insurance: name and address of insurance company, policy number, benefits provided, insured parties, amount of coverage, amount of premium, source of funds used to pay premiums, date premiums are due.
- Fire/homeowner insurance on residence or vacation home: name and address of insurance company, policy number, insured parties, premises insured, face amount, amount of premium, source of funds used to pay premiums, date premiums are due, assignability of policy, other benefits.
- Vehicle insurance: name and address of insurance company, policy number, insured parties, vehicle insured, face amount, amount of premium, source of funds used to pay premiums, date premiums are due, assignability of policy, other benefits.
- Boat insurance: name and address of insurance company, policy number, insured parties, vehicle insured, face amount, amount of premium, source of funds used to pay premiums, date premiums are due, assignability of policy, other benefits.
- Disability insurance: name and address of insurance company, policy number, benefits provided, insured parties, beneficiaries (state whether beneficiaries can be changed), face amount, amount of premiums, source of funds used to pay premiums, date premiums are due, assignability of policy.

XIX. MISCELLANEOUS INCOME (Address the following topics for each source of income listed: name and address of payor, dates of receipt, source of the funds, and reason payments are made.)

- Social security income (client? spouse?).
- Unemployment compensation income (client? spouse?).
- Workers' compensation income (client? spouse?).
- Income from veterans benefits (client? spouse?).
- Public assistance, e.g., TANF (client? spouse?).
- Anticipated tax refund (client? spouse?).
- Income from annuity (client? spouse?).
- Income from trusts (client? spouse?).
- Income from alimony/maintenance obligation (client? spouse?).
- Income from book or patent royalties (client? spouse?).
- Income from rental property (client? spouse?).
- Income from personal loans (client? spouse?).
- Gift from client to spouse.
- Gift from spouse to client.
- Other income (client? spouse?).

XX. INSURANCE OR COURT CLAIMS (For each question, explain the extent to which the recovery sought is designed, at least in part, to redress a loss of income or damage to property acquired during the marriage)

- Has the client or spouse filed, or does either expect to file, a claim against an insurance company, e.g., a claim arising out of a recent automobile accident? State the circumstances.
- Is the client or spouse now the plaintiff in a civil suit? State the circumstances.
- Does the client or spouse expect to file a claim in court? State the circumstances.

XXI. FREQUENTLY OVERLOOKED ASSETS

- Frequent flier points.
- Hotel discount program based on accumulated points.
- Credit card cash or discount program based on accumulated points.
- Department store discount program based on accumulated points.
- Unused season tickets; the right to purchase season tickets at a discount.
- Accumulated equity in a car lease.
- Expected medical reimbursement.
- Unused sick leave.
- Lottery tickets purchased during the marriage that may produce winnings in the future.

XXII. LIABILITIES (Address the following topics for each liability listed: nature of debt or other kind of liability, name and address of creditors, name of debtors, loan number, date liability was incurred, source of funds in the past and currently used to pay it, reason debt was incurred, original amount of the debt, amount outstanding, date and amount of next payment, whether the client or spouse can increase the amount of the debt on his or her own.)

- Mortgage on primary residence.
- Mortgage on second home or vacation home.
- Mortgage on business property.

• Anticipated court damage awards may be marital property that can be divided upon divorce, depending on whether the amount received is personal to the victim (e.g., pain and suffering) or is designed to replace income that would have been earned during the marriage. (See chapter 17.)

- Mechanic's lien.
- Credit cards.
- Charge cards.
- Car loan.
- Boat loan.
- Education loan.
- Loan against cash value of life insurance policy.
- Loan from a friend.
- Other notes.
- Court judgment for money in which the client or spouse is or will be a defendant or may otherwise be responsible for the judgment. State the circumstances.
- Bankruptcy payments (e.g., under a Chapter 13 bankruptcy).

XXIII. TAX RETURNS (Address the following topics for the last three years in which returns were filed: gross income, taxable income, amount due, source of funds used to pay the amount due, accountant or attorney who helped prepare the return, extent to which the client or spouse was involved in the preparation of the return, location of a copy of the return.)

- Federal income tax return.
- Federal corporate (or other business) tax return.
- State income tax return.
- State corporate (or other business) tax return.
- City or other local tax return.
- City or other local corporate (or other business) tax return.
- Gift tax return.
- Estate tax return.

• Under the innocent spouse doctrine, a spouse might not be liable for the delinquent taxes that result from a tax return prepared by the other spouse. (See chapter 11.)

XXIV. OTHER FINANCIAL DATA

- Insurance premiums, education costs, or other expenses paid by a third party (e.g., a relative) on behalf of spouse or client.
- Record of charitable contributions (cash and in-kind) made by spouse or client.
- Evidence of loans made by spouse or client that are not being collected.
- Written family budgets.
- Newspaper or other media stories on spouse or client.
- Family or business photographs of spouse or client in settings of wealth.

XXV. ASSETS OF THE CHILDREN

- Do any of the children own property in their own name, e.g., cash, securities, land?
- How was this property acquired? Gift by whom? Purchase by child?
- Who controls this property? A guardian or custodian? A trustee?
- Has the client, the spouse, or anyone else used or consumed any of this property?
- When will the child have unrestricted access to this property?

XXVI. PERSONS FAMILIAR WITH CLIENT'S AFFAIRS AND SPOUSE'S AFFAIRS (Address the following topics for each person listed: name and address, dates hired or consulted, whether hired by client or spouse, fees paid, kinds of financial or other records he or she now possesses, etc.)

- Attorneys.
- Accountants.
- Real estate agents or brokers.
- Insurance agents.
- Bankers.
- Stockbrokers.
- Relatives.
- Friends.
- Clergy.
- Doctors.
- Others.

This checklist is not the only place in the book where there are guidelines on fact gathering. Throughout many of the remaining chapters, you will find interviewing and investigation checklists that pertain to specific issues under discussion in a chapter. In chapter 8, there is an extensive set of interrogatories that are designed to pry information from an opposing party. See also the technique of fact particularization discussed in Appendix A prior to the general instructions for the investigation and interviewing assignments. There is overlap among these different avenues of fact gathering, but family law is a fact-intensive area of the law. Many facts are often needed to resolve the variety of issues that can arise in a family law case. We need as much guidance as possible to achieve factual comprehensiveness.

ASSIGNMENT 3.2

Interview a married person. Cover the questions outlined in this chapter as well as any additional questions you think should be included. Tell the person you interview:

a. To assume he or she is about to file for divorce and has hired the law firm where you work as a paralegal.
b. To assume the spouses acquired considerable wealth during the marriage.
c. To make up answers to all the questions you ask.

(See General Instructions for the Interview Assignment in Appendix A. Instructions 5 and 6 in those General Instructions do not apply to this assignment.)

ASSIGNMENT 3.3

Your instructor will play the role of a new client in the office where you work as a paralegal. Assume that you have been asked to conduct a comprehensive interview of this client in order to compile a family history. The client is a spouse in a marriage where there are substantial personal and business assets over which the spouses are expected to have some bitter disputes. They are also expected to contest the custody of their two minor children. The marriage was the second marriage for both parties. To date the client has not been asked to bring anything to the interview. You must let the client know what you want him or her to bring to you in subsequent meetings.

Everyone in the class will play the role of interviewer. Raise your hand when you have questions. Everyone should ask numerous questions in this potentially complex case. (You do not have to follow the outline of questions in Exhibit 3.3 in the chapter.) Take detailed notes on the questions and answers, regardless of who asks the questions. Do not limit your notes to the answers to the questions you ask.

If you feel that another student failed to elicit sufficient detail on a question, re-ask the question in your own way to try to obtain greater detail.

After the interview, prepare a detailed report (sometimes called an *intake memorandum*) on what you learned from the interview. Use headings for different categories of data. Choose an overall organization for the report that you feel would best facilitate reading. The format of the beginning of the report should be as follows:

INTER-OFFICE MEMORANDUM
TO: [name of your instructor]
FROM: [your name]
DATE: [date(s) of the interview]
RE: Comprehensive Interview of [name of client]

(See General Instructions for the Interview Assignment in Appendix A.)

SUMMARY

In light of the potential complexity of a family law case, a law office may want to compile a comprehensive family history, particularly in contested cases that involve relatively large sums of money. The history is collected primarily by legal interviewing and investigation. Because clients are not always sure what they want, sensitivity is needed in providing explanations and options. Often they are confused about the law. Early on, the office must make sure that accepting a case will not involve an unethical conflict of interest.

After a new client has been accepted and the retainer is signed, the office begins its collection of the family history. The client is told what documents he or she should bring to the office. Any emergency concerns (e.g., physical safety) are dealt with soon after the client arrives. Facts are collected on the marriage, its deterioration, prior contracts between the spouses, expenses, health history, wills, trusts, children, businesses, employment history, stocks, bonds, other personal property, insurance, debts and liabilities, contributions each made to the career of the other, real property, and tax returns. The client is also asked for a list of names of people familiar with the life and affairs of both spouses.

KEY CHAPTER TERMINOLOGY

contested
retainer
letter of nonengagement
letter of authorization
meritorious

ETHICS IN PRACTICE

You are a paralegal working at a law office of Smith and Smith. You have referred a client to the firm. The client is a close friend of yours. During an interview, the client asks you whether a wife is ever obligated to pay alimony to a husband. Last week, you happened to be discussing the same topic with your attorney supervisor. You tell the client what the attorney told you; namely, that either spouse can be liable for alimony. Any ethical problems?

ON THE NET: MORE ON COMPREHENSIVE FACT GATHERING AND CLIENT RELATIONS

Fact Investigation and Evidence
http://www.tiac.net/users/tillers

Legal and Factual Research on the Internet
http://www.virtualchase.com/legalresearcher/index.html

Retainer: Client Rights and Responsibilities
http://www.courts.state.ny.us/clientsrr.htm

CHAPTER

PREMARITAL AGREEMENTS AND COHABITATION AGREEMENTS

CHAPTER OUTLINE

KINDS OF AGREEMENTS

We need to distinguish the different kinds of agreements that can be entered by adult parties who are living together in an intimate relationship or who are about to enter or exit such a relationship. The categories of agreements are summarized in Exhibit 4.1. Our main concerns in this chapter are the premarital agreement and the cohabitation agreement. We will consider the others later in the book.

PREMARITAL AGREEMENTS

A *premarital agreement* is a contract between prospective spouses made in contemplation of marriage and to be effective upon marriage. More specifically, it is a contract made by two individuals who are about to be married that covers spousal support, property division, and related matters in the event of the separation of the parties, the death of one of them, or the dissolution of the marriage by divorce or annulment. Of course, the marriage itself is a contract. A premarital agreement, in effect, is a supplemental contract that helps define some of the terms of the marriage contract.

Why, you might ask, would two individuals about to enter the blissful state of marriage discuss such matters as "who gets what" if they ever divorce? The kinds of people who tend to make premarital agreements:

- are older
- have substantial property of their own
- have an interest in a family-run business
- have children and perhaps grandchildren from prior marriages

Exhibit 4.1 Kinds of Agreements

Kind	Definition	Example
Cohabitation Agreement	A contract made by two individuals who intend to stay unmarried indefinitely that covers financial and related matters while living together, upon separation, or upon the death of one of them.	Ed and Claire meet at a bank where they work. After dating several years, they decide to live together. Although they give birth to a child, they do not want to be married. They enter an agreement that specifies what property is separately owned and how they will divide property purchased with joint funds in the event of a separation.
Premarital Agreement (also called prenuptial agreement (a "prenup") or antenuptial agreement)	A contract made by two individuals who are about to be married that covers spousal support, property division, and related matters in the event of the separation of the parties, the death of one of them, or the dissolution of the marriage by divorce or annulment.	Jim and Mary want to marry. Each has a child from a prior marriage. Before the wedding, they enter an agreement that specifies the property each brings to the marriage as separate property. The agreement states that neither will have any rights in this property; it will go to the children from their prior marriages. In addition, the agreement states that all income earned by a party during the marriage shall be the separate property of that party rather than marital or community property.
Postnuptial Agreement ("postnup"; also called a midmarriage or midnuptial agreement)	A contract made by two individuals while they are married that covers financial and related matters. The parties may have no intention of separating. If they have this intention, the agreement is called a separation agreement.	While happily married, George and Helen enter an agreement whereby George lends Helen $5,000 at 5% interest. She is to make monthly payments of $300. (To make this loan, George uses money he recently inherited from his mother.)
Separation Agreement	A contract made by two married individuals who have separated or are about to separate that covers support, custody, property division, and other terms of their separation.	Sam and Jessica have separated. In anticipation of their divorce, they enter an agreement that specifies how their marital property will be divided, who will have custody of their children, and what their support obligations will be. Later they will ask the divorce court to approve this agreement.

Such individuals may want to make clear that the new spouse is not to have any claim on designated property, or that the children of the former marriage have first claim to property acquired before the second marriage.

Another large category of couples favoring premarital agreements are young professionals, particularly those in their early thirties, with separate careers, who may have lived together before marriage. Although the women's movement of the 1980s and 1990s did not crusade in favor of premarital agreements, the "protect yourself" message of this movement certainly helped increase the popularity of premarital agreements among brides-to-be. Finally, the skyrocketing divorce rate has made more and more couples aware of the need for preplanning for the possible crisis of separation and dissolution. One preplanning tool that is available is the premarital agreement.

Parties cannot, however, completely reshape the nature of their marital status through a contract. Although premarital agreements are favored by the courts, there are limitations and requirements we need to explore.

Valid Contract

States differ on the requirements for a valid premarital agreement. (For a general overview of the elements of a contract, see the beginning of chapter 5.) In most states the agreement must be in writing. The parties must have legal capacity to enter a binding contract and must sign voluntarily. Fraud or duress will invalidate the agreement. An additional requirement in a few states is that the contract be notarized. The **consideration** for the agreement is the mutual promise of the parties to enter the marriage. To avoid litigation over the

consideration
Whatever the parties are mutually promising or exchanging in their agreement.

"It's a prenuptial agreement, silly! I'm asking you to *marry* me!"

Source: Mark Hannabury, 90 Case and Comment 34 (Mar.–Apr. 1985). Reprinted with permission.

niceties of the law of consideration, however, many states provide that such an agreement is enforceable without consideration.

ASSIGNMENT 4.1

What are the requirements for entering a valid premarital agreement in your state? (See General Instructions for the State-Code Assignment in Appendix A.)

Disclosure of Assets

waiver
Giving up a right or privilege by explicitly rejecting it or by failing to take appropriate steps to claim it at the proper time.

One of the main objectives of a premarital agreement is to take away rights that spouses would otherwise have in each other's assets. This is done by a **waiver** of such rights. For a waiver to make sense, you must have knowledge of the other person's assets and debts. This raises a number of questions:

- Do the parties have a duty to make a disclosure of their assets and debts to each other before signing the premarital agreement?
- If so, how detailed must this disclosure be?
- Can the parties waive their right to have this disclosure?

Most states require disclosure, but allow parties to waive their right to receive it. Of course, a party is not entitled to disclosure if he or she already has knowledge of the other party's wealth or net worth. When disclosure is required, states differ on how much disclosure is necessary. Some insist on a full and frank disclosure. In other states, it is enough to provide a general picture of one's financial worth. Careful attorneys will always try to provide maximum disclosure, so as to rebut any later claim by a spouse that he or she did not know the scope of the other spouse's wealth when the premarital agreement was signed. Furthermore, such attorneys will make sure the assets that are disclosed are not undervalued. Often the agreement includes a clause that says full disclosure has been made. This clause, however, is not always controlling, particularly if it can be shown that the party was tricked or forced into signing the entire agreement.

Fairness and Unconscionability

A few states require the agreement to be fair to both parties. There was a time when society viewed women as vulnerable and in need of special protection. There was almost a presumption that a woman's prospective husband would try to take advantage of her through the premarital agreement. Courts that took this view of the status of women tended to scrutinize such agreements to make sure they were fair to the prospective bride.

The women's movement has helped change this perspective. There is a greater degree of equality between the sexes. Consequently, if a woman makes a bad bargain in a premarital agreement, most courts are inclined to force her to live with it so long as:

- there was adequate disclosure of the identity and value of the other's assets and debts
- there was no fraud or duress
- there was an opportunity to seek advice from independent counsel or financial advisers
- there is no danger of her becoming a public charge and going on welfare because of how little the premarital agreement provided.

Of course, the same is true of males of modest means who later regret signing premarital agreements with relatively wealthy women.

Cautious attorneys advise their clients to give their prospective spouses sufficient time to study and think about the premarital agreement before signing. Waiting until the morning of the wedding to bring up the subject of a premarital agreement is not wise, particularly if the parties have substantially different education and business backgrounds. The more immature a person is in age and in worldly matters, the more time he or she needs to consider the agreement and to consult with independent experts or friends who are able to explain (1) the present and future financial worth of his or her prospective spouse and (2) what the premarital agreement is asking him or her to waive.

What if the agreement is substantially unfair to one of the parties, such as by granting him or her few property rights and no support from the other in the event of a separation or divorce? Shockingly unfair agreements are considered **unconscionable.** Will a court enforce an unconscionable premarital agreement? The answer may depend, in part, on whether there was adequate disclosure prior to signing.

unconscionable
Shocking to the conscience; substantially unfair.

Almost half of the states have adopted the Uniform Premarital Agreement Act. Under § 6 of that act, there are two major reasons a court will refuse to enforce a premarital agreement. First, the agreement was not entered voluntarily, a topic we will examine at length in the *Bonds* case. Second, the agreement is unconscionable *and* there was inadequate disclosure of assets. Note the language of the act:

> § 6. An agreement is not enforceable if the party against whom enforcement is sought proves that:
> (a) [he or she] did not execute the agreement voluntarily; or
> (b) the agreement was unconscionable when it was executed and, before execution of the agreement, that party:
>> (i) was not provided a fair and reasonable disclosure of the property or financial obligations of the other party,
>> (ii) did not voluntarily and expressly waive, in writing, any right to disclosure of the property or financial obligations of the other party beyond the disclosure provided, and
>> (3) did not have, or reasonably could not have had, an adequate knowledge of the property and financial obligations of the other party.

Hence, in these states, the court *will* enforce an unconscionable agreement if it was voluntarily entered with adequate disclosure.

Yet there are limits. Most courts do not want to see spouses become destitute as a result of what they voluntarily gave up in a premarital agreement. Furthermore, even if an agreement was fair at the time it was entered, circumstances may have changed since that date so that it is no longer fair.

> *Norm and Irene enter a premarital agreement in which they waive all rights they have in each other's separate property. In the event of a divorce, the agreement provides that Norm will pay Irene support of $500 a month for two years. A year before the parties divorce, Irene is diagnosed with cancer. She will need substantially more than $500 a month for support. Norm has resources to pay her more than what the premarital agreement provides. If he does not do so, Irene will need public assistance.*

To avoid this unconscionable result, some courts will be inclined to disregard the spousal support clause in the premarital agreement and order Norm to pay Irene additional support. The enforceability of this part of the agreement will be judged as of the date of the separation or divorce, not the date the agreement was signed.

confidential relationship
A relationship of trust in which one person has a duty to act for the benefit of another.

fiduciary
Pertaining to the high standard of care that must be exercised on behalf of another.

When individuals have a **confidential relationship,** they owe each other a duty of full disclosure and fair dealing. (This duty is sometimes referred to as a **fiduciary** duty.) They cannot take advantage of each other. Examples of individuals who have a confidential relationship include attorney and client, banker and depositor, and husband and wife. What about individuals engaged to be married—prospective spouses—who are preparing a premarital agreement? Some states say that they also have a confidential relationship. Courts in such states tend to scrutinize premarital agreements carefully and to invalidate provisions that are unfair to one of the parties. Indeed, if one side receives an advantage in the agreement, a presumption may arise that the advantage was obtained by undue influence. Most states, however, say that there is no confidential relationship between individuals about to be married. The duty of disclosure still exists in such states, but not at the level that would be required if they had a confidential relationship.

ASSIGNMENT 4.2

a. Jim and Mary are about to be married. Mary is a wealthy actress. Jim is a struggling artist. Both agree that it would be a good idea to have a premarital agreement. Mary suggests that Jim make an appointment to visit her tax preparer, whom Mary will instruct to give Jim a complete understanding of her assets. Laughing, Jim replies, "Not necessary. I'm insulted at the suggestion, my love." A year after the marriage, the parties divorce. Mary seeks to apply the premarital agreement, which provides that Jim is not entitled to support nor to any of Mary's property in the event of a divorce. Jim argues that the agreement is unenforceable. Discuss whether he is correct. (See General Instructions for the Legal Analysis Assignment in Appendix A.)

b. Do women have enough equality in today's society that they should be forced to live with agreements that, in hindsight, they should not have made? Is it more demeaning to a woman to rescue her from a bad agreement or to force her to live in drastically poorer economic circumstances because of the premarital agreement she signed?

public policy
The principles inherent in the customs, morals, and notions of justice that prevail in a state; the foundation of public laws; the principles that are naturally and inherently right and just.

Public Policy

Care must be taken to avoid provisions in a premarital agreement that are illegal because they are against **public policy.** For example, the parties cannot agree in advance that neither will ever make a claim on the other for the support of any children they might have together. The livelihood of children cannot be contracted away by such a clause. So, too, it would be improper to agree never to bring a future divorce action or other suit against the other side. It is against public policy to discourage the use of the courts in this way, as legitimate grievances might go unheard.

ASSIGNMENT 4.3

Would the following provisions in a premarital agreement be legal in your state? Explain why. (See General Instructions for the Court-Opinion Assignment in Appendix A.)

a. A clause designating how much support one spouse will receive from the other during the marriage.
b. A clause stating that the husband will never have to wash the dishes.
c. A clause stating that the children from a prior marriage will not live with the parties.
d. A clause stating that any children born to the couple will not attend formal services of any religion.
e. A clause stating a minimum number of times that the parties will engage in sexual intercourse per month.

Very often the premarital agreement will specify alimony and other property rights in the event of a divorce. Many courts once considered such provisions to be against public policy because they *facilitate* (or encourage) *divorce.* The theory is that a party will be more inclined to seek a divorce if he or she knows what funds or other property will be available upon divorce, particularly, of course, if the financial terms upon divorce are favorable. Most courts, however, are moving away from this position. Divorces are no longer difficult to obtain in view of the coming of no-fault divorce laws. There is less pressure from society to keep marriages together at all costs. A spouse who wants a divorce can obtain one with relative ease and probably does not need the inducement of a favorable premarital agreement to end the marriage. Hence, most (but by no means all) courts uphold provisions in premarital agreements that provide a designated amount of alimony or, indeed, that provide no alimony in the event of a divorce.

As indicated, however, this approach is not taken in all states. Some courts refuse to enforce *any* premarital agreement that tries to define rights in the event of a divorce. They will enforce only non-divorce clauses such as one covering the disposition of property upon death. Other courts distinguish between an alimony-support clause and a property-division clause in a premarital agreement. When the parties eventually divorce and one of them tries to enforce the premarital agreement, such courts are more likely to enforce the property-division clause than the alimony-support clause.

ASSIGNMENT 4.4

The property division clause in the premarital agreement of George and Jane provides that in the event of a divorce George will receive $750,000 and Jane will receive all other property acquired during the marriage. Is this clause legal? (See the General Instructions for the Legal-Analysis Assignment in Appendix A.)

Death clauses in premarital agreements are less controversial. Parties often agree to give up the rights they may have (e.g., dower, see chapter 8) in the estate of their deceased spouse. If the premarital agreement is not otherwise invalid, such terms are usually upheld by the courts.

Some premarital agreements try to regulate very specific and sensitive aspects of the marriage relationship. For example, there might be a clause on which household chores the husband is expected to perform or how frequently the parties will engage in sexual intercourse. Although such clauses are not illegal, their practical effect is questionable, as it is unlikely that a court would become involved in enforcing terms of this nature.

The Uniform Premarital Agreement Act has a very liberal view of what the parties can cover in an antenuptial agreement. Section 3 of the act provides as follows:

> (a) Parties to a premarital agreement may contract with respect to:
> (1) the rights and obligations of each of the parties in any of the property of either or both of them whenever and wherever acquired or located;
> (2) the right to buy, sell, use, transfer, exchange, abandon, lease, consume, expend, assign, create a security interest in, mortgage, encumber, dispose of, or otherwise manage and control property;
> (3) the disposition of property upon separation, marital dissolution, death, or the occurrence or nonoccurrence of any other event;
> (4) the modification or elimination of spousal support;
> (5) the making of a will, trust, or other arrangement to carry out the provisions of the agreement;
> (6) the ownership rights in and disposition of the death benefit from a life insurance policy;
> (7) the choice of law governing the construction of the agreement; and
> (8) any other matter, including their personal rights and obligations, not in violation of public policy or a statute imposing a criminal penalty.
>
> (b) The right of a child to support may not be adversely affected by a premarital agreement.

Interviewing and Investigation Checklist

Factors Relevant to the Validity of the Premarital Agreement

(C = client; D = defendant/spouse)

Legal Interviewing Questions

1. On what date did you begin discussing the premarital agreement?
2. Whose idea was it to have an agreement?
3. On what date did you first see the agreement?
4. Who actually wrote the agreement?
5. Did you read the agreement? If so, how carefully?
6. Did you understand everything in the agreement?
7. Describe in detail what you thought was in the agreement.
8. Did you sign the agreement? If so, why?
9. Were any changes made in the agreement? If so, describe the circumstances, the nature of each change, who proposed it, etc.
10. Do you recall anything said during the discussions on the agreement that was different from what was eventually written down?
11. Was anyone present at the time you discussed or signed the agreement?
12. Where is the agreement kept? Were you given a copy at the time you signed?
13. Before you signed the agreement, did you consult with anyone, e.g., attorney, accountant, relative?
14. If you did consult with anyone, describe that person's relationship, if any, with D.
15. What were you told by the individuals with whom you consulted? Did they think it was wise for you to sign the agreement? Why or why not?
16. How old were you when you signed the agreement? How old was D?
17. How much did you know about D's background before you agreed to marry? What generally did you think D's wealth and standard of living were?
18. How did you obtain this knowledge?
19. While you were considering the premarital agreement, describe what you specifically knew about the following: D's bank accounts (savings, checking, trust), insurance policies, home ownership, business property, salary, investments (e.g., stocks, bonds), rental income, royalty income, inheritances (recent or expected), cars, planes, boats, etc. Also, what did you know about D's debts and other liabilities? For each of the above items about which you had knowledge, state how you obtained the knowledge.
20. When did you first learn that D owned (______) at the time you signed the agreement? (Insert

items in parentheses that C learned about only after the agreement was signed.)

21. Do you think you were given an honest accounting of all D's assets at the time you signed? Why or why not?
22. Do you think the agreement you signed was fair to you and to the children you and D eventually had? Why or why not?

Possible Investigation Tasks

- Obtain copies of the premarital agreement and of drafts of the agreement, if any, reflecting changes.
- Contact and interview anyone who has knowledge of or was present during the discussions and/or signing of the agreement.
- Try to obtain bank records, tax records, etc., that would give some indication of the wealth and standard of living of D and of C at the time they signed the premarital agreement.
- Prepare an inventory of every asset that C *thought* D owned at the time the agreement was signed, and an inventory of every asset your investigation has revealed D *in fact* owned at the time of the signing.

Independent Counsel and Voluntariness

What happens if a party signs a premarital agreement without the benefit of independent counsel? Is it strong evidence that the agreement could not have been voluntarily entered? The recent celebrated case of *In re Marriage of Bonds* answered this question. A multimillionaire baseball player, Barry Bonds, entered a premarital agreement with his prospective wife, Sun Bonds. Paragraph 10 of the agreement provided:

> 10. CONTROL AND EARNINGS OF BOTH HUSBAND AND WIFE DURING MARRIAGE. We agree that all the earnings and accumulations resulting from the other's personal services, skill, efforts and work, together with all property acquired with funds and income derived therefrom, shall be the separate property of that spouse.

This clause meant that Sun Bonds would have no marital rights in Barry Bonds's baseball salary, clearly the largest asset in the coming marriage. She did not have independent counsel when she signed the agreement.

The case arose in California, a community property state in which each spouse has a 50 percent interest in marital property such as a spouse's salary, regardless of which spouse earned the salary. A valid premarital agreement can change this rule. If the *Bonds* case had arisen in a noncommunity property state, the same issue would have had to be decided. The question before the court would still be whether the absence of independent counsel rendered the premarital agreement involuntary and therefore unenforceable.

As you read *In re Marriage of Bonds,* notice the extensive factual detail provided by the court. This detail comes from the evidence that both sides presented during the trial. This factual detail will give you some idea of the extent of interviewing and investigation that attorneys and their paralegals must undertake in such cases.

CASE

In re Marriage of Bonds

24 Cal. 4th 1, 5 P.3d 815 (2000)
Supreme Court of California

Background: *At the time Barry Bonds married Susann (Sun) Bonds, he was earning $106,000 a year with the Pittsburgh Pirates. At the time of his divorce, he was earning millions a year with the San Francisco Giants. Before they married, they signed a premarital agreement prepared by Barry's counsel in which she*

continued

CASE

In re Marriage of Bonds—*Continued*

waived any interest in his earnings during the marriage. Sun Bonds did not have independent counsel and she argued that the agreement was invalid because she did not sign it voluntarily. The trial court found that Sun entered the agreement voluntarily with a full understanding of its terms. Sun appealed to the Court of Appeal, which reversed and directed a retrial on the issue of voluntariness. Barry has now appealed to the California Supreme Court.

Decision on Appeal: *The Court of Appeal is reversed. There is substantial evidence that Sun Bonds signed voluntarily despite the lack of independent counsel.*

Opinion of the Court

Chief Justice GEORGE delivered the opinion of the court: . . .

Sun and Barry met in Montreal in the summer of 1987 and maintained a relationship during ensuing months through telephone contacts. In October 1987, at Barry's invitation, Sun visited him for 10 days at his home in Phoenix, Arizona. In November 1987, Sun moved to Phoenix to take up residence with Barry and, one week later, the two became engaged to be married. In January 1988, they decided to marry before the commencement of professional baseball's spring training. On February 5, 1988, in Phoenix, the parties entered into a written premarital agreement in which each party waived any interest in the earnings and acquisitions of the other party during marriage. . . . That same day, they flew to Las Vegas, and were married the following day.

Each of the parties then was 23 years of age. Barry, who had attended college for three years and who had begun his career in professional baseball in 1985, had a contract to play for the Pittsburgh Pirates. His annual salary at the time of the marriage ceremony was approximately $106,000. Sun had emigrated to Canada from Sweden in 1985, had worked as a waitress and bartender, and had undertaken some training as a cosmetologist, having expressed an interest in embarking upon a career as a makeup artist for celebrity clients. Although her native language was Swedish, she had used both French and English in her employment, education, and personal relationships when she lived in Canada. She was unemployed at the time she entered into the premarital agreement.

[Barry sought a dissolution of the marriage in May of 1994. Sun was awarded custody of their two minor children and child support] in the amount of $10,000 per month per child. Spousal support was awarded in the amount of $10,000 per month, to terminate December 30, 1998. Only the first issue—the validity of the premarital agreement—is before this court.

Barry testified that he was aware of teammates and other persons who had undergone bitter marital dissolution proceedings involving the division of property, and recalled that from the beginning of his relationship with Sun he told her that he believed his earnings and acquisitions during marriage should be his own. He informed her he would not marry without a premarital agreement, and she had no objection. He also recalled that from the beginning of the relationship, Sun agreed that their earnings and acquisitions should be separate, saying "what's mine is mine, what's yours is yours." Indeed, she informed him that this was the practice with respect to marital property in Sweden. She stated that she planned to pursue a career and wished to be financially independent. Sun knew that Barry did not anticipate that she would shoulder her living expenses while she was not employed. She was not, in fact, employed during the marriage. Barry testified that he and Sun had no difficulty communicating.

Although Barry testified that he had previous experience working with lawyers in the course of baseball contract negotiations and the purchase of real property, his testimony at trial did not demonstrate an understanding of the legal fine points of the agreement.

Sun's testimony at trial differed from Barry's in material respects. She testified that her English language skills in 1987 and 1988 were limited. Out of pride, she did not disclose to Barry that she often did not understand him. She testified that she and Barry never discussed money or property during the relationship that preceded their marriage. She agreed that she had expressed interest in a career as a cosmetologist and had said she wished to be financially independent. She had very few assets when she took up residence with Barry, and he paid for all their needs. Their wedding arrangements were very informal, with no written invitations or caterer, and only Barry's parents and a couple of friends, including Barry's godfather Willie Mays, were invited to attend. No marriage license or venue had been arranged in advance of their arrival in Las Vegas.

Several persons testified as to the circumstances surrounding the signing of the premarital agreement. Sun testified that on the evening before the premarital agreement was signed, Barry first informed her that they needed to go the following day to the offices of his lawyers, Leonard Brown and his associate Sabinus Megwa. She was uncertain, however, whether Barry made any reference to a premarital agreement. She testified that only at the parking lot of the law office where the agreement was to be entered into did she learn, from Barry's financial advisor, Mel Wilcox, that Barry would not marry her unless she signed a premarital agreement. She was not upset. She was surprised, however, because Barry never had said that signing the agreement was a precondition to marriage. She did not question Barry or anyone else on this point. She was under the impression that Barry wished to retain separate ownership of property he owned before the marriage, and that this was the sole object of the premarital agreement. She was unaware the agreement would affect her future and was not concerned about the matter, because she was nervous and excited about getting married and trusted Barry. Wilcox's statement had little effect on her, because she had no question but that she and Barry were to be married the following day.

Sun recalled having to hurry to arrive at the lawyers' office in time both to accomplish their business there and make the scheduled departure of the airplane to Las Vegas so that she and Barry could marry the next day. Sun recalled that once they arrived at the lawyers' office on February 5, 1988, she, her friend Margareta Forsberg, Barry, and Barry's financial advisor Mel Wilcox were present in a conference room. She did not recall asking questions or her friend asking questions, nor did she recall that any changes were made to the agreement. She declared that her English language skills were limited at the time and she did not understand the agreement, but she did not ask questions of anyone other than Margareta Forsberg or ask for more time, because she did not want to miss her flight and she was focused on the forthcoming marriage ceremony. She did not believe that Barry understood the agreement either. Forsberg was unable to assist her. Sun did not recall the lawyers telling her that she should retain her own lawyer, that they were representing Barry and not her, that the applicable community property law provided that a spouse has an interest in the earnings and in acquisitions of the other spouse during marriage, or that she would be waiving this right if she signed the agreement. The lawyers may have mentioned the possibility of her being represented by her own lawyer, but she did not believe she needed one. She did not inform anyone at the meeting that she was concerned about the agreement; the meeting and discussion were not cut short, and no one forced her to sign the agreement.

Forsberg, a native of Sweden and 51 years of age at the time the agreement was signed, confirmed that she was present when attorneys Brown and Megwa explained the agreement, that Wilcox also was present, that no changes to the agreement were made at Sun's or Forsberg's request, and that she had been unable to answer Sun's questions or explain to Sun the terminology used in the agreement. She confirmed that Sun's English was limited, that the lawyers had explained the agreement, and that Sun never stated that she was considering not signing the agreement, that she did not understand it, or that she was not signing of her own free will. Sun never said that Barry threatened her or forced her to sign, that she wanted to consult independent counsel concerning the agreement, or that she felt pressured. Forsberg understood that Brown and Megwa were Barry's attorneys, not Sun's. She testified that when the attorneys explained the agreement, she did not recall any discussion of Sun's community property rights.

Barry and other witnesses offered a different picture of the circumstances leading to the signing of the premarital agreement, an account found by the trial court to be more credible in material respects, as reflected in its statement of decision. Barry and his attorney Brown recalled that approximately two weeks before the parties signed the formal agreement, they discussed with Sun the drafting of an agreement to keep earnings and acquisitions separate. Brown testified that he told Sun at this meeting that he represented Barry and that it might be in her best interest to obtain independent counsel.

Barry, Brown, and Megwa testified that Wilcox was not present at the February 5, 1988, meeting, which lasted between one and two hours, and that at the meeting the attorneys informed Sun of her right to independent counsel. All three recalled that Sun stated she did not want her own counsel, and Megwa recalled explaining that he and Brown did not represent her. Additionally, all three recalled that the attorneys read the agreement to her paragraph by paragraph and explained it as they went through it, also informing her of a spouse's basic community property rights in earnings and acquisitions and that Sun would be waiving these rights. Megwa recalled it was clearly explained that Barry's income and acquisitions during the marriage would remain Barry's separate property, and he recalled that Sun stated that such arrangements were the practice in Sweden. Furthermore, Barry and the two attorneys each confirmed that Sun and Forsberg asked questions during the meeting and were left alone on several occasions to discuss its terms, that Sun did not exhibit any confusion, and that Sun indicated she understood the agreement. They also testified that changes were

continued

CASE

In re Marriage of Bonds—*Continued*

made to the agreement at Sun's behest. Brown and Megwa experienced no difficulty in communicating with Sun, found her confident and happy, and had no indication that she was nervous or confused, intimidated, or pressured. No threat was uttered that unless she signed the agreement, the wedding would be cancelled, nor did they hear her express any reservations about signing the agreement. Additionally, legal secretary Illa Washington recalled that Wilcox waited in another room while the agreement was discussed, that Sun asked questions and that changes were made to the agreement at her behest, that Sun was informed she could secure independent counsel, that Sun said she understood the contract and did not want to consult another attorney, and that she appeared to understand the discussions and to feel comfortable and confident. . . .

[The trial court concluded that Barry had demonstrated by clear and convincing evidence that the agreement and its execution were free from the taint of fraud, coercion, or undue influence and that Sun entered the agreement with full knowledge of the property involved and her rights therein. The court of appeal reversed and directed a retrial on the issue of voluntariness. The court stressed that Sun lacked independent counsel and had not waived counsel effectively. It asserted that attorneys Brown and Megwa failed to explain that Sun's interests conflicted with Barry's, failed to urge her to retain separate counsel, and may have led Sun to believe they actually represented her interests as they explained the agreement paragraph by paragraph. The court of appeal concluded that the trial court erred in failing to give proper weight to the circumstance that Sun was not represented by independent counsel. It also pointed to Sun's limited English-language skills and lack of "legal or business sophistication," and stated that she "received no explanation of the legal consequences to her ensuing from signing the contract" and "was told there would be 'no marriage' if she did not immediately sign the agreement." It also referred to typographical errors and omissions in the agreement, the imminence of the wedding and the inconvenience and embarrassment of canceling it, Sun's asserted lack of understanding that she was waiving her statutory right to a community property interest in Barry's earnings, and the absence of an attorney acting as an advocate on her behalf.]

Pursuant to Family Code section 1615 [based on the Uniform Premarital Agreement Act], a premarital agreement will be enforced unless the party resisting enforcement of the agreement can demonstrate either (1) that he or she did not enter into the contract voluntarily, or (2) that the contract was unconscionable when entered into and that he or she did not have actual or constructive knowledge of the assets and obligations of the other party and did not voluntarily waive knowledge of such assets and obligations. In the present case, the trial court found no lack of knowledge regarding the nature of the parties' assets, a necessary predicate to considering the issue of unconscionability, and the Court of Appeal accepted the trial court's determination on this point. We do not reconsider this factual determination, and thus the question of unconscionability is not before us. . . . [T]he only issue we face concerns the trial court's determination that Sun entered into the agreement voluntarily. . . .

[Family Code § 1615 does not define] the term "voluntarily." . . . *Black's Law Dictionary* defines "voluntarily" as "Done by design. . . . Intentionally and without coercion." (Black's Law Dict. (6th ed. 1990) p. 1575.) The same source defines "voluntary" as "Proceeding from the free and unrestrained will of the person. Produced in or by an act of choice. Resulting from free choice, without compulsion or solicitation. The word, especially in statutes, often implies knowledge of essential facts." (Ibid.) The *Oxford English Dictionary* defines "voluntarily" as "[o]f one's own free will or accord; without compulsion, constraint, or undue influence by others; freely, willingly." (19 *Oxford English Dict.* (2d ed. 1989) p. 753.) . . .

[A number of factors are relevant to the issue of voluntariness. A court should examine whether the evidence indicates coercion or lack of knowledge and consider] the impact upon the parties of such factors as the coercion that may arise from the proximity of execution of the agreement to the wedding, or from surprise in the presentation of the agreement; the presence or absence of independent counsel or of an opportunity to consult independent counsel; inequality of bargaining power in some cases indicated by the relative age and sophistication of the parties; whether there was full disclosure of assets; and the parties' understanding of the rights being waived under the agreement or at least their awareness of the intent of the agreement. . . . [T]he parties' general understanding of the effect of the agreement constitutes a factor for the court to consider in determining whether the parties entered into the agreement voluntarily. . . .

In *In re Marriage of Dawley,* 17 Cal. 3d 342, 131 Cal. Rptr. 3, 551 P.2d 323, we rejected the wife's claim that a premarital agreement waiving community property rights had been obtained through undue influence, pointing out that in the particular case the pressure to marry created by an unplanned pregnancy fell equally on both the parties, that both parties were educated and employed, and that the party challenging the agreement did not rely upon the other party's advice, but consulted her own attorney. [See also] *La Liberty v. La Liberty,* (1932) 127 Cal. App. 669, 16 P.2d 681 (rejecting lack of independent counsel as a basis for rescission, given the parties' apparent understanding of the meaning of the premarital agreement.) . . .

We have considered the range of factors that may be relevant to establish the involuntariness of a premarital agreement in order to consider whether the Court of Appeal erred in according such great weight to one factor—the presence or absence of independent counsel for each party. . . .

[Nothing in our statute] makes the absence of assistance of independent legal counsel a condition for the unenforceability of a premarital agreement. . . . [The presence of independent counsel or a reasonable opportunity to consult counsel is] merely one factor among several that a court should consider in examining a challenge to the voluntariness of a premarital agreement. . . .

[W]e conclude that the trial court's determination that Sun voluntarily entered into the premarital agreement in the present case is supported by substantial evidence. . . .

The Court of Appeal held the trial court erred in finding the parties' agreement to be voluntary. The appellate court stressed the absence of counsel for Sun, and . . . pointed to Sun's limited English language skills and lack of "legal or business sophistication," stated that she "received no explanation of the legal consequences to her ensuing from signing the contract" and "was told there would be 'no marriage' if she did not immediately sign the agreement." It also referred to typographical errors and omissions in the agreement, the imminence of the wedding and the inconvenience and embarrassment of cancelling it, and Sun's asserted lack of understanding that she was waiving her statutory right to a community property interest in Barry's earnings.

The trial court, however, determined that Sun entered into the premarital contract voluntarily, without being subject to fraud, coercion, or undue influence, and with full understanding of the terms and effect of the agreement. . . . It determined that [Barry] had demonstrated by clear and convincing evidence that the agreement had been entered into voluntarily.

The trial court made specific findings of fact regarding the factors we have identified as relevant to the determination of voluntariness. These findings are supported by substantial evidence and should have been accepted by the Court of Appeal. . . .

The trial court determined that there had been no coercion. It declared that Sun had not been subjected to any threats, that she had not been forced to sign the agreement, and that she never expressed any reluctance to sign the agreement. It found that the temporal proximity of the wedding to the signing of the agreement was not coercive, because under the particular circumstances of the case, including the small number of guests and the informality of the wedding arrangements, little embarrassment would have followed from postponement of the wedding. It found that the presentation of the agreement did not come as a surprise to Sun, noting that she was aware of Barry's desire to "protect his present property and future earnings," and that she had been aware for at least a week before the parties signed the formal premarital agreement that one was planned.

These findings are supported by substantial evidence. Several witnesses, including Sun herself, stated that she was not threatened. The witnesses were unanimous in observing that Sun expressed no reluctance to sign the agreement, and they observed in addition that she appeared calm, happy, and confident as she participated in discussions of the agreement. Attorney Brown testified that Sun had indicated a desire at their first meeting to enter into the agreement, and that during the discussion preceding execution of the document, she stated that she understood the agreement. As the trial court determined, although the wedding between Sun and Barry was planned for the day following the signing of the agreement, the wedding was impromptu—the parties had not secured a license or a place to be married, and the few family members and close friends who were invited could have changed their plans without difficulty. (For example, guests were not arriving from Sweden.) In view of these circumstances, the evidence supported the inference, drawn by the trial court, that the coercive force of the normal desire to avoid social embarrassment or humiliation was diminished or absent. Finally, Barry's testimony that the parties early in their relationship had discussed their desire to keep separate their property and earnings, in addition to the testimony of Barry and Brown that they had met with Sun at least one week before the document was signed to discuss the need for an agreement, and the evidence establishing that Sun understood and concurred in the agreement, constituted substantial evidence to support the trial court's

continued

CASE

In re Marriage of Bonds—*Continued*

conclusion that Sun was not subjected to the type of coercion that may arise from the surprise and confusion caused by a last-minute presentation of a new plan to keep earnings and property separate during marriage. In this connection, certain statements in the opinion rendered by the Court of Appeal . . .—that Sun was subjected to aggressive threats from financial advisor Mel Wilcox[;] that the temporal proximity of the wedding was coercive under the circumstances of this case; and that defects in the text of the agreement indicate it was prepared in a rush, came as a surprise when presented, and was impossible to understand—are inconsistent with factual determinations made by the trial court that we have determined are supported by substantial evidence.

With respect to the presence of independent counsel, although Sun lacked legal counsel, the trial court determined that she had a reasonable opportunity to obtain counsel. The trial court stated: "Respondent had sufficient awareness and understanding of her right to, and need for, independent counsel. Respondent also had an adequate and reasonable opportunity to obtain independent counsel prior to execution of the Agreement. Respondent was advised at a meeting with Attorney Brown at least one week prior to execution of the Agreement that she had the right to have an attorney represent her and that Attorneys Brown and Megwa represented Petitioner, not Respondent. On at least two occasions during the February 5, 1988, meeting, Respondent was told that she could have separate counsel if she chose. Respondent declined. Respondent was capable of understanding this admonition."

These factual findings are supported by substantial evidence. Brown testified that at the meeting that preceded the February 5, 1988, meeting at which the premarital agreement was executed, both Sun and Barry indicated they wished to enter into a premarital agreement, and that Brown informed Sun that he represented Barry and that therefore it might be in her best interest to have her own attorney. She declined. Brown testified that at the February 5, 1988, session he explained the basics of community property law, telling Sun that she would be disavowing the protection of community property law by agreeing that income and acquisitions during marriage would be separate property. He informed her of her right to separate counsel, and told both parties that the agreement did not have to be signed that day. He again informed Sun that he represented Barry. He testified that Sun stated that it was not necessary for her to have counsel, and that she said she understood how the contract affected her interests under the community property law. Attorney Megwa also testified that the attorneys discussed basic community property law with Sun and told her that she had a right to have her own attorney and that she did not have to sign the agreement. He testified that the subject of her obtaining her own counsel came up at least three times during the February 5, 1988, meeting, and that she stated explicitly that she did not wish to submit the agreement to separate counsel for review. Megwa testified that he had cautioned Sun that she should not sign the agreement (which she had reviewed herself and which then had been explained to her clause by clause) unless it reflected her intentions, and that she said she understood the agreement.

The Court of Appeal . . . rejected the conclusion of the trial court that Sun understood why she should consult separate counsel. This determination by the appellate court contradicts the specific finding of the trial court that Sun understood what was at stake. The trial court's finding is supported by the language of the agreement itself, including the indication in paragraph 10 that the earnings and accumulations of each spouse "during marriage" would be separate property, and additional language stating that "[w]e desire by this instrument to agree as to the treatment of separate and community property *after* the marriage. . . ." (Italics added.) The trial court's finding also was supported by evidence establishing that the attorneys explained to Sun the rights she would have under community property law. In addition, Barry testified that ever since the issue first came up at the beginning of the relationship, Sun had agreed that the parties' earnings and acquisitions should be separate. Further, the attorneys testified that during the February 5, 1988, meeting, Sun stated her intent to keep marital property separate. These circumstances establish that Sun did not forgo separate legal advice out of ignorance. Instead, she declined to invoke her interests under the community property law because she agreed, for her own reasons, that Barry's and her earnings and acquisitions after marriage should be separate property.

The Court of Appeal . . . surmised that Sun did not have a reasonable opportunity to consult counsel because a copy of the agreement was not provided in advance of the February 5, 1988, meeting, and because Sun had insufficient funds to retain counsel and was not informed that Barry would pay for independent counsel's services. Again, this determination is contradicted by the conclusion of the trial court that Sun had "an adequate and reasonable opportunity to obtain independent counsel prior to execution of the Agreement." The trial court's determination was supported by evidence that Sun had been told about the agreement and her potential need for counsel at least a week before the document was executed and that she was told at the February 5, 1988, meeting that she could consult separate counsel and was not required to sign the contract that day. Additionally, there was evidence supporting the inference that she declined counsel because she understood and agreed with the terms of the agreement, and not because she had insufficient funds to employ counsel. . . .

With respect to the question of inequality of bargaining power, the trial court determined that Sun was intelligent and, evidently not crediting her claim that limited English made her unable to understand the import of the agreement or the explanations offered by Barry's counsel, found that she was capable of understanding the agreement and the explanations proffered by Barry's attorneys. There is ample evidence to support the trial court's determination regarding Sun's English-language skills, in view of the circumstances that for two years prior to marriage she had undertaken employment and education in a trade that required such skills, and before meeting Barry had maintained close personal relationships with persons speaking only English. In addition, Barry and his witnesses all testified that Sun appeared to have no language problems at the time she signed the agreement. Brown and Megwa testified that Sun indicated at the February 5, 1988, meeting that she understood the agreement, and indeed the contract contains a paragraph indicating that the parties attest that they "fully understand [ ]" the terms of the agreement. The trial court's findings with respect to the notice and opportunity Sun received to obtain independent counsel at least one week before the agreement was executed, as well as evidence indicating Sun long had known and agreed that the marriage would entail separation of earnings and acquisitions, tend to undercut any inference that coercion arose from unequal bargaining power, including Barry's somewhat greater sophistication and the involvement of two attorneys and a financial advisor on Barry's behalf. In addition, although these persons represented Barry, there is substantial evidence that they did not pressure Sun or even urge her to sign the agreement. Further, although Barry had three years of college studies as well as some experience in negotiating contracts, while Sun had only recently passed her high school equivalency exam (in English) and had little commercial experience, there is evidence that Barry did not understand the legal fine points of the agreement any more than Sun did. In addition, the basic purport of the agreement—that the parties would hold their earnings and accumulations during marriage as separate property, thereby giving up the protection of marital property law—was a relatively simple concept that did not require great legal sophistication to comprehend and that was, as the trial court found, understood by Sun. Finally, we observe that the evidence supports the inference that Sun was intrepid rather than a person whose will is easily overborne. She emigrated from her homeland at a young age, found employment and friends in a new country using two languages other than her native tongue, and in two years moved to yet another country, expressing the desire to take up a career and declaring to Barry that she "didn't want his money." These circumstances support the inference that any inequality in bargaining power—arising primarily from the absence of independent counsel who could have advised Sun not to sign the agreement or urged Barry to abandon the idea of keeping his earnings separate—was not coercive.

With respect to full disclosure of the property involved, the trial court found that Sun was aware of what separate property was held by Barry prior to the marriage, and as the Court of Appeal noted, she failed to identify any property of which she later became aware that was not on the list of property referred to by the parties when they executed the contract. The trial court also determined that Sun was aware of what was at stake—of what normally would be community property, namely the earnings and acquisitions of the parties during marriage. Substantial evidence supports this conclusion, including Sun's statements to Barry before marriage, the terms used in the contract, and Brown and Megwa's testimony that they painstakingly explained this matter to Sun.

With respect to the question of knowledge, as already explained it is evident that the trial court was impressed with the extent of Sun's awareness. The trial court did not credit her claim that before the premarital agreement was presented to her, the parties never had discussed keeping their earnings and acquisitions separate during marriage. Nor did the trial court credit her claim that the subject and content of the agreement came as a surprise to her, or that she did not understand that absent the agreement, she would be entitled to share in Barry's earnings and acquisitions during marriage. The finding that she was sufficiently aware of her statutory rights and how the agreement "adversely affected these rights" is supported by the testimony of Barry, Brown, and Megwa that the attorneys explained

continued

CASE

In re Marriage of Bonds—*Continued*

these matters before Sun signed the agreement. In addition, as noted, Barry testified that he and Sun agreed long before their marriage that their earnings and acquisitions would remain separate. . . .

The factors we have identified in assessing the voluntariness of the agreement entered into between Barry and Sun are not rigidly separate considerations; rather the presence of one factor may influence the weight to be given evidence considered primarily under another factor. In this respect, the trial court's finding that Sun had advance knowledge of the meaning and intent of the agreement and what was at stake for her is influential, as we have seen, in considering some of the other factors.

In considering evidence that Sun responded to Barry's suggestion that she secure independent counsel with the observation that she did not need counsel because she had nothing, the Court of Appeal . . . drew the inference least in support of the judgment—namely, that this statement indicated Sun did not understand that she did have property interests at stake in the form of the community property rights that would accrue to her under applicable statutes, in the absence of a premarital agreement. We believe that this was error on the part of the appellate court, because substantial evidence supported the trial court's determination to the contrary. It is clear from the testimony of Brown and Megwa that, even if Sun did not peruse the entire document herself, they read it to her paragraph by paragraph, thoroughly explaining the matter to her. Barry's testimony further established that he and Sun had agreed from the beginning of their relationship that each would forgo any interest in the other's earnings and acquisitions during marriage.

Family Code section 1615 places on the party seeking to avoid a premarital agreement the burden of demonstrating that the agreement was involuntary. The trial court determined that Sun did not carry her burden, and we believe that its factual findings in support of this conclusion are supported by substantial evidence.

The judgment of the Court of Appeal is reversed. . . .

ASSIGNMENT 4.5

a. Make a list of every fact that helps support the conclusion that the agreement was signed involuntarily. For each fact, state why.

b. Make a list of every fact that helps support the conclusion that the agreement was signed voluntarily. For each fact, state why.

c. Assess the voluntariness of the premarital agreement in (i)–(iv). Assume in each instance that the parties did not have independent counsel.

(i) Harry presented Linda with the premarital agreement for the first time at the jewelry store where they were buying a ring the day before the wedding. Immediately after the wedding, they were scheduled to begin an expensive honeymoon cruise.

(ii) Sam presented Mary with the premarital agreement for the first time two weeks before the wedding, just after Mary's elderly and frail parents arrived for the wedding from abroad.

(iii) When Diane signed the premarital agreement, she was a pregnant teenager, anxious about the legitimacy of her child. Her husband-to-be and the father of the child, Bill, was an older man.

(iv) The spouse signing the premarital agreement was a paralegal.

d. Should the law *require* each party to have his or her own independent counsel in order for the premarital agreement to be valid?

e. Do you think that there should be any difference between determining the voluntariness of a confession in a criminal case and the voluntariness of a premarital agreement in a civil case? Why or why not?

Drafting Guidelines

At the end of this section on premarital agreements, you will find a series of sample clauses for such agreements. See also the drafting guidelines in the following checklist.

Premarital Agreements: A Checklist of Drafting Guidelines

Ensuring the Enforceability of a Premarital Agreement

(FH = future husband; FW = future wife)

Although all the steps listed in this checklist may not be required in your state, they will help ensure the enforceability of the agreement. This checklist assumes that the attorney drafting the agreement represents the prospective husband, who is going to enter the marriage with considerably more wealth than the prospective wife.

Preparation

- Research the requirements for premarital agreements in the state (e.g., whether they must be subscribed, acknowledged, notarized, or recorded).
- Weeks (and, if possible, months) before the marriage, notify the FW when the agreement will be prepared and that she should obtain independent counsel.
- The greater the disparity in the age, wealth, education, and business experience of the FH and FW, the more time the FW should be given to study the agreement.
- Make sure the FW is old enough to have the legal capacity to enter a valid contract in the state.
- Determine whether the FW has ever been treated for mental illness. If she has, determine whether a current mental health evaluation is feasible to assess FW's present capacity to understand the agreement.
- Prepare a list of all currently owned assets of each party with the exact or approximate market value of each asset. (Include real property, jewelry, household furnishings, stocks, bonds, other securities, and cash.) This list should be referred to in the agreement, shown to the FW and to her independent counsel, and attached to the agreement.
- Prepare a list of all known future assets that each party expects to acquire during the marriage, with the exact or approximate market value of each asset. (Include future employment contracts, options, and anticipated purchases.) This list should be referred to in the agreement, shown to the FW and to her independent counsel, and attached to the agreement.
- Hire an accountant to prepare a financial statement of the FH detailing assets and liabilities. This statement should be referred to in the agreement, shown to the FW and to her independent counsel, and attached to the agreement.
- Obtain copies of recent personal tax returns, business tax returns, existing contracts of employment, deeds, purchase agreements, credit card bills, pension statements, and brokerage reports. These documents should be made available to the FW and to her independent counsel.
- Verify the accuracy of the names, addresses, and relationships of every individual to be mentioned in the agreement.

Participants and Their Roles

- The FH's attorney, financial advisor, and other experts who have any communication with the FW should make clear to the FW that they represent the FH only and should not be relied on to protect the interests of the FW.
- If needed, suggestions should be made to the FW about where she can find independent counsel and other experts who have never had any business or social dealings with the FH.
- If needed, funds should be made available to the FW to hire independent counsel or other experts.
- If no independent counsel of the FW is used, representatives of the FH will explain the terms of the agreement to the FW. When doing so, they should again remind the FW that their sole role is to protect the best interests of the FH.
- If English is the second language of the FW, arrange for a translator to be present. Encourage the FW to select this translator.
- There should be at least two witnesses present who will witness the execution of the agreement. (Paralegals are sometimes asked to act as witnesses to such documents.)

Content of the Agreement

- State the reasons the parties are entering the agreement.
- For each party, include a separate list of the names, addresses, and titles, if any, of every individual who helped the party prepare and understand the agreement.
- State whether the assets of the FH and of the FW that are now separate property will remain separate.
- State whether the appreciation of separate property will constitute separate property.
- List FH's existing children, other relatives, or friends and specify what assets they will be given to the exclusion of FW.
- List FW's existing children, other relatives, or friends and specify what assets they will be given to the exclusion of FH.
- List the documents that were shown to, read by, and understood by FW (e.g., lists of the assets, copies of tax returns, and financial statements). State which of these documents are attached to the agreement.

continued

Premarital Agreements: A Checklist—*Continued*

- Briefly summarize the major property and support rights that FW and FH would have upon dissolution of a marriage or upon the death of either *in the absence of a premarital agreement* (e.g., the right to an equitable share in all marital property, the right to alimony, and the right to elect against the will of a deceased spouse). Then include a statement that the parties understand that by signing the premarital agreement, they are waiving these rights.
- State whether there is a business or property that FH will have the right to manage and dispose of without the consent or participation of FW.
- State whether FW will own and be entitled to the death benefits of specific life insurance policies.
- Indicate which state's law will govern the interpretation and enforcement of the agreement.
- State whether arbitration will be used if FW and FH have disagreements over the agreement and whether the arbitrator's findings can be appealed.
- State the method FH and FW will use to modify or terminate the agreement during the marriage.
- Do not ask for a waiver of disclosure of assets.
- Do not ask for a waiver of mutual support during the marriage.
- Do not ask for a waiver of child support.
- Do not ask for a waiver of the right to seek custody or visitation.
- Do not provide that substantial property will be transferred to FW in the event the marriage is dissolved.
- Do not specify a date on which the prospective marriage will be dissolved.
- If the parties are of child-bearing age, do not state that either or both will not have children.
- State that each party will keep the contents of the agreement confidential.

Signing the Agreement

- Videotape the session, particularly while FW is explaining why she is signing; whom she relied upon in accepting the terms of the agreement; her understanding of FH's present and future assets; her understanding of what she is waiving in the agreement; and, if she does not have independent counsel, why she chose not to have such counsel.
- FH and FW should sign every page of the agreement.
- The signatures should be notarized.
- Any changes to the agreement should be dated and signed by the parties in the margin next to the change.

ASSIGNMENT 4.6

a. Find an opinion written by a court in your state that discusses the fairness or reasonableness of a premarital agreement. Give the facts and result of the opinion. If no such opinion exists in your state, try to find one written by a court in a neighboring state. According to the opinion, what standards are used in the state to assess the enforceability of the agreement? (See General Instructions for the Court-Opinion Assignment in Appendix A.)

b. Pretend you are about to be married. Draft a premarital agreement for you and your future spouse. You can assume anything you want (within reason) about the financial affairs and interests of your spouse-to-be and yourself. Number each clause of the agreement separately and consecutively. Try to anticipate as many difficulties as possible that could arise during the marriage and state in the agreement how you want them resolved. (See General Instructions for the Agreement-Drafting Assignment in Appendix A.)

c. After your instructor makes note of the fact that you have drafted an agreement, you will be asked to exchange agreements with another member of the class. You are to analyze the agreement written by your classmate. Go through each numbered clause in the agreement and determine whether it is valid or invalid according to the standards identified in this chapter and/or according to the law governing premarital agreements in your state. When you cannot apply a standard, in whole or in part, because you need more facts, simply list the factual questions to which you would like answers in order to be able to assess the validity of the clause in question. (See General Instructions for the Legal-Analysis Assignment in Appendix A.)

Pre-Civil Union Agreements

In chapter 5 we will discuss gay marriages and the substitute created in Vermont called the **civil union** relationship. Gay marriages are not legal in the United States today. However, the civil union relationship in Vermont is designed to provide same-sex couples with state benefits that are equal to those available in Vermont marriages. One of the benefits of a Vermont marriage is the right to enter a premarital agreement that will alter most of the spousal support and property rights that normally apply to a marriage in the event of the death of one of the spouses or the dissolution of the marriage. Because those in a Vermont civil union are to have rights equal to those of spouses in a Vermont marriage, one would expect that the parties contemplating a civil union should be able to enter a pre-civil union agreement that defines rights in the event of the death of one of the parties or the dissolution of the union. The civil union status, however, is relatively new, and therefore there is little case law interpreting such agreements.

civil union
A same-sex legal relationship in Vermont that has the same benefits, protections, and responsibilities under Vermont law that are granted to spouses in a marriage.

CLAUSES IN PREMARITAL AGREEMENTS

Here are some sample clauses used in several premarital agreements. Note the variety of phrasing used in different agreements to cover the same topic. Margin comments are provided to highlight important themes in the clauses. For terms you do not understand in the clauses, consult the glossary at the end of the book.

SAMPLE PREMARITAL AGREEMENT CLAUSES

I

Release of Husband's Rights in Wife's Property

Agreement made this ______ day of ______, 20______, between John Day, of ______, and Jane Kent of ______.

Whereas a marriage is shortly to be solemnized between the parties hereto;

Whereas Jane Kent now owns a large amount of property and expects to acquire from time to time additional property under a trust established for her by her father, ______;

Whereas John Day has agreed that all of the property now or in the future owned by Jane Kent, or her estate, shall be free of all rights that he might acquire by reason of his marriage to her;

Whereas both parties have made a full and complete disclosure of all their assets and liabilities and have attached a detailed schedule of these assets and liabilities to this agreement as Attachments A and B.

It is agreed as follows:

- *This disclosure clause takes the added precaution of listing assets as attachments to the agreement itself.*

Wife Retains Full Control of Property

1. Jane Kent shall have full right and authority, in all respects the same as she would have if unmarried, to use, enjoy, manage, convey, mortgage, and dispose of all of her present and future property and estate, of every kind and character, including the right and power to dispose of same by last will and testament.

Husband Releases All Right in His Wife's Property

2. John Day releases to Jane Kent, her heirs, legal representatives and assigns, every right, claim, and estate, actual, inchoate, or contingent, that he might have in respect to said property by reason of his marriage to Jane Kent.

Deceased Minor Child's Property

3. In the event any child of said marriage shall survive Jane Kent and shall then die a minor, John Day releases every right, claim, and estate he might inherit by reason of death of such minor child, and agrees that the property of such minor child shall be subject to any bequest or devise thereof made by Jane Kent.

continued

Sample Premarital Agreement Clauses—*Continued*

Additional Instruments

4. John Day further agrees that upon the request of Jane Kent he will execute, acknowledge and deliver any additional instruments that may reasonably be necessary to carry out more effectually the purpose of this agreement.

Representatives Bound

This agreement shall bind the parties and their heirs, legal representatives and assigns.

In Witness Whereof, etc.

II
Clause Releasing Husband's Interest in Wife's Property for a Lump Sum Payable on Wife's Death

Now, therefore *[Wife]* agrees that she will, upon her death, cause to be paid to *[Husband,]* if he is then living, $______, within one year after her death; and *[Husband]* agrees that he will, upon the death of *[Wife,]* take the said $______ in full of all rights of curtesy, homestead, survivorship, inheritance, separate maintenance, widower's award, or otherwise in or to her estate, and in full of all other rights, interests, claims or allowances which he might be entitled to but for this agreement, and that on payment to him of the $______ he will release, quitclaim and discharge to her representatives or heirs all rights of curtesy, homestead, survivorship, inheritance, separate maintenance, widower's award, and all other rights, claims or interests which he might have in her estate but for this agreement.

III
Release of Wife's Interest in Husband's Property—Present Payment of a Lump Sum

Agreement made this day ______ day of ______, 20______, between Alex Fin, of ______, and Mary Sims, of ______, witnesseth:

Whereas the parties contemplate entering into marriage relations:

Whereas Alex Fin is the owner of property listed on the memorandum attached hereto; and

Whereas Alex Fin desires to make suitable provision for Mary Sims in lieu of dower or other interest in his property which she otherwise might have.

Now, therefore, the parties agree as follows:

Payment of Lump Sum

1. Alex Fin agrees to pay to Mary Sims, immediately after the solemnization of said marriage, the sum of ______ dollars, the said sum to be her sole and separate property.

Wife Releases Rights in Husband's Property

2. Mary Sims agrees that she will accept the said sum in lieu of any and all claims of dower, inheritance and descent in and to the property of Alex Fin, now owned or that may hereafter be acquired by him, and in lieu of any and all other claims which might otherwise arise or accrue to her by reason of said marriage.

Management of Lump Sum

3. In view of the nature of the property set forth in the memorandum attached hereto, the nature and extent of which property is fully understood by Mary Sims, it is the desire of Mary Sims, and it is therefore agreed, that Alex Fin shall take over the management of the ______ dollars this day given by him to the end that its value may be preserved and made productive.

- *Mary is agreeing to accept a lump sum in exchange for an interest in Alex's property, but she is agreeing to let him manage this lump sum.*

Wife to Join in Conveyances

4. Mary Sims agrees that upon the request of Alex Fin, she will execute all and any proper instruments of conveyance in order to enable Alex Fin to sell or convey real estate now owned or afterward acquired by him.

In Witness Whereof, *etc.*

IV
Release of Marital Rights in Husband's Estate—Payment of Lump Sum Out of Husband's Estate

This agreement, made this ______ day of ______, 20______, between Albert Smith, of ______, and Joan May, of ______.

Whereas, a marriage is about to be solemnized between the parties to this agreement, who have made a full disclosure to each other as to their property, and are desirous that Joan May should have a cash payment instead of an interest in the estate of Albert Smith.

Now, therefore, if Joan May survives Albert Smith, Joan May agrees to accept from the estate of Albert Smith the sum of ______ dollars in lieu of dower and her distributive share of the personal property, and Albert Smith shall hold all the real estate which he now owns or may hereafter acquire free from any claim of dower, inchoate or otherwise; in consideration whereof Albert Smith agrees that Joan May shall be paid said sum of ______ dollars as soon after his decease as may be practicable.

In Witness Whereof, *etc.*

V
Clause Providing for Monthly Payment to Wife After Husband's Death

Now, therefore, the Husband agrees that the representative of his estate shall pay to the Wife the sum of ______ dollars ($______), payable as follows: ______ dollars ($______) ______ days after the decease of the Husband and a like amount each ______ days thereafter, until the full sum is paid in full, which cash payment shall be a lien on any real estate owned by the Husband at the time of his decease, provided, however, that at his option the Husband, during his life, may purchase an annuity for a like sum payable in monthly installments in any good and solvent insurance company, which annuity shall be received by the Wife as a substitute for said cash payment. Provided also that if the Wife shall predecease the Husband, this agreement shall terminate upon her death.

• *This clause provides security (the lien or an annuity) for the payments to be made to the wife upon the death of the husband.*

VI
Release of Husband's Interest in Wife's Estate and Limiting Wife's Interest in Husband's Estate

Whereas, ______, of ______, herein called the Husband, and ______, of ______, herein called the Wife, contemplate entering into marriage relations; and whereas, the Husband has a large estate and has children by a former marriage; and whereas, the Wife is possessed of property in her own right and has a child by a former marriage; and whereas, the said parties desire to prescribe, limit, and determine the interest and control which each of them may have in the estate of the other party; therefore the following agreement is entered into:

Know all men by these presents: That we, ______ and ______, being about to enter into the marriage relations, do hereby agree:

Husband Releases His Rights in Wife's Estate

1. In the event of the death of the Wife during the continuance of said marriage relations, the Husband surviving her, then the Husband shall receive from the estate of the Wife the sum of five dollars; such sum when paid by the executors or administrators of the estate of the Wife to be in full for all claims and demands of every kind and character which the Husband shall have against the estate of the wife.

• *The token payment of five dollars is the equivalent of the husband's agreement to renounce any claim to his wife's estate. This small amount is inserted so that no one can later claim that the parties forgot to provide for the husband's claim against his wife's estate.*

Wife Limits Her Rights in Husband's Estate

2. In the event of the death of the Husband during the said marriage relations, the Wife agrees that her claim upon the estate of the Husband shall be limited to $______, and a payment by the executors or the administrators of the estate of the Husband to the Wife, her heirs or legal representatives, of the sum of $______ shall be in full for all claims and demands of every kind and character which the Wife shall have against the estate of the Husband.

During Marriage Each to Have Full Control of Own Property

3. During the continuance of said marriage relations, each of the parties is to have full right to own, control, and dispose of his or her separate property the same as if the marriage relations did not exist, and each of the parties is to have full right to dispose of and sell any and all real or personal property now or hereafter owned by each of them without the other party joining, and said transfer by either of the parties to this contract shall convey the same title that said transfer would convey had the marriage relations not existed. This contract limits the right of either party to participate in the estate of the other, whether the marriage relation is terminated by death or legal proceedings.

Purpose of Contract to Limit Rights

4. The purpose of this agreement is to define and limit the claims and demands which each of the parties shall have against the estate of the other. Should either party die during the pendency of this contract, or should the contract be terminated by legal proceedings, the claims herein stipulated and defined shall be the limit which either party may have against the other party or his or her estate.

• *Here the parties are waiving the right to detailed disclosure of each other's assets. They declare "general knowledge" to be sufficient.*

Contract Made with Full Knowledge

5. This agreement is entered into with full knowledge that each of the parties has a separate estate, and no claim or demand can be predicated upon the fact that there has been any misrepresentation or concealment as to the amount and condition of said separate estate, it being expressly agreed that each of the parties considers the amount hereinabove fixed to be sufficient participation in the estate of the other, and

continued

SAMPLE PREMARITAL AGREEMENT CLAUSES—*CONTINUED*

it being expressly stated that each of the parties has sufficient general knowledge of the condition of the estate of the other to justify making and entering into this agreement.

In Witness Whereof, *etc.*

VII
Each Relinquishing Interest in Other's Property

Agreement made the ______ day of ______, 20______, between Ed Gray, of ______, and Grace Kay, of ______.

Whereas, the parties contemplate entering into the marriage relation with each other, and both are severally possessed of real and personal property in his and her own right, and each have children by former marriages, all of said children being of age and possessed of means of support independent of their parents, and it is desired by the parties that their marriage shall not in any way change their legal right, or that of their children and heirs, in the property of each of them.

Therefore it is agreed:

Home

1. Ed Gray agrees that he will provide during the continuance of the marriage a home for Grace Kay, and that the two children of Grace Kay may reside in such home with their mother so long as said children remain unmarried.

• *The agreement makes specific provision for children of a prior marriage.*

Husband Releases Rights in Wife's Property

2. Ed Gray agrees, in case he survives Grace Kay, that he will make no claim to any part of her estate as surviving husband; that in consideration of said marriage, he waives and relinquishes all right of curtesy or other right in and to the property, real or personal, which Grace Kay now owns or may hereafter acquire.

Wife Releases Rights in Husband's Property

3. Grace Kay agrees, in case she survives Ed Gray, that she will make no claim to any part of his estate as surviving wife; that in consideration of said marriage she waives and relinquishes all claims to dower, homestead, widow's award, or other right in and to the property, real or personal, which Ed Gray now owns or may hereafter acquire.

Intent That Marriage Shall Not Affect Property

4. It is declared that by virtue of said marriage neither one shall have or acquire any right, title, or claim in and to the real or personal estate of the other, but that the estate of each shall descend to his or her heirs at law, legatees, or devisees, as may be prescribed by his or her last will and testament or by the law of the state in force, as though no marriage had taken place between them.

Agreement to Join in Conveyances

5. It is agreed that in case either of the parties desires to mortgage, sell or convey his or her real or personal estate, each one will join in the deed of conveyance or mortgage, as may be necessary to make the same effectual.

Full Disclosure between the Parties

6. It is further agreed that this agreement is entered into with a full knowledge on the part of each party as to the extent and probable value of the estate of the other and of all the rights conferred by law upon each in the estate of the other by virtue of said proposed marriage, but it is their desire that their respective rights to each other's estate shall be fixed by this agreement, which shall be binding upon their respective heirs and legal representatives.

In Witness Whereof, *etc.*

VIII
Each Relinquishing Interest in Other's Property

This Agreement made the ______ day of ______, 20______, between Paul Oran, of ______, and Diane Leno of ______.

Whereas the parties contemplate legal marriage under the laws of the State of ______; and

Whereas, it is their mutual desire to enter into this agreement whereby they will regulate their relationships toward each other with respect to the property each of them owns and in which each of them has an interest.

Now, therefore, it is agreed as follows:

1. That all properties of any kind or nature, real, personal or mixed, wherever the same may be found, which belong to each party, shall be and forever remain the personal estate of said party, including all interest, rents and profits which may accrue therefrom.

2. That each party shall have at all times the full right and authority, in all respects the same as each would have if not married, to use, enjoy, manage, convey and encumber such property as may belong to him or her.

3. That each party may make such disposition of his or her property as the case may be, by gift or will during his or her lifetime, as each sees fit; and in the event of the death of one of the parties, the survivor shall have no interest in the property of the estate of the other, either by way of inheritance, succession, family allowance or homestead.

4. That each party, in the event of a separation, shall have no right as against the other by way of claims for support, alimony, attorney fees, costs, or division of property.

In Witness Whereof, *etc.*

IX

Each Relinquishing Interest in Other's Property

This agreement is made the ______ day of ______, 20______, between ______, of ______, and ______, of ______.

Whereas, a marriage is intended to be shortly after the date hereof solemnized between the said ______ and ______; and

Whereas, each of the parties is possessed of considerable property, and has made a full and frank disclosure to the other in relation to its character and amount, and they have been advised as to their respective rights therein in the event of their marriage and in the absence of any agreement between them:

Now, therefore, the *[bridegroom]* and *[bride],* hereby declare it to be their intention that during their marriage each of them shall be and continue completely independent of the other as regards the enjoyment and disposal of all property, whether owned by either of them at the commencement of the marriage or coming to them or either of them during the marriage. Accordingly, they agree that all property belonging to either of them at the commencement of the marriage or coming to either of them during the marriage shall be enjoyed by him or her, and be subject to the dispositions of him or her, as his or her separate property, and after the death of either it shall be free from any claim by the other on account of dower, curtesy, or other statutory right, in the same manner as if the marriage had never been celebrated.

In Witness Whereof, *etc.*

X

Pooling of Property

This agreement made this the ______ day of ______, 20______, between ______, of ______, and ______, of ______.

Whereas, the parties are contemplating marriage and establishing a home together; and

Whereas, the parties upon their marriage desire to pool their resources for the benefit of each other; and

Whereas, this agreement is made in order to avoid any future conflict as to their rights and interests in said property.

Now, therefore, the parties agree as follows:

1. The parties shall enter into the marriage relation and live together as husband and wife.

2. On or before the date of marriage, all property belonging to the parties, including bonds, bank accounts and realty, shall be reissued, redeposited and deeds drawn so that each party shall be the joint owner, with right of survivorship, of all of the property at present owned and held by the parties individually.

3. Each party obligates himself or herself to purchase and hold all property, present and future, jointly with the other party and agrees to execute any instrument necessary to convey, sell, or encumber any property, real or personal, when it is to the best interest of both parties that same be conveyed, sold, or encumbered.

4. At the death of either party the property belonging to both shall become the absolute property of the other, free from claims of all other persons. To make effective this section of the agreement a joint will of the parties is made and is placed in their safe deposit box in the ______ Bank in the City of ______, ______.

- *The parties are agreeing that the separate property they are bringing into the marriage shall be converted into marital property.*
- *The parties are agreeing to the preparation of a joint will.*

5. Should either party file a divorce against the other, then the party so filing shall by such filing forfeit to the other all right, title, and interest in all the property, real, personal or mixed, jointly held and owned by them.

6. The parties agree that the original of this instrument shall be deposited in escrow with ______ to be held by him.

7. This agreement cannot be revoked except by written consent of both parties and the holder in escrow shall not deliver the original to anyone except a court of competent jurisdiction or to the parties to this instrument upon their mutual demand for the surrender thereof.

8. This agreement is made in triplicate with each party hereto retaining a copy thereof, but the copy shall not be used in evidence or serve any legal purpose whatsoever if the original is available.

In Witness Whereof, *etc.*

Source: B. Stone, *Modern Legal Forms* § 4.1ff., p. 274ff. (rev. 2d ed., West Group, 1995). Reprinted with permission of West Group.

COHABITATION AGREEMENTS

Compare the following two situations:

> *Jim hires Mary as a maid in his house. She receives weekly compensation plus room and board. For a three-month period Jim fails to pay Mary's wages, even though she faithfully performs all of her duties. During this period, Jim seduces Mary. Mary sues Jim for* breach of contract *due to nonpayment of wages.*
>
> *Bob is a prostitute. Linda hires Bob for an evening but refuses to pay him his fee the next morning. Bob sues Linda for* breach of contract *due to nonpayment of the fee.*

The result in the second situation is clear. Bob cannot sue Linda for breach of contract. A contract for sex is not enforceable in court. Linda promised to pay money for sex. Bob promised and provided sexual services. This was the consideration he gave in the bargain. But sex for hire is illegal in most states. In fact, **fornication** and **adultery** are crimes in some states even if no payment is involved. Bob's consideration was **meretricious** sexual services and, as such, cannot be the basis of a valid contract.

fornication
Sexual relations between unmarried persons or between persons who are not married to each other.

adultery
Sexual relations between a married person and someone other than his or her spouse.

meretricious
Pertaining to unlawful sexual relations; vulgar or tawdry.

The result in the first situation above should also be clear. Mary has a valid claim for breach of contract. Her agreement to have a sexual relationship with Jim is incidental and, therefore, irrelevant to her right to collect compensation due her as a maid. She did not sell sexual services to Jim. There is no indication in the facts that the parties bargained for sexual services or that she engaged in sex in exchange for anything from Jim (e.g., continued employment, a raise in pay, lighter work duties). Their sexual involvement with each other is a **severable** part of their relationship and should not affect her main claim. Something is severable when what remains after it is removed can survive without it. (The opposite of severable is *essential* or *indispensable.*)

severable
Removable without destroying what remains.

Now we come to a more difficult case:

> *Dan and Helen meet in college. They soon start living together. They move into an apartment, pool their resources, have children, etc. Twenty years after they entered this relationship, they decide to separate. Helen now sues Dan for a share of the property acquired during the time they lived together. At no time did they ever marry.*

The fact that Dan and Helen never married does not affect their obligation to support their children, as we shall see in chapter 10. But what about Dan and Helen themselves? They **cohabited** and never married. They built a relationship, acquired property together, and helped each other over a long period of time. Do they have any support or property rights in each other now that they have separated?

cohabited
Lived together as husband and wife whether or not they were married. Also defined as setting up the same household in an emotional and sexual relationship whether or not they ever marry. The noun is *cohabitation.*

This is not an academic question. The Bureau of the Census says that between 1960 and 1997, the number of "unmarried-couple households" in America increased from 439,000 to more than 4.1 million. This category consists of two unrelated adults of the opposite sex who share a housing unit. The Bureau of the Census refers to these unmarried heterosexuals as **POSSLQs** (pronounced *possle-kews*), an acronym that stands for *p*eople (or *p*ersons) of the *o*pposite *s*ex [who are] *s*haring *l*iving *q*uarters. Furthermore, an additional 1.5 million households consist of two unrelated adults of the same sex.[1]

POSSLQs
Acronym for "people (or persons) of the opposite sex [who are] sharing living quarters."

[1] These are not all homosexual-couple households. The count includes some couples who are not cohabiting (e.g., those that include a roommate, a boarder, or a paid employee). In the future, the Census Bureau will use a new category of "unmarried partner," which is a person who is not related to the householder, who shares living quarters, and who has a close personal relationship with the householder.

For years, the law has denied any rights to an unmarried person who makes financial claims based upon a period of cohabitation. The main reasons for this denial are as follows:

- To grant financial or property rights to unmarried persons would treat them as if they were married. Our laws favor the institution of marriage. To recognize unmarried relationships would denigrate marriage and discourage people from entering it.
- Most states have abolished common law marriage, as we will see in chapter 5. To allow substantial financial rights to be awarded upon the termination of an unmarried relationship would be the equivalent of giving the relationship the status of a common law marriage.
- Sexual relations are legal and morally acceptable within marriage. If the law recognizes unmarried cohabitation, then illicit sex is being condoned.

These arguments are still dominant forces in many states. In 1976, however, a major decision came from California: *Marvin v. Marvin,* 18 Cal. 3d 660, 557 P.2d 106, 134 Cal. Rptr. 815 (1976). This case held that parties living together would not be denied a remedy in court upon their separation solely because they never married. Although all states have not followed *Marvin,* the decision has had a major impact in this still-developing area of the law.

The parties in *Marvin* lived together for seven years without marrying.[2] The plaintiff alleged that she entered an oral agreement with the defendant that provided (1) that he would support her, and (2) that while "the parties lived together they would combine their efforts and earnings and would share equally any and all property accumulated as a result of their efforts whether individual or combined." She further alleged that she agreed to give up her career as a singer in order to devote full time to the defendant as a companion, homemaker, housekeeper, and cook. During the seven years that they were together, the defendant accumulated in his name more than $1 million in property. When they separated, she sued for her share of this property.

The media viewed her case as an alimony action between two unmarried "ex-pals" and dubbed it a **palimony** suit. Palimony, however, is not a legal term. The word *alimony* should not be associated with this kind of case. Alimony is a court-imposed obligation of support that grows out of a failed marital relationship. There was no marital relationship in the *Marvin* case.

palimony
A nonlegal term for payments made by one nonmarried party to another after they cease living together, usually because they entered an express or implied contract to do so while they were cohabiting.

One of the first hurdles for the plaintiff in *Marvin* was the problem of "meretricious sexual services." The defendant argued that even if a contract did exist (which he denied), it was unenforceable because it involved an illicit relationship. The parties were not married but were engaging in sexual relations. The court, however, ruled that

> [A] contract is unenforceable only *to the extent* that it *explicitly* rests upon the immoral and illicit consideration of meretricious sexual services. . . . The fact that a man and woman live together without marriage, and engage in a sexual relationship, does not in itself invalidate agreements between them relating to their earnings, property, or expenses.[3]

The agreement will be invalidated only if sex is an express condition of the relationship. If the sexual aspect of their relationship is severable from their agreements or understandings on earnings, property, and expenses, the agreements or understandings will be enforced. An example of an *un*enforceable agreement would be a promise by a man to provide for a woman in his will in exchange for her agreeing to live with him for the purpose of bearing his

---

[2]The parties were Michelle Marvin (formerly Michelle Triola) and Lee Marvin, a famous actor. Although they never married, Michelle changed her last name to Marvin.
[3]*Marvin v. Marvin,* 557 P.2d at 112, 113.

children. This agreement is *explicitly* based on a sexual relationship. Thus sex in such a case cannot be separated from the agreement and is *not* severable.

The next problem faced by the plaintiff in *Marvin* was the theory of *recovery.* Married parties have financial rights in each other because of their *marital status,* which gives rise to duties imposed by law. What about unmarried parties? The *Marvin* court suggested several theories of recovery for such individuals:

- Express contract
- Implied contract
- Quasi contract
- Trust
- Partnership
- Joint venture
- Putative spouse doctrine

Before we examine these theories, three points must be emphasized. First, as indicated earlier, not all states agree with the *Marvin* doctrine that there are circumstances when unmarried cohabiting parties should be given a remedy upon separation. Second, in states that follow *Marvin,* there is disagreement over how many of the items in the preceding list of remedies will be accepted. Some states accept all of them and are even willing to explore others to achieve justice in particular situations. In contrast, there are states in which the only theory that will be accepted is an express contract. Third, all of the theories will be to no avail, even in states that follow *Marvin,* if it can be shown that meretricious sexual services were at the heart of the relationship and cannot be separated (are not severable) from the other aspects of the relationship.

Express Contract

In an express cohabitation agreement or contract, the parties expressly tell each other what is being "bargained" for (e.g., household services in exchange for a one-half interest in a house to be purchased, or companion services [nonsexual] in exchange for support during the time they live together). There must be an offer, acceptance, and legal consideration. (*Consideration* is whatever the parties are mutually promising or exchanging.) Although this is the cleanest theory of recovery, it is often difficult to prove. Rarely will the parties have the foresight to commit their agreement to writing, and it is equally rare for witnesses to be present when the parties make their express agreement. Ultimately the case will turn on which party the court believes.

Implied Contract

implied contract
A contract that is not created by an express agreement between the parties but is inferred as a matter of reason and justice from their conduct and the surrounding circumstances.

Another remedy is to sue under a theory of **implied contract,** also called an *implied in fact contract.* This kind of contract exists when a reasonable person would conclude that the parties had a tacit understanding that they had a contractual relationship even though its terms were never expressly discussed. Consider the following example:

> *Someone delivers bottled milk to your door daily, which you never ordered. You consume the milk every day, place the empty bottles at the front door, exchange greetings with the delivery person, never demand that the deliveries stop, etc.*

At the end of the month when you receive the bill for the milk, you will not be able to hide behind the fact that you never expressly ordered the milk. Under traditional contract principles, you have entered an "implied contract" to buy the milk, which is as binding as an express contract. Unless the state has enacted special laws to change these principles, you must pay for the milk.

In the case of unmarried individuals living together, we must similarly determine whether an implied contract existed. Was it clear by the conduct of the parties that they were entering an agreement? Was it obvious under the circumstances that they were exchanging something? Did both sides expect "compensation" in some form for what they were doing? If so, an implied contract existed, which can be as enforceable as an express contract.

Quasi Contract

A **quasi contract** is also called an *implied in law contract.* Although called a contract, it is a legal fiction because it does not involve an express agreement and we cannot reasonably infer that the parties had an agreement in mind. The doctrine of quasi contract is simply a device designed by the courts to prevent **unjust enrichment.**[4] An example might be a doctor who provides medical care to an unconscious motorist on the road. The doctor can recover the reasonable cost of medical services under a quasi contract theory even though the motorist never expressly or impliedly asked for such services. Another example might be a man who arranges for a foreign woman to come to this country to live in his home and provide domestic services. Assume there was no express or implied understanding between them that she would be paid. If what she provided was not meretricious, the law might obligate him to pay the reasonable value of her services, less the value of any support she received from him during the time they were together. The court's objective would be to avoid unjust enrichment. A court might reach a similar result when unmarried cohabitants separate.

quasi contract
A contract created by law to avoid unjust enrichment.

unjust enrichment
Receiving property or benefit from another when in fairness and equity the recipient should make restitution of the property or provide compensation for the benefit, even though there was no express or implied promise to do so.

Trust

A **trust** is another option to consider. At times, the law will hold that a trust is implied. Assume that Tim and Sandra, an unmarried couple, decide to buy a house. They use the funds in a joint account to which both contribute equally. The deed to the house is taken in Tim's name so that he has legal title. On such facts, a court will impose an implied trust for Sandra's benefit. She will be entitled to a half-interest in the house through the trust. A theory of implied trust might also be possible if Sandra contributed services rather than money toward the purchase of the property. A court would have to decide what her interest in the property should be in light of the nature and value of these services.

Another example of a trust that is imposed by law is called a **constructive trust.** Assume that a party obtains title to property through fraud or an abuse of confidence. The funds used to purchase the property come from the other party. A court will impose a constructive trust on the property if this is necessary to avoid the unjust enrichment of the person who obtained title in this way. This person will be deemed to be holding the property for the benefit of the party defrauded or otherwise taken advantage of.

trust
A legal entity that exists when one person holds property for the benefit of another.

constructive trust
A trust created by operation of law against one who has obtained legal possession of property (or legal rights to property) through fraud, duress, abuse of confidence, or other unconscionable conduct.

Partnership

A court might find that an unmarried couple entered the equivalent of a **partnership** and thereby acquired rights and obligations in the property involved in the partnership.

partnership
A voluntary contract between two (or more) persons to use their resources in a business or other venture, with the understanding that they will proportionately share losses and profits.

Joint Venture

A **joint venture** is like a partnership, but on a more limited scale. A court might use the joint venture theory to cover some of the common enterprises

joint venture
An express or implied agreement to participate in a common enterprise in which the parties have a mutual right of control.

[4]In a suit that asserts the existence of a quasi contract, the amount of recovery awarded a victorious plaintiff is measured by what is called *quantum meruit,* which means "as much as he deserves."

entered into by two unmarried individuals while living together (e.g., the purchase of a home). Once a joint venture is established, the parties have legally enforceable rights in the fruits of their endeavors.

Putative Spouse Doctrine

putative spouse
A person who reasonably believed he or she entered a valid marriage even though there was a legal impediment that made the marriage unlawful.

In limited circumstances, a party might have the rights of a **putative spouse.** This occurs when the parties attempt to enter a marital relationship, but a legal *impediment* to the formation of the marriage exists (e.g., one of the parties is underage or is married to someone else). If at least one of the parties is ignorant of this impediment, the law will treat the "marriage" as otherwise valid. Upon separation, the innocent party might be entitled to the reasonable value of the services rendered while together, or a share of the property accumulated by their joint efforts.

CASE

Hewitt v. Hewitt

77 Ill. 2d 49, 394 N.E.2d 1204, 3 A.L.R. 4th 1 (1979)
Supreme Court of Illinois

Background: *Victoria Hewitt met Robert Hewitt in college. When she became pregnant, he told her they were husband and wife and that no formal ceremony was necessary. He said he would "share his life, his future, his earnings and his property" with her. They announced to their parents that they were married and held themselves out as husband and wife. She helped him in his education and business. During fifteen years together, they had three children. They never entered a ceremonial marriage. (Since 1905 Illinois has not allowed common law marriages.*) Upon their separation, she sued him for "an equal share of the profits and properties accumulated" while together. The circuit court dismissed her complaint. She appealed. The lower appellate court reversed and ruled that she could sue him for violating an express oral contract. Robert then appealed. The case is now on appeal before the Supreme Court of Illinois.*

Decision on Appeal: *Judgment for Robert. It is against public policy in Illinois to enforce property rights of unmarried cohabitants.*

Opinion of the Court:

Justice UNDERWOOD delivered the opinion of the court. . . .

In finding that plaintiff's complaint stated a cause of action on an express oral contract, the appellate court adopted the reasoning of the California Supreme Court in the widely publicized case of *Marvin v. Marvin* (1976), 18 Cal. 3d 660, 134 Cal. Rptr. 815, 557 P.2d 106, . . . The issue of unmarried cohabitants' mutual property rights, however, . . . cannot appropriately be characterized solely in terms of contract law, nor is it limited to considerations of equity or fairness as between the parties to such relationships. There are major public policy questions involved in determining whether, under what circumstances, and to what extent it is desirable to accord some type of legal status to claims arising from such relationships. Of substantially greater importance than the rights of the immediate parties is the impact of such recognition upon our society and the institution of marriage. Will the fact that legal rights closely resembling those arising from conventional marriages can be acquired by those who deliberately choose to enter into what have heretofore been commonly referred to as "illicit" or "meretricious" relationships encourage formation of such relationships and weaken marriage as the foundation of our family-based society? In the event of death shall the survivor have the status of a surviving spouse for purposes of inheritance, wrongful death actions, workmen's compensation, etc.? And still more importantly: what of the children born of such relationships? What are their support and inheritance rights and by what standards are custody questions resolved? What of the sociological and psychological effects upon them of that type of environment? Does not the recognition of legally enforceable property and custody rights emanating from nonmarital cohabitation in practical effect equate with the legalization of common law marriage at least in the circumstances of this case? And, in summary, have the increasing numbers of unmarried cohabitants and changing mores of our society reached the point at which the general welfare of the citizens of this State

*A common law marriage is a marriage of two people who agree to be married, cohabit, and hold themselves out as husband and wife even though they do not go through a traditional ceremonial marriage. See chapter 5.

is best served by a return to something resembling the judicially created common law marriage our legislature outlawed in 1905?

Illinois' public policy regarding agreements such as the one alleged here was implemented long ago in *Wallace v. Rappleye* (1882), 103 Ill. 229, 249, where this court said: "An agreement in consideration of future illicit cohabitation between the plaintiffs is void." . . . It is true, of course, that cohabitation by the parties may not prevent them from forming valid contracts about independent matters, for which it is said the sexual relations do not form part of the consideration. (*Restatement of Contracts* secs. 589, 597 (1932). . . .)

The real thrust of plaintiff's argument here is that we should abandon the rule of illegality because of certain changes in societal norms and attitudes. It is urged that social mores have changed radically in recent years, rendering this principle of law archaic. It is said that because there are so many unmarried cohabitants today the courts must confer a legal status on such relationships. . . . If this is to be the result, however, it would seem more candid to acknowledge the return of varying forms of common law marriage than to continue displaying the naivete we believe involved in the assertion that there are involved in these relationships contracts separate and independent from the sexual activity, and the assumption that those contracts would have been entered into or would continue without that activity. . . .

[J]udicial recognition of mutual property rights between unmarried cohabitants would, in our opinion, clearly violate the policy of our recently enacted Illinois Marriage and Dissolution of Marriage Act . . . "[to] strengthen and preserve the integrity of marriage and safeguard family relationships." (Ill. Rev. Stat. 1977, ch. 40, par. 102.) We cannot confidently say that judicial recognition of property rights between unmarried cohabitants will not make that alternative to marriage more attractive by allowing the parties to engage in such relationships with greater security. . . .

The policy of the Act gives the State a strong continuing interest in the institution of marriage and prevents the marriage relation from becoming in effect a private contract terminable at will. This seems to us another indication that public policy disfavors private contractual alternatives to marriage. . . .

[W]e believe that these questions are appropriately within the province of the legislature, and that, if there is to be a change in the law of this State on this matter, it is for the legislature and not the courts to bring about that change. We accordingly hold that plaintiff's claims are unenforceable for the reason that they contravene the public policy, implicit in the statutory scheme of the Illinois Marriage and Dissolution of Marriage Act, disfavoring the grant of mutually enforceable property rights to knowingly unmarried cohabitants.

Appellate court reversed; circuit court affirmed.

CASE

Watts v. Watts

137 Wis. 2d 506, 405 N.W.2d 303 (1987)
Supreme Court of Wisconsin

Background: *Sue Watts alleges that she quit her job and abandoned her career in exchange for James Watts's promise to take care of her. For twelve years, they raised a family and worked in a family business together. They never married. (Common law marriages are not allowed in Wisconsin.) When the relationship deteriorated, she sued him in circuit court for her share of the property they had accumulated. Among her legal theories were breach of contract, constructive trust, and unjust enrichment. The circuit court dismissed the case, arguing that the legislature, not the court, should provide relief to parties who have accumulated property in nonmarital cohabitation relationships. The case is now on appeal before the Supreme Court of Wisconsin.*

Decision on Appeal: *Reversed. Sue Watts should be allowed to bring her claims against James.*

Opinion of the Court:

Justice ABRAHAMSON delivered the opinion of the court. . . .

Nonmarital cohabitation does not render every agreement between the cohabiting parties illegal. . . . The plaintiff alleges that during the parties' relationship, and because of her domestic and business contributions, the business and personal wealth of the couple increased. Furthermore, the plaintiff alleges that she never received any compensation for these contributions to the relationship and that the defendant indicated to the plaintiff both orally and through his conduct that he considered her to be his wife and that she would share equally in the increased wealth.

The plaintiff asserts that since the breakdown of the relationship the defendant has refused to share

continued

CASE

Watts v. Watts—*Continued*

equally with her the wealth accumulated through their joint efforts or to compensate her in any way for her contributions to the relationship. . . . [H]er claim . . . is that she and the defendant had a contract to share equally the property accumulated during their relationship. The essence of the complaint is that the parties had a contract, either an express or implied in fact contract, which the defendant breached.

Wisconsin courts have long recognized the importance of freedom of contract and have endeavored to protect the right to contract. A contract will not be enforced, however, if it violates public policy. A declaration that the contract is against public policy should be made only after a careful balancing, in the light of all the circumstances, of the interest in enforcing a particular promise against the policy against enforcement. Courts should be reluctant to frustrate a party's reasonable expectations without a corresponding benefit to be gained in deterring "misconduct" or avoiding inappropriate use of the judicial system. *Merten v. Nathan,* 108 Wis. 2d 205, 211, 321 N.W.2d 173, 177 (1982); *Restatement (Second) of Contracts,* Section 178 comments b and e (1981).

The defendant appears to attack the plaintiff's contract theory on three grounds. First, the defendant apparently asserts that the court's recognition of plaintiff's contract claim for a share of the parties' property contravenes the Wisconsin Family Code. Second, the defendant asserts that the legislature, not the courts, should determine the property and contract rights of unmarried cohabiting parties. Third, the defendant intimates that the parties' relationship was immoral and illegal and that any recognition of a contract between the parties or plaintiff's claim for a share of the property accumulated during the cohabitation contravenes public policy.

The defendant rests his argument that judicial recognition of a contract between unmarried cohabitants for property division violates the Wisconsin Family Code on *Hewitt v. Hewitt,* 77 Ill. 2d 49, 394 N.E.2d 1204, 3 A.L.R. 4th 1 (1979). In *Hewitt* the Illinois Supreme Court concluded that judicial recognition of mutual property rights between unmarried cohabitants would violate the policy of the Illinois Marriage and Dissolution Act because enhancing the attractiveness of a private arrangement contravenes the Act's policy of strengthening and preserving the integrity of marriage. The Illinois court concluded that allowing such a contract claim would weaken the sanctity of marriage, put in doubt the rights of inheritance, and open the door to false pretenses of marriage. . . .

The defendant has failed to persuade this court that enforcing an express or implied in fact contract between these parties would in fact violate the Wisconsin Family Code. The Family Code, chs. 765–68, Stats. 1985–86, is intended to promote the institution of marriage and the family. We find no indication, however, that the Wisconsin legislature intended the Family Code to restrict in any way a court's resolution of property or contract disputes between unmarried cohabitants.

The defendant also urges that if the court is not willing to say that the Family Code proscribes contracts between unmarried cohabiting parties, then the court should refuse to resolve the contract and property rights of unmarried cohabitants without legislative guidance. The defendant asserts that this court should conclude, as the *Hewitt* court did, that the task of determining the rights of cohabiting parties is too complex and difficult for the court and should be left to the legislature. We are not persuaded by the defendant's argument. Courts have traditionally developed principles of contract and property law through the case-by-case method of the common law. While ultimately the legislature may resolve the problems raised by unmarried cohabiting parties, we are not persuaded that the court should refrain from resolving such disputes until the legislature gives us direction. . . .

We turn to the defendant's third point, namely, that any contract between the parties regarding property division contravenes public policy because the contract is based on immoral or illegal sexual activity. . . . Courts have generally refused to enforce contracts for which the sole consideration is sexual relations, sometimes referred to as "meretricious" relationships. See *In Matter of Estate of Steffes,* 95 Wis. 2d 490, 514, 290 N.W.2d 697 (1980), citing *Restatement of Contracts,* Section 589 (1932). Courts distinguish, however, between contracts that are explicitly and inseparably founded on sexual services and those that are not. This court, and numerous other courts, have concluded that "a bargain between two people is not illegal merely because there is an illicit relationship between the two so long as the bargain is independent of the illicit relationship and the illicit relationship does not constitute any part of the consideration bargained for and is not a condition of the bargain." *Steffes,* supra, 95 Wis. 2d at 514, 290 N.W.2d 697.

While not condoning the illicit sexual relationship of the parties, many courts have recognized that the result of a court's refusal to enforce contract and property rights between unmarried cohabitants is that one party keeps all or most of the assets accumulated during the relationship, while the other party, no more or less "guilty," is deprived of property which he or she has helped to accumulate. See e.g., *Marvin v. Marvin,* 18 Cal. 3d 660, 682, 134 Cal. Rptr. 815, 830, 557 P.2d 106, 121 (1976).

The *Hewitt* decision, which leaves one party to the relationship enriched at the expense of the other party who had contributed to the acquisition of the property, has often been criticized by courts and commentators as being unduly harsh. Moreover, courts recognize that their refusal to enforce what are in other contexts clearly lawful promises will not undo the parties' relationship and may not discourage others from entering into such relationships. *Tyranski v. Piggins,* 44 Mich. App. 570, 577, 205 N.W.2d 595 (1973). A harsh, per se rule that the contract and property rights of unmarried cohabiting parties will not be recognized might actually encourage a partner with greater income potential to avoid marriage in order to retain all accumulated assets, leaving the other party with nothing.

In this case, the plaintiff has alleged many facts independent from the parties' physical relationship which, if proven, would establish an express contract or an implied in fact contract that the parties agreed to share the property accumulated during the relationship. The plaintiff has alleged that she quit her job and abandoned her career training upon the defendant's promise to take care of her. A change in one party's circumstances in performance of the agreement may imply an agreement between the parties. *Steffes,* supra, 95 Wis. 2d at 504, 290 N.W.2d 697; *Tyranski,* supra, 44 Mich. App. at 574, 205 N.W.2d at 597. In addition, the plaintiff alleges that she performed housekeeping, childbearing, childrearing, and other services related to the maintenance of the parties' home, in addition to various services for the defendant's business and her own business, for which she received no compensation. Courts have recognized that money, property, or services (including housekeeping or childrearing) may constitute adequate consideration independent of the parties' sexual relationship to support an agreement to share or transfer property. See *Tyranski,* supra, 44 Mich. App. at 574, 205 N.W.2d at 597; *Steffes,* supra 95 Wis. 2d at 501, 290 N.W.2d 697.*

According to the plaintiff's complaint, the parties cohabited for more than twelve years, held joint bank accounts, made joint purchases, filed joint income tax returns, and were listed as husband and wife on other legal documents. Courts have held that such a relationship and "joint acts of a financial nature can give rise to an inference that the parties intended to share equally." *Beal v. Beal,* 282 Or. 115, 122, 577 P.2d 507, 510 (1978). The joint ownership of property and the filing of joint income tax returns strongly implies that the parties intended their relationship to be in the nature of a joint enterprise, financially as well as personally.

Having reviewed the complaint and surveyed the law in this and other jurisdictions, we hold that the Family Code does not preclude an unmarried cohabitant from asserting contract and property claims against the other party to the cohabitation. We further conclude that public policy does not necessarily preclude an unmarried cohabitant from asserting a contract claim against the other party to the cohabitation so long as the claim exists independently of the sexual relationship and is supported by separate consideration. Accordingly, we conclude that the plaintiff in this case has pleaded the facts necessary to state a claim for damages resulting from the defendant's breach of an express or an implied in fact contract to share with the plaintiff the property accumulated through the efforts of both parties during their relationship. . . . [W]e do not judge the merits of the plaintiff's claim; we merely hold that she be given her day in court to prove her claim. . . .

The plaintiff's [next] theory of recovery involves unjust enrichment. Essentially, she alleges that the defendant accepted and retained the benefit of services she provided knowing that she expected to share equally in the wealth accumulated during their relationship. She argues that it is unfair for the defendant to retain all the assets they accumulated under these circumstances and that a constructive trust should be imposed on the property as a result of the defendant's unjust enrichment. . . .

Unlike claims for breach of an express or implied in fact contract, a claim of unjust enrichment does not arise out of an agreement entered into by the parties. Rather, an action for recovery based upon unjust enrichment is grounded on the moral principle that one who has received a benefit has a duty to make

---

*Until recently, the prevailing view was that services performed in the context of a "family or marriage relationship" were presumed gratuitous. However, that presumption was rebuttable. In *Steffes,* we held the presumption to be irrelevant where the plaintiff can show either an express or implied agreement to pay for those services, even where the plaintiff has rendered them "with a sense of affection, devotion and duty." Id. 95 Wis. 2d at 503, 290 N.W.2d at 703–704. For a discussion of the evolution of thought regarding the economic value of homemaking services by cohabitants, see Bruch, *Property Rights of De Facto Spouses Including Thoughts on the Value of Homemakers' Services,* 10 Family Law Quarterly 101, 110–14 (Summer 1976).

continued

CASE

Watts v. Watts—*Continued*

restitution where retaining such a benefit would be unjust. *Puttkammer v. Minth,* 83 Wis. 2d 686, 689, 266 N.W.2d 361, 363 (1978).

Because no express or implied in fact agreement exists between the parties, recovery based upon unjust enrichment is sometimes referred to as "quasi contract," or contract "implied in law" rather than "implied in fact." Quasi contracts are obligations created by law to prevent injustice. *Shulse v. City of Mayville,* 223 Wis. 624, 632, 271 N.W. 643 (1937).

In Wisconsin, an action for unjust enrichment, or quasi contract, is based upon proof of three elements: (1) a benefit conferred on the defendant by the plaintiff, (2) appreciation or knowledge by the defendant of the benefit, and (3) acceptance or retention of the benefit by the defendant under circumstances making it inequitable for the defendant to retain the benefit. . . .

As part of his general argument, the defendant claims that the court should leave the parties to an illicit relationship such as the one in this case essentially as they are found, providing no relief at all to either party. For support, the defendant relies heavily on *Hewitt v. Hewitt,* supra, to argue that courts should provide no relief whatsoever to unmarried cohabitants until the legislature provides specifically for it.

As we have discussed previously, allowing no relief at all to one party in a so-called "illicit" relationship effectively provides total relief to the other, by leaving that party owner of all the assets acquired through the efforts of both. Yet it cannot seriously be argued that the party retaining all the assets is less "guilty" than the other. Such a result is contrary to the principles of equity. Many courts have held, and we now so hold, that unmarried cohabitants may raise claims based upon unjust enrichment following the termination of their relationships where one of the parties attempts to retain an unreasonable amount of the property acquired through the efforts of both.

In this case, the plaintiff alleges that she contributed both property and services to the parties' relationship. She claims that because of these contributions the parties' assets increased, but that she was never compensated for her contributions. She further alleges that the defendant, knowing that the plaintiff expected to share in the property accumulated, "accepted the services rendered to him by the plaintiff" and that it would be unfair under the circumstances to allow him to retain everything while she receives nothing. We conclude that the facts alleged are sufficient to state a claim for recovery based upon unjust enrichment.

As part of the plaintiff's unjust enrichment claim, she has asked that a constructive trust be imposed on the assets that the defendant acquired during their relationship. A constructive trust is an equitable device created by law to prevent unjust enrichment. *Wilharms v. Wilharms,* 93 Wis. 2d 671, 678, 287 N.W.2d 779, 783 (1980). To state a claim on the theory of constructive trust the complaint must state facts sufficient to show (1) unjust enrichment and (2) abuse of a confidential relationship or some other form of unconscionable conduct. The latter element can be inferred from allegations in the complaint which show, for example, a family relationship, a close personal relationship, or the parties' mutual trust. These facts are alleged in this complaint or may be inferred. *Gorski v. Gorski,* 82 Wis. 2d 248, 254–55, 262 N.W.2d 120 (1978). Therefore, we hold that if the plaintiff can prove the elements of unjust enrichment to the satisfaction of the circuit court, she will be entitled to demonstrate further that a constructive trust should be imposed as a remedy. . . .

In summary, we hold that the plaintiff's complaint has stated a claim upon which relief may be granted. . . . Accordingly, we reverse the judgment of the circuit court, and remand the cause to the circuit court for further proceedings consistent with this opinion.

ASSIGNMENT 4.7

a. Why did the *Hewitt* court rule that cohabitation agreements were illegal? Why did the *Watts* court rule that they can be legal?

b. Which opinion was correctly decided, *Hewitt* or *Watts?*

c. Assume that James Watts died without leaving a will while he still had a good relationship with Sue Watts. Would she be able to claim a share of his estate as one of his heirs?

d. How would the facts of *Hewitt* be resolved in your state? How would the facts of *Watts* be resolved in your state? (See General Instructions for the Court-Opinion Assignment in Appendix A.)

ASSIGNMENT 4.8

a. Helen Smith and Sam Jones live together in your state. They are not married and do not intend to become married. They would like to enter a contract that spells out their rights and responsibilities. Specifically, they want to make clear that the house in which they both live belongs to Helen even though Sam has done extensive remodeling work on it. They each have separate bank accounts and one joint account. They want to make clear that only the funds in the joint account belong to both of them equally. Next year they hope to have or adopt a child. In either event, they want the contract to specify that the child will be given the surname, "Smith-Jones," a combination of their own last names. Draft a contract for them. Include any other clauses you think appropriate (e.g., on making wills, the duration of the contract, on the education and religion of children). (See General Instructions for the Agreement-Drafting Assignment in Appendix A.)

b. Tom and George are gay. They live together. George agrees to support Tom while the latter completes engineering school, at which time Tom will support George while the latter completes law school. After Tom obtains his engineering degree, he leaves George. George now sues Tom for the amount of money that would have been provided as support while George attended law school. What result? (See General Instructions for the Legal-Analysis Assignment in Appendix A.)

c. Richard and Lea have lived together for ten years without being married. This month, they separated. They never entered a formal contract, but Lea says that they had an informal understanding that they would equally divide everything acquired during their relationship together. Lea sues Richard for one-half of all property so acquired. You work for the law firm that represents Lea. Draft a set of interrogatories for Lea that will be sent to Richard in which you seek information that would be relevant to Lea's action. (See General Instructions for the Interrogatories Assignment in Appendix A.)

Interviewing and Investigation Checklist

Factors Relevant to the Property Rights of Unmarried Couples

Legal Interviewing Questions

1. When and how did the two of you meet?
2. When did you begin living together?
3. Why did the two of you decide to do this? What exactly did you say to each other about your relationship at the time?
4. Did you discuss the living arrangement together? If so, what was said?
5. What was said or implied about the sexual relationship between you? Describe this relationship. Was there ever any express or implied understanding that either of you would provide sex in exchange for other services, for money, or for other property? If sexual relations had not been a part of your relationship, would you have still lived together?
6. What was your understanding about the following matters: rent, house purchase, house payments, furniture payments, food, clothing, medical bills?
7. Did you agree to keep separate or joint bank accounts? Why?
8. What other commitments were made, if any? For example, was there any agreement on providing support, making a will, having children, giving each other property or shares in property? Were any of these commitments put in writing?
9. Did you ever discuss marriage? If so, what was said by both of you on the topic?
10. What did you give up in order to live with him or her? Did he or she understand this? How do you know?
11. What did he or she give up in order to live with you?
12. What other promises were made or implied between you? Why were they made?
13. How did you introduce each other to others?
14. Did you help each other in your businesses? If so, how?

continued

Interviewing and Investigation Checklist—*Continued*

15. What were your roles in the house? How were these roles decided upon? Through agreement? Explain.
16. Did he or she ever pay you for anything you did? Did you ever pay him or her? Explain the circumstances.
17. If no payment was ever made, was payment expected in the future? Explain.
18. Were the two of you "faithful" to each other? Did either of you ever date others? Explain.
19. Did you use each other's money for any purpose? If so, explain the circumstances. If not, why not?

Possible Investigation Tasks

- Obtain copies of bank statements, deeds for property acquired while the parties were together, loan applications, tax returns, etc.
- Interview persons who knew the parties.
- Contact professional housekeeping companies to determine the going rate for housekeeping services.

SAMPLE COHABITATION AGREEMENT

I
Intention of the Parties

_______ and _______ declare that they are not married to each other, but they are living together under the same roof, and by this agreement intend to protect and define each other's rights pertaining to future services rendered, earnings, accumulated property and furnishings and other matters that may be contained herein. It is expressly set forth herein that the consent of either party to cohabit sexually with the other is not a consideration, either in whole or in part, for the making of this agreement. It is further expressly set forth herein that the general purpose of this agreement is that the earnings, accumulations and property of each party herein shall be the separate property of the person who earns or acquires said property, and shall not be deemed community property, joint property, common law property or otherwise giving the non-earning or non-acquiring party an interest in same.

• *The parties want to make clear that their sexual relationship is not the essence of their relationship and of their agreement.*

II
Representations to the Public

It is agreed that should either or both of the parties to this agreement represent to the public, in whatever manner, that they are husband and wife, that said representation shall be for social convenience only, and shall in no way imply that sexual services are a consideration for any party of this agreement, nor shall it imply that sexual cohabitation is taking place.

• *If parties hold themselves out to be husband and wife, a court might conclude that they have entered a common law marriage if such marriages are allowed in the state where they live or where they spend significant time. (See chapter 5.) See, however, clause XIII, in which they explicitly disclaim an intent to enter a common law marriage.*

III
Property, Earnings, and Accumulations

It is agreed that all property of any nature or in any place, including but not limited to the earnings and income resulting from the personal services, skill, effort, and work of either party to this agreement, whether acquired before or during the term of this agreement, or acquired by either one of them by purchase, gift or inheritance during the said term, shall be the separate property of the respective party, and that neither party shall have any interest in, and both parties hereby waive any right or interest he or she may have in the property of the other.

IV
Services Rendered

It is agreed that whatever household, homemaking, or other domestic work and services that either party may contribute to the other or to their common domicile shall be voluntary, free, and without compensation, and each party agrees that work of this nature is done without expectation of monetary or other reward from the other party.

• *Note that clause IV does not cover business or professional services they render to each other. Such services are covered in clause IX.*

V
Debts and Obligations

It is agreed that all debts and obligations acquired by either party which is to the benefit of that party shall be the debt or obligation of that party only, and that the other shall not be liable for same. Should one party be forced to pay a debt rightfully belonging to and benefiting the other, the other promises to reimburse, indemnify and hold harmless the one who has paid said debt or obligation.

Those debts and obligations which are to the benefit of both parties, such as utilities, garbage, local telephone service, rent, and renter's insurance shall be paid in such sums and in such proportion by each party as shall be mutually agreeable.

VI
Money Loaned

All money, with the exception of mortgage or rent payments, transferred by one party to the other, either directly or to an account, obligation, or purchase of the other, shall be deemed a loan to the other, unless otherwise stated in writing. This shall include such things as downpayments on a home or vehicle, and deposits in either party's separate bank account.

VII
Rented Premises

It is agreed that should the parties share rented premises, said rented premises shall "belong" to the person who first rented the same, and should the parties separate, the second one shall leave taking only such belongings as he or she owned prior to moving in or purchased while living together.

If the parties both rent the premises from the beginning, then it is agreed that they will have a third person flip a coin to see who "owns" the premises, and the winner will have the option to remain while the loser leaves.

VIII
Rent or Mortgage

It is agreed that the parties may split the rent or mortgage payments in whatever proportion they choose, each contributing such sum as is mutually agreeable. It is also agreed that if one party contributes to the mortgage payment of a premises belonging to or being purchased in the name of the other party, that such contribution shall be deemed rent only, and shall be non-refundable and shall not create in the person who is living in the premises owned or being purchased by the other, any interest in said property or in the equity therein.

IX
Business Arrangements

A. It is agreed that should one party hereto contribute services, labor, or effort to a business enterprise belonging to the other, that the party contributing said services, labor or effort shall not acquire by reason thereof any interest in, ownership of, or claim to said business enterprise, nor shall said person be compensated in any way for said services, labor, or effort, unless the terms of said compensation are expressly agreed to by both parties.

B. Should the parties share services, labor or effort in a jointly owned business enterprise the relative interests of each party shall be apportioned according to a separate partnership agreement, or, if there is no express agreement, then in proportion that each contributed thereto.

C. It is agreed that the business known as ______ is the individual and separate business of *[Name of Owner]*, and is not to be deemed a jointly owned business of both parties.

X
Separate Accounts

In conformity with the intentions of the parties set forth herein, both parties agree to maintain separate bank accounts, insurance accounts (except "renter's" insurance to insure the contents of an apartment, house, etc., which the parties may jointly hold), tax returns, credit accounts, credit union accounts, medical accounts, automobile registration and ownership, and deeds to property, and to make all purchases of personal property, including furniture, appliances, records, books, works of art, stereo equipment, etc., separate, in order to avoid confusion as to the ownership of same, and also in order to avoid nullifying the general intent of this agreement.

XI
Duration of This Agreement

This agreement shall remain in effect from the date the parties start cohabiting until either party leaves or removes himself or herself from the common domicile with the intention not to return, or until they marry, or until they make a new written agreement that is contrary to the terms of this agreement.

XII
Attorney Fees and Costs

Each party agrees to act in good faith with the provisions of this agreement, and should one party breach the agreement or fail to act in good faith therewith, such party agrees to pay to the other such attorney fees and costs as may be reasonable in order to properly enforce the provisions herein.

continued

SAMPLE COHABITATION AGREEMENT—*CONTINUED*

XIII
No Common Law Marriage Intended

Even though the parties hereto are cohabiting under the same roof and may give the appearance of being married, or from time to time represent to the public that they are husband and wife, they do not intend by such acts to acquire the status of "common law" marriage, and expressly state herein that this is not an agreement to marry, that they are not now married, and that they understand they are not married to each other during the term of this agreement.

XIV
Waiver of Support

Both parties waive and relinquish any and all rights to "alimony," "spousal support," or other separate maintenance from the other in the event of a termination of their living together arrangement.

Dated: ______

____
[Name and Signature of Party]

____
[Name and Signature of Party]

Witnesses:

____

____

Notary Public:

______________________ (Seal)

My commission expires ______

Source: W. Mulloy, *West's Legal Forms* § 3.54, pp. 225–29 (2d ed., West Group, 1983). Reprinted with permission of West Group.

SUMMARY

The four main kinds of agreements parties enter before and after marriage are cohabitation agreement, premarital agreement, postnuptial agreement, and separation agreement. A premarital agreement is a contract made by two individuals who are about to be married that covers spousal support, property division, and related matters in the event of the separation of the parties, the death of one of them, or the dissolution of the marriage by divorce or annulment. To be enforceable, the agreement must meet the requirements for a valid contract, must be based on disclosure of assets, must not be unconscionable, and must not be against public policy.

A cohabitation agreement is a contract between two unmarried parties (who intend to remain unmarried) covering financial and related matters while they live together, upon separation, or upon death. Some states will enforce such agreements so long as they are not based solely on meretricious sexual services, or so long as the sexual aspect of their agreement is severable from the rest of the agreement. When one party sues the other for breaching the agreement, the media's misleading phrase for the litigation is palimony suit.

If the aggrieved party cannot establish the existence of an express or implied cohabitation contract, other theories might be used by the court to avoid the unfairness of one of the parties walking away from the relationship with nothing. These theories include quasi contract, trust, partnership, joint venture, and the putative-spouse doctrine.

KEY CHAPTER TERMINOLOGY

cohabitation agreement
premarital agreement
postnuptial agreement
separation agreement
consideration
waiver
unconscionable
confidential relationship
fiduciary
public policy
civil union
fornication
adultery
meretricious
severable
cohabited
POSSLQs
palimony
implied contract
quasi contract
unjust enrichment
trust
constructive trust
partnership
joint venture
putative spouse

ETHICS IN PRACTICE

You are a paralegal working at the law office of Paul Smith, Esq. Alice Henderson has asked the firm to write a cohabitation agreement for her and her boyfriend, Fred Lincoln. Both Alice and Fred come to the firm's office, where Paul Smith describes the agreement that he has drafted for them, telling them that it is a standard agreement considered fair to both parties. Alice and Fred are happy with the agreement and sign it. Any ethical problems?

ON THE NET: PREMARITAL AGREEMENTS AND COHABITATION

FormDepot: Antenuptial Agreement
http://www.formdepot.com/forms/clf/clf5.html

Jewish Law: Suggested Antenuptial Agreement
http://www.jlaw.com/Articles/antenuptial_agreement4.html

Premarital Agreements Online
http://www.edisso.com/antenup.htm

Divorce Source (click your state; type "antenuptial" or "cohabitation")
http://www.divorcesource.com

Alternatives to Marriage Project
http://www.unmarried.org

Family Law Advisor: Cohabitation Agreements
http://www.divorcenet.com/co/co%2Dart03.html

Unmarried Couples and the Law
http://www.palimony.com

CHAPTER 5

TRADITIONAL MARRIAGE AND ALTERNATIVES

CHAPTER OUTLINE

LEGAL ISSUES PRIOR TO MARRIAGE

Before we examine the question of who can enter a marriage and the availability of alternatives to marriage, we will explore two important issues that can arise when a contemplated marriage does not occur. First, can someone be sued for failing to fulfill a promise to marry? If so, what is the theory of the suit—what is the cause of action? Second, if both parties agree to call off the marriage, what happens to engagement and wedding gifts that have already been exchanged? Finally, we need to look at whether a promise *not* to marry is enforceable.

Breach of Promise to Marry

Just under half the states allow one person to sue another for breach of promise to marry. Twenty-seven states and the District of Columbia have abolished this action.[1] The decision to maintain or to abolish the action has been the subject of considerable debate.

Over 100,000 engagements are broken each year. This can be a costly experience. In some cities, "traditional weddings can cost as much as $50,000 or $100,000, and as the wedding day approaches, less and less of the expense of the event can be recovered if the event is canceled." In New York City, for example, many caterers and hotels charge for services and rooms that cannot be

[1]The following have abolished it by statute or court opinion: Alabama, California, Colorado, Connecticut, Delaware, District of Columbia, Florida, Indiana, Kentucky, Maine, Maryland, Massachusetts, Michigan, Minnesota, Montana, Nevada, New Hampshire, New Jersey, New York, North Dakota, Ohio, Pennsylvania, Utah, Vermont, Virginia, West Virginia, Wisconsin, and Wyoming.

rebooked when canceled with less than six months' notice.[2] When faced with such costs, some victims of broken engagements sue for breach of **contract** or, more specifically, for breach of promise to marry.

contract
An agreement that a court will enforce.

For centuries, one of the sacred principles in law has been the stability of contracts. An organized society depends on the faithful performance of contractual commitments. Hence courts are available to force parties to abide by their contracts. In the business world, thousands of contracts are made every hour. Merchants invest large amounts of money and other resources in reliance on these contracts. Consequently, the law will not allow a merchant to avoid performing its contract simply because it is now having second thoughts about the agreement reached or because it can now obtain a better deal elsewhere. But does the sacred principle of contractual stability apply to broken promises to marry? Should courts be used to force parties to honor such contracts? Before answering these questions, let's review the major components or elements of a contract:

Elements of a Contract

- There must be an offer.
- There must be an acceptance of the offer.
- There must be **consideration.** (Consideration is something of value that is exchanged, e.g., an exchange of money for services, an exchange of promises to do something or to refrain from doing something.)

consideration
Something of value that is exchanged between the parties.

In addition, the parties must have the **capacity** to enter a contract. Finally, some contracts may have to be in writing to comply with the **statute of frauds.**

capacity
The legal power to do something.

statute of frauds
The requirement that certain kinds of contracts be in writing in order to be enforceable.

Must be in writing.

About 1/2 the states let you sue for being left at the alter. Usually can only sue for what you have spent in preparing for the wedding.

John, age thirty-four, has been dating Mary, an independently wealthy woman of thirty-three. She proposes, John accepts, and they both agree on a wedding date. The next day Mary changes her mind and tells John that she no longer wants to marry him. Does a contract exist that is enforceable by John against Mary? Each of the elements needs to be examined:

1. Offer. *Mary offered to marry John.*
2. Acceptance. *John agreed to marry her (he accepted her offer).*
3. Consideration. *Something of value was exchanged by both parties; they both exchanged* promises *to marry each other. This mutual* exchange of promises *was the consideration for the contract.*

There is no indication that John or Mary lacked the capacity to enter a contract. For example, neither appeared to be mentally ill (incapable of understanding the nature of the agreement) or a minor (below the minimum age for entering an agreement he or she can be forced to perform). John and Mary's agreement does not appear to have been in writing. Does this violate the statute of frauds? In most states, mutual promises to marry do *not* have to be in writing to be enforceable. In these states, the statute of frauds does not apply to this type of contract.

All of the requirements for a contract, therefore, appear to have been met. Does John have a **cause of action** against Mary? Years ago the answer was yes. The suit for breach of promise to marry was referred to as a **heart balm action.**

cause of action
An allegation of facts that gives a party a right to judicial relief.

heart balm action
An action based on a broken heart (e.g., breach of promise to marry, alienation of affections).

The tide, however, has begun to turn against heart balm actions. As indicated, twenty-eight jurisdictions have abolished the action. When the abolition has been accomplished by statute, it is called a **heart balm statute.** (In chapter 17 on torts, we will see that a state's heart balm action may also abolish

heart balm statute
A statute (sometimes called an anti–heart balm statute) that abolishes heart balm actions.

---

[2]Keith Bradsher, *Modern Tale of Woe: Being Left at the Altar,* N.Y. Times, Mar. 7, 1990, at B8.

closely related causes of action, such as alienation of affections, criminal conversation, and seduction of a minor.) Here, for example, is the language of a heart balm statute in one state:

> No action may be brought upon any cause arising from alienation of affections or from breach of a promise to marry.[3]

These statutes were enacted for a number of reasons. The emotions involving a refusal to marry are usually so personal, intense, and possibly bitter that a court did not appear to be a proper setting to handle them. Furthermore, many feel that engaged persons should be allowed to correct their mistakes without fear of a lawsuit. As one judge said, the "courtroom scene" should not be "transposed into a grotesque marketplace whose wares would be the exposure of heart-rending episodes of wounded pride, which should be best kept private rather than public."[4] Courts were also afraid of being flooded with breach-of-promise lawsuits, particularly by unscrupulous "gold diggers and blackmailers" who use the threat of publicity to force a settlement.[5]

Another criticism of heart balm actions is the difficulty of designing an appropriate **remedy** for the aggrieved party. In the business world, one of the possible remedies for a breach of contract is **specific performance.** For the marriage contract that is breached, the remedy of specific performance would mean that the court would force the reluctant party to go through with the marriage contract. The obviously unacceptable concept of a compulsory marriage under these circumstances led many states to abolish the cause of action altogether. Another possible remedy is the payment of **damages** caused by the breach. But what should the damages be, and are the problems involved in calculating them so great that we should abolish heart balm actions altogether? These are some of the concerns addressed in the *Stanard* opinion.

remedy
The method or means by which a court or other body will enforce a right or compensate someone for a violation of a right.

specific performance
A remedy for breach of contract that forces the wrongdoing party to complete the contract as promised.

damages
Money paid because of a wrongful injury or loss to person or property.

[3]Connecticut General Statutes Annotated § 52-572b.
[4]*Friedman v. Geller,* 368 N.Y.S.2d 980, 983 (Civil Court, City of New York 1975).
[5]*Prosser & Keeton on Torts* 929 (5th ed. 1984).

CASE

Stanard v. Bolin

88 Wash. 2d 614, 565 P.2d 94 (1977)
Supreme Court of Washington

Background: *During their courtship, defendant assured plaintiff that he was worth in excess of $2 million, that he was planning to retire in two years, and that the two of them would then travel. He promised plaintiff that she would never have to work again and that he would see to the support of her two teenage boys. He also promised that the plaintiff's mother would never be in need. After he proposed, the parties found a suitable home for their residence and signed the purchase agreement as husband and wife. At the insistence of defendant, plaintiff placed her home on the market for sale and sold most of her furniture at a public auction. The parties set the wedding date, reserved a church, and hired a minister to perform the service. Dresses for plaintiff, her mother, and the matron of honor were ordered, and a reception was arranged at a local establishment. The parties began informally announcing their plans to a wide circle of friends. After the wedding date was set, plaintiff's employer hired another person and asked plaintiff to assist in teaching the new employee the duties of her job. A month before the wedding, defendant informed plaintiff that he would not marry her. This came as a great shock to plaintiff and caused her to become ill and to lose sleep and weight. She sought medical advice and was treated by her physician. Plaintiff also had to take her home off the market and repurchase furniture at a cost in excess of what she received for her older furniture. In addition, plaintiff was forced to cancel all wedding plans and reservations, return wedding gifts, and explain to her friends, family, and neighbors what had happened.*

Plaintiff sued the defendant for breach of promise to marry. In her first claim for relief, she sought damages to compensate her for her pain, impairment to health, humiliation, and embarrassment. Her second claim sought damages to compensate her for her loss of expected financial security. Washington State does not have a heart balm statute. Yet the trial court concluded on its own that such a lawsuit would be against public policy and dismissed the case. Plaintiff is now appealing before the Supreme Court of Washington.

Decision on Appeal: *The trial court is reversed. The plaintiff should be allowed to sue for breach of promise, although there are limitations on the kind of damages that can be awarded.*

Opinion of the Court:

Justice HAMILTON delivered the opinion of the court.

This appeal presents the question of whether the . . . action for breach of promise to marry should be abolished. . . . Although the action is treated as arising from the breach of a contract (the contract being the mutual promises to marry), the damages allowable more closely resemble a tort action. [If the action is allowed,] the plaintiff may recover for loss to reputation, mental anguish, and injury to health, in addition to recovering for expenditures made in preparation for the marriage and loss of the pecuniary and social advantages which the promised marriage offered. In addition, some states allow aggravated damages for seduction under promise to marry and for attacks by the defendant on the plaintiff's character. Furthermore, some states allow punitive damages when the defendant's acts were malicious or fraudulent. . . .

When two persons agree to marry, they should realize that certain actions will be taken during the engagement period in reliance on the mutual promises to marry. Rings will be purchased, wedding dresses and other formal attire will be ordered or reserved, and honeymoon plans with their attendant expenses will be made. Wedding plans such as the rental of a church, the engagement of a minister, the printing of wedding invitations, and so on, will commence. It is also likely that the parties will make plans for their future residence, such as purchasing a house, buying furniture, and the like. Further, at the time the parties decide to marry, they should realize that their plans and visions of future happiness will be communicated to friends and relatives and that wedding gifts soon will be arriving. When the plans to marry are abruptly ended, it is certainly foreseeable that the party who was unaware that the future marriage would not take place will have expended some sums of money and will suffer some forms of mental anguish, loss to reputation, and injury to health. We do not feel these injuries should go unanswered merely because the breach-of-promise-to-marry action may be subject to abuses; rather, an attempt should be made to eradicate the abuses from the action.

One major abuse of the action is allowing the plaintiff to bring in evidence of the defendant's wealth and social position. This evidence is admissible under the theory that the plaintiff should be compensated for what she or he has lost by not marrying the defendant. See, e.g., *Bundy v. Dickinson*, 108 Wash. 52, 182 P. 947 (1919).

Although damages for loss of expected financial and social position more closely resemble the contract theory of recovery than the other elements of damages for breach of promise to marry, we do not believe these damages are justified in light of modern society's concept of marriage. Although it may have been that marriages were contracted for material reasons in 17th Century England, marriages today generally are not considered property transactions, but are, in the words of Professor Clark, "the result of that complex experience called being in love." H. Clark, *The Law of Domestic Relations in the United States* 2 (1968) (hereafter cited as Clark). A person generally does not choose a marriage partner on the basis of financial and social gain; hence, the plaintiff should not be compensated for losing an expectation which he or she did not have in the first place. Further, the breach-of-promise-to-marry action is based on injuries to the plaintiff, and evidence of the defendant's wealth tends to misdirect the jury's attention when assessing the plaintiff's damages towards an examination of the defendant's wealth rather than the plaintiff's injuries . . . We conclude that damages for loss of expected financial and social position should no longer be recoverable under the breach-of-promise-to-marry actions. This means that evidence of the defendant's wealth and social position becomes immaterial in assessing the plaintiff's damages.

Other damages subject to criticism are those damages given for mental anguish, loss to reputation, and injury to health. It is argued that these injuries are "so vague and so little capable of measurement in dollars that they give free rein to the jury's passions, prejudices and sympathies." See Clark, supra at 12. This argument has little merit, for it places no faith in the jury's ability to evaluate objectively the evidence regarding plaintiff's injuries and render a just verdict. If a jury's verdict is tainted by passion or prejudice, or is otherwise excessive, the trial court and the appellate court have the power to reduce the

continued

CASE

Stanard v. Bolin—*Continued*

award or order a new trial. See *Hogenson v. Service Armament Co.,* 77 Wash. 2d 209, 461 P.2d 311 (1969). Lack of ability to quantify damages in exact dollar amounts does not justify abolishing the breach-of-promise-to-marry action. In her complaint plaintiff alleged that she had suffered pain, impairment to health, humiliation, and embarrassment as a result of the defendant's breach of his promise to marry. If this is true . . . , then she is entitled to compensation for these injuries.

As for retaining aggravated damages for seduction under a promise to marry, and the like, since plaintiff here was not seeking aggravated damages, we leave a decision on aggravated damages for a future case in which the issue for these damages arises. Also, we note that although other states allow punitive damages, these damages are not allowed in this state because they are not authorized by statute. See *Steele v. Johnson,* 76 Wash. 2d 750, 458 P.2d 889 (1969).

We also do not believe the action should be abolished so that engaged persons are free from compulsion to choose whether to end an engagement. Although the policy of the state should not be to encourage a person to marry when he or she has begun to have second thoughts about a prospective mate, it is also the policy of the state to afford an avenue of redress for injuries suffered due to the actions of another. . . .

The judgment of the trial court is reversed on plaintiff's first claim for relief, and remanded for further proceedings consistent with this opinion. The judgment is affirmed on plaintiff's second claim for relief, which sought damages for loss of prospective economical and social advantage.

ASSIGNMENT 5.1

a. Give (i) specific examples of evidence of damages you think the plaintiff will try to introduce at the new trial and (ii) specific examples of evidence of damages she will be forbidden to introduce.

b. Do you agree with the result reached by the court in *Stanard?* Why or why not? Is marriage a property transaction today?

ASSIGNMENT 5.2

a. Does your state code contain a heart balm statute for breach of contract to marry? If so, give its citation and summarize what it says. (See General Instructions for the State-Code Assignment in Appendix A.)

b. Find a court opinion written by one of your state courts that tells whether a heart balm action for breach of contract to marry can be brought. Briefly state the facts and conclusion of this opinion. (See General Instructions for the Court-Opinion Assignment in Appendix A.)

ASSIGNMENT 5.3

Assume that you live in a state where heart balm actions can be brought. Dan asks Carol to marry him. Carol says yes. The date is set for the wedding. Two weeks before the wedding, Carol learns that Dan has just married Linda. At the time Dan was engaged to Carol, Carol was already married to Bill, but Dan did not know this. Carol was in the process of divorcing Bill and hoped the divorce would be finalized before her marriage to Dan. Carol wanted to wait until the divorce was final before telling Dan about the prior marriage and divorce. Dan did not learn about any of this until after his marriage to Linda. When Carol's divorce to Bill became final, she sued Dan. The cause of action stated in Carol's complaint against Dan is breach of promise to marry. Should Carol be allowed to bring this action? Why or why not? (See General Instructions for the Legal-Analysis Assignment in Appendix A.)

Assume that a woman lives in a state where it is still possible to sue for breach of promise to marry. Today even these states would not grant her the remedy of specific performance if she won. No court will order a marriage to occur. What then does a court victory mean? What can she recover? What are her damages? Four aspects of damages are possible:

1. **Compensatory damages.** For example:
   - Out-of-pocket expenses. Money spent by the plaintiff in purchasing a trousseau, renting a hall, purchasing rings, etc.
   - Loss of income. The plaintiff may have lost income by leaving a job in order to marry the defendant.
   - Physical and mental health deterioration due to worry, publicity, and humiliation.
   - Injury to the plaintiff's reputation and chances of obtaining a new marriage proposal.
   - Destroyed financial expectations. If the defendant was wealthy and the plaintiff was poor, the plaintiff has obviously lost a great deal in terms of potential standard of living. Note, however, that most states would agree with the *Stanard* opinion in not allowing damages for this kind of loss.
2. **Aggravated damages.** For example:
   - Sexual intercourse due to seduction.
   - Pregnancy, miscarriage.
   - An unusual degree of publicity and resulting humiliation.
3. **Punitive damages.** For example:
   - Deceit. The defendant never intended to marry the plaintiff in spite of the promise made.
   - Malice. The defendant wanted to hurt and humiliate the plaintiff, or the defendant recklessly disregarded the impact of the breach of promise.
4. **Mitigating circumstances.** For example:
   - Plaintiff never loved the defendant. Plaintiff was trying to marry for money only.
   - Plaintiff was unchaste before meeting the defendant.
   - Defendant broke the promise to marry, but with some sensitivity to the feelings of the plaintiff.

compensatory damages
Money to restore the injured party to the position he or she was in before the injury or loss; money to make the aggrieved party whole.

aggravated damages
Money paid to cover special circumstances that justify an increase in the amount paid.

punitive damages
(also called exemplary damages) Money paid to punish the wrongdoer and to deter others from similar wrongdoing.

mitigating circumstances
Facts that in fairness justify a reduction in damages because of the conduct of the aggrieved party.

At one time, juries returned very high verdicts against defendants in breach-of-promise actions (e.g., $250,000). More recently, however, the trend has been toward smaller verdicts. Some states will limit damage awards to out-of-pocket losses (e.g., the cost of wedding preparation) and will not compensate the victim for more speculative harm such as that caused by humiliation.

Interviewing and Investigation Checklist

In a State That Allows Suits for Breach of the Promise to Marry (C = client; D = defendant)

Legal Interviewing Questions

1. On what date did you and D first agree to be married?
2. Where were you at the time of this agreement? Were you in this state? If not, what state?
3. How old were you at the time? How old was D?
4. What specific language did D use when he or she promised to marry you? What specific language did you use when you accepted? (Try to obtain exact quotations.)
5. Who were the first people you told? Did you and D tell them together?
6. Was a date set for a wedding? If so, what date? If not, why not?
7. Were any preparations made (e.g., church selected or caterer ordered)?

continued

Interviewing and Investigation Checklist—*Continued*

8. Did D send you any letters ("love letters") about the engagement? Did you send D any?
9. Did D ever repeat his or her promise to marry you? If so, under what circumstances?
10. What other actions did D take to indicate to you that D wanted to marry you? How much time did you spend together? Did you live together? (Where? How long?) Did you talk about children? Did you meet each other's parents?
11. When did you first learn that D no longer wished to marry you? What specifically was said and done?
12. What reason did D give?
13. What did you say or do when you learned about this? Did you give any indication to D that you did not want to marry D? Were you angry? How were your feelings expressed?
14. Was there anything about *your* life prior to the time that D promised to marry you that D did not know but that D now feels you should have revealed, e.g., information about a prior marriage, your age, your prior sex life?
15. What expenses did you incur to prepare for the wedding (e.g., clothes, church, rings)?
16. Were you employed before the engagement? Did you leave your job? How did the cancellation of the marriage affect your job, if at all?
17. Describe your standard of living before the cancellation (e.g., kind of dwelling, car, travel, entertainment interests).
18. Describe D's standard of living.
19. If D had married you, describe what you think your financial standing and standard of living would have been.
20. Describe the effect of D's breach of promise on your physical and mental health (e.g., did you lose any sleep, were there any special mental problems?).
21. When D broke the promise to marry you, who knew about it? Was there any publicity?
22. Were you humiliated? Describe the reasons why.
23. Since D broke the engagement, have you dated others? When they find out about the broken engagement, what is their reaction? Do you think your chances of marrying in the future are diminished because of D's breach of promise? Why?
24. Did you have sexual relations with D? Were you seduced by D? Did D impregnate you? (If so, inquire into pregnancy problems, abortion, miscarriage, delivery, etc.)
25. Do you have any reason to believe that at the time D promised to marry you, D never intended to fulfill this promise? Explain.
26. Do you have any reason to believe D wanted to hurt you? Explain.
27. Could D say that you never loved D?
28. Did D ever give you any gifts?
29. For each gift received, describe the gift and the date you were told about it. Specify whether the gift was received before or after the engagement.
30. Has D ever given you gifts on special occasions such as birthdays; holidays such as Easter, Christmas, or Chanukah; or recognition days such as the day you won a race or other prize? Describe all such gifts.
31. What were D's exact words when D gave you each gift? What did you say to D?
32. When did each gift come into your possession?
33. Answer questions 28–32 for any gifts you gave D.
34. Did you or D receive any shower gifts or wedding gifts from others before the engagement was broken? Explain.

Possible Investigation Tasks

- Try to contact people who may have heard about D's promise to marry C. Obtain witness statements.
- Locate all letters from D to C.
- Locate all receipts of expenses resulting from wedding preparations. If not available, contact merchants and others to whom money was paid in order to obtain new receipts or copies.
- Obtain financial records, e.g., bank statements, to show C's financial worth and standard of living before the engagement was broken. Try to obtain the same kind of records for D.
- Obtain medical records to document the physical and mental strain C experienced when D broke the promise to marry (e.g., hospital records, doctor bills).
- Determine what kind of publicity, if any, accompanied the news that D broke the engagement (e.g., newspaper clippings).
- Attempt to determine whether D had broken any other marriage engagements.
- Draft an inventory of every gift in any way connected with D's relationship with C. For each gift, identify the donor, donee, date of the gift, kind and value of the gift, circumstances surrounding the gift, present location of the gift, etc.

fraud
Knowingly making a false statement of present fact with the intention that the plaintiff rely on the statement. The plaintiff's reasonable reliance on the statement harms him or her.

Fraud

Where a heart balm statute exists, some plaintiffs have tried to get around it by bringing a *tort* cause of action for **fraud** rather than the breach-of-contract cause of action.

Elements of the Tort of Fraud
(Sometimes called misrepresentation or deceit)

- There must be a *false* statement of present fact by the defendant (D).
- The D must *know* that it is false.
- The D must *intend* that the plaintiff (P) rely upon the statement.
- The P must *rely* on the statement of the D and be reasonable in so relying.
- The P must suffer *harm* due to the reliance.

Here is an example of how a fraud cause of action might arise out of a broken engagement.

> *Don tells Phyllis that he wants to marry her. At the time he makes this statement of fact, it is* false *because Don never wants to marry her. He knows he is lying. His goal—his* intention*—is to obtain a loan of $25,000 from her. He knows that without a marriage proposal, she will refuse. She believes he wants to marry her and lends him the money in* reliance *on his promise of marriage. Soon thereafter she learns that he never wanted to marry her and that he has spent most of the money she lent him. Her reliance on his promise has led to the* harm *of losing $25,000.*

Each of the elements of fraud exists in this case. Suppose, however, that Phyllis and Don live in a state that has abolished the breach-of-contract cause of action. Can she overcome this obstacle by suing Don for fraud? The answer depends on whether the legislature intended the heart balm statute to eliminate both causes of action even though the act may specifically mention only the contract action. Some states allow the fraud action. Others have said that the heart balm statute eliminates both the contract *and* the fraud action.

Intentional Infliction of Emotional Distress

Another tort action some plaintiffs have tried to bring is **intentional infliction of emotional distress.** The plaintiff must convince a court that the heart balm statute does not bar this action as well. If this can be done, the next step is to prove that he or she was the victim of particularly shocking conduct by the defendant. For example, a man knows his fiancée is emotionally unstable because she is a former mental patient. He proposes marriage for the sole purpose of humiliating her by changing his mind just after she makes elaborate, public, and expensive wedding plans. A state might conclude that this is sufficiently outrageous and shocking conduct. A more common change-of-mind case, on the other hand, would probably not be enough for this tort, no matter how upset the jilted party becomes. The behavior of the culprit must shock the conscience.

intentional infliction of emotional distress
Intentionally causing severe emotional distress by extreme or outrageous conduct.

We will return to the tort of intentional infliction of emotional distress in chapter 17, when we study the case of *Hakkila v. Hakkila,* which resolved the question of whether this tort could be brought against a spouse in a divorce action.

Gifts

It is not commonly known that once a gift is made, it is **irrevocable**—the **donor** cannot reclaim the gift from the *donee.* For a gift to be irrevocable, all of the elements of a gift must be present:

irrevocable
That which cannot be revoked or recalled.

donor
The person who gives a gift. The *donee* receives it.

Elements of an Irrevocable Gift

- There must be a *delivery* of the property.[6]
- The transfer must be *voluntary.*

[6]The delivery of the gift of a house or of the contents of a safe deposit box can be accomplished by a symbolic act such as giving the donee the key to the house or box.

- The donor must intend to relinquish *title* and *control* of or dominion over what is given.
- There must be *no consideration* such as a cash payment for the gift.
- The donor must intend that the gift take effect *immediately;* there must be a *present* intention to give an *unconditional* gift.
- The donee must *accept* the gift.

If Pat says to Bill, "I'll give you my car next year," no gift has been given. There was no intent that an immediate transfer occur. There was also no delivery. If Pat says to Bill, "You have borrowed my pen; maybe I'll give it to you tomorrow," again there is no gift, since there was no intent by Pat to relinquish her title and dominion over the pen now. This is so even though Bill already had possession of the pen.

Suppose that Pat says to Bill, "I'll give you this desk if it rains tomorrow." No gift has occurred because a condition exists that must be fulfilled before the gift becomes effective (i.e., it must rain tomorrow). There is no present intention to relinquish title and dominion. Suppose that Frank and Judy exchange engagement rings after they both agree to be married. One or both of them then change their minds. Did a legally binding gift occur? It appears that all of the elements of a binding gift existed, so either Frank or Judy can refuse to return the ring. Yet, should we not *infer* a condition that the parties intended the gift to be binding only if the marriage took place? They never explicitly said this to each other, but it is reasonable to infer that this is what they had in mind. This is what they would have intended if they had thought about it. Courts often find that such an *implied intention* exists, thereby requiring a return of premarital gifts.

Examine the following sequence of events:

January 1, 2000:	Mary and Bob meet.
January 2, 2000:	On a date at a restaurant, Bob gives Mary a bracelet.
March 13, 2000:	Mary and Bob become engaged; he gives her an engagement ring. The marriage date will be November 7, 2000.
March 26, 2000:	This is Mary's birthday; Bob gives Mary a new car.
June 5, 2000:	Bob and Mary change their minds about marriage.

Bob wants the bracelet, ring, and car back. When Mary refuses, Bob sues her, contending in court that the elements of a gift were not present when he gave Mary the items because he intended that she keep them only if they married. Should the court infer this condition of marriage? The answer depends on Bob's intention *at the time* he gave each of the items to Mary.

At the time the bracelet was given, the parties were not engaged. A jury might conclude that Bob's intent was to please Mary, but not necessarily to win her hand in marriage. The bracelet was given the day after they met, when it is unlikely that marriage was on anyone's mind. It would be rare, therefore, for a court to rule that the gift of the bracelet was conditional and force Mary to return it.[7] The birthday gift of the car is the most troublesome item. Again, the central question is, What was Bob's intent at the time he gave her the car? Mary would argue that no condition of marriage was attached to the gift. She would say that a birthday gift would have been given whether or not they were engaged. Bob, on the other hand, would argue that the extraordinary cost of a new car is strong evidence that it would not have been given as a birthday gift unconnected with the impending marriage. His argument is probably correct. Do you agree?

---

[7]On the other hand, the facts show that two months after the bracelet was given, the parties became engaged. This short time period does raise the possibility, however slight, that marriage *was* on Bob's mind when he gave Mary the bracelet (i.e., that the gift was conditional). More facts would be needed in order to determine whether this argument has merit.

ASSIGNMENT 5.4

What further facts would you seek in order to assess whether the car was a gift in the case of Bob and Mary above? (See General Instructions for the Investigation-Strategy Assignment in Appendix A.)

What about the engagement ring? When the decision to break the engagement is mutual, most courts say that a condition of marriage was implied and, therefore, the ring must be returned. Suppose, however, that one of the parties unilaterally breaks the engagement without any plausible reason or justification. This person is considered to be at fault. Must the ring be returned in such a case? Some courts will order the return of the ring if the person receiving it (the *donee*) is the one who broke the engagement without justification, but not if he or she is the "innocent" party. Other courts, however, will order the return of the ring regardless of who was at fault. When a court examines wrongdoing in reaching a decision, it is using *fault-based* analysis. When a court makes its decision regardless of who was the "bad guy" or wrongdoer, it is using *no-fault* analysis. Here, with a touch of humor, is an example of a court using fault-based analysis:

> A gift given by a man to a woman on condition that she embark on the sea of matrimony with him is no different from a gift based on the condition that the donee sail on any other sea. If, after receiving the provisional gift, the donee refuses to leave the harbor,—if the anchor of contractual performance sticks in the sands of irresolution and procrastination—the gift must be restored to the donor. A fortiori would this be true when the donee not only refuses to sail with the donor, but, on the contrary, walks up the gangplank of another ship arm in arm with the donor's rival.[8]

Third parties (e.g., relatives and friends) often send gifts in contemplation of the coming marriage. When the marriage does not take place, these parties can force a return of the gifts, since courts almost always will conclude that such gifts were conditional.

Earlier we saw that some states passed heart balm statutes that abolished the cause of action for breach of promise to marry. Some of these statutes are worded so broadly that courts might interpret them to mean that *any* cause of action growing out of a broken engagement will not be allowed, including a cause of action to obtain the return of conditional gifts.

ASSIGNMENT 5.5

Examine the following sequence of events:

February 13, 2000:	Jim says to Bob, "Please introduce me to Joan. I want to meet her because I know that she is the girl I want to spend the rest of my life with." Bob does so. Jim is so happy that he gives Bob a gold wristwatch and says to him, "I want you to have this. Thanks for being my friend. I want you to wear this watch to my wedding some day."
March 1, 2000:	Joan brings Jim home to meet her mother. When the evening is over, Jim gives Joan's mother an expensive family Bible.
June 23, 2000:	Jim loans Joan $1,000 to pay a medical bill of Joan's youngest brother, giving her one year to pay back the loan without interest.

continued

[8]*Pavlicic v. Vogtsberger,* 390 Pa. 502, 136 A.2d 127, 130 (1957).

July 23, 2000:	Joan pays back the $1,000.
September 5, 2000:	They agree to marry. The wedding date is to be February 18, 2001. On the day that they agree to marry, Jim gives Joan a diamond bracelet, saying, "I want you to have this no matter what happens."
December 14, 2000:	They both agree to break the engagement.

Jim asks Bob for the wristwatch back. Bob refuses. Jim asks Joan's mother for the Bible back. The mother refuses. Jim asks Joan for one month's interest at 10 percent on the $1,000 loan and also asks for the bracelet back. Joan refuses both requests.

a. Assume that the law office where you work represents Jim. Conduct a legal interview of Jim. (See General Instructions for the Interview Assignment in Appendix A.)
b. Can Jim obtain any of these items from Bob, the mother, or Joan? (See General Instructions for the Legal-Analysis Assignment in Appendix A.)
c. Draft a complaint against Joan in which Jim seeks the return of the bracelet and one month's interest. (See General Instructions for the Complaint-Drafting Assignment in Appendix A.)
d. Prepare a flowchart of the steps necessary to litigate the matter raised in the complaint that you drafted in (c) above. (See General Instructions for the Flowchart Assignment in Appendix A.)

Contracts Restraining Marriage

In this section, we consider contracts of private parties that have the effect of restraining marriage. The law looks with disfavor on attempts to limit the right to marry, even with the consent of the person subject to the limitation. Not all restrictions, however, are invalid. A distinction must be made between a *general restraint* on marriage and a *reasonable limitation* on marriage.

General Restraint

A **general restraint on marriage** is a total or near total prohibition against marriage and is unenforceable. For example:

- In exchange for a large sum of money to be given to her by her father, Mary agrees never to marry.
- As John goes off to war, Jane says, "It is you that I want to marry, and even if you don't want to marry me, even if you marry someone else, even if you die, I promise you that I will never marry anyone else as long as I live." John leaves without promising to marry Jane.

Mary's father cannot sue her to hold her to her agreement never to marry, nor can Jane be sued by John for breach of her promise should she marry someone other than him. People may decide on their own never to marry, but no court will force them to abide by that decision.

The John/Jane agreement is unenforceable for another reason. You will recall that for a contract to exist, there must be consideration. Jane's consideration was her promise never to marry anyone but John. John, however, gave no consideration in exchange. Hence, Jane's promise is unenforceable because she received no consideration; there was no contract to breach.

Reasonable Limitation

A **reasonable limitation on marriage** is one that (1) is a partial rather than a general prohibition, (2) serves what the court feels is a useful purpose, and (3) is not otherwise illegal. Consider the following situations:

- John enters a contract in which he promises that he will never marry a woman who is not of his religious faith.
- Mary enters a contract in which she promises never to marry anyone who has a criminal record.
- Jane enters a contract in which she promises that she will not marry before she turns eighteen, and that she will obtain the permission of her parent if she decides to marry between the ages of eighteen and twenty-one.
- Linda enters a contract in which she promises that she will not marry until she completes her college education.

Assume that John, Mary, Jane, and Linda received consideration (e.g., cash) in exchange for their promises. Are the promises enforceable? If John, Mary, Jane, and Linda later decide to marry, contrary to their promises, can they be forced through litigation to return whatever consideration they received as a remedy for their breach of promise? Not all states answer this question in the same way, but generally the answer is yes. The restraints on marriage to which they agreed are enforceable. All of the restraints are *partial:* they do not totally prohibit marriage or come near such a total prohibition. All of the restraints arguably serve a *useful purpose:* to protect a person or a valuable tradition. There is no *illegality* evident in any of the restraints, e.g., no one is being asked to refrain from marriage in order to engage in adultery or fornication (which are crimes in some states). Hence, all of the restraints could be considered reasonable limitations on one's right to marry and are enforceable in most states.

Suppose schoolteachers sign a contract containing a clause that they will quit if they marry. This is not a general restraint on marriage, but is it enforceable as a reasonable limitation? Is there a useful or beneficial purpose to the restriction? Many courts have said yes, although this conclusion has been criticized. Can you see any useful purpose in forcing a teacher to resign under these circumstances? Do not answer this question by saying that people should be forced to do what they have agreed to do. Answer it on the basis of whether you think any person, tradition, value, etc., is being protected by holding the teacher to his or her contract.

Thus far we have been examining *contracts* that restrain marriage. Suppose, however, that the attempted restriction on marriage came as a condition attached to a *gift* rather than through a contract. For example:

- In Bob's will, he promises to give $100,000 to Fran so long as she remains unmarried. When Bob dies, Fran is not married. She is given the **bequest** of $100,000. One year later Fran marries. Bob's estate brings a suit against Fran to have the money returned.
- John has a deed drafted that states, "I convey all my property to my widowed sister, Joan, to be owned and used by her until she remarries, at which time all remaining property shall go to the Red Cross."

bequest
A gift of personal property in a will.

The same rules on marriage restrictions should apply to such gifts as apply to contracts. If a person is going to lose a substantial gift upon marriage, the gift obviously operates to restrain marriage. In theory, the same rules do apply. In fact, however, some courts are more inclined to find the restrictions to be reasonable (and hence enforceable) when gifts are involved than when the restraint is embodied in a contract.

ASSIGNMENT 5.6

Closely examine each of the following situations. Determine which restraints on marriage, if any, are enforceable. Give specific reasons you think the restraint is or is not enforceable. (See General Instructions for the Legal-Analysis Assignment in Appendix A.)

continued

a. John is married to Brenda. John enters a contract with Brenda's father stating that if children are born from the marriage and if Brenda dies before John, John will never remarry. In exchange, John is given the father's large farm to live on for life rent-free. Children are born, and Brenda does die first. John marries Patricia. Brenda's father then sues to evict John from the farm. Does John have a defense to this suit?

b. Joan enters a contract with her aunt stating that she will not have children before she turns twenty-one. In exchange, Joan is given a sum of money when she signs the contract. Before she turns twenty-one, Joan has a baby (out of wedlock). The aunt sues Joan for breach of contract. Does Joan have a defense?

c. Fred enters a contract with his father in which the father agrees to pay for Fred's entire medical education if Fred agrees to marry a doctor or a medical student if he decides to marry. When Fred becomes a doctor, he marries Sue, an electrician. The father sues Fred for the cost of the medical education. Does Fred have a defense?

d. Bill and Jean are not married. They live together, sharing bed and board. They enter a contract by which Jean promises to continue to live with Bill and to care for him. Bill agrees to place $500 per month in a bank account for Jean so long as she carries out her promise. Jean cannot receive the money until Bill dies. Also, if she marries before Bill dies, she forfeits the right to all the money in the account. After living with Bill for twenty years, Jean leaves him to marry Tom. Can Jean sue Bill to recover $120,000 (plus interest), the amount in the account at the time she married Tom?

INTRODUCTION TO MARRIAGE

> Marriage is a coming together for better or for worse, hopefully enduring and intimate to the degree of being sacred. It is an association that promotes a way of life, not causes; a harmony in living, not political faiths; a bilateral loyalty, not commercial or social projects. Yet it is an association for as noble a purpose as any involved in our prior decisions.[9]

We now begin our examination of the law governing the formation of marriages. Approximately 110.6 million adults (56 percent of the adult population) are married and living with their spouse. Every year over 2.3 million adults join the ranks of the married. Most of the new marriages consist of men and women marrying for the first time. Yet an increasing number of individuals are entering second and third marriages, as we saw in chapter 4. Recently, a confused minister accidently asked the bride, "Do you take this man to be your first husband?"[10] Perhaps more indicative of the changing landscape is a cartoon in *The New Yorker* in which the minister solemnly proclaims to the couple, "I pronounce you husband and wife of the opposite sex."[11] While at the present time, no state allows same-sex marriages, recent court opinions brought two states dramatically close to authorizing them. In the meantime, new legal relationships have been created that provide some of the characteristics of a marriage. These will be some of the themes we will be studying in the remainder of the chapter.

---

[9] *Griswold v. Connecticut,* 381 U.S. 479, 486, 85 S. Ct. 1678, 1682, 14 L. Ed. 2d 510 (1965) (Douglas, J.).

[10] Laura Peterson, *Divorce,* N.Y. Times, May 5, 1996, at 8.

[11] JBH, *The New Yorker,* June 10, 1996, at 32.

AM I MARRIED?: HOW THE MARRIAGE ISSUE IS RAISED

A client is not likely to walk into a law office and ask, "Am I married?" The existence of a marriage becomes an issue when the client is trying to obtain some other objective, such as seeking

- a divorce (you can't divorce someone to whom you are not married)
- pension benefits as the surviving spouse of a deceased employee
- social security survivor benefits through a deceased spouse
- workers' compensation death benefits as the surviving spouse of an employee fatally injured on the job
- assets as the spouse of a deceased person who died **intestate**
- assets under a clause in a will that gives property "to my wife" or "to my husband"
- a **forced share** of a deceased spouse's estate
- **dower** or **curtesy** rights
- entrance to the United States (or avoidance of deportation) as a result of being married to a U.S. citizen
- The right to assert in a criminal case the **privilege for marital communications,** also called the husband-wife privilege.

intestate
Dying without leaving a valid will.

forced share
A designated share of a deceased spouse's estate that goes to the surviving spouse despite what the will of the deceased spouse gave the surviving spouse.

dower
A widow's right to the lifetime use of one-third of the land her deceased husband owned during the marriage.

curtesy
A husband's right to the lifetime use of all the land his deceased wife owned during the marriage (if issue were born of the marriage.)

privilege for marital communications
One spouse cannot disclose in court any confidential communications that occurred between the spouses during the marriage. (This privilege does not apply when the spouses are suing each other.)

miscegenation
Mixing the races. The marriage or cohabitation of persons of different races.

CONSTITUTIONAL LIMITATION ON MARRIAGE RESTRICTIONS

Marital status may be achieved through one of two possible methods: ceremonial marriage or common law marriage. As we shall see, however, most states have abolished common law marriage.

The United States Supreme Court has held that marriage is a fundamental right. Consequently, a state is limited in its power to regulate one's right to marry. For example, a state cannot prohibit **miscegenation.** Nor can it withhold a marriage license pending proof that child-support payments (from an earlier marriage) are being met, and proof that any children due such payments are not likely to become public charges. Only "reasonable regulations that do not significantly interfere with decisions to enter into the marital relationship may legitimately by imposed."[12] The United States Supreme Court held in *Zablocki v. Redhail* that the restriction based on child-support payments was not reasonable. *Zablocki's* insistence on reasonable restrictions that do not significantly interfere with the decision to marry is a major *constitutional* limitation on marriage restrictions. Whenever the government passes a statute or administrative regulation that makes it impossible or more difficult for someone to marry, the question arises as to whether the restriction violates *Zablocki.*

States have imposed two major kinds of requirements for entering marriage: (1) technical or formal requirements for ceremonial marriages (e.g., obtaining a license) and (2) more basic requirements relating to the intent and capacity to marry that apply to both ceremonial and common law marriages (e.g., being of minimum age to marry and not being too closely related to the person you want to marry). The latter requirements will be discussed in chapter 6. Here our focus is primarily on the technical or formal requirements.

---

[12]*Zablocki v. Redhail,* 434 U.S. 374, 386, 98 S. Ct. 673, 681, 54 L. Ed. 2d 618 (1978).

CEREMONIAL MARRIAGE

ceremonial marriage
A marriage that is entered in compliance with the statutory requirements (e.g., obtaining a marriage license, having the marriage performed [i.e., solemnized] by an authorized person).

The requirements for a **ceremonial marriage,** found within the statutory code of your state, usually specify the following:

- Marriage license (Exhibit 5.1) (both parties may be required to apply for the license in person)
- Ceremony performed by an authorized person (Exhibit 5.2)
- Witnesses to the ceremony (Exhibit 5.2)
- Waiting period
- Recording of the license (by the person performing the ceremony) in a designated public office following the ceremony

Exhibit 5.1 A Marriage License

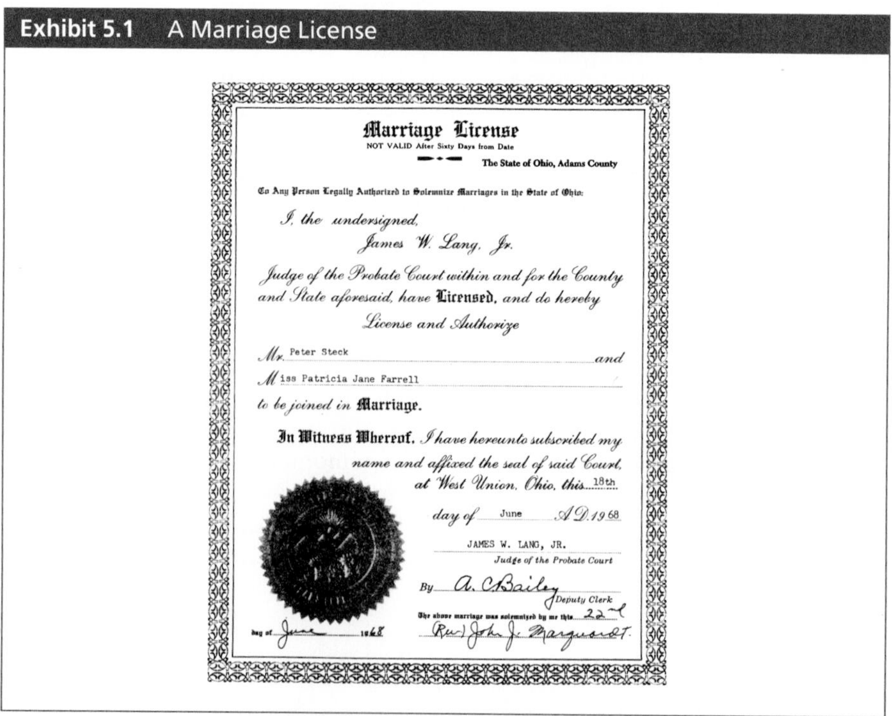

Marriage License
NOT VALID After Sixty Days from Date

The State of Ohio, Adams County

To Any Person Legally Authorized to Solemnize Marriages in the State of Ohio:

I, the undersigned,
James W. Lang, Jr.
Judge of the Probate Court within and for the County and State aforesaid, have **Licensed**, *and do hereby License and Authorize*

Mr. Peter Steck *and*
*M*iss Patricia Jane Farrell
to be joined in **Marriage.**

In Witness Whereof. *I have hereunto subscribed my name and affixed the seal of said Court, at West Union, Ohio, this* 18th *day of* June *A.D. 19*68

JAMES W. LANG, JR.
Judge of the Probate Court

By A. C. Bailey *Deputy Clerk*

The above marriage was solemnized by me this 22nd day of June 1968

Rev. John J. Marquardt

Exhibit 5.2 Authorization to Celebrate or Witness a Marriage

Number ________.
To __________, authorized to celebrate (or witness) marriages in the state of __________, greeting:

You are hereby authorized to celebrate (or witness) the rites of marriage between __________, of __________, and __________, of __________, and having done so, you are commanded to make return of the same to the clerk's office of ____________________ within ten days under a penalty of fifty dollars for default therein.

Witness my hand and seal of said court this ________ day of ________, anno Domini ________.

____________________ Clerk.
By ____________________ Assistant Clerk.

Number ________.
I, __________, who have been duly authorized to celebrate (or witness) the rites of marriage in the state of __________ do hereby certify that, by authority of a license of corresponding number herewith, I solemnized (or witnessed) the marriage of __________ and __________, named therein, on the __________ day of __________, at __________, in said state.

States can differ in their requirements. Not all states, for example, require a blood test. A license may be good for sixty days in one state, whereas in another state the license may expire if the parties are not married within ninety days. In one state, a license may be useable in any county of the state, whereas in another state the parties may have to be married in the county where they obtained the license. States may also have different requirements for the format of the ceremony, although in most states all that is required is for the parties to declare in the presence of the clergy member, judge, or other marrying official that they take each other as husband and wife.

There is no requirement that one party take the other's surname. While it is traditional for women to take their husband's last name, there is nothing to prevent her from keeping her own name or using a hyphenated name consisting of the surnames of both spouses. (In New York, parties are given specific notice that marriage does not automatically change anyone's name.) When the parties apply for the marriage license, they simply indicate what surname they will use. Name changes are allowed so long as a person is consistent in using a name and is not trying to defraud anyone such as creditors.[13]

ASSIGNMENT 5.7

Go to your state statutory code and identify all of the technical requirements for entering a ceremonial marriage (e.g., obtaining a license, paying a fee). (See General Instructions for the State-Code Assignment in Appendix A.)

ASSIGNMENT 5.8

In Assignment 5.7, you identified all of the requirements for a ceremonial marriage in your state. In this assignment, you are to interview someone who was married in your state in order to determine whether all the requirements for a ceremonial marriage were met. You may interview your spouse or a married

continued

[13]The same flexibility is usually applied when someone wants to change his or her name by using the separate change-of-name court procedure that is available in most states. See also chapter 12 on the legal rights of women.

relative, friend, classmate, etc. Before you conduct the interview, draft a checklist of questions necessary to determine if the marriage is in compliance with state requirements. (These should be questions that could be part of a manual.) Make notes of the interviewee's answers. For all answers, ask the interviewee if any documents or other evidence exists to substantiate (or corroborate) information given. (See General Instructions for the Checklist-Formulation Assignment in Appendix A.) Hand in to your instructor a written account of the interview (including the questions you asked). Remember that one of the primary characteristics of such written work products should be specificity; the details of names, addresses, dates, who said what, etc., can be critical. (See General Instructions for the Interview Assignment in Appendix A.)

Suppose that the technical requirements for a ceremonial marriage have been violated. What consequences follow?

Assume, for example, that a statute requires a ten-day waiting period between the date of the issuing of the license and the date of the ceremony. Joe and Mary want to marry right away. They find a minister who marries them on the same day they obtained the license. Are they validly married? In most states, the marriage is valid even when there has been a failure to comply with one of the requirements discussed in this chapter for a ceremonial marriage. In such states, noncompliance with the requirements for a ceremonial marriage cannot later be used as a ground for annulment or divorce. Keep in mind, however, that we are *not* discussing age or relationship requirements that involve the *legal capacity* of parties to marry nor are we discussing requirements relating to *intent to marry.* Violations of such requirements can indeed be grounds for annulment or divorce, as we will see in the next chapter.

While noncompliance with technical requirements does not affect the validity of a marriage in most states, other consequences may result. The parties,

Over 2,000 followers of Rev. Sun Myung Moon go through a ceremonial marriage in Madison Square Garden, New York City. (Courtesy of AP/Wide World Photos.)

for example, might be prosecuted for perjury if they falsified public documents in applying for the marriage. The person who performed the marriage ceremony without the authority to do so might be subjected to a fine. Other sanctions similar to these might also apply.

ASSIGNMENT 5.9

a. In your state, is the validity of the marriage affected by a violation of any of the technical requirements for a ceremonial marriage that you identified in Assignment 5.7?

b. What penalties can be imposed for the violation of any of the technical requirements for a ceremonial marriage in your state?

To answer the above two questions, you may have to check both statutory law and case law. See General Instructions for the State-Code Assignment and for the Court-Opinion Assignment in Appendix A.

ASSIGNMENT 5.10

Suppose that a statute in a state provides as follows:

> **§ 10** No marriage shall be invalid on account of want of authority in any person solemnizing the same if consummated with the full belief on the part of the persons so married, or either of them, that they were lawfully joined in marriage.

George and Linda read a newspaper article stating that five of seven ministers connected with the Triple Faith Church in their state had been fined for illegally performing marriage ceremonies. A week later they are married by Rev. Smith, who is in charge of Triple Faith Church but who has no authority to marry anyone. Can the validity of their marriage be called into question under § 10? (See General Instructions for the Legal-Analysis Assignment in Appendix A.)

Is physical presence of the bride and groom at the ceremony one of the requirements for a ceremonial marriage? You might think so, but most states allow a **proxy marriage,** in which the ceremony takes place with one or both parties being absent (e.g., the groom is overseas). A third-party agent must be given the authority to act on behalf of the missing party or parties during the ceremony. Where proxy marriages are allowed, there is a danger of abuse, particularly in immigration cases. An American citizen may enter a proxy marriage with someone who lives abroad and thereby try to qualify that person for entry status as the spouse of a citizen. It may not succeed. Immigration law provides:

proxy marriage
The performance of a valid marriage through agents because one or both of the prospective spouses are absent.

> The term "spouse," "wife," or "husband" does not include a spouse, wife, or husband by reason of any marriage ceremony where the contracting parties thereto are not physically present in the presence of each other, unless the marriage shall have been consummated.[14]

Note, however, that the marriage might still be valid under state law.

COVENANT MARRIAGE

The high divorce rate has led some reformers to propose making marriage more difficult to enter and to dissolve. To achieve this goal, several states are experimenting with a new category of marriage called **covenant marriage.** In

covenant marriage
A form of marriage that requires proof of premarital counseling, a promise to seek marital counseling when needed during the marriage, and proof of marital fault to dissolve.

---

[14] 8 U.S.C.A. § 1101(a)(35).

1997, for example, Louisiana instituted a two-tiered system of marriage. Couples that want to marry are forced to choose the kind of marriage they want:

- *covenant marriage:* a marriage that cannot be dissolved without proof of marital fault such as adultery or spousal abuse; to obtain the marriage license, the parties must obtain premarital counseling and promise to seek counseling when needed during the marriage
- *conventional or standard marriage:* a marriage that can be dissolved without proof of marital fault; to enter the marriage, premarital counseling is not required

As we will see in chapter 7, one of the major reforms in family law has been the abolition of the fault grounds of divorce. Covenant marriage reintroduces fault into the dissolution of marriages.

A covenant marriage is more difficult to enter not only because the parties are required to obtain premarital counseling, but also because they must take the time at the outset to decide how easily they want to be able to dissolve the marriage. If, for example, the man wants a conventional marriage, his fiancée might ask him why he wants a marriage that is so easy to get out of. This frank discussion may lead to a decision to cancel the marriage or at least to postpone it until they can both have a more serious discussion about the institution of marriage. Through such discussions, potentially weak marriages might be avoided.

When a couple selects a covenant marriage, it must submit an affidavit from a therapist, minister, or other member of the clergy that he or she has given the couple counseling on the "nature and purpose" of marriage. The couple must also sign a statement that says:

> We do solemnly declare that marriage is a covenant between a man and a woman who agree to live together as husband and wife for so long as they both may live. We have chosen each other carefully and disclosed to one another everything which could adversely affect the decision to enter into this marriage. We have received premarital counseling on the nature, purposes, and responsibilities of marriage. We have read the Covenant Marriage Act, and we understand that a Covenant Marriage is for life. If we experience marital difficulties, we commit ourselves to take all reasonable efforts to preserve our marriage, including marital counseling. With full knowledge of what this commitment means, we do hereby declare that our marriage will be bound by Louisiana law on Covenant Marriages and we promise to love, honor, and care for one another as husband and wife for the rest of our lives.[15]

The commitment to remain married "for the rest of our lives" does not mean that divorce has been abolished. Divorce is possible, but only on specified fault grounds. In Louisiana, these are adultery, a sentence of death or imprisonment for a felony, abandonment of the matrimonial domicile for a year, physical or sexual abuse, and living separate and apart continuously without reconciliation for a period of two years. Fault is *not* required to dissolve a conventional Louisiana marriage. Such a marriage can be dissolved simply by a showing that the parties have lived separate and apart for six months.

Will covenant marriages reduce the rate of divorce? It is too early to tell. There is enough enthusiasm over this possibility, however, that many states are now considering covenant marriage programs such as Louisiana's.

ASSIGNMENT 5.11

a. Does your state allow covenant marriage? If so, describe its components. (See General Instructions for the State-Code Assignment in Appendix A.)

---

[15] Louisiana Revised Statutes Annotated tit. 9, § 273.

b. Explain why you think it is a good or bad idea for every state to force couples to choose between conventional and covenant marriages.
c. Explain why you think it is a good or bad idea for every state to abolish conventional marriages and to require every marriage to be a covenant marriage.

COMMON LAW MARRIAGE

When parties enter a valid **common law marriage,** the marriage is as valid as a ceremonial marriage. Children born during a common law marriage, for example, are legitimate. To end such a marriage, one of the parties must die, or they both must go through a divorce proceeding in the same manner as any other married couple seeking to dissolve a marriage.

common law marriage
The marriage of two people who agree to be married, cohabit, and hold themselves out as husband and wife even though they do not go through a ceremonial marriage. (In Texas, a common law marriage is called an *informal marriage.*)

Most states have abolished common law marriages. Twelve states and the District of Columbia still recognize them (see Exhibit 5.3). Even in states that have abolished common law marriages, however, it is important to know something about them for the following reasons:

1. Parties may enter a common law marriage in a state where such marriages are valid and then move to another state that has abolished such marriages. Under traditional **conflict of law** principles, as we shall see, the second state may have to recognize the marriage as valid. In our highly mobile society, parties who live together should be aware that if they travel through states that recognize common law marriages for vacations or for other temporary purposes, one of the parties might

conflict of law
An inconsistency between the laws of different legal systems such as two states or two countries.

Exhibit 5.3 Common Law Marriage

State	Valid in State?	State	Valid in State?
Alabama	Yes	Nebraska	Not after 1923
Alaska	Not after 1/1/64	Nevada	Not after 3/29/43
Arizona	No	New Hampshire	Yes (but only for inheritance or to claim death benefits)
Arkansas	No		
California	Not after 1895		
Colorado	Yes		
Connecticut	No	New Jersey	Not after 1/12/39
Delaware	No	New Mexico	No
District of Columbia	Yes	New York	Not after 4/29/33
Florida	Not after 1/1/68	North Carolina	No
Georgia	Not after 1/1/97	North Dakota	No
Hawaii	No	Ohio	Not after 10/10/91
Idaho	Not after 1/1/96	Oklahoma	Yes
Illinois	Not after 1905	Oregon	No
Indiana	Not after 1/1/58	Pennsylvania	Yes
Iowa	Yes	Rhode Island	Yes
Kansas	Yes	South Carolina	Yes
Kentucky	No	South Dakota	Not after 7/1/59
Louisiana	No	Tennessee	No
Maine	No	Texas	Yes
Maryland	No	Utah	Yes
Massachusetts	No	Vermont	No
Michigan	Not after 1/1/57	Virginia	No
Minnesota	Not after 4/26/41	Washington	No
Mississippi	Not after 4/5/56	West Virginia	No
Missouri	Not after 3/3/21	Wisconsin	Not after 1913
Montana	Yes	Wyoming	No

Source: U.S. Department of Labor, Women's Bureau.

later try to claim that they entered a common law marriage in such a state.

2. It may be that your state once recognized common law marriages as valid, but then, as of a certain date, abolished all such marriages for the future. A number of people may still live in your state who entered valid common law marriages before the law was changed, and hence, their marriages are still valid.

ASSIGNMENT 5.12

Does your state have a statute abolishing common law marriages? If so, what is its effective date? If not, check court opinions to determine whether common law marriages are valid in your state. Give the full citation to the statute or case that you rely on. (See General Instructions for the State-Code Assignment and General Instructions for the Court-Opinion Assignment in Appendix A.)

What conditions must exist for a common law marriage to be valid in states that recognize such marriages? Not all states have the same requirements. Generally, however, the following conditions must be met.

Common Law Marriage

- The parties must have legal capacity to marry.
- There must be an intent to marry and a present agreement to enter a marital relationship—to become husband and wife to each other. (Some states require an express agreement; others allow the agreement to be inferred from the manner in which the man and woman relate to each other.)
- The parties must actually live together as husband and wife (i.e., there must be cohabitation). In some states, cohabitation must include sexual relations. In other states, however, living openly together as husband and wife is sufficient even if the relationship was never consummated, particularly if illness prevented consummation. (Note that consummation is never a requirement for a valid ceremonial marriage.)
- There must be an openness about the relationship; the parties must make representations to the world that they are husband and wife. (See interviewing questions in checklist below.)

A popular misconception about common law marriages is that the parties must live together for seven years before the marriage becomes legal. There is no such time requirement.

In some states, the courts are reluctant to find all the above elements present in a particular case. Common law marriages may be disfavored by the court *even in a state where such marriages are legal.* It is too easy to fabricate a claim that the parties married, particularly after one of them has died. While millions of adults live together in an intimate relationship, their goals or intent is not always clear. In many of these relationships, neither party may want a marriage, although in some, one of the adults may have this intention or hope. Courts generally require strong evidence that the parties had the intent to marry before concluding that a common law marriage was entered. According to one court, the "mutual understanding or consent must be conveyed with such a demonstration of intent and with such clarity on the part of the parties that marriage does not creep up on either of them and catch them unawares. One cannot be married unwittingly or accidentally."[16]

---

[16] *Collier v. City of Milford,* 537 A.2d 474, 478–79 (Conn. 1981).

Interviewing and Investigation Checklist

Factors Relevant to the Formation of a Common Law Marriage between C (Client) and D (Defendant)

Legal Interviewing Questions

1. On what date did you first meet D?
2. When did the two of you first begin talking about living together? Describe the circumstances. Who said what, etc.?
3. Did you or D ever discuss with anyone else your plans to live together?
4. On what date did you actually move in together? How long have you been living together?
5. Have you and D had sexual relations? If so, when was the first time?
6. In whose name was the lease to the apartment or the deed to the house in which you lived?
7. Do you have separate or joint bank accounts? If joint, what names appear on the account?
8. Who pays the rent or the mortgage?
9. Who pays the utility bills?
10. Who pays the food bills?
11. Since you have been living together, have you filed separate or joint tax returns?
12. Have you ever made a written or oral agreement that you and D were going to be married?
13. Why didn't you and D have a marriage ceremony?
14. Did you ever introduce each other as "my husband" or "my wife"?
15. Name any relatives, neighbors, business associates, friends, etc., who think of you and D as husband and wife.
16. Did you and D ever discuss making individual or joint wills? Do you have them? Did you contact any attorneys about them? If so, what are their names and addresses?
17. Did you and D ever separate for any period of time? If so, describe the circumstances.
18. Did you and D ever have or adopt any children? If so, what last name did the children have?
19. On insurance policies, is either of you the beneficiary? How is the premium paid?
20. During your life with D, what other indications exist that the two of you treated each other as husband and wife?
21. Have the two of you ever spent significant time in Alabama, Colorado, the District of Columbia, Iowa, Kansas, Montana, New Hampshire, Oklahoma, Pennsylvania, Rhode Island, South Carolina, Texas, or Utah (states that recognize common law marriage; see Exhibit 5.3)? If so, describe the circumstances.

Possible Investigation Tasks

- Obtain a copy of the lease or deed.
- Obtain copies of bills, receipts, tax returns, etc., to determine how the names of C and D appear on them.
- Obtain copies of any agreements between C and D.
- Interview anyone C indicates would think of C and D as husband and wife.
- Obtain birth certificates of children, if any.

Two situations remain to be considered: *conflict of law* and *impediment removal.*

Conflict of Law

Bill and Pat live in State X, where common law marriages are legal. They enter such a marriage. Then they move to State Y, where common law marriages have been abolished. A child is born to them in State Y. Bill is injured on the job and dies. Pat claims workers' compensation benefits as the "wife" of Bill. Will State Y recognize Pat as married to Bill? Is their child legitimate?

The law of State X is inconsistent with the law of State Y on the validity of common law marriages. A conflict of law problem exists whenever a court must decide between inconsistent laws of different legal systems. There are conflict of law principles that guide a court in deciding which law to choose. In the case of marriages, the traditional "conflicts" principle is that the validity of a marriage is governed by the law of the place where the parties entered or contracted it.

Pat and Bill's marriage was contracted in State X, where it is valid. Since the marriage was valid where it was contracted, State Y will accept the marriage as valid (even though it would have been invalid had they tried to enter it in State Y). Pat is married to Bill and their child is legitimate. (In chapter 6, we will discuss the problem of parties moving to another state *solely* to take advantage of its more lenient marriage laws and returning to their original state after the marriage.)

Impediment Removal

In 1979, Ernestine enters a valid ceremonial marriage with John. They begin having marital troubles and separate. In 1985, Ernestine and Henry begin living together. Ernestine does not divorce John. She and Henry cohabitate and hold each other out as husband and wife in a state where common law marriages are valid. Except for the existence of the 1979 marriage to John, it is clear that Ernestine and Henry would have a valid common law marriage. In 1991, John obtains a divorce from Ernestine. Henry and Ernestine continue to live together in the same manner as they had since 1985. In 1999, Henry dies. Ernestine claims death benefits under the Workers' Compensation Act as his surviving "wife." Was she ever married to Henry?

impediment
A legal obstacle that prevents the formation of a valid marriage or other contract.

Ernestine and Henry never entered a ceremonial marriage. Until 1991, a serious **impediment** existed to their being able to marry: Ernestine was already married to someone else. When the marriage was dissolved by the divorce in 1991, the impediment was removed. The issue is (1) whether Ernestine and Henry would be considered to have entered a valid common law marriage at the time the impediment was removed, or (2) whether at that time they would have had to enter a *new* common law marriage agreement, express or implied. In most states, a new agreement would not be necessary. An earlier agreement to marry (by common law) will carry forward to the time the impediment is removed so long as the parties have continued to live together openly as husband and wife. Accordingly, Ernestine automatically became the wife of Henry when the impediment of the prior marriage was removed, since she and Henry continued to live together openly as husband and wife after that time. As one court explains:

> It is not to be expected that parties once having agreed to be married will deem it necessary to agree to do so again when an earlier marriage is terminated or some other bar to union is eliminated.[17]

In the states that reach this conclusion, it makes no difference that either or both of the parties knew of the impediment at the time they initially agreed to live as husband and wife.

ASSIGNMENT 5.13

Examine the following sequence of events:

- Ann and Rich meet in State Y where they agree to live together as husband and wife forever. They do not want to go through a marriage ceremony, but they agree to be married and openly represent themselves as such. State Y does not recognize common law marriages.
- Rich accepts a job offer in State X, where common law marriages are legal, and they both move there.
- After three years in State X, Rich and Ann move back to State Y. One year later Rich dies. In his will, he leaves all his property "to my wife." Ann is not mentioned by name in his will.

---

[17]*Matthews v. Britton,* 303 F.2d 408, 409 (D.C. Cir. 1962).

- From the time they met until the time of Rich's death, they lived together as husband and wife, and everyone who knew them thought of them as such.

a. Can Ann claim anything under the will? State Y provides tax benefits to "widows." Can Ann claim these benefits? (See the General Instructions for the Legal-Analysis Assignment in Appendix A.)
b. What further information would you like to have about this case? (See the General Instructions for the Investigation-Strategy Assignment in Appendix A.)

ASSIGNMENT 5.14

Vivian Hildenbrand and Tom Hildenbrand began living together in Oregon in 1975 and continuously did so until Tom's death in 1984. During this time, pursuant to mutual agreement, they cohabited and held themselves out as husband and wife, but never went through a marriage ceremony. They purchased real property in their joint names as husband and wife. On four different occasions, they went on vacation fishing trips to a resort in Montana, where they registered as husband and wife, held themselves out as such, and lived together during their stay. Two trips in 1977 were of three days' duration each. Two trips were of seven days' duration each, one in 1978 and one in 1979. Oregon does not recognize common law marriages; Montana does.

a. Were the parties married in 1984? (See General Instructions for the Legal-Analysis Assignment in Appendix A.)
b. Assume that Tom Hildenbrand died while he was working for the Oregon XYZ Chemical Company, due to an on-the-job accident. Vivian claims Oregon workers' compensation benefits. The state Workers' Compensation Board denies these benefits on the ground that she was not his wife. Draft a complaint for Vivian against the board. (See General Instructions for the Complaint-Drafting Assignment in Appendix A.)

ASSIGNMENT 5.15

a. Why do you think most states have abolished common law marriages?
b. What is the feminist argument in favor of allowing common law marriages? See Cynthia Grant Bowman, *A Feminist Proposal to Bring Back Common Law Marriage*, 75 Oregon Law Review 709 (1996).

PUTATIVE MARRIAGE

In chapter 4, we saw that some courts will treat unmarried parties as **putative spouses** for purposes of providing limited rights. Only a few states recognize putative marriages, however, and the requirements for establishing them are very strict:

putative spouse
A person who reasonably believed he or she entered a valid marriage even though there was a legal impediment that made the marriage unlawful.

> A putative marriage is one which has been contracted in good faith and in ignorance of some existing impediment on the part of at least one of the contracting parties. Three circumstances must occur to constitute this species of marriage: (1) There must be bona fides. At least one of the parties must have been ignorant of the impediment, not only at the time of the marriage, but must also have continued ignorant of it during his or her life. (2) The marriage must be duly solemnized. (3) The marriage must have been considered lawful in the estimation of the parties or of that party who alleges the bona fides.[18]

[18] *United States Fidelity & Guarantee Co. v. Henderson,* 53 S.W.2d 811, 816 (Tex. Civ. App. 1932).

An example might be a woman who goes through a marriage ceremony in good faith and does not find out until after her "husband" dies that he never even tried to obtain a divorce from his first wife, who is still alive. In the few states that recognize putative marriages, such a woman would be given some protection (e.g., she would be awarded the reasonable value of the services she rendered or a share of the property the parties accumulated during the relationship).[19] Note, however, that only the innocent party can benefit from the putative marriage. If the woman had died first in our example, her bigamist "husband" could not claim benefits as her putative spouse.

SAME-SEX RELATIONSHIPS

Can a man marry a man? Can a woman marry a woman? Until recently, marriage statutes did not specifically prohibit same-sex marriages. Yet even without such a prohibition, courts have consistently held that a marriage cannot exist without a man and a woman.

The Netherlands is the only country in the world that allows same-sex marriages. The law authorizing such marriages became effective in 2001. At least one partner must be a Dutch citizen or resident, a requirement that also applies to heterosexual couples entering marriage in the Netherlands.

Proponents of same-sex marriages in America have attempted a number of strategies—all without success:

1. *Equal protection.* Opposite-sex couples have the right to marry. Is the denial of this right to same-sex couples a violation of the equal protection of the law? In the *federal* constitution, section 1 of the Fourteenth Amendment provides that "[n]o State shall . . . deny to any person within its jurisdiction the equal protection of the laws." No federal court, however, has held that the denial of same-sex marriage is unconstitutional under the Fourteenth Amendment. Every *state* constitution has its own equal protection clause or one closely equivalent. No state court, however, has held that the denial of same-sex marriages violates the state constitution. Yet two states—Hawaii and Vermont—came very close, as we will see.
2. *Fundamental right to marry.* Earlier in the chapter, we saw that in *Zablocki v. Redhail* the United States Supreme Court held that only "reasonable regulations that do not significantly interfere with decisions to enter into the marital relationship may legitimately be imposed." The reason is that marriage is a fundamental right. No court, however, has yet held that the prohibition against same-sex marriages is unreasonable.
3. *Common law marriage.* If gay people cannot enter ceremonial marriages, can they enter a common law marriage if all of the conditions for such a marriage are present (e.g., open cohabitation, intent to marry)? No. Where this theory has been used, the courts have still insisted on a man-woman relationship.

---

[19]Some states have enacted the Uniform Marriage and Divorce Act, which provides in section 209 that "[a]ny person who has cohabited with another to whom he is not legally married in the good faith belief that he was married to that person is a putative spouse until knowledge of the fact that he is not legally married terminates his status and prevents acquisition of further rights. A putative spouse acquires the rights conferred upon a legal spouse, including the right to maintenance following termination of his status, whether or not the marriage is prohibited (Section 207) or declared invalid (Section 208). If there is a legal spouse or other putative spouses, rights acquired by a putative spouse do not supersede the rights of the legal spouse or those acquired by other putative spouses, but the court shall apportion property, maintenance, and support rights among the claimants as appropriate in the circumstances and in the interests of justice."

4. *Putative spouse doctrine.* Here the parties acknowledge a legal impediment to the marriage (namely that they were not an opposite-sex couple) but argue that they had a good faith belief that they were legally married. Courts, however, have said that homosexuals could not possibly have such a good faith belief.

In many states, homosexual conduct among adults is a crime even if it is consensual. In *Bowers v. Hardwick,* the United States Supreme Court has held that it is constitutional for states to impose criminal penalties for such conduct.[20] Such states obviously have little sympathy for the argument that homosexuals should be allowed to marry.

Suppose that one of the parties is a transsexual (an individual, usually a man, who has had a sex-change or reassignment surgery). Can such an individual marry a man? Most courts would not permit the marriage, arguing that both parties to the marriage must have been *born* members of the opposite sex. A recent case considered the related issue of whether a transsexual man ("Christie") who underwent sex reassignment surgery can be considered the surviving spouse of a recently deceased male patient. He and Christie had previously gone through a ceremonial "marriage." A Texas Court of Appeals held that "Christie cannot be married to another male" and, therefore, cannot be a surviving spouse.[21] A few courts, however, have taken the opposite position and have allowed transsexuals to marry in such cases.

A number of other special circumstances need to be considered in this area of the law:

- Two homosexuals can enter a *Marvin*-type contract, in which they agree to live together and share property acquired during the relationship. The major issue (as in a heterosexual relationship) is whether sexual services were an integral and inseparable part of the agreement. If so, as we saw in chapter 4, the contract will not be enforced.
- In some states, a gay adult can adopt another gay adult (see chapter 15).
- Assume that two lesbians live together. One is artificially inseminated and bears a child. In a few states, the other lesbian may be able to adopt the child, who then has two legal parents of the same sex (see chapter 16).
- In the above situation, if the other lesbian does not adopt the child and the adults separate, can the other lesbian be granted visitation rights? As we will see in chapter 9 on child custody, the United States Supreme Court in the 2000 case of *Troxel v. Granville*[22] held that the visitation by nonparents (e.g., grandparents) must not interfere with the primary right of fit custodial parents to raise their children. Hence, if a fit or competent natural mother objects to visitation by her ex–lesbian lover, it is unlikely that a court will order the visitation. Would it make any difference if the two women had entered a *co-parenting* agreement in which they agreed to raise and support the child together? Probably not, although the answer is unclear. The question has not yet arisen since the United States Supreme Court wrote its pro–natural parent decision of *Troxel v. Granville.*
- Some universities have allowed gay student couples to live in *married* student housing.
- An increasing number of large corporations (e.g., Levi Strauss & Co. and Walt Disney Co.) offer health insurance coverage and other benefits to partners of their homosexual employees. The Levi plan applies to any worker who lives and shares finances with an unmarried lover.

---

[20]478 U.S. 186, 106 S. Ct. 2841, 92 L. Ed. 2d 140 (1986).
[21]*Littleton v. Prange,* 9 S.W.3d 223 (Tex. App. 1999).
[22]530 U.S. 57, 120 S. Ct. 2054, 147 L. Ed. 2d 49 (2000).

- Rent-control laws in New York City limit the right of a landlord to evict "the surviving spouse of the deceased tenant or some other member of the deceased tenant's family who has been living with the tenant." In a highly publicized case, the New York State Court of Appeals ruled that a man whose male lover died of AIDS was a "family" member of the deceased within the meaning of this law and therefore was entitled to remain in the apartment.[23]
- Over twenty-five cities and counties give marriagelike benefits to same-sex couples and to unmarried opposite-sex couples. The couples are called **domestic partners.** Opposite-sex couples may seek this status because they do not want to marry but would like the benefits provided by a formal domestic partnership. Same-sex couples may seek the status not only because they want to receive the benefits but also because domestic partnership is the closest status to marriage they are allowed to achieve. Some of the benefits include hospital visitation rights, bereavement leave from work, and health insurance benefits. For example, a hospital will have to include domestic partners among the individuals who are allowed to visit patients. Prior to the creation of the domestic partnership relationship, hospitals could limit visitors to spouses and relatives. Who can register as a domestic partner? Not all cities and counties have the same rules. The program might be limited to municipal employees or extend to everyone. New York City's law covers both categories:

domestic partners
Individuals in a same-sex relationship (or in an unmarried opposite-sex relationship) who are emotionally and financially interdependent and also meet the requirements for registering their relationship with the government so that they can receive specified marriagelike benefits.

> A domestic partnership may be registered by two people who meet all of the following conditions:
>
> 1. Either: (a) both persons are residents of the city of New York or (b) at least one partner is employed by the city of New York on the date of registration;
> 2. Both persons are eighteen years of age or older;
> 3. Neither of the persons is married;
> 4. Neither of the persons is a party to another domestic partnership, or has been a party to another domestic partnership within the six months immediately prior to registration;
> 5. The persons are not related to each other by blood in a manner that would bar their marriage in the state of New York;
> 6. The persons have a close and committed personal relationship, live together and have been living together on a continuous basis.[24]

Eligibility in New York City is not limited to same-sex couples. All that is required is that the individuals "have a close and committed personal relationship" and have been living together on a "continuous basis." Once a domestic partnership is formed, it continues until one or both of the parties file a formal notice of termination with the government. One of the first *statewide* domestic partnership programs was created in California. See Exhibits 5.4 and 5.5 for the forms used to declare and terminate a California domestic partnership. The criteria in California are listed at the top of Exhibit 5.4. Note that in addition to same-sex couples, the status can be used by any couple (same-sex or opposite-sex) if both members are over sixty-two and are eligible for certain social security programs.

As indicated, no state has yet taken the drastic step of legalizing same-sex marriages. While domestic partnership is a step in that direction, married couples possess many rights that domestic partners do not enjoy. For example, if one domestic partner dies without leaving a valid will (i.e., dies intestate), the surviving partner receives nothing from the deceased partner's estate, whereas

---

[23] *Braschi v. Stahl,* 74 N.Y.2d 201, 543 N.E.2d 49, 544 N.Y.S.2d 784 (1989).
[24] New York City Code § 3-241.

Exhibit 5.4 Declaration of Domestic Partnership

State of California
Bill Jones
Secretary of State

FILE NO: ____________________

(Office Use Only)

DECLARATION OF DOMESTIC PARTNERSHIP

(Family Code Section 298)

Instructions:

1. **Complete and mail to: Secretary of State, P.O. Box 944225, Sacramento, CA 94244-2250 (916) 653-4984**
2. **Include filing fee of $10.00**

We the undersigned, do declare that we meet the requirements of Section 297 at this time:

We share a common residence;
We agree to be jointly responsible for each other's basic living expenses incurred during our domestic partnership;
Neither of us is married or a member of another domestic partnership;
We are not related by blood in a way that would prevent us from being married to each other in this state;
We are both at least 18 years of age;
We are both members of the same sex or we are both over the age of 62 and meet the eligibility criteria under Title II of the Social Security Act as defined in 42 U.S.C. Section 402(a) for old-age insurance benefits or Title XVI of the Social Security Act as defined in 42 U.S.C Section 1381 for aged individuals;
We are both capable of consenting to the domestic partnership;
Neither of us has previously filed a Declaration of Domestic Partnership with the Secretary of State pursuant to Division 2.5 of the Family Code that has not been terminated under Section 299 of the Family Code.

The representations herein are true, correct and contain no material omissions of fact to our best knowledge and belief. Sign and print complete name (if not printed legibly, application will be rejected.) Signatures of <u>both</u> partners must be notarized.

____________________	____________________		
Signature	(Last)	(First)	(Middle)
Signature	(Last)	(First)	(Middle)
Common Residence Address	City	State	Zip Code
Mailing Address	City	State	Zip Code

NOTARIZATION IS REQUIRED
State of California
County of ____________________

On ____________________, before me, ____________________, personally appeared ____________________
personally known to me (or proved to me on the basis of satisfactory evidence) to be the person(s) whose name(s) are subscribed to the within instrument and acknowledged to me that he/she/they executed the same in his/her/their authorized capacity(ies), and that by his/her/their signature(s) on the instrument the person(s) executed the instrument.

____
Signature of Notary Public

[PLACE NOTARY SEAL HERE]

Exhibit 5.5 Notice of Termination of Domestic Partnership

State of California
Bill Jones
Secretary of State

FILE NO: ____________________

(Office Use Only)

NOTICE OF TERMINATION OF DOMESTIC PARTNERSHIP
(Family Code Section 299)

Instructions:

1. **Complete and send by <u>CERTIFIED</u> mail to:**
   Secretary of State
   P.O. Box 944225
   Sacramento, CA 94244-2250
   (916) 653-4984
2. **There is no fee for filings this Notice of Termination**

I, the undersigned, do declare that:

Former Partner:______________________________________ and I are no longer Domestic Partners.
(Last) (First) (Middle)

Secretary of State File Number: ______________________________.

If termination is caused by death or marriage of the domestic partner please indicate the date of the death or the marriage: ______________________.
(month/day/year)

This date shall be the actual termination date for the Domestic Partnership as provided in Family Code Section 299.

______________________________ ____
Signature (Last) (First) (Middle)

____
Mailing Address City State Zip Code

NOTARIZATION IS REQUIRED
State of California
County of ______________________

On ______________________ before me, ______________________________, personally appeared

____

____

personally known to me (or proved to me on the basis of satisfactory evidence) to be the person whose name is subscribed to the within instrument and acknowledged to me that he/she executed the same in his/her authorized capacity, and that by his/her signature on the instrument the person executed the instrument.

____
Signature of Notary Public [PLACE NOTARY SEAL HERE]

a surviving spouse automatically receives a significant share of the deceased spouse's estate. (See the right of election against a will in chapter 8.)

In the 1990s, however, two thunderbolts came from the states of Hawaii and Vermont. Many thought that the day of same-sex marriages had arrived. While this did not happen, the states came very close.

Hawaii

In Hawaii, the landmark gay-rights opinion written by the Hawaii Supreme Court was *Baehr v. Lewin.*[25] This case did not say that same-sex couples have the right to marry. Yet it did hold that the denial of this right *might* constitute a denial of the equal protection of the law under the *state* constitution of Hawaii. The case arose when three same-sex couples sued the state after they were denied a marriage license. The lower court dismissed the case on the ground that the Hawaii Revised Statutes (HRS) did not authorize same-sex marriage. The couples then appealed to the Hawaii Supreme Court, which wrote *Baehr v. Lewin.*

The *Baehr* opinion covered two main state constitutional principles: privacy and equal protection under the state constitution:

- *Privacy:* There is an express right to privacy in the Hawaii Constitution. Section 6 of the Hawaii Constitution says; "The right . . . to privacy is recognized." Does this right include a fundamental right of same-sex couples to marry? The court's answer was no. Same-sex marriage is not included within the principle of privacy or within the related principles of liberty and justice under the state constitution:

  > [W]e do not believe that a right to same-sex marriage is so rooted in the traditions and collective conscience of our people that failure to recognize it would violate the fundamental principles of liberty and justice that lie at the base of all our civil and political institutions. Neither do we believe that a right to same-sex marriage is implicit in the concept of ordered liberty, such that neither liberty nor justice would exist if it were sacrificed. Accordingly, we hold that the applicant couples do not have a fundamental constitutional right to same-sex marriage arising out of the right to privacy or otherwise.[26]

- *Equal protection:* State governments have the right to regulate marriage. For example, the state can pass statutes that designate who is eligible to marry and what rights married couples have in marital property upon divorce. But there are limits on a state's authority to write such statutes. A state cannot pass a statute that violates the constitution. Did Hawaii do that here? Section 5 of the Hawaii Constitution contains the state's equal protection clause. It says

  > No person shall be . . . denied the equal protection of the laws, nor be denied the enjoyment of the person's civil rights or be discriminated against in the exercise thereof because of race, religion, sex, or ancestry.

  This section prohibits the state from passing statutes that discriminate against any person in the exercise of his or her civil rights on the basis of sex. The Hawaii Revised Statutes (HRS) discriminate on the basis of sex by granting opposite-sex couples (but not same-sex couples) the status of marriage along with the rights and responsibilities of this status. Does this discrimination in the HRS violate the equal protection clause in section 5 of the Hawaii Constitution?

---

[25] 74 Haw. 530, 852 P.2d 44 (1993).
[26] Id. At 557, 852 P.2d at 65.

rational basis test
Discrimination in a law is constitutional if the law rationally furthers a legitimate state interest.

strict scrutiny test
Discrimination in a law is presumed to be unconstitutional unless the state shows compelling state interests that justify the discrimination and also shows that the law is narrowly drawn to avoid unnecessary abridgments of constitutional rights.

Whenever a court is deciding whether discrimination in a statute is unconstitutional because of an alleged denial of equal protection, it applies a test or standard. There are two main tests: the rational basis test and the strict scrutiny test. The **rational basis test** says that discrimination in the statute is constitutional if the statute rationally furthers a legitimate state interest. On the other hand, the **strict scrutiny test,** which is more difficult to meet, presumes that the statute is unconstitutional unless the state shows compelling state interests that justify the discrimination and also shows that the statute is narrowly drawn to avoid unnecessary abridgments of constitutional rights. The strict scrutiny test is often applied when the discrimination encroaches on a fundamental right or is against what is called a "suspect class" such as a racial group. (The word "suspect" derives from the conclusion that certain kinds of discrimination create classifications that are inherently suspect or questionable.)

The *Baehr* court had to decide which of these tests to apply in determining whether the HRS unconstitutionally deny same-sex couples the equal protection of the law. The court chose the strict scrutiny test. Hence it sent the case back to the lower court for a new trial. At the new trial, the HRS discrimination is presumed to be unconstitutional. The state must show that there are compelling state interests that justify the discrimination against same-sex couples in the HRS and that the statute is narrowly drawn to avoid unnecessary abridgments of constitutional rights.

Keep in mind that the court is applying the equal protection clause in the *state* constitution. No controlling federal court opinion has ever reached the same conclusion when interpreting the equal protection clause in the United States Constitution. Yet a state constitution can be broader and more generous than the federal constitution. "[T]his court is free to accord greater protection to Hawaii's citizens under the state constitution than are recognized under the *United States Constitution.*"[27]

The drama of the *Baehr* court's opinion was clear. While the court did not authorize same-sex marriage, it did rule that the denial of same-sex marriage is presumed to be unconstitutional. This decision made international news. Many gay activists were ecstatic. On the other hand, to say that conservatives in Hawaii and in the nation were alarmed would be an understatement.

The fear of opponents in other states was that if Hawaii eventually authorizes same-sex marriage, other states might be forced to recognize such marriages within their own state. Here is how this could happen. Assume that State X allows same-sex marriage:

> *Ted and Bob marry in State X. They then move to State Y, where they continue to live together. Bob dies. Ted now goes to a court in State Y and asks for a share of Bob's estate as his "spouse." Or assume that after they move to State Y, they decide to separate. They go to a Y state court and ask for a "divorce" and an order dividing their "marital" property. In either event, the Y state court must decide whether to recognize the marriage entered in State X.*

Assume that under the law of State Y same-sex marriages are not allowed. What law does the Y state court apply? Its own or that of State X? This is a conflict of law question.

As we will see in chapter 6, the traditional conflict of law rule is that the validity of a marriage is determined by the law of the state in which the marriage was entered or contracted. Another state will recognize that marriage *unless* to do so would violate a strong public policy of the state asked to recognize

---

[27]Id at 576, 852 P.2d at 65.

it. Under this rule, State Y would be required to recognize the same-sex marriage entered in State X unless State Y determined that to do so would violate a strong public policy of State Y. While, in our example, same-sex marriages are not allowed in State Y, there may be no clear declaration in the law of State Y that recognizing such a marriage entered elsewhere would violate a strong public policy of State Y. In this climate of uncertainty, a Y state court might recognize Ted and Bob's State X marriage.

The problem is further compounded by the **full faith and credit clause** in Article IV of the United States Constitution, which provides that "Full Faith and Credit shall be given in each State to the public Acts, Records, and judicial Proceedings of every other State." Assume that Ted and Bob have a judgment from a court in State X that declares their marriage legal under the law of State X. Would other states be required to give full faith and credit (i.e., to recognize) the judgment of this State X court? There is no clear answer to this question, since no state has allowed same-sex marriage. The recognition issue, therefore, has not been tested in the courts.

full faith and credit clause
Article IV of the *United States Constitution* provides that "Full Faith and Credit shall be given in each State to the public Acts, Records, and judicial Proceedings of every other State."

While legal scholars and activists throughout the country were debating these recognition issues, the *Baehr* case was still in progress. Recall that the Hawaii Supreme Court sent the case back to a lower court to determine whether the state could justify its discrimination against same-sex couples. Politicians in the Hawaii legislature, however, decided not to await the outcome of the litigation. In response to one of the objections of the *Baehr* court that same-sex couples were denied many of the benefits of married couples, the Hawaii legislature passed the Reciprocal Beneficiaries Act. This law allowed same-sex couples to register as *reciprocal beneficiaries*—Hawaii's version of domestic partnership. Registered couples were given a number of rights that once were available only to married couples.

More important, the legislature and the state voters overwhelmingly approved a constitutional amendment that gave the legislature the authority to limit marriage to opposite-sex couples. The legislature then passed such a statute, which said that a valid marriage contract "shall be only between a man and a woman."[28] Hence the voters and the legislature did an end run around the Hawaii Supreme Court. Discrimination against same-sex marriage now had constitutional *approval,* since the constitution gave the legislature the power to ban same-sex marriages. There was no point, therefore, in continuing the *Baehr* litigation. Even though a lower court in the *Baehr* litigation ruled in favor of the same-sex couples, further litigation was now moot. The case was dismissed.

Opponents of same-sex marriage across the country expressed a collective sigh of relief. There was no longer a possibility that their state might be forced to recognize a Hawaiian same-sex marriage. But if Hawaii came this close, what if another state actually authorized such marriages? Rather than wait, over thirty-five state legislatures enacted statutes banning same-sex marriages and making clear that it is against the state's strong public policy to recognize such marriages entered in other states. A story in the *New York Times* on this development was titled "Fearing a Toehold for Gay Marriages, Conservatives Rush to Bar the Door."[29] At the federal level, Congress passed, and President Bill Clinton signed, the **Defense of Marriage Act (DOMA),** which said that a state is not required to give full faith and credit to a same-sex marriage entered in another state:

Defense of Marriage Act (DOMA)
A federal statute that says one state is not required to give full faith and credit to a same-sex marriage entered in another state.

> No State, territory, or possession of the United States, or Indian tribe, shall be required to give effect to any public act, record, or judicial proceeding of any other State, territory, possession, or tribe respecting a relationship between

---

[28]Hawaii Revised Statutes § 572-1.

[29]N.Y. Times, Mar. 3, 1996, at A7.

> persons of the same sex that is treated as a marriage under the laws of such other State, territory, possession, or tribe, or a right or claim arising from such relationship.[30]

If a state wants to recognize another state's same-sex marriage, it can, but DOMA says that this recognition is not required. DOMA does not say that same-sex marriages are illegal. It simply provides that one state cannot be forced to recognize such a marriage if another state ever allows one. The state statutes declaring that it is against the state's strong public policy to recognize out-of-state same-sex marriages became known as **mini-DOMAs** or baby-DOMAs.

mini-DOMA
A statute of a state declaring that its strong public policy is not to recognize any same-sex marriage that might be validly entered in another state.

ASSIGNMENT 5.16

Does your state have a mini-DOMA? If so, what does it say? (See General Instructions for the State-Code Assignment in Appendix A.)

Will the federal DOMA and the mini-DOMAs of the states work? The answer is not clear. The United States Supreme Court might eventually rule that such laws are unconstitutional. At the present time, we do not know whether any legislature has the constitutional power to limit the scope of the full faith and credit clause of the United States Constitution in the way that DOMA does. We will eventually find out, but only when some state in the country legitimizes same-sex marriages. When a same-sex couple marries in such a state and moves to another state seeking recognition and enforcement of their marriage, the other state might say that DOMA gives it the right to refuse. This will eventually require the United States Supreme Court to decide whether DOMA is constitutional.

Vermont

The next state to enter the fray was Vermont. Courts in Vermont, like those in Hawaii, recognize that there is no right to same-sex marriage under the United States Constitution. Yet, since a state is free to give more generous protection under its state constitution than is provided under the federal Constitution, the question in Vermont is whether the denial of same-sex marriage is a violation of the Vermont Constitution. This is the issue raised in one of the most significant cases in the history of family law, *Baker v. State.*

CASE

Baker v. State

744 A.2d 864, 81 A.L.R. 5th 627 (1999)
Supreme Court of Vermont

Background: *Three same-sex couples applied for a marriage license in Vermont. They were told that they were ineligible under Vermont Statutes Annotated because marriage is limited to a man and woman. The couples then sued. They asserted that the refusal to grant the license violated Vermont statutes and the common benefits clause of the Vermont Constitution. The superior court dismissed their complaint and ruled that the marriage statutes could not be interpreted to permit the issuance of a license to same-sex couples. The trial court further ruled that the marriage statutes were constitutional because they rationally furthered the state's interest in promoting "the link between procreation and child rearing." The couples appealed this judgment*

[30] 28 U.S.C. § 1738C.

against them. The case is now before the Supreme Court of Vermont.

Decision of the Court: *The superior court judgment is reversed. Vermont marriage statutes were not intended to apply to same-sex couples. This exclusion of same-sex couples from benefits and protections incident to marriage violates the common benefits clause of the Vermont Constitution. To exclude the classification of same-sex couples from the marriage statutes is not reasonably related to any state governmental purpose. The Vermont legislature is directed to allow same-sex couples to marry* or *to establish a separate legal relationship that gives such couples the same state benefits and protections enjoyed by opposite-sex married couples.*

Opinion of the Court:

Chief Justice AMESTOY delivered the opinion of the court:

May the State of Vermont exclude same-sex couples from the benefits and protections that its laws provide to opposite-sex married couples? That is the fundamental question we address in this appeal, a question that the Court well knows arouses deeply-felt religious, moral, and political beliefs. Our constitutional responsibility to consider the legal merits of issues properly before us provides no exception for the controversial case. The issue before the Court, moreover, does not turn on the religious or moral debate over intimate same-sex relationships, but rather on the statutory and constitutional basis for the exclusion of same-sex couples from the secular benefits and protections offered married couples.

We conclude that under the Common Benefits Clause of the Vermont Constitution, which, in pertinent part, reads,

> That government is, or ought to be, instituted for the common benefit, protection, and security of the people, nation, or community, and not for the particular emolument or advantage of any single person, family, or set of persons, who are a part only of that community. . . . chapter I, article 7,

plaintiffs may not be deprived of the statutory benefits and protections afforded persons of the opposite sex who choose to marry. We hold that the State is constitutionally required to extend to same-sex couples the common benefits and protections that flow from marriage under Vermont law. Whether this ultimately takes the form of inclusion within the marriage laws themselves or a parallel "domestic partnership" system or some equivalent statutory alternative, rests with the Legislature. Whatever system is chosen, however, must conform with the constitutional imperative to afford all Vermonters the common benefit, protection, and security of the law.

Plaintiffs are three same-sex couples who have lived together in committed relationships for periods ranging from four to twenty-five years. Two of the couples have raised children together. Each couple applied for a marriage license from their respective town clerk, and each was refused a license as ineligible under the applicable state marriage laws. Plaintiffs thereupon filed this lawsuit. . . .

The Statutory Claim

[The court first rejects the claim of the plaintiffs that the Vermont marriage statutes can be interpreted to allow the issuance of marriage licenses to same-sex couples.] Although it is not necessarily the only possible definition, there is no doubt that the plain and ordinary meaning of "marriage" is the union of one man and one woman as husband and wife. See *Webster's New International Dictionary* 1506 (2d ed. 1955) (marriage consists of state of "being united to a person . . . of the opposite sex as husband or wife"). . . . Plaintiffs . . . argue, nevertheless, that the underlying purpose of marriage is to protect and encourage the union of committed couples and that, absent an explicit legislative prohibition, the statutes should be interpreted broadly to include committed same-sex couples. Plaintiffs rely principally on our decision in *In re B.L.V.B.,* 160 Vt. 368, 628 A.2d 1271 (1993). There, we held that a woman who was co-parenting the two children of her same-sex partner could adopt the children without terminating the natural mother's parental rights. Although the statute provided generally that an adoption deprived the natural parents of their legal rights, it contained an exception where the adoption was by the "spouse" of the natural parent. See id. at 370, 628 A.2d at 1273 (citing 15 V.S.A. § 448). Technically, therefore, the exception was inapplicable. We concluded, however, that the purpose of the law was not to restrict the exception to legally married couples, but to safeguard the child, and that to apply the literal language of the statute in these circumstances would defeat the statutory purpose and "reach an absurd result." Id. at 371, 628 A.2d at 1273. Although the Legislature had undoubtedly not even considered same-sex unions when the law was enacted in 1945, our interpretation was consistent with its "general intent and spirit." Id. at 373, 628 A.2d at 1274.

Contrary to plaintiffs' claim, *B.L.V.B.* does not control our conclusion here. We are not dealing in this case with a narrow statutory exception requiring a broader reading than its literal words would permit in order to avoid a result plainly at odds with the leg-

continued

CASE

Baker v. State—*Continued*

islative purpose. Unlike *B.L.V.B.*, it is far from clear that limiting marriage to opposite-sex couples violates the Legislature's "intent and spirit." Rather, the evidence demonstrates a clear legislative assumption that marriage under our statutory scheme consists of a union between a man and a woman. Accordingly, we reject plaintiffs' claim that they were entitled to a license under the statutory scheme governing marriage.

The Constitutional Claim

Assuming that the marriage statutes preclude their eligibility for a marriage license, plaintiffs contend that the exclusion violates their right to the common benefit and protection of the law guaranteed by Chapter I, Article 7 of the Vermont Constitution. They note that in denying them access to a civil marriage license, the law effectively excludes them from a broad array of legal benefits and protections incident to the marital relation, including access to a spouse's medical, life, and disability insurance, hospital visitation and other medical decisionmaking privileges, spousal support, intestate succession, homestead protections, and many other statutory protections. They claim the trial court erred in upholding the law on the basis that it reasonably served the State's interest in promoting the "link between procreation and child rearing." They argue that the large number of married couples without children, and the increasing incidence of same-sex couples with children, undermines the State's rationale. They note that Vermont law affirmatively guarantees the right to adopt and raise children regardless of the sex of the parents, see 15A V.S.A. § 1-102, and challenge the logic of a legislative scheme that recognizes the rights of same-sex partners as parents, yet denies them—and their children—the same security as spouses. . . .

[U]nder Article 7 . . . legislative classifications must "reasonably relate to a legitimate public purpose." *Choquette v. Perrault*, 153 Vt. 45, 52, 569 A.2d 459 (1989). . . . [A]ny exclusion from the general benefit and protection of the law [must] bear a just and reasonable relation to the legislative goals. *State v. Ludlow Supermarkets, Inc.*, 141 Vt. 261, 268, 448 A.2d 791, 795 (1982). . . . *MacCallum v. Seymour's Administrator*, 165 Vt. 452, 686 A.2d 935 (1996), . . . involved an Article 7 challenge to an intestacy statute that denied an adopted person's right of inheritance from collateral kin. . . . [A]lthough the State proffered at least a conceivable purpose for the legislative distinction between natural and adopted children, we held that the classification was unreasonable, explaining that "[a]dopted persons have historically been a target of discrimination," id. at 459, 686 A.2d at 939, and that however reasonable the classification when originally enacted, it represented an "outdated" distinction today. Id. at 460, 686 A.2d at 939. Thus, while deferential to the historical purpose underlying the classification, we demanded that it bear a reasonable and just relation to the governmental objective in light of contemporary conditions. . . .

When a statute is challenged under Article 7, we first define that "part of the community" disadvantaged by the law. We examine the statutory basis that distinguishes those protected by the law from those excluded from the state's protection. . . . We look next to the government's purpose in drawing a classification that includes some members of the community within the scope of the challenged law but excludes others. Consistent with Article 7's guiding principle of affording the protection and benefit of the law to all members of the Vermont community, we examine the nature of the classification to determine whether it is reasonably necessary to accomplish the State's claimed objectives.

We must ultimately ascertain whether the omission of a part of the community from the benefit, protection and security of the challenged law bears a reasonable and just relation to the governmental purpose. Consistent with the core presumption of inclusion, factors to be considered in this determination may include: (1) the significance of the benefits and protections of the challenged law; (2) whether the omission of members of the community from the benefits and protections of the challenged law promotes the government's stated goals; and (3) whether the classification is significantly underinclusive or overinclusive. . . .

The first step in our analysis is to identify the nature of the statutory classification. As noted, the marriage statutes apply expressly to opposite-sex couples. Thus, the statutes exclude anyone who wishes to marry someone of the same sex. . . . Next, we must identify the governmental purpose or purposes to be served by the statutory classification. The principal purpose the State advances in support of the excluding same-sex couples from the legal benefits of marriage is the government's interest in "furthering the link between procreation and child rearing." The State has a strong interest, it argues, in promoting a permanent commitment between couples who have children to ensure that their offspring are considered legitimate and receive ongoing parental support. The

State contends, further, that the Legislature could reasonably believe that sanctioning same-sex unions "would diminish society's perception of the link between procreation and child rearing . . . [and] advance the notion that fathers or mothers . . . are mere surplusage to the functions of procreation and child rearing." The State argues that since same-sex couples cannot conceive a child on their own, state-sanctioned same-sex unions "could be seen by the Legislature to separate further the connection between procreation and parental responsibilities for raising children." Hence, the Legislature is justified, the State concludes, "in using the marriage statutes to send a public message that procreation and child rearing are intertwined."

Do these concerns represent valid public interests that are reasonably furthered by the exclusion of same-sex couples from the benefits and protections that flow from the marital relation? It is beyond dispute that the State has a legitimate and long-standing interest in promoting a permanent commitment between couples for the security of their children. It is equally undeniable that the State's interest has been advanced by extending formal public sanction and protection to the union, or marriage, of those couples considered capable of having children, i.e., men and women. And there is no doubt that the overwhelming majority of births today continue to result from natural conception between one man and one woman. See J. Robertson, *Assisted Reproductive Technology and the Family,* 47 Hastings L. J. 911, 911–12 (1996) (noting the number of births resulting from assisted-reproductive technology, which remain small compared to overall number of births).

It is equally undisputed that many opposite-sex couples marry for reasons unrelated to procreation, that some of these couples never intend to have children, and that others are incapable of having children. Therefore, if the purpose of the statutory exclusion of same-sex couples is to "further [ ] the link between procreation and child rearing," it is significantly underinclusive. The law extends the benefits and protections of marriage to many persons with no logical connection to the stated governmental goal.

Furthermore, while accurate statistics are difficult to obtain, there is no dispute that a significant number of children today are actually being raised by same-sex parents, and that increasing numbers of children are being conceived by such parents through a variety of assisted-reproductive techniques. See D. Flaks, et al., *Lesbians Choosing Motherhood: A Comparative Study of Lesbian and Heterosexual Parents and Their Children,* 31 Dev. Psychol. 105, 105 (1995) (citing estimates that between 1.5 and 5 million lesbian mothers resided with their children in United States between 1989 and 1990, and that thousands of lesbian mothers have chosen motherhood through donor insemination or adoption); G. Green & F. Bozett, *Lesbian Mothers and Gay Fathers,* in Homosexuality: Research Implications for Public Policy 197, 198 (J. Gonsiorek et al. eds., 1991) (estimating that numbers of children of either gay fathers or lesbian mothers range between six and fourteen million); C. Patterson, *Children of the Lesbian Baby Boom: Behavioral Adjustment, Self-Concepts, and Sex Role Identity,* in Lesbian and Gay Psychology (B. Greene et al. eds., 1994) (observing that although precise estimates are difficult, number of families with lesbian mothers is growing); E. Shapiro & L. Schultz, *Single-Sex Families: The Impact of Birth Innovations Upon Traditional Family Notions,* 24 J. Fam. L. 271, 281 (1985) ("[I]t is a fact that children are being born to single-sex families on a biological basis, and that they are being so born in considerable numbers.").

Thus, with or without the marriage sanction, the reality today is that increasing numbers of same-sex couples are employing increasingly efficient assisted-reproductive techniques to conceive and raise children. See L. Ikemoto, *The In/Fertile, the Too Fertile, and the Dysfertile,* 47 Hastings L. J. 1007, 1056 & n. 170 (1996). The Vermont Legislature has not only recognized this reality, but has acted affirmatively to remove legal barriers so that same-sex couples may legally adopt and rear the children conceived through such efforts. See 15A V.S.A. § 1–102(b) (allowing partner of biological parent to adopt if in child's best interest without reference to sex). The state has also acted to expand the domestic relations laws to safeguard the interests of same-sex parents and their children when such couples terminate their domestic relationship. See 15A V.S.A. § 1–112 (vesting family court with jurisdiction over parental rights and responsibilities, parent-child contact, and child support when unmarried persons who have adopted minor child "terminate their domestic relationship").

Therefore, to the extent that the state's purpose in licensing civil marriage was, and is, to legitimize children and provide for their security, the statutes plainly exclude many same-sex couples who are no different from opposite-sex couples with respect to these objectives. If anything, the exclusion of same-sex couples from the legal protections incident to marriage exposes their children to the precise risks that the State argues the marriage laws are designed to secure against. In short, the marital exclusion treats persons who are similarly situated for purposes of the law, differently.

continued

CASE

Baker v. State—*Continued*

The State also argues that because same-sex couples cannot conceive a child on their own, their exclusion promotes a "perception of the link between procreation and child rearing," and that to discard it would "advance the notion that mothers and fathers . . . are mere surplusage to the functions of procreation and child rearing." Apart from the bare assertion, the State offers no persuasive reasoning to support these claims. Indeed, it is undisputed that most of those who utilize nontraditional means of conception are infertile married couples, see Shapiro and Schultz, supra, at 275, and that many assisted-reproductive techniques involve only one of the married partner's genetic material, the other being supplied by a third party through sperm, egg, or embryo donation. See E. May, *Barren in the Promised Land: Childless Americans and the Pursuit of Happiness* 217, 242 (1995); Robertson, supra, at 911–12, 922–27. The State does not suggest that the use of these technologies undermines a married couple's sense of parental responsibility, or fosters the perception that they are "mere surplusage" to the conception and parenting of the child so conceived. Nor does it even remotely suggest that access to such techniques ought to be restricted as a matter of public policy to "send a public message that procreation and child rearing are intertwined." Accordingly, there is no reasonable basis to conclude that a same-sex couple's use of the same technologies would undermine the bonds of parenthood, or society's perception of parenthood.

The question thus becomes whether the exclusion of a relatively small but significant number of otherwise qualified same-sex couples from the same legal benefits and protections afforded their opposite-sex counterparts contravenes the mandates of Article 7. It is, of course, well settled that statutes are not necessarily unconstitutional because they fail to extend legal protection to all who are similarly situated. See *Benning v. State,* 161 Vt. 472, 486, 641 A.2d 757, 764 (1994) ("A statute need not regulate the whole of a field to pass constitutional muster."). Courts have upheld underinclusive statutes out of a recognition that, for reasons of pragmatism or administrative convenience, the legislature may choose to address problems incrementally. . . . The State does not contend, however, that the same-sex exclusion is necessary as a matter of pragmatism or administrative convenience. We turn, accordingly, from the principal justifications advanced by the State to the interests asserted by plaintiffs. . . .

[I]n determining whether a statutory exclusion reasonably relates to the governmental purpose it is appropriate to consider the history and significance of the benefits denied. . . . What do these considerations reveal about the benefits and protections at issue here? In *Loving v. Virginia,* 388 U.S. 1, 12, 87 S. Ct. 1817, 18 L. Ed. 2d 1010 (1967), the United States Supreme Court, striking down Virginia's anti-miscegenation law, observed that "[t]he freedom to marry has long been recognized as one of the vital personal rights." The Court's point was clear; access to a civil marriage license and the multitude of legal benefits, protections, and obligations that flow from it significantly enhance the quality of life in our society.

The Supreme Court's observations in *Loving* merely acknowledged what many states, including Vermont, had long recognized. One hundred thirty-seven years before *Loving,* this Court characterized the reciprocal rights and responsibilities flowing from the marriage laws as "the natural rights of human nature." See *Overseers of the Poor of the Town of Newbury v. Overseers of the Poor of the Town of Brunswick,* 2 Vt. 151, 159 (1829).

While the laws relating to marriage have undergone many changes during the last century, largely toward the goal of equalizing the status of husbands and wives, the benefits of marriage have not diminished in value. On the contrary, the benefits and protections incident to a marriage license under Vermont law have never been greater. They include, for example, the right to receive a portion of the estate of a spouse who dies intestate and protection against disinheritance through elective share provisions, under 14 V.S.A. §§ 401–404, 551; preference in being appointed as the personal representative of a spouse who dies intestate, under 14 V.S.A. § 903; the right to bring a lawsuit for the wrongful death of a spouse, under 14 V.S.A. § 1492; the right to bring an action for loss of consortium, under 12 V.S.A. § 5431; the right to workers' compensation survivor benefits under 21 V.S.A. § 632; the right to spousal benefits statutorily guaranteed to public employees, including health, life, disability, and accident insurance, under 3 V.S.A. § 631; the opportunity to be covered as a spouse under group life insurance policies issued to an employee, under 8 V.S.A. § 3811; the opportunity to be covered as the insured's spouse under an individual health insurance policy, under 8 V.S.A. § 4063; the right to claim an evidentiary privilege for marital communications, under V.R.E. 504; homestead rights and protections, under 27 V.S.A.

§§ 105–108, 141–142; the presumption of joint ownership of property and the concomitant right of survivorship, under 27 V.S.A. § 2; hospital visitation and other rights incident to the medical treatment of a family member, under 18 V.S.A. § 1852; and the right to receive, and the obligation to provide, spousal support, maintenance, and property division in the event of separation or divorce, under 15 V.S.A. §§ 751–752. Other courts and commentators have noted the collection of rights, powers, privileges, and responsibilities triggered by marriage. See generally *Baehr v. Lewin,* 74 Haw. 530, 852 P.2d 44, 59 (1993); D. Chambers, *What If? The Legal Consequences of Marriage and the Legal Needs of Lesbian and Gay Male Couples,* 95 Mich. L. Rev. 447, passim (1996); J. Robbennolt & M. Johnson, *Legal Planning for Unmarried Committed Partners: Empirical Lessons for a Preventive and Therapeutic Approach,* 41 Ariz. L. Rev. 417, passim (1999); J. Trosino, *American Wedding: Same-Sex Marriage and the Miscegenation Analogy,* 73 B.U. L. Rev. 93, 96 (1993).

While other statutes could be added to this list, the point is clear. The legal benefits and protections flowing from a marriage license are of such significance that any statutory exclusion must necessarily be grounded on public concerns of sufficient weight, cogency, and authority that the justice of the deprivation cannot seriously be questioned. Considered in light of the extreme logical disjunction between the classification and the stated purposes of the law—protecting children and "furthering the link between procreation and child rearing"—the exclusion falls substantially short of this standard. The laudable governmental goal of promoting a commitment between married couples to promote the security of their children and the community as a whole provides no reasonable basis for denying the legal benefits and protections of marriage to same-sex couples, who are no differently situated with respect to this goal than their opposite-sex counterparts. Promoting a link between procreation and childrearing similarly fails to support the exclusion. We turn, accordingly, to the remaining interests identified by the State in support of the statutory exclusion.

The State asserts that a number of additional rationales could support a legislative decision to exclude same-sex partners from the statutory benefits and protections of marriage. Among these are the State's purported interests in "promoting child rearing in a setting that provides both male and female role models," minimizing the legal complications of surrogacy contracts and sperm donors, "bridging differences" between the sexes, discouraging marriages of convenience for tax, housing or other benefits, maintaining uniformity with marriage laws in other states, and generally protecting marriage from "destabilizing changes." The most substantive of the State's remaining claims relates to the issue of childrearing. It is conceivable that the Legislature could conclude that opposite-sex partners offer advantages in this area, although we note that child-development experts disagree and the answer is decidedly uncertain. The argument, however, contains a more fundamental flaw, and that is the Legislature's endorsement of a policy diametrically at odds with the State's claim. In 1996, the Vermont General Assembly enacted, and the Governor signed, a law removing all prior legal barriers to the adoption of children by same-sex couples. See 15A V.S.A. § 1–102. At the same time, the Legislature provided additional legal protections in the form of court-ordered child support and parent-child contact in the event that same-sex parents dissolved their "domestic relationship." Id. § 1–112. In light of these express policy choices, the State's arguments that Vermont public policy favors opposite-sex over same-sex parents or disfavors the use of artificial reproductive technologies are patently without substance.

Similarly, the State's argument that Vermont's marriage laws serve a substantial governmental interest in maintaining uniformity with other jurisdictions cannot be reconciled with Vermont's recognition of unions, such as first-cousin marriages, not uniformly sanctioned in other states. See 15 V.S.A. §§ 1–2 (consanguinity statutes do not exclude first cousins); 1 H. Clark, *The Law of Domestic Relations in the United States* § 2.9, at 153–54 (2d ed. 1987) (noting states that prohibit first-cousin marriage). In an analogous context, Vermont has sanctioned adoptions by same-sex partners, see 15A V.S.A. § 1–102, notwithstanding the fact that many states have not. See generally Annotation, *Adoption of Child By Same-Sex Partners,* 27 A.L.R.5th 54, 68–72 (1995). Thus, the State's claim that Vermont's marriage laws were adopted because the Legislature sought to conform to those of the other forty-nine states is not only speculative, but refuted by two relevant legislative choices which demonstrate that uniformity with other jurisdictions has not been a governmental purpose.

The State's remaining claims (e.g., recognition of same-sex unions might foster marriages of convenience or otherwise affect the institution in "unpredictable" ways) may be plausible forecasts as to what the future may hold, but cannot reasonably be construed to provide a reasonable and just basis for the

continued

CASE

Baker v. State—*Continued*

statutory exclusion. The State's conjectures are not, in any event, susceptible to empirical proof before they occur.[1]

Finally, it is suggested that the long history of official intolerance of intimate same-sex relationships cannot be reconciled with an interpretation of Article 7 that would give state-sanctioned benefits and protection to individuals of the same sex who commit to a permanent domestic relationship. We find the argument to be unpersuasive for several reasons. First, to the extent that state action historically has been motivated by an animus against a class, that history cannot provide a legitimate basis for continued unequal application of the law. See *MacCallum,* 165 Vt. at 459–60, 686 A.2d at 939 (holding that although adopted persons had "historically been a target of discrimination," social prejudices failed to support their continued exclusion from intestacy law). As we observed recently in *Brigham v. State,* 166 Vt. 246, 267, 692 A.2d 384, 396 (1997), "equal protection of the laws cannot be limited by eighteenth-century standards." Second, whatever claim may be made in light of the undeniable fact that federal and state statutes—including those in Vermont—have historically disfavored same-sex relationships, more recent legislation plainly undermines the contention. See, e.g., Laws of Vermont, 1977, No. 51, §§ 2, 3 (repealing former § 2603 of Title 13, which criminalized fellatio). In 1992, Vermont was one of the first states to enact statewide legislation prohibiting discrimination in employment, housing, and other services based on sexual orientation. See 21 V.S.A. § 495 (employment); 9 V.S.A. § 4503 (housing); 8 V.S.A. § 4724 (insurance); 9 V.S.A. § 4502 (public accommodations). Sexual orientation is among the categories specifically protected against hate-motivated crimes in Vermont. See 13 V.S.A. § 1455. Furthermore, as noted earlier, recent enactments of the General Assembly have removed barriers to adoption by same-sex couples, and have extended legal rights and protections to such couples who dissolve their "domestic relationship." See 15A V.S.A. §§ 1–102, 1–112.

Thus, viewed in the light of history, logic, and experience, we conclude that none of the interests asserted by the State provides a reasonable and just basis for the continued exclusion of same-sex couples from the benefits incident to a civil marriage license under Vermont law. Accordingly, in the faith that a case beyond the imagining of the framers of our Constitution may, nevertheless, be safely anchored in the values that infused it, we find a constitutional obligation to extend to plaintiffs the common benefit, protection, and security that Vermont law provides opposite-sex married couples. It remains only to determine the appropriate means and scope of relief compelled by this constitutional mandate.

It is important to state clearly the parameters of today's ruling. Although plaintiffs sought . . . relief designed to secure a marriage license, their claims and arguments here have focused primarily upon the consequences of official exclusion from the statutory benefits, protections, and security incident to marriage under Vermont law. While some future case may attempt to establish that—notwithstanding equal benefits and protections under Vermont law—the denial of a marriage license operates per se to deny constitutionally-protected rights, that is not the claim we address today.

We hold only that plaintiffs are entitled under Chapter I, Article 7, of the Vermont Constitution to obtain the same benefits and protections afforded by Vermont law to married opposite-sex couples. We do not purport to infringe upon the prerogatives of the Legislature to craft an appropriate means of addressing this constitutional mandate, other than to note that the record here refers to a number of potentially constitutional statutory schemes from other jurisdictions. These include what are typically referred to as "domestic partnership" or "registered partnership" acts, which generally establish an alternative legal status to marriage for same-sex couples, impose similar formal requirements and limitations, create a parallel licensing or registration scheme, and extend all or most of the same rights and obligations provided by the law to married partners. See . . . C. Christensen, *If Not Marriage? On Securing Gay and Lesbian Family Values by a "Simulacrum of Marriage",* 66 Fordham L. Rev. 1699, 1734–45 (1998) (discussing various domestic and foreign domestic partnership acts); A. Friedman, *Same-Sex Marriage and the Right to Privacy: Abandoning Scriptural, Canonical, and Natural Law Based Definitions of Marriage,* 35 How. L. J. 173, 217–20 n. 237 (1992) (reprinting Denmark's "Registered Partnership Act"); see gener-

---

[1]It would, for example, serve no useful purpose to remand this matter for hearings on whether marriages of convenience (i.e., unions for the purpose of obtaining certain statutory benefits) would result from providing same-sex couples with the statutory benefits and protections accorded opposite-sex couples under marriage laws. For the reasons we have stated in this opinion, it is not a failure of proof that is fatal to the State's arguments, it is a failure of logic.

ally Note, *A More Perfect Union: A Legal and Social Analysis of Domestic Partnership Ordinances,* 92 Colum. L. Rev. 1164 (1992) (discussing local domestic partnership laws); M. Pedersen, *Denmark: Homosexual Marriage and New Rules Regarding Separation and Divorce,* 30 J. Fam. L. 289 (1992) (discussing amendments to Denmark's Registered Partnership Act); M. Roth, *The Norwegian Act on Registered Partnership for Homosexual Couples,* 35 J. Fam. L. 467 (1997) (discussing Norway's Act on Registered Partnership for Homosexual Couples). We do not intend specifically to endorse any one or all of the referenced acts, particularly in view of the significant benefits omitted from several of the laws.

Further, while the State's prediction of "destabilization" cannot be a ground for denying relief, it is not altogether irrelevant. A sudden change in the marriage laws or the statutory benefits traditionally incidental to marriage may have disruptive and unforeseen consequences. Absent legislative guidelines defining the status and rights of same-sex couples, consistent with constitutional requirements, uncertainty and confusion could result. Therefore, we hold that the current statutory scheme shall remain in effect for a reasonable period of time to enable the Legislature to consider and enact implementing legislation in an orderly and expeditious fashion. . . . In the event that the benefits and protections in question are not statutorily granted, plaintiffs may petition this Court to order the remedy they originally sought.

Conclusion

While many have noted the symbolic or spiritual significance of the marital relation, it is plaintiffs' claim to the secular benefits and protections of a singularly human relationship that, in our view, characterizes this case. The State's interest in extending official recognition and legal protection to the professed commitment of two individuals to a lasting relationship of mutual affection is predicated on the belief that legal support of a couple's commitment provides stability for the individuals, their family, and the broader community. Although plaintiffs' interest in seeking state recognition and protection of their mutual commitment may—in view of divorce statistics—represent "the triumph of hope over experience,"[2] the essential aspect of their claim is simply and fundamentally for inclusion in the family of state-sanctioned human relations.

The past provides many instances where the law refused to see a human being when it should have. See, e.g., *Dred Scott v. Sandford,* 60 U.S. (19 How.) 393, 407 15 L. Ed. 691 (1857) (concluding that African slaves and their descendants had "no rights which the white man was bound to respect"). The future may provide instances where the law will be asked to see a human when it should not. See, e.g., G. Smith, *Judicial Decisionmaking in the Age of Biotechnology,* 13 Notre Dame J. Ethics & Pub. Policy 93, 114 (1999) (noting concerns that genetically engineering humans may threaten very nature of human individuality and identity). The challenge for future generations will be to define what is most essentially human. The extension of the Common Benefits Clause to acknowledge plaintiffs as Vermonters who seek nothing more, nor less, than legal protection and security for their avowed commitment to an intimate and lasting human relationship is simply, when all is said and done, a recognition of our common humanity.

The judgment of the superior court upholding the constitutionality of the Vermont marriage statutes under Chapter I, Article 7 of the Vermont Constitution is reversed. The effect of the Court's decision is suspended, and jurisdiction is retained in this Court, to permit the Legislature to consider and enact legislation consistent with the constitutional mandate described herein.

[2] J. Boswell, *Life of Johnson* (1791) (reprinted in *Bartlett's Familiar Quotations* 54 (15th ed. 1989)).

ASSIGNMENT 5.17

a. Why did the court rule that the Vermont marriage statutes violated the state constitution?
b. Did the court rule that same-sex couples must be allowed to marry? If not, under what circumstances might it reach this result?
c. The court discussed its adoption decision of *In re B.L.V.B.* What did *In re B.L.V.B.* decide? What argument did the plaintiffs make on the basis of *In re B.L.V.B.?* Do you agree with this argument?
d. Is there sex discrimination in the Vermont marriage laws?

ASSIGNMENT 5.18

a. What rights and protections does the *Baker v. Vermont* court say are given to married, opposite-sex couples in Vermont?
b. Which of these rights and protections are offered married couples in your state? (See General Instructions for the State-Code Assignment in Appendix A.)

civil union
A same-sex legal relationship in Vermont that has the same benefits, protections, and responsibilities under Vermont law that are granted to spouses in a marriage.

reciprocal beneficiaries relationship
A form of domestic partnership in Vermont for parties related by blood who are ineligible to form a civil union or marriage with each other.

Following *Baker v. Vermont,* there was extensive debate throughout the state on whether the legislature should allow same-sex couples to marry or should give them the same rights and protections in a different legal relationship. The legislature chose that latter route. Effective July 1, 2000, same-sex couples were allowed to enter a **civil union** with the same benefits, protections, and responsibilities under Vermont law that are granted to spouses in a marriage.[31] (See Exhibit 5.6 for the Vermont license and certificate of civil union.) Vermont also created a less formal relationship called a **reciprocal beneficiaries relationship,** a form of domestic partnership for parties related by blood who are not eligible to enter a civil union with each other. This relationship is designed to give the parties rights such as hospital visitation and medical decision making, but not the full spouselike rights of a civil union.

To be joined in civil union, a couple must;

- be eighteen years of age or older
- be of the same sex and therefore ineligible to enter a Vermont marriage
- be of sound mind (not be non compos mentis)
- not be a party to a marriage, reciprocal beneficiary relationship, or another civil union (note that a married person whose spouse has died can enter a civil union)
- not be close family members (you cannot enter a civil union with your parent, grandparent, sibling, child, grandchild, niece, nephew, uncle, aunt, or first cousin)

Non-Vermont residents can obtain a Vermont civil union. A couple from another state can come to Vermont and enter a civil union.

In the new terminology of the day, parties to a civil union (CU) become "CU-ed" instead of married, or they become "all-but-married." Civil unions are ceremonial relationships, just as the vast majority of marriages are ceremonial. The civil union ceremony must be presided over by a judge, justice of the peace, or authorized member of the clergy. The Vermont Secretary of State provides an example of how the ceremony might occur:

Suggested Civil Union Ceremony

JUSTICE OF THE PEACE: We are here to join ______ and ______ in civil union. Will you ______ have ______ to be united as one in your civil union? Will you ______ have ______ to be united as one in your civil union?

RESPONSE OF EACH: I will.

JUSTICE OF THE PEACE: Then each in turn will repeat after me: "I ______ take you ______ to be my spouse in our civil union, to have and to hold from this day on, for better, for worse, for richer, for poorer, to love and to cherish forever."

(If rings are used, each in turn says, as the ring is put on): "With this ring I join with you in this our civil union."

JUSTICE OF THE PEACE: By the power vested in me by the State of Vermont, I hereby join you in civil union.

[31] 15 Vermont Statutes Annotated (V.S.A.) § 1204; 18 V.S.A. § 5163.

Exhibit 5.6 Vermont License and Certificate of Civil Union

DEPARTMENT OF HEALTH

VERMONT LICENSE AND CERTIFICATE OF CIVIL UNION

LOCAL FILE NUMBER

STATE FILE NUMBER

TYPE OR PRINT IN BLACK INK. SEE MANUAL FOR INSTRUCTIONS.

PARTY A

1. NAME *(First, Middle, Last)*	1b. MAIDEN SURNAME *(If Applicable)*	1c. DATE OF BIRTH *(Month, Day, Year)*

2. SEX	3. MAILING ADDRESS *(Street and Number or Rural Route Number, City or Town, State, Zip Code)*

4a. USUAL RESIDENCE – STATE	4b. CITY OR TOWN	5. BIRTHPLACE *(State or Foreign Country)*

6a. FATHER'S NAME *(First, Middle, Last)*	6b. BIRTHPLACE *(State or Foreign Country)*	7a. MOTHER'S NAME *(First, Middle, Maiden Surname)*	7b. Birthplace *(State or Foreign Country)*

PARTY B

8a. NAME *(First, Middle, Last)*	8b. MAIDEN SURNAME *(If Applicable)*	8c. DATE OF BIRTH *(Month, Day, Year)*

9. SEX	10. MAILING ADDRESS *(Street and Number or Rural Route Number, City or Town, State, Zip Code)*

11a. USUAL RESIDENCE – STATE	11b. CITY OR TOWN	12. BIRTHPLACE *(State or Foreign Country)*

13a. FATHER'S NAME *(First, Middle, Last)*	13b. BIRTHPLACE *(State or Foreign Country)*	14a. MOTHER'S NAME *(First, Middle, Maiden Surname)*	14b. Birthplace *(State or Foreign Country)*

APPLICANTS

We hereby certify that the information provided is correct to the best of our knowledge and belief and that we are free to form a civil union under the laws of Vermont.

15a. SIGNATURE	15b. DATE SIGNED	15c. SIGNATURE	15d. DATE SIGNED

CERTIFICATION

I hereby certify that the above named persons have made oath to the truth of the facts stated in the foregoing declaration and complied with the civil union laws of the State of Vermont.

16a. DATE ON WHICH LICENSE WAS ISSUED *(Month, Day, Year)*

16b. TOWN CLERK *(Signature)*

16c. TOWN OR CITY

16d. THIS LICENSE IS VALID FROM ____________ (DATE)

TO ____________ (DATE) UNLESS WAIVED BY A VERMONT COURT

OFFICIANT *(See instructions on back)*

This license authorizes the establishment of a civil union IN VERMONT ONLY of the above named parties by any person duly authorized to certify a civil union.

17a. I CERTIFY THAT THE ABOVE PERSONS ESTABLISHED A CIVIL UNION ON *(Month, Day, Year)* DATE >	17b. IN THE CITY OR TOWN OF

17c. SIGNATURE OF OFFICIANT

17d. NAME *(Type/Print)*	17e. TITLE

17f. ADDRESS OF OFFICIANT *(Street and Number or Rural Route Number, City or Town, State, Zip Code)*

REGISTRATION

18a. CLERK'S SIGNATURE	18b. DATE RECEIVED BY LOCAL REGISTRAR

19a. TRUE COPY – (Clerk's Signature) *(To be signed by Registrar on copy only)* Attest:	19b. TOWN	19c. DATE

CONFIDENTIAL INFORMATION. THE INFORMATION BELOW MUST BE COMPLETED. IT WILL NOT APPEAR ON CERTIFIED COPIES OF THE RECORD.

PARTY A

20. NAME		IF PREVIOUSLY MARRIED OR IN A CIVIL UNION		EDUCATION *(Specify only highest grade completed)*	
		LAST MARRIAGE OR CIVIL UNION ENDED BY	DATE	Elementary or Secondary (0-12)	College (1-4 OR 5+)
21. RACE – *White, Black, American Indian, etc. (Specify)*	22. TOTAL NO. OF CIVIL UNIONS OR MARRIAGES INCLUDING THIS ONE	☐ DEATH ☐ DISSOLUTION ☐ DIVORCE ☐ ANNULMENT 23a.	MONTH YEAR 23b.	24.	

PARTY B

25. NAME		IF PREVIOUSLY MARRIED OR IN A CIVIL UNION		EDUCATION *(Specify only highest grade completed)*	
		LAST MARRIAGE OR CIVIL UNION ENDED BY	DATE	Elementary or Secondary (0-12)	College (1-4 OR 5+)
26. RACE – *White, Black, American Indian, etc. (Specify)*	27. TOTAL NO. OF CIVIL UNIONS OR MARRIAGES INCLUDING THIS ONE	☐ DEATH ☐ DISSOLUTION ☐ DIVORCE ☐ ANNULMENT 28a.	MONTH YEAR 28b.	29.	

Once a civil union is formed, the parties have rights and duties such as:

- a mutual obligation to support each other;
- the right to inherit from each other under the laws of intestate succession if the deceased dies without a valid will;
- the same rights of hospital visitation and medical decisionmaking as married couples enjoy;
- the right to own property in a tenancy by the entirety (a form of joint ownership previously limited to husbands and wives); and
- the right not to be forced to give testimony against each other (comparable to the marital communication privilege of married couples)

The parties can also enter the equivalent of an antenuptial or premarital agreement before they enter the civil union in order to change some of the terms, conditions, or effects of their civil union. (On premarital agreements, see chapter 4.) Parties to a civil union are included within the definition of spouse, family, dependent, or next of kin whenever these terms are mentioned in Vermont law.

It is as difficult to dissolve a civil union as a marriage. A party to a civil union must petition the Family Court for the dissolution and follow the same procedures as those used to dissolve a marriage.

The civil union relationship creates rights under *state* law. It does not change *federal* rights in areas such as social security benefits, immigration requirements, and federal income or estate tax benefits and obligations. There are over 1,000 federal laws in which a person's marital status affects whether he or she is entitled to a federal benefit or must comply with a federal obligation. If these laws do not apply to single individuals, they would also not apply to a couple joined in a Vermont civil union. Furthermore, Congress has no interest in changing its own laws to allow same-sex couples to have the benefits of marriage under federal law. Congress recently passed a statute that makes this abundantly clear:

> In determining the meaning of any Act of Congress, or of any ruling, regulation, or interpretation of the various administrative bureaus and agencies of the United States, the word "marriage" means only a legal union between one man and one woman as husband and wife, and the word "spouse" refers only to a person of the opposite sex who is a husband or a wife.[32]

What will happen when parties who have a Vermont civil union move to another state and ask the new state to recognize or enforce their legal relationship? Suppose that a Vermont court renders a judgment that a particular civil union is valid and one or both of the parties then ask a court in another state to enforce that Vermont judgment. We do not know whether another state will be required to give full faith and credit to the Vermont judgment. (See the earlier discussion of full faith and credit and the Hawaii case of *Baehr v. Lewin.*) We should know relatively soon, however, since approximately two-thirds of the first 2,300 civil unions in Vermont were granted to couples who were not Vermont residents. They came to Vermont to enter the relationship and then returned to their home state. According to one report, "Gay and lesbian lawyers across the country are bracing for a wave of litigation over the status of same-sex couples whose relationships have been given a new legal status in the state of Vermont."[33]

---

[32]1 U.S.C. § 7.

[33]Shannon Duffy, *Pushing the States on Gay Unions,* National Law Journal, Nov. 27, 2000.

SUMMARY

When two people promise to marry each other, a contract is created so long as the elements of a valid contract exist—offer, acceptance, and consideration. Years ago, if one of the parties refused to enter the marriage, and thereby breached the contract, the other party could bring a heart balm cause of action for breach of promise to marry. Just under half the states, however, have abolished this contract action because of the difficulty of assessing damages, the danger of blackmail, and the inappropriateness of trying to force someone to enter a marriage he or she no longer wants.

Fraud is an alternative cause of action a plaintiff might try to bring against a defendant who reneges on a promise to marry. The elements of fraud are as follows: a deliberately false statement of present fact by the defendant, intent to have the plaintiff rely on the statement, actual reliance by the plaintiff on the statement, and resulting harm. Not all states, however, allow a fraud suit. They have interpreted the heart balm statute as abolishing both the contract action and the fraud action. Another possibility is the tort of intentional infliction of emotional distress, but it, too, might not be permitted in a state with a heart balm statute.

In states where a suit is possible, the usual remedy is for the plaintiff to seek compensatory damages. The damage award may be increased by aggravated damages for special circumstances, or by punitive or exemplary damages intended to punish the defendant and deter others from similar conduct. Mitigating circumstances, on the other hand, will decrease the award.

When a planned marriage does not occur, any gifts that have already been exchanged are irrevocable, provided all the elements of a gift exist: delivery, voluntary transfer, intent to relinquish title and control, no consideration, intent to have the gift take effect immediately, and acceptance by the donee. If, however, a court concludes that the donor would not have made the gift except for the anticipation of marriage, the gift is considered conditional and thus must be returned. Some states, however, will reach this result with respect to engagement rings only if the engagement was broken by the donee without justification.

A contract that imposes a total or a near total prohibition on marriage is an unenforceable, general restraint on marriage. On the other hand, contracts that impose reasonable limitations on one's right to marry can be enforceable.

Marriage is a fundamental right. Government can impose only reasonable restrictions that interfere with the decision to marry. Many material benefits derive from being married, particularly when a spouse dies (e.g., social security and pension benefits). To claim these benefits, one must establish the existence of a valid ceremonial marriage or, in states that allow them, a valid common law marriage.

States differ on the requirements that must be fulfilled to enter a ceremonial marriage. In many states, the requirements include obtaining a license, waiting a designated period of time, having the ceremony performed by an authorized person, having witnesses to the ceremony, and recording the license in the proper public office. Yet in most states, the failure to comply with such requirements is not a ground for an annulment.

A covenant marriage is a form of marriage that requires proof of premarital counseling, a promise to seek marital counseling when needed during the marriage, and proof of marital fault to dissolve. A couple that chooses a traditional marriage can dissolve it without proof of marital fault.

In states where common law marriages are still possible, the requirements are a present agreement to enter a marital relationship, living together as husband and wife (cohabitation), and an openness about living together as husband and wife. As with ceremonial marriages, the parties must have the legal capacity to marry and must intend to marry. The latter conditions will be considered in chapter 6.

The validity of a marriage is governed by the state in which it was entered or contracted. Hence, if a couple enters a common law marriage in a state where it is valid but moves to a state where such marriages have been abolished, the latter state will recognize the marriage as valid.

Occasionally, an impediment exists to an otherwise valid common law marriage (e.g., one of the parties is still married to someone else). If the impediment is removed while the parties are still openly living together, a valid common law marriage will be established as of the date of the removal.

Same-sex marriages are invalid in every American state. No legislature has passed a statute recognizing them, and all of the arguments made in court to force recognition have been unsuccessful. In some states, however, homosexuals have achieved limited rights in this area (e.g., to enter contracts governing nonsexual aspects of living together, to adopt a gay adult, and to register as "domestic partners" for purposes of being entitled to bereavement leave upon the death of one of the partners).

In Hawaii, a court held that the denial of same-sex marriage might violate the state constitution if the state could not show that there were compelling state interests to justify the discrimination and that the discrimination was narrowly drawn to avoid unnecessary abridgments of constitutional rights. Before this litigation was resolved, it was rendered moot when the Hawaii legislature banned same-sex marriage after the voters approved a constitutional amendment supporting such a ban. Defense of marriage acts (DOMAs) were passed by many states and by Congress to prevent required recognition of out-of-state same-sex marriages if any state ever authorizes them. In Vermont, the exclusion of same-sex couples from the benefits and protections of marriage was held to violate the state constitution. The Vermont legislature then created the civil union relationship, with all the state benefits and protections enjoyed by married couples.

KEY CHAPTER TERMINOLOGY

contract
consideration
capacity
statute of frauds
cause of action
heart balm action
heart balm statute
remedy
specific performance
damages
compensatory damages
aggravated damages
punitive damages
mitigating circumstances
fraud
intentional infliction of emotional distress
irrevocable
donor
donee
general restraint on marriage
reasonable limitation on marriage
bequest
intestate
forced share
dower
curtesy
privilege for marital communications
miscegenation
ceremonial marriage
proxy marriage
covenant marriage
common law marriage
conflict of law
impediment
putative spouse
domestic partners
rational basis test
strict scrutiny test
full faith and credit clause
Defense of Marriage Act (DOMA)
mini-DOMA
civil union
reciprocal beneficiaries relationship

ETHICS IN PRACTICE

Mary and Ted live in Louisiana. They want to enter a covenant marriage. They visit Rev. Sharon Fox for the required premarital counseling. Reverend Fox is also a part-time paralegal. The couple spends two hours with Rev. Fox. She spends over half this time answering questions from Ted and Mary about the grounds for divorce of a covenant marriage, the kind of testimony that will be admissible in court to prove marital fault, and the court that can grant such a divorce. Reverend Fox did the best she could in answering these questions. Any ethical problems?

ON THE NET: MORE ON MARRIAGE FORMATION

Vermont Secretary of State Guide to Civil Unions
http://www.sec.state.vt.us/pubs/civilunions.htm#intro

Lambda Legal Defense Fund: State-by-State Family Laws Affecting Gays and Lesbians (e.g., domestic partnership law)
http://www.lambdalegal.org/cgi-bin/pages/states

Hawaii Same-Sex Marriage Issue
http://www.hawaiilawyer.com/same_sex/samesex.htm

Common Law Marriage
http://www.law.cornell.edu/topics/Table_Marriage.htm
http://www.nolo.com/encyclopedia/faqs/mlt/sp8.html#FAQ-508

Domestic Partnership Organizing Manual
http://www.ngltf.org/library/dp_pub.htm

Covenant Marriage Links
http://www.divorcereform.org/cov.html

CHAPTER 6

ANNULMENT

CHAPTER OUTLINE

ANNULMENT, DIVORCE, AND LEGAL SEPARATION

annulment
A declaration by a court that a valid marriage never existed.

divorce
A declaration by a court that a marriage has been dissolved so that the parties are no longer married to each other.

legal separation
A declaration by a court that parties can live separately and apart even though they are still married to each other.

An **annulment** is a declaration by a court that a valid marriage never existed despite the fact that the parties may have obtained a marriage license, gone through a ceremony, lived together, and perhaps had children together over a period of many years. A **divorce,** on the other hand, is a dissolution of a marriage that once validly existed. In a divorce, there is something to dissolve. An annulment is simply a judicial statement or declaration that no marital relationship ever existed. A divorce is granted because of facts that occurred after the marriage was entered. An annulment is granted because of facts in existence at the time the parties attempted to enter the marriage.[1] A **legal separation** (also called a judicial separation) is a declaration by a court that the spouses can live separately and apart even though they remain married. The legal separation ends the "bed and board" relationship but not the marriage relationship. If the parties want to remarry, they must obtain an annulment or a divorce.

[1]There are a few exceptions to this. In New York, for example, one of the grounds for annulment is that an individual "[h]as been incurably mentally ill for a period of five years or more" and was in this condition at the time of the annulment trial even if the five years occurred after the marriage was entered. New York Domestic Relations Law § 7(5). It is rare, however, for an annulment ground to pertain to facts that occur after a marriage is entered.

Not many annulments are granted in American courts today, although they are available in every state. This was not so years ago, when divorce was more difficult to obtain than it is today. In the current era of no-fault divorce, parties are less likely to seek an annulment, since a divorce is relatively easy to obtain, as we will see in the next chapter. Yet for several reasons, we still need to study annulment carefully. First, clients are sometimes confused about annulment, particularly the distinction between divorce and annulment. (Some Catholics are also unclear about the distinction between civil annulment and church annulment.) Without an understanding of annulment law, a law office will not be able to clear up such confusion. Second, anyone conducting a legal interview or investigation needs to be alert to those facts that might trigger the availability of an annulment so that it can be presented to the client as an option along with divorce and legal separation. Third, one of the current hot button issues is gay civil unions and, perhaps one day, same-sex marriages. The conflict of law topics that we will discuss in this chapter are directly relevant to the issue of whether a state must recognize such unions or marriages entered in another state.

States use different terminology to describe the proceeding that is our central concern in this chapter:

- action for annulment
- petition for annulment
- suit to annul
- libel for annulment
- action for a declaration of invalidity
- action for a judgment of nullity
- petition to issue a judgment of nullity
- action for a declaratory judgment that the marriage is invalid
- action to declare a marriage void
- action to declare the nullity of a void marriage
- action to affirm the validity of a marriage

It is technically incorrect to refer to an "annulled marriage." The word "marriage" means the legal union of two persons as husband and wife. To bring an action to "annul a marriage" means that you are seeking to invalidate something that never existed. It would be more logical to say that you are seeking to "annul an attempted marriage." Because of habit and convenience, however, phrases such as "annulled marriage" are widely used throughout family law in spite of the slight lapse in logic this language entails.

THE VOID/VOIDABLE DISTINCTION

Certain grounds for annulment will render the marriage void, while other grounds will render it only voidable. *Void* means the marriage is invalid whether or not any court declares its invalidity. *Voidable* means the marriage is invalid only if a court declares that it is invalid. This distinction can be critical, as we will see in the *Miller* opinion later in the chapter.

Assume that two individuals have a **voidable marriage,** but that they die without anyone bringing an annulment action or challenging their marriage in any way. The practical effect of this inaction is that the entire world treats the marriage as if it were valid. In effect, there is no practical difference between a marriage that complies with all the legal requirements and a voidable marriage that no one ever challenges. Suppose, however, an annulment action *is* brought and a court declares a voidable marriage to be invalid. In most cases, the invalidity "relates back" to the time when the parties tried to enter the marriage. The invalidity does not begin on the date the court declares the marriage

voidable marriage
A marriage that is invalid only if someone challenges it and a court declares it invalid.

void marriage
A marriage that is invalid whether or not a court declares it so.

void ab initio
Invalid from the very beginning.

ratification
Approval retroactively by agreement, conduct, or any inaction that can reasonably be interpreted as an approval. The verb is *ratify.*

invalid. A **void marriage** is considered **void ab initio.** If a marriage is void, there is no need to bring a court action to seek a declaration that it is invalid. Nevertheless, parties will usually want a court declaration in order to remove any doubt that the marriage is invalid.

Occasionally, the conduct of a party will prevent him or her from being able to use an otherwise available ground for annulment. Suppose, for example, that Mary freely cohabits with Ted in spite of her discovery that he fraudulently tricked her into the marriage. In some states, her conduct constitutes a **ratification** of the marriage, which will prevent her from obtaining an annulment on the ground of fraud. In effect, the invalid marriage is retroactively validated. In general, void marriages cannot be ratified, but voidable ones often can. This is another reason it is important to know which grounds for annulment render a marriage void and which render it voidable.

WHO CAN SUE?

standing
The right to bring a case and seek relief from a court.

estopped
Prevented from asserting a right or a defense because it would be unfair or inequitable to do so.

dirty hands
Wrongdoing or other inappropriate behavior that would make it unfair or inequitable to allow a person to assert a right or a defense he or she would normally have.

As we study each of the grounds for annulment, one of the questions we must ask is, Who can be the plaintiff to bring the annulment action? The wrongdoer (i.e., the party who knowingly did the act that constituted the ground for the annulment) is *not* always allowed to bring the action. This party may lack **standing** to bring the action. If the *innocent* party refuses to bring the action, it may be that the marriage can never be annulled. In such cases, the wrongdoing party, in effect, is prevented (sometimes called **estopped**) from getting out of what might clearly be an invalid marriage. Such a marriage is sometimes referred to as a *marriage by estoppel.* The wrongdoing party has **dirty hands** and should not be allowed to "profit" from this wrongdoing through a court action seeking an annulment. When will a wrongdoing party be estopped from bringing the annulment action? The answer often depends on whether the marriage is void or voidable.

Finally, for some grounds, a parent or legal guardian of the innocent spouse may have independent standing to bring the annulment action even if the innocent spouse is either unwilling to sue or incapable of doing so.

OVERVIEW OF GROUNDS FOR ANNULMENT

grounds
Acceptable reasons for seeking a particular result.

There are two main categories of **grounds** for annulment. First, we examine those that relate to a party's *legal capacity* to marry:

- Preexisting marriage.
- Improper relationship by blood or by marriage
- Nonage
- Physical disabilities

Second, we will turn to those that focus on whether a party with legal capacity to marry formed the requisite *intent* to marry:

- Sham marriages
- Mental disabilities
- Duress
- Fraud

ASSIGNMENT 6.1

List the grounds for annulment in your state. (See General Instructions for the State-Code Assignment in Appendix A.)

GROUNDS RELATING TO THE LEGAL CAPACITY TO MARRY

Prior Existing Marriage (Bigamy)

Here we will consider both the criminal and the civil consequences of **bigamy,** which is entering or attempting to enter a second marriage when a prior marriage is still valid. If someone tries to live with more than one spouse simultaneously, it is **polygamy.**[2]

bigamy
Entering or attempting to enter a second marriage when a prior marriage is still valid.

polygamy
(1) Multiple simultaneous marriages; (2) having more than one wife at the same time.

CRIME Entering a second marriage or even attempting to enter such a marriage when the first marriage has not ended by death, annulment, or divorce is a crime in most states, usually a misdemeanor.

In some states, if a spouse has disappeared for a designated number of years, he or she will be presumed dead. This presumption is the foundation for what is called the **Enoch Arden defense,** which will defeat a bigamy prosecution following a second marriage. The elements of this defense usually include a minimum time during which the spouse has been missing (often five years) and diligence in trying to locate him or her before remarrying. The name of the defense comes from the narrative poem *Enoch Arden,* by Alfred Lord Tennyson, about a sailor who returned to his home years after being shipwrecked to discover that his wife had married again.

Enoch Arden defense
The presumption that a spouse is dead after being missing for a designated number of years.

ANNULMENT: THE CIVIL ACTION Our next concern is the existence of a prior undissolved marriage as a ground for an annulment of a second marriage. In most states, a bigamous marriage is void; in only a few states is it voidable.

When a claim is made in an annulment proceeding that a second marriage is invalid because of a prior undissolved marriage, a common response or defense to this claim is that the *first* marriage was never valid or that this earlier marriage ended in divorce or annulment. Yet marriage records, particularly old ones, are sometimes difficult to obtain, and for common law marriages, there are no records. Consequently, proving the status of a prior marriage can be a monumental task. Was it properly contracted? Was it dissolved? To assist parties in this difficult situation, the law has created a number of **rebuttable presumptions,** including the following:

rebuttable presumption
A presumption is an assumption of fact that can be drawn when another fact or set of facts is established. The presumption is rebuttable if a party can introduce evidence to try to show that the assumption is false.

- A marriage is presumed to be valid.
- When there has been more than one marriage, the latest marriage is presumed to be valid.

The effect of the second presumption is that the court will treat the first marriage as having been dissolved by the death of the first spouse, by divorce, or by annulment. Note, however, that the presumption is *rebuttable,* which means that the party seeking to annul the second marriage can attempt to rebut (i.e., attack) the presumption by introducing evidence (1) that the first spouse is still alive or (2) that the first marriage was *not* dissolved by divorce or annulment. The presumption favoring the validity of the latest marriage is so strong, however, that some states require considerable proof to overcome or rebut it.

Finally, we need to consider the impact of *Enoch Arden* in annulment cases. We have already looked at Enoch Arden as a defense to a criminal prosecution for bigamy. We now examine the consequences of Enoch Arden for the

---

[2] *Polygamy* means "multiple simultaneous marriages." Sometimes, however, the word *polygamy* is used more narrowly to mean having more than one wife at the same time, while *polyandry* means having more than one husband at the same time. Polygamy was once legal in Utah. As a condition of statehood, however, Utah outlawed the practice in 1896. Nevertheless, the practice continues in that state. "[S]tate officials estimate that as many as 50,000 people are part of families with more than one wife." M. Janofsky, *Trial Opens in Rare Case of a Utahan Charged With Polygamy,* N.Y. Times, May 15, 2001, at A12.

second marriage in a civil annulment proceeding. Paul marries Cynthia. Cynthia disappears. Paul has not heard from her for fifteen years in spite of all his efforts to locate her. Paul then marries Mary in the honest belief that his first wife is dead. Mary does not know anything about Cynthia. Suddenly Cynthia reappears, and Mary learns about the first marriage. Mary immediately brings an action against Paul to annul her marriage to him on the ground of a prior existing marriage (bigamy). The question is whether Paul can raise the defense of Enoch Arden. Can Paul contest the annulment action against him by arguing that he had a right to presume that his first wife was dead? States differ in their answer to this question. Here are some of the different approaches:

- Enoch Arden applies only to criminal prosecutions for bigamy; the presumption of death does not apply to annulment proceedings.
- Enoch Arden does apply to annulment proceedings; the missing spouse is presumed dead. The second marriage is valid and cannot be annulled even if the missing spouse later appears.
- Enoch Arden does apply to annulment proceedings; the missing spouse is presumed dead. If, however, the missing spouse later appears, the second marriage can be annulled. Hence the Enoch Arden defense is effective only if the missing spouse stays missing.

Summary of Ground for Annulment: Prior Existing Marriage

Definition: Entering a marriage when a prior valid marriage has not been dissolved by divorce, annulment, or the death of the first spouse.

Void or voidable: In most states, the establishment of this ground renders the second marriage void.

Who can sue: In most states, either party to the second marriage can bring the annulment action on this ground; both have standing.

Major defenses:

1. The first spouse is dead or presumed dead (Enoch Arden).
2. The first marriage was not validly entered.
3. The first marriage ended by divorce or annulment.
4. The plaintiff has "dirty hands" (available in a few states).

Is this annulment ground also a ground for divorce? Yes, in some states.

Consanguinity and Affinity Limitations

consanguinity
Relationship by blood.

affinity
Relationship by marriage.

There are two ways that you can be related to someone: by **consanguinity** (blood) and by **affinity** (marriage).

Examples of a marriage of individuals related by consanguinity would be:

- Father marries his daughter.
- Sister marries her brother.

Examples of a marriage of individuals related by affinity would be:

- Man marries his son's former wife.
- Woman marries her stepfather.

State statutes prohibit certain individuals related by consanguinity or related by affinity from marrying. Violating these prohibitions can be a ground for annulment of the marriage.

Incest
Sexual intercourse between two people who are too closely related to each other as defined by statute.

States generally agree that sexual relations in certain relationships constitute **incest:** marriage of parent and child, brother and sister, grandparent and grandchild, etc. Some disagreement exists on whether this is also true of cousin-cousin marriages and affinity relationships. The *crime* of incest is committed mainly by designated individuals related by consanguinity. Surprisingly, however, the crime can also be committed in some states by designated individuals related by affinity.

ASSIGNMENT 6.2

In the following list, you will find pairs of individuals. For each pair, check your state code and answer three questions: Can the individuals marry? If the marriage is prohibited, is it void or voidable? What code section gives you the answer? (See General Instructions for the State-Code Assignment in Appendix A.)

	Can They Marry?	Void or Voidable?	Code Section
a. Mother/son	________	________	________
b. Father/daughter	________	________	________
c. Brother/sister	________	________	________
d. Grandparent/grandchild	________	________	________
e. Uncle/niece or aunt/nephew	________	________	________
f. First cousin/first cousin	________	________	________
g. Second cousin/second cousin	________	________	________
h. Half brother/half sister	________	________	________
i. Father-in-law/daughter-in-law or mother-in-law/son-in-law	________	________	________
j. Brother-in-law/sister-in-law	________	________	________
k. Stepparent/stepchild	________	________	________
l. Adoptive parent/adoptive child	________	________	________
m. Godparent/godchild	________	________	________

(If your state code does not provide a direct answer to any of the above questions, you may have to check court opinions. See General Instructions for the Court-Opinion Assignment in Appendix A.)

Notes on Consanguinity and Affinity

1. Assume that a prohibition to a marriage exists because of an affinity relationship between the parties. What happens to the prohibition when the marriage ends by the death of the spouse who created the affinity relationship for the other spouse? Can the surviving spouse *then* marry his or her in-laws? (For example, John is the father-in-law of Mary, who is married to John's son Bill. After Bill dies, John marries Mary.) Some states allow such marriages, while others maintain the prohibition even after the death of the spouse who created the affinity relationship for the other spouse.
2. The Uniform Marriage and Divorce Act (§ 207) would prohibit all marriages between ancestors and descendants, brother-sister marriages, and adopted brother-sister marriages; it would permit first-cousin marriages and all affinity marriages.
3. States differ on whether two adopted children in the same family can marry.
4. The Supreme Court has held that marriage is a fundamental right and only "reasonable regulations" that interfere with the decision to enter a marriage can be imposed.[3] It is anticipated that some of the rules mentioned above regarding who can marry will be challenged as unreasonable regulations—particularly the rules prohibiting the marriage of individuals related by affinity.

---

[3]*Zablocki v. Redhail,* 434 U.S. 374, 98 S. Ct. 673, 54 L. Ed. 2d 618 (1978). See Constitutional Limitations on Marriage Restrictions in Chapter 5.

Summary of Ground for Annulment: Prohibited Consanguinity or Affinity Relationship

Definition: State statutes provide that persons lack the legal capacity to marry if they are related by consanguinity (blood) or by affinity (marriage) in the manner specified in those statutes.

Void or voidable: In most states, the prohibited marriage is void.

Who can sue: Either party can be the plaintiff in the annulment action; both have standing.

Major defenses:

1. The parties are not prohibitively related by blood or marriage.
2. The spouse who created the affinity relationship for the other spouse has died (this defense is available only for affinity relationships and only in some states).

Is this annulment ground also a ground for divorce? Yes, in most states.

Nonage

nonage
Below the required minimum age to enter a designated relationship or to perform a particular task.

In order to marry, a party must be a certain minimum age. Marrying below that age constitutes the ground of **nonage.** The minimum age may differ, however, depending upon whether:

- Parental consent exists.
- The female is already pregnant.
- A child has already been born out of wedlock.

In some states, a court may have the power to authorize a marriage of parties under age even if a parent or guardian has refused to consent to the marriage. In these states, the court will consider factors such as the maturity of the parties, their financial resources, and whether children (to be born or already born) would be illegitimate if the marriage were not authorized. Still another variation found in some states is that the courts have the authority to require that underage individuals go through premarital counseling as a condition of their being able to marry.

At one time, states imposed different age requirements for males and females. This has been changed either by statute or by a court ruling that this kind of sex discrimination is unconstitutional.

If an underage child marries, he or she can sue for annulment, as can the person he or she attempted to marry. A parent or legal guardian also has standing to seek the annulment in most states even if the minor does not want the annulment. There are, however, time limits. The annulment cannot be brought if the parties cohabitate after the child reaches the statutory minimum age. Such conduct constitutes a ratification of the marriage.

ASSIGNMENT 6.3

What age restrictions apply to marriages in your state? (See General Instructions for the State-Code Assignment in Appendix A.)

Summary of Ground for Annulment: Nonage

Definition: At the time of the marriage, one or both of the parties were under the minimum age to marry set by statute.

Void or voidable: In most states, the marriage is voidable.

Who can sue: Either party in most states. In some states, the parent or legal guardian of the underaged party also has standing.

Major defenses:

1. The parties were of the correct statutory age at the time of the marriage.
2. The underaged party affirmed or ratified the marriage by cohabitation after that party reached the statutory minimum age.
3. Even though the parties failed to obtain parental consent as specified in the statute, the absence of this consent is not a ground for annulment. (Note, however, that this defense is available only in some states.)

Is this annulment also a ground for divorce? Yes, in some states.

Physical Disabilities

The major physical incapacities or disabilities mentioned in marriage statutes are communicable venereal disease and incurable **impotence,** the inability to have sexual intercourse. Some statutes also include conditions such as epilepsy and pulmonary tuberculosis in advanced stages.

impotence
The inability to have sexual intercourse, often due to an inability to achieve or maintain an erection.

States sometimes have a statutory requirement that parties contemplating marriage go through a medical examination as a condition of obtaining a marriage license. An important objective of this exam is to determine whether either or both of the parties have communicable venereal disease. Suppose that either or both of the parties do have such a disease at the time of their marriage. It may be that the medical exam failed to show this, or that they failed to take the exam (and entered a common law marriage in a state where such marriages are valid), or that they were able to falsify the results of the medical exam. States differ as to the consequences of marrying where one or both of the parties have the disease. While the marriage is valid in most states, in several states the marriage is not valid, and a ground for annulment can arise as a result. Furthermore, a state may make it a crime knowingly to marry or have sexual intercourse with someone who has an infectious venereal disease.

An allegation of impotence can raise several issues:

- Inability to **copulate**—incurable
- Inability to copulate—curable
- **Sterility**—infertility
- Refusal to have sexual intercourse

copulate
To engage in sexual intercourse.

sterility
Inability to have children; infertile.

In most states, only the first situation—an incurable inability to copulate—is a ground for annulment. The standard for incurability is not the impossibility of a cure; rather, it is the present unlikelihood of a cure. The standard for copulation is the ability to perform the physical sex act naturally, without pain or harm to the other spouse. The "mere" fact that a spouse does not derive pleasure from the act is not what is meant by an inability to copulate. The *refusal* to copulate is not an inability to copulate, although the refusal is sometimes used as an indication of (i.e., as evidence of) the inability to copulate. In most states, it makes no difference whether the inability is due to physical (organic) causes or to psychogenic causes, nor does it matter that the person is impotent only with his or her spouse. If normal coitus is not possible with one's spouse, whatever the cause, the ground exists.

It is a defense to an annulment action that the party seeking the annulment knew of the party's impotence at the time of the marriage and yet still went through with the marriage. Finally, time limits may exist for bringing the action on this ground. For example, a state may bar the action if it is not brought within a designated number of years (e.g., four or five years) after the marriage was entered.

Note on Testing for HIV

Some states require applicants for marriage to be given information about the human immunodeficiency virus (HIV) and acquired immunodeficiency syndrome (AIDS). West Virginia, for example, requires that "[e]very person who is empowered to issue a marriage license shall, at the time of issuance thereof, distribute to the applicants for the license, information concerning acquired immunodeficiency syndrome (AIDS) and inform them of the availability of HIV-related testing and counseling."[4] In other states, the applicant must sign a statement that he or she has been offered a list of sites in the state that offer HIV tests. At one time, Illinois went even further by requiring that every applicant be actually tested "to determine whether either of the parties to the proposed marriage has been exposed to human immunodeficiency virus (HIV) or any other identified causative agent of acquired immunodeficiency syndrome (AIDS)."[5] During the first six months of the program, the number of marriage licenses issued in Illinois dropped by 22.5 percent, and the number of licenses issued to Illinois residents in surrounding states increased significantly.[6] Rather than bother with the test, many couples simply crossed state lines to obtain their marriage license. Consequently, Illinois abolished its program of mandatory testing.

ASSIGNMENT 6.4

a. Should Illinois have abolished its program of mandatory testing for HIV?
b. Should Congress pass a federal law requiring every state to impose mandatory HIV testing? What problems would such a law solve and cause?

Summary of Ground for Annulment: Physical Disabilities (Impotence)

Definition: The incurable inability to copulate without pain or harm to the spouse.

Void or voidable: Voidable.

Who can sue: Either party; both have standing.

Major defenses:

1. The impotence is curable.
2. The nonimpotent party knew of the other's impotence at the time of the marriage.
3. The plaintiff waited too long to bring the annulment action on this ground.

Is this annulment ground also a ground for divorce? Yes, in some states.

Homosexual "Marriages"

Since people of the same sex cannot legally marry, a traditional annulment can never be an issue; there is no accepted marital union to annul. See the earlier discussion of homosexual "marriages" in chapter 5. The dramatic creation of same-sex civil unions in Vermont, however, has created new annulment laws. A person in Vermont, for example, cannot enter a marriage if he or she is still in an undissolved civil union. "Marriages contracted while either party has a living spouse or a living party to a civil union shall be void."[7] Also, civil unions cannot be entered with close family members such a parent or a sibling. Couples in a civil union must be given rights under state law equal to those enjoyed by married couples. "The law of domestic relations, *including annulment,* separation and divorce, child custody and sup-

[4]West Virginia Code § 16-3C-2 (1966).
[5]Illinois Revised Statutes ch. 40, § 204(b).
[6]B. Turnock & C. Kelly, *Mandatory Premarital Testing . . .* , 261 Journal of the American Medical Association 3415 (June 15, 1989).
[7]Vermont Statutes Annotated tit. 15, § 4.

port, and property division and maintenance shall apply to parties to a civil union."[8] Hence the panoply of annulment laws governing marriages also applies to Vermont civil unions.

GROUNDS RELATING TO THE INTENT TO MARRY

Sham Marriages

An essential element of a marriage contract is the intent to enter a marriage. With this in mind, examine the following "marriages":

- Dennis and Janet enter a marriage solely to obtain permanent resident alien status for Dennis, who is not a U.S. citizen. Janet is a citizen. Dennis wants to use his marriage status to avoid deportation by immigration officials.
- Edna dares Stanley to marry her following a college party. After a great deal of laughing and boasting, they go through all the formalities (obtaining a license, having the blood test, etc.) and complete the marriage ceremony.
- Frank and Helen have an affair. Helen becomes pregnant. Neither wants the child to be born illegitimate. They never want to live together but decide to be married solely for the purpose of having the child born legitimate. They agree that the child will live with Helen.
- Robin and Ken have been dating for a number of months. They decide to get married "just to try it out." They feel this is a modern and rational way of determining whether they will want to stay together, forever. Both fully understand that there will be "no hard feelings" if either of them wants to dissolve the marriage after six months.

All four of the above couples go through all the steps required to become married. To any reasonable outside observer of their outward actions, nothing unusual is happening. They all intended to go through a marriage ceremony; they all intended to go through the outward appearances of entering a marriage contract. Subjectively, however, they all had "hidden agendas."

According to traditional contract principles, if individuals give clear outward manifestations of mutual assent to enter a contract, the law will bind them to their contract even though their unspoken motive was *not* to enter a binding contract. Most courts, however, apply a different principle to marriage contracts than to other contracts. The first three couples above engaged in totally **sham** marriages. The parties never intended to live together as husband and wife; they had a limited purpose of avoiding deportation, displaying braggadocio, or "giving a name" to a child. Most courts would declare such marriages to be void and would grant an annulment to either party so long as the parties did not **consummate** their union or otherwise cohabit *after* the marriage. Suppose, however, that the couples in these three cases lived together as husband and wife even for a short period after the marriage. Most courts would be reluctant to declare the marriage void. The subsequent **cohabitation** would be some evidence that at the time they entered the marriage they *did* intend to live as husband and wife. The central question is, What intention did the parties have at the time they entered the marriage? Did they intend to be married or not? It is, of course, very difficult to get into their heads to find out what they were thinking. Hence the law must rely on objective conduct as evidence of intent. If parties cohabit after marriage, this is certainly some evidence that they intended to be married at the time they appeared to enter a marriage contract.

sham
Pretended, false, empty.

consummate
To engage in sexual intercourse for the first time as spouses.

cohabitation
Living together as husband and wife whether or not the parties are married.

[8] Id. § 1204(d) (emphasis added).

In the first three hypothetical cases, assume that the couples did not cohabit after they entered the marriage. Most courts would, therefore, find that at the time they entered the marriage contract, they did not have the intention to be married (i.e., to assume the duties of a marriage). It should be pointed out, however, that some courts apply a *different* rule and would hold that the marriage is valid whether or not cohabitation followed the marriage ceremony—so long as the parties went through all the proper procedures to be married. While such states would refuse to allow the parties to annul their marriage, this does not mean that the parties would be forced to stay married. It simply means that if they wanted to dissolve the marriage, they would have to go through a divorce.

What about the fourth hypothetical case, in which the parties entered a *trial marriage?* The fact that the parties cohabited is evidence that they intended to be married at the time they entered the marriage contract. Most courts would find that this marriage is valid and deny an annulment to anyone who later claims that the parties never intended to assume the marital status. It cannot be said that they married in jest or that they married for a limited purpose. The fact that they did not promise to live together forever as husband and wife does not mean that they lacked the intent to be married at the time they entered the marriage.

Summary of Ground for Annulment: Sham Marriage

Definition: The absence of an intention to marry in spite of the fact that the parties voluntarily went through all the formalities of a marriage.

Void or voidable: Void.

Who can sue: Either party; both have standing.

Major defense: The parties did have the intention to marry at the time they entered the marriage ceremony. A major item of evidence that this intention existed is that they cohabited after the ceremony. (*Note:* In some states, the annulment will be denied if the parties went through all the outward formalities of the marriage no matter what their unspoken objective was.)

Is this annulment ground also a ground for divorce? Usually not.

ASSIGNMENT 6.5

a. Elaine is twenty years old, and Philip, a bachelor, is seventy-five. Philip asks Elaine to marry him. Philip has terminal cancer and wants to die a married man. He and Elaine know that he probably has less than six months to live and that he will spend the rest of his life in a hospital bed. Under their arrangement, she does not have to continue as his wife after six months if he is still alive. They go through all the formal requirements to be married. On the day after the marriage ceremony, Elaine changes her mind and wants to end the marriage. Can she obtain an annulment? (See General Instructions for the Legal-Analysis Assignment in Appendix A.)

b. Interview Elaine. (See General Instructions for the Interview Assignment in Appendix A.)

c. Draft a complaint for Elaine for her annulment action. (See General Instructions for the Complaint-Drafting Assignment in Appendix A.)

d. Draft a set of interrogatories from Philip to Elaine. (See General Instructions for the Interrogatory Assignment in Appendix A.)

In the *Miller* case, which we will now read, a party was alleged to have entered a common law marriage to avoid prosecution for a crime. Even if your state does not recognize common law marriages (see chapter 5), the case is important because the issue would be the same if he entered a ceremonial marriage in order avoid criminal prosecution. The case raises the question of what to do when someone has multiple purposes or intentions when entering a marriage.

CASE

In the Interest of Melissa Miller

301 Pa. Super. 511, 448 A.2d 25 (1982)
Superior Court of Pennsylvania.

Background: *Edward Christoph is a thirty-six-year-old English teacher who began a romantic relationship with one of his eighth grade students, Melissa Miller (also called Missy). She was fourteen years old at the time. Her mother had been having difficulty with her at home. Melissa would sneak out of the house through her bedroom window in the early morning hours and stay away for three or four hours. Her mother found letters to Melissa from Christoph that said, "You gave yourself fully," and "I love you." When the police began investigating Christoph for sexual involvement with a minor, he consulted an attorney who advised him how to enter a common law marriage. He then entered a common law marriage with Melissa. (Common law marriages are allowed in Pennsylvania. Though you must be sixteen to enter a ceremonial marriage, the age of consent to enter a common law marriage in the state is seven.) The mother asked the state to declare Melissa to be a dependent child because of her incorrigibility. The juvenile division of the lower court did so and ordered her placed in a foster home. Since Christoph's motive in marrying Melissa was to avoid criminal prosecution, the court also invalidated the common law marriage. Melissa, as appellant, is now appealing this decision in the Superior Court of Pennsylvania. She does not want the marriage invalidated.*

Decision on Appeal: *Reversed. The common law marriage was valid. Melissa should not have been declared a dependent child.*

Opinion of the Court:

Judge SPAETH delivered the opinion of the court. . . .

Mr. Christoph testified that his motive [in entering the common law marriage] was that appellant should "be my wife" and that his understanding, when he told her this, was that no criminal charges were going to be brought against him:

> Q. What did you say to Melissa . . . on that occasion? A. I said, "I marry you, Melissa." . . .
> Q. And what did you intend when you said you married her? A. I intended that she be my wife.
> Q. And as your wife, what was your intention towards her? A. To take her home to live with me as my wife.
> Q. Did you recognize any responsibility when you said these words? A. Yes.
> Q. What were the responsibilities that you recognized? A. To take her, provide a home and all the necessities that you would normally provide for your wife.
> Q. Mr. Christoph, at the time this alleged marriage is to have taken place between you and Missy, do you know—were you aware of the fact that the police were investigating you? A. I had talked to the police at the time, yes.
> Q. Were you afraid that charges would be filed against you by the police as a result of your involvement with Missy. A. No.
> Q. You were not afraid of that? A. No.
> Q. The crime, corrupting the moral[s] of minors, have you ever heard of that at the time you got married to Missy? A. Yes, I did.
> Q. Did you have any concerns at the time this alleged marriage is to have taken place with you being charged by the police. A. No.
> Q. Why not? A. Because when I talked to Detective Slupski he said . . he was going to recommend to the D.A. that no charges be brought. . . .

It is true, as the lower court states in its opinion, that Mr. Christoph's sister, Virginia Byers, who was a witness to the marriage ceremony, testified that "one of Mr. Christoph's express motives in marrying Melissa Miller was to avoid criminal prosecution.". . . However, the sister also testified that another of Mr. Christoph's motives was that he loved appellant. . . .

. . . It seems to us that the fairest inference to be drawn from the evidence is that Mr. Christoph may have had at least two motives for marrying appellant—his love for her, and his desire to avoid criminal prosecution for his relationship with her. We find no support in the record for the lower court's assignment of priority to the second of these motives.

We may, however, put aside any difficulty with the inferences drawn by the lower court. Accepting

continued

CASE

In the Interest of Melissa Miller—*Continued*

the lower court's finding that Mr. Christoph married appellant to avoid criminal prosecution, still, we are unable to uphold its order. For contrary to the court's opinion, such a motive does not invalidate a common law marriage.

The controlling decision is *Estate of Gower,* 445 Pa. 554, 284 A.2d 742 (1971). In *Gower,* as here, the parties had by words in the present tense expressed their intent to marry one another. The lower court nevertheless held the marriage invalid because the appellant's motive in entering into the marriage was to avoid conscription for military service. Reversing, the Supreme Court held that "[t]he reason or motive underlying a decision to marry is not relevant to a finding of the *intention* to marry." Id. at 557, 284 A.2d at 744. (emphasis in original). Therefore, the appellant's motive to avoid conscription could not "render[ ] invalid his otherwise valid common law marriage." Id.

The record here establishes—and the lower court did not question—appellant's and Mr. Christoph's *intention* to marry. The fact—as the lower court found it to be—that Mr. Christoph's *motive* was to avoid prosecution could not render invalid their otherwise valid common law marriage. . . .

[T]here is a distinction, in both the common law and the Pennsylvania Divorce Code, Act of April 2, 1980, P.L. 63, Act No. 26, 23 P.S. § 101 et seq., between a void marriage and a voidable marriage. The Code provides the following grounds for annulment or invalidity of void marriages, in Section 204:

> (a) . . . (3) Where either party to such marriage was incapable of consenting by reason of insanity or serious mental disorder, or otherwise lacked capacity to consent or did not intend to assent to such marriage. . . .

The Code provides the following grounds for annulment of voidable marriages, in Section 205:

> (a) . . . (1) Where either party to such marriage was under 16 years of age, unless such marriage was expressly authorized by a judge of the court. . . . (5) Where one party was induced to enter into such marriage due to the fraud, duress, coercion, or force attributable to the other party . . .
>
> (b) In all such cases of marriages which are voidable, either party thereto may seek and obtain an annulment of such marriage, but unless and until such decree is obtained from a court of competent jurisdiction, such marriage shall be valid and subsisting. The validity of such a voidable marriage shall not be subject to attack or question by any person if it is subsequently confirmed by the parties thereto or if either party has died.

Section 203 of the Code authorizes a proceeding for the annulment of both void and voidable marriages: In all cases where a supposed or alleged marriage shall have been contracted which is void or voidable under this act or under applicable law, either party to such supposed or alleged marriage may bring an action in annulment to have it declared null and void in accordance with the procedures provided for under this act and the Rules of Civil Procedure. . . .

Section 204(a)(3) . . . makes a marriage void only where one of the parties "lacked capacity to consent or did not intend to assent" to the marriage. Since here neither party lacked capacity and both intended to assent, the section is inapplicable. The lower court's finding that "[Mr. Christoph's] sole purpose was to practice a fraud upon this Court and upon [appellant]" does not bring the marriage within Section 204(a)(3). For marriages induced by fraud are dealt with explicitly in Section 205(a)(5), which concerns voidable marriages.*

The distinction between a void marriage and a voidable marriage is not merely a matter of semantics. The Divorce Code, like the common law, provides that a voidable marriage may be annulled only by "either party thereto" and is "valid and subsisting" "unless and until" challenged by one of them. Section 205(b); Perlberger, *Pennsylvania Divorce Code* § 3.2.3 (1980) ("the legislature has expressly declared this crucial distinction between void and voidable marriages by enactment of section 205(b)"). If indeed appellant was induced to enter into marriage by Mr. Christoph's fraud, their marriage is not, as the lower court held, void, but voidable. In that event, appellant may seek to have it annulled. Not only, however, does she not make such a request; she has appealed to this court asking that her marriage be upheld.

We have not overlooked the arguments of counsel for appellant's mother, urging that we re-examine the doctrine of common law marriage, and either abolish it or align the age of consent to that required for statutory marriage. However, we have declined previous opportunities to abolish or modify the doctrine of common law marriage. . . . Past efforts in the Legislature to abolish common law marriage have failed. . . . The Marriage Law, Act of August 22, 1953, P.L. 1344, 48 P.S. § 1–23, explicitly preserves the right to contract a common law marriage, providing that "[n]othing herein shall be construed to change the existing law with regard to common law marriage." This remains the legislative intent. . . .

In conclusion, we wish to note that neither have we overlooked the anguish that this marriage has caused appellant's mother. We may hope that her fears are unfounded, as they may be, for the most devoted mother is sometimes mistaken about what is good for her child. But if we knew that the marriage would prove unhappy and short, that would not deflect us from our decision. Our responsibility is to interpret and apply the law. If a marriage is lawful, that is the end of our inquiry. For as judges, we are agents of the State, and whether a lawful marriage is happy or unhappy is none of the State's affair.

Reversed.

*We note that counsel for appellant's mother urges an entirely different reason for the application of section 204(a)(3), arguing that appellant lacked the capacity to consent to the marriage because she was under sixteen, as required by The Marriage Law, Act of Aug. 22, 1953, P.L. 1344, 48 P.S. § 1–1 et seq. However, the statutory age requirement is not applicable to common law marriages. *Buradus v. General Cement Products Co.,* 356 Pa. 349, 52 A.2d 205 (1949). Appellant did not lack capacity to consent to a common law marriage. . . .

ASSIGNMENT 6.6

a. Why couldn't this marriage be annulled?

b. Assume that Edward Christoph files for divorce the day after the statute of limitations for corrupting the morals of a minor expires. If Melissa Miller then filed for an annulment, do you think Judge Spaeth would have reached a different result?

Mental Disabilities

Two related reasons have been attributed to the existence of *mental disability* as a ground for annulment. First, it is designed to prevent people from marrying who are incapable of understanding the nature and responsibilities of the marriage relationship. Second, it is designed to prevent or at least discourage such individuals from reproducing, since it is argued that many mentally ill parents are likely to be poor parents and their children are likely to become public charges.

Mental disability has been very difficult to define. Various state statutes use different terms to describe this condition: insane, want of understanding, unsound mind, idiot, weak-minded, feebleminded, mentally retarded, lack of mental capacity, imbecile, lunatic, incapable of consenting to a marriage, mentally ill, legally incompetent, mental defective, etc. One court provided the following definition:

> While there has been a hesitancy on the part of the courts to judicially define the phrase "unsound mind," it is established that such term has reference to the mental capacity of the parties at the very moment of inception of the marriage contract. Ordinarily, lack of mental capacity, which renders a party incapable of entering into a valid marriage contract, must be such that it deprives him of the ability to understand the objects of marriage, its ensuing duties and undertakings, its responsibilities and relationship. There is a general agreement of the authorities that the terms "unsound mind" and "lack of mental capacity" carry greater import than eccentricity or mere weakness of mind or dullness of intellect.[9]

Not all states would agree with every aspect of this definition of mental disability, although in general it is consistent with the definitions used by most courts.

Suppose that a person is intoxicated or under the influence of drugs at the time the marriage contract is entered. In most states, this, too, would be a ground for annulment if the alcohol or drugs rendered the person incapable of understanding the marriage contract.

[9]*Johnson v. Johnson,* 104 N.W.2d 8, 14 (N.D. 1960).

While the issue of mental health usually arises in annulment actions—when someone is trying to dissolve the marriage—it also becomes relevant in some states at the license stage. Before a state official can issue a license to marry, he or she may be required by statute to inquire into the prior mental difficulties, if any, of the applicants for the license (e.g., to ask whether either applicant has ever been in a mental institution). At one time, the license to marry in these states could be denied to any mentally disabled person unless that person was sterilized or the woman involved in the proposed marriage was over forty-five years old. (For more on sterilization, see chapter 12.) It is generally conceded, however, that these license restrictions have been ineffective in preventing the marriage of people with serious mental problems. They are also of questionable constitutionality in view of the ruling of the United States Supreme Court that any state regulation that interferes with the decision to marry must be "reasonable."[10]

Whenever the mental health question arises (at the license stage or as part of an annulment proceeding), it is often very difficult to prove that the "right" amount of mental illness is present. All individuals are presumed to be sane unless the contrary has been demonstrated. Suppose that someone was once committed to a mental institution and, upon release, seeks to be married. Surely, the fact of prior institutionalization does not conclusively prove that the person is *presently* incapable of understanding the marriage contract and the marriage relationship at the time he or she attempts to marry.

lucid interval
A period of time during which a person has the mental capacity to understand what he or she is doing. The lucid interval occurs between periods of mental illness.

Assume that a person is mentally disabled but marries during a brief period of mental health before relapsing again to his or her prior state of mental disability. The marriage took place during what is called a **lucid interval,** and many states will validate such a marriage if there was cohabitation. Furthermore, some states will deny the annulment if the parties freely cohabited during a lucid interval at any time *after* the marriage was entered even if one or both parties were not "lucid" at the time of the marriage. The problems of trying to prove that any "interval" was "lucid" can be enormous, however.

Summary of Ground for Annulment: Mental Disability

Definition: The inability to understand the marriage contract and the duties of marriage at the time the parties attempt to enter the marriage due to mental illness, the influence of alcohol, or the influence of drugs.

Void or voidable: Voidable in most states.

Who can sue: In some states, only the mentally ill person (or his or her parent, guardian, or conservator) can sue for the annulment. In other states, only the mentally healthy person can sue. In many states, either can sue; both have standing.

Major defenses:

1. The person was never mentally disabled.
2. The marriage occurred during a lucid interval.
3. After the marriage began, there was a lucid interval during which the parties freely cohabited.
4. The plaintiff has no standing to bring this annulment action.

Is this annulment ground also a ground for divorce? Yes, in most states, if the mental disability arises after the marriage commences.

Notes on Mental Illness

1. A state may have one standard of mental illness that will disable a person from being able to marry, another standard that will disable a person from being able to enter an ordinary business contract, and still another standard that will disable a person from being able to write a will.

[10] *Zablocki v. Redhail,* 434 U.S. 374, 98 S. Ct. 673, 54 L. Ed. 2d 618 (1978). For more on the *Zablocki* decision, see chapter 5.

2. Mental illness is, of course, also relevant in criminal proceedings where the defense of *insanity* is often raised in an attempt to relieve a defendant of criminal responsibility for what was done. Within criminal law, a great debate has always existed as to the definition of insanity. The *M'Naghten* "right-wrong" test is as follows: "[A]t the time of the committing of the act, the party accused was laboring under such a defect of reason, from disease of the mind, as not to know the nature and quality of the act he was doing, or if he did know it, that he did not know he was doing what was wrong."[11] The *Durham* "diseased mind" test is as follows: "[A]n accused is not criminally responsible if his unlawful act was the product of mental disease or mental defect."[12] The Model Penal Code test is stated in § 4.01: "A person is not responsible for criminal conduct if at the time of such conduct as a result of mental disease or defect he lacks substantial capacity either to appreciate the criminality (wrongfulness) of his conduct or to conform his conduct to the requirements of the law."

Duress

If someone has been forced to consent to marry, it clearly cannot be said that that person had the requisite *intent* to be married. The major question of **duress** is what kind of force will be sufficient to constitute a ground for annulment. Applying physical force or threatening its use is clearly sufficient. If an individual is faced with a choice between a wedding and a funeral, and chooses the wedding, the resulting marriage will be annulled as one induced by duress. The same is true if the choice is between bodily harm and marriage. Suppose, however, that the choice does not involve violence or the threat of violence. The most common example is as follows:

duress
Coercion; acting under the pressure of an unlawful act or threat.

> *George is courting Linda. They have had sexual relations several times. Linda announces that she is pregnant. Linda's father is furious at George and threatens to "turn him in" to the county district attorney to prosecute him for the crimes of seduction and bastardy. (If Linda is underage, the charge of statutory rape may be involved as well.) Furthermore, Linda and her father will sue George in the county civil court for support of the child. On the other hand, no criminal prosecution will be brought and no civil action will be initiated if George agrees to marry Linda. George agrees, and the "shotgun wedding" promptly takes place. After the wedding, it becomes clear that Linda was not pregnant; everyone made an honest mistake. George then brings an action to annul the marriage on the ground of duress.*

Here the threat is of criminal prosecution and of bringing a civil support action. If such threats are made *maliciously*, they will constitute duress and be a ground for annulment. The threat is malicious if it has no basis in fact. If the threats are made in the good faith belief that the court action could be won, the threats are not malicious, and no annulment action can be based on them.

In most states, marriages induced by duress are voidable rather than void, but only the innocent party will have standing to bring the annulment action on that ground. If, however, this innocent party voluntarily cohabited with the "guilty" party (i.e., the one who did the coercing) after the effects of the duress have worn off, then the annulment action will be denied on the theory that the marriage has been ratified.

---

[11] *M'Naghten's Case,* 10 Clark & F. 200, 8 Eng. Rep. 718 (1843).
[12] *Durham v. United States,* 214 F.2d 862, 874–75 (D.C. Cir. 1954). See also *United States v. Brawner,* 471 F.2d 969 (D.C. Cir. 1972).

ASSIGNMENT 6.7

Do you think that any of the following marriages could be annulled on the ground of duress? (See General Instructions for the Legal-Analysis Assignment in Appendix A.)

a. Rita married Dan after Dan threatened to kill Rita's second cousin if she did not marry him. The only reason Rita married Dan was to save her cousin's life.
b. Tom married Edna after Tom's very domineering father ordered him to marry her. Tom had been in ill health lately. Tom married Edna solely because he has never been able to say no to his father.
c. Paula married Charles after Paula's mother threatened suicide if Paula would not marry him. Paula married Charles solely to prevent this suicide.

Summary of Ground for Annulment: Duress

Definition: The consent to marry was induced by (a) physical violence, or (b) threats of physical violence, or (c) malicious or groundless threats of criminal prosecution, or (d) malicious or groundless threats of civil litigation.

Void or voidable: Voidable in most states.

Who can sue: The party who was coerced. In some states, his or her parent or guardian also has standing.

Major defenses:

1. There was no physical violence or threat of it.
2. The plaintiff did not believe the threat of violence and hence was not coerced by it.
3. There was no threat of criminal prosecution or of civil litigation.
4. The threat of criminal prosecution or of civil litigation was not malicious; it was made in the good faith belief that it could be won.
5. This is the wrong plaintiff (e.g., this plaintiff has "dirty hands" and lacks standing, since this is the party who used duress).
6. The plaintiff freely cohabited with the defendant after the effect of the duress had gone (ratification).

Is this annulment ground also a ground for divorce? Yes, in some states.

Fraud

fraud
Knowingly making a false statement of present fact with the intention that the plaintiff rely on the statement. The plaintiff is harmed by his or her reasonable reliance on the statement.

The theory behind **fraud** as a ground for annulment is that if a party consents to a marriage where fraud is involved, the consent is not real. A party does not have an *intent to marry* if the marriage has a foundation in fraud. The party intends one thing and gets another! Generally, for this ground to succeed, the defendant must intentionally misrepresent or conceal an important fact and the person deceived must reasonably rely upon this fact in the decision to enter the marriage.

Not every fraudulent representation will be sufficient to grant an annulment. As one court put it:

> [T]he fact that a brunette turned to a blond overnight, or that the beautiful teeth were discovered to be false, or the ruddy pink complexion gave way suddenly to pallor, or that a woman misstated her age or was not in perfect health, would lead no court to annul the marriage for fraud.[13]

essentials test
Did the matter go to the heart or essence of the relationship?

What kind of fraud *is* ground for an annulment? Most courts have used an **essentials test:** The fraud must involve the essentials of the marital relationship, usually defined as those aspects of the marriage that relate to having future sexual relations and having children. An example would be a man who misrepresents his intention to have children.

A few states use broader tests for fraud, which can make annulment easier to obtain on this ground. For example, the state might grant the annul-

[13] P. Ryan & D. Granfield, *Domestic Relations* 136 (1963).

ment if the fraud pertains to any matter that is *vital* to the marriage relationship. Some states use the **materiality test.** Under this standard, the fraud must be material, meaning "but for" the fraudulent representation (whether or not it relates to having future sexual relations and having children) the person deceived would not have entered the marriage. Under this broader test, the failure to disclose an out-of-wedlock child, for example, might be found to be material if the person deceived would not have entered the marriage if this fact had been known. Note, however, that this deception does not pertain to the essentials of marriage, since already being a parent does not necessarily interfere with having future sexual relations and having children together. Hence under the narrower essentials test, the annulment might be denied.

materiality test
If a specific event had not occurred, would the result have been different?

If children have been born from the union, courts sometimes strain the application of the test for fraud in order to deny the annulment, since preserving the marriage may be the only way to legitimize the children in some states. Also, if the marriage has never been consummated, courts tend to be more liberal in finding fraud. Oddly, a few courts treat an unconsummated marriage as little more than an engagement to be married.

The state of mind of the deceiving party is critical. In most states, there must be an *intentional misrepresentation* of fact or an *intentional concealment* of fact. Consider the following methods by which false facts are communicated:

Forms of Communication

1. Just before their marriage, Joe tells Mary that he is anxious to have children with her. In fact, he intends to remain celibate after their marriage.	1. Joe's statement about children is an *intentional misrepresentation* of fact.
2. Joe says nothing about his planned celibacy, since he knows that if he tells Mary, she will not marry him. He says nothing about children or celibacy, and the subject never comes up prior to their marriage.	2. Joe's silence is an *intentional concealment* of fact.
3. Joe does not tell Mary that he intended to remain celibate because he incorrectly assumed that Mary already knew.	3. Joe's silence is an *innocent* (or *good faith*) *nondisclosure* of fact.
4. Just before their marriage, Joe tells Mary that since he is physically unable to have sexual intercourse, he will have to stay celibate. To his surprise, Joe later finds out that he is not impotent.	4. Joe's statement is an *innocent* (or *good faith*) *misrepresentation* of fact.
5. One hour after Joe marries Mary, he gets on a bus and disappears forever. They never had sexual intercourse before or after marriage and never discussed the subject.	5. From Joe's conduct, we can draw an *inference* that at the time he married Mary, he probably never intended to consummate the marriage.

Generally, only the first, second, and fifth forms of communication mentioned in the above chart will support an annulment on the ground of fraud. *Innocent nondisclosure* or *innocent misrepresentation* will not be sufficient in most states. It should be pointed out, however, that in some states the innocence of the communication is not relevant so long as the other elements of fraud are present.

Summary of Ground for Annulment: Fraud

Definition: The intentional misrepresentation or concealment of a fact that is essential or material to the marriage and that the person deceived reasonably relies on in the decision to enter the marriage.

Void or voidable: Voidable in most states.

Who can sue: The innocent party. In some states, his or her parent or guardian also has standing.

Major defenses:

1. The fraud was not about an essential fact.
2. The fraud was not material: the plaintiff did not rely on the fraud in his or her initial decision to marry.
3. The fraud arose after the marriage was entered (again, no reliance).
4. The plaintiff may have relied on the fraud, but he or she was unreasonable in doing so.
5. After plaintiff discovered the fraud, he or she consummated the marriage or otherwise freely cohabited with the fraudulent party (ratification).
6. The misrepresentation or nondisclosure was innocent—made in good faith with no intention to deceive.
7. This plaintiff has no standing to bring the annulment action, since the plaintiff was the deceiver.
8. This plaintiff has "dirty hands" (e.g., in a case involving fraud relating to pregnancy, the plaintiff had premarital sex with the defendant).

Is this annulment ground also a ground for divorce? Yes, in a few states.

I Take This Man for Richer Only: Who Wants to Marry a Multimillionaire?

In February 2000, television viewers watched *Who Wants to Marry a Multimillionaire?* on Fox TV, a live broadcast from Las Vegas. On the program, a bachelor selected a bride from among fifty contestants he had never met. Immediately after his selection, marriage vows were exchanged before 23 million viewers. Apparently, however, the honeymoon of the instant bride and groom did not go well. Soon after the newlyweds returned, she asked a Nevada court for an annulment based on fraud. They had not consummated their relationship. The bride became disenchanted when she learned that a prior girlfriend had obtained a restraining order against him for domestic violence. His failure to disclose his "history of problems with prior girlfriends," she told the court, constituted fraud. This was not a particularly strong argument, however, since she knew that one of the show's main attractions was that she was willing to take her chances. If she did not have all the facts needed to make the marriage decision, she arguably was willfully ignorant.

Nevertheless, the court granted the annulment. As a condition of appearing on the show, the bachelor and all the contestants signed individual premarital agreements in which they agreed not to challenge any annulment action that might be filed in the future. In granting the annulment, however, the court did not base its decision on this agreement. Indeed, it is doubtful that such agreements are enforceable. As a matter of public policy, courts do not want to encourage the dissolution of marriages by the device of an agreement. (See chapter 4 on premarital agreements.) Why then was the annulment granted, particularly since the factual basis for fraud was relatively weak? The answer is not clear. First of all, the Nevada hearing was uncontested. The husband neither appeared nor was represented by counsel. Hence there was no opposition to the petition to annul on the ground of fraud. Nor did anyone appeal. There was no written opinion in which the trial judge laid out his rationale for granting the annulment. Some have speculated that the judge may have been influenced by the negative public outcry over what had taken place.

Of course, if the annulment had been denied, the parties would not have been forced to stay married. The option of divorce would have been readily available. The annulment appeared to have been the best way for the country to get this embarrassing incident behind it as quickly as possible.

ASSIGNMENT 6.8

a. Do you think the annulment could have been granted on the ground that the marriage was a sham?

b. Later we will study no-fault divorce, in which marital fault is no longer relevant to the granting of divorce. Is there any reason why we should not have a system of no-fault annulment?

c. Is it relevant that the winning contestant agreed to pose for *Playboy* soon after the annulment was granted?

Note on Church Annulment

The Roman Catholic Church has its own separate system of annulment. The church does not recognize divorce. Nor does it recognize the annulments discussed in this chapter that are granted by the civil courts. Having a civil annulment does not automatically lead to a church annulment. In the eyes of the church, the only way to terminate a marriage (other than by the death of one of the parties) is by seeking a petition of nullity in a canon law church court, which declares the marriage "null." Technically, the church does not dissolve the marriage. Rather, it makes a judicial finding that a valid sacramental marriage was not created or entered on the wedding day. This will allow a Catholic to remarry in the church, to receive communion, and to participate in all the other sacraments. Full participation is denied a Catholic who remarries without obtaining a church annulment—even if he or she obtained a civil annulment.

The main ground for a church annulment is defective consent, usually due to "lack of due discretion" or "lack of due competence." A primary focus of the church court is whether the parties entered the marriage through a free act of the will with the intention to accept the essential elements of marriage: permanence, fidelity, and conjugal love that is open to children. Among the factors that can interfere with this intention are duress, fraud, conditions to one's consent, and psychological problems such as mental illness.[14]

To initiate a church annulment, the petitioner pays a processing fee (approximately $500) in order to have a formal hearing presided over by a tribunal judge. An advocate presents the case of the petitioner seeking the annulment. Also present is a "defender of the bond," who monitors the proceeding to ensure that rights are protected and church law properly observed. The hierarchy in Rome has criticized American bishops for allowing too many church annulments. Over 50,000 annulments are granted each year in the 119 dioceses of the United States. This constitutes 80 percent of the annulments granted by the church worldwide.

CONFLICT OF LAW

The conflict of law question requires us to compare the law of two states. In annulment cases, the law that exists where the parties were married (the *state of celebration*) may have to be compared with the law that exists where the parties now live (the state of **domicile** or **domiciliary state**). The question arises as follows:

> *Jim and Jane marry in State X, where their marriage is valid. They then move to State Y. If they had married in State Y, their marriage would not have been valid. Jim sues Jane in State Y for an annulment. What*

domicile
The place where a person has been physically present with the intent to make that place a permanent home; the place to which one intends to return when away.

domiciliary state
The state where a person is domiciled. (This person is referred to as the domiciliary.)

[14]Rev. Michael Smith Foster, How Is a Marriage Declared Null? <http://www.rcab.org/marriageglobe.html> (Apr. 20, 1997) (site visited Aug. 22, 2000).

annulment law does the court in State Y apply—the law of State X or the law of State Y?

State X is the state of celebration or the state of contract (i.e., the state where the parties entered the marriage contract). State Y is the domiciliary state (i.e., the state where the parties are now domiciled). The state where the parties file the suit is called the **forum** state. (Forum also refers to the court or tribunal hearing the case.) In our example, State Y is both the domiciliary state and the forum state.

forum
(1) The place where the parties are presently litigating their dispute. (2) A court or tribunal hearing a case.

intestate
Die without leaving a valid will.

To place this problem in a concrete perspective, assume that Jim dies **intestate.** Assume further that he has children from a prior marriage but had no children with his second spouse, Jane. Under the intestacy laws of most states, his spouse and children receive designated portions of his estate. If there is no spouse, the children obviously have more of an estate to share. Hence it is in the interest of the children to claim that Jane cannot be the surviving spouse of Jim because they were never validly married. The success of this claim may depend on which law applies—that of State X or State Y.

Before examining the question of what law applies, we need to keep in mind the public policy favoring marriages. Legislatures and courts tend to look for reasons to validate a marriage, rather than creating circumstances that make it easy to invalidate it. This is all the more so if the parties have lived together for a long time and if children are in the picture. We have already seen that the law has imposed a presumption that a marriage is valid. The public policy favoring marriage, however, is not absolute. Other public policies must also be taken into account. The conflict of law rules are a product of a clash of public policies.

General Conflict of Law Rule in Annulment Actions If the marriage is valid in the state of celebration (even though it would have been invalid if it had been contracted in the domiciliary state), the marriage will be recognized as valid in the domiciliary state *unless* the recognition of the marriage would violate some strong public policy of the domiciliary state.

Thus, in the case of Jim and Jane above, the general rule would mean that State Y would apply the law of State X unless to do so would violate some strong public policy of State Y. Assuming that no such policy would be violated, the annulment would be denied, since the marriage was valid in the state of celebration, State X. Assuming, however, that a strong public policy is involved, State Y would apply its own law and grant the annulment.

What do we mean by a strong public policy, the violation of which would cause a domiciliary state to apply its own marriage law? Some states say that if the marriage would have been *void* (as opposed to merely voidable) had it been contracted in the domiciliary state, then the latter state will not recognize the marriage even though the state of celebration recognizes the marriage as valid. In other words, it is against the strong public policy of a domiciliary state to recognize what it considers a void marriage even though other states consider the marriage valid.

A marriage that the domiciliary state would consider bigamous or incestuous is usually not recognized. In such cases, the domiciliary state will apply its own marriage law and grant the annulment even though the marriage may have been valid in the state of celebration. When other grounds for annulment are involved, states differ as to whether they, as domiciliary states, will apply their own marriage law or that of the state of celebration.

As we saw in chapter 5, no state has yet allowed same-sex marriages. When the first state does so, however, we will have to face the question of whether another state will recognize the validity of such marriages. The answer will depend on whether the state considers such marriages to be against its strong public policy. Today the overwhelming number of states do. Most states have passed laws that ban same-sex marriages and that declare it is against the state's public policy to recognize such marriages entered in other states. Furthermore, the federal Defense of Marriage Act (DOMA) specifically provides that a state is not required to recognize (i.e., to give full faith and credit to) same-sex marriages that may be valid in the state of celebration. As we also saw in chapter 5, however, the constitutionality of DOMA is in doubt.

What about the civil union status of same-sex couples in Vermont? Such couples are given the same state rights that Vermont gives heterosexual married couples. For example, assume that Ted and Bob form a civil union in Vermont. Ted has the right to be supported by Bob, and vice versa. They move to New Hampshire and separate. Can either of them bring an action in a New Hampshire state court to enforce this right of support? We do not know the answer to such a question, since the civil union status in Vermont is so new. It has not been tested across state lines. The probability, however, is that another state will refuse to enforce the marriagelike rights and duties of a Vermont civil union. A state such as New Hampshire might take the position that it is against its strong public policy to recognize not only same-sex marriages but also same-sex relationships that are intended to be the equivalent of marriage.

Marriage-Evasion Statutes

Suppose that a man and woman live in a state where they cannot marry (e.g., they are underage). They move from their domiciliary state to another state *solely* for the purpose of entering or contracting a marriage, since they can validly marry under the laws of the latter state (e.g., they are not underage in this state). They then move back to their domiciliary state. If an annulment action is brought in the domiciliary state, what law will be applied? The marriage law of the domiciliary state or that of the state of celebration? If the annulment action is brought in the state of celebration, what law will be applied? Again, the conflict of law question becomes critical because the annulment will be granted or denied depending upon which state's marriage law governs. Note that the man and woman went to the state of celebration in order to *evade* the marriage laws of the domiciliary state. Several states have enacted *marriage-evasion* statutes to cover this situation. In such states, the choice of law depends upon the presence or absence of an intent to evade. The statute might provide that the domiciliary state will refuse to recognize the marriage if the parties went to the state of celebration for the purpose of evading the marriage laws of the domiciliary state to which they returned. It is sometimes very difficult to prove whether the parties went to the other state with the intent to evade the marriage laws of their domiciliary state. It may depend on circumstantial evidence such as how long they remained in the state of celebration and whether they returned to their initial domiciliary state or established a domicile in another state altogether. The interviewing and investigation checklist below is designed to assist you in collecting evidence on intent:

Interviewing and Investigation Checklist

Factors Relevant to the Intent to Evade the Marriage Laws*

(Assume that the parties are from State Y but were married in State X.)

Legal Interviewing Questions

1. How long have the two of you lived in State Y?
2. Why didn't you marry in State Y?
3. When did you decide to go to State X?
4. Have you or D ever lived in State X?
5. Do you or D have any relatives in State X?
6. Were you or D born in State X?
7. On what date did you and D go to State X?
8. Did you sell your home or move out of your apartment in State Y?
9. When you left State Y, did you intend to come back?

continued

Interviewing and Investigation Checklist—*Continued*

10. After you arrived in State X, when did you apply for a marriage license?
11. On what date were you married?
12. While you were in State X, where did you stay? Did you have all your clothes and furniture with you?
13. Who attended the wedding ceremony in State X?
14. Did you and D have sexual relations in State X?
15. Did you or D work in State X?
16. How long did you and D stay in State X?
17. Did you and D vote or pay taxes in State X?
18. Did you and D open a checking account in any bank in State X?
19. Where did you and D go after you left State X?

Possible Investigation Tasks

- Obtain copies of all records that tend to establish the kind of contact the parties had with State X (e.g., motel receipts, bank statements, rent receipts, employment records).
- Interview friends, relatives, and associates of the parties to determine what light they can shed on the intent of the parties in going to State X.

*See also the interviewing and investigation checklist for establishing domicile in chapter 7.

Thus far our main focus has been on marriages that are valid in the state of celebration but invalid and annullable in the domiciliary state if they had been contracted in the latter state (see Exhibit 6.1). Suppose, however, that the marriage was invalid in the state of celebration. The parties then move to a new state where they establish a domicile. If they had been married in their new domicile state, their marriage would have been valid. An annulment action is brought in their new domicile state (Exhibit 6.2).

Our question now becomes, If a marriage is invalid where contracted, can it ever be considered valid in any other state? Will a present domiciliary state validate a marriage that is invalid according to the law of the state of celebration? Surprisingly, the answer is often yes. In some states, a domiciliary state will deny an annulment of a marriage that would have been valid if contracted in the domiciliary state but that is clearly invalid in the state where it was actually contracted. Such states take this position, in part, because of the public policy (and indeed the presumption) favoring the validity of marriages.

Exhibit 6.1 Marriages Valid in State of Celebration

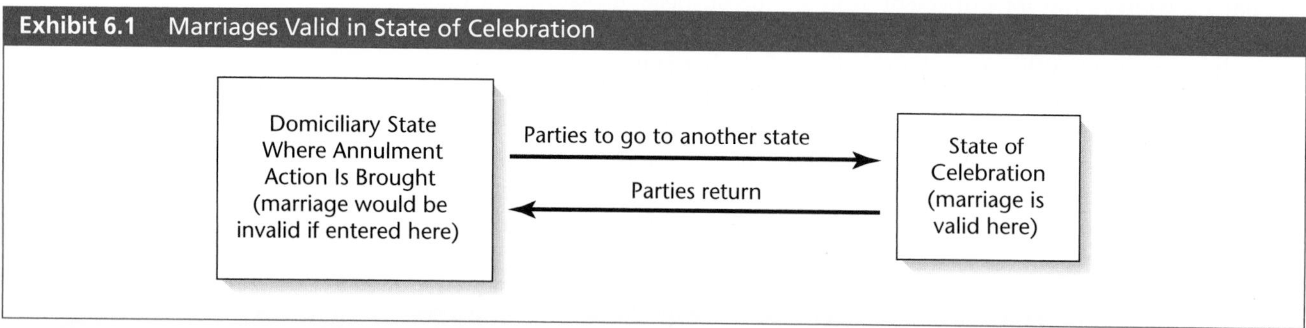

Exhibit 6.2 Marriages Invalid in State of Celebration

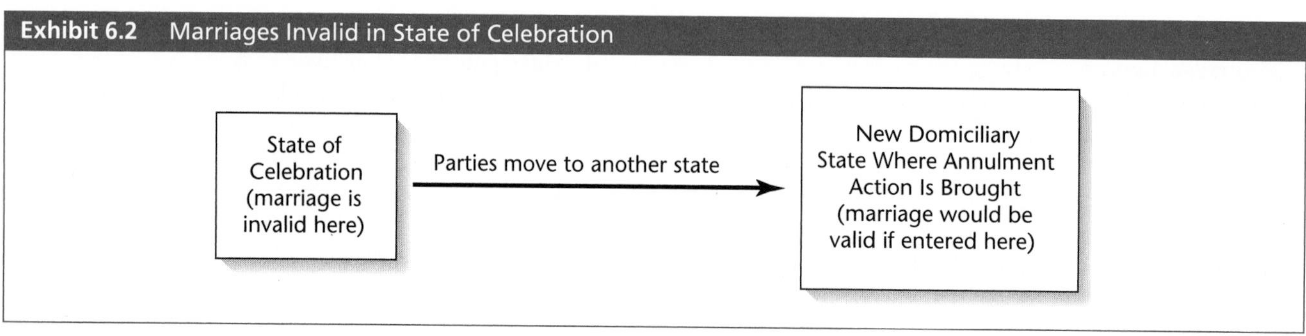

ASSIGNMENT 6.9

a. Is there a statute in your state that deals with marriages contracted out of state? If so, give its citation and state how it handles such marriages. (See General Instructions for the State-Code Assignment in Appendix A.)

b. Find a court opinion written by a state court in your state that involved an annulment action brought in your state concerning a marriage that was contracted in another state. (If no such action has ever been brought in your state, pick an opinion from any state.) Answer the following questions about the opinion you found:

1. In what state was the marriage contracted?
2. What was the alleged ground for the annulment?
3. What marriage law was applied in the opinion?
4. What reason did the court give for applying that law?
5. Was the annulment granted? Why or why not? (See the General Instructions for the Court-Opinion Assignment in Appendix A.)

CONSEQUENCES OF AN ANNULMENT DECREE

In theory, an annulled marriage never existed. The major question that always arises as a result of this theory is, What effect does the annulment have on events occurring after the "marriage"?

The old rule was that once a marriage was declared invalid, the declaration "related back" to the time the parties attempted to enter the marriage. This relation-back doctrine meant that the annulment decree was retroactive. The doctrine, when strictly applied, resulted in some very harsh consequences. Children born to parents before their marriage was annulled were, in effect, born out of wedlock and were illegitimate. Suppose that a woman lives with a man for forty years before their marriage is annulled. She would not be entitled to any alimony or support payments, since a man has no duty to support someone who was never his wife! Clearly, these were unfair consequences, and all states took steps to offset them. What follows is an overview of the present law in this area.

Legitimacy of Children from an Annulled Marriage

Most states have passed statutes that **legitimize** children from an annulled marriage. Some of the statutes, however, are not absolute (e.g., the statute might say that the children are legitimate only if one or both of the parents honestly believed that their marriage was valid when they entered it, or the statute might legitimize all the children born from an annulled marriage *except* when the annulment was granted on the ground of a prior existing marriage [bigamy]).

legitimize
To formally declare that children born out of wedlock are legitimate.

Alimony and Disposition of Property Acquired before the Marriage Was Annulled

In some states, alimony cannot be awarded in annulment proceedings. In other states, however, statutes have been passed that allow alimony in such actions. This includes temporary alimony pending the final outcome of the action and permanent alimony following the annulment decree. It may be, however, that alimony will be denied to the "guilty" party (e.g., the party who committed the fraud or who forced the other party to enter the marriage).

Another limitation on alimony in some states is that only defendants can receive it. By definition, the plaintiff seeking the annulment is saying that no marriage ever existed. A few courts say that it is inconsistent for the plaintiff to take this position and also to ask for alimony.

Where alimony is authorized, attorney fees might also be awarded. If so, the spouse able to pay, usually the husband, must pay the fees of the attorney for the other spouse in defending or initiating the annulment action.

Suppose it is clear in a particular state that alimony cannot be awarded in the annulment action. Courts have devised various theories to provide other kinds of relief such as allowing a party to bring a suit on a theory of *quasi contract* to prevent *unjust enrichment.* Under this theory, the party may be able to recover the reasonable value of the goods and services provided during the relationship. Other theories that might allow a division of property acquired during the relationship include *partnership, joint venture,* and *putative spouse.* For a discussion of these theories, see chapter 4, where we discussed similar theories to obtain relief for parties who cohabited but never tried to marry.

Problems of Revival

Bob is validly married to Elaine. They go through a valid divorce proceeding, which provides that Bob will pay Elaine alimony until she remarries. One year later Elaine marries Bill; Bob stops his alimony payments. Two years later Elaine's marriage to Bill is annulled.

In this case, what is Bob's obligation to pay alimony to Elaine? Several possibilities exist:

- Bob does not have to resume paying alimony; his obligation ceased forever when Elaine married Bill; the fact that the second marriage was annulled is irrelevant.
- Bob does not have to resume paying alimony; *Bill* must start paying alimony if the state authorizes alimony in annulment actions.
- Bob must resume paying alimony from the date of the annulment decree; the annulment of the second marriage *revived* his alimony obligation.
- Bob must resume paying alimony for the future and for the time during which Elaine was married to Bill; the annulment *revived* the alimony obligation.

The last option is the most logical. Since the technical effect of an annulment decree is to say that the marriage never existed, this decree should be retroactive to the date when the parties entered the marriage that was later annulled. While the last option is perhaps the most logical of the four presented, it is arguably as unfair to Bob as the first option is unfair to Elaine. States take different positions on this problem. Most states, however, adopt the second or third option mentioned above.

Custody and Child Support

When children are involved, whether considered legitimate or not, courts will make temporary and permanent custody decisions in the annulment proceeding. Furthermore, child-support orders are inevitable when the children are minors. Hence the fact that the marriage is terminated by annulment usually has little effect on the need of the court to make custody and child-support orders (see chapters 9 and 10).

Inheritance

testate
Die leaving a valid will.

If a spouse dies **testate** (with a valid will), he or she can leave property to the surviving spouse. Suppose, however, that the marriage is annulled before the spouse died and that the will was never changed. In most states, an annulment (or a divorce) automatically revokes gifts to a surviving spouse unless the will specifically says otherwise. Also automatically revoked is the appointment of the surviving spouse as executor, trustee, conservator, or guardian.

Assume that one of the spouses of the annulled marriage dies *intestate* (without a valid will). In this event, the state's intestacy laws operate to determine who inherits the property of the deceased. The intestacy statute will usually provide that so much of the deceased's property will go to the surviving spouse, so much to the children, etc. If the marriage has already been annulled, there will be no surviving spouse to take a spouse's intestate share of the decedent's estate. An annulment (as well as a divorce) terminates mutual intestate rights of former spouses.

Workers' Compensation Benefits

Assume that a spouse is receiving workers' compensation benefits following the death of her husband, but that these benefits will cease when she remarries. If the second marriage is annulled, will the workers' compensation benefits be revived? Courts differ in answering this question. Some revive the benefits; some do not.

Criminal Law Consequences

> *Ed marries Diane. He leaves her without obtaining a divorce. He now marries Claire. This marriage is then annulled. He is charged with the crime of bigamy.*

Can Ed use the defense that his marriage with Claire was annulled and, therefore, he was never married to Claire?

Most of the cases that have answered this question have said that the subsequent annulment is *not* a defense to the bigamy charge.

Interspousal Immunity in Tort Actions

As we shall see in chapter 17, spouses may have the benefit of an **interspousal tort immunity** that prevents certain kinds of tort litigation between spouses. For example, assume George assaults his wife, Paulene, in a state where the immunity applies. She would not be able to sue him for the tort of assault. (She might be able to initiate a *criminal* action against him for the crime of assault and battery, but she could not bring a *civil* assault action against him.) An annulment of the marriage would not change this result. Even if George's marriage with Paulene was later annulled, she would still not be able to bring this tort action against him for conduct that occurred while they were together. The annulment does not wipe out the impact of the interspousal tort immunity.

interspousal tort immunity
One spouse cannot sue another for designated torts that grow out of the marriage relationship.

Privilege for Marital Communications

At common law, one spouse was not allowed to give testimony concerning *confidential communications* exchanged between the spouses during the marriage. The details of this prohibition will be explained in chapter 7. For now, our question is as follows:

> *Sam is married to Helen. Their marriage is annulled. A year later Sam is sued by a neighbor who claims that Sam negligently damaged the neighbor's property. The alleged damage was inflicted while Sam was still married to Helen. At the trial, the neighbor calls Helen as a witness and asks her to testify about what Sam told her concerning the incident while they were still living together. According to the privilege for marital communications, Helen would be prohibited from testifying about what she and her husband told each other during the marriage. Their marriage, however, was annulled, so that in the eyes of the law they were never married. Does this change the rule on the privilege? Can Helen give this testimony?*

The answer is not clear; few cases have considered the issue. Of those that have, some have concluded that the annulment does not destroy the privilege, while others have reached the opposite conclusion.

Tax Return Status

A husband and wife can file a joint return so long as they were married during the taxable year. Suppose, however, that after ten years of marriage and ten years of filing joint returns, the marriage is annulled. Must the parties now file *amended* returns for each of those ten years? Should the returns now be filed as separate returns rather than joint ones, again on the theory that the annulment meant the parties were never validly married? According to the Internal Revenue Service:

> You are considered unmarried for the whole year [if you have] . . . obtained a decree of annulment which holds that no valid marriage ever existed. You must file amended returns [claiming an unmarried status] for all tax years affected by the annulment not closed by the [three-year] period of limitations.[15]

ASSIGNMENT 6.10

Answer the following questions by examining the statutory code of your state.

a. Is there a statute on whether children of annulled marriages are legitimate? If so, give the citation to the statute and explain how it resolves the question.
b. Is there a statute on whether temporary and permanent alimony can be granted in annulment proceedings? If so, give the citation to the statute and explain how it resolves the question.

(See General Instructions for the State-Code Assignment in Appendix A.)

ASSIGNMENT 6.11

How would the following two problems be resolved in your state? You may have to check both statutory law and case law. (See General Instructions for the State-Code Assignment and General Instructions for the Court-Opinion Assignment in Appendix A.)

a. Fred and Jill are married. Fred is killed in an automobile accident with the ABC Tire Company. Jill brings a wrongful death action against the ABC Tire Company. The attorney of ABC learns that Jill was married to someone else at the time she married Fred. The attorney claims that Jill cannot bring the wrongful death action, since she was never validly married to Fred.
b. Bob and Mary are married. Bob dies intestate. Mary claims Bob's estate (i.e., his property) pursuant to the state's intestate law. Bob's only other living relative, Fred, claims that he is entitled to Bob's estate. Fred argues that Mary is not entitled to any of Bob's property because the marriage between Bob and Mary was invalid and should be annulled.

ASSIGNMENT 6.12

a. What is the name of the court in your state that can hear annulment actions?
b. How does this court acquire jurisdiction over the subject matter of annulment actions (e.g., residence or domicile requirements, place of celebration, etc.)?
c. To what court(s) can a party appeal a trial court judgment on annulment?

(See General Instructions for the State-Code Assignment in Appendix A.)

---

[15]Internal Revenue Service, Publication 504, *Tax Information for Divorced or Separated Individuals* 2 (1999 ed.).

ASSIGNMENT 6.13

Prepare a flowchart of annulment litigation in your state. (See General Instructions for the Flowchart Assignment in Appendix A.)

SUMMARY

A divorce is a termination of a valid marriage. An annulment is a declaration that the parties were never married, whether they lived together (and acted as if they were married) for thirty minutes or for thirty years after the "marriage" ceremony. To obtain an annulment, a party must establish grounds and must have standing. Two categories of grounds exist: grounds relating to the legal capacity to marry and grounds relating to the intent to marry. Some of these grounds will render the marriage void, while others will render it voidable.

There are four grounds relating to the legal capacity to marry:

1. *Prior existing marriage.* At the time of the marriage, a prior marriage had not been terminated.
2. *Consanguinity and affinity.* The parties married in violation of a prohibition against the marriage of certain categories of individuals who are already related to each other.
3. *Nonage.* A party was underage at the time of the marriage.
4. *Physical disabilities.* A party had a specified disease or was impotent at the time of the marriage.

There are four grounds relating to the intent to marry:

1. *Sham marriage.* The parties never intended to live together as husband and wife.
2. *Mental disability.* At the time of the marriage, a party was incapable of understanding the nature of the marriage relationship.
3. *Duress.* A party was forced into the marriage.
4. *Fraud.* A party intentionally misrepresented or concealed certain facts from the other party that were either essential to the marriage or material to the decision to enter the marriage.

Under conflict of law principles:

1. A marriage will be considered valid in a domiciliary state if (a) the marriage is valid according to the state where it was contracted and (b) recognizing the validity of the marriage would not violate any strong public policy of the domiciliary state. If both conditions are met, the domiciliary state will deny the annulment even though the marriage could have been annulled if it had been contracted in the domiciliary state. (Many states have passed laws saying that same-sex marriage, if ever allowed in another state, is against the strong public policy of their state and hence would not be enforced.)
2. Generally, if a marriage would have been void had it been contracted in the domiciliary state, the latter state will not apply the law of the state of celebration, where the marriage is valid.
3. Some states have statutes that invalidate marriages contracted in other states solely to evade the domiciliary state's marriage laws.
4. Some states have statutes that invalidate marriages contracted in their own state solely to evade the marriage laws of other states.
5. Some states will validate a marriage contracted in another state (even though the marriage is invalid in the state where it was contracted) so long as the marriage would have been valid if it had been contracted in the state where the parties are now domiciled. In effect, this state will

deny the annulment even though the state of celebration would have granted it.

In an annulment proceeding, the court must award custody of the children and provide for their support. Children born from an annulled marriage are usually considered legitimate. If the state does not allow alimony, the court may use a theory such as quasi contract to divide property acquired during the time the parties were together.

Suppose a divorced spouse remarries and thereby loses certain benefits granted by the divorce. But the second marriage is annulled. States do not always agree on whether the divorce benefits are revived. Revival issues might also arise in cases that involve inheritance, bigamy, tort liability, evidence, and income tax status.

KEY CHAPTER TERMINOLOGY

annulment
divorce
legal separation
voidable marriage
void marriage
void ab initio
ratification
standing
estopped
dirty hands
grounds
bigamy
polygamy
Enoch Arden defense
rebuttable presumption
consanguinity
affinity
incest
nonage
impotence
copulate
sterility
sham
consummate
cohabitation
lucid interval
duress
fraud
essentials test
materiality test
domicile
domiciliary state
forum
intestate
legitimize
testate
interspousal tort immunity

ETHICS IN PRACTICE

You are a paralegal working at a law office that is representing Mary Smith in her annulment action against Paul Smith. The case is uncontested. Both parties want the annulment. After a state trial court grants the annulment, Paul Smith asks you to represent him as an independent paralegal in the petition he now wants to file for an annulment from the Catholic Church. Are there any ethical problems in your doing so?

ON THE NET: MORE ON ANNULMENT

Annulments in the Catholic Church
http://www.rcab.org/marriage.html

Attorney Site: Information on Annulment
http://www.boumanlaw.com/annulment.htm

Court Information on Annulment (Georgia)
http://www.fultonfamilydivision.com/publications/annulment.html

Independent Paralegal: Divorce and Annulments
http://businesses.msn.com/legalservicesprovider

Nolo's Legal Encyclopedia: Annulment
http://www.nolo.com/encyclopedia/articles/div/sp18.html

Who Wants to Marry a Multimillionaire? Who Wants to Annul?
http://www-cgi.cnn.com/2000/LAW/07/columns/fl.grossman.annulment.07.11

CHAPTER 7

DIVORCE GROUNDS AND PROCEDURE

CHAPTER OUTLINE

HISTORICAL BACKGROUND

In order to obtain a divorce that dissolves the marital relationship, specified reasons must exit. These reasons, called **grounds,** are spelled out in statutes. The two categories of grounds are no-fault and fault. The major **no-fault grounds** are as follows:

- Living apart
- Incompatibility
- Irreconcilable differences, irremediable breakdown

When a divorce is granted on a no-fault ground, marital misconduct is, in most respects, irrelevant. The divorce statute might provide that "evidence of specific acts of misconduct shall be improper and inadmissible, except where child custody is in issue and such evidence is relevant." A divorce sought on a no-fault ground, therefore, will not involve cross-examination designed to ferret out the blameworthy party. A famous attorney, looking back over his long career, recalled the time when an indignant woman accused of infidelity broke

grounds
Acceptable reasons for seeking a particular result.

no-fault grounds
Reasons for granting a divorce that do not require proof that either spouse committed marital wrongs.

down on the witness stand and screamed, "What you say isn't true. I've been faithful to my husband dozens of times."[1] No-fault grounds have made such testimony highly unlikely.

This does not mean, however, that *fault* grounds have been abolished. They still exist in most states. The availability of no-fault grounds, however, and their ease of use have meant that the fault grounds are not often used. The major fault grounds are as follows:

- Adultery
- Cruelty
- Desertion

Although these are the main three, a number of other fault grounds also exist in most states.

covenant marriage
A form of marriage that requires proof of premarital counseling, a promise to seek marital counseling when needed during the marriage, and proof of marital fault to dissolve.

There is one notable exception to the decline in the use of fault grounds. A number of states are experimenting with a new marriage option called a **covenant marriage.** Couples in states like Louisiana have a choice between a conventional marriage and a covenant marriage. Divorce from a conventional marriage is no-fault, whereas divorce from a covenant marriage requires proof of marital fault such as adultery, physical or sexual abuse (cruelty), and abandonment (desertion). Spouses in a covenant marriage must also make a commitment to obtain counseling before and during the marriage. Reformers hope that the availability of this new option will encourage couples to engage in more serious planning before entering the state of marriage. For more on covenant marriages, see chapter 5.

For many years, fault grounds were the only grounds for divorce, the premise being that a marriage should not be terminated unless there was evidence of serious wrongdoing by one of the spouses—blame had to be established. Many believed that such stringent divorce laws would help prevent the failure of marriages. In colonial America, it was common to deny the guilty spouse the right of remarriage if a divorce was granted. The payment of alimony was sometimes used to punish the guilty spouse rather than as a way to help the other become reestablished. In short, guilt, wrongdoing, and punishment were predominant themes of our divorce laws. (Exhibit 7.1 shows how the divorce rate has changed since 1940.)

uncontested
Not disputed; not challenged.

During this period of fault-based divorce, the system was frequently criticized as irrelevant and encouraging fraud. Over 90 percent of the divorces were **uncontested,** meaning that there was no dispute between the parties. Since both spouses wanted the divorce, they rarely spent much time fighting

[1]Erie Pace, *Louis Nizer, Lawyer to the Famous, Dies at 92,* N.Y. Times, Nov. 11, 1994, at A15.

Exhibit 7.1 Divorce Rate

Year	Number of Divorces	Rate/1000 Total Population
1998	1,135,000	4.2
1997	1,142,000	4.3
1996	1,158,000	4.4
1990	1,175,000	4.7
1980	1,182,000	5.2
1970	773,000	3.7
1960	393,000	2.2
1950	385,000	2.6
1940	293,000	2.2

Source: Monthly Vital Statistics Report, Vol. 47, No. 21; National Center for Health Statistics <http://www.cdc.gov/nchs/fastats/divorce.htm>; F. Cox, *Human Intimacy* 484 (8th ed. 1999).

each other about whether adultery, cruelty, or other fault grounds existed. In fact, parties often flagrantly lied to the courts about the facts of their case in order to quickly establish that fault did exist. While such **collusion** was obviously illegal, the parties were seldom caught. Since both sides wanted the divorce, there was little incentive to reveal the truth. The system also encouraged **migratory divorces,** where one of the parties would "migrate," or travel, to another state solely to take advantage of its more lenient divorce laws. Some of these states gained the reputation of being divorce mills.

collusion
An agreement between spouses in a divorce proceeding that one or both will lie to the court to facilitate the obtaining of the divorce.

migratory divorce
A divorce obtained in a state to which one or both spouses traveled before returning to their original state.

Reform was obviously needed. In 1969, California enacted the first no-fault divorce law in the country. Soon other states followed. Today no-fault grounds (or their equivalent) exist in every state. Some states have eliminated the word "divorce" and replaced it with the word **dissolution** as a symbolic gesture that a new day has arrived.

dissolution
A divorce; a court's termination of a marriage.

Not everyone, however, is happy with the shift to no-fault divorce. There are conservatives who regret that marriage is now so easy to dissolve. No-fault divorce has also removed an emotional outlet. There are some clients who want and need the opportunity to tell the world about the abuse they have received from their spouse. They become frustrated when they learn that they cannot do so in divorce court. In this sense, no-fault divorce prevents some spouses from attaining "emotional closure" through the divorce.[2]

ASSIGNMENT 7.1

a. In your state code, find the statute that lists the grounds for divorce. Give the citation to this statute and list all the grounds for divorce provided therein. (See General Instructions for the State-Code Assignment in Appendix A.)

b. For each ground of divorce identified in part (a), draft a checklist of questions to help determine whether those grounds exist. (See General Instructions for the Checklist-Formulation Assignment in Appendix A.)

NO-FAULT GROUNDS FOR DIVORCE

Living Apart

Living "separate and apart" is a ground for divorce in many states. The statutes authorizing this ground of **living apart** must be carefully read, since slight differences in wording may account for major differences in meaning. Most statutes require that the parties live separate and apart for a designated period of consecutive time, as outlined below. Some states impose additional and more restrictive requirements. For example, living separate and apart may have to be pursuant to a court order or a separation agreement, or it may have to be consensual or "voluntary."

living apart
A no-fault ground of divorce that exists when the spouses live separately for a designated period of consecutive time.

TIME In all states where living apart is a ground, the statute requires that the parties live apart for a designated period of time, ranging from six months to three years. The purpose of the time limitation is, in effect, to force the parties to think seriously about whether a reconciliation is possible.

CONSECUTIVENESS The separated time must be consecutive. Off-and-on separations do not qualify if one of the separations does not last the requisite length of time. This is true even if the total time spent apart from the intermittent separations exceeds the minimum required. Furthermore, the qualifying period of separation must continue right up to the time one of the spouses

[2]Brae Canlen, *No More Mrs. Nice Guy,* California Lawyer 51, 95 (Apr. 1994).

brings the divorce action on the ground of living apart. Hence, if the parties reconcile and resume cohabitation, even if only temporarily, the period of separation will not be considered consecutive. If, following cohabitation, the parties separate again, the requisite consecutiveness of the period of living apart will be calculated as of the time when the most recent cohabitation ended.

CONSENT Several states require that the period of separation be consensual or voluntary on the part of *both* spouses. Thus, if one spouse is drafted into the service or is hospitalized for an extended period of time, the separation is surely not by consent.

Sometimes the *cause* of the separation may be relevant to its voluntariness. Suppose, for example, that Bob deserts his wife Linda and they live apart for a period in excess of that required by the statute. Arguably, the parties did not separate voluntarily; they separated as a result of the *fault* of Bob. Some states will deny the divorce on the ground of living apart because the separation was not voluntary. Others will deny the divorce on this ground only when the plaintiff seeking the divorce is the "guilty" party. Most states, however, will grant the divorce to either party on the basis that voluntariness and marital fault are irrelevant so long as there was a living apart for the requisite period of time.

Interviewing and Investigation Checklist

Divorce on the Ground of Living Apart
Legal Interviewing Questions

1. How long have you lived apart?
2. On what date did you separate?
3. Since that date, what contact have you had with D (defendant)?
4. Have you ever asked D to live with you again? Has D ever asked you?
5. Have you had sexual intercourse with D since you separated?
6. Describe the circumstances of your separation with D.
7. When you separated, did you intend a permanent separation? If so, what indications of this did you give?
8. Did D intend a permanent separation? If so, what indications did D give?
9. What was the condition of your marriage at the time of separation?
10. Did you leave D? Did D leave you? Did you both leave at the same time by mutual agreement?
11. When the separation occurred, did either of you protest? Were you or D dissatisfied with the separation?
12. Since you separated, has either of you asked or suggested that the two of you get back together again? If so, what was the response of the other?
13. Has either of you obtained a judicial separation or a decree of separate maintenance? If so, when? Have you been living separate since that time? Have both of you abided by the terms of the judicial separation or of the maintenance decree?
14. Are you now living separate from D?
15. Since you separated, at what address have you lived? (Same question about D.)
16. Do you and D have a separation agreement? If so, when was it signed?

Possible Investigation Tasks

- Collect evidence that the parties have lived separate and apart (e.g., rent receipts from the apartments of the client and of D, copies of separate utility bills).
- Obtain witness statements from people aware of the separation.

ASSIGNMENT 7.2

Assume that a statute provides that one of the grounds for divorce is voluntary separation for a period of two consecutive years. This living-apart ground is the only one authorized in the state. Could a divorce be granted on the ground of living apart in the following three situations? (See General Instructions for the Legal-Analysis Assignment in Appendix A.)

a. Fred and Gail are married. On June 10, 1995, they agree to separate. Fred moves out. On May 15, 1997, when he learns that she is thinking about filing for divorce, he calls Gail and pleads with her to let him come back. She refuses. On July 25, 1997, she files for divorce on the ground of living apart.

b. Tom and Diane are married. On November 1, 1995, Diane deserts Tom. Tom did not want her to go. On March 13, 1996, Tom meets Karen. They begin seeing each other regularly. On June 14, 1996, Tom tells Karen that he hopes he never sees Diane again. On December 28, 1997, Tom files for divorce on the ground of living apart.

c. Bill and Susan are married. For over three years, they have been living separate lives due to marital difficulties, although they have continued to live in the same house. They have separate bedrooms and rarely have anything to do with each other. One of them files an action for divorce on the ground of living apart.

ASSIGNMENT 7.3

a. In your answer to Assignment 7.1, you made a list of the grounds for divorce in your state. If one of the grounds for divorce in your state is living apart, determine whether the divorce actions sought above in Assignment 7.2(a), (b), and (c) would be granted in your state. (See General Instructions for the Legal-Analysis Assignment in Appendix A.) Try to find opinions written by courts in your state that have interpreted the law governing the same facts as, or facts similar to, those involving Fred and Gail, Tom and Diane, and Bill and Susan. (See General Instructions for the State-Code Assignment and General Instructions for the Court-Opinion Assignment in Appendix A.)

b. Pick one of the three fact situations involved in Assignment 7.2. Draft a complaint for the party seeking the divorce. (See General Instructions for the Complaint-Drafting Assignment in Appendix A.)

As we shall see, many states allow parties to seek a *judicial separation,* which is a court authorization that the parties can live separate lives under specified terms (e.g., alimony, custody order). In some states, this judicial separation can be *converted* into a divorce after a designated period of time. Similarly, a decree of *separate maintenance* (spousal support) can often be converted into a divorce after this period of time.

Summary of Ground for Divorce: Living Apart

Definition: Living separate and apart for a designated, consecutive period of time. (In some states, the separation must be mutual and voluntary.)

Who can sue: In most states, either party. In a few states, the party at fault (i.e., the party who wrongfully caused the separation) cannot bring the divorce action.

Major defenses:

1. The parties have never separated.
2. The parties have not been separated for the period designated in the statute.
3. The parties reconciled and cohabitated before the statutory period was over (i.e., the separation was not consecutive).
4. The separation was not voluntary (this defense is available in only a few states).
5. The agreement to separate was obtained by fraud or duress.
6. The court lacks jurisdiction (discussed later in this chapter).
7. Res judicata (discussed later in this chapter).

Is this also a ground for annulment? No.

Is this also a ground for judicial separation? Yes, in many states.

Is this also a ground for separate maintenance? Yes, in many states.

Incompatibility

incompatibility
Such discord exists between the spouses that it is impossible for them to live together in a normal marital relationship.

Some states list **incompatibility** as a ground for divorce. Courts often say that "petty quarrels" and "minor bickerings" are not enough to grant the divorce on this ground. There must be such rift or discord that it is impossible to live together in a normal marital relationship. For most of the states that have this ground, fault is not an issue; the plaintiff does not have to show that the defendant was at fault in causing the incompatibility, and the defendant cannot defend the action by introducing evidence that the plaintiff committed marital wrongs. In a few states, however, the courts *are* concerned about the fault of the defendant and the plaintiff.

Suppose that the plaintiff alleges that the parties are incompatible. Can the defendant defend by disagreeing? Do *both* husband and wife have to feel that it is impossible to live together? Assuming that the plaintiff is able to establish that more than "petty quarrels" are involved, most courts will grant the divorce to the plaintiff even though the defendant insists that they can still work it out. Each state's statute, however, must be carefully examined to determine whether this is a proper interpretation.

The ground of incompatibility and the ground of cruelty appear to be rather similar. Even though cruelty is a fault ground, while incompatibility is not, the same or a similar kind of evidence is used to establish both grounds. The major difference in most states is that for cruelty, unlike incompatibility, the plaintiff must show that the acts of the defendant endangered the plaintiff's physical health.

Interviewing and Investigation Checklist

Divorce on the Ground of Incompatibility

(This checklist is also relevant to the breakdown ground, discussed next.)

Legal Interviewing Questions

1. Are you and D (defendant) now living together? If not, how long have you been separated?
2. Have you ever sued D or been sued by D for separate maintenance or for a judicial separation? If so, what was the result?
3. Describe your relationship with D at its worst.
4. How often did you argue? Were the arguments intense or bitter? Explain.
5. Did you or D ever call the police?
6. Did you or D receive medical attention as a result of your arguments or fights?
7. Did you or D have a drinking or drug problem?
8. How did D act toward the children? What is your relationship with them?
9. How would you describe your sexual relationship with D?
10. Do you feel that there is any possibility that you and D could reconcile your differences?
11. Do you think D feels that the two of you can solve the problems in the marriage?
12. Have you or D ever sought counseling or therapy of any kind?
13. Are you now interested in any such help in order to try to save the marriage? Do you feel it would work? How do you think D feels about this?

Possible Investigation Tasks

- Obtain copy of judicial separation judgment, separate maintenance decree, police reports, hospital records, if any.

ASSIGNMENT 7.4

a. Is incompatibility a ground for divorce in your state? If so, what is the exact language of this ground in the statute? (See General Instructions for the State-Code Assignment in Appendix A.)

b. One married partner says to the other, "I no longer love you." By definition, are they incompatible for purposes of this ground for divorce? (See General Instructions for the Legal-Analysis Assignment in Appendix A.)

Summary of Ground for Divorce: Incompatibility

Definition: The impossibility of two parties being able to continue to live together in a normal marital relationship because of severe conflicts or personality differences.

Who can sue: Either party in most states.

Major defenses:
1. The differences between the parties are only minor.
2. The defendant was not at fault in causing the incompatibility (this defense is *not* available in most states).
3. The court lacks jurisdiction.
4. Res judicata.

Is this also a ground for annulment? No.

Is this also a ground for judicial separation? Yes, in many states.

Is this also a ground for separate maintenance? Yes, in many states.

Irreconcilable Differences, Irremediable Breakdown

The newest and most popular version of the no-fault ground for divorce adopted in many states provides that the marriage can be dissolved for **irreconcilable differences** that have caused the *irremediable breakdown* of the marriage. The goal of the legislatures that have enacted this ground has been to focus on the central question of whether it makes any sense to continue the marriage. The statutes often have similar language and content. For example:

irreconcilable differences
Such discord exists between the spouses that the marriage has undergone an irremediable breakdown.

- Discord or conflict of personalities that destroys the legitimate ends of marriage and prevents any reasonable expectation of reconciliation
- Irretrievable breakdown of the marriage
- Breakdown of the marriage to such an extent that the legitimate objects of marriage have been destroyed and there remains no reasonable likelihood that the marriage can be preserved
- Substantial reasons for not continuing the marriage
- Insupportability, where discord or conflict of personalities destroys the legitimate ends of the marital relationship and prevents any reasonable expectation of reconciliation

This ground for divorce is obviously quite similar to the incompatibility ground just considered.

What happens if the defendant denies that the breakdown of the marriage is irremediable and feels that marriage counseling would help? In most states, this is simply one item of evidence that the court must consider in deciding whether remediation is possible. It is likely, however, that if one party absolutely refuses to participate in any reconciliation efforts, the court will conclude that the breakdown of the marriage is total even if the other party expresses a conciliatory attitude. Again, the language of individual statutes would have to be examined on this issue.

If the court concludes that there is a reasonable possibility of reconciliation, its options may be limited to delaying the divorce proceedings—granting a stay—for a limited number of days (e.g., thirty) to give the parties additional time to try to work out their difficulties.

Interviewing and Investigation Checklist

Divorce on the Ground of Irremediable Breakdown

Legal Interviewing Questions

1. How long have you been married to defendant (D)? How many children do you have?
2. How does D get along with the children?
3. How often do you and D communicate meaningfully?
4. Does D insult you, ridicule your religion, your political views, your family?
5. Does D do this in front of anyone? Who else knows that D does this? How do they know?
6. Have your friends, relatives, or associates told you that D has ridiculed or criticized you behind your back?
7. Do you think that D has ever tried to turn the children against you? If so, how do you know? What specifically have the children or others said or done to make you think so?
8. Does D drink or use drugs? If so, how much, how often, and how has it affected your marriage?
9. Has D ever hit you? If so, describe the circumstances. How often has D done this? Did the children see it? Has anyone else ever seen it?
10. Were there any other major events or scenes that were unpleasant for you? If so, describe them.
11. How would you describe your sexual relationship with D?
12. Has D ever accused you of infidelity?
13. Does D stay away from home often? Does D ever not come home at night?
14. Have you ever had to call the police because of what D did?
15. Has D ever sued you, or have you ever sued D?
16. How often do you fight or argue with D?
17. Is D now living with you? If not, explain the circumstances of the separation.
18. Has D's behavior affected your health in any way? Have you had to see a doctor?
19. Have you seen or have you considered seeing a psychiatrist or some other person in the field of mental health?
20. Have you ever experienced any behavior like this before?
21. How was your health before D started behaving this way?
22. Do you have any difficulty sleeping?
23. Do you have any difficulty doing your regular work because of D?
24. What is D's opinion of you as a spouse?
25. Do you think that you will ever be able to live in harmony with D? Explain why or why not.
26. Does D think the two of you will ever be able to get back together again? Explain why or why not.

Possible Investigation Tasks

- Obtain all of client's (C's) medical records, if any, from doctors, hospitals, etc., that have treated C as a result of what D has done.
- If the children are old and mature enough, interview them to see how they viewed D's relationship with C and, specifically, how D treated them.
- Obtain police records, if any, resulting from any fights or disturbances.

ASSIGNMENT 7.5

a. Is irreconcilable differences or irremediable breakdown a ground for divorce in your state? If so, what is the exact language of this ground in the statute? (See General Instructions for the State-Code Assignment in Appendix A.)

b. Dan and Helen were married in your state. Helen does not want to be married anymore. She loves Dan and enjoys being his wife, but simply wants to live alone indefinitely. Dan does not want a divorce. Can she obtain a divorce in your state? (See General Instructions for the State-Code Assignment and the Court-Opinion Assignment in Appendix A.)

Summary of Ground for Divorce: Irreconcilable Differences, Irremediable Breakdown

Definition: The breakdown of the marriage to the point where the conflicts between the spouses are beyond any reasonable hope of reconciliation.

Who can sue: Either party.

Major defenses:

1. The breakdown is remediable.

2. The court lacks jurisdiction.
3. Res judicata.

Is this also a ground for annulment? No.

Is this also a ground for judicial separation? Yes, in many states.

Is this also a ground for separate maintenance? Yes, in many states.

FAULT GROUNDS FOR DIVORCE

Although fault grounds are less often considered in today's courts, they remain in force. They include:

- Adultery
- Cruelty
- Desertion
- Others

Adultery

Adultery is voluntary sexual intercourse between a married person and someone to whom he or she is not married. This person is called the **co-respondent.** The intercourse is not voluntary, of course, if the defendant is raped or if the defendant is insane at the time. Since direct evidence of adultery is seldom available, circumstantial evidence must be relied upon. Specifically, the plaintiff must prove that the defendant had the *opportunity* and the *inclination* to commit adultery. **Corroboration** is often required to support the plaintiff's testimony.

adultery
Voluntary sexual intercourse between a married person and someone to whom he or she is not married.

co-respondent
The person who allegedly had voluntary sexual intercourse with a spouse charged with adultery.

corroboration
Additional evidence of a point beyond that offered by the person asserting the point.

Notes on Sexual Relations as a Crime and as a Tort

1. In most states, adultery (as defined above), fornication, and illicit cohabitation are crimes. **Fornication** is sexual intercourse between unmarried persons. **Illicit cohabitation** is fornication between two individuals who live together. It is rare, however, for the state to prosecute anyone for these crimes.
2. **Criminal conversation** is a tort brought against a third party who has had sexual intercourse (committed adultery) with the plaintiff's spouse (see chapter 17).

fornication
Sexual intercourse between unmarried persons.

illicit cohabitation
Fornication between two persons who live together.

criminal conversation
A tort committed by a person who has sexual relations with the plaintiff's spouse.

ASSIGNMENT 7.6

Is adultery, fornication, or illicit cohabitation a crime in your state? If so, what are their elements? (See General Instructions for the State-Code Assignment in Appendix A.)

Cruelty

In most marriage ceremonies, the parties take each other "for better or worse." This concept was viewed quite literally early in our history, particularly when the woman was the one claiming to have received too much of the "worse." It was expected that a good deal of fighting, nagging, and mutual abuse would occur within the institution of marriage. The concept of permitting the marriage to be dissolved because of "mere" cruelty or indignities was alien to our legal system for a long time. The change in the law came slowly. When **cruelty** was allowed as a ground for divorce, the statute would often require that it be "extreme" or "inhuman" before the divorce could be granted.

cruelty
The infliction of serious physical or mental suffering on another.

Furthermore, some states limited the ground to actual or threatened *physical* violence. Later, *mental anguish* came to be recognized as a form of cruelty and indignity, but there was often a requirement that the psychological cruelty result in some impairment of the plaintiff's health. Some courts will accept a minimal health impairment (e.g., a loss of sleep). Other courts require more serious impairment. Whether a court will accept a minimum impairment or will require something close to hospitalization, most courts have insisted on at least some physical effect from the cruelty. Only a few states will authorize a divorce on the ground of cruelty or indignity where the mental suffering does not produce physical symptoms.

Desertion

desertion
One spouse voluntarily but without justification leaves another (who does not consent to the departure) for an uninterrupted period of time with the intent not to return to resume cohabitation.

constructive desertion
The conduct of the spouse who stayed home justified the other spouse's departure; or the spouse who stayed home refuses a sincere offer of reconciliation from the other spouse who initially left without justification.

Desertion (also called *abandonment*) occurs when (1) one spouse voluntarily leaves another, (2) for an uninterrupted statutory period of time (e.g., two years), (3) with the intent not to return to resume cohabitation, and when (4) the separation occurred without the consent of the other spouse and (5) there was no justification or reasonable cause for the separation. **Constructive desertion** exists when the conduct of the spouse who stayed home justified the other spouse's departure or when the spouse who stayed home refuses a sincere offer of reconciliation (within the statutory period) from the other spouse who initially left without justification. In effect, the spouse who stayed home becomes the deserter! The spouse who left would be allowed to sue the other spouse for divorce on the ground of desertion.

Others

A number of closely related and sometimes overlapping grounds exist in some states. Here is a partial list (some of which are also grounds for annulment):

- Bigamy
- Impotence
- Nonage
- Fraud
- Duress
- Incest
- Imprisonment for three consecutive years
- Conviction of a serious crime
- Insanity; mental incapacity for three years
- Habitual drunkenness
- Drug addiction
- Nonsupport
- Unexplained absence
- Neglect of duty
- Obtaining an out-of-state divorce that is invalid
- Venereal disease or AIDS
- Unchastity
- Pregnancy by someone else at the time of the marriage
- Treatment injurious to health
- Deviant sexual conduct
- Any other cause deemed by the court sufficient, if satisfied that the parties can no longer live together

DEFENSES TO THE FAULT GROUNDS FOR DIVORCE

The basic defenses to the fault grounds for divorce may be defined as follows:

- **Collusion** Parties to a divorce committed fraud on the court by agreeing on a story to be told to the court by one or both parties even though both know the story is untrue.
- **Connivance** There was a willingness or a consent by one spouse that the marital wrong be done by the other spouse.
- **Condonation** There was an express or implied forgiveness by the innocent spouse of the marital fault committed by the other spouse.
- **Recrimination** The party seeking the divorce (the plaintiff) has also committed a serious marital wrong.
- **Provocation** The plaintiff incited the acts constituting the marital wrong by the other spouse.

These defenses are rarely used today, however, since the fault grounds are themselves seldom used.

Note on Religious Divorces

> When a man hath taken a wife, and married her, and it come to pass that she find no favor in his eyes, because he hath found some uncleanliness in her: then let him write her a bill of divorcement, and give it in her hand, and send her out of his house. *Deuteronomy* 24:1 (King James)

A Jewish couple that wants a religious divorce can go to a special court called a *Beth Din,* presided over by a rabbi who is aided by scribes and authorized witnesses. There the husband delivers a document called a **get,** or bill of divorcement, to his wife. Fault does not have to be shown. Both the husband and the wife must consent to the divorce, but it is the husband who gives the get and the wife who receives it. In New York, a religious divorce is allowed only if a secular (i.e., civil) divorce or annulment is under way or has already been granted. If a Jewish man has a civil divorce but not a religious divorce, he can still be remarried by a rabbi. But a Jewish woman without a get—even if divorced in a civil court—is called an *agunah,* or abandoned wife, and cannot be remarried by a rabbi.[3] Agunah Inc. is an organization of Orthodox Jewish women "chained to dead marriages" because their husbands refuse to grant them a Jewish divorce or get.[4] Some rabbis allege that increasing numbers of husbands try to withhold the get as a bargaining chip to obtain reduced support payments or better custody rights. If the husband disappears, the wife's plight is even more desperate. Rabbi Shlomo Klein, based in Israel, travels the world in search of such husbands in order to pressure them into signing the divorce.[5]

get
A bill of divorcement in a Jewish divorce.

A Muslim divorce is traditionally performed by a husband pronouncing the word **Talak** (I divorce you) three times. The wife need not be present, although one Islamic court recently ruled that sending her an e-mail announcing the Talak is not sufficient. In some countries, the process is public. In Pakistan, for example, the husband must notify the chairman of an arbitration council that he has pronounced the Talak. The council will then attempt to reconcile the parties. If this fails, the divorce becomes absolute ninety days after the husband pronounced the Talak. In Egypt, the husband must pronounce the Talak in the presence of two witnesses, who are usually officers of a special court.[6] If a wife wants a divorce, she must go to court and prove that her husband has mistreated her. Wives are not often successful. A recent change in Egyptian law allows a woman to obtain a divorce without proving mistreatment. She must, however, return her dowry and agree that there will be no alimony.

Talak
"I divorce you." Words spoken by a husband to his wife in a Muslim divorce.

---

[3]M. Markoff, *How Couples "Get" a Religious Divorce,* National Law Journal, Aug. 15, 1988, at 8.
[4]Rivka Haut, *Letter to the Editor,* N.Y. Times, Oct. 12, 1994, at A18.
[5]John Donnelly, *Rabbi Is an Unorthodox Manhunter,* San Diego Union Tribune, Oct. 28, 1995, at A-22.
[6]*The Religious Effect of Religious Divorces,* 37 Modern Law Review 611-13 (1974).

JUDICIAL SEPARATION

judicial separation
A declaration by a court that parties can live separate and apart even though they are still married to each other.

A **judicial separation** is a decree by a court that two people can live separately—from bed and board—while still remaining husband and wife. The decree also establishes the rights and obligations of the parties while they are separated. A judicial separation is also known as a:

- Legal separation
- Limited divorce
- Divorce a mensa et thoro
- Separation from bed and board
- Divorce from bed and board

Parties subject to a judicial separation are not free to remarry. The marriage relationship remains until it is dissolved by the death of one of the parties, by annulment, or by an absolute divorce, or a *divorce a vinculo matrimonii,* as the "full" divorce is called.

Perhaps the main function of a judicial separation is to secure support from the other spouse. In this sense, an action for judicial separation is very similar to an action for separate maintenance, to be discussed in the next section. For religious or family reasons, the parties may not wish to end the marriage by obtaining a divorce. A conservative Catholic, for example, may believe that it is morally wrong to obtain a divorce. Or a spouse may not be emotionally ready to accept the finality of a divorce. Yet the spouse may be in need of support for medical or other reasons. In such cases, judicial separation is an option in many states.

We should distinguish a judicial separation from a *separation agreement.* The latter is a private contract between a husband and wife. The agreement may or may not become part of (i.e., be incorporated and merged in) the judicial separation decree or the absolute divorce decree if one is later sought. Also, it is important that the words "separated" and "separation" be used carefully. Alone, these words mean simply a *physical* separation between the husband and wife. If, however, a court-sanctioned or court-ordered separation is involved, then the reference should be to a *legal* or *judicial* separation.

To obtain a judicial separation, *grounds* must be established in the same manner as grounds must be established to obtain an absolute divorce. In fact, the grounds for judicial separation are often very similar, if not identical, to the grounds for an absolute divorce (e.g., no-fault grounds such as incompatibility or irretrievable breakdown and fault grounds such as adultery or cruelty).

ASSIGNMENT 7.7

a. Does your state have an action for a judicial separation?
b. If so, what is the action called?
c. What is the citation of the statute authorizing this action?
d. What are the grounds in your state for a judicial separation?
e. Are there any grounds for judicial separation that are *not* grounds for divorce?
f. What defenses exist for an action for judicial separation?

(See General Instructions for the State-Code Assignment and General Instructions for the Court-Opinion Assignment in Appendix A.)

In a judicial separation decree, the court can award alimony and can issue custody and child support orders, all of which are enforceable through traditional execution and contempt remedies. If the parties have drafted a separation agreement, the court will consider incorporating and merging the terms of this agreement into the judicial separation decree. (For a further discussion of incorporation and merger into a court decree, see "Power to Modify" in chapter 8.) The separation agreement, of course, will reflect the wishes of the parties on the critical issues of alimony, property division, child custody, and child support.

After a judicial separation decree has been rendered, the fact that the parties reconcile and resume cohabitation does not mean that the decree becomes inoperative. It remains effective until a court declares otherwise. Hence a husband who is under an order to pay alimony to his wife pursuant to a judicial separation decree must continue to pay alimony even though the parties have subsequently reconciled and are living together again. To be relieved of this obligation, a petition must be made to the court to change the decree.

The major consequence of a judicial separation decree in many states is its *conversion* feature. The decree can be converted into a divorce—an absolute divorce. In effect, the existence of the judicial separation decree for a designated period of time can become a ground for a divorce.

ASSIGNMENT 7.8

Prepare a flowchart of the procedural steps that are necessary for a judicial separation in your state. (See General Instructions for the Flowchart Assignment in Appendix A.)

SEPARATE MAINTENANCE

separate maintenance
Court-ordered spousal support while the spouses are separated.

An action for **separate maintenance** (sometimes called an action for *support*) is a proceeding brought by a spouse to secure support. The action is usually filed by wives, but an increasing number of husbands are seeking spousal support by this route. Like the judicial separation decree, a separate maintenance decree does not alter the marital status of the parties; they remain married to each other while living separately. To the extent that both decrees resolve the problem of support, there is very little practical difference between them.

Since the main objective of the separate maintenance action is to reach the property (e.g., cash, land) of the defendant for purposes of support, the court must have personal jurisdiction over the defendant (see chapter 10). In general, property division is not resolved by the court in a decree of separate maintenance. If the parties cannot agree on how their marital property should be divided, they need to seek other avenues of relief such as a divorce or judicial separation.

The major ground for a separate maintenance decree is the refusal of one spouse to support the other without just cause. In addition, most states provide that all of the grounds for divorce will also be grounds for a separate maintenance award. Furthermore, in a divorce action, if the court refuses to grant either party a divorce, it usually can still enter an order for separate maintenance.

If the plaintiff refuses a good faith offer by the defendant to reconcile, the plaintiff becomes a wrongdoer, which in some states may justify the defendant in refusing to provide support. If the separate maintenance action is still pending, the plaintiff will lose it. If a separate maintenance decree has already been awarded, the defendant may be able to discontinue making payments under it.

The court determines the amount and form of a separate maintenance award in the same way that it makes the alimony determination in a divorce (see chapter 8). If needed, the court can also make child-support and child-custody decisions in the separate maintenance action.

Separate maintenance decrees can be enforced in the same manner as alimony awards in divorce decrees (e.g., contempt, execution [see chapters 8 and 10]).

ASSIGNMENT 7.9

a. Does your state have an action for separate maintenance or its equivalent? If so, on what grounds will the action be granted?
b. Prepare a flowchart of all the procedural steps required in a proceeding for separate maintenance or its equivalent.

(See General Instructions for the State-Code Assignment, for the Court-Opinion Assignment, and for the Flowchart Assignment in Appendix A).

INTRODUCTION TO DIVORCE PROCEDURE

As indicated earlier, over 90 percent of divorce cases are uncontested, since the parties are in agreement on the termination of the marital relationship, alimony, property division, child custody, and child support. In such cases, divorce procedure is often relatively simple. In some states, short-term marriages with no children and no significant property to divide can be dissolved under an expedited procedure, often involving few or no trips to the court other than to file court documents such as a divorce petition and a statement of assets and debts. If, however, the bitterness of the past has not subsided and agreements have not been reached, the technicalities of procedure can occupy center stage in costly and complicated proceedings.

The following terms are often used in connection with divorce procedure:

- **Migratory Divorce** A divorce obtained in a state to which one or both spouses traveled before returning to their original state. The husband and/or wife travels (migrates) to another state in order to obtain a divorce—usually because it is procedurally easier to divorce there. He or she establishes domicile in the state, obtains the divorce, and then returns to the "home" state, where at some point there will be an attempt to enforce the "foreign" divorce judgment. If the domicile was valid, this divorce is entitled to full faith and credit (i.e., it must be enforced) by the home state or any other state.
- **Foreign Divorce** A divorce decree obtained in a state other than the state where an attempt is made to enforce that decree. For example, a divorce decree that is granted in Iowa or in France would be a foreign divorce when an attempt is made to enforce it in New York.
- **"Quickie" Divorce** A migratory divorce obtained in what is often called a *divorce mill* state (i.e., a state where the procedural requirements for divorce are very slight in order to encourage out-of-state citizens to come in for a divorce and, while there, to spend some tourist dollars).
- **Collusive Divorce** A divorce that results from an agreement or "conspiracy" between a husband and wife to commit fraud on the court by falsely letting it appear that they qualify procedurally or substantively for a divorce.
- **Default Divorce** A divorce granted to the plaintiff because the defendant failed to appear to answer the complaint of the plaintiff. (In most states, the divorce is not granted automatically; the plaintiff must still establish grounds for the divorce.)
- **Divisible Divorce** A divorce judgment that is enforceable only in part. A divorce judgment can (1) dissolve the marriage, (2) award spousal support, (3) award child support, (4) divide marital property,

and (5) award child custody. As we will see, a court needs more than one kind of jurisdiction to accomplish all of these objectives. The court may try to accomplish all five, but only that part of the judgment for which it had proper jurisdiction is enforceable. In other words, the judgment is *divisible* into the parts for which the court had proper jurisdiction and the parts for which it did not. For example, assume that a court dissolves the marriage and awards child support. If the court had the right kind of jurisdiction to dissolve the marriage, but did not have the right kind of jurisdiction to award child support, then only the part of the judgment that dissolved the marriage is enforceable. Another state would not have to give full faith and credit to the child-support award but would have to give such credit to the dissolution itself.

- **Bifurcated Divorce** A case in which the dissolution of the marriage—the divorce itself—is tried separately from other issues in the marriage such as the division of property. Suppose, for example, that the parties have a bitter and complicated dispute over business assets and pension rights. Rather than waiting until these issues are resolved, the court may have the power to dissolve the marriage now in one proceeding and then resolve the economic issues in a separate proceeding. This allows the parties to get on with their lives (e.g., to marry someone else) much sooner than would otherwise be possible. A bifurcated divorce is similar to a divisible divorce in that both tell us that the divorce has separate parts. A divisible divorce means that not all parts are entitled to full faith and credit. A bifurcated divorce means that the parts are resolved in separate proceedings.
- **Bilateral Divorce** A divorce granted by a court when both parties were present before the court.
- **Ex Parte Divorce** A divorce granted by a court when only one party (the plaintiff) was present before the court. The court did not have personal jurisdiction over the defendant.
- **Dual Divorce** A divorce granted to both husband and wife. A court might award the divorce decree to one party only—to the plaintiff or to the defendant, if the latter has filed a counterclaim for divorce against the plaintiff. A dual divorce, however, is granted to *both* parties.
- **Uncontested Divorce** A divorce granted to parties who had no disagreements. The defendant does not appear at the divorce proceeding (see *default divorce* above) or appears without disputing any of the plaintiff's claims.
- **Contested Divorce** A divorce granted after the defendant appeared and disputed some or all of the claims made by the plaintiff at the divorce proceeding.
- **Divorce a Mensa et Thoro** A *judicial separation;* a *limited divorce.* The parties are not free to remarry, since they are still married after receiving this kind of "divorce."
- **Limited Divorce** A *judicial separation;* a *divorce a mensa et thoro.*
- **Divorce a Vinculo Matrimonii** An *absolute divorce.* The parties are no longer married. They are free to remarry.

One of our objectives in the remainder of this chapter is to have you prepare a flowchart of divorce procedure for your state. There will be a number of individual assignments to be answered mainly by reference to the state code and court rules of your state and, to a lesser degree, by reference to court opinions of your state. The answers to these assignments on pieces of the procedural picture will be used to complete divorce flowchart Assignment 7.29 on pages 222 and 223 of this chapter.

DOMICILE

The word *domicile* is often confused with the word *residence.* Many divorce statutes use the word *residence* even though the meaning intended is *domicile.* Except for such oddities, there are distinct differences between the two words:

- **Residence** The place where someone is living at a particular time. A person can have many residences (e.g., a home in the city, plus a beach house, plus an apartment in another state or country).
- **Domicile** The place (1) where someone has physically been (2) with the intention to make that place his or her permanent home, or with no intention to make any other place a permanent home. It is the place to which one would intend to return when away. With rare exceptions, a person can have only one domicile.

It is important to be able to determine where one's domicile is, particularly in our mobile society. Here are two specific reasons why:

- A court does not have divorce jurisdiction to dissolve a marriage unless one or both spouses are domiciled in the state where that court sits.
- Liability for inheritance taxes may depend upon the domicile of the decedent at the time of death.

emancipated
Legally independent of one's parent or legal guardian.

operation of law
A result occurs by operation of law when it happens because the law mandates the result, not because a party agrees to produce the result.

domicile by choice
A domicile chosen by a person with the capacity to choose. A person's *domicile of origin* is the place of his or her birth.

Generally, children cannot acquire a domicile of their own until they reach majority (e.g., eighteen years of age) or become otherwise **emancipated.** In effect, a child acquires a domicile by **operation of law** rather than by choice. The law operates to impose a domicile on the child regardless of what the child may want (if the child is old enough to form any opinion at all). The domicile of a child is the domicile of its parents. If they are separated, the child's domicile is that of the parent who has legal custody.

An emancipated child and an adult can pick any domicile they want **(domicile by choice)** so long as they are physically present in a place and have the intention to make it their permanent home at the time of their presence there. This intention can sometimes be very difficult to prove. Intention is a state of mind, and the only way to determine a state of mind is by interpreting external acts.

Verbal statements are not necessarily conclusive evidence of a person's state of mind. Suppose, for example, that Bill is domiciled in Ohio and, while visiting California, becomes violently ill. He knows that if he dies domiciled in California, his beneficiaries will pay a lower inheritance tax than if he had died domiciled in Ohio. While lying in a California sick bed just before he dies, Bill openly says, "I hereby declare that I intend California to be my permanent home." This statement in itself fails to prove that Bill was domiciled in California at the time of his death. Other evidence may show that he made the statement simply to give the appearance of changing his domicile and that, if he had regained his health, he would have returned to Ohio. If so, his domicile at death is Ohio in spite of his declaration, since he never actually intended to make California his permanent home.

The following chart seeks to identify some of the factors courts will consider in determining whether the requisite state of mind or intention existed:

Interviewing and Investigation Checklist

How to Determine When a Person Has Established a Domicile

Legal Interviewing Questions

1. When did you come to the state?
2. How often have you been in the state in the past? (Describe the details of your contacts with the state.)
3. Why did you come to the state?
4. Was your intention to stay there for a short period of time? A long period of time? Indefinitely? Forever?
5. While you were in the state, did you also have homes elsewhere in the state, and/or in another state, and/or in another country? If so, give details (e.g., addresses, how long you spent at each home, etc.).
6. Where do you consider your permanent home to be?
7. Have you ever changed your permanent home in the past? (If so, give details.)
8. Do you own a home in the state? Do you rent a home or apartment? How long have you had the home or apartment? Do you own any other land?
9. Where are you registered to vote?
10. Where is your job or business?
11. In what state is your car registered?
12. What state issued your driver's license?
13. In what states do you have bank accounts?
14. In what states do you have club memberships?
15. In what states are your pets licensed?
16. In what state do you attend church or synogogue?
17. Did you change your will to mention your new state?
18. When you register at hotels, what address do you give?
19. What is your address according to the credit card companies you use?
20. Where do your relatives live?

Possible Investigation Tasks

- Interview persons with whom the client may have discussed the move to the state (e.g., relatives, neighbors, business associates).
- Obtain copies of records that would indicate the extent of contact with the state (e.g., state tax returns, bank statements, land ownership papers, leases, hotel receipts, voting records, library cards).

In some states—Florida, for example—it is possible to make a formal declaration, or affidavit, of domicile that is filed with an official government body (Exhibit 7.2).

ASSIGNMENT 7.10

a. For purposes of obtaining a divorce, how is domicile determined in your state? (See General Instructions for the State-Code Assignment and General Instructions for the Court-Opinion Assignment in Appendix A.)

b. Using the index volume(s) of your state code, find as many references as you can to *domicile* (up to a maximum of five). Briefly state the context in which the word is used in each of the statutes to which you were referred by the index.

ASSIGNMENT 7.11

Try to find an individual (e.g., relative, friend, classmate) who now lives, or who in the past lived, in more than one state at the same time (e.g., for business purposes, for school purposes, for vacation purposes, etc.). Interview this individual with the objective of determining where his or her domicile is (or was). List all the facts that would tend to show that the person's domicile was in one state, and then list all the facts that would tend to show that his or her domicile was in another state. (See General Instructions for the Interview Assignment in Appendix A.)

ASSIGNMENT 7.12

In each of the following situations, determine in what state the person was domiciled at the time of death. (See General Instructions for the Legal-Analysis Assignment in Appendix A.)

a. While living in Illinois, Fred hears about a high-paying job in Alaska. He decides to move to Alaska, since he no longer wants to live in Illinois. He sells everything he owns in Illinois and rents an apartment in Alaska. There he discovers jobs are not easy to find. He decides to leave if he cannot find a job in three months. If this happens, he arranges to move in with his sister in New Mexico. Before the three months are over, Fred dies jobless in Alaska.

b. Gloria lives in New York because she attends New York University. Her husband lives in Montana. Gloria plans to rejoin her husband in Montana when she finishes school in six months. Two months before graduation, her husband decides to move to Oregon. Gloria is opposed to the move and tells him that she will not rejoin him if he does not return to Montana. Her husband refuses to move back to Montana. One month before graduation, Gloria dies in New York.

Exhibit 7.2 Declaration of Domicile

DECLARATION OF DOMICILE

TO THE STATE OF FLORIDA AND COUNTY OF ________________ :

This is my Declaration of Domicile in the State of Florida that I am filing this day in accordance, and in conformity with Section 222.17, Florida Statutes.

I, ____, was formerly a legal resident of

________________________ (City) ________________________ (State), and I resided at ________________________________ (Street and Number)

____,

however, I have changed my domicile to and am and have been a bona fide resident of the State of Florida since the __________ day of ________, 19 __________________ . I now reside at __________ ____________________,
________________ County, Florida, and this statement is to be taken as my declaration of actual legal residence and permanent domicile in this State and County to the exclusion of all others, and I will comply with all requirements of legal residents of Florida.

I understand that as a legal resident of Florida: I am subject to intangible taxes; I must purchase Florida license plates for motor vehicles, if any, owned by me and/or my spouse; I must vote in the precinct of my legal domicile (if I vote), and that my estate will be probated in the Florida Courts.

I was born in the U.S.A.: Yes ______ No ______ Place of Birth: ________________________

Naturalized citizen—Where: ________________ — Date ________________ No. ________________

Permanent Visa: Yes ______ No ______ Date ________________ No. ________________

Sworn and subscribed before me this ______ day of

________________________________, A.D. 20 ___ .

PAUL F. HARTSFIELD, Clerk of Circuit Court

By ________________________________
Deputy Clerk

____
Signature

____
(Mailing Address)

(To be executed and filed with Clerk of Circuit Court)

Penalty for perjury—up to 20 years in state prison—(Section 837.01, Florida Statutes)

JURISDICTION

Before discussing the nature of jurisdiction, some definitions that apply to this area of the law must be examined:

- **Adversarial Hearing** Both the plaintiff and the defendant appear at the hearing or other court proceeding to contest all the issues.
- **Ex Parte Hearing** Only one party appears at the hearing or other court proceeding; the defendant is not present.
- **Direct Attack vs. Collateral Attack** Two kinds of challenges or attacks can be made on a judgment: direct and collateral. The difference depends on when the attack is made and on what kind of court proceeding the challenge is raised in. Assume, for example, that Mary goes to a state trial court to sue Ed for child support. He does not appear in the action. Mary wins a judgment. But Ed refuses to pay any child support under the judgment. He believes the trial court lacked personal jurisdiction to render its child-support judgment against him. If he raises this challenge to the judgment in a normal appeal immediately after the trial court rendered its judgment, he would be bringing a *direct attack* against the judgment. Suppose, however, that the time for bringing a normal appeal has passed. In the same state or in a different state, Mary brings a separate suit against Ed to enforce the child-support judgment. In this new suit, Ed says the child-support judgment is invalid because the court that rendered it lacked personal jurisdiction over him. This is a *collateral attack* against the judgment. In general, an attack against a judgment is collateral when it is brought in a court proceeding that is outside the normal appeal process.
- **Res Judicata** When a judgment on its merits has been rendered, the parties cannot relitigate the same dispute (i.e., the same cause of action); the parties have already had their day in court.
- **Estop or Estoppel** Stop or prevent.
- **Equitable Estoppel** Equitable estoppel means that a party will be prevented from doing something because it would be unfair to allow him or her to do it. A party will be *equitably estopped* from attacking the validity of a judgment—even a clearly invalid judgment—when:
  - that party obtained the judgment or participated in obtaining it, *or*
  - that party relied on the judgment by accepting benefits based on it, *or*
  - that party caused another person to rely on the judgment to the detriment of the other person.
- **Foreign** Another state or country. A foreign divorce decree, for example, is one rendered by a state other than the state where one of the parties is now seeking to enforce the decree.
- **Forum State** The state in which the parties are now litigating a case.
- **Full Faith and Credit** Under Article IV of the U.S. Constitution, a valid public act of one state must be recognized and enforced by other states. Hence a judgment of divorce granted by a state with proper jurisdiction must be recognized by every other state (i.e., it must be given full faith and credit by other states).
- **Service of Process** Providing a formal notice to a defendant that orders him or her to appear in court to answer allegations in claims made by a plaintiff. The notice must be delivered in a manner prescribed by law.
- **Substituted Service** Service of process other than by handing the process documents to the defendant in person (e.g., service by mail, service by publication in a local newspaper).

jurisdiction
(1) The geographic area over which a particular court has authority. (2) The power of a court to act.

The word **jurisdiction** has two main meanings: a *geographic* meaning and a *power* meaning. A specific geographic area of the country is referred to as the jurisdiction. A Nevada state court, for example, will often refer to its entire state as "this jurisdiction." The more significant definition of the word, which we will examine below, relates to power—the power of a court to resolve a particular controversy. If a citizen of Maine wrote to a California court and asked for a divorce through the mail, the California court would be without jurisdiction (without power) to enter a divorce decree if the husband and wife never had any contact with that state. As we will see in a moment, there are three kinds or categories of power jurisdiction: subject matter jurisdiction, in rem jurisdiction, and personal jurisdiction.

Our study of jurisdiction will focus on the different attacks or challenges a party will often try to assert against the jurisdiction of a divorce court. In particular, we will examine the following themes:

- Kinds of jurisdiction
- What part of the divorce decree is being attacked
- Who is attacking the divorce decree
- In what court the divorce decree is being attacked
- How jurisdiction is acquired

To a very large extent, the success of a jurisdictional attack on a divorce decree depends on the kind of jurisdiction involved, the part of the divorce decree being attacked, and the identity of the person bringing the attack. We now turn to a discussion of these critical factors.

Kinds of Jurisdiction

domestic relations exception
Federal courts do not have subject matter jurisdiction over divorce, alimony, or child-custody cases even if there is diversity of citizenship among the parties.

res
A thing, object, or status.

1. **Subject matter jurisdiction:** The power of the court to hear cases of this kind. A criminal law court would not have subject matter jurisdiction to hear a divorce case. Similarly, a divorce decree rendered by a court without subject matter jurisdiction over divorces is void. In some states, divorce and other family law cases are heard in a special division or section of the trial courts. Other states have established separate family law or domestic relations courts that have subject matter jurisdiction in this area of the law.

   The vast majority of family law cases are heard in state courts. In the main, federal courts do not have subject matter jurisdiction over such cases. When parties are citizens of different states, the federal courts have diversity jurisdiction, but under the **domestic relations exception,** federal courts will not hear divorce, alimony, or child-custody cases even if the parties are from different states. Federal courts will, however, hear some family tort cases (e.g., one spouse sues another for fraud) and some child-support enforcement cases (a father is prosecuted for failure to pay child support) when the parties involved are from different states. Such cases, however, are relatively rare.
2. **In rem jurisdiction:** The power of the court to make a decision affecting the **res,** which is a thing, object, or status. In divorce actions, the *res* is the marriage status, which is "located" in any state where one or both of the spouses are domiciled. A state with in rem jurisdiction because of this domicile has the power to terminate the marriage. (Another kind of jurisdiction is *personal* jurisdiction over the defendant. If a court with in rem jurisdiction does not have personal jurisdiction, it will not have the power to grant alimony, child support, or a property division; it can only dissolve the marriage.) A court lacks in rem jurisdiction if it renders a divorce judgment when neither party was domiciled in that state. Such a judgment is not entitled to full faith and credit (see discussion below); therefore, another state is not required to enforce the divorce judgment.

3. **Personal jurisdiction** (also called *in personam jurisdiction*): The power of the court over the person of the defendant. If a court has personal jurisdiction over a defendant, it can order him or her to pay alimony and child support and can divide the marital property. If a court makes such an order without personal jurisdiction, the order can be attacked on jurisdictional grounds; it is not entitled to full faith and credit.

Exhibit 7.3 summarizes the kinds of divorce jurisdiction.

Exhibit 7.3 Kinds of Divorce Jurisdiction

KIND OF JURISDICTION A COURT CAN HAVE	HOW THIS KIND OF JURISDICTION IS ACQUIRED	POWER THIS KIND OF JURISDICTION GIVES THE COURT
Subject matter jurisdiction	A state statute or constitutional provision gives the court the power to hear cases involving the subject matter of divorce.	The court can hear divorce cases.
In rem jurisdiction	One or both of the spouses are domiciled in the state.	The court can dissolve the marriage.
Personal jurisdiction	Process is personally delivered to the defendant—service of process. (Alternatives may include substituted service, the long-arm statute, etc.)	The court can order the defendant to comply with alimony, child-support, or property division obligations.

(The special problems involved in acquiring jurisdiction to render child-custody decisions are discussed in chapter 9.)

Part of Divorce Decree Being Attacked

Here are the parts of a divorce judgment that could be attacked and a review of the kinds of jurisdiction needed for each part:

1. *Dissolution of the marriage.* For a court to have jurisdiction to dissolve a marriage, one or both of the spouses must be domiciled in the state. When this is so, the court has in rem jurisdiction, which is all that is needed to dissolve the marriage. Personal jurisdiction of both parties is not needed.
2. *Alimony, child support, and property division.* Alimony, child support, and property division cannot be ordered by the court unless it has personal jurisdiction over the defendant. Hence it is possible for the court to have jurisdiction to dissolve the marriage (because of domicile) but not have jurisdiction to make alimony, child-support, and property division awards (because the plaintiff was not able to take the necessary steps, such as service of process, to give the court personal jurisdiction over the defendant). This is the concept of the *divisible divorce*—a divorce that is effective for some purposes but not for others.
3. *Child custody.* On the jurisdictional requirements to make a child-custody award, see chapter 9.

Person Attacking Divorce Decree

1. *The person who obtained the divorce decree.* A person should not be allowed to attack a divorce decree on jurisdictional grounds if that person was the plaintiff in the action that resulted in the decree. This person will be estopped in any action to deny the validity of the divorce decree. The same result will occur if this person helped his or her spouse obtain the divorce decree or received benefits because of the decree. The

effect of this rule, sometimes known as *equitable estoppel,* is to prevent a person from attacking a divorce decree even though the decree is clearly invalid. Note, however, that a few courts do not follow this rule and *will* allow a person to attack a divorce decree he or she participated in obtaining.

2. *The person against whom the divorce decree was obtained.* If the person now attacking the divorce decree on jurisdictional grounds was the defendant in the action that led to the divorce decree *and made a personal appearance* in that divorce action, he or she will not be allowed to attack the decree. He or she should have raised the jurisdictional attack in the original divorce action.

   If the original divorce decree was obtained *ex parte* (i.e., no appearance by the defendant), the defendant *will* be able to attack the decree on jurisdictional grounds, such as by asserting that the plaintiff was not domiciled in the state that granted the divorce or that the court granting the divorce decree had no subject matter jurisdiction.

   If the person against whom the divorce decree was obtained has accepted the benefits of the decree (e.g., alimony payments), many courts will estop that person from now attacking the decree on jurisdictional grounds.

   If the person against whom the divorce was obtained has remarried, he or she will be estopped from claiming that the second marriage is invalid because of jurisdictional defects in the divorce decree on the first marriage. Some states, however, will allow the jurisdictional attack (e.g., no domicile) on the divorce if the person making the attack did not know about the jurisdictional defect at the time.

3. *A person who was not a party to the divorce action.* A second spouse who was not a party to the prior divorce action cannot challenge the validity of that divorce on jurisdictional grounds. This second spouse relied on the validity of the divorce when he or she entered the marriage and should not now be allowed to upset the validity of that marriage by challenging the validity of the divorce.

   A child of the parties of the prior divorce action cannot challenge the validity of the divorce decree on jurisdictional grounds if that child's parent would have been estopped from bringing the challenge.

Court in Which Divorce Decree Is Being Attacked

Many of the disputes in this area arise when a divorce decree is obtained in one state and brought to another state for enforcement. Is the *forum state* (where enforcement of the divorce decree is being sought) required to give *full faith and credit* to the foreign divorce? The answer may depend on which of the three aspects of the divorce decree a party is attempting to enforce:

1. *The dissolution of the marriage.* If either the plaintiff or the defendant was domiciled in the state where the divorce was granted, every other state must give full faith and credit to the part of the divorce decree that dissolved the marriage. The forum state must decide for itself whether there was a valid domicile in the foreign state. The person attacking the foreign divorce decree has the burden of proving the jurisdictional defect, namely, the absence of domicile in the foreign state.
2. *Alimony, child-support, and property division awards.* If the state where the divorce was obtained did not have personal jurisdiction over the defendant, then that state's award of alimony, child support, and property division is *not* entitled to full faith and credit in another state. Again, we see the divisible-divorce concept: only part of the divorce decree is recognized in another state if the court had jurisdiction to dissolve the

marriage because of domicile but had no jurisdiction to grant alimony, child support, and a property division due to the absence of personal jurisdiction over the defendant. (In chapter 10, we will examine some of the special rules enacted by Congress and the states to acquire personal jurisdiction over a parent who has not paid child support.)

3. *Custody award.* See chapter 9 for an overview of the requirements for jurisdiction to grant or modify a child-custody decree.

How Jurisdiction Is Acquired

1. *Subject matter jurisdiction.* The only way a court can acquire subject matter jurisdiction over a divorce is by a special statute or constitutional provision giving the court the power to hear this kind of case. A divorce decree rendered by a court without subject matter jurisdiction over divorces is void.
2. *In rem jurisdiction.* All that is needed for a court to acquire in rem jurisdiction is the domicile of at least one of the spouses in the state. The case can proceed so long as reasonable notice of the action is given to the defendant. If the defendant is not domiciled in the state, notice can be by substituted service (e.g., mail, publication of notice in a newspaper).
3. *Personal jurisdiction.* A court can acquire personal jurisdiction over the defendant in several ways:

   a. Personal service of process on the defendant in the state. This is effective whether or not the defendant is domiciled in the state.[7]

   b. Consent. The defendant can always consent to personal jurisdiction simply by appearing in the action and defending the entire case. But if the defendant is a nondomiciliary, he or she can appear solely to contest the jurisdictional issue without being subjected to full personal jurisdiction. *Any* appearance by a *domiciliary,* however, will confer full personal jurisdiction on the court.

   c. Substituted service (e.g., mail, publication in a newspaper). Substituted service of process will confer personal jurisdiction if the defendant is domiciled in the state. For nondomiciliaries, see the following discussion on the long-arm statute.

   d. Long-arm statute. This is used to acquire personal jurisdiction over a defendant who is not domiciled in the state. This defendant must have sufficient minimum contacts with the state so that it is reasonable and fair to require the defendant to appear and be subjected to full personal jurisdiction in the state. What constitutes sufficient minimum contacts to meet this standard has not been answered clearly by the courts. Here are some of the factors that a court will consider, no one of which is necessarily conclusive: the defendant was domiciled in the state at one time before he or she left, the defendant cohabitated with his or her spouse in the state before the defendant left the state, the defendant visits the state, the defendant arranges for schooling for his or her children in the state, etc. In addition to these minimum contacts, the defendant must be given reasonable notice of the action. The Uniform Interstate Family Support

---

[7]The United States Supreme Court has said: "Among the most firmly established principles of personal jurisdiction in American tradition is that the courts of a State have jurisdiction over nonresidents who are physically present in the State. The view developed early that each State had the power to hale before its courts any individual who could be found within its borders, and that once having acquired jurisdiction over such a person by properly serving him with process, the State could retain jurisdiction to enter judgment against him, no matter how fleeting his visit." *Burnham v. Superior Court of California,* 495 U.S. 604, 610, 110 S. Ct. 2105, 2110, 109 L. Ed. 2d 631 (1990).

Act (UIFSA) expands the scope of the long-arm statute in order to facilitate enforcement of interstate child-support and spousal-support orders. UIFSA will be discussed in chapter 10.

Jurisdictional Analysis: Examples

Here are some examples of how divorce jurisdiction is determined:

1. *Tom and Mary are married. Both are domiciled in Massachusetts. Mary moves to Ohio, which is now her state of domicile. She obtains a divorce decree from an Ohio state court. The decree awards Mary $500 a month alimony. Tom was notified of the action by mail but did not appear. He has had no contacts with Ohio. Mary travels to Massachusetts and brings an action against Tom to enforce the alimony award of the Ohio court.*

Jurisdictional Analysis

- The Ohio court had jurisdiction to dissolve the marriage because of Mary's domicile in Ohio. This part of the divorce decree is entitled to full faith and credit in Massachusetts (i.e., Massachusetts *must* recognize this aspect of the Ohio divorce decree if Massachusetts determines that Mary was in fact domiciled in Ohio at the time of the divorce decree).
- The Ohio court did not have jurisdiction to render an alimony award, since it did not have personal jurisdiction over Tom. This part of the divorce decree is not entitled to full faith and credit in Massachusetts (i.e., the Massachusetts court does not have to enforce the Ohio alimony award).
- Suppose that Tom had an out-of-state divorce in a state where he alone was domiciled. Suppose further that the divorce decree provided that Mary was *not* entitled to alimony. If this court did not have personal jurisdiction over Mary, she would not be bound by the no-alimony decision even though she would be bound by the decision dissolving the marriage.

2. *Bill and Pat are married in New Jersey. Bill brings a successful divorce action against Pat in a New Jersey state court. Bill is awarded the divorce. Pat was not served with process or notified in any way of this divorce action. Bill then marries Linda. Linda and Bill begin having marital difficulties. They separate. Linda brings a support action (separate-maintenance action) against Bill. Bill's defense is that he is not married to Linda because his divorce with Pat was invalid due to the fact that Pat had no notice of the divorce action.*

Jurisdictional Analysis

- Bill is raising a collateral attack against the divorce decree. He is attacking the jurisdiction of the court to award the divorce because Pat had no notice of the divorce action.
- Bill is the person who obtained the divorce decree. In most states, he will be estopped from attacking the decree on jurisdictional grounds. Whether or not the court in fact had jurisdiction to render the divorce decree, Bill will not be allowed to challenge it. He relied on the divorce and took the benefits of the divorce when he married Linda. He should not be allowed to attack the very thing he helped accomplish.

3. *Joe and Helen are married in Texas. Helen goes to New Mexico and obtains a divorce decree against Joe. Joe knows about the action but does not appear. Helen has never been domiciled in New Mexico.*

Joe marries Paulene. When Helen dies, Joe claims part of her estate. His position is that he is her surviving husband because the New Mexico court had no jurisdiction to divorce them, since neither was ever domiciled there.

Jurisdictional Analysis

- Joe was not the party who sought the New Mexico divorce. The divorce proceeding was ex parte. Normally, he would be allowed to attack the divorce decree on the ground that no one was domiciled in New Mexico at the time of the divorce.
- But Joe relied upon the divorce and accepted its benefits by marrying Paulene. It would be inconsistent to allow him to change his mind now, and it could be unfair to Paulene. Hence Joe will be estopped from attacking the divorce on jurisdictional grounds.

ASSIGNMENT 7.13

John and Sandra were married in Florida but live in Georgia. Sandra returns to Florida with their two children. John never goes back to Florida. He often calls his children on the phone, and they come to visit him pursuant to arrangements he makes with Sandra. Once he asked his mother to go to Florida to look after the children while Sandra was sick. Sandra files for a divorce in Florida. John does not appear, although he is given notice of the action. (Florida has a long-arm statute.) Sandra is granted the divorce and $840 as her share of the proceeds from the sale of a used car purchased during the marriage and stored in John's garage. No alimony or child support is awarded. She later travels to Georgia and asks a Georgia court to enforce the property division order on the car, which John has been ignoring. What result? (See General Instructions for the Legal-Analysis Assignment in Appendix A.) What would the result be in your state? Check your state code and court opinions. (See General Instructions for the State-Code Assignment and General Instructions for the Court-Opinion Assignment in Appendix A.)

The remaining assignments in this section focus on the mechanics of jurisdiction—specifically, what courts have subject matter jurisdiction over divorce and what the residency requirements and service of process rules are for your state.

ASSIGNMENT 7.14

Identify each court in your state with subject matter jurisdiction over divorces. Write your answer in step 1 of the Divorce Litigation Flowchart in Assignment 7.29 at the end of the chapter. (See General Instructions for the State-Code Assignment in Appendix A.)

Venue

Venue refers to the place of the trial. Within a state, it may be that the divorce action could be brought in a number of different counties or districts because each one of them has or could acquire the necessary jurisdiction. The *choice of venue* is the choice of one county or district among several where the trial could be held. The state's statutory code will specify the requirements for the selection of venue. The requirements often relate to the residence (usually meaning domicile) of the plaintiff or defendant. For example, the statute might specify that a divorce action should be filed in the county in which the plaintiff has been a resident (meaning domiciliary) for three months preceding the commencement of the action.

venue
The place of the trial. The county, district, or state where the trial is held.

ASSIGNMENT 7.15

a. In a divorce action in your state, how is venue determined? Write your answer in step 2 at the end of the chapter. (See General Instructions for the State-Code Assignment in Appendix A.)
b. If your state code uses the word *residence* in its divorce statute without defining it, find a court opinion in your state that does define it. (See General Instructions for the Court-Opinion Assignment in Appendix A.)

ASSIGNMENT 7.16

Tara, a member of the armed services, is temporarily stationed in your state. She and her husband, George, are domiciled in another state. Under what circumstances, if any, can Tara obtain a divorce in your state? Assume that George has never been in your state. (See General Instructions for the State-Code Assignment in Appendix A.)

PRETRIAL MATTERS

Pleadings

pleadings
The formal documents that contain allegations and responses of parties in litigation.

complaint
The pleading filed by one party against another that states a grievance (called a cause of action) and thereby commences a lawsuit on that grievance.

summons
The formal notice from the court that informs the defendant a lawsuit has been filed and that orders the defendant to appear and answer the allegations of the plaintiff.

in forma pauperis
As a poor person (allowing the waiver of court fees).

answer
The pleading filed in response to a complaint.

counterclaim
A claim made by a defendant against a plaintiff.

Pleadings are the formal documents that contain allegations and responses of parties in litigation. In a divorce case, the main pleading is the **complaint,** also called the *petition.* The complaint states the nature of the action, the basis of the court's jurisdiction, the alleged grounds for the divorce, the relief sought, etc. (See Exhibit 7.4 for a sample divorce complaint.) There are a number of assignments in this book that ask you to draft a complaint. The general instructions for this assignment are found in Appendix A. Review these instructions now. They provide a good overview of the law governing complaints.

The lawsuit begins when the plaintiff files the complaint with the court (along with the appropriate filing fee) and completes service of process on the defendant. The main method of completing service of process is by handing the complaint and the **summons** to the defendant in person. In some cases, substituted service, such as publication in a newspaper, is allowed. (See Exhibit 7.5 for a sample summons.) The summons is the formal notice from the court that informs the defendant a lawsuit has been filed and that orders the defendant to appear and answer the allegations of the plaintiff. If the plaintiff is poor, he or she can apply to the court for a waiver of fees in order to proceed **in forma pauperis** (as a poor person).

The response of the defendant is the **answer,** which is the pleading filed by the defendant that responds to the complaint filed by the plaintiff. In most states, the defendant can raise his or her own claim (called a **counterclaim**) against the plaintiff in the answer. Hence, when the plaintiff asks for a divorce in the complaint, the defendant's answer can ask also for a divorce in a counterclaim.

ASSIGNMENT 7.17

Answer the following questions by examining your statutory code. Your answers will also become part of the Divorce Litigation Flowchart at the end of this chapter. (See General Instructions for the State-Code Assignment in Appendix A.)

a. What must a complaint for divorce contain? Write your response in step 3 at the end of the chapter.
b. Must the complaint be subscribed and/or verified? If so, by whom? Write your response in step 4 at the end of the chapter.

Exhibit 7.4 Basic Structure of a Divorce Complaint

Caption

STATE OF ___________
COUNTY OF ___________
FAMILY COURT BRANCH

Mary Smith, Plaintiff
v. Civil Action No. ___________
Fred Smith, Defendant

Commencement

COMPLAINT FOR ABSOLUTE DIVORCE

The plaintiff, through her attorney, alleges:

(1) The jurisdiction of this court is based upon section _______ , title _______ of the State Code (1978).

(2) The plaintiff is fifty years old.

(3) The plaintiff is a resident of the State of ___________ , County of ___________ . She has resided here for five years immediately preceding the filing of this complaint.

(4) The parties were married on March 13, 1983, in the State of ___________ , County of _______ .

Body

(5) There are no children born of this marriage.

(6) The plaintiff and defendant lived and cohabitated together from the date of their marriage until February 2, 1999, at which time they both agreed to separate because of mutual incompatibility. This separation has continued voluntarily and without cohabitation for more than two years until the present time.

(7) Since the separation, the plaintiff has resided at ___________________________________ , and the defendant has resided at ___________________________________ .

(8) There is no reasonable likelihood of reconciliation.

Prayer for Relief

WHEREFORE, the plaintiff PRAYS:

(1) For an absolute divorce.
(2) For alimony and a division of property.
(3) For restoration of her maiden name.
(4) For reasonable attorney's fees and costs.
(5) For such other relief as this Court may deem just and proper.

___________________________ ___________________________
Linda Stout Mary Smith, Plaintiff
Attorney for Plaintiff
234 Main St.
___________ , ___________ 07237

Verification

STATE of ___________
COUNTY of ___________

Mary Smith, being first duly sworn on oath according to law, deposes and says that she has read the foregoing complaint by her subscribed and that the matters stated therein are true to the best of her knowledge, information, and belief.

____
Mary Smith

Subscribed and sworn to before me on this _________ day of ___________________ , 20 ___

____
Notary Public

My commission expires ___________

c. Where is the complaint served and filed? Write your response in step 5 at the end of the chapter.

d. What is the fee for filing a divorce complaint in your state? Write your answer in step 6 at the end of the chapter.

e. What happens if a party seeking a divorce cannot afford the filing fee or any court costs? Can he or she proceed as a poor person and thereby have these fees and costs waived?

f. Who may serve process in your state? Write your answer in step 7 at the end of the chapter.

g. How is personal service made on an individual? Write your answer in step 8 at the end of the chapter.

h. In a divorce action, when can substituted service be used?

Exhibit 7.5 Divorce Summons

STATE OF MAINE
CUMBERLAND COUNTY

SUPERIOR COURT
Civil Action, Docket Number ______

A.B., Plaintiff
of Bath,
Sagadahoc County,
v.
C.D., Defendant
of Portland,
Cumberland County,

To the Defendant ________________ :

The Plaintiff ______________ has begun a divorce action against you in this Court. If you wish to oppose the divorce, you or your attorney must prepare and file a written Answer to the attached Complaint within 20 days from the day this summons was served upon you. You or your attorney must file your Answer by delivering it in person or by mail to the office of the Clerk of the Superior Court, Cumberland County Courthouse, 142 Federal Street, Portland, Maine. On or before the day you file your Answer, you or your attorney must mail a copy of your Answer to the Plaintiff's attorney, whose name and address appear below.

IMPORTANT WARNING: IF YOU FAIL TO FILE AN ANSWER WITHIN THE TIME STATED ABOVE, OR IF, AFTER YOU FILE YOUR ANSWER, YOU FAIL TO APPEAR AT ANY TIME THE COURT NOTIFIES YOU TO DO SO, A JUDGMENT MAY IN YOUR ABSENCE BE ENTERED AGAINST YOU FOR THE DIVORCE. IF AN ORDER FOR PAYMENT OF MONEY IS ENTERED AGAINST YOU, YOUR EMPLOYER MAY BE ORDERED TO PAY PART OF YOUR WAGES TO THE PLAINTIFF OR YOUR PERSONAL PROPERTY, INCLUDING BANK ACCOUNTS, AND YOUR REAL ESTATE MAY BE TAKEN TO SATISFY THE JUDGMENT. IF YOU INTEND TO OPPOSE THE DIVORCE, DO NOT FAIL TO ANSWER WITHIN THE REQUIRED TIME.

If you believe you have a defense to the Plaintiff's Complaint or if you believe you have a claim of your own against the Plaintiff, you should talk to a lawyer.

[Seal of the Court]

Dated ______________________________

____
Clerk of Said Superior Court

Served on ______________________________
Date

____
Name of Plaintiff's Attorney

____
Address

____
Deputy Sheriff

____
Telephone

i. How is substituted service made? By publication of a notice? By posting a notice? By other methods? Summarize your answer in step 9 at the end of the chapter.

j. How is proof of service made? Write your answer in step 10 at the end of the chapter.

k. Does your state have a long-arm statute for divorce actions? If so, when can it be used?

l. How many days does the defendant have to answer the complaint? Write your response in step 11 at the end of the chapter.

m. Must the answer be subscribed and/or verified? If so, by whom? Write your response in step 12 at the end of the chapter.

n. Must the defendant specifically plead all available *affirmative defenses* (i.e., those defenses that raise facts not stated in the complaint) in the answer? Write your response in step 13 at the end of the chapter.

o. Where and how is the answer served and filed? Write your response in step 14 at the end of the chapter.

p. How many days does the plaintiff have to reply to any counterclaims of the defendant? Write your response in step 15 at the end of the chapter.

q. Where and how is the reply of the plaintiff served and filed? Write your response in step 16 at the end of the chapter.

In some states, it is possible to obtain a divorce primarily through the mail without going through elaborate court procedures. Such a divorce is often referred to as a *summary dissolution* (see Exhibit 7.6) or a *simplified dissolution*. The requirements for taking advantage of this option are quite strict. In California, for example, the couple must be childless, be married for five years or less, have no interest in real property (other than a lease on a residence), waive any rights to spousal support, etc. In short, there must be very little need for courts, attorneys, and the protection of the legal system. The less conflict between parties over children, property, and support, the easier it is to obtain a divorce.

A party who represents himself or herself in a divorce action (summary or traditional) is proceeding **pro se.**

pro se
On one's own behalf. Representing oneself.

Guardian Ad Litem

If the husband or wife is a minor or if the defendant is insane at the time of the divorce action, the court may require that the individual be represented by a **guardian ad litem** or *conservator* to ensure that the interests of the individual are protected during the proceeding. In a disputed child-custody case, the state might appoint a guardian ad litem to represent the child.

guardian ad litem
A special guardian appointed by the court to represent the interests of another.

ASSIGNMENT 7.18

Under what circumstances can a guardian ad litem be appointed in a divorce action in your state? Write your answer in step 17 at the end of the chapter. (See General Instructions for the State-Code Assignment in Appendix A.)

Waiting Period

Some states have a compulsory *waiting period* or "cooling-off" period (e.g., sixty days) that usually begins to run from the time the divorce complaint is filed. During this period of time, no further proceedings are held in the hope that tempers might calm down, producing an atmosphere of reconciliation.

ASSIGNMENT 7.19

Is there a waiting period in your state? If so, how long is it and when does it begin to run? Write your answer in step 18 at the end of the chapter. (See General Instructions for the State-Code Assignment in Appendix A.)

Discovery

Divorce cases can involve many facts, particularly when custody and finances are in dispute. "Usually the parties have numerous assets and liabilities that need to be documented, discovered, and produced for review in order to settle or try cases."[8] **Discovery** consists of pretrial devices that parties can use to help prepare for settlement or trial. The major discovery devices are as follows:

discovery
Steps that a party can take before trial to obtain information from the other side in order to prepare for settlement or trial.

- **Interrogatories** Interrogatories are a written set of factual questions sent by one party to another before a trial begins. For an example of a set of interrogatories, see Exhibit 8.2 in chapter 8.
- **Deposition** A deposition is an in-person question-and-answer session conducted outside the courtroom (e.g., in one of the attorney's offices). The person questioned is said to be *deposed.*
- **Request for Admissions** If a party believes that there will be no dispute over a certain fact at trial, it can request that the other party admit

[8]Lindi Massey, *Discovery: Just What Are You Looking For?*, 9 Legal Assistant Today 128 (July/Aug. 1992).

Exhibit 7.6 Joint Petition for Summary Dissolution of Marriage

3-57

ATTORNEY OR PARTY WITHOUT ATTORNEY *(Name and Address):* TELEPHONE NO. ATTORNEY FOR *(Name):*	***FOR COURT USE ONLY***
SUPERIOR COURT OF CALIFORNIA, COUNTY OF STREET ADDRESS: MAILING ADDRESS: CITY AND ZIP CODE: BRANCH NAME:	
MARRIAGE OF HUSBAND: WIFE:	
JOINT PETITION FOR SUMMARY DISSOLUTION OF MARRIAGE	CASE NUMBER:

We petition for a summary dissolution of marriage and declare that all the following conditions exist on the date this petition is filled with the court:

1. We have read and understand the Summary Dissolution Information booklet.
2. We were married on *(date):*
   [A SUMMARY DISSOLUTION OF YOUR MARRIAGE WILL NOT BE GRANTED IF YOU FILE THIS PETITION MORE THAN FIVE YEARS AFTER THE DATE OF YOUR MARRIAGE.]
3. One of us has lived in California for at least six months and in the county of filing for at least three months preceding the date of filing.
4. There are no minor children born of our relationship before or during our marriage or adopted by us during our marriage and the wife, to her knowledge, is not pregnant.
5. Neither of us has an interest in any real property anywhere. *(You may have a lease for a residence in which one of you lives. It must terminate within a year from the date of filing this petition. The lease must not include an option to purchase.)*
6. Except for obligations with respect to automobiles, on obligations either or both of us incurred during our marriage, we owe no more than $4,000.
7. The total fair market value of community property assets, excluding all encumbrances and automobiles, is less than $14,000.
8. Neither of us has separate property assets, excluding all encumbrances and automobiles, in excess of $14,000.
9. *(Check whichever statement is true)*
   a. ☐ We have no community assets or liabilities.
   b. ☐ We have signed an agreement listing and dividing all our community assets and liabilities and have signed all papers necessary to carry out our agreement. A copy of our agreement is attached to this petition.
10. Irreconcilable differences have caused the irremediable breakdown of our marriage and each of us wishes to have the court dissolve our marriage without our appearance before a judge.
11. ☐ Wife desires to have her former name restored. Her former name is *(specify name):*
12. Upon entry of final judgment of summary dissolution of marriage, we each give up our rights as follows:
    a. to appeal, and
    b. to move for a new trial.
13. EACH OF US FOREVER GIVES UP ANY RIGHT TO SPOUSAL SUPPORT FROM THE OTHER.
14. We stipulate that this matter may be determined by a commissioner sitting as a temporary judge.

(i.e., stipulate) the fact. This will avoid the expense and delay of proving the fact at trial. The party can also be asked to admit that a specific document is genuine. The other party, of course, need not make the admission if it feels that there is some dispute over the fact.

- **Mental or Physical Examination** If the mental or physical condition of a party is relevant to the litigation, many courts can order him or her to undergo an examination. If paternity is at issue, for example, the court might order a man to undergo a blood-grouping or DNA test.
- **Request for Production** One party can ask another to allow the inspection, testing, or copying of documents or other tangible things relevant to the case (e.g., tax returns, credit card receipts, diaries, business records).

One of the best ways to prepare for discovery is to study the *inventory of assets and liabilities* that both parties must provide each other and file with the court at the beginning of a divorce case. The inventory lists all the assets and debts that each spouse says are relevant to the support and property division issues in the case. The other side may be unclear, incomplete, and occasionally deceptive about what it reveals in the inventory or about what it omits. Any item on the inventory can often provide the basis for using a variety of discovery devices. Suppose, for example, that the inventory says a spouse owns a car that was a gift from that spouse's parent. You can draft interrogatory questions about the value of the car, its date and model, the date the spouse obtained it, the reason it was allegedly given as a gift, etc. The same types of questions can be prepared in the event that this spouse is deposed. You will also want to see the title document for the car in order to check names and dates of transfer on it. This could be done by making a request for production of the title or, if the spouse is going to be deposed, by asking him or her to bring the title document to the deposition. (A command to produce documents or other items is called a *subpoena duces tecum.*)

Another excellent source of ideas for what to pursue through the various discovery devices is what the client tells the office about the other spouse and the marriage. See the extensive checklist of client questions in chapter 3 on compiling a family history.

There are some limitations on the use of the discovery devices. For example, most states have restrictions on who can be deposed and on the number of interrogatories one divorce party can send another.

ASSIGNMENT 7.20

Answer the following questions for a divorce action after examining your statutory code and your court rules. (See General Instructions for the State-Code Assignment in Appendix A.)

a. Who can be deposed? When must a deposition be requested? How must the request be made? Write your response in step 19 at the end of the chapter.
b. Are there any restrictions on the use of depositions in divorce actions? Write your response in step 20 at the end of the chapter.
c. When and on whom can interrogatories be filed? Write your response in step 21 at the end of the chapter.
d. When must interrogatories be answered? Write your response in step 22 at the end of the chapter.
e. When can a request for admissions be made? Write your response in step 23 at the end of the chapter.
f. When will a court order a physical or mental examination? Write your response in step 24 at the end of the chapter.
g. What sanctions can be imposed if a party improperly refuses to comply with valid discovery requests? Summarize your response in step 25 at the end of the chapter.

ASSIGNMENT 7.21

Pick any well-known married couple in the media. Assume that they are getting a divorce and that you work for the law firm that is representing the wife. You are asked to draft a set of interrogatories meant to elicit as much relevant information as possible about the husband's personal and business finances. The information will be used in the firm's representation of the wife on alimony and property division issues. Draft the interrogatories. (See General Instructions for the Interrogatories Assignment in Appendix A.)

Preliminary Orders

pendente lite
While the litigation is going on.

Obtaining a divorce can be time-consuming even when the matter is uncontested. The court's calendar may be so crowded that it may take months to have the case heard. If the case is contested and some bitterness exists between the parties, the litigation can seemingly be endless. While the litigation is going on (or to use the Latin phrase, **pendente lite**), the court may be asked to issue a number of *preliminary* orders (sometimes called temporary orders), which remain in effect only until final determinations are made later:

- Granting physical and legal custody of the children
- Granting exclusive occupancy of the marital home to the custodial parent
- Granting a child-support order
- Granting alimony
- Granting attorney's fees and related court costs in the divorce action
- Enjoining (preventing) one spouse from bothering or molesting the other spouse and children
- Enjoining a spouse from transferring any property, which might make it unavailable for property division or for the support of the other spouse and children
- Appointing a receiver over a spouse's property until the court decides what his or her obligations are to the other spouse and children
- Enjoining the parties from changing any insurance policies
- Ordering an inventory and appraisal of all family assets and debts
- Granting control of any business operated by one or both spouses
- Enjoining the defendant from leaving the state or the country
- Enjoining either spouse from taking the children out of the state
- Enjoining the defendant from obtaining a foreign divorce

Specific requests for orders such as these do not always have to be made; the orders may be automatic. For example, a state might provide that once the divorce action begins and service of process is made, the parties are automatically restrained from transferring marital property, canceling insurance that now benefits family members, and removing minor children from the state.

ASSIGNMENT 7.22

In a divorce action in your state, what preliminary orders can be granted by the court pendente lite? Summarize your response in step 26 at the end of the chapter. (See General Instructions for the State-Code Assignment in Appendix A.)

For an example of a request for preliminary or temporary orders, see Exhibit 7.7.

Exhibit 7.7 Motion and Affidavit for Temporary Alimony, Maintenance of Support, or Custody of Minor Children

SUPERIOR COURT OF THE DISTRICT OF COLUMBIA
FAMILY DIVISION
DOMESTIC RELATIONS BRANCH

-- *Plaintiff*
v. } Jacket No. --
-- *Defendant*

MOTION AND AFFIDAVIT

Note:
FINANCIAL STATEMENT REQUIRED FILL OUT AND ATTACH HERETO.

For ☐ TEMPORARY ALIMONY, MAINTENANCE OR SUPPORT
☐ TEMPORARY CUSTODY OF MINOR CHILDREN

Now comes ☐ Plaintiff ☐ Defendant and moves the Court that -- (name)

be required to pay such amount as seems just and reasonable for the support and maintenance of

the ☐ Plaintiff ☐ Defendant (and ------------------------ minor children) pending the final disposition of this cause (and

to award ☐ her ☐ him the temporary custody of said minor children). Note: *Strike out portions of the preceding that do not apply.*

The following facts are submitted in support of the above motion:

1. Marriage:	Date:	Place:	2. Are you agreeable to a reconciliation: ☐ Yes ☐ No

3. Children by this marriage:		Living with			Amounts Contributed to family
Name	Age	Name	Address	Relation	

4. WIFE	5. HUSBAND
Age: Married before: ☐ Yes—How terminated? ☐ No	Age: Married before: ☐ Yes—How terminated? ☐ No
Occupation: Employer:	Occupation: Employer:
Living with — Name: Relation: Address:	Living with — Name: Relation: Address:
6. Wife asks for support of self (and ---- minor children): Amount: $ Per ☐ Week ☐ Month	7. Husband willing to contribute as such support: Amount: $ Per: ☐ Week ☐ Month
8. Husband's support to family: Before Separation: $ After Separation: $	9. Previous divorce proceedings between parties. ☐ Yes ☐ No Alimony awarded: ☐ Yes ☐ No
10. Juvenile Court proceedings: ☐ Yes ☐ No Explain:	11. Remarks

TRIAL

voir dire
Jury selection.

preponderance of evidence
A standard of proof that is met if the evidence shows it is more likely than not that an alleged fact is true or false as alleged.

privilege for marital communications
One spouse cannot disclose in court any confidential communications that occurred between the spouses during the marriage.

default judgment
A judgment rendered when the other side failed to appear.

Some states do not permit jury trials in divorce cases. If there is no jury, the judge decides the questions of fact as well as the questions of law. If a jury trial is allowed, the jurors are selected through a procedure known as **voir dire.** During this procedure, the lawyers and/or judge asks questions of prospective jurors to assess their eligibility to sit on the jury.

A trial is designed to be a single proceeding in which all divorce issues are resolved. As mentioned earlier, however, some states have the power to conduct *bifurcated divorce* proceedings, in which the dissolution of the marriage is resolved in one proceeding and the more complicated financial or final custody issues are resolved in a separate, later proceeding.

The attorneys begin the trial by making opening statements outlining the evidence they intend to try to prove during the trial. The plaintiff's side will usually present its case first. The attorney will call the plaintiff's witnesses and directly examine them. The other side can cross-examine these witnesses. Physical evidence such as documents is introduced as exhibits. Some evidence may have to be corroborated, meaning that additional evidence must be introduced to support the position taken by the party. The plaintiff's side will "rest" its case after presenting all of its witnesses and evidence. The defendant's attorney then begins his or her case through direct examination of witnesses, introduction of exhibits, etc.

When a party has the burden of proving a fact, the standard of proof is usually a **preponderance of evidence:** the fact finder must be able to say from the evidence introduced and found admissible that it is *more likely than not* that the fact has been established as claimed. Occasionally, however, the law requires a fact to meet a higher standard of proof (e.g., clear and convincing evidence). Who has the burden of proof? In general, the party asserting a fact has the burden of proof on that fact. For example, a spouse who claims that the other spouse has a hidden bank account and physically assaulted the children has the burden of proof on these facts.

Within the marriage, there is a **privilege for marital communications,** which prevents one spouse from testifying about confidential communications between the spouses during the marriage. This privilege, however, does not apply to:

- Criminal proceedings in which one spouse is alleged to have committed a crime against the other or against the children
- Civil cases between the spouses such as a divorce action

The privilege is limited to cases in which a third party is suing one or both of the spouses and attempts to introduce into evidence what one spouse may have said to the other. Such evidence is inadmissible.

A **default judgment** can be entered against a defendant who fails to appear. The plaintiff, however, is still required to introduce evidence to establish his or her case. Unlike other civil proceedings, the default judgment is not automatic.

ASSIGNMENT 7.23

Answer the following questions after examining your state code and court rules. (See General Instructions for the State-Code Assignment in Appendix A.)

a. In a divorce action, what evidence, if any, must be corroborated? Write your response in step 27 at the end of the chapter.

b. In a divorce action, are there any limitations on testimony that one spouse can give against the other? Write your answer in step 28 at the end of the chapter.

c. Can there be a jury trial in a divorce case? If so, when must the request for one be made? Write your response in step 29 at the end of the chapter.
d. What happens if the defendant fails to appear? Can there be a default judgment? Write your response in step 30 at the end of the chapter.

ASSIGNMENT 7.24

In your state, can one spouse use wiretap evidence against the other spouse at the divorce hearing (e.g., the wife taps her husband's phone and wants to introduce into evidence the conversation he had with his business partner about large assets that he has previously denied he owned). Check the code of your state as well as the federal code: the United States Code or the United States Code Annotated or the United States Code Service. (See General Instructions for the State-Code Assignment in Appendix A.)

ASSIGNMENT 7.25

In Assignment 7.14, you identified what court(s) in your state have the power to grant divorce. Attend a divorce hearing in one of these courts and answer the following questions concerning what you observe:

a. What court heard the case?
b. What was the name of the case?
c. Were both sides represented by counsel?
d. Were both parties present?
e. What kind of evidence, if any, was introduced?

ALTERNATIVE DISPUTE RESOLUTION (ADR)

There are alternatives to traditional litigation of a family law dispute in court, or at least alternatives that can be attempted before resorting to traditional litigation. All states encourage the use of alternative dispute resolution (ADR). In Texas, for example, a party seeking a divorce is asked to sign a statement that he or she has been informed of the availability of ADR. The major ADR programs are as follows.

Arbitration

In **arbitration,** both sides agree to submit their dispute to a neutral third person, who will listen to the evidence and make a decision. This individual is usually a professional arbitrator hired through an organization such as the American Arbitration Association. An arbitration proceeding is not as formal as a court trial. Generally, the decision of an arbitrator is not appealable to a court. If a party is dissatisfied, he or she must go to court and start all over again.

arbitration
The process of submitting a dispute to a third party outside the judicial system, who will render a decision that resolves the dispute.

Rent-a-Judge

When parties rent a judge, they are using another form of arbitration. A retired judge is hired by both sides to listen to the evidence and to make a decision that has no more or less validity than any other arbitrator's decision.

Mediation

In **mediation,** both sides agree to submit their dispute to a neutral third person, who will try to help the disputants reach a resolution on their own. In

mediation
The process of submitting a dispute to a third party outside the judicial system, who will help the parties reach their own resolution of the dispute. The mediator will not render a decision that resolves the dispute.

some states, mediation is mandatory; the parties are required to try to work out their differences before final action by the court. During the preliminary stages of the case, the judge might order the parties to attend mediation within the family court services unit of the court itself. This is particularly true when the judge learns that the parties do not agree on custody and visitation issues. The mediator does not render a decision, although occasionally he or she may make suggestions or recommendations to the parties and ultimately to the court.

Med-Arb

First, mediation is tried. Those issues that could not be mediated are then resolved through arbitration. Often the same person serves as mediator and arbitrator in a Med-Arb proceeding.

Revelations of a Family Law Mediator: What Goes On behind Closed Doors to Help Divorcing Couples Reach Agreement?

by Joshua Kadish

Oregon State Bar Bulletin 27 (February/March 1992).

Over the past seven or eight years, I have mediated a substantial number of family law cases. My office mates often inquire, "Just what happens behind those closed doors, anyway?" "What was the loud screaming about, followed by hysterical laughter and silence?" "How do you get these embattled couples to agree on anything if they hate each other so much?" I usually parry these questions with a crafty smile and a muttered, "I have my ways . . ." as I scuttle down the hallway.

Bowing to pressure from various fronts, I have decided that the time has come to tell all. What follows is fiction, which I hope reveals the truth.

Fred and Wilma were a young couple in the process of divorcing. They had significant disagreement about custody of their two children, ages 1½ and 6. Both had consulted with attorneys and, after receiving estimates of the cost of a custody battle, had followed their attorneys' recommendation to at least try mediation. Wilma had called me to set up an appointment, and at the appointed hour I ushered them into my office.

My office is somewhat different from many lawyers' offices. I do have a desk in one corner. Most of the office is given over to a sitting area consisting of a large, comfortable couch and two chairs grouped around a coffee table. I always let the couple enter my office first and seat themselves as they wish. Depending upon how they arrange themselves, I can get a preliminary idea of how hotly the battle is raging. Some couples will sit together on the couch. Most position themselves as far away from each other as possible. Fred and Wilma put a good deal of distance between themselves.

After we were settled, I spent a few minutes describing mediation to them. First, my job was to remain neutral and to help them reach agreements for themselves. My job was not to reach decisions for them. Second, what transpired in the mediation sessions was confidential and would not later be disclosed in a courtroom. Third, the process was voluntary and anyone was free to terminate the mediation at any time. Fourth, we would consider the interests of their children to be of paramount importance.

Without looking at either one of them, I then asked them to tell me about their current situation while I studiously looked down at my legal pad. I like to see who will start talking first. This gives me a clue about where the balance of power may lie in the relationship. I am always concerned about one party overpowering the other in mediation.

Fred started talking. Speaking angrily, he told me about their 10-year marriage, the two children and Wilma's affair and withdrawal from the marriage. He stated that although he worked hard, he spent more than an average amount of time caring for the children. He felt that in having an affair, Wilma had proved herself to be an unstable person and that he would be a preferable custodial parent. He pointed out that Wilma had worked during the course of the marriage and that parenting duties had been shared between them more or less equally.

During the course of his statement, Wilma had interrupted Fred to point out that although she had had an affair, it occurred after they had separated and that Fred had been emotionally distant and withdrawn from the marriage for a number of years. Her statement ignited a loud argument between them. I let them argue for a minute or two to get a sense of their style of arguing. This argument was a well-rehearsed one which they must have been through a hundred times. As each one spoke, I could see that neither party was listening but was marshaling arguments with which to respond, making sure that his or her position was well defended.

I interrupted the argument by stating that I suspected they had had this argument before. This brought a slightly sheepish smile to both faces. Humor is often useful in easing tension and getting people on another track. I then borrowed an idea from an excellent mediator, John Haynes, and asked each of them to take a few minutes to think about what was the absolute worst outcome they could imagine in mediation. By asking this question, I wanted to get them further off the track they had been racing down and to give them a few minutes to calm down. After a few minutes, I asked each to answer. Fred said he was afraid of losing everything, including his children. Wilma stated that she was afraid of the same thing.

I remarked that it was interesting that they were both afraid of exactly the same thing, specifically a loss of their children to the other party. I then asked whether it would be possible for them to agree that whatever the outcome of mediation was, it would not result in a complete loss of the children to the other person. They both indicated that they would agree to this.

From that point, the atmosphere eased considerably. Both Fred and Wilma had dramatically realized that each was concerned about exactly the same thing. When people realize that they have the same concerns, it makes them feel closer or at least less adversarial. Moreover, they had been able to reach their first agreement. They realized they had a common interest in not becoming estranged from their children and that they could agree this would not be a result of the mediation.

I then asked what the current situation was regarding the children. Fred stated that he had moved out and was living in a small apartment. He was seeing the children every other weekend. However, he emphasized that he was a very involved father and he wanted the children to spend at least half of their time with him on an alternating weekly basis. Wilma thought this would be bad for the children. She wanted them to be at home with her and see Fred every other weekend. She clearly wished to be the primary parent and felt that the children needed a mother's love. She was quite concerned about the children being in Fred's care for more than one overnight at a time. Fred interrupted her to state that he felt he was just as good a parent as she was. Wilma responded by telling an anecdote about Fred forgetting to feed the children lunch about three weeks ago.

Again, I interrupted. Taking a bit of a risk, I asked whether each parent thought the children loved and needed the other parent. Again, each parent responded affirmatively. My asking this question had the effect of derailing the disagreement and again bringing Fred and Wilma back to some common ground of understanding. Most parents will at least admit the children love and need the other parent.

The next task was to help Fred and Wilma learn to listen to each other and to start separating their positions from their interests. I asked them each if they thought they could state what the other person's position was regarding custody and visitation and the reasons for it. Fred thought he could, but when he tried, Wilma felt he was inaccurate. I then asked Wilma to tell him again what she was concerned about, which she did. Fred was then able to repeat Wilma's position back to her. We then reversed the process, and after a couple of tries, Wilma was able to state Fred's concerns back to him.

This is a simple technique known as "active listening" which I borrowed from the field of psychology. It is not too difficult to learn the rudiments, particularly when you are married to a clinical psychologist, as I am. The goal in active listening is to make each person feel understood. There is great power in helping each party feel his or her position is genuinely understood by the other person. In most marital disputes, as one party talks, the other party is not listening, but is preparing arguments to respond to the other. This results in long, well worked out and pointless disputes. Active listening slows the pace down and helps couples improve their communication; if you are assured that you will be listened to, you will be much more likely to be able to listen to another.

At this point Fred and Wilma understood not only each other's positions, but the interests and reasons behind the positions. Wilma was concerned about being separated from the children for too many overnight periods in a row. Fred was concerned about long periods of time going by without seeing the children. I pointed out that although their positions (alternating weekly versus every other weekend visitation) conflicted, their interests did not necessarily conflict. Perhaps it would be possible to work out a schedule where Fred saw the children frequently, but not for a long string of overnights. Perhaps every other weekend visitation with some shorter but frequent midweek visitations, plus frequent telephone contact would be acceptable.

I then hauled out a blank calendar. Using the calendar as the focus of discussion, we worked out a visitation schedule that seemed acceptable to both of them. During this discussion, I emphasized to them that they were fortunate to have the opportunity to experiment with different patterns of visitation because it is very difficult to sit in a room and decide what will and will not work in the long run. I suggested that they should commit to trying a certain pattern of visitation for perhaps two months and also commit to reviewing it and altering it as indicated by their needs and the children's.

By finally working out a schedule, I was trying to do several things. First, I was trying to show them that in some ways their interests could be meshed. Second, big problems can be broken down into small, manageable pieces. Rather than creating a visitation schedule which was engraved in stone and would last for the next 20 years, they could try something for two months. Finally, I had introduced the idea of experimentation and flexibility. They could adjust the situation based upon how they and the children actually reacted to the plan.

I ended the session by telling them I would write their agreement in memo form, which they could review with their attorneys. I then asked each of them to comment on the process of the session. Did either of them have any concerns about what had happened? What did they like about the session? What could we do differently next time when we moved to a discussion of financial issues? I try to make people feel that they are in control of the process. Fred and Wilma both stated that they were pleased with the session and surprised that they had been able to reach agreement. Fred asked how I had done it. "I have my ways . . ." I muttered as I ushered them to the door.

DIVORCE JUDGMENT

interlocutory
Not final; interim.

An **interlocutory** decree (or a *decree nisi*) is one that will not become final until the passage of a specified period of time. In some states, after the court has reached its decision to grant a divorce, an interlocutory decree of divorce will be issued. During the period that this decree is in force, the parties are still married. The divorce decree could be set aside if the parties reconcile.

In many states, the parties may not remarry while the trial court's divorce judgment is being appealed. Finally, in a few states, even a final divorce judgment will not automatically enable a party to remarry. The court may have the power to prohibit one or both of the parties from remarrying for a period of time.

An absolute, or final, judgment (as opposed to an interlocutory judgment) will determine whether the marriage is dissolved. If it is, the divorce may be granted to the plaintiff, or to both parties (dual divorce) if both initially filed for the divorce. The judgment will also resolve the questions of alimony, child custody, child support, and property division. (All of this, of course, assumes that the court had proper jurisdiction to make these determinations as outlined earlier.) In addition, the judgment will often restore the woman's maiden name, if that is her wish, and determine what the surname of the children will be as part of the custody decision.

Exhibit 7.8 shows a notice of entry of judgment, and Exhibit 7.9 shows a record of dissolution of marriage.

ASSIGNMENT 7.26

Answer the following questions after examining your state code. (See General Instructions for the State-Code Assignment in Appendix A.)

a. Is there an interlocutory decree or a decree nisi in your state? If so, how long is it effective and how does the divorce become final? Write your answer in step 31 at the end of the chapter.

b. While the divorce decree is being appealed, can the parties remarry?

c. To what court can the divorce decree be appealed? Write your answer in step 32 at the end of the chapter.

d. How many days does a party have to appeal? Write your answer in step 33 at the end of the chapter.

e. Where and how is the notice of appeal served and filed? Write your answer in step 34 at the end of the chapter.

Exhibit 7.8 Notice of Entry of Judgment

3-41

ATTORNEY OR PARTY WITHOUT ATTORNEY *(Name and Address):* TELEPHONE NO. ATTORNEY FOR *(Name):*	***FOR COURT USE ONLY***
SUPERIOR COURT OF CALIFORNIA, COUNTY OF STREET ADDRESS: MAILING ADDRESS: CITY AND ZIP CODE: BRANCH NAME:	
MARRIAGE OF PETITIONER: RESPONDENT:	
NOTICE OF ENTRY OF JUDGMENT	CASE NUMBER:

You are notified that the following judgment was entered on *(date):*

1. ☐ Dissolution of Marriage
2. ☐ Dissolution of Marriage — Status only
3. ☐ Dissolution of Marriage — Reserving Jurisdiction over Termination of Marital status
4. ☐ Legal Separation
5. ☐ Nullity
6. ☐ Other *(specify):*

Date: Clerk, by ______________________, Deputy

— NOTICE TO ATTORNEY OF RECORD OR PARTY WITHOUT ATTORNEY —
Pursuant to the provisions of Code of Civil Procedure section 1952, if no appeal is filed the court may order the exhibits destroyed or otherwise disposed of after 60 days from the expiration of the appeal time.

Effective date of termination of marital status (specify):
WARNING: NEITHER PARTY MAY REMARRY UNTIL THE EFFECTIVE DATE OF THE TERMINATION OF MARITAL STATUS AS SHOWN IN THIS BOX.

CLERK'S CERTIFICATE OF MAILING

I certify that I am not a party to this cause and that a true copy of the Notice of Entry of judgment was mailed first class, postage fully prepaid, in a sealed envelope addressed as shown below, and that the notice was mailed

at (place): California,

on (date):

Date: Clerk, by ______________________, Deputy

Exhibit 7.9 Record of Dissolution of Marriage

OREGON DEPARTMENT OF HUMAN RESOURCES
HEALTH DIVISION
Vital Records Unit
RECORD OF DISSOLUTION OF MARRIAGE, OR ANNULMENT

SAMPLE

CO. FILE NO.________________

136- State File Number

TYPE OR PRINT PLAINLY IN BLACK INK

HUSBAND

1. HUSBAND'S NAME (*First, Middle, Last*)		
2. RESIDENCE OR LEGAL ADDRESS — STREET AND NUMBER / CITY OR TOWN / COUNTY / STATE		
3. SOCIAL SECURITY NUMBER (*Optional*)	4. BIRTHPLACE (*State or Foreign Country*)	5. DATE OF BIRTH (*Month, Day, Year*)

WIFE

6a. WIFE'S NAME (*First, Middle, Last*)		6b. MAIDEN SURNAME
7. FORMER LEGAL NAMES (IF ANY) — (1) / (2) / (3)		
8. RESIDENCE OR LEGAL ADDRESS — STREET AND NUMBER / CITY OR TOWN / COUNTY / STATE		
9. SOCIAL SECURITY NUMBER (*Optional*)	10. BIRTHPLACE (*State or Foreign Country*)	13. DATE OF BIRTH (*Month, Day, Year*)

MARRIAGE

12a. PLACE OF THIS MARRIAGE - CITY, TOWN OR LOCATION	12b. COUNTY	12c. STATE OR FOREIGN COUNTRY	13. DATE OF THIS MARRIAGE (*Month, Day, Year*)
14. DATE COUPLE LAST RESIDED IN SAME HOUSEHOLD (*Month, Day, Year*)	15. NUMBER OF CHILDREN UNDER 18 IN THIS HOUSEHOLD AS OF THE DATE IN ITEM 14 Number ________ ☐ None	16. PETITIONER ☐ Husband ☐ Wife ☐ Both	

ATTORNEY

17a. NAME OF PETITIONER'S ATTORNEY (*Type/Print*)	17b. ADDRESS (*Street and Number or Rural Route Number, City or Town, State, Zip Code*)
18a. NAME OF RESPONDENT'S ATTORNEY (*Type/Print*)	18b. ADDRESS (*Street and Number or Rural Route Number, City or Town, State, Zip Code*)

DECREE

19. MARRIAGE OF THE ABOVE NAMED PERSONS WAS DISSOLVED ON: (*Month, Day, Year*)	20. TYPE OF DECREE DISSOLUTION OF MARRIAGE ☐ Annulment ☐	21. DATE DECREE BECOMES EFFECTIVE (*Month, Day, Year*)
22. NUMBER OF CHILDREN UNDER 18 WHOSE PHYSICAL CUSTODY WAS AWARDED TO Husband ________ Wife ________ Joint (Husband/Wife) ________ ☐ No children	23. COUNTY OF DECREE	24. TITLE OF COURT
25. SIGNATURE OF COURT OFFICIAL	26. TITLE OF COURT OFFICIAL	27. DATE SIGNED (*Month, Day, Year*)

ORS 432.010 REQUIRED STATISTICAL INFORMATION. THE INFORMATION BELOW WILL NOT APPEAR ON CERTIFIED COPIES OF THE RECORD.

	28. NUMBER OF THIS MARRIAGE—First, Second, etc. (*Specify below*)	29. IF PREVIOUSLY MARRIED, LAST MARRIAGE ENDED: By Death, Divorce, Dissolution, or Annulment (*Specify below*)	29. Date (*Month, Day, Year*)	30. RACE - *American Indian, Black, White etc. (specify below)*	31. EDUCATION (*Specify only highest grade completed*): Elementary/Secondary (0–12)	31. College (1–4 or 5 +)
HUSBAND	28a.	29a.	29b.	30a.	31a.	
WIFE	28b.	29c.	29d.	30b.	31b.	

THE PETITIONER OR LEGAL REPRESENTATIVE OF THE PETITIONER IS RESPONSIBLE FOR COMPLETING THE PERSONAL INFORMATION ON THIS FORM AND SHALL PRESENT THIS FORM TO THE CLERK OF THE COURT WITH THE PETITION.
IN ALL CASES THE COMPLETED RECORD SHALL BE A PREREQUISITE TO THE GRANTING OF THE FINAL DECREE

45-5 (2-89)

ENFORCEMENT OF DIVORCE JUDGMENT

Most of the controversy involving the enforcement of a divorce judgment has centered on enforcing support and custody orders, particularly across state lines. These topics will be examined at length in chapters 9 and 10. What follows are some general observations about enforcement options that are often available.

Civil Contempt

A delinquent party who must pay a money judgment (e.g., an alimony order) is called the *judgment debtor.* The person in whose favor the judgment is rendered is the *judgment creditor.* For disobeying the order, the judgment debtor can be held in civil contempt, for which he or she will be jailed until complying with the order. This remedy, however, is not used if the judgment debtor does not have the present financial ability to pay. Inability to pay does not mean burdensome or inconvenient to pay. Using all resources currently available or those that could become available with reasonable effort, he or she must be able to comply with the payment order. (Exhibit 7.10 shows an affidavit in support of a motion to punish for contempt.)

Contempt is generally not available to enforce property division orders. The latter are more often enforced by execution, attachment, posting security, receivership, and constructive trust, which are discussed below.

Execution

A judgment is *executed* when the court orders the sheriff to carry it out by seizing the property of the judgment debtor, selling it, and turning the proceeds over to the judgment creditor. This is done pursuant to a **writ of execution.**

writ of execution
A document directing a court officer to seize the property of someone who lost a judgment, sell it, and pay the winner of the judgment.

Execution is usually possible only with respect to support orders that are *final* and *nonmodifiable.* Such orders can become final and nonmodifiable in two ways:

- In some states, each unpaid installment automatically becomes a final and nonmodifiable judgment of nonpayment to which execution will be available.
- In other states, each unpaid installment does not become a final and nonmodifiable judgment of nonsupport until the wife makes a specific application for such a judgment and one is entered. Execution is available only after the judgment is so entered or docketed.

As we will see in chapter 10, federal law places severe restrictions on the ability of a court to modify child-support arrearages retroactively.

Garnishment

When **garnishment** is used, the court authorizes the judgment creditor to reach money or other property of the judgment debtor that is in the hands of a third party (e.g., the employer or bank of the judgment debtor).

garnishment
A process whereby a debtor's property under the control of another is given to a third person to whom the debtor owes a debt.

Attachment

Property of the judgment debtor is *attached* when the court authorizes its seizure to bring it under the control of the court so that it can be used to satisfy a judgment.

Posting Security

The court may require the judgment debtor to provide insurance or to post a bond (i.e., *post security*), which will be forfeited if he or she fails to obey the judgment.

Exhibit 7.10 Affidavit in Support of Motion to Punish for Contempt

SUPREME COURT OF THE STATE OF NEW YORK
COUNTY OF ____________

__________, Plaintiff,

-against-

__________, Defendant,

AFFIDAVIT IN SUPPORT OF MOTION TO PUNISH FOR CONTEMPT

Index No. __________

STATE OF NEW YORK
COUNTY OF __________ } ss.:

______________, being duly sworn, deposes and says:

That I am the plaintiff in the above entitled action and make this application to punish the defendant for contempt of Court for willfully neglecting and refusing to comply with the Judgment of this Court dated ________, 20 ___, directing the defendant, among other things, to pay to the plaintiff the sum of _______ ($ _______) Dollars per week as alimony, plus the sum of ________ ($ _______) Dollars per week per child for the maintenance and support of the infant children __________, __________, and __________, for a total sum of ________ ($ ________) Dollars per week by check or money order at the residence of the plaintiff.

That hereto annexed is a copy of the Judgment of Divorce herein. That the defendant was duly personally served with a copy of said Judgment on the ________ day of ________, 20 ___.

That defendant has failed, neglected, and refused to pay me the amounts of money set forth in said Judgment of Divorce during the period commencing __________, 20 ___ to date.

That the above named defendant has willfully neglected and failed to comply with said Judgment of this Court and he is now in arrears in the sum of ________ ($________) Dollars, and no part of which has been paid although duly demanded. That the neglect and refusal of the above named defendant to comply with said judgment of the Court was calculated to and did defeat, impair, impede, and prejudice the rights and remedies of the above named plaintiff.

That the arrears are computed as follows:

DATE	AMOUNT DUE	AMOUNT PAID	ARREARS
________	$ ________	$ ________	$ ________
________	$ ________	none	$ ________
________	$ ________	$ ________	$ ________
________	$ ________	none	$ ________
________	$ ________	none	$ ________
________	$ ________	$ ________	$ ________
________	$ ________	none	$ ________
________	$ ________	$ ________	$ ________
________	$ ________	none	$ ________
________	$ ________	$ ________	$ ________
________	$ ________	none	$ ________
		TOTAL ARREARS	$ ________

That total arrears are therefore due me in the sum of _______ ($ _______) Dollars.

That it is respectfully submitted that the defendant deliberately does this to defeat and prejudice the rights and remedies of myself and my infant children.

That defendant is employed as a school teacher with the same position that he held at the time of the trial on _______, 20 ___, which was only _______ months ago. His income is at least as much as he was earning then, if not more. The defendant is also engaged in private tutoring.

That no order of sequestration has been made herein for the reason that there is no property to sequestrate.

That no bond or security has been given for the payment of said alimony.

That the plaintiff has been unable to obtain steady employment and is in dire financial straits by reason of the defendant's willful refusal to comply with said Judgment of Divorce.

That no previous application for the relief herein prayed for has been made.

That the reason that an order to show cause herein is requested is that the same is required on an application of this matter by virtue of section 245 of the Domestic Relations Law.

WHEREFORE, an order to show cause is respectfully prayed requiring the defendant to show cause why he should not be punished for contempt for willfully disobeying the Judgment of this Court.

[*Signature*] ______________________

[*Type Name of Deponent*]

Source: J. Marvins, *McKinney's Forms* 13:131A (1976).

Receivership

The court can appoint a *receiver* over some or all the judgment debtor's property to prevent him or her from squandering it or otherwise making it unavailable to satisfy the judgment.

Constructive Trust

The court could impose a trust on property that the judgment debtor conveys to a "friendly" third party (e.g., the judgment debtor's mother) in an effort to make it appear that he or she no longer owns the property. A **constructive trust** is a trust created by the law, rather than by the parties, in order to prevent a serious inequity or injustice.

constructive trust
A trust created by operation of law against one who has obtained legal possession of property (or legal rights to property) through fraud, duress, abuse of confidence, or other unconscionable conduct.

ASSIGNMENT 7.27

Answer the following questions after examining your state code. (See General Instructions for the State-Code Assignment in Appendix A.)

a. What procedures must be followed to seek enforcement of a divorce order by contempt? Write your answer in step 35 at the end of the chapter.
b. What procedures must be followed to set aside a divorce judgment on the ground that it was obtained by fraud? Write your answer in step 36 at the end of the chapter.

CIVIL UNIONS

In chapter 5, we saw that Vermont created the new legal relationship called the **civil union** for same-sex couples. It is an alternative to traditional marriage, which continues to be limited to opposite-sex couples. One of the major characteristics of the civil union is that it creates all the rights and obligations of marriage; the two relationships are treated equally. This includes divorce or dissolution of the relationship. The steps to dissolve a Vermont marriage are the same as the steps to dissolve a civil union:

civil union
A same-sex legal relationship in Vermont that grants the same benefits, protections, and responsibilities under Vermont law that are granted to spouses in a marriage.

> **Dissolution of civil unions** The family court shall have jurisdiction over all proceedings relating to the dissolution of civil unions. The dissolution of civil unions shall follow the same procedures and be subject to the same substantive rights and obligations that are involved in the dissolution of marriage in accordance with chapter 11 of this title, including any residency requirements.[9]

ASSIGNMENT 7.28

Interview a paralegal, attorney, or legal secretary who has been involved in divorce actions in your state. (See General Instructions for the Systems Assignment in Appendix A.)

a. Approximately how many divorce cases have you worked on?
b. How many of them have been uncontested?
c. Approximately how long does it take to process an uncomplicated, uncontested divorce?
d. Is there a difference between working on a divorce case and working on another kind of case in the law office? If so, what is the difference?

continued

[9]Vermont Statutes Annotated tit. 15, § 1206.

e. What are the major steps for processing a divorce action in this state? What documents have to be filed? What court appearances must be made? Etc.
f. What formbook, manual, or other legal treatise do you use, if any, that is helpful? Who is the publisher?
g. Does your office have its own internal manual that covers any aspect of divorce practice?
h. In a divorce action, what is the division of labor among the attorney, the paralegal, and the legal secretary?
i. What computer software, if any, is used? What is its function and how useful is it? What would the office have to do if such software did not exist?

ASSIGNMENT 7.29

Divorce Litigation Flowchart for Your State

(Fill in each step after checking the law of your state, particularly your state statutory code. You may also need to refer to court rules and judicial opinions. See General Instructions for the Flowchart Assignment in Appendix A. For each step, cite the statute, court rule, or other law that you are relying upon as authority for your answer.)

Step 1 Name the court or courts that have subject matter jurisdiction over divorces.
Citation:
Step 2 How is venue determined in a divorce action?
Citation:
Step 3 What must a complaint for divorce contain?
Citation:
Step 4 Must the complaint be subscribed and/or verified? If so, by whom?
Citation:
Step 5 Where is the complaint served and filed?
Citation:
Step 6 What is the filing fee for a divorce?
Citation:
Step 7 Who may serve process?
Citation:
Step 8 How is personal service made on an individual?
Citation:
Step 9 In divorce actions, how is substituted service made?
Citation:
Step 10 How is proof of service made?
Citation:
Step 11 How many days does the defendant have to answer the complaint?
Citation:
Step 12 Must the defendant's answer be subscribed and/or verified? If so, by whom?
Citation:
Step 13 Must the defendant specifically plead all available affirmative defenses in the answer?
Citation:
Step 14 Where and how is the answer served and filed?
Citation:
Step 15 How many days does the plaintiff have to reply to any counterclaims of the defendant?
Citation:

Step 16 Where and how is the reply of the plaintiff served and filed?
Citation:
Step 17 When can a guardian ad litem be appointed in a divorce action?
Citation:
Step 18 Is there a waiting period? If so, how long is it and when does it begin to run?
Citation:
Step 19 Who can be deposed? When must a deposition be requested? How is the request made?
Citation:
Step 20 Are there any restrictions on the use of depositions in divorce actions?
Citation:
Step 21 When and on whom can interrogatories be filed?
Citation:
Step 22 When must interrogatories be answered?
Citation:
Step 23 When can a request for admissions be made?
Citation:
Step 24 When will a court order a physical or mental examination?
Citation:
Step 25 Summarize the sanctions that can be imposed if a party improperly refuses to comply with valid discovery requests.
Citation:
Step 26 In a divorce action, summarize the preliminary orders that can be granted by the court pendente lite.
Citation:
Step 27 In a divorce action, what evidence, if any, must be corroborated?
Citation:
Step 28 Are there any limitations on testimony that one spouse can give against the other?
Citation:
Step 29 Can there be a jury trial in a divorce case? If so, when must the request for one be made?
Citation:
Step 30 What happens if the defendant fails to appear? Can there be a default judgment?
Citation:
Step 31 Is there an interlocutory decree or decree nisi? If so, how long is it effective, and how does the divorce become final?
Citation:
Step 32 To what court can the divorce decree be appealed?
Citation:
Step 33 How many days does a party have to appeal?
Citation:
Step 34 Where and how is the notice of appeal served and filed?
Citation:
Step 35 Summarize the procedures that must be followed to seek enforcement of a divorce order by contempt.
Citation:
Step 36 Summarize the procedures that must be followed to set aside a divorce judgment on the ground of fraud.
Citation:

SUMMARY

The three major court proceedings that can be used when a marriage is disintegrating are divorce, judicial separation, and separate maintenance. Grounds must exist before parties can use any of these three actions.

There are three major no-fault grounds for divorce: living apart, incompatibility, and irreconcilable differences that cause the irremediable breakdown of the marriage. The major fault grounds for divorce are adultery, cruelty, and desertion. Fault grounds, and the defenses to them are less commonly used today. To dissolve a covenant marriage, however, proof of marital fault is required.

Actions for judicial separation and separate maintenance are primarily designed to secure spousal support in a marriage that will continue to exist, at least for the time being.

A person's residence is the place where he or she is living at a particular time. Domicile is the place where a person has been physically present with the intent to make that place a permanent home; it is the place to which one intends to return when away. In divorce laws, however, the word *residence* often has the meaning of domicile.

A divorce decree is divisible when only part of it is enforceable. The decree will dissolve the marriage. This part of the decree is enforceable if the court had in rem jurisdiction. If the court also orders alimony, child support, or property division without having personal jurisdiction over the defendant, this part of the decree is not enforceable. There are times, however, when a party with a valid jurisdictional challenge to a divorce decree will be estopped from bringing the challenge.

Once a court grants a divorce, one of the major concerns of the judgment debtor is how to enforce it. The remedies that are often available include civil contempt, execution, garnishment, attachment, posting security, receivership, and constructive trust.

KEY CHAPTER TERMINOLOGY

grounds
no-fault grounds
covenant marriage
uncontested
collusion
migratory divorce
dissolution
living apart
incompatibility
irreconcilable differences
adultery
co-respondent
corroboration
fornication
illicit cohabitation
criminal conversation
cruelty
desertion
constructive desertion
connivance
condonation
recrimination
provocation
get
Talak
judicial separation
separate maintenance
foreign divorce
"quickie" divorce
collusive divorce
default divorce
divisible divorce
bilateral divorce
ex parte divorce
dual divorce
uncontested divorce
contested divorce
divorce a mensa et thoro
limited divorce
divorce a vinculo matrimonii
residence
domicile
emancipated
operation of law
domicile by choice
adversarial hearing
ex parte hearing
direct attack
collateral attack
res judicata
estoppel
equitable estoppel
foreign
forum state
full faith and credit
service of process
substituted service
jurisdiction
subject matter jurisdiction
domestic relations exception
in rem jurisdiction
res
personal jurisdiction
venue
pleadings
complaint
summons
in forma pauperis
answer
counterclaim
pro se
guardian ad litem
discovery
interrogatories
deposition

request for admissions
mental or physical examination
request for production
pendente lite
voir dire
preponderance of evidence
privilege for marital communications
default judgment
arbitration
mediation
interlocutory
writ of execution
garnishment
constructive trust
civil union

ETHICS IN PRACTICE

You are a paralegal working at the law office of Smith & Smith. The office represents David Gerry in a divorce action against his wife, Lena Gerry. One of the disputes is how to divide business assets acquired during the marriage. In an effort to pressure Lena to divide the assets in his favor, David tells his attorney to request sole physical and legal custody of their two children even though David has no desire to raise the children. He knows, however, that Lena is terrified at the thought of losing sole custody herself. David wants his attorney to engage in extensive discovery (depositions, interrogatories, etc.) on the custody issue for the sole purpose of wearing Lena down in the hope that she will reduce her claims on the business assets. Any ethical problems?

ON THE NET: MORE ON DIVORCE GROUNDS AND PROCEDURE

Divorce Manual (American Academy of Matrimonial Lawyers)
http://www.aaml.org/Manual.htm

The Messy Steps of Divorce (Prairielaw)
http://www.prairielaw.com/articles/article.asp?channelid=2&articleid=1259

Divorce Law Information
http://www.divorcelawinfo.com

Divorce Mediation
http://www.divorceinfo.com/mediation.htm

American Values Organization: The Unexpected Legacy of Divorce
http://www.americanvalues.org/html/bk_the_unexpected_legacy_of_di.shtml

The Agunah Problem in Jewish Divorce
http://users.aol.com/agunah/index.htm

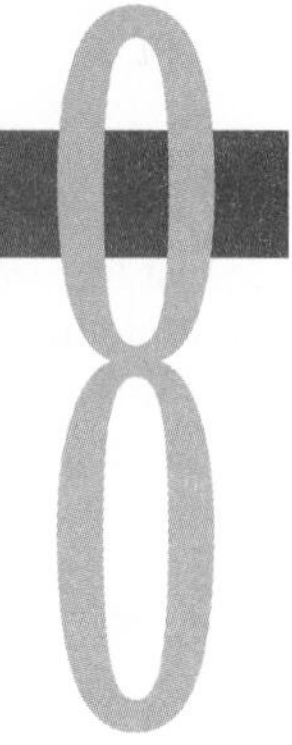

CHAPTER

SPOUSAL SUPPORT, PROPERTY DIVISION, AND THE SEPARATION AGREEMENT

CHAPTER OUTLINE

Chapter 8 begins our comprehensive study of the separation agreement. Our primary themes in the chapter will be spousal support and property division—two major components of the separation agreement. Some of chapter 9 (on child custody), chapter 10 (on child support), and chapter 11 (on taxation) also cover parts of the separation agreement. Chapter 8, however, examines the document as a whole, setting the stage for the other chapters. Our focus throughout will be on the nature of the separation agreement, the drafting options available, and the response of a court *when the parties are not able to reach an agreement.*

SEPARATION AGREEMENTS AND LITIGATION

separation agreement
A contract by two married individuals who have separated or are about to separate that covers support, custody, property division, and other terms of their separation.

A **separation agreement** is a contract entered into by spouses who have separated or who are about to separate. The contract covers the terms of their separation. (See Exhibit 4.1 in chapter 4 for a chart comparing the functions of separation agreements, premarital agreements, postnuptial agreements, and cohabitation agreements.) Parties to a separation agreement have one of three possible objectives, at least initially. First, they may intend to dissolve the marriage through a divorce. Most spouses have this objective. Second, if they do not want a divorce, they may seek a legal separation, also called a judicial separation or limited divorce (see chapter 7). Parties with a legal separation cannot remarry, since their marriage has not been dissolved. Third, they may simply want to remain separated without seeking a divorce or legal separation at the present time. Whatever the goal, spouses can use the separation agreement to specify how they propose to settle the questions of custody, support, and property division, and all other terms of their separation.

Separation agreements find their way into court in the following kinds of situations:

- One party sues the other for breach of contract (i.e., for violation of the separation agreement); the plaintiff in this suit wants the separation agreement enforced.
- The parties file for a divorce and ask the court either (1) to approve the terms of the separation agreement or (2) to approve the terms *and* to incorporate them into the divorce decree so that the decree and the agreement become merged.
- After the divorce, one of the parties brings a suit to set aside the separation agreement (e.g., because it was induced by fraud).

The law encourages parties to enter separation agreements. So long as certain basic public policies (to be discussed below) are not violated, the law gives a great deal of leeway to the parties to resolve their difficulties and, in effect, to decide what their relationship will be upon separation. The role of the attorney and paralegal is to assist the client in this endeavor.

A high priority of the family law practitioner must always be to avoid litigation, since it is often time-consuming, expensive, and emotionally draining for everyone involved. The marital breakdown of the parties was probably a most painful experience for the entire family. Litigation tends to remind the parties of old sores and to keep the bitterness alive. While an effective separation agreement will not guarantee harmony between the spouses, it can help keep their disputes on a constructive level.

NEGOTIATION FACTORS

An effective separation agreement is achieved through bargaining or negotiation by the parties on their own or, more commonly, through attorneys representing them. What is an effective separation agreement? Obviously, this will vary according to individual circumstances. Nevertheless, some general observations can be made about the characteristics of an effective separation agreement. See Exhibit 8.1.

Exhibit 8.1 Characteristics of an Effective Separation Agreement

1. *Comprehensive.* It covers all major matters. Should a problem arise months or years later, the parties will not have to say, "We never thought of that when we drafted the agreement."

2. *Fair.* If the agreement is not fair to both sides, it may be unworkable, which will force the parties into expensive and potentially bitter litigation. Hence the worst kind of legal assistance a law office can provide is to "outsmart" the other side into "giving up" almost everything. Little is accomplished by winning the war, but losing the peace. "You gain no advantage in depriving your ex-spouse of what he/she is entitled to. Remember, your ex-spouse has the ability to make your life miserable." Mississippi State Bar, Family Law Section, Consumers Guide to Divorce 4 (1990).

3. *Accurate.* The agreement should accurately reflect the intentions of the parties. What they orally agreed to do in formal or informal bargaining sessions should be stated in the written agreement. No clause in the agreement should ever prompt one of the parties to exclaim, "That's not what we agreed to do!"

4. *Legal.* Certain things can and cannot be done in a separation agreement; the agreement must not attempt to do anything that is illegal.

5. *Readable.* The agreement should be written in language that the parties can understand without having to hire or rehire an attorney every time a question arises.

CHECKLISTS FOR THE PREPARATION OF A SEPARATION AGREEMENT

Before an intelligent separation agreement can be drafted, a great deal of information is needed. First of all, a series of detailed lists should be compiled on the following items:

- All prior agreements between husband and wife (e.g., premarital agreement, postnuptial agreements such as a loan between the spouses)
- All property held by the husband in his separate name
- All property held by the wife in her separate name
- All property in one person's name that really "belongs" to the other
- All property held jointly—in both names
- All property acquired during the marriage before the date of the separation
- All property acquired by husband or wife after the date of the separation
- All contracts for the purchase or sale of real property
- All insurance policies currently in force
- All debts currently outstanding, with an indication of who incurred each one
- All income from any source earned by the husband
- All income from any source earned by the wife
- Projected future income of both parties (e.g., salary, dividends, interest, pension rights, royalties, loans that will be repaid, future trust income, expected inheritance)
- All present and projected living expenses of the husband
- All present and projected living expenses of the wife
- All present and projected living expenses of the children

In addition to such lists, the following data should be collected:

- Names and addresses of both spouses and of the children
- Data on all prior litigation, if any, between the parties
- Name and address of present attorney of other spouse
- Names and addresses of prior attorneys, if any, retained by either party
- Copies of tax returns filed during the marriage
- Character references (if needed on questions of custody or credibility)
- Names and addresses of individuals who might serve as arbitrators or mediators
- Documentation of prior indebtedness
- Copy of will(s) currently in force, if any

Chapter 3, on compiling a family history, includes a great many categories of questions that should provide much of this background information within the knowledge of the client. The interrogatories in the next section focus on obtaining information from the *opposing* spouse and are also designed to identify critical information needed to negotiate and draft a separation agreement.

Here is a checklist covering individual clauses of a separation agreement. The checklist is an overview of topics that need to be considered by the parties and that we will consider in chapters 8, 9, 10, and 11. Some of the headings in the checklist are commonly used in the separation agreement itself.

1. *Alimony:*
   - Who pays
   - How much
   - Method of payment
   - Frequency of payment
   - Whether it terminates on the remarriage or the death of either spouse
   - Whether it fluctuates with income of payor
   - Whether it is modifiable
   - Security for payment
   - Method of enforcement
   - Tax consequences
2. *Child support:*
   - Who pays
   - How much (check the mandatory child support guidelines)
   - Whether amount of child support is modifiable
   - Method of payment
   - Security for payment
   - Frequency of payment
   - Whether it terminates when a child reaches a certain age
   - Whether it terminates if the child is otherwise emancipated
   - Day care expenses
   - Education expenses covering private schools, college, etc.
   - Tax consequences
3. *Custody:*
   - Custody options: physical custody (sole or joint) and legal custody (sole or joint)
   - Method of communicating/consulting on major child rearing decisions such as health and education (if parties have joint legal custody)
   - Visitation rights of noncustodial parent
   - Visitation rights of others (e.g., grandparent)
   - Summer vacations and special holidays
   - Transportation expenses
   - Permissible removal of child from the state on a temporary or permanent basis
   - Changing the last name of the child
   - The child's participation in religious activity
4. *Health expenses of custodial parent and children:*
   - Medical
   - Dental
   - Drugs
   - Special needs
   - Expenses not covered by insurance
5. *Insurance:*
   - Life
   - Health
   - Automobile

- Disability
- Homeowner's

6. *Estate documents:*
    - Wills already in existence (individual or mutual): changes needed
    - Family trust: changes needed
    - Trust accounts for children
7. *Debts still to be paid:*
    - Incurred by whom
    - Who pays
8. *Personal property:*
    - Cash
    - Joint and separate bank accounts (savings, checking, certificates of deposit, etc.)
    - Stocks, bonds, mutual funds, other kinds of securities
    - Motor vehicles
    - Works of art
    - Household furniture
    - Jewelry
    - Rights to receive money in the future (e.g., retirement pay, stock options, royalties, rents, court judgment awards)
9. *Real property:*
    - Residence
    - Vacation home
    - Business real estate
    - Tax shelters
    - Leases
10. *Income tax returns*
11. *Attorney fees and court costs*
12. *Incorporation of separation agreement into divorce decree (merger)*
13. *Arbitration or mediation (for disputes over the interpretation of any terms of the agreement)*
14. *What happens to agreement if parties reconcile*

UNCOVERING FINANCIAL ASSETS

Gaining access to all the personal and financial information needed to negotiate a separation agreement or to prepare for trial is not always easy. In fact, one of the major reasons separation agreements are later challenged is that one of the parties did not have or was not given a complete inventory of the other spouse's financial assets before signing. In chapter 7, we examined discovery devices that are designed to help an office obtain this kind of information. One of the devices is **interrogatories,** which can be particularly effective when seeking financial assets.

interrogatories
A written set of factual questions sent by one party to another before a trial begins.

In Exhibit 8.2, you will find a set of interrogatories directed at the spouse of a client. Read these interrogatories to increase your understanding of the potential complexity of someone's financial affairs. As you read the questions, make careful note of the categories of financial data sought and the comprehensiveness of the questions. A paralegal must pursue the same kind of information with the same comprehensiveness when given interviewing and investigative tasks designed to help the office identify the financial assets of a client's spouse.

Uncovering financial assets is primarily a document hunt. Here is a list of the documents that the interrogatories in Exhibit 8.2 sought copies of:

- Medical reports
- Physician letters
- Canceled rent checks

- Lease or rental agreements
- Real estate closing statements
- Deeds
- Real estate appraisals
- Real estate mortgages
- Real estate tax bills
- Contracts to buy real estate
- Contracts to sell real estate
- Pay stubs
- W-2 forms
- Employment contracts
- Car lease agreements
- Deferred compensation agreements
- Account statements for deferred compensation
- Federal income tax returns
- State tax returns
- Local tax returns
- 1099 tax forms for miscellaneous income
- Partnership agreements
- Partnership tax returns
- Articles of incorporation
- Corporate tax returns
- Bank account statements
- Appraisals of livestock
- Appraisals of jewelry
- Appraisals of other collectibles
- Royalty statements
- Securities account statements
- Gift tax returns
- Trust instruments
- Trustee accounting reports
- Pension account statements
- Credit card statements
- Financial statements
- Loan applications

Some of the documents only indirectly relate to someone's financial worth. Knowing a person's medical history, for example, is some evidence of whether health problems interfere with an ability to earn income.

Often a spouse will not be forthcoming about his or her financial worth. Indeed, considerable asset hiding may have taken place and may still be going on. One divorced author advises, "Clean out your bank account before she does it for you. Hide your assets."[1] How does a law office penetrate this wall of resistance? Most states require divorcing parties to disclose their assets and liabilities to each other. The failure to do so can be penalized by the court. (In one case, for example, a court awarded the husband 100 percent of his wife's $1,336,000 lottery prize because she concealed it from him before the divorce became final.) States often have official disclosure forms on which spouses must provide net worth statements covering assets and liabilities. Yet such requirements do not guarantee compliance. Law firms must take the initiative in uncovering assets. The starting point is knowing where to look. The interrogatories in Exhibit 8.2 (along with the other discovery devices outlined in chapter 7) provide an excellent roadmap of where an aggressive, competent law office will look for assets. The financial information revealed by these efforts becomes the foundation of an honest separation agreement.

---

[1]John Tayor, Falling, p. 5 (1999).

Exhibit 8.2 Interrogatories

The plaintiff requests that the defendant answer under oath, in accordance with Section ______, the following interrogatories:

Notes: (i) Where a question or a part of a question is inapplicable, indicate why.
(ii) If facts occurring after the date these interrogatories are answered would change any of the answers provided, notify the plaintiff in writing of such changes.

1. State your full name, age, residence and post office address, home telephone number, social security number, business addresses, business phone numbers, personal and business e-mail addresses, and personal and business WWW addresses.
2. State:
   (a) The names, birth dates, and present addresses of all children born or adopted during the marriage, indicating whether any children are emancipated and who has physical and legal custody of each unemancipated child.
   (b) Whether any dependent child is in need of unusual or extraordinary medical or mental care or has special financial needs, giving a detailed description of the condition that requires such care and the treatment required, to the best of your knowledge, including, but not limited to:
      (i) Nature of treatment;
      (ii) Name of treating doctors and/or other professionals;
      (iii) Cost of care; and
      (iv) Estimated length of treatment (attach copies of medical reports or physician letters).
3. As to yourself, state:
   (a) Your present health;
   (b) Whether you have any need of unusual or extraordinary medical care or special financial needs;
   (c) Your educational background, giving all schools attended, years of attendance, and any degrees conferred, as well as any special training courses and employment skills;
   (d) If you were married at the time you attended school or any special training course, indicate whether your spouse contributed to the cost of your education and/or support and living expenses and the amount thereof, and, if your spouse did not contribute to these, who paid for your education and/or support and living expenses;
   (e) If you own or have been granted a license to practice any profession or other occupation in this or any other state, indicate the nature of such license(s) and the approximate monetary value of each license.
4. If you have any disability(ies) that at any time renders or rendered you unable to perform work or limits or limited your ability to perform work, whether now, in the past, or in the future, state:
   (a) The nature of the disability(ies);
   (b) The name and address of each treating physician for the past ten years for said disability(ies);
   (c) The frequency of said treatment;
   (d) The cost of said treatment;
   (e) The nature of said treatment;
   (f) The method of payment for said treatment, including the name of the payor.
   *Attach any medical reports concerning the disability(ies).

PRIMARY AND MARITAL RESIDENCES

5. State your primary residence addresses for the past five (5) years, up to the present time, indicating periods of residence at each address.
6. If you are not currently residing with your spouse, state the names, ages, and relationship to you of those persons with whom you reside at the above address, either on a permanent or on a periodic basis.
7. If your primary residence is rented or leased, state:
   (a) The monthly rental and term of the lease or agreement;
   (b) To whom the rent is paid, including name and address;
   (c) Whether any other persons are contributing to rental payments, the amount of the contribution, and the names of any such persons.
   *Attach copies of canceled rent checks for the last twelve (12) months and a copy of your lease or rental agreement.
8. If your present primary residence is owned by you, state:
   (a) The date the residence was acquired;
   (b) From whom it was purchased;
   (c) The purchase price;
   (d) The amount of the down payment;
   (e) The source of the down payment, showing contribution by both spouses, as well as any other persons;
   (f) The amount of the original mortgage(s);
   (g) The amount of the mortgage(s) as of the date of the separation of the parties;
   (h) The amount of the mortgage(s) at the present time if different from (f) or (g) above;
   (i) The name and address of the mortgagee(s) and the mortgage number(s), if any;
   (j) The market value of the property at the time of the separation of the parties;
   (k) The present market value of the property, if different from (j) above;
   (l) The tax basis of the property when acquired;
   (m) The adjusted tax basis of the property at the time of the separation of the parties;
   (n) The current adjusted tax basis, if different from your answer to (m) above;
   (o) The nature and dollar amount of any liens or other encumbrances on the property not indicated in previous answers;

(p) The current assessed valuation assigned the property for real property taxation purposes.
*Attach copies of closing statements, deeds, and appraisals, and mortgages, as well as the most recent bill or bills for real estate taxes.

9. If the residence referred to in question 8 above is not the "marital residence," then supply the same information as requested in questions 8(a) through 8(p) above for the "marital residence."
*Attach copies of closing statements, deeds, and appraisals, as well as the most recent bill or bills for real estate taxes.
10. Who has been paying the mortgage and/or tax payments from the date of the separation of the parties?

OTHER REAL ESTATE

11. If you have an interest in any real property other than indicated in the previous section, for each such piece of real property, state:
(a) Street address, county, and state where the property is located;
(b) Type of property, deed references, and the nature of your interest in the property (full or partial; type of tenancy; restraints on alienation);
(c) Zoning of the property;
(d) Date property was acquired;
(e) From whom it was purchased;
(f) The amount of the down payment;
(g) The source of the down payment, showing the contribution of both spouses and others;
(h) The amount of the original mortgage(s);
(i) The purchase price;
(j) The amount of the mortgage(s) as of the date of the separation of the parties;
(k) The amount of the present mortgage(s);
(l) The name and address of the mortgagee(s) and the mortgage number(s), if any;
(m) The present market value of the property;
(n) The nature and dollar amount of any liens or other encumbrances on the property that are not listed in a previous answer;
(o) The names and addresses of all co-owners and the nature of their interest in the property;
(p) Itemize all operation expenses, including but not limited to taxes, mortgage payments, insurance, fuel oil, gas, electric, water, and maintenance;
(q) The present assessed valuation assigned the property for real property taxation purposes;
(r) The exact nature and extent of your interest, if not listed in question 11(b);
(s) The tax basis of the property when acquired;
(t) The adjusted tax basis at the time of the separation of the parties;
(u) The names and mailing addresses of all tenants and occupants and the annual and/or monthly rental paid by each, and their relationship to you (e.g., relative, friend), if any;
(v) The source and amount of any income produced by the property, if not previously indicated.
*Attach copies of the closing statements, deeds, and appraisals.
12. If you have sold or otherwise disposed of any real property in which you have had an interest during your marriage (including periods of separation), state for each property, in detail, the same information as asked in interrogatory 11 above.
*Attach copies of each closing statement and deed.
13. If you have executed any contracts to buy or sell real property during your marriage (including periods of separation), indicate the location of the property, terms of the sale, whether you were the purchaser or seller, and the name of the other party or parties.
*Attach a copy of each such contract.
14. If you are the holder of an interest in any real property not disclosed in a previous interrogatory, state for each:
(a) The type of such property (whether real or personal);
(b) The location of such property;
(c) The date acquired;
(d) The net monthly rental to you from each piece of property;
(e) The gross monthly rental to you from each piece of property;
(f) The present value of such property.

INCOME AND EMPLOYMENT

15. State the names, addresses, and telephone numbers of all employers for the last ten (10) years and give the dates of such employment, position held, salary, other compensation, and reason for termination.
16. As to your present employment, state:
(a) Name and address of your employer;
(b) Type of work performed, position held, and nature of work or business in which your employer is engaged;
(c) Amount of time you have been employed in your present job;
(d) Hours of employment;
(e) Rate of pay or earnings, gross and net average weekly salary, wages, commissions, overtime pay, bonuses, and gratuities.
*Attach copies of all evidence of above payments, including pay stubs, W-2 forms, etc., for the past twelve months.
17. State what benefits your employer provides for you and/or your family inclusive but not limited to all of the following. Include a brief description of the benefit and whether your family is a beneficiary of the particular benefit:
(a) Health insurance plan;
(b) Life insurance;

continued

Exhibit 8.2 Interrogatories—*Continued*

(c) Pension, profit sharing, or retirement income program;
(d) Expense and/or drawing accounts;
(e) Credit cards (include reimbursement for business expenses placed on your personal credit cards);
(f) Disability insurance;
(g) Stock purchase options;
(h) Indicate whether you are required to pay for all or any part of the benefits listed in this interrogatory and the amount of those payments and/or contributions.

18. If you are furnished with a vehicle by any person, employer, or other entity, state:
    (a) The year, make, model, and license number;
    (b) The name and address of the legal owner;
    (c) The name and address of the registered owner;
    (d) The date you were furnished with such vehicle or replacement vehicle;
    (e) The amount paid for gas, repairs, maintenance, and insurance by you personally and by anyone other than yourself. Indicate whether you are reimbursed directly or indirectly for the expenses paid by you personally.
    *If this vehicle is leased, attach a copy of said lease.
19. Describe any other property or other benefit furnished to you as a result of your present employment.
20. State and itemize all deductions taken from your gross weekly earnings or other emoluments, including but not limited to taxes, insurance, savings, loans, pensions, profit sharing, dues, and stock options.
21. State if you have an employment contract with any company, corporation, partnership, and/or individual at the present time or have had one at any time during the last three (3) years. If there is or was such a contract of employment, state the terms thereof, or if written, attach a copy hereto.
22. As a result of your employment at any time during the marriage, are you entitled to receive any monies from any deferred compensation agreement? If so, for each agreement state:
    (a) The date such agreement was made or, if in writing, executed. If written, attach a copy.
    (b) The parties making or executing such agreement.
    (c) The amount you are to receive under such deferred compensation agreement and when you are to receive same. Attach account statements or other evidence of such payment.
23. State whether you have filed federal, state, and/or local income tax returns during the last five (5) years. If so, indicate the years during which they were filed and whether federal, state, or local.
    *Attach copies of all returns filed during the past five (5) years.
24. State in which bank savings account or checking account your salary, bonus, or other compensation is deposited, giving the name of the bank, branch, and account number. If said salary, bonus, or other compensation checks are cashed or negotiated rather than deposited, indicate the name and branch of the bank(s) or other institutions where said checks are regularly cashed or negotiated.
25. State whether you have received or are receiving any form of compensation, monetary or otherwise, from any work and/or services performed for other individuals, companies, corporations, and/or partnerships outside the business in which you are regularly engaged. If so, state:
    (a) The name and address of the individual, company, corporation, and/or partnership from whom you are receiving or have received such compensation during the last five (5) years;
    (b) The amount of the compensation received;
    (c) The nature of the services rendered by you for said compensation.
    *Attach copies of all 1099 tax forms covering "miscellaneous income" received as a result of such work and/or services during the last five (5) years.
26. State whether your salary or other compensation will increase during the next year and/or contract period as a result of any union contract and/or employment contract, or as the result of any regular incremental increase, or as a result of a promotion you have received that is not yet effective.
27. Itemize all income benefits and other emoluments not already included in your answers to the preceding interrogatories, including but not limited to any other sources of income such as pensions, annuities, inheritances, retirement plans, social security benefits, military and/or veteran's benefits, lottery prizes, bank interest and dividends, showing the source, amount, and frequency of payment of each. Indicate whether each income benefit and/or other emolument is taxable or nontaxable.

SELF-EMPLOYMENT

28. If you are self-employed or conduct a business or profession as a sole proprietor, partner, or corporation, state the type of entity it is. (For purposes of this question, a corporation includes any corporation in which your interest exceeds twenty percent (20%) of the outstanding stock.)
29. If a partnership, list the names and addresses of all partners, their relationship to you, and the extent of their interest and yours in the partnership.
    *Attach copies of any partnership agreements in effect at any time during the last five (5) years and all partnership tax returns filed during this period.
30. If a corporation, list the names and addresses of all directors, officers, and shareholders and the percentage of outstanding shares held by each. If any of the foregoing people are related to you, indicate the relationship.
    *Attach copies of the articles of incorporation and all corporate tax returns filed by the corporation during the past five (5) years.
31. State whether you have had an ownership interest(s) in any other corporation, partnership, proprietorship, limited venture, or other business during the course of the marriage. If so, state:
    (a) The nature of such interest(s);
    (b) The market value of such interest(s);

(c) The position held by you with respect to such interest(s) including whether you were an officer, director, partner, etc.;
(d) The date of acquisition of your interest(s) and the market value of said interest(s) when acquired;
(e) The value of said interest(s) on the date of your marriage if such interest(s) were acquired before your marriage;
(f) The date of termination of your ownership interest(s), if terminated;
(g) The total sale price of the business enterprise, if sold or transferred;
(h) The amount of the compensation received by you and the form of the compensation if other than cash or negotiable instrument as a result of the sale or transfer;
(i) The terms of each agreement of sale or transfer;
(j) The income received by you from the business during the last year prior to the sale or transfer.

32. State for each business, partnership, corporation, or other business entity in which you have an interest, the following:
(a) The amount of your contribution to the original capitalization;
(b) The amount of your contribution for any additional capitalization or loans to the business entity;
(c) The source from which monies were taken for capitalization and/or loans;
(d) The market value of the business entity at the time of the separation of the parties;
(e) The present market value of the business entity if different than (d) above;
(f) The market value of your share of the business entity at the time of the separation of the parties if different than (d) above;
(g) The present market value of your share of the business entity if different than (f) above;
(h) The market value of your share of the total value of the business entity at the time of your marriage;
(i) Amount of loans and/or reimbursement of capitalization paid you by the business entity at any time during the past five (5) years; indicate the amount received, the date received, and the disposition of the proceeds;
(j) The present amount maintained in the capital account;
(k) The name and address of all banks or other institutions in which the business entity has or has had, during the past five (5) years, checking, savings, or other accounts, the account number of each account, the amount presently contained in each, the amount contained in each at the time of the separation of the parties, and the amount contained in each six (6) months prior to the separation of the parties. If an account was closed prior to the time periods mentioned in this question, that is, prior to six (6) months before the separation of the parties, indicate the amounts in each such account for a three (3) year period prior to the closing of the account. State the destination of the amount in the account when closed;
(l) The total value of your capital account;
(m) The total value of all accounts receivable;
(n) The dollar value of all work in progress;
(o) The appreciation in the true worth of all tangible personal assets over and above book value;
(p) The total dollar amount of accounts payable;
(q) A list of all liabilities.

33. State the name and address of the following:
(a) All personal and business accountants consulted during the last five (5) years;
(b) All personal, business, or corporate attorneys consulted during the past five (5) years;
(c) Your stockbroker(s);
(d) Your investment advisor(s).

PERSONAL ASSETS

34. Itemize all accounts in banks or other institutions, time deposits, certificates of deposit, savings clubs, Christmas clubs, and checking accounts in your name or in which you have an interest presently or have had an interest during the past five (5) years, stating for each:
(a) The name and address of each depository;
(b) The balance in those accounts as of the date of the separation of the parties;
(c) The present balance;
(d) The balance four (4) months prior to the separation of the parties;
(e) If there are any differences among your answers to (b), (c), and (d) above, specify when the withdrawals were made, who received the benefit of the withdrawals, who made the withdrawals, and where the proceeds of the withdrawals went;
(f) The name and address in which each account is registered, account numbers, and the present location and custodian of the deposit books, check registers, and certificates.
*Attach copies of the monthly statements of such accounts for the past five (5) years and copies of savings account books or savings books and check registers.

35. State whether you have a safe deposit box either in your name individually, or in the name of a partnership, corporation, or other business entity to which you have access, stating the following:
(a) The location of the box and box number;
(b) The name in which it is registered and who, in addition to yourself, has access to the box;
(c) List the contents of said box in which you claim an interest.

36. If you have any cash in your possession or under your control in excess of one hundred dollars ($100), specify:
(a) The amount of the cash;
(b) Where it is located;
(c) The source of said cash.

37. For each vehicle of any nature in which you have any interest, including, but not limited to, automobiles, trucks, campers, mobile homes, motorcycles, snowmobiles, boats, and airplanes, state:
(a) The nature of each vehicle;
(b) Your interest therein;

continued

Exhibit 8.2 Interrogatories—*Continued*

(c) The name in which the vehicle is registered;
(d) The make, model, and year of each;
(e) The price paid, the date acquired, and the source of the funds used;
(f) The principal operator of the vehicle since its purchase;
(g) The present location of the vehicle;
(h) The names and addresses of any co-owners;
(i) The present value of the vehicle.

38. State whether you own any horses or other animals with a value in excess of two hundred fifty dollars ($250). If so, state:
    (a) The date of purchase, the purchase price, and the source of the funds used;
    (b) The type of animals;
    (c) The market value of the animals at the time of the separation of the parties;
    (d) Their present market value if different from (c)
    (e) The names and addresses of any co-owners and the percentage of their interest.
    *Attach copies of any appraisals of the animals.
39. List all household goods, furniture, jewelry, and furs with a value in excess of two hundred fifty dollars ($250), in which you have an interest, stating for each:
    (a) The nature of each;
    (b) Your interest therein;
    (c) The price paid, the date acquired, and the source of the funds used;
    (d) The present value of the asset;
    (e) Whether the asset is "marital property," "separate property," or "community property." If you claim the asset is separate property, state your reasons therefor.
    *Attach copies of any appraisals of the jewelry or other personal property.
40. State whether you own or have an interest in any collections or hobbies, including, but not limited to, art, stamps, coins, precious metals, antiques, books, and collectibles with an aggregate value in excess of two hundred fifty dollars ($250). If so, state:
    (a) The nature of each;
    (b) Your interest therein and the interest of any co-owners. Also state the names and addresses of all co-owners and their relationship to you;
    (c) A complete itemization of each such collection, showing the price paid, the date acquired, and the source of the funds used;
    (d) The present value of each element of the asset (an "element" means a unit capable of being sold by itself);
    (e) If owned prior to the marriage, the value of each such element at the time of the marriage.
    *Attach copies of any appraisals of the collectibles.
41. State whether you are receiving or are entitled to receive any royalty income. If so, state:
    (a) The basis for such income, including the nature of any composition, copyright, work, or patent from which such income arose;
    (b) The amount of such income during the past five (5) years;
    (c) The terms of any agreement in relation to such composition, copyright, work, or patent.
    *Attach copies of any royalty statements or other invoices verifying such income.
42. State whether you have any legal actions pending for money damages, or whether you are entitled to receive any legal settlements or insurance recoveries. If so, state:
    (a) The amount of money you are demanding in your pleadings, or to which you are entitled as an insurance recovery or legal settlement;
    (b) The court in which the action is or was pending, the caption of the case, and the index or docket number;
    (c) Whether any other persons have an interest in the insurance recovery, legal settlement, or pending action and, if so, state their name, address, and the nature of their interest;
    (d) The circumstances resulting in your becoming entitled to the insurance recovery or legal settlement, or the circumstances leading to the commencement of the legal action.
43. State whether you have any HR10 or IRA agreements. If so, state:
    (a) The date of the creation of each such plan;
    (b) The amounts contributed by you or on your behalf to each such plan;
    (c) The current value of your account under each such plan.
    *Attach copies of the last three account statements for each plan.
44. State whether you are entitled to receive, or have received during the past five (5) years, any gambling awards or prizes, indicating the nature thereof, the amount, when you are to receive the same, and the date you became entitled to the award or prize.
45. State the names and addresses of all persons who owe you money if not indicated in previous interrogatories. Also state as to each:
    (a) The amount thereof;
    (b) When said sum is due;
    (c) The nature of the transaction that entitled you to receive the money and when the transaction took place.

STOCK ASSETS

46. Itemize all shares of stock, securities, bonds, mortgages, and other investments, other than real estate revealed in previous interrogatories, stating for each:
    (a) The identity of each item, indicating the type and amount of shares;
    (b) Whose name they are registered in, the names of any co-owners, their interest therein, and their relationship to you;

(c) The source of the monies from which you purchased the item;
(d) The original price of each item;
(e) The market value of each item at the time of the separation of the parties;
(f) The present market value of each item if different from (e) above;
(g) The amount of any dividends or other distribution received;
(h) The present location and custodian of all certificates or evidences of such investments.
*Attach hereto monthly statements of these securities for the past five (5) years.

47. State whether any of the shares of stock owned by you and listed in any of your previous answers to interrogatories is subject to any cross purchase or redemption agreement. If so, state:
(a) The date of such agreements;
(b) The parties to such agreements;
(c) The event that will bring about the sale or transfer under the agreement;
(d) The sale price under the agreement.

48. Itemize all shares of stock, securities, bonds, mortgages, and other investments, other than real estate and business entities previously listed in your name or in which you have an interest, which you have sold in the last five (5) years, stating for each:
(a) The identity of each item, indicating the type and amount of shares;
(b) Whose name they were registered in, including the names of any co-owners, their interest therein, and their relationship to you;
(c) The source of the monies from which you purchased each item;
(d) The original price of each item and date of purchase;
(e) The market value at the time of the separation of the parties;
(f) The amount of dividends or other distribution received;
(g) The date each was sold or transferred;
(h) To whom each was sold or transferred;
(i) The amount received for each such sale or transfer;
(j) The disposition and destination of the proceeds of said sale;
(k) If applicable, the value of each such item at the time of your marriage.

49. Itemize all shares of stock, securities, bonds, mortgages, and other investments purchased by you but held nominally by third persons, stating for each:
(a) The manner in which the person is holding said investment;
(b) The identity of each item as to type and amount of shares;
(c) Whose name they are registered in, including the names of any co-owners, their interest therein, and their relationship to you;
(d) The source of the monies from which you purchased each item;
(e) The original price of each item;
(f) The market value at the time of the separation of the parties;
(g) The present market value of each item;
(h) The value, if applicable, at the time of your marriage;
(i) The present location and custodian of all certificates or evidence of such investments;
(j) The amount of dividends or other distribution received.
*Attach monthly statements of these securities for the past three (3) years.

50. Are you the holder of any mortgages, accounts receivable, notes, or other evidence of indebtedness not indicated in your answer to previous interrogatories? If so, for each such instrument, state:
(a) The type of instrument;
(b) The date of maturity of such instrument;
(c) The amount of interest payable to you under such instrument;
(d) The nature of the sale or transaction (including the type of merchandise sold) from which the said instrument arose;
(e) The date the instrument was acquired by you.

51. State whether you have any money invested in any business ventures not covered in previous interrogatories. For each such investment, state:
(a) The nature of such investment;
(b) Your share of the interest therein;
(c) The original cost of such investment and the source of monies used for said investment;
(d) The amount of income yielded from the said investment;
(e) The present value of said investment.

52. If, during the course of your marriage, you have received any inheritances, state:
(a) From whom you inherited;
(b) The nature and amount of the inheritance;
(c) The disposition of any of the assets of the inheritance, tracing them to the time of the separation of the parties;
(d) The value of the inheritance at the time of the separation of the parties;
(e) The present value of the inheritance.

53. State whether you expect to receive any future inheritances. If so, state:
(a) From whom you expect to inherit;
(b) The nature and amount of inheritance.

54. State whether you have, during the last five (5) years, sold or transferred any interest in personal property valued in excess of two hundred fifty dollars ($250), and for each such sale or transfer, state:
(a) The nature of the property;

continued

Exhibit 8.2 Interrogatories—*Continued*

(b) The date of the sale or transfer;
(c) The method of transfer;
(d) The name and address of each purchaser or person receiving title;
(e) The amount received for said transfer or sale;
(f) The disposition of the proceeds of said sale or transfer.

55. State whether you have made any gift of any money or other personal property to friends, relatives, or anyone else during the past five (5) years of a value in excess of two hundred fifty dollars ($250). If so, state:
(a) The name and address of said person and the relationship of that person to you;
(b) The nature and value of the gift or the amount of money given;
(c) The date each gift was given;
(d) The reason for such gift.
*Attach copies of all gift tax returns filed.

TRUSTS

56. State whether you are the grantor, beneficiary, or holder of a power of appointment for any trust created by you, the members of your family, or any other persons or corporations. If so, for each trust, state:
(a) The date of the trust instrument;
(b) The name of the settlor;
(c) The name of the beneficiary(ies);
(d) The present amount of the trust corpus;
(e) The amount of the trust corpus at the time of the separation of the parties;
(f) The amount of the trust corpus at the time of your marriage, if applicable.
(g) Any restrictions on alienation to which such corpus is subject;
(h) The terms of the trust instrument;
(i) The income earned by the trust during the past five (5) years.
*If there is a trust instrument, attach a copy. If the trustee has rendered an accounting during the past five (5) years, attach a copy.

57. List any and all property, assets, or other things of a value in excess of two hundred fifty dollars ($250) that you hold in trust for anyone, stating as to each:
(a) The description of the property, its location, the name and address of the person for whom you hold same, and his or her relationship to you;
(b) The conditions or terms of the trust, including the amounts you are paid as commissions or other compensation for holding such property;
(c) How such property was acquired by you and whether you paid any part of the consideration therefor.

58. List all property or other things of value of any nature or kind with a value in excess of two hundred fifty dollars ($250) that is held in trust for you or that is in the care or custody of another person, corporation, or entity for you, stating for each:
(a) The nature of the property or other thing of value, its location, and custodian;
(b) The name and address of the trustee, if different than above;
(c) The conditions or terms of the trust;
(d) How such property or other thing of value was acquired and who paid the consideration therefor;
(e) The original cost;
(f) The value at the time of the separation of the parties;
(g) The present value if different than (f) above.
*Attach copies of any trust instruments or writings evidencing the above.

INSURANCE

59. List each life insurance policy, annuity policy, disability policy, or other form of insurance not disclosed in a previous interrogatory, stating for each:
(a) The name and address of the insurance company;
(b) The policy number;
(c) The type of policy;
(d) The name and address of the owner of the policy;
(e) The name and address of the present beneficiaries of the policy;
(f) If there has been a change of beneficiary in the last five (5) years, give the date of each change and the name and address of each former beneficiary;
(g) The date the policy was issued;
(h) The face amount of the policy;
(i) The annual premium and the name and address of the person paying the premium currently and for the past five (5) years;
(j) The cash surrender value of said policy;
(k) If any loans have been taken out against the policy, the date of each such loan, the person making such loan, the amount of the loan, and the purpose for which the proceeds were utilized;
(l) If said policy has been assigned, the date of the assignment and the name and address of each assignee;
(m) The present custodian of the policy;
(n) If any policy is supplied by an employer, whether it is a condition of employment and under what conditions it terminates.

60. State whether you have surrendered, transferred, or in any way terminated any form of insurance policy for the last five (5) years. If so, state:

(a) The name and address of the insurance company;
(b) The number of the policy;
(c) The type of policy;
(d) The name and address of the last or current owner of the policy;
(e) The name and address of the last or present beneficiary of the policy;
(f) The face amount of the policy;
(g) The cash surrender value of the policy at present or just prior to its being surrendered, transferred, or terminated;
(h) The person transferring, surrendering, or terminating said policy;
(i) If any cash was realized from the said transfer, termination, or surrender, the amount realized and for what purposes the proceeds were used.

PENSION AND DISABILITY

61. State whether you are entitled to any pension, profit sharing, or retirement plan. If so, state:
   (a) The nature of the plan;
   (b) The name and address of the entity or person providing the plan;
   (c) Whether your interest in the plan is vested and, if not, the date and conditions under which the plan will vest;
   (d) Whether the plan is contributory or noncontributory and, if contributory, the amount you contributed during the marriage;
   (e) The amount you earned in the plan during the marriage;
   (f) If you have the right to withdraw any monies from the plan, how much money you may withdraw and when;
   (g) If you have withdrawn or borrowed any monies from the plan, indicate when and how much was borrowed and whether the money must be returned or repaid;
   (h) If there are any survivor benefits, give a brief description thereof.
   *Attach copies of all account statements, reports, or other writings concerning the plan(s) that are in your possession or readily available from your employer or pension payor.
62. If you are entitled to any disability benefits, state:
   (a) The nature of the disability;
   (b) The dollar amount of the award;
   (c) The date of payment of the award;
   (d) Whether there are any survivor benefits, giving a brief description thereof;
   (e) Whether any benefits or awards are presently being claimed by you, litigated, or reviewed, indicating the amount thereof if not included above.

EXPENSES

63. Itemize your average monthly expenses in detail [see chart below]. If any of the expenses include support of any other person outside your immediate family, set forth the name and address of such person and the portion of each expense attributable to each such person supported. (*NOTE:* All weekly expenses must be multiplied by 4.333 to obtain the monthly expense.) If certain expenses are paid by your employer, your spouse, or another party, so indicate by footnoting.

* * * * *

MONTHLY BUDGET EXPENSE
(interrogatory 63)

Food ____________
Clothing ____________
Mortgage(s) ____________
Property taxes ____________
Rent ____________
Utilities ____________
Fuel oil ____________
Telephone ____________
Garbage collection ____________
Water ____________
Plumbing ____________
Electrician ____________
Doctors ____________
Dentists ____________
Orthodontists ____________
Psychiatrists ____________
Attorney fees ____________
Drugs ____________
Hair care ____________
Dry cleaners ____________
Laundry ____________
Veterinarian ____________
Newspapers ____________
Magazines ____________
Internet service provider ____________

Insurance ____________
  Homeowner ____________
  Renter ____________
  Automobile ____________
  Life ____________
  Hospitalization ____________
  Floater ____________
  Umbrella ____________
  Disability ____________
  Other ____________
Professional dues ____________
Club dues ____________
Babysitters ____________
Domestics ____________
Burglar alarm service ____________
Voluntary support payments ____________
Court-ordered support payments ____________
Past due installment obligations ____________
  Credit cards ____________
  Auto loans ____________
  Personal loans ____________
  Charge accounts ____________
Credit card fees ____________
Education ____________

continued

Exhibit 8.2 Interrogatories—*Continued*

Allowances __________
Sports & hobbies __________
Dancing lessons __________
Music lessons __________
Sport lessons __________
Auto expenses __________
  Gas __________
  Maintenance __________
  Commuting __________
  Parking __________
  License & registration __________
  Transportation __________
Camp __________
Household improvements __________
Household repairs __________
Apartment maintenance __________
Garden maintenance __________
Pool maintenance __________
Termite/pest service __________
Tree service __________
Water softener __________
Furniture & appliances __________
Furnishings __________
Contributions __________

Vacations __________
Christmas presents __________
Chanukah presents __________
Other presents __________
Entertainment __________
Misc. spending money __________
Cable TV __________
Emergencies __________

DETAIL ALL OTHER EXPENSES BELOW:

____
____
____
____
____
____

TOTAL MONTHLY EXPENSES __________

64. State whether anyone contributes to your support, income, or living expenses who has not been included in your answers to a previous interrogatory. If so, state:
    (a) The person's name and address;
    (b) The person's relationship to you;
    (c) The amount of support, income, or living expenses received by you during the last five (5) years and the frequency of said support, income, or living expenses;
    (d) The reason for said support;
    (e) The nature of said support.

LIABILITIES

65. Set forth a list of all credit card balances, stating:
    (a) The name of the obligor;
    (b) The total amount due at the present time and the amount due at the time of the separation of the parties;
    (c) The minimum monthly payment;
    (d) The name in which the card is listed and the names of all persons entitled to use the card;
    (e) The exact nature of the charges for which the money is owed;
    (f) Who incurred each obligation.
    *Attach copies of all credit card statements for the past twelve (12) months.
66. Set forth in detail any outstanding obligations, including mortgages, conditional sales contracts, contract obligations, promissory notes, or government agency loans not included in your answers to any previous interrogatories, stating for each:
    (a) Whether the obligation is individual, joint, or joint and several;
    (b) The name and address of each creditor and that creditor's relationship to you;
    (c) The form of the obligation;
    (d) The date the obligation was incurred;
    (e) The consideration received for the obligation;
    (f) A description of any security given for the obligation;
    (g) The amount of the original obligation;
    (h) The date of interest on the obligation;
    (i) The present unpaid balance of the obligation;
    (j) The date and the amount of each installment repayment due;
    (k) An itemization of the disposition of the funds received for which the obligation was incurred.
67. List all judgments outstanding against you or your spouse not included in your answer to a previous interrogatory, and for each state:
    (a) The names of the parties and their respective attorneys;
    (b) The courts in which the judgments were entered and the index or docket number assigned to each case;
    (c) The amount of each judgment.
68. If there is a wage execution, judgment, or order to pay out of income and earnings, state:
    (a) How much is taken from your earnings each week;
    (b) The name and address of obligors and their relationship to you;
    (c) The balance due.
69. State the nature of any lien or security interest not indicated in your answer to a previous interrogatory to which any of the assets listed by you in previous interrogatories are subject, indicating for each:
    (a) The name and address of the holder thereof;
    (b) The holder's relationship to you;

(c) The amount and frequency of the payments you make thereon;
(d) The balance due.

MISCELLANEOUS

70. If any money, property, and/or asset was acquired by you either before the marriage or after the separation of the parties, state for each with a value in excess of two hundred fifty dollars ($250) the following:
(a) The nature of the property;
(b) The date acquired;
(c) The source of the acquisition;
(d) Your interest therein;
(e) The present market value.
71. If any other money, property, or assets described in the above interrogatory were sold, transferred, or disposed of, state for each:
(a) The manner of the disposition;
(b) The date of the disposition;
(c) To whom sold, transferred, or disposed and their relationship to you;
(d) The amount received.
72. List all gifts received by you from your spouse with a value in excess of one hundred dollars ($100), giving for each:
(a) The date received;
(b) The nature of the gift;
(c) The market value of the gift when given, and currently.
73. List all gifts received by you from your family, your spouse's family, or any other party or entity, with a value in excess of one hundred dollars ($100), giving for each:
(a) The name of the donor and the relationship of the donor to you;
(b) The date received;
(c) The nature of the gift;
(d) The market value of the gift when given, and currently.
74. If you have prepared a financial statement of your assets and liabilities, either individually or for any business in which you have an interest within the past five (5) years, state:
(a) The dates of all such statements;
(b) The name and address of the person, firm, company, partnership, corporation, or entity for whom they were prepared;
(c) The name and address of all persons who worked on the preparation of such statements.
*Attach copies of all such financial statements.
75. State what counsel fees you have paid or agreed to pay for services rendered in connection with the separation of the parties.
76. State whether you have made application for any loans with any lending institutions, individuals, companies, or corporations during the past five (5) years. If so, state for each:
(a) The name and address of the lending institution, individual, company, or corporation;
(b) The date of the application;
(c) The amount of the loan;
(d) Whether your application was approved or denied.
*Attach a copy of all such loan applications.

THE BEGINNING OF THE SEPARATION AGREEMENT

On the assumption that the law firm now has a comprehensive picture of the assets of the client (see chapter 3) and of the opposing spouse (see interrogatories in Exhibit 8.2), we turn to the separation agreement itself.

Exhibit 8.3, on page 242, presents some sample introductory clauses sometimes found in separation agreements. It is good practice in the drafting of a separation agreement to number each paragraph separately (1, 2, 3, etc.) after the introductory clauses and to use headings for each major topic (e.g., alimony, custody).

A number of issues relating to the introductory clauses in Exhibit 8.3 need to be discussed:

- Public policy and collusion
- Capacity to contract
- Duress and fraud
- Consideration

Public Policy and Collusion

The agreement in Exhibit 8.3 between Fred and Linda Jones is careful to point out that a separation has already occurred. When parties are still living

Exhibit 8.3 Sample Introductory Clauses in a Separation Agreement

Separation Agreement

THIS AGREEMENT is entered on this ______ day of ______, 20___, by Fred Jones (referred to in this agreement as the Husband), residing at __________, and by Linda Jones (referred to in this agreement as the Wife), residing at __________.

Witnesseth:

WHEREAS, the parties were married on ______, 19___ in the state of ______________, city of ______, and

WHEREAS, ______ children were born of this marriage: (here list each child with dates of birth)

WHEREAS, as a result of irreconcilable marital disputes, the parties have been voluntarily living apart since ______, 20___ which both parties feel is in their own best interests and that of their children, and

WHEREAS, both parties wish to enter this agreement for the purpose of settling all custody, support, and property rights between them, and any other matter pertaining to their marriage relationship, and

WHEREAS, both parties acknowledge that they have had separate and independent legal advice from counsel of their own choosing on the advisability of entering this agreement, that they have not been coerced or pressured into entering the agreement, and that they voluntarily decide to enter it.

NOW THEREFORE, in consideration of the promises and the mutual commitments contained in this agreement, the parties agree as follows:

[the full text of the agreement goes here in numbered paragraphs; sample clauses are found at the end of this chapter.]

together despite their decision to separate, the law operates on the assumption that there is still hope. By definition, a separation agreement attempts to provide *benefits* to the parties in the form of money, freedom, etc. The very existence of such an agreement is viewed as an *inducement* to obtain a divorce unless the parties have already separated or are about to do so shortly. A separation agreement between two parties who are still living together and who intend to remain together indefinitely might be declared unenforceable. It would be the equivalent of one spouse saying to another, "If you leave me now, I'll give you $25,000." The agreement is invalid because it is **conducive to divorce.** This is against **public policy.**

conducive to divorce
Tending to encourage or contribute to divorce.

public policy
The principles inherent in the customs, morals, and notions of justice that prevail in a state. The foundation of public laws. The principles that are naturally and inherently right and just.

Another kind of illegal agreement is an attempted "private divorce." Suppose a husband and wife enter the following brief separation agreement:

> "We hereby declare that our marriage is over and that we will have nothing to do with each other henceforth. As we part, we ask nothing of each other."

Assume further that this agreement is not shown to anyone. To permit parties to make such a contract would be to enable them to "divorce" themselves without the involvement of a court. At the time the parties attempted to enter this contract, it may have seemed fair and sensible. Suppose, however, that months or years later, the wife finds herself destitute. If she sues her husband for support or alimony, he cannot defend the action by raising her contract commitment not to ask anything of him. If either of them later tries to marry someone else, he or she will have no defense against a charge of bigamy.

collusion
(1) An agreement to commit fraud. (2) An agreement between a husband and wife in a divorce proceeding that one or both will lie to the court to facilitate obtaining the divorce.

A more serious kind of illegal agreement between husband and wife is **collusion.** An example of this category of fraudulent agreement would be a plaintiff who falsely asserts that the defendant deserted her on a certain date and a defendant who falsely admits to this or remains silent even though he knows that the assertion is false. Their *collusive* objective is usually to *facilitate* the granting of the divorce. Before no-fault divorce became part of our legal system (see chapter 7), this kind of falsehood was common. Another example is a clause in a separation agreement providing that if either party later seeks a divorce, the other party promises not to appear or not to raise any defenses to the divorce action even if the parties know that such defenses exist. Such an agreement would be invalid because it is collusive, improperly inducing divorce.

The rule that separation agreements are invalid if they are conducive to divorce has been criticized as unrealistic, since it is difficult to imagine a mutually acceptable separation agreement involving future divorce that does *not* in some way facilitate or encourage the parties to go through with the divorce. Nevertheless, courts continue to watch for improper facilitation and collusion. The coming of no-fault divorce has lessened a court's inclination to invalidate a separation agreement for these reasons. Since divorce has been made much easier to obtain because of no-fault grounds, courts are more reluctant to try to save the marriage at all costs and more willing to let the separation agreement be the vehicle through which the parties confront the inevitable. This is not to say that courts will no longer be concerned with collusion and agreements that are conducive to divorce. These prohibitions are still on the books. The atmosphere, however, has changed with no-fault. Most of the court decisions on these prohibitions were handed down before the arrival of no-fault. It is questionable how willing courts are to follow all of those decisions today.

Below are a series of clauses sometimes found in separation agreements, with comments on how the courts have treated the issues of divorce facilitation and collusion raised by the clauses.

> "The wife agrees that she will file for a divorce against the husband within three months."
>
> "None of the terms of this separation agreement shall be effective unless and until either of the parties is granted a divorce."

The first clause is invalid; a party cannot promise to file for a divorce. The clause does not merely encourage divorce; it makes it almost inevitable. The second clause appears to be as bad as or worse than the first. Neither of the parties will obtain any of the benefits in the separation agreement unless one of them obtains a divorce. Arguably, this clause encourages one of the parties to file for divorce and the other party to refrain from contesting the divorce. Oddly, however, the courts have not interpreted the second clause in this way. It *is* legal to condition the entire separation agreement on the granting of a divorce. The logic of this result is not entirely clear, but the courts so hold.

> "The wife agrees that if the husband files for divorce, she will not raise any defenses to his action."
>
> "In the event that the wife travels to another state to file for divorce, the husband agrees to go to that state, appear in the action, and participate therein."

The first clause is collusive. If a party has a defense, it is improper to agree not to assert it. Even if you are not sure whether you have a defense, it is collusive to agree in advance to refrain from asserting whatever defense you *might* have. Courts consider this as improper as an agreement to destroy or to conceal important evidence.

The second clause is more troublesome. Here the parties are clearly contemplating an out-of-state divorce, perhaps because they both realize that they would have difficulty establishing the grounds for divorce in their own state. Such **migratory divorces** were once quite common. Is a clause conducive to divorce if it obligates the defendant to appear in the foreign divorce action? Some states think that it is and would invalidate the agreement. Other states, however, would uphold the agreement.

migratory divorce
A divorce obtained in a state to which one or both parties traveled before returning to their original state.

ASSIGNMENT 8.1

Determine whether any of the following clauses improperly facilitates divorce or is collusive. (See General Instructions for the Legal-Analysis Assignment in Appendix A.)

a. "In the event that the wife files a divorce action, the husband agrees not to file any defenses to said action if and only if it is clear to both parties that the husband has no defense."
b. "In the event that the wife files a divorce action, the husband will pay in advance all expenses incurred by the wife in bringing said action."
c. "In the event that the wife files for a judicial separation, for separate maintenance, or for an annulment, the husband agrees to cooperate fully in the wife's action."

ASSIGNMENT 8.2

a. Locate a digest containing small paragraph summaries of court opinions from your state. Find those parts of the digest that deal with separation agreements. List any ten key topics and numbers that cover any aspect of separation agreements.
b. Are there statutes in your state code dealing with separation agreements? If so, briefly summarize any five. (See General Instructions for the State-Code Assignment in Appendix A.)

Capacity to Contract

There was a time in our history when the very thought of a wife entering a contract with her husband was anathema. A married woman lacked the *capacity to contract* with her husband. At common law, the husband and wife were one, and "the one" was the husband. You cannot make a contract with yourself. This rule, of course, has been changed. A wife can enter a contract such as a separation agreement with her husband. While such contracts can be entered, the Internal Revenue Service and the husband's creditors are often suspicious of husband-wife contracts, especially when the result is to place property purchased by the husband in the name of the wife.

Today the major question of capacity involves mental health. A separation agreement is invalid if either party lacked the capacity to understand the agreement and the consequences of signing it. The traditional test is as follows: the person must understand the nature and consequences of his or her act at the time of the transaction. This understanding may not exist due to insanity, mental retardation, senility, temporary delirium due to an accident, intoxication, drug addition, etc.

Duress and Fraud

In the excerpt from the Jones separation agreement in Exhibit 8.3, you will note that several times at the beginning of the agreement the parties mention that they are entering it "voluntarily." According to traditional contract principles, if a party enters a contract because of **duress,** it will not be enforced. Suppose that a wife is physically threatened if she does not sign the separation agreement. Clearly, the agreement would not be valid. The husband could not sue her for breaching it or attempt to enforce it in any other way.

duress
Coercion; acting under the pressure of an unlawful act or threat.

Of course, simply because the separation agreement says that the parties enter it "voluntarily" does not necessarily mean that no duress existed. Either spouse could have been forced to say the agreement was signed "voluntarily." But to have the agreement say that it was "voluntarily" signed is at least *some* indication (however slight) that no duress existed. An **aggrieved** party can still introduce evidence to the contrary.

aggrieved
Injured or wronged; the person injured or wronged.

During discussions and negotiations, if a spouse lies about a major asset that he or she possesses, the separation agreement must be set aside for **fraud.** If the spouse fails to disclose or undervalues major assets, many courts will again invalidate the agreement unless its terms are deemed to be fair to the other spouse.

fraud
Knowingly making a false statement of present fact with the intention that the plaintiff rely on the statement. The plaintiff's reasonable reliance on the statement harms him or her.

Suppose that after signing the separation agreement, a party becomes destitute or near-destitute. Some courts will intervene and not allow him or her to suffer the consequences of a bad bargain in the separation agreement, even if there was no clear evidence of duress or fraud. At one time, many courts presumed that a husband took unfair advantage of his wife unless he demonstrated otherwise. These courts did not allow the husband to treat his wife **at arm's length** as he would a competitor in a commercial transaction. The women's movement has helped change this attitude. Courts no longer so blatantly protect women. Both sides will be forced to live with the agreement they signed, particularly if there was full disclosure of assets and no duress or fraud, both had the opportunity to seek independent advice before they signed, and neither is about to become a public charge.

at arm's length
As between two strangers who are looking out for their own self-interests. At a distance; without trusting the other's fairness; free of personal bias or control.

The last WHEREAS clause in the beginning of the Jones separation agreement in Exhibit 8.3 states that both Fred and Linda had the benefit of separate legal advice on the advantages and disadvantages of signing the agreement. As indicated, this fact can be very significant in a court's deliberation on whether to set the agreement aside on a ground such as duress. It is relatively difficult to challenge the validity of a separation agreement that was signed after both sides had the benefit of their own attorney—even though the spouse with most of the resources may have had to pay for both attorneys.

The following case of *Bell v. Bell* contains some of the factors that a court might consider when the validity of a separation agreement is called into question because of duress or other improper conduct:

CASE

Bell v. Bell

38 Md. App. 10, 379 A.2d 419 (1977)
Court of Special Appeals of Maryland

Background: *Diane and Stanley Bell entered a separation agreement and executed eleven deeds pursuant to the agreement. Diane asked the circuit court to cancel the agreement and the deeds on the ground that they were obtained by duress and undue influence. The chancellor in the circuit court denied this request. The case is now on appeal before the Court of Special Appeals of Maryland where Diane is the appellant and Stanley is the appellee.*

Decision on Appeal: *Decree of circuit court affirmed. The separation agreement and deeds should not be set aside.*

Opinion of the Court:

Justice THOMPSON delivered the opinion of the court. . . .

The facts that gave rise to this suit are as follows. Diane Bell consulted an attorney in July of 1975, concerning the preparation of a separation agreement. The agreement was prepared and Mrs. Bell presented it to Mr. Bell at home on the morning of August 27, 1975. After examining the agreement at his place of business Mr. Bell inserted several changes and gave it to his secretary for retyping. Two significant changes were made in the agreement. The original provided for child support in the amount of $700 per month. This figure in the amended agreement was reduced to $300. Mr. Bell's agreement also provided for the disposition of the eleven houses owned by the parties as tenants by the entireties. Under his agreement Mrs. Bell was to receive one of the houses while he retained the other ten. After his agreement was completed he telephoned the appellant and asked her to come to his office in Wheaton to sign the agreement. At that time no mention was made of the changes.

When Mrs. Bell arrived, Mr. Bell suggested that they go to the nearby offices of Ralph Duane Real Estate Co. so that they could discuss the agreement in pri-

continued

CASE

Bell v. Bell—*Continued*

vate. Prior to Mrs. Bell's arrival Mr. Bell had prepared a series of sixteen 3 × 5 cards containing phrases such as "the man," "the kids," "his carrier," "your name," and "Ingrid (accessory)." During the course of the meeting he used these cards to inform the appellant of an investigation of her activities by private detectives and his knowledge of her adulterous affair with a police lieutenant. He also informed her that he knew that many of the contacts occurred at the apartment of her friend, Ingrid Gibson. He then presented his version of the separation agreement and made it clear that unless she signed it he would reveal her relationship to the Internal Affairs section of the police department and to the newspapers. Several times during the course of the conversation Mrs. Bell threatened to leave or requested an opportunity to consult with her attorney, but on each occasion, Mr. Bell threatened to "start the ball rolling" if such attempts were made before the agreement was signed. Mr. Bell placed a tape recorder in the office and recorded the entire conversation without the knowledge of Mrs. Bell. The tape was introduced into evidence.

After Mrs. Bell registered several protests, she read through the agreement and negotiated with Mr. Bell to make several changes. Among these changes was the receipt of a total of $15,000 in cash in addition to the one house. Under the agreement that was signed Mr. Bell received approximately $163,000 worth of property that was previously owned as tenants by the entireties while Mrs. Bell settled for approximately $45,000 in cash and property.*

The appellant argues that a confidential relationship existed between the parties and the burden was on the appellee to show the agreement was fair in all respects. In order to establish a confidential relationship one must show that by virtue of the relationship between them, he is justified in assuming the other party will not act in a manner inconsistent with his welfare. Unlike many jurisdictions, Maryland does not presume the existence of a confidential relationship in transactions between husband and wife. . . . In Maryland there has been a presumption that the husband is the dominant figure in the marriage. In *Manos v. Papachrist,* 199 Md. 257, 262, 86 A.2d 474, 476 (1951), the Court noted:

> "Ordinarily the relationship of husband and wife is a confidential one. Of course, in any given case it is a question of fact whether the marital relationship is such as to give the husband dominance over his wife or to put him in a position where words of persuasion have undue weight. Generally, however, on account of the natural dominance of the husband over the wife, and the confidence and trust usually incident to their marriage, a court of equity will investigate a gift from a wife to her husband with utmost care, especially where it strips her of all her property; and the burden of proof is on the husband to show that there was no abuse of confidence, but that the gift was fair in all respects, was fully understood, and was not induced by fraud or undue influence."

We noted the questionable foundation upon which this presumption rests in light of Article 46 of the Maryland Declaration of Rights, better known as the Equal Rights Amendment, in *Trupp v. Wolff,* 24 Md. App. 588, n. 15, 335 A.2d 171 (1975). . . . Since that decision, the Court of Appeals has held that sex classifications are no longer permissible under the amendment. . . . Consequently, the presumption of dominance cannot stand.

When the presumption is disregarded the question of whether a confidential relationship exists between husband and wife becomes a question of fact. Among the various factors to be considered in determining whether a confidential relationship exists are the age, mental condition, education, business experience, state of health, and degree of dependence of the spouse in question. . . .

The testimony shows that Mrs. Bell was born in Europe, moved to this country when she was eleven years old, and left school at the age of fifteen. Although she is employed as a beautician, she has relatively little experience or expertise in business matters. On the other hand, Mr. Bell is an experienced businessman, possesses a real estate license, and has a college degree. The chancellor considered these facts, but found that no confidential relationship existed primarily because Mrs. Bell negotiated several changes in the agreement and questioned other provisions, as is clearly shown by the tape recording. He found there was a lack of trust and confidence in the other party necessary to the establishment of a confidential relationship. We are unable to say his decision on this issue was clearly erroneous. Md. Rule 1086.

Absent proof of a confidential relationship between the parties, separation agreements, not disclosing any injustice or inequity on their face, are presumptively valid and the burden is on the party challenging the agreement to show its execution resulted from coercion, fraud, or mistake. *Cronin v. Hebditch,* 195 Md. 607, 74 A.2d 50 (1950). . . .

*The property Mr. Bell received had a gross value of $597,000 but was subject to mortgages totaling $434,339.

The only inequity claimed by the appellant is that she relinquished her one half interest in approximately $210,000 worth of real estate for approximately $45,000 in property and cash. This disparity in consideration is not sufficient to show that the agreement was unjust or inequitable. The cases which have found agreements to be unjust or inequitable on their face involved agreements that were completely lacking in any reasonable consideration. *Cronin v. Hebditch,* supra; *Eaton v. Eaton,* 34 Md. App. 157, 366 A.2d 121 (1976). In *Cronin* the wife signed an agreement releasing all her rights in property totalling more than $700,000 for a mere $10,000 and the Court of Appeals voided the agreement. More recently, in *Eaton* we struck down an agreement in which rights in $200,000 to $250,000 worth of property were released for $4,300. There we said:

> "'[The] defendant in this case has ostensibly purchased far more cheaply than a Court of Equity can condone all of the plaintiff's rights "of whatsoever kind or nature originating in and growing out of the marriage status." ' " 34 Md. App. at 162, 366 A.2d at 124.

As we are unable to say the agreement in question was lacking in any reasonable consideration, *Cronin* and *Eaton* cannot be used to relieve the appellant from proving the agreement was the product of duress or undue influence.*

The appellant's claim of duress or undue influence rests on the threats of Stanley Bell to notify the Internal Affairs section of the Police Department and the newspapers of her adulterous relationship unless the agreement was signed. Mr. Bell also stated that such disclosures would ruin the career of her lover and Ingrid Gibson, as well as her reputation in the community. The chancellor construed these statements as being no more than a threat to institute a divorce action on the grounds of adultery.

In order to establish duress there must be a wrongful act which deprives a person of the exercise of his free will. . . . Although we have found no Maryland case discussing the issue whether a threat to institute a civil suit can furnish a legally sufficient basis for duress, the question has been considered by a number of courts in other jurisdictions. Under these cases such suits do not form a legally sufficient basis for duress where the threat to institute the suit is made in good faith. . . . The courts have stated the assertion of a claim with the knowledge there is no reasonable belief of success or that it is false, amounts to bad faith and is a sufficient basis for a claim of duress. . . . Even though a particular act is legal, if it is wrongful in the moral sense a number of authorities have held that it can be used to establish a claim of duress. . . . *Link v. Link,* 278 N.C. 181, 179 S.E.2d 697 (1971).

The appellant argues that a threatened civil suit can be wrongful in a moral sense where it is used to coerce a settlement in a transaction unrelated to the subject matter of the suit. In support of this argument she relies on *Link v. Link,* supra. In *Link* the husband threatened to institute divorce proceedings against the wife and seek custody of their children unless the wife signed an agreement transferring her individual property to the husband. In deciding the case the Court noted the general rule that threats to institute civil proceedings are not wrongful but went on to state:

> "The law with reference to duress has, however, undergone an evolution favorable to the victim of oppressive action or threats. The weight of modern authority supports the rule, which we here adopt, that the act done or threatened may be wrongful even though not unlawful, per se; and that the threat to institute legal proceedings, criminal or civil, which might be justifiable, per se, becomes wrongful, within the meaning of this rule, if made with the corrupt intent to coerce a transaction grossly unfair to the victim and not related to the subject of such proceedings." 179 S.E.2d at 705. . . .

We find the reasoning of *Link* to be persuasive. Applying this approach to the case before us we think there was a legally sufficient basis for a finding of duress.

Mr. Bell threatened an action for divorce on the grounds of adultery to force a property settlement between the parties. Although the threatened action and the separation agreement both relate to the marital status of the parties, their substance is significantly different. . . . Mr. Bell's threats of a civil suit for divorce were unrelated to the dispute over the property and were made to obtain Mrs. Bell's signature on an agreement.

Even though the chancellor concluded that there was no wrongful conduct he went on to note in his

continued

---

*We are aware that some cases in other jurisdictions have created a presumption of invalidity where the consideration given is grossly disproportionate to the consideration received or is otherwise unfair. See *Le Bert-Francis v. Le Bert-Francis,* 194 A.2d 662 (D.C. 1963) (where separation agreement is unfair it is presumed to be invalid and the burden is on the party seeking to enforce it to prove otherwise); *Demaggio v. Demaggio,* 317 So. 2d 848 (Fla. App. 1975) (presumption of fraud created where agreement was grossly disproportionate, husband concealed assets, and wife was unrepresented by counsel); *Davis v. Davis,* 24 Ohio Misc. 17, 258 N.E.2d 277 (1970) (where provisions are disproportionate burden is on party seeking to uphold agreement to show there was full disclosure and the agreement was signed voluntarily).

In the absence of a confidential relationship, we see no reason to shift the burden of proof because the parties were husband and wife and one of them made a bargain which now seems unfair, but is not grossly unfair.

CASE

Bell v. Bell—*Continued*

opinion that even if the actions were considered wrongful, they did not deprive Mrs. Bell of her free will. . . . In support of this finding he noted that Mrs. Bell actively negotiated with Mr. Bell concerning various provisions in the agreement. At one point in the conversation she stated: "Umm, I'm just trying to get you know as much as I can which is, you have to admit, you'd do the same thing." Although there was testimony that Mrs. Bell was extremely upset after the agreement was signed, there was other testimony to the contrary. The chancellor considered this evidence and concluded:

> "[T]he negotiations and the tenor of the parties' meeting indicate quite clearly that the Plaintiff, in order to avoid an embarrassing incident involving her and close friends, freely and voluntarily negotiated with her husband."

The question of whether Mrs. Bell was deprived of her free will was one of fact and as there is ample evidence to support this finding, we are unable to say it was clearly erroneous. . . . In other words, there is no rule of law that precludes a woman from giving away a substantial portion of her property to save her reputation, if it is her voluntary act. Although on the evidence we may have found the act involuntary, we must accept the chancellor's findings because of his superior position to make this subtle distinction. . . .

[T]he chancellor found on the merits that the appellant did not act under duress or undue influence. We have accepted his finding because there was evidence to support it. . . .

DECREE AFFIRMED.

APPELLANT TO PAY THE COSTS.

ASSIGNMENT 8.3

a. Was Diane Bell coerced into signing the separation agreement? Was there coercion?

b. Conduct a debate in class on whether the separation agreement should have been enforced. Assume that there is a higher court in Maryland and that Diane appeals to this higher court. Make arguments to this court on behalf of Diane and on behalf of Stanley.

c. Assume that the facts of *Bell v. Bell* arose in your state. How would the case be decided? (If your state is Maryland, answer this question based on the law of any other state. See General Instructions for the Court-Opinion Assignment in Appendix A.)

d. Does a separation agreement have to be fair to both parties to be enforceable in your state? Check the statutes and the court opinions of your state. (See General Instructions for the State-Code Assignment and General Instructions for the Court-Opinion Assignment in Appendix A.)

Consideration

consideration
Something of value that is exchanged between the parties (e.g., an exchange of promises to do something or to refrain from doing something).

Contracts must be supported by **consideration** to be valid. The separation agreement is a set of promises by the parties of what they will do. The exchange of these promises (some of which may have already been performed, at least in part, at the time the agreement is signed) is the consideration for the separation agreement. A wife's promise to relinquish all claims she may have against her husband's estate when he dies is an example of her consideration to him. A husband's promise to transfer to his wife full title to land he solely owns is an example of his consideration to her.

We have already seen, however, that certain kinds of consideration are improper. A couple, for example, cannot exchange promises that one party will file for divorce and the other party will refrain from asserting any defenses he or she might have. Such consideration is illegal because it is conducive to divorce and may be collusive.

Perhaps the main consideration in the separation agreement is the separation itself. A husband and wife have the right to live with each other as husband and wife (i.e., the right of cohabitation). By reason of the separation agreement, the parties promise each other that they will never again claim this cohabitation right.

ALIMONY PAYMENTS AND PROPERTY DIVISION: INTRODUCTION

We now begin our coverage of **alimony** and **property division.** These two concepts are sometimes confused. A separation agreement (or a court opinion) may refer to a property division but mean *both* support and property division. In part, the confusion may be due to the fact that in the minds of the husband and wife, there is not always a clear distinction between these two concepts.

Exhibit 8.4 presents some major consequences of the distinction between alimony and property division. These consequences must be understood before examining the options available to the parties in drafting those clauses of the separation agreement that cover alimony and property division.

alimony
The amount of money or other property paid in fulfillment of a duty to support one's spouse after a separation or divorce.

property division
The distribution of property accumulated by spouses as a result of their joint efforts during the marriage. (Sometimes referred to as a **property settlement.**)

Exhibit 8.4 Alimony and Property Division Terms of a Separation Agreement

Alimony	Property Division
Effect of Bankruptcy	
If the spouse with the obligation to pay alimony goes into bankruptcy, his or her obligation to pay alimony is *not* discharged. All unpaid or delinquent alimony debts are still owed.	Under certain circumstances, a spouse may be able to discharge his or her property division debt through bankruptcy.
Effect of Remarriage and Death	
If the person receiving alimony (the payee) remarries, the alimony payments stop unless the separation agreement specifically provides otherwise. If the person paying alimony (the payor) remarries, the alimony payments to the first spouse must continue unless a court provides otherwise. If the payee or the payor dies, alimony payments cease unless the separation agreement specifically provides otherwise.	The remarriage or death of either party does not affect the terms of the property division. All remaining obligations under the property division must be fulfilled regardless of who remarries or dies.
Availability of Contempt	
If a party fails to fulfill an alimony obligation and falls into arrears, the power of the court to punish for contempt can be used as an enforcement device if the separation agreement has been incorporated and merged into a later divorce decree.	If either party fails to fulfill the obligations under the property division, states differ on whether the contempt power of the court can be used as an enforcement device. Many states say that they cannot, except for violation of a court order to transfer property.
The Court's Power to Modify Terms	
A court may have the power to modify the alimony term of a separation agreement if there has been a substantial change of circumstances of a continuing nature.	If either party later becomes dissatisfied with the terms of an otherwise valid property division, the court will rarely, if ever, modify those terms.

continued

Exhibit 8.4 Alimony and Property Division Terms of a Separation Agreement—*Continued*

Federal Income Tax Treatment

Alimony	Property Division
Alimony payments are includible in the gross income of the payee and are deductible for the payor. (See chapter 11.)	Transfers of property incident to a divorce are not reportable as income by the transferee or deductible by the transferor. The basis of the property in the hands of the transferee is the same as the transferor's basis.

Effect of Bankruptcy

arrears
Payments that are due but have not been made. (Also called **arrearages.**)

outstanding
Unpaid.

discharged
Released; forgiven so that the debt is no longer owed.

Under most forms of bankruptcy, citizens can eliminate all or most of their debts in order to make a fresh start. If a husband has fallen behind on his obligation under a separation agreement or a divorce decree, all **arrears** constitute a debt to his wife. Each time an alimony payment becomes due, a new debt is created. All **outstanding** obligations under a property division agreement are also debts. When a debtor goes into bankruptcy, some of his or her debts are **discharged.** Which ones? The Bankruptcy Act of Congress provides as follows:

> A discharge . . . does not discharge an individual debtor from any debt . . . to a spouse, former spouse, or child of the debtor, for alimony to, maintenance for, or support of such spouse or child, in connection with a separation agreement, divorce decree or other order of a court of record. . . .[2]

Hence debts in the nature of spousal or child support survive bankruptcy; they are not discharged. Property division debts, however, are treated differently. In general, they also are not dischargeable. But under two special circumstances, they *are* dischargeable: first, when the spouse who owes the obligation (the debtor) proves that he or she does not have enough assets to pay the property division debt plus all his or her other legitimate debts; second, when the debtor proves that the benefit of discharging the property division debt outweighs the harm or detriment that this discharge would cause the other spouse.[3]

This has a number of practical consequences. Assume that the husband is in serious financial difficulty and that bankruptcy is a possibility (a fact that must be carefully investigated by the attorney and paralegal representing the wife). The wife may be advised in the negotiation stage of the separation agreement to accept a small property division in exchange for a high amount of alimony. In the event that a bankruptcy does occur, she does not want to take the risk that he will be able to prove to the Bankruptcy Court that he fits within one of the two special circumstances that allow a discharge of property division debts. If he can, she loses everything still owed under the property division, whereas the alimony debt always survives the bankruptcy.

The specter of bankruptcy is real. Between 20 and 30 percent of all bankruptcies are precipitated by the financial fallout of divorce. An overriding question that must be asked about every bargained-for benefit in a property division is, What are the chances of being able to collect this?

---

[2] 11 U.S.C.A. § 523(a)(5).

[3] 11 U.S.C.A. § 523(a)(15): An individual debtor will not be discharged from any nonsupport debt incurred by the debtor in the course of a divorce or separation or in connection with a separation agreement unless:

(A) the debtor does not have the ability to pay such debt from income or property of the debtor not reasonably necessary to be expended for the maintenance or support of the debtor or a dependent of the debtor and, if the debtor is engaged in a business, for the payment of expenditures necessary for the continuation, preservation, and operation of such business; or

(B) discharging such debt would result in a benefit to the debtor that outweighs the detrimental consequences to a spouse, former spouse, or child of the debtor. . . .

Effect of Remarriage and Death

Normally, a spouse will want to stop paying alimony in the event that the receiving spouse (the payee) remarries. But alimony that ends upon the payee's remarriage can be an incentive *not* to remarry. To offset this, the separation agreement might provide reduced alimony payments if the payee remarries. Absent such an agreement, alimony ends upon the payee's remarriage.

If the paying spouse (the payor) remarries, his or her alimony obligation continues unless modified by a court.

If either party dies, alimony payments cease unless the separation agreement specifically provides otherwise. The separation agreement, for example, could provide that the alimony payments will continue after the death of the payor, at which time the payee would collect the alimony from the payor's **estate** or from a trust fund set up by the payor. Furthermore, the payor might take out a life insurance policy payable to the payee upon the death of the payor. This, in effect, continues some measure of support for the payee after the payor dies. Absent such provisions, the death of the payor terminates the alimony obligation in most states.

estate
All the property left by the deceased. After being used to pay debts, this property is distributed to those entitled under the will or the intestacy laws.

The situation is entirely different with respect to property division commitments; they continue no matter who dies or remarries. For example, as part of a property division (having nothing to do with support), John agrees to pay Mary $25,000. After John has paid Mary $1,000 of this amount, he dies. Mary can make a claim against John's estate for $24,000. If Mary dies after John has paid the $1,000, her heirs can require John to pay the remaining $24,000 to it (i.e., to Mary's estate) for distribution according to Mary's will or according to the laws of intestacy. The same is true if either party remarries. The funds or other property owed under the property division clauses of the separation agreement remain due and owing no matter who remarries.

Availability of Contempt

When one of the parties breaches a term of the separation agreement, ensuing legal action may depend upon whether the agreement is incorporated and merged into a subsequent divorce decree. If it is not, the regular breach-of-contract remedies are available (e.g., suit for damages, suit to rescind the contract). The sanctions for **contempt** (e.g., fine, prison) are *not* available. To some extent, the picture changes if the divorce decree incorporates and merges with the separation agreement. Alimony provisions *can* be enforced by the contempt powers of the court when incorporation and merger have occurred. States differ on whether the property division terms of a separation agreement can also be enforced by contempt. Many states say that it cannot. The sanction of contempt, however, is usually available when a party has violated a specific court order to transfer property.

contempt
Obstructing or assailing the authority or dignity of the court such as by intentionally violating a court order.

Court's Power to Modify Terms

A court will rarely, if ever, modify the property division term of a separation agreement. It may, however, have the power to modify alimony terms, particularly where a change in circumstances seriously affects the need of the recipient or the ability of the payor to pay. We will consider alimony modification in greater detail later in the chapter.

Federal Income Tax Treatment

The federal tax implications of alimony and property division in a separation agreement will be treated in detail in chapter 11.

Distinguishing between Alimony and Property Division

As you can see, it can make a great deal of difference whether a term of a separation agreement is classified as alimony or as property division. The classification hinges on the intent of the parties at the time they entered the separation agreement. For example, did the parties intend a five-year annual payment of $50,000 to be alimony or property division? Unfortunately, it is often difficult to answer this question. As indicated earlier, the parties may either be confused about the distinction or pay no attention to it. At a later date, however, when the parties realize the importance of the distinction (e.g., at tax time or when bankruptcy occurs), they will probably make conflicting claims about what their intentions were. It is the court's job to turn the clock back to when they were negotiating the separation agreement and determine what their intent was at that time. Note that the test is *not* what the payee actually uses the money or other property for. Proof that a payment was used for rent and groceries, for example, does not show that the payment was alimony. The test is the intent of the parties at the time of the agreement—*before the money or other property is used.*

When faced with the need to decide whether a transfer is alimony or property division, the court will consider a number of factors:

- Labels used in the agreement
- Contingencies
- Method of payment
- The nature of what is transferred

Usually, none of these factors is conclusive by itself. All of them must be considered. One of the factors may clearly indicate an intent that a term is alimony. If, however, the other factors clearly suggest that the term is part of the property division, the court may conclude that it is the latter. Unhappily, the factors do not always point in the same direction.

Labels Used in the Agreement Sometimes the separation agreement will explicitly label a provision as "alimony" or as a "property settlement" or "property division." These labels, however, do not always control. For example, suppose that an annual payment of $10,000 given to the wife is labeled "Property Division." If it is otherwise clear to the court that this money was in the nature of support, the court will classify it as alimony in spite of the label.

contingent
Conditional; dependent on something that may not happen.

Contingencies Terms that are **contingent** on the occurrences of certain events are often interpreted as alimony rather than as a property division (e.g., $10,000 a year to the wife until she remarries or dies). The presence of such contingencies suggests an intent to provide support while needed rather than an intent to divide property.

Method of Payment A term may provide a single *lump-sum payment* (e.g., $10,000), a *periodic payment* (e.g., $10,000 a year), or a *fluctuating payment* (e.g., $10,000 a year to be increased or decreased depending upon earnings in a particular year). Single lump-sum payments often suggest a property division. Periodic and fluctuating payments often suggest alimony.

The Nature of What Is Transferred A conveyance of property other than cash (e.g., a house, a one-half interest in a business) often suggests a property division. Cash alone, however, usually suggests alimony.

Again, these are only guides. All of the circumstances must be examined in order to determine the intent of the parties. It may be that a court will conclude that a transfer of a house was intended as alimony or support. The court might also conclude that a single lump-sum payment was intended as alimony. While a court will be inclined to rule otherwise in these examples, specific proof of intent will control.

ALIMONY

We will now examine individual clauses in the separation agreement, starting with alimony. Keep in mind, however, that no individual clause of a separation agreement can be fully understood in isolation. The negotiation process involves a large variety of factors. A party may agree to a term in the agreement not so much because that term in and of itself gives the party what he or she wants, but rather because the party decided to concede that term in order to gain another term (e.g., a wife may accept a lower alimony provision in exchange for the husband's agreement to the term giving her sole physical and legal custody of their child). This is the nature of the bargaining process.

Alimony, as we have seen, is the amount of money or other property paid in fulfillment of a duty to support one's spouse after a separation or divorce. (Later, in chapter 11 on taxation, we will see that the Internal Revenue Service has its own definition of alimony.) Other terms used for alimony include *maintenance, separate maintenance,* and *spousal support.*

Traditionally, it was the husband's duty to support the wife. Today, however, the duty is mutual in the sense that it will be imposed on the party who has the resources for the benefit of the party in need. To impose the duty only on a man would amount to unconstitutional sex discrimination in violation of the equal protection clause of the U.S. Constitution and in violation of many state constitutions. In the vast majority of situations, however, it is the woman who is the recipient of support through a separation agreement and/or through a court order.

First, we will examine some of the major negotiating options that must be considered in drafting the support provisions of the separation agreement. Then we turn to how a court will handle spousal support if the parties have not been able to negotiate an agreement.

Support Provisions in a Separation Agreement

Initial Decision The first decision the spouses must make is whether either should receive alimony. As we will see, alimony is less common today than it was before the law of property division was changed to become fairer to both parties. Assume, however, that the parties have decided that one of them will receive alimony. The separation agreement must then address a number of important issues to which we now turn.

Periodic Payments or Lump Sum? In a few states, it is illegal for a husband and wife to agree on a lump-sum payment (sometimes called **alimony in gross**) in satisfaction of the support duty. In most states, however, it is permissible. From the perspective of the recipient, collectibility is an important factor in deciding whether to seek a single lump-sum alimony payment. The wife may find it safer to take the lump-sum payment now rather than hassle with installment or periodic payments if there is any likelihood that the husband will fall behind in his payments. It can be expensive and psychologically draining to have to go after a delinquent former husband.

alimony in gross
A lump-sum payment of alimony.

Fixed or Fluctuating Periodic Payments?

If periodic payments are agreed to, a number of questions need to be considered and resolved. Should the payments have a fixed dollar amount (e.g., $700 per month)? On what day of the month is each payment due? Another major option is the flexible periodic payment. The amount of the payment may fluctuate up or down depending upon the income of the husband, of the wife, or of both. An alimony payment of 25 percent of the husband's earnings, for example, provides an automatic fluctuating standard.

MEDICAL AND DENTAL EXPENSES Does the alimony payment cover medical, dental, or mental health expenses (e.g., psychiatrist)? If not, do the parties want to include a term in the separation agreement on how these expenses are to be covered? They must also consider the tax consequences of paying these expenses (see chapter 11).

payor
One who makes a payment of money or is obligated to do so.

payee
One to whom money is paid or is to be paid.

LIFE INSURANCE Even though the duty of support usually ends at the death of the **payor** or of the **payee,** the parties might agree that the support payments will continue after the payor dies. If so, one way to do this is through a life insurance policy on the life of the party with the support duty. The beneficiary would be the other spouse and/or the children. If a life insurance policy already exists, the parties may decide to include a term in the separation agreement that requires a spouse to continue paying the premiums, to increase the amount of the policy, to name the other spouse as the irrevocable beneficiary, etc. The agreement should also specify whether an existing policy remains in force if either side remarries. If no life insurance policy exists, the parties need to decide whether to take one out.

TERMINATION OF SUPPORT PAYMENTS The circumstances that will terminate the support obligation should be explicitly spelled out in the separation agreement. For example, it might say that payments end when:

- The payee dies.
- The payor dies.
- The payee remarries. (If the second marriage is later annulled, states differ on whether the original support obligations of the first husband revive. See chapter 6.)
- The payee begins cohabiting with someone of the opposite sex.
- The payee fails to abide by the custody terms of the separation agreement.
- The payee competes with the payor in business. (In most states, however, such a term will *not* be enforced, since a payee's support payments cannot be conditioned on something that is not reasonably related to the marriage relationship.)

Of course, the separation agreement can provide the opposite. It may specify, for example, that the support payments will *continue* when:

- The payor dies. (The payor's estate would then have the obligation to continue the support payments. Life insurance is often used as a method of continuing support payments after the payor's death.)
- The payee remarries. (Rather than continuing the support payments in full after the payee remarries, the separation agreement usually provides for a reduced support payment. Some payors fear that if the total support payment ends upon remarriage, the payee will have little incentive to remarry.)

The termination of alimony payments does not affect arrears (i.e., unpaid back payments). All delinquent payments that accrued before the support obligation terminated must be paid. If they terminated upon the death of the ex-husband, for example, all payments he failed to make before he died can be enforced against his estate.

SECURITY When a payor fails to make a support payment, the payee can sue, but this is hardly an adequate remedy. Litigation can be expensive, lengthy, and emotionally draining. The Uniform Interstate Family Support Act (UIFSA) does make it easier to collect support through administrative and judicial tribunals, particularly in cases where the delinquent spouse is in another state. Nevertheless, the process is still time-consuming and somewhat cumbersome. (We will discuss the UIFSA at length in chapter 10 on child support.) The best way for a payee to avoid litigation is to be given *security* for the performance of the support obligation within the separation agreement itself. This security can be provided in a number of forms:

1. **Escrow.** The payor deposits a sum of money with an escrow agent (e.g., a bank), with instructions to pay the payee a designated amount of money in the event that the payor falls behind in a payment.
2. **Surety bond.** The payor gives the payee a surety bond. The payor pays premiums to the surety company. The surety company guarantees that if the payor fails to fulfill the support obligation, the company will fulfill it up to the amount of the bond.
3. **Annuity.** The payor purchases an annuity contract that provides a fixed income to the payee (annuitant) in the amount of the support obligation.
4. **Trust.** The payor transfers property (e.g., cash) to a trustee (e.g., a bank) with instructions to pay a fixed income to the payee (the beneficiary) in the amount of the support obligation.

The last two forms of security do not depend upon a breach by the payor of the support obligation clause of a separation agreement in order to come into effect.

escrow
Property is delivered by one person to another who will hold it until a designated condition or contingency occurs; then the property is delivered to the person for whose benefit the escrow was established.

surety bond
An obligation by a guarantor to pay a second party if a third party defaults in its obligation to the second party.

annuity
A fixed sum payable to an individual at specified intervals for a limited period of time or for life.

trust
A method of holding property by which legal title is given to one party (the trustee) for the benefit of another (the beneficiary).

Court-Ordered Alimony in the Absence of a Separation Agreement

Assume that the parties cannot agree on how much alimony or maintenance should be paid or on whether there should be any alimony at all. How will the court resolve the issue of alimony? There was a time in our history when courts gave substantial alimony awards to wives, particularly when the husband tended to control the family finances and to place all property in his name alone. Today, large alimony awards are less common because reforms in the law of property division have placed women in a less vulnerable position. Indeed, many courts will not address the alimony question until after they have divided the marital property. This division will be critical to obtaining a realistic assessment of a spouse's need for support.

Even when the need for alimony is clear, the trend is toward an award of **rehabilitative alimony** (also called *durational maintenance*), which is an award of support payments to a spouse for a limited time to allow him or her to return to financial self-sufficiency through employment or job training. How long should this take? The answer, of course, depends on the payee's skills and health and on the state of the economy. It also depends on whether the payee must spend time raising children. California says that alimony should be provided for a "reasonable time." In general, this has been interpreted to mean one-half the length of the marriage, although a shorter or longer time can be ordered.[4]

rehabilitative alimony
Support payments to a former spouse limited to the time needed to return to financial self-sufficiency through employment or job training.

In some states, alimony cannot be granted for more than a specific number of years (e.g., three years in Texas) except in extreme cases. Permanent or lifetime alimony is rare. It may require a ruling that health reasons or other

[4]California Family Code § 4320.

circumstances make it impossible for a spouse to become self-sufficient. Hostility toward long-term alimony can be found in the observation sometimes heard from judges that a failed marriage should not be turned into a "ticket for a lifetime pension."

The modern view on court-ordered alimony or maintenance is expressed in section 308(b) of the Uniform Marriage and Divorce Act, which some states have adopted:

> The maintenance order shall be in amounts and for periods of time the court deems just, without regard to marital misconduct, and after considering all relevant factors including:
>
> (1) the financial resources of the party seeking maintenance, including marital property apportioned to him, his ability to meet his needs independently, and the extent to which a provision for support of a child living with the party includes a sum for that party as custodian;
>
> (2) the time necessary to acquire sufficient education or training to enable the party seeking maintenance to find appropriate employment;
>
> (3) the standard of living established during the marriage;
>
> (4) the duration of the marriage;
>
> (5) the age and the physical and emotional condition of the spouse seeking maintenance; and
>
> (6) the ability of the spouse from whom maintenance is sought to meet his needs while meeting those of the spouse seeking maintenance.

Some states add a catchall factor that allows a court to consider anything else that the court deems "necessary to do equity and justice between the parties."

Courts will want to know what standard of living the spouses enjoyed during the marriage. While maintaining this standard may no longer be financially possible for both parties, the court will often use this standard as the starting point in its deliberations on alimony. The resources and earning capacities of both parties must be considered. Resources consist of independently owned assets (e.g., an inheritance from one's relative) as well as the share of the marital assets each will receive in the property division. As indicated earlier, a person's present and future earning capacity is affected by age, health, and other responsibilities such as raising children. The test for calculating income is not a person's actual earnings; it is his or her realistic earning potential now and in the future. A spouse cannot plead poverty that could be substantially eliminated by using available or obtainable employment skills. Nor can a spouse create self-imposed poverty by squandering or dissipating assets, as we will see later when we study dissipation in the case of *Gastineau v. Gastineau.* The length of the marriage is also an important factor. Spouses in marriages that lasted less than two years often receive no alimony or relatively modest rehabilitative alimony.

Most courts will take into account the tax consequences of the payment and receipt of alimony. As we will see in chapter 11, alimony is taxable to the payee and deductible by the payor.

Note that section 308(b) of the Uniform Marriage and Divorce Act says that alimony should be awarded "without regard to marital misconduct." Most courts follow this guideline, but some do not. There are courts that will increase the amount of alimony to be paid by a spouse who has committed domestic violence or other marital fault. And there are a few courts that will decrease the amount of alimony to be paid to a spouse who wrongfully interferes with the payor's child visitation rights.

Suppose that during the marriage one spouse takes care of the children or postpones his or her entry into the work force in order to help the other spouse obtain an education and build a career. In some states, this will lead to a larger alimony award for the sacrificing spouse. Technically, however, helping the other spouse build a career is more appropriately considered when dividing the marital assets in the property division stage of the divorce. Of course, delayed education or sacrificed job opportunities are certainly relevant to a person's current ability to earn a living and therefore to his or her current need for support.

States differ on when a court will order the termination of alimony. It could be upon the death of the payor or of the payee, upon the remarriage of the payee, or upon the cohabitation of the payee with a member of the opposite sex. When termination can result from cohabitation, the termination might be automatic or might simply constitute some evidence that the payee no longer needs alimony. In the latter event, the payee would be able to introduce evidence that cohabitation has not changed the need for alimony.

ASSIGNMENT 8.4

Answer the following questions after examining your state code. Also check state court opinions of your state if you cannot find an answer in the code. (See General Instructions for the State-Code and Court-Opinion Assignments in Appendix A.)

a. What standards will a court use in awarding alimony? For example, is marital fault relevant?
b. When can alimony be awarded to a man?
c. Are there any limitations on the form that alimony can take (e.g., periodic payments, lump sum, etc.)?
d. When alimony is awarded, is it always for an indefinite period? If not, under what circumstances can it be for a fixed period?
e. If the court denies the divorce to both parties, can alimony still be awarded?

ASSIGNMENT 8.5

a. Find an opinion decided within the last ten years by a court in your state that awarded alimony to a woman. List all the considerations that the court used in making its alimony decision. Try to find an opinion in which the court mentioned a specific dollar amount as alimony. If you cannot find such an opinion written by a court sitting in your state, select a neighboring state.
b. Repeat the assignment, except this time find an opinion in which the court awarded alimony to a man.
c. Are the two opinions consistent with each other? Explain.

ASSIGNMENT 8.6

A former secretary petitions a court for alimony. She tells the court that she will return to work as a secretary, but still needs alimony. Her husband, however, argues that she is capable of earning a higher salary as a paralegal. Assuming he is correct, under what circumstances should the court refuse to take into account the higher salary that she could earn as a paralegal? See *Crabill v. Crabill,* 119 Md. App. 249, 704 A.2d 532 (Court of Special Appeals 1998).

PROPERTY DIVISION: GENERAL PRINCIPLES

Categorizing Property

To understand property division, we need to explore three preliminary questions:

1. What kinds of property do the parties have?
2. How and when was the property acquired? Is it separate or marital property?
3. How is the property held? Who has title?

real property
Land and anything permanently attached to the land.

personal property
Movable property; any property other than real property.

tangible
Pertaining to a physical form; able to be made contact with through the senses such as touch.

intangible
Pertaining to that which does not have a physical form.

What Kinds of Property Do the Parties Have? **Real property** can include a main home, a vacation home, land and building used in a business, a condominium, etc. **Personal property** consists of cars, boats, cash, stocks, bonds, royalties, furniture, jewelry, art objects, books, records, clothes, photographic equipment, sports equipment, pets, business supplies (inventory), credits, accounts receivable, exclusive options to buy, insurance policies, etc. Some of these items are **tangible** (e.g., cars, cash) and others are **intangible** (e.g., stocks, bonds). Intangible property consists primarily of a right to something. There may be a document that is evidence of the right such as a stock certificate, but the right itself is by definition without physical form.

Later, we will examine three categories of personal property that have generated considerable controversy in recent years: pensions, professional degrees, and the goodwill of a business or profession.

How and When Was the Property Acquired? Is it Separate or Marital Property? Real and personal property can be acquired in a variety of ways:

bequest
A gift of personal property in a will.

devise
A gift of real property in a will.

intestate succession
Obtaining the property from a deceased who died without leaving a valid will. The persons entitled to this property are identified in the statute on intestate distribution.

- As a gift to one of the spouses
- As a gift to both of the spouses
- As a **bequest** to one or both spouses
- As a **devise** to one or both spouses
- Through **intestate succession** to one of the spouses
- Through funds from the salary or investments of one of the spouses
- Through funds from the salaries or investments of both of the spouses

The acquisition of property through any of these methods could have occurred during three possible periods of time:

- before the marriage,
- during the marriage before the parties separated, or
- during the marriage after the parties separated.

When interviewing a client or conducting an investigation about assets, it is important to place each acquisition within one of these three periods of time. Once property is acquired, it may appreciate in value. If so, it is also important to know during which of the three periods of time the appreciation occurred.

separate property
Property one spouse acquired before the marriage by any means and property he or she acquired during the marriage by gift, will, or intestate succession.

All property a spouse acquired before the marriage is **separate property.** The same is true of property a spouse acquires during the marriage by gift, will, or intestate succession. For example:

- a car a spouse bought before the marriage
- a gift of jewelry to a spouse from his or her aunt before or during the marriage
- a spouse's inheritance of stock from the will of his or her father who died before or during the marriage

Separate property also includes any property acquired during the marriage in exchange for separate property. An example would be the purchase of a car during the marriage using funds that a spouse earned before the marriage.

marital property
Nonseparate property acquired by a spouse during the marriage and the appreciation of separate property that occurred during the marriage.

In general, **marital property** is all nonseparate property. Specifically, marital property includes property acquired by either spouse during the marriage such as salaries, a home, and lottery winnings. Marital property also includes the appreciation (i.e., increase in value) of separate property that occurred during the marriage. (In some states, marital property is called *community property,* a special concept that we will examine in the next section.)

The distinction between separate and marital property is sometimes difficult to make, particularly when the parties mix or commingle assets in one account. For example:

Before Mary married Ted, she had her own $10,000 checking account. After the marriage, she and Ted opened a joint checking account. Into this account Mary deposits the $10,000 she brought into the marriage and they both start depositing their paychecks.

There has been a **commingling** of property. The pre-marriage $10,000 (clearly separate property) has been deposited into the same account as the post-marriage paychecks of both spouses (clearly marital property). A court may treat all commingled property as marital property unless the party claiming part of the account as separate property can trace the existence of the separate property with adequate records or other evidence—an increasingly difficult task as time passes. Unless separate property can be adequately traced, the court will probably treat all the commingled property as marital property or at least presume that the parties intended it to be marital property.

commingling
Placing funds from different sources into the same account.

Compounding the problem, when one spouse brings separate property into a marriage (e.g., car, jewelry) that the other spouse makes extensive use of, a claim is sometimes asserted that a gift of the separate property was made to the other spouse during the marriage.

How Is the Property Held? Who Has Title? Property can be held in a number of ways:

1. *Legal title in name of one spouse only.* The title to the property is in the name of only one of the parties. This could be because the property was purchased with the separate funds of that one spouse. Or it may be that the property was purchased with the funds of one spouse but placed in the name of the other spouse (perhaps in an attempt to insulate the property from the claims of the creditors of the spouse who purchased the property). Finally, title may be in the name of one spouse even though both contributed funds for its purchase.
2. *Joint tenancy.* In a **joint tenancy,** each joint tenant owns and has an equal right to possess the entire property. They do not each own a piece of the property; each joint tenant owns it all. When one joint tenant dies, his or her interest passes to the surviving joint tenants by the **right of survivorship.**
3. *Tenancy by the entirety.* A **tenancy by the entirety** is a joint tenancy held by a married couple. (In Vermont, while same-sex couples cannot marry, they can enter a civil union, which allows them to hold property as tenants by the entirety. See chapter 5 on civil unions.)
4. *Tenancy in common.* In a **tenancy in common,** all parties have a right to possession of the property, but their shares in the property may not be equal. There is no right of survivorship. When one tenant dies, the property goes to whomever the deceased designated by will or to the heirs of the deceased by intestate succession if the deceased died without leaving a valid will. Hence, a major distinction between (1) a joint tenancy and a tenancy by the entirety and (2) a tenancy in common is that the property of a deceased tenant passes through the estate of that tenant only in the case of a tenancy in common. In the other tenancies, the property passes immediately to the surviving tenant(s) by **operation of law.**
5. *Community property.* States fall into two broad categories:
   - **community property** states, in which each spouse has a one-half interest in all marital property; upon divorce, community property is divided equally
   - **common law property** states, in which property can be owned by the spouse who earned it; upon divorce, marital property is divided equitably, which may or may not be an equal division

joint tenancy
Property that is owned equally by two or more persons with the *right of survivorship.*

right of survivorship
When one owner dies, his or her share goes to the other owners; it does not go through the estate of the deceased owner.

tenancy by the entirety
A joint tenancy held by a husband and wife.

tenancy in common
Property owned by two or more persons in shares that may or may not be equal, with no right of survivorship.

operation of law
Automatically because of the law. (A result occurs by operation of law when it happens because the law mandates the result, not because a party agrees to produce the result.)

community property
Property in which each spouse has a one-half interest because it was acquired during the marriage regardless of who earned it or who has title to it. Community property also includes separate property that the parties have agreed to treat as community property.

common law property
Property acquired during the marriage that can be owned by the spouse who earned it.

Not all states use the same terminology; considerable variation exists among the states. Most states have common law property systems in one form or another. Various forms of community property systems exist in nine states: Arizona, California, Idaho, Louisiana, Nevada, New Mexico, Texas, Washington, and Wisconsin. For an overview of how property is divided in common law property and community property states, see Exhibit 8.5.

Community property (originally a Spanish legal concept) is property in which each spouse has a one-half interest because the property was acquired during the marriage regardless of who earned the property or who has title to it. Community property, of course, does not include property that one spouse acquires by gift, will, or intestate succession during the marriage. These items constitute separate property. Spouses can enter agreements in which they decide to treat community property as separate property or to treat separate property as community property. (The voluntary change of separate property into community property or vice versa is called **transmutation.**)

transmutation
The voluntary change of separate property into community property or community property into separate property.

The underlying principle of community property is that the efforts of both spouses contributed to the acquisition of property during the marriage. One spouse, for example, could not have gone to the office each day to work if the other spouse had not stayed home to take care of the household, which could include child rearing, home economics, and social outreach. (This point of view also exists in most common law property states, although the consequence is not necessarily an equal division of marital property.) When property is acquired during the marriage in a community property state, there is a presumption that it is community property. This presumption can be rebutted by showing that it was acquired by one spouse alone through gift, will, or intestate succession. In general, husbands and wives have an equal right to manage community property during the marriage. One spouse cannot sell community property without the consent of the other. The spouses owe each other the **fiduciary** duties of good faith and fair treatment in handling community property.

fiduciary
Pertaining to the high standard of care that must be exercised on behalf of another.

Community property states do not always categorize property in the same way. In Texas, for example, an award of damages received for personal injury

Exhibit 8.5 Property Division upon Divorce

Kind of Property	Distribution in Common Law Property States	Distribution in Community Property States
Property acquired before marriage	This is separate property. In most states, all of it goes to the spouse who acquired it unless he or she agrees otherwise.	This is separate property. All of it goes to the spouse who acquired it unless he or she agrees otherwise.
Property acquired by one spouse during marriage by gift, will, or intestate succession	This is separate property. In most states, all of it goes to the spouse who acquired it unless he or she agrees otherwise.	This is separate property. All of it goes to the spouse who acquired it unless he or she agrees otherwise.
Property acquired or earned by either spouse during the marriage (other than what only one spouse received by gift, will, or intestate succession)	If the spouses cannot agree, each gets a fair (equitable) share, which may or may not be equal.	Property is split fifty/fifty between the spouses unless they agree otherwise.
Increased value (appreciation) of separate or marital property that occurs during marriage	If the spouses cannot agree, each gets a fair (equitable) share of the amount of the appreciation, which may or may not be equal.	Appreciation is split fifty/fifty between the spouses unless they agree otherwise.

is separate property, and an award covering medical expenses and loss of earnings is community property. Other community property states, however, treat the entire recovery as community property. (For more on when damages can be divided upon divorce, see chapter 17 on torts.) States also differ on how to categorize property purchased by one spouse before marriage but paid for in part after marriage with community funds.

In our mobile society, categorization problems can exist when a married couple moves from a common law property state to a community property state, acquiring marital property in each. In such cases, California has created a category of property called **quasi-community property.** This is property acquired by the couple in a noncommunity state that would have been community property if the couple had acquired it in California. Quasi-community property is divided in the same manner as community property in California.

quasi-community property
Property acquired during the marriage in a noncommunity state that would have been community property if it had been acquired in a community property state.

What Property Is Divided and Who Gets What?

Spouses dissolving their marriage are generally free to divide property in any way they want within their separation agreement. A spouse, for example, can give his or her separate property to the other spouse. Or both may decide that specific marital property (including community property) will go entirely to one of the parties. Bargaining is the order of the day. If the parties entered a valid premarital (antenuptial) agreement, its terms may specify what property was brought into the marriage as separate property and how property acquired during the marriage should be divided (see chapter 4).

If the parties cannot agree, the court will impose a property division on them. (The court's decision is called a *distributive award* in New York.) A central theme of the division is that marriage is an economic partnership in which each spouse made personal sacrifices and provided major financial contributions that were either direct (e.g., earning a salary) or indirect (e.g., taking care of the children to allow the other spouse to spend the day earning a salary).

In community property states, as indicated, each spouse receives a 50 percent interest in all property the court classifies as community property. In common law property states, the general principle of division is **equitable distribution,** which is a fair, but not necessarily equal, division of all marital property. In general, a division of property is fair when it is "proportionate" to the contributions made by each party to the acquisition of that property. While there are important theoretical differences between property division in community property states and property division in common law property states, the practical results are often similar. The reason is that a judge in a common law property state will often be inclined to order a fifty/fifty division of the marital property unless such a division would be inequitable. (A statute in one common law property state provides that "[a]ll marital property shall be distributed one-half (1/2) to each party unless the court finds such a division to be inequitable."[5])

equitable distribution
The fair, but not necessarily equal, division of all marital property in a common law property state.

Here are some of the factors a court in a common law property state will consider in determining the fairness and equitableness of a property division:

- The length of the marriage
- Who earned the asset
- What the other party did to contribute to the household while the asset was being earned

---

[5]Arkansas Code of 1987 Annotated § 9-12-315.

- Any interruption in the educational opportunities or personal career of either party, particularly the one who stayed home to take care of the children
- The age and health of both parties
- The need of the party with physical custody of the children to use the marital home
- The desirability of keeping any asset (e.g., a business) intact
- The income and property of both at the time the marriage was entered and at the time the divorce action was filed
- The probable future financial circumstances of each party; the employability of each party
- Whether either party has been granted alimony or maintenance
- Any intentional dissipation of marital assets
- The tax consequences of the property division
- Any other factor that should be considered in order to achieve justice and fairness in the division

A court's inclination to an equal division of marital property is even stronger in those states in which long-term alimony is generally unavailable.

Marital fault—who caused the marriage to break up—is not a factor in the property division. Under section 307 of the Uniform Marriage and Divorce Act, property is to be divided "without regard to marital misconduct."

Courts must sometimes be concerned about safety. If domestic violence existed during the marriage, it would obviously be unwise to divide a two-story home by allowing former spouses to live on separate floors. In a recent case calling for the wisdom of Solomon, a judge had to decide how to divide season tickets to New York Knicks basketball games. Both spouses were passionate fans. The option of giving them each one ticket to every game was unacceptable, since this would mean they would have to sit together. "This court will not compel them to team up once again at courtside." The judge decided to give the husband both tickets to every even-numbered game and the wife both tickets to every odd-numbered game. Each spouse could then take someone else to the game and avoid having to face the other in the already emotionally charged environment of many professional basketball games.

By definition, separate property is not divided, although there are exceptions to this rule. A few states will divide *all* property whether it is marital or separate. A court may have discretion to reach a party's separate property where it determines that the division of the marital property alone would be unfair. States that allow a court to divide all property are sometimes called "all-property," "kitchen sink," or "hotchpot" states. **Hotchpot** means mixing or blending all property, however acquired, to achieve greater equality.

hotchpot
Mixing or blending all property, however acquired, to achieve greater equality.

Once the decision is made on how to divide the property in a community property state or a common law property state, the next concern is to identify the most *practical* way to accomplish the division. Cash, of course, is easy to split (e.g., a 60/40 percent division of a bank account in a common law property state or a 50/50 percent division in a community property state). Not so for the division of homes, vehicles, and businesses. They cannot be conveniently chopped up. Sometimes it is practical to sell an asset and divide the proceeds according to the allocation that applies. When this is not practical, other options are negotiated and/or ordered by the court:

- The wife will keep the house, and the husband will keep the car and his business.
- The wife will live in the house, but the husband will retain a designated amount of the equity in the house, which must be paid to him if the house is sold.

- The wife receives $250,000 as a lump-sum payment, and the husband receives everything else.

Many factors can play a role in the negotiations. For example, the wife may agree to a lower property division in exchange for the husband's agreement to let her have custody of the children. She may agree to a higher alimony award in exchange for a relatively lower property division out of fear that he is on the brink of bankruptcy (in which the property division debts, but not the alimony debts, might be discharged). He may be able to convince her to take more alimony and less property so that he can take advantage of the alimony tax deduction. She may agree even though she must pay taxes on the alimony received. They both know that his higher income would cause the same money to be taxed at a higher rate. He may find ways to compensate her for this in other terms of the separation agreement.

ASSIGNMENT 8.7

When parties are not able to agree on a property division, what standards will a court in your state use to do it for them? Under what circumstances, if any, can a court divide separate property? (See General Instructions for the State-Code Assignment in Appendix A.)

Dissipation

As we saw when discussing alimony, a spouse cannot avoid a support obligation by voluntarily becoming poor. The amount of the obligation will be based on earning capacity, not necessarily actual earnings. A similar principle is at work in the property division. One spouse cannot squander—**dissipate**—marital property so that there is nothing left to divide in the separation agreement. These concerns are at the heart of the *Gastineau* decision, to which we now turn.

dissipate
Waste, destroy, or squander.

CASE

Gastineau v. Gastineau

151 Misc. 2d 813, 573 N.Y.S.2d 819 (1991)
New York Supreme Court, Suffolk County

Background: *Marcus Gastineau was a professional football player for the New York Jets. His wife, Lisa, sued him for divorce and charged that he dissipated some of the marital assets. While the trial was in progress (i.e., pendente lite), the court ordered Marcus to make payments to Lisa to cover expenses. He fell $71,707 behind in these payments. The court then ordered the sequestration of his net severance pay of $83,000. This removed it from his possession and control until the court rendered its decision.*

Decision: *Marcus dissipated marital assets. In the equitable distribution of the marital assets, a court can treat dissipated assets as if they still exist.*

Opinion of the Court:

Justice LEIS delivered the opinion of the court.

This action for divorce, equitable distribution and other ancillary relief was tried on February 25, 28, March 5, and 6, 1991. The Plaintiff, Lisa Gastineau, is represented by counsel. The Defendant, Marcus Gastineau appeared pro se. . . .

The parties were married in December of 1979. This action was commenced in September 1986. Consequently, this is a marriage of short duration. The Plaintiff is thirty-one years old and the Defendant is thirty-four. The parties have one child, Brittany, born on 11/6/82.

At the beginning of the trial the Plaintiff testified as to specific allegations of cruel and inhuman treatment allegedly committed by the Defendant. The Defendant remained mute, neither admitting

continued

CASE

Gastineau v. Gastineau—*Continued*

nor denying these allegations. The Court thereupon granted the Plaintiff a divorce based on cruel and inhuman treatment [Domestic Relations Law (DRL) § 170(1)].

The parties married just after Marc Gastineau had been drafted by the New York Jets to play professional football. The Plaintiff, at that time, was a sophomore at the University of Alabama. The Plaintiff never completed her college education, nor did she work during the course of the marriage.

In 1982, when Brittany was born, the parties purchased a house in Huntington, New York for $99,000.00. In addition to the purchase price, the Plaintiff and Defendant spent another $250,000.00 for landscaping and other renovations. This money came from the Defendant's earnings as a professional football player.

According to the uncontroverted testimony of the Plaintiff, in 1979 (the Defendant's first year in professional football) the Defendant earned a salary of $55,000.00. In his second year, 1980, the Defendant's salary was approximately $75,000.00. In 1981 it was approximately $95,000.00 and in 1982 he earned approximately $250,000.00. The Defendant's tax returns (which were not available for the years 1979 through 1982) indicate that the Defendant earned $423,291.00 in 1983, $488,994.00 in 1984, $858,035.00 in 1985, $595,127.00 in 1986, $953,531.00 in 1987 and in 1988, his last year with the New York Jets, his contract salary was $775,000.00 plus $50,000.00 in bonuses. It must be noted that in most years the Defendant earned monies in excess of his contract salary as a result of promotions, advertisements and bonuses.

In 1985 the parties purchased a home in Scottsdale, Arizona for $550,000.00. During the course of the parties' marriage Plaintiff and Defendant acquired many luxury items including a power boat, a BMW, a Corvette, a Rolls Royce, a Porche, a Mercedes and two motorcycles. They continually had a housekeeper who not only cleaned the house but prepared the parties' meals. In addition, the parties frequently dined out at expensive restaurants. The Plaintiff testified that as a result of this life style she has become accustomed to buying only the most expensive clothes and going to the best of restaurants.

In 1988 the Defendant began an illicit relationship with Brigitte Nielsen. When Ms. Nielsen was diagnosed as having cancer the Defendant testified that he could no longer concentrate on playing football. At that time the Defendant was under contract with the New York Jets at a salary of $775,000.00. He left professional football in October 1988 (breaking his contract) after the sixth game of the 1988 season. The Defendant went to Arizona and remained with Ms. Nielsen while she underwent treatment for cancer.

Regardless of whether the Defendant wanted to be with his girl friend while she underwent treatment for cancer, he had a responsibility to support his wife and child. The Court cannot condone Mr. Gastineau's walking away from a lucrative football contract when the result is that his wife and child are deprived of adequate support.

According to the testimony adduced at trial, there are sixteen games per season in the NFL. Players are paid one-sixteenth of their contract salary at the end of each game. Based on the Defendant's salary for 1988 ($775,000.00), he received $48,437.00 per game. The Defendant played six games in the 1988 season and received approximately $290,622.00 plus $50,000.00 in bonuses. He was entitled to an additional $484,437.00 for the ten games remaining in the season. This Court finds that by walking away from his 1988–89 contract with the NFL the Defendant dissipated a marital asset in the amount of $484,437.00 (DRL § 236(B)(5)(d)(11)).*

Whether or not the Defendant would have been offered a contract by the New York Jets for the 1989/90 football season if he had not broken his 1988/89 contract is pure speculation. In professional football there are no guarantees. Variables such as age, how an athlete plays, the ability of other players seeking to fill his position, as well as possible injuries sustained during the season, make it impossible to determine with certainty whether or not the Defendant would have been re-signed by the New York Jets had he finished the 1988/89 season. It must also be noted that there has been no testimony offered by the Plaintiff to establish that the Defendant would have been re-signed by the New York Jets for the 1989/90 season had he not broken his contract.

The speculative nature of the Defendant's future in professional football is highlighted by the fact that

*["5. a. Except where the parties have provided in an agreement for the disposition of their property . . . the court . . . shall determine the respective rights of the parties in their separate or marital property, and shall provide for the disposition thereof in the final judgment. . . . d. In determining an equitable disposition of property. . ., the court shall consider: . . . (11) the wasteful dissipation of assets by either spouse. . . ."]

in 1989 he tried out for the San Diego Chargers, the LA Raiders and the Minnesota Vikings, without success. The New York Jets also refused to offer him a contract. In 1990 the Defendant did acquire a position with the British Colombia Lions in the Canadian Football League at a salary of $75,000.00. He was cut, however, less than half way through the season. The Defendant played five of the 18 scheduled games and was paid approximately $20,000.00. The Defendant's performance in the Canadian Football League lends credence to his claim that he no longer has the capacity to earn the monies that he once made as a professional football player. Under these circumstances the court is limited to considering the dissipation of a marital asset valued at $484,437.00, to wit: the remaining amount of money that the Defendant was eligible to collect pursuant to his 1988/89 contract.

While Defendant admits that he has name recognition, he claims that his name has a negative rather than a positive connotation. The Defendant testified that because of his antics on the field (such as his victory dance after sacking a quarterback), the fact that he crossed picket lines during the NFL player's strike and because he walked away from his professional football career, his name has no value for promotions or endorsements. There has been no evidence presented to the contrary by the Plaintiff.

The Defendant testified that his chances of obtaining employment with a professional football team are almost nil. Although he is presently attempting to obtain a position at a Jack LaLanne Health Spa he could not provide details as to the potential salary. The Defendant has also attempted to enter professional boxing. No testimony has been elicited by the Plaintiff, however, as to the Defendant's financial potential as a professional boxer. Since the Defendant left professional football he has not worked or earned any money (except for the $20,000.00 that he earned when he played football in Canada). According to the Defendant, Ms. Nielsen paid for all of the Defendant's expenses during the period of time that they lived together.

After the Defendant failed to appear for a number of court dates and also failed to comply with this Court's pendente lite order, the Court directed that the Defendant's NFL severance pay be sequestered pursuant to DRL § 243 and the Plaintiff be appointed receiver and sequestrator of said funds (which amounted to approximately $83,000.00 after deducting taxes).

According to Plaintiff the entire $83,000.00 (reflecting the Defendant's total net severance pay from the NFL) was spent by her as follows: Thirty-two thousand dollars ($32,000.00) was used to pay mortgage arrears on the Huntington house (which still has approximately $15,000.00 outstanding in arrears), $22,000.00 went to the Plaintiff's attorneys, $15,000.00 went to repay loans taken out by the Plaintiff to pay necessary expenses and the rest, approximately $14,000.00, went for landscaping, medical insurance, electricity, fuel oil, telephone bills, dental and doctor bills.

Primary Marital Assets

With all of the money that the Defendant earned throughout the course of his professional football career he has retained only three significant marital assets. (1) The Huntington house, which has been valued at approximately $429,000.00 and has an outstanding mortgage of $150,000.00. (2) A house located in the state of Arizona which was purchased for approximately $550,000.00 and has a $420,000.00 mortgage (which in all probability will be sold at foreclosure); (3) The Defendant's severance pay from the NFL of approximately $83,000.00.

It is clear that the Defendant has also dissipated a marital asset worth approximately $324,573.00 (to wit: $484,437.00 the Defendant was entitled to receive pursuant to his 1988/89 contract tax effected by 33%, reflecting approximate federal and state income tax). Although neither the Plaintiff nor the Defendant attempted to tax effect this dissipated marital asset, it is clear that the Defendant would not have actually received $484,437.00 had he finished the 1988/89 season. The Court therefore, on its own, has tax effected this amount by 33%, approximately what the defendant would have paid in federal and state taxes had he actually received the $484,437.00. In this regard the Court has considered the tax returns of the parties (which are in evidence) with reference to their tax consequences and takes judicial notice of the fact that compensation for service constitutes income (IRC [26 USC] § 61(a)(1)) which is taxable (IRC [26 USC] §§ 1 and 63); New York Tax Law § 620 et seq., *Richardson on Evidence* §§ 17 and 18 [10th Ed.].

Equitable Distribution

It is a guiding principle of equitable distribution that parties are entitled to receive equitable awards which are proportionate to their contributions, whether direct or indirect, to the marriage, *Ullah v. Ullah,* 555 N.Y.S.2d 834 (2nd Dep't 1990).

In this case, the Plaintiff testified that during the course of the marriage she supervised the renovations made on the Huntington house, traveled with the Defendant wherever he trained and, with the assistance of a full-time nanny, raised and cared for their child.

continued

CASE

Gastineau v. Gastineau—*Continued*

This is not a long term marriage, and there has been minimal testimony elicited concerning the Plaintiff's direct or indirect contributions to the Defendant's acquisition of marital assets. Although it was the defendant's own athletic abilities and disciplined training which made it possible for him to obtain and retain his position as a professional football player, equity dictates, under the facts of this case, that the Plaintiff receive one-third of the marital assets. The Defendant's decision to voluntarily terminate his contract with the New York Jets, depriving Plaintiff and the parties' child of the standard of living to which they had become accustomed, his failure to obtain meaningful employment thereafter and the indirect contributions made by the Plaintiff during the course of the marriage warrant an award to the Plaintiff of one third of the parties' marital assets. The Court is also mindful of the fact that during the years of the Defendant's greatest productivity, the Plaintiff enjoyed the fruits of Defendant's labors to the fullest (*Parlow v. Parlow,* 548 N.Y.S.2d 373 (Sup. Ct. Westchester Co. 1989)), unlike the landmark *O'Brien* case (*O'Brien v. O'Brien,* 66 N.Y.2d 576, 498 N.Y.S.2d 743, 489 N.E.2d 712 (1985)), where a newly licensed professional discarded his wife after she provided years of contributions to the attainment of his medical license.

There are only two marital assets to be considered in granting Plaintiff her one-third distributive award, (1) the Huntington house, and (2) the $324,573.00 dissipated marital asset. The Arizona house has no equity.

The Huntington house is valued at $429,000.00. It has a $150,000.00 mortgage with $15,000.00 owed in back mortgage payments. It thus has an equity of $264,000.00. One third of the equity would entitle the Plaintiff to $87,120.00. When one adds $107,109.00 (1/3 of the $324,573.00 tax effected marital asset which was dissipated), the Plaintiff would be entitled to $194,229.00. This would encompass Plaintiff's 1/3 distributive award of the parties' sole remaining marital asset (the Huntington house) and her 1/3 share of the marital asset dissipated by the Defendant. If one adds this $194,229.00 to the arrears owed by the Defendant on the pendente lite order ($71,707.00) Plaintiff could be awarded the total equity ($264,000.00) in the Huntington house in full satisfaction of her one-third distributive award of the parties' marital assets and still have approximately $1,936.00 remaining as a credit. The Court awards Plaintiff the Huntington house and grants her a Judgment for $1,936.00 for the remaining arrears owed to her.

Neither side has offered proof as to the present value of the Arizona house or the extent of arrears on mortgage payments (*Gluck v. Gluck,* 520 N.Y.S.2d 581 (2nd Dep't 1987)). It would appear however, that there is no equity remaining in the Arizona house. The Court awards the Arizona house to the Defendant. The Court directs that each party take whatever steps are required to effect the transfer of the deed to the real property awarded to the other party so as to convey title to said property in said other's name alone.

ASSIGNMENT 8.8

a. Who was treated unfairly by the *Gastineau* case: Marcus? Lisa? Neither? Was her one-third share too high, too low, or just right? Have a debate in class on this question. (Note that this case did not cover child support. The court must make a separate decision on who pays child support and how much.)

b. How much would Lisa have gotten if New York were a community property state?

Pensions, Degrees, and Goodwill

Three recent areas of contention involving property division are pensions, professional degrees (or occupational licenses), and the goodwill of a business. Until fairly recently, parties negotiating a separation agreement did *not* include these items in their bargaining. They were either considered too intangible or simply assumed to belong to one of the parties separately, usually the husband. Litigation and legislation, however, have forced drastic changes in these views. As a result, the negotiations for a separation agreement now regularly take account of these items in one way or another.

Dividing a Pension

Many workers are covered by pension plans at work. Employer-sponsored plans may be financed entirely by the employer or by the employer with employee contributions. There are two main kinds of pension plans, the **defined-benefit plan** and the **defined-contribution plan.**

- **Defined-Benefit Plan** The amount of the benefit is fixed, but not the amount of the contribution. The formula for such plans usually gears the benefits to years of service and earnings (e.g., a benefit of $10 a month for each year of employment) or a stated dollar amount.
- **Defined-Contribution Plan** Each employee has his or her own individual account such as a 401(k) plan. The amount of the contribution is generally fixed, but the amount of the benefit is not. Such plans usually involve profit-sharing, stock-bonus, or money-purchase arrangements where the employer's contribution (usually a percentage of profits) is divided among the participants based on the individual's wages and/or years of service and accumulations in the individual's pension account. The eventual benefit is determined by the amount of total contributions and investment earnings in the years during which the employee is covered. The existence of individual accounts makes defined-contribution plans easier to divide than defined-benefit plans.

Accumulated benefits in these plans are not **vested** until the employee has a nonforfeitable right to receive the benefits, whether or not the employee leaves the job before retirement.

vested
Fixed so that it cannot be taken away by future events or conditions; accrued so that you now have a right to present or future possession or enjoyment.

Can pension benefits be divided upon divorce? Assume that a wife stayed home to care for the children while her husband worked. Is she entitled to any of his pension benefits? The question is important because retirement benefits may be the largest portion of the marital estate in many marriages.

Yes, pension benefits can be reached. This can occur in two ways. First, the parties might agree on how to divide the pension. If so, their separation agreement would specify how they would accomplish this. They might, for example, each receive an agreed-upon percentage of every pension payout. This agreement would then be embodied in a court order that would be presented to the employer. Alternatively, one spouse might agree to relinquish all right to the other spouse's pension in exchange for a lump-sum cash payment or in exchange for some other benefit sought in the divorce. Second, if the parties cannot agree on how to divide a pension, a court can order the division of the pension.

The order of a court to divide a pension (whether agreed upon by the parties or forced upon them by a court) is contained in what is called a **qualified domestic relations order (QDRO).** It orders an employer (or an employer's pension administrator) to divide the pension in a specified manner. Under a QDRO, a spouse, ex-spouse, or child can receive some or all of an employee's pension benefits. Any one of these individuals can become an **alternate payee** under the pension plan. While a QDRO is a method of dividing a pension for purposes of a property division, the QDRO can also be used to collect spousal support obligations (alimony) or child support obligations (see chapter 10 on child support).

qualified domestic relations order
A court order that allows a nonemployee to reach pension benefits of an employee or former employee to satisfy a support or other marital obligation to the nonemployee.

alternate payee
A nonemployee entitled to receive pension benefits of an employee or former employee pursuant to a qualified domestic relations order.

The use of QDROs to divide pensions represents a dramatic change in the law. Before 1984, when QDROs were created, individuals other than the employee could not demand that pension benefits be paid directly to them. QDROs have now made this practice commonplace. Exhibit 8.6 presents an example of a typical QDRO provided by an employer as guidance to its employees in drafting proposed QDROs to be signed by a judge. The example assumes that the alternate payee will receive one-half of the employee's pension benefits. It is certainly possible, however, for a different allocation to be ordered.

How much does the nonemployee receive from the employee's pension fund? What amount or percentage will be ordered in the QDRO? As indicated,

Exhibit 8.6 Qualified Domestic Relations Order (QDRO)

This sample QDRO is provided by Apex Company, Inc., to its employees as an example of an order the company will treat as a QDRO. The company does not give individual tax advice or advice about the marital property rights of either party.

1. Pursuant to Section 414(p) of the Internal Revenue Code, this qualified domestic relations order ("Order") assigns a portion of the benefits payable in the Apex Company, Inc. Annuity Plan ("the Plan") from ____[Member's Name]____ (Member No. __________) to ___[Spouse's Name]__ in recognition of the existence of his/her marital rights in ___[Member's Name] retirement benefits.

2. The Member in the Plan is ____[Member's Name]____, whose last known mailing address is __________, Social Security No. __________.

3. The Alternate Payee is ___[Spouse's Name]___, whose last known mailing address is __________, Social Security No. __________.

[Use the following paragraph if the Member is not already receiving retirement benefits:]

4. Apex Company, Inc. is hereby ORDERED to assign a portion of the accumulations so that each party as of the date of the assignment has a retirement account of approximately the same value. The date of assignment is __________.

[Use the following paragraph if the Member is already receiving retirement benefits:]

4. Apex Company, Inc. is hereby ORDERED to make monthly payments equal to one-half of the amount payable to ___[Member's Name]__ directly to ___[Spouse's Name]__. These direct payments to ___[Spouse's Name]__ shall be made beginning after the date of this order and ending at ___[Member's Name]___ 's death.

5. This qualified domestic relations order is not intended to require the Plan to provide any type or form of benefits or any option not otherwise provided by the Plan, nor shall this Order require the Plan to provide for increased benefits not required by the Plan. This Order does not require the Plan to provide benefits to the Alternate Payee that are required to be paid to another Alternate Payee under another order previously determined to be a qualified domestic relations order.

6. All benefits payable under the Apex Company, Inc. Annuity Plan other than those payable to ___[Spouse's Name]___ shall be payable to ___[Member's Name]__ in such manner and form as he/she may elect in his/her sole and undivided discretion, subject only to plan requirements.

7. ___[Spouse's Name]__ is ORDERED AND DECREED to report any retirement payments received on any applicable income tax return. The Plan Administrator of Apex Company, Inc. is authorized to issue the appropriate Internal Revenue Form for any direct payment made to ___[Spouse's Name]___.

8. While it is anticipated that the Plan Administrator will pay directly to ____[Spouse's Name]____ the benefit awarded to her, ___[Member's Name]__ is designated a constructive trustee to the extent he receives any retirement benefits under the Plan that are due to ___[Spouse's Name]__ but paid to ___[Member's Name]__. ___[Member's Name]__ is ORDERED AND DECREED to pay the benefit defined above directly to ___[Spouse's Name]__ within three days after receipt by him.

____________________ ____________________

[NAME OF COURT] [NAME OF JUDGE]

the parties can negotiate this in their separation agreement. If they cannot reach an agreement, the court will decide. It is possible for an alternate payee to receive up to 100 percent of the employee's pension benefits.

Employees and employers do not like QDROs—the former because they had thought their pension could never be touched by anyone, and the latter because of the extra administrative burden imposed. During negotiations, the employee will usually try to get the other side to accept some other benefit in lieu of asking the court for a QDRO. If, however, nothing else of comparable value is available, dividing pension benefits through a QDRO is unavoidable. (In chapter 10, we will consider a similar device called a qualified medical child support order—QMCSO—that covers health insurance for children.)

A great deal depends on the *value* of the employee's pension plan. Without knowing this value, the negotiations are meaningless. Yet determining value can be a complex undertaking, often requiring the services of actuarial and accounting specialists. Value will depend on factors such as:

- Type of pension plan
- Amount contributed to the plan by the employee and by the employer
- How benefits are determined (e.g., when they accrue or are vested)
- Age of employee
- Employee's earliest retirement date
- Employee's life expectancy

Information about a particular pension plan can be obtained from the employer or the administrator hired by the employer to manage employee-benefit programs such as pensions. Request a copy of the "plan document," the overview called the "summary plan description," and a statement describing the employee's vested benefits under the plan. If a law firm is seeking these documents on behalf of a client, written authorization from the client to obtain the documents would be submitted along with the request.

Often the parties must calculate the **present value** of a benefit. Assume that at the beginning of the year you become entitled to $1,000 at the end of the year. On January 1, you are *not* given $1,000; you are given the present value of $1,000. The present value of $1,000 is $909.09 if we assume that you could invest $909.09 in a local bank (or in some other safe investment entity) at 10 percent simple interest. If you brought $909.09 to a bank and opened an account paying 10 percent simple interest, at the end of the year you would have $1,000. When a court distributes a benefit such as a portion of a pension, what is actually received may be the present value of the benefit, calculated in this way. If a 10 percent rate of interest is too high in today's market, the parties will have to assume a lower interest percentage and a higher present value. At 5 percent interest, for example, the present value of $1,000 is $952.38.

present value
The amount of money an individual would have to be given now to produce or generate a certain amount of money in a designated period of time.

QDROs are complex instruments because pension plans are often complex. There are law firms that specialize in pension valuation and division. An attorney at one such firm claims that many attorneys are failing to provide competent representation in this area of practice. Flawed retirement-plan paperwork is a "ticking time bomb waiting to go off" in thousands of divorce cases across the country.[6]

A number of companies have been formed that help parties value pensions. One such company is Legal Economic Evaluations, Inc., whose application is presented in Exhibit 8.7.

ASSIGNMENT 8.9

Find a friend or relative who works at a place where he or she is covered by a pension. Assume that you work at an office where your friend or relative is a client who is seeking a divorce in which one of the issues is the division of pension benefits. (If you are covered by an employee pension plan, use yourself as the client in this assignment.)

Your supervisor asks you to do two things. First, obtain as much information as you can about the client's pension (e.g., the kind of plan it is, when benefits become available). Second, obtain an employer-approved copy of a sample QDRO. Ask the client to call the personnel office at work in order to speak to the "plan administrator" (the person in charge of administering the pension plan) and request the information and the sample.

Prepare a report that summarizes the plan's features, pointing out whatever you think will be relevant to later negotiations on dividing the pension benefits. (You can change the name of your friend or relative.) Attach the copy of the sample QDRO to your report.

Social security benefits, unlike private pensions, are not divisible marital property. Divorced spouses, however, are entitled to collect social security benefits based upon the former spouse's earning record if the marriage lasted at least ten years immediately before the divorce became final. The divorced spouse seeking benefits through this route must be at least sixty-two years old.

Dividing a Degree

Bill and Pat are married in 1973. While Bill goes through college, medical school, and internship to become a doctor, Pat works full-time to support

[6]Lynn Asinof, *Divorcing? Attend to the Nest Egg,* Wall Street Journal, Nov. 13, 2000, at c1.

Exhibit 8.7 Pension Valuation Form

Legal Economic Evaluations
1000 Elwell Ct #203 Palo Alto, CA 94303 Phone (800) 221-6826 Fax: (650) 969-0266

DEFINED BENEFIT PENSION VALUATION FORM

Attorney / Mediator / Other Mailing Information

Name: ____ Firm: ____

Street Address: ____ City: ____

State: ____ ZIP: ____

Phone: ____ FAX: ____

Case Information

Pensioner Name: ____

Gender: ○ Male ○ Female

Date of Birth: ____

Employer: ____

Name of Plan:

Date entered Plan: ____

Is the Pensioner still employed? ○ Yes ○ No

If no, date of termination: ____

Spouse's Name: ____ Date of Birth: ____

Date of Marriage: ____

Date spouse's interest in pension ends: ____

(Date of separation, filing, dissolution or trial, as appropriate in your state)

If the pensioner is already receiving benefits, how much are they? $____ When did they begin? ____

Please Describe any Survivors Benefits: ____

Please enclose a copy of the pension plan booklet and a copy of the pensioner's most recent benefit statement.

Is the Pensioner employed by a government agency or school district?

○ Yes ○ No

If "YES", please list the gross base pay for the current year and each of the previous three years.

Current Year: ____ Previous three years:

Year: ____ Salary: $____

Year: ____ Salary: $____

Year: ____ Salary: $____

In addition to the present value of the pension, do you wish us to show the marital interest based on the ratio of service during the marriage to the total plan service. (Also known as the "Time Rule" or "Coverture Percentage")?

○ Yes ○ No

Does the pensioner have any life-threatening illnesses?

○ Yes ○ No

If "YES", please describe below:

____

Payment Information

Please submit a check for $150 payable to Legal Economic Evaluations, Inc.
We make no attempt to independently verify your data.
The accuracy of our report depends upon the validity and completeness of the data submitted with this form.

Source: Legal Economic Evaluations, Inc., (800) 221-6826, econeval@legaleconomic.com.

the two of them. On the day he obtains his license to practice medicine, they decide to divorce. During the long years of Bill's education, they have accumulated almost no property. Pat earns $25,000 a year at her job. Since she is fully capable of supporting herself, the court decides that she should receive no alimony. They have no children.

Many would consider it an outrage that Pat walks away from the marriage with nothing. She is not eligible for alimony, and there is no tangible property to divide. He walks away with a professional degree and a doctor's license ready to embark on a lucrative career. Courts have slowly come to the realization that the supporting spouse should be given a remedy in such a situation.

In our example, what financial factors are involved?

1. The amount Pat contributed to Bill's support while he was in school
2. The amount Pat contributed to the payment of Bill's education expenses

3. The amount Bill would have contributed to the marriage if he had worked during these years rather than going to school
4. Any increased earnings Pat would have had if she had taken a different job (e.g., by moving to a different location)
5. Any increased earnings Pat would have had if she had continued her education rather than working to support Bill through his education
6. The increased standard of living Pat would have enjoyed due to Bill's expected high earnings if they had stayed married
7. The share of his increased earnings to which Pat would have been entitled if they had stayed married

Some courts will consider only items (1) and (2) in providing Pat with a remedy. As a matter of equity, she is entitled only to **restitution**—a return of what she contributed while Bill was acquiring his degree and license. Such courts do not consider a degree and license to be divisible property. They are personal to the holder. Under this view, it logically follows that she is not entitled to a share of his increased earnings as a result of the degree and license. All of the above items (1–7) are taken into consideration in deciding the question of *spousal support*. Increased earnings as a result of the degree and license are taken into consideration because one of the factors in an alimony or maintenance decree is the spouse's ability to pay. The problem, however, is that the wife may not be eligible for alimony because of her own employability. Nor can equity be done by giving the wife a generous share of tangible property, since no such property may have been accumulated due to the fact that the husband had high educational expenses and little or no income of his own. In such situations, one minimal remedy is a direct award for items (1) and (2) above, which again amounts to little more than restitution. A few courts, however, will deny even this remedy, taking the position that the wife, in effect, was making a gift of her money and other resources to the husband during his education.

restitution
An equitable remedy in which a person is restored to his or her original position prior to the loss or injury. Restoring to the plaintiff the value of what he or she parted with.

A growing number of cases, however, have ruled that the degree and license *do* constitute divisible marital property and that more than restitution is called for. The *Woodworth* case is one example:

CASE

Woodworth v. Woodworth

126 Mich. App. 258, 337 N.W.2d 332 (1983)
Court of Appeals of Michigan

Background: *While Michael Woodworth went through law school, his wife, Ann, was a nursery school teacher. In their divorce action, she claimed that his law degree was a marital asset that should be divided. The trial court agreed. It valued the degree at $20,000 and ruled that he must pay her $2,000 per year for ten years. The case is now on appeal before the Court of Appeals of Michigan. On appeal, Michael is the plaintiff and Ann is the defendant.*

Decision on Appeal: *A former husband's law degree, which was the end product of a concerted family effort, was marital property subject to distribution upon divorce. The case is remanded to the trial court to recalculate the value of the degree.*

Opinion of the Court:

Judge BURNS delivered the opinion of the court.

On January 6, 1982, the parties' divorce was finalized. Both parties appeal as of right.

The parties were married on June 27, 1970, after plaintiff had graduated from Central Michigan University with a bachelor's degree in secondary education and defendant had graduated from Lansing Community College with an associates degree. They then moved to Jonesville, where plaintiff worked as a teacher and coach for the high school and defendant worked as a nursery school teacher in Hillsdale. In

continued

CASE

Woodworth v. Woodworth—*Continued*

Summary of Earnings During the Marriage

Year	Plaintiff		Defendant	
1970	$ 2,591	Jonesville HS teacher/coach	$ 1,422	Nursery School Teacher
			$ 2,549	Grant Company (clerk)
1971	$ 7,989	Teacher	$ 4,236	Teacher
	$ 410	St. Anthony Ch. (instructor)	$ 280	St. Anthony Ch. (instructor)
1972	$ 9,691	Teacher	$ 2,525	Teacher
1973	$ 6,557	Teacher	$ 986	Bank Teller
1974	$ 2,483	Legal Aid (student lawyer)	$ 6,572	Bank Teller
1975	$ 2,588	Legal Aid (student lawyer)	$ 1,050	Bank Teller
			$ 8,191	Dept/Social Services (case worker)
1976	$ 6,342	Court of Appeals (attorney)	$10,276	Dept/Social Services (case worker)
1977	$12,493	Court of Appeals (attorney)	$ 1,586	Dept/Social Services (case worker)†
	$ 5,595	Assistant Prosecuting Attorney		
1978	$21,085	Assistant Prosecuting Attorney	$—0—	
1979	$27,247	Assistant Prosecuting Attorney	$—0—	
1980	$ 2,057	Assistant Prosecuting Attorney	$—0—	
	$30,000	Private Practice		

†Defendant quit this job in January after the parties' third child was born.

the Fall of 1973, they sold their house, quit their jobs,* and moved to Detroit, where plaintiff attended Wayne State Law School. Three years later, they moved to Lansing where plaintiff took and passed the bar exam and accepted a job as a research attorney with the Court of Appeals. Plaintiff is now a partner in a Lansing law firm.

For all intents and purposes, the marriage ended on August 25, 1980, when the parties separated. The [chart above] summarizes each party's earnings during the marriage.

The basic issue in this case is whether or not plaintiff's law degree is marital property subject to distribution. The trial court held that it was, valued it at $20,000, and awarded this amount to defendant in payments of $2,000 over ten years. Plaintiff contends that his law degree is not such a marital asset. We disagree.

The facts reveal that plaintiff's law degree was the end product of a concerted family effort. Both parties planned their family life around the effort to attain plaintiff's degree. Toward this end, the family divided the daily tasks encountered in living. While the law degree did not preempt all other facets of their lives, it did become the main focus and goal of their activities. Plaintiff left his job at Jonesville and the family relocated to Detroit so that plaintiff could attend law school. In Detroit, defendant sought and obtained full time employment to support the family.

We conclude, therefore, that plaintiff's law degree was the result of mutual sacrifice and effort by both plaintiff and defendant. While plaintiff studied and attended classes, defendant carried her share of the burden as well as sharing vicariously in the stress of the [law school] experience known as the "paper chase."

We believe that fairness dictates that the spouse who did not earn an advanced degree be compensated whenever the advanced degree is the product of such concerted family investment. The degree holder has expended great effort to obtain the degree not only for him or herself, but also to benefit the family as a whole. The other spouse has shared in this effort and contributed in other ways as well, not merely as a gift to the student spouse nor merely to share individually in the benefits but to help the marital unit as a whole. . . .

We are aware that numerous other cases have held that an advanced degree is not a marital asset and may be considered only (if at all) in determining alimony.

However, we reject the reasons given in these cases to support their conclusions. The cases first contend that an advanced degree is simply not "property":

> "An educational degree, such as an M.B.A., is simply not encompassed by the broad views of the concept of 'property'. It does not have an exchange value or any objective transferable value on an open market. It is personal to the holder. It terminates on death of the holder and is not inheritable. It cannot be assigned, sold, transferred, conveyed, or pledged. An advanced degree is a cumulative product of many years of previous education,

*Defendant had already quit her job the year before after the parties' first child was born.

combined with diligence and hard work. It may not be acquired by the mere expenditure of money. It is simply an intellectual achievement that may potentially assist in the future acquisition of property. In our view, it has none of the attributes of property in the usual sense of that term." *Graham v. Graham,* 194 Colo. 432, 374 P.2d 75 (1978).

Yet whether or not an advanced degree can physically or metaphysically be defined as "property" is beside the point. Courts must instead focus on the most equitable solution to dissolving the marriage and dividing among the respective parties what they have.

> "[T]he student spouse will walk away with a degree and the supporting spouse will depart with little more than the knowledge that he or she has substantially contributed toward the attainment of that degree." Comment, *The Interest of the Community in a Professional Education,* 10 Cal. West. L. Rev. 590 (1974).

In *DeLa Rosa v. DeLa Rosa,* 309 N.W.2d 758, (1981), the Minnesota Supreme Court added:

> "[O]ne spouse has forgone the immediate enjoyment of earned income to enable the other to pursue an advanced education on a full time basis. Typically, this sacrifice is made with the expectation that the parties will enjoy a higher standard of living in the future."

Where, as in this case, the family goal of obtaining the law degree was the purpose of the substantial contribution and sacrifice, both the degree holder and his or her spouse are entitled to share in the fruits of the degree. The trial judge recognized as much:

> "Here the plaintiff quit his job and entered law school. The defendant secured employment so plaintiff could become a professional with far greater earning capacity than he had, which would benefit him and their children. To permit this, upon divorce, to benefit only the party who secured the professional degree is unconscionable."

The next argument is that a marriage is not a commercial enterprise and that neither spouse's expectations are necessarily going to be met after the divorce:

> "I do not believe that a spouse who works and contributes to the education of the other spouse during marriage normally does so in the expectation of compensation." *Sullivan v. Sullivan,* 184 Cal. Rptr. 801 (1982) (Kaufman, P. J., concurring).

Furthermore:

> "They do not nor do they expect to pay each other for their respective contributions in any commercial sense. Rather, they work together, in both income and nonincome producing ways, in their joint, mutual and individual interests.
>
> "The termination of the marriage represents, if nothing else, the disappointment of expectations, financial and nonfinancial, which were hoped to be achieved by and during the continuation of the relationship. It does not, however, in our view, represent a commercial investment loss. Recompense for the disappointed expectations resulting from the failure of the marital entity to survive cannot, therefore, be made to the spouses on a strictly commercial basis which, after the fact seeks to assign monetary values to the contributions consensually made by each of the spouses during the marriage. . . .
>
> "If the plan fails by reason of the termination of the marriage, we do not regard the supporting spouse's consequent loss of expectation by itself as any more compensable or demanding of solicitude than the loss of expectations of any other spouse who, in the hope and anticipation of the endurance of the relationship in its commitments, has invested a portion of his or her life, youth, energy and labor in a failed marriage." *Mahoney v. Mahoney,* 182 N.J. Super. 612–614, 442 A.2d 1062 (1982).

We agree that a marriage is not intrinsically a commercial enterprise. Instead, it is a relationship sanctioned by law governed at its essence by fidelity and troth. Neither partner usually expects to be compensated for his or her efforts. But that consideration does not end the discussion. We are not presently concerned with how best to characterize a marriage while it endures. Instead, we are concerned with how best to distribute between the parties what they have once the marriage has for all intents and purposes dissolved. In other words:

> "To allow a student spouse . . . to leave a marriage with all the benefits of additional education and a professional license without compensation to the spouse who bore much of the burdens incident to procuring these would be unfair. . . ." *O'Brien v. O'Brien,* 452 N.Y.S.2d 801, 805 (1982).

Furthermore, we also agree that divorce courts cannot recompense expectations. However, we are not talking about an expectation here. Defendant is

continued

CASE

Woodworth v. Woodworth—*Continued*

not asking us to compensate for a failed expectation that her husband would become a wealthy lawyer and subsequently support her for the rest of her life. Instead, she is merely seeking her share of the fruits of a degree which she helped him earn. We fail to see the difference between compensating her for a degree which she helped him earn and compensating her for a house in his name which her earnings helped him buy.

The third argument against including an advanced degree as marital property is that its valuation is too speculative. In *Lesman v. Lesman,* 452 N.Y.S.2d 938-939 (1982), the Court stated:

> "Gross inequities may result from predicating distribution awards upon the speculative expectations of enhanced future earnings, since distributive awards, unlike maintenance, once fixed may not be modified to meet future realities. It is almost impossible to predict what amount of enhanced earnings, if any, will result from a professional education. The degree of financial success attained by those holding a professional degree varies greatly. Some, even, may earn less from their professional practices than they could have earned from non-professional work. Moreover, others, due to choice or factors beyond their control, may never practice their professions."

Michigan has already recognized that:

> "Interests which are contingent upon the happening of an event which may or may not occur are not distributable. The party seeking to include the interest in the marital estate bears the burdens of proving a reasonably ascertainable value; if the burden is not met, the interest should not be considered an asset subject to distribution." *Miller v. Miller,* 83 Mich. App. 672, 677, 269 N.W.2d 264 (1978).

However, future earnings due to an advanced degree are not "too speculative." While a degree holder spouse might change professions, earn less than projected at trial, or even die, courts have proved adept at measuring future earnings in such contexts as personal injury, wrongful death, and workers' compensation actions. In fact, pain and suffering, professional goodwill and mental distress, within these general legal issues, have similar valuation "problems". . . . We, therefore, do not believe that the *Miller* contingency caveat applies to future earnings.

The last argument is that these matters are best considered when awarding alimony rather than when distributing the property. . . . A trial judge is given wide discretion in awarding alimony. . . . However, alimony is basically for the other spouse's support. The considerations for whether or not a spouse is entitled to support are different than for dividing the marital property. *McLain v. McLain,* 108 Mich. App. 166, 310 N.W.2d 316 (1981), listed eleven factors that the trial judge is to consider in determining whether or not to award alimony. Some of these deal with the parties' financial condition and their ability to support themselves. If the spouse has already supported the other spouse through graduate school, he or she is quite possibly already presently capable of supporting him or herself. Furthermore, M.C.L.A. [Michigan Compiled Laws Annotated] § 552.13; M.S.A. [Michigan Statutes Annotated] § 25.93 gave the trial court discretion to end alimony if the spouse receiving it remarries. We do not believe that the trial judge should be allowed to deprive the spouse who does not have an advanced degree of the fruits of the marriage and award it all to the other spouse merely because he or she has remarried. Such a situation would necessarily cause that spouse to think twice about remarrying.

Having determined that the defendant is entitled to compensation in this case, we must next determine how she is to be compensated. Two basic methods have been proposed—a percentage share of the present value of the future earnings attributable to the degree or restitution.

[Some courts limit] the recovery to restitution for any money given to the student spouse to earn the degree. While this solution may be equitable in some circumstances, we do not believe that restitution is an adequate remedy in this case. Limiting the recovery to restitution "would provide [the supporting spouse] no realization of [his or] her expectation of economic benefit from the career for which the education laid the foundation." Pinnel, *Divorce After Professional School: Education and Future Earning Capacity May Be Marital Property,* 44 Mo.L.Rev. 329, 335 (1979). Clearly, in this case, the degree was a family investment, rather than a gift or a benefit to the degree holder alone. Treating the degree as such a gift would unjustly enrich the degree holder to the extent that the degree's value exceeds its cost. . . . We note that this case does not involve the situation where both parties simultaneously earned substantially similar advanced degrees during the marriage. In such a situation, equity suggests that the parties have already amply compensated each other.

The trial court in this case valued plaintiff's law degree at $20,000 and ruled that plaintiff must pay defendant $2,000 per year for ten years. We are unable to determine how this value was reached and therefore, remand to the trial court to permit that court to revalue the degree in light of the following factors: the length of the marriage after the degree was obtained, the sources and extent of financial support given plaintiff during his years in law school, and the overall division of the parties' marital property. In determining the degree's present value, the trial court should estimate what the person holding the degree is likely to make in that particular job market and subtract from that what he or she would probably have earned without the degree. . . . The ultimate objective in a property distribution is to be fair. . . . Both parties may present new evidence on these matters and the degree's valuation.

One of the tragedies of this divorce, as in so many others, is that what used to be financially adequate is no longer enough. As the trial court aptly stated: "The tablecloths . . . will not cover both tables." We, therefore, note that the trial court has discretion to order that the payments be made on an installment basis. . . . If the trial court should order such a payment schedule, the trial court should also consider the possibility of insuring these payments by a life insurance policy on plaintiff's life benefitting defendant.

Plaintiff has also appealed the overall property division while defendant has cross-appealed from the alimony determination. If the trial court alters the value placed on plaintiff's law degree, the property division and alimony award must also be reassessed. We, therefore, refrain from addressing these issues at this time.

Pursuant to GCR [General Court Rules] 1963, 726.1, we order plaintiff to pay defendant reasonable attorney fees for this appeal. Costs to defendant.

Remanded with instructions to proceed in a manner consistent with this opinion. We do not retain jurisdiction.

ASSIGNMENT 8.10

a. Was *Woodworth v. Woodworth* correctly decided? Why or why not?

b. Frank and Elaine are married in your state. Both work at low-paying jobs at a fast-food restaurant. Elaine wishes to become a paralegal, and Frank would like to become an electrician. A local institute has a one-year paralegal training program and a nine-month electrician training program. Frank and Elaine decide that only one of them can go to school at a time. Frank volunteers to let Elaine go first, keeping his job at the restaurant to support them both while she is at the institute. A month before Elaine is scheduled to graduate, Frank has a serious accident at the restaurant. He will not recover fully from his injury or be able to go to school for at least five years. When Elaine is graduated, she obtains a good job as a paralegal. The parties seek a divorce a month after graduation. There are no children from the marriage, and no tangible property to divide. In the divorce proceeding, Frank tells the court that the only asset that can be divided is Elaine's paralegal certificate. He asks the court to award him a percentage of the earnings that Elaine will have during the next five years as a paralegal.

   i. How would *Woodworth v. Woodworth* apply to this case?

   ii. How would your state resolve the case of Elaine and Frank? (See General Instructions for the Court-Opinion Assignment in Appendix A.)

Dividing a Business

When a divorce occurs, one of the assets to be divided may be a business that either was acquired during the marriage or was acquired before the marriage but developed or expanded during the marriage. The business could be a large corporation, a small sole proprietorship, a partnership, a law practice, a medical practice, etc. (Our focus here is a functioning business rather than a degree or license that will allow one to operate a business in the future.) Business appraisers are often hired to place a value on the business. In addition to plant and equipment, a number of intangible items must be valuated (e.g., patents, trademarks, employment agreements, copyrights, securities, and goodwill).

Many standard business documents[7] must be collected when valuing a business. For example:

- Federal, state, and local income tax returns for the last five years
- Annual and interim financial statements
- Bank statements
- Depreciation schedules
- Articles of incorporation and bylaws or partnership agreements, including amendments
- Minutes of meetings of shareholders and directors
- Buy/sell agreements of shareholders or partners, including amendments
- Loan applications
- W-2 statements (or the equivalent) for the highest paid employees
- Leases
- Production schedules
- Inventory reports
- Management reports
- Billing records

goodwill
The favorable reputation of a business that causes it to generate additional business.

One aspect of a business that is sometimes particularly difficult to evaluate is its **goodwill.** Because of goodwill, the company is expected to have earnings beyond what is considered normal for the type of business involved. Individuals providing services, such as accountants and lawyers, may also have goodwill:

> If you are a lawyer facing divorce, it is open season on your practice. . . . Like it or not, law practices and lawyer's goodwill are assets. That you can't sell your practice doesn't mean it has no value. And there are almost no legal limits on the methods an appraiser may use in assigning a value to a law practice. . . . One approach is called the excess earnings method. An appraiser looks at published surveys to find the average income for a lawyer of your experience and type of practice, then compares your earnings with the average. If your earnings are higher than the average, the increment is said to be attributable to goodwill. If your ability to attract clients and collect substantial fees from them brings you more income than you would earn working for an average salary, you have built real goodwill.[8]

If goodwill was developed during the marriage, the spouse who stayed at home may be deemed to have contributed to it (as well as to the rest of the business). In community property states, spouses have a fifty/fifty interest in the portion of the business (including goodwill) that materialized during the marriage. In other states, the court might reach a different allocation based on its determination of what would be equitable.

The fact that a business (with or without goodwill) is a divisible part of the marital estate does not necessarily mean that upon divorce the business must be sold so that the proceeds can be physically divided. The separation agreement may provide, for example, that the husband gives the wife $150,000 in exchange for the release of any interest that the wife may have in his business—or vice versa if she is the one primarily responsible for the business. Similarly, a court may order such an exchange if the parties are not able to agree on dividing the business in their separation agreement.

ASSIGNMENT 8.11

Does your state have any statutes on the division of (a) a pension, (b) a degree or license, (c) a business or profession, or (d) goodwill following a divorce? If so, briefly summarize their terms. (See General Instructions for the State-Code Assignment in Appendix A.)

---

[7]Part of the following list comes from Business Valuation Research, Inc., of Seattle, Washington.
[8]Gabrielson & Walker, *Surviving Your Own Divorce,* California Lawyer 76 (June 1987).

INSURANCE

A number of insurance questions must be considered by the parties:

- What kinds of insurance do the parties now have?
- How have the insurance premiums been paid?
- Following the separation, what will happen to the policies?
- Is there a need for additional insurance?

Several different kinds of insurance policies could be in effect at the time the parties draft the separation agreement:

- Life insurance
- Homeowners' insurance
- Hospitalization or other medical insurance
- Liability insurance (for business)
- Car insurance
- Umbrella insurance

Each kind of policy should be carefully identified with notations as to how much the premiums are, who has paid them, who the beneficiaries are, whether the beneficiaries can be changed and, if so, by whom, etc. Unfortunately, parties often neglect such important details. Insurance policies can be as crucial as other "property" items that must be divided or otherwise negotiated as part of the separation agreement. The parties may opt to leave the policies as they are with no changes. This is fine if it is a conscious decision of *both* parties after *all* the facts are known about each policy, the tax consequences are explained, and the economic advantages and disadvantages of the various ways of handling each policy are discussed.

As we have seen, one spouse usually has no obligation to support the other spouse or the children after the payor spouse dies. The latter, however, may want to assume this obligation voluntarily. Life insurance on the payor's life, with the beneficiaries being the other spouse and/or the children, is a common way of doing this. If such a life insurance policy already exists, then the payor may agree to keep it effective (e.g., pay the premiums) after the separation. The payee and children, however, may not gain much protection from such an agreement if the payor can change the beneficiaries. Hence, as part of the bargaining process, the payee may ask that the designation of the beneficiaries be made irrevocable.

DEBTS

The parties must discuss how to handle:

- Debts outstanding (i.e., unpaid) at the time the separation agreement is signed
- Debts incurred after the separation agreement is signed

A great variety of debts may be outstanding:

- Debts between the spouses (e.g., a loan made by one spouse to the other during the marriage)
- Business debts incurred by the husband
- Family debts incurred by the husband
- Business debts incurred by the wife
- Family debts incurred by the wife
- Business or family debts incurred by both the husband and the wife (i.e., the debts are in both names so that there is **joint and several liability**

joint and several liability
More than one person is legally responsible. They are responsible together and individually for the entire amount.

on the debts, meaning that a creditor could sue the husband and wife *together* on the debt, or could sue *either* the husband or the wife for payment of the whole debt).

The parties must decide who is going to pay what debts; the separation agreement should specifically reflect what they have decided. The extent to which the parties are in debt is relevant to (1) the necessity of using present cash and other resources to pay these debts, (2) the availability of resources to support spouse and children, and (3) the possibility of bankruptcy now or in the immediate future.

Divorce often leads to massive financial upheaval for one or both spouses. The option of bankruptcy must be kept in mind throughout the negotiations for the separation agreement. A wife, for example, should not have the attitude that her husband's debts are "his problem." His bankruptcy might cause her to lose whatever he still owes her under the property division agreement. (As we have seen, however, a bankruptcy would not discharge alimony and child support obligations. See Exhibit 8.4.)

As to future debts (i.e., those incurred after the separation agreement is signed), the normal expectation of the parties is that they will pay their own debts. (A cautious spouse, however, will not only cancel all joint credit cards but also notify known creditors that future debts will be the sole responsibility of the spouse incurring the debts.) Except for the obligations that arise out of the separation agreement itself, the parties are on their own. A clause should be inserted in the agreement providing that each party promises not to attempt to use the credit of the other.

TAXES

In chapter 11, we will discuss the tax consequences of divorce. Our focus here is on the question of who pays the taxes and who will be able to take advantage of certain tax benefits. The following are the kinds of situations the parties need to anticipate:

- If the Internal Revenue Service (IRS) assesses a tax deficiency and penalty for a prior year during which the parties filed a joint return, who pays the deficiency and penalty?
- If the parties file their last joint return in the current tax year, and then, many months later, the IRS assesses a tax deficiency and penalty on that last tax return, who pays this deficiency and penalty?
- In the year in which the separation agreement is signed, if the parties file separate returns, with whose resources are each person's taxes paid?
- In the current year and in future years, who takes the tax deduction for the payment of interest on the mortgage and for the payment of property taxes on the home where the children and the custodial parent continue to live?
- In the current year and in future years, who takes the tax exemption for each of the dependent children?
- What happens to any tax refunds for the current tax year and for any prior year?

During a marriage, the couple's tax returns are often prepared by the husband with minimal involvement of the wife. This does not necessarily relieve her from liability for tax errors or fraud committed by her husband, although, as we will see in chapter 11, a spouse might be able to obtain relief as an "innocent spouse." In the negotiations for the separation agreement, the wife might ask the husband to insert a clause that he will **indemnify** the wife

indemnify
To compensate another for any loss or expense incurred.

against any tax deficiencies and penalties that may arise out of the joint returns filed in any year during their marriage. Under such a clause, he will have to pay the entire deficiency and penalty for which they both may be jointly and severally liable.

The parties must also agree on how tax refunds, if any, are to be divided. Such refunds are usually payable by government check to both of the parties. Two signatures are required on such checks. Another concern is that the IRS might institute an audit years after a particular return is filed. It is a good idea to insert a clause in the separation agreement that both parties agree to cooperate with each other in responding to the issues raised during any possible audits in the future.

There are laws on who can receive the tax benefits of exemptions and deductions from alimony, interest payments, and property tax payments. The parties do not have total freedom in deciding who can use these tax benefits. The point, however, is that one of the parties will be entitled to the benefits. This is an economic advantage that should be taken into consideration in the overall evaluation of who is getting what from the separation agreement. The separation agreement may specify a dollar amount to be transferred pursuant to a support clause or a property division clause. If, however, all the tax factors have not been considered, the parties may later be surprised by the discrepancy between such stated dollar figures and the *real* amounts that they receive and pay out. To **tax effect** a clause in a separation agreement means to determine the tax consequences of that clause.

tax effect
(a) To determine the tax consequences of something; (b) the tax consequences of something.

WILLS

The parties must consider a number of questions involving wills and estates:

- Do the spouses already have wills naming each other as beneficiary? If so, are these wills to be changed? In most states, a divorce automatically revokes gifts to a surviving spouse unless the will specifically says otherwise. Nevertheless, the parties may want to make this explicit in their separation agreement and also cover the period between separation and the issuance of the final divorce decree.
- Have they named each other as **executor** of their estates? If so, is this to be changed?
- Is the husband going to agree to leave his wife and/or children something in his will? If so, and this requires a change in his will, when is this change to be made?
- Is either spouse mentioned as a beneficiary in the will of a relative of the other spouse? If so, is this likely to be changed?

When a spouse dies, the surviving spouse has important rights in the property of the deceased spouse, sometimes in spite of what the latter intended or provided for in a will. Assume that a spouse dies **testate,** leaving nothing to the surviving spouse. In most states, a surviving spouse who is dissatisfied with a will can **elect against the will** and receive a **forced share** of the deceased's property. This share is often the same share that the surviving spouse would have received if the deceased had died **intestate.**

The separation agreement should specify what happens to the right to elect against a will and similar rights such as **dower** and **curtesy.** The normal provision is that each side *releases* all such rights in the other's property.

executor
The person designated in a will to carry out the terms of the will and handle related matters.

testate
Die leaving a valid will.

elect against the will
To obtain a designated share of a deceased spouse's estate in spite of what the latter provided or failed to provide for the surviving spouse in a will.

forced share
The share of a deceased spouse's estate that the surviving spouse elects to receive in spite of what the deceased provided or failed to provide for the surviving spouse in a will.

intestate
Die without leaving a valid will.

dower
The right of a widow to the lifetime use of one-third of the land her deceased husband owned during the marriage.

curtesy
The right of a husband to the lifetime use of all the land his deceased wife owned during the marriage (if issue were born of the marriage).

MISCELLANEOUS PROVISIONS

A number of other items need to be considered:

Legal Expenses

One spouse is often ordered by the court to pay the attorney fees of the other in a divorce action. The parties may want to specify this in the separation agreement itself. They should consider not only the legal costs (counsel fees, filing fees, etc.) of a potential divorce but also the legal costs incurred in connection with the preparation of the separation agreement itself. Of course, if both have adequate resources of their own, the parties may agree (and the court will probably order) that they pay their own legal bills.

Nonmolestation Clause

nonmolestation clause
A clause in an agreement that the parties will not bother each other.

Most separation agreements contain a **nonmolestation clause,** in which both parties agree, in effect, to leave each other alone. Specifically, they will not try to live with the other person, interfere with each other's lifestyle, or bother each other in any way. This does not necessarily mean that they cannot have any future contact with each other. If, for example, one spouse has physical custody of the children, communication may be necessary in order to make visitation arrangements.

MODIFICATION OF THE SEPARATION AGREEMENT

Generally, a court has no power to alter the terms of a valid contract. A separation agreement is a contract. Can its terms be modified? Clearly, the parties to any contract can mutually agree to modify its terms. But can the court *force* a modification on the parties when only one party wants it?

The answer may depend on which terms of the separation agreement are in question. *Property division* terms, as indicated earlier, are rarely modifiable (see Exhibit 8.4). *Child-custody* and *child-support* terms, however, are almost always modifiable according to the court's perception of the best interests of the child (see chapters 9 and 10 for special rules on when a court in one state has jurisdiction to modify the child-custody order or child-support order of another state). Can *alimony* or spousal support terms be modified by a court?

First, consider two extreme and relatively rare circumstances where the court can modify spousal-support terms:

- The separation agreement itself includes a provision allowing a court to modify its terms.
- The needy spouse has become so destitute that he or she will become a public charge unless a modification is ordered.

If neither of these situations exists, can the court order a modification of the spousal-support terms of the separation agreement? This involves two separate questions: Does the court have the power to modify, and if so, when will it exercise this power?

Power to Modify

In a few states, a court has no power to modify a spousal-support term unless the parties have agreed in the separation agreement to allow the court to do so. Most states, however, will allow their courts to modify a separation agreement even if it expressly says that modification is not allowed. A number of theories have been advanced to support this view. Some states hold that the separation agreement is merely advisory to the court and that as a matter of public policy, the court cannot allow the question of support to be determined solely by the parties. The state as a whole has an interest in seeing to it that this sensitive question is properly resolved. What the parties have agreed upon will be a factor in the court's determination, but it will not be the controlling factor. Other states advance the theory of merger. When a court accepts the terms of a separation agreement, it can *incorporate* and *merge* them into the divorce decree. The agreement loses its separate identity. The question is not whether the separation agreement can be modified, but whether the decree can be modified. Courts are much less reluctant to modify their own decrees than they are to modify the private contracts of parties. Under the merger doctrine, the contract no longer exists. Suppose, however, that a court incorporates but does *not* merge the separation agreement into the decree. Here the court simply refers to the separation agreement in its decree and usually approves the spousal-support terms the parties agreed to. Since there is no merger, the separation agreement remains as an independent—and nonmodifiable—contract.

Exercising the Power to Modify

Assuming the court has the power to modify spousal-support orders, when will the court use it? The general rule is that a modification will be ordered only when there has been a substantial change of circumstances of a continuing nature that is not due to voluntary action or inaction of the parties. Furthermore, some courts limit the exercise of their modification power to periodic or ongoing alimony payments; they will not modify a *lump-sum* support award.

> *Tom and Mary enter a separation agreement that is approved, incorporated, and merged by the court in its divorce decree. Tom is required to pay Mary $750 a month alimony. Assume that Tom comes to the court a year later seeking a decrease, and/or Mary comes seeking an increase.*

Unfortunately, courts are not always consistent as to when they will allow a modification in such a case. Consider the following circumstances:

1. *The ex-husband becomes sick and earns substantially less.* Most courts would modify the decree to lessen the amount he must pay—at least during the period when his earning capacity is affected by the illness.
2. *The ex-husband suddenly starts earning a great deal more.* The ex-wife will usually not be able to increase her alimony award simply because her ex-husband becomes more wealthy than he was at the time of the divorce decree. The result might be different if she can show that the *original* alimony award was inadequate due to his weaker earning capacity at that time.
3. *The ex-wife violates the terms of the separation agreement relating to the visitation rights of the ex-husband/father.* A few courts feel that alimony payments and visitation rights are interdependent. If the ex-wife interferes with the father's visitation rights with the children, these courts will reduce or terminate her alimony. For such a result, however, the interference must be substantial.
4. *The ex-wife cohabits with a member of the opposite sex.* In many states, such cohabitation can lead to a termination or other modification of alimony, particularly if the cohabitation is ongoing and open. (The statute authorizing this is sometimes called the "live-in-lover" statute.) The ex-wife probably has a decreased need for alimony due to the new living arrangement. Of course, the main reason an ex-husband will

petition the court for modification is his suspicion that his alimony payments are helping to support the new lover.

5. *The ex-husband wants to retire, change jobs, or go back to school.* When his income is reduced in this way, the courts will consider a downward modification of the alimony obligation only if the proposed change in lifestyle is made in good faith and not simply as a way to avoid paying the original amount of alimony. A rich executive, for example, cannot "drop out" and become a poor farmer. Such an executive, however, may be able to take a lower paying job if this is required for his health.
6. *The ex-husband remarries.* In most states, his alimony obligation to his first wife is not affected by his remarriage. A few states, however, will consider a reduction if it is clear that he cannot meet the burden of supporting two families, particularly when there are children from the second marriage.
7. *The ex-wife remarries.* If the ex-wife remarries, most courts will terminate the ex-husband's alimony obligation unless the parties agreed in the separation agreement that alimony would continue in some form after she remarried.
8. *The ex-husband dies.* Alimony ends upon the death of the ex-husband unless the separation agreement provides for its continuance and/or the divorce decree imposes his obligation on the ex-husband's estate.

ASSIGNMENT 8.12

Find authority (e.g., a statute or a court opinion) in your state for the court's power to modify an alimony award. When will such a modification be made? (See also General Instructions for the State-Code Assignment and the Court-Opinion Assignment in Appendix A.)

ASSIGNMENT 8.13

Karen and Jim obtain a divorce decree that awards Karen $500 a month in alimony "until she dies or remarries." A year after the divorce decree becomes final, Karen marries Paul. Jim stops the alimony payments. A year later this marriage to Paul is annulled. Karen now wants Jim to resume paying her $500 a month alimony and to pay her $6,000 to cover the period when she was "married" to Paul ($500 × 12). What result? (See General Instructions for the Legal-Analysis Assignment in Appendix A.)

ARBITRATION AND MEDIATION

arbitration

The process of submitting a dispute to a third party outside the judicial system who will render a decision that resolves the dispute.

mediation

The process of submitting a dispute to a third party outside the judicial system who will help the parties reach their own resolution of the dispute. The mediator will not render a decision that resolves the dispute.

Many separation agreements contain a clause providing that disputes arising in the future about the agreement will be subject to **arbitration.** This is a method of alternative dispute resolution (ADR), which operates outside the judicial system. ADR is an alternative to litigation. When the ADR method is arbitration, the parties hire an arbitrator, who will examine all the evidence and render a decision on the dispute that the parties submit for resolution. Normally, a professional arbitration organization, such as the American Arbitration Association, is specified as the arbitrator who will resolve the dispute. A professional group, however, is not necessary. The parties may select a mutually trusted friend or associate as the arbitrator. The agreement should specify who the arbitrator will be and who will pay the arbitration expenses.

Another ADR method is **mediation,** which also operates outside the judicial system as an alternative to litigation. Unlike an arbitrator, a mediator does not make a decision. The mediator tries to guide the parties to reach a decision *on their own* in much the same manner as a labor mediator tries to assist union and management to reach a settlement. If mediation does not work, the parties either agree to submit the dispute to an arbitrator or are forced to litigate it in court. For more on mediation and how it can be used elsewhere in the divorce process, see the section on alternative dispute resolution on page 213 in chapter 7.

RECONCILIATION

What happens if the parties become reconciled to each other after they execute the separation agreement but before they divorce? They certainly have the power to cancel or rescind their contract so long as both do so voluntarily. If it is clear that they want to cancel, no problem exists. Legally, the separation agreement goes out of existence. The problem arises when the parties say nothing about the separation agreement after they reconcile and resume cohabitation. Sometime thereafter the parties separate again, and one of them tries to enforce the separation agreement, while the other argues that it no longer exists. Courts handle the problem in different ways:

- The reconciliation will cancel the alimony or spousal-support terms of the separation agreement, but will not cancel the property division terms.
- The reconciliation will cancel the **executory** (unperformed) terms of the separation agreement, but will not cancel the executed (already performed) terms.

executory
Unperformed as yet.

The case is somewhat more complicated if a divorce decree exists that orders the parties to pay alimony or to divide the marital property. The parties cannot cancel a court decree simply by reconciling. They must go back to court and petition for changes in the decree that reflect their resumed relationship.

Reconciliation usually means the full and unconditional resumption of the marital relationship; occasional or casual contact will not suffice. The intent must be to abandon the separation agreement and to resume the marital relationship permanently.

Interviewing and Investigation Checklist

Have the Parties Reconciled?

Legal Interviewing Questions

1. On what date did you both sign the separation agreement?
2. When did you stop living together?
3. Where did you both live when you were separated?
4. Was the separation bitter? Describe the circumstances of the separation.
5. After you signed the separation agreement, when did the two of you have your first contact? Describe the circumstances.
6. Have the two of you had sexual intercourse with each other since the separation agreement was signed? How often?
7. Did you ever discuss getting back together again? If so, describe the circumstances (e.g., who initiated the discussion, was there any reluctance)?
8. During this period, did the two of you abide by the terms of the separation agreement? Explain.
9. Did you move in together? If so, where did you both stay? Did one of you give up a house or apartment in order to live together?
10. Did you discuss what to do with the separation agreement?
11. Did the two of you assume that it was no longer effective?
12. After you came together again, did either of you continue abiding by any of the terms of the separation agreement?

continued

Interviewing and Investigation Checklist—*Continued*

13. Did either of you give back whatever he or she received under the terms of the separation agreement?
14. When you resumed the relationship, did you feel that the reunion was going to be permanent? What do you think your spouse felt about it?
15. Did either of you attach any conditions to resuming the relationship?
16. What have the two of you done since you came together again to indicate that you both considered each other to be husband and wife (e.g., both sign joint tax returns, make joint purchases, spend a lot of time together in public, etc.)?
17. Have you separated again? If so, describe the circumstances of the most recent separation.

Possible Investigation Tasks

- Interview people who know the plaintiff (P) and defendant (D) well to find out what they know about the alleged reconciliation.
- Obtain any documents executed after the separation agreement was signed that may indicate the extent to which P and D did things together during this time (e.g., rent receipts with both of their names on them, opening or continuing joint checking or savings accounts).

ASSIGNMENT 8.14

Tom and Mary execute a separation agreement on February 17, 1998, in which they mutually release all rights (dower, curtesy, election, etc.) in each other's estate. They ceased living together on February 2, 1998. On March 13, 1998, Tom moves out of the city. On the next day, he makes a long distance call to Mary in which he says, "This is ridiculous. Why don't you come live with me? You know I still love you." Mary answers, "I guess you're right, but if we are going to live together again, I want you to come back here." Tom then says, "I'm sure we can work that out." They agree to meet the next week to discuss it further. Before they meet, Tom dies. Tom's will makes no provision for Mary. Mary now seeks a forced share of his estate, electing against his will. What result? At the time of Tom's death, he was still married to Mary. (See General Instructions for the Legal-Analysis Assignment in Appendix A.)

COMPUTER HELP

Computer companies have designed software to assist the law office in managing the large volume of data involved in the negotiation of a separation agreement. For example, Exhibit 8.8 presents a screen from PROPertizer™, which helps provide real property and pension calculations in divorce cases. The screen shows the equity of specific property that is calculated on the basis of its fair market value and encumbrances. A single keystroke or mouse-click assigns items to one or both spouses, automatically displaying recalculations as the office formulates and reformulates proposals during bargaining for the separation agreement.

For more information on computer use in other areas of a family law practice, see the software on designing joint custody schedules in Exhibit 9.1 of chapter 9 (page 307) and the Internet online worksheets for the calculation of child support in Exhibit 10.1 of chapter 10 (page 357).

Many software programs have the ability to turn financial data into interesting and effective graphics presentations. For example, the first charts in Exhibit 8.9 compare the income of a husband and wife over a seven-year period. Other charts in Exhibit 8.9 depict bank deposits and withdrawals over a twelve-month period. A dry listing of numbers can come alive when used in conjunction with such charts.

Exhibit 8.8 Data Input Screen of PROPertizer™

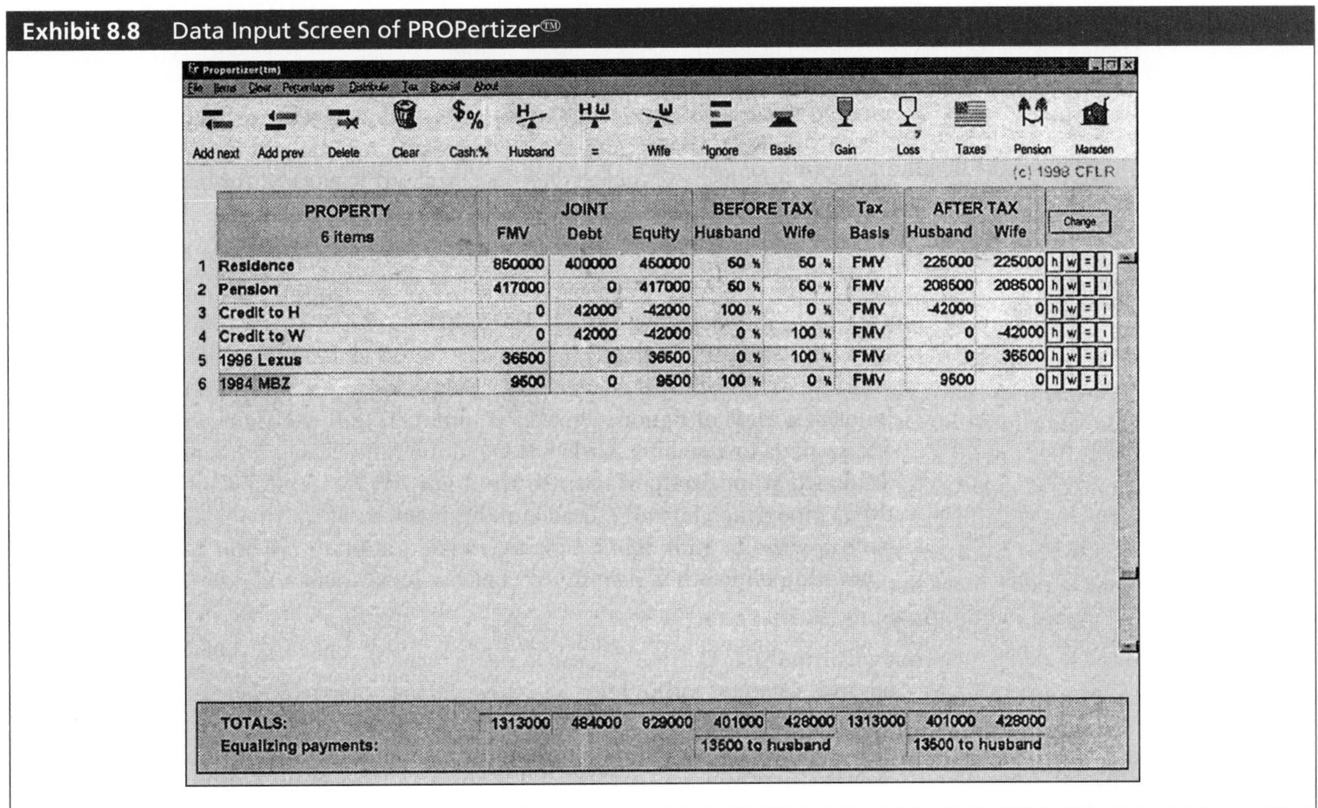

	PROPERTY 6 items	FMV	JOINT Debt	Equity	BEFORE TAX Husband	Wife	Tax Basis	AFTER TAX Husband	Wife
1	Residence	850000	400000	450000	50 %	50 %	FMV	225000	225000
2	Pension	417000	0	417000	50 %	50 %	FMV	208500	208500
3	Credit to H	0	42000	-42000	100 %	0 %	FMV	-42000	0
4	Credit to W	0	42000	-42000	0 %	100 %	FMV	0	-42000
5	1996 Lexus	36500	0	36500	0 %	100 %	FMV	0	36500
6	1984 MBZ	9500	0	9500	100 %	0 %	FMV	9500	0
	TOTALS:	1313000	484000	829000	401000	428000	1313000	401000	428000
	Equalizing payments:				13500 to husband			13500 to husband	

Source: PROPertizer™, California Family Law Report, Inc., P.O. Box 5917, Sausalito, CA 94966-5917, www.cflr.com, (415) 332-9000.

ASSIGNMENT 8.15

Contact a lawyer or paralegal who works in a law office that practices family law in whole or part, and find out what computer software programs they use on family law cases other than basic word-processing programs used in any kind of case. Write a report about one such program, including its name, functions, cost, level of difficulty, and strengths and weaknesses. Try to obtain the address and phone number of the company that wrote the program. (Perhaps you can write the company and ask for promotional literature on the product. Use its 800 number, if available.)

Exhibit 8.9 Graphics Presentations: Seven-Year Comparative Income; 2002 Deposits and Withdrawals (Husband vs. Wife)

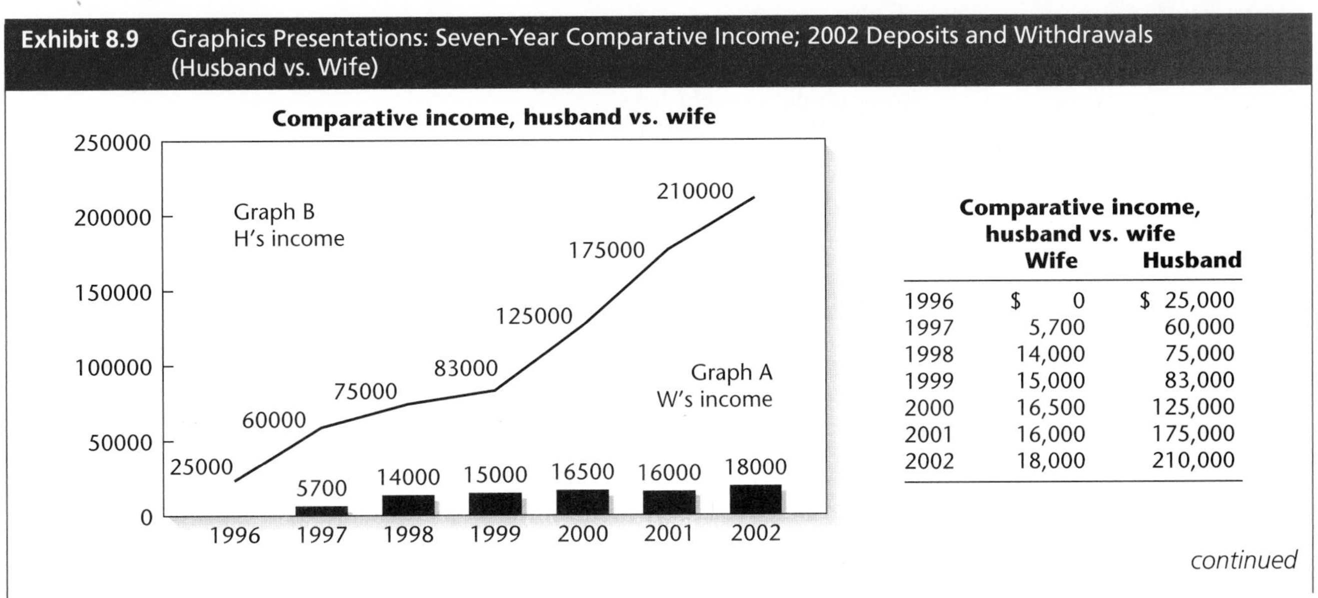

Comparative income, husband vs. wife

	Wife	Husband
1996	$ 0	$ 25,000
1997	5,700	60,000
1998	14,000	75,000
1999	15,000	83,000
2000	16,500	125,000
2001	16,000	175,000
2002	18,000	210,000

continued

Exhibit 8.9 Graphics Presentations: Seven-Year Comparative Income; 2002 Deposits and Withdrawals (Husband vs. Wife)—*Continued*

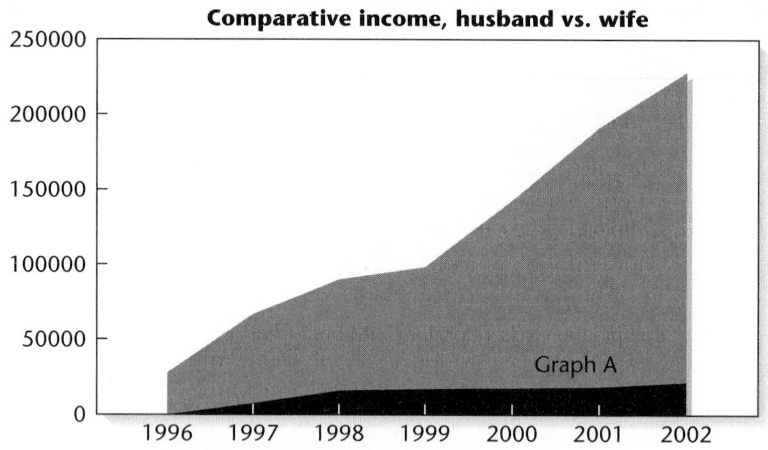

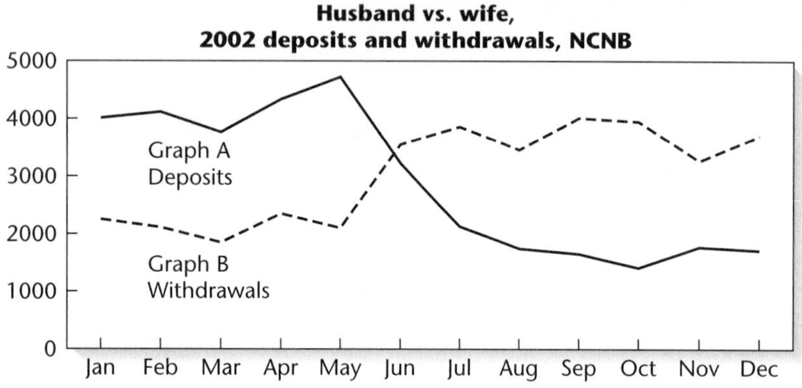

Bank account

2002	Deposit	W/D
Jan	$4,010	$2,270
Feb	4,120	2,120
Mar	3,755	1,850
Apr	4,305	2,310
May	4,700	2,080
Jun	3,210	3,550
Jul	2,102	3,810
Aug	1,721	3,420
Sep	1,595	3,985
Oct	1,380	3,880
Nov	1,750	3,225
Dec	1,660	3,660

Source: Kenneth Raggio, *Lawyer-Proof Presentation Graphics,* 12 Family Advocate 41 (Summer 1989).

SAMPLE SEPARATION AGREEMENT CLAUSES

B. Stone, Modern Legal Forms
§ 4515ff., p. 274ff. West Group (1977)

I

Separation Agreement—Significant Clauses*

Agreement made this 19th day of November, 19______, between John Jones, presently residing at 10 South Street, ______, hereinafter sometimes referred to as "the Husband," and Mary Jones, presently residing at 25 North Street, ______, hereinafter sometimes referred to as "the Wife."

• *The beginning of the agreement lays out its purpose and identifies all family members involved.*

Witnesseth:

Whereas, the parties are husband and wife and were married in ______, on June 15, 19______, and

Whereas, there are two children of the marriage, namely a daughter, Elizabeth Ann Jones, hereinafter referred to as "Elizabeth," born on April 1, 19______, and a son, William Roe Jones, hereinafter referred to as "William," born on August 15, 19______ and

---

*From a lecture by John Scully, Jr., on *Significant Clauses in a Separation Agreement,* published in 7 Record of the Bar Association of the City of New York 236–50.

Whereas, in consequence of disputes and irreconcilable differences, the parties have separated, and are now living separate and apart, and intend to continue to live separate and apart for the rest of their natural lives; and

Whereas the parties desire to confirm their separation and make arrangements in connection therewith, including the settlement of all questions relating to their property rights, the custody of their children (which the parties recognize as paramount), and other rights and obligations growing out of the marriage relation;

Now, Therefore, in consideration of the premises and of the mutual covenants and undertakings herein set forth, the parties covenant and agree as follows:

• *The consideration for the agreement is the mutual exchange of promises ("covenants").*

Separation

1. The parties may and shall at all times hereafter live and continue to live separate and apart for the rest of their natural lives. Each shall be free from interference, authority and control, direct or indirect, by the other as fully as if he or she were single and unmarried. Subject to the provisions of this agreement, each may reside at such place or places as he or she may select. The parties shall not molest each other or compel or endeavor to compel the other to cohabit or dwell with him or her, by any legal or other proceedings for the restoration of conjugal rights or otherwise.

• *Paragraph 1 contains the nonmolestation clause.*

Wife's Debts

2. The Wife covenants and represents that she has not heretofore incurred or contracted, nor will she at any time in the future incur or contract, any debt, charge or liability whatsoever for which the Husband, his legal representatives, or his property or estate is now or may become liable, and the Wife further covenants at all times to keep the Husband free, harmless and indemnified of and from any and all debts, charges and liabilities heretofore and hereafter contracted by her.

Mutual Release

3. Subject to the provisions of this agreement, each party has remised, released and forever discharged and by these presents does for himself or herself, and his or her heirs, legal representatives, executors, administrators and assigns, remise, release and forever discharge the other of and from all cause or causes of action, claims, rights or demands whatsoever, in law or in equity, which either of the parties hereto ever had or now has against the other, except any or all cause or causes of action for divorce.

Waivers of Claims against Estate

4. Subject to the provisions of this agreement, each of the parties may in any way dispose of his or her property of whatsoever nature, real or personal, and each of the parties hereto, for himself or herself, and for his or her heirs, legal representatives, executors, administrators and assigns, hereby waive any right of election which he or she may have or hereafter acquire regarding the estate of the other, or to take against any last will and testament of the other, whether heretofore or hereafter executed, and renounces and releases all interest, right or claim of right to dower, or otherwise, that he or she now has or might otherwise have against the other, on the property of whatsoever nature, real or personal, of the other, under or by virtue of the laws of any State or country, and each will at the request of the other, or his or her legal representatives, executors, administrators and assigns, execute, acknowledge and deliver any and all deeds, releases, or any other instruments necessary to bar, release or extinguish such interests, rights and claims, or which may be helpful for the proper carrying into effect of any of the provisions of this agreement. Each of the parties renounces and relinquishes any and all claims and rights that he or she may have or may hereafter acquire to act as executor or administrator of the other party's estate.

• *If the parties die while still married, one can elect against whatever the will of the other provides for the spouse. Paragraph 4 waives this right.*

• *In paragraph 4, each party promises to prepare whatever documents are needed in the future to carry out the agreement. See also paragraph 12.*

Division of Personal Property

5. The parties have heretofore divided their personal property to their mutual satisfaction. Henceforth, each of the parties shall own, have and enjoy, independently of any claim or right of the other party, all items of personal property of every kind, nature and description and wheresoever situate, which are now owned or held by or which may hereafter belong or come to the Husband or the Wife, with the full power to the Husband or the Wife to dispose of same as fully and effectually, in all respects and for all purposes, as if he or she were unmarried.

Custody of Children

6. (a) The Wife shall have sole custody of Elizabeth and shall have sole custody of William, except that the Husband may at his option have the custody of either child or both, concurrently or at different or overlapping periods, as follows:

(1) between the 1st day of June and the 30th day of September in each year for a continuous period not to exceed three months; and

(2) during the Christmas holidays each year, for a period of not more than 5 days; and

(3) during the Easter school vacations, for a period of not more than 5 days; and

continued

SAMPLE SEPARATION AGREEMENT CLAUSES—*CONTINUED*

(4) for one weekend, consisting of Saturday and Sunday, in each calendar month.

(b) The Husband shall exercise his option by notifying the Wife in writing of his intention so to do at least 30 days before the beginning of any such period referred to in subparagraph (1) of paragraph 6(a) and at least 10 days before the beginning of any such period referred to in subparagraphs (2), (3) or (4) of paragraph 6(a).

(c) It is the Husband's intent to exercise the right of custody each year and from time to time, but the Husband's custody as provided in subparagraph 6(a) shall be entirely optional with him and his waiver thereof on any occasion, and for any reason, shall not constitute a waiver of his right to insist thereafter upon compliance with the provision thereof.

(d) The Husband shall have the right to meet with the children at any time on reasonable notice, and the Wife shall afford the Husband the opportunity to do so.

(e) Neither the Husband nor the Wife shall have the right to take or send the children or either of them outside of the continental territorial limits of the United States of America without obtaining the prior written consent of the other.

(f) Each of the parties agrees to keep the other informed at all times of the whereabouts of the children while the children or either of them are with the Husband or Wife respectively, and they mutually agree that if either of them has knowledge of any illness or accident or other circumstances seriously affecting the health or welfare of either of the children, the Husband or the Wife, as the case may be, will promptly notify the other of such circumstances.

(g) The parties shall consult with each other with respect to the education and religious training of the children, their illnesses and operations (except in emergencies), their welfare and other matters of similar importance affecting the children, whose well-being, education and development shall at all times be the paramount consideration of the Husband and the Wife.

(h) The parties shall exert every reasonable effort to maintain free access and unhampered contact between the children and each of the parties, and to foster a feeling of affection between the children and the other party. Neither party shall do anything which may estrange either child from the other party, or injure the opinion of the children as to their mother or father, or which may hamper the free and natural development of either child's love and respect for the other party.

• *Paragraph 6(d) is a catchall visitation clause ("at any time"). This is in addition to the specific times listed in paragraph 6(a).*

• *It is apparently not a violation of paragraph 6(e) to take a child out of the state without permission.*

• *Paragraph 6(h) requires each parent to "foster a feeling of affection" in the children for the other. Later, in chapter 9, we will see that the case of Schutz v. Schutz raised the question of whether this kind of commitment is enforceable.*

• *Paragraph 7 provides that alimony ends if the wife remarries.*

Support of Wife and Children

7. If the Wife has not remarried (should the parties be divorced), the Husband shall make the following payments to the Wife for her life and for the support and maintenance of the Wife and for the support, maintenance and education of the children:

(a) Wife ______________________ (b) Children ______________________.

Wife's Counsel Fees

8. The Husband will pay the reasonable counsel fees and legal expenses of the Wife in connection with negotiation and preparation of this agreement.

Acceptance and Release by Wife

9. The Wife recognizes and acknowledges that the foregoing provisions for her benefit are satisfactory and that they are reasonable and adequate for her support and maintenance, past, present and future, and in keeping with her accustomed mode of living, reasonable requirements and station in life. The Wife accordingly releases and discharges the Husband, absolutely and forever, for the rest of her life from any and all claims and demands, past, present and future for alimony or for any provision for maintenance and support except as contained in this agreement.

Subsequent Divorce

10. In the event that an action for divorce is instituted at any time hereafter by either party against the other in this or any other state or country, the parties hereto agree that they shall be bound by all the terms of this agreement and this agreement shall *not* be merged in any decree or judgment that may be granted in such action but shall survive the same and shall be forever binding and conclusive on the parties and nothing herein contained shall be construed to prevent the decree of judgment in any such action from incorporating in full or in substance the terms of this agreement.

• *As stated in paragraph 10, the parties want the separation agreement to survive divorce as a separate contract; they do not want it merged into the divorce decree.*

Entire Agreement

11. Both the legal and practical effect of this agreement in each and every respect and the financial status of the parties has been fully explained to both parties by their respective counsel and they both acknowledge that it is a fair agreement and is not the result of any fraud, duress, or undue influence exercised by either party upon the other or by any other person or persons upon either, and they further agree that this agreement contains the entire understanding of the parties. There are no representations, promises, warranties, convenants, or undertakings other than those expressly set forth herein.

Additional Instruments

12. Each of the parties agrees further at any time and from time to time to make, execute, and deliver all instruments necessary to effectuate the provisions of this agreement.

Notices

13. For the purpose of this agreement, all notices or other communications given or made hereunder shall, until written notice to the contrary, be given or mailed to the Wife at 25 North Street, ______, and to the Husband at 10 South Street, ______.

Each party shall at all times keep the other party informed of his or her place of residence and business and shall promptly notify the other party of any change, giving the address of any new place of residence or business.

Situs

14. All matters affecting the interpretation of this agreement and the rights of the parties hereto shall be governed by the laws of the State of ______.

Binding Effect

15. All the provisions of this agreement shall be binding upon the respective heirs, next of kin, executors, administrators, and assigns of the parties hereto.

Counterparts

16. This agreement shall be executed in triplicate, each of which so executed shall be deemed an original and shall constitute one and the same agreement.

In Witness Whereof, the parties hereto have hereunto set their respective hands and seals and initialed each page of this agreement the day and year first above written.

Witnesses:

______________________ . ______________________ . [L.S.]

______________________ . ______________________ . [L.S.]

[Add acknowledgments]

II

Separation Agreement—Fixed Monthly Payments—Custody and Support of Children

This Agreement is made the ______ day of ______, 20___, between ______, herein called the Husband, and ______, his wife, herein called the Wife.

Whereas the Husband and Wife were married on the ______ day of ______, 20______, and have two children, ______ and ______;

Whereas differences have arisen between the Husband and Wife as the result of which they are now living separate and apart;

Whereas the Husband and Wife have entered into this Agreement freely, with the advice of counsel, and acknowledge that its provisions are fair.

The parties agree as follows:

• *This agreement, like the prior one, is careful to point out that the parties are no longer living together*

Separation

1. The Husband and Wife may live apart from each other as if they were unmarried. Each shall be free from the control of the other and may reside at such place as he or she shall think fit.

No Interference

2. The Husband and Wife will not in any manner annoy, molest, or disturb the other, or compel or endeavor to compel the other to cohabit or dwell with him or her.

Wife's Debts

3. The Wife will at all times keep the Husband indemnified against all debts and liabilities she may hereafter contract and from all actions, claims, demands, costs, damages, and expenses on account thereof. In case the Husband shall at any time be called on to and shall pay any debt or debts she may hereafter contract, then it shall be lawful for the Husband to retain out of the next amount payable to the Wife hereunder the amount of such debt or debts with all costs and expenses he may incur on account thereof.

Division of Household Goods

4. The Husband and Wife have divided between them to their mutual satisfaction the personal effects, household furniture and furnishings, and all other articles of personal property used by them in common, in accordance with the Schedule attached hereto.

• *Note the different phrasing used in this agreement and in the prior one to accomplish the same objectives. Different attorneys prefer different language.*

• *Paragraph 4 refers to an attachment to this agreement called a schedule, which lists specific property that has been divided.*

continued

Sample Separation Agreement Clauses—*Continued*

Transfer of Home

5. The Husband has conveyed to the Wife by deed, executed, acknowledged, and delivered simultaneously with the execution of this Agreement, the property which was the former home of the parties and in which the Wife now resides.

Support of Wife

6. The Husband shall during the life of the Wife and until she remarries pay to the Wife, or to such person as she shall from time to time appoint in writing, the yearly sum of _______ dollars by equal monthly payments beginning on the _______ day of _______, 20___, for the support and maintenance of herself.

Custody of the Children in Wife

7. The Wife shall have the sole custody and control of the children, _______ and _______, without any interference on the part of the Husband except as herein provided.

Right of Husband to Visit Children

8. The Husband shall have the right to visit the children or either of them one day every two weeks if he so desires at reasonable times and places. Further, the Husband shall at his option have the custody of the children or either of them during the summer school holidays for a continuous period of one month.

Duty to the Wife to Care for Children

9. The Wife shall properly care for, educate, and maintain the children until they respectively reach the age of 18 years.

Support of Children

10. The Husband shall pay to the Wife as long as she shall have custody of the children or either of them the sum of _______ dollars each month beginning on the _______ day of _______, 20___, for the support and education of each child so in the custody of the Wife until such child reaches the age of 18 years.

Mutual Release

11. Except as herein otherwise provided, the Husband and Wife release and forever discharge the other of and from all causes of action, claims, rights, or demands whatsoever in law or in equity which either of the parties hereto ever had or now has against the other except all causes of action for divorce.

Subsequent Divorce

12. If the Husband and Wife shall hereafter apply for a divorce and the court shall grant the same, this Agreement shall be submitted to the court for approval. If it is approved by the court, the terms thereof shall be carried into and merge with the decree of divorce and operate as a final determination of the property rights of the parties.

- *Unlike the prior agreement, the parties agree in paragraph 12 that they want this agreement to merge into the divorce decree so that it loses its separate identity.*

Wife's Attorney's Fees

13. The Husband shall pay to _______ the sum of _______ dollars for his services as attorney to the Wife in connection with the negotiation and preparation of this Agreement.

Additional Instruments

14. The Husband and Wife shall at the request of the other execute, acknowledge, and deliver to the other party any and all further instruments that may be reasonably required to give full force and effect to the provisions of this Agreement.

Binding Effect

15. This Agreement shall be binding on the heirs, executors, administrators, and assigns of the parties hereto.

In witness whereof the parties have signed and sealed this Agreement.

_________________________ *[Seal]*
_________________________ *[Seal]*

[Add acknowledgments]

III
Separation Agreement—Dismissal of Pending Action for Separation—Lump Sum Cash and Property Settlement—No Children

This agreement, made this _______ day of _______, 20___, between _______, the Husband and _______, the Wife.

Whereas, the parties were married on _______ day of _______, 20___, and thereafter, on or about the _______ day of _______, 20___, separated and have since lived apart;

Whereas, an action was instituted by the Wife against the Husband in the _______ Court of _______, for a separation and provision for the maintenance of the Wife;

Whereas, the parties have agreed upon what is a reasonable provision for the support and maintenance of the Wife, past, present, and for the remainder of her natural life; and

Whereas, the parties have agreed on a reasonable and just disposal of all of the property of the Husband, free and discharged of any and all past, present, and future claims, demands, charges, dower estate rights, interests, liens, or other property rights of any kind whatsoever of the Wife.

Now, therefore, the parties agree as follows:

Separation

1. The parties agree to continue to live separate and apart from each other the same as if unmarried. Each may reside from time to time at such place or places, and, conduct, carry on and engage in any employment, business, or trade he or she shall deem fit, free from any control, restraint, or interference direct or indirect by the other.

Dismissal of Action

2. The parties agree that the said action for separation and maintenance now pending in the _______ Court shall be immediately dismissed without costs to either party.

Wife's Support

3. Simultaneously with the signing of this agreement the Husband agrees to pay to the Wife the sum of _______ dollars, and to pay her attorney's bills and court disbursements in said action, amounting to _______ dollars, and further to convey to her by warranty deed the following described property: *[Description]*. It is understood that said money and property is given to the Wife for her support and maintenance. The Wife agrees that such provision is ample and will in fact provide her with a support and maintenance befitting her station in life, and she accepts said money and property in full satisfaction and in lieu of support and maintenance by the Husband during her life.

No Future Liability

4. Neither party shall contract any debts in the name of the other, or in any way attempt to charge the other with liability therefor, nor will either party claim or demand maintenance or support from the other.

Each Spouse Releases Right in Property of Deceased Spouse

5. The Wife agrees that the estate of the Husband, after the payment of the consideration herein mentioned to the Wife, shall belong to the person or persons who would have become entitled thereto if the Wife had died during the lifetime of the Husband; and the Wife further agrees that she will permit any will of the Husband to be probated, and allow administration upon his personal estate to be taken out by the person or persons who would have been entitled so to do, had the Wife died during the lifetime of the Husband. The Husband agrees that the estate of the Wife, including the consideration herein mentioned, shall belong to the person or persons who would have become entitled thereto if the Husband had died during the lifetime of the Wife; and the Husband further agrees that he will permit any will of the Wife to be probated, and allow administration upon her personal estate to be taken out by the person or persons who would have been entitled so to do, had the Husband died during the lifetime of the Wife.

Further Assurance

6. The parties shall make, execute, and deliver any and all such further assurances as the other of the parties shall reasonably require, for the purpose of giving full effect to the provisions of this agreement.

Effect of Divorce

7. The Wife agrees that in case the marriage between the parties should be dissolved by order of a court, then the consideration passing to the Wife under this agreement shall stand as full satisfaction and

- *In the case referred to in paragraph 2, the wife sued for a legal separation and support (maintenance). The husband has apparently convinced her to drop that action and accept the support provided in this agreement.*
- *Note that in paragraph 3 they are labeling the transfer of the property (via a warranty deed) as support. On the tax implications of this, see chapter 11.*

continued

Sample Separation Agreement Clauses—*Continued*

discharge of alimony, counsel fees, and other claims and demands that might be made by the Wife against the Husband for any cause whatever.

In Witness Whereof, *etc.*

[Signatures]

IV
Separation Agreement Incident to Divorce Action—Lump Sum Cash Settlement—No Children

This agreement made ______, 20___, between ______, the Husband, and ______, the Wife.

Whereas on ______, 20___, the parties were married in ______ County, ______, and lived together as husband and wife until ______, 20___, and have reached the conclusion that it will be impossible for them to continue to live together;

Whereas a bill for divorce has been prepared and the parties are desirous of settling any and all claims for alimony that the Wife might have against the Husband; and

Whereas each party acknowledges that this agreement has been entered into freely with full knowledge of the facts, and each party believes that under the circumstances the sum of $______ is a fair and adequate settlement of all alimony;

Now, therefore, in consideration of the payment to the Wife of the sum of $______, the receipt of which is hereby acknowledged, the Wife does hereby release the Husband from any and all claims, now and hereafter, that might arise by way of alimony. The said settlement of alimony is hereby accepted as a full release of any and all liability, present and future, in so far as any alimony or property adjustment between the Husband and the Wife is concerned.

The foregoing settlement is approved by the undersigned ______ as attorney for the Wife.

In Witness Whereof, *etc.*

[Signatures]

V
Separation Agreement—Divorce Action Pending—Fixed Monthly Payments—Deposit of Property to Secure Such Payments—Release of Wife's Interest in Community Property—No Children*

This agreement made this ______ day of ______, 20___, between ______, herein called the Husband, and ______, herein called the Wife.

Whereas, the parties were united in marriage at ______, on the ______ day of ______, 20___, and lived together as husband and wife until the ______ day of ______, 20___; and

Whereas, during the time the parties lived together as husband and wife they acquired certain real and personal property which comprises their community estate and which is not susceptible of partition; and

• *The parties do not want all their property sold so that the cash proceeds can be divided. The wife has agreed to accept a monthly sum of money in exchange for releasing all her rights in the property to her husband.*

Whereas, on the ______ day of ______, 20___, the Wife filed her petition in the ______ Court of ______ County, ______, praying that the marriage relation between herself and the Husband be dissolved, and the parties have agreed that in the event said marriage relation is dissolved by judgment of said Court as prayed for in said petition, in lieu of a partition of said community estate the Husband shall pay to the Wife the sum of ______ dollars per month so long as she shall live, and the Wife shall transfer, assign, and convey to the Husband all her right, title, and interest in and to said community estate;

---

*Adapted from the record in *Farrell v. Commissioner of Internal Revenue,* 134 F.2d 193 (C.C.A. Tex. 1943), a proceeding to collect a deficiency in income taxes from one of the parties to this agreement.

The community property released in this contract consisted in part of oil leases that subsequently turned out to be very valuable. Shortly after this agreement was executed, Mrs. Farrell secured a divorce from her husband and the decree embodied the terms of the contract with respect to the monthly payments and the transfer of the community interest to the husband. Four days later she married again.

About two years later she brought suit in the Texas courts to have the property provisions of the divorce decree set aside on the ground that she was induced to enter into this agreement by fraud. The Court of Civil Appeals in *Burguieres v. Farrell,* 85 S.W.2d 952 (Tex. Civ. App. 1935) upheld the agreement, holding that the entire transaction was fair, that the wife was fully informed and there was no fraud.

Now, therefore, it is agreed as follows:

1. The Husband agrees to pay to the Wife the sum of ______ dollars on the first day of ______, 20___, and the sum of ______ dollars on the first day of each and every month thereafter so long as she shall live, said payments to be made by the Husband to the ______ National Bank of ______, with instructions to said bank to promptly pay the same to the Wife. For the purpose of guaranteeing such payments the Husband shall deposit with said bank the sum of ______ dollars in cash and ______ shares of the capital stock of ______ Corporation, of the approximate present value of ______ dollars; provided that the Husband shall have the right at any time to withdraw such shares of stock upon depositing with said bank the further sum of ______ dollars in cash in lieu thereof; and provided further that in the event the Husband shall fail to make any of the payments herein provided for, said ______ bank shall have the right to sell said shares of stock for cash and make such payments to the Wife out of such fund, and in such event the Wife shall have the right to require the Husband to deposit the amount of such payment or payments with said bank in order that such fund shall at all times be maintained at the sum of ______ dollars or at the sum of ______ dollars and said ______ shares of the capital stock of ______ Corporation.

• According to paragraph 1, specific shares of stock are deposited as security for the monthly payments. The husband, however, can replace the stock with cash.

2. The Wife agrees that all property, belonging to the community estate of the parties, shall be and become the separate property of the Husband, and any and all rights, title, and interest in and to said property now belonging to the Wife, or which might be claimed by her, shall be, and the same hereby is, transferred, assigned, and conveyed to the Husband, free from any and all liens or claims on the part of the Wife, and the Wife further agrees that she will, upon demand, execute and deliver to the Husband proper deeds, assignments, or conveyances for any and all of such property conveying the title therein to the Husband.

• In paragraph 2, the wife agrees that community property shall become separate property (transmutation).

In Witness Whereof, *etc.*

VI
Separation Agreement—Divorce Action Pending—Lump Sum and Fixed Monthly Payments to Wife—Transfer of Community Property to Husband—Custody and Support of Children

This agreement made the ______ day of ______, 20___, between ______, herein called the Husband, and ______, herein called the Wife.

Whereas, disputes have arisen between the parties, and by reason thereof they have agreed to live separate and apart from each other during their natural lives; and

Whereas, the Husband as plaintiff filed a suit for divorce in the ______ Court of ______ County, ______, numbered ______ on the docket of said Court, which suit is now pending, and the Wife has filed her cross-action for divorce in said suit, and regardless of the outcome of the trial thereof, the parties recognize that their differences are so great that a reconciliation is impossible; and

Whereas, the Husband has furnished to the Wife a list of all principal assets and liabilities as of ______, 20___, and has also furnished additional information as to change of assets and liabilities as of this date, and the Wife has investigated and appraised these assets and liabilities with the aid of her legal counsel and is thoroughly conversant with all facts; and

Whereas, the parties desire to completely and forever settle their property rights in and to their community property, which is all of the property that either of them possesses.

• The parties say that reconciliation is impossible—one of the conditions of this no-fault ground for divorce. See chapter 7.

The parties agree as follows:

Separation

1. They shall live separate and apart from each other the remainder of their natural lives, and neither shall have any right in any way to control the personal actions or conduct of the other, or to complain about such actions or conduct except in so far as the same may affect the right of custody of their children, and neither shall in any way molest, disturb, or trouble the other.

Alimony to Wife

2. In full, final, and complete settlement of all the rights of the Wife in and to the community property of the parties, as well as any and all other claims which she may now or hereafter have against the Husband arising out of the marriage relationship, the Husband has paid and promises to pay to the Wife the following amounts:

(a) *Lump Sum Payment.* The Husband has this day paid to the Wife the sum of $______, receipt of which is hereby acknowledged.

(b) *Fixed Monthly Payments.* The Husband promises to pay to the Wife at ______, the sum of $______ per month for ______ years, the first payment being due ______ and one payment being due on the ______ day of each month thereafter for ______ full years. Such payments may be made by check mailed to the Wife on or before the due dates, addressed to the last address that the Wife may have given in writing to the Husband.

continued

Sample Separation Agreement Clauses—*Continued*

(c) *Insurance Policies to Secure Monthly Payments.* The Husband shall at all times carry life insurance in solvent companies, payable to the Wife as beneficiary, for the amount of the then unpaid installments hereinabove provided, discounted at ______ per cent per year compounded for the period of prepayment; and upon the Husband's death, the Wife shall accept payment of said insurance money in full payment and satisfaction of all of the then unpaid monthly payments provided for in paragraph (b) hereof. The husband shall have the right to discharge his obligations under said paragraph (b) at any time after the expiration of ______ years from this date by paying the value of unmatured installments discounted at ______ per cent per year compounded for the period of prepayment.

• In paragraph 2(c), the wife receives security in the form of a life insurance policy.

(d) *Upon Death of Wife, Wife's Monthly Payments to Be Made to Children.* Should the Wife die before the monthly installments are all paid, the then remaining installments shall be paid as they mature to the ______ children of the parties in equal parts, or to their guardian if they are then minors.

(e) *Transfer to Wife of Personal Belongings.* The Wife shall have as her property all of the silverware, dishes, glassware, linens, rugs, drapes, furniture, pictures, and furnishings now in the home at ______, except [*description*], which excepted articles shall belong to the husband. The Wife shall vacate the home on or before ______, 20______, but agrees that the husband may keep all of her said personal property in the home until ______, 20______, at which time she shall remove the same, provided however that if the home is sold at an earlier date she shall upon demand remove her personal property.

Transfer of Community Property to Husband

3. All other property, rights, claims, and choses in action belonging to the Husband or to their community estate, whether or not herein specifically mentioned, shall belong absolutely to the Husband, as his separate property, and the Wife agrees to execute to the Husband upon demand general warranty deeds covering her interest in all real property owned by them and bills of sale or other conveyances of title to such personal property. The principal items of property to be conveyed are as follows: [*description*].

Wife's Debts

4. The Wife agrees to pay promptly all bills incurred by her since ______, 20______. Should the Wife fail to pay any of such bills, and demand for payment is made on the Husband, he may pay same and deduct the amount so paid from the monthly payments owing by him to the Wife.

Community Debts

5. The Husband agrees to pay all of the community indebtedness of the parties not herein assumed by the Wife.

Custody of Children

6. The two children, ______ and ______, shall remain with the Wife, subject to the orders of the Court as is provided by law in such cases. The Husband shall have the right to visit his children and to have their company and companionship at reasonable times to be arranged.

Support of Children

7. The Husband shall pay to the Wife the sum of $______ per month for each child on the first day of each month for the support and maintenance of the two children, which payments shall continue until the Husband's legal obligation to support them ends, or until changed as to amount by agreement of the parties or by order of the Court. Such payments shall cover all living expenses of the children that could be chargeable to the Husband, except tuition to schools to be selected by agreement of the parties which the Husband shall also pay, and such medical expenses as the Husband may first approve in writing. If one or both of the children shall at any time, by agreement of the parties, be sent to boarding schools or to summer camps, the Husband shall pay their reasonable expenses while there, but during such times he shall not be required to make the monthly payments otherwise required to be made to the Wife for their support and maintenance.

• In paragraph 7, the parties specify the amount of child support, which they can change later by agreement. As we will see in chapter 10, however, the parties cannot agree on an amount that is lower than that required by the child support guidelines in the state.

Mutual Release

8. In consideration of the payments now made and agreed to be hereafter made, the parties do each declare this to be a full, final, and complete settlement of all of their property rights, and each party does hereby release and relinquish to the other all of his or her rights, title, claim, interest, and demand, accrued or accruing in and to the property of the other whether now in being or hereafter acquired; and this shall be a full and complete settlement of the controversy over the property rights of the parties, involved in cause No. ______ in the ______ Court of ______ County, and, except for the right of either party to prosecute his or her suit for complete divorce, this settlement shall be a bar to any suit at law or otherwise for anything growing out of the marriage relation of the parties as well as the property rights of the one against the other.

Witness our hands, in triplicate, at ______, this ______ day of ______, 20___.

____
____

Witness:

____
____

[Add Acknowledgments]

VII
Separation Agreement—Divorce Action Pending—Alimony Based on Oil Royalties—Custody and Support of Child

This agreement, made this ______ day of ______, 20______, between ______, of ______, herein called the Husband, and ______, of ______, herein called the Wife, witnesseth:

Whereas, the parties are husband and wife, but are now living separate and apart from each other, and it is their intention to continue to live separate and apart; and,

Whereas, the Wife has this day instituted suit for divorce against the Husband in the ______ Court of ______ County, ______, under cause numbered ______ in said Court, and has asked that she be awarded the custody, care, control, and education of ______, minor child of the parties and for the ratification and approval of this property settlement and agreement concerning the support and maintenance of said child; and,

Whereas, the parties have this day reached a satisfactory agreement between themselves out of Court concerning the custody, support, and maintenance of said child, and the support, maintenance, and alimony of the Wife, as well as for a division of and settlement of property rights, claims, or demands of any nature, either past, present, or future, as hereinafter set out.

Now, therefore, the parties agree as follows:

Custody of Child

1. The Wife is to have the care, custody, and control of ______, minor child of the parties, subject to the approval of the ______ Court of ______ County, ______, subject to any future orders of said Court concerning the custody of said child and subject to the right of the Husband to visit said child at any and all reasonable times and occasions; and the Wife, subject to the conditions hereinafter stated, accepts the custody of said child and agrees to properly care for, support, rear, train, and educate said child to the best of her ability, it being understood that the Wife shall have the right to select the residence for said child at whatsoever place within the State of ______ she may desire, but that she will inform the Husband of any change in said place of residence.

Support of Wife and Child

2. *The Husband shall turn over to the Wife for the support of and maintenance of herself and* ______, minor child of the parties, until such time as the Wife may remarry, all of the proceeds arising from his interest in oil and gas royalties from wells now producing, and one half of all of the proceeds arising from his interest in oil and gas royalties from any wells which may be hereafter drilled upon any and all land now owned by the Husband, or in which he may own any interest, either legal or equitable, said land being particularly described as follows: [*Here describe*].

Remarriage or Death of Wife

3. It is further agreed that in the event of the remarriage of the Wife to any person other than the Husband during the lifetime of ______, minor child of the parties, then all of said oil and gas royalties, oil and gas runs, or proceeds from same arising from said lands shall be paid to said child, or to her duly appointed guardian. In the event the Husband and the Wife remarry each other, or in the event the Wife marries someone other than the Husband during the lifetime of said child, and said child thereafter dies, or in the event of the remarriage of the Wife after the death of said child, or in the event of the death of the Wife at any time, then immediately upon the happening thereof, the Husband shall be entitled to, and shall have and receive all such oil and gas royalties, oil and gas runs, or other proceeds arising from the same not already paid over to the Wife or to said child under this agreement; and the Wife agrees that in the event of any such remarriage she will promptly make, execute, and deliver any necessary and proper transfer orders, division orders, or other instruments necessary to enable such person as is entitled thereto under this agreement to collect and receive same, and that in the event she should refuse or neglect to do so, then this instrument shall be treated and construed as a compliance and assignment of said interests, runs, and royalties.

continued

Sample Separation Agreement Clauses—*Continued*

Sale of Royalty Interest

4. It is further agreed that the Husband shall have the full and unrestricted use of all of the lands in any manner acquired by him and the rents and profits thereof, except the royalties and oil and gas runs above mentioned, but that in the event of the sale by the Husband of any of said real estate herein described during the lifetime of ______, minor child of the parties, the Husband shall pay over to said child, or to her duly appointed guardian, for her use, support, maintenance and education, one third of any and all sums realized from the sale of any or all of said property and that the Wife will, upon request, join with the Husband, or will execute, acknowledge, and deliver any and all necessary and proper instruments in writing to effectuate the sale and conveyance of any such property; it being understood, however, that nothing in this paragraph shall be construed as conferring the right upon the Husband to make any sale or conveyance of any oil or gas royalty in, to, or under any of the land above described, but that said oil and gas royalty interests in said land shall be held for the use, support, and maintenance of the Wife and said child, as herein provided.

Release by Wife

5. The Wife agrees that she will not at any time undertake to hold the Husband liable for, or undertake to collect from him any sums for alimony, court costs, attorneys' fees, support, and maintenance for herself or said child, and that this agreement may be pleaded in any suit as a defense to any action for alimony, court costs, attorneys' fees, support, and maintenance.

Witness our signatures in duplicate the day and year above written.

____

____

[Add acknowledgements]

____

The following agreement is presented by the court as a guide to couples who want to draft their own agreement in a relatively uncomplicated case.

Sample Property Agreement

California Judicial Council Form Manual
3-99 to 3-82 (Jan. 1988)

I. We are Waldo P. Smedlap, hereafter called Husband, and Lydia T. Smedlap, hereafter called Wife.[1] We were married on October 7, 1978 and separated on December 5, 1979. Because irreconcilable differences have caused the permanent breakdown of our marriage,[2] we have made this agreement together to settle once and for all what we owe to each other and what we can expect from each other. Each of us states here that nothing has been held back, that we have honestly included everything we could think of in listing the money and goods that we own; and each of us states here that we believe the other one has been open and honest in writing this agreement. And each of us agrees to sign and exchange any papers that might be needed to complete this agreement.

Each of us also understands that even after a Joint Petition for Summary Dissolution is filed, this entire agreement will be cancelled if either of us revokes the Dissolution Proceeding.[3]

II. Division of Community Property[4]
We divided our community property as follows:

1. Husband transfers to Wife as her sole and separate property:
   A. All household furniture and furnishings located at her apartment at 180 Needlepoint Way, San Francisco.[5]
   B. All rights to cash in savings account #08-73412-085 at Home Savings.
   C. All cash value in life insurance policy #798567 Sun Valley Life Insurance, insuring life of Wife.
   D. All retirement and pension plan benefits earned by Wife during marriage.
   E. 2 U.S. Savings Bond Series E.
   F. Wife's jewelry.
   G. 1972 Chevrolet 4-door sedan, License No. EXL 129.
2. Wife transfers to Husband as his sole and separate property:
   A. All household furniture and furnishings located at his apartment on 222 Bond Street, San Francisco.
   B. All retirement and pension plan benefits earned by Husband during the marriage.
   C. Season tickets to Golden State Terriers Basketball games.
   D. 1 stereo set.

- *[1]Wherever the word Husband appears anywhere in this agreement, it will stand for Waldo P. Smedlap; wherever the word Wife appears, it will stand for Lydia T. Smedlap.*
- *[2]This means that there are problems in your marriage which you think can never be solved. Irreconcilable differences are the only legal grounds for getting a Summary Dissolution.*
- *[3]This means that the property agreement is a part of the divorce proceedings. If either of you decides to stop the Dissolution proceedings by turning in a Notice of Revocation of Summary Dissolution, this entire agreement will be cancelled.*
- *[4]Community property is property which you own as a couple. If you have no community property, replace part II with the simple statement, "We have no community property."*
- *[5]If furniture and household goods in one apartment are to be divided, then they may have to be listed item by item.*

E. 1 set of Jack Nicklaus golf clubs.
F. 1 RAC color television.
G. 1973 Ford station wagon License No. EPX 758.
H. 1 pet parrot named Arthur, plus cage and parrot food.
I. All rights to cash in Checking Account #1721-319748-07, Bank of America.

III. Division of Community Property (Debts)[6]

1. Husband shall pay the following debts and will not at any time hold Wife responsible for them:
   A. Master Charge account #417-38159 208-094.
   B. Debt to Dr. R. C. Himple.
   C. Debt to Sam's Drugs.
   D. Debt to U.C. Berkeley for college education loan to Husband.[7]
2. Wife shall pay the following debts and will not at any time hold Husband responsible for them:
   A. Cogwell's charge account #808921.
   B. Debt to Wife's parents, Mr. and Mrs. Joseph Smith.
   C. Debt to Green's Furniture.
   D. Debt to Dr. Irving Roberts.

IV. Waiver of Spousal Support[8]
Each of us waives any claim for spousal support now and for all time.

V. Dated: ______________________ Dated: ______________________

______________________ ______________________

Waldo P. Smedlap Lydia T. Smedlap

- *[6]If you have no unpaid debts, replace part III with the simple statement, "We have no unpaid community obligations."*
- *[7]A general rule for dividing debts is to give the debt over to the person who benefited most from the item. In the sample agreement, since the Husband received the education, you could agree that he should pay off the loan.*
- *[8]In this clause you are giving up the right to have your spouse support you.*

ASSIGNMENT 8.16

Two members of the class will role-play in front of the rest of the class a negotiation session involving a husband and wife who want to enter a separation agreement. They have two children, ages two and three. Each member of the class (including the two role-players) will draft a separation agreement based upon the understandings reached at the negotiation session. The role-players can make up the facts as they go along, e.g., names of the parties, addresses, kinds of assets involved. Use the checklist on pages 229-230 as an overview of the topics to be negotiated. In the negotiation session, the role-players should not act hostile toward each other. They should be courteous but anxious to protect their own rights. Finally, they should not leave any matters unresolved—everything should result in some form of agreement through the process of bargaining and negotiation. The separation agreement that results from this session should conform to the standards for an effective separation agreement outlined in Exhibit 8.1. (See General Instructions for the Agreement-Drafting Assignment in Appendix A.)

SUMMARY

A separation agreement is a contract entered into by spouses who are about to separate, covering the terms of their separation. A major goal of the law office is to prepare an effective separation agreement that will avoid litigation. The first step is the collection of extensive information, particularly financial information pertaining to everyone involved. Elaborate checklists can be helpful in this effort, as well as detailed interrogatories sent to the other spouse.

For a separation agreement to be valid, the parties must have the capacity to contract. The agreement must not violate public policy by inducing the parties to divorce, and it must not be the product of collusion, duress, or fraud. Finally, the consideration for the agreement must be proper.

The separation agreement should clearly distinguish alimony from property division. The distinction can be relevant in a number of areas (e.g., the effect of bankruptcy, the effect of remarriage and death, the availability of enforcement by contempt, the power of the court to modify terms, and federal tax treatment). The distinction is not simply a matter of labels. The question is, What did the parties intend?

In negotiating alimony, the parties should consider a number of factors (e.g., method of payment, coverage, relationship to child support, modification, termination, and security). The principal focus of the court will be the needs of the recipient, the length of the marriage, and the ability of the payor to pay. Courts are inclined to grant alimony for a limited period such as the time needed to become self-sufficient (rehabilitative alimony). In most states, marital fault is not relevant.

In negotiating property division, the first step is to categorize all the property to be divided as personal or real. What resources were used to acquire it? How is title held? Separate property is property that one spouse acquired before the marriage by any means and property that he or she acquired during the marriage by gift, will, or intestate succession. Marital property is all nonseparate property acquired by a spouse during the marriage and the appreciation of separate property that occurred during the marriage. The division that is made depends on the bargaining process and on whether the parties live in a community property state (fifty/fifty division) or in a common law property state (equitable distribution). A spouse will be assumed to be in possession of whatever cash or other marital property he or she dissipates. Pension assets can be divided, particularly through a qualified domestic relations order (QDRO). Businesses are also divisible, including their goodwill. Not all states agree, however, as to whether a license or degree can be divided.

The parties need to consider the continuation of insurance policies, the payment of debts incurred before and after the separation agreement is signed, the payment of taxes, whether wills need to be changed, the payment of attorney fees, and the need for a nonmolestation clause.

Child-custody and child-support terms of a separation agreement are often modifiable by a court, unlike property division terms. Spousal-support terms can be modifiable, particularly if the separation agreement has been incorporated and merged into the divorce decree

When problems arise that involve an interpretation of the separation agreement, the parties may decide to submit the controversy to arbitration or mediation in lieu of litigation. If the parties reconcile and resume cohabitation after they sign the separation agreement, the spousal-support terms (but not the property division terms) are automatically canceled in some states. In others, both support and property division terms are canceled if they are executory. If there is a court order on any aspect of the divorce, the reconciled parties may have to return to court and petition the court to change the order.

KEY CHAPTER TERMINOLOGY

separation agreement
interrogatories
conducive to divorce
public policy
collusion
migratory divorce
duress
aggrieved
fraud
at arm's length
consideration
alimony
property division
property settlement
arrears
arrearages
outstanding
discharged
estate
contempt
contingent
alimony in gross
payor
payee
escrow
surety bond
annuity
trust
rehabilitative alimony
real property
personal property
tangible
intangible
bequest
devise
intestate succession
separate property
marital property
commingling
joint tenancy
right of survivorship
tenancy by the entirety
tenancy in common
operation of law
community property
common law property
transmutation
fiduciary
quasi-community property
equitable distribution
hotchpot
dissipate
defined-benefit plan
defined-contribution plan
vested
qualified domestic relations order (QDRO)
alternate payee
present value
restitution
goodwill
joint and several liability
indemnify
tax effect
executor
testate
elect against the will
forced share
intestate
dower
curtesy
nonmolestation clause
arbitration
mediation
executory

ETHICS IN PRACTICE

You are a paralegal working at the law office of James & James. The law firm represents the husband in a divorce action. One of the largest assets in the marriage is the husband's pension. The wife's attorney, however, fails to inquire into the pension because this attorney mistakenly believes that pensions are not divisible as marital property. Since the wife's attorney does not mention it, James & James is silent about the pension. Consequently, the final divorce decree does not divide the pension. Any ethical problems?

ON THE NET: MORE ON SPOUSAL SUPPORT, PROPERTY DIVISION, AND SEPARATION AGREEMENTS

Legal Café: Spousal Support and Alimony
http://www.courttv.com/legalcafe/family/spousal/spousal_background.html

Property Division in the Fifty States
http://www.abanet.org/family/familylaw/table5.html

Alimony/Spousal Support in the Fifty States
http://www.abanet.org/family/familylaw/table1.html

U.S. Department of Labor: The Division of Pensions through Qualified Domestic Relations Orders (QDROs)
http://www.dol.gov/dol/pwba/public/pubs/qdro.htm

CHILD CUSTODY

CHAPTER OUTLINE

INTRODUCTION

> Then the king said, "Bring me a sword." So they brought a sword for the king. He then gave an order: "Cut the living child in two and give half to one and half to the other." 1 *Kings* 3:24–25 (NIV)

In most divorce cases, there is little or no dispute over who should have custody of the children. Since the parents agree on custody and visitation, they simply ask the court to approve the arrangement they work out. In the vast majority of cases, the court will do so.

When there is a dispute, however, it can be intense. Judges, forced into the role of King Solomon, say that child custody is one of the most painful issues they face. "We are asked to play God, a role we are neither trained nor prepared for," lamented a family law judge. Sometimes the bitterness between parents in custody battles can be extraordinary. In one case, the child tragically died in the midst of his parents' marital difficulties. This did not stop the rancor. The divorcing parents could not agree on who should control the disposition of their son's body. In a decision "reminiscent of Solomon," the judge ruled that if they could not agree on who should bury their son, he would order the body cremated and each given "half the ashes."[1] While not all cases

---

[1]Chicago Daily Law Bulletin, July 21, 1978, at 1; Harry Krause et al., Family Law 628 (4th ed. 1998).

are this rancorous, it does demonstrate the level of hostility that is possible. In this chapter, we will explore the spectrum of child-custody cases, from those in which the parties are in agreement to those in which their disagreement is little short of open warfare.

In our early history, child-custody disputes were rare because the wishes of the father were almost always followed. If he wanted custody upon divorce, the courts gave it to him. A radical change occurred in the early nineteenth century, when the courts began awarding custody based on a determination of the **best interests of the child.**[2] The new standard, however, was controversial, since the courts often presumed that it was in the best interest of a young child to be placed with the mother. (This presumption was called the **tender years presumption.**) Critics argued that the effect of the presumption was to replace a father-dominated system with a mother-dominated one. Today, gender-based presumptions have been abolished or declared unconstitutional as a denial of the equal protection of the law. Courts still apply the best-interests-of-the-child standard, but without using presumptions that favor one gender over the other. Nevertheless, mothers continue to be granted custody in the overwhelming majority of cases—about 90 percent. Later, we will examine some of the explanations for this reality when we take a closer look at the tender years presumption and its replacement.

best interests of the child
A standard of decision based on what would best serve the child's welfare.

tender years presumption
Mothers should be awarded custody of their young children, since they are more likely to be better off raised by their mothers than by their fathers.

KINDS OF CUSTODY

A distinction needs to be made between physical custody and legal custody:

- **Physical custody** (sometimes called *residential custody*) is the right to decide where the child will reside. The phrase also refers to the actual residence of the child. The parent with physical custody is called the **custodial parent** (or sometimes the *residential parent*). The other parent is called the *noncustodial parent.* While the child does not live with a noncustodial parent, the latter often has the right of visitation.
- **Legal custody** is the right to make the major child rearing decisions on health, education, religion, discipline, and general welfare.

physical custody
(a) The right to decide where the child will reside; (b) the actual residence of the child.

custodial parent
The parent with physical custody.

legal custody
The right to make the major child rearing decisions on health, education, religion, discipline, and general welfare

If only one parent is granted both kinds of custody, he or she has *sole physical custody* and *sole legal custody.* This phrase is more accurate than the phrase "sole custody." If you are told that a parent has sole custody, you need to determine whether this includes both physical and legal custody.

If *both* parents are granted physical and legal custody, they have **joint physical custody** and **joint legal custody.** This phrase is more accurate than the phrase "joint custody" or the more modern phrase "shared parenting." If you are told that parents have joint custody or that they share the task of parenting, you need to determine whether this includes both physical and legal custody. Joint physical custody means that the child spends alternating, but not necessarily equal, periods of time in the homes of the mother and father. Joint legal custody means that the mother and father must agree on the major child rearing decisions such as where the child will go to school or whether he or she will have a medical operation.

joint physical custody
The right of both parents to have the child reside with both for alternating (but not necessarily equal) periods of time.

joint legal custody
The right of both parents to make the major child rearing decisions on health, education, religion, discipline, and general welfare.

For example:

Ten-year old Helen Teller lives year-round with Grace Teller, her mother. Helen's father, Peter Teller, lives in a different state, a thousand miles away. Grace and Peter regularly talk on the phone about all the major decisions in Helen's life. No decision is made unless both agree.

---

[2] Carl Schneider & Margaret Brinig, An Invitation to Family Law 62 (1996).

In this example, Grace and Peter have joint legal custody, and Grace has sole physical custody.

When the parents have more than one child, courts try to place all the children with the same parent in order to foster sibling bonding. If this is not possible, the custody arrangement in which siblings are placed with different parents is called **split custody.**

split custody
Siblings are in the physical custody of different parents.

States do not always use the same terminology for custody. In Texas, for example, the word *conservatorship* is used in place of *custody.* The person with primary responsibility for raising the child is called the *managing conservator.* Also, some states prefer the phrase "parenting plan" or "co-parenting plan" to the phrase "custody arrangement."

Finally, it should be pointed out that the categories of custody we have been discussing can be somewhat fluid in practice in spite of what was originally agreed upon by the parents or imposed by a court. Suppose, for example, that the father begins to withdraw after having difficulties with the mother in working out their joint physical and joint legal custody arrangement. After a while, the mother may find herself with sole physical and sole legal custody. Or, in a case where the mother begins with sole physical custody, the father's visitation might become much more extensive than contemplated because of an illness of the mother. In effect, the father finds himself having sole physical custody. Such rearranging may occur without formal changes in the custody clauses of the original separation agreement. And unless child support becomes an issue, the courts may never become aware of these informal adjustments.

We turn now to the custody decision itself—both when the parties are able to reach agreement in their separation agreement and when the custody decision is forced upon them because of their inability to agree.

SEPARATION AGREEMENT

Custody

In attempting to negotiate the custody term of a separation agreement, the parties must consider many circumstances:

- The kind of custody they want.
- The age and health of the child.
- The age and health of the parents. Which parent is physically and mentally more able to care for the child on a day-to-day basis?
- The parent with whom the child has spent the most time up to now. With whom are the emotional attachments the strongest?
- Which parent must work full-time?
- The availability of backup assistance (e.g., from grandparents or close friends who can help in emergencies).
- The availability of day care facilities.
- How will the major decisions on the child's welfare be made (e.g., whether to transfer schools, whether to have an operation)? Must one parent consult the other on such matters? Is joint consent ever needed? Is such consent practical?
- The religious upbringing of the child.
- The child's surname. Can the name be changed if the mother remarries?
- Can the child be moved from the area?
- Who would receive custody if both parents died?
- If disputes arise between the parents concerning custody, how are they to be resolved? Arbitration? Mediation?
- What happens if one parent violates the agreement on custody? For example, the custodial parent interferes with the visitation rights of the noncustodial parent. Can the latter stop paying alimony?

- Mutual respect. Do the parties specifically agree to encourage the child to love both parents?

In the most common custody arrangement used today, the mother receives sole physical and sole legal custody. Parents do not often use joint physical custody because of the disruptive impact on a child of constantly changing households. The arrangement might work if the child is very young, the parents live close to each other, and the parents are relatively well-to-do. In most cases, however, joint physical custody is not practical. Also, if either of the parties ever applies for public assistance, joint physical custody might raise questions about eligibility. For example, under the federal program for Temporary Assistance for Needy Families (TANF), benefits may depend in part on having an eligible child in the home. A parent may have difficulty meeting this requirement if the child spends long alternating periods with the other parent. Joint *legal* custody, on the other hand, is more common. In approximately 20 percent of separations and divorces, the parents have joint legal custody, with one parent having sole physical custody.[3]

Some states use a presumption that joint legal custody is in the best interests of the child and should be ordered unless the facts of the case demonstrate that this arrangement would not work. Advocates of joint custody claim that it is psychologically the most healthy alternative for the child. It arguably produces less hostility between parents, less hostility between child and individual parent, less confusion in values for the child, less sexual stereotyping of parental roles (one parent "works," the other raises the children), less manipulation of the child by one or both parents, less manipulation of one or both parents by the child, etc. Joint custody arrangements also dramatically increase the likelihood that child support will be consistently paid. Critics, however, argue that the decision on joint custody should be approached with great caution, since it will work only in exceptional circumstances. The parents have just separated. In this environment, it is doubtful that they will be able to cooperate in the manner called for by a joint legal custody arrangement. A study of 700 divorce cases in Massachusetts concluded that couples with joint legal custody are more than twice as likely to reopen lawsuits over child care arrangements than couples where only one parent had custody. In addition, it is by no means clear that a child is more likely to be better off when living under a joint custody arrangement. Recent studies have found no difference in a child's development under joint custody and under more traditional sole custody arrangements.[4]

The following factors are relevant to a decision on whether joint legal custody will work. Any one of these factors might tip the scale *against* its feasibility.

- Is each parent fit and mentally stable?
- Do both parents agree to joint legal custody, or is one or both hesitant or opposed?
- Have the parents demonstrated that they are able to communicate at least to the extent necessary to reach shared decisions in the child's best interests?
- Is joint custody in accord with the child's wishes, or does the child have strong opposition to such an arrangement?

Unfortunately, parents do not always have the welfare of the child in mind when negotiating the custody term of the separation agreement. For example, a father's request for joint custody may be no more than a bargaining chip to pressure the mother to agree to a property settlement that favors the father. If she agrees to the property settlement he wants, he will not challenge the sole custody she wants.

---

[3]Scott Coltrane & Randall Collins, Sociology of Marriage and the Family 530 (2001).

[4]Mary Ann Lamanna and Agnes Riedmann, Marriages and Families 481 (2000).

Visitation

In negotiating visitation rights in a separation agreement, a number of details must be worked out:

- When can the noncustodial parent have the child visit? Alternating weekends? School vacations? Holidays? Which ones? How much advance notice is needed if additional time is desired?
- At what time is the child to be picked up and returned?
- Can the noncustodial parent take the child on long trips? Is the consent of the custodial parent needed?
- Can the custodial parent move out of the area even though this makes visitation more burdensome and costly? Should a clause be inserted that the permission of the noncustodial parent is needed before the child can be moved more than a specified number of miles away?
- Who pays the transportation costs, if any, when the child visits the noncustodial parents?
- Is the noncustodial parent required to be available for visits? Will it be a violation of the separation agreement if he or she does *not* visit? Or is visitation at the sole discretion of the noncustodial parent?
- When the noncustodial parent decides not to visit at a given time, must he or she notify the custodial parent in advance, or attempt to?
- Do any third parties have visitation rights (e.g., grandparents)?
- If disputes arise between parents on visitation, how are they resolved? Arbitration? Mediation?
- What happens if one of the parties violates the agreement on visitation?
- Does this breach justify nonperformance by the other party of another term of the separation agreement (e.g., alimony payments)?

There are two major choices in selecting visitation times. The parties can simply state in their separation agreement that visitation will be at "reasonable" times to be mutually agreed upon by the parties in the future, with adequate advance notice to be given by the noncustodial parent when he or she wants visitation. Alternatively, the agreement can spell out precise times for visitation. The following article advocates the latter position in cases where both parents have relatively stable work schedules.

Fixing Definite Schedules

The Matrimonial Strategist 2 (May 1983)

The traumatic and emotional issues that often dominate determination of custody and visitation . . . rights of parents of minor children continue to provoke much litigation. This has perhaps been measurably improved by constructive mediation efforts that have now been initiated by many courts of this country.

As much as it would be preferable to maintain a degree of flexibility in allowing parents to agree on reasonable visitation rights, it is the opinion of most family-law practitioners that it is more important to fix visitation or shared physical custody rights as specifically as possible. . . . This will minimize friction and ensuing disputes between parents who are frequently in a hostile posture to begin with. When visitation rights are set down with particularity, it is more likely that arguments will be discouraged, and less likely that the custodial parent will attempt to limit or defeat the noncustodial parent's visitation rights.

Problems Can Arise

In certain situations, though, specifying visitation rights . . . can lead to problems for parents and child. For example, if a non-custodial parent has an occupation or job with defined hours during the week and regular vacations every year, specificity is fine. But, if the non-custodial parent has an occupation or profession which frequently requires travel, or in which the work requirements do not permit vacations to be planned in advance, specifying rigid visitation rights can often lead to conflict. Such situations should be resolved by tailor-made provisions in the separation agreement.

It is clear that regularity and consistency of visits . . . is better for children because it promotes stability and security of the children's lives, as well as for the parents. However, as with all theories of custody and visitation, even these theories are now being challenged, as exemplified by the continued stress on joint legal and physical custody arrangements. . . .

In a typically traditional visitation arrangement the following schedule has been found reasonably effective in agreements. As with all example clauses, it should be varied or modified by the attorneys and parties to comport with the facts and circumstances of a given case.

SAMPLE VISITATION SCHEDULE:
CUSTODY AND VISITATION RIGHTS

Custody of the minor children, Jane X and Joe X, is awarded *Wife.*

I. **Husband** shall have the children with him at the following times:

A. Regular Visitation:

1. On alternate weekends from seven (7:00) p.m. Friday to seven (7:00) p.m. Sunday, commencing Friday, ______, 20XX.
2. The entire month of July, 20XX, the entire month of August, the following year, and alternating July and August in subsequent years.

B. Holidays and Special Days:

1. Lincoln's Birthday, 20XX, from seven (7:00) p.m. the day before said holiday to seven (7:00) p.m. the day of said holiday, and thereafter on alternate years.
2. Washington's Birthday, 20XX, from seven (7:00) p.m. the day before said holiday to seven (7:00) p.m. the day of said holiday, and thereafter on alternate years.
3. Memorial Day, 20XX, from seven (7:00) p.m. the day before said holiday to seven (7:00) p.m. the day of said holiday, and thereafter on alternate years.
4. Independence Day, 20XX, from seven (7:00) p.m. the day before said holiday to seven (7:00) p.m. the day of said holiday, and thereafter on alternate years.
5. Labor Day, 20XX, from seven (7:00) p.m. the day before said holiday to seven (7:00) p.m. the day of said holiday, and thereafter on alternate years.
6. Columbus Day, 20XX, from seven (7:00) p.m. the day before said holiday to seven (7:00) p.m. the day of said holiday, and thereafter on alternate years.
7. Veterans Day, 20XX, from seven (7:00) p.m. the day before said holiday to seven (7:00) p.m. the day of said holiday, and thereafter on alternate years.
8. Thanksgiving Day, 20XX, from seven (7:00) p.m. the day before said holiday to seven (7:00) p.m. the day of said holiday, and thereafter on alternate years.
9. Christmas, 20XX, the first week of the Christmas school vacation, commencing seven (7:00) p.m. the last day of school before the vacation and ending at eleven (11:00) a.m. Christmas Day, and thereafter on alternate years.
10. Christmas Day, 20XX, the second week of Christmas school vacation, commencing eleven (11:00) a.m. Christmas Day to five (5:00) p.m. New Year's Day, and thereafter on alternate years.
11. The entire Easter school vacation in the year 20XX, including Easter Sunday, commencing seven (7:00) p.m. the last day of school before the vacation and ending at seven (7:00) p.m. the day before school resumes, and thereafter during the Easter vacation on alternate years.
12. On the children's birthdays in the year 20XX, and thereafter on alternate years.
13. Every Father's Day.
14. On Husband's birthday
15. Religious Holidays (where applicable):

a. Good Friday of 20XX, from noon (12:00) p.m. to six (6:00) p.m. of said day, and thereafter on alternate years, or
b. The first day of the Jewish Holidays of Yom Kippur, Rosh Hashannah and Passover during 20XX, commencing at five (5:00) p.m. on the eve of each such day and terminating at seven (7:00) p.m. on such day, and thereafter on alternate years.

II. **Wife** shall have the children with her on the holidays and special days listed in Clause I-B in the years alternate to the years in which Husband has the children with him pursuant to Clause I-B; Wife shall also have the children on every Mother's Day and on Wife's birthday.

[*Editor's Note: A common variation would be to split the holidays between Husband and Wife and have them switch halves in alternate years. Another suggested addition if the children are young is Halloween in alternating years.*]

III. **Priorities:**

The rights of Wife under Clause II shall override the regular visitation rights of Husband set

continued

Fixing Definite Schedules—*Continued*

forth in Clause I-A, in the event of conflict between Clause I-A and Clause II, except that Husband shall not be limited in his right to take the children out of the Home-City area during the period set forth in Clause I-A2 above, even though Wife shall thereby be deprived of the right she would otherwise have under Clause II to have the children with her during said period. In the event of conflict between Clause I-B and Clause II, the rights of Husband under Clause I-B shall override the rights of Wife under Clause II.

[*Editor's Note: The significance of Clause III cannot be overrated. A key function of any drafter is to avoid argument over meaning and intention. A provision establishing a hierarchy of clauses will help avoid problems.*]

Negotiating a mutually acceptable custody and visitation plan is not always easy. "For many family law practitioners, the seemingly endless wrangling over days and even hours is one of the most time-consuming but least rewarding parts of custody practice."[5] Computer programs exist to help parties plan and understand timesharing schedules. This can be particularly helpful in cases where the family has more than one child. Joint custody options in such cases can be complex. Computer programs can generate color-coded calendar graphics to help the parties visualize what is involved.

For an example of such a graphic from a popular computer program, see Exhibit 9.1. Kidmate is designed to help parents plan and visualize custody and visitation options. In this example, the mother and father have joint physical and joint legal custody. There is also an additional caretaker (AC), a boarding school, in the example. Four children are involved: Michael (Mic), Stephanie (Ste), Claire (Cla), and Richard (Ric). The mother and father have been negotiating a possible schedule through their attorneys. The latest proposal under consideration is Proposal Number 3. One of the attorneys then used Kidmate to give the parents a graphic picture of what the schedule would look like for one month, December, under this proposal.

ASSIGNMENT 9.1

Richard and Helen Dowd have been married for six years. They are both financial consultants who work out of their home. They have one child, Kevin, aged four. Recently, they decided to separate. Draft a joint custody agreement for them. Assume that both want to be active in raising Kevin. (See General Instructions for the Agreement-Drafting Assignment in Appendix A.)

CONTESTED CUSTODY: INTRODUCTION

If the parties are able to agree on issues of custody and visitation, they place their agreement in writing, usually in the separation agreement. A court will accept the terms if it finds that they are in the best interests of the child. If, however, the parties cannot agree, the decision will be imposed on them by the court.

[5]James E. Manhood, *Kidmate Simplifies Custody Scheduling for Lawyers, Clients,* 16 Matrimonial Strategist 5 (Aug. 1998).

Exhibit 9.1 Example of Computer-Assisted Custody and Visitation Planning

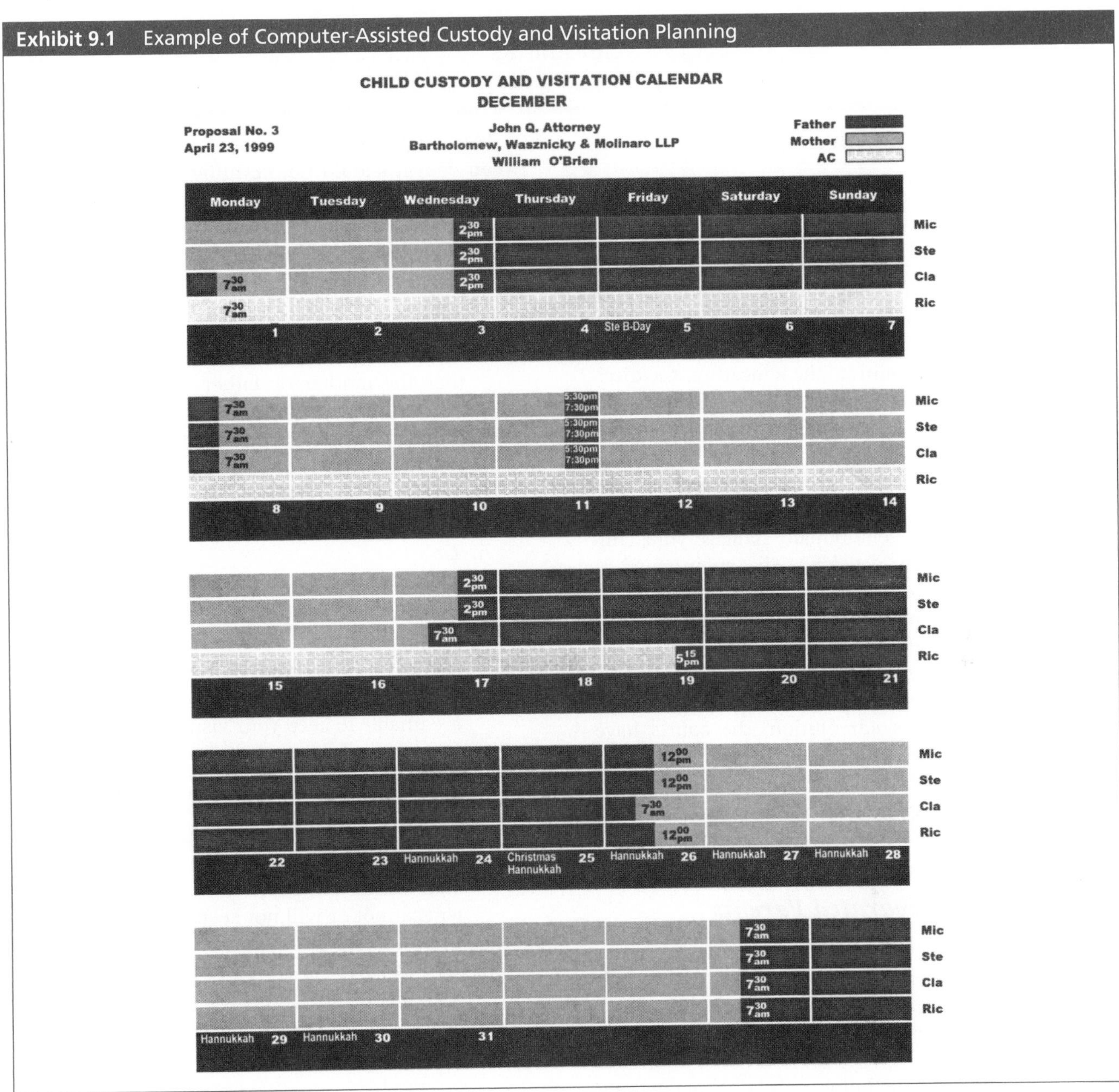

Source: Kidmate, Lapin Agile Software, Inc.

In **contested** custody cases, many courts require the parties to attend parenting classes. (Some states mandate such classes for all divorcing parties with children even if they have reached agreement on the custody issues.) For example, Tarrant County, Texas, requires attendance at a four-hour seminar on how parents can help their children cope with separation and visitation. Using video and role-playing, the seminar emphasizes the emotional harm that fighting parents can continue to inflict on their children.

contested
Disputed; challenged. (If the parties agree on how to resolve an issue, it is an *uncontested* issue.)

Most courts have guidelines they distribute to the parties on the effect of divorce on children. Sometimes these guidelines are made part of the court's custody decree. Before examining how courts make the custody decision in contested cases, we should examine some of these guidelines. The following (written on the assumption that the mother is awarded custody) are used in Wisconsin.

Guidelines

Dade County Family Court Counseling Service Staff, Madison, Wisconsin

Relation toward Children

Although the court does have the power to dissolve the bonds of matrimony, the court does not have the power to dissolve the bonds that exist between you as parents and your children. Both of you, therefore, are to continue your responsibility to emotionally support your children. You are to cooperate in the duty and right of each other to love those children. By love, the court means the training, the education, the disciplining and motivation of those children. Cooperation means to present the other party to the children with an attitude of respect either for the mother or for the father. Neither of you should in any way downplay, belittle or criticize the other in the presence of those children because you may emotionally damage your children and/or you may develop a disappointment or hatred in the minds of those children for the party that attempts to belittle or demean the other in the presence of those children. It is of utmost importance you both recognize your children's right to love both parents without fear of being disloyal to either one of you.

In support of this admonition, the courts have drafted written guidelines on your future conduct relating to the best interest of your children. I sincerely urge that you preserve them, periodically read them and always be guided by them.

Guidelines for Separated Parents

As you know, your children are usually the losers when their parents separate. They are deprived of full-time, proper guidance that two parents can give—guidance and direction essential to their moral and spiritual growth.

It is highly desirable that you abstain from making unkind remarks about each other. Recognize that such remarks are not about a former spouse but are about a parent of your children. Such comments reflect adversely upon the children.

It is urged that both parties cooperate to the end that mutual decisions concerning the interest of the children can be made objectively. Parents should remember that the mother who has custody should urge the children to find time to be with the father and encourage them to realize that their father has affection for them and contributes to their support. The father should recognize that his plans for visitation must be adjusted from time to time in order to accommodate the planned activities of the child. Visitation should be a pleasant experience rather than a duty. Cooperation in giving notice and promptness in maintaining hours of visitation are important to avoid ruffled feelings.

Although there is probably some bitterness between you, it should not be inflicted upon your children. In every child's mind there must and should be an image of two good parents. Your future conduct with your children will be helpful to them if you will follow these suggestion.

i. *Do Not's*

   a. Do not poison your child's mind against either the mother or father by discussing their shortcomings.
   b. Do not use your visitation as an excuse to continue the arguments with your spouse.
   c. Do not visit your children if you have been drinking.

ii. *Do's*

   a. Be discreet when you expose your children to [anyone] with whom you may be emotionally involved.
   b. Visit your children only at reasonable hours.
   c. Notify your spouse as soon as possible if you are unable to keep your visitation. It's unfair to keep your children waiting—and worse to disappoint them by not coming at all.
   d. Make your visitation as pleasant as possible for your children by not questioning them regarding the activities of your spouse and by not making extravagant promises which you know you cannot or will not keep.
   e. Minimize the amount of time the children are in the care of strangers and relatives.
   f. Always work for the spiritual well-being, health, happiness and safety of your children.

iii. *General*

   a. The parent with whom the children live must prepare them both physically and mentally for the visitation. The children should be available at the time mutually agreed upon.
   b. If one parent has plans for the children that conflict with the visitation and these plans are in the best interests of the children, be adults and work out the problem together.
   c. Arrangements should be made through visitation to provide the mother with some time "away" from the family. She needs the time for relaxation and recreation. Upon her return, she will be refreshed and better prepared to resume her role as mother and head of the household. Therefore, provide for extended periods of visitation such as weekends and vacations.

Bill of Rights for Children in Divorce Action

1. The right to be treated as important human beings, with unique feelings, ideas and desires and not as a source of argument between parents.
2. The right to a continuing relationship with both parents and the freedom to receive love from and express love for both.
3. The right to express love and affection for each parent without having to stifle that love because of fear of disapproval by the other parent.
4. The right to know that their parents' decision to divorce is not their responsibility and that they will live with one parent and will visit the other parent.
5. The right to continuing care and guidance from both parents.
6. The right to honest answers to questions about the changing family relationships.
7. The right to know and appreciate what is good in each parent without one parent degrading the other.
8. The right to have a relaxed, secure relationship with both parents without being placed in a position to manipulate one parent against the other.
9. The right to have the custodial parent not undermine visitation by suggesting tempting alternatives or by threatening to withhold visitation as a punishment for the children's wrongdoing.
10. The right to be able to experience regular and consistent visitation and the right to know the reason for a cancelled visit.

Most courts force parents into **mediation** to try to construct a workable custody plan they both can support. The mediator is a private counselor or a trained government employee in the family services division of the court who meets with the parents to try to help them reach agreement. The mediator does not force a decision on them. While he or she may ultimately recommend a custody/visitation arrangement to the court, the primary objective of mediation is to pressure the parents to reach their own agreement, which they can take before the judge for approval. On the mediation process, see page 214.

mediation
The process of submitting a dispute to a third party (other than a judge) who will help the parties reach their own resolution of the dispute.

PARENT VS. PARENT

First, we consider the custody decision when the dispute is between the two *biological parents* who cannot agree on custody. The standard used by the court, as we have seen, is the best interests of the child. The main participants are the mother and her attorney against the father and his attorney. (The parent with all or most of the financial resources will often be ordered to pay the reasonable attorney fees of the other parent if the latter does not have sufficient resources to hire one.) In most states, the court has the power to appoint *separate* counsel for the child. A **guardian ad litem** is an individual (often an attorney, although in some states it can be a social worker) who is appointed to represent the interests of a third party—here, the child. This individual will act independently of the attorneys for the parents.

guardian ad litem
A special guardian appointed by the court to represent the interests of another.

SD doesn't usually do ↑

How does the court decide who receives custody? What factors go into the decision? Earlier in this chapter, we presented a list of factors that parties negotiating a separation agreement must consider in arriving at a mutually acceptable custody arrangement. A court will usually consider these same factors in rendering a custody decision when the parties have not been able to reach agreement or in deciding whether to approve a custody arrangement that they have agreed upon. We will examine the factors through the following themes:

- Court discretion
- Stability
- Availability
- Emotional ties
- Legal preferences

- Morality and lifestyle
- Domestic violence
- Religion
- Race
- Wishes of the child
- Expert witnesses

Court Discretion

Of necessity, trial judges are given great discretion in making the custody decision. Unlike determining child support (see chapter 10), there are no formulas the court can use to reach the custody decision. The standard is very broad: the best interests of the child. Inevitably, the judge's personal views and philosophy of life help shape his or her concept of what is in the best interests of a child (e.g., views on the traditional family, alternate lifestyles, working women, child discipline). Of course, a judge would never admit that he or she is following his or her own personal views and philosophy; judges are supposed to be guided by "the law" and not by their individual biases. In reality, however, they are guided by both.

Stability

By far the most important consideration is stability. Courts are inclined to award custody to the parent who will cause the least amount of disruption to the disintegrating life of the child. The loss of a household with two functioning parents is a shattering experience for most children. They will need as much stability as possible in their living arrangement, schooling, religious practice, access to relatives and friends, etc. While their lives will never be the same again, a court will want to know how each parent proposes to maintain maximum stability and continuity in these areas. Each parent should submit to the court a "parenting plan" that will attempt to demonstrate how the parent proposes to meet the needs of the child, the most important of which is the preservation of as much stability as is possible under the circumstances.

Availability

Which parent will be available to spend the time required to respond to the day-to-day needs of the child? There is a danger that the child will feel abandoned and responsible for the divorce. To offset this danger, it is important that at least one of the parents be available to the child to provide reassurance and comfort. The court will want to know which parent in the past:

- Took the child to doctor's appointments
- Met with teachers
- Took the child to church or synagogue
- Helped with homework
- Attended school plays with the child
- Involved the child in athletic activities
- Arranged and attended birthday parties
- Changed diapers
- Stayed up with the sick child during the night

An office representing a parent seeking custody should make sure that he or she is able to answer questions such as the following during a deposition or on the witness stand at trial:

- What is the name of the child's pediatrician?
- When was the last time the child saw the pediatrician and for what reason?
- What is the name of the child's dentist?

- When was the last time the child saw the dentist and for what reason?
- Does the child have nightmares? If so, about what?
- What television programs do you watch with the child?
- What is the name of one of the child's main teachers? What does this teacher think are the child's strengths and weaknesses as a student?
- In what subject has the child received his or her best grade and worst grade?
- What are the names of some of the child's friends at school?
- What are the names of some of the child's friends at home?

A parent may not be able to answer all of these questions from direct knowledge because he or she is at work most of the day. Yet a responsible parent would be interested enough in the child to find out answers to such questions by talking with the other parent and with the child.

For the future, the court will want to know what plan each parent has to meet the future day-to-day needs. The health, age, and employment responsibilities of each parent are obviously relevant to this plan.

Immediately after the separation, it is common for one of the parents to have temporary custody. Upon filing for divorce, the court may formally order a temporary-custody arrangement (with visitation rights) pending the final court proceeding, which may take place months later. During this interval, the court will inquire into the amount and kind of contact each parent had with the child. Again, the above list of questions becomes important, particularly with respect to the parent who moved out. How much time has this parent spent with the child? Have letters and gifts been sent? What about visits and telephone calls? To what extent has this parent gone out of his or her way to be with the child?

Emotional Ties

Closely related to time availability is the emotional relationship that has developed in the past between a parent and child and the future prospects for this development. Which parent has been sensitive or insensitive to the psychological crisis that the child has experienced and will probably continue to experience because of the divorce? Of particular importance is the extent to which one parent has tried and succeeded in fostering the child's love for the *other* parent. A qualification to become a custodial parent is the ability and inclination to cooperate in arranging visitations by the other parent. Hence a major issue will be which parent can separate his or her own needs and lingering bitterness from the need of the child to maintain emotional ties with both parents. (Children who have been pressured by one parent to be hostile toward the other might suffer from what is called the **parental alienation syndrome.**)

parental alienation syndrome
A disorder suffered by some children at the center of a custody dispute. They idealize one parent while expressing hatred for the other, even though the relationship with both parents was relatively positive before the dispute.

A number of other factors are relevant to the emotional needs of the child:

- The level of education of the parent
- The psychological health of the parent: Has the parent been in therapy for any reason? Has it been helpful? What is the parent's attitude about seeking such help? Positive? Realistic? Does the parent think that the *other* parent is the only one who needs help?
- The stability of the parent's prior work history
- Views on discipline, TV watching, studying, religious activities, cleaning the child's room, etc.
- How siblings get along in the home
- General home and neighborhood environment: Cramped apartment conditions? Residential area? Easy accessibility to school, friends, and recreational facilities?

Also, does the parent seeking sole custody plan to move from the area? If so, into what kind of environment? How will the proposed move affect the other parent's ability to visit the child? Depending upon the circumstances of the case, a court might award custody to a parent on condition that he or she *not* move out of a designated area without the consent of the other parent.

CASE

Schutz v. Schutz

581 So. 2d 1290 (1991)
Supreme Court of Florida

Background: *Following a divorce, custody was eventually given to the mother, Laurel Schutz (the petitioner). When the trial court became concerned that the children had negative feelings toward their father, Richard Schutz (the respondent), it ordered Laurel to do everything in her power to create in the minds of the children a loving feeling toward their father. Laurel objected that this interfered with her First Amendment free speech rights and appealed. The case is now on appeal before the Supreme Court of Florida.*

Decision on Appeal: *Judgment affirmed. The order did not violate the First Amendment rights of Laurel Schutz.*

Opinion of the Court:

Justice KOGAN delivered the opinion of the court. . . .

[T]he petitioner contends [that the order] requires her to affirmatively express feelings and beliefs which she does not have in violation of her first amendment right of free expression. . . . A final judgment dissolving the six-year marriage of petitioner, Laurel Schutz (mother) and respondent, Richard R. Schutz (father) was entered by the trial court on November 13, 1978. Although custody of the parties' minor children was originally granted to the father, the final judgment was later modified in 1979. Under the modified judgment, the mother was awarded sole custody of the children, and the father was both granted visitation rights and ordered to pay child support.

As noted by the trial court, the ongoing "acrimony and animosity between the adult parties" is clear from the record. The trial court found that in February 1981 the mother moved with the children from Miami to Georgia without notifying the father. After moving, the mother advised the father of their new address and phone number. Although the father and children corresponded after the move, he found an empty house on the three occasions when he traveled to Georgia to visit the children. The father was not notified that after only seven months in Georgia the mother and children had returned to Miami. Four years later in 1985, upon discovering the children's whereabouts, the father visited the children only to find that they "hated, despised, and feared" him due to his failure to support or visit them. After this visit, numerous motions concerning visitation, custody and support were filed by the parties.

After a final hearing on the motions, the trial court found that "the cause of the blind, brainwashed, bigoted belligerence of the children toward the father grew from the soil nurtured, watered and tilled by the mother." The court further found that "the mother breached every duty she owed as the custodial parent to the noncustodial parent of instilling love, respect and feeling in the children for their father." The trial court's findings are supported by substantial competent evidence.

Based on these findings, the trial court ordered the mother "to do everything in her power to create in the minds of [the children] a loving, caring feeling toward the father . . . [and] to convince the children that it is the mother's desire that they see their father and love their father." The court further ordered that breach of the obligation imposed "either in words, actions, demeanor, implication or otherwise" would result in the "severest penalties . . . , including contempt, imprisonment, loss of residential custody or any combination thereof." . . .

We begin our analysis by noting our agreement with the district courts of appeal that have found a custodial parent has an affirmative obligation to encourage and nurture the relationship between the child and the noncustodial parent. See *Gardner v. Gardner,* 494 So. 2d 500, 502 (Fla. 4th DCA 1986), appeal dismissed, 504 So. 2d 767 (Fla. 1987); *In re Adoption of Braithwaite,* 409 So. 2d 1178, 1180 (Fla. 5th DCA 1982). This duty is owed to both the noncustodial parent and the child. This obligation may be met by encouraging the child to interact with the noncustodial parent, taking good faith measures to ensure that the child visit and otherwise have frequent and continuing contact with the noncustodial parent and refraining from doing anything likely to undermine the relationship naturally fostered by such interaction.

Consistent with this obligation, we read the challenged portion of the order at issue to require nothing more of the mother than a good faith effort to take those measures necessary to restore and promote the frequent and continuing positive interaction (e.g., visitation, phone calls, letters) between the children and their father and to refrain from doing or saying anything likely to defeat that end. There is no requirement that petitioner express opinions that she does not hold, a practice disallowed by the first amendment. *Coca-Cola Co. v. Department of Citrus,* 406 So. 2d 1079, 1087 (Fla. 1981) ("the state may never force one to adopt or express a particular opinion") . . . ; see *Wooley v. Maynard,* 430 U.S. 705, 97 S. Ct. 1428, 51 L. Ed. 2d 752 (1977) (states' interest insufficient to outweigh individual's first amendment right to avoid being courier of state motto); *West Virginia State Board of Education v. Barnette,* 319 U.S. 624, 642, 63 S. Ct. 1178, 1187, 87 L. Ed. 1628 (1943) (state cannot "prescribe . . . matters of opinion or force citizens to confess by word or act their faith therein").

Under this construction of the order, any burden on the mother's first amendment rights is merely "incidental."* Therefore, the order may be sustained against a first amendment challenge if "it furthers an important or substantial governmental interest . . . and if the incidental restriction on alleged First Amendment freedoms is no greater than is essential to the furtherance of that interest." *United States v. O'Brien,* 391 U.S. 367, 377, 88 S. Ct. 1673, 1679, 20 L. Ed. 2d 672 (1968). Accordingly, we must balance the mother's right of free expression against the state's parens patriae interest in assuring the well-being of the parties' minor children. However, as with all matters involving custody of minor children, the interests of the father and of the children, which here happen to parallel those of the state, must also factor into the equation.

In this case, the court, acting on behalf of the state as parens patriae, sought to resolve the dispute between the parties in accordance with the best interests of their children by attempting to restore a meaningful relationship between the children and their father by assuring them unhampered, frequent and continuing contact with him. See § 61.13(2)(b)1, Florida Statues (1985) (the court shall determine all matters relating to custody of minor children in accordance with the best interests of each child and it is the public policy of this state to assure a minor child frequent and continuing contact with both parents after marriage has been dissolved); id. § 61.13(3) (a) ("frequent and continuing contact with the nonresidential parent" is generally considered to be in best interest of child). In resolving the matter, the court also properly considered the father's constitutionally protected "inherent right" to a meaningful relationship with his children,** a personal interest which in this case is consistent with the state's interest in promoting meaningful family relationships. See id. § 61.001(2) (a) (one of the purposes of chapter 61 is to "safeguard meaningful family relationships").

There is no question that the state's interest in restoring a meaningful relationship between the parties' children and their father, thereby promoting the best interests of the children, is at the very least substantial. Likewise, any restriction placed on the mother's freedom of expression is essential to the furtherance of the state's interests because affirmative measures taken by the mother to encourage meaningful interaction between the children and their father would be for naught if she were allowed to contradict those measures by word or deed.

Moreover, as evinced by this record, the mother as custodial parent has the ability to undermine the association to which both the father and the parties' children are entitled. *Frazier v. Frazier,* 109 Fla. 164, 169, 147 So. 464, 466 (1933) (recognizing a noncustodial parent's "inherent right" to "enjoy the society and association of [his or her] offspring, with reasonable opportunity to impress upon them a father's or a mother's love and affection in their upbringing"); § 61.13(2) (b)1 (minor child is assured frequent and continuing contact with both parents). Therefore, not only is the incidental burden placed on her right of free expression essential to the furtherance of the state's interests as expressed in chapter 61, but also it is necessary to protect the rights of the children and their father to the meaningful relationship that the order seeks to restore.

Accordingly, construing the order as we do, we find no abuse of discretion by the trial court, nor impermissible burden on the petitioner's first amendment rights. . . . [T]he result reached is approved.

It is so ordered.

---

*The burden is "incidental" because the state interests which are furthered by the order are "unrelated to the suppression of free expression." *United States v. O'Brien,* 391 U.S. 367, 377, 88 S. Ct. 1673, 1679, 20 L. Ed. 2d 672 (1968).

****Frazier v. Frazier,** 109 Fla. 164, 172, 147 So. 464, 467 (1933) (noncustodial father is "entitled to have and enjoy [child's] society for a reasonably sufficient length of time each year to enable him to inculcate in her mind a spirit of love, affection and respect for her father," if such is not contrary to best interest of child); see *Michael H. v. Gerald D.,* 491 U.S. 110, 109 S. Ct. 2333, 2342, 105 L. Ed. 2d 91 (1989) (parent-child relationship which develops within the unitary family is constitutionally protected); *Quilloin v. Walcott,* 434 U.S. 246, 254–55, 98 S. Ct. 549, 554–55, 54 L. Ed. 2d 511 (1978) ("the relationship between parent and child is constitutionally protected").

ASSIGNMENT 9.2

a. The mother was ordered to "promote the frequent and continuing positive interaction" between the children and the father. Wouldn't this promotion constitute an expression of opinion by the mother? If so, isn't she being required to "express opinions that she does not hold," which the court said would violate the First Amendment?
b. Would the court have reached the same result if the mother was ordered to tell the children every day "Your father is a good man"?
c. Keeping in mind that the mother continues to be bitter about the father, give five examples of things she could say about the father to the children that would promote positive feelings about him without constituting opinions that she does not hold.
d. Would the mother violate the order if she refused to ever mention the father in the presence of the children?
e. What are the father's options if, a year after this case, he concludes that the children "still hate me"?

Legal Preferences

As indicated earlier, at one time many courts presumed that it was in the best interests of a young child to be with its mother rather than its father. This tender years presumption was justified on the basis of biological dependence, socialization patterns, and tradition. "There is but a twilight zone between a mother's love and the atmosphere of heaven, and all things being equal, no child should be deprived of that maternal influence."[6] A very strong case had to be made against the mother to overcome the presumption (e.g., proof that she was unfit).

Today the presumption no longer exists—at least formally. Fathers successfully argued that this gender-based presumption is an unconstitutional violation of the equal protection of the law. Male anger and frustration over the presumption were main reasons for the growth of the men's rights movement. As a result, more fathers today are granted custody. Yet this is so in relatively few cases even though the number of father-only households has increased from 900,000 in 1970 to 2,200,000 in 2000. Mothers continue to be granted custody approximately 90 percent of the time. The cases in which fathers tend to be successful are those in which they are seeking custody of an older male child. At one time, courts established a presumption that it was in the best interests of an older boy to be with his father. This gender-based presumption, however, is as constitutionally suspect as the tender years presumption. No court today would openly acknowledge that it is using a pro-father presumption when the custody of an older male is in dispute.

A number of reasons account for the high percentage of cases in which the mother is granted custody. Perhaps the primary reason is the fact that many fathers simply do not ask for custody. Becoming a full-time, at-home parent does not fit into the life plan of large numbers of men, particularly if it means significant interference with their occupation. Arguably, another major reason is that fathers are still handicapped by the tender years presumption in spite of its formal abolition. Most of the judges now sitting on the bench grew up with full-time moms at home. Some experts feel it is difficult for these judges to accept the notion of giving sole custody to working fathers. But new judges are on the way. It "will take a generation of judges who are brought up by, or married to career women" before there is more sympathy for granting custody to working parents—particularly fathers.[7]

---

[6] *Tuter v. Tuter,* 120 S.W.2d 203, 205 (Mo. App. 1938).
[7] Jan Hoffman, *Divorced Fathers Make Gains in Battles to Increase Rights,* N.Y. Times, Apr. 26, 1995, at A11.

In place of the tender years presumption, many courts have substituted a **primary caregiver presumption,** by which the court presumes that custody should go to the parent who has been the primary person taking care of the child over the years. This, of course, means that the mother continues to receive sole custody in most cases, since she is usually the one who stays home to care of the child. Even when both the mother and the father work outside the home, the mother is more likely to be awarded custody as the primary caregiver or caretaker. Some, therefore, have argued that this presumption is another disguise for the tender years presumption.

primary caregiver presumption
The primary person who has taken care of the child should have custody.

A less controversial presumption is that brothers and sisters are best kept together with the same parent whenever possible. (In effect, this was a presumption that split custody was *not* in the best interests of the children.) Finally, courts widely accept the idea that the preference of older, more mature children as to their own custody should be given great, though not necessarily controlling, weight.

Morality and Lifestyle

Just as marital fault or misconduct should not be a factor in deciding whether to grant a divorce (see chapter 7), it should not determine who receives custody—unless the fault affects the child. According to one court:

> A judge should not base his decision upon [a] disapproval of the morals or other personal characteristics of a parent that do not harm the child. . . . We do not mean to suggest that a person's associational or even sexual conduct may not be relevant in deciding a custody dispute where there is compelling evidence that such conduct has a significant bearing upon the welfare of the children.[8]

Assume that Bill and Mary are married with one child, Alice. After Mary and Bill separate, Mary and Alice move into an apartment where Mary begins living with her boyfriend. In the divorce proceeding, Bill argues that he should have sole custody because Mary is living in "illicit cohabitation" with her boyfriend. This argument will lose unless Bill can show that Mary's relationship with her boyfriend is having a detrimental effect on Alice. An example would be evidence that Alice is becoming emotionally upset because of the boyfriend's presence in the home and that this is negatively affecting her schoolwork. If the relationship is not affecting Alice, the presence of the boyfriend will not be relevant to the determination of custody despite Bill's plea that his daughter should not be exposed to the "sin and immorality" of Mary's conduct.

This result should also apply if the parent seeking custody has a homosexual partner in the home. A court will want to know if the couple is discreet in the expression of their mutual affection. If sexuality is flaunted, whether heterosexual or homosexual, a court is likely to conclude that a child will be adversely affected. Courts have granted custody to a gay parent when all of the factors point to a healthy home environment for the child and there is no evidence that the homosexuality will have an adverse impact on the child. At one time, there was fear that a parent's homosexuality would cause the child to be homosexual. Many studies have rejected this conclusion, particularly since a child's sexual preference is developed during its infancy and very early years. This is usually well before the homosexual parent seeks custody. It must be acknowledged, however, that a gay parent has a substantial uphill battle in gaining custody (or in keeping custody if the homosexuality is revealed only after the parent has been awarded custody). Gay parents have been most successful in winning custody when the heterosexual parent is either no longer available

---

[8] *Wellman v. Wellman,* 104 Cal. App. 3d 992, 998, 164 Cal. Rptr. 148, 151–52 (1980).

or demonstrably unfit. In such cases, the homosexual parent wins by default unless his or her conduct is so offensive that the court will grant custody to neither biological parent.

Domestic Violence

A court is obviously unlikely to grant custody to a parent who has a history of child abuse—physical, emotional, or sexual. (Later, in the *Allen* case, we will examine the impact of an allegation of sexual abuse of a child.) What about domestic violence between the parents? Most courts take the position that a parent who commits spousal abuse is not necessarily an unfit parent. The court will want to know what effect the abuse has had on the child. Evidence of spousal abuse could be damaging if it was consistently committed in front of the child or if the anger and violence seriously disturbed the child's ability to function normally. It is possible, however, for the offending parent to show that the abuse has been isolated and has not affected the home environment of the child. It may also help if this parent can show that he or she is seeking psychological counseling for anger control.

Religion

Under our Constitution, a court cannot favor one religion over another or prefer organized religion over less orthodox forms of religious beliefs. To do so could amount to an unconstitutional "establishment" of religion. The state must remain neutral. In the law of custody, the question is what effect the practice of religion is likely to have on the child, not which religion is preferable or correct according to the judge's personal standards, or according to the standards of the majority in the community, or according to "respectable" minorities in the community. The court will want to know what religion, if any, the child has practiced to date. Continuity is highly desirable. Also, will the practice of a particular religion tend to take the child away from other activities? For example, will the child be asked to spend long hours in door-to-door selling of religious literature and hence be unable to attend regular school? If so, the court will be reluctant to award custody to the parent who would require this of the child.

ASSIGNMENT 9.3

When Helen married John, she converted from Catholicism to his religion, Judaism. Neither Helen nor John was a very religious person, however. To a moderate extent, their two children were raised in the Jewish faith. The couple divorced when the children were ages four and five. Because of John's job, he could not be the sole custodian of the children. Hence he agreed that Helen receive sole custody. But he asked the court to order Helen to continue raising the children in the Jewish faith.

a. Under what circumstances do you think a court can grant this request, so that, in effect, John will be granted *spiritual custody* of the children even though physical custody and legal custody (in all matters except religion) will be granted to Helen? (See General instructions for the Legal-Analysis Assignment in Appendix A.)

b. Suppose that Helen returns to her original religion and starts taking the children to Catholic mass. What options does John have in your state? (See General Instructions for the State-Code Assignment in Appendix A.)

Race

A child's ethnic and cultural heritage is important. Suppose, for example, that a child has been raised in the Mexican American community. If possible, a court will want to grant custody to the parent who will help the child maintain his or her contacts with this community. Race, however, cannot be the sole factor that determines custody. Assume, for example, that a divorced white parent asks a court for custody because the other parent has married a black person. A court cannot grant custody for this reason. It would be an unconstitutional denial of the equal protection of the law.[9]

Wishes of the Child

Older children are almost always asked where they would want to live. Courts are understandably reluctant, however, to ask young children to take sides in custody disputes. If this becomes common practice, there would be an incentive for both parents to pressure the child to express preferences. If, however, the court is convinced that the child is mature enough to state a rational preference and that doing so would not harm the child, evidence of such a preference will be admissible. Great caution must be used in questioning the child. The judge may decide to speak to the child outside the formal courtroom (with the attorneys but not the parents present), or the judge may allow a professional (e.g., child psychologist, social worker) to interview the child at home.

Expert Witnesses

Psychologists, psychiatrists, social workers, and other experts can be called as expert witnesses by either parent to testify on the child's home environment and emotional development, the mental stability of the parents, the suitability of various custody plans, etc. Either parent, or the guardian ad litem for the child, can make a motion that the court order a custody evaluation by an expert. An example of a custody-evaluation report by such an expert is provided in Exhibit 9.2.

---

[9] *Palmore v. Sidoni,* 466 U.S. 429, 104 S. Ct. 1879, 80 L. Ed. 2d 421 (1984).

Exhibit 9.2 Sample Custody Evaluation by an Expert

Psychiatric Custody Evaluation

August 25, 1991

Honorable James K. O'Brien
Supreme Court of New York
New York County
60 Centre Street
New York, New York 10007

Re: Johnson v. Johnson
Docket No. M-3784-91

Dear Judge O'Brien:

This report is submitted in compliance with your court order dated June 9, 1991, requesting that I conduct an evaluation of the Johnson family in order to provide the court with information that would be useful to it in deciding which of the Johnson parents should have custody of their children Tara, Elaine, and Charles.

My findings and recommendations are based on interviews conducted as itemized below:

July 6, 1991	Mrs. Carol Johnson and Mr. Frank Johnson, seen jointly	2 hours
July 7, 1991	Mr. Frank Johnson	1 hour
July 11, 1991	Mrs. Carol Johnson	1 hour
July 13, 1991	Tara Johnson	1 ½ hours
July 14, 1991	Mr. Frank Johnson	1 hour
July 20, 1991	Mrs. Carol Johnson	1 hour
July 21, 1991	Charles Johnson	¾ hour
	Elaine Johnson	¾ hour
July 22, 1991	Tara Johnson	½ hour
	Mrs. Carol Johnson and Tara Johnson, seen jointly	½ hour

continued

Exhibit 9.2 Sample Custody Evaluation by an Expert—*Continued*

Date	Persons seen	Time
July 24, 1991	Mrs. Carol Johnson	1 hour
July 27, 1991	Mrs. Carol Johnson and Mr. Frank Johnson, seen jointly	1 hour
Aug. 3, 1991	Elaine Johnson	¾ hour
Aug. 4, 1991	Tara Johnson	¼ hour
	Mr. Frank Johnson and Tara Johnson, seen jointly	½ hour
Aug. 10, 1991	Tara Johnson	
	Mr. Frank Johnson and Mrs. Carol Johnson, seen jointly	¾ hour
Aug. 11, 1991	Tara Johnson	
	Elaine Johnson	
	Charles Johnson	
	Mrs. Carol Johnson and Mr. Frank Johnson, seen jointly	¾ hour
Aug. 14, 1991	Tara Johnson	
	Elaine Johnson	
	Charles Johnson	
	Mrs. Carol Johnson and Mr. Frank Johnson, seen jointly	1 hour
		16 hours

In addition, on Aug. 16, 1991, Mr. and Mrs. Johnson were seen together for the purpose of my presenting these findings and recommendations to them. This interview lasted two hours, bringing to 18 the total number of hours spent with the Johnson family in association with this evaluation.

Mr. Frank Johnson, an airline pilot, is 43 years old. His first wife died soon after the delivery of Tara, who is now 16 years of age. He married Mrs. Carol Johnson when Tara was 2 years old. Mrs. Johnson, a housewife, who was formerly an elementary school teacher, is now 40. Her first marriage ended in divorce. A child of this relationship died soon after birth. There are two children of the Johnson marriage: Elaine, 11 and Charles, 7. Mrs. Johnson adopted her stepdaughter Tara in July 1990. In October 1990, Mr. Johnson initiated divorce proceedings because he felt that his wife no longer respected him and that she was a poor mother for the children, especially his daughter Tara. However, Mr. and Mrs. Johnson are still occupying the same domicile.

Both parents are requesting custody of all three children. It is this examiner's recommendation that Mr. Frank Johnson be granted custody of Tara and that Mrs. Carol Johnson be granted custody of Elaine and Charles. The observations that have led me to these conclusions will be divided into four categories: 1) Mr. Frank Johnson's assets as a parent, 2) Mr. Frank Johnson's liabilities as a parent, 3) Mrs. Carol Johnson's assets as a parent, and 4) Mrs. Carol Johnson's liabilities as a parent. Following these four presentations I will comment further on the way in which my observations brought about the aforementioned recommendations. Although much information was obtained in the course of the evaluation, only those items specifically pertinent to the custody consideration will be included in this report.

Mr. Frank Johnson's Assets as a Parent

Mr. Frank Johnson is Tara's biological father. The special psychological tie that this engenders is not enjoyed by Mrs. Carol Johnson and Tara. It is not the genetic bond per se that is crucial here; rather, it is the psychological attachment that such a bond elicits. Mr. Johnson had already started to develop a psychological tie with Tara while his first wife was pregnant with her. He was actually present at her birth and assumed an active role in her rearing—almost from birth because of the illness and early death of his first wife. This situation prevailed until the time of his marriage to Mrs. Johnson when Tara was 2 years of age. Although Mrs. Johnson has been Tara's primary caretaker since then, Mr. Johnson's early involvement with Tara during these crucial years of her development contributes to a very strong psychological tie between them that has continued up to the present time.

My observations have convinced me, and both parents agree, that at this time, Tara has a closer relationship with her father than her mother. Her relationship with Mrs. Johnson at this time is characteristically a difficult one in that there are frequent battles and power struggles. Although Tara is not completely free of such involvement with her father, such hostile interaction is far less common. In my interviews with Mr. Johnson and Tara, I found her to be far more friendly with him than I observed her to be with Mrs. Johnson in my joint interviews with them.

In every interview, both alone and in joint sessions with various members of the family, Tara openly and unswervingly stated that she wished to live with her father: "I want to live with my father. I am closer to him." "When I was younger, my mother did more things; but since I'm older, my father does more things." "My father listens to what I say; my mother doesn't."

Mr. Johnson and Tara both utilize a similar method of communication. Neither feels a strong need to give confirmation of examples to general statements that they make, and they are therefore comfortable with one another. Mrs. Johnson, on the other hand, is much more specific in her communications and this is a source of difficulty, not only in her relationship with Tara, but in her relationship with her husband as well.

All five family members agree that Mr. Johnson spends significant time with Charles, involved in typical father-son activities, sports, games, etc. It is also apparent that Charles has a strong masculine identification and this arose, in part, from his modeling himself after his father.

Mr. Frank Johnson's Liabilities as a Parent

Mr. Johnson states that he would not have involved himself in the custody evaluation conducted by this examiner if he had to contribute to its financing. Accordingly, Mrs. Johnson assumed the total financial obligation for this evaluation. I conclude from this that with regard to this particular criterion for comparing the parents, Mr. Johnson's position is less strong than Mrs. Johnson's.

On many occasions Mr. Johnson made general comments about his superiority over his wife with regard to parental capacity. For example, "She's a very poor mother," "She neglects the children," and "If you had all the information you would see that I'm a better parent." However, it was extremely difficult to elicit from Mr. Johnson specific examples of incidents that would substantiate these statements. I not only considered this to be a manifestation of Mr. Johnson's problem in accurately communicating, but also considered it to be a deficiency in his position. One cannot be convinced of the strength of such statements if no examples can be provided to substantiate them.

In the hope that I might get more specific information from Mr. Johnson I asked him, on at least three occasions, to write a list of specifics that might help corroborate some of his allegations. He came to three subsequent interviews without having written anything in response to my invitation. I consider such failure to reflect a compromise in his motivation for gaining custody of the three children. When he did finally submit such a list it was far less comprehensive than that which was submitted by Mrs. Johnson and in addition, the issues raised had far less significance, e.g., "She's late once in a while," "She's sometimes forgetful," and "She doesn't like playing baseball with Charles."

Although I described Mr. Johnson's communication problem as a factor supporting his gaining custody of Tara, I would consider it a liability with regard to his gaining custody of Elaine and Charles. Tara (possibly on a genetic basis) communicates in a similar way and so, as mentioned, is comfortable with her father when they communicate. Elaine and Charles, however, appear to be identifying with their mother with regard to communication accuracy. Accordingly, intensive exposure to Mr. Johnson might compromise what I consider a healthier communicative pattern.

Mr. Johnson's profession as an airline pilot has not enabled him to have predictable hours. Not only is his schedule variable, but there are times when he is required to work on an emergency basis. All three children agree that Mrs. Johnson is more predictably present. Mr. Johnson's irregular schedule is not a significant problem for Tara who, at 16, is fairly independent and would not suffer significantly from her father's schedule. The younger children, however, are still in need of predictability of parental presence and Mr. Johnson has not demonstrated his capacity to provide such predictability. In my final interview with Mr. Johnson he stated that he would change his work pattern to be available to his children during non-school hours. Mrs. Johnson was very dubious that this could be arranged because his job does not allow such flexibility. Both parents agreed, however, that it had not occurred in the past and that such predictability was not taking place at the time of this evaluation.

Both Charles and Elaine stated that they wanted to live with their mother and not live with their father. Charles stated, "I want to be with my mother. I'd be alone when my father goes to work." Elaine stated, "I want to live with my mother. I'm closer to my mother. I'm not as close to my father."

In a session in which I was discussing his future plans with Mr. Johnson, he stated that he was considering moving to California because he could earn more money there by supplementing his income with certain business ventures that he had been invited to participate in. He stated also that he would still move even if he were only to be granted custody of Tara. Although I appreciate that a higher income could provide Mr. Johnson's children with greater financial flexibility, I believe that the disadvantages of such a move would far outweigh its advantages from their point of view. Specifically, the extra advantages they might enjoy from such a move would be more than offset by the even greater absence of their father who, his liabilities notwithstanding, is still an important figure for them.

In an interview in which I discussed with Mr. Johnson how he would react to the various custodial decisions, he was far more upset about the prospect of losing Tara than he was about the possibility of losing Charles and Elaine. In fact, he appeared to be accepting of the fact that Elaine would go to her mother. Although somewhat distressed about the possibility of Charles' living with his mother, he did not show the same degree of distress as his wife over the prospect of losing the younger two children.

Mrs. Carol Johnson's Assets as a Parent

Mrs. Carol Johnson was far more committed to the custody evaluation than her husband. As mentioned, she was willing to make the financial sacrifices involved in the evaluation. I consider this to be a factor reflecting greater motivation than her husband for gaining custody of the children. Mrs. Johnson is more available to the children during non-school hours than her husband and this is one element in her favor regarding gaining custody, especially of the younger children. Mrs. Johnson is a more accurate and clearer communicator than her husband and this is an asset. As mentioned, the younger children do not seem to have been affected by their father's communication difficulty. Having them live with him might result in their acquiring this maladaptive trait.

During her pregnancy with Elaine, Mrs. Johnson suffered with toxemia and associated high blood pressure and convulsions. Most physicians generally discourage women with this disorder from becoming pregnant again because it is genuinely life endangering. However, Mrs. Johnson did wish to have a third child, primarily because her husband, she states, was so desirous of having a son. Her pregnancy with Charles was complicated by the exacerbation of a preexisting asthmatic condition from which she states that she almost died. A less maternal woman would not have become pregnant again.

Elaine stated on many occasions, and in every interview, both alone and with other family members, that she wished to live with her mother: "I'm closer to my mother," "She's home more than my father," "They call my father to do things at work all the time," and "My mother has more feelings for me than my father."

Charles also, both in individual session and in joint interviews, emphatically stated that he wished to live with his mother: "I want to stay with my mother because she doesn't work as much as my father." "If you get sick the father might not know what to do, but the mother does." "My mother knows how to take care of me." "She doesn't work that much." "She reads me books more than my father."

On one occasion Mr. Johnson stated: "Carol is closer to Elaine than I am. They are similar. They're both sore losers. Both get emotional if they don't have their way." Mrs. Carol Johnson agrees that she and her daughter Elaine have these traits, but not to the degree described by her husband. Although there are certainly negative elements regarding the reasons why Mr. Johnson sees Elaine to be closer to his wife, this statement is an admission of his recognition of this preference of Elaine for her mother. The situation is analogous to Mr. Johnson's involvement with Tara. They are closer to one another, yet maladaptive and undesirable factors are contributing to the closeness.

Mrs. Carol Johnson's Liabilities as a Parent

Tara is not Mrs. Johnson's biological daughter. Although she has raised Tara from her infancy, as if she were her own biological child, and although she has adopted her, Mrs. Johnson is at a certain disadvantage regarding the development of a strong psychological parent-child tie. As mentioned, I believe that a biological relationship increases the strength of the psychological bond. Accordingly, Mrs. Johnson is at a disadvantage when compared to Mr. Johnson regarding this aspect of the custody consideration.

continued

Exhibit 9.2 Sample Custody Evaluation by an Expert—*Continued*

Mrs. Johnson and Tara have a poor relationship at this point. In my interviews with Mrs. Johnson and Tara I found the latter to view her mother scornfully and to be openly resentful of her authority. On one occasion Tara said: "She has a lot of nerve telling me what to do." Were this an isolated statement, it would probably not have much significance. However, all agreed that it epitomized her general attitude toward her mother. Although some of the scornful attitude Tara exhibits toward her mother can be viewed as age-appropriate, I believe the extent goes beyond what is to be expected for teen-agers.

Mrs. Johnson cannot provide Charles with the same kind of father model and father-type involvement that her husband can. Although she claims an interest in sports and a greater degree of facility than the average woman, it is still clear that her husband has been far more involved in this type of activity with his son than has Mrs. Johnson.

Mr. Johnson accuses Mrs. Johnson of being excessively punitive and too strong a disciplinarian. Mrs. Johnson claims that her husband is too lax with the children and does not implement proper disciplinary measures. I believe that it is most likely that Mrs. Johnson is a little too punitive and that Mr. Johnson is a little too lenient. However, neither parent exhibits these difficulties to a degree that would be significantly injurious to the children, nor would I consider this to be a factor compromising either of their capacities as parents. It is probable, however, that these differences are playing a role in Tara's antagonism to her mother and her gravitating toward her father.

In every interview, both individual and joint, Tara openly stated that she wished to live with her father. "I would be very unhappy if the judge made me go with my mother." "He can't make me live with my mother. I'd run away to my father if he did."

Conclusions and Recommendations

Weighing the above factors as best I can, I believe that the evidence is strongly in favor of Mr. Johnson being given custody of Tara. I believe, also, that the above evidence strongly supports the conclusion that Elaine should be given to Mrs. Johnson. Although there are certain arguments supporting Mr. Johnson's gaining custody of Charles, I believe that these are greatly outweighed by arguments in favor of Mrs. Johnson's gaining custody. Were the court to conclude that Tara would be better off living with Mrs. Johnson, I believe that there would be a continuation of the present hostilities, and this could be disruptive to the healthy psychological development of the younger children—if they were exposed to such hostile interactions over a long period. I believe that if Mr. Johnson were to be granted custody of Elaine and Charles it is most likely that they would suffer psychological damage. All things considered, I believe he is the less preferable parent for the young children and, if they had to live with him, they would suffer emotional deprivations that could contribute to the development of psychiatric disorders.

Richard A. Gardner, M.D.

Source: R. Gardner, M.D., *Family Evaluation in Child Custody Litigation,* 318–25 (1982).

ASSIGNMENT 9.4

a. What standards exist in your state to guide the judge on the decision to grant custody when the dispute is between the two biological parents? (See General Instructions for the State-Code Assignment in Appendix A.)

b. Find an opinion written by a court in your state in which the court granted custody to one of the parents following a divorce or legal separation. Pick an opinion in which both parents sought sole custody. State the factors that the court used in making this decision. Why did the judge decide not to give custody to the other parent? Do you agree with the judge's decision on the custody issue? Are there other facts about the case that you would like to know, but were not provided in the opinion? Do you think the investigators for each side did a good job of gathering all the facts? (See General Instructions for the Court-Opinion Assignment in Appendix A.)

COURT DECISION ON VISITATION

Introduction

Courts want to preserve as much of the child's relationship with both parents as possible. Hence visitation rights are almost always granted to the noncustodial parent even if they must be exercised in the presence of third parties (see the discussion of *supervised visitation* below). Failing to grant such rights would be a step in the direction of terminating the parental rights of that parent (see chapter 15). Moreover, as indicated earlier, one of the criteria that a court will use in awarding sole custody to a parent is whether the latter will cooperate in the exercise of visitation rights by the other parent. Custodial parents who fail to provide such cooperation are sometimes dealt with harshly by the court (e.g., transferring custody to the other parent, issuing contempt orders). It is never permissible, however, for the noncustodial parent to terminate child-support payments in retaliation for the custodial parent's violation of visitation rights.

Whenever possible, the court will favor frequent and regular visitation by the noncustodial parent (e.g., every other weekend, alternating holidays, substantial summer vacation time). When the custody battle is between two relatively fit parents, the court is even more inclined to grant greater visitation rights to the loser.

An essential component of successful visitation in most cases is physical proximity between the child and the noncustodial parent. A great deal of litigation has centered on the right of the custodial parent to move the child substantial distances away. Some courts flatly forbid such moving. A few states have statutes that cover this problem. For example:

> The custodial parent shall not move the residence of the child to another state except upon order of the court or with the consent of the noncustodial parent, when the noncustodial parent has been given visitation rights by the decree.[10]

In extreme cases, the court might order the custodial parent to post a bond to secure compliance with the visitation rights of the noncustodial parent.

Third-Party Visitation

Another issue that is occasionally litigated is whether *third parties* can be given rights of visitation (e.g., grandparents, former stepparents). Factors considered by the court in deciding this question include:

- The language of the statute in the state that governs who can visit. A court will want to know if it has statutory power to grant visitation rights to third parties.
- Whether the child has lived with the third party for a substantial period of time in the past or has otherwise formed close emotional ties with the third party.

If a court has the power to grant visitation rights to someone other than biological parents the standard the court will use in deciding whether to exercise this power is the best interests of the child.

The visitation rights of third parties, however, cannot substantially interfere with the primary right of fit custodial parents to raise their children. Some third-party visitation statutes go too far. At one time, for example, Washington state had a statute that allowed "[a]ny person" "at any time" to petition the court for visitation, which could be granted if the court felt it would be in the best interests of child. The statute gave no special consideration or weight to the opinion of the parents on whether third-party visitation should be allowed. When a parent opposed such visitation, for example, the statute did not say that the third party had to overcome a presumption that the parent's opposition was valid. The statute gave no such presumption of validity to the parent's views.

This statute was called "breathtakingly broad" and declared unconstitutional by the United States Supreme Court in the case of *Troxel v. Granville.*[11] Tommie Granville and Brad Troxel were the unmarried parents of Isabelle and Natalie Troxel. After the parents separated, Brad lived with his parents, Jenifer and Gary Troxel, the girls' paternal grandparents. Brad regularly brought his daughters to his parents' home for weekend visits. When Brad committed suicide, the grandparents continued to see the girls on a regular

---

[10]Minnesota Statutes Annotated § 518.175(3).

[11]530 U.S. 57, 120 S. Ct. 2054, 147 L. Ed. 2d 49 (2000).

basis. Tommie Granville, however, informed the Troxels that she wished to limit their visitation with her daughters to one short visit per month. The grandparents used the Washington state statute to petition to the court for two weekends of overnight visitation per month and two weeks each summer. Over the objection of Granville, the court granted them one weekend per month, one week during the summer, and four hours on both of the grandparents' birthdays. Granville's appeal eventually reached the United States Supreme Court.

The Court began its analysis by acknowledging the changing reality of family life in America:

> The demographic changes of the past century make it difficult to speak of an average American family. The composition of families varies greatly from household to household. While many children may have two married parents and grandparents who visit regularly, many other children are raised in single-parent households. In 1996, children living with only one parent accounted for 28 percent of all children under age 18 in the United States. U.S. Dept. of Commerce, Bureau of Census, Current Population Reports, *1997 Population Profile of the United States* 27 (1998). Understandably, in these single-parent households, persons outside the nuclear family are called upon with increasing frequency to assist in the everyday tasks of child rearing. In many cases, grandparents play an important role. For example, in 1998, approximately 4 million children—or 5.6 percent of all children under age 18—lived in the household of their grandparents. U.S. Dept. of Commerce, Bureau of Census, Current Population Reports, *Marital Status and Living Arrangements: March 1998* (Update), p. i (1998).[12]

The Court specified that if a fit parent is present in the home, his or her right to raise a child is entitled to constitutional protection. The due process clause of the Fourteenth Amendment to the United States Constitution gives parents the fundamental right to make decisions concerning the care, custody, and control of their children:

> The Fourteenth Amendment provides that no State shall "deprive any person of life, liberty, or property, without due process of law." We have long recognized that the Amendment's Due Process Clause . . . "guarantees more than fair process." *Washington v. Glucksberg,* 521 U.S. 702, 719, 117 S. Ct. 2258 (1997). The Clause also includes a substantive component that "provides heightened protection against government interference with certain fundamental rights and liberty interests." Id., at 720, 117 S. Ct. 2258. . . . The liberty interest at issue in this case—the interest of parents in the care, custody, and control of their children—is perhaps the oldest of the fundamental liberty interests recognized by this Court. More than 75 years ago, in *Meyer v. Nebraska,* 262 U.S. 390, 399, 401, 43 S. Ct. 625 (1923), we held that the "liberty" protected by the Due Process Clause includes the right of parents to "establish a home and bring up children" and "to control the education of their own." Two years later, in *Pierce v. Society of Sisters,* 268 U.S. 510, 534–535, 45 S. Ct. 571 (1925), we again held that the "liberty of parents and guardians" includes the right "to direct the upbringing and education of children under their control."[13]

There was no indication in this case that Granville was an unfit parent. When fit parents make a decision in raising their child, they are entitled to a presumption that the decision is in the child's best interests. The presumption means that the decision controls unless someone proves that the decision is not in the best interests of the child. It is not enough to show that another decision is a good idea.

Granville was not given the benefit of this presumption. Her opposition to the grandparents' request was given no "special weight." The judge simply dis-

---

[12]Id. at 64, 120 S. Ct. at 2059.
[13]Id. at 65, 120 S. Ct. at 2060.

agreed with her on whether more extensive visitation with the paternal grandparents was in the best interests of the children. This troubled the United States Supreme Court:

> [S]o long as a parent adequately cares for his or her children (i.e., is fit), there will normally be no reason for the State to inject itself into the private realm of the family to further question the ability of that parent to make the best decisions concerning the rearing of that parent's children. . . . [T]he Due Process Clause does not permit a State to infringe on the fundamental right of parents to make childrearing decisions simply because a state judge believes a "better" decision could be made.[14]

While the Court ruled that a fit parent must be given the presumption of correctness, the Court did not clarify what kind of evidence would overcome this presumption. The Court left this question for another day. Hence, while we do not know the precise scope of the constitutional right of parents to raise their children, we do know that the Court will take a dim view of any effort by the state to interfere with the child rearing decisions of a fit parent.

Supervised Visitation

Finally, we need to consider **supervised visitation**—visitation of a child in the presence of a third party, someone other than the custodial parent. In some cases, a custodial parent will ask the court to deny all visitation rights to the other parent because of a fear that the child might be taken out of the state or country or might be physically or emotionally harmed by unrestricted visitation. As indicated, courts are very reluctant to deny all visitation rights to a parent. If the court is convinced that unrestricted visitation would not be in the best interests of the child, supervised visitation is a possible alternative. When used, the custodial parent usually takes the child to a facility that is equipped to monitor visitation in a safe environment. The facility might be a government agency or, more commonly, a private nonprofit group (e.g., a unit of the YWCA) that charges a fee for its services. After the custodial parent drops off the child and leaves, the noncustodial parent has a visit of several hours (as designated by the court order) in rooms available in the facility. The custodial parent then returns to pick up the child. Supervised visitation can also occur in less formal settings such as the home of a relative that both parents trust. It is more common, however, for supervised visitation to occur at a facility that is professionally organized to offer such visitation.

supervised visitation
Visitation of a child in the presence of an adult other than the custodial parent.

ASSIGNMENT 9.5

Flora Smith and Harry Smith have one child, ten-year-old Mary Smith. Flora and Harry are separated. Flora wants supervised visitation of Mary by Harry Smith because he often misses child-support payments and has a girlfriend who is an alcoholic. Flora is afraid that if Harry takes Mary to his home, she will be exposed to drinking. How should the court rule? (See General Instructions for the Legal-Analysis Assignment in Appendix A.)

THE NEW "TERROR WEAPON"

I had to face the fact that for one year [during the exercise of unsupervised visitation rights by the father], I sent my child off to her rapist.[15]

---

[14] Id. at 68, 72–73, 120 S. Ct. at 2061, 2063–64.
[15] M. Szegedy-Maszak, *Who's to Judge,* N.Y. Times Magazine, May 21, 1989, at 28.

> For many parents engaged in seriously contested child custody disputes, false allegations of child abuse have become an effective weapon for achieving an advantage in court.[16]

In alarming numbers, parents are being accused of sexually abusing their children, usually during visitation. The issue can also arise during an initial custody proceeding where one parent claims that the other committed sex abuse during the marriage, and hence should not be granted custody, or should not be granted visitation rights in unsupervised settings.

The level of bitterness generated by this accusation is incredibly high. It is the equivalent of a declaration of total war between the parties. The chances of reaching a settlement or of mediating the custody dispute—or anything else that is contested—often vanish the moment the accusation is made. Protracted and costly litigation is all but inevitable.

Nor does litigation always resolve the matter. Assume that a mother with sole custody is turned down when she asks a court to terminate the father's right to visit the child because of an allegation of child abuse. The court finds the evidence of abuse to be insufficient and orders a continuation of visitation. Unable to accept this result, the mother goes underground out of desperation and a total loss of faith in the legal system. She flees with the child, or she turns the child over to sympathetic third parties who agree to keep the child hidden from the authorities. The child might be moved from one "safe house" to another to avoid detection. This underground network consists of a core of dedicated women who at one time were in a similar predicament or who are former child-abuse victims themselves.

If the mother remains behind, she is hauled back into court. If she refuses to obey an order to produce the child, she faces an array of possible sanctions, including imprisonment for civil contempt or even prosecution for criminal kidnaping. Unfortunately, the media have an excessive interest in cases of this kind. Once reporters and cameras become involved, a circus atmosphere tends to develop.

Attorneys can find themselves in delicate situations. The first question they face is whether to take the case. When an alleged child abuser—usually the father—seeks representation, the attorney understands the father's need for a vigorous defense. What if he didn't do it? Yet attorneys tend to place cases of this kind in a different category. Many need to believe in his innocence before they will take the case. According to a prominent matrimonial attorney, "I have a higher duty to make sure some wacko doesn't get custody of his child." Before proceeding, therefore, the attorney might ask him to:

- Take a lie detector test
- Take the **Minnesota Multiphasic Personality Inventory Test (MMPI),** which may reveal whether someone has a propensity to lie and is the kind of person who statistically is likely to be a child abuser
- Be evaluated by a knowledgeable psychologist or psychiatrist

Some attorneys have even insisted that the father undergo hypnosis as a further aid in trying to assess the truth of the allegation.

Attorneys representing the mother face similar concerns. Is she telling the truth? Is she exaggerating, knowingly or otherwise? Is she trying to seek some other strategic advantage from the father, e.g., more financial support, custody blackmail? What advice should the attorney give her when she first reveals the charge of sexual abuse, particularly when the evidence of abuse is not overwhelming? Should she be advised to go public with the charge? As indicated, the consequences of doing so—and of not doing so—can be enormous. Bitter litigation is almost assured. What if the attorney talks her out of going

[16]C. Gordon, *False Allegations of Abuse in Child Custody Disputes,* 2 Minnesota Family Law Journal 225 (1985).

public with the charge in order to settle the case through negotiation, "and a month or two later something terrible happens"? Faced, therefore, with a need to know if the accusation is true, the attorney may ask *her* to take a polygraph test or an MMPI test, or to undergo an independent evaluation by a psychologist or psychiatrist.

Other attorneys disagree with this approach. They do not think that clients should be subject to such mistrust by their own attorney. And they fail to see much value in some of the devices used to assess the truth. Some typical comments from such attorneys are that professionals "trained in sexual abuse are wrong very often"; "Frankly, I trust my horse sense more than I trust psychiatrists"; and "There is no research that says the polygraph or MMPI is of any use."[17]

Of course, attorneys for both sides will have to interview the child. This can be a very delicate task. There is a danger of emotional damage every time the child is forced to focus on the events in question. Even though children are generally truthful, many are susceptible to suggestion and manipulation. Very often the charge is made that the child has been "brainwashed" into believing that abuse did or did not occur. Clearly, the child needs protection. A separate attorney (guardian ad litem) is usually appointed by the court to represent the child in the litigation. Guidelines may exist in the state on who can interview the child and in what setting. Trained child counselors are commonly used. Using special, anatomically correct dolls, the counselor will ask the child to describe what happened. These interviews are usually videotaped. When the time comes for a court hearing, the judge will often interview the child outside the courtroom (e.g., in the judge's chambers without either parent present).

ASSIGNMENT 9.6

Diane and George are the parents of Mary. When the child is two years old, the parents divorce. The decree awards Diane sole custody with visitation rights to George (on alternating weekends). Diane soon suspects that George is sexually abusing Mary during the visits. Answer the following questions for your state. (See General Instructions for the State-Code Assignment and General Instructions for the Court-Opinion Assignment in Appendix A.)

a. What options does Diane have?
b. Under what circumstances can the child be interviewed about the alleged molestation? Are there any restrictions on such interviews?
c. Can Diane be jailed for contempt of court if she refuses to obey an order to disclose Mary's location following a court decision that there was no sexual abuse by George? If so, for how long? Indefinitely?

CASE

Allen v. Farrow

197 A.D.2d 327, 611 N.Y.S.2d 859 (1994)
Supreme Court, Appellate Division, New York

Background: *Woody Allen is an internationally famous director and actor. His custody case generated widespread publicity. When it was over, Allen commented, "I was on the cover of every magazine, and magazines all over the world. I couldn't believe the amount of interest."*[18] *His opponent in the case was Mia Farrow, an actress who starred in thirteen of his movies. Allen had a romantic relationship with Farrow. She was formerly married to singer Frank Sinatra and conductor*

continued

[17]Fisk, *Abuse: The New Weapon,* National Law Journal, July 17, 1989, at 20.
[18]N.Y. Times, Sept. 29, 2000, at A58.

CASE

Allen v. Farrow—*Continued*

Andre Previn. (With Previn she had six children, three biological and three adopted. One of the adopted children was Soon-Yi Previn.) Farrow and Allen never married, but they had a child together, Satchel Farrow, and Allen adopted two of Farrow's other children, Moses Amadeus Farrow and Dylan O'Sullivan Farrow. The relationship between Allen and Farrow fell apart when Allen began a romantic relationship with Soon-Yi when she was nineteen or twenty-one years old. (There is some doubt about her date of birth in Korea.) At the time the affair began, Allen was fifty-seven years old. Farrow discovered the relationship after finding sexually explicit pictures that Allen took of Soon-Yi. Farrow also accused Allen of sexually abusing Dylan. (He was never criminally prosecuted for this charge.) A drawn-out, well-financed, and highly publicized custody trial ensued. Allen (the petitioner) went to court asking for custody of Satchel, Moses, and Dylan or for better visitation than Farrow was allowing him. He objected to supervised visitation. The trial court denied his request. Farrow (the respondent) was granted custody and counsel fees. Allen's visitation with the three children was severely limited: (1) He was granted supervised visitation with Satchel for two hours, three times a week. (2) Visitation with Dylan was to be "conducted in a therapeutic context" until the therapist recommends to the court that other visitation is appropriate. (3) Moses, now fifteen years old, refused to see Allen and the court refused to force him to do so. Allen has now appealed to the Supreme Court, Appellate Division.

Decision on Appeal: *The decision of the trial court in Farrow's favor on custody, visitation, and counsel fees is affirmed.*

Opinion of the Court:

Justice ROSS delivered the opinion of the court. . . .

The petitioner and the respondent have brought themselves to this unhappy juncture primarily as a result of two recent events. These are, Mr. Allen's affair with Soon-Yi Previn and the alleged sexual abuse of Dylan O'Sullivan Farrow by Mr. Allen. While the parties had difficulties which grew during Ms. Farrow's pregnancy with Satchel, it was the discovery of the relationship between Mr. Allen and Ms. Previn that intensified Ms. Farrow's concerns about Mr. Allen's behavior toward Dylan, and resulted in the retention of counsel by both parties. While various aspects of this matter remain unclear, it is evident that each party assigns the blame for the current state of affairs to the other.

The parties' respective arguments are very clear. The petitioner maintains that he was forced to commence this proceeding in order to preserve his parental rights to the three infant children, because the respondent commenced and continues to engage in a campaign to alienate him from his children and to ultimately defeat his legal rights to them. The petitioner contends, inter alia, that the respondent seeks to accomplish her goals primarily through manipulation of the children's perceptions of him. He wishes to obtain custody, ostensibly to counteract the detrimental psychological effects the respondent's actions have had on his children, and to provide them with a more stable atmosphere in which to develop. Mr. Allen specifically denies the allegations that he sexually abused Dylan and characterizes them as part of Ms. Farrow's extreme overreaction to his admitted relationship with Ms. [Soon-Yi] Previn.

The respondent maintains that the petitioner has shown no genuine parental interest in, nor any regard for, the children's welfare and that any interest he has shown has been inappropriate and even harmful. Respondent cites the fact that the petitioner has commenced and maintained an intimate sexual relationship with her daughter Soon-Yi Previn, which he has refused to curtail, despite the obvious ill effects it has had on all of the children and the especially profound effect it has had on Moses. It is also contended that petitioner has at best, an inappropriately intense interest in, and at worst, an abusive relationship with, the parties' daughter Dylan. Further, the respondent maintains that petitioner's contact with the parties' biological son, Satchel, is harmful to the child in that petitioner represents an emotional threat and has on at least one occasion threatened physical harm. Respondent contends that the petitioner's only motive in commencing this proceeding was to retaliate against the allegations of child sexual abuse made against him by Ms. Farrow.

Certain salient facts concerning both Mr. Allen's and Ms. Farrow's relationships to their children and to each other are not disputed. Review of these facts in an objective manner and the conclusions that flow from them, demonstrate that the determination of the [trial] court as to both custody and visitation is amply supported by the record before this Court.

From the inception of Mr. Allen's relationship with Ms. Farrow in 1980, until a few months after the adoption of Dylan O'Sullivan Farrow on June 11, 1985, Mr. Allen wanted nothing to do with Ms. Farrow's children. Although Mr. Allen and Ms. Farrow attempted for approximately six months to have a child of their own, Mr. Allen did so apparently only after Ms. Farrow promised to assume full responsibility for the child. Following the adoption however, Mr. Allen became interested in developing a relationship with the newly adopted Dylan. While previously he rarely spent time in the respondent's apartment, after the adoption of Dylan he went to the respondent's Manhattan apartment more often, visited Ms. Farrow's Connecticut home and even accompanied the Farrow family on vacations to Europe. Allen also developed a relationship with Moses Farrow, who had been adopted by the respondent in 1980 and was seven years old at the time of Dylan's adoption. However, Allen remained distant from Farrow's other six children.

In 1986 Ms. Farrow expressed a desire to adopt another child. Mr. Allen, while not enthusiastic at the prospect of the adoption of Dylan in 1985, was much more amenable to the idea in 1986. Before the adoption could be completed Ms. Farrow became pregnant with the parties' son Satchel. While the petitioner testified that he was happy at the idea of becoming a father, the record supports the finding that Mr. Allen showed little or no interest in the pregnancy. It is not disputed that Ms. Farrow began to withdraw from Mr. Allen during the pregnancy and that afterwards she did not wish Satchel to become attached to Mr. Allen.

According to Mr. Allen, Ms. Farrow became inordinately attached to the newborn Satchel to the exclusion of the other children. He viewed this as especially harmful to Dylan and began spending more time with her, ostensibly to make up for the lack of attention shown her by Ms. Farrow after the birth of Satchel. Mr. Allen maintains that his interest in and affection for Dylan always has been paternal in nature and never sexual. The various psychiatric experts who testified or otherwise provided reports did not conclude that Allen's behavior toward Dylan prior to August of 1992 was explicitly sexual in nature. However, the clear consensus was that his interest in Dylan was abnormally intense in that he made inordinate demands on her time and focused on her to the exclusion of Satchel and Moses even when they were present.

The record demonstrates that Ms. Farrow expressed concern to Allen about his relationship with Dylan, and that Allen expressed his concern to Ms. Farrow about her relationship with Satchel. In 1990 both Dylan and Satchel were evaluated by clinical psychologists. Dr. Coates began treatment of Satchel in 1990. In April of 1991 Dylan was referred to Dr. Schultz, a clinical psychologist specializing in the treatment of young children with serious emotional problems.

In 1990 at about the same time that the parties were growing distant from each other and expressing their concerns about the other's relationship with their youngest children, Mr. Allen began acknowledging Farrow's daughter Soon-Yi Previn. Previously he treated Ms. Previn in the same way he treated Ms. Farrow's other children from her prior marriage, rarely even speaking to them. In September of 1991 Ms. Previn began to attend Drew College in New Jersey. In December 1991 two events coincided. Mr. Allen's adoptions of Dylan and Moses were finalized and Mr. Allen began his sexual relationship with their sister Soon-Yi Previn.

In January of 1992, Mr. Allen took the photographs of Ms. Previn, which were discovered on the mantelpiece in his apartment by Ms. Farrow and were introduced into evidence at the [trial court] proceeding. Mr. Allen in his trial testimony stated that he took the photos at Ms. Previn's suggestion and that he considered them erotic and not pornographic. We have viewed the photographs and do not share Mr. Allen's characterization of them. We find the fact that Mr. Allen took them at a time when he was formally assuming a legal responsibility for two of Ms. Previn's siblings to be totally unacceptable. The distinction Mr. Allen makes between Ms. Farrow's [older adopted children] and Dylan, Satchel and Moses is lost on this Court. The children themselves do not draw the same distinction that Mr. Allen does. This is sadly demonstrated by the profound effect his relationship with Ms. Previn has had on the entire family.

Allen's testimony that the photographs of Ms. Previn ". . . were taken, as I said before, between two consenting adults wanting to do this . . ." demonstrates a chosen ignorance of his and Ms. Previn's relationships to Ms. Farrow, his three children and Ms. Previn's other siblings. His continuation of the relationship, viewed in the best possible light, shows a distinct absence of judgment. It demonstrates to this Court Mr. Allen's tendency to place inappropriate emphasis on his own wants and needs and to minimize and even ignore those of his children. At the very minimum, it demonstrates an absence of any parenting skills.

We recognize Mr. Allen's acknowledgment of the pain his relationship with Ms. Previn has caused the family. We also note his testimony that he tried to insulate the rest of the family from the "dispute" that resulted, and tried to "de-escalate the situation" by attempting to "placate" Ms. Farrow. It is true that Ms. Farrow's failure to conceal her feelings from the rest of the family and the acting out of her feelings of betrayal and anger toward Mr. Allen enhanced

continued

CASE

Allen v. Farrow—*Continued*

the effect of the situation on the rest of her family. We note though that the reasons for her behavior, however prolonged and extreme, are clearly visible in the record. On the other hand the record contains no acceptable explanation for Allen's commencement of the sexual relationship with Ms. Previn at the time he was adopting Moses, or for the continuation of that relationship at the time he was supposedly experiencing the joys of fatherhood.

While the petitioner's testimony regarding his attempts to de-escalate the dispute and to insulate the family from it, displays a measure of concern for his three children, it is clear that he should have realized the inevitable consequences of his actions well before his relationship with Ms. Previn became intimate. Allen's various inconsistent statements to Farrow of his intentions regarding Ms. Previn and his attempt to have Dr. Schultz explain the relationship to Dylan in such a manner as to exonerate himself from any wrong doing, make it difficult for this Court to find that his expressed concern for the welfare of the family is genuine.

As we noted above, Mr. Allen maintains that Ms. Farrow's allegations concerning the sexual abuse of Dylan were fabricated by Ms. Farrow both as a result of her rage over his relationship with Ms. Previn and as part of her continued plan to alienate him from his children. However, our review of the record militates against a finding that Ms. Farrow fabricated the allegations without any basis. . . . [There is evidence to] suggest that the abuse did occur. While the evidence in support of the allegations remains inconclusive, it is clear that the investigation of the charges in and of itself could not have left Dylan unaffected.

Any determination of issues of child custody or visitation must serve the best interests of the child and that which will best promote the child's welfare (*Domestic Relations Law* § 70; *Eschbach v. Eschbach,* 56 N.Y.2d 167, 171). . . . It was noted by the [trial] court that the psychiatric experts agreed that Mr. Allen may be able to fulfill a positive role in Dylan's therapy. We note specifically the opinion of Dr. Brodzinsky, the impartial expert called by both parties, who concluded that contact with Mr. Allen is necessary to Dylan's future development, but that initially any such visitation should be conducted in a therapeutic context. The [trial] court structured that visitation accordingly and provided that a further review of Allen's visitation with Dylan would be considered after an evaluation of Dylan's progress.

Although the investigation of the abuse allegations have not resulted in a conclusive finding, all of the evidence received at trial supports the determination as to custody and visitation with respect to this child. There would be no beneficial purpose served in disturbing the custody arrangement. Moreover, even if the abuse did not occur, it is evident that there are issues concerning Mr. Allen's inappropriately intense relationship with this child that can be resolved only in a therapeutic setting. At the very least, the process of investigation itself has left the relationship between Mr. Allen and Dylan severely damaged. The consensus is that both Mr. Allen and Ms. Farrow need to be involved in the recovery process. The provision for further review of the visitation arrangement embodied in the trial court's decision adequately protects the petitioner's rights and interests at this time.

With respect to Satchel, the [trial] court denied the petitioner's request for unsupervised visitation. While the court stated that it was not concerned for Satchel's physical safety, it was concerned by Mr. Allen's "demonstrated inability to understand the impact that his words and deeds have upon the emotional well being of the children". We agree. The record supports the conclusion that Mr. Allen may, if unsupervised, influence Satchel inappropriately, and disregard the impact exposure to Mr. Allen's relationship with Satchel's sister, Ms. Previn, would have on the child. His failure to understand the effect of such exposure upon Satchel as well as upon his other children is evidenced by his statement on direct examination in which he stated:

> If you ask me personally, I would say the children, the children adore Soon Yi, they adore me, they would be delighted, if you asked me this personally, I would say they would be delighted and have fun with us, being taken places with us. But, I don't want to give you my amateur opinion on that. That's how I feel. And I know it counts for very little.

The record indicates that Ms. Previn when not at college spends most of her time with Mr. Allen. Contact between Ms. Previn and her siblings in the context of the relationship with Mr. Allen would be virtually unavoidable even if Mr. Allen chose to insulate his children from the relationship. Expert medical testimony indicated that it would be harmful for Ms. Previn not to be reintegrated into the family. However, the inquiry here concerns the best interests of Dylan, Moses and Satchel. Their best interests would be clearly be served by contact with their sister Soon-Yi, personally and not in Mr. Allen's presence. Seeing both Ms. Previn and Mr. Allen together in the unsupervised context envisioned by Mr. Allen would, at this early stage, certainly be detrimental to the best interests of the children. It has been held that the desires of the child are to be considered, but that it must be kept in mind that those desires can be manipulated (*Friederwitzer v. Friederwitzer,* 55 N.Y.2d 89, 94). In considering the custody and visitation decision concerning Moses, who is now a teenager, we cannot ignore his expressed desires. The record shows that he had a beneficial relationship with the petitioner prior to the events of December 1991. However, that relationship has been gravely damaged. While Moses' feelings were certainly affected by his mother's obvious pain and anger, we concluded that it would not be in Moses' best interests to be compelled to see Mr. Allen, if he does not wish to.

Therefore, we hold that in view of the totality of the circumstances, the best interests of these children would be served by remaining together in the custody of Ms. Farrow, with the parties abiding by the visitation schedule established by the trial court.

With respect to the award of counsel fees we note that the record demonstrates that Mr. Allen's resources far outpace those of Ms. Farrow. Additionally, we note the relative lack of merit of Mr. Allen's position in commencing this proceeding for custody. It became apparent, during oral argument, that there was serious doubt that Mr. Allen truly desired custody. It has been held that "in exercising its discretionary power to award counsel fees, a court should review the financial circumstances of both parties together with all the other circumstances of the case, which may include the relative merit of the parties' positions" (*DeCabrera v. Cabrera-Rosete,* 70 N.Y.2d 879, 881). We find no abuse of discretion in the court's award of counsel fees in this case.

Accordingly, the judgment [below] . . . , which, inter alia, denied the petitioner Woody Allen's request for custody of Moses Amadeus Farrow, Dylan O'Sullivan Farrow, and Satchel Farrow, set forth the terms of visitation between the petitioner and his children and awarded Ms. Farrow counsel fees, is affirmed in all respects, without costs.

CARRO, Justice (dissenting in part).

I agree with the majority's conclusions, except for the affirmance of the order of visitation with respect to Mr. Allen's son Satchel, which I find unduly restrictive.

There is strong evidence in the record from neutral observers that Mr. Allen and Satchel basically have a warm and loving father-son relationship, but that their relationship is in jeopardy, in large measure because Mr. Allen is being estranged and alienated from his son by the current custody and visitation arrangement. Frances Greenberg and Virginia Lehman, two independent social workers employed to oversee visitation with Satchel, testified how "Mr. Allen would welcome Satchel by hugging him, telling him how much he loved him, and how much he missed him." Also described by both supervisors "was a kind of sequence that Mr. Allen might say, I love you as much as the river, and Satchel would say something to the effect that I love you as much as New York City . . . then Mr. Allen might say, I love you as much as the stars, and Satchel would say, I love you as much as the universe." Sadly, there was also testimony from those witnesses that Satchel had told Mr. Allen: "I like you, but I am not supposed to love you;" that when Mr. Allen asked Satchel if he would send him a postcard from a planned trip to California with Ms. Farrow, Satchel said "I can't [because] Mommy won't let me;" and on one occasion when Satchel indicated that he wanted to stay with Mr. Allen longer than the allotted two-hour visit, "Satchel did say he could not stay longer, that his mother had told him that two hours was sufficient." Perhaps most distressing, Satchel "indicated to Mr. Allen that he was seeing a doctor that was going to help him not to see Mr. Allen anymore, and he indicated that he was supposed to be seeing this doctor perhaps eight or ten times, at the end of which he would no longer have to see Mr. Allen."

In contrast to what apparently is being expressed by Ms. Farrow about Mr. Allen to Satchel, Mr. Allen has been reported to say only positive things to Satchel about Ms. Farrow, and conveys only loving regards to Moses and Dylan through Satchel. Thus I find little evidence in the record to support the majority's conclusion that "Mr. Allen may, if unsupervised, influence Satchel inappropriately, and disregard the impact exposure to Mr. Allen's relationship with Satchel's sister, Ms. Previn, would have on the child."

The majority's quotation of Mr. Allen's testimony with respect to Soon-Yi in support of its conclusion respecting visitation should be viewed in the context of Dr. David Brodzinsky's testimony. Dr. Brodzinsky is an expert in adoption with considerable experience in court-related evaluations of custody and visitation disputes. . . . It was his clinical judgment that Mr. Allen had more awareness of the consequences of his actions than he was able to articulate in the adversarial process, and he was optimistic about Mr. Allen's ability to accept his share of responsibility for what had taken place in light of his love for his children, his capacity for perspective-taking and empathy, and his motivation and openness toward the ongoing therapeutic process. In

continued

CASE

Allen v. Farrow—*Continued*

addition, Dr. Susan Coates, Satchel's therapist until December 1992, and the only expert to testify about Satchel's mental health, stated that Mr. Allen's parental relationship with Satchel was essential to Satchel's healthy development. . . .

I do not believe that Mr. Allen's visitation with Satchel for a mere two hours, three times a week, under supervision, is reasonable and meaningful under the circumstances, or that exceptional circumstances are presented that warrant such significant restriction on visitation with Satchel. Mr. Allen and Satchel clearly need substantial quality time together to nurture and renew their bonds and to foster a warm and loving father-son relationship. Obviously this cannot occur overnight; but more significantly, it is almost inconceivable that it will occur even over an extended period of time if visitation is limited to three two-hour periods per week under the supervision of strangers, as ordered by the trial court and affirmed by the majority. Accordingly I would modify the judgment appealed from to provide that Mr. Allen shall have unsupervised visitation with Satchel for four hours, three times weekly, plus alternate Saturdays and Sundays for the entire day, plus alternate holidays to be agreed upon by the parties.

ASSIGNMENT 9.7

a. Was Allen denied custody because of his immoral behavior?

b. (i) For Allen, prepare a list of factual allegations that support his position that he should be given custody rather than Farrow. (ii) For Farrow, prepare a list of factual allegations that support her position that she should be given custody rather than Allen. (iii) In class, be prepared to be called upon to debate who should have custody.

c. Is it relevant that Allen married Soon-Yi soon after the case?

d. What responsibility, if any, did the court assign to the behavior of Mia Farrow? Did she help cause Allen's deterioration with the children?

e. If Allen is correct that Farrow has poisoned his relationship with the children, wouldn't keeping him away from them reward her efforts?

f. The court said Allen agreed to have a biological child "apparently only after Ms. Farrow promised to assume full responsibility for the child." If Farrow did make this promise, what legal effect do you think it would have? For example, would it affect Allen's duty of child support?

g. The dissent says that in the "clinical judgment" of Dr. Brodzinsky, an adoption expert, "Allen had more awareness of the consequences of his actions than he was able to articulate in the adversarial process." What do you think Brodzinsky meant? Do you think a courtroom is the best place to resolve disputed custody cases? Is there an alternative?

BIOLOGICAL PARENT VS. PSYCHOLOGICAL PARENT

Thus far our main focus has been the custody dispute where the main combatants are the two biological parents. Suppose, however, that the dispute is between one biological parent and a third party such as a/an:

- Grandparent
- Other relative
- Former lover/stepparent (who never adopted the child)
- Foster parent (who is temporarily caring for the child at the request of the state)
- Neighbor
- Friend

Assume that the other biological parent is out of the picture because he or she has died, has disappeared, or does not care. The third party is usually someone with whom the child has established close emotional ties. Frequently, the child has lived with the third party for a substantial period of time. This may have occurred for a number of reasons:

- The biological parent was ill, out of the state, out of work, etc.
- The biological parent was in prison.
- The state asked the third party to care for the child temporarily as a foster parent (see chapter 14).
- The child could not stay at home because of marital difficulties between the biological parents.
- The biological parent was in school for substantial periods of time.
- The biological parent once considered giving the child up for adoption.

Third parties who have formed such emotional ties with a child are referred to as **psychological parents.**[19]

psychological parent
An adult who is not legally responsible for the care of a child, but who has formed a substantial emotional bond with the child.

There are two main schools of thought among courts when the custody dispute is between a biological parent and a psychological parent:

1. It is in the best interests of the child to be placed with its biological parent (this is a strong presumption).
2. It is in the best interests of the child to be placed with the adult who will provide the most wholesome, stable environment.

The emphasis of the first approach is on parental rights: unless you can show that the biological parent is *unfit,* he or she has the right to custody. The emphasis of the second approach is on the child's needs. Most states follow the first approach. In these states, the question is not whether the biological parent or the psychological parent can provide the best home for the child. The question is whether it is clear that placement with the biological parent would be harmful to the child. While the child may suffer some damage if his or her relationship with the psychological parent is severed, this does not necessarily overcome the biological parent's overriding right to have the child. The law is very reluctant to take children away from their natural parents because of a determination that someone else could do a better job raising them.

In practice, courts sometimes tend to blur the two approaches listed above. While maintaining allegiance to the doctrine of parental rights, the court might still undertake a comparison between the benefits to the child of living with the biological parent and the benefits of living with the psychological parent. When the benefits to be derived from the latter are overwhelming, the court might be more inclined to find unfitness in the biological parent or to conclude that giving custody to the biological parent would be detrimental to the child. The interpretation of the evidence can be very subjective. There is often enough data to support any conclusion the court wants to reach. A person's mistakes in raising children can be viewed either as an inability to be a competent parent or as an inevitable component of the nearly impossible job of parenting in today's society.

ASSIGNMENT 9.8

a. Are there any statutes in your state on how the court is to resolve a custody dispute between a biological parent and a psychological parent? If so, what do they say? (See General Instructions for the State-Code Assignment in Appendix A.)

continued

[19]See J. Goldstein, A. Freud, & A. Solnit, Beyond the Best Interests of the Child (1979).

b. Find an opinion written by a court in your state in which the dispute was between a biological parent and a psychological parent. Who won? Why? What standards did the judge apply? Were there other facts about the case that you wish the court had provided? If so, what facts and why would you want them? (See General Instructions for the Court-Opinion Assignment in Appendix A.)

c. Make up a fact situation involving a custody dispute between a biological parent and a psychological parent. *Make it a close case.* Include facts that would strongly favor each side. Now write a memorandum in which you discuss the law that would apply in your state to your case. Assume that you are working for the office that represents the psychological parent. (See General Instructions for the Legal-Analysis Assignment in Appendix A.)

CHANGING THE CHILD'S SURNAME

Once the court decides who receives custody, the custodial parent might request that the surname of the child be changed. For example, a mother might ask that the child's surname be changed to her maiden name or to a hyphenated surname that combines the father's surname and her maiden name. This change-of-name request might also be made at a later time in a separate proceeding. Assume that since birth the child has had the surname of the noncustodial parent. The court must determine whether the change is in the best interests of the child. The following excerpt from a court opinion explains the factors that most courts would consider in applying this standard:

> We first note that neither parent has a superior right to determine the initial surname their child shall bear. . . . However, once a surname has been selected for the child, be it the maternal, paternal, or some combination of the child's parents' surnames, a change in the child's surname should be granted only when the change promotes the child's best interests. In determining the child's best interests, the trial court may consider, but its consideration is not limited to, the following factors: the child's preference; . . . the effect of the change of the child's surname on the preservation and the development of the child's relationship with each parent; the length of time the child has borne a given name; the degree of community respect associated with the present and the proposed surname; and the difficulties, harassment or embarrassment, that the child may experience from bearing the present or the proposed surname.[20]

The court stressed what when the noncustodial parent objects to the change, the evidence that the change is in the best interests of the child should be "clear and compelling."

MODIFICATION OF THE CUSTODY ORDER BY THE STATE THAT ISSUED THE ORDER

In this section, we consider the modification of a custody order by the *same* state that issued the order. Assume that the court has jurisdiction to issue and modify custody orders. (We will focus on jurisdiction in the next section when we examine child snatching and special interstate problems.) While our discussion will focus on the two biological parents, the same principles apply no matter who is given custody by the original order.

---

[20]In re Saxton, 309 N.W.2d 298, 301 (Minn. 1981).

Two reasons justify a court in modifying its own custody order:

- There has been a significant change in circumstances since the original order, or
- Relevant facts were not made available to the court at the time of its original order.

In either situation, new facts are now before the court. The question becomes whether it is in the best interests of the child for the court to change its mind and award custody to the other parent. Given the disruption of such a change, the answer is no unless the new facts *substantially* alter the court's perception of the child's welfare. For example:

- The custodial parent has been neglecting or abusing the child.
- The custodial parent has moved from the area, contrary to the court's order, thus making visitation extremely difficult or impossible.
- The custodial parent has adopted an unorthodox lifestyle that has negatively affected the child's physical or moral development (or there is a danger that this lifestyle will have this effect).

It is not enough that the custodial parent has experienced hard times such as sickness or loss of a part-time job since the original order. Nor is it enough to show that mistakes have been made in raising the children. To justify a modification, the adverse circumstances or mistakes must be (1) ongoing, (2) relatively permanent, (3) serious, and (4) detrimental to the children. For an argument by a noncustodial parent on why custody should be changed, see the affidavit in support of a motion to modify custody in Exhibit 9.3.

Exhibit 9.3 Affidavit in Support of a Motion to Modify a Custody Decree

AFFIDAVIT IN SUPPORT
Index No. 3

STATE OF NEW YORK } ss.
COUNTY OF ______________

______________________, being duly sworn, deposes and says:

1. I am the defendant herein. This affidavit is submitted in support of an application for reconsideration of the decision of the court made in this action on _______, 20 _______, insofar as custody of my children is concerned.

2. Custody of the children has been awarded to my ex-wife, plaintiff. I did not contest her claim in the divorce. When I reported this to the children, they became extremely upset. My son told me that he did not want to live with his mother and that he felt it was unfair for a boy of his age to be forced to live with a parent contrary to his desires. My daughter had a similar reaction.

3. I tried to convey the situation to the Court by an informal application of reconsideration, on the strength of simple notes written to the Court by my children. My attorney advised me that the Court would not alter its determination.

4. I love my children very much. A history of prior proceedings between my wife and myself indicates that she had been awarded custody of the children under a Family Court order several years ago. At that time, she lived with the children in our house in Peekskill. I paid support, as directed for the children and my wife, and for the upkeep of the house. About two years ago my wife ousted my son from the house and sent him to live with me. At that time, I occupied a small apartment in Peekskill so that I could be near the children. I would see them quite often and would take them to school on many mornings. When my son came to me, I made room for him and we lived together until my daughter came to live with us about a year ago. We made room for her. My wife made no objections to the children living with me and made no attempts to get them to come back to her. While we all lived in my small apartment, my wife continued to live in the Peekskill house all by herself. I continued paying the upkeep on the house, although my wife permitted it to fall into a state of deteriorating disrepair. I contributed to her support.

5. I took care of my children as best I could. They were grown and attended school most of the day. In the evening we enjoyed a family life. We were together on the week-ends. There were many week-ends when their mother would not attempt to spend any time with them. My son stayed away from the Peekskill house. My daughter visited there with her mother on occasion. I know that on many occasions my wife stayed away from the Peekskill house for days at a time.

6. I have devoted my non-working hours to my children. I altered my schedule so that I would see them off to school each morning when I was not away from the City. If I was to be away, I would arrange adult supervision. I worked with my children on their homework and on anything else where they sought my participation. We shopped together and played together. My children were encouraged to maintain their friendships and to bring their friends to our home. Because of cramped quarters, my children would often visit with their friends and I encouraged them to maintain relationships with companions of their respective ages. I shared their problems and their joys. I tried to set responsible examples for them. My son had demonstrated to me that he is growing

continued

Exhibit 9.3 Affidavit in Support of a Motion to Modify a Custody Decree—*Continued*

into a responsible young man who aspires to attend Massachusetts Institute of Technology. I am proud of his seriousness and of his healthy outlook in times like this. I have tried to maintain a closely knit family between my children and myself so that they should know the advantages of love, companionship, and security. I know that they did not find any such relationship at their mother's bosom.

7. My children have revealed to me that they were wrong in not having made a definite choice during this interview with the court on the matter of their preference of a home. I understand that they will still love their mother and I have not attempted to sway them from that plateau. They told me that they wanted the court to decide the problem for them and that they had hoped that they could be the force which could solve the rift between plaintiff and myself. They were unaware that at the time of the interview, my wife's prayer for divorce had already been granted. My son told me that he indicated to the court that he preferred to live with me although he did not state, unequivocally, that he did not desire to live with his mother.

8. I gather from my children's reaction and from what they have told me that they misunderstood what was required of them during their interview with the court. I submit that another interview should be granted if the court feels that my children's affidavits are insufficient to establish their desires. Had I not seen the effect of the custody decision on my children and had they not indicated their grief over it, I would sit back and abide by the will of the court.

9. I seriously question my wife's fitness as our children's custodian. She voluntarily relinquished their custody, as aforesaid. Under adverse living conditions (cramped quarters), my children have thrived and demonstrated a progression toward adulthood. I believe that my wife's having been competitive instead of being cooperative with the children operated to compromise their welfare. I believe that using the children as a pawn has lost our children's respect. I feel that my pleasures must be subservient to the welfare of my children. They deserve as real a home as can be possible under the circumstances. They are entitled to eat a meal in peace and one which shows concern in its preparation. I believe that the children deserve some security in the knowledge that they have the genuine care and love of a parent. I believe that they cannot get this from their mother.

10. WHEREFORE, I respectfully pray that this application be granted and that upon reconsideration I be awarded custody of my children.

[*Signature*]

____

Source: J. Marino, McKinney's Forms, Form 14:24B and 14:33A (West 1976).

ASSIGNMENT 9.9

a. Are there any statutes in your state specifying the conditions for modifying a custody order that was issued within your state? If so, what are they? (See General Instructions for the State-Code Assignment in Appendix A.)

b. Find an opinion in which a custody order issued in your state was modified by a court in your state. What was the modification? Why was it ordered? What standards did the court use? Were there other factors about the case that you would have liked to have had? If so, what facts and why would you want to know about them? (See General Instructions for the Court-Opinion Assignment in Appendix A.)

c. Make up a fact situation involving a case in which sole custody was granted to one parent, but the other parent is now seeking a modification. *Make it a close case.* Include facts that support a modification and facts that support a continuation of the status quo. Now write a memorandum in which you discuss the law that would apply in your state to your case. Assume that you are working for the office that represents the party who wants to prevent the other side from modifying the order. (See General Instructions for the Legal-Analysis Assignment in Appendix A.)

d. Read Exhibit 9.3 containing an affidavit in support of a motion to modify a custody decree. Do you think the court should reconsider the custody order as requested? What further facts, if any, would you like to have? (See General Instructions for the Investigation-Strategy Assignment in Appendix A.)

JURISDICTIONAL PROBLEMS AND CHILD SNATCHING

We have been discussing the modification of a child-custody order by the state that issued the order. Suppose, however, that a party tries to have the order modified by *another* state. Consider the following sequence:

> *Dan and Ellen are divorced in New York where they live. Ellen receives custody of their child. Dan moves to Delaware. During a visit of the child in Delaware, Dan petitions a Delaware court for a modification of the New York custody order. Ellen does not appear in the Delaware proceeding. Dan tells the Delaware court a horror story about the child's life with Ellen in New York. The Delaware court modifies the New York order on the basis of changed circumstances, awarding custody to Dan.*

Or worse:

> *Dan and Ellen's child is playing in the yard of a New York school. Dan takes the child from the yard and goes to Delaware without telling Ellen. Dan petitions a Delaware court for a modification of the New York custody order. If he loses, he tries again in Florida. If he loses, he tries again in another state until he finds a court that will grant him custody.*

The latter situation involves what has been commonly called *child snatching.* The parent "grabs" the child and then "shops" for a favorable forum **(forum shopping).** For years, the problem reached epidemic proportions.

forum shopping
Seeking a court that will be favorable to you. Traveling from court to court until you find one that will provide a favorable ruling.

Courts are caught in a dilemma. When a custody order is made, it is not a final determination by the court. Custody orders are always modifiable on the basis of changed circumstances that affect the welfare of the child. This rule is designed to help the child by making the court always available to protect the child. Under the traditional rule, if an order is not final, it is not entitled to *full faith and credit* by another state (i.e., another state is not required to abide by it). Hence other states are free to reexamine the case to determine whether new circumstances warrant a modification. To maintain flexibility, states require very little to trigger their jurisdiction to hear a custody case (e.g., the domicile or mere presence of the child in the state along with one of the parents). The result is chaos: scandalous child snatching and unseemly forum shopping.

The question, therefore, is how to cut down or eliminate child snatching and forum shopping without taking away the flexibility that courts need to act in the best interests of the child. One solution is to enact uniform statutes in every state that would clarify what can and cannot be done when a child is taken across state lines. State legislatures, however, tend to be protective of their independence and often resist the enactment of uniform legislation. This resistance changed relatively quickly after a top-rated television program *(60 Minutes)* gave dramatic exposure to the problem of child snatching and forum shopping. The publicity helped enact a state uniform law and a federal kidnaping law:

- The *Uniform Child Custody Jurisdiction and Enforcement Act*
- The *Parental Kidnaping Prevention Act*

Uniform Child Custody Jurisdiction and Enforcement Act

The **Uniform Child Custody Jurisdiction and Enforcement Act (UCCJEA)** is designed to avoid jurisdictional competition and conflict among state courts that can arise when parents shift children from state to state in search of a favorable custody decision. The UCCJEA is a revision of the Uniform Child Custody Jurisdiction Act (UCCJA), which was an earlier attempt to remedy the problem. Eventually, every state is expected to adopt the UCCJEA.

Two important questions are covered in the UCCJEA:

- When does a court in the state have the power or jurisdiction to make the *initial* decision on child custody?
- When will a court modify a custody order of another state?

Jurisdiction to Make the Initial Child-Custody Decision

Under the UCCJEA, mere physical presence of the child in the state is *not* sufficient to give the state jurisdiction to enter an initial custody order. Nor is the mere physical presence of a parent sufficient. There are three major foundations for custody jurisdiction under the UCCJEA:

- Home state custody jurisdiction
- Significant connection/substantial evidence (sc/se) custody jurisdiction
- Temporary emergency custody jurisdiction

home state
The state where the child has lived with a parent for at least six consecutive months immediately before the custody case begins in court, or since birth if the child is less than six months old.

Home state custody jurisdiction is the most important and has ultimate priority. It is based on where the child has lived for the last six months with a parent before the custody case began. For a summary of the three categories of child custody jurisdiction under the UCCJEA, see Exhibit 9.4.

Exhibit 9.4 Jurisdiction to Make an Initial Custody Decision under the Uniform Child Custody Jurisdiction and Enforcement Act (UCCJEA)

1. *Home state custody jurisdiction*

—This state is the home state of the child. A home state is the state in which the child has lived with a parent* for at least six consecutive months immediately before the custody case is commenced in court. If the child is less than six months old, the home state is the state where the child has lived since birth. (Temporary absences count as part of the six months or as part of the time since birth.) *Or*
—This state *was* the home state of the child within six months before the custody case was begun and the child is now absent from the state, but a parent continues to live in this state.

2. *Significant connection/substantial evidence (sc/se) custody jurisdiction*

—No other state is the home state of the child (or if another state is the home state, it has declined to exercise the custody jurisdiction that it has). *And*
—The child and at least one parent have a *significant connection* with this state other than mere presence in this state. *And*
—There is *substantial evidence* in this state concerning the child's care, protection, training, and personal relationships.

3. *Temporary emergency custody jurisdiction*

—The child is present in the state. *And*
—The child has been abandoned or there is an emergency requiring protection of the child because the child, a sibling, or a parent is being mistreated or abused or threatened with mistreatment or abuse (domestic violence).
—*Note:* Temporary emergency custody jurisdiction can be exercised by a state that does not have home state or sc/se jurisdiction. The need to protect the child takes precedence. But the custody order made by a court with temporary emergency jurisdiction will remain in effect only until a state with home state or sc/se jurisdiction intervenes. Hence temporary emergency jurisdiction has a lower priority than home state jurisdiction or sc/se jurisdiction.

*Or anyone acting as a parent.

inconvenient forum
The state or jurisdiction where it is not as convenient to litigate a matter as another state or jurisdiction.

Assume that a court has jurisdiction to make the initial custody decision because it is the home state or the state with sc/se. Nevertheless, this court may decline to exercise this jurisdiction because it determines that it is an **inconvenient forum.** The state may determine that another state is a more convenient forum and defer to it. How does a state decide whether it is an inconvenient forum? There is no rigid formula. It will consider a number of factors. Assume, for example, that Oregon has home state jurisdiction, but that one of the parents is asking a Tennessee court to make the initial custody decision.

Here are some of the factors an Oregon court will consider in determining whether Tennessee is a more convenient forum for the parties to litigate the custody matter:

- *Domestic violence.* If domestic violence has been committed or threatened in Tennessee, an Oregon court might decide that Tennessee is in the best position to protect the parties. If so, Tennessee would be the most convenient state to make the custody decision.
- *Length of time the child has been outside the state.* If the child has spent more of its life in Tennessee than in Oregon, an Oregon court might decide that Tennessee is the most convenient state to make the custody decision.
- *Relative financial circumstances of the parties.* If litigating the custody case in Oregon would impose extreme financial burdens on the party in Tennessee and if the party in Oregon would have the financial resources to litigate in Tennessee, then an Oregon court might decide that Tennessee would be the most convenient forum to make the custody decision.
- *Nature and location of the evidence.* If the important evidence needed to resolve the custody matter (including the testimony of the child) is in Tennessee, then an Oregon court might decide that Tennessee would be the most convenient forum to make the custody decision.

The decision is discretionary with Oregon. In our example, it has home state custody jurisdiction and has the right to exercise it. The UCCJEA encourages, but does not require, such a state to relinquish its jurisdiction if it decides that another state would be a more convenient place—forum—to render the custody decision.

ASSIGNMENT 9.10

a. Fred and Jane were married in Iowa on January 1, 2000. On March 13, 2000, they had a child, Bob. From the first day of their marriage, however, they began having marital difficulties. On July 4, 2000, Fred moved to California. Bob continued to live with his mother in Iowa. By mutual agreement, Fred can occasionally take the child to California for visits. After a scheduled one-day visit on November 5, 2000, Fred decides not to return the child. He keeps Bob until November 1, 2001, when he returns him to Jane. Fred then joins the Army. When he returns on October 6, 2003, he discovers that Jane has been beating Bob.

Assume that both Iowa and California have enacted the UCCJEA. Which state would have jurisdiction to determine the custody of Bob on the following dates:

April 4, 2000
November 6, 2000
January 1, 2001
December 1, 2001
October 6, 2003

See General Instructions for the Legal-Analysis Assignment in Appendix A.

b. Interview Fred. See General Instructions for the Interviewing Assignment in Appendix A.

Jurisdiction to Modify a Custody Order of Another State

Thus far we have examined the jurisdiction of a state to make an *initial* custody order. We have addressed the questions of when a court has jurisdiction to decide the custody question for the first time, and if more than one state is involved, which is the most convenient forum. We now turn to the question,

When does one state have jurisdiction to modify a custody order of another state?

exclusive, continuing jurisdiction
The authority of a court, obtained by compliance with the UCCJEA, to make all initial and modifying custody decisions in a case to the exclusion of courts in any other state.

The guiding principle is that once a court has made an initial custody order under the UCCJEA, that court has **exclusive, continuing jurisdiction** (ecj) over the case. *Continuing* means that the case is kept open; *exclusive* means that no other court has authority to act in the case. Hence a court in State X cannot modify a child custody order issued in State Y if State Y has ecj because of compliance with the UCCJEA.

Another state can modify State Y's order only if State Y loses its ecj. There are two circumstances under which a state can lose its ecj:

- First, when the child and its parents no longer reside in the state ("parent" under the UCCJEA always includes anyone acting as a parent);
- Second, when the court with ecj determines that the child and parents do not have a significant connection to the state and that substantial evidence is no longer available in the state concerning the child's care, protection, training, and personal relationships.

Suppose, for example, that Connecticut issues an initial custody order and has ecj. The dissatisfied parent then takes the child to Maine. Can a Maine court modify the Connecticut order? Not if one of the parents remains in Connecticut. The dissatisfied parent would have to go back to Connecticut to ask the Connecticut court to modify its order or to ask the Connecticut court to declare that the child and parents do not have a significant connection to Connecticut and that substantial evidence on the child's welfare is no longer available in Connecticut.

An exception exists when there is an emergency, but only on a temporary basis. A state court with temporary emergency custody jurisdiction (see Exhibit 9.4) can modify the custody decision of any other court if the child is present in the state and has been abandoned or if there is an emergency requiring protection of the child because the child, a sibling, or a parent is being mistreated or abused or threatened with mistreatment or abuse (domestic violence). If a Maine court concluded that it had temporary emergency jurisdiction because of abandonment or violence in Maine, the Maine court could issue a custody order that would have the effect of modifying the Connecticut order. (A Maine court, for example, might issue a protective or restraining order keeping a violent parent away from the child until a further hearing is held.) As indicated in Exhibit 9.4, however, temporary emergency jurisdiction *is temporary*. A court with home state or sc/se jurisdiction—Connecticut in our example—can step in and change (modify) the temporary emergency custody order of Maine.

There is another circumstance in which Connecticut might yield to Maine. As we saw earlier, a state with proper custody jurisdiction under the UCCJEA can always make a determination that another state is a more convenient forum and thereby relinquish its jurisdiction. If Connecticut decides that it is an inconvenient forum and that Maine is a more convenient forum, Maine would thereby obtain full jurisdiction to act in the case.

dirty hands
Wrongdoing or other inappropriate behavior that would make it unfair or inequitable to allow a person to assert a right or defense he or she would normally have.

When a parent has **dirty hands,** a court might decline to exercise its jurisdiction if doing so would not harm the child. Suppose, for example, that a parent engages in blatant forum shopping by moving a child from state to state for the sole purpose of trying to find a friendly court. In the unlikely event that this parent eventually finds a court that has jurisdiction under the UCCJEA, this court can decline to take the case because of the parent's dirty hands. But the court will make such a decision only if it determines that the refusal to take the case would not harm the child.

ASSIGNMENT 9.11

a. Ted and Ursula Jackson have one child, Sam. Sam was born on March 13, 2000, in State A, where everyone has lived since the beginning of 2000. Upon discovering that Ted is having an affair with an office worker, Ursula on May 1, 2000, takes Sam to State B, where her parents live. On May 1, 2000, could Ted go to a court in State A to obtain a custody order? Could Ursula obtain one in State B on May 1, 2000?

b. Assume that Ursula eventually obtains a custody order in State B. Assume further that State B had proper jurisdiction to issue this order. Under what circumstances, if any, could Ted obtain a modification of this order in a court in State A?

(See General Instructions for the Legal-Analysis Assignment in Appendix A.)

ASSIGNMENT 9.12

a. Find a court opinion in your state in which your state refused to modify the custody order of another state. Why did it refuse?

b. Find a court opinion of your state in which your state modified the custody order of another state. Why did it do so? (See General Instructions for the Court-Opinion Assignment in Appendix A.)

c. Is the opinion you discussed in part (a) consistent with the opinion you discussed in part (b)?

Parental Kidnaping Prevention Act

Thus far we have been talking about *state* laws on child custody jurisdiction. There is also a *federal* statute designed to combat child snatching and forum shopping: the **Parental Kidnaping Prevention Act (PKPA).** Congress was concerned that the lack of nationwide consistency in state custody laws contributed to a tendency of parties "to frequently resort to the seizure, restraint, concealment, and interstate transportation of children, the disregard of court orders, excessive relitigation of cases, obtaining of conflicting orders by the courts, . . . and interstate travel and communication that is so expensive and time consuming." To help combat this problem, Congress enacted the PKPA. As indicated earlier, all states are eventually expected to adopt the UCCJEA. When they do, there will not be as great a need for the PKPA, since the UCCJEA (unlike its predecessor, the UCCJA) establishes clear guidelines on when a state can issue or modify a child-custody order. Until the UCCJEA is adopted everywhere, however, the PKPA can help reduce child snatching and forum shopping.

The PKPA addresses the question of when one state *must* enforce (without modification) the custody decree of another state. Phrased another way, when must one state give *full faith and credit* to the custody decree of another state? First, the state that rendered the custody decree must have had jurisdiction according to its own laws. Additionally, one of the following conditions must be met as of the time the state rendered its custody decree:

> (A) such state (i) is the home State of the child on the date of the commencement of the proceeding, or (ii) had been the child's home State within six months before the date of the commencement of the proceeding and the child is absent from such State because of his removal or retention by a contestant or for other reasons, and a contestant continues to live in such State;
>
> (B)(i) it appears that no other State would have jurisdiction under subparagraph (A), and (ii) it is in the best interest of the child that a court of such State assume jurisdiction because (I) the child and his parents, or the

child and at least one contestant, have a significant connection with such State other than mere physical presence in such State, and (II) there is available in such State substantial evidence concerning the child's present or future care, protection, training, and personal relationships;

(C) the child is physically present in such State and (i) the child has been abandoned, or (ii) it is necessary in an emergency to protect the child because he has been subjected to or threatened with mistreatment or abuse;

(D)(i) it appears that no other State would have jurisdiction under subparagraph (A), (B), (C), or (E), or another State has declined to exercise jurisdiction on the ground that the State whose jurisdiction is in issue is the more appropriate forum to determine the custody of the child, and (ii) it is in the best interest of the child that such court assume jurisdiction; or

(E) the court has continuing jurisdiction. . . .

In these circumstances, the custody order shall be given full faith and credit by another state. Another state "shall not modify" it. Once a court has proper jurisdiction to render a custody decree, this jurisdiction continues so long as this state remains the residence of the child *or* of any party claiming a right to custody.

Congress also made available to the states the *Federal Parent Locator Service,* which will help to locate an absent parent or child for the purpose of enforcing laws on the unlawful taking or restraint of a child or for the purpose of making or enforcing a child-custody determination. Previously, this service has been used mainly in child-support cases (see chapter 10).

Finally, the PKPA expressly declared the intent of Congress that the federal Fugitive Felon Act applies to state felony cases involving parental kidnaping and interstate or international flight to avoid prosecution. The state prosecutor may formally present a request to the local U.S. Attorney for a federal unlawful flight to avoid prosecution (UFAP) warrant.

ASSIGNMENT 9.13

Is it a crime for a parent in your state to take his or her child from the other parent without the consent of the latter? Check the statutes and cases of your state. (See General Instructions for the State-Code Assignment and General Instructions for the Court-Opinion Assignment in Appendix A.)

CHILDREN ABROAD: SPECIAL PROBLEMS

The following material deals with child abduction over international borders. As we have seen, parental kidnaping within the United States can lead to complex jurisdictional problems. These problems multiply when the child is taken out of the country.

International Parental Child Abduction

United States Department of State
Office of Children's Issues (1997)

Introduction

When a U.S. citizen child is abducted abroad, the U.S. State Department's Office of Children's Issues (CI) works with U.S. embassies and consulates abroad to assist the child and left-behind parent in a number of ways. Since the late 1970's, we have been contacted in the cases of approximately 11,000 American children who were either abducted from the United States or prevented from returning to the United States by one of their parents. Despite the fact that children are taken across international borders, child custody disputes remain fundamentally private legal matters between the parents involved, over which the Department of State has no jurisdiction. If a child custody dispute cannot be settled amicably between the parties, it often must be resolved by judicial proceedings in the country where the child is located. You, as the deprived parent, must direct the search and recovery operation yourself.

Cross-Cultural Marriages: Should You or Your Child Visit the Country of the Other Parent?

Many cases of international parental child abduction are actually cases in which the child traveled to a foreign country with the approval of both parents but was later prevented from returning to the United States. While these cases are not abductions, but wrongful retentions, they are just as troubling to a child. Sometimes the marriage is neither broken nor troubled, but the foreign parent, upon returning to his or her country of origin, decides not to return to the U.S. or to allow the child to do so. A person who has assimilated a second culture may find a return to his or her roots traumatic and may feel a pull to shift loyalties back to the original culture. A person's personality may change when he or she returns to the place where he or she grew up. In some traditional societies, children must have their father's permission and a woman must have her husband's permission to travel. If you are a woman, to prevent your own or your child's detention abroad, find out about the laws and traditions of the country you plan to visit or to allow your child to visit, and consider carefully the effect that a return to his roots might have on your husband.

Precautions That Any Vulnerable Parent Should Take

In international parental child abduction, an ounce of prevention is worth a pound of cure. Be alert to the possibility and be prepared—keep a list of the addresses and telephone numbers of the other parent's relatives, friends, and business associates both here and abroad. Keep a record of important information on the other parent, including these numbers: passport, social security, bank account, driver's license, and auto license. In addition, keep a written description of your child, including hair and eye color, height, weight, and any special physical characteristics. Take color photographs of your child every six months. If your child should be abducted, this information could be vital in locating your child. The National Center for Missing and Exploited Children (NCMEC, 1-800-843-5678) suggests that you teach your child to use the telephone; practice making collect calls; and instruct him or her to call home immediately if anything unusual happens. If you feel your child is vulnerable to abduction, get professional counseling. Do not merely tell a friend or relative about your fears.

The Importance of a Custody Decree

Under the laws of many American states and many foreign countries, if there is no decree of custody prior to an abduction, both parents are considered to have equal legal custody of their child. If you are contemplating divorce or separation, or are divorced or separated, or even if you were never legally married to the other parent, obtain a decree of sole custody or a decree that prohibits the travel of your child without your permission or that of the court as soon as possible. If you have or would prefer to have a joint custody decree, make certain that it prohibits your child from traveling abroad without your permission or that of the court. Obtain several certified copies of your custody decree from the court that issued it. Give a copy to your child's school and advise school personnel to whom your child may be released.

U.S. Passports

From the Department of State, you may learn whether your child has been issued a U.S. passport. You may also ask that your child's name be entered into the State Department's passport name check system. This will enable the Department to notify you or your attorney if an application for a U.S. passport for the child is received anywhere in the United States or at any U.S. embassy or consulate abroad. If you have a court order that either grants you sole custody or prohibits your child from traveling without your permission or the permission of the court, the Department may also refuse to issue a U.S. passport for your child. The Department may not, however, revoke a passport that has already been issued to the child.

Foreign Passports—The Problem of Dual Nationality

Many U.S. citizen children who fall victim to international parental abduction possess dual nationality. While the Department of State will make every effort to avoid issuing a U.S. passport if the custodial parent has provided a custody decree, the Department cannot prevent embassies and consulates of other countries in the United States from issuing their passports to children who are also their nationals. You can, however, ask a foreign embassy or consulate not to issue a passport to your child. Send the embassy or consulate a written request, along with certified complete copies of any court orders addressing custody or the overseas travel of your child that you have. In your

continued

International Parental Child Abduction—*Continued*

letter, inform them that you are sending a copy of this request to the U.S. Department of State. If your child is only a U.S. citizen, you can request that no visa for that country be issued in his or her U.S. passport. No international law requires compliance with such requests, but some countries may comply voluntarily.

International Parental Kidnapping Crime Act

The IPKCA makes it a Federal offense to remove a child from the United States or retain a child (who has been in the United States) outside the United States with intent to obstruct the exercise of parental rights (custody or visitation). The FBI is responsible for investigating the IPKCA. Once a warrant has been issued for the abductor's arrest, you can ask local law enforcement authorities or the FBI to enter the abductor's name in the "wanted persons" section of the National Crime Information Center (NCIC) computer and the INTERPOL system.

Contact the National Center for Missing and Exploited Children (NCMEC)

With the searching parent's permission, the child's photograph and description may be circulated to the media in the country to which you believe the child may have been taken. At the same time that you report your child missing, you should contact a lawyer to obtain a custody decree if you do not already have one. In many states, a parent can obtain a temporary custody decree if the other parent has taken their child.

What the State Department Can Do:

- assist parents in filing an application with foreign authorities for return of the child if the Hague Convention on the Civil Aspects of International Child Abduction applies (see below);
- attempt, in other cases, to locate, visit and report on the child's general welfare;
- provide the left-behind parent with information on the country to which the child was abducted, including its legal system, family laws, and a list of attorneys there willing to accept American clients;
- provide a point of contact for the left-behind parent at a difficult time;
- monitor judicial or administrative proceedings overseas;
- assist parents in contacting local officials in foreign countries or contact them on the parent's behalf;
- provide information concerning the need for use of federal warrants against an abducting parent, passport revocation, and extradition from a foreign country to effect return of a child to the U.S.; and
- alert foreign authorities to any evidence of child abuse or neglect.

What the State Department Cannot Do:

- intervene in private legal matters between the parents;
- enforce an American custody agreement overseas (U.S. custody decrees are not automatically enforceable outside of U.S. boundaries);
- force another country to decide a custody case or enforce its laws in a particular way;
- assist the left-behind parent in violating foreign laws or reabduction of a child to the United States;
- pay legal or other expenses;
- act as a lawyer or represent parents in court;
- translate documents

The Hague Convention

The most difficult and frustrating element for most parents whose child has been abducted abroad is that U.S. laws and court orders are not usually recognized in the foreign country and therefore are not directly enforceable abroad. Each sovereign country has jurisdiction within its own territory and over persons present within its borders, and no country can force another to decide cases or enforce laws within its confines in a particular way.

The Hague Convention on the Civil Aspects of International Child Abduction is a treaty that seeks to deter international child abduction. It applies to abductions or wrongful retentions between party countries. As of January 1, 1997, the Convention is in effect between the United States and Argentina, Australia, Austria, Bahamas, Belize, Bosnia-Herzegovina, Burkina Faso, Canada, Chile, Colombia, Croatia, Cyprus, Czech Republic, Denmark, Ecuador, Finland, former Yugoslav Republic of Macedonia, France, Germany, Greece, Honduras, Hungary, Iceland, Ireland, Israel, Italy, Luxembourg, Mauritius, Mexico, Monaco, Netherlands, New Zealand, Norway, Panama, Poland, Portugal, Romania, St. Kitts & Nevis, Slovenia, Spain, Sweden, Switzerland, United Kingdom, Venezuela, and Zimbabwe.

What Is Covered by the Convention

The Hague Convention is a private civil legal mechanism available to parents seeking the return of, or access to, their child. As a private civil law mechanism, the parents, not the governments, are parties to the legal action. The countries that are parties to the Convention have agreed that, subject to certain limited exceptions and conditions outlined below, a child who is habitually resident in one country that is a party to the Convention and who is removed to or retained in another country that is party to the Convention in breach of the left-behind parent's custody rights shall be promptly returned to the country of habitual residence. The Convention also provides a means for helping parents to exercise visitation rights abroad. There is a treaty obligation to return an abducted child below the age of 16 if application is made within one year from the date of the wrongful removal or retention, unless one of the exceptions to return applies. After one year, the court may still be obligated to order the child returned unless the person resisting return demonstrates that the child is settled in the new environment. A court may refuse to order a child returned if there is a grave risk that the child would be exposed to physical or psychological harm or otherwise placed in an intolerable situation in his or her country of habitual residence. A court may also decline to return the child if the child objects to being returned and has reached an age and degree of maturity at which the court can take account of the child's views. Finally, the return of the child may be refused if the return would violate the fundamental principles of human rights and freedoms of the country where the child is being held. These exceptions have been interpreted narrowly by courts in the United States and by some other countries party to the Convention.

Where to Go for Assistance

Office of Children's Issues (CI)
Overseas Citizens Services
Department of State
2201 C Street, N.W., Room 4817
Washington, D.C. 20520-4818
202-736-7000
http://travel.state.gov
http://travel.state.gov/int'lchildabduction.html

National Center for Missing and Exploited Children (NCMEC)
[See Appendix I for the address and World Wide Web site.]

SUMMARY

Legal custody and physical custody can be given to one parent or to both parents. In negotiating custody and visitation terms of a separation agreement, many factors need to be considered, such as the age and health of the parents and child, the emotional attachments of the child, the work schedules of the parents, etc. If negotiations fail and the parties cannot agree, litigation is necessary. This can be a stressful experience, not only for the parents but also for the person caught in the middle—the child.

The court has considerable discretion in resolving a custody battle between two biological parents according to the standard of the best interests of the child. It will consider a number of relevant factors such as stability in the child's life, availability to respond to the child's day-to-day needs, emotional ties that have already developed, etc. At one time, courts applied evidentiary guidelines such as the presumption that a child of tender years is better off with his or her mother. Today courts reject gender-based presumptions, although fathers continue to complain that the mother is still given an undue preference.

The moral values and lifestyles of the parent seeking custody are generally not considered by the court unless they affect the welfare of the child. Domestic violence that affects the child's welfare is also a factor. If the parents practice different religions, the court cannot prefer one religion over another, but can consider what effect the practice of a particular religion will have on the child. To the extent possible, the court will try to maintain continuity in the child's cultural development. The custody decision cannot be based on race. If the child is old enough to express a preference, it will be considered. Often the court will also consider the testimony of expert witnesses.

The court will generally favor liberal visitation rights for the noncustodial parent. Occasionally, such rights will be granted to individuals other than biological parents (e.g., grandparents), if doing so does not interfere with the constitutional right of a fit parent to make child rearing decisions. One of the most distressing issues in this area is the charge by the custodial parent that the child has been sexually molested during visitation. Such an allegation may lead to a denial of visitation or to visitation only when supervised by another adult, usually a professional.

When the custody battle is between a biological parent and a nonparent (often called a psychological parent), the biological parent usually wins unless he or she can be shown to be unfit. If the parents disagree on whether the child's surname should be changed, the court will resolve the issue on the basis of whether the change is in the best interests of the child.

Occasionally, it is in the best interests of the child for a court to modify an earlier custody decision because of changed circumstances. Frantic parents will sometimes engage in child snatching and forum shopping in order to find a court that will make a modification order. To cut down on this practice, two important laws have been enacted: the state Uniform Child Custody Jurisdiction and Enforcement Act and the federal Parental Kidnaping Prevention Act. The primary tool used by these statutes to cut down on forum shopping is to give priority to the child's home state among possible competing states that could be asked to issue or modify a custody decision. When the child has been taken to a foreign country, the aid of the Hague Convention on Child Abduction might be enlisted.

KEY CHAPTER TERMINOLOGY

best interests of the child
tender years presumption
physical custody
custodial parent
legal custody
joint physical custody
joint legal custody
split custody
contested
mediation
guardian ad litem
parental alienation syndrome
primary caregiver presumption
supervised visitation
Minnesota Multiphasic Personality Index Test (MMPI)
psychological parent
forum shopping
Uniform Child Custody Jurisdiction and Enforcement Act (UCCJEA)
home state
inconvenient forum
exclusive, continuing jurisdiction
dirty hands
Parental Kidnaping Prevention Act (PKPA)

ETHICS IN PRACTICE

You are a paralegal working at the law office of Harris and Harris, which represents William Norton in a custody dispute with his wife, Irene Norton. Irene is represented by Davis & Davis. Your supervisor asks you to prepare some interrogatories to be sent to Irene about her employment. You are not sure whether to include questions about her pension plan. Before you write any pension questions, you call Irene and ask her if she has a pension plan at her work. She is very cooperative, telling you that she does not have a pension. You then go back to drafting the interrogatories. Any ethical problems?

ON THE NET: MORE ON CHILD CUSTODY

Professional Academy of Custody Evaluators (PACE)
http://www.pace-custody.org/home.html

Kidmate (joint custody software)
http://www.kidmate.com

Win Child Custody (how to win or defend custody cases)
http://www.winchildcustody.com

Kidshare (software tool for negotiating child custody)
http://www.kidshare.com

Abuse-Excuse (unfounded claims of child abuse)
http://www.abuse-excuse.com

DadsDivorce
http://www.dadsdivorce.com

CHAPTER 10

CHILD SUPPORT

CHAPTER OUTLINE

INTRODUCTION

As we have seen, family law is primarily governed by state law. One of the rallying cries of states' rights enthusiasts is that we don't want federal courts telling us when someone can be divorced or adopted. By and large, state control over family law has remained intact. This was also true of the law of child support until the 1970s, when Congress began passing laws that offered funding to states that complied with federal standards for the enforcement of child-support orders. This led to major changes in every state. One of the most significant was to require employers to withhold child-support payments from the paychecks of delinquent parents, usually noncustodial parents who did not have physical custody of their children. Congress determined that letting every state design its own child-support system was not working in light of the growing number of children living in poverty and the enormity of the cost assumed by welfare agencies (primarily financed with federal funds) when noncustodial parents abandoned their child-support obligations. While the changes have dramatically increased child-support collection, the problem has not been solved. The average amount of child support received by a custodial parent is $3,543 per year.[1] This covers less than half of a child's support needs.

---

[1]Statistical Abstract of the United States: 1998, table 632.

We begin our examination of child support with an overview of the considerations facing a divorcing couple in their separation agreement—before child-support agencies and the courts become involved.

SEPARATION AGREEMENT

When the parties are negotiating the child-support terms of a separation agreement, they need to consider a wide range of factors:

- According to state guidelines, what is the minimum amount of child support that must be paid to the custodial parent? Do the parents want to exceed the minimum? If they have the resources to meet the minimum, they cannot agree to a child-support amount that is *lower* than what the guidelines mandate. (Yet there is a danger that a parent might agree to accept a very modest amount of child support out of fear that the other parent will contest custody or will commit physical violence.) When the separation agreement eventually comes before the court for approval, the child-support terms will be rejected if they fall below the minimum specified by the guidelines, which we will consider in detail later. Parents cannot bargain away the basic need of their children for support.
- What standard of living was the child accustomed to during the marriage?
- Do the providers of support have the financial resources to maintain this standard of living?
- What are the tax considerations? First, unlike alimony, child-support payments are not deductible by the provider (see chapter 11). Consequently, the provider or payor may try to convince the other parent to agree to a lower child-support payment in exchange for a higher alimony payment in order to take advantage of the deduction. Alimony payments, unlike child-support payments, are taxable to the recipient. Hence, the alimony recipient (payee) will usually want some other benefit to compensate for the increased taxes that will result from agreeing to the higher alimony and lower child-support payments (e.g., some extra benefit in the property division terms of the separation agreement). Second, which parent will claim the child as a dependency exemption? If the noncustodial parent wants to claim the child, the custodial parent must agree to cooperate by telling the Internal Revenue Service (IRS) that he or she is releasing the exemption. The separation agreement should specify how the parents propose to handle this tax benefit.

- On what day is each payment to be made?
- How many payments are to be made? One covering everyday expenses and a separate one covering large, emergency expenses (e.g., hospitalization)?
- Will there be security for the payments (e.g., a trust account, an escrow account that can be used in the event of nonpayment)?
- Is the child to be covered by medical insurance? If so, who pays the premiums?
- When the provider dies, is his or her estate obligated to continue payments? If so, must the provider's will so state?
- Is the child to be the beneficiary of a life insurance policy on the life of the provider? If so, for how much, who pays the premiums, and can the beneficiaries be changed by the provider? Does the payment of premiums (and hence the insurance coverage) end when the child reaches the age of majority?

- Is there an escalation clause? Do the support payments fluctuate with the income of either of the parents?
- Do the support payments fluctuate with the income of the child (e.g., summer jobs, inheritance)?
- Do they fluctuate in relationship to the Consumer Price Index?
- Do the payments end or change when the child reaches a certain age, marries, moves out of the house, or becomes disabled?
- What educational expenses will be covered by the provider? Tutors, preparatory school, college, graduate/professional school, room, board, books, transportation, entertainment expenses while at school, etc.?
- Is the amount of child support reduced for every day the child spends overnight visiting the noncustodial parent (or a relative of the noncustodial parent)? If so, is the reduction a dollar amount or a percentage of each payment?
- When the child is away at school, does the provider have to continue sending child-support payments to the custodial parent? Are payments reduced during these periods? If so, by how much?
- Do school payments go to the custodial parent or directly to a child away at school?
- If disputes arise between the parents concerning child-support payments, what happens? Arbitration? Mediation?

As indicated, parents cannot agree to support a child at an amount lower than the minimum required by state guidelines. Also, many states do not allow parents to agree that child support will be paid as a one-time, lump-sum payment. Attempts to remove a parent's *continuing* obligation of support are void in such states. The case of *Straub v. B.M.T.* presents an even more extreme example of what parents cannot attempt to accomplish through agreement.

CASE

Straub v. B.M.T.

626 N.E.2d 848 (1993)
Court of Appeals of Indiana

Background: *Edward Straub and Francine Todd are having an affair. Straub impregnates her after she agreed not to hold him responsible for children born from the union. But three years after the birth of a child to them (referred to as B.M.T. by the court), Todd sued Straub for child support. The trial court ordered him to pay $130 per week. Straub appealed. The case is now on appeal before the Court of Appeals of Indiana.*

Decision on Appeal: *Affirmed. The agreement to relieve a father of financial responsibility was void as a matter of public policy.*

Opinion of the Court:

Judge MILLER delivered the opinion of the court. . . .

Straub and Todd began dating in 1985 when both were teachers at the same elementary school. In late 1986, Todd [aged 33] discussed her desire to have a child with Straub after her doctor informed her that artificial insemination would not work. Straub told Todd that he did not want the responsibility of another family due to his age [58] and the fact that he already had children from a previous marriage. However, when Todd threatened to end their relationship, he agreed to try to impregnate her providing she would sign a "hold harmless" agreement. On December 15, 1986, Straub presented Todd with a holographic agreement purporting to hold Straub harmless from financial and emotional support of a child which might result from the couple's sexual relations. . . . That document, Petitioner's Exhibit #8, reads in its entirety as follows:

> "To Whom it may concern. I Francine Todd in sound mind & fore thought have decided not to marry, but would like to have a baby of my own. . . . I have approached several men who will not be held responsible financially or emotionally who's [sic] names will be kept secret for life. Signed *Francine Todd*. . . .

Edward continued to have sexual relations with Francine after the child's birth but did not establish a relationship with the child. He stopped seeing Francine after she filed this action. . . .

I. Is the Agreement against Indiana's Public Policy?

Indiana has long recognized the obligation of both parents to support their children. In *Matter of M.D.H.* (1982), Ind. App., 437 N.E.2d 119, 126, the court noted that current statutory provisions relating to support orders for legitimate and illegitimate children are virtually identical. The court stated, "[A] parent's obligation to support his minor child, legitimate or illegitimate, is *a basic tenet recognized in this state by statutes* that provide civil and criminal sanctions against parents who neglect such duty. . . ." Id. at 127 (emphasis added).* . . .

Straub first claims that "fundamental contract principles" allow him to contract around his statutory and common-law duty to provide support to his daughter. . . . It is well settled that a parent cannot, by his own contract, relieve himself of the legal obligation to support his minor children. In *Ort v. Schage* (1991), Ind. App., 580 N.E.2d 335, we held that an agreement to forego court ordered child support even in exchange for a benefit (social security payments) to the child is unenforceable because a parent has no right to contract away a child's support benefits. *Pickett v. Pickett* (1984), Ind. App., 470 N.E.2d 751. . . .

Public policy considerations mandate that the state take an active interest in providing for the welfare of illegitimate children in order to avoid placing an undue financial burden on its taxpayers. "The duty of parents to provide necessary support, care, and maintenance for their children, although arising out of the fact of their relationship, may be rested upon the interest of the state as *parens patriae* of children and of the community at large in preventing them from becoming a public burden, and is, therefore, a duty not only to themselves, but to the public as well. This duty is at the same time a legal and natural obligation, *the consistent enforcement of which is equally essential to the well-being of the state, the morals of the community, and the development of the individual.*" 59 *Am. Jur. 2d* Parent and Child § 51 (emphasis added). . . .

Finally, Straub argues that the agreement signed by Todd should be enforced because he was acting merely as a "sperm donor." He argues that we should follow cases from other jurisdictions which look to the pre-conception intent of the parties involved in deciding whether to enforce their agreement.

*Ind. Code 35-46-1-5(a) provides: A person who knowingly or intentionally fails to provide support to his dependent child commits nonsupport of a child, a Class D felony.

Straub's Brief at 25–27 citing *Davis v. Davis* (1993), Tenn., 842 S.W.2d 588.† We are not persuaded.

We first note, of course, arguing that Straub's and Todd's relationship was that of a sperm donor and donee ignores the facts. It is undisputed that Straub and Todd had an ongoing affair, one which began before Todd decided to become pregnant and only ended three years after B.M.T.'s birth when she decided to have a second child by Straub—after Straub had married someone else. Secondly, both parties testified, and the trial court found, that Straub and Todd continued to have intercourse after Todd became pregnant with B.M.T. and their relationship continued for a number of years after B.M.T.'s birth. We know of no medical requirements—or of any sperm donor program—that continues to give insemination injections after the donee becomes pregnant. . . . The trial court did not err in finding Straub's and Todd's agreement was void because it is against Indiana's public policy.

II. Indemnification

Straub argues that he should be indemnified against any support claims because: 1) Todd is capable of supporting the child on her own; and 2) the "economic injury" to Straub due to her "breach of contract" would exceed $100,000.00. Because this argument merely seeks to circumvent public policy, it too must fail. First, because the agreement between the parties is void, there is no enforceable contract to breach. Second, Todd's present ability to care for the child on her own and the cost of the support to Straub do not change the law—Straub must provide his share of his daughter's support as determined by the trial court under the Guidelines, which take into account both parent's incomes.** . . .

†If we were to accept Straub's argument, this type of contract would arguably be binding in a variety of situations. For example, a couple desirous of having a child, but for some reason—religious or otherwise—feels the child should be born in wedlock, could enter into a valid and binding antenuptial agreement absolving one of the parents from the duty to support the child after divorce. Similarly, an agreement made after marriage (and in contemplation of divorce) would also be binding.

**We must be ever mindful of the best interests of this child. Thus, B.M.T. has a right to more than the basic necessities of life. Specifically, she has a right to the lifestyle that her parent's combined income will furnish. This right may not be contracted away by her parents, and to do so is a violation of public policy. However, while we are not able to address every factual possibility, we recognize an exception may lie where the custodial parent is so affluent as to render the contribution of the non-custodial parent's income irrelevant to the child's lifestyle. In that case, the child's lifestyle may not be an issue, and it might be argued that the parents would not be contracting away the best interests of the child. Here, however, because Todd's only apparent income is her salary for teaching school, this appears to be a typical case wherein the child is entitled to the lifestyle that the combination of her parent's incomes will afford.

continued

CASE

Straub v. B.M.T.—*Continued*

The judgment of the trial court is affirmed.

Judge CONOVER, dissenting. . . .

Todd, an unmarried adult female teacher, wanted to have a child but did not want to remarry to accomplish that end. When she was medically advised artificial insemination would not work in her case, she asked her current lover Straub, a 56 year old adult male teacher, to cease using condoms during intercourse and impregnate her. Straub already had raised 5 children of his own. While willing to help, Straub neither wanted to raise another child nor assume the financial obligations concomitant with child rearing. Straub told Todd he would accommodate her if he could be free of the obligation to support the child-to-be and his name as inseminator would remain a secret. Agreeing, Todd, an employed teacher fully capable of supporting the child, signed a written agreement to that effect that Straub had prepared. In the normal course of things thereafter, Todd became pregnant. Three years after the child was born, Todd changed her mind. . . .

Today, the general public almost universally looks with understanding and approval upon a single woman's desire to bear and nurture a child without male interference. A financially responsible modern woman, at her option, has an unqualified right to do so, it perceives. In other words, our declarations on this subject are currently incorrect. They reflect policy which has been dead since the 1960's. Accordingly, they must be changed, in my view, because we are subject to the public's will in such matters.

I find no better statement of the vagaries of public policy than this: Public policy has been described as a will-o'-the-wisp of the law which varies and changes with the interests, habits, needs, sentiments, and fashions of the day; the public policy of one generation may not, under changed conditions, be the public policy of another. Thus, the very reverse of that which is public policy at one time may become public policy at another time. Hence, no fixed rules can be given by which to determine what is public policy for all time. When an alteration of public policy on any given point of general interest has actually taken place, and such alteration is indicated by long-continued change of conduct on the part of the people affected and has become practically universal, the court may recognize the fact and declare the public policy accordingly. . . .

I believe this change in public policy is readily discernible. . . . [A]n Indiana woman in this modern age has had an inalienable right to contract in any manner she chooses in the pursuit of her happiness. . . . Since the last obstructions to contractual equality due to womanhood have been removed, women are now irrevocably bound to perform the obligations they incur when contracting just as men are. Courts have neither the right nor the power in the name of public policy to intervene simply because the contracting woman with the benefit of hindsight determines she has made a bad bargain by entering into a contract of this kind. The courts now must leave the parties where they find them in such cases.

Thus, in my opinion, the contract in question is valid and enforceable because it is conversant with current public policy. Todd had an absolute right to contract with Straub as she did, and is absolutely bound by the obligations she incurred under that contract. . . . Todd is gainfully employed and fully capable of providing for all the needs of the child she so desperately wanted. Under current public policy, the contract she signed here is valid and enforceable. Neither the legislature nor the judiciary can act to impair the obligations she incurred thereunder because the record demonstrates the child will never become a ward of the state.

I would reverse.

ASSIGNMENT 10.1

a. Did this court hold that it would have reached a different result if Todd had been rich?

b. Who is correct? Judge Miller or Judge Conover? Is the majority opinion anti-woman?

c. As we will see in chapter 13 on paternity, a sperm donor who is not married to the mother is not considered the father of the child and, therefore, has no support obligation. Why didn't this rule apply in the *Straub* case?

d. In the discussion of the *Marvin v. Marvin* case in chapter 4 on cohabitation agreements, we learned that sexual intercourse cannot be a valid consideration for an enforceable contract. In the *Straub* case, was sexual intercourse consideration for the agreement between Straub and Todd? If so, is this another reason their agreement is invalid?

e. George and Helen are not married but are living together. George impregnates Helen. He asks her to have an abortion. She refuses. When the child is born, can she force George to support it? Would it make any difference if Helen became pregnant after lying to George about using contraceptives? (See General Instructions for the Legal-Analysis Agreement in Appendix A.)

JURISDICTION AND THE UNIFORM INTERSTATE FAMILY SUPPORT ACT

If the parents are married and are in the process of seeking a divorce, the custodial parent might ask a court for an award of temporary child support **pendente lite**—while the case is being resolved in court. At the conclusion of the case, the court will decide on permanent child support. What are the jurisdictional requirements for obtaining and enforcing a temporary or permanent child-support order?

pendente lite
While the litigation is going on.

As we learned in chapter 7, a divorce judgment can accomplish five objectives: (1) dissolve the marriage, (2) award spousal support, (3) award child support, (4) divide marital property, and (5) award child custody. The court needs more than one kind of jurisdiction to accomplish these objectives. (The kinds of divorce jurisdiction are summarized in Exhibit 7.3 in chapter 7.) Our focus here is the kind of jurisdiction needed for child support.

To award child support, the court needs **personal jurisdiction** (sometimes called *in personam jurisdiction*) over the defendant. If a court makes an order of child support against someone over whom it does not have personal jurisdiction, a court in another state does not have to enforce it (i.e., the support order is not entitled to full faith and credit).

personal jurisdiction
The power of a court to render a decision that binds an individual defendant.

How does a court acquire personal jurisdiction over a noncustodial parent in order to issue an enforceable child-support order? If the defendant is a resident of the state, the most common method is to hand deliver the divorce complaint and court summons to the defendant. This delivery is called personal or actual *service of process*. If the resident defendant cannot be found in the state, substituted service of process might be authorized such as service by mail.

A more serious problem is collecting child support from a *nonresident* parent. Approximately 34 percent of child-support cases are against parents who live in a state that is different from the state of the child and custodial parent. Efforts to collect child support from out-of-state parents have generally been ineffective. While 34 percent of cases involve an out-of-state parent, only 8 percent of all collections come from such parents. One reason for this poor record has been the difficulty of obtaining personal jurisdiction over the nonresident parent and the lack of uniformity in child support laws among the states. According to one court:

> [The] lack of uniformity in the laws regarding child support orders encouraged noncustodial parents to relocate to other states to avoid the jurisdiction of the courts of the home state. This contributed to the relatively low levels of child support payments in interstate cases and to inequities in child support payment levels that are based solely on the noncustodial parent's choice of residence.[2]

To help combat the problem, every state has recently enacted the **Uniform Interstate Family Support Act (UIFSA)** to govern many aspects of out-of-

Uniform Interstate Family Support Act (UIFSA)
A state law on establishing and enforcing support obligations against someone who does not live in the same state as the person to whom the support is owed.

[2] *Day v. Child Support Enforcement Division,* 272 Mont. 170, 900 P.2d 296, 300 (1995).

state support cases. Under the UIFSA, there are seven main ways a state can acquire personal jurisdiction over a nonresident defendant:

1. The nonresident is personally served within the state;
2. The nonresident submits to the jurisdiction of this state by consent, by entering a general appearance, or by filing a responsive document having the effect of waiving any contest to personal jurisdiction;
3. The nonresident resided with the child in this state;
4. The nonresident resided in this state and provided prenatal expenses or support for the child;
5. The child resides in this state as a result of the acts or directives of the nonresident;
6. The nonresident engaged in sexual intercourse in this state and the child may have been conceived by that act of intercourse;
7. The nonresident asserted parentage in the state such as through the putative father registry (see chapter 13).[3]

If nonresidents are not personally served within the state or if they do not consent to the court's jurisdiction (the first two conditions), they must have at least minimum contact with the state. Otherwise, the state cannot assert personal jurisdiction over the nonresident. Note the examples of minimum contacts listed in the UIFSA: residing in the state with the child at one time, arranging for the child to reside in the state, and engaging in sexual intercourse in the state that may have led to the conception of the child. Because these contacts with the state are considered sufficiently *purposeful,* it is fair and reasonable for a court in that state to resolve (i.e., to adjudicate) disputes arising out of those contacts. An example of such a dispute is whether the nonresident is the child's father and, therefore, should pay child support. The personal jurisdiction that a state acquires over a nonresident defendant because of his or her purposeful contact with that state is called **long-arm jurisdiction.** A statute authorizing it is called a long-arm statute. The state extends its "arm" of power across state lines to assert personal jurisdiction over someone who in fairness should answer to the authority of the court because of his or her sufficiently purposeful contacts with that state.[4]

long-arm jurisdiction
The personal jurisdiction that a state acquires over a nonresident defendant because of his or her purposeful contact with the state.

Let's examine two case examples:

> ***CASE I.*** *Ted and Wilma live in New York, where they were married. While on a two-week vacation in Maine, they conceive their only child, Mary. Upon returning to New York, they decide to separate. Wilma and Mary move to Maine. Except for the two-week vacation, Ted has never been to Maine. Before Wilma leaves, he tells her that if she moves to Maine, he will have nothing to do with her or Mary. She goes anyway, and Ted carries out his threat of having no contact with either. He never pays child support. After establishing domicile in Maine, Wilma obtains a divorce and a child-support order from a Maine court. Ted is never served in Maine and does not appear in Wilma's divorce action. He knows about the case because Wilma has mailed him all the divorce pleadings to which he never responds.*

Wilma's domicile in Maine gave the Maine court jurisdiction to dissolve the marriage. (See Exhibit 7.3 in chapter 7.) Under the UIFSA, Maine also had personal jurisdiction over Ted to make the child-support order. Ted's act of sexual intercourse in Maine leading to conception was a sufficiently pur-

---

[3] 9 Uniform Laws Annotated pt. 1, § 201 (Supp. 1996). An eighth basis of personal jurisdiction under the UIFSA is a catch-all option: "any other basis consistent with the constitutions of this state and the United States for the exercise of personal jurisdiction."

[4] The long-arm jurisdiction provisions of the UIFSA can also be used in the enforcement of *spousal* support orders against obligor spouses who live in another state. (See chapter 8.)

poseful contact with the state of Maine to give it personal jurisdiction over him.

Once personal jurisdiction is acquired over a nonresident in this way, issues such as paternity and child support can be resolved. Under the UIFSA, special rules exist in conducting the proceeding against the nonresident. For example, the Maine court can accept testimony from witnesses in New York by telephone, video, or other electronic means. Also, assuming Ted continues to refuse to come to Maine, a Maine court can ask a New York court to force Ted to submit to discovery on issues such as his financial resources.

Once Wilma has a valid Maine child-support order, she has two main enforcement choices. First, she can take the expensive and cumbersome (but traditional) step of traveling to New York in order to ask the New York court system to enforce her Maine order. Such travel, however, is impractical for most custodial parents. The same is true of hiring a New York attorney. Second, the UIFSA allows her to use a special *registration* procedure to enforce the Maine order in New York. Without traveling to New York, she can use a government child-support agency in Maine (called a **IV-D agency**) to help her send the Maine order to the appropriate tribunal in New York for the purpose of registering the order. (As we will see later, there is a IV-D agency in every state.) Once registered in New York, her order can then be enforced in the same manner as a New York order can be enforced against a New York resident with the help of a New York IV-D agency. Hence the UIFSA registration procedure has allowed a Maine resident (Wilma) to obtain and enforce a Maine support order against a New York resident (Ted) even though the process never required Wilma to travel to New York and never required Ted to travel to Maine. This efficiency was one of the main reasons the UIFSA was enacted.

IV-D agency
A state agency that attempts to enforce child-support obligations. (The name of these agencies comes from the fact that they were proposed in title IV-D of the Social Security Act.)

In our example, Maine is the **initiating state**—the state in which a support case is filed in order to forward it to another state. New York is the **responding state**—the state to which the case was forwarded for a response. A responding state can enforce, but cannot modify, an order registered from an initiating state.

initiating state
The state in which a support case is filed in order to forward it to another state (called the responding state) for enforcement proceedings under the UIFSA.

responding state
The state to which a support case is forwarded from an initiating state for enforcement proceedings under the UIFSA.

Suppose, however, that Maine *cannot* obtain personal jurisdiction over Ted under the long-arm provisions of the UIFSA. Let's change some of the facts of our example:

> ***CASE II.*** *Ted and Wilma live in New York, where they were married and where their only child, Mary, was conceived and born. They decide to separate. Wilma and Mary move to Maine. Ted has never been to Maine. Before Wilma leaves, he tells her that if she moves to Maine, he will have nothing to do with her or Mary. She goes anyway, and Ted carries out his threat of having no contact with either. He never pays child support. After establishing domicile in Maine, Wilma obtains a divorce and a child-support order from a Maine court. Ted is never served in Maine and does not appear in Wilma's divorce action. He knows about the case because Mary has mailed him all the divorce pleadings to which he never responds.*

The major fact difference between case I and case II is that Mary was not conceived in Maine. Reread the seven ways for a state to obtain personal jurisdiction over a nonresident under the UIFSA. *None* of them applies to Ted in case II. He was not personally served in Maine, he never consented to Maine jurisdiction, he never lived in Maine with his child, he never sent any child support to Maine, he never arranged for his daughter to live in Maine, he never had sexual intercourse in Maine, and he never asserted his parentage in Maine. Therefore, a Maine court could not obtain personal jurisdiction over Ted by the long-arm method in case II, and Wilma cannot use the efficient and inexpensive registration process in New York.

In case II, the Maine court's dissolution of the marriage is valid and enforceable because Wilma's domicile in Maine gave the court jurisdiction to dissolve the marriage. The Maine court also issued a child-support order against Ted. *This order, however, is not enforceable and not entitled to full faith and credit, since it was issued against a defendant over whom the court did not have personal jurisdiction.* This is an example of **divisible divorce,** which we studied in chapter 7; only part of the divorce judgment is enforceable.

divisible divorce
A divorce decree that is enforceable in another state only in part.

If Wilma wants child support from Ted, she will need a child-support order *from a New York court.* Obtaining a support order from a Maine court and registering it in New York for enforcement will not work, since Maine cannot obtain personal jurisdiction over Ted. Can New York obtain personal jurisdiction over Ted? Yes. This is relatively easy, since Ted is a New York resident.

To obtain a New York support order, does Wilma have to travel to New York and hire a New York attorney? Fortunately, under the UIFSA, the answer is no. Another efficient and inexpensive process is available to her. Here are the steps involved:

- Wilma files a petition for child support in Maine.
- A Maine IV-D agency helps her forward the petition to New York.
- New York obtains personal jurisdiction over Ted, a New York resident (e.g., by service of process in person or substituted service).
- New York conducts an administrative or judicial proceeding on issues such as paternity and child support.
- A New York IV-D agency uses its collection powers to force Ted to pay his support obligation.

In case II, Maine again is the initiating state and New York is the responding state. Everything is handled on Wilma's behalf by the IV-D agency in Maine and the IV-D agency in New York. At no time is Wilma required to appear in New York. Her testimony can be received in New York by telephone, video, or other electronic means.

Note the difference between case I and case II:

- Case I: A Maine support order is enforced against a New York resident in New York by the registration process.
- Case II: A New York support order is enforced against a New York resident in New York.

The difference is based on which state could obtain personal jurisdiction over Ted.

If Wilma does not want the IV-D agency to act on her behalf in Maine or New York, she can hire a private attorney to represent her. The role of the IV-D agency would then be to assist any attorney she decides to hire.

In our mobile society, parties move often. In such an environment, one judge commented that child-support orders can "proliferate like mushrooms."[5] Defendants such as Ted might start traveling to different states in order to try to find a court that will modify the child-support order against them. The UIFSA tries to prevent this.

Once a court issues a valid support order under the UIFSA, that court has **continuing, exclusive jurisdiction (cej)** over the case. This means that no other state can modify the order. A state retains its cej so long as the custodial parent (e.g., Wilma) or the noncustodial parent (e.g., Ted) or the child (e.g., Mary) continues to reside in the state. If they all leave the state, the court loses its cej, and another state can acquire cej over the case. (Another way for a court to lose its cej is if all the parties agree that another state can have cej to modify the order.)

continuing, exclusive jurisdiction (cej)
Once a court acquires proper jurisdiction to make an order, the case remains open and only that court can modify the order.

If, in spite of these rules, the parties have generated competing support orders from courts that have jurisdiction or if the parties seek simultaneous support orders in different states, the UIFSA gives preference to the order issued

[5]Thomas J. Devine, *From the Bench,* 24 Vermont Bar Journal & Law Digest 10 (Mar. 1998).

in the **home state.** This is the state in which a child has lived with a parent[6] for at least six consecutive months immediately before the support case was filed. If the child is less than six months old, the home state is the state in which the child has lived since birth with the parent. Periods of temporary absence are counted as part of the six months or the time since birth.[7] (As we saw in chapter 9, the home state is also the basis of determining child-custody jurisdiction in interstate cases.)

home state
The state where the child has lived with a parent for at least six consecutive months immediately before the case begins in court, or since birth if the child is less than six months old.

If a court has the authority to modify a child-support order, under what circumstances will it do so? We will examine this question in some depth later in the chapter.

WHO PAYS AND HOW MUCH?

The traditional rule was that only the father had the legal duty to support his children. Today each parent has an equal duty of support regardless of who has physical custody (the right to decide where the child resides) or who has legal custody (the right to make the major child rearing decisions on health, education, religion, discipline, and general welfare). A parent who does not have physical or legal custody has the same duty of support as the parent with both physical and legal custody. The essential question is, Who has the ability to pay? The mother, the father, or both? In practice, it is usually the father who is ordered to pay. He is the one who often controls most of the financial resources. If, however, the mother also has a salary or other available resources, she will be asked to contribute her proportionate share of the child's support.

What about a stepparent (someone who has married one of the natural parents)? If the stepparent has adopted the child formally or equitably (see chapter 15), there is a duty to support the child even after the marriage ends in divorce. Without adoption, however, most states say that the stepparent has no duty of support unless he or she has agreed otherwise.

How much child support do the parents owe? A child has many needs that must be paid for: shelter, food, clothing, education, medical care, transportation, recreation, etc. A court will consider a number of factors in determining the amount of child support. These factors are quite similar to what the parties must assess on this issue in their separation agreement:

- State guidelines—the most important (see discussion below).
- Standard of living enjoyed by child before the separation or divorce.
- Child's age.
- Child's own income or other financial resources (e.g., from a trust fund set up by a relative, from part-time employment).
- Income or other financial resources of custodial parent.
- Income or other financial resources of noncustodial parent.
- Earning potential of both parents.
- Child's need and capacity for education, including higher education.
- Financial needs of noncustodial parent.
- Responsibility of noncustodial parent to support others (e.g., a second family from a second marriage).

Note that marital fault is not on the list. Which parent was at fault in "causing" the divorce is not relevant and should not be considered in assessing the need for child support.

---

[6]Or a person acting as a parent.

[7]To further prevent proliferating child-support orders, Congress passed the Full Faith and Credit for Child Support Orders Act (FFCCSOA), 28 U.S.C. § 1738B, which requires states to enforce (i.e., give full faith and credit to) and not modify valid child support orders of other states except in limited circumstances.

child-support guidelines
A required method of determining the amount of child support that must be paid.

Every state has adopted **child-support guidelines** for the determination of child support by its courts. The guidelines establish a rebuttable presumption on the amount of child support that should be awarded:

> There shall be a rebuttable presumption . . . that the amount of the award which would result from the application of such guidelines is the correct amount of child support to be awarded. A written finding or specific finding on the record that the application of the guidelines would be unjust or inappropriate in a particular case, as determined under criteria established by the State, shall be sufficient to rebut the presumption in that case.[8]

While the guidelines are not the same in every state, many states have based their guidelines on the *income shares model,* which operates on the principle that the children should receive the same proportion of parental income that they would have received had the parents lived together. Studies have shown that individuals tend to spend money on their children in proportion to their income, and not solely on need. Child support is calculated as a *share* of each parent's income that would have been spent on the children if the parents and children were living in the same household. The calculation of these shares is based on the best available economic data on the amount of money ordinarily spent on children by their families in the United States. This amount is then adjusted to the cost of living for a particular state.

If a state does not use the income shares model in its guidelines, it will use one of several alternative models. Under the *percentage-of-obligor-income model,* the amount of child support is based on the number of children and a fixed percentage of the obligor's gross income. (An **obligor** is someone with a legal obligation. The **obligee** is the person to whom that legal obligation is owed.) For example, child support might be 17 percent of the obligor's gross income if there is one child, 25 percent if there are two children, 29 percent if there are three children, etc. Other models include the *Melson-Delaware model* and the *equal-living standard.* There may also be variations among states using the same model. For example, some states using the percentage-of-obligor-income model take a percentage of the obligor's after-tax (net) income rather than a percentage of his or her gross income.

obligor
One who has a legal obligation.

obligee
The person to whom a legal obligation is owed.

Whatever model a state uses, adjustments can be made when the parties have joint physical custody of the child or when a child has special medical or child care needs. There may also be separate guidelines when the combined incomes of the parents exceed a high amount, such as $100,000.

The calculation of child support under the guidelines is relatively mechanical. A number of commercial software companies sell computer programs that can be used to determine the amount of child support that should be due under the guidelines used by a particular state. Several IV-D agencies have placed calculation worksheets on their World Wide Web pages. This allows custodial parents, noncustodial parents, and others to enter their own financial data to determine the amount of child support that a IV-D agency or a court would impose. In Exhibit 10.1, there are examples of online worksheets from the Web pages of two state IV-D agencies.

Cost of College

A good deal of litigation has centered on the issue of educational expenses, particularly higher education. Does a divorced parent have a duty to send his or her child to college? Arguments *against* imposing this duty are as follows:

- A parent's support duty is limited to providing the necessities to the child (e.g., food, shelter, clothing). A large percentage of Americans do not attend college. It, therefore, is a luxury, not a necessity.

---

[8] 42 U.S.C.A. § 667(b)(2).

Exhibit 10.1 Examples of Online Worksheets to Calculate Child Support

Colorado Child Support Guidelines

Worksheet A—Sole Physical Custody

	Mother	Father	Combined
Noncustodial Parent	○ Mother	⊙ Father	
Number of Children	One Child ▼		
Monthly Gross Income	$	$	
Preexisting Child Support	$	$	
Maintenance Paid	$	$	
Responsibility for Other Children	$	$	
Monthly Adjusted Gross Income	$	$	$
Percentage Share	%	%	
Basic Obligation Adjustments			$
Child Care Costs (work related) **(will compute tax credit)**	$	$	
Health Insurance Premium Costs	$	$	
Extraordinary Medical Expenses	$	$	
Extraordinary Expenses	$	$	
Extraordinary Adjustments	$	$	
Total Adjustments	$	$	$
Total Obligation			$
Each Parent's Share	$	$	
Suggested Amount	$	$	

Colorado: <www.childsupport.state.co.us/gwsa.htm>

Massachusetts Child Support Guidelines

Calculation Worksheet - Short Form

BASIC ORDER

a) Non-custodial gross weekly income (less prior support orders actually paid, for child/family other than the family seeking this order)

b) % of gross/number of children (from Chart A - Basic Order) %

c) % increase for age (from Chart B - Age Differential) %

If custodial parent makes $15,000 or less please skip (d, e, and f).

d) Custodial parent gross (annual) income

e) Less day care cost (annual)

f) Non-custodial gross (annual) income

g) Less 50% weekly cost by noncustodial parent of family group health insurance [under the provisions of section G(1)]

Click "Calculate" for your Basic Order amount **Calculate** **Reset**

WEEKLY SUPPORT ORDER $

OPTIONAL SUPPORT CALCULATOR

a) Please enter your current weekly child support payment.

b) Please enter the amount from the "WEEKLY SUPPORT ORDER" above.

Calculate

Reset

The % difference of your current weekly child support payment and the calculated weekly support order from above. %

If you used this worksheet for the purpose of seeking modification, this is the percentage difference between your current obligation and what your obligation might be (based solely on the data you have just entered).

Massachusetts: <www.state.ma.us/cse/programs/employer/Quick.htm>

- A parent's support duty terminates when the child reaches the age of majority in the state (e.g., eighteen). Children in college will be over the age of majority during some or most of their college years.
- Children of parents who are still married have no right to force their parents to send them to college. Why should children of divorced parents have the right to be sent to college?

Some states, however, have rejected these arguments and have required the divorced parent to pay for a college education as part of the child-support payments if the parent has the ability to pay and the child has the capacity to go to college. Several arguments support this position:

- In today's society, college is not a luxury. A college degree, at least the first one, is a necessity.
- A parent's duty to provide child support does not terminate in all cases when the child reaches majority. For example, a physically or mentally disabled child may have to be supported indefinitely. Some courts take the position that the support duty continues so long as the child's need for support continues (i.e., so long as the child remains dependent). This includes the period when the child is in college.
- It is true that married parents have no obligation to send their children to college. But there is a strong likelihood they will do so if they have the means and their children have the ability. When the court requires a divorced parent to send his or her children to college, the same tests are applied: ability to pay and capacity to learn. Thus, the court, in effect, is simply trying to equalize the position of children of divorced parents with that of children of married parents.

The Second Family

Another area of controversy concerns the noncustodial parent's responsibility of supporting others. Should the amount of child support be less because this parent has since taken on the responsibility of supporting a second family? Suppose there is a remarriage with someone who already has children and/or they have additional children of their own. The old view was that the parent's primary responsibility was to the first family. No adjustment would be made because the parent has voluntarily taken on additional support obligations. Many courts, however, no longer take this hard line. While they will not permit the parent to leave the first family destitute, they will take into consideration the fact that a second family has substantially affected the parent's ability to support the first. Given this reality, an appropriate adjustment will be made. It must be emphasized, however, that not all courts are this understanding. Some continue to adhere to the old view.

ASSIGNMENT 10.2

a. How does a court determine the amount of child support in your state? Describe the main features of whatever guidelines exist and explain how they are used.

b. Make up a fact situation involving two parents (John Smith and Mary Smith) and one infant child (Billy Smith). Your facts should include the income and resources available to each parent. (i) How much would each parent owe in child support in your state? (ii) On the Internet, use the online worksheets of any two states to determine how much the Smiths would owe in child support in each state. Again, make up any financial facts that you need, but be sure to use the same facts each time you make a calculation for the Smiths.

c. Under what circumstances, if any, does a noncustodial parent have an obligation to pay for his or her child's college education in your state?

To answer questions a, b(i), and c, check your state code and opinions of courts in your state. (See General Instructions for the State-Code Assignment and General Instructions for the Court-Opinion Assignment in Appendix A.)

MODIFICATION OF CHILD-SUPPORT ORDERS

Earlier we discussed the procedural law of jurisdiction needed to impose or modify a child-support order. Now we examine the substantive law of modification itself. Assume that a court has jurisdiction to modify. When will it use that jurisdiction to make an actual modification?

The standard rule is that a child-support order can be modified on the basis of a substantial change of circumstances that has arisen since the court granted the order. The changed circumstances must be serious enough to warrant the conclusion that the original award has become inequitable (e.g., the child's welfare will be jeopardized if the child-support award is not increased due to an unexpected illness of the child, requiring costly medical care). Alternatively, the child-support award can be decreased if it is clear that the need no longer exists at all or to the same degree (e.g., if the child has acquired independent resources or moved out on his or her own). A recent federal law allows the parties to request a review of a child-support order every three years (or such shorter cycle as a state deems appropriate) to make sure that the order complies with the guidelines and to add cost-of-living adjustments as needed.[9]

Frequently, the custodial parent claims that child support should be increased because the noncustodial parent's ability to pay has increased since the time of the original order (e.g., by obtaining a much better paying job). This is a ground to increase child support only when it is clear that the original decree was inadequate to meet the needs of the child. At the time of the original decree, a lesser amount may have been awarded because of an inability to pay more *at that time.* Hence a later modification upward is simply a way for the court to correct an initially inadequate award. Since many initial awards *are* inadequate, courts are inclined to grant the modification.

Note that we have been discussing the modification of *future* child support payments. What about **arrearages?** Can a court modify a delinquent obligation? There was a time when courts were sympathetic to requests by delinquent obligors to forgive past due debts, particularly when the court was convinced that future obligations would be met. Congress changed this in 1986 when the Bradley Amendment banned retroactive modification of child-support arrearages in most cases.[10]

arrearage
Payments that are due but have not been made (also called **arrears**).

What happens when the noncustodial parent seeks a modification downward because he or she can no longer afford the amount originally awarded? If the circumstances that caused this change are beyond the control of the parent (e.g., a long illness), the courts will be sympathetic. Suppose, however, that the change is voluntary. For example:

> *At the time of a 2000 child-support order, Dan was a fifty-year-old sales manager earning $120,000 a year. The order required him to pay his ex-wife $3,000 a month in child support. In 2001, Dan decides to go to evening law school. He quits his job as a sales manager and takes a part-time job as an investigator earning $10,000 a year. He then petitions the court to modify his child-support payments to $250 a month.*

In many courts, Dan's petition would be denied because he has not lost the *capacity* to earn a high salary. Self-imposed poverty is not a ground to reduce child support in such courts. Other courts are not this dogmatic. They will grant the modification petition if:

- The child will not be left in a destitute condition and
- The petitioner is acting in good faith.

[9] 42 U.S.C.A. § 666(a)(10).
[10] 42 U.S.C.A. § 666(a)(9).

The court will want to know whether a legitimate change of career or change of lifestyle is involved. Is it the kind of change that the party would probably have made if the marriage had not ended? If so, the court will be inclined to grant a modification downward, so long as the child is not seriously harmed thereby. On the other hand, is the parent acting out of *bad faith* or malice (e.g., to make life more miserable for the custodial parent)? If so, the modification request will be denied.

imputed income
Income that will be assumed to be available regardless of whether it is actually available.

When parents improperly reduce their income capacity, a court can treat the amount of the reduction as if it is income that was actually earned. This **imputed income** will be used in the calculation of the amount of child support that is owed.

CASE

Goldberger v. Goldberger

96 Md. App. 313, 624 A.2d 1328 (1993)
Court of Special Appeals of Maryland

Background: *The Circuit Court awarded Esther Goldberger a divorce from Aron Goldberger and custody of their six children: Chana Frumit, Mamele, Meir, Chaim Tzvi, Eliezer, and Yaacov. The court also ordered Aron to pay $4,066 per month in child support for the six children. It found that he had impoverished himself voluntarily and that his potential income was $60,000 per year. The court based this figure on the amount of money others had contributed to his litigation expenses. The case is now on appeal before the Court of Special Appeals of Maryland. Aron is the appellant and Esther is the appellee.*

Decision on Appeal: *Affirmed in part; reversed in part. The trial court correctly concluded that Aron voluntarily impoverished himself but failed to properly calculate the amount he should pay for child support.*

Opinion of the Court:

Judge LEVITZ delivered the opinion of the court.

The odyssey of the young children of Aron and Esther Goldberger has led them from Lakewood, New Jersey, to Israel, to Belgium and England, and finally to Baltimore, Maryland. These children have been the subject of the attention of various courts including: The High Court of Justice, Family Division, London, England; the Ecclesiastical Court of the Chief Rabbi of London (Beth Din); and, finally, the Circuit Court for Baltimore City. [Eight judges of the Circuit Court (nearly 30% of the Bench) have been involved in the case to date.]

Prior to the trial of this matter before the Circuit Court, the parties and their children had been examined and evaluated by ten physicians or psychologists. When the trial began, Esther and Aron Goldberger were fighting only about the custody of their children and related matters of support and visitation. Allegations of sexual child abuse, kidnapping, insanity and unfitness were made by one or the other of the parents. Other extended family members were brought into the conflict and took an active part in it. Since both parties are devout Orthodox Jews, noted Rabbis in this country and in Europe and Israel were consulted by the parties for advice, guidance and support. . . .

[T]he evidence revealed that appellant was 32 years old and healthy, with many years of higher education. It was undisputed that appellant had earned no actual income, as he had never worked at any income-producing vocation. Appellant planned his life to be a permanent Torah/Talmudic student.* He was a student before he was married and before any of his children were born. Appellant testified that he studies "for the sake of studying, which is a positive commandment to study the Torah for the sake of studying it." Further, appellant testified that it was his intention to continue his life of study forever: ". . . I should continue to study the rest of my life, to always be in studying. . . ." Throughout his life appellant has been supported by others, first, his parents, thereafter, his father-in-law, and most recently, friends in the Orthodox community. Nevertheless, appellant fathered six children whom he has refused to support, arguing that he has no means to support and never will have the means to provide support.†

---

*The Torah is the "fundamental" law of the Jewish people. It consists of the five books of Moses (the Pentateuch): Genesis, Exodus, Leviticus, Numbers and Deuteronomy. It is considered to be of divine origin. The Talmud is an exposition of the fundamental oral and written law. It contains the rabbinic interpretation of the "fundamental" and "common" law.

†Rabbi Jacob ben Asher (1270–1340), known as the "Ba'al Ha Turim" and considered one of the great authorities on Jewish Law, stated in his authoritative digest, "A man can be forced to work in order to maintain his wife and infant children." Tur, Even Ha'ezec 70. Horwitz, *Spirit of Jewish Law.* Central Book Co. 1973.

A life devoted to study is viewed by many in the Orthodox community as a true luxury that very few can enjoy.** Unfortunately for the appellant's children, permanent Torah/Talmudic students must depend on the charity of others to provide the necessities of life. Those who support a Torah student have no legal obligation to continue such support in either duration or amount.

Nevertheless, through a network of family and Orthodox communities in Europe and the United States, approximately $180,000 had been contributed to appellant over a three year period to enable him to pursue his custody claim. Approximately $3,000 of that sum was once used to purge appellant of contempt for failing to pay child support.

Based on these facts, the court determined (1) that appellant had voluntarily impoverished himself, and (2) that his potential income was equivalent to the money that had been contributed by others to his cause. It therefore regarded his income, for purposes of paying child support as $60,000 per year and ordered that he pay $4,066 per month for the support of his six children. Appellant challenges both the finding of voluntary impoverishment and the calculation of potential income.

The obligation of parents to support their minor children has been consistently upheld by the Court of Appeals of Maryland. In *Carroll County v. Edelman,* 320 Md. 150, 577 A.2d 14, 23 (1990), the Court stated,

> Parenthood is both a biological and a legal status. By nature and by law, it confers rights and imposes duties. One of the most basic of these is the obligation of the parent to support the child until the law determines that he is able to care for himself. . . .

The legislature of Maryland has made it a crime for parents to fail to support their minor children. Md. Code Ann., Fam. Law § 10-203 (1991). . . .

In view of the above authorities, there can be no question that appellant has a legal obligation to financially support his children until they reach the age of legal majority. The more difficult question is how to calculate the proper amount of that support. Fortunately, that question has been answered by the Legislature of Maryland. Md. Code Ann., Fam. Law § 12-202(a)(1) (1991) states, "[I]n any proceeding to establish or modify child support, whether pendente lite or permanent, the court shall use the child support guidelines set forth in this subtitle." In order to use the guidelines as required by § 12-202(a)(1), it is necessary to calculate the income of the parents. "Income" is defined in § 12-201(b) of the Family Law Article as: (1) actual income of a parent, if the parent is employed to full capacity; or (2) potential income of a parent, if the parent is voluntarily impoverished.

The legislature's purpose in including potential income was to implement state and federal policy of requiring adequate support by precluding parents from avoiding their obligation by deliberately not earning what they could earn.

While the Code does not define the term "voluntarily impoverished," in *John O. v. Jane O.,* 90 Md. App. 406, 601 A.2d 149 (1992), we had occasion to address the meaning of that term. We noted that neither the Legislature nor the Courts in existing case law had defined what "voluntarily impoverished" meant. We noted that no clear definition was found in any Maryland resource materials. Accordingly, we looked to the dictionary definitions of the words "voluntarily" and "impoverished." We noted that "voluntarily" means "done by design or intention; proceeding from the free and unrestrained will of the person; produced in or by act of choice. . . ." "Impoverished" means "to make poor, reduce to poverty or to deprive . . . of resources, etc." . . .

The issue of voluntary impoverishment most often arises in the context of a parent who reduces his or her level of income to avoid paying support by quitting, retiring or changing jobs. The intent of the parent in those cases is often important in determining whether there has been voluntary impoverishment. Was the job changed for the purpose of avoiding the support obligation and, therefore, voluntary, or was it for reasons beyond the control of the parent, and thus involuntary? . . . A parent who chooses a life of poverty before having children and makes a deliberate choice not to alter that status after having children is . . . "voluntarily impoverished." Whether the voluntary impoverishment is for the purpose of avoiding child support or because the parent simply has chosen a frugal lifestyle for another reason, doesn't affect that parent's obligation to the child. Although the parent can choose to live in poverty, that parent cannot obligate the child to go without the necessities of life. A parent who brings a child into this world must support that child, if he has or reasonably could obtain, the means to do so. The law requires that parent to alter his or her previously chosen lifestyle if necessary to enable the parent to meet his or her support obligation.

Accordingly, we now hold that, for purposes of the child support guidelines, a parent shall be consid-

continued

**Even Teveya, the fictional lead character of *Fiddler on the Roof,* recognizes that a life of study is a luxury when he sings, *"If I were a rich man. . . .* Wouldn't have to work hard. . . . I'd discuss the Holy books with the learned men seven hours every day; that would be the sweetest thing of all." (Emphasis added).

CASE

Goldberger v. Goldberger—*Continued*

ered "voluntarily impoverished" whenever the parent has made the free and conscious choice, not compelled by factors beyond his or her control, to render himself or herself without adequate resources. To determine whether a parent has freely been made poor or deprived of resources the trial court should look to the factors enunciated in *John O. v. Jane O.,* 90 Md. App. 406, at 422:

1. his or her current physical condition;
2. his or her respective level of education;
3. the timing of any change in employment or financial circumstances relative to the divorce proceedings;
4. the relationship of the parties prior to the divorce proceedings;
5. his or her efforts to find and retain employment;
6. his or her efforts to secure retraining if that is needed;
7. whether he or she has ever withheld support;
8. his or her past work history;
9. the area in which the parties live and the status of the job market there; and
10. any other considerations presented by either party.

Based on a review of the evidence before the circuit court, there was no error in finding that appellant was "voluntarily impoverished."

Once a court determines that a parent is voluntarily impoverished, the court must then determine the amount of potential income to attribute to that parent in order to calculate the support dictated by the guidelines. Some of the factors the court should consider in determining the amount of potential income include:

1. age;
2. mental and physical condition;
3. assets;
4. educational background, special training or skills;
5. prior earnings;
6. efforts to find and retain employment;
7. the status of the job market in the area where the parent lives;
8. actual income from any source;
9. any other factor bearing on the parent's ability to obtain funds for child support.

After the court determines the amount of potential income to attribute to the parent, the court should calculate the amount of support by using the standardized worksheet authorized in Family Law § 12–203(a) and the schedule listed in Family Law § 12–204(e). Once the guideline support figure is determined, the court must then determine whether the presumptive correctness of the guideline support figure has been overcome by evidence that application of the guidelines would be unjust or inappropriate. Md. Code Ann., Fam. Law § 12–202(a)(2) (1991).

Unfortunately, the court below erred in determining that appellant's potential income was $60,000 per year, based solely on his ability to raise funds to support and carry on this litigation. Although the court may consider the ability of appellant to persuade others to provide him with funds to pay child support in the future, the court cannot assume this will occur merely because appellant has been able to convince others to support this litigation up until now. The court needs to hear testimony and make findings regarding the factors relating to potential income previously enunciated. No such findings were made in this case. After calculating the guidelines using appellant's realistic potential income, the court must decide whether the presumptive correctness of the guidelines has been overcome. Accordingly, this matter must be remanded to the trial court for such determinations. . . .

We vacate the court's child support order and remand the matter to the trial court to recalculate the appellant's child support obligation in light of this opinion. Judgment affirmed in part and vacated in part. Appellant to pay the costs.

ASSIGNMENT 10.3

a. Did the court violate Aron Goldberger's First Amendment right to freedom of religion by forcing him to pay child support?

b. Assume you work for the law firm that represents Esther Goldberger. To determine how much child support Aron should pay, what facts would you investigate as a result of the *Goldberger* opinion? (See General Instructions for the Investigation-Strategy Assignment in Appendix A.)

We saw in chapter 8 that separation agreements are often sloppily written in that they fail to distinguish between property division terms (which are not modifiable by a court) and support terms (which are). For example, suppose that the parties agree to give the "wife the exclusive use of the marital home until the youngest child reaches the age of twenty-one." Is this a division of property or a child-support term? If it is the former, then the husband cannot modify it on the basis of changed circumstances (e.g., her remarriage). If it is a child-support term, then a modification is possible. Most courts would interpret the above clause as a child-support term, since it is tied to a period of time when the child would most likely need support. Yet a court *could* rule the other way. Needless litigation often results from poor drafting. (For a discussion of when the Internal Revenue Service will treat a payment as child support *for tax purposes,* see chapter 11.)

ASSIGNMENT 10.4

a. What standards apply to a request to modify child-support payments in your state? (See General Instructions for the State-Code Assignment in Appendix A.)

b. Sara pays her ex-husband, Harry, $800 a month in child support under a 1995 court order that granted custody to Harry but gave liberal visitation rights to Sara. Due to continuing bitterness, Harry refuses to allow Sara to see their child. Sara then petitions the court to reduce her child-support payments. How would her request for a modification be handled in your state? (See General Instructions for the Court-Opinion Assignment in Appendix A.)

c. Reread the facts involving Dan, the former sales manager who wants to go to law school (see the facts of Dan's case in the text just before the *Goldberger* case). How would this request for a modification be handled in your state? (See General Instructions for the Court-Opinion Assignment in Appendix A.)

ENFORCEMENT OF CHILD-SUPPORT ORDERS

Introduction

Nonpayment of child support has reached epidemic proportions. Every year billions of dollars go uncollected. The Census Bureau found that in 1997 and 1998:

- 14 million parents had custody of 22.9 million children (under the age of twenty-one) whose other parent lived elsewhere (1998).
- Mothers were the custodial parents in 85.1 percent of families and fathers in 14.9 percent (1998).[11]
- 7 million custodial parents had child-support agreements or court awards (1998).
- 6.6 million custodial parents had no child-support agreement or court award (many felt that one was not needed, or that the noncustodial parent could not pay, or that the noncustodial parent paid what he or she could) (1998).
- Custodial parents with child-support agreements or awards were scheduled to receive $29.1 billion; the total amount actually paid was $17.1 billion, or 58.8 percent of the amount due (1997).
- Custodial parents without child-support awards received $2.1 billion (1997).

[11]Since the vast majority of custodial parents are mothers, we will often refer to the noncustodial parent/obligor as the father, although the same rules apply when the obligor is the mother.

- 34.1 percent of all custodial parents participated in at least one public assistance program—medicaid, food stamps, general assistance, TANF (Temporary Assistance for Needy Families), or AFDC (Aid to Families with Dependent Children, a program that was eventually replaced by TANF) (1997).
- 28.9 percent of custodial parents and their children lived below the poverty line or threshold (1997).
- Approximately 40 percent of custodial parents received all the child-support payments that were due (1997).
- Approximately 25 percent of custodial parents received partial child support payments (1997).
- Between a quarter and a third of all custodial parents received no child support (1997).
- The average amount of child support received by custodial mothers during the year was $3,700 (1997).
- The average amount of child support received by custodial fathers during the year was $3,300 (1997).
- The amount of child support actually received covers less than half of the child's support needs (1998).[12]

As indicated at the beginning of this chapter, Congress decided that the efforts of state governments to collect child support were inadequate. Federal legislation was needed to create national standards of enforcement, particularly in light of the federal tax dollars that had to be spent on welfare programs when parents failed to pay child support.

Congress added title IV-D to the Social Security Act to encourage the creation of new child-support enforcement agencies and new enforcement tools that can be used in every state.[13] Each state now has such an agency. States might use different names for them such as Child Support Enforcement Division or Office of Recovery Services. Collectively, they are known as *IV-D agencies,* since they were proposed in title IV-D of the Social Security Act. (The address and World Wide Web site of the central IV-D agency in each state are listed in Appendix E.)

Any custodial parent with a child under eighteen is eligible for the services of a IV-D agency. The parent does not have to be receiving public assistance through a program such as TANF. Those not receiving public assistance, however, may be charged a nominal fee for the services of the IV-D agency. These services can be substantial, as we saw when discussing jurisdiction problems in cases involving nonresident parents, and, as we will see in greater detail shortly, IV-D agencies have state-of-the-art facilities. For example, when a IV-D agency collects child support from an obligor, the agency can deposit the funds directly into the bank account of the obligee through electronic funds transfer (EFT). In addition to child support, an IV-D agency can help secure health insurance for the child through the group health policy of the employer of the obligor. Exhibit 10.2 contains the application for the services of a IV-D agency in one state.

ASSIGNMENT 10.5

What is the name of the IV-D agency in your state? Contact the closest branch. Ask for a copy of a brochure describing its services. Summarize them.

---

[12]Child Support for Custodial Mothers and Fathers 1997 (U.S. Census Bureau, Current Population Reports, Oct. 2000), <http://www.census.gov/prod/www/abs/custody.html>; Statistical Abstract of the United States: 1998, table 632.

[13]42 U.S.C.A. §§ 651-65.

Exhibit 10.2 Application for Child-Support Enforcement Services from IV-D Agency

Massachusetts Department of Revenue
Child Support Enforcement Division

Application for
Child Support Enforcement Services

• • • •

Absent Parent Background and Financial Information:

a. Is the absent parent currently married? Yes ☐ No ☐ Don't Know ☐
(If no or don't know, skip to question #b.)
What is his or her spouse's name? ____________________
Does his or her spouse work? Yes ☐ No ☐ Don't Know ☐
If yes, where does she or he work, if you know? ____________________
What is her or his income $ __________ per __________ Don't Know ☐
(Week, Month, or Year)

b. If not married, does the absent parent share his or her household with another adult?
Yes ☐ No ☐ Don't Know ☐

c. Does the absent parent have any children who are not also your children?
Yes ☐ No ☐ Don't Know ☐
If yes, please list their names and ages here, along with the name of the adult with whom they live.

Name	Age	Living With:

d. Is the absent parent providing support for children who are not also your children?
Yes ☐ No ☐ Don't Know ☐
If yes, how much is he/she paying? $ __________ per __________ Don't Know ☐
(Week, Month or Year)

e. To your knowledge, does the absent parent have any of the following sources of income?

Type of Income	Amount (if known)		Week/Month/Year
Worker's compensation	$ ______	per	______
Unemployment compensation	______		______
Social Security retirement (over 62, green check)	______		______
Other pension	______		______
Social Security disability (green check)	______		______
Supplemental Security Income (SSI) (gold check)	______		______
Other disability	______		______
Welfare	______		______
Veteran's benefits	______		______
Commissions	______		______
Trust income	______		______
Rental income (from houses/apartments he or she owns)	______		______
Annuities	______		______
Interest income	______		______
Dividend income	______		______

f. To your knowledge, does he or she have—or has he or she ever had in the last three years:

	Yes	No	When	Amount
Royalties	☐	☐	20__	$ ______
Severance pay	☐	☐	20__	______
Capital gains	☐	☐	20__	______
Prizes and awards	☐	☐	20__	______
Lottery winnings	☐	☐	20__	______
Gambling winnings	☐	☐	20__	______
Bonuses	☐	☐	20__	______

g. Does the absent parent:
Own any houses or other real estate? Yes ☐ No ☐ Don't Know ☐
If yes, please describe and indicate location if you can. ____________________

Own any motor vehicle? Yes ☐ No ☐ Don't Know ☐
If yes, for each vehicle, please identify the model, color, state where it is registered, and license plate number, if you can.
____
____

continued

Exhibit 10.2 Application for Child-Support Enforcement Services from IV-D Agency—*Continued*

Own a boat? Yes ☐ No ☐ Don't Know ☐
If yes, please indicate the registration number, if you can. ______
Where is it moored? ______
City or Town State

Own any stocks or bonds? Yes ☐ No ☐ Don't Know ☐

If yes, please use a separate sheet of paper to identify the name and address of the absent parent's stock broker and list any stocks and/or bonds owned by the absent parent if that information is available to you. Indicate the name of the company, the number of shares, and the date the stock was purchased, if possible.

Have any bank accounts? Yes ☐ No ☐ Don't Know ☐

List the name(s) of the bank(s), location(s), and type(s) of account(s) if that information is available to you.

Bank Name	Location	Type of Account

If you need additional space, please continue on a separate piece of paper.

Have any credit cards? Yes ☐ No ☐ Don't Know ☐

If yes, please list the names of the companies and account numbers if that information is available to you.

Credit Company	Account Number

Have any outstanding loans? Yes ☐ No ☐ Don't Know ☐

If yes, please identify the name of the bank(s) or financial institution(s), location(s) and account number(s).

Lending Institution	Location	Account Number
	City/Town State	
	City/Town State	

h. Have you ever filed a joint income tax return with the absent parent? Yes ☐ No ☐

If yes, for which state(s) and for what year(s)?

State Tax Years
______ 19 ___ to 20 ___ If you filed a joint *federal* return, for what years? 19 ___ to 20 ___

i. Does the absent parent have any disabilities or handicaps? Yes ☐ No ☐ Don't Know ☐

j. Does the absent parent have a driver's license? Yes ☐ No ☐ Don't Know ☐
If yes, from what state? ______ What is the license number? ______ Don't Know ☐

k. Does the absent parent have any trade or commercial licenses? Yes ☐ No ☐ Don't Know ☐
If yes, what sort of license is it? ______

From what state was it issued? ______

l. Has the absent parent ever belonged to any labor unions? Yes ☐ No ☐ Don't Know ☐
If yes, enter the name of the union, local number, city and state.

m. Does the absent parent go by any other names or aliases? Yes ☐ No ☐ Don't Know ☐
If yes, please identify. ______

n. Has the absent parent ever been a member of the armed forces? Yes ☐ No ☐ Don't Know ☐
If yes, what branch of service? ______

__/__/__	__/__/__	______	______
Date Entered	Date Discharged	Service Number	Last Duty Station

o. What high school, trade school and/or college did the absent parent attend? Please indicate the name and address of each school, the dates attended and the degree earned.

Name	Address	Dates of Attendance	Degree

Please attach an additional piece of paper if you need more space.

p. Does the absent parent have a criminal record?

Yes ☐ No ☐ Don't Know ☐ If yes,in which state? ______

q. Please identify the names and addresses of as many of the absent parent's past employers as you can. (Do not include the most recent employer which you have already identified earlier.)

Name	Address

Please attach an additional piece of paper if you need more space.

r. What are the names of the absent parent's parents? (Please indicate their names even if they are deceased.)

Father's Name

Street or P.O. Box

City State Zip

Telephone

Mother's Maiden Name

Street or P.O. Box

City State Zip

Telephone

s. Please provide the names and addresses of others who might know the whereabouts of the absent parent.

Name Relationship Phone

Street or P.O. Box City State Zip

Name Relationship Phone

Street or P.O. Box City State Zip

Source: Massachusetts Department of Revenue Child Support Enforcement Division.

If a woman is receiving public assistance, she must cooperate with the IV-D agency to establish paternity and collect child support. If, however, she can show "good cause," she is relieved of this requirement. An example of good cause is that she faces a serious threat of physical violence if she cooperates.

A woman on public assistance must **assign** or transfer her support rights to the state IV-D agency or other county welfare agency that attempts to collect support from the father. This simply means that she gives the agency the right to keep any support money that it collects on her behalf. This money is then

assign
To transfer rights or property.

used to offset the TANF money she receives on an ongoing basis for herself and her children. If she fails to cooperate in assigning these rights, her share of the TANF benefits can be terminated, and the TANF benefits of her children can be sent to some other responsible adult who will agree to make them available for the children.

One of the valuable services provided by the IV-D agency is its attempt to keep careful records on when the noncustodial parent pays and fails to pay child support. (Each state has a State Case Registry [SCR], which contains a record of every support order entered or modified in the state and a State Disbursement Unit [SDU], which acts as a centralized collection center in the state.) The IV-D agencies can be quite persistent in going after the noncustodial parent through automatic billing, telephone reminders, delinquency notices, etc. Other enforcement tools are also available through the IV-D agency as outlined below.

A new *federal* agency was created to coordinate, evaluate, and assist state IV-D agencies—the Office of Child Support Enforcement (OCSE) within the U.S. Department of Health and Human Services. For the home page of the OCSE on the Internet, see Exhibit 1.11 on page 25 in chapter 1.

But first things first. A very large number of noncustodial parents simply disappear. Problem number one is to *find* the noncustodial parent in order to obtain a child-support order and/or in order to enforce it. Another service provided by the IV-D agency is its **State Parent Locator Service (SPLS).** At the national level, there is a comparable **Federal Parent Locator Service (FPLS),** which operates through the Office of Child Support Enforcement. The FPLS includes a National Directory of New Hires (NDNH), which, as we will see, collects data on newly hired employees throughout the country. The FPLS also has a Federal Case Registry (FCR), which contains data received from each state's State Case Registry (SCR) on the child-support orders being enforced by IV-D agencies in every state. The centralization of data within these entities has been very helpful in the search for parents within a state and across state lines.

State Parent Locator Service (SPLS)
A state government agency that helps locate parents who fail to pay child support.

Federal Parent Locator Service (FPLS)
A federal government agency that helps locate parents who fail to pay child support, particularly in interstate cases. The FPLS can also help in parental kidnaping cases.

The starting point in the search is the custodial parent who is asked to provide the following leads to the IV-D agency on the whereabouts of the noncustodial parent:

- Social security number (check old state and federal tax returns, hospital records, police records, bank accounts, insurance policies, credit cards, loan applications, pay slips, union records, etc.)
- Last known residential address
- Current or recent employer's name and address
- Prior employers' names and addresses
- Place of birth
- Names and addresses of relatives and friends
- Local clubs and organizations to which he once belonged
- Local banks, public utilities, and other creditors he may have had or now has

The State Parent Locator Service (SPLS) of the IV-D agency will use the leads provided by the custodial parent to try to locate the noncustodial parent. It will check the records of other state agencies for a current address (e.g., Department of Motor Vehicle Registration, Unemployment Compensation Commission, Tax Department, and prisons). If the noncustodial parent has moved to another state, the IV-D agency in that state can be asked to provide comparable search services, or the Federal Parent Locator Service (FPLS) can be asked to help. The FPLS can search its records on newly hired employees throughout the country as well as the records of federal agencies such as the Internal Revenue Service, the Social Security Administration, and the Department of Defense.

The success of the SPLS and the FPLS in finding noncustodial parents has in large measure been due to the centralization and computerization of data on parents and children involved in child-support cases. The computer databases of state and federal child-support agencies are linked in order to facilitate matches between child-support orders and obligors. These agencies, however, must be careful about the locator information they release, particularly in cases where domestic violence against a spouse or child is a reasonable possibility. Without safeguards, for example, a husband might be able to use available locator services to find a wife or child who is in hiding because of his abuse. In a system containing millions of records, this is a distinct possibility. To prevent it from happening, a "flag" called a **family violence indicator (FVI)** is placed on the name of a person who has been abused or threatened with abuse. The victim might have an order of protection in effect against the abuser or might simply have told the IV-D agency of the danger of family violence. This leads to the placement of a flag on her name and that of her children. States are prohibited from releasing information on the whereabouts of a "flagged" parent or child to someone who has committed or threatened domestic violence. Furthermore, the address of a victim is shielded or otherwise blocked out in the maze of paperwork that will eventually be exchanged in the enforcement of a child-support order. Access to locator information such as addresses is highly restricted once a victim is flagged with an FVI.

family violence indicator (FVI)
A designation placed on a participant in a child-support case indicating that he or she may be a victim of child abuse or domestic violence.

ASSIGNMENT 10.6

How does the State Parent Locator Service of the IV-D agency in your state operate? Describe how the service functions. (See General Instructions for the State-Code Assignment in Appendix A.)

Every state is required to have expedited paternity procedures, including standard forms in maternity wards on which unwed fathers are encouraged to acknowledge paternity voluntarily immediately after birth. (See Exhibit 13.5 in chapter 13 for an example of such a form.) In 1998, over 614,000 in-hospital paternities were voluntarily acknowledged. Where needed, the IV-D agency will help a mother obtain a court order establishing paternity. The total number of paternities established and acknowledged in 1998 was 1.5 million.

Once paternity has been established and a child-support order obtained, how is the order enforced? Some of the major enforcement mechanisms include:

- Civil contempt proceeding
- Execution
- Prosecution for criminal nonsupport
- Income withholding
- New hire reporting
- License denial or revocation
- Passport denial
- Federal tax refund offset
- Unemployment compensation intercept
- Qualified domestic relations order (QDRO)
- Qualified medical child support order (QMSCO)
- Credit bureau referral (credit clouding)
- Financial institution data match ("freeze and seize")
- Posting security
- Protective order

Civil Contempt Proceeding

contempt
Obstructing or assailing the authority or dignity of the court.

Contempt of court exists when the authority or dignity of the court is obstructed or assailed. The most glaring example is an intentional violation of a court order. There are two kinds of contempt proceedings, civil and criminal, both of which can lead to the jailing of the offender. The purpose of a *civil contempt* proceeding is to compel future compliance with the court order, whereas the purpose of a *criminal contempt* proceeding is to punish the offender. Criminal contempt in child-support cases is rare because of the cumbersome nature of any criminal proceeding.

When civil contempt occurs in child-support cases, the offender is jailed until he agrees to comply with the court order. Suppose, however, that the offender has no resources and thus cannot comply. In effect, such a person would be imprisoned because of his poverty. This is illegal. Imprisonment for debt is unconstitutional because it amounts to a sentence for an indefinite period beyond the control of the offender. To bypass this constitutional prohibition, a court must determine that the offender has the *present ability* to pay the child-support debt but simply refuses to do so. Such an individual is in control of how long the sentence will be. In effect, the keys to jail are in his own pocket. Release occurs when he pays the child-support debt. As one court recently said, "There is no constitutional impediment to imposition of contempt sanctions on a parent for violation of a judicial child support order when the parent's financial inability to comply with the order is the result of the parent's willful failure to seek and accept available employment that is commensurate with his or her skills and ability."[14]

In addition to jailing the obligor, most courts have the power to order the less drastic sanction of imposing a fine when the obligor is found to be in civil contempt.

ASSIGNMENT 10.7

What steps must be taken in your state to use a civil contempt proceeding to enforce a child-support order? (See General Instruction for the Flowchart Assignment in Appendix A.)

Execution

writ of execution
A document directing a court officer to seize the property of someone who lost a judgment, sell it, and pay the winner of the judgment.

lien
An encumbrance or claim on property imposed as security for the payment of a debt.

Once an obligor fails to pay a judgment ordering child support, the sheriff can be ordered to seize the personal or real property of the obligor in the state. All of this occurs through a **writ of execution.** Its initial effect is to create a **lien** on the property that prevents the obligor from disposing of it. The property seized can then be sold by the sheriff. The proceeds from this *forced sale* are used to pay the judgment and the expenses of the execution. Not all property of the obligor, however, is subject to execution in every state. Certain property (e.g., clothes and cars) may be exempt from execution.

Prosecution for Criminal Nonsupport

In most states, the willful failure to support a child is a *state* crime for which the obligor can be prosecuted. There must be an ability to provide support before the obligor can be tried and convicted of *criminal nonsupport* or desertion. The range of punishment includes probation, fine, and imprisonment. Except for relatively wealthy offenders, imprisonment is seldom an effective method of enforcing child support. Most obligors are wage earners, and once they are jailed, their primary source of income obviously dries up. One way out of this dilemma is for the judge to agree to suspend the imposition of the jail sentence on condition that the obligor fulfill the support obligation, including the payment of arrearages. The obligor would be placed on *probation* under this condition.

---

[14]*Moss v. Superior Court,* 950 P.2d 59, 62, 71 Cal. Rptr. 2d 215, 218 (1998).

The threat of prosecution has encouraged some delinquent obligors to come forward. Several states have launched highly publicized amnesty programs (see Exhibit 10.3). Some states post "wanted lists" containing the pictures of individuals who have been convicted of the willful failure to pay child support or for whom arrest warrants have been issued because of the amount of child support owed. (See, for example, the wanted list for Berks County, Pennsylvania, at www.drs.berks.pa.us/bw_photos.htm.)

Exhibit 10.3 Amnesty Ad Placed in Sports Section of Local Newspaper

DO YOU OWE CHILD SUPPORT?
—Has your luck run out?—

Beginning Monday morning, December 6, a substantial number of Kansas City area parents who have failed to make their court-ordered child support payments will be arrested, jailed, and prosecuted. Could you be one of those parents?

Rather than gamble, you can receive amnesty from criminal prosecution by coming in person to the child support enforcement office at 1805 Grand Avenue in Kansas City and making immediate payment arrangements. You only have until this Friday at 5 p.m. Next Monday, you may be in jail, and then it will be too late.

Come in—let's talk.

Missouri Division of Child Support Enforcement
1805 Grand Ave., Suite 300
Kansas City, MO

ASSIGNMENT 10.8

a. Is it a crime in your state to fail to pay child support? If so, quote the essential elements of the crime. (See General Instructions for the State-Code Assignment in Appendix A.)
b. Prepare a list of questions you would ask in order to help determine whether this crime was committed. (See General Instructions for the Investigation-Strategy Assignment in Appendix A.)
c. What steps must be taken in your state to prosecute someone for violating this crime? (See General Instructions for the Flowchart Assignment in Appendix A.)
d. On the Internet, find a wanted poster containing the facts of an individual wanted for the criminal failure to pay child support. What information does the site give about the individual? What is the address of the site?

The failure to pay child support can also be a *federal* crime under the Deadbeat Parents Punishment Act. A sentence of between six months and two years can be imposed when the obligor:

> (1) willfully fails to pay a support obligation with respect to a child who resides in another State, if such obligation has remained unpaid for a period longer than 1 year, or is greater than $5,000;
> (2) travels in interstate or foreign commerce with the intent to evade a support obligation, if such obligation has remained unpaid for a period longer than 1 year, or is greater than $5,000; or
> (3) willfully fails to pay a support obligation with respect to a child who resides in another State, if such obligation has remained unpaid for a period longer than 2 years, or is greater than $10,000. . . .[15]

[15]18 U.S.C.A. § 228.

To be prosecuted under this act, the obligor must be financially able to pay the child support that is due. Federal prosecutors in the United States Attorney's Office, however, are reluctant to bring a case until civil and criminal remedies at the *state* level have been tried. Furthermore, federal prosecutors will give priority to cases (1) where there is a pattern of moving from state to state to avoid payment, (2) where there is a pattern of deception such as the use of a false name or a false social security number, (3) where there is failure to make support payments after being held in contempt of court, and (4) where failure to make support payments is connected to another federal offense such as bankruptcy fraud.

The creation of federal crimes in this area by Congress has been criticized as inappropriately "federalizing" family law. For example, the chief justice of the United States Supreme Court, William H. Rehnquist, has complained that Congress is enacting too many federal crimes to cover conduct that should be the exclusive domain of the state criminal justice system. One of the examples he cites is the federal crime of failing to pay child support for a child living in another state.

Income Withholding

One of the most successful enforcement programs is *income withholding*, which is a mandatory, automatic deduction from the paycheck of an obligor who falls behind in child-support payments. Nearly 60 percent of all child support is collected by employers through this method. An income withholding order can be sent to employers in any state where the obligor works. In addition to wages, employers can withhold commissions and retirement payments. Each pay period, the employer deducts a specified amount and sends it to the IV-D agency, to the court, or, in some cases, to the custodial parent. The process begins when the IV-D agency sends the employer an order/notice to withhold income for child support.

The order/notice can also include a requirement that the employer enroll the employee's children in health insurance coverage made available to its employees. There is a box on the order/notice that says, "If checked, you are required to enroll the child(ren) identified above in any health insurance coverage available through the employee's/obligor's employment." The employer cannot deny coverage for children simply because they may no longer live with the employee. (See also the discussion below on the qualified medical child support order or QMCSO, a formal method of accomplishing the same objective of health coverage for children.)

Employers must comply with all the requirements listed in the order/notice. They can be fined or otherwise sanctioned for failure to withhold income or to include the children in the company health insurance plan. Most states allow employers to charge an employee an administrative fee for processing the withholding, but they cannot fire or discipline the employee because of withholding.

If the employee quits or is terminated by the employer for a legitimate reason, the employer must send the IV-D agency or court a notice giving the date of termination, the employee's last known home address, and the new employer's address. A form to provide this notice of termination is found on the reverse side of the original order/notice to withhold income for child support received by the employer.

Here are the guidelines sent to employers on their responsibilities.

Income Withholding for Support: Employer Guidelines

What is the maximum amount of money that may be withheld from an employee's paycheck?

The upper limit on what may be withheld is based on the Federal Consumer Credit Protection Act (CCPA). The federal withholding limits for child support are based on the disposable earnings of the obligor (i.e., the employee). The federal CCPA limit is 50 percent of the disposable earnings if the employee lives with and supports a second family and 60 percent if the employee does not support a second family. These limits increase to 55 percent and 65 percent, respectively, if the employee owes arrearages that are 12 weeks or more past due. (States may choose a lower limit.) Check with your state to determine exact limits. About two-thirds of the states use the federal limits, and about one-third cap the withholding at 50 percent regardless of second families or age of arrearages.)

Income withholding requires extra paper work on our part. May I charge a processing fee to the employees?

Most states allow you to charge an administrative fee for processing the income withholding. Contact your local or state child support enforcement agency (also called the IV-D agency) to learn what the administrative fee is in your state.

Some of our employees already have income attachments against their paychecks. How do we handle these attachments and child support withholdings?

Child support withholdings take priority over all other claims against the same income except federal tax liens that were served before the child support order was served. Only after satisfying the child support obligation (to the CCPA-maximum-allowed limit) may you honor the other income attachments.

How soon do we need to send the child support payment that we have withheld from an employee's paycheck?

You need to send payment of the withheld income within seven business days of paying wages to the employee. Your state may set a shorter time limit for making payment.

Where are payments sent?

Each state has a State Disbursement Unit (SDU) for the collection and disbursement of child support payments for all IV-D cases (cases enforced by a child support agency) and for all private child support orders issued.

We received an income withholding Order/Notice from a child support agency in another state. Must we send payments directly to the other state?

Yes. An employer is required to honor income withholding Orders/Notice from another state as long as the order appears to be "regular on its face."

What if my employee tells me the amount being claimed is the wrong amount and/or that I do not need to withhold?

If your employee disputes the income withholding notice, the employee should contact the child support enforcement agency or court, not his or her employer. Until you are otherwise notified by an amended Order/Notice, you should proceed with the withholding Order/Notice as issued.

Our company has an employee who has remarried and now has a child by his second wife. He told us that we should reduce the amount of the child support he is paying to his first wife because of this second family. Who makes the decision in this kind of situation?

The court or child support enforcement agency makes the decision to change an income withholding order. You must continue withholding according to a valid withholding Order/Notice until you receive notification in writing from the child support agency or court issuing the Order/Notice that a change is necessary. It is up to the employee to notify the child support agency or court of the change in his/her family situation so that the agency or court can then issue a revised Order/Notice (with a lower maximum withholding amount) to your company.

What if I fire or lay off my employee or the employee quits after I begin withholding child support?

Report the termination of employment. Complete the back of the Order/Notice and send it to the child support enforcement agency or court. Notify them of the employee's last known address and, if you know it, the name and address of the new employer.

garnishment
A process whereby a debtor's property under the control of another is given to a third person to whom the debtor owes a debt.

Income withholding is similar to the more traditional **garnishment** process, under which a third party (e.g., a bank or employer) who owes the obligor money or other property is ordered by a court to turn it over to a debtor of the obligor, such as the custodial parent. Garnishment, however, is usually less effective than income withholding because of the more cumbersome procedures for instituting garnishment and the restrictions that may exist on how long it can be in effect.

ASSIGNMENT 10.9

a. Who can use income withholding in your state through the state IV-D agency? How does this enforcement mechanism operate?
b. Compare income withholding to the garnishment process in your state. How do they differ?

(See General Instructions for the State-Code Assignment in Appendix A.)

New Hire Reporting

Employers are required to report information about all newly hired employees to a State Directory of New Hires (SDNH) shortly after the hire date. (In many states, it is twenty days.) The "New Hire" report from the employer must provide the employee's name, address, and social security number as listed on his or her W-4 form. The SDNH will then match this data against its child-support records to locate delinquent parents so that income withholding orders can be issued. To help locate parents in other states, the SDNH submits its data to the National Directory of New Hires (NDNH), which is a national database that is part of the Federal Parent Locator Service (FPLS). To help locate parents who have moved across state lines, the NDNH compiles new hire and quarterly wage data from every state and federal agency and also unemployment insurance data from every state. The NDNH is an important locator tool, since a large percentage of child-support cases involve noncustodial parents who do not live in the same state as their children.

The new hire program has been quite successful. In the first two years of its operation, over 2.8 million delinquent parents were uncovered. There have been side benefits as well. Citizens collecting unemployment compensation should not be working full-time. Yet the new hire program has found thousands who have been fraudulently collecting unemployment benefits while employed. In 1998, for example, Pennsylvania alone identified 4,289 overpayments in unemployment with a dollar value of $2.3 million. Among the new hires, the government has also found numerous individuals who are in default on their student loans. Their names have been shared with the United States Department of Education, which has initiated successful loan collection efforts. Clearly, the benefits of the new hire program have extended beyond improved child-support collection.

License Denial or Revocation

To engage in certain occupations, a person must obtain a license from the state. Examples include plumber, hairdresser, real estate broker, accountant, electrician, teacher, doctor, and attorney. Many states will deny an initial application for a license, deny an application for a renewal of a license, or revoke the license of a parent who is delinquent in making child-support payments. In Illinois, for example, the license statute that applies to attorneys provides as follows:

> No person shall be granted a license or renewal authorized by this Act who is more than 30 days delinquent in complying with a child support order. . . .[16]

[16] 705 Illinois Compiled Statutes Annotated § 205/1.

Many states will also revoke or suspend a delinquent obligor's *driver's* license or vehicle registration. One state sends him or her an "intent to revoke" letter. If the child-support debt is not satisfied, an investigator locates the car or other vehicle, removes the license plate, and leaves a bright orange decal on the driver's side window explaining the seizure and the steps to take through the IV-D agency to have the license plate restored.

ASSIGNMENT 10.10

Under the state code of your state, can licenses be revoked for the failure to pay child support? If so, what licenses? What are the conditions that will trigger a revocation? (See General Instructions for the State-Code Assignment in Appendix A.)

Passport Denial

Individuals who owe over $5,000 in child support can have their passport application denied. In addition, the United States secretary of state, the federal official in charge of the Passport Office, can take action to revoke or restrict a passport previously issued to those who have this amount of child-support debt.

Federal Tax Refund Offset Program

The Federal Tax Refund Offset Program collects past due child-support payments out of the tax refunds of parents who have been ordered to pay child support. Each year state IV-D agencies submit to the IRS the names, social security numbers, and amounts of past due child support owed by parents. The IRS then determines whether these individuals are scheduled to receive tax refunds on their returns. If so, the IRS sends them an offset notification that informs them of the proposed offset and gives them an opportunity to pay the past due amount or to contest the amount with the IV-D agency. (See Exhibit 10.4.) Since 1982, almost 10 million tax refunds have been intercepted, and over $6 billion has been collected. In 2000, $1.4 billion was collected. The average tax refund amount is $721. In addition, a program exists to intercept and offset tax refunds due on *state* returns.

Unemployment Compensation Intercept

The unemployment compensation benefits of the obligor can be intercepted to meet ongoing (not just past due) child-support payments. This method of withholding enables the IV-D agency to collect at least some support from an unemployed obligor. Nothing is left to chance. Computers at the unemployment compensation agency and at the IV-D agency communicate with each other to identify delinquent parents who have applied for or who are eligible for unemployment compensation. An investigator from the IV-D agency will then contact the surprised obligor. It may even be possible to intercept benefits across state lines pursuant to reciprocal agreements among cooperating states. (In most states, a similar intercept program can reach an obligor's workers' compensation benefits.)

Qualified Domestic Relations Order

Very often an obligor will have pension and other retirement benefit plans through an employer. A special court order, called a **qualified domestic relations order (QDRO),** allows someone other than the obligor to reach some or all of these benefits in order to meet a support obligation of the obligor, such as child support. The child becomes an *alternate payee* under these plans. This

qualified domestic relations order (QDRO)
A court order that allows a nonemployee to reach pension benefits of an employee or former employee in order to satisfy a marital obligation to the nonemployee.

Exhibit 10.4 Notice of Collection of Income Tax Refund

Department of the Treasury
Internal Revenue Service

If you have any questions, refer to this information:

Date of This Notice: January 4, 2003
Social Security Number: 215-32-2726
Document Locator Number:
Form Tax Year Ended: 2001

Call:

Sam Jones
999 Peachtree Street
Doraville, CO 99999

or

Write: Chief, Taxpayer Assistance Section
Internal Revenue Service Center

If you write, be sure to attach this notice.

THIS IS TO INFORM YOU THAT THE AGENCY NAMED BELOW HAS CONTACTED US REGARDING AN OUTSTANDING DEBT YOU HAVE WITH THEM.

UNDER AUTHORITY OF SECTION 6402(c) OF THE INTERNAL REVENUE CODE, ANY OVERPAYMENT OF YOUR FEDERAL INCOME TAX WILL BE APPLIED TO THAT OBLIGATION BEFORE ANY AMOUNT CAN BE REFUNDED OR APPLIED TO ESTIMATED TAX. IF YOU HAVE ANY QUESTIONS ABOUT THE OBLIGATION OR BELIEVE IT IS IN ERROR, YOU SHOULD CONTACT THAT AGENCY IMMEDIATELY.

NAME OF AGENCY

DEPT. OF SOCIAL SERVICES
DIV. OF INCOME AND SUPPORT
CHILD SUPPORT ENFORCEMENT
1575 OBLIGATION STREET
TIMBUKTU, CO 92037

CONTACT: CHILD SUPPORT
PHONE: 619-456-9103

person cannot receive benefits under the plan that the obligor would not have been able to receive. For example, if the obligor is not entitled to a lump-sum payment, the child as alternate payee is also subject to this limitation. (For an example of a QDRO in which a spouse is the alternate payee, see Exhibit 8.6 on page 268 in chapter 8.)

Qualified Medical Child Support Order

Many children of noncustodial parents have no health insurance. Assume that such a parent is working for a company that has a group health plan. But the parent either refuses to add the child to the plan, or the insurance company tells the parent that the child is ineligible because he or she does not live with the parent, does not live in the insurer's service area, is not claimed as a dependent on the parent's tax return, or was born to unmarried parents. In 1993, Congress passed a law that made it illegal for insurance companies to use such reasons to deny coverage to children. A court order can now be obtained to require coverage. It is called the **qualified medical child support order (QMCSO).** The child becomes an *alternate recipient* under the health plan. The employer can deduct the cost of adding the child to the plan from the parent's pay. In 1998, Congress made QMCSOs easier to implement. As we saw earlier, employers can now be required to include a noncustodial parent's children in company health plans. This requirement is included in the order/notice to withhold income for child support sent to an employer.

qualified medical child support order (QMCSO)
A court order requiring that a group health plan provide benefits for the child of a parent covered under the plan.

Credit Bureau Referral (Credit Clouding)

An obligor may be warned that a credit bureau (e.g., TRW, Trans Union, CBI-Equifax) will be notified of a delinquency in making child-support payments unless the delinquency is eliminated by payment or unless satisfactory arrangements are made to pay the debt. Once the computers of a credit bureau have information on such payment problems, a "cloud" on the obligor's credit rating is created *(credit clouding)*, which notifies potential creditors that the obligor may be a bad credit risk. This method of pressuring compliance with child-support obligations is particularly effective with self-employed obligors, who often do not have regular wages that can be subjected to income withholding or garnishment. Many states now routinely report child-support debts to credit bureaus.

Financial Institution Data Match ("Freeze and Seize")

State IV-D agencies can attach and seize ("freeze and seize") the accounts of delinquent parents in financial institutions that operate in more than one state. The accounts can include savings, checking, time deposit, and money-market mutual fund accounts at large banks, credit unions, and money-market mutual funds. The IV-D agency issues a lien or levy on the account. A lien, as we saw earlier, is an encumbrance or claim on property that is imposed as security for the payment of a debt. The lien impedes the debtor's ability to transfer the property. The debtor must satisfy the lien before the property may be sold or transferred. A **levy** is an actual collection or seizure of the property. Liens and levies are governed by state law. Some states, for example, require a minimum dollar amount of child-support debt before a lien can be imposed.

levy
The collection or seizure of property by a marshal or sheriff with a writ of execution.

Posting Security

In some cases, a noncustodial parent may be asked to post security in the form of a bond or other guarantee that will cover future support obligations.

Protective Order

Some men do not react kindly to requests from the mothers of their children that they meet their child-support obligations. Occasionally, they may even physically assault the mother or threaten to do so. The police may be called in, although some have complained that the police do not take so-called domestic disputes seriously. Usually the woman can obtain through the local prosecutor or district attorney a **protective order,** which threatens the man with arrest and jail unless he stays away from the children and their mother. (For an example of a protective order, see Exhibit 12.2 in chapter 12.)

protective order
A court order designed to protect a person from harm or harassment.

IMPROPER ENFORCEMENT

There are limits to what a state can do to enforce a child-support order. As we have seen, a state cannot imprison parents for failure to pay child support when they do not have the financial resources or capability to make such payments. Some states have tried to enforce support obligations through their marriage license statutes. One state refused to issue marriage licenses to individuals who had failed to support their children in the custody of someone else. As we saw in chapter 5 on marriage formation, however, the United States Supreme Court has held that this method of child-support enforcement is invalid because it is an unconstitutional interference with the fundamental right to marry.[17]

Although the failure to pay child support cannot be used to interfere with the right to marry, can such failure be used to interfere with the right to pro-

[17] *Zablocki v. Redhail,* 434 U.S. 374, 98 S. Ct. 673, 54 L. Ed. 2d 618 (1978).

create? Can the state say to a "deadbeat dad": Stop having more children until you pay for the ones you already have? The United States Supreme Court has not yet answered this question. In 2001, however, the Supreme Court of Wisconsin answered it in the affirmative. The Wisconsin court held that a father who intentionally refused to pay child support can be required to avoid having another child until he makes sufficient efforts to support his current children.[18] David Oakley was convicted of intentionally failing to support the nine children he fathered with four different women, even though nothing prevented him from obtaining gainful employment. He could have been sent to prison for eight years. Instead, the court released him on probation under the condition that he avoid fathering another child until he complied with his support obligation to the nine he had already fathered. He faced eight years in prison if he violated this condition. Oakley argued that the condition violated his fundamental right to procreate. The court acknowledged "the fundamental liberty interest of a citizen to choose whether or not to procreate."[19] Yet the court said the interest had not been violated in this case. Oakley was a convicted felon and, therefore, he was subject to more restrictions than ordinary citizens. Furthermore, the condition was reasonably related to his rehabilitation. To avoid eight years of prison (where he would face a total ban on his right to procreate), he merely had to make the efforts required by law to support his current children. The condition simply required him to avoid creating another victim of willful nonsupport.

The vote of the Wisconsin justices upholding the probation condition was 4–3. The dissenters were concerned that the right to have children was based on a parent's financial resources. One dissenter said that the condition "is basically a compulsory, state-sponsored, court-enforced financial test for future parenthood."[20] Another dissenter commented that the condition creates a strong incentive for Oakley to demand an abortion from any woman he impregnates in the future. An attorney for the American Civil Liberties Union called the decision "a dangerous precedent" in the area of reproductive rights.[21] The case received widespread publicity. Some of the news accounts thought it relevant to point out that the four justices in the majority were male and that the three dissenters were female.

NECESSARIES

necessaries
The basic items needed by family members to maintain a standard of living.

A seldom used method for a wife and child to obtain support is to go to merchants, make purchases of **necessaries,** and charge them to the credit of the nonsupporting husband/father. The latter must pay the bills, whether or not he knows about them or authorizes them so long as:

- They are in fact for necessaries and
- The husband/father has not already provided them for the family

Since the definition of necessaries is not precise and since a merchant has difficulty knowing whether a husband/father has already made provision for the necessaries of his family, few merchants are willing to extend credit in these circumstances without express authorization from the husband/father. Some states, however, have eliminated the requirement that there be evidence of a failure of the husband/father to provide necessaries before his credit can be charged.

---

[18] *State v. Oakley,* 629 N.W.2d 200 (WI 2001).
[19] 629 N.W.2d at 207.
[20] 629 N.W.2d at 221.
[21] T. Lewin, *Father Owing Child Support Loses a Right to Procreate,* N.Y. Times, July 12, 2001, at A14.

What are necessaries? Generally, they encompass what is needed and appropriate to maintain the family at the standard of living to which it has been accustomed (e.g., home, food, clothing, furniture, medical care). The educational expenses of minor children are necessaries. A college education, on the other hand, is not in many states.

Originally, the doctrine of necessaries applied against the husband only. At common law, a wife was not responsible for necessaries furnished to her child or husband. Today states have either extended the doctrine so that it now applies equally to both spouses or they have abolished the doctrine altogether.

SUMMARY

Child support is heavily influenced by federal law. When parents are negotiating the child-support terms of their separation agreement, they must consider a number of factors such as child-support guidelines, tax considerations, and methods of payment. Parents cannot agree to an amount of child support that will fall below the minimum required in the state.

A child-support order requires personal jurisdiction over the defendant/obligor. The Uniform Interstate Family Support Act (UIFSA) allows a state to obtain personal jurisdiction over a nonresident by the long-arm method. The resident parent can then enforce the order by registering it in the state of the defendant/obligor. If the resident state cannot obtain personal jurisdiction over the obligor, the custodial parent can use the services of IV-D agencies to obtain and enforce an order in the state of the obligor. A state with a valid order under the UIFSA has continuing, exclusive jurisdiction over the case so that another state cannot modify the order. If there is a conflict in orders, the order of the home state has priority.

Both parents have an equal obligation to pay child support. The amount of child support is determined primarily by the child-support guidelines of each state. States differ on whether a parent has an obligation to pay for a child's college education and on the impact of the obligor's start of a second family.

Child-support orders cannot be modified unless there is a substantial change of circumstances since the original order. No modification will be ordered if a parent voluntarily reduces his or her income-earning capacity in order to avoid paying support, nor will there be a modification if it results in the child becoming destitute.

Each state has a IV-D agency to assist custodial parents in obtaining and enforcing child-support orders. Locator services will help find missing noncustodial parents. An order can be enforced by civil contempt and by prosecution for criminal nonsupport if the obligor has the financial means or capacity to pay the support obligation. A writ of execution can be used to place a lien on the obligor's property. Income withholding is the most effective enforcement device. Employers are required to deduct support payments from the obligor's paycheck and to enroll the obligor's children in available company health insurance plans. Employers must notify the state every time they hire a new employee; the names of these new employees are then matched with a list of delinquent obligors. Delinquent parents can be denied licenses, have licenses revoked, and have passports denied. Payments can be taken out of an obligor's tax refund and unemployment compensation funds. Pensions can be reached through a qualified domestic relations order, and health benefits can be obtained through a qualified medical child support order. Credit bureaus can be notified of nonpayment by an obligor. Accounts in interstate financial institutions can be seized. Obligors can be required to post security for future payments. Protective orders are available if violence has been committed or is threatened against the child or custodial parent. Some states allow one spouse to charge the credit of the other for necessaries such as food for the spouse and child. Efforts to collect child support, however, cannot interfere with an obligor's fundamental right to marry.

KEY CHAPTER TERMINOLOGY

pendente lite
personal jurisdiction
Uniform Interstate Family Support Act (UIFSA)
long-arm jurisdiction
IV-D agency
initiating state
responding state
divisible divorce
continuing, exclusive jurisdiction (cej)
home state
child-support guidelines
obligor
obligee
arrearage
arrears
imputed income
assign
State Parent Locator Service (SPLS)
Federal Parent Locator Service (FPLS)
family violence indicator (FVI)
contempt
writ of execution
lien
garnishment
qualified domestic relations order (QDRO)
qualified medical child support order (QMCSO)
levy
protective order
necessaries

ETHICS IN PRACTICE

You are a paralegal working at the law office of Helen Farrell, Esq. Claire Richardson asks Farrell to represent her in a child-support case. The court ordered the father of their child to pay $1,000 a month in child support. He is currently $25,000 in arrears. Farrell agrees to take the case. Her fee will be 40 percent of whatever amount of the arrears she collects. In addition, she will receive 10 percent of every future monthly child-support payment. Any ethical problems?

ON THE NET: MORE ON CHILD SUPPORT

Support Guidelines
http://www.supportguidelines.com

State Child Support Agencies
http://www.acf.dhhs.gov/programs/cse/extinf.htm#exta

Alliance for Non-Custodial Parents Rights (Child Support)
http://www.ancpr.org

Missing Dads (search for delinquent parents)
http://www.missingdads.com

online Support Calculators/Worksheets in Selected States

California:
http://www.pegasussoft.com/homepage.htm

Massachusetts:
http://www.divorcenet.com//worksheet.html
http://www.state.ma.us/cse/programs/employer/Quick.htm

Ohio:
http://www.alllaw.com/calculators/Childsupport/ohio

Utah:
http://www.lawutah.com/gb/docs/Calc.htm

Vermont:
http://www.state.vt.us./courts/csguide.htm

CHAPTER

Tax Consequences of Separation and Divorce

CHAPTER OUTLINE

THE ROLE OF TAX LAW IN THE BARGAINING PROCESS

Tax law should play a major role in the representation of divorce clients. Clauses in a separation agreement, for example, may have a distorted relationship to the real world of dollars and cents if their tax consequences are not assessed (and, to the extent possible, *bargained for*) before the agreement is signed. Income that once supported one household must now support two (or more) households. Careful tax planning can help accomplish this objective.

We need to examine the three major financial components of a separation and divorce: alimony, child support, and property division. In general, the tax law governing these categories is as follows:

- The person who pays alimony (the payor) can deduct it.
- The person who receives alimony (the recipient or payee) must report it as income and pay taxes on it.
- Child-support payments are not deductible to the payor or reportable as income by the recipient.
- Payments pursuant to a property division are not deductible to the payor or reportable as income by the recipient.

Since alimony is deductible, but child-support and property division payments are not, attempts are sometimes made to disguise child-support or property division payments as alimony. Why would alimony recipients agree to the disguise in view of the fact that they would have to pay taxes on the alimony received? In the bargaining process, they may be given some other benefit in the separation agreement in exchange for cooperation in disguising child-support or property division payments as alimony. The effort, however, may not work. A major theme of this chapter is determining when the Internal Revenue Service (IRS) will challenge the disguise.

ALIMONY

adjusted gross income (AGI) The total amount of income received by a taxpayer less allowed deductions.

Alimony payments are:

- Reported as taxable income on line 11 of the recipient's 1040 return (see Exhibit 11.1) and
- Deducted from gross income on line 31a of the payor's 1040 return to obtain the latter's **adjusted gross income (AGI)** (refer again to Exhibit 11.1)

Exhibit 11.1 1040 Income Tax Form

Form **1040** Department of the Treasury—Internal Revenue Service **U.S. Individual Income Tax Return 2000** (99) IRS Use Only—Do not write or staple in this space.

For the year Jan. 1–Dec. 31, 2000, or other tax year beginning , 2000, ending , 20 OMB No. 1545-0074

Label (See instructions on page 19.) **Use the IRS label.** Otherwise, please print or type. LABEL HERE

Your first name and initial | Last name | **Your social security number**

If a joint return, spouse's first name and initial | Last name | **Spouse's social security number**

Home address (number and street). If you have a P.O. box, see page 19. | Apt. no.

City, town or post office, state, and ZIP code. If you have a foreign address, see page 19.

▲ Important! ▲ You **must** enter your SSN(s) above.

Presidential Election Campaign (See page 19.) **Note.** Checking "Yes" will not change your tax or reduce your refund. Do you, or your spouse if filing a joint return, want $3 to go to this fund? ▶ You ☐Yes ☐No Spouse ☐Yes ☐No

Filing Status

Check only one box.

1 ☐ Single
2 ☐ Married filing joint return (even if only one had income)
3 ☐ Married filing separate return. Enter spouse's social security no. above and full name here. ▶
4 ☐ Head of household (with qualifying person). (See page 19.) If the qualifying person is a child but not your dependent, enter this child's name here. ▶
5 ☐ Qualifying widow(er) with dependent child (year spouse died ▶). (See page 19.)

Exemptions

6a ☐ **Yourself.** If your parent (or someone else) can claim you as a dependent on his or her tax return, **do not** check box 6a
b ☐ **Spouse**
c **Dependents:**

(1) First name Last name	(2) Dependent's social security number	(3) Dependent's relationship to you	(4) ✓ if qualifying child for child tax credit (see page 20)
			☐
			☐
			☐
			☐
			☐
			☐

If more than six dependents, see page 20.

d Total number of exemptions claimed

No. of boxes checked on 6a and 6b ____
No. of your children on 6c who:
• lived with you ____
• did not live with you due to divorce or separation (see page 20) ____
Dependents on 6c not entered above ____
Add numbers entered on lines above ▶ ☐

Income

Attach Forms W-2 and W-2G here. Also attach Form(s) 1099-R if tax was withheld.

If you did not get a W-2, see page 21.

Enclose, but do not attach, any payment. Also, please use **Form 1040-V.**

7 Wages, salaries, tips, etc. Attach Form(s) W-2 — 7
8a **Taxable** interest. Attach Schedule B if required — 8a
b **Tax-exempt** interest. **Do not** include on line 8a — 8b
9 Ordinary dividends. Attach Schedule B if required — 9
10 Taxable refunds, credits, or offsets of state and local income taxes (see page 22) — 10
11 Alimony received — 11
12 Business income or (loss). Attach Schedule C or C-EZ — 12
13 Capital gain or (loss). Attach Schedule D if required. If not required, check here ▶ ☐ — 13
14 Other gains or (losses). Attach Form 4797 — 14
15a Total IRA distributions 15a — b Taxable amount (see page 23) — 15b
16a Total pensions and annuities 16a — b Taxable amount (see page 23) — 16b
17 Rental real estate, royalties, partnerships, S corporations, trusts, etc. Attach Schedule E — 17
18 Farm income or (loss). Attach Schedule F — 18
19 Unemployment compensation — 19
20a Social security benefits 20a — b Taxable amount (see page 25) — 20b
21 Other income. List type and amount (see page 25) — 21
22 Add the amounts in the far right column for lines 7 through 21. This is your **total income** ▶ — 22

Recipient reports alimony as income on line 11.

Adjusted Gross Income

23 IRA deduction (see page 27) — 23
24 Student loan interest deduction (see page 27) — 24
25 Medical savings account deduction. Attach Form 8853 — 25
26 Moving expenses. Attach Form 3903 — 26
27 One-half of self-employment tax. Attach Schedule SE — 27
28 Self-employed health insurance deduction (see page 29) — 28
29 Self-employed SEP, SIMPLE, and qualified plans — 29
30 Penalty on early withdrawal of savings — 30
31a Alimony paid b Recipient's SSN ▶ — 31a
32 Add lines 23 through 31a — 32
33 Subtract line 32 from line 22. This is your **adjusted gross income** ▶ — 33

Payor reports alimony payments as an adjustment to income on line 31a and gives the recipient's social security number on line 31b. Alimony is deducted from gross income to obtain the taxpayer's adjusted gross income.

For Disclosure, Privacy Act, and Paperwork Reduction Act Notice, see page 56. Cat. No. 11320B Form **1040** (2000)

Since the deduction comes through the determination of adjusted gross income, there is no need to itemize deductions in order to take advantage of it.

Note that line 31b in Exhibit 11.1 requires the payor to give the social security number of the recipient. Failure to do so can result in a $50 penalty and a disallowance of the deduction. Providing this information will make it easier for the IRS to check its own records to make sure that the recipient is reporting as income what the payor is deducting as alimony.

Deductible Alimony: The Seven Tests

When does a payment qualify as alimony for tax purposes? When it meets the seven requirements for alimony listed in Exhibit 11.2. A more thorough discussion of each requirement follows:

- Divorce or separation agreement
- No joint return
- Parties are not members of the same household
- Payment in cash
- No payment after death of recipient
- Payment is not improperly disguised child support
- Parties have not exercised nonalimony option

Exhibit 11.2 Requirements for Deductible Alimony

A payment qualifies as alimony when:

1. The payment is to a spouse or former spouse under a divorce decree or separation agreement.
2. The parties do not file a joint tax return with each other.
3. The parties are not members of the same household when the payment is made. (This third requirement applies only if the parties are legally separated under a decree of divorce or separate maintenance.)
4. The payment is in cash.
5. There is no obligation to make any payment (in cash or other property) after the death of the recipient.
6. The payment is not improperly disguised child support.
7. The parties have not exercised the option of treating qualifying alimony payments as nonalimony.

Divorce or Separation Agreement The payment must be to a spouse or former spouse pursuant to and required by a divorce decree or a separation agreement.[1] The decree does not have to be final. A payment ordered by an *interlocutory* (interim or nonfinal) decree or a decree *pendente lite* (while awaiting the court's final decree) can also qualify.

If a spouse makes an *additional* payment beyond what is required by the divorce or separation agreement, the additional payment is not alimony for tax purposes.

> *A 1999 separation agreement requires Linda to pay her ex-husband, Fred, a total of $1,000 per month in alimony. Assume that this amount fulfills all the requirements of deductible alimony. Hence, Linda can deduct each $1,000 payment and Fred must report it as income. During the last seven months of the year, Linda decides to increase her alimony*

[1]The rules also apply to payments pursuant to a decree of separate maintenance and a decree of annulment. The rules are limited to payments made after 1984. Different rules apply to payments made before 1985.

payments to $3,000 each month in order to cover some extra expenses Fred is incurring.

Linda may *not* deduct the extra $14,000 ($2,000 × 7 months) she voluntarily added, and Fred does not have to report this $14,000 as income on his return. This is so even if state law considers the entire $3,000 payment each month to be alimony. Under *federal tax* law, voluntary alimony payments are not deductible.

No Joint Return The parties must not file a joint tax return with each other at the time the attempt is made to deduct the alimony.

Parties Are Not Members of the Same Household If the parties have been separated under a decree of divorce or separate maintenance, they must not be members of the same household when the alimony payment is made. Living in separate rooms is not enough; the parties must not be living in the same physical home or apartment. There is, however, a one-month grace period. If one of the parties is planning to move and in fact does move within one month of the payment, it *is* deductible even though they were living together when the payment was made.

Jack and Tara live at 100 Elm Street. They are divorced on January 1, 2000. Under the divorce decree, Jack is obligated to pay Tara $500 a month in alimony on the first of each month. He makes his first payment January 1, 2000. He moves out of the Elm Street house on February 15, 2000.

The January 1, 2000, payment is *not* deductible. Since the parties have a divorce decree, they must not be living in the same household at the time of the alimony payment. Jack and Tara were both living at 100 Elm Street—the same household—at the time of that payment. The one-month grace period does not apply, since Jack did not move out within a month of this payment. If he had left earlier (e.g., January 29, 2000), the payment *would* have been deductible. Of course, the February 1, 2000, payment and all payments after February 15, 2000 (when they opened separate households), are deductible if the other requirements for deductible alimony are met.[2]

Payment in Cash Only *cash* payments, including checks and money orders, qualify.

Under the terms of a separation agreement and divorce decree, Bob:

- *Gives Mary, his ex-wife, a car*
- *Paints her house*
- *Lets her use his mother's house*
- *Gives her stocks, bonds, or an annuity contract*

The value of these items cannot be deducted as alimony, since they are not in cash.

Can cash payments made by the payor *to a third party* be deducted as alimony?

Bob sends $1,000 to Mary's landlord to pay her rent. He also sends $800 to Mary's college to cover part of her tuition costs and $750 to Mary's bank to pay the mortgage on the vacation house she owns.

---

[2]There is an exception to the same-household rule. If the parties are not legally separated under a decree of divorce or separate maintenance, but make a payment pursuant to a separation agreement, support decree, or other court order, the payment may qualify as alimony even if the parties are members of the same household when the payment is made.

Can Bob deduct any of these payments as alimony, and does Mary have to report them as income? The answer is yes if the cash payment to the third party is required by the divorce decree or by the separation agreement and meets all other requirements for deductible alimony. Also, cash payments made to a third party at the written request of a spouse can qualify as alimony if the following conditions are met:

- The payments to the third party are in lieu of payments of alimony directly to the spouse;
- The written request says that both spouses intend the payments to be treated as alimony; and
- The payor receives the written request before filing the return that seeks the alimony deduction for the payments to the third party.

Suppose that the third party is an insurance company.

Bob pays an annual premium of $1,700 on a life insurance policy on his life, with Mary as the beneficiary.

Can he deduct these premiums as alimony? The answer is yes, but only if:

- The payor (Bob) is obligated to make these premium payments by the divorce decree or separation agreement and
- The beneficiary (Mary) *owns* the policy so that the payor cannot change the beneficiary.

No Payment after Death of Recipient If the payor is obligated (under the divorce decree or separation agreement) to make payments after the death of the recipient, none of the payments made after *or before* the death of the recipient qualifies as alimony. Here the IRS is trying to catch a blatant and improper attempt to disguise property division as alimony in order to take advantage of a deduction.

Under the terms of a separation agreement, Bob agrees to pay Mary $10,000 a year "in alimony" for fifteen years. If Mary dies within the fifteen years, Bob will make the remaining annual payments to Mary's estate. In the twelfth year of the agreement, after Bob has paid Mary $120,000 (12 years × $10,000), Mary dies. For the next three years, Bob makes the remaining annual payments, totaling $30,000 (3 years × $10,000), to Mary's estate.

All of the payments made by Bob—the entire $150,000 covering the periods before and after Mary's death—will be disallowed as alimony. It makes no difference that the separation agreement called the payments "alimony." To qualify as deductible alimony, one of the tests is that the payor must have no liability for payments after the death of the recipient.

Most debts continue in effect after the death of either party. If, for example, I pay you $3,500 to buy your car and you die before delivering the car to me, it is clear that your obligation to give me the car survives your death. Your estate would have to give me the car. The same is true of a property division debt. Assume that Bob is obligated under a property division agreement to transfer a house to Mary, his ex-wife. If Bob dies before making this transfer, his estate can be forced to complete the transfer to Mary. Property division debts survive the death of either party. Alimony is different. It is very rare for a "real" alimony debt to continue after the death of the recipient. After the recipient dies, he or she does not need alimony! Whenever the payor must make payments beyond the death of the recipient, the payments are really part of a property division.

At the time of their separation, Mary had a separate career in which she earned a high salary. Bob owned a going business valued at $400,000, *which he started when he married Mary. Bob and Mary agreed that she should have a substantial share of this business as part of the property division between them. But Bob does not want to sell the business in order to give Mary her share. In the negotiations, Mary asks for $150,000, payable immediately. Bob agrees that $150,000 is a fair amount, but he doesn't have it. Hence he counters by offering her $200,000 payable over ten years in $20,000 annual payments to be labeled as "alimony" in their separation agreement. If Mary dies within the ten years, Bob will make the annual payments to Mary's estate. The extra $50,000 is added to offset the fact that Mary will have to wait in order to receive all her money and will have to pay income tax on whatever Bob declares as deductible alimony.*

Again, this arrangement will not work. There are ways to disguise property division as alimony, but this is not one of them. The $200,000 can never be deductible alimony, since the parties planned to continue the payments after the death of the recipient.

The IRS will reach the same conclusion if the payor agrees to make a substitute payment to a third party upon the death of the recipient or a lump-sum payment to the estate of the recipient after his or her death.

PAYMENT IS IMPROPERLY DISGUISED CHILD SUPPORT Child support is neither deductible by the payor nor includible in the income of the recipient. But what is child support? This question is easy to answer if the divorce decree or separation agreement specifically designates or fixes a payment (or part of a payment) as child support.

Under the terms of a divorce decree, Jane must pay Harry $2,000 a month, of which $1,600 is designated for the support of their child in the custody of Harry.

The $1,600 has been fixed as child support. Hence it is not deductible by Jane or includible in the income of Harry. This remains true even if the amount so designated varies from time to time.

Suppose, however, payments are made to the parent with custody of the children, but the parties say nothing about child support in their separation agreement. Assume that there is as yet no divorce decree. In the separation agreement, the payments are labeled "alimony." In such a case, the IRS will suspect that the parties are trying to disguise child-support payments as alimony in order to trigger a deduction for the payor. The suspicion will be even stronger if the payments are to be *reduced* upon the happening of certain events or contingencies that relate to the child's need for support.

Under the terms of a separation agreement, Bill will pay Grace $2,000 a month "in alimony," which will be reduced to $800 a month when their child leaves the household and obtains a job.

The parties are trying to disguise $1,200 a month as alimony, although it is fairly obvious that this amount is child support. Otherwise, why would the parties reduce the payment at a time when the child would no longer need support? There is no other reason for the parties to add such a **contingency.** The device will not work.

contingency
An event that may or may not occur.

The IRS will conclude that a payment is child support rather than alimony when the amount of the payment is to be reduced:

1. On the happening of a contingency relating to the child or
2. At a time that can be clearly associated with a contingency relating to the child.

A contingency relates to a child when the contingency depends on an event that relates to that child.

The separation agreement of Bill and Mary Smith says that an "alimony" payment from Bill to Mary will be reduced by a designated amount when their son, Bob, does any of the following:

- *Dies*
- *Marries*
- *Leaves school*
- *Leaves home (temporarily or permanently)*
- *Gains employment*
- *Attains a specified income level*
- *Reaches a specified age (see discussion below, however, on reductions that occur at the age of majority)*

Since each of these contingencies depends on an event that obviously relates to the child, no alimony deduction is allowed.

A payor will often want to reduce a payment when the child reaches the age of majority, which is usually eighteen under state law. Will the IRS treat this reduction as an indication that alimony is being improperly disguised as child support? From what we have said thus far, one would expect the answer to be an unqualified "yes." But this is not necessarily so. The rule is as follows:

> The IRS will *presume* that a payment is child support if the reduction is to occur not more than six months before or after the child reaches the age of majority in the state.

Thus, if the reduction is to occur *more* than six months before or after the child reaches the age of majority, it can be treated as alimony.

Leo, Elaine, and their son, Fred, live in a state where the age of majority is eighteen. Fred was born on March 13, 1982. Leo and Elaine are divorced on January 12, 2000. Under the terms of the divorce decree, Elaine gets custody of Fred, and Leo must pay Elaine $2,000 a month in "alimony" until July 13, 2000, when the monthly payments are reduced to $1,200.

On these facts, the IRS will presume that the amount of the reduction is child support. Fred reaches the age of majority on March 13, 2000, when he turns eighteen. The reduction occurs on July 13, 2000, four months afterward. Since this reduction occurs not more than six months after the child reaches the age of majority, the presumption of child support applies.[3] The IRS will presume that the amount of the reduction ($800) is child support.

Same facts as above example involving Leo, Elaine, and Fred except that the reduction is to occur on March 13, 2001.

On these facts, the presumption of child support does not apply. The reduction occurs one year after Fred reaches the age of majority, which of course is more than six months. The entire $2,000 can be deductible alimony.

PARTIES HAVE NOT EXERCISED NONALIMONY OPTION Assume that all of the first six tests for determining alimony (see Exhibit 11.2) are met by the parties. As a result, the payor can deduct the payments and the recipient must include them in income. But suppose the parties do *not* want the payments to be deductible/includible. It may be, for example, that both parties are in the same tax bracket and hence neither would benefit significantly more than the other by having the tax alimony rules apply. They can decide to treat otherwise qualifying alimony payments as *nonalimony.* This is done by including a provision

---

[3]This presumption can be rebutted by showing that the time at which the payments are to be reduced was determined independently of any contingencies relating to the children. For example, the payment period might be one customarily provided in the state, such as a period equal to one-half the duration of the marriage.

in the separation agreement or by asking the court to include a provision in the divorce decree that the payments will *not* be deductible to the payor and will be excludible from the income of the recipient.

This designation of nondeductibility/nonincludibility must be attached to the recipient's tax return for every year in which it is effective.

The Recapture Rule: Front Loading of Payments

A common tactic of a party who wants to try to disguise property division payments as alimony is to make substantial payments shortly after the divorce or separation (i.e., to **front load** the payments).

front load
To make substantial "alimony" payments shortly after the separation or divorce.

Jim runs a cleaning business, which he developed during his marriage to Pat. The value of the business is $234,000 on the date of their divorce. During their negotiations for the separation agreement, they both agree that each should receive a one-half share ($117,000) of the business, which Jim wants to continue to run after the divorce. They are clearly thinking about a property division. Of course, any payments pursuant to a property division are not deductible. Jim suggests a different route: he will pay Pat the following amounts of "alimony" during the first three years of their separation:

Year	*Amount Paid*
1999	*$50,000*
2000	*$39,000*
2001	*$28,000*

In return, Pat will give Jim a release of her interest in the business.

Jim has front loaded the payments of the $117,000 he agreed to give Pat. Note that the bulk of the payments come at the beginning of the three-year period. Will the IRS accept this arrangement and allow Jim to take an alimony deduction in each of the three years? The governing rule is as follows:

> Alimony must be recaptured in the third year if (1) the alimony paid in the third year decreases by more than $15,000 from the second year or (2) the alimony paid in the second and third years decreases significantly from the amount paid in the first year.[4]

This is known as the **recapture rule.** To determine the amount to be recaptured, you use the worksheet in Exhibit 11.3. In our example, the amount to be recaptured is $1,500.

recapture rule
Tax liability will be recalculated when the parties improperly front load "alimony" deductions.

How does the recapture occur? The payor must now declare as taxable income the amounts improperly deducted as alimony. Since the recipient paid taxes on the amounts improperly deducted by the payor, the recipient is now allowed to deduct those amounts.

Payor: Of the amounts Jim deducted, $1,500 must be recaptured on line 11 of his 2001 return. Line 11 now says "Alimony received" (see Exhibit 11.1). Jim must cross out the word *received* and write in the word *recapture,* so that line 11 will now read "Alimony recapture." Once $1,500 is entered in this way, it becomes taxable income. On the dotted line of line 11, Jim must also enter the recipient's (Pat's) name and social security number.

Recipient: Pat can now deduct the recaptured $1,500 on line 31a of her 2001 return. Line 31a now says "Alimony paid" (see Exhibit 11.1). She

[4]When figuring decreases in alimony, do not include the following amounts: payments made under a temporary support order; payments required over a period of at least three calendar years of a fixed part of income from a business or property, or from compensation for employment or from self-employment; or payments that decrease because of the death of either spouse or the remarriage of the spouse receiving the payments.

Exhibit 11.3 Recapture Worksheet

Note: Do not enter less than zero on any line.

Line			
1. Alimony paid in 2nd year		**1.** 39,000	
2. Alimony paid in 3rd year	**2.** 28,000		
3. Floor	**3.** $15,000		
4. Add lines 2 and 3		**4.** 43,000	
5. Subtract line 4 from line 1			**5.** 0
6. Alimony paid in 1st year		**6.** 50,000	
7. Adjusted alimony paid in 2nd year (line 1 less line 5)	**7.** 39,000		
8. Alimony paid in 3rd year	**8.** 28,000		
9. Add lines 7 and 8	**9.** 67,000		
10. Divide line 9 by 2	**10.** 33,500		
11. Floor	**11.** $15,000		
12. Add lines 10 and 11		**12.** 48,500	
13. Subtract line 12 from line 6			**13.** 1,500
14. **Recaptured alimony.** Add lines 5 and 13			***14.** 1,500

*If you deducted alimony paid, report this amount as income on line 11, Form 1040. If you reported alimony received, deduct this amount on line 31a, Form 1040.

must cross out the word *paid* and write in the word *recapture,* so that line 31a will now read "Alimony recapture." Once entered in this way, the amount is deducted in calculating her adjusted gross income. On line 31b, she must also enter Jim's social security number.

The recapture rule is not limited to cases where the parties are trying to disguise property division as alimony. The rule applies to excessive reductions in the second or third year for other reasons as well. Suppose, for example, that there was a significant reduction in the third year simply because the payor could not raise the agreed-upon amount in that year. The excess must still be recaptured if the calculations in Exhibit 11.3 call for it.

PROPERTY DIVISION

In this section, our focus will be the division of marital property between spouses. Before discussing the tax consequences of such a property division, we will review some basic terminology.

Tom buys a house in 1980 for $60,000. He spends $10,000 to add a new room. In 1991, he sells the house to a stranger for $100,000.

- ***Transferor*** *The person who transfers property. Tom is the transferor.*
- ***Transferee*** *The person to whom property is transferred. The stranger is the transferee.*
- ***Appreciation*** *An increase in value. Tom's house appreciated by $40,000 (from $60,000 to $100,000). He has made a profit, called a* gain. *The gain, however is* not *$40,000. See the definition for* adjusted basis *below.*
- ***Depreciation*** *A decrease in value. If the highest price Tom could have obtained for his house had been $55,000, the house would have depreciated by $5,000.*
- ***Realize*** *To benefit from or receive. Normally,* income, gain, *or* loss *is realized when it is received. If Tom could sell his house for*

$100,000, but he decides not to do so, he has not realized any income. He has a "paper" gain only. He does not have to pay taxes on a gain until he has realized a gain, such as by selling the house.

- ***Fair Market Value*** *The price that could be obtained in an open market between a willing buyer and a willing seller dealing* at arm's length. *A sale between a parent and a child will usually not be at fair market value, since the fact that they are related will probably affect the price paid. It is possible for a happily married husband and wife to sell things to each other at fair market value, but the likelihood is that they will not. In our example, Tom sold his house for $100,000 to a stranger. There is no indication that the buyer or seller was pressured into the transaction or that either had any special relationship with each other that might have affected the price or the terms of the deal. The price paid, therefore, was the fair market value.*
- ***Basis*** *The initial capital investment, usually the cost of the property. Tom's basis in his house is $60,000.*
- ***Adjusted Basis*** *The basis of the property after adjustments are made. The basis is either adjusted upward (increased) by the amount of* capital improvements *(i.e., structural improvements on the property) or adjusted downward. Tom added a room to his house—a structural improvement. His basis ($60,000) is increased by the amount of the capital expenditure ($10,000), giving him an adjusted basis of $70,000.*

When Tom sold his house for $100,000, he *realized* income. To determine whether he realized a gain or profit, we need to compare this figure with his adjusted basis. The amount of gain for tax purposes is determined as follows:

SALE PRICE − ADJUSTED BASIS = TAXABLE GAIN
($100,000) ($70,000) ($30,000)

Tom must declare this gain of $30,000 on his tax return. Of course, if the sale price had been *less* than the adjusted basis, he would have realized a loss. If, for example, he had sold the house for $65,000, his loss would have been $5,000 ($70,000 − $65,000).

Tax Consequences of a Property Division

A property division can be in cash or in other property. To illustrate:

CASH: *Ex-wife receives a lump sum of $50,000 (or five yearly payments of $10,000) in exchange for the release of any rights she may have in property acquired during the marriage.*
Other Property: *Ex-wife receives the marital home, and ex-husband receives stocks and the family business. They both release any rights they may have in property acquired during the marriage.*

Cash property divisions rarely pose difficulties unless the parties are trying to disguise property division as alimony in order to take advantage of the deductibility of alimony. We already discussed when such attempts will be unsuccessful. A true property division in cash is a nontaxable event; nothing is deducted and nothing is included in the income of either party. The IRS will assume that what was exchanged was of equal value.

Suppose, however, that property other than cash is transferred in a property division and that the property so transferred had *appreciated* in value since the time it had been acquired.

Tom buys a house in 1980 for $60,000. He spends $10,000 to add a new room. In 1991, on the date of his divorce, he transfers the house to his wife,

Tara, as part of a property division that they negotiated. Tara releases any rights (e.g., dower) that she may have in his property. On the date of the transfer, the fair market value of the house is $100,000.

Tom's adjusted basis in the house was $70,000 (his purchase price of $60,000 plus the capital improvement of $10,000). If Tom had transferred the house to a stranger for $100,000, he would have realized a gain of $30,000 ($100,000 less his adjusted basis of $70,000). The picture is dramatically different, however, when property is transferred to a spouse because of a divorce.

Two important questions need to be raised:

1. When *appreciated* property is transferred as part of a property division, is any gain or loss realized?
2. What is the transferee's basis in appreciated property that is transferred as part of a property division?

The answer to the first question is no. The IRS will not recognize any gain or loss upon the transfer of appreciated property because of a divorce. In the Tom/Tara example, therefore, Tom does not realize a gain even though he transferred to Tara a $100,000 house in which his adjusted basis was $70,000.[5] The answer to the second question is that the basis of the transferee is the same as the adjusted basis of the transferor at the time of the transfer. Hence Tara's basis in the house when she receives it is $70,000—Tom's adjusted basis when he transferred it to her as part of the divorce.

Assume that a week after Tara receives the house, she sells it to a stranger for $105,000. On these facts, she would realize a gain of $35,000, since her basis in the house is $70,000, its adjusted basis when she received it from Tom.

SALE PRICE	– ADJUSTED BASIS	= TAXABLE GAIN
($105,000)	($70,000)	($35,000)

Needless to say, it is essential that a spouse know the adjusted basis of the property in the hands of the other spouse before accepting that property as part of a property division. It is meaningless, for example, to be told that property is "worth $150,000" on the market unless you are also told what the adjusted basis of that property is. Furthermore, the law office representing the transferee must insist that the transferor turn over records that will allow the transferee to determine the adjusted basis of the property. This could include a copy of the original purchase contract and all contractor bills or statements that will prove what capital improvements were made to the property. Without such records, the transferee will not be able to tell the IRS, perhaps years later, what the adjusted basis of the property is.

These rules do not apply to every transfer of property between ex-spouses. We turn now to those that are covered.

Property Transfers Covered

In general, the tax rules governing a property division apply to property transfers that are *incident to a divorce.* A property transfer is incident to a divorce when the transfer:

- Occurs within one year after the date on which the marriage ends *or*
- Is related to the ending of the marriage

---

[5]The rule was otherwise before 1984, when gain was recognized when appreciated property was transferred because of a divorce. Transferors complained bitterly. They could not claim a deduction (since the property division was not alimony), and they had to pay taxes on paper gains due to the appreciation. This was the ruling of *United States v. Davis,* 370 U.S. 65 (1962). Congress changed the law in 1984, however, so that gains and losses were no longer recognized in property divisions due to a divorce. The change negated the ruling of *United States v. Davis.*

A property transfer is related to the ending of the marriage *if* it occurs within six years after the date on which the marriage ends *and* is made under the original or a modified divorce or separation instrument.

A property transfer that is not made under a divorce or separation instrument or that does not occur within six years after the end of the marriage is *presumed* to be unrelated to the ending of the marriage unless the parties can show that some business or legal factors prevented an earlier transfer of the property and that the transfer was made promptly after these factors were taken care of.

Gabe solely owns a garage and a residence. He and his wife, Janet, are divorced on January 10, 1985. Pursuant to a property division that is spelled out in their separation agreement, Gabe will keep the residence but will transfer the garage to Janet on March 13, 1992.

Was the transfer of the garage incident to a divorce? It did not occur within a year of the ending of the marriage. But was it related to the ending of the marriage? It did not occur within six years of the ending of the marriage. The transfer was made just over seven years after the divorce. We are not told why the parties waited this long after the divorce, but there is no evidence of business or legal factors that prevented an earlier transfer. Hence the IRS will *presume* that the transfer was not related to the ending of the marriage. This means that Janet's basis in the garage will be its fair market value on March 13, 1992, not whatever Gabe's adjusted basis in it was.

Exhibit 11.4 contains a summary of the tax rules we have discussed thus far.

Exhibit 11.4 Tax Treatment of Payments and Transfers Pursuant to Divorce Agreements and Decrees

	Payor	Recipient
Alimony	Deduction from income.	Included in income.
Alimony recapture	Included in income in the third year	Deducted from income in the third year.
Child support	Not deductible.	Not includible in income.
Property settlement	Not included in income. Not deductible.	Not included in income. Not deductible; basis for the property is the same as the transferor's adjusted basis if the transfer is incident to a divorce.

Source: West's Federal Taxation: Individual Income Taxes, 4–22 (1994).

LEGAL AND RELATED FEES IN OBTAINING A DIVORCE

Obtaining a divorce can be expensive. In addition to attorney fees, one or both parties may have to hire an accountant, actuary, and appraiser. Only two types of such fees are deductible:

- Fees paid for *tax* advice in connection with a divorce
- Fees paid to obtain *alimony* included in gross income

Other fees are not deductible. For example, you cannot deduct legal fees paid to negotiate the most advantageous or financially beneficial property division.

Bills from professionals received by a taxpayer should include a breakdown showing the amount charged for each service performed.

For legal representation in divorce case	*$9,000*
For tax advice in connection with the divorce	*800*
Total bill	*$9,800*
Only $800 is deductible.	

For legal representation in divorce case	*$6,500*
For legal representation in obtaining alimony	*1,200*
Total bill	*$7,700*
Only $1,200 is deductible.	

To deduct fees for these services, the taxpayer must itemize deductions in the year claimed. They go on Schedule A of the 1040 return under Miscellaneous Deductions. As such, they are subject to the 2 percent limit of adjusted gross income.

INNOCENT SPOUSE RELIEF

What happens when the IRS determines that taxes and penalties are due on prior returns of spouses who have just divorced? Who pays? Frequently, one of the spouses simply signed the return prepared by the other spouse with little knowledge of the sources of income that was reported on the return—or that should have been reported on the return. (While the less-involved spouse can be the husband or the wife, the following discussion will assume it is the homemaker/wife, since this is the most common situation.) When the IRS audits the return, the ex-wife says, "I was not involved in his business; I just signed what he told me to sign; I never kept any of the records." At one time, the rule was that the signers of a joint return are jointly *and individually* responsible for taxes and penalties even if they later divorce and even if a separation agreement or divorce court decree says that only the husband will be responsible for all taxes and penalties due on a prior return. This meant that the IRS could still demand payment from the wife. This could create a substantial hardship when the husband is unwilling or unable to pay due to obstinacy, disappearance, or financial setbacks.

Recently, Congress changed the law to provide some relief to the innocent spouse in such cases. It is called **innocent spouse relief.** She must be able to prove that at the time she signed the return, she did not know and had no reason to know that her husband understated the taxes that were due. The IRS will decide whether, under all the facts and circumstances of the case, it would be unfair to hold her responsible for the understatement of tax due on the return.

innocent spouse relief
A former spouse will not be liable for taxes and penalties owed on prior joint returns if he or she can prove that at the time he or she signed the return, he or she did not know and had no reason to know that the other spouse understated the taxes due. The IRS must conclude that under all the facts and circumstances of the case it would be unfair to hold the innocent spouse responsible for the understatement of tax on the return.

MARRIAGE PENALTY

When most of the income in a marriage is earned by one of the spouses, less tax is paid if the couple files a joint return than if each files an individual return on his or her separate income. This is sometimes called a marriage bonus. If, however, the spouses earn roughly the same income, they often pay more taxes when filing a joint return than if they file as single taxpayers. The reason is that their combined incomes push the couple into a higher income bracket than they would be in if they remained single. This is called the **marriage penalty**—the increased taxes that a two-income couple pays when filing a joint return. In 1999, 25 million couples paid an average marriage penalty of $1,141 on their returns. Good accountants advise high-earning individuals to delay their marriage, if possible, until the

marriage penalty
If both spouses earn substantially the same income, they pay more taxes when filing a joint return than they would if they could file as single taxpayers.

beginning of the next year so that they can take advantage of the lower taxes each will pay on the individual return he or she files in the last year of single status. Indeed, there are couples who avoid marriage altogether in part because it is cheaper simply to live together. Some couples divorce every year and remarry at the beginning of the following year to avoid the marriage penalty! (A taxpayer's filing status is determined at the end of the year.) The courts, however, have agreed with the IRS that this divorce-remarriage tax avoidance strategy is illegal. For years, Congress has debated the elimination of the marriage penalty paid by two-income couples. This has been difficult to accomplish because of the complexity of the tax code, the wrangling of politics, and honest disagreement over the best way to eliminate the penalty. In 2001, Congress finally enacted legislation to address the problem. Relief for the two-income couple, however, does not begin until 2005 when partial relief is phased in. Complete elimination of the penalty does not occur until 2008.

ASSIGNMENT 11.1

John and Carol are divorced on September 1, 1991. Their separation agreement requires John to pay Carol $500 a month for her support until she dies. Use the guidelines of this chapter to answer the following questions, which present a number of variations in the case of John and Carol. (See General Instructions for the Legal-Analysis Assignment in Appendix A.)

a. Carol has an automobile accident. To help her with medical bills, John sends her a check for $900 with the following note: "Here's my monthly $500 payment plus an extra $400 alimony to help you with your medical bills." Can John deduct the entire $900 as alimony?

b. A year after the divorce, Carol has trouble paying her state income tax bill of $1,200. John wants to give her a gift of $1,200 in addition to his regular $500 monthly alimony. He sends $1,200 to the state tax department on her behalf. Can John deduct the $1,200 as alimony?

c. Assume that in the September 1, 1991 divorce, Carol is awarded $1,500 a month in alimony, effective immediately and payable on the first of each month. John makes a payment on September 1, 1991, and on October 1, 1991. During this time, John lived in the basement of their home, which has a separate entrance. He moves into his own apartment in another town on October 25, 1991. Which of the following 1991 payments, if any, are deductible: $1,500 (on September 1) and $1,500 (on October 1)?

d. Assume that under the divorce decree, John must make annual alimony payments to Carol of $30,000, ending on the earlier of the expiration of fifteen years or the death of Carol. If Carol dies before the expiration of the fifteen-year period, John must pay Carol's estate the difference between the total amount he would have paid her if she survived and the amount actually paid. Carol dies after the tenth year in which payments are made. John now pays her estate $150,000 ($450,000 − $300,000). How much of the $300,000 paid before her death is deductible alimony? How much of the $150,000 lump sum is deductible alimony?

e. Assume that under the terms of the separation agreement, John will pay Carol $200 a month in child support for their teenage child, Nancy, and $900 a month as alimony. If Nancy marries, however, the $900 payment will be reduced to $400 a month. What is deductible?

f. Assume that under the terms of the separation agreement, John will pay Carol $200 a month as child support for their only child, Nancy, and $900 a month as alimony. While Nancy is away at boarding school, however, the $900 payment will be reduced to $400 a month. What is deductible?

ASSIGNMENT 11.2

a. Greg was born on July 31, 1980. He is the only child of Bill and Karen. Under the terms of their separation agreement, which becomes effective on December 5, 1995, Bill is to have custody of Greg, and Karen is to pay him $4,000 a month in alimony. The agreement specifies that "none of the alimony is to be used for child support." On April 15, 1998, the alimony payment is to be reduced to $2,200 a month. What will be deductible in 1998?

b. Millie pays Paul the following amounts of alimony under the terms of her 1987 divorce decree:

Year	*Amount*
1987	$25,000
1988	4,000
1989	4,000

What amounts, if any, must be recaptured?

c. Under a 1989 separation agreement and divorce decree, Helen transfers a building she solely owns to her ex-husband, Ken, in exchange for his release of any rights he has in other property that Helen acquired during the marriage. The transfer is made on the day of the divorce. Helen had bought the building in 1986 for $1,000,000. In 1987, she made $200,000 worth of capital improvements in the building. Its fair market value on the date she transfers it to Ken is $1,500,000. A week later, however, the market crashes, and Ken is forced to sell the building for $800,000. What are the tax consequences of these transactions?

d. Dan and Karen are negotiating a separation agreement in contemplation of a divorce that they expect to occur within six months of today's date. Karen wants $1,000 a month in alimony, and she wants Dan to pay all of her legal fees. Dan agrees to do so. Assume that there will be no difficulty deducting the $1,000 a month under the alimony rules. Dan would also like to deduct what he pays for her legal fees, which are anticipated to be $12,000, of which $3,000 will be for obtaining alimony from Dan. What options exist for Dan?

SUMMARY

Tax consequences should be a part of the negotiation process in a separation and divorce.

If seven tests are met, alimony can be deducted by the payor but then must be declared as income by the recipient:

1. The payment must be to a spouse or former spouse and must be required by a divorce decree or separation agreement.
2. The parties must not file a joint tax return with each other.
3. The parties must not be members of the same household if they are separated under a decree of divorce or separate maintenance.
4. The payment must be in cash.
5. The payor must be under no obligation to make payments after the death of the recipient.
6. The payment must not be improperly disguised child support.
7. The parties must not elect to treat qualifying alimony payments as nonalimony.

If substantial payments are made within three years after a divorce or separation, the IRS will suspect that the parties are trying to disguise nondeductible, property division payments as deductible alimony payments. Such excessive front loading may result in a recalculation of taxes paid in the third year in order to recapture improper deductions for alimony.

In a property division incident to a divorce, property is transferred from one ex-spouse to the other. The property can be cash (e.g., $50,000) or noncash (e.g., a house). When there is a transfer of cash, none of it is deducted by the transferor, and none of it is included in the income of the transferee. When there is a transfer of noncash property that has appreciated in value, the following rules apply:

1. The transferor does not deduct anything.
2. The transferee does not include anything in income.
3. The transferor does not pay taxes on the amount of the appreciation.
4. The basis of the property in the hands of the transferee is the adjusted basis that the property had in the hands of the transferor.

A fee paid to your own attorney, accountant, or other professional is deductible if paid to obtain tax advice in connection with a divorce or if paid to help you obtain alimony that is included in gross income.

A former spouse will not be liable for taxes and penalties owed on prior joint returns if he or she can prove that at the time he or she signed the return, he or she did not know and had no reason to know that the other spouse understated the tax due and if the IRS concludes that it would be unfair to hold this spouse responsible for the understatement of tax on the return. If both spouses earn substantially the same income, they often pay more taxes when filing a joint return than they would if they could file as single taxpayers.

KEY CHAPTER TERMINOLOGY

adjusted gross income (AGI)
contingency
front load
recapture rule
transferor
transferee
appreciation
depreciation
realize
fair market value
basis
adjusted basis
innocent spouse relief
marriage penalty

ETHICS IN PRACTICE

You are a paralegal working at a law office that is representing David Harrison, a wealthy landowner whom everyone knows because of his exposure in the media. He is challenging the IRS's rejection of his claim of the deductibility of over $2 million in alimony. You work on this case because your supervising attorney is the main tax attorney at the firm. One day after work you return home looking tired. Your spouse asks you if you have had a bad day. You respond, "The Harrison case is driving me crazy; there is a good chance he may lose his $2 million deduction." Any ethical problems?

ON THE NET: MORE ON TAXATION AND FAMILY LAW

DivorceInfo: Taxes in Divorce
http://www.divorceinfo.com/taxes.htm

Tax Resources on the Web
http://pages.prodigy.net/agkalman/aklaw.htm#div

Tax Help and Education: Alimony Paid
http://www.irs.ustreas.gov/plain/tax_edu/teletax/tc452.html

Spousal Tax Relief Eligibility Explorer
http://www.irs.gov/ind_info/s_tree/index.html

CHAPTER 12

THE LEGAL RIGHTS OF WOMEN

CHAPTER OUTLINE

> Man is, or should be, woman's protector and defender. The natural and proper timidity and delicacy which belongs to the female sex evidently unfits it for many of the occupations of civil life. The constitution of the family organization, which is founded in the divine ordinance, as well as in the nature of things, indicates the domestic sphere as that which properly belongs to the domain and function of womanhood. . . . The paramount destiny and mission of woman are to fulfill the noble and benign offices of wife and mother. This is the law of the Creator. *Bradwell v. Illinois,* 83 U.S. (16 Wall.) 130, 140–41, 21 L. Ed. 442 (1872).

> No longer is the female destined solely for the home and the rearing of the family, and only the male for the marketplace, and the world of ideas. *Stanton v. Stanton,* 412 U.S. 7, 15, 95 S. Ct. 1373, 1378, 43 L. Ed. 2d 688 (1975).

THE STATUS OF WOMEN AT COMMON LAW

Today a married woman would consider it condescending to be told that she has the right to:

- Make her own will
- Own her own property
- Make a contract in her own name
- Be a juror
- Vote
- Bring a suit and be sued
- Execute a deed
- Keep her own earnings

There was a time in our history, however, when a married woman could engage in none of these activities, at least not without the consent of her husband. For example, she could not bring a suit against a third party unless her husband agreed to join in it. Upon marriage, any personal property that she owned automatically became her husband's. If she committed a crime in the presence of her husband, the law assumed that he forced her to commit it. If she worked outside the home, her husband was entitled to her earnings. In large measure, a married woman was the property of her husband. In short, at common law, the husband and wife were considered one person, and the one person was the husband.[1]

While a great deal has happened to change the status of married women, not all sex discrimination has been eliminated.

OWNING AND DISPOSING OF PROPERTY

married women's property acts
Statutes removing all or most of the legal disabilities imposed on women as to the disposition of their property.

Most states have enacted **married women's property acts,** which remove the disabilities married women suffered at common law. Under the terms of most of these statutes, women are given the right to own and dispose of property in the same manner as men. Without such laws, a woman would not have a separate legal existence.

ASSIGNMENT 12.1

Mary and Thad are married. Mary is a doctor and Thad is an architect. Before the marriage, Thad incurred a $35,000 debt at a local bank for his own education expenses. He is now in default on the loan. To collect this debt in your state, can the bank reach a vacation home that is solely owned by Mary? (See General Instructions for the State-Code Assignment and for the Court-Opinion Assignment in Appendix A.) Answer this question based on the following assumptions:

a. Mary acquired title to the vacation home as an inheritance from her uncle before she married Thad.
b. Mary acquired title to the vacation home as an inheritance from her uncle during her marriage to Thad.
c. Mary acquired title to the vacation home by buying it from a stranger solely from her own earnings as a doctor during her marriage to Thad.
d. Mary acquired title to the vacation home by buying it from Thad for $1 during the marriage. Thad inherited it from his mother before he married Mary. The sale to Mary was made just before Thad discovered that he was going to default on the bank loan. (See the next section on "Contracts and Conveyances.")

CONTRACTS AND CONVEYANCES

conveyance
The transfer of an interest in land.

Today women have the power to enter into all forms of contracts and **conveyances** in their own names, independent of their husbands. If, however, both spouses own property together, the wife normally must have the consent of her husband—and vice versa—to convey the property to someone else.

---

[1]An unmarried woman at common law was not as restricted, since she could own property and enter into contracts in her own name. But she could not vote or serve on juries, and her inheritance rights were limited. H. Clark, The Law of Domestic Relations in the United States § 8.1, p. 498 (practitioner's ed. 2d ed. 1987).

What about contracts and conveyances between the spouses? Are there any restrictions on the ability of one spouse to enter into agreements with the other while they are in a ongoing marriage? Such agreements are often referred to as **postnuptial agreements.** (On the various categories of agreements that are possible, see Exhibit 4.1 in chapter 4.) If the spouses are still living together, there are some restrictions on what they can do in a postnuptial agreement. For example, they cannot contract away their obligation to support each other (although this will be possible in a separation agreement, as we saw in chapter 8).

postnuptial agreement
An agreement between spouses while they are married. If they are separated or contemplating a separation or divorce, the agreement is called a separation agreement.

Courts tend to be very suspicious of conveyances of property between husband and wife. Suppose, for example, that a husband transfers all his property into his wife's name, for which she pays nothing, so that when he is sued by his creditors, he technically does not own any assets from which they can satisfy their claims. Since the transfer was made to avoid an obligation to a creditor, it is a **fraudulent transfer** and, if challenged, would be invalidated by a court.

fraudulent transfer
A transfer made to avoid an obligation to a creditor.

Two other situations can cause difficulty:

- The husband buys property with his separate funds but places the title in his wife's name. (Assume this is not a fraudulent transfer—he is not trying to defraud his creditors.)
- The wife buys property with her separate funds but places the title in her husband's name. (Again, assume no intent to defraud her creditors.)

Not all courts treat these two situations alike. In the first, most courts presume that the husband intended to make a gift of the property to his wife. In the second circumstance, however, there are some courts that do *not* presume a gift of the wife to her husband. Rather, they presume that the husband is holding the property in trust for his wife. Arguably, treating husbands and wives differently in this regard is an unconstitutional discrimination based on sex, and some courts have so held. The better rule is to presume that whatever *either* spouse contributes to the purchase price is a gift to the other spouse unless it is clear that they had a different intention.

ASSIGNMENT 12.2

For the following questions, you will need to consult the statutory code of your state and/or the opinions of courts in your state. (See General Instructions for the State-Code Assignment and for the Court-Opinion Assignment in Appendix A.)

a. In your state, is there a Married Women's Property Act or an equivalent statute? If so, what is the citation?
b. Is the consent of the husband required when his wife wishes to convey her separately owned property to a third person?
c. What restrictions, if any, exist in your state on the capacity of one spouse to enter into a contract with the other?
d. Suppose that a wife worked for her husband in the latter's business in your state. Does the husband have to pay her, or would such work be considered part of the "services" that she owes him?

DEATH OF THE HUSBAND

Dower

dower
The right of a widow to the lifetime use of one-third of the land her deceased husband owned during the marriage.

At common law, when a husband died, the surviving wife was given the protection of **dower,** although not all states defined dower in the same way. In many states, it was the right of a surviving wife to use one-third of all the real

forced share
The share of a deceased spouse's estate that a surviving spouse elects to receive in spite of what the deceased provided or failed to provide for the surviving spouse in a will.

right of election
The right to take a designated share of a deceased spouse's estate in spite of what the latter provided or failed to provide for the surviving spouse in a will.

intestate
Dying without leaving a valid will.

estate her deceased husband owned during the marriage.[2] The practical impact of this law was that the husband could not sell or give his property to others without accounting for her dower right. Very often she was paid to "waive her dower rights" so that others could obtain clear title to this property.[3]

Right of Election

Dower has been abolished in most states. In its place, the wife is given a share of her deceased husband's estate, often called a **forced share** because she can elect to take it in place of, and in spite of, what he gives her in his will. In exercising this **right of election,** she usually receives whatever the state would have provided for her if her husband had died **intestate.** (When a wife dies, her husband has a corresponding right of election against her will.)

ASSIGNMENT 12.3

For the following questions, examine the statutory code of your state. (See General Instructions for the State-Code Assignment in Appendix A.)

a. Has a dower been abolished in your state? If so, give the citation to the statute that abolished it.
b. If a widow is not satisfied with the property left her in the will of her deceased husband, what can she do in your state? Can she elect against the will?
c. If her husband dies intestate, what proportion of his estate will his widow receive in your state?
d. Does curtesy still exist in your state (see footnote 3)? If so, what is it? If not, what has replaced it?

NAME

Many women change their surname to that of their husband at the time of marriage. This is done for one of two reasons:

- The law of the state gives her a choice on keeping her maiden name or taking her husband's name, and she chooses the latter.
- The law of the state gives her a choice that she does not know about; she uses her husband's name simply because that is the custom.

At one time, the law of some states *required* her to use her husband's name. Such laws either have been repealed or are clearly subject to constitutional attack, since husbands are not required to take the name of their wife and no rational reason exists for the distinction. If she decides not to use her husband's name, she does not have to go through any special steps to exercise this choice. Once she is married, she simply continues using her maiden name, or she starts using a totally new name. For example, she may select a hybrid or combination name consisting of her maiden name and her husband's name. In such states, her legal name is whatever name she uses after her marriage so long as she is not trying to defraud anyone (e.g., to make it difficult for her creditors to locate her) and so long as her use of the name is exclusive and consistent.

In a divorce proceeding, all courts will grant her request that she be allowed to resume her maiden name or to use another name. Suppose, however,

---

[2]Some states imposed the requirement that she die leaving issue capable of inheriting the estate.
[3]The corresponding right of the husband was called *curtesy*. At common law, if a wife died, the surviving husband had the right to the lifetime use of *all* the land his deceased wife owned during the marriage if issue were born of the marriage.

that she asks the court to change the name of the children of the marriage. She may want them to have her new name or to take the name of the man she will marry when the divorce is final. Courts will not automatically grant such a request. They will want to be sure that the change would be in the best interests of the child.

Independent of marriage or divorce, every state has a statutory procedure that must be used when citizens (male or female) wish to change their names. This *change-of-name* procedure involves several steps (e.g., filing a petition to change one's name in the appropriate state court, stating the reasons for the change, paying a fee to the court, and publishing a notice of the court proceeding in a local newspaper). The process is usually not complicated so long as the court is convinced that the name change will not mislead anyone who may need to contact the individual (e.g., police officials, a former spouse, creditors).

ASSIGNMENT 12.4

For most of the following assignments, you will need to examine your state statutory code. You may also need to check opinions written by your state courts. (See General Instructions for the State-Code Assignment and for the Court-Opinion Assignment in Appendix A.)

a. When a woman marries in your state, does she have to take her husband's name?

b. After a divorce, how can a woman change her name to her maiden name?

c. Make a list of three different administrative agencies situated in your state that require some kind of application to be filled out (e.g., for a driver's license, for state employment, for food stamps, for workers' compensation). When Alice Kelly marries Peter Burke on March 1, 2001, she takes the name Alice Burke. On June 15, 2001, she wants to apply for benefits at the three agencies you selected. She wants to apply as Alice Kelly. Can she? Assume that she and Peter separate on June 1, 2001, and that she thinks she may divorce him someday. Contact each agency to find out if she can apply in her maiden name.

d. Prepare a flowchart of all the steps that an individual must go through to change his or her name in your state through the appropriate statutory procedure. (See General Instructions for the Flowchart Assignment in Appendix A.)

e. Assume that you want to change your name. Pick a new name. Draft all the necessary court papers to acquire your new name via the statutory procedure outlined in the flowchart prepared in part (d).

f. Mary Jones marries Tom Smith in your state. Her name then becomes Mary Smith. They have one child, Paul Smith. Tom abandons Mary. Can Mary have Paul's name changed to Paul Jones in your state? Assume that Paul is five years old and that Mary does not want to bring a divorce proceeding against Tom.

CREDIT

The federal Equal Credit Opportunity Act prohibits discrimination on the basis of sex or marital status in a credit application.[4] Creditors such as banks, finance companies, and department stores that violate the prohibition can be liable for damages, attorney fees, and court costs.

---

[4]Or on the basis of race, color, religion, national origin, or age. 15 U.S.C.A. § 1691.

- When you apply for credit, a creditor must not:

  1. Discourage you from applying because of your sex or marital status;
  2. Ask about your marital status if you are applying for a separate, unsecured account (note, however, that a creditor may ask for your marital status if you live in a community property state: Arizona, California, Idaho, Louisiana, Nevada, New Mexico, Texas, and Washington; also, in every state, a creditor may ask about your marital status if you apply for a joint account or one secured by property);
  3. Request information about your spouse except when your spouse is applying with you, when your spouse will be allowed to use the account, when you are relying on your spouse's income or on alimony or child-support income from a former spouse, or when you reside in a community property state;
  4. Inquire about your plans for having or raising children;
  5. Ask if you receive alimony, child-support, or separate maintenance payments (unless you are first told that you do not have to provide this information) if you will not be relying on these payments to obtain credit; (note, however, that a creditor may ask if *you* have to pay alimony, child-support, or separate maintenance payments);

- When evaluating your income, a creditor must not:

  1. Discount income because of your sex or marital status (for example, a creditor cannot count a man's salary at 100 percent and a woman's at 75 percent);
  2. Assume that a woman of childbearing age will stop working to raise children;
  3. Refuse your request that regular alimony, child-support, or separate maintenance payments be considered (note, however, that a creditor may ask you to prove you have received this income consistently);

- You also have the right to:

  1. Have credit in your birth name (Mary Smith), your first and your spouse's last name (Mary Jones), or your first name and a combined last name (Mary Smith-Jones);
  2. Obtain credit without a cosigner if you meet the creditor's standards;
  3. Have a cosigner other than your spouse if you legitimately need a cosigner;
  4. Keep your own accounts after you change your name, change your marital status, reach a certain age, or retire unless the creditor has evidence that you are not willing or able to pay;

- If you suspect discrimination:

  1. Complain to the creditor; make it known you are aware of your rights under the law;
  2. Report violations to the appropriate government agency (if you are denied credit, the creditor must give you the name and address of the agency to contact);
  3. check with your state attorney general to see if the creditor violated state equal credit opportunity laws and, if so, whether the state will prosecute the creditor;
  4. bring a case in federal district court;
  5. join with others and file a class action suit (recovery could include punitive damages of up to $500,000 or 1 percent of the creditor's net worth, whichever is less).[5]

---

[5]Federal Trade Commission, Equal Credit Opportunity (Mar. 1998); see <http://www.ftc.gov/bcp/conline/pubs/credit/ecoa.htm>.

EMPLOYMENT

Job Discrimination

There are many laws that in theory have eliminated job discrimination against women. The equal protection clause of the United States Constitution provides that:

> No State shall . . . deny to any person within its jurisdiction the equal protection of the laws.

If a state passes a law that treats women differently from men, it will be invalidated unless there is a reasonable purpose for the differentiation. Only *unreasonable* discrimination violates the Constitution. Title VII of the 1964 Civil Rights Act provides that:

> It shall be an unlawful employment practice for an employer . . . to fail or refuse to hire or to discharge any individual, or otherwise to discriminate against any individual with respect to his compensation, terms, conditions, or privileges of employment, because of such individual's . . . sex. . . .[6]

Again, this does not mean that all sex discrimination in employment is illegal. Job-related sex discrimination is permitted if sex is a **bona fide occupational qualification (BFOQ),** meaning that sex discrimination is reasonably necessary to the operation of a particular business or enterprise. For example, it would be proper for a state prison to exclude women from being guards in all-male prisons where a significant number of the inmates are convicted sex offenders. It is reasonable to anticipate that some of the inmates would attack the female guards, creating a security problem. In this instance, the discrimination based on sex (i.e., being a male) in an all-male prison would be a BFOQ. An even clearer example of a BFOQ would be an acting job that required someone to play a mother. On the other hand, a BFOQ does *not* exist simply because customers or co-workers prefer a person of a particular sex to fill a position.

bona fide occupational qualification (BFOQ)
Sex discrimination that is reasonably necessary for the operation of a particular business or enterprise.

An employer cannot refuse to hire a woman because of her pregnancy-related condition so long as she is able to perform the major functions necessary to the job. Also, an employer may not terminate workers because of pregnancy, force them to go on leave at an arbitrary point during pregnancy if they are still able to work, or penalize them in reinstatement rights, including credit for previous service, accrued retirement benefits, and accumulated seniority.

Finally, the law has begun to address the issue of pay disparity between men and women. The "median working man earns 59% more, in an average year, than the median working woman."[7] One of the major statutes covering the problem is the Equal Pay Act. This law prohibits employers from discriminating in pay because of sex if the job performed by men and women requires equal skill, effort, and responsibility under similar working conditions. There can, however, be pay differences based on seniority or merit.

It is illegal for an employer to retaliate against an employee who files a charge of employment discrimination.

Sexual Harassment

Sexual harassment is an unlawful employment practice under Title VII of the Civil Rights Act. There are two major kinds of sexual harassment:

> *Quid pro quo harassment:* Submission to or rejection of unwelcome sexual conduct is used as an explicit or implicit basis for employment decisions such as promotion or other job-related benefits.

---

[6]42 U.S.C.A. § 2000e-2(a)(1) (1974).
[7]Editorial, *New Numbers to Crunch,* N.Y. Times, Aug. 9, 2001, at A23

Hostile environment harassment: Pervasive unwelcome sexual conduct or sex-based ridicule that unreasonably interferes with an individual's job performance or that creates an intimidating, hostile, or offensive working environment, even if no tangible or economic consequences result.

An example of the latter would be an office that is significantly pervaded by sexual commentary, dirty jokes, offensive pictures, or generalized sexual conduct even if there is no direct trading of sexual favors for employment benefits.[8]

An employer must actively combat sexual harassment by:

- Establishing a written policy against sexual harassment and distributing it throughout the office
- Investigating all accusations of sexual harassment promptly
- Establishing appropriate sanctions for employees who commit sexual harassment
- Informing employees of their right to raise a charge of sexual harassment under Title VII
- Informing employees how to raise a charge of sexual harassment under Title VII

It is not a defense for an employer to say that it did not know that one of its employees engaged in sexual harassment of another employee or that the harassment took place in spite of a company policy forbidding it. If it *should have known of the harassing conduct,* the employer must take immediate and appropriate corrective action, which usually entails more than merely telling all employees not to engage in sexual harassment.

Enforcement

The Equal Employment Opportunity Commission (EEOC) is a federal agency with the primary responsibility of enforcing Title VII of the Civil Rights Act. A charge of employment discrimination (see Exhibit 12.1) can be made to the EEOC in its offices throughout the country.

Most states have a *fair employment practices* (FEP) law that also provides protection against sex discrimination in employment. A complaint can be initiated at an EEOC office or at the state or city agency that administers the local FEP law.

The major complaint leveled against the laws outlawing sex discrimination in employment is that they have been very inadequately enforced. The law of discrimination can be complex and confusing. Bringing a discrimination case is usually time-consuming and expensive. Many feel we have a long way to go before the problem is solved.

SEXUALITY AND REPRODUCTIVE RIGHTS

Topics relevant to a discussion of sexuality and reproductive rights include:

- Contraception
- Sterilization
- Abortion
- New routes to motherhood
- Lesbianism

[8]Wapner, *Sexual Harassment in the Law Firm,* 16 Law Practice Management 42, 43 (Sept. 1990); Smith, *Sexual Harassment Discussed at Litigation Sectional,* MALA Advance 19 (Minnesota Association of Legal Assistants, Summer 1989); 29 C.F.R. § 1604.11(a)(3); 47 Federal Register 74,676 (Nov. 10, 1980).

Exhibit 12.1 Charge of Discrimination

CHARGE OF DISCRIMINATION This form is affected by the Privacy Act of 1974; see Privacy Act Statement on reverse before completing this form.		ENTER CHARGE NUMBER ☐ FEPA ☐ EEOC
____________________________ and EEOC (*State or local agency, if any*)		
NAME (*Indicate Mr., Ms., or Mrs.*)		HOME TELEPHONE NO. (*Include Area Code*)
STREET ADDRESS	CITY, STATE AND ZIP CODE	COUNTY
NAMED IS THE EMPLOYER, LABOR ORGANIZATION, EMPLOYMENT AGENCY, APPRENTICESHIP COMMITTEE, STATE OR LOCAL GOVERNMENT AGENCY WHO DISCRIMINATED AGAINST ME (*If more than one list below.*)		
NAME	NO. OF EMPLOYEES/MEMBERS	TELEPHONE NUMBER (*Include Area Code*)
STREET ADDRESS		CITY, STATE AND ZIP CODE
NAME		TELEPHONE NUMBER (*Include Area Code*)
STREET ADDRESS		CITY, STATE AND ZIP CODE
CAUSE OF DISCRIMINATION BASED ON (*Check appropriate box(es)*) ☐ RACE ☐ COLOR ☐ SEX ☐ RELIGION ☐ NATIONAL ORIGIN ☐ AGE ☐ RETALIATION ☐ OTHER (*Specify*)		DATE MOST RECENT OR CONTINUING DISCRIMINATION TOOK PLACE (*Month, day, year*)
THE PARTICULARS ARE (*If additional space is needed, attached extra sheet(s)*):		
■ I also want this charge filed with the EEOC. I will advise the agencies if I change my address or telephone number and I will cooperate fully with them in the processing of my charge in accordance with their procedures.		NOTARY—(When necessary to meet State and Local Requirements) I swear or affirm that I have read the above charge and that it is true to the best of my knowledge, information and belief.
I declare under penalty of perjury that the foregoing is true and correct. Date Charging Party (*Signature*)		SIGNATURE OF COMPLAINANT SUBSCRIBED AND SWORN TO BEFORE ME THIS DATE (Day, month, and year)
EEOC FORM 5. PREVIOUS EDITIONS OF THIS FORM ARE OBSOLETE AND MUST NOT BE USED. MAR 84		FILE COPY

The first three topics are discussed below. New routes to motherhood, such as surrogate motherhood, in vitro fertilization, and similar themes, are examined in chapter 16. Legal problems involving homosexuality and lesbianism are covered in chapter 5 on marriage and chapter 15 on adoption.

Contraception

Married and unmarried individuals cannot be denied access to contraceptives. "If the right of privacy means anything, it is the right of the *individual,* married or single, to be free from unwarranted governmental intrusion into matters so fundamentally affecting a person as the decision whether to bear or beget a child."[9]

Sterilization

Some states have laws that authorize the forced sterilization of persons who are legally considered mentally retarded or insane in order to prevent them from reproducing. Over sixty years ago, the United States Supreme Court decided that a state could legally sterilize a person it termed "feeble-minded." The woman in question was an institutionalized eighteen-year-old who was the daughter of a feeble-minded woman in the same institution; the eighteen-year-old had already had a baby that was feeble-minded. In an infamous passage, Justice Oliver Wendell Holmes in *Buck v. Bell* said, "Three generations of imbeciles are enough."[10] Since forced sterilization is rarely, if ever, practiced today, the courts have not had a chance to rule on the constitutionality of the practice under modern interpretations of the U.S. Constitution. If, however, the United States Supreme Court had such a case before it today, it would probably overrule *Buck v. Bell.*

Abortion

In the early 1970s, abortion was a crime in every state. It was permitted only when the health of the woman necessitated it (usually to preserve her life) or when special circumstances warranted it (e.g., when the pregnancy was caused by rape or incest).

In 1973, the law was dramatically changed by the landmark case of *Roe v. Wade,*[11] in which the United States Supreme Court held that a pregnant woman's *right to privacy* included the right to terminate her pregnancy. The ruling in *Roe* was later modified by the 1992 case of *Planned Parenthood of Southeastern Pennsylvania v. Casey.* Before examining *Casey,* however, we need to look at what *Roe* said.

In *Roe v. Wade,* the Court did not conclude that the right to have an abortion was absolute. The extent of the right depended on the stage of a woman's pregnancy:

1. For the stage prior to approximately the end of the first trimester, the abortion decision and its effectuation must be left to the medical judgment of the pregnant woman's attending physician.
2. For the stage subsequent to approximately the end of the first trimester, the state, in promoting its interests in the health of the mother, may, if it chooses, regulate the abortion procedure in ways that are reasonably related to maternal health.
3. For the stage subsequent to viability, the state in promoting its interest in the potentiality of human life may, if it chooses, regulate, and even proscribe, abortion except where it is necessary, in appropriate medical judgment, for the preservation of the life or health of the mother.

A major theme of *Roe* was that the state should not be regulating abortions until **viability** unless the regulations were clearly necessary to protect the

viability
The stage of fetal development when the life of an unborn child may be continued indefinitely outside the womb by natural or artificial life-support systems.

[9] *Eisenstadt v. Baird,* 405 U.S. 438, 453, 92 S. Ct. 1029, 1038, 31 L. Ed. 2d 349 (1972) (italics in original).

[10] *Buck v. Bell,* 274 U.S. 200, 207, 47 S. Ct. 584, 585, 71 L. Ed. 1000 (1927).

[11] 410 U.S. 113, 93 S. Ct. 705, 35 L. Ed. 2d 147 (1973).

health of the mother. If this necessity did not exist, the state could not prohibit a woman from obtaining an abortion during the first trimester when a fetus is not viable. *Roe* held that to deny her this right would infringe upon her constitutional right to privacy. Different considerations applied during the next twelve weeks—the second trimester. Between the end of the first trimester and the beginning of the child's viability (a child is usually considered viable after about six months), the state could regulate medical procedures to make sure that abortions are performed safely but could not prohibit abortions altogether. Once the child is viable—during the third trimester—abortions could be prohibited unless they were necessary to preserve the life or health of the mother.

The Court later reinforced *Roe* by holding that a wife may have an abortion without the consent of her husband.

Some limits, however, were upheld. For example, if a poor woman wanted an abortion for nonhealth reasons (i.e., a nontherapeutic abortion), the state was *not required* to pay for it, although a number of states decided to set aside funds for such abortions. Also, if a pregnant minor was living with and dependent on her parents, it was permissible for a state to require that the parents be notified of, and give their consent to, the child's desire to have an abortion—so long as the girl had the opportunity to go to court to try to convince a judge (in what is called a "bypass proceeding") that she was a mature minor and that therefore parental notice and consent were not needed in her particular case.

These restrictions on *Roe*, however, did not significantly limit the number of abortions performed in America—approximately 1.5 million a year. The Supreme Court acknowledged that abortion continued to be "the most politically divisive domestic issue of our time." Some activists argued for a constitutional amendment that would return us to the pre-*Roe* days, when states could extensively outlaw abortion. As it became clear that these efforts would not succeed, many wondered whether the appointment of conservatives to the Supreme Court by Presidents Reagan and Bush, Sr., would lead to an overruling of *Roe* by the Court itself. The burning question of the day was whether there were now enough votes on the Court to abandon *Roe*. The answer came in the opinion of *Planned Parenthood of Southeastern Pennsylvania v. Casey*, 505 U.S. 833, 112 S. Ct. 2791, 120 L. Ed. 2d 674 (1992).

Casey did not overrule *Roe*. Rather, it reaffirmed *Roe* and, in the process, laid out three principles:

1. Before viability, a woman has a right to choose to terminate her pregnancy.
2. A law that imposes an *undue burden* on a woman's decision before viability is unconstitutional. An undue burden exists when the purpose or effect of the state's regulation is to place a substantial obstacle in the path of a woman seeking an abortion of a nonviable fetus.
3. After viability, the state, in promoting its interest in the potentiality of human life, may, if it chooses, regulate, and even prohibit, abortions except where an abortion is medically necessary to preserve the life or health of the mother.

The due process clause of the Fourteenth Amendment declares that no state shall "deprive any person of life, liberty, or property, without due process of law." The basis of a woman's right to terminate her pregnancy is the protection of "liberty" in the Fourteenth Amendment. But every restriction on this liberty is not unconstitutional.

The key test continues to be viability. In *Roe*, the Court used a trimester analysis as a guide in the determination of viability. In *Casey*, the Court decided to reject this analysis as too rigid. In the future, the question of when a child is able to survive outside the womb will be determined by the facts of medicine and science rather than by rigid assumptions of what is possible during the trimesters of pregnancy.

Before viability, a state cannot place "undue burdens" on the right to seek an abortion. The state can pass laws designed to encourage women to choose childbirth over abortion and laws designed to further her health or safety so long as these laws do not present "substantial obstacles" in the path of her decision to abort a nonviable fetus.

Using these tests, the Court in *Casey* reached the following conclusions about specific laws enacted by the state of Pennsylvania:

- It is *not* an undue burden on the right to abortion for a state to require (except in a medical emergency) that at least twenty-four hours before performing an abortion a physician give a woman information about the nature of the procedure, the health risks of abortion and of childbirth, the probable gestational age of her unborn child, available medical assistance for childbirth, methods of obtaining child support from the father, and a list of agencies that provide adoption and other services as alternatives to abortion. Providing this information is not a substantial obstacle because the information allows women to give informed consent to whatever decision they make.
- It *is* an undue burden on the right to abortion for a state to require (except in a medical emergency) that no physician perform an abortion on a married woman without receiving a signed statement from the woman that she has notified her spouse that she is about to undergo an abortion. This is a substantial obstacle because many women may not seek an abortion due to a fear of psychological and physical abuse from their husband if they tell him about their plan to have an abortion. Furthermore, a woman does not need her husband's consent to undergo an abortion. Since he does not have a veto, notifying him about the planned abortion is not necessary.

Another controversial decision involved a Nebraska statute that outlawed "partial birth abortion," which the statute defined as "an abortion procedure in which the person performing the abortion partially delivers vaginally a living unborn child before killing the unborn child and completing the delivery." In *Stenberg v. Carhart,*[12] the Court held that this statute was unconstitutional. First, it did not make an exception for preserving the health of the mother. Second, the statute placed an undue burden on the right to choose an abortion because it applied to a dilation and evacuation (D&E) procedure as well as to a dilation and extraction (D&X) procedure. Proponents of abortion rights hailed the decision; critics were appalled. One of the dissenting justices said that *Stenberg* will become as infamous as the Court's *Dred Scott* decision (protecting the rights of slave owners) and the *Korematsu* decision (allowing the internment of Japanese Americans during World War II). It is still true that abortion is "the most politically divisive issue of our time."

THE BATTERED WIFE

The statistics on violence against women in America are staggering:

- Approximately 4 million women are battered each year by their husbands or partners.
- Over 1 million women seek medical assistance each year for injuries caused by their husbands or partners.
- Up to 50 percent of homeless women and children are fleeing domestic violence.

---

[12]530 U.S. 914, 120 S. Ct. 2597, 147 L. Ed. 2d 743 (2000).

- Three out of four American women will be victims of violent crimes sometime during their life.
- Violence is the leading cause of injuries to women ages fifteen to forty-four.
- Between 2,000 and 4,000 women die every year from domestic abuse.
- Close to half a million girls now in high school will be raped before they finish high school.
- The country spends $5 to $10 billion a year on health care, criminal justice, and other social costs of domestic violence.[13]

As alarming as these statistics are, the numbers are considered low because violence against women, particularly domestic violence, is one of the most unreported crimes in the country. Approximately one out of every 100 perpetrators of domestic violence is arrested.

At one time in our history, wives were considered the property of their husbands. This reality encouraged the use of violence against wives. Indeed, there was religious and legal approval for a husband's use of force against his wife. Around 1475, for example, Friar Cherubino of Siena compiled the following *Rules of Marriage:*

> When you see your wife commit an offense, don't rush at her with insults and violent blows. . . . Scold her sharply and terrify her. And if this still doesn't work . . . take up a stick and beat her soundly, for it is better to punish the body and correct the soul than to damage the soul and spare the body. . . . Then readily beat her, not in rage but out of charity and concern for her soul, so that the beating will redound to your merit and her good.[14]

Hence wife beating was acceptable and indeed was considered a duty of the husband. Society even condoned a particular weapon for the deed: a "rod not thicker than his thumb" or a stick that was not too thick to pass through a wedding ring![15]

---

[13]Summarized from *United States v. Morrison,* 120 S. Ct. 1740, 1761 (2000) (Souter, J., dissenting); H. R. Rep. No. 395, 103d Cong. (1993); E. Schneider, Legal Reform Efforts for Battered Women: Past, Present, and Future (July 1990).

[14]Quoted in T. Davidson, Conjugal Crime 99 (1978).

[15]United States Commission on Civil Rights, Under the Rule of Thumb: Battered Women and the Administration of Justice 2 (Jan. 1982).

CASE

State v. Black

Supreme Court of North Carolina
60 N.C. 262 (1 Win. 266) (1864)

A husband cannot be convicted of battery on his wife, unless he inflicts a permanent injury, or uses such excessive violence or cruelty, as indicates malignity or vindictiveness: and it makes no difference that the husband and wife are living separate by agreement.

This was an indictment of assault and battery, tried before BAILEY, Judge, at—Term of Ashe Superior Court, 1864.

The defendant was indicted for an assault on Tamsey Black, his wife. The evidence showed, that the defendant and his wife lived separate from one another. The defendant was passing by the house of one Koonce, where his wife then resided, when she called to him in an angry manner and asked him, if he had patched Sal Daly's bonnet. (Sal Daly being a woman of ill-fame.)

She then went into the house, and defendant followed her and asked her what she wanted, when she repeated her question about the bonnet. Angry words then passed between them. He accused her of connection with a negro man, and she called him a

continued

CASE

State v. Black—*Continued*

hog thief, whereupon the defendant seized her by her hair, and pulled her down upon the floor, and held her there for sometime. He gave her no blows, but she stated on the trial, that her head was considerably hurt, and that her throat was injured, and continued sore for several months, but that he did not choke her, nor attempt to do so. At the trial she was entirely recovered. After she got up from the floor, she continued her abuse of him. A verdict of guilty was entered, subject to the opinion of the Court. The Judge, being of opinion with the State, gave judgment accordingly.

Winston, Sr., for the State

No counsel for the defendant in this Court.

PEARSON, C. J. A husband is responsible for the acts of his wife, and he is required to govern his household, and for that purpose, the law permits him to use towards his wife such a degree of force, as is necessary to control an unruly temper, and make her behave herself; and unless some permanent injury is inflicted, or there be an excess of violence, or such a degree of cruelty as shows that it is inflicted to gratify his own bad passions, the law will not invade the domestic forum, to go behind the curtain. It prefers to leave the parties to themselves, as the best mode of inducing them to make the matter up and live together as man and wife should.

Certainly, the exposure of a scene like that set out in this case, can do no good. In respect to the parties, a public exhibition in the Court House of such quarrels and fights between man and wife, widens the breach, makes a reconciliation almost impossible, and encourages insubordination; and in respect to the public, it has a pernicious tendency: so, . . . such matters are excluded from the Courts, unless there is a permanent injury or excessive violence or cruelty indicating malignity and vindictiveness.

In this case the wife commenced the quarrel. The husband, in a passion provoked by excessive abuse, pulled her upon the floor by the hair, but restrained himself, did not strike a blow, and she admits he did not choke her, and she continued to abuse him after she got up. Upon this state of facts the jury ought to have been charged in favor of the defendant. *State v. Pendergrass,* 18 N. C., 365; *Joyner v. Joyner,* 59 N. C., 322.

It was insisted by Mr. Winston that, admitting such to be the law when the husband and wife lived together, it did not apply when, as in the case, they were living apart. They may be so when there is a divorce "from bed and board," because the law then recognizes and allows the separation, but it can take no notice of a private agreement to live separate. The husband is still responsible for her acts, and the marriage relation and its incidents remain unaffected.

This decision must be certified to the Superior Court of law for Ashe County, that it may proceed according to law.

Eventually, laws were passed outlawing wife beating. Yet the crime continues at an alarming rate today. As indicated, women frequently do not report such violence, particularly when they are still living with their abuser/husband. Furthermore, when a woman does report the incident to the authorities, she often is not taken seriously. Many complain that the police handle violence in a "domestic quarrel" differently, that is, less seriously, from an assault on the street between strangers. Politically active women's groups have campaigned for a change in the attitude and policies of courts, legislatures, and law enforcement agencies. In addition, they have fought for the creation of shelters to which battered women can flee.

injunction
A court order requiring a person to do or to refrain from doing a particular thing.

ex parte
With only one party (usually the plaintiff or petitioner) present when court action is requested.

If a woman is persistent and desperate enough, her main remedy is to go to court to ask for an **injunction.** In this situation, the injunction is to stop abusing the plaintiff and/or her children. Depending on the state, the injunction is called a *restraining order,* a *protective order,* or a *protection from abuse* (PFA) *order* (see Exhibit 12.2). For purposes of obtaining the injunction, abuse is often defined as attempting to cause bodily injury or intentionally, knowingly, or recklessly causing bodily injury, or by threat of force placing another person in fear of imminent serious physical harm. The first step in obtaining the injunction is often the filing of an application for a temporary injunction based on actual or threatened abuse. The petitioner files the application **ex parte,** meaning that only one party is before the court. A judge (or sometimes a clerk)

Exhibit 12.2 Protective Order

3-116.3

SUPERIOR COURT OF CALIFORNIA, COUNTY OF STREET ADDRESS: MAILING ADDRESS: CITY AND ZIP CODE: BRANCH NAME:	*FOR COURT USE ONLY*
PROTECTED PERSON (NAME):	
RESTRAINED PERSON (NAME):	
EMERGENCY PROTECTIVE ORDER / COURT CASE NUMBER:	

1. **THIS EMERGENCY PROTECTIVE ORDER WILL EXPIRE AT 5 P.M. ON:** ☐ (INSERT DATE OF NEXT COURT DAY)
2. Reasonable grounds appear that an immediate danger of domestic violence exists and this order should be issued
   a. AGAINST RESTRAINED PERSON (name): ______
   b. WHO must not contact, molest, attack, strike, threaten, sexually assault, batter, telephone, or otherwise harass or disturb the peace of the protected person
      (1) ☐ or the peace of the following family or household members (*names*): ______
   c. ☐ WHO must stay away from the protected person at least (*yards*): ______
   d. ☐ WHO must move out and not return to the residence at (*address*): ______
3. ☐ Temporary custody of the following minor children is given to the protected person:
   Children (*names and ages*): ______
4. ☐ The protected person has been given a copy of this order, the application, and instructions about how to get a more permanent order.
5. Date: ☐
6. **Law Enforcement Officer:** ...... (PRINT NAME) ► ______ (SIGNATURE)
   a. Badge No.: ______ b. Incident Case No.: ______
   c. Agency: ______ d. Telephone No.: ______
7. **Service of this order and application on the restrained person was completed as follows:**

	Date	**Time**	**Signature**
a. ☐ I orally advised person of contents:			
b. ☐ I personally gave person copies:			

DESCRIPTION OF RESTRAINED PERSON (fill out what you know)

(1) approximate age:	(4) weight:	(7) vehicle make:
(2) race:	(5) hair color:	(8) vehicle model:
(3) height:	(6) eye color:	(9) vehicle license no.:

(10) other distinguishing features: ______

VIOLATION OF THIS ORDER IS A MISDEMEANOR PUNISHABLE BY A $1000 FINE, SIX MONTHS IN JAIL, OR BOTH. THIS ORDER SHALL BE ENFORCED BY ALL LAW ENFORCEMENT OFFICERS IN THE STATE OF CALIFORNIA.

(See reverse for important notices)

Form Adopted by Rule 1295.95
Judicial Council of California
1295.95 (New July 1, 1988)

Emergency Protective Order
(Domestic Violence Prevention)

Code of Civil Procedure, § 546(b)

WHITE copy to court, CANARY to restrained person, PINK to protected person

can issue the temporary injunction. The order is served on the defendant, who is ordered to stay a designated number of feet away from the petitioner. A date is set for a hearing at which both sides can address the question of whether the injunction should be made permanent, which usually means being in effect for a year or more. The woman is urged to carry the temporary or permanent injunction with her at all times so that she can show it to the police in the event that the defendant violates its terms.

In addition to the civil remedy of an injunction, a woman can ask the state to prosecute the defendant for a crime (e.g., assault, aggravated assault, battery, aggravated battery, reckless conduct, disorderly conduct, harassment). Some states have special crimes that specifically cover violence committed by one family member against another such as spouse-against-spouse crime.

A major attempt to address the problem at the national level occurred when Congress passed the Violence Against Women Act (VAWA), which established a federal civil rights cause of action for victims of violence motivated by "animus" toward the victim's gender. The United States Supreme Court, however, struck down this statute as an unconstitutional exercise of the commerce clause.[16] Part of the Court's reasoning was its hesitancy to impose additional federal laws in the area of family relations. In our legal system, the primary responsibility for regulating domestic relations rests with the state governments. (This is one of the reasons, for example, that divorces are obtained in state courts, not federal courts. See chapter 7.)

Another attempt by Congress to regulate gender-related violence was its passage of the Free Access to Clinic Entrances Act (FACE), which gives a cause of action to anyone who is the victim of assault or other attack while seeking "reproductive health services," such as an abortion.[17] In view of the Court's rejection of VAWA, however, it is unclear whether FACE will eventually be held to be an unconstitutional intrusion by Congress on the right of the states to regulate family law.

Later, in chapter 17, we will examine whether a spouse who is the victim of domestic violence can bring a traditional personal injury *tort* action against the other spouse in a state court.

Some women have taken the extreme step of killing the husband who has been abusing them. Does this killing constitute the crime of murder or manslaughter? In part, the answer depends on when the killing occurs. Compare the predicament of the women in the following two situations. Assume that both women had been physically abused by their husband or boyfriend for years:

> Carol is being physically attacked by her husband, who is coming at her with a knife. As he approaches, Carol shoots him.
>
> Hours after being beaten by her boyfriend, Helen takes a gun to his bedroom and shoots him while he is asleep.

It is highly unlikely that Carol has committed a crime. She is protected by the traditional defense of *self-defense.* Citizens can use deadly force that they reasonably believe is necessary to protect themselves from imminent death or serious bodily injury.

What about Helen? Unless she can prove temporary insanity, she must establish the elements of self-defense to avoid conviction. But she apparently was not in *imminent* danger at the time she shot her boyfriend. Arguably, for example, she could have left the home while he was sleeping if she felt that he

---

[16]The Court held that gender violence did not have a substantial enough effect on interstate commerce to justify the regulation of such violence through the VAWA. *United States v. Morrison,* 529 U.S. 598, 120 S. Ct. 1740, 146 L. Ed. 2d 658 (2000).

[17]18 U.S.C.A. § 248.

might kill or maim her once he awoke. Women in Helen's situation have been prosecuted for crimes such as manslaughter and murder.

In these prosecutions, a novel argument that is often raised by the woman is the battered wife syndrome or, more broadly, the **battered woman syndrome.** She claims that she acted out of a *psychological paralysis.* A variety of circumstances combined to block all apparent avenues of escape: financial dependence, loneliness, guilt, shame, and fear of reprisal from her husband or boyfriend.[18] From this state of "learned helplessness," she kills him. This argument is not an independent defense; it is an argument designed to bolster the self-defense argument. More accurately, it is an attempt to broaden the definition of *imminent danger* in self-defense. To a woman subjected to the psychological terror and paralysis of long-term abuse, the danger from her husband or boyfriend is real and close at hand. At any moment, his behavior might trigger a flashback in her mind to an earlier beating, causing her to honestly believe that she is in immediate danger.

battered woman syndrome
Psychological helplessness because of a woman's financial dependence, loneliness, guilt, shame, and fear of reprisal from her husband or boyfriend who has repeatedly battered her in the past.

Prosecutors are not sympathetic to the battered-woman-syndrome argument. They say it is too easy to exaggerate the extent of the abuse and, more important, the extent to which the abuse resulted in such a state of paralysis that the wife felt her only way to protect herself—immediately—was to kill her husband. Some courts, however, are at least willing to listen to testimony on the syndrome. This has been very helpful for the defendant because when jurors hear this testimony, they are often reluctant to return guilty verdicts even if the traditional elements of self-defense that the judge instructs them to apply do not warrant verdicts of not guilty. Prosecutors are aware of this reluctance, and, therefore, many are more inclined to bring charges on lesser crimes such as voluntary manslaughter and, in some instances, not to bring any charges. Hence while prosecutors may deride the battered woman syndrome as an "abuse excuse," raising the syndrome defense can still be an important part of defense strategy.

ASSIGNMENT 12.5

For the following questions, see General Instructions for the State-Code Assignment in Appendix A.

a. In your state, if a wife is threatened with violence, what remedies does she have?
b. When, if ever, can an injunction or protective order be issued when the defendant is not present in court (i.e., ex parte)?
c. Without justification, a husband stabs his wife, but does not kill her. What are the possible crimes the husband can be charged with in your state?

ASSIGNMENT 12.6

Prepare a flowchart on obtaining an injunction (or restraining order) against violence threatened by a husband against his wife in your state. (See General Instructions for the Flowchart Assignment in Appendix A.)

ASSIGNMENT 12.7

a. Do you think that a court encourages killing when it allows evidence of the battered woman syndrome to be introduced in trials of women who kill their spouses or boyfriends? Explain why or why not.
b. Do you think it is possible for a battered *man* syndrome to exist? Explain why or why not.

---

[18]M. Buda & T. Butler, *The Battered Wife Syndrome,* 23 Journal of Family Law 359 (1984–85).

MARITAL RAPE

The common law rule was that a husband cannot rape his wife. The "husband cannot be guilty of rape committed by himself upon his lawful wife, for by their mutual matrimonial consent and contract, the wife hath given up herself in this kind unto her husband which she cannot retract."[19] This view is still the law in some states. Most states, however, allow prosecution if the couple is living apart and a petition has been filed for divorce or separate maintenance. The reluctance of courts and legislatures to allow the criminal law of rape to apply to married couples is in part based on a fear that a wife will lie about whether she consented to sexual intercourse. As we will see in the case of *Warren v. State,* however, this fear is unfounded.

[19]1 M. Hale, The History of the Pleas of the Crown 629 (1736).

CASE

Warren v. State

255 Ga. 151, 336 S.E.2d 221 (1985)
Supreme Court of Georgia

Background: *Daniel Steven Warren was indicted for rape and sodomy of his wife while they were still living together. He moved to dismiss the indictment on the ground that a husband cannot be convicted of committing these crimes against his wife. The motion was denied. He then appealed to the Supreme Court of Georgia where he is the appellant.*

Decision on Appeal: *Affirmed. There is no exception for husbands.*

Opinion of the Court:

Justice Smith delivered the opinion of the court.

"When a woman says I do, does she give up her right to say I won't?"* This question does not pose the real question, because rape† and aggravated sodomy are not sexual acts of an ardent husband performed upon an initially apathetic wife, they are acts of violence that are accompanied with physical and mental abuse and often leave the victim with physical and psychological damage that is almost always long lasting. Thus we find the more appropriate question: When a woman says "I do" in Georgia does she give up her right to State protection from the violent acts of rape and aggravated sodomy performed by her husband[?] The answer is no. We affirm. . . .

The appellant asserts that there exists within the rape statute an implicit marital exclusion that makes it legally impossible for a husband to be guilty of raping his wife. Until the late 1970's there was no real examination of this apparently widely held belief. Within the last few years several jurisdictions have been faced with similar issues and they have decided that under certain circumstances a husband can be held criminally liable for raping his wife.

What is behind the theory and belief that a husband could not be guilty of raping his wife? There are various explanations for the rule and all of them flow from the common law attitude toward women, the status of women and marriage.

Perhaps the most often used basis for the marital rape exemption is the view set out by Lord Hale in

*Griffin, *In 44 States, It's Legal to Rape Your Wife,* 21 Student Lawyer. Another question posed is: "But if you can't rape your wife, who[m] can you rape?" Freeman, *"But If You Can't Rape Your Wife, Who[m] Can You Rape?": The Marital Rape Exemption Re-examined,* 15 Family Law Quarterly (1981).

†"As one author has observed, people have 'trouble with rape' because: [T]he mention of rape makes us all uneasy—for different reasons depending on who we are. It makes men uneasiest of all perhaps, and usually brings forth an initial response of nervous laughter or guffaw-evoking jokes. After all, as far as the normal, but uninformed, man knows, rape is something he might suddenly do himself some night if life becomes too dull. It isn't, of course, but he knows too little about it to realize that. On the other hand, the thoughtful normal man, after hearing the details of a forcible rape, finds it difficult to believe. . . . He knows that all thoughts of sex—which he equates with fun, romance, and mutual admiration—would leave him if the woman were *really* struggling to get free. . . . He does not realize that, to the rapist, the act is not 'love,' nor ardor, and usually not even passion; it is a way of debasing and degrading a woman. . . ." (Emphasis in original.) Massaro, *Experts, Psychology, Credibility, and Rape: The Rape Trauma Syndrome Issue and Its Implications for Expert Psychological Testimony,* 69 Minn. Law Review 395, 399 n. 27 (1985).

1 Hale P.C. 629. It is known as Lord Hale's contractual theory. The statement attributed to Lord Hale used to support the theory is: "but a husband cannot be guilty of a rape committed by himself upon his lawful wife, for by their mutual matrimonial consent and contract the wife hath given up herself in this kind unto her husband which she cannot retract."

There is some thought that the foundation of his theory might well have been the subsequent marriage doctrine of English law, wherein the perpetrator could, by marrying his victim, avoid rape charges. It was thus argued as a corollary, rape within the marital relationship would result in the same immunity. Another theory stemming from medieval times is that of a wife being the husband's chattel or property. Since a married woman was part of her husband's property, nothing more than a chattel, rape was nothing more than a man making use of his own property. A third theory is the unity in marriage or unity of person theory that held the very being or legal existence of a woman was suspended during marriage, or at least was incorporated and consolidated into that of her husband. In view of the fact that there was only one legal being, the husband, he could not be convicted of raping himself.

These three theories have been used to support the marital rape exemption. Others have tried to fill the chasm between these three theories with justifications for continuing the exemption in the face of changes in the recognition of women, their status, and the status of marriage. Some of the justifications include: Prevention of fabricated charges; Preventing wives from using rape charges for revenge; Preventing state intervention into marriage so that possible reconciliation will not be thwarted. A closer examination of the theories and justifications indicates that they are no longer valid, if they ever had any validity.

Hale's implied consent theory was created at a time when marriages were irrevocable and when all wives promised to "love, honor, and obey" and all husbands promised to "love, cherish, and protect until death do us part." Wives were subservient to their husbands, her identity was merged into his, her property became his property, and she took his name for her own.

There have been dramatic changes in women's rights and the status of women and marriage. Today our State Constitution provides that, "no person shall be deprived of life, *liberty,* or property except by due process," (Emphasis supplied.) Art. I, § I, Par. I, and "protection to *person* and property is the paramount duty of government and shall be impartial and complete. No person shall be denied the equal protection of the laws." (Emphasis supplied.) Art. I, § I, Par. II. Our state Constitution also provides that each spouse has a right to retain his or her own property. Art. I, § I, Par. XXVII. Our statutory laws provide that, "[t]he rights of citizens include, *without limitation,* the following: (1) The right of *personal security,* [and] (2) The right of personal liberty . . ." (Emphasis supplied.) OCGA § 1–2–6. Women in Georgia "are entitled to the privilege of the elective franchise and have the right to hold any civil office or perform any civil function as fully and completely as do male citizens." OCGA § 1–2–7. Couples who contemplate marriage today may choose either spouse's surname or a combination of both names for their married surname, OCGA § 19–3–33.1. No longer is a wife's domicile presumed to be that of her husband, OCGA § 19–2–3 and no longer is the husband head of the family with the wife subject to him. OCGA § 19–3–8. Marriages are revocable without fault by either party, OCGA § 19–5–3(13); either party, not just the husband, can be required to pay alimony upon divorce, OCGA § 19–6–1; and both parties have a joint and several duty to provide for the maintenance, protection, and education of their children, OCGA § 19–7–2. Couples may write antenuptial agreements in which they are able to decide, prior to marriage, future settlements, OCGA § 19–3–62; and our legislature has recognized that there can be violence in modern family life and it has enacted special laws to protect family members who live in the same household from one another's violent acts, Ga.L. 1981, 880; OCGA § 19–13–1 et seq. . . .

One would be hard pressed to argue that a husband can rape his wife because she is his chattel. Even in the darkest days of slavery when slaves were also considered chattel, rape was defined as "the carnal knowledge of a female whether free or slave, forcibly and against her will." Georgia Code, § 4248 (1863). Both the chattel and unity of identity rationales have been cast aside. "Nowhere in the common law world—[or] in any modern society—is a woman regarded as chattel or demeaned—by denial of a separate legal identity and the dignity associated with recognition as a whole human being." *Trammel v. United States,* 445 U.S. 40, 52, 100 S. Ct. 906, 913 (1980).

We find that none of the theories have any validity. The justifications likewise are without efficacy. There is no other crime we can think of in which all of the victims are denied protection simply because someone might fabricate a charge; there is no evidence

continued

CASE

Warren v. State—*Continued*

that wives have flooded the district attorneys with revenge filled trumped-up charges,[‡] and once a marital relationship is at the point where a husband rapes his wife, state intervention is needed for the wife's protection.

There never has been an expressly stated marital exemption included in the Georgia rape statute. Furthermore, our statute never included the word "unlawful" which has been widely recognized as signifying the incorporation of the common law spousal exclusion. A reading of the statute indicates that there is no marital exclusion. "A person commits the offense of rape when he has carnal knowledge of a female forcibly and against her will." OCGA § 16–6–1. . . .

Judgment affirmed.

[‡]"'[E]mbittered and vengeful wives are not rushing to their District Attorney to falsely claim rape in order to gain leverage on their husbands in a divorce. Victims are very reluctant to report the crime.' . . ." *People v. De Stefano,* 467 N.Y.S.2d 506, 515 (Co. Ct. 1983). Furthermore, studies show that the average person finds alleged husband-wife rapes the lowest in credibility, 69 Minn. Law Review n. 63 at 408, and juries convict only 3 of 42 rape suspects in simple rapes, i.e., where there is only one assailant, he is known by the victim, and there is no evidence of extrinsic violence. 69 Minn. Law Review 395, n. 52 at 405.

ASSIGNMENT 12.8

a. The Georgia statute says: "A person commits the offense of rape when he has carnal knowledge of a female forcibly and against her will." OCGA § 16–6–1. The court in *Warren* suggests that there might be an argument that the statute excludes husbands if the word "unlawful" appeared in the statute. What is this argument? Assume the statute read, "A person commits the offense of rape when he has *unlawful* carnal knowledge of a female forcibly and against her will."

b. Under what circumstances, if any, can a husband be guilty of raping his wife in your state? (See General Instructions for the State-Code Assignment and the Court-Opinion Assignment in Appendix A.)

CLIENT SENSITIVITY

A law office may become involved in domestic violence cases in a number of ways. In a divorce case, for example, there may have been violence or a threat of violence during the marriage. A criminal case may have begun when the police were called because of violence committed in the home. Attorneys and paralegals may be involved in a pro bono project in which they give free legal services to victims of domestic violence. (For a dramatic description of one paralegal's participation in such a pro bono program, see Exhibit 12.3.)

Exhibit 12.3 A Paralegal's Experience with Domestic Violence Cases

Protection from Abuse Program
by Laurie R. Mansell, RP, Senior Paralegal
Equitable Resources, Inc.

I can still clearly remember my first day as a pro bono volunteer with the Protection From Abuse Program (PFA) in Allegheny County, PA. I entered the PFA area of the City-County Building clutching a binder of sample forms, sweating profusely from nervousness and feeling very scared.

The PFA area is an austere section just off the elevators on the eighth floor that has been partitioned off and "decorated" with old, well-worn government issue tables and chairs. There is one desk, and that is reserved for a volunteer. A sheriff's deputy sits on a plastic chair by the pay phone in case trouble breaks out between petitioners, which does happen. And did I mention that the building has no air conditioning and an overzealous heating system?

I had received my required one hour of training (from whence came the binder of forms) from the PFA coordinator of the Pittsburgh Paralegal Association. For some six years, the Association has participated in the PFA program, which is run by Allegheny County in conjunction with Neighborhood Legal Services and the women's shelters in the area.

I had decided to volunteer one Monday a month. We were told at training that Monday is the worst day, especially following a three-day holiday weekend or a weekend sporting event. The session lasts from 9:00 to 11:00 a.m. each day, Monday through Friday. If someone needs a PFA over the weekend or in the evening, he or she has to go to night court and obtain an emergency PFA until the program's office opens on Monday—thus the Monday crowd.

When I first arrived, I thought, how bad could this be? Well, on my first day, there were 50 petitioners. The PFA program had one paid advocate and three or four volunteer advocates who are trained counselors. These volunteer advocates show up, unpaid, day in and day out. And then, there was me. I leave you to count the odds.

In Pennsylvania, abuse is considered to have occurred if there is a family or sexual relationship between the parties and the abuse is imminent. So it is important first to establish that a family or sexual relationship exists. For example, a roommate cannot apply for a PFA against another roommate if there is no sexual relationship. If the defendant is a minor, the matter is referred to juvenile court. If the plaintiff is a juvenile, a parent or guardian must complete the paperwork on his or her behalf.

It is important to make sure that the abuse was very recent, usually within the last few days. Otherwise, the judge will dismiss the allegation as not meeting the imminency test. If the abuse did not happen recently, the plaintiff would have to show a good reason for the delay in applying for the PFA, such as being hospitalized or perhaps having to flee the area.

I can remember bumbling my way through that first day, trying desperately to help and worrying that I would get something wrong and ruin someone's chances of getting his or her PFA. I think I spent more time frantically searching through my reference binder and asking questions of the advocates than I did helping the clients.

Even now after two years of PFA volunteering, I have never stopped being nervous. It is a big responsibility to help someone to fill out a complaint that will be read by a judge, and these people desperately need help. Most of the petitioners are women, but a few men come in. Usually the men are there petitioning for a PFA at the same time their wives or girlfriends are petitioning for a PFA against them. It is very important to note that it is considered a conflict of interest for us to assist them both with their complaints, no matter how dispassionate we may feel or act.

It is also crucial to point out that at no time do we give legal advice even though we are asked. I explain to the people that I am not an attorney and refer them to Neighborhood Legal Services. . . .

For this reason, when I became the Pittsburgh Paralegal Association's PFA coordinator, I made nametags for paralegal volunteers with the Association's name on top and the first name of the paralegal below. This gave a clear message as to who we are. For safety's sake, we put only first names on the nametags so volunteers could not be contacted outside of the program.

The petitioners who come in go through a full day of paperwork and hearings before—if they are lucky and if they get a sympathetic judge—they obtain a temporary PFA. The temporary PFA is good for ten days, at which time a hearing of both parties is held to determine whether a permanent PFA, good for one year, should be issued. The volunteer's role is to help an applicant get a temporary PFA.

Many of the women come in exhausted. They have been up all night and have their children with them. I finally brought in coloring books and crayons so the children could have something to do for the two hours that the parent is filling out paperwork.

And the paperwork (five to six forms) is daunting, I can assure you. Some petitioners are illiterate. We are encouraged to have petitioners complete the paperwork themselves, mainly because there just are not enough volunteers to go around. If we do end up writing the actual description of the incident, we have to initial our description and have the petitioner read and initial it as well. This is to ensure that the petitioner will not tell the judge that he or she was unaware of what we wrote. The petitioner must initial the description to show he or she has read the description and agrees that it is accurate.

The stories the women tell are chilling. One woman's boyfriend held her by the neck from a third story apartment building. Another woman had gasoline poured down her throat and suffered permanent physical damage. One woman's fingernails were ripped off, and she could not even hold a pen. Sometimes these women are harassed at work or by telephone with as many as 30 or 40 calls during the night. Often their lives are threatened. Many are raising four or five children on $500 a month. I cannot tell you how fortunate and how humble I felt each time I left the PFA office.

The experience gave me a whole new perspective on life and the use of my paralegal skills. Often when I would finish working with these women, they would have tears in their eyes as they thanked me for my help. They gratefully acknowledged that they could never have completed the forms without help. I am listening to them and trying to help them, and they appreciate that.

While the training session is essential, going and doing (i.e., on-the-job experience) are the best lessons. I encourage all paralegals to become involved in pro bono activity. You will never find a better or more rewarding way to use your skills. As few as two hours a month (if your employer is a concern, the time is easily made up) is not too much to ask—particularly considering the satisfaction you receive in return.

When working with a victim of domestic violence, special sensitivity is required. The following guidelines in handling such cases assume that the victim is a woman and the perpetrator or batterer is a man, although similar guidelines apply if the roles are reversed or if the violence is being committed within a same-sex relationship.

- *Focus on immediate safety needs.* The client may be in immediate danger. The batterer, for example, may be following or stalking the client. Ask the client if she is safe at the present moment. Are the children safe? If danger exists, suggest to the client that she consider calling the police or the emergency 911 phone number from your office. Ask if the batterer knows where the client is. Does she have any relatives where she can safely stay? Is the client interested in staying at a woman's shelter for the night? In short, before exploring the niceties of the law and legal procedures with the client, focus on any immediate safety concerns.

- *Know the community resources for battered women.* Someone in the city or county has probably already compiled a list of resources for domestic violence victims such as counseling, hotline numbers, overnight shelters, battered women's support groups, hospitals, emergency financial assistance from public welfare agencies, and information on obtaining a restraining order or a protective order. To find such a list, contact the police department, the district attorney, the mayor's office, a local public library, Catholic Charities, the Salvation Army, the YWCA, and any special offices or task forces on women's issues. Also check the Internet. You need to know where victims can turn for social, psychological, financial, and security assistance. In the unlikely event that this list does not exist where you live, start compiling your own.
- *Avoid being judgmental.* You may not approve of some of the client's decisions. You may think she has helped cause her own predicament. You may be shocked if you learn that the client has regularly returned to the batterer after repeated incidents of violence over a long period of time. This is not the time to judge the morality or wisdom of the client's life choices. This is not the time for a lecture or sermon.
- *Understand the client's point of view.* The client may feel afraid, ashamed, confused, angry, or even guilty about the violence that has occurred. When you speak to her, she may be exhausted from being up all night on the run from her abuser, trying to protect herself and her children. She may be in physical pain. The crisis brought on by violence may be overwhelming. It is extremely important that you exhibit concern and understanding. The client may not be capable at the moment of grasping technical legal concepts. She needs information, but perhaps most of all, she needs a sympathetic ear.
- *Take the client seriously.* If the client says there is danger, believe it. Too often society does not take domestic violence seriously. The police, for example, may feel that nothing more than a "lover's quarrel" is taking place. Their attitude might be "just go back and work things out." Many victims of domestic violence have been subjected to this attitude often. They should not find it in a law office.
- *Leave the critical decisions to the client.* It is the client's life that is on the line. Every decision she makes, including contacting the police, has the potential of escalating the violence when the batterer finds out what she has done. Let the client make the decisions. Provide options and information on the pros and cons of each option. Help the client think through the safety and other consequences of each step.
- *Alert the client to the danger of false security.* A restraining order or a protective order is a court document that orders the batterer to stay away from the victim and authorizes the police to arrest the batterer if he violates its terms. But these orders are not self-executing. Many batterers are not intimidated by them. In fact, such an order may provoke the batterer to further violence. Hence clients should not feel 100 percent safe simply because they have the court order. They should carry it with them at all times but not have a false sense of security about it. Clients still need to take active steps to protect themselves such as locating safe places to stay. In a crisis, a 911 call will probably be much more effective than showing the batterer another copy of the order.
- *Do not leave phone messages that will alert the batterer.* If the batterer does not know that the victim is seeking legal help, he may become enraged

when he finds out. Ask the client if it is safe to call her at home and leave a message. When you leave a message, it may not be wise to indicate that you are calling from a law office. It may also be unsafe to leave a phone number. If the batterer hears the message, he may call the number and find out you were calling from a law office. Arrange with the client ahead of time how to reach you so that you do not have to leave too much identifying information in a phone message. Alternatively, ask the client if she has a relative or close friend with whom messages can be left safely.

- *Help the client develop a safety plan.* When the client leaves the office, she should have identified the locations and situations that are likely to lead to further violence. Help the client prepare a safety plan that will address these potential sources of further violence. The plan should outline how the client will try to avoid further violence (e.g., where to stay away from, what to avoid saying if/when she sees the batterer again) and what she will do if the violence recurs (e.g., what emergency phone numbers to call, where to take the children). While every eventuality cannot be predicted,a safety plan should be able to cover the major vulnerabilities in the client's life and give her some direction on how to respond to them.

SUMMARY

Historically, a married woman had very few rights independent of her husband. Today her situation is very different. For example, her right to own and dispose of property and to enter contracts is now equal to that of her husband. There are some restrictions on contracts and conveyances between spouses (e.g., they cannot enter a contract to provide services and support if they are still living together, and they cannot transfer property to each other in order to defraud creditors). However, these restrictions apply equally to husbands and wives.

When a husband dies, his wife has a right of dower in his property. Many states have replaced this with a right to elect a forced share of his estate. In most states, the wife is not required to take her husband's surname upon marriage, nor is she required to keep it upon divorce if she used it when married.

An applicant for credit cannot be discriminated against on the basis of sex or marital status. Sex discrimination in employment is illegal unless sex is a bona fide occupational qualification. Salaries cannot be determined on the basis of gender. Certain forms of pregnancy-related discrimination and sexual harassment are also prohibited. These laws are enforced by the federal Equal Employment Opportunity Commission and by state agencies that administer rules on fair employment practices.

In the area of sexuality and reproductive rights, neither men nor women can be denied access to contraceptives. But they can be subjected to forced sterilization if they are mentally retarded or insane. A state cannot place undue burdens on a woman's right to an abortion before viability.

Wife beating is a major problem in our society in spite of the laws against it and the availability of restraining orders and protective orders to keep the offending husband or boyfriend away. A few women have taken the drastic step of killing their abuser. In such cases, the defense of the battered woman syndrome is sometimes raised within the context of self-defense.

Finally, marital rape is not a crime in every state, although most states allow prosecution if the parties are separated and a petition has been filed for divorce or separate maintenance.

KEY CHAPTER TERMINOLOGY

married women's property acts
conveyance
postnuptial agreement
fraudulent transfer
dower
curtesy
forced share
right of election
intestate
bona fide occupational qualification (BFOQ)
quid pro quo harassment
hostile environment harassment
Roe v. Wade
viability
injunction
ex parte
battered woman syndrome

ETHICS IN PRACTICE

You are a paralegal who works in the office of Linda Williams, who is defending Richard Summer against a charge of raping his girlfriend. Linda asks you to do some paralegal work on the case. You have never told anyone that you were a rape victim ten years ago. The rape was never reported. Any ethical problems?

ON THE NET: LEGAL RIGHTS OF WOMEN

Equal Employment Opportunity Commission (job discrimination)
http://www.eeoc.gov

CataLaw: Women, Gender and Law
http://www.catalaw.com/topics/Women.shtml

Civil Remedies for Domestic Violence Victims
http://www.smith-lawfirm.com/domestic_violence_article.html

Civil Remedies for Victims of Sexual Abuse
http://www.smith-lawfirm.com/remedies.html

National Organization for Women
http://www.now.org

CHAPTER 13

ILLEGITIMACY AND PATERNITY PROCEEDINGS

CHAPTER OUTLINE

ILLEGITIMACY

> The status of illegitimacy has expressed through the ages society's condemnation of irresponsible liaisons beyond the bonds of marriage. But visiting this condemnation on the head of an infant is illogical and unjust. Moreover, imposing disabilities on the illegitimate child is contrary to the basic concept of our system that legal burdens should bear some relationship to individual responsibility or wrongdoing. Obviously, no child is responsible for his birth and penalizing the illegitimate child is an ineffectual—as well as an unjust—way of deterring the parent. Courts are powerless to prevent the social opprobium suffered by these hapless children, but the Equal Protection Clause does enable us to strike down discriminatory laws relating to status of birth where . . . the classification is justified by no legitimate state interest. . . .[1]

A legitimate child is a child born to parents who are married. The test is birth, not conception. A child conceived by an unmarried couple is legitimate if the parents are married at the time of the birth. An illegitimate child is one born outside of marriage. As of the late 1990s, a third of all children were born to unmarried women. At one time, the legal term for this person was *bastard.* The predominant term today is *illegitimate child.* There are some states, however, that have begun to use less harsh terms such as nonmarital child, child of an informal relationship, and child with no presumed father.

At common law, the illegitimate child was **filius nullius,** the child of nobody. The central disability imposed by this status was that the child born out of wedlock had no right to inherit from either parent. In addition, the child was prohibited from entering certain professions and, except in some ecclesiastical (church) courts, had no right to be supported by the father. Fortunately, the pronounced discrimination that has existed for centuries between the legitimate and the illegitimate child is eroding. States that have adopted the Uniform Parentage Act have abolished the distinction between legitimate and illegitimate children. ("The parent and child relationship extends equally to every

filius nullius
An illegitimate child—"the son [or child] of no one."

[1] *Weber v. Casualty & Surety Co.,* 406 U.S. 164, 175, 92 S. Ct. 1400, 1406, 31 L. Ed. 2d 768 (1972).

child and to every parent, regardless of the marital status of the parents." § 2.) In many states, however, some discrimination still exists.

Inheritance

intestate
Die without leaving a valid will.

Most states have passed statutes permitting an illegitimate child to inherit from its mother when the latter dies **intestate.** Some states tried to prevent the child from inheriting from its father who dies intestate, but such laws have been declared unconstitutional.[2] Yet restrictions on inheritance do exist. For example, assume that an illegitimate child waits until after his or her father dies before declaring that a parent-child relationship existed. Some states would not allow such a child to inherit, insisting that paternity must be determined by a court *before* death as a condition of inheriting from an intestate parent. This requirement is considered reasonable because it helps prevent false or fraudulent inheritance claims against the estate of an alleged parent who is now deceased.

Testate Distribution

testate
Die leaving a valid will.

Assume that the father of an illegitimate child dies **testate** and that a clause in the will gives property "to my children" or "to my heirs." If the father has legitimate and illegitimate children living when he dies, the question sometimes arises as to whether he intended "children" or "heirs" to include his illegitimate children. To resolve this question of intent, the court must look at all of the circumstances (e.g., how much contact the illegitimate child had with the father at the time the father wrote the will and at the time he died). A surprisingly large number of cases exist in which the court concluded that the illegitimate child was *not* included in the meaning of "children" or "heirs."

Support

Today both parents have an equal obligation to support their children, whether legitimate or illegitimate (see chapter 10). The support duty is not limited to biological or adoptive parents. A man can have a duty to support a child to whom he is not biologically related and whom he never adopted. As we will see, this result is due to the effect of the presumption of legitimacy.

Wrongful Death

When a parent dies due to the wrongful act of another, who can sue? Legitimate and illegitimate children have an equal right to bring wrongful death actions against defendants who have caused the death of one or both parents.

Workers' Compensation

When a parent dies from an injury on the job, the workers' compensation laws of the state permit the children of the deceased to recover benefits. If the state gives a preference to legitimate children over illegitimate children in claiming these benefits, the state is unconstitutionally denying equal protection of the law to the illegitimate children.

Social Security

Social security laws discriminate against illegitimate children in various phases of the social security system. Some of these discriminatory provisions have been declared unconstitutional, yet others have been allowed to stand.

---

[2] *Trimble v. Gordon,* 430 U.S. 762, 97 S. Ct. 1459, 52 L. Ed. 2d 31 (1977). Cf. *Labine v. Vincent,* 401 U.S. 532, 91 S. Ct. 1017, 28 L. Ed. 2d 288 (1971).

While it is unconstitutional to deny social security survivorship benefits to a child solely because that child is illegitimate, it may be permissible to impose greater procedural burdens on illegitimate children than on legitimate children in applying for benefits. Suppose, for example, that a child applies for survivorship benefits following the death of his or her father. To be eligible, the child must have been "dependent" on the deceased father. An illegitimate child can be forced to *prove* that he or she was dependent on the father, whereas no such requirement will be imposed on a legitimate child—the law will *presume* that the legitimate child was dependent on the father without requiring specific proof of it. The difference in treatment is considered reasonable, since illegitimate children are generally less likely to be dependent on their father than legitimate children.

Artificial Insemination

Assume that a woman is fertile but cannot conceive a child with her partner through sexual intercourse. His sperm may have poor motility. The couple might try **artificial insemination.** A physician injects sperm into the woman's vagina during a time she is ovulating. A single woman or a lesbian couple might also consider this option, using sperm that is purchased anonymously from a commercial sperm bank or that is donated by a known male. A gay male couple who wants a biological child would have to use the services of a surrogate mother. We will study surrogacy arrangements in chapter 16.

artificial insemination
The impregnation of a woman by a method other than sexual intercourse.

There are three main kinds of artificial insemination that married couples consider:

1. Artificial insemination with the semen of the husband (AIH)
2. Artificial insemination with the semen of a third-party donor (AID)
3. Artificial insemination in which the semen of the husband is mixed (confused) with that of a third-party donor (AIC)

The advantage in AIH is that the physician may be able to use "better" or concentrated sperm of the husband. One of the psychological advantages of AIC is the knowledge that the child *might* have been fathered by the husband.

In cases where the donor is clearly the mother's husband (AIH), the child is legitimate, and the husband has full parental rights and responsibilities. At one time, there was some doubt about the legitimacy of a child born through AID or AIC. Today there is no longer any doubt when the husband consents to an AID or AIC procedure. Under section 5(a) and (b) of the Uniform Parentage Act:

> If, under the supervision of a licensed physician and with the [written] consent of her husband, a wife is inseminated artificially with semen donated by a man not her husband, the husband is treated in law as if he were the natural father of a child thereby conceived [and] the donor of semen is treated in law as if he were not the natural father of a child thereby conceived.

Many states have adopted this statute or one similar to it.

The legal rights and responsibilities of a sperm donor are not as clear, however, when artificial insemination is used by a lesbian couple or a single heterosexual woman. Not many cases on this issue have been litigated. The few that do exist say a donor of semen to someone other than his wife has no parental rights to a child conceived through artificial insemination unless the donor and the woman have entered into a written contract to the contrary or the donor has begun to establish a bonding relationship with the child.

Sperm banks have become big business. Ads for donors often appear in college newspapers and on the World Wide Web. Since sperm is frequently sold to the banks, it is more accurate to call the men sperm vendors than sperm donors. The system has worked well, but not without controversy. One sperm bank tried to recruit Nobel Prize winners as sperm donors. Not many came forward. Critics ridiculed the bank as elitist genetic engineering. It is no longer in existence. In 1992, a Virginia fertility doctor was arrested after it was discovered that he was using his own sperm to impregnate his patients through artificial insemination. Prosecutors said that he may have fathered up to seventy-five children. In 1991, a white woman gave birth to a black child after the sperm bank accidently injected her with the sperm of a black man. And in 2000, a trial court ordered a sperm bank to reveal the identity of "Donor 276" when it became clear that the child born with his sperm had a genetic disease. There was no allegation in the case that the donor lied about his medical condition when he agreed to donate. Nor was there an allegation that the donee (the mother) was not given sufficient information about the risks of artificial insemination. Doctors simply wanted more information about the father to help them in their diagnosis and treatment of the child.

Finally, what happens when artificial insemination occurs after the death of the father? In 1991, Judith Hart applied for social security survivorship benefits for her young daughter. On the application form, she was asked, "What was your relationship to the child's father at the time of conception?" She answered, "widow." She had been artificially inseminated with her husband's sperm three months after he died of cancer. (His sperm was frozen before he started chemotherapy, which would probably have left him sterile.) The child was not alive at the time of her father's death. Survivorship benefits, therefore, were initially denied because she could not be considered a surviving dependent. After extensive publicity and just before an appeal was about to begin in court, the Social Security Administration reversed its position and allowed the child to receive survivorship benefits of $700 a month.

ASSIGNMENT 13.1

Answer the following questions by examining your state code. (See General Instructions for the State-Code Assignment in Appendix A.)

a. What are the inheritance rights of an illegitimate child in your state? From whom can an illegitimate child inherit?
b. Who can inherit from an illegitimate child?
c. Is a child born through artificial insemination legitimate?

LEGITIMATION AND PATERNITY

legitimation
The steps that enable an illegitimate child to become a legitimate child.

paternity proceeding
A formal process to determine whether a particular man is the biological father of a particular child.

Legitimation confers the status of legitimacy on an illegitimate child. A major reason parties go through legitimation is to clarify and assure rights of inheritance. A **paternity proceeding** is a process by which the fatherhood of a child is determined. In most states, a finding of paternity does not necessarily lead to the legitimation of the child.

Legitimation

States have different methods by which illegitimate children can be legitimated:

- *Acknowledgment.* The father publicly recognizes or acknowledges the illegitimate child as his. States differ on how this acknowledgment must take place. In some states, it must be in writing and witnessed. (For a form acknowledging parentage that is used in many maternity wards, see Exhibit 13.5 at the end of the chapter.) In some states, a written acknowledgment of paternity is not required if the man's activities strongly indicate that he is the father of the child (e.g., the father treats the child the same as the children who were born legitimate).

- *Marriage.* If the mother and father of the illegitimate child marry, the child is often automatically legitimated.
- *Combination of acknowledgment and marriage.* Some states require marriage of the parents and some form of acknowledgment by the father.
- *Legitimation proceeding.* A few states have special proceedings by which illegitimate children can be legitimated.
- *Paternity proceedings.* Although most paternity proceedings deal with fatherhood only, in a few states a finding of paternity also legitimates the child.
- *Legitimation by birth.* In some states, all children are legitimate whether or not their parents were married at the time of birth.

As indicated earlier, children of annulled marriages are considered legitimate according to special statutes, even though technically the parents were not validly married at the time the children were born (see chapter 6).

ASSIGNMENT 13.2

In what way(s) can an illegitimate child be legitimated in your state? (See General Instructions for the State-Code Assignment in Appendix A.)

Paternity

A major method by which a father is forced to support his illegitimate child is through a paternity proceeding, sometimes called a **filiation** proceeding, a suit to determine parentage, or, in our early history, a bastardy proceeding. Once fatherhood is determined, the support obligation is imposed. Most paternity proceedings in the country today are instigated by the state to try to recover some of the welfare or public assistance money paid to custodial parents. These parents are required to cooperate in instituting paternity proceedings. The program has been very successful. In 1998, paternities were established and acknowledged for over 1.5 million children with the help of state child-support agencies that exist in every state. This is triple the number obtained in 1992.

filiation
(1) A judicial determination of paternity; (2) the relation of child to father.

The starting point in establishing paternity is to obtain detailed facts from the mother. The questionnaire in Exhibit 13.1 has this objective.

Exhibit 13.1 Paternity Questionnaire

1. Your full name ______
   Your social security number ______
   Your address ______
   Your home phone ______ Your work phone ______
   Your date of birth ______
   With whom are you living: ______
2. List two people who will always know where you live:
   Name ______ Name ______
   Address ______ Address ______
   ______ ______
   Phone ______ Phone ______
3. Give the following information regarding the father of your child:
   Full name ______
   Address ______
   Date of birth ______ Social security number ______
   Home phone ______ Work phone ______
   Do you have a picture of the father: ______
4. Child's name ______ Child's date of birth ______ Child's sex ______
5. Do you have a picture of the child: ______
6. Does the child look like the father: ______

continued

Exhibit 13.1 Paternity Questionnaire—*Continued*

7. Does the child have the same coloring: ______
8. When and where did you meet the father: ______
9. When did you begin dating the father: ______
10. Did you ever live with the father: ______ If so, where and when: ______
Address ______ Phone ______
11. Others who knew you were living together:
Name ______ Name ______
Relationship to you ______ Relationship to you ______
Address ______ Address ______
Phone ______ Phone ______
12. When did you first have sexual relations with the father: ______
13. When did you last have sexual relations with him: ______
14. Where was the child conceived? (Where did you get pregnant):
City ______ County ______ State ______
15. Date father was told that you were pregnant: ______
16. Who told the father that you were pregnant: ______
17. What did he say when he was told you were pregnant: ______
18. Was a father listed on your child's birth certificate: ______ Did he sign it: ______
19. If no father was listed, explain why the father was not named on the birth certificate: ______
20. Write anything the father said suggesting to you that he is the child's father such as "Isn't our baby cute," or "I am glad you had my baby."
______
21. Did the father sign any papers or write any letters suggesting he is your baby's father: ______
22. What did he sign: ______ Where: ______
23. Did the father offer to help pay for an abortion? If so, briefly explain what he said, when, where, and if anyone else was present:
______
24. Did the father ever give or offer to give you money for the child? If so, how much and when: ______
25. Did the father ever buy the child gifts? If so, list the gifts and dates given: ______
26. Did you ever tell anyone that the father of your child is someone other than the man you are naming on this form: ______
If so, whom did you tell: ______
27. What was said (include name of other man named): ______
28. Give the names, addresses, and phone numbers of all witnesses who may be called to testify who have:
   a. Seen you and the father together during the time of conception (8–10 months prior to birth).
   b. Seen you and the father kissing, necking, or petting, or are aware of or have knowledge of any intimate relations you had with the alleged father.
   c. Heard the father make a statement to anyone about you getting an abortion or helping pay for an abortion.
   d. Heard the father make a statement to anyone suggesting or admitting he was the father of the child. (Indicate for each witness briefly what his or her testimony would be.)
   Name ______ Phone ______
   Address ______
   Testimony ______
   Name ______ Phone ______
   Address ______
   Testimony ______
29. Answer these questions for the 8th month before the birth (one month pregnant):
   a. Month ______ Year ______
   b. Were you having sex with the father: ______
   c. How frequently did you have intercourse: ______
   d. Did you use birth control on any occasion: ______
   e. Did the father use birth control on any occasion: ______
   f. Did you have sex with any other men during that month: ______
   If so, list their names, addresses, or other information that may be helpful in locating them.
   Name ______ Address ______
   Phone ______
   Name ______ Address ______
   Phone ______
30. Answer these questions for the 7th month before the birth (two months pregnant):
   a. Month ______ Year ______
   b. Were you having sex with the father: ______
   c. How frequently did you have intercourse: ______

d. Did you use birth control on any occasion: ______
e. Did the father use birth control on any occasion: ______
f. Did you have sex with any other men during that month: ______
If so, list their names, addresses, or other information that may be helpful in locating them.
Name ______ Address ______
Phone ______
Name ______ Address ______
Phone ______

31. Answer these questions for the 11th month before the birth (two months before you became pregnant):
a. Month ______ Year ______
b. Were you having sex with the father: ______
c. How frequently did you have intercourse: ______
d. Did you use birth control on any occasion: ______
e. Did the father use birth control on any occasion: ______
f. Did you have sex with any other men during that month: ______
If so, list their names, addresses, or other information that may be helpful in locating them.
Name ______ Address ______
Phone ______
Name ______ Address ______
Phone ______

32. Answer these questions for the 10th month before the birth (one month before you came became pregnant):
a. Month ______ Year ______
b. Were you having sex with the father: ______
c. How frequently did you have intercourse: ______
d. Did you use birth control on any occasion: ______
e. Did the father use birth control on any occasion: ______
f. Did you have sex with any other men during that month: ______
If so, list their names, addresses, or other information that may be helpful in locating them.
Name ______ Address ______
Phone ______
Name ______ Address ______
Phone ______

33. Answer these questions for the 9th month before the birth (the month you became pregnant):
a. Month ______ Year ______
b. Were you having sex with the father: ______
c. How frequently did you have intercourse: ______
d. Did you use birth control on any occasion: ______
e. Did the father use birth control on any occasion: ______
f. Did you have sex with any other men during that month: ______
If so, list their names and addresses, or other information that may be helpful in locating them.
Name ______ Address ______
Phone ______
Name ______ Address ______
Phone ______

34. Are you presently married: ______ If so, give name of husband. ______
35. Date of marriage ______ Place of marriage ______
36. Were you married at any time between one year before and one year after the birth of the child? ______
If so give name of each husband, date, and place of marriage, and, if applicable, the date and place of divorce or annulment:
Name ______ Date of marriage ______
Place ______ Date of divorce/annulment ______
Name ______ Date of marriage ______
Place ______ Date of divorce/annulment ______
37. On what date did your last menstrual flow begin before the birth of your child: ______
38. On what date did your last menstrual flow end before the birth of your child: ______
39. Do you have a calendar or other records showing these dates: ______
40. Do you have a diary or other written records of the dates you had intercourse with your child's father: ______
41. Name of doctor who cared for you before the child was born: ______
42. Name of doctor who cared for child after birth: ______
43. Address: ______
44. Circle one: Child premature, overdue, or normal term.
45. Exact due date ______ Birth weight ______
46. Who paid for the birth of the child:
Self ______ Medicaid ______ Other (please name) ______
47. Name of hospital in which child was born: ______
______

continued

Exhibit 13.1 Paternity Questionnaire—*Continued*

State of)
) ss.
County of)

____________________, being duly sworn states that she has read the above document and that the statements contained therein are true to the best of her knowledge.

____
Signature

____
Date

Subscribed and sworn to before me this __________ day of __________, 20_____

____
Notary Public

Resides at: ____________________
My Commission Expires: ____________________

putative
Alleged or reputed.

guardian ad litem
A special guardian appointed by the court to represent the interests of another.

The paternity proceeding itself looks a good deal like a criminal proceeding in some states. A warrant is issued for the arrest of the **putative** (i.e., alleged) father, the jury renders a guilty or not guilty verdict, etc. In most states, however, the proceeding is civil rather than criminal. Paternity must be established by a preponderance of the evidence, although a few states require proof by a higher standard—clear and convincing evidence. There is an eighteen-year statute of limitations so that the paternity action can be brought at any time before the child reaches the age of majority.

The mother (on her own or at the prompting of the welfare department) usually initiates the paternity proceeding, although the child is often also given standing to sue through a specially appointed representative (e.g., a **guardian ad litem**). (Exhibit 13.2 shows an example of a paternity petition.) When the mother brings the action, it is important to know whether the child was made a party to the proceeding and was represented. If not, then in some states, the child will not be bound by the judgment.

Exhibit 13.2 Paternity Petition

FAMILY COURT OF
COUNTY OF

. . . .

In the Matter of a Paternity Proceeding

____________________ Petitioner,

—against—

____________________ Respondent,

. . . .

Docket No.
PATERNITY PETITION
(Parent)

TO THE FAMILY COURT:

The undersigned Petitioner respectfully shows that:

1. Petitioner resides at ____________________.
2. Petitioner had sexual intercourse with the above named Respondent (on several occasions covering a period of time beginning on or about the ______ day of __________, 20_____, and ending on or about the ______ day of ________, 20____, and as a result thereof (Petitioner) became pregnant.
3. *(a) (Petitioner) gave birth to a (male) (female) child out of wedlock on the _____ day of _____, 20_____, at _____.
   *(b) (Petitioner) is now pregnant with a child who is likely to be born out of wedlock.
4. (Respondent) who resides at _____ is the father of the child.
5. (Respondent) (has acknowledged) (acknowledges) paternity of the child (in writing) (and) (by furnishing support).
6. No previous application has been made to any court or judge for the relief sought herein (except ____________________.)

WHEREFORE, Petitioner prays that this Court issue a summons or warrant requiring the Respondent to show cause why the Court should not enter a declaration of paternity, an order of support, and such other and further relief as may be appropriate under the circumstances.

____
Petitioner

Dated: __________, 20_____.

*Alternative allegations.

> *Mary, the mother of Sam, brings a paternity proceeding against Kevin, alleging he is the father of Sam. Sam is not made a party to the proceeding. A guardian ad litem is not appointed for him, and he is not otherwise represented in court. The court finds that Kevin is not the father of Sam. Ten years later Sam brings his own action against Kevin for support, alleging that he is the son of Kevin.*

Is Sam's support action ten years later barred by the defense of **res judicata?** That is, was the fatherhood issue already resolved in the paternity proceeding? States differ in their answer to this question. Many will bar the later suit of the child only if the latter was a party to the earlier case that decided the fatherhood issue. In such states, Sam *would* be able to relitigate the paternity issue against Kevin, since he was not represented on his own or through a guardian ad litem in the proceeding ten years earlier.

res judicata
When a judgment on the merits has been rendered, the parties cannot relitigate the same dispute; they have already had their day in court.

A related question is whether the mother can enter a settlement with the putative father under which she agrees to drop the paternity proceeding in exchange for the defendant's agreement to pay a certain amount for the support of the child and for the mother's expenses in giving birth to the child. In some states, it is illegal to enter into such an agreement. In states where this type of settlement is permitted, the child must be represented and/or the settlement must be approved by the court.

The paternity proceeding requires **personal jurisdiction** over the defendant—putative father (see chapter 7). This generally means that service of process must be made on the defendant in person within the forum state (i.e., the state where the paternity proceeding is being brought). If the defendant is not a resident of the forum state, personal jurisdiction over him may be obtainable under the state's **long-arm statute** on the ground that he engaged in sexual intercourse in the state, which may have led to the conception of the child. For other grounds, see the discussion of the Uniform Interstate Family Support Act (UIFSA) on page 351 in chapter 10.

personal jurisdiction
The power of a court to render a decision that binds an individual defendant.

long-arm statute
A law that gives a court personal jurisdiction over a nonresident because of his or her purposeful contact with the state.

Once the trial on the paternity issue begins, the defendant may be faced with a *presumption of legitimacy.* This presumption has been called "one of the strongest and most persuasive known to the law."[3] A child born to a married woman is presumed to be legitimate unless conclusively proven otherwise. This means that if the defendant is the husband of the mother and denies paternity, he must introduce very strong evidence that he is not the father (e.g., evidence that he is sterile). At one time, neither spouse could introduce evidence that he or she had no sexual intercourse around the time of conception (i.e., evidence of nonaccess) if such evidence would tend to "bastardize" or "illegitimize" the child. This was known as **Lord Mansfield's rule.** Hence, if a defendant had not had sexual intercourse with his wife in years, he could not give testimony or introduce other evidence to this effect if it would tend to bastardize the mother's recently born child.

Lord Mansfield's rule
The testimony of either spouse is inadmissible on the question of whether the husband had access to the wife at the time of conception if such evidence would tend to bastardize (i.e., declare illegitimate) the child.

Most states still apply the presumption of legitimacy but have abolished or substantially limited Lord Mansfield's rule. The modern version of the presumption is found in the Uniform Parentage Act. In states that have adopted this act, a man is presumed to be the natural father of a child (and will be referred to as the *presumed father*) if he and the child's natural mother are married to each other and the child is born during the marriage, or within 300 days after the marriage is terminated.[4] The presumption can be rebutted or overcome but only by clear and convincing evidence.

[3] *In re Findlay,* 170 N.E. 471, 472 (N.Y. 1930).

[4] In addition, the husband is the presumed father if, while the child is under the age of majority, the husband receives the child into his home and openly holds out the child as his natural child. Under certain conditions, the same is true for a child born within a marriage that can be or has been annulled.

In most cases, the presumed father will be trying to overcome the presumption that he is the biological father by using blood tests and other evidence that we will consider later. Suppose, however, that a *third party* wants to prove that he is the biological father.

> *Ted and Helen are married. Helen gives birth to Mary while having an affair with a neighbor. Ted is the presumed father because the child was born during his marriage with Helen. The neighbor now wants to go to court to prove that he is in fact the biological father so that he can have custody or visitation rights. Ted objects, since he wants to raise Mary as his own.*

standing
The right to bring a case and seek relief from a court.

States differ on whether a third party such as the neighbor would have **standing** to prove to a court that he is in fact the biological father of the child. Some states will give him standing but may impose a time limit within which he must bring the suit to establish his paternity (e.g., within two years after the birth of the child). Other states would deny him standing. The United States Supreme Court has held that it is constitutional for a state to favor a husband (the presumed father) over a biological father and deny standing to the latter.[5] In this case, the plaintiff, Michael, sought to establish paternity to a child born to a woman who was married to another man. Despite the fact that blood tests indicated a 98.07 percent probability that Michael was the father and the fact that Michael had established a relationship with the child, the Court upheld the rights of the husband as the presumed father and denied Michael any rights.

We turn now to an examination of the kind of evidence that can be considered by a court in cases where standing is not an issue. In most of these cases, an unmarried man is trying to prove that he is not the father, or a married man (the presumed father) is trying to overcome the presumption that he is.

The discovery of human blood groups and types has been of great assistance in paternity cases because they:

- Can be determined at birth or shortly thereafter
- Remain constant throughout an individual's life
- Are inherited

In 1981, the United States Supreme Court commented on the operation and effectiveness of blood group tests as follows:

> If the blood groups and types of the mother and child are known, the possible and *impossible* blood groups and types of the true father can be determined under the rules of inheritance. For example, a group AB child cannot have a group O parent, but can have a group A, B, or AB parent. Similarly, a child cannot be type M unless one or both parents are type M, and the factor rh′ cannot appear in the blood of a child unless present in the blood of one or both parents. . . . Since millions of men belong to the possible groups and types, a blood grouping test cannot conclusively establish paternity. However, it can demonstrate *non-paternity,* such as where the alleged father belongs to group O and the child is group AB. It is a negative rather than an affirmative test with the potential to scientifically exclude the paternity of a falsely accused putative father.
>
> The ability of blood grouping tests to exonerate innocent putative fathers was confirmed by a 1976 report developed jointly by the American Bar Association and the American Medical Association. Miale, Jennings, Rettberg, Sell & Krause, *Joint AMA–ABA Guidelines: Present Status of Serologic Testing in Problems of Disputed Parentage,* 10 Family L. Q. 247 (Fall 1976). The joint report recommended the use of seven blood test "systems"—ABO, Rh, MNS, Kell, Duffy, Kidd, and HLA—when investigating questions of paternity. . . . These

[5] *Michael H. v. Gerald D.,* 491 U.S. 110, 109 S. Ct. 2333, 105 L. Ed. 2d 91 (1989).

> systems were found to . . . provide a 91% cumulative probability of negating paternity for erroneously accused Negro men and 93% for white men. . . .
>
> The effectiveness of the seven systems attests the probative value of blood test evidence in paternity cases. The importance of that scientific evidence is heightened because "[t]here are seldom accurate or reliable eye witnesses since the sexual activities usually take place in intimate and private surroundings, and the self-serving testimony of a party is of questionable reliability." Larson, *Blood Test Exclusion Procedures in Paternity Litigation: The Uniform Acts and Beyond,* 13 J. Family L. 713 [1974].[6]

Since 1981, when the preceding commentary was written, the effectiveness of scientific testing has increased significantly. Today newly discovered serologic and statistical methods have made major changes in the law of evidence in this area. A "wider range of genetic tests have come to be admissible, and not merely to demonstrate that it is biologically impossible for a particular man to be the father, but also to show that it is highly probable that a specific man *is* the father."[7] The tests are used to indicate the likelihood or probability of paternity of a man who is not excluded by the tests:

> The test results will establish whether your client is excluded as being the father of the child; or if not, what is the probability or likelihood of his being the actual father. If the client is excluded by the blood test, then the case has ended and the mother will have to accuse some other man as being the father. If your client is not excluded, the probability or likelihood of his paternity will be mathematically determined. The likelihood that he is the actual father is then compared statistically to that of a fictional man who is assumed to have had sexual intercourse with the mother and who is assumed not to be excluded by the test. These results are expressed in the form of a "paternity index" and in the form of a "probability of paternity." For example, the paternity index would be expressed as (53 to 1) fifty-three to one; that is, the putative father is fifty-three times more likely to have fathered the child than some other man who could have had intercourse with the mother and who would not be excluded by the blood test. The "probability of paternity" is generally expressed in a percentage figure; for example, 98.15%.[8]

The newest scientific breakthrough in paternity identification is called **DNA testing.** This test is performed on genetic material known as deoxyribonucleic acid—DNA. The success of the test is due to the fact that the configuration of DNA is different in virtually all individuals except identical twins. DNA, the "blueprint of life," determines each person's unique genetic individuality. "The chances that two unrelated persons will have the same DNA are 1 in a quadrillion. Even with siblings (except identical twins), the chances are 1 in ten trillion."[9] To begin the test, the most common procedure is to remove DNA from cells obtained in a blood sample of a mother, child, and possible father. An alternative to drawing blood is to use a "buccal swab." To obtain cells by this method (most often used on small children), a cotton swab is rubbed on the inside of a person's cheeks. See Exhibit 13.3 for a description of how DNA identity testing works and Exhibit 13.4 for a sample test report. The cost of testing a mother, child, and possible father by a DNA testing laboratory is approximately $500. The results will often state that:

DNA testing
Genetic testing on deoxyribonucleic acid removed from cells.

- The tested man is not the biological father of the child or
- The probability is greater than 99.9 percent that the tested man is the biological father of the child in comparison to the general population of men of the same race.

---

[6]*Little v. Streater,* 451 U.S. 1, 8, 101 S. Ct. 2202, 2206, 68 L. Ed. 2d 627 (1981).
[7]D. Kaye & R. Kanwischer, *Admissibility of Genetic Testing in Paternity Litigation,* 22 Family Law Quarterly 109, 109–10 (1988).
[8]Neubaum, *Defense of Paternity Cases,* 92 Case & Comment, July–Aug. 1987, at 38–39.
[9]Office of Child Support Enforcement, DNA Profiling 64–6 (3d ed. 1990).

Exhibit 13.3 How DNA Identity Testing Works

Testing Technical Information

A sample is collected from the mother, child and alleged father for DNA parentage testing. Single parent testing (the child and the alleged father only) may also be performed. The genetic material itself is directly examined in DNA parentage testing.

What Are Genes?

The human body consists of trillions of cells. Most of these cells have a nucleus or center. The nucleus contains genes, the fundamental units of our heredity. These genes are grouped into separate bundles called chromosomes. We have forty-six chromosomes inside every cell in our body. Twenty-three of these chromosomes came from the biological mother and twenty-three came from the biological father. Chromosomes are named by a letter "D" followed by a number [i.e., chromosome #1 is named D1; and chromosome #2 is named D2, etc.]. Genes are named by the number of the chromosome they inhabit. A DNA Parentage Testing report identifies the genes that were analyzed during the process of testing. When the test results refer to D2S44, you know that the gene analyzed was on chromosome #2 at locus 44.

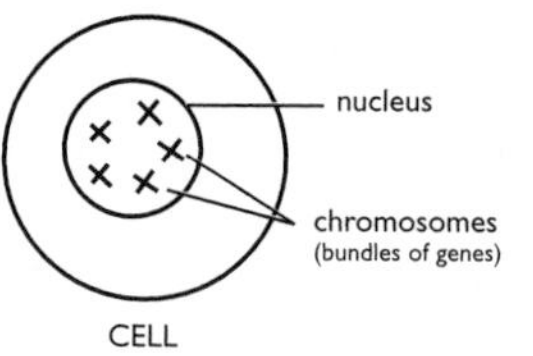

The Chemistry of Genes

Twenty-six letters of the alphabet are the basic units of our English language. Words and sentences are formed from these 26 letters. Genes on the other hand are formed from only 4 chemicals, or bases. These bases are named: (1) adenine, (2) cytosine, (3) guanine, and (4) thymine. Like the letters of the alphabet that form sentences, these 4 bases form long gene fragments called deoxyribonucleic acid—DNA. We can measure the length of the gene fragments by the number of bases they have. When you see the gene fragment on your DNA Parentage Test report, if it is 2.34 kilobases, that means the gene fragment consists of 2,340 bases [kilobase = 1,000 bases].

All children have a biological mother and a biological father. For each gene in the child, there is one genetic variant size that came from the father and one genetic variant size that came from the mother. A DNA Parentage Test determines and examines the genetic variant sizes (i.e. allele sizes) found in the mother, the child and the alleged father.

In the sample report shown, the upper gene fragment in the child (3.76-kb size) matches the upper gene fragment size of the mother. The child received the lower gene fragment (1.46-kb size) from his/her biological father.

The alleged father #1 has gene fragment sizes different from those found in the child. Therefore, the alleged father #1 cannot be the child's biological father. The alleged father #2 has the same gene size fragment as that found in the child (i.e., 1.46 kb). He could be the child's biological father. The probability that he is the child's biological father depends on the frequency with which this gene fragment is found in the male population. The fewer men who have this gene fragment size, the greater probability that the tested man is the biological father of the child.

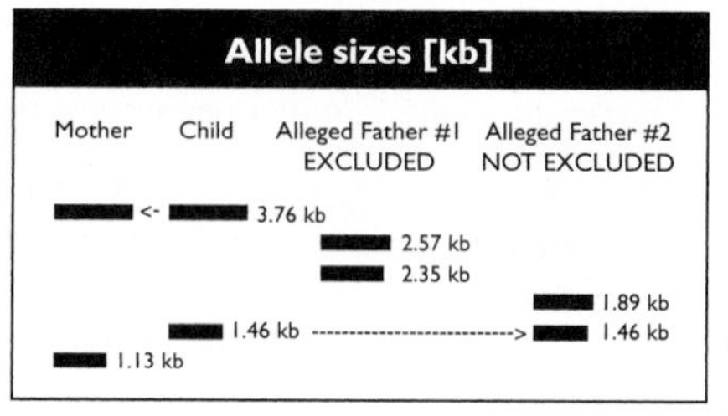

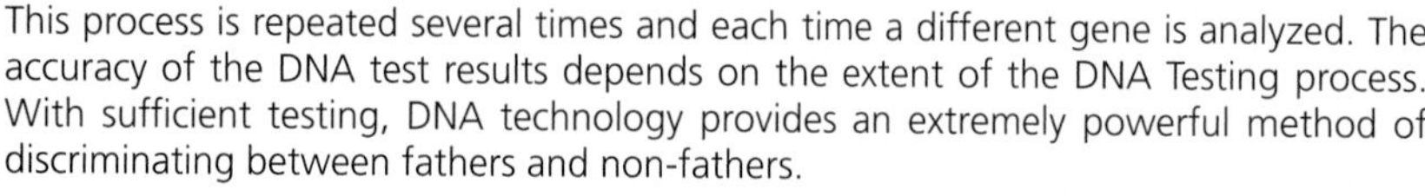
This process is repeated several times and each time a different gene is analyzed. The accuracy of the DNA test results depends on the extent of the DNA Testing process. With sufficient testing, DNA technology provides an extremely powerful method of discriminating between fathers and non-fathers.

Source: Genetica, DNA Laboratories, Inc., 8740 Montgomery Road, Cincinnati, OH 45236, www.genetica.com, identity @genetica.com, (800) 433-6848.

One consequence of the effectiveness of all of these tests is that most disputed paternity cases today are resolved on the basis of the tests rather than by trial. Testing can be expensive, however. If the putative father is indigent, the state must pay for the tests. If he refuses to undergo the tests, many states will either force him to be tested or allow the trial court to take his refusal into consideration in making the paternity decision. The strong implication of such a refusal is that he has something to hide. Many states provide state-appointed counsel for the putative father in these proceedings.

ASSIGNMENT 13.3

a. In what way(s) can the fatherhood of a child be determined by a court in your state?

b. Select the main way that fatherhood is established in your state (e.g., a paternity proceeding), and prepare a flowchart of all the procedural steps of the process.

Exhibit 13.4 Sample DNA Test Result

the GENETICA DNA Test™

No. 87237 4321	MOTHER	CHILD	ALLEGED FATHER
Patient Name	XXXXX	XXXXX	XXXXX
Date of Birth	7/2/1974	7/12/2000	3/18/1973
Race	Caucasian		Caucasian
Date Collected	1/1/2001	1/1/2001	1/1/2001
Test Number	**87237-1**	**87237-2**	**87237-3**
Genetic Systems Tested	Allele Sizes (kilobases)	Allele Sizes (kilobases)	Allele Sizes (kilobases)
D2S44 SLI106 - Hae III PI **16.10**	2.35 2.24	3.21 2.35	3.21 1.35
D4S163 SLI604 - Hae III PI **8.70**	6.02 4.52	6.02 4.88	8.26 4.88
D6S132 SLI1090 - Hae III PI **6.68**	4.49 3.31	4.49 1.88	3.78 1.88
D7S467 SLI989 - Hae III PI **74.00**	5.18 4.67	4.67 2.68	4.36 2.68
D10S28 SLI917 - Hae III PI **24.60**	3.81 1.80	3.81 1.68	1.68 1.59

SAMPLE

Interpretation: Combined Parentage Index **1,703,289** Probability of Parentage **99.9999%**

The alleged father, XXXXX, cannot be excluded as the biological father of the child named XXXXX. Based on testing results obtained from analyses of 5 different DNA probes, the probability of paternity is 99.9999%. This probability of paternity is calculated by comparing to an untested, unrelated man of the North American Caucasian population (assumes prior probability equals .50). The GENETICA DNA Test excluded greater than 99.99% of the male population from the possibility of being the biological father of the tested child.

COURT/ADMIN Case No.: **XXXX-XX** Report Date **1/3/2001**

Subscribed and sworn before me on 5/10/2001.

I, Elizabeth Panke, M.D., Ph.D., verify that the interpretation of results is correct as reported, and the above testing was conducted in accordance with the recommended guidelines for DNA testing set forth by AABB.

Source: Genetica, DNA Laboratories, Inc., 8740 Montgomery Road, Cincinnati, OH 45236, www.genetica.com, identity@genetica.com, (800) 433-6848.

c. What is the statute of limitations for paternity actions in your state?
d. What is the standard of proof in paternity cases in your state? Does paternity have to be proven by a "preponderance of the evidence," by "clear and convincing evidence," "beyond a reasonable doubt," or by some other standard?
e. How, if at all, can blood grouping, DNA, or similar tests be used in your state?
f. Can a polygraph test be used?
g. Does Lord Mansfield's rule apply in your state?

(See General Instructions for the State-Code Assignment, General Instructions for the Flowchart Assignment, and General Instructions for the Court-Opinion Assignment in Appendix A.)

Of course, not every father must be dragged into court in order to establish paternity. In every state, maternity wards have forms on which fathers and mothers are asked to sign a voluntary recognition of parentage. (See Exhibit 13.5 for an example of such a form that can be used in hospitals or elsewhere.)

Before signing, the parents are told that they have a duty to support the child and that the signed form is the legal equivalent of a court order determining parentage. Months or years later a man who has signed the form will have a difficult time establishing that he is not the father. (See also the putative father registry in Exhibit 15.5 of chapter 15, containing a form that is used if an unwed father wants to acknowledge paternity so that he will be notified if someone in the future petitions to adopt his child.)

Exhibit 13.5 Voluntary Recognition of Parentage

Voluntary Recognition of Parentage

For use of State Registrar Only

Instructions: Fill this out in blue or black ink. Press hard, using a ballpoint pen. Do not cross out words or make corrections.

Form Completed at:
☐ Hospital
☐ County Office
☐ State Registrar
☐ State Human Ser. Off.
☐ Other

Complete all Requested Information Before Signing this Form

Child and Parents' Information

Important: Use the same name that is on your child's birth certificate. If you want to change your child's last name to the father's last name, mark this box. ☐

Child's Name (first)	Middle	Last	Date of Birth (month/day/year)
Place of Birth (city/county/state/country)			

Father's Name (first/middle/last)	
Date of Birth (month/day/year)	Place of Birth (state)
Address	
City/State/Zip	
Social Security Number	Over 18 ☐ yes ☐ No

Mother's Name (first/middle/last)	
Date of Birth (month/day/year)	Place of Birth (state)
Address	
City/State/Zip	
Social Security Number	Over 18 ☐ yes ☐ No

Parent's Statement:

Under oath, I state that:

- I have been told about the Recognition of Parentage and understand my rights and responsibilities created and waived by signing this form.
- I have a copy of *Being a Legal Father: Parentage Information for Mothers and Fathers*. I read the booklet or had someone else read it to me, and viewed the videotape.
- I acknowledge that we are the biological parents of the child named in this Recognition of Parentage.
- I understand that this Recognition of Parentage does not give custody or visitation to the legal father. However, this Recognition of Parentage gives the father the right to ask the court for custody or visitation.
- I accept responsibility to provide financial support for my child. I understand that financial support can include payments for child support, medical support, and child care support starting from my child's birth until a court order for support ends.
- I understand that both parents have the right to all notices of any adoption proceedings.
- I understand that this is a legal document. If we are both age 18 or older when we sign this form, this Recognition of Parentage is the same as a court order determining the legal relationship between a father and child.
- I understand that if either of us is under age 18 when we sign this form, this Recognition of Parentage is only a presumption of paternity. I understand that this Recognition of Parentage will be the same as a court order determining the legal relationship between a father and child six months after the youngest of us turns 18. If I want to stop this Recognition of Parentage from becoming a legal document, I understand that I must take legal action before the six months ends.
- I understand that either of us can cancel this Recognition of Parentage by stating in writing that, "I am revoking the Recognition of Parentage." I understand that I must sign the Revocation in front of a Notary Public and that I must file the Revocation with the Office of the State Registrar within 60 days after I complete this Recognition of Parentage form. If I have not filed a Revocation within 60 days and still want to cancel this Recognition of Parentage, I understand that I will need to take legal action to request a change to any of the information in this Recognition of Parentage.
- To the best of my knowledge, the above information is true.
- I am signing this form voluntarily. No one forced me to sign this Recognition of Parentage.

Signature of Father X
Subscribed and sworn to before me this ________day of ______________________, 20_____
Notary Public Signature
My commission expires:

Signature of Mother X
Subscribed and sworn to before me this ________day of ______________________, 20_____
Notary Public Signature
My commission expires:

☐ Husband's Non-Paternity Statement Attached

Important Information

Waiver of Rights

Important: By signing this Recognition of Parentage form, you give up rights listed below:

- The right to have blood or genetic testing to prove that the man is the biological father of the child.
- The right to have an attorney represent you. The court will provide an attorney for parents who meet income standards and cannot afford to pay an attorney.
- The right to a trial to determine if the man is the biological father of the child.
- The right to cross-examine witnesses at a trial.
- The right to testify about who is the biological father of the child.

Custody Issues

When a child is born to parents who are not married to each other the law gives custody of the child to the mother. If the father wants a different custody arrangement, he must go to court. If the parents cannot agree about visitation, the father will need to go to court. If you have any questions, please contact an attorney.

CASE

Pettinato v. Pettinato

582 A.2d 909 (1990)
Supreme Court of Rhode Island

Background: *Gregory Pettinato sued Susanne Pettinato for divorce and custody of their son Gregory, Jr. During the litigation, she denied that he was the father. The Family Court granted the divorce and gave custody to the father. The case is now on appeal brought by Susanne before the Supreme Court of Rhode Island.*

Decision on Appeal: *Affirmed. Susanne is estopped from denying Gregory's paternity.*

Opinion of the Court:

Justice Shea delivered the opinion of the court. . . .

Although many of the facts were disputed, it appears that a relationship developed between Gregory and Susanne in the fall of 1984. The parties disagreed about the date when they began sexual relations. However, it is undisputed that the parties were engaging in sexual relations by February 1985. Susanne testified that she did not engage in sexual relations with Gregory between February 14, 1985, and April 7, 1985. During that period she traveled to Florida for two weeks. Moreover, Susanne testified, she did not speak with Gregory until after November

1985 when she returned to Rhode Island from her second trip to Florida.

Susanne gave birth to Gregory, Jr., on January 5, 1986. Despite the parties' discrepancies regarding events leading to the child's birth, Gregory was named as the child's father on the birth certificate filed on January 13, 1986.

Susanne testified that she told Gregory while in the hospital after giving birth that Gregory, Jr., was the child of the man she had stayed with while in Florida. Gregory disputed this testimony. He testified that Susanne telephoned him in April 1985, informed him of her pregnancy, and stated that he, Gregory, was the father. Gregory first became aware of Susanne's denial of his paternity at the time of this divorce action when she filed her answers to interrogatories.

The evidence established that the parties had a fairly nomadic existence after the birth of Gregory, Jr. For approximately one month after the child's birth, Susanne and the child lived at her parents' home. Gregory was forbidden by her parents to visit Susanne or Gregory, Jr., although the parties would arrange to meet at a friend's house without the knowledge of Susanne's parents. Thereafter, Susanne and the child shared a rented apartment with a friend for approximately three months before moving into an apartment with Gregory.

Gregory, Susanne, and Gregory, Jr., lived in an apartment from May 1986 until October 1986. All three then moved into Gregory's parents' home in October 1986. Gregory and Susanne married on December 21, 1986. Gregory testified that he married Susanne because he "thought it would be the proper thing to do to make a family and be on our own together and bring up our child." The parties remained at his parents' home until Susanne moved out on April 26, 1987. Susanne initially left Gregory, Jr., with Gregory and his parents. Susanne testified, however, that the Cranston police retrieved Gregory, Jr., the next day and brought the child to her at a friend's home. . . .

Over the objections of Gregory, the court heard testimony from Marjorie Kimball, a medical technologist at the Rhode Island Blood Center. Kimball testified that she performed genetic blood testing on Gregory, Susanne, and Gregory, Jr. As a result of this genetic blood testing, Kimball concluded that it was not possible for Gregory to be the biological father of Gregory, Jr.

The trial justice issued an interlocutory decision pending entry of final judgment on October 11, 1988. He granted the petition of Gregory for an absolute divorce and awarded Gregory permanent custody of Gregory, Jr., subject to all reasonable rights of visitation for Susanne. In his decision the trial justice based the award on the care given Gregory, Jr., by Gregory, the length of time Gregory, Jr., spent with Gregory, and the bonding that had occurred between Gregory, Jr., and Gregory. . . .

On appeal Susanne argues that the trial justice improperly overlooked and/or misconceived the expert testimony regarding the genetic blood testing that excluded Gregory as the biological father of Gregory, Jr. Susanne contends that as the natural parent of Gregory, Jr., she is entitled to custody of the child absent a showing of unfitness. . . .

In this case we consider for the first time the rights of parents whose legal presumption of paternity is later challenged during a divorce proceeding. It is undisputed that Gregory is the presumptive natural father of Gregory, Jr. . . . § 15–8–3 Presumption of paternity:

> (a) A man is to be the natural father of a child if: . . . (3) After the child's birth, he and the child's natural mother have married, or attempted to marry, each other by a marriage solemnized in apparent compliance with law, although the attempted marriage could be declared invalid, and: (i) He has acknowledged his paternity of the child in writing filed with the clerk of the [F]amily [C]ourt; or (ii) With his consent, he is named as the child's father on the child's birth certificate; or, (iii) He is obligated to support the child under a written voluntary promise or by court order; (4) He acknowledges his paternity of the child in a writing filed with the clerk of the [F]amily [C]ourt, who shall promptly inform the mother of the filing of the acknowledgement, and she does not dispute the acknowledgement, within a reasonable time after being informed thereof, in a writing filed with the clerk of the [F]amily [C]ourt. If another man is presumed under this section to be the child's father, acknowledgement may be effected only with the written consent of the presumed father or after the presumption has been rebutted.
>
> (b) A presumption under this section may be rebutted in an appropriate action only by clear and convincing evidence. If two (2) or more presumptions arise which conflict with each other, the presumption which on its facts is founded on the weightier considerations of policy and logic controls. The presumption is rebutted by a court decree establishing paternity of the child by another man.

Susanne admits that Gregory has met the requirements of § 15–8–3(a)(3)(ii). The parties married after Gregory, Jr.'s birth, and with his consent Gregory was named as the child's father on the birth

continued

CASE

Pettinato v. Pettinato—*Continued*

certificate. Nevertheless, Susanne contends, the results of the genetic blood testing that excluded Gregory as the biological father provide the "clear and convincing" evidence required by § 15–8–3(b) to rebut the presumption of Gregory's paternity.

We are concerned about the situation before the court wherein a mother can tell a man that he is the father of her child, marry him and live together as a family, and then illegitimize the child during a divorce proceeding by attacking the legal presumption of paternity that she helped to bring about. The situation before us is a matter of first impression in this state. After reviewing the conclusions arrived at by other states that have considered this issue, we have reached the conclusion that Susanne may not defeat Gregory's legal presumption of paternity.

We are of the opinion that a mother should be equitably estopped from using the genetic blood testing permitted by § 15–8–11 to disestablish a child's paternity in connection with a routine divorce proceeding. The underlying rationale of the equitable-estoppel doctrine is that "under certain circumstances, a person might be estopped from challenging paternity where that person has by his or her conduct accepted a given person as father of the child." *John M. v. Paula T.,* 524 Pa. 306, 318, 571 A.2d 1380, 1386 (1990). Where the equitable-estoppel doctrine is operative, evidence of genetic blood tests is considered irrelevant in a divorce proceeding wherein the basic issue is the termination of the marriage bond—not the paternity of a child. "[T]he law will not permit a person in these situations to challenge the status which he or she has previously accepted [or created]." Id.

The circumstances of the case before us, in our opinion, compel the application of the equitable-estoppel doctrine. Gregory has represented himself to be and has been accepted as Gregory, Jr.'s natural father. He married Susanne, believing her representation that the child was his child. He married her with the intention that the couple would raise their child in a family unit. Gregory consented to being named as the father on Gregory, Jr.'s birth certificate. The three lived together and represented themselves to the community as a family. Susanne never questioned Gregory's paternity until after he commenced divorce proceedings that followed her leaving him. At the time he filed for divorce, Susanne had become pregnant again but not by Gregory.

Taken together, this court's adherence to the statutory presumption of paternity in § 15–8–3(a)(3)(ii) and the court's application of the equitable-estoppel doctrine lead to the same point: the genetic blood test results offered into evidence were not relevant because legal paternity had been established and biological paternity was not at issue. *Scott v. Mershon,* 394 Pa. Super. 411, 417–418, 576 A.2d 67, 71 (1990). Therefore, the genetic blood test results disestablishing Gregory's paternity should not have been admitted. We reject Susanne's contention that the trial justice overlooked and/or misconceived the expert testimony regarding genetic blood testing. That testimony should have been excluded as irrelevant on Gregory's objection to its admission. . . .

For these reasons the defendant's appeal is denied and dismissed, the judgment appealed from is affirmed, and the papers of the case are remanded to the Family Court.

ASSIGNMENT 13.4

a. What is the difference between legal paternity and biological paternity? Why was the distinction important in *Pettinato?*

b. Assume that the paternity issue is not raised in the divorce case and that Susanne is granted custody of the son. Years later Gregory refuses to pay child support. He wants to introduce evidence of the genetic blood tests that prove he is not the father. Can he introduce this evidence?

c. In chapter 9 on child custody, we discussed at length the recent United States Supreme Court case of *Troxel v. Granville,* which said that a parent has a fundamental constitutional right to raise his or her child against the wishes of a grandparent or other nonparent. Was Susanne Pettinato's fundamental constitutional right as a parent violated in *Pettinato v. Pettinato?* Phrased another way, is *Pettinato v. Pettinato* consistent with *Troxel v. Granville?*

SUMMARY

At one time, an illegitimate child had very few rights. This situation has changed, although the discrimination has not been entirely eliminated. An illegitimate child can now fully inherit from his or her father who dies intestate. Some states insist, however, that paternity be established before the parent dies. If the parent dies testate, leaving property "to my children" or "to my heirs," the answer to the question of whether illegitimate children were included in these phrases depends on the intent of the parent.

Legitimate and illegitimate children have the same right to be supported, to bring wrongful-death actions because of the death of a parent, and to receive workers' compensation benefits if the parent dies on the job. To obtain social security benefits, however, an illegitimate child must prove he or she was dependent on a deceased father, whereas the law presumes the dependence of a legitimate child.

In most states, when a child is born through artificial insemination with the semen of a man other than the husband, the latter has a duty to support the child, and the child is considered legitimate if the husband consented to the insemination.

Legitimation can occur in a number of ways: acknowledgment of paternity, marriage of the mother and father, legitimation proceeding, paternity proceeding, etc. In some states, all children are legitimate regardless of whether the mother and father ever married.

A major function of a paternity proceeding is to establish a father's duty of support. For this purpose, the court must have personal jurisdiction over him. The child should be joined as a party in the proceeding to ensure that the judgment will be binding on the child. If the defendant is married to the mother, he may face a number of evidentiary obstacles at the trial (e.g., the presumption of legitimacy and Lord Mansfield's rule). Some states deny standing to a man who wants to prove that he is the father of a child born to a woman married to another man. A state can subordinate his rights as a biological father to the rights of the husband as the presumed father even if the husband could not possibly be the father. Traditional blood group testing can help establish the nonpaternity, though not the paternity, of a particular defendant. More modern scientific techniques, however, claim the ability to establish the high probability of paternity.

All states allow a father to file a paternity acknowledgment in the hospital at the birth of his child.

KEY CHAPTER TERMINOLOGY

filius nullius
intestate
testate
artificial insemination
legitimation
paternity proceeding
filiation
putative
guardian ad litem
res judicata
personal jurisdiction
long-arm statute
Lord Mansfield's rule
standing
DNA testing

ETHICS IN PRACTICE

You are a paralegal working at the law office of James Adams, Esq. On November 10, 2000, Adams is assigned by the court to represent John Edwinson against whom a paternity petition has been filed. There is a hearing scheduled for March 13, 2001. Edwinson is not a cooperative client. He frequently misses appointments at the law firm office. Frustrated, Adams sends Edwinson a short letter on March 1, 2001, that says, "Due to your noncooperation, I am withdrawing from the case as your representative effective immediately." Any ethical problems?

ON THE NET: MORE ON ILLEGITIMACY AND PATERNITY

DNA Diagnostic Center (paternity testing)
http://www.dnacenter.com

Gene Tree Inc. Paternity Testing
http://www.genetree.com

Community Legal Education: How Is Paternity Established?
http://mnlegalservices.org/publications/fact_sheets/b3.html

Slater & Zurz (law firm specializing in paternity cases)
http://www.slater-zurz.com/FAM-8.HTM

CHAPTER 14

The Legal Status of Children

CHAPTER OUTLINE

AGE OF MAJORITY AND EMANCIPATION

In most states and for most purposes, an adult is an individual who is eighteen years of age or older. A **minor** is anyone under eighteen. At this age, *majority* is achieved. There was a time, however, when the age of majority was twenty-one, and in some states, it still is. Furthermore, a person may be a minor for one purpose, but not for another. Hence one cannot always rely on eighteen as the critical age to determine rights and obligations. Three questions must always be asked:

minor
Someone under the age of majority, which is usually eighteen.

1. What is the individual trying to do (e.g., vote, drive, enter a contract, avoid a contract)?
2. Does the state set a specific age as the minimum for that task or objective?
3. Has the individual been emancipated? If so, does the emancipation mean that the person is no longer a minor for purposes of that particular task or objective?

Emancipation is the loss of a parent's legal control over a child. Children can be emancipated before the age of majority if certain events take place that clearly indicate they are living independently of their parents with the consent of the latter. Such events include marriage, entering military service, abandonment by the parents, an explicit agreement between the parents and the child that the latter can live independently, etc.

emancipation
Becoming legally independent of one's parent or legal guardian.

In most states, a child can petition a court for an order or declaration of emancipation when the consent of the parents cannot be obtained. The child must be a minimum age (sixteen in many states) before making such a petition. In addition, most states require the applicant to prove that he or she is financially self-sufficient. This requirement is particularly important in cases where the parents might be pressuring or forcing the child to seek emancipation. Since one of the consequences of emancipation is that the parents are no longer obligated to support the child, some parents might be tempted to precipitate emancipation in order to avoid their support obligation. A court will not be interested in allowing an impoverished minor to be emancipated from relatively well-to-do parents when there is a good likelihood that the child will end up on public assistance.

There are some age requirements that are imposed regardless of whether emancipation has occurred. For example, a seventeen-year-old emancipated person must wait until he or she is eighteen to vote or twenty-one to purchase alcoholic beverages in most states. As indicated, we must examine what the person is specifically trying to do and determine the requirements for that task. Emancipation may not be enough to meet those requirements.

ASSIGNMENT 14.1

a. Find one opinion written by a court in your state in which the court held that emancipation had occurred. State the facts of the opinion. What specific events led the court to conclude that emancipation had occurred? (See General Instructions for the Court-Opinion Assignment in Appendix A.)

b. Draft a flowchart of the procedural steps involved in petitioning a court for an order or declaration of emancipation in your state. (See General Instructions for the Flowchart Assignment in Appendix A.)

CONTRACTS

disaffirm
To repudiate.

voidable
That which can be invalidated.

Minors are allowed to **disaffirm** and, in effect, to walk away from most of the contracts they enter. This, of course, is one of the reasons merchants usually refuse to enter contracts with minors unless a parent or other financially responsible adult co-signs. Contracts that a minor can disaffirm are **voidable,** meaning that they can be invalidated by choice. A voidable contract, however, is valid and enforceable unless and until it is canceled.

> *Tom is fifteen years of age—clearly a minor. He goes to the ABC Truck Co. and purchases a truck. The sales contract calls for a small down payment (which Tom pays) with the remainder to be paid in installments—on credit. Six months later Tom changes his mind about the truck and decides to take it back to the dealer. The truck is still in good working order.*

If Tom were an adult, he would be bound by his contract. Once an adult and a merchant enter a contract, they both are bound by it. Neither party can rescind a contract simply because of a change of mind. The difference in our example is that Tom is a minor. Most states give minors the right to disaffirm such contracts so long as they do so while they are still minors or within a reasonable time (e.g., several months) after they have reached majority. In Tom's case, this would mean that he is not bound by the contract to buy the truck. He can take it back and perhaps even force the company to return whatever money he paid on it. In some states, however, the merchant can keep all or part of the purchase price paid thus far to cover depreciation resulting from the minor's use of the item.

Why are minors given this right to disaffirm? The objective of the law is to protect young people from their immaturity. Merchants are on notice that if they deal with minors, they do so at their own risk.

This does not mean that every contract of a minor is invalid. If the minor does not disaffirm, the contract is valid and can be enforced against the minor. Similarly, if a minor tries to disaffirm too late, the contract will be enforced. Suppose that Tom tried to disaffirm the truck contract when he was twenty years old in a state where the age of majority is eighteen. It won't work. He must disaffirm *before* he reaches majority or within a *reasonable* time thereafter.

What happens if the minor commits fraud to induce the merchant to enter a contract (e.g., lies about his or her age through a forged birth certificate)? Some courts take the position that such wrongdoing by the minor **estops** him or her from being able to disaffirm. Other courts, however, argue that the policy of protecting minors against their own immaturity is so strong that even their own fraud will not destroy their right to disaffirm.

estop
To be prevented from asserting a right or a defense because it would be unfair or inequitable to do so.

Special statutes have been passed in many states to limit the minor's right to disaffirm, particularly with respect to certain kinds of contracts. In several states, for example, some employment contracts, such as sports and show business contracts, are binding on minors. Similarly, contractual arrangements with banks and other lending institutions cannot be disaffirmed in many states. Finally, when a minor makes a contract with a merchant for **necessaries** such as food or clothing (see chapter 10), the contract can rarely be fully disaffirmed. If the minor disaffirms a contract for necessaries, he or she may still be liable for the reasonable value of the goods or services provided but not necessarily for the amount of the purchase price the minor initially agreed to pay.

necessaries
The basic items needed by family members to maintain a standard of living.

When a guardian has been appointed over a minor and the guardian enters a contract on behalf of that minor, the contract generally cannot be disaffirmed by the minor. Suppose, for example, that a minor is involved in litigation and an offer of settlement is made. A settlement is a contract. If a court appoints a **guardian ad litem** who negotiates a settlement contract on behalf of the minor, which the court finds is fair, the minor cannot later disaffirm the settlement.

guardian ad litem
A special guardian appointed by the court to represent the interests of another.

Most states have enacted the Uniform Gifts to Minors Act. Under this statute, gifts of certain kinds of property (e.g., securities) can be made to minors through custodians of the property. The custodian can sell the property on behalf of the minor. Contracts made by the custodian for this purpose cannot be disaffirmed by the minor.

Suppose that a minor has become emancipated before reaching the age of majority (e.g., by marrying or by being abandoned by the parents). Does this end the child's power to disaffirm? There is no absolute answer to this question. A minor so emancipated may be denied the power to disaffirm in some states, while in others, it will not affect the power.

ASSIGNMENT 14.2

Answer the following questions by examining the statutory code of your state or the opinions of the courts in your state. (See General Instructions for the State-Code Assignment and the Court-Opinion Assignment in Appendix A.)

a. What is the minimum age to enter a contract that cannot be disaffirmed in your state?
b. Are there specific kinds of contracts a minor cannot disaffirm in your state? If so, what are they?
c. Does lying about his or her age in entering a contract affect the minor's power to disaffirm the contract in your state? If so, how?
d. Is a minor required to return the goods purchased from a merchant as a condition of exercising the power to disaffirm?
e. Does your state have the Uniform Gifts to Minors Act? If so, give the citation and briefly explain how it works.

ASSIGNMENT 14.3

George is a wealthy thirteen-year-old who owns an expensive painting. He signs a contract to exchange the painting for a valuable horse owned by Helen, an equally wealthy twelve-year-old. Both George and Helen are represented by

continued

their separate attorneys during the negotiations on the contract. Once the contract is signed and the items are exchanged, what rights do George and Helen have? Assume that there are no problems with the quality and condition of the painting and the horse. (See General Instructions for the Legal-Analysis Assignment in Appendix A.)

PROPERTY AND EARNINGS

A minor can own real property and most personal property in his or her own name. The parents of a minor do not own and cannot dispose of the minor's property. Earnings are an exception. A minor does *not* have a right to keep his or her own earnings. The parent with the duty to support the child has a right to keep the child's earnings. Since a mother and father are both obligated to support their child, they are equally entitled to the child's earnings. In most states, if a child is employed, the employer must pay wages directly to the child unless one of the parents instructs the employer to pay the parent. Once a child has been emancipated (e.g., by express agreement with the parents, by marriage, by abandonment by the parents), the parents are no longer entitled to the child's earnings.

DOMICILE

domicile
For adults, domicile is the place where they have been physically present with the intent to make that place a permanent home.

The **domicile** of a minor is the domicile of the parents—even in some instances when the minor lives in a different state from the parents. With parental consent, however, a minor can acquire his or her own separate domicile. Similarly, if a minor who has not yet reached the age of majority is emancipated, most states give that individual the power to acquire his or her own domicile.

ESTATES

States have specified a minimum age for a person to have the legal capacity to dispose of his or her property by a will. Some states have different minimum ages for the disposition of personal property (e.g., clothes, cash) and of real property (e.g., land). In a few states, the emancipation of the minor by his or her marriage will enable the minor to make a valid will before reaching the minimum age.

If the parent of a minor dies, the court will appoint a guardian over the person and/or estate of the minor. This person is called a general guardian, a guardian of the estate, or a guardian ad litem. It is this guardian's duty to:

- Manage the minor's property
- Collect funds due the minor
- Sell, lease, or mortgage the minor's property (with the approval of the court)
- Invest the minor's funds
- Pay the minor's debts
- Support the minor from the minor's funds
- Represent the minor in court when needed

estate
All the assets or property of a person that is available to satisfy that person's obligations.

For such services, the minor must pay the guardian a fee, which might be a percentage of the minor's **estate.** If the guardian is not an attorney and legal services are required, the guardian will hire an attorney on behalf of the minor.

ASSIGNMENT 14.4

Answer the following questions by examining the statutory code of your state and/or the opinions of the courts of your state. (See General Instructions for the State-Code Assignment and General Instructions for the Court-Opinion Assignment in Appendix A.)

a. What is the minimum age for an individual to execute a valid will in your state?
b. When a minor dies without leaving a valid will (i.e., dies intestate), what happens to his or her property?
c. What happens to the estate of a minor when his or her parents die? Is a guardian appointed? What are the duties of this person?

EDUCATION

School attendance is compulsory for children up to a designated age, usually sixteen. The school does not have to be public if an alternate private school (or home-schooling arrangement) meets minimum educational standards.

Children at home can be subject to corporal (i.e., physical) punishment by their parents so long as the punishment does not constitute abuse. Teachers are **in loco parentis,** which means that they stand in the place of parents. As such, teachers can also impose corporal punishment on children if reasonably necessary for proper education and discipline. Subjecting children to such punishment is *not* considered cruel and unusual punishment under the Constitution.

in loco parentis
Standing in the place of (and able to exercise some of the rights of) parents.

A student cannot be expelled or given a long-term suspension from school without being accorded certain procedural rights. For example:

- The right to receive written notice of the charges against him or her
- The right to a hearing on the charges to determine whether they are valid
- The right to an impartial hearing officer (The latter cannot be directly involved in the matter. For example, the teacher who brought the charges against the student cannot be the hearing officer.)
- The right to be represented by counsel at the hearing
- The right to present evidence and to confront the accuser at the hearing

If the student is faced with a less severe punishment, such as a short-term suspension, all of these procedural rights are not provided. The student has a right to know the basis of the charges and the right to respond to them, but not necessarily to a hearing with legal representation.

NEGLECT AND ABUSE

Statutes exist to protect children who have been neglected or abused by their parents. **Neglect** is often defined as failing to give support, education, medical care, or other care necessary for the child's welfare (e.g., the refusal of a parent to give a child a needed operation, leaving a young child unattended at home for a long period of time). **Abuse** consists of physically harming a child other than by accident. For statistics on the scope of child neglect and abuse, see Exhibit 14.1. Note that these statistics are limited to cases that are reported and investigated. The numbers would be considerably higher if unreported cases were added.

neglect
The failure to provide support, medical care, education, moral example, or discipline.

abuse
Physically harming a person other than by accident.

Exhibit 14.1 Statistics on Child Abuse and Neglect

Item	1990		1995		1996		1997	
	Number	Percent	Number	Percent	Number	Percent	Number	Percent
TYPES OF SUBSTANTIATED MALTREATMENT								
Victims total	**690,658**	**(X)**	**970,285**	**(X)**	**969,018**	**(X)**	**798,358**	**(X)**
Neglect	338,770	49.1	507,015	52.3	500,032	51.6	436,630	54.7
Physical abuse	186,801	27.0	237,840	24.5	229,332	23.7	195,517	24.5
Sexual abuse	119,506	17.3	122,964	12.7	119,397	12.3	97,425	12.2
Emotional maltreatment	45,621	6.6	42,051	4.3	55,473	5.7	49,146	6.2
Medical neglect	(NA)	(NA)	28,541	2.9	25,758	2.7	18,866	2.4

[Based on reports alleging child abuse and neglect that were referred for investigation by the respective child protective services agency in each state.]

By State: 1997

State	Population under 18 years old	Reports: Number of reports[1]	Reports: Number of children subject of a report	Investigation disposition, number of children substantiated[2]
U.S.	**69,527,944**	**1,941,253**	**2,700,369**	**889,665**
AL	1,071,708	[3]25,626	37,873	19,489
AK	188,329	11,616	11,616	9,017
AZ	1,278,063	38,229	80,622	24,005
AR	662,692	21,671	36,340	5,109
CA	8,951,653	380,528	480,443	174,170
CO	1,015,529	30,647	18,893	5,532
CT	792,161	29,676	34,152	18,178
DE	177,411	6,659	9,657	4,416
DC	107,204	4,656	11,518	5,341
FL	3,471,316	124,810	186,726	79,785
GA	1,987,811	48,770	79,848	45,504
HI	302,592	[3]4,218	4,221	2,559
ID	351,352	12,144	32,522	8,283
IL	3,174,223	66,613	115,344	38,936
IN	1,497,455	31,483	47,170	15,624
IA	725,325	(NA)	(NA)	(NA)
KS	687,931	31,451	45,459	18,592
KY	961,202	[3]45,001	45,001	20,783
LA	1,190,878	27,908	46,287	14,825
ME	297,266	4,591	10,041	3,746
MD	1,268,552	30,330	48,528	14,198
MA	1,451,374	37,722	64,008	29,815
MI	2,504,757	59,829	147,628	20,654
MN	1,250,685	17,358	26,252	10,777
MS	752,998	17,869	(NA)	(NA)

State	Population under 18 years old	Reports: Number of reports[1]	Reports: Number of children subject of a report	Investigation disposition, number of children substantiated[2]
MO	1,406,425	51,151	80,185	15,845
MT	229,530	10,885	21,568	3,611
NE	444,681	8,140	16,654	4,054
NV	442,856	14,685	(NA)	(NA)
NH	296,090	6,429	9,015	1,092
NJ	1,987,124	[3]70,024	70,024	10,982
NM	499,322	18,224	23,454	8,213
NY	4,560,031	141,482	234,205	72,000
NC	1,873,403	[3]104,950	104,950	33,347
ND	165,208	4,219	6,870	(NA)
OH	2,838,641	(NA)	(NA)	(NA)
OK	878,305	33,375	51,001	13,800
OR	810,699	17,187	27,499	9,742
PA	2,864,082	[3]22,688	22,688	5,691
RI	233,654	8,486	10,182	3,481
SC	955,641	20,573	39,333	8,684
SD	197,338	[4]5,441	4,874	2,491
TN	1,324,789	[3]32,383	32,383	10,803
TX	5,577,135	109,598	162,974	39,638
UT	688,077	17,044	27,219	9,356
VT	145,519	2,223	2,309	1,041
VA	1,644,386	33,273	51,227	10,025
WA	1,454,654	35,838	38,200	21,806
WV	411,746	17,579	(NA)	(NA)
WI	1,346,376	[3]43,406	43,406	14,625
WY	131,765	2,565	(NA)	(NA)

NA Not available. [1]Except as noted, reports are on incident/family based basis or based on number of reported incidents regardless of the number of children involved in the incidents. [2]Type of investigation disposition that determines that there is sufficient evidence under state law to conclude that maltreatment occurred or that the child is at risk of maltreatment. [3]Child-based report that enumerates each child who is a subject of a report. [4]South Dakota has both child and incident based reports.

Sources: U.S. Department of Health and Human Services, National Center on Child Abuse and Neglect, National Child Abuse and Neglect Data System, Child Maltreatment 1997: Reports from the States to the National Child Abuse and Neglect System (Apr. 1999); Statistical Abstract of the United States 230 (1999).

Early in our history, children were considered the property of their parents. In Colonial Massachusetts, a law based on the Book of Deuteronomy said that if a child "disobeyed his father's voice, he could be put to death."[1] In a nineteenth-century case, a sixteen-year-old daughter told the court that her father:

> was a man of bad temper and frequently whipped her without any cause; that on one occasion he whipped her at the gate in front of his house, giving her about twenty-five blows with a switch, or small limb, about the size of one's thumb or forefinger, with such force as to raise whelks upon her back, and then going into the house, he soon returned and gave her five blows more with the same switch, choked her, and threw her violently to the ground, causing a dislocation of her thumb joint; that she had given him no offence; that she did not know for what she was beaten, nor did he give her any reason for it during the time. No permanent injury was inflicted upon her person.

The court refused to "interfere in the domestic government of families" by punishing a parent for correcting his child, however severe or unmerited the punishment, unless it produces permanent injury or is inflicted from malicious motives.[2]

Today our laws are much more sensitive to child abuse and neglect. Specific statutes exist defining the scope of child abuse and neglect. A network of public and private institutions has been created to respond to suspected abuse or neglect. The most dramatic development has been the passage of mandatory reporting laws in every state. Under these laws, designated professionals such as teachers, doctors, nurses, social workers, day care workers, and counselors are required to report suspected child abuse or neglect to the police, child protective services, or other child welfare authorities. Here is an example of a statute that imposes this requirement:

> [A]ny child care custodian, health practitioner, employee of a child protective agency, child visitation monitor, firefighter, animal control officer, or humane society officer who has knowledge of or observes a child, in his or her professional capacity or within the scope of his or her employment, whom he or she knows or reasonably suspects has been the victim of child abuse or neglect, shall report the known or suspected instance of child abuse to a child protective agency immediately or as soon as practically possible by telephone and shall prepare and send a written report thereof within 36 hours of receiving the information concerning the incident. . . . For the purposes of this article, "reasonable suspicion" means that it is objectively reasonable for a person to entertain a suspicion, based upon facts that could cause a reasonable person in a like position, drawing, when appropriate, on his or her training and experience, to suspect child abuse or neglect.[3]

The failure to make a required report can result in criminal penalties and civil liability. Compulsory reporting has dramatically increased the number of reported cases. In 1963, about 150,000 were reported; in 1997, as you can see from Exhibit 14.1, there were 2.7 million reported cases. Once a case is reported, the police or agency will conduct an investigation and, if appropriate, will refer the case to the courts.

If a court finds that a child has been neglected or abused, a number of options are usually available. Criminal penalties might be imposed. The court may have the power to terminate the parent's parental rights (see chapter 15), or the child may be placed in the custody of the state's child welfare agency for foster care placement.

---

[1] Walter Weyrauch et al., Family Law 949 (1994).

[2] *State v. Jones,* 95 N.C. 188, 1886 WL 1152, at 1 (1886).

[3] California Penal Code § 11166.

ASSIGNMENT 14.5

Answer the following questions after examining your state statutory code. (See General Instructions for the State-Code Assignment in Appendix A.)

a. What is the state-code definition of a neglected, abandoned, dependent, or abused child in your state?
b. What court has subject matter jurisdiction to determine whether a child is neglected, abandoned, dependent, or abused?
c. What can the court do once it determines that such a child exists?

ASSIGNMENT 14.6

a. Prepare a checklist of questions you could use to help determine whether a child has been neglected, abandoned, etc. (See General Instructions for the Checklist-Formulation Assignment in Appendix A.)
b. Draft a flowchart of the procedural steps that are necessary in your state to determine whether a child has been neglected, abandoned, etc. (See General Instructions for the Flowchart Assignment in Appendix A.)

DELINQUENCY

At common law, a minor below the age of seven was incapable of committing a crime—or so the law conclusively presumed. Evidence that such a child was in fact capable of committing a crime was inadmissible. A minor between the ages of seven and fourteen could be guilty of a crime if the prosecutor could show that the minor was mature enough to have formed the criminal intent necessary for the particular crime. A rebuttable presumption existed that a minor between these ages could *not* possess the requisite criminal intent. This simply meant that the court would assume the absence of this intent unless the prosecutor affirmatively proved otherwise. Minors over fourteen were treated and tried the same as adults.

juvenile delinquent
A young person under a designated age whose conduct would constitute a crime if committed by an adult.

In the early part of the twentieth century, a trend developed to remove the stigma of criminality from the misconduct of minors. Juvenile courts were created. Terms such as **juvenile delinquent,** PINS (Person In Need of Supervision), MINS (Minor In Need of Supervision), and CHIPS (Child In Need of Protection and Services) began to be widely used. A juvenile delinquent is a person under a certain age (e.g., sixteen) whose conduct would constitute a crime if performed by an adult. A PINS, MINS, or CHIPS is a person who has committed a so-called *status offense,* which in this context means noncriminal misconduct by a person under a certain age. Examples of such offenses include habitual truancy from school and incorrigibility at home. When a juvenile court decides that a child fits into one of these special categories, it has a number of options, including sending the child home with a warning, institutionalization in a juvenile facility, probation under the supervision of a youth counselor, and **foster home** placement.

foster home
A temporary home for a child when his or her own family cannot provide care and when adoption either is not possible at the present time or is under consideration.

While this system of special treatment is now widely used, it has been criticized as too lenient, particularly when the child commits a serious act such as homicide or sexual assault. Experts say that hundreds of children under age twelve commit homicides each year.[4] When a child of a specified age is accused of particularly heinous conduct of this kind, many states give a judge discretion in deciding whether the case should be handled in a juvenile court or whether the regular criminal adult courts should take over.

---

[4]C. Anderson, *Grown-Up Crime, Boy Defendant,* 75 American Bar Association Journal 27, 27 (Nov. 1989).

ASSIGNMENT 14.7

Most of the following questions can be answered by examining your state statutory code. (See General Instructions for the State-Code Assignment in Appendix A.)

a. What is a juvenile delinquent in your state?
b. What court has subject matter jurisdiction to determine juvenile delinquency?
c. Is any classification other than juvenile delinquent used in your state to describe a minor who has misbehaved (e.g., the classification of PINS)? If so, define the classification.
d. Once a minor has been found to be a juvenile delinquent, what disposition options are available to the court in your state?
e. Under what circumstances, if any, can a child be prosecuted in an adult criminal court?
f. Draft a flowchart of the procedural steps required in your state to process a juvenile delinquency case. (See General Instructions for the Flowchart Assignment in Appendix A.)

SUMMARY

The age of majority is eighteen, but a state may impose different age requirements for performing different activities. Emancipation before the age of majority can make a minor eligible for some of these activities.

A number of special laws apply to minors. For example, they have the right to disaffirm contracts they have entered. They can own real and personal property in their own name, but unless they have been emancipated, their parents have a right to keep their earnings. Also, minors cannot acquire their own domicile without parental consent, and in most states, an unemancipated minor is ineligible to make a will. If the parents of a minor die, the court will appoint a guardian to oversee his or her affairs.

School is compulsory until a designated age. Teachers stand in the place of parents and, as such, can impose reasonable corporal punishment. However, students are entitled to certain procedural rights (e.g., a hearing) if the school wants to expel or suspend them long term.

When a parent neglects or abuses a child, the state has a number of options (e.g., criminal prosecution, foster home placement, and termination of parental rights). In all states, suspected child abuse or neglect must be reported when observed by designated individuals. A child below the age of seven cannot commit a crime, but one between seven and fourteen can be prosecuted if the state can overcome the presumption that such a child is not old enough to form the necessary criminal intent. A modern tendency is to treat misbehaving children as juvenile delinquents or as persons in need of supervision rather than as defendants in criminal courts.

KEY CHAPTER TERMINOLOGY

minor
emancipation
disaffirm
voidable
estop
necessaries
guardian ad litem
domicile
estate
in loco parentis
neglect
abuse
juvenile delinquent
foster home

ETHICS IN PRACTICE

You are a paralegal working at the law office of Daniel Britton, Esq. At a Halloween party, you begin talking to a sixteen-year-old guest. The guest tells you he is having troubles at home. You tell him about applying for emancipation and explain how it is accomplished. You also give him your business card. Any ethical problems?

ON THE NET: MORE ON CHILDREN AND THE LAW

Child Abuse Prevention Network
http://child.cornell.edu

National Clearinghouse on Child Abuse and Neglect
http://www.calib.com/nccanch

Teenparents: Emancipation
http://www.teenparents.org/emancipation.html

Child Law Watch
http://www.child-law-watch.net

CHAPTER 15

ADOPTION

CHAPTER OUTLINE

INTRODUCTION

A number of important terms should be defined and distinguished before discussing the subject of adoption.

- **Custody** The control and care of an individual.
- **Guardianship** The legal right to the custody of an individual.
- **Ward** An individual who is under guardianship.
- **Termination of Parental Rights (TPR)** A judicial declaration that ends the legal relationship between parent and child. The parent no longer has any right to participate in decisions affecting the welfare of the child and no longer has any duties toward the child.
- **Adoption** The legal process by which an adoptive parent assumes the rights and duties of a natural (i.e., biological) parent.
- **Paternity** The biological fatherhood of a child.
- **Foster Care** A child welfare service that provides shelter and substitute family care when a child's own family cannot care for it. Foster care is designed to last for a temporary period during which adoption is neither desirable nor possible, or during the period when adoption is under consideration.
- **Stepparent** A person who marries the natural mother or father of a child, but is not one of the child's natural parents. For example, assume that Ted and Mary marry each other. It is the second marriage for both. Ted has a son, Bill, from his first marriage. Mary has a daughter, Alice, from her first marriage. Ted is the natural father of Bill and the

stepfather of Alice. Mary is the natural mother of Alice and the stepmother of Bill. If Mary adopts Bill, and Ted adopts Alice, they become *adoptive parents;* they will no longer be stepparents.

ASSIGNMENT 15.1

a. Find statutes or court opinions that define the words *custody* and *guardianship* in your state. For each word, try to find at least one statute or opinion that defines the word. If either or both words have more than one meaning in your state, give each meaning. (See General Instructions for the State-Code Assignment and General Instructions for the Court-Opinion Assignment in Appendix A.)

b. Prepare a flowchart of guardianship procedures in your state involving a minor child. If there is more than one kind of such guardianship in your state, select any one. (See General Instructions for the Flowchart Assignment in Appendix A.)

c. Draft a custody agreement under which your best friend agrees to care for your child while you are in the hospital for six months. (See General Instructions for the Agreement-Drafting Assignment in Appendix A.)

Adoption establishes a permanent, legal parent-child relationship between the child and a person who is not the natural parent of the child. (Between 2 and 4 percent of children in the country today live with adoptive parents. See Exhibit 15.1.) In many states, an adoption leads to the reissuance of the child's birth certificate, listing the adoptive parent as the "mother" or "father" of the child. The relationship is permanent in that only the court can end the relationship by terminating the parental rights of the adoptive parent. Even the divorce or death of the adoptive parent does not end the relationship. Assume, for example, that Tom marries Linda and then adopts her son, Dave, by a previous marriage. If Tom subsequently divorces Linda, he does not cease to be Dave's parent. His obligation to support Dave, for example, continues after the divorce. Similarly, when Tom dies, Dave can inherit from Tom as if he were a natural child of Tom. In this sense, the parent-child relationship continues even after the death of the adoptive parent.

Exhibit 15.1 Adoption Statistics

Number of adopted children in the country: approximately 1 million
Number of children adopted in 1992 (the last year for which complete statistics are available): 127,441

- 42% were stepparent or relative adoptions
- 15.5% were adoptions of children in foster care
- 5% were adoptions of foreign children
- 8% were transracial adoptions
- 37.5% were adoptions handled by private agencies or independent practitioners such as attorneys

Ages of the children adopted:

- under 1 year: 2%
- 1–5 years: 46%
- 6–10 years: 37%
- 11–15 years: 14%
- 16–18 years: 2%

Categories of families adopting:

- married couples: 66%
- unmarried couples: 2%
- single females: 30%
- single males: 2%

Couples seeking to adopt:

- for every actual adoption, there are approximately 5 to 6 couples seeking to adopt
- over 1 million couples compete for 30,000 white infants each year (adoption agencies sometimes refer to such children born in this country as DWIs—domestic white infants)

Waiting time to adopt:
- healthy infant: 1 to 7 years
- international: 6 to 18 months

Adoption expenses (general):
- domestic public agency adoption: $0 to $4,000
- domestic private agency adoption: $4,000 to $30,000
- domestic independent adoption: $8,000 to $30,000+
- international adoption (private agency or independent): $7,000 to $25,000+

Adoption expenses (specifics):
- attorney fees: $1,200 to $2,500
- maternity home-care during third trimester and postdelivery: $6,000
- prenatal and hospital care (normal delivery): $6,000
- prenatal and hospital care (Caesarean Section): $9,000
- prenatal and hospital care (major complications): $100,000
- preadoption foster care if infant does not go directly from hospital to adoptive parents: $650
- home study and post-placement evaluation visits: $2,500
- other costs (travel, phone, insurance): $2,000 to $6,000
- additional costs of international adoption: $7,000 to $10,000

Number of children adopted from other countries:
- 1990: 7,093
- 1995: 9,679
- 1999: 16,396 (the largest numbers came from Russia, 4,348; China, 4,101; Korea, 2,008; and Guatemala, 1,002)

Percentage of unmarried women who place their babies for adoption:
- 1998: under 2%
- before 1973 (the year abortion was legalized): 9%

Women who place their babies for adoption:
- 19% of white women (from 1965 to 1972)
- 1.7% of white women (from 1989 to 1995)
- under 1% of black women (a number that has remained constant)
- under 2% of Latina women (a number that has remained constant)

Foster care children in 1999:
- total number: 547,000
- number needing adoptive families: 117,000
- number of children in foster care adopted by a single adoptive parent: 34%
- length of wait for adoptive families: between 3.5 and 5.5 years
- average (mean) age of children in foster care: 9 years
- average (mean) time in foster care: 33 months

Federal tax credit for expenses to adopt an eligible child:
- up to $5,000
- for a child with special needs: $6,000

Percentage of public and private agency adoptions in 1991 in which the birth parent(s) met with the adoptive couple: 69%

Number of adopted adults who search for their biological parents: between 2% to 4%

Sources: National Adoption Information Clearinghouse; U.S. Department of Health and Human Services; North American Council on Adoptable Children; Voluntary Cooperative Information System; U.S. Immigration and Naturalization Service; U.S. Department of State; National Center for Health Statistics; Adoptive Families of America; National Endowment for Financial Education; National Council for Adoption; Evan B. Donaldson Adoption Institute, http://www.adoptioninstitute.org/research/ressta.html.

KINDS OF ADOPTION

The three main kinds of adoption are agency adoption, independent adoption, and black market adoption. A fourth, equitable adoption, will be considered later in the chapter.

Agency Adoption

In an **agency adoption** (also called an *authorized agency adoption* or a *public adoption*), the child is placed for adoption by the public agency that is responsible for adoptions or by a private adoption agency that is either licensed by the state or in compliance with state standards. There are two main circumstances in which such agencies become involved. First, the parent (usually the mother) voluntarily transfers the child to the agency by executing a formal

agency adoption
An adoption in which a child is placed for adoption by a public agency responsible for adoptions or by an approved private adoption agency.

surrender document that relinquishes all parental rights in the child. Second, a court terminates the parental rights of a parent because of abandonment, abuse, or neglect, and asks the agency to place the child for adoption.

Independent/Private Adoption

independent adoption
An adoption in which a child is placed for adoption by its natural parent, often with the help of facilitators.

In an **independent adoption** (also called a *private adoption*), a natural parent places the child for adoption with the adoptive parents. This "direct placement" often occurs with the help of intermediaries acting as consultants or "facilitators" who help bring the biological parents and the adoptive parents together. The intermediary can be an attorney, doctor, or member of the clergy. Also selling their services are photographers and Web designers who will help childless couples design their own Web site as part of their search for pregnant mothers thinking about adoption. (In your Yellow Pages, check the listings under "Adoption Services.") Several insurance companies sell adoption cancellation insurance to recover expenses incurred if a birth mother changes her mind. Other available resources include numerous support groups, adoptive parent groups, and adoption exchanges that operate out of living rooms and office buildings. (An adoption exchange is an organization that seeks adoptive parents for foster care or special care children.) In states where ads are legal, you will find ads directed at young, unmarried pregnant women ("Loving couple wishes to adopt your child."). The ads are placed in newspapers, in bus shelters, on billboards, in newsletters, on fast-food paper bags, and on the World Wide Web.

As with agency adoptions, a court must give its approval to the independent adoption. Furthermore, the state may require an agency to investigate the prospective adoption and file a report (a home study), which is considered by the court. In most states, the court must approve the fees that have been paid or claimed in the case. It should be noted that in an independent adoption, the level of involvement by the agency is far less extensive and intrusive than in a traditional agency adoption, where the agency supervises the entire process.

Most, but not all, independent adoptions are initiated by a stepparent or by someone who is otherwise already related to the child. (See Exhibit 15.1.) Yet many independent adoptions occur when no such relationship exists.

Here is an example of how an independent adoption might occur:

> *When Ralph and Nancy Smith discovered that they were infertile, they decided to adopt. Several visits to adoption agencies, however, were quite discouraging. One agency had a long waiting list of couples seeking to adopt healthy, white infants; it was not taking any new applications. Another accepted their application, but warned that the process might take up to five years, with no guarantee that a child would eventually become available. Nationally, hundreds of thousands of women are waiting to adopt a relatively small number of healthy, white infants. The small number of available children is due to the widespread use of abortion and the declining social stigma attached to the single-parent motherhood.*
>
> *Acting on the advice of a friend, the Smiths then tried the alternative of an independent adoption. They placed personal ads in newspapers and magazines seeking to contact an unwed pregnant woman willing to relinquish her child for adoption. They created their own Web page containing photographs and video clips of their home life in order to give a birth mother an idea of what life would be like for her child if she chose the Smiths as adoptive parents. They also sent their résumé and letters of inquiry to doctors, members of the clergy, and attorneys specializing in independent adoptions. In some cities, the Yellow Pages had listings for attorneys with this specialty. Their efforts were finally successful when an attorney led them to Diane Kline, a seventeen-year-old pregnant girl. The Smiths prepared a scrapbook on their life, which Diane reviewed along*

> *with their Web page. She then interviewed the Smiths and decided to allow them to adopt her child. The Smiths paid the attorney's fees, Diane's medical bills, the cost of her psychological counseling, travel expenses, and living expenses related to the delivery of the baby. Diane signed a consent form relinquishing her rights in the baby and agreeing to the adoption by the Smiths, who formally applied to the court for the adoption. A social worker at a local agency investigated the case and made a home-study report to the court, which then issued an order authorizing the adoption.*

In this example, the natural mother had personal contact with the adoptive parents. This occurs in 69 percent of adoptions, as indicated in Exhibit 15.1. When anonymity is desired, it can easily be arranged. Anonymity most often occurs in agency adoptions.

Note that the money paid by the Smiths covered medical, legal, and related expenses. Other payments would be illegal. Assume, for example, that Diane had hesitated about going through with the adoption and the Smiths had offered her $10,000 above expenses. This could constitute illegal *baby buying,* turning an independent adoption into a **black market adoption.** Such a payment to a birth parent, to an attorney, or to anyone is illegal. A person may pay those expenses that are naturally and reasonably connected with the adoption, so long as no cash or other consideration is given to induce someone to participate in the adoption. (The separate but related problems of surrogate motherhood will be considered in the next chapter.)

black market adoption
An adoption that involves a payment beyond reasonable expenses in order to facilitate the adoption.

In some states, independent adoptions are more common than agency adoptions. Critics argue that illegal payments are frequent and that the lack of safeguards in independent adoptions can lead to disastrous consequences. A dramatic example occurred in 1988 when a New York City attorney was convicted in the battery death of a six-year-old girl who had been placed in his care so that he might arrange an independent adoption. The attorney had kept the child—and then abused her—when prospective adoptive parents failed to pay his fee for the adoption. Proponents of independent adoptions view this case as an aberration and maintain that the vast majority of independent adoptions are legal and are adequately supervised.

Black Market Adoption

Frustration with agency adoptions leads to the alternative of independent adoptions. And frustration with both kinds of legal adoptions leads to *black market adoptions,* which involve a payment beyond reasonable expenses.

An adoption becomes baby buying when the payment is for finding or placing a child rather than for reasonable expenses. (See Exhibit 15.6 at the end of this chapter.) The most blatant example is the *baby broker,* who financially entices women to give up their children and then charges adoptive parents a large "fee" for arranging the adoption. In 1990, a typical black market adoption cost up to $50,000.

It is difficult to know how many independent adoptions turn into black market adoptions, since the participants have an interest in keeping quiet about the illegal payment. While accepting a fee for "finding a baby" or "placing a child" for adoption is illegal, it is not always easy to distinguish such fees from the legitimate payment of reasonable fees connected with the cost of adoption services. To discourage illegal payments, most states require the adoptive parent to file with the court a list of all expenditures pertaining to the adoption. This, however, has not stopped black market adoptions, and critics argue that the only way to do so is to eliminate independent adoptions so that all adoptions will be more adequately supervised by traditional public and private agencies.

Other abuses can also occur. In Los Angeles, the police recently arrested a woman for promising her unborn child to seven couples seeking to adopt. She was charged with adoption fraud. Another woman was charged with child abandonment when she tried to place her son for adoption with someone she met on eBay, the Internet auction site. In a case that received international publicity, a facilitator used her Internet service to collect thousands of dollars from two separate adoptive couples, one in America and one in England. Neither couple knew the other existed.[1] In the midst of the chaos, the natural mother changed her mind about wanting to go through with the adoption.

ASSIGNMENT 15.2

Answer the following questions based on your state code. (See General Instructions for the State-Code Assignment in Appendix A.)

a. Are independent or private adoptions allowed in your state? If so, how do they differ from agency adoptions? In what ways does the state try to prevent "baby buying"?
b. Is it a crime to "buy" a baby? If so, how is this crime committed?

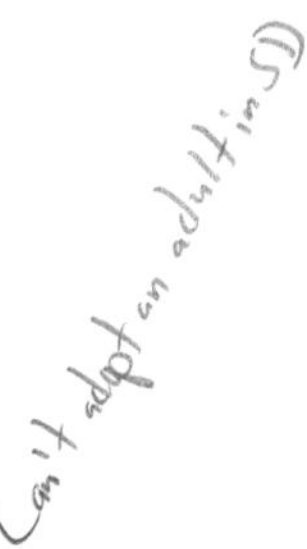

WHO MAY BE ADOPTED?

In the vast majority of cases, the person adopted (called the *adoptee*) is a child, usually an infant. Yet in most states it is possible for one adult to adopt another adult. The most common reason for this practice is that the adoptive parent wants to give the adopted adult rights of inheritance from the adoptive parent. In effect, the latter is naming an heir. In ancient Greece and Rome, perpetuating the family line by designating an heir was the main purpose of adoption.

Suppose, however, that a homosexual wants to adopt his or her homosexual partner? Most adoption statutes appear to be broad enough to allow it, but not many courts have had occasion to consider the issue. Those that have are split. Delaware allowed it as a way to "formalize the close emotional relationship" of the two men involved.[2] New York took the opposite position. The "sexual intimacy" between such individuals "is utterly repugnant to the relationship between child and parent in our society, and . . . a patently incongruous application of our adoptive laws."[3]

ASSIGNMENT 15.3

Can one adult adopt another adult in your state? If so, can one homosexual adult adopt another? (Check your state code and cases, interpreting the relevant provisions. See General Instructions for the State-Code Assignment and General Instructions for the Court-Opinion Assignment in Appendix A.)

WHO MAY ADOPT?

The petitioners (i.e., the persons seeking to become the adoptive parents) will be granted the adoption if it is in "the best interests of the child." Such a broad standard gives the judge a good deal of discretion. In addition to relying

---

[1]Tamar Lewin, *At Core of Adoption Dispute Is Crazy Quilt of State Laws,* N.Y. Times, Jan. 19, 2001, at A12.
[2]*In re Adoption of Swanson,* 623 A.2d 1095, 1096 (Del. 1993).
[3]*In the Matter of Robert Paul P.,* 63 N.Y.2d 233, 236, 471 N.E.2d 424, 425, 481 N.Y.S.2d 652, 653 (1984).

on the adoption agency's investigation report, the judge will consider a number of factors, no one of which is usually controlling.

1. *Age of petitioner.* Most states require the petitioner to be an adult. The preference is for someone who is not unusually older than the child. A court would be reluctant, for example, to allow a seventy-five-year-old to adopt an infant, unless special circumstances warranted it.
2. *Marital status of petitioner.* While many states allow single persons to adopt, the preference is for someone who is married. His or her spouse is usually required to join in the petition.
3. *Health of petitioner.* Adoptive parents are not expected to be physically and emotionally perfect. If a particular disability will not seriously interfere with the raising of the child, it will not by itself bar the adoption.
4. *Race.* Most judges and adoption agencies prefer that the race of the adoptive parents be the same as that of the child. At one time, some states imposed time periods during which the search for adoptive parents had to be limited to adoptive parents of the same race. The problem, however, was that there were not enough same-race adoptive parents available. The net effect was to lengthen the time children had to wait to be adopted. In an attempt to remedy the problem, Congress passed a statute on "interethnic adoption." It prohibits the delay or denial of adoptions on account of race:

    > A person or government that is involved in adoption or foster care placements may not (A) deny to any individual the opportunity to become an adoptive or a foster parent, on the basis of the race, color, or national origin of the individual, or of the child, involved; or (B) delay or deny the placement of a child for adoption or into foster care, on the basis of the race, color, or national origin of the adoptive or foster parent, or the child, involved.[4]

    American Indians, however, are treated differently. Congress has determined that

    > an alarmingly high percentage of Indian families are broken up by the removal, often unwarranted, of their children from them by nontribal public and private agencies and that an alarmingly high percentage of such children are placed in non-Indian foster and adoptive homes and institutions."[5]

    Consequently, the adoption of Indian children by non-Indians today is relatively rare.
5. *Religion.* When possible or practicable, the religion of the adoptive parents should be the same as the religion of the natural parents. Interfaith adoptions, though allowed, are generally not encouraged.
6. *Wishes of the child.* The court will consider the opinion of the prospective adoptee if he or she is old enough to communicate a preference.
7. *Economic status.* The adoptive parents must have the financial means to care for the child. The court will examine their current financial status and prospects for the future in light of the child's support needs.
8. *Home environment and morality.* The goal is for the child to be brought up in a wholesome, loving home where values are important and where the child will be nurtured to his or her potential. Illegal or conspicuously unorthodox lifestyles are frowned upon.

Earlier we saw that states differ on whether to allow the adoption of a homosexual adult by another homosexual. There is also disagreement about adoption of minors by homosexuals.

---

[4] 42 U.S.C.A. § 1996b.
[5] 25 U.S.C.A. § 1901.

A gay or lesbian person who petitions for adoption could fall into one of several categories. He or she might:

- Live alone and hence seek to become the sole parent
- Live with a same-sex partner who is a biological parent of the child (this would be a **second-parent adoption**)
- Live with a same-sex partner who is not a biological parent of the child, so that both would petition the court for adoption (they would be seeking to co-adopt as joint petitioners)

second-parent adoption
The adoption of a child by a partner (or cohabitant) of a natural parent who does not give up his or her own parental rights.

When a court receives a petition from a homosexual to adopt a minor, it could reach one of four conclusions about the adoption statutes in the state:

- They explicitly ban such adoptions;
- They do not explicitly ban such adoptions, but the court interprets the statutes to include such a ban;
- They explicitly authorize such adoptions; or
- They do not explicitly authorize such adoptions, but the court interprets the statutes to allow them.

In most states, adoption statutes do not explicitly ban adoptions by gays and lesbians. Florida is an exception:

> No person eligible to adopt under this statute may adopt if that person is a homosexual.[6]

Similarly, in Denmark, a country otherwise known for its liberal laws on same-sex relationships, adoption of minors by homosexuals is not allowed. New Hampshire once had a similar ban but recently repealed it. The state legislatures of many other states have considered writing such bans into their statutes, but to date, none has been enacted into law.

In Vermont (the state that gave us the civil union we examined in chapter 5), the law is quite different:

> (a) [A]ny person may adopt or be adopted by another person for the purpose of creating the relationship of parent and child between them.
>
> (b) If a family unit consists of a parent and the parent's partner, and adoption is in the best interest of the child, the partner of a parent may adopt a child of the parent.[7]

This statute has been interpreted as a law "removing all prior legal barriers to the adoption of children by same-sex couples."[8]

New York State has an administrative regulation that has the same effect:

> Applicants shall not be rejected solely on the basis of homosexuality. A decision to accept or reject when homosexuality is at issue shall be made on the basis of individual factors as explored and found in the adoption study process as it relates to the best interests of adoptive children.[9]

States reach different conclusions when their adoption statutes or regulations neither explicitly ban nor explicitly authorize such adoptions. Some state courts have concluded that the language of their statute is broad enough to include homosexual adoptive parents. Courts in other states have ruled that the definition of adoptive parent intended by the legislature could not have included homosexuals.

If a court concludes that adoption by a homosexual petitioner can be valid, it will then proceed to the question of whether the adoption petition in the par-

[6]Florida Statutes Annotated § 63.042(3).
[7]Vermont Statutes Annotated § 1–102.
[8]*Baker v. State,* 744 A.2d 864, 884–85 (1999).
[9]New York Compilation of Codes, Rules & Regulations title 18, § 421.16.

ticular case before it is in the best interests of the child. In applying the best-interests standard, courts examine some of the same factors we looked at in chapter 9 on child custody. The court will want to know if the petitioner's sexual activity is likely to have any adverse effect on the child. In most cases, the answer is no if such activity takes place discreetly and in private. Research suggests that children develop their sexual orientation independent of that of their parents.[10] A number of courts are impressed by this research.

In general, a court will tend to favor the adoption of a child who has already begun to bond with a prospective adoptive parent. A lesbian, for example, may be petitioning to adopt a child she has helped raise since its birth by her lesbian partner through artificial insemination. By granting the adoption, the court is recognizing that the child is already in a co-parenting family. Weighing in favor of the adoption is the fact that the biological parent wants it to occur. Every state allows a stepparent to adopt the children of his or her spouse. Some courts have said that adoption by a gay or lesbian who has been acting as a co-parent is the "functional equivalent" of a stepparent adoption.

Finally, a court will want to assess the options available. Suppose, for example, a child has medical problems or other special needs. The future may consist of institutionalization or long-term foster care. In such a case, the court may be favorably disposed to the alternative of adoption by a caring, competent adult who happens to be homosexual—even if this adult has no significant other.

This is not to say that the courts are anxious to grant adoption petitions filed by homosexuals. In many courts, quite the contrary is true. Yet there are courts that take these petitions seriously. Slowly, an increasing number of judges are examining each case on its merits rather than rejecting them out of hand because of the sexual orientation of the petitioner.

ASSIGNMENT 15.4

To answer questions a–f, check your state code and court opinions. (See General Instructions for the State-Code Assignment and the Court-Opinion Assignment in Appendix A.)

a. In your state, who is eligible to adopt children? Who is not eligible?
b. What standards exist to guide a judge's decision in your state on whether to approve a particular adoption?
c. Mary Jones is a Baptist. She wants to place her one-year-old child for adoption. Mr. and Mrs. Johnson want to adopt the child and file the appropriate petition to do so in your state. The Johnsons are Jewish. Mary Jones consents to the adoption. What effect, if any, will the religious differences between Mary Jones and the Johnsons have on the adoption? Assume that Mary has no objection to the child's being raised in the Jewish faith.
d. Same facts as in part (c) above except that the Johnsons are professed atheists. Mary Jones does not care.
e. Can a homosexual adopt a minor in your state?
f. Under what circumstances, if any, can a single person—an adult who lives alone—adopt a minor in your state?
g. Both Paul and Helen Smith are deaf and mute. They wish to adopt the infant daughter of Helen's best friend, a widow who just died. Prepare an investigation strategy to collect evidence relevant to whether the adoption should be permitted. (See General Instructions for the Investigation-Strategy Assignment in Appendix A.)

---

[10]Steve Susoeff, *Assessing Children's Best Interests When a Parent Is Gay or Lesbian: Toward a Rational Custody Standard,* 32 UCLA Law Review 852, 882 (1985).

ASSIGNMENT 15.5

a. Contact a *private* agency in your state involved in adoption placement. Ask the agency what criteria it uses in recommending an adoption. Also, ask the agency to send you any available literature that lists such standards (e.g., pamphlets, applications). Compare these standards with your answers to the questions in the preceding assignment (15.4). Does the agency's practice conform with the standards of the law of your state?

b. Same question as in part (a) above except that this time a *public* agency should be contacted.

(*Note:* Let your teacher know in advance which private and public agencies you propose to contact. The teacher may want to coordinate the contacts so that no single agency receives more than its share of contacts from the class.)

ADOPTION PROCEDURE

It is not easy to adopt a child. Elaborate procedures have been created to protect the interests of the child, the natural parents, and the adoptive parents. When the most-sought-after babies (i.e., healthy, white infants) are in short supply, the temptation to "buy" a baby on the black market is heightened. One way to try to control this is by increasing procedural safeguards in the process. Fewer safeguards, however, are usually needed in stepparent adoptions of children who will continue to live with a natural parent. A stepparent is someone who has married one of the natural parents of the child. In stepparent adoptions, courts may have discretion to use expedited adoption procedures such as waiving the home study. Some states, however, will not streamline the process in this way unless the natural parent has been married to the stepparent for at least a year.

Jurisdiction and Venue

subject matter jurisdiction
The power of the court to hear a particular category or kind of case.

choice of venue
The selection of the court to try the case when more than one court has subject matter jurisdiction to hear that kind of case.

Subject matter jurisdiction refers to the power of the court to hear a particular kind of case. Not every court in a state has subject matter jurisdiction to issue adoption decrees. The state constitution or state statutes will designate one or perhaps two courts that have authority to hear adoption cases (e.g., the state family court, probate court, surrogate court, or juvenile court). There are also specifications for selecting the county or district in which the adoption proceeding must be brought. The selection is referred to as the **choice of venue.** It will often depend on the residence (usually meaning domicile) of one or more of the participants, usually the natural parents, the adoptive parents, or the child.

ASSIGNMENT 15.6

a. What court or courts in your state have the power to hear adoption cases?

b. In what county or section of your state must the adoption proceeding be initiated? Does your answer depend upon the residence or domicile of any of the participants? If so, what is the definition of residence or domicile?

(To answer the above questions, you may have to check your state constitution, state statutory code, and perhaps opinions of your state courts. See General Instructions for the State-Code Assignment in Appendix A.)

Petition

petition
A formal request that the court take some action.

States differ on the form and content of the adoption **petition** filed by the adoptive parents to begin the adoption proceeding. The petition will contain such data as the names of the petitioners; their ages; whether they are married and, if so, whether they are living together; the name, age, and religion of the child, etc. While the natural parents play a large role in the adoption proceeding, not all states require that they be mentioned in the petition itself. (For an example of the format of a petition, see Exhibit 15.2.)

Exhibit 15.2 Adoption Petition

FAMILY COURT OF THE STATE OF ____________________
COUNTY OF ____________________

In the Matter of the
Adoption by

________________ of ________________

a minor having the first
name of

whose last name is contained
in the Schedule annexed to
the Petition herein.

Index No.

PETITION
(Agency)

TO THE FAMILY COURT:

1. (a) The name and place of residence of the petitioning adoptive mother is:
Name:
Address:
She is (of full age) (a minor), born on
She is (unmarried) (married to
and they are living together as husband and wife).
Her religious faith is
Her occupation is
and her approximate annual income is $
(b) The name and place of residence of the petitioning adoptive father is:
Name:
Address:
He is (of full age) (a minor), born on
He is (unmarried) (married to
and they are living together as husband and wife).
His religious faith is
His occupation is
and his approximate annual income is $

2. As nearly as can be ascertained, the full name, date and place of birth of the (male) (female) adoptive child are set forth in the Schedule annexed to this Petition and verified by a duly constituted official of an authorized agency.

3. (a) As nearly as can be ascertained, the religious faith of the adoptive child is
(b) As nearly as can be ascertained, the religious faith of the natural parents of the adoptive child is

4. The manner in which the adoptive parents obtained the adoptive child is as follows:

5. The adoptive child has resided continuously with the adoptive parents since

6. The name by which the adoptive child is to be known is

7. The consent of the above-mentioned authorized agency has been duly executed and is filed herewith. The consent of the natural parents of the adoptive child is not required because

8. No previous application has been made to any court or judge for the relief sought herein.

9. The adoptive child has not been previously adopted.

10. To the best of petitioners' information and belief, there are no persons other than those hereinbefore mentioned interested in this proceeding.

11. WHEREFORE, your petitioners pray for an order approving the adoption of the aforesaid adoptive child by the above named adoptive parents and directing that the said adoptive child shall be regarded and treated in all respects as the child of the said adoptive parents and directing that the name of the said adoptive child be changed as specified in paragraph 6 above and that henceforth (s)he shall be known by that name.

Source: 1 Guide to American Law 103 (1983).

ASSIGNMENT 15.7

a. What must a petition for adoption contain in your state? Must it name the natural parents? (See General Instructions for the State-Code Assignment in Appendix A.)
b. Draft an adoption petition. Assume that you are seeking to adopt the one-year-old baby of a woman who has recently been hospitalized. This friend has no other relatives. The natural father of the child is no longer alive. You can make up facts you need to draft the petition. (Although an adoption petition is not a complaint, you may find some of the suggestions on drafting complaints to be useful. See Exhibit 7.4.)

Notice

Due process of law requires that both natural parents be given *notice* of the petition to adopt the child by the prospective adoptive parents. (Later, when we study the Baby Richard and Baby Jessica cases, we will see the importance of this requirement.) The preferred method of providing notice is to personally serve the natural parents with process within the state where the adoption petition is brought. If this is not possible, the court may allow substituted service (e.g., by registered mail or publication in a newspaper).

There was a time when the father of an illegitimate child was not entitled to notice of the adoption proceeding; only the mother of such a child was given notice. The situation has changed, however, due to recent decisions of the United States Supreme Court. While the full scope of the rights of the father of an illegitimate child has not yet been fully defined by the courts, it is clear that he can no longer be ignored in the adoption process. As we shall see, however, there is a difference between a parent's right to notice of the adoption proceeding and a parent's right to prevent the adoption by refusing to consent to it.

ASSIGNMENT 15.8

a. In your state, who must receive notice of an adoption proceeding?
b. When can substituted service of process (e.g., by mail, publication) be used in your state for persons who must receive notice of adoption proceedings?

(See General Instructions for the State-Code Assignment and General Instructions for the Court-Opinion Assignment in Appendix A.)

Interstate Compact on the Placement of Children

The **Interstate Compact on the Placement of Children** (ICPC) governs adoptions of a child born or living in one state (called the *sending state*) who will be adopted by someone in another state (called the *receiving state*). The ICPC does not cover all interstate adoptions. It applies mainly to so-called stranger adoptions—those undertaken by individuals other than relatives, guardians, or stepparents.

To coordinate the adoption, an ICPC office is established in each state. When a court approves the adoption, the ICPC office in the sending state gives written notice to the ICPC office in the receiving state of the proposed adoption. The notice provides identifying information about the child, the child's parents or guardians, and the person, agency, or institution with whom the child is to be placed. Also included are a statement of reasons for the proposed placement and "evidence of the authority pursuant to which the placement is proposed to be made." The receiving state ICPC office reviews this information. If approved, it submits to the sending state ICPC office a written notice that "the proposed placement does not appear to be contrary to the best interests of the child." The parties are then given permission to bring the child across state lines so that the placement can occur. A violation of these ICPC requirements can result in a voiding of the adoption.

ASSIGNMENT 15.9

A couple in a neighboring state seeks to adopt a child in your state. The couple is not related to the child and has never seen the child. Assuming that a court in your state is prepared to approve the adoption, draft a flowchart of the procedural steps involved under the Interstate Compact on the Placement of Children. (See General Instructions for the Flowchart Assignment in Appendix A.)

Consent

Adoption occurs in essentially two ways: with or without the consent of the natural parents. When consent is necessary, the state's statute will usually specify the manner in which the consent must be given (e.g., whether it must be witnessed, whether it must be in writing, whether the formalities for consent differ for agency adoptions as opposed to independent adoptions, whether the consent form must mention the names of the parties seeking to adopt the child, etc.). Women who change their mind about giving up their baby often claim that they were coerced into consenting. In one case, the woman alleged that she was pressured to choose the adoptive parents while she was in labor and to sign the adoption papers while she was under the influence of the sedative Demerol. To combat such problems, some states say that the consent is not valid if it is obtained prior to the birth of the child. Many states say that it cannot be obtained until at least seventy-two hours after birth. Once the consent is validly given, the mother has a period of time (e.g., ten days) during which she has the right to change her mind and revoke the consent. See Exhibit 15.3 for an example of a consent form.

Exhibit 15.3 Consent Form

CONSENT TO ADOPTION

We, the undersigned, being the father and mother, respectively, of ______________, who was born on ______, 20___, in ______________ County, California, and being the persons entitled to the sole custody of said child do hereby give our full and free consent to the adoption of said child by ______________ and ______________, his wife, and do hereby relinquish to said persons forever all of our rights to the care, custody, control, services, and earnings of said child.

Each of us hereby promises that, as soon as adoption proceedings are commenced in the state of ______________, we will properly execute any further instruments or papers necessary to effectuate the adoption of said child by said persons.

Each of us hereby authorizes said persons, or either of them, to procure and provide any and all medical, hospital, dental, and other care needed for said child, it being understood by us that said persons have agreed to, and will pay, such expenses without seeking reimbursement from us prior to the adoption of said child.

Each of us fully understands that, upon the signing of this instrument, we have irrevocably relinquished and waived all right to withdraw the consent and authority herein given.

DATED: ________, 20___.

____
[Name and Signature of Party]

____
[Name and Signature of Party]

Witnesses:

____

____

Notary Public: (SEAL)

____

My commission expires ________

Source: D. Adams, California Code Forms (1960).

unfit
Demonstrating abuse or neglect that is substantially detrimental to a child.

Both natural parents must consent to the adoption unless the parental rights of one or both of them have been formally terminated because of unfitness. An **unfit** parent loses the power to veto the adoption. As indicated earlier, the father of an illegitimate child has a right to present his views on the propriety of the proposed adoption. He must be given notice of the adoption proceeding unless he has abandoned the child. If he has lived with his illegitimate child, supported him or her, or otherwise maintained close contacts with the child, a court will grant him the same rights as the mother. He *will* be allowed to veto the proposed adoption.

In some states, the child to be adopted—the adoptee—must consent to the adoption if he or she has reached a specified age (e.g., twelve or fourteen) unless the court determines that it would not be in the child's best interests to ask the child. If the prospective adoptive parent is married, the consent of his or her spouse may be needed even if this spouse is not also adopting the child.

Often a child welfare agency will place the child in a foster home. Foster parents cannot prevent the adoption of the child by someone else. As we saw in Exhibit 15.1, a great many children spend a great deal of time in foster care. Critics have argued that the foster care system is overly concerned with the rights of the natural parents from whom the child had been taken. While waiting to determine whether reunion with the natural parents was possible, many children languished for years in multiple foster homes. In 1997, Congress passed the Adoption and Safe Families Act (ASFA).[11] This law had the effect of speeding up adoptions of children in foster care by forcing states to hold regularly scheduled hearings on whether reunion with the natural parents is feasible and safe and, if not, whether termination of parental rights is warranted.

Once it is determined that adoption is appropriate, foster parents cannot prevent the adoption. The consent of foster parents to the adoption is not necessary. This does not mean that the foster parents can be ignored entirely. When an agency attempts to remove the child from the foster home, many states give the foster parents the right to object to the removal and to present their arguments against the removal. While foster parents may be given a right to be heard on the removal, they cannot veto the adoption of the child.

ASSIGNMENT 15.10

a. Give the citation to the statute that contains the formalities necessary for consent to adoption in your state.
b. Who must give consent?
c. Is it necessary to obtain the consent of a natural parent who is mentally ill?
d. Is it necessary to obtain the consent of a natural parent who previously was *not* awarded custody of the child in a divorce proceeding?
e. Is there a minimum age for giving consent? Can a parent who is a minor consent or withhold consent to adoption of his or her child?
f. When, if ever, must the child consent to his or her own adoption?
g. In what form or with what formalities must the consent be given? Does your answer differ for a public agency adoption as opposed to an independent adoption? If so, explain the difference.
h. Does the consent form have to name the prospective adoptive parents?

(See General Instructions for the State-Code Assignment in Appendix A. You may also need to check court opinions for some of the above questions. See General Instructions for the Court-Opinion Assignment in Appendix A.)

[11] 42 U.S.C.A. § 671.

ASSIGNMENT 15.11

In Assignment 15.7, part (b), you drafted an adoption petition based primarily on facts that you invented yourself. Using those facts, draft a consent form (to be signed by the mother) that complies with the statutory requirements for consent in your state.

Once a natural parent consents to the adoption, can the consent be changed, assuming that it was given according to the requisite formalities? When the adoptive decree has been entered, most states will *not* allow the consent to be revoked, but some states permit revocation beforehand if:

1. The court determines that the revocation would be in the best interests of the child.
2. The court determines that the consent was obtained by fraud, duress, or undue pressure.

See Exhibit 15.4 for an example of a notice of hearing on revocation.

Typically about 30 days to revoke

Exhibit 15.4 Notice of Hearing on Issue of Revocation of Adoption

STATE OF NEW YORK
__________ COURT
COUNTY OF __________
ADDRESS __________

In the Matter of the Adoption of
____
Adoptive Child

NOTICE OF HEARING ON ISSUE OF REVOCATION AND DISPOSITION AS TO CUSTODY, PRIVATE PLACEMENT ADOPTION

PLEASE TAKE NOTICE that the ______ Court, ______ County, New York, on the ______ day of ______, 20__ at ______ o'clock or as soon thereafter as counsel can be heard, will hear and determine whether the revocation of consent of the parent in the above entitled matter shall be permitted and, in any event, hear and determine what disposition should be made with respect to the custody of said child.

____
Chief Clerk of the ______ Court

To: ____________________
Adoptive Parents

____
Parents

____________________, Esq.
Attorney for Adoptive Parent(s)

____________________, Esq.
Attorney for Parent(s)

____
Law Guardian

Source: West's McKinney's Forms, New York § 22:24 (1986).

ASSIGNMENT 15.12

When, if ever, can consent to adoption be revoked in your state? (See General Instructions for the State-Code Assignment in Appendix A. You may also have to check court opinions of your state if no statutes on revocation exist. See General Instructions for the Court-Opinion Assignment in Appendix A.)

Involuntary Termination of Parental Rights

It would be illogical to permit a natural parent to prevent the adoption of his or her child by withholding consent if that parent has abandoned the child. Many statutes, therefore, provide that abandonment as well as extreme cruelty, conviction of certain crimes, or willful neglect will mean that the consent of a parent engaged in such conduct is not necessary. The difficulty, however, is the absence of any clear definition of terms such as abandonment and extreme cruelty. Many courts have taken the position that a parent does not lose the right to withhold consent to an adoption unless the parent's conduct demonstrates *a clear intention to relinquish all parental duties.* Nonsupport in itself, for example, may not be enough if the parent has made some effort to see the child, at least occasionally.

As demonstrated in the following checklist, many factors are relevant to the question of whether a parent had the *intention to abandon* or otherwise relinquish all rights in the child. A court will consider all of these factors in combination; no one factor is usually determinative.

Interviewing and Investigation Checklist

Factors Relevant to Whether an Intent to Abandon the Child Existed

Legal Interviewing Questions

1. How old are you now?
2. With whom is your child living?
3. Is the person who is caring for the child your relative, a friend, a stranger?
4. How did the child get there?
5. How long has the child been there?
6. When is the last time you saw the child?
7. How often do you see your child per month?
8. How many times do you speak to your child on the phone per month?
9. How often do you write to your child?
10. Did you ever say to anyone that you did not want your child or that you wanted your child to find a home with someone else? If so, explain.
11. Did you ever say to anyone that you wanted your child to live with someone else temporarily until you got back on your feet again? If so, explain.
12. Have you ever placed your child with a public or private adoption agency? Have you ever discussed adoption with anyone? If so, explain.
13. Have you ever been charged with neglecting, abandoning, or failing to support your child? If so, explain.
14. Has your child ever been taken from you for any period of time? If so, explain.
15. Have you ever been found by a court to be mentally ill?
16. How much have you contributed to the support of your child while you were not living with the child?
17. Did you give the child any presents? If so, what were they and when did you give them?
18. While your child was not with you, did you ever speak to the child's teachers or doctors? If so, explain how often you did so and the circumstances involved.
19. Were you on public assistance while the child was not living with you? If so, what did you tell the public assistance workers about the child?
20. How well is the child being treated now?
21. Could anyone claim that the child lived under immoral or unhealthy circumstances while away from you and that you knew of these circumstances?
22. Has the child ever been charged with juvenile delinquency? Has the child ever been declared a person in need of supervision (PINS)?

Possible Investigation Tasks

- Find and interview relatives, friends, and strangers who knew that the client visited the child.
- Find and interview anyone with whom the client may have discussed the reasons for leaving the child with someone else.
- Prepare an inventory of all the money and other property given by the client for the support of the child while the child was living with someone else.
- Collect receipts (e.g., canceled check stubs) for all funds given by the client for such support.
- Locate all relevant court records, if any (e.g., custody order in divorce proceeding, neglect or juvenile delinquency petitions and orders).
- Interview state agencies that have been involved with the child. Determine how responsive the client has been to the efforts of the agency to help the child and the client.

To take the drastic step of ordering an involuntary termination of parental rights, there must be clear and convincing evidence that the parent is unfit. It is not enough to show that the parent has psychological or financial problems, or that there are potential adoptive parents waiting in the wings who can provide the child with a superior home environment. There must be a specific demonstration of unfitness through abandonment, willful neglect, etc.

The parent can be represented by counsel at the termination proceeding. There is, however, no automatic right to state-appointed counsel if the parent cannot afford to pay one. A court must decide on a case-by-case basis whether an indigent parent needs free counsel because of the complexity of the case. A parent who loses in the trial court and wishes to appeal the termination of parental rights must be given a free transcript if he or she cannot afford the cost of the transcript, which can amount to several thousand dollars.

If parental rights are terminated and there are adoptive parents available, a separate adoption procedure will take place. Of course, the parent whose rights have been terminated is not asked to consent to the adoption.

ASSIGNMENT 15.13

a. When is the consent of a natural parent *not* necessary in your state for the adoption of his or her child?
b. Is there a proceeding to terminate the parental rights in your state that is separate from the adoption process? If so, explain.
c. When will parental rights be terminated in your state? What are the grounds? What standard of proof must be met? Clear and convincing evidence?
d. Who can initiate a petition to terminate parental rights in your state? (See General Instructions for the State-Code Assignment in Appendix A.)
e. Prepare a flowchart of all the procedural steps necessary to terminate parental rights in your state. (See General Instructions for the Flowchart Assignment in Appendix A.)

ASSIGNMENT 15.14

Mary is the mother of two children. She is convicted of murdering her husband, their father. What facts do you think need to be investigated in order to determine whether Mary's parental rights should be terminated? (See General Instructions for the Investigation-Strategy Assignment in Appendix A.)

Placement

Before ruling on a petition for adoption, the court, as indicated, will ask a public or private child welfare agency to investigate the case through a home study and make a recommendation to the court. The agency, in effect, assumes a role that is very similar to that of a social worker or a probation officer in many juvenile delinquency cases.

ASSIGNMENT 15.15

a. What is the role of child welfare agencies in your state after an adoption petition has been filed?
b. Once an agency files a report in your state containing the results of its investigation and its recommendation on the proposed adoption, who has access to the report? Can the prospective adoptive parents have access to it? Can they (through their attorney) question the person who wrote the report?

(See General Instructions for the State-Code Assignment in Appendix A. You may also need to check court opinions of your state. See General Instructions for the Court-Opinion Assignment in Appendix A.)

Can Children Divorce Their Parents?

unemancipated
Legally dependent on one's parent or legal guardian.

No. It is, of course, logically impossible to divorce someone to whom you are not married. The concept of parental divorce was created by the media in the Florida case of *Gregory K. v. Rachel K.* Gregory was an eleven-year-old **unemancipated** child who asked a court to terminate the rights of his natural mother so that his foster parents could adopt him. Since he was the party who initiated the action, the media described him as a child who wanted to "divorce" his parents. The *trial* court allowed him to bring the action, terminated the parental rights of his mother, and granted the adoption.

The decision sparked considerable controversy. Some hailed it as the beginning of a major child's rights movement, comparing Gregory to the black woman who began the civil rights movement by refusing to give up her seat on the bus. "Gregory is the Rosa Parks of the youth rights movement," according to the chairperson of the National Child Rights Alliance.[12] Others were deeply disturbed by the decision. They thought it would open a floodgate of litigation brought by disgruntled children against their parents. A presidential candidate lamented that "kids would be suing their parents for being told to do their homework or take out the trash."[13]

nonage
Below the required minimum age to enter a desired relationship or perform a particular task.

standing
The right to bring a case and seek relief from a court.

On appeal, however, the Florida Court of Appeals ruled it was an error for the trial court to allow Gregory to initiate the termination action. A minor suffers the disability of **nonage** and hence does not have **standing** to ask a court to terminate the rights of his or her natural parents. Yet the court agreed that the parental rights of Gregory's mother should be terminated. When Gregory filed his petition, his foster parent simultaneously brought his own petition to terminate the rights of Gregory's natural mother on the ground that she had abandoned him. Foster parents *do* have standing in Florida to bring such petitions, and in this case, the adult's termination petition had merit. Hence, although Gregory eventually obtained the result he wanted (termination of parental rights plus adoption), the court, in effect, shut the door to comparable actions initiated by children in the future. "Courts historically have recognized that unemancipated minors do not have the legal capacity to initiate legal proceedings in their own names."[14]

Challenges to the Adoption Decree

interlocutory
Not final; interim.

In many states, an adoption decree does not become final immediately. An **interlocutory** (temporary) decree of adoption is first issued, which becomes final after a set period of time. During the interlocutory period, the child is placed with the adoptive parents. Since it would be very unhealthy for the child to be moved from place to place as legal battles continue to rage among any combination of adoptive parents, natural parents, and agencies, there are time limitations within which challenges to the adoption decree must be brought (e.g., two years).

ASSIGNMENT 15.16

a. Is there an interlocutory period in your state that must pass before the adoption can become final? If so, how long is it?
b. After the trial court in your state issues a final adoption decree, to what court can the decree be appealed?

continued

[12]M. Hansen, *Boy Wants "Divorce" from Parents,* 78 American Bar Association Journal 24 (July 1992).
[13]M. Hansen, *Boy Wins "Divorce" from Mom,* 78 American Bar Association Journal 16 (Dec. 1992).
[14]*Kingsley v. Kingsley,* 623 So. 2d 780, 783 (Fla. Dist. Ct. App. 1993).

c. If someone wants to challenge an adoption decree in your state, within what period of time must the challenge be brought? What happens if the challenge is not brought within this time?

(See General Instructions for the State-Code Assignment in Appendix A. You may also need to check the court rules of your state courts, and perhaps court opinions as well. See General Instructions for the Court-Opinion Assignment in Appendix A.)

d. Draft a flowchart of all the procedural steps involved in an adoption proceeding in your state. (See General Instructions for the Flowchart Assignment in Appendix A.)

"Journalistic Terrorism"

We turn now to one of the more dramatic cases in the history of family law—the Illinois case of Baby Richard: *In re Petition of Doe.* Before the glare of cameras and national media, a four-year-old boy was taken from his adoptive parents and turned over to his natural father, Otakar Kirchner, whom the boy had never met. One newspaper account said the biological father "took physical custody of the sobbing child as he frantically reached for his adoptive mother in front of the house where the boy had lived since he was four days

The day of reckoning. Baby Richard is carried away to a new home by his biological father, Otakar Kirchner, as the child cries and reaches for his adoptive mother. (Courtesy of AP/Wide World Photos.)

old."[15] The public's reaction was intense. Newspapers, newscasts, and talk shows gave the story extensive coverage. The case was called "nightmarish," "monstrous," "absolutely horrible," and "state sanctioned child abuse." The governor of Illinois said that Baby Richard was being "brutally, tragically torn away from the only parents he has ever known." The opinion in *In re Petition of Doe* was written by Justice Heiple. When it was published, he was denounced. One columnist, Bob Greene, was particularly critical. Justice Heiple took the highly unusual step of responding to this criticism in the supplemental opinion he wrote denying a rehearing of the case. He referred to the criticism as "journalistic terrorism." As we study *In re Petition of Doe,* you need to decide for yourself to what extent the case demonstrates a collapse of the legal system.

[15] *Unnecessary Cruelty,* San Diego Union-Tribune, May 4, 1995, at B-12.

CASE

In re Petition of Doe & Doe to Adopt Baby Boy Janikova

159 Ill. 2d 347, 638 N.E.2d 181 (1994)
Supreme Court of Illinois
June 16, 1994
Supplemental Opinion on Denial of Rehearing
July 12, 1994

Background: *Baby Boy Janikova (known in the media as Baby Richard) lived for three years with John and Jane Doe, his adoptive parents. The Supreme Court of Illinois then ruled that he had been improperly adopted and ordered him returned. He was four years old by the time the order was finally carried out.*

Daniella Janikova and Otakar Kirchner were not married when their son, Baby Boy Janikova, was born. Otakar was out of the country at the time. Four days after the birth, Daniella consented to have the baby adopted by John and Jane Doe. Daniella did not tell Otakar about the adoption by the Does. In fact, she told him the baby was born dead. Fifty-seven days after the boy's birth, Otakar learned the truth. Within two weeks, he challenged the legality of the adoption on the ground that he did not consent to it. Lengthy litigation and media attention followed. The trial court found that Otakar was unfit because he did not show sufficient interest in the child during the first thirty days of the child's life, and therefore his consent to the adoption was not required. On appeal before the appellate court, Justice Rizzi affirmed, ruling that the adoption was in the best interests of the child. The case is now on appeal before the Supreme Court of Illinois. (During the litigation, Daniella married Otakar and, therefore, now joins him in seeking to revoke the adoption.)

Decision on Appeal: *Reversed. Justice Heiple of the Supreme Court held that the adoption was invalid because it violated the rights of the natural father. The use of the best-interests-of-the-child standard by Justice Rizzi in the appellate court "grossly misstated the law."*

Opinion of the Court:

Justice HEIPLE delivered the opinion of the court. . . .

Otakar and Daniella began living together in the fall of 1989, and Daniella became pregnant in June of 1990. For the first eight months of her pregnancy, Otakar provided for all of her expenses.

In late January 1991, Otakar went to his native Czechoslovakia to attend to his gravely ill grandmother for two weeks. During this time, Daniella received a phone call from Otakar's aunt saying that Otakar had resumed a former romantic relationship with another woman.

Because of this unsettling news, Daniella left their shared apartment, refused to talk with Otakar on his return, and gave birth to the child at a different hospital than where they had originally planned. She gave her consent to the adoption of the child by the Does, telling them and their attorney that she knew who the father was but would not furnish his name. Daniella and her uncle warded off Otakar's persistent inquiries about the child by telling him that the child had died shortly after birth.

Otakar found out that the child was alive and had been placed for adoption 57 days after the child was born. He then began the instant proceedings by filing an appearance contesting the Does' adoption of his son. . . . [T]he trial court ruled that Otakar was an unfit parent under section 1 of the Adoption Act (750 ILCS 50/1 (West 1992)) because he had not shown a reasonable degree of interest in the child within the first 30 days of his life. Therefore, the father's consent was unnecessary under section 8 of the Act (750 ILCS 50/8 (West 1992)).

The finding that the father had not shown a reasonable degree of interest in the child is not supported by the evidence. In fact, he made various attempts to locate the child, all of which were either frustrated or blocked by the actions of the mother. Further, the mother was aided by the attorney for the adoptive parents, who failed to make any effort to ascertain the name or address of the father despite the fact that the mother indicated she knew who he was. Under the circumstances, the father had no opportunity to discharge any familial duty.

In the opinion below, the appellate court, wholly missing the threshold issue in this case, dwelt on the best interests of the child. Since, however, the father's parental interest was improperly terminated, there was no occasion to reach the factor of the child's best interests. That point should never have been reached and need never have been discussed.

Unfortunately, over three years have elapsed since the birth of the baby who is the subject of these proceedings. To the extent that it is relevant to assign fault in this case, the fault here lies initially with the mother, who fraudulently tried to deprive the father of his rights, and secondly, with the adoptive parents and their attorney, who proceeded with the adoption when they knew that a real father was out there who had been denied knowledge of his baby's existence. When the father entered his appearance in the adoption proceedings 57 days after the baby's birth and demanded his rights as a father, the petitioners should have relinquished the baby at that time. It was their decision to prolong this litigation through a lengthy, and ultimately fruitless, appeal.

The adoption laws of Illinois are neither complex nor difficult of application. Those laws intentionally place the burden of proof on the adoptive parents in establishing both the relinquishment and/or unfitness of the natural parents and, coincidentally, the fitness and the right to adopt of the adoptive parents. In addition, Illinois law requires a good-faith effort to notify the natural parents of the adoption proceedings. These laws are designed to protect natural parents in their preemptive rights to their own children wholly apart from any consideration of the so-called best interests of the child. If it were otherwise, few parents would be secure in the custody of their own children. If best interests of the child were a sufficient qualification to determine child custody, anyone with superior income, intelligence, education, etc., might challenge and deprive the parents of their right to their own children. The law is otherwise and was not complied with in this case.

Accordingly, we reverse.

Supplemental Opinion Upon Denial of Rehearing

Justice HEIPLE, writing in support of the denial of rehearing:

On Thursday, June 16, 1994, this court reversed a decision by a divided appellate court which had affirmed certain adoption proceedings in the circuit court of Cook County. Our reversal was the result of the failure of the courts below to correctly apply Illinois law in terminating the natural father's parental rights. This cause is now before the court on petitions for rehearing filed by the adoptive parents and the guardian ad litem for the child. The following is offered in support of today's order denying rehearing.

I have been a judge for over 23 years. In that time, I have seldom before worked on a case that involved the spread of so much misinformation, nor one which dealt with as straightforward an application of law to fact.

[A] . . . conspiracy was undertaken to deny the natural father any knowledge of his son's existence. It began when the biological mother, 8½ months pregnant, was misinformed that the father, her fiance, had left her for another woman. She left their shared home and, at the encouragement of a social worker, agreed to give up her child. The social worker called her personal attorney, who contacted the adoptive mother (that attorney's friend and employee). At the behest of the adoptive parents and their attorney, the mother gave birth at a different hospital than she and the father had planned to avoid the father's intervention; the mother surrendered the baby to strangers four days after his birth; and then falsely told the father that the child had died. All of this occurred in the space of less than three weeks.

The father did not believe the mother, and he immediately began an intensive and persistent search and inquiry to learn the truth and locate the child. On the 57th day following the child's birth, the father learned of his son's existence and of the pending adoption. On that day, he hired a lawyer and contested the adoption of his son by strangers. One may reasonably ask, What more could he have done? What more should he have done? The answer is that he did all that he could and should do.

The . . . adoptive parents should have relinquished the baby at that time. That is to say, on the 57th day. Instead of that, however, they were able to

continued

CASE

In re Petition of Doe & Doe to Adopt Baby Boy Janikova—*Continued*

procure an entirely erroneous ruling from a trial judge that allowed the adoption to go forward. The father's only remedy at that stage was a legal appeal which he took. He is not the cause of the delay in this case. It was the adoptive parents' decision to prolong this litigation through a long and ultimately fruitless appeal. Now, the view has been expressed that the passage of time warrants their retention of the child; that it would not be fair to the child to return him to his natural parents, now married to each other, after the adoptive parents have delayed justice past the child's third birthday.

For a fuller and more detailed account of the father's efforts and the underlying facts, one may refer to the dissenting opinion authored by Justice Tully in the appellate court decision rendered below. (254 Ill. App. 3d 405, 418, 627 N.E.2d 648 (Tully, P. J., dissenting).) As noted by Justice Tully, Justice Rizzi, writing the majority opinion for himself and Justice Cerda, "patently distorted and slanted the facts on a number of important points." I would further add that Justice Rizzi grossly misstated the law.

If, as stated by Justice Rizzi, the best interests of the child is to be the determining factor in child custody cases (254 Ill. App. 3d at 412), persons seeking babies to adopt might profitably frequent grocery stores and snatch babies from carts when the parent is looking the other way. Then, if custody proceedings can be delayed long enough, they can assert that they have a nicer home, a superior education, a better job or whatever, and that the best interests of the child are with the baby snatchers. Children of parents living in public housing or other conditions deemed less than affluent and children with single parents might be considered particularly fair game. The law, thankfully, is otherwise.

In 1972, the United States Supreme Court, in the case of *Stanley v. Illinois* (1972), 405 U.S. 645, 92 S. Ct. 1208, 31 L. Ed. 2d 551 ruled that unmarried fathers cannot be treated differently than unmarried mothers or married parents when determining their rights to the custody of their children. The courts of Illinois are bound by that decision. Subsequently, in 1990, a unanimous Illinois Supreme Court pointed out that when ruling on parental unfitness, a court is not to consider the child's best interests, since the child's welfare is not relevant in judging the fitness of the natural parent; that only after the parent is found by clear and convincing evidence to be unfit does the court proceed to consider the child's best interest and whether that interest would be served if the child were adopted by the petitioners. *In re Adoption of Syck* (1990), 138 Ill. 2d 255, 276–78, 562 N.E.2d 174.

Under Illinois law, a parent may be divested of his parental rights either voluntarily (e.g., consenting to an adoption (see Ill. Rev. Stat. 1991, ch. 40, par. 1513)) or involuntarily (e.g., finding of abuse, abandonment, neglect or lack of sufficient interest (see Ill. Rev. Stat. 1991, ch. 40, par. 1510)). . . . [T]he adoption laws of Illinois are neither complex nor difficult of application. These laws intentionally place the burden of proof on the adoptive parents. In addition, Illinois law requires a good-faith effort to notify the natural father of the adoption proceedings. (Ill. Rev. Stat. 1991, ch. 40, par. 1509.) We call this due process of law. In the case at hand, both the adoptive parents and their attorney knew that a real father existed whose name was known to the mother but who refused to disclose it. Under these circumstances, the adoptive parents proceeded at their peril.

The best interest of the child standard is not to be denigrated. It is real. However, it is not triggered until it has been validly determined that the child is available for adoption. And, a child is not available for adoption until the rights of his natural parents have been properly terminated. Any judge, lawyer, or guardian ad litem who has even the most cursory familiarity with adoption laws knows that. Justice Rizzi, if he is to be taken at face value, does not know that.

Columnist Bob Greene apparently does not care. Rather, columnist Greene has used this unfortunate controversy to stimulate readership and generate a series of syndicated newspaper columns in the Chicago Tribune and other papers that are both false and misleading. In so doing, he has wrongfully cried "fire" in a crowded theatre, and has needlessly alarmed other adoptive parents into ill-founded concerns that their own adoption proceedings may be in jeopardy. In support of his position, Greene has stirred up contempt against the Supreme Court as an institution, concluding one of his columns by referring to all of the Justices with the curse, "Damn them all." Chicago Tribune, June 19, 1994, page 1.

Greene's implicit objective is to secure justice for a child. With that ethical and moral imperative, of course, no one could disagree. Greene, however, elevates himself above the facts, above the law, and above the Supreme Court of Illinois. He arrogates to himself the right to decide the case.

In support of his objective, Greene brings to bear the tools of the demagogue, namely, incomplete information, falsity, half-truths, character assassination and spurious argumentation. He has conducted a steady assault on my abilities as a judge, headlining one of his columns "The Sloppiness of Justice Heiple." Another was entitled "Supreme Injustice for a Little Boy." He has shown my picture in his columns with bylines reading, respectively, "Justice Heiple: Ruling takes boy from home," and "James D. Heiple: No justice for a child."

Make no mistake about it. These are acts of journalistic terrorism. These columns are designed to discredit me as a judge and the Supreme Court as a dispenser of justice by stirring up disrespect and hatred among the general population.

Lest we forget the place from which he comes, let us remind ourselves that Greene is a journalist with a product to sell. He writes columns for a living. His income is dependent on writing and selling his columns to newspapers. He cannot secure either sales or earnings by writing on subjects that lack impact or drama. So, he must seek out subjects that are capable of generating wide public interest. An adoption case involving two sets of parents contesting for the custody of a three-year-old boy is a ready-made subject for this type of journalist. So far, so good.

The trouble with Greene's treatment of the subject, however, is that his columns have been biased, false and misleading. They have also been destructive to the cause of justice both in this case and in the wider perspective. Part of Greene's fury may be attributable to the fact that he staked out his views on this case in a published column that appeared on August 22, 1993. (Chicago Tribune, August 22, 1993, page 1.) Subsequently, on June 16, 1994, the Supreme Court had the audacity to base its decision on the law rather than on his newspaper column. So much for his self-possessed moralizing.

That Greene has succeeded to a limited degree cannot be denied. I have, indeed, received several pieces of hate mail with such epithets as idiot, jerk, etc. The Governor, in a crass political move, announced his attempt to intervene in the case. And the General Assembly, without meaningful debate of consideration, rushed into law a constitutionally infirm statute with the goal of changing the Supreme Court's decision.

Both the Governor and the members of the General Assembly who supported this bill might be well advised to return to the classroom and take up Civics 101. The Governor, for his part, has no understanding of this case and no interest either public or private in its outcome. The legislature is not given the authority to decide private disputes between litigants. Neither does it sit as a super court to review unpopular decisions of the Supreme Court. We have three branches of government in this land. They are designated as the legislative, the executive and the judicial. Legislative adjudication of private disputes went by the wayside generations ago. Moreover, this case cannot be decided by public clamor generated by an irresponsible journalist. Neither can it be decided by its popularity or lack thereof. This case can only be decided by a court of law. That is a judicial function pure and simple. For the Supreme Court to surrender to this assault would be to surrender its independence, its integrity and its reason for being. In so doing, neither justice to the litigants nor the public interest would be served. Under the circumstances, this case looms even larger than the child or the two sets of contesting parents.

Many law suits are painful matters. This case is no exception. Capital cases, for instance, demand the forfeiture of the life of the defendant. Damage suits take money away from some people and give it to others. No one ever claimed that both sides walk away from a law suit with smiles on their faces. No member of this court ever entertained any thought that the decision it rendered in this case would be easy to accept by the losing litigants. Such an event would be incredible.

As for the child, age three, it is to be expected that there would be an initial shock, even a longing for a time in the absence of the persons whom he had viewed as parents. This trauma will be overcome, however, as it is every day across this land by children who suddenly find their parents separated by divorce or loss to them through death. It will not be an insurmountable trauma for a three-year-old child to be returned, at last, to his natural parents who want to raise him as their own. It will work itself out in the fullness of time. As for the adoptive parents, they will have to live with their pain and the knowledge that they wrongfully deprived a father of his child past the child's third birthday. They and their lawyer brought it on themselves.

This much is clear. Adoptive parents who comply with the law may feel secure in their adoptions. Natural parents may feel secure in their right to raise their own children. If there is a tragedy in this case, as has been suggested, then that tragedy is the wrongful breakup of a natural family and the keeping of a child by strangers without right. We must remember that the purpose of an adoption is to provide a home for a child, not a child for a home.

ASSIGNMENT 15.17

a. Someone obviously made a major blunder in this case. From infancy, Baby Richard lived with one set of adults. Years later he is forced to live with other adults. Who does Justice Heiple say is to blame? Why? Which of the following cast of characters do *you* think is to blame and why: the natural mother, her attorney, the relatives of the natural mother, her social worker, the natural father, his attorney, the adoptive parents, their attorney, Baby Richard's guardian ad litem, the trial court (which granted the adoption), the appellate court (which said it was in the best interests of the child that he go with the Does), the Supreme Court of Illinois (which gave the child to his natural father)?

b. What do you think of the quality of the legal representation given to the Does by their attorney?

c. In chapter 9 we learned that custody decisions are based on the best interests of the child. Did this case say that the best interests of the child are irrelevant?

d. What do you think could have been done to avoid this tragedy?

e. Is it relevant that Daniella married Otakar and therefore agreed with him that the adoption should be set aside?

f. Do you think it was wise for Justice Heiple to attack Bob Greene as a journalistic terrorist?

g. Justice Heiple said, "It will not be an insurmountable trauma for a three-year-old child to be returned, at last, to his natural parents who want to raise him as their own." Do you agree? If Justice Heiple thought the trauma *would be* insurmountable, would he have ruled differently? Recall that he said the best interests of the child were irrelevant in this case.

h. Rich and Paula Davis are the natural parents of John. Following a divorce, Rich is granted custody of John. Rich illegally takes John to another state, where his girlfriend adopts him. During the adoption proceeding, Rich falsely tells the court that John's mother, Paula, is dead. Paula, therefore, never receives notice of the adoption proceeding. Years later, after the passing of the statute of limitations, Paula learns about the adoption for the first time. Can she still challenge the adoption? How would this case be decided in Illinois in view of *In re Petition of Doe?*

Baby Jessica

The Baby Jessica case is another highly publicized example of a biological father successfully challenging an adoption on the basis of the biological mother's lies. Cara Clausen gave birth to Baby Jessica in Iowa. Within days of the birth, she put her up for adoption to Jan and Roberta DeBoer, who took her to Michigan. In the adoption proceedings, Cara lied about who the biological father was. Three weeks later she had a change of heart and told the biological father, Dan Schmidt, what had happened. He then sought to get Baby Jessica back from the adoptive parents. He argued that he never consented to the adoption and was never found to be unfit. After two and a half years of litigation, the Iowa and Michigan courts nullified the adoption and ordered Baby Jessica returned.[16] The federal courts refused to change this result. In *DeBoer v. DeBoer,* the United States Supreme Court said, "Neither Iowa law, Michigan law, nor federal law authorizes unrelated persons to retain custody of a child whose natural parents have not been found to be unfit simply because they may be better able to provide for her future and her education. '[C]ourts are not free to take children from parents simply by deciding another home appears more advantageous.' "[17]

---

[16]See *In re Baby Girl Clausen,* 502 N.W.2d 649 (Mich. 1993); *In the Interest of B.G.C.,* 496 N.W.2d 239 (Iowa 1992).

[17]509 U.S. 1301, 1302, 114 S. Ct. 1, 2, 125 L. Ed. 2d 755 (1993).

Putative Father Registry

How do we protect the rights of an unmarried father who does not become aware of the adoption of his child until it is too late to intervene? How can we prevent heart-rending scenes of children being forced from their adoptive parents and returned to their biological father—sometimes years after their placement with the adoptive parents? The father needs notice of the proposed adoption so that he has time to intervene. Yet he cannot be given notice if the mother lies about who the father is or where he can be found.

One approach in many states has been to establish a **putative father registry.** A putative father is the alleged or reputed father of a child. He will be given notice of the proposed adoption of his child (which would include the termination of his parental rights) if he registers with the putative father registry within a specific time frame. By registering, he announces his intent to assert his rights and responsibilities as a parent. The failure to register may preclude his right to notice of the adoption proceedings. For an example of a putative father registry, see Exhibit 15.5.

putative father registry
A place where the father of a child can register so that he can be notified of a proposed adoption of the child.

Exhibit 15.5 Putative Father Registry

The **Putative Father Registry** is a confidential file maintained in Albany to register fathers of children born out of wedlock.

PURPOSE

The Putative Father Registry was developed to ensure that, if an individual has registered (or has been registered by a court) as the father of a particular child, he will receive legal notice if that child is to be adopted. Additionally, registration provides such a child the right of inheritance in the event of the death of an out of wedlock father. A father may be registered for both purposes provided he follows the instructions in this leaflet.

REGISTRATION

The attached form, called "An Instrument to Acknowledge Paternity of An Out of Wedlock Child," must be filled out in the presence of a witness and signed and notarized before it is returned to the address indicated. Once it is received it will be filed in the Putative Father Registry. The New York State Department of Social Services shall, upon request from any court or authorized agency, provide the names and addresses of persons listed with the registry. The department will not divulge this information to any other party.

The mother and other legal guardian of the child, (if any) will be contacted by registered mail to notify her (them) that a registration has been received.

INSTRUMENT TO ACKNOWLEDGE PATERNITY OF AN OUT OF WEDLOCK CHILD
(pursuant to Section 4–1.2 of New York Estates, Powers and Trust Law)

COMPLETE THIS SECTION

I ______________ (NAME OF FATHER), residing at ______________ (ADDRESS)
______________ (TOWN) ______ (STATE) ______ (ZIP CODE) hereby acknowledge that I am the natural father of
______________ (NAME OF CHILD) born on ______ (DATE OF BIRTH) in ______ (TOWN) ______ (STATE) ______ (ZIP CODE).
The natural mother of the child ______________ (CHILD'S NAME) is ______________ (NAME OF NATURAL MOTHER) who resides
at ______________
Witness ______________ (SIGNATURE) ______________ (NATURAL FATHER (SIGNATURE))
______________ (ADDRESS)
______ (TOWN) ______ (STATE) ______ (ZIP CODE)

STATE OF NEW YORK
COUNTY OF ______________

On the ______ (DAY) day of ______ (MONTH) ______ (YEAR), before me came
______________ (NATURAL FATHER) to me known to be the individual described herein and who executed the foregoing instrument, and acknowledges to me that he executed same.

______________ (NOTARY PUBLIC)

STATE OF NEW YORK
COUNTY OF ______________

This instrument must be filed with the New York State Department of Social Services, Putative Father Register, 40 North Pearl Street, Albany, New York 12243, within sixty days after it is completed. The natural mother indicated on this instrument will be sent notification of this acknowledgement within seven days after its filing.

The registry is by no means a perfect solution. It can work well when the man knows about the registry and knows he has impregnated an unmarried woman. Difficulties arise when the woman with whom he is intimate does not tell him she is pregnant or falsely tells him that she had an abortion. Realistically, the only way he can protect his rights is to register every time he has sexual relations with an unmarried woman. Some states are unsympathetic to the man who says, "I didn't know." A Utah statute, for example, provides that "[a]n unmarried biological father, by virtue of the fact that he has engaged in a sexual relationship with a woman, is deemed to be on notice that a pregnancy and an adoption proceeding regarding that child may occur, and has a duty to protect his own rights and interests."[18] The burden, therefore, is on the man to find out whether he is about to become or has become a father and, if so, to take steps to protect his rights such as by helping to arrange prenatal and delivery care, paying child support, petitioning a court for an order of paternity, or making sure his name is on the birth certificate. If in doubt, register! Whether this approach violates the constitutional rights of the father is unclear. This is an area of the law in which we can expect continued litigation.

ASSIGNMENT 15.18

Under what circumstances will an unmarried man be given notice of an adoption proceeding for his child in your state? (See General Instructions for the State-Code and Court-Opinion Assignments in Appendix A.)

CONSEQUENCES OF ADOPTION

Once the adoption becomes final, the adopted child and the adoptive parents have almost all the rights and obligations toward each other that natural parents and children have toward each other. The major exception involves the death of a relative of the adoptive parent.

Kevin is the adopted child of Paul. Paul's brother, Bill, dies intestate (i.e., without leaving a valid will). Can Kevin inherit from Bill?

In some states, the answer is no: an adopted child cannot take an intestate share of a relative of its adoptive parents. Other states do not impose this limitation.

In most other respects, an adopted child is treated the same as a natural child:

- Adopted children can take the name of their adoptive parents.
- The birth certificate can be changed to reflect the new parents.
- Adopted children can inherit from their adoptive parents who die intestate. In a few states, adopted children can also inherit from their natural parents who die intestate. Natural parents, however, cannot inherit from a child who dies intestate if he or she has been adopted by someone else. There are no restrictions on who can be beneficiaries under a will if any of these individuals dies testate (i.e., leaving a valid will).
- Adoptive parents have a right to the services and earnings of the adopted children.
- Adoptive parents must support adopted children.
- Adopted children are entitled to workers' compensation benefits due to an on-the-job injury of their adoptive parent.
- If an adoptive parent dies with a will leaving property to "my heirs" or to "my children" or to "my issue," without mentioning any individuals

[18]Utah Statutes § 78–30–4.13.

by name, most (but not all) courts are inclined to conclude that the intention of the deceased adoptive parent was to include adopted children as well as natural children within the designation of "heirs," "children," or "issue."

- An adoptive parent (with no biological connection to the child) has priority over biological grandparents when the adoptive parent objects to their visitation.

ASSIGNMENT 15.19

a. What rights and obligations are assumed by adoptive parents and children in your state?

b. In the example immediately above involving Kevin, Paul, and Bill, could Kevin inherit from Bill in your state?

c. Assume that Kevin's natural parent dies intestate. Can Kevin inherit from his natural parent in your state?

d. Helen is the natural child of George and Sally; Bob is their adopted child. Can Helen and Bob marry in your state?

(Check statutes and cases on the above questions. See General Instructions for the State-Code Assignment and General Instructions for the Court-Opinion Assignment in Appendix A.)

CONFIDENTIALITY

In recent years, there has been great controversy over whether adopted children have a right to discover the identity of their natural parents. The traditional answer has been no. Once the adoption becomes final, the record is sealed. The data within it is confidential. There are, however, limited exceptions to this rule. If *good cause* can be shown, access to part of the adoption records may be allowed. For example, an adopted child may need medical or genetic information on its natural parents to help treat diseases that might be hereditary. Similarly, the adopted child may need some information about the identity of his or her natural parents to avoid unknowingly marrying a natural brother or sister. Access to such information, however, is the exception. It is rare that identifying information is released. The norm is nonidentifying information consisting of social or medical facts that would not allow positive identification of any person who was a party to the adoption. The need for information must be great. Many courts have held that it is not enough for the adopted child to prove that he or she is experiencing emotional distress due to not knowing the identity of his or her natural parents.

While many states continue to follow this narrow approach on confidentiality, there is a trend in the other direction. Some states have broadened the categories of nonidentifying information they will release without compromising anonymity. In one recent case, for example, an adult adoptee was allowed to discover information on the race of the birth parents, the general health of the adoptee at the time of the adoption, the reasons assigned for the adoption, and the length of time the adoptee was in the custody of her adoptive parents prior to the adoption.[19] A few states (e.g., Kansas and Alaska) have created a system of complete openness. Adult adoptees, without restriction, can see their adoption records or original birth certificate. Reform in most other states has not been this radical.

Some states have created a **reunion registry,** which contains identifying information about adoptees and biological parents. There are two kinds of

reunion registry
A central adoption file that could be used to release identifying information about, and allow contact between, adult adoptees and biological parents.

---

[19] *Appeal of Jo Ann Kasparek,* 653 A.2d 1254 (Pa. Super. Ct. 1995).

registries: passive and active. A *passive registry* (also called a *mutual consent registry*) requires both the adoptee and the biological parent to register their consent to release identifying information. When both have registered and a match is made, an agency employee contacts both. An *active registry* does not require both the adoptee and the biological parent to register their consent to release information. Once one of them registers, an agency official will contact the other to determine his or her wishes for the release of information. Some states allow the use of a **contact veto,** which gives permission to release identifying information from adoption records but prohibits contact between the parties. In a few states, the release of information also requires the consent of the adoptive parents. Biological fathers can use the registry, but most states condition such use on the fathers' acknowledgment of paternity.

contact veto
A denial of consent to have contact between the adoptee and the biological parent, although permission for the release of identifying information might be given.

Some independent or private adoptions give the participants the option of maintaining limited contact between the natural parent and the child after the adoption. These are called **open adoptions,** involving an exchange of identifying information or face-to-face meetings. Some believe that such adoptions should be discouraged. Young women "are finding it harder to get on with their lives. . . ." "They start living for the photos that the adoptive parents send them every month." Adoptive parents sometimes "find themselves not only raising a new baby but providing counseling for the birth mother who often finds it difficult to break her bond with the child."[20] Not many adoptive parents, therefore, pursue open adoptions. Exhibit 15.6 provides a state-by-state overview of adoption rules including confidentiality.

open adoption
An adoption in which the natural parent maintains certain kinds of contact with his or her child after the adoption.

[20]Council of State Governments, *Adoption,* State Government News, Sept. 1989, at 31.

Exhibit 15.6 Regulation of Adoption

	Is Independent Adoption Legal?	Can a Profit-Making Organization Be Licensed to Provide Children?	What Is the Length of Time between Filing for and Finalizing an Adoption?	How Soon after Birth Can a Mother Consent to Adoption?	How Long Is she Given to Revoke Her Consent?*	What Are the Legal Penalties for Baby Selling and for Baby Buying?	Are Sealed Records Available to Adult Adoptees?
Alabama	Yes†	Yes	6 months	Anytime	5 days	Maximum 3 months in jail and/or $100 fine	Yes**
Alaska	Yes	Yes	Varies	Anytime	10 days	No defined penalties; judge decides	Yes
Arizona	Yes	Yes	6 months	72 hours	No time	6 months to 1.9 years in prison and/or $1,000 to $150,000 fine	No
Arkansas	Yes	Yes	6 months	24 hours	10 days	Felony: 3–10 years in prison	No**
California	Yes†	No	Usually 6–12 months	After hospital discharge†	90 days in a direct placement	Misdemeanor: local D.A. decides penalty	No
Colorado	Yes†	Yes	6 months	Anytime in court	No time	Felony: 4–16 years in prison and/or up to $750,000 fine	No**
Connecticut	No	No	1 year after placement	48 hours	Up to final decree	Felony: 1–5 years in prison and/or $5,000 fine	No**
Delaware	No	Yes	2–30 days	Anytime once drug-free	Until parental rights ended	No defined penalties; judge decides	No
D.C.	Yes	Yes	6–12 months	Anytime	10 days	90 days in jail and/or $300 fine	No
Florida	Yes	No	At least 30 days	Anytime	No time	Felony: maximum 5 years in prison	No

Georgia	Yes[†]	No	At least 60 days	Anytime†	10 days	Felony: maximum 10 years in prison and/or $1,000 fine	No
Hawaii	Yes	No	Varies (131-day average)	Anytime	Until placement	No defined penalties; judge decides	No
Idaho	Yes	Yes	30 days	Anytime	No time	Felony: maximum 14 years in prison and/or $5,000 fine	No**
Illinois	Yes	Yes	6 months	72 hours	3 days	Felony: 1–3 years in prison and/or $10,000 fine	No**
Indiana	Yes	Yes	Varies	Anytime	No time	Felony: maximum 2 years in prison and/or $10,000 fine	No**
Iowa	Yes	Yes	6 months from placement	72 hours	Until parental rights ended	30 days in jail and/or $100 fine	No
Kansas	Yes	Yes	At least 30 days	12 hours	No time	No defined penalties; judge decides	Yes
Kentucky	Yes[†]	Yes	Usually within 180 days	72 hours	20 days	6 months in prison and/or $500 to $2,000 fine	No**
Louisiana	Yes	Yes	6–12 months	5 days	5 days	Felony: maximum 5 years in prison and/or $5,000 fine	No**
Maine	Yes	Yes	Varies, a week to several months	Anytime	3 days	No defined penalties; judge decides	No**
Maryland	Yes	Yes	2–6 months	Anytime	30 days	Maximum 3 months in jail and/or $100 fine	No**
Massachusetts	No	No	Varies	4 days	No time	2½–5 years in jail and/or $5,000 to $30,000 fine	No
Michigan	No	Yes	1 year	Anytime	No time	Maximum 90 days in jail and/or $100 fine	No
Minnesota	No[†]	No	At least 3 months	72 hours	10 working days	Maximum 90 days in jail and/or $700 fine	No**
Mississippi	Yes	Yes	0–6 months	72 hours	No time	Maximum 5 years in prison and/or $5,000 fine	No
Missouri	Yes	Yes	9 months	48 hours	Until adoption hearing	Felony: maximum 7 years in prison and/or $5,000 fine	No**
Montana	Yes[†]	No	No time set	72 hours	No time	Maximum fine: $1,000	No
Nebraska	Yes[†]	Yes	6 months	Anytime	No time	Maximum 3 months in jail and/or $500 fine	No**
Nevada	Yes	No	6 months	72 hours	No time	1–6 years in prison and/or a maximum $5,000 fine	No**
New Hampshire	Yes	No	At least 6 months	72 hours	No time	No defined penalties; judge decides	No
New Jersey	Yes	No	At least 6 months	72 hours	No time	3–5 years in prison and/or $7,500 fine	No**
New Mexico	Yes	Yes	90–180 days from placement	48 hours	No time	Maximum fine: $500	No
New York	Yes	No	6 months	Anytime	45 days	No defined penalties; judge decides	No**
North Carolina	Yes[†]	Yes	1 year	Anytime	varies	Misdemeanor: court decides penalty	No
North Dakota	No	Yes	At least 6 months	72 hours	Until adoption is final	Felony: maximum 5 years in prison and/or $5,000 fine	No**
Ohio	Yes	Yes	6 months	72 hours	Until adoption is final	Maximum 6 months in jail and/or $500 to $1,000 fine	No
Oklahoma	Yes	No	6 months	Anytime	No time	Minimum 1 year in jail	No

continued

Exhibit 15.6 Regulation of Adoption—*Continued*

	Is Independent Adoption Legal?	Can a Profit-Making Organization Be Licensed to Provide Children?	What Is the Length of Time between Filing for and Finalizing an Adoption?	How Soon after Birth Can a Mother Consent to Adoption?	How Long Is she Given to Revoke Her Consent?*	What Are the Legal Penalties for Baby Selling and for Baby Buying?	Are Sealed Records Available to Adult Adoptees?
Oregon	Yes	Yes	About 90 days	24 hours	No time	No defined penalties; judge decides	No**
Pennsylvania	Yes	Yes	No set time	72 hours	Until court's order	Maximum 5 years in prison and/or $10,000 fine	No**
Rhode Island	Yes	No	At least 6 months	15 days	15 days†	No defined penalties; judge decides	Yes†
South Carolina	Yes	Yes	90–365 days	Anytime	No time	Felony: maximum 10 years in prison and/or $10,000 fine	No**
South Dakota	Yes	Yes	6 months, 10 days	5 days	30-day appeal period	Felony: maximum 2 years in prison and/or $2,000 fine	No**
Tennessee	Yes	No	6 months	4 days	10 days	Felony: 1–10 years in prison	No**
Texas	Yes	Yes†	6 months	2 days	10 days†	Felony: 2–10 years in prison and/or $5,000 fine	No**
Utah	Yes	Yes	At least 6 months	24 hours	No time	Must forfeit payment and pay $10,000 maximum fine	No**
Vermont	Yes	No	6 months from placement	72 hours	21 days	No defined penalties; judge decides	No
Virginia	Yes†	Yes	0–12 months	Anytime; effective in 10 days	15–25 days	No defined penalties; judge decides	No
Washington	Yes	Yes	No set time	Before birth†	Until court's order	Felony: maximum 5 years in prison and/or $10,000 fine	No
West Virginia	Yes	Yes	At least 6 months	72 hours	No time	No defined penalties; judge decides	No
Wisconsin	Yes†	Yes	At least 6 months	Anytime in court	No time	Felony: maximum 2 years in prison and/or $10,000 fine	No**
Wyoming	Yes	Yes	6 months	Anytime	No time†	No defined penalties; judge decides	No

Source: © 1989 by the National Committee for Adoption, Inc. From *Adoption Factbook,* available from the Committee at P.O. Box 33366, Washington, DC 20033.

Note: Adoptions of American Indians are governed by the federal Indian Child Welfare Act, which prevents a mother from signing consent papers until 10 days after birth and allows her to revoke her consent until an adoption is final.

*Assuming no fraud, duress, or coercion is proved.

**Information may be obtained through a voluntary state registry or adoption agency.

†With restrictions or exceptions.

ASSIGNMENT 15.20

Under what circumstances, if any, can an adopted child gain access to adoption records in your state? What kind of information can be obtained? Is it possible to find out whether the mother was married when the child was born? (See General Instructions for the State-Code Assignment in Appendix A. You may also have to check court opinions. See General Instructions for the Court-Opinion Assignment in Appendix A.)

EQUITABLE ADOPTION

Assume that John Smith enters a contract with Mary Jones to adopt Mary's child, Bill, but fails to perform the contract. Such contracts are occasionally in writing but more often are simply oral understandings between parties who know each other very well. Assume further that John takes custody of Bill, treats him as a member of his family, but never goes through formal adoption procedures as he had promised. John then dies intestate (i.e., without leaving a valid will). Technically, Bill cannot inherit from John because the adoption never took place. This argument might be used by John's natural children to prevent an unadopted child—Bill—from sharing in the estate.

Many feel that it would be unfair to deny the child inheritance benefits simply because the deceased failed to abide by the agreement to adopt. To avoid the unfairness, some courts conclude that such a child was adopted under the doctrine of **equitable adoption** (also called *de facto adoption*) and hence is entitled to the inheritance rights of adopted children. The doctrine is also referred to as *adoption by estoppel;* challengers will be estopped (i.e., prevented) from denying that such a child has been adopted. Since, however, it is relatively easy (and tempting) for someone to claim that a deceased person agreed to an adoption that never took place, a court may require that the agreement to adopt be proven by clear and convincing evidence rather than by the lower standard of preponderance of the evidence.

equitable adoption
For purposes of inheritance, a child will be considered the adopted child of a person who made a contract to adopt the child but failed to go through the formal adoption procedures.

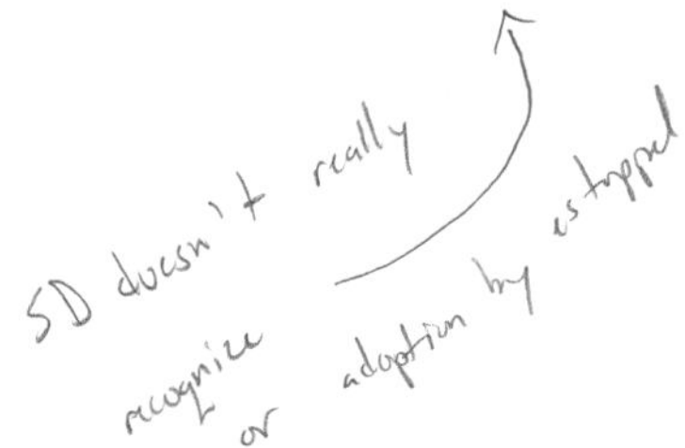

Some courts will grant inheritance rights *even if there was no initial agreement to adopt.* If clear evidence exists that the deceased treated the child as his or her own in every way, a court might rule that a contract to adopt was *implied.* When the deceased dies intestate, equitable adoption status will be accorded the child so that he or she will have full inheritance rights from the deceased.

ASSIGNMENT 15.21

To what extent, if at all, does your state recognize equitable adoption or adoption by estoppel? (See General Instructions for the Court-Opinion Assignment in Appendix A.)

ASSIGNMENT 15.22

Contact a paralegal, an attorney, or a legal secretary in your state who has worked on adoption cases in the past. Obtain answers to the following questions. (See General Instructions for the Systems Assignment in Appendix A.)

1. How many adoption cases have you worked on?
2. How many of them have been uncontested?
3. Approximately how long does it take to process an uncomplicated, uncontested adoption?
4. Is there a difference between working on an adoption case and working on another kind of case in the law office? If so, what is the difference?
5. What are the major steps for processing an adoption in this state? What documents must be filed? What court appearances must be made? Etc.
6. What formbook or other treatise do you use, if any, that is helpful? What software?
7. Does your office have its own internal manual that covers any aspect of adoption practice?
8. In an adoption case, what is the division of labor among the attorney, the paralegal, and the legal secretary?

WRONGFUL ADOPTION

wrongful adoption
A tort action seeking damages for wrongfully stating or failing to disclose to prospective adoptive parents available facts on the health or other condition of the adoptee that would be relevant to the decision on whether to adopt.

For a discussion of the tort of **wrongful adoption,** covering the failure to disclose relevant information to the adoptive parents, see chapter 17.

SUMMARY

There are three main kinds of adoptions. First is an agency adoption, where a child is placed for adoption by a private or public agency. Second is an independent/private adoption, where a natural parent places a child for adoption with the adoptive parents, often through an intermediary such as an attorney and after an investigation by an adoption agency. In such an arrangement, any payment to the natural mother beyond covering her expenses constitutes illegal baby buying. Third is a black market adoption, where illegal payments are made to the natural mother beyond her expenses.

A court will allow an adoption if it is in the best interests of the child. In making this determination, a number of factors are considered: the petitioner's age, marital status, health, religion, economic status, home environment, and lifestyle. Race can be considered, but it cannot be the reason for the delay or denial of an adoption. If the child is old enough, his or her preference will usually be considered. States differ on whether homosexuals can adopt minors or homosexual adults.

An adoption must follow strict procedures. The court must have subject matter jurisdiction. Proper venue must be selected. The petition must contain the required information. The natural parents must be notified of the proceeding and must consent to the adoption unless their parental rights have been terminated because of conduct that clearly demonstrates an intention to relinquish parental duties. The Interstate Compact on the Placement of Children facilitates interstate adoptions. The Adoption and Safe Families Act requires regularly scheduled hearings on whether children in foster homes can be returned to their natural parents.

A child does not have standing to petition a court to terminate the parental rights of his or her parent. Under certain circumstances, a parent will be given the right to revoke an earlier consent to the adoption. An agency investigates the prospective adoptive parents and reports back to the court. An interlocutory decree of adoption is then made by the court, which becomes final within a designated period of time. If a father wants to be notified of the proposed adoption of the child he had with an unmarried woman, he must register with the putative father registry.

Once the adoption becomes final, the adopted child is treated the same as a natural child with respect to inheritance rights, support rights, etc. In a traditional adoption, the records are sealed, and matters such as the identity of the natural parents are kept confidential except in relatively rare circumstances. Some states have created active or passive reunion registries that can be the basis of the release of identifying information about adoptees and biological parents. In an open adoption, there may be varying degrees of contact between a natural parent and the child after the adoption becomes final.

An equitable adoption occurs when a person dies before fulfilling a contract to adopt a child and when unfairness can be avoided only by treating the child as having been adopted for purposes of inheritance. The failure of an adoption agency to give available information about the health of the prospective adoptee might constitute the tort of wrongful adoption.

KEY CHAPTER TERMINOLOGY

custody
guardianship
ward
termination of parental rights
adoption
paternity
foster care
stepparent
agency adoption
independent adoption
black market adoption
second-parent adoption
subject matter jurisdiction
choice of venue
petition
Interstate Compact on the Placement of Children
unfit
unemancipated
nonage
standing
interlocutory
putative father registry
reunion registry
contact veto
open adoption
equitable adoption
wrongful adoption

ETHICS IN PRACTICE

You are a paralegal working at the law office of Daniel Johnson. The office takes adoption cases. While working on one of these cases, you learn that Mr. Johnson has told the birth mother that she can have a job as receptionist at the law firm if she agrees to give up her baby for adoption to one of the firm's clients. You are asked to interview the birth mother for this job. During the interview, you learn that she is clearly not qualified for the job and that the only reason she is giving up her baby for adoption is that she needs the job. You do not say anything to anyone about her suitability for the job or her hesitancy about going through with the adoption. Any ethical problems?

ON THE NET: MORE ON ADOPTION

National Adoption Information Clearinghouse
http://www.calib.com/naic/index.htm

Adoption and Foster Care: Analysis and Reporting System
http://www.acf.dhhs.gov/programs/cb/afcars/index.html

Adoption Resource Guide
http://www.wendys.com/community/adoption/resource_guide.html

Evan B. Donaldson Adoption Institute
http://www.adoptioninstitute.org

Adoption Reunion Registry (Georgia)
www.georgiaagape.org/adoptioninfo/adoptionreunion.htm

National Council for Adoption
http://www.ncfa-usa.org

American Academy of Adoption Attorneys
http://adoptionattorneys.org

Putative Father Registry (Illinois)
http://www.state.il.us/dcfs/putative.htm

CHAPTER

THE NEW SCIENCE OF MOTHERHOOD

CHAPTER OUTLINE

INTRODUCTION

Between 10 and 15 percent of couples trying to conceive—approximately 5 million couples—have fertility problems. Infertility exists when a couple has not conceived in over a year in spite of having sexual relations without contraceptives. Male infertility accounts for about a third of the cases due to low sperm count, poor semen motility, and the effects of sexually transmitted diseases. Female infertility accounts for about another third due to blocked fallopian tubes, dysfunctional ovaries, hormonal imbalance, and the effects of sexually transmitted diseases. The other third is due to combined male and female problems and to unknown causes.

assisted reproductive technologies (ART)
Treatments or procedures in which eggs are surgically removed from a woman's ovaries and combined with sperm to help a woman become pregnant.

One of the methods of treatment is called **assisted reproductive technologies (ART),** which bypass sexual intercourse. ART consists of treatments or procedures in which eggs are surgically removed from a woman's ovaries and combined with sperm to help a woman become pregnant. (See Exhibit 16.1 for definitions of the relevant terminology.) In 1996, approximately 65,000 ART treatment cycles were carried out at 300 programs in the United States.[1] This is an area in which the science of motherhood (called by some the "ovarian Olympics") is moving much faster than the law. Increasingly, courts are faced with legal issues for which there are no precedents.

[1] Carl Coleman, *Procreative Liberty. . .*, 84 Minnesota Law Review 55, 58 (1999).

Exhibit 16.1 Terminology: The Biology of Reproduction

cervix The narrow, outer end of the uterus; the part of the uterus that protrudes into the cavity of the vagina.

cryopreservation Freezing embryos for transfer or implantation at a later time.

conception Fertilization; the union of a sperm and an ovum; the formation of a viable zygote by the union of a sperm and an ovum.

egg An unfertilized female reproductive cell; also called an *ovum* or *oocyte*.

embryo An egg that has been fertilized by a sperm in the early stage of development; the product of conception from the second to the eighth week of pregnancy.

fallopian tube The passageway for the eggs from the ovary to the uterus; also called *uterine tube* or *oviduct*.

fertilization Conception; the initial union of a sperm and an ovum (egg) that becomes an embryo.

fetus A developing organism—the unborn offspring—from the eighth week after conception until birth.

gamete A reproductive cell, either a sperm or an egg; a reproductive cell with a specified number of chromosomes; a mature sperm or egg that is capable of fusing with the gamete of the opposite sex to produce a fertilized egg.

gene A hereditary unit on a chromosome; an element of the germ plasm that has a specific hereditary function determined by a DNA sequence.

genetic Pertaining to genes.

gestation Pregnancy; the period of development in the uterus from conception to birth.

gonad A gland that produces gametes. Gonads include an ovary and a testis.

oocyte The female reproductive cell, also called an *egg*.

ovum An egg; a female reproductive cell. (Plural, *ova*.)

ovary One of the two female sex or reproductive glands that produce eggs; female sex cells.

ovulation The release of a mature egg from the ovary.

ovum A female gamete or reproductive cell.

pregnancy The period of development of the fetus from conception to birth.

preembryo (pre-embryo) The four to eight-cell stage of a developing fertilized egg. ("The term 'pre-embryo' refers to that period of development from the end of the process of fertilization until the appearance of a single primitive streak, a period that lasts approximately fourteen days." Howard Jones, *And Just What Is a Pre-Embryo?,* 52 Fertility & Sterility 189, 190 (1989).)

pre-zygote An egg that has been penetrated by sperm but has not yet joined genetic material; also called a *preembryo*. The embryo proper develops only after implantation.

procreate To reproduce, to bring forth offspring.

semen Sperm and other secretions expelled through the male reproductive tract.

sperm The male gamete or reproductive cell; a mature male germ cell.

uterus A hollow, pear-shaped organ that holds a fertilized ovum during pregnancy.

viable Able to live outside the womb indefinitely; able to live outside the womb indefinitely by natural or artificial means.

zygote A cell formed by the union of a male sex cell and a female sex cell.

The largest category of ART methods (70 percent) is **in vitro fertilization (IVF),** sometimes referred to as fertilization "in a glass" or conception "in a test tube." IVF consists of the surgical removal of a woman's eggs, their fertilization with a man's sperm in a petri dish in a laboratory, and the transfer of the resulting embryo into the uterus through the cervix. The cost of each IVF cycle can be between $8,000 and $10,000. Over 300,000 children in the world have been born through IVF since 1978, when the first child, Louise Brown, was born in England using this method. In the United States, over 45,000 babies have been born using IVF since it was first introduced in 1981.[2]

in vitro fertilization (IVF)
The surgical removal of a woman's eggs and their fertilization with a man's sperm in the laboratory.

Here is how a recent court opinion described the IVF procedure:

[2]American Society for Reproductive Medicine, http://www.asrm.com/Patients/faqs.html.

> IVF involves injecting the woman with fertility drugs in order to stimulate production of eggs which can be surgically retrieved or harvested. After the eggs are removed, they are combined in a petri dish with sperm produced by the man, on the same day as the egg removal, in an effort to fertilize the eggs. If fertilization between any of the eggs and sperm occurs, preembryos are formed that are held in a petri dish for one or two days until a decision can be made as to which preembryos will be used immediately and which will be frozen and stored by the clinic for later use. Preembryos that are to be utilized immediately are not frozen.[3]

In most IVF procedures, the fertilized egg is implanted in the uterus of the woman from whom the egg was taken. (If they are transferred to the uterus of *another* woman, a surrogacy arrangement is involved, as we will see later.)

Suppose that a woman's eggs are not usable. Assume that she is able to carry a child, but not with her own egg. One of her options is to be implanted with the egg of someone else—an *egg donor*—with whom her husband's sperm is joined via IVF. Just as high-quality sperm donors are in demand (see chapter 13 on paternity), so, too, there is competition for egg donors that meet certain criteria. Ads are placed in college newspapers that urge female students to "donate eggs to pay for college." More dramatically, in 1999, the following ad was placed in several Ivy League college newspapers such as those at Harvard and Yale:

EGG DONOR NEEDED
Large Financial Incentive
Intelligent, Athletic Egg Donor Needed
for Loving Family
You must be at least 5′10″
Have a 1400 SAT score
$50,000
Free Medical Screening
All Expenses Paid

The ad was eventually given national publicity and generated hundreds of responses from women claiming to meet the requisite qualifications. Soon thereafter another ad appeared that sought a "Caucasian" with "proven college level athletic ability." The price for the right woman was $100,000. A more typical fee for an egg donor would be in the range of $2,000 to $3,000. For an example of a fertility service that offers to find sperm and egg donors (with or without their photographs), see the Options National Fertility Register on the Internet at http://www.fertilityoptions.com.

In addition to IVF, other major ART methods include:

- *Artificial insemination:* using a catheter (tube) to inject semen through the cervix directly into the uterus without sexual contact; the semen can be from the father or from a donor (see the discussion of artificial insemination at the beginning of chapter 13).
- *Gamete intrafallopian transfer (GIFT):* surgically removing eggs from a woman's ovary, combining the eggs with sperm, and, using a laparoscope, placing the unfertilized eggs and the sperm directly into the fallopian tube, where they will fertilize and travel into the uterus.
- *Zygote intrafallopian transfer (ZIFT):* surgically removing eggs from a woman's ovary, fertilizing them with a man's sperm in a laboratory, and transferring the resulting zygote directly into the fallopian tube through a small incision in her abdomen (combining IVF and GIFT).
- *Embryo transplant:* placing a fertile woman's embryo (an egg that has been fertilized via IVF) into the uterus of an infertile woman (this method is also called *embryo transfer, ovum transfer,* or *ovum transplant*).

---

[3] *A.Z. v. B.Z.,* 431 Mass. 150, 152, 725 N.E.2d 1051, 1053 (2000).

As indicated, the new science of motherhood has generated many legal issues of first impression—those that the courts have had to face for the first time. Among the areas of controversy have been the status of frozen embryos in a divorce, the ethical propriety of stem-cell research, and the legality of surrogacy contracts.

THE STATUS OF FROZEN EMBRYOS

Some embryos resulting from in vitro fertilization are not immediately implanted into the uterus. Through cryopreservation, embryos can be frozen for transfer or implantation at a later time. Between 80,000 and 100,000 frozen embryos or preembryos are in storage throughout the country.

Suppose that a husband and wife file for divorce before all their frozen embryos are used. Who receives "custody" of the embryos? Who "owns" them? Are they subject to property division along with everything else the parties acquired during the marriage?

The problem arises when the divorcing parties disagree about what should be done with the embryos. Suppose that the husband wants them destroyed because he does not want to become the father of a child with his soon-to-be ex-wife, but she wants them kept alive so that they can be implanted in her at a later time. Can he be forced to become a father against his will? In a different context, the courts have held that a man cannot force a woman whom he has impregnated to have an abortion. Can he force a laboratory to destroy a frozen embryo that the woman wants to preserve?

The first major case in this area of the law arose in Tennessee: *Davis v. Davis.*[4] Junior Lewis Davis sought a divorce from his wife, Mary Sue Davis. The parties were able to agree on all the terms of dissolution except one. Who was to have custody of seven frozen embryos (referred to by the court as preembryos) stored in a Knoxville fertility clinic that had attempted to assist the Davises in achieving a much-wanted pregnancy during a happier period of their relationship? Mary did not want to use the frozen embryos herself but wanted to donate them to a childless couple. Junior was adamantly opposed to such donation; he wanted the embryos destroyed. When the Davises enrolled in the IVF program at the Knoxville clinic, the agreement they signed did not specify what disposition should be made of any unused embryos in the cryopreservation facility. Nor were there any Tennessee statutes on what to do in this situation.

The Tennessee court decided to establish its own guidelines on what to do when parties cannot agree:

- The party wishing to avoid procreation should ordinarily prevail, assuming the other party has a reasonable possibility of achieving parenthood by means other than the use of the frozen embryos in question.
- If no other reasonable alternatives exist, the argument in favor of using the embryos to achieve pregnancy should be considered.
- If, however, the party seeking control of the embryos intends merely to donate them to another couple, the objecting party has the greater interest and should prevail.

Using these guidelines in the *Davis* case, Junior Lewis Davis prevailed, since Mary Sue Davis did not want to use the embryos herself. The embryos should be discarded.

A much different result would have been reached if the *Davis* case had arisen in Louisiana. A statute in Louisiana specifies that a "human embryo" is

---

[4] 842 S.W.2d 588 (Tenn. 1992).

a fertilized "human" ovum "with certain rights granted by law." The principles laid out in the Louisiana statute are as follows:

- "A viable in vitro fertilized human ovum is a juridical person which shall not be intentionally destroyed."
- If the IVF patients "renounce, by notarial act, their parental rights for in utero implantation, then the in vitro fertilized human ovum shall be available for adoptive implantation in accordance with written procedures of the facility where it is housed or stored."
- The in vitro fertilization patients may renounce their parental rights in favor of another married couple, but only if the other couple is willing and able to receive the in vitro fertilized ovum.
- No compensation shall be paid or received by either couple to renounce parental rights.
- Disputes between parties should be resolved in the "best interest" of the in vitro fertilized ovum.[5]

Hence in the dispute between Mary Sue Davis (who wanted to keep the embryos alive for adoption) and Junior Lewis Davis (who wanted them destroyed), Mary Sue would have won if the case had been brought in Louisiana. It could hardly be said that the "best interest" of the embryos would be to destroy them.

As a result of the difficulties that arose in the *Davis* case, IVF contracts that couples sign with fertility clinics today almost always specify what should happen to unused frozen embryos or preembryos. (Florida *requires* couples to execute a written agreement on how "eggs, sperm, and preembryos" are to be disposed of in the event of death, divorce, or other unforeseen event.[6] Courts are generally inclined to enforce such an agreement unless they are faced with a statute as stringent as Louisiana's.

In a recent New York case, the parties underwent ten unsuccessful attempts to have a child through IVF at a cost in excess of $75,000. The agreement they signed said, "In the event that we no longer wish to initiate a pregnancy or are unable to make a decision" on the disposition of their frozen preembryos, they should be donated to the IVF clinic for research purposes and then disposed of by the clinic. After the parties divorced, the ex-wife wanted the preembryos implanted in her, claiming that it would be her only chance for genetic motherhood. The ex-husband, however, objected and asked the court to enforce the agreement so that the IVF clinic would dispose of them. The court ruled that the agreement was binding and should be enforced.[7]

While most states (other than Louisiana) would follow this position, there are limitations. In a Massachusetts case, for example, the court said that it will not enforce an agreement on the disposition of frozen preembryos if it has the effect of forcing one of the parties to become a parent against his or her will. The ex-wife in the case wanted to use the preembryos for implantation. The ex-husband objected. The court ruled in his favor even though the agreement they signed appeared to favor the option she now wanted. The court said that it

> would not enforce an agreement that would compel one donor to become a parent against his or her will. As a matter of public policy, we conclude that forced procreation is not an area amenable to judicial enforcement. . . . We would not order either a husband or a wife to do what is necessary to conceive a child or to prevent conception, any more than we would order either party to do what is necessary to make the other happy.[8]

---

[5]Louisiana Statutes Annotated §§ 121-31.
[6]Florida Statutes Annotated § 742.17.
[7]*Kass v. Kass,* 91 N.Y.2d 554, 696 N.E.2d 174, 673 N.Y.S.2d 350 (1998).
[8]*A.Z. v. B.Z.,* 431 Mass. 150, 159, 161, 725 N.E.2d 1051, 1057-58 (2000).

ASSIGNMENT 16.1

George's will leaves his girlfriend fifteen tubes of his frozen sperm, stating that he hopes his girlfriend will have his child. After his death, an older child from a previous marriage objects to this clause in the will and wants the court to order the sperm destroyed.

a. How should the court rule? (See General Instructions for the Legal-Analysis Assignment in Appendix A.)
b. If this case arose in your state, how would a court in your state rule? Check statutes and case law. (See General Instructions for the State-Code and Court-Opinion Assignments in Appendix A.)

STEM-CELL RESEARCH

The human embryo contains *stem cells* that can grow into (i.e., differentiate into) other cells that make up the heart, brain, kidney, and other organs. In a laboratory, stem cells can be removed from the embryo and grown into *cell lines* that multiply indefinitely. These laboratory-grown cells have the potential of being used to repair or replace damaged tissue or organs and to treat or cure numerous diseases such as Alzheimer's. To remove stem cells for this purpose, however, the embryo must be destroyed. Opponents argue that the human embryo is the earliest stage of human life and, therefore, must be protected. Some church leaders and pro-life activists believe it is morally wrong to destroy embryos because life begins at fertilization.

Scientists have two main sources of embryos from which they can extract stem cells:

- Embryos produced for in vitro fertilization (IVF) procedures but that are scheduled for destruction because the couples no longer need or want them
- Embryos produced for the sole purpose of scientific research rather than for use in IVF procedures

Conservatives oppose the destruction of both categories of embryos. They consider the latter particularly heinous since the embryos that are destroyed are not surplus embryos. Rather, they are created from donated eggs and sperm for the express purpose of medical experimentation.

Others, however, take the position that embryos not needed for IVF and already scheduled for destruction should be available for research. This is the official policy of the United States government in its guidelines on research projects that can receive federal funding. It will not fund research on embryos created solely for medical research.

Stem cells are not limited to embryos. Adult stem cells can be found in blood, skeletal muscle, skin, and elsewhere. These cells can be extracted without destroying anything. Yet adult stem cells are more difficult than embryonic stem cells to grow in the laboratory. Also, embryonic stem cells are considered more versatile and promising for medical research.

Although the government will not fund research on embryos created solely for research, there is nothing to prevent private industry from conducting such research on its own. Some fear that even more drastic research is taking place. In his address to the nation announcing the federal government's policy on funding embryonic stem cell research, President George W. Bush said:

> As the discoveries of modern science create tremendous hope, they also lay vast ethical mine fields. As the genius of science extends the horizons of what we can do, we increasingly confront complex questions about what we should

do. We have arrived at that brave new world that seemed so distant in 1932, when Aldous Huxley wrote about human beings created in test tubes in what he called a "hatchery."

In recent weeks, we learned that scientists have created human embryos in test tubes solely to experiment on them. This is deeply troubling, and a warning sign that should prompt all of us to think through these issues very carefully.

Embryonic stem cell research is at the leading edge of a series of moral hazards. The initial stem cell researcher was at first reluctant to begin his research, fearing it might be used for human cloning. Scientists have already cloned a sheep. Researchers are telling us the next step could be to clone human beings to create individual designer stem cells, essentially to grow another you, to be available in case you need another heart or lung or liver.

I strongly oppose human cloning, as do most Americans. We recoil at the idea of growing human beings for spare body parts, or creating life for our convenience. And while we must devote enormous energy to conquering disease, it is equally important that we pay attention to the moral concerns raised by the new frontier of human embryo stem cell research. Even the most noble ends do not justify any means.[9]

ASSIGNMENT 16.2

Do you agree with the federal government's decision not to fund research on embryos that are created solely for medical science? Should there be limitations imposed on private funding of such research?

SURROGACY CONTRACTS

surrogate mother
A woman who is artificially inseminated with the semen of a man who is not her husband, with the understanding that she will surrender the baby at birth to the father and his wife.

broker
An individual who coordinates various service providers needed to accomplish a legal objective such as an adoption.

One of the most dramatic developments in this area of the law has been the use of a **surrogate mother.** She is a woman who arranges to become pregnant, usually by artificial insemination, so that she can give the child to an infertile woman to raise. We do not have accurate statistics on the number of births that occur through the use of a surrogate. In 1993, the Center for Surrogate Parenting estimated that 4,000 surrogate births had occurred in the United States.[10] There is a great deal of media interest in surrogacy, particularly when something goes wrong, such as the refusal of the surrogate to relinquish the child. The number of surrogate births is probably increasing every year, as evidenced by the large number of World Wide Web sites devoted to attorneys, doctors, agencies, and other intermediaries who are available to bring all the parties together and perform the various services that are required for the process. (An individual who coordinates the required service providers is called a **broker.**)

The Bible contains one of the earliest records of surrogacy when Abram's wife gave him her slave girl:

> Abram's wife Sarai had not born him any children. But she had an Egyptian slave girl named Hagar, and so she said to Abram, "The Lord has kept me from having children. Why don't you sleep with my slave girl? Perhaps she can have a child for me." *Genesis* 16:1–2 (NIV).

Today surrogates offer their services by using the assisted reproductive technologies (ART) summarized at the beginning of the chapter, particularly IVF. The natural insemination method used by Abram and Hagar is relatively rare.

There are two major categories of surrogates:

---

[9]President George W. Bush, www.whitehouse.gov/news/releases/2001/08/20010809-2.html.
[10]Marsha Garrison, *Law Making for Baby Making,* 113 Harvard Law Review 835, 851 (2000).

- The surrogate who supplies the egg and, therefore, is genetically related to the child (this category of surrogate is sometimes called the *genetic mother*)
- The surrogate who carries an embryo that was formed from the egg of another woman; since someone else's fertilized egg was implanted in the surrogate's uterus, the surrogate is not genetically related to the child (this category of surrogate is sometimes called a *gestational carrier, a gestational surrogate,* or a *surrogate host*)

Surrogacy comes into existence by agreement. An unpregnant woman enters a contract to become pregnant, to give birth to a child, and then to relinquish all parental rights to the couple (usually a husband and wife), who will then adopt the child. The couple agrees to pay her medical and related expenses. In addition, some surrogates are paid a fee, often between $10,000 and $20,000. When a fee is to be paid, critics of surrogacy contracts deride the arrangement as a "womb for hire."

Unfortunately, surrogacy contracts do not always operate as planned. Suppose, for example, that the surrogate mother changes her mind and refuses to relinquish the child upon birth? What law applies? Different states answer this question differently. In some states, surrogacy contracts are illegal. In New York, for example, "[s]urrogate parenting contracts are hereby declared contrary to the public policy of this state, and are void and unenforceable."[11] In such states, it is against public policy to give birth to a child with the sole purpose of surrendering it for adoption. Some states also object to the payment of an adoption fee other than to cover the expenses involved, as we saw in chapter 15 on adoption. The following report provides an overview of how the courts and legislatures have attempted to respond to this new area of the law.

[11]McKinney's Domestic Relations Law § 122.

Surrogate Parenting

D. Bennett, *Surrogate Parenting* (1988) (Background Paper 88-2 prepared for the Legislative Counsel Bureau of Nevada)

I. Introduction

In March 1987, the nation's attention focused on a breach of contract battle underway in New Jersey. The contract in question was between Elizabeth and William Stern and Mary Beth Whitehead (now Mary Beth Whitehead-Gould). The Sterns had contracted with Ms. Whitehead in 1985 to act as a surrogate mother. [Under the terms of the contract, Ms. Whitehead was to be artificially inseminated with Mr. Stern's sperm, become pregnant, give birth to a baby, turn it over to the Sterns, and cooperate in the termination of her parental rights. Mrs. Stern would then adopt the baby.] Upon the birth of the baby—known as Baby M in the case—Ms. Whitehead reconsidered and refused to relinquish her parental rights. The Sterns then sued in an attempt to hold Ms. Whitehead to the terms of the contract.

On March 31, 1987, a New Jersey trial court upheld the contract, granted permanent custody to the Sterns, permitted Mrs. Stern to adopt the child, and denied any rights to Ms. Whitehead. On February 3, 1988, the New Jersey Supreme Court approved only the custody portion of the lower court's decision, ruling that surrogate parenting contracts fall under the New Jersey "baby-selling" statutes and are therefore illegal.[1] [In spite of the illegality of the contract, the court ruled that it would be in the best interests of Baby M to be in the custody of her biological father and his wife.]

The publicity surrounding this case led to a flurry of activity in legislative bodies around the country as pro- and anti-surrogacy groups attempted to sway policymaking bodies to one side or the other. . . .

II. Definitions

Although the term surrogate parenting has become widely used since the Baby M case, it can refer to

[1]*In the Matter of Baby M,* 109 N.J. 396, 537 A.2d 1227 (1988).

continued

Surrogate Parenting—*Continued*

more than one method of achieving parenthood. In addition, the parties involved in a surrogacy contract may not necessarily be limited to a married couple contracting with a single woman. The parties could involve a married surrogate mother, a single father, or single-sex couples. However, for ease of discussion, . . . the terms "married couple," "husband," and "wife" will be used, keeping in mind that a broader definition may apply to these words.

A. Methods

Four general methods of surrogate parenting are recognized. These methods are:

1. *Artificial Insemination by Husband (AIH).* The AIH method is an arrangement in which the surrogate, a woman other than the wife of the sperm donor, is artificially inseminated with the sperm of the husband of a married couple.
2. In Vitro Fertilization (IVF). In vitro fertilization is a process by which a sperm and an egg are joined in a laboratory and the fertilized egg is implanted in the surrogate.
3. *Artificial Insemination by Donor (AID[1]).* The AID[1] method is a technique in which the surrogate is artificially inseminated with the sperm of a donor other than the contracting male. Such sperm is typically a specimen obtained from a sperm bank.*
4. *Natural Insemination (NI).* The NI method involves a situation where sexual intercourse occurs between the surrogate and the husband of a married couple.

Of the four methods, AIH is the most common and NI is the least. Sometimes the IVF and AID[1] methods are chosen in surrogate parenting situations, but not as frequently as AIH. . . . Because AIH is the most common method chosen in surrogate parenting agreements, the definition will be applied to the term surrogate parenting in this [discussion].

B. Agreements

The agreement between the surrogate mother and the intended parents takes one of two forms: (1) commercial; or (2) noncommercial. Both agreements involve similar factors. A couple contracts with a woman to bear a child for them. The woman agrees to be artificially inseminated with the husband's sperm, carry the child to term and surrender her parental rights to the biological father upon the birth of the child.

Once the husband has full parental rights to the child [upon birth], the wife (technically the child's stepmother) begins adoption proceedings. Some . . . [states allow] the wife to forgo formal adoption procedures and obtain a substitute birth certificate from a court of competent jurisdiction. In return, the couple agrees to pay all of the surrogate's medical expenses and other necessary expenses (e.g., maternity clothing).

The difference between a commercial and a noncommercial agreement centers on whether a fee is paid to the surrogate mother. If a fee—usually around $10,000—is paid, then the agreement is considered to be commercial. However, many surrogacy agreements are between family members or friends and do not involve the payment of a fee. These agreements are the noncommercial contracts.

A major argument in the courts and the legislatures involves the nature of this fee. Is it a fee for the surrogate mother's services or is it a fee in exchange for the surrender of her parental rights? . . .

Another factor in surrogacy contracts is the broker. Either a private agency or a lawyer, the broker is a third party who coordinates a surrogate parenting agreement. Although a broker receives a fee (in the $10,000–$20,000 range), a broker could be used in both commercial and noncommercial arrangements. However, most arrangements made through a broker include a fee paid to the surrogate mother.

III. Reasons for Choosing Surrogate Parenting Agreements

According to a study of surrogacy recently completed in Wisconsin, the demand for surrogate mothers stems primarily from female infertility. The National Center for Health Statistics estimates that 10 to 15 percent of all married couples are infertile (defined as partners who are sexually active, not using contraception, and unable to conceive after at least one year). The Center excludes the surgically sterile from its statistics. The Wisconsin study also cites evidence that suggests the number of infertile women is on the increase due to the use of intrauterine birth control devices, greater incidence of sexually transmitted diseases, previous abortions and the postponement of childbearing to establish careers. Studies indicate that women who delay having children have a greater risk of being infertile, bearing children with birth defects, and/or being physically impaired. The most common treatments for female infertility are drugs and surgery. Until recently, when these treatments failed, adoption

*AID[2] is a technique in which the *wife* is artificially inseminated with the sperm of a donor other than her husband. Such sperm is also typically a specimen obtained from a sperm bank.

of an unrelated child was the only alternative available.

Couples who want children, but cannot conceive, usually consider adoption. The Wisconsin study noted that, despite a marked increase in the number of live births to single women, fewer unrelated individuals are adopted. Adoption experts believe that the increasing willingness of single mothers to keep their children is a significant factor in limiting the number of infants available for adoption. The stigma once attached to single mothers has diminished. Peers and relatives often encourage single mothers to keep their babies. Medical personnel and social workers are less likely to encourage women to give babies up for adoption.

Laws have changed in recent years to allow single mothers more time to make or revoke a decision to allow adoption. Consequently, couples often cite long waiting periods and other obstacles to adoption (such as the age limit placed on prospective parents) as reasons for seeking surrogate mothers. [R. Roe, *Childbearing by Contract 4* (Wisconsin Legislative Bureau, Mar. 1988).]

Not all couples who contract with a surrogate have failed at adoption. Some couples would rather be childless than adopt an unrelated child. For such families, a genetic link to their child is of primary importance. For example, William Stern lost most of his family in Adolf Hitler's holocaust and wanted a child biologically linked to him. Newspaper interviews of intended fathers confirm the importance some of them place on a biological link when seeking surrogates. One father favored a surrogate birth because "that child will be biologically half-mine" while another father stated that "we believe strongly in heredity."

IV. Major Arguments for and against Surrogate Parenting

A review of the literature on surrogate parenting reveals several common policy positions on each side of this issue.

A. Supporting Arguments

Those who support surrogacy contracts and the regulation of them generally cite the following:

- A limitation placed on the fees charged by brokers and the licensing and regulation of brokers will ensure competency, honesty and legitimacy in this process.
- Due to the ever-decreasing number of babies available for adoption and the ever-increasing technology in the area of human reproduction, couples who desperately want children will continue to seek out surrogate mothers. Consequently, some form of protection must be provided for the couple, the surrogate mother, and the resulting child.
- Proper examination of both couple and surrogate as provided in state law would ensure:
  1. That the couple is emotionally and financially ready to bear the responsibility of parenthood.
  2. That the couple is truly in need of this service, such as when the wife is unable to carry a child to term.
  3. That the woman who will bear the child is emotionally, physically, and psychologically able to carry the child and to give up her rights to the child at birth.

The majority of surrogate contracts are completed without [controversy]. Only a small percentage of surrogate mothers have refused to surrender the resulting babies. . . .

B. Opposing Arguments

Those people who advocate a ban on surrogacy contracts argue that:

- Children will be psychologically damaged when they discover that they were "bought."
- Surrogate parenting arrangements are in violation of the Thirteenth Amendment of the United States Constitution, which applies to slavery and can be interpreted to forbid the buying and selling of people.
- Surrogate parenting will become another form of economic exploitation of rich people over poor. As exemplified by the Baby M affair, the adoptive couples tend to have an economic and educational advantage over the surrogate. [A] study of potential and existing surrogate mothers also indicates that most of the women are unemployed or on some form of public assistance and only have a high school diploma. Thus, surrogate parenting arrangements will serve to create a class of "womb-sellers."
- There are plenty of nonwhite babies, older children, and special needs children available for adoption.
- Women will be forced—not because they choose, but because the contract requires—to abort fetuses upon demand or to become pregnant again in the case of a miscarriage.

V. Issues in State Law

According to the Wisconsin study of surrogacy, court decisions and discussions of surrogacy indicated that four existing areas of law affect surrogate parenting agreements. These areas are (1) adoption and termination of parental rights; (2) artificial insemination and legal paternity; (3) child custody; and (4) contracts. . . .

continued

Surrogate Parenting—*Continued*

A. Adoption Laws

Two aspects of many state adoption laws may restrict or prevent surrogate parenting agreements. One forbids compensation in exchange for the consent to an adoption, and the other forbids consent to an adoption to be given prior to the birth of the child.

At least 24 states . . . prohibit the payment of compensation for adoptions. Often called baby-selling laws, these statutes range from those prohibiting all payments to those allowing payment of certain expenses. Nevada, for example, forbids the payment of a fee in return for the mother's agreement to terminate her parental rights of the child.

While surrogacy opponents favor the use of adoption statutes to control it, proponents maintain that modern anti-baby-selling laws predate surrogate parenting and were designed to protect unwed mothers. Under a surrogacy agreement, the intended father is also the biological father; therefore, how can he buy his own child? Also, proponents argue surrogates have voluntarily agreed to surrender the child. She is not doing so under pregnancy related stress. Finally, the fees are paid primarily to replace lost work time or pain and suffering.

All 50 states . . . have laws that prohibit a mother from granting consent to adoption before a child's birth or for some period of time after birth. Waiting periods range up to as much as 20 days (Pennsylvania). A mother's consent to surrender a newborn for adoption is not valid in Nevada until at least 72 hours after birth.

However, as with baby-selling laws, consent laws were designed to protect unwed mothers. The decisions facing an unwed mother are not like those facing the surrogate mother who has voluntarily chosen to bear children for another couple.

B. Paternity Laws

Paternity laws may also affect surrogate arrangements. Some states retain the common law rule that the husband of a woman who gives birth to a child is presumed to be the father. Courts in many of these states will not admit evidence to the contrary. A majority of states now allow a rebuttal to the presumption of paternity, but place a strict burden of proof on the contending party. . . .

Surrogate supporters argue that paternity laws were designed to protect the child, particularly the rights to inheritance, and were not drafted in anticipation of surrogate parenting arrangements. Rights and duties outlined in surrogate agreements fall on the natural father and would secure the child's rights. Critics point out that paternity determinations are made by courts and do not necessarily give custody to one party or the other.

Paternity laws could also affect surrogate arrangements based on the reliance on artificial insemination. Since most surrogate mothers are artificially inseminated, laws on that subject might be relevant. At least 30 states . . . have laws that presume that the husband of the woman being inseminated is the child's father and that relieves the sperm donor of any legal obligation.

Although some critics approve applying artificial insemination law to surrogate agreements, others find the analogy suspect and open to court challenge.

C. Custody Issues

The traditional basis for custody decisions is a determination of the best interest of the child. The standards for judging the suitability of intended parents include marital and family status, mental and physical health, income and property, any history of child abuse or neglect and other relevant facts. In the case of Baby M, custody of the child was awarded to the Sterns because the court felt it was in the best interest of the child. Ms. Whitehead's divorce after 13 years of marriage and subsequent marriage to the father of her unborn child 2 weeks after the divorce were key factors in the court's decision.

A spokesperson for the National Committee for Adoption objects to surrogate contracts because they are not required to take into account the best interest of the child. Unlike normal adoption proceedings, no one screens intended parents. Currently, surrogacy agreements require nothing more than the financial ability to hire a lawyer and pay the surrogate mother.

Supporters of surrogate agreements argue that intended parents should receive the same treatment as ordinary parents, since the only qualification they lack is the physical ability to have children. Supporters also maintain that surrogate agreements are inherently in the best interest of the child because the intended parents have given much thought to their actions and decided that they truly want a child. Adoption proceedings, on the other hand, were devised to provide a permanent home for a child who otherwise would not have one. In a surrogate agreement, the child's home is provided by contract.

D. Contractual Duties

Existing federal and state contract laws do not address the issues of the surrogate's liability or acceptable remedies in case of breach of contract, nor do they address the responsibilities of the intended parents.

Contracts impose a number of duties on one or both of the intended parents. These duties include the payment of expenses and fees and the assumption of responsibility for the child at birth. If the birth mother performs as agreed, does she have recourse if the other party refuses to pay all or part of the expenses and fees? What happens if the intended parents refuse to take the child? Can the surrogate mother sue the natural father for child support?

Some of these issues are already facing state courts. For example, in Texas, a 24-year-old surrogate mother died of heart failure in her eighth month of pregnancy; and in Washington, D.C., a baby born through a surrogate agreement was diagnosed as having acquired immune deficiency syndrome (AIDS). Now, neither the surrogate mother nor contracting parents want the AIDS baby. These issues were not previously addressed in the contracts.

Enforcement of a surrogate mother's duties are even more difficult. She agrees to be inseminated, bear a child and surrender all parental rights. She is also to refrain from sexual intercourse during the insemination period and has the duty to refrain from activities that may harm the fetus. If medical clauses are included in the contract, what recourse do the intended parents have if the surrogate refuses to follow them? If she refuses the insemination, are any expenses refunded to the intended parents? If the surrogate chooses to have an abortion in the first trimester, which is legally her right, can the intended parents sue for expenses? Can they sue for damages if the surrogate decides to keep the child?

Even if the surrogate agreement clears all other legal hurdles, many questions remain about the responsibilities of each party to the contract.

VI. State Regulation

States differ on how to handle surrogacy contracts:

- Some states are silent on the subject. No statutes exist, and no cases have yet been litigated in the courts.
- A few states have outright bans on all commercial and noncommercial surrogacy contracts.
- Some states prohibit commercial surrogacy contracts.
- Some states prohibit fees to the surrogate beyond the expenses involved.
- Some states prohibit fees to [a broker or] intermediary, the person who facilitates the surrogacy arrangement such as by bringing the surrogate and couple together.
- Some states allow surrogacy contracts, but closely regulate the process including medical and psychological screening, home studies, the payment of fees, time periods within which the surrogate can change her mind, the identification of the legal parents, etc.

In August 1988, the National Conference of Commissioners on Uniform State Laws drafted and approved for use in all state legislatures the Uniform Status of Children of Assisted Conception Act. The model act provides two alternatives for consideration by state legislatures: one to regulate surrogate parenting agreements (Alternative A), and the other to ban the agreements (Alternative B). (See Exhibit 16.2.)

Alternative A would allow surrogate parenting contracts and provides a regulatory framework. A court hearing would be held at which both parties would be required to submit medical evidence to prove that the would-be mother cannot bear her own child and that the surrogate mother is mentally and physically fit to bear the child. The proposal also would allow the surrogate mother to pull out of the agreement up to 180 days into her pregnancy.

The opposing language in the act (Alternative B) simply bans all surrogate parenting agreements. It does not make any distinction between commercial and noncommercial contracts; all such contracts are void.

Exhibit 16.2 Uniform Status of Children of Assisted Conception Act

National Conference of Commissioners on Uniform State Laws (1988)

Section 1. Definitions

In this [Act]:

(1) **"Assisted conception"** means a pregnancy resulting from (i) fertilizing an egg of a woman with sperm of a man by means other than sexual intercourse or (ii) implanting an embryo, but the term does not include the pregnancy of a wife resulting from fertilizing her egg with sperm of her husband.

(2) **"Donor"** means an individual [other than a surrogate] who produces egg or sperm used for assisted conception, whether or not payment is made for the egg or sperm used, but does not include a woman who gives birth to a resulting child.

continued

Exhibit 16.2 Uniform Status of Children of Assisted Conception Act—*Continued*

[(3) **"Intended parents"** means a man and woman, married to each other, who enter into an agreement under this [Act] providing that they will be the parents of a child born to a surrogate through assisted conception using egg or sperm of one or both of the intended parents.]
(4) **"Surrogate"** means an adult woman who enters into an agreement to bear a child conceived through assisted conception for intended parents. . . .

Section 2. Maternity

[Except as provided in Sections 5 through 9,] a woman who gives birth to a child is the child's mother. . . .

Section 3. Assisted Conception by Married Woman

[Except as provided in Sections 5 through 9,] the husband of a woman who bears a child through assisted conception is the father of the child, notwithstanding a declaration of invalidity or annulment of the marriage obtained after the assisted conception, unless within two years after learning of the child's birth he commences an action in which the mother and child are parties and in which it is determined that he did not consent to the assisted conception.

Section 4. Parental Status of Donors and Deceased Individuals

[Except as otherwise provided in Sections 5 through 9:]
(a) A donor is not a parent of a child conceived through assisted conception.
(b) An individual who dies before implantation of an embryo, or before a child is conceived other than through sexual intercourse, using the individual's egg sperm, is not a parent of the resulting child. . . .

Alternative A

Comment

A state that chooses Alternative A should also consider Section 1(3) and the bracketed language in Sections 1(2), 2, 3, and 4.

[Secton 5. Surrogacy Agreement

(a) A surrogate, her husband, if she is married, and intended parents may enter into a written agreement whereby the surrogate relinquishes all her rights and duties as a parent of a child to be conceived through assisted conception, and the intended parents may become the parents of the child pursuant to Section 8.
(b) If the agreement is not approved by the court under Section 6 before conception, the agreement is void and the surrogate is the mother of a resulting child and the surrogate's husband, if a party to the agreement, is the father of the child. If the surrogate's husband is not a party to the agreement or the surrogate is unmarried, paternity of the child is governed by [the Uniform Parentage Act]. . . .

Section 6. Petition and Hearing for Approval of Surrogacy Agreement

(a) The intended parents and the surrogate may file a petition in the [appropriate court] to approve a surrogacy agreement if one of them is a resident of this State. The surrogate's husband, if she is married, must join in the petition. A copy of the agreement must be attached to the petition. The court shall name a [guardian ad litem] to represent the interests of a child to be conceived by the surrogate through assisted conception and [shall] [may] appoint counsel to represent the surrogate.
(b) The court shall hold a hearing on the petition and shall enter an order approving the surrogacy agreement, authorizing assisted conception for a period of 12 months after the date of the order, declaring the intended parents to be the parents of a child to be conceived through assisted conception pursuant to the agreement and discharging the guardian ad litem and attorney for the surrogate, upon finding that:

(1) the court has jurisdiction and all parties have submitted to its jurisdiction under subsection (e) and have agreed that the law of this State governs all matters arising under this [Act] and the agreement;
(2) the intended mother is unable to bear a child or is unable to do so without unreasonable risk to an unborn child or to the physical or mental health of the intended mother or child, and the finding is supported by medical evidence;
(3) The [relevant child-welfare agency] has made a home study of the intended parents and the surrogate and a copy of the report of the home study has been filed with the court;
(4) the intended parents, the surrogate, and the surrogate's husband, if she is married, meet the standards of fitness applicable to adoptive parents in this State;
(5) all parties have voluntarily entered into the agreement and understand its terms, nature, and meaning, and the effect of the proceeding;
(6) the surrogate has had at least one pregnancy and delivery and bearing another child will not pose an unreasonable risk to the unborn child or to the physical or mental health of the surrogate or the child, and this finding is supported by medical evidence;
(7) all parties have received counseling concerning the effect of the surrogacy by [a qualified health-care professional or social worker] and a report containing conclusions about the capacity of the parties to enter into and fulfill the agreement has been filed with the court;
(8) a report of the results of any medical or psychological examination or genetic screening agreed to by the parties or required by law has been filed with the court and made available to the parties;
(9) adequate provision has been made for all reasonable health-care costs associated with the surrogacy until the child's birth including responsibility for those costs if the agreement is terminated pursuant to Section 7; and
(10) the agreement will not be substantially detrimental to the interest of any of the affected individuals.

(c) Unless otherwise provided in the surrogacy agreement, all court costs, attorney's fees, and other costs and expenses associated with the proceeding must be assessed against the intended parents.
(d) Notwithstanding any other law concerning judicial proceedings or vital statistics, the court shall conduct all hearings and proceedings under this section in camera. The court shall keep all records of the proceedings confidential and subject to inspection under the same standards applicable to adoptions. At the request of any party, the court shall take steps necessary to ensure that the identities of the parties are not disclosed.
(e) The court conducting the proceedings has exclusive and continuing jurisdiction of all matters arising out of the surrogacy until a child born after entry of an order under this section is 180 days old. . . .

Section 7. Termination of Surrogacy Agreement

(a) After entry of an order under Section 6, but before the surrogate becomes pregnant through assisted conception, the court for cause, or the surrogate, her husband, or the intended parents may terminate the surrogacy agreement by giving written notice of termination to all other parties and filing notice of the termination with the court. Thereupon, the court shall vacate the order entered under Section 6.
(b) A surrogate who has provided an egg for the assisted conception pursuant to an agreement approved under Section 6 may terminate the agreement by filing written notice with the court within 180 days after the last insemination pursuant to the agreement. Upon finding, after notice to the parties to the agreement and hearing, that the surrogate has voluntarily terminated the agreement and understands the nature, meaning, and effect of the termination, the court shall vacate the order entered under Section 6.
(c) The surrogate is not liable to the intended parents for terminating the agreement pursuant to this section. . . .

Section 8. Parentage under Approved Surrogacy Agreement

(a) The following rules of parentage apply to surrogacy agreements approved under Section 6:
(1) Upon birth of a child to the surrogate, the intended parents are the parents of the child and the surrogate and her husband, if she is married, are not parents of the child unless the court vacates the order pursuant to Section 7(b).
(2) If, after notice of termination by the surrogate, the court vacates the order under Section 7(b) the surrogate is the mother of a resulting child, and her husband, if a party to the agreement, is the father. If the surrogate's husband is not a party to the agreement or the surrogate is unmarried, paternity of the child is governed by [the Uniform Parentage Act].
(b) Upon birth of the child, the intended parents shall file a written notice with the court that a child has been born to the surrogate within 300 days after assisted conception. Thereupon, the court shall enter an order directing the [Department of Vital Statistics] to issue a new birth certificate naming the intended parents as parents and to seal the original birth certificate in the records of the [Department of Vital Statistics]. . . .

Section 9. Surrogacy: Miscellaneous Provisions

(a) A surrogacy agreement that is the basis of an order under Section 6 may provide for the payment of consideration.
(b) A surrogacy agreement may not limit the right of the surrogate to make decisions regarding her health care or that of the embryo or fetus.
(c) After the entry of an order under Section 6, marriage of the surrogate does not affect the validity of the order, and her husband's consent to the surrogacy agreement is not required, nor is he the father of a resulting child.
(d) A child born to a surrogate within 300 days after assisted conception pursuant to an order under Section 6 is presumed to result from the assisted conception. The presumption is conclusive as to all persons who have notice of the birth and who do not commence within 180 days after notice, an action to assert the contrary in which the child and the parties to the agreement are named as parties. The action must be commenced in the court that issued the order under Section 6.
(e) A health-care provider is not liable for recognizing the surrogate as the mother before receipt of a copy of the order entered under Section 6 or for recognizing the intended parents as parents after receipt of an order entered under Section 6. . . .]

[End of Alternative A]

Alternative B

Surrogate Agreements

An agreement in which a woman agrees to become a surrogate or to relinquish her rights and duties as parent of a child thereafter conceived through assisted conception is void. However, she is the mother of a resulting child, and her husband, if a party to the agreement, is the father of the child. If her husband is not a party to the agreement or the surrogate is unmarried, paternity of the child is governed by [the Uniform Parentage Act].] . . .

[End of Alternative B]

ASSIGNMENT 16.3

a. Should surrogacy contracts be banned? If not, what kind of regulation is needed? Do you favor the regulation in Alternative A of the Uniform Status of Children of Assisted Conception Act? Why?

b. Do you approve of an advertisement such as the following one placed in the want ad section of the newspaper along with ads for accountants and truck drivers:

continued

CASH AVAILABLE NOW. Married or single women needed as surrogate mothers for couples unable to have children. Conception to be by artificial insemination. We pay well! Contact the Infertility Clinic today.

c. What is the current law in your state on the validity of surrogacy contracts? (See General Instructions for the State-Code Assignment and General Instructions for the Court-Opinion Assignment in Appendix A.)

CASE

Johnson v. Calvert

5 Cal. 4th 84, 851 P.2d 776, 19 Cal. Rptr. 2d 494 (1993)
Supreme Court of California

Background: *This is a case of* ***gestational surrogacy*** *in which the sperm and egg of a couple are combined in vitro in a laboratory and the resulting embryo is then implanted in a surrogate mother who carries the child to term. The surrogate mother gives birth to a child with whom she has no genetic relationship.*

Anna Johnson, a licensed vocational nurse, agreed to become a gestational surrogate. An embryo created by the sperm and egg of Mark and Crispina Calvert was implanted in Johnson. The agreement, however, fell apart while Johnson was still pregnant. Crispina Calvert and Anna Johnson filed separate actions to be declared the mother of the child who was eventually born. (Anna named the child Matthew; the Calverts named him Christopher.) The cases were consolidated. The trial court ruled that Mark and Crispina were the child's "genetic, biological and natural" father and mother. It called Anna a "genetic stranger" to the child. The Court of Appeal affirmed. The case is now on appeal before the Supreme Court of California.

Decision on Appeal: *Judgment affirmed. In a gestational surrogacy contract, the natural mother of the child is the woman whose intent was to raise the child as her own. Only Crispina had this intent.*

Opinion of the Court:

Justice PANELLI delivered the opinion of the court.

In this case we address several of the legal questions raised by recent advances in reproductive technology. When, pursuant to a surrogacy agreement, a zygote* formed of the gametes† of a husband and wife is implanted in the uterus of another woman, who carries the resulting fetus to term and gives birth to a child not genetically related to her, who is the child's "natural mother" under California law? . . . And is such an agreement barred by any public policy of this state? We conclude that the husband and wife are the child's natural parents, and that this result does not offend . . . public policy.

Mark and Crispina Calvert are a married couple who desired to have a child. Crispina was forced to undergo a hysterectomy in 1984. Her ovaries remained capable of producing eggs, however, and the couple eventually considered surrogacy. In 1989 Anna Johnson heard about Crispina's plight from a coworker and offered to serve as a surrogate for the Calverts.

On January 15, 1990, Mark, Crispina, and Anna signed a contract providing that an embryo created by the sperm of Mark and the egg of Crispina would be implanted in Anna and the child born would be taken into Mark and Crispina's home "as their child." Anna agreed she would relinquish "all parental rights" to the child in favor of Mark and Crispina. In return, Mark and Crispina would pay Anna $10,000 in a series of installments, the last to be paid six weeks after the child's birth. Mark and Crispina were also to pay for a $200,000 life insurance policy on Anna's life. The zygote was implanted on January 19, 1990. Less than a month later, an ultrasound test confirmed Anna was pregnant.

Unfortunately, relations deteriorated between the two sides. Mark learned that Anna had not disclosed she had suffered several stillbirths and miscarriages. Anna felt Mark and Crispina did not do enough to obtain the required insurance policy. She also felt abandoned during an onset of premature labor in June. In July 1990, Anna sent Mark and Crispina a letter demanding the balance of the payments due her or else she would refuse to give up the child. The following month, Mark and Crispina responded with a lawsuit, seeking a declaration they were the legal parents of the unborn child. Anna filed her own action to be declared the mother of the child, and the two cases were eventually consolidated. . . .

*An organism produced by the union of two gametes. (McGraw-Hill Dict. of Scientific and Technical Terms (4th ed. 1989) p. 783.)

†A cell that participates in fertilization and development of a new organism, also known as a germ cell or sex cell. (McGraw-Hill Dict. of Scientific and Technical Terms, supra, p. 2087.)

The child was born on September 19, 1990, and blood samples were obtained from both Anna and the child for analysis. The blood test results excluded Anna as the genetic mother. The parties agreed to a court order providing that the child would remain with Mark and Crispina on a temporary basis with visits by Anna.

At trial in October 1990, the parties stipulated that Mark and Crispina were the child's genetic parents. After hearing evidence and arguments, the trial court ruled that Mark and Crispina were the child's "genetic, biological and natural" father and mother, that Anna had no "parental" rights to the child, and that the surrogacy contract was legal and enforceable against Anna's claims. The court also terminated the order allowing visitation. Anna appealed from the trial court's judgment. The Court of Appeal for the Fourth District, Division Three, affirmed. We granted review. . . .

[In California, there are two kinds of evidence that can be used to establish the existence of a parent-child relationship: evidence on who gave birth to the child, and genetic evidence derived from blood testing. Our statutes do not say what a court must do when the two kinds of evidence lead to conflicting results. There is] . . . undisputed evidence that Anna, not Crispina, gave birth to the child and that Crispina, not Anna, is genetically related to him. Both women thus have adduced evidence of a mother and child relationship. . . . Yet for any child California law recognizes only one natural mother, despite advances in reproductive technology rendering a different outcome biologically possible.** . . .

Because two women each have presented acceptable proof of maternity, we do not believe this case can be decided without enquiring into the parties' intentions as manifested in the surrogacy agreement. Mark and Crispina are a couple who desired to have a child of their own genetic stock but are physically unable to do so without the help of reproductive technology. They affirmatively intended the birth of the child, and took the steps necessary to effect in vitro fertilization. But for their acted-on intention, the child would not exist. Anna agreed to facilitate the procreation of Mark's and Crispina's child. The parties' aim was to bring Mark's and Crispina's child into the world, not for Mark and Crispina to donate a zygote to Anna. Crispina from the outset intended to be the child's mother. Although the gestative function Anna performed was necessary to bring about the child's birth, it is safe to say that Anna would not have been given the opportunity to gestate or deliver the child had she, prior to implantation of the zygote, manifested her own intent to be the child's mother. No reason appears why Anna's later change of heart should vitiate the determination that Crispina is the child's natural mother.

We conclude that although [California law] recognizes both genetic consanguinity and giving birth as means of establishing a mother and child relationship, when the two means do not coincide in one woman, she who intended to procreate the child—that is, she who intended to bring about the birth of a child that she intended to raise as her own—is the natural mother under California law.†† . . .

Our conclusion finds support in the writings of several legal commentators. . . . (See Shultz, *Reproductive Technology and Intent-Based Parenthood: An Opportunity for Gender Neutrality* (1990) Wis. L. Rev. 297 [Schultz].) "Within the context of artificial reproductive techniques," Professor Schultz argues, "intentions that are voluntarily chosen, deliberate, express and bargained-for ought presumptively to determine legal parenthood." (Id., at p. 323.) . . . Moreover, as Professor Shultz recognizes, the interests of children, particularly at the outset of their lives, are "[un]likely to run contrary to those of adults who choose to bring them into being." (Id., at p. 397.) Thus, "[h]onoring the plans and expectations of adults who will be responsible for a child's welfare is likely to correlate significantly with positive outcomes for parents and children alike." (Ibid.)

Under Anna [Johnson's view,] a woman who agreed to gestate a fetus genetically related to the intending parents would, contrary to her expectations, be held to be the child's natural mother, with all the responsibilities that ruling would entail, if the intending mother declined to accept the child after its birth. In what we must hope will be the extremely rare situation in which neither the gestator nor the woman who provided the ovum for fertilization is willing to assume custody of the child after birth, a rule recognizing the intending parents as the child's

**We decline to accept the contention of amicus curiae the American Civil Liberties Union (ACLU) that we should find the child has two mothers. Even though rising divorce rates have made multiple parent arrangements common in our society, we see no compelling reason to recognize such a situation here. The Calverts are the genetic and intending parents of their son and have provided him, by all accounts, with a stable, intact, and nurturing home. To recognize parental rights in a third party with whom the Calvert family has had little contact since shortly after the child's birth would diminish Crispina's role as mother.

††Thus, under our analysis, in a true "egg donation" situation, where a woman gestates and gives birth to a child formed from the egg of another woman with the intent to raise the child as her own, the birth mother is the natural mother under California law. . . .

continued

CASE

Johnson v. Calvert—*Continued*

legal, natural parents should best promote certainty and stability for the child.

In deciding the issue of maternity . . . we have felt free to take into account the parties' intentions, as expressed in the surrogacy contract, because in our view the agreement is not, on its face, inconsistent with public policy. . . .

Anna urges that surrogacy contracts violate several social policies. Relying on her contention that she is the child's legal, natural mother, she cites the public policy embodied in Penal Code section 273, prohibiting the payment for consent to adoptions of a child.*** She argues further that the policies underlying the adoption laws of this state are violated by the surrogacy contract because it in effect constitutes a prebirth waiver of her parental rights.

We disagree. Gestational surrogacy differs in crucial respects from adoption and so is not subject to the adoption statutes. The parties voluntarily agreed to participate in in vitro fertilization and related medical procedures before the child was conceived; at the time when Anna entered into the contract, therefore, she was not vulnerable to financial inducements to part with her own expected offspring. As discussed above, Anna was not the genetic mother of the child. The payments to Anna under the contract were meant to compensate her for her services in gestating the fetus and undergoing labor, rather than for giving up "parental" rights to the child. Payments were due both during the pregnancy and after the child's birth. We are, accordingly, unpersuaded that the contract used in this case violates the public policies embodied in Penal Code section 273 and the adoption statutes. For the same reasons, we conclude these contracts do not implicate the policies underlying the statutes governing termination of parental rights. . . .

It has been suggested that gestational surrogacy may run afoul of prohibitions on involuntary servitude. (See U.S. Const., Amend. XIII; Cal. Const., art. I, § 6; Pen. Code, § 181.) Involuntary servitude has been recognized in cases of criminal punishment for refusal to work. (*Pollack v. Williams* (1944) 322 U.S. 4, 18; see, generally, 7 Witkin, *Summary of Cal. Law* (9th ed. 1988) Constitutional Law, §§ 411–414, pp. 591–596.) We see no potential for that evil in the contract at issue here, and extrinsic evidence of coercion or duress is utterly lacking. We note that although at one point the contract purports to give Mark and Crispina the sole right to determine whether to abort the pregnancy, at another point it acknowledges: "All parties understand that a pregnant woman has the absolute right to abort or not abort any fetus she is carrying. Any promise to the contrary is unenforceable." We therefore need not determine the validity of a surrogacy contract purporting to deprive the gestator of her freedom to terminate the pregnancy.

Finally, Anna and some commentators have expressed concern that surrogacy contracts tend to exploit or dehumanize women, especially women of lower economic status. Anna's objections center around the psychological harm she asserts may result from the gestator's relinquishing the child to whom she has given birth. Some have also cautioned that the practice of surrogacy may encourage society to view children as commodities, subject to trade at their parents' will.

We are all too aware that the proper forum for resolution of this issue is the Legislature, where empirical data, largely lacking from this record, can be studied and rules of general applicability developed. However, in light of our responsibility to decide this case, we have considered as best we can its possible consequences.

We are unpersuaded that gestational surrogacy arrangements are so likely to cause the untoward results Anna cites as to demand their invalidation on public policy grounds. Although common sense suggests that women of lesser means serve as surrogate mothers more often than do wealthy women, there has been no proof that surrogacy contracts exploit poor women to any greater degree than economic

***Penal Code section 273 provides, in pertinent part, as follows: "(a) It is a misdemeanor for any person or agency to offer to pay money or anything of value, or to pay money or anything of value, to a parent for the placement for adoption, for the consent to an adoption, or for cooperation in the completion of an adoption of his or her child. (b) This section does not make it unlawful to pay the maternity-connected medical or hospital and necessary living expenses of the mother preceding and during confinement as an act of charity, as long as the payment is not contingent upon placement of the child for adoption, consent to the adoption, or cooperation in the completion of the adoption." See also Penal Code section 181, which provides: "Every person who holds, or attempts to hold, any person in involuntary servitude, or assumes, or attempts to assume, rights of ownership over any person, or who sells, or attempts to sell, any person to another, or receives money or anything of value, in consideration of placing any person in the custody, or under the power or control of another, or who buys, or attempts to buy, any person, or pays money, or delivers anything of value, to another, in consideration of having any person placed in his custody, or under his power or control, or who knowingly aids or assists in any manner anyone thus offending, is punishable by imprisonment in the state prison for two, three, or four years."

necessity in general exploits them by inducing them to accept lower-paid or otherwise undesirable employment. We are likewise unpersuaded by the claim that surrogacy will foster the attitude that children are mere commodities; no evidence is offered to support it. The limited data available seem to reflect an absence of significant adverse effects of surrogacy on all participants.

The argument that a woman cannot knowingly and intelligently agree to gestate and deliver a baby for intending parents carries overtones of the reasoning that for centuries prevented women from attaining equal economic rights and professional status under the law. To resurrect this view is both to foreclose a personal and economic choice on the part of the surrogate mother, and to deny intending parents what may be their only means of procreating a child of their own genetic stock. Certainly in the present case it cannot seriously be argued that Anna, a licensed vocational nurse who had done well in school and who had previously borne a child, lacked the intellectual wherewithal or life experience necessary to make an informed decision to enter into the surrogacy contract. . . .

The judgment of the Court of Appeal is affirmed.

ASSIGNMENT 16.4

a. Isn't it true that the child in the *Johnson* case has three biological parents, two of whom are mothers? Why couldn't there be a three-parent solution to this case?
b. Do you think a gestational mother can bond with her child prenatally? If so, would this be relevant to Anna Johnson's claim to be declared the natural or legal mother?
c. Do you think that a gestational mother makes a substantial or significant contribution to the birth of a child? If so, why not determine who the legal/natural parent is on the basis of whether it would be in the best interests of the child to be with the gestational mother or with the intended genetic mother? Since both have serious claims, why shouldn't the test be: Who would make the better parent?
d. Assume that California had adopted the Uniform Status of Children of Assisted Conception Act (Alternative A). How would the *Johnson* case have been decided under this Act?

Not all courts agree with the intent test used in the *Johnson* case. Similar facts arose in the Ohio case of *Belsito v. Clark.*[12] An embryo from the sperm and ovum of a husband and wife was transferred to a gestational mother (referred to in the opinion as the "surrogate host"). The wife asked the hospital to list her as the mother on the birth certificate. The hospital refused, telling her that the woman who gave birth to the child must be listed as the mother on the birth certificate. Furthermore, since the father was not married to the birth mother, the child would be considered illegitimate. The husband and wife then asked a court to declare them the genetic and natural parents of the child so that they could both be listed on the birth certificate as the natural parents of a legitimate child. (The birth mother was the wife's sister, who was not being compensated for carrying the child. Although the birth mother was related to the child as an aunt, she was not a "genetic provider.") The *Belsito* court was faced with the same questions as the *Johnson* court: Who is the mother of the child? The woman who provided the genetic link via the egg or the woman who gave birth? While the *Belsito* court and the *Johnson* court both concluded that the woman who provided the genetic link is the mother, the *Belsito* court refused to use the intent test to reach its conclusion. The following excerpt from *Belsito v. Clark* explains the court's reasoning:

> In *Johnson v. Calvert* (1993), 851 P.2d 776, the facts are very similar to this case, with a married couple supplying the egg and sperm and a surrogate

[12] 644 N.E.2d 760 (Ohio C.P. 1994).

agreeing to carry and deliver the child. . . . The court in *Johnson* looked for the intent to procreate and to raise the child, in order to identify the natural mother. Since the genetic mother in *Johnson* intended to procreate, she was the natural parent. The *Johnson* court discarded both genetics and birth as the primary means of identifying the natural maternal parent, and replaced both with a test that involves intent of the parties. . . .

[We do not find the *Johnson* case] to be persuasive. . . . Intent can be difficult to prove. Even when the parties have a written agreement, disagreements as to intent can arise. In addition, in certain fact patterns when intent is clear, the *Johnson* test of intent to procreate and raise the child may bring about unacceptable results. As an example, who is the natural parent if both a nongenetic-providing surrogate and the female genetic provider agree that they both intend to procreate and raise the child? It is apparent that the *Johnson* test presents problems when applied. . . .

[In addition, it] has long been recognized that, as a matter of public policy, the state will not enforce or encourage private agreements or contracts to give up parental rights. . . . See *Matter of Baby M.* (1988), 109 N.J. 396, 537 A.2d 1227. . . . Through the intent to procreate, the *Johnson* case allows the nongenetic carrier/surrogate to be designated as the natural mother. The possibility of recognition as a parent means that a potential right is implicit in any agreement or contract to act as gestational surrogate. A surrogate who chooses not to be the natural parent forfeits her right to be considered the natural and legal parent. Because a fee is often involved in a surrogacy service, that assent amounts to selling a parental right, and is in contradiction to the public policy against private contracts to surrender parental rights.

[The intent test also conflicts with] the underlying public policy of adoption law. Adoption laws of Ohio have long required that a relinquishing natural mother be given an unpressured opportunity before a disinterested magistrate to surrender her parental rights. R.C. 3107.08. Considering the substantial rights involved, the possible financial pressures, and the value our society places on procreation, the need for such procedures is evident.

In addition to protecting the interest of the mother, adoption law has attempted to protect the interest of the child. By agreement or otherwise, the natural mother is not free to surrender her child to whomever she wishes. Through the use of its parens patriae powers, the state closely supervises the process, and ultimately selects or approves of the new parents. . . . The underlying public policy is to provide for the best interest of the child: to ensure that the abandoned child is not given to persons who will abuse or neglect the child, but will be placed in a home with caring and competent parents. . . .

The *Johnson* court's formulation of the intent-to-procreate test does not . . . provide a means to review and ensure the suitability of the gestational surrogate or her spouse as parents. In addition, because it is based on private agreement or intent that has not been sanctioned by a court proceeding, it raises the question of future legal challenges, and thus undermines the stability of the child-parent relationship. The *Johnson* intent formulation ignores those concerns and relies on the whims of private intent and agreement. It is, in effect, a private adoption process that is readily subject to all the defects and pressures of such a process. . . .

[T]here is abundant precedent for using the genetics test for identifying a natural parent. For the best interest of the child and society, there are strong arguments to recognize the genetic parent as the natural parent. The genetic parent can guide the child from experience through the strengths and weaknesses of a common ancestry of genetic traits. Because that test has served so well, it should remain the primary test for determining the natural parent, or parents, in nongenetic-providing surrogacy cases. . . . When dealing with a nongenetic-providing surrogate, such a rule minimizes or avoids the question of the surrogate selling her right to be determined the natural parent. . . . In addition, given the relative certainty of DNA blood testing, such a foundation or test for parental identity would be simpler to apply and more certain in results than a *Johnson*-type intent test. . . .

In conclusion, under Ohio law, when a child is delivered by a gestational surrogate who has been impregnated through the process of in vitro fertilization, the natural parents of the child shall be identified by a determination as to which individuals have provided the genetic imprint for that child. If the individuals who have been identified as the genetic parents have not relinquished or waived their rights to assume the legal status of natural parents, they shall be considered the natural and legal parents of that child.[13]

ASSIGNMENT 16.5

a. Which court is correct? The *Johnson* court or the *Belsito* court? Why?

b. Mary and Beverly are a lesbian couple. Each wants to give birth to and to raise a child together. Mary becomes pregnant and gives birth to a child whose genetic parents are an anonymous sperm donor and Beverly, who provided the egg that was implanted in Mary after in vitro fertilization. Who should be declared the mother?

SUMMARY

A major method of treatment for infertility is assisted reproductive technologies (ART), in which eggs are removed from a woman's ovaries and combined with sperm to help a woman become pregnant. ART includes in vitro fertilization (IVF), artificial insemination, gamete intrafallopian transfer (GIFT), zygote intrafallopian transfer (ZIFT), and embryo transplant.

States do not agree on what to do with frozen embryos after a couple divorces or separates. Louisiana will not allow the embryos to be destroyed. Other states will try to abide by the contract the couple signed on what to do with the frozen embryos. If there is no such contract, Tennessee gives preference to the party who wants to avoid procreation unless the other party does not have a reasonable chance of procreating without the frozen embryos. A Massachusetts court was reluctant to enforce any agreement that had the effect of compelling someone to be a parent against his or her will. Stem cells in human embryos hold great promise for medical research. The country is divided, however, on the ethical propriety of destroying embryos in order to extract such cells. The federal government will not fund research on embryos that are created solely for medical science, although private funding for such research is allowed.

Under a surrogacy contract, an unpregnant woman enters a contract to become pregnant, to give birth to a child, and then to relinquish all parental rights to the couple who will then adopt the child. If the surrogate supplies the egg, she is genetically related to the child, the genetic mother. If the surrogate carries an embryo that was formed from the egg of another woman, the surrogate is not genetically related to the child; she is the gestational carrier, gestational surrogate, or surrogate host.

Those who argue that surrogate contracts should be legalized point out that since society cannot stop the practice of surrogacy, it would be better to regulate it to ensure competency and honesty in the process. Those who would ban surrogate contracts denounce the very notion of "buying and selling babies" in an atmosphere of exploitation.

Numerous questions arise as the topic of surrogacy comes before the legislatures of the country. For example, if a surrogate mother is paid as she goes through adoption, has there been a violation of the law that prohibits paying

[13]Id. at 764–67.

someone to consent to an adoption? Under current paternity laws, is the husband of the surrogate mother presumed to be the father of the child that she is under contract to allow another man to adopt? On the ultimate question of custody, what assurances exist that giving the child to the couple that hires the surrogate mother will always be in the best interests of the child? Also, numerous enforcement questions must be addressed when it becomes clear that one of the parties to the surrogate contract refuses to go along with its terms, or when something happens that is not covered in the terms of the contract (e.g., the surrogate mother gives birth to a baby with AIDS).

State legislatures have handled such questions in different ways, including the following: doing nothing; prohibiting surrogate contracts; permitting such contracts, but regulating them; and finally, giving serious consideration to a new model act called the *Uniform Status of Children of Assisted Conception Act* proposed by the National Conference of Commissioners on Uniform State Laws.

Courts must sometimes determine who is the natural mother of a child when the contestants are the woman who provided the ovum (egg) for the child and is thereby genetically related to the child and the woman (surrogate) who gave birth to the child to which she has no genetic link. Some courts say that the natural mother is the woman who had the intent to procreate and to raise the child even if she has no genetic link to the child. Other courts say that the natural mother is the woman who has the genetic link to the child.

KEY CHAPTER TERMINOLOGY

assisted reproductive technologies (ART)
in vitro fertilization (IVF)
surrogate mother
broker
Uniform Status of Children of Assisted Conception Act
assisted conception
gestational surrogacy

ETHICS IN PRACTICE

You are a paralegal working at the law office of Franklin & Franklin. One of the clients at the office is a biotechnology company. When you learn that the company is about to announce the discovery of a new fertility drug, you buy 1,000 shares of its stock. Any ethical problems?

ON THE NET: MORE ON SURROGACY AND ASSISTED CONCEPTION

American Society for Reproductive Medicine
http://www.asrm.org

Surrogate Mothers Online
http://www.surromomsonline.com/articles/index.htm

The InterNational Council on Infertility Information Dissemination
http://www.inciid.org

OPTS, Inc., the Organization of Parents through Surrogacy
http://www.opts.com

Options National Fertility Register
http://www.fertilityoptions.com

Growing Generations: Surrogacy for the Gay Community
http://www.growinggenerations.com

Resolve: The National Infertility Association
http://www.resolve.org

CHAPTER 17

TORTS AND FAMILY LAW

CHAPTER OUTLINE

INTRODUCTION

tort
A civil wrong that has caused harm to person or property for which a court will provide a remedy.

Tort law is becoming increasingly important in the practice of family law. For example, one of the most-talked-about tort cases of 1997 was the million-dollar verdict won by an ex-wife against a paramour for the tort of alienation of affections. Most attorneys thought this tort was a relic of a forgotten age. Not so in North Carolina, where the ex-wife successfully argued that her ex-husband's secretary enticed him into an affair by wearing tight skirts and joining him on business trips.[1] Also, more and more courts are allowing spouses to sue each other for torts committed during the marriage. Many states allow tort claims to be brought in the divorce action. In a world of no-fault divorce, this has the effect of reintroducing concepts of fault and blame, which are central to the resolution of most tort claims.

There are two main categories of tort cases that we need to consider: those in which spouses or other family members bring tort actions against each other and those in which one or both spouses sue someone else for a tort that has seriously affected the family.

Before we begin, we should briefly cover a property division issue that can arise over the proceeds of a tort settlement or judgment. Assume, for example, that Ted is injured in an automobile accident caused by the negligence of a truck driver. He sues this driver for the tort of negligence and wins $100,000 in damages. Before the money is collected, however, Ted and his wife file for divorce. The question is whether the $100,000 is marital property subject to property division in the divorce.

The answer may depend on what the damages were awarded for. They might cover economic losses, such as lost income, and noneconomic losses,

[1] Karen S. Peterson, *Million-Dollar Message from Ex-Wife,* USA Today, Aug. 8, 1997, at 1D, 2D.

such as pain and suffering. A court may conclude that noneconomic damages are personal to the injured party and, therefore, not subject to property division. The money received for such losses cannot be said to have been a product of the marriage relationship. Economic damages, on the other hand, are arguably different. The other spouse can rightfully claim that economic damages replace the income that both spouses would have enjoyed if the tort had not been committed. Hence economic damages should be classified as marital property and subject to property division. Many states have adopted this reasoning, although all have not done so. There are some states that consider all personal injury awards to be marital property. For an extensive discussion of the general topic of property division, see chapter 8.

INTRAFAMILY TORTS

Torts committed by one spouse against another are sometimes called *domestic torts* or *interspousal torts.* The broader term for torts within the family committed by spouses, parents, children, or other family members is **intrafamily torts** (also called *intrafamilial torts*). Historically, an **immunity** existed for such torts. The effect of the immunity was to prevent someone from being sued for his or her wrongful conduct. An immunity between spouses is called *interspousal tort immunity.* The more general phrase covering spouses and all other family members is *intrafamily tort immunity.*

Courts have always been reluctant to permit tort actions among any combination of husband, wife, and **unemancipated** child. (A child is unemancipated while still legally dependent on his or her parent or legal guardian; a child is **emancipated** by becoming legally independent such as by marrying or obtaining a court order of emancipation.) This reluctance is based on the theory that family harmony will be threatened if members know that they can sue each other in tort. If the family carries **liability insurance,** there is also fear that family members will fraudulently try to collect under the policy by fabricating tort actions against each other. Furthermore, courts simply did not want to become involved. According to an 1877 opinion, "[I]t is better to draw the curtain, shut out the public gaze, and leave the parties to forgive and forget."[2] At common law, a more technical reason was given for why husbands and wives could not sue each other. The husband and wife were considered to be one person, and that one person was the husband. Hence to allow a suit between spouses would theoretically amount to one person suing himself. With the passage of the Married Women's Property Acts (see chapter 12) and the enforcement of the laws against sex discrimination, a wife now has her separate identity so that she can sue and be sued like anyone else.

Reform in the law, however, has not meant that intrafamily tort immunity no longer exists. A distinction must be made between suits against the person (such as battery) and suits against property (such as conversion). For torts *against property,* most states allow suits between spouses and between parent and child. Many states, however, retain the immunity in some form when the suit involves a tort *against the person.* The state of law is outlined in Exhibit 17.1.

intrafamily tort
A tort committed by one family member against another.

immunity
A defense that prevents someone from being sued for what would otherwise be wrongful conduct.

unemancipated
Still under the legal control of a parent or legal guardian.

emancipated
Having a legal status that is independent of one's parent or legal guardian.

liability insurance
Insurance that pays the liability that is incurred by an insured to a third party.

[2] *Abbott v. Abbott,* 67 Me. 304, 307 (1877).

Exhibit 17.1 Intrafamily Torts

Spouse against Spouse

1. In most states, spouses can sue each other for intentional or negligent injury to their property (e.g., negligence, trespass, conversion).
2. In some states, spouses cannot sue each other for intentional or negligent injury to their person—a personal tort action (e.g., negligence, assault, battery).
3. Some states will permit personal tort actions if the man and woman are divorced or if the tort is covered by liability insurance.
4. Some states will permit intentional tort actions against the person to be brought by spouses against each other, but continue to forbid negligence actions for injury to the person.

Child against Parent(s)

1. In all states, a child can sue the parent for intentional or negligent injury caused by the parent to the child's property (e.g., negligence, trespass, conversion).
2. In many states, a child cannot sue a parent for intentional or negligent injury caused by the parent to the child's person (e.g., negligence, assault, battery), particularly in cases where the parent was disciplining the child. Parents have a privilege to discipline their children.
3. If the child is emancipated (e.g., married, member of the armed forces, self-supporting), the child in all states can sue the parent for intentional or negligent injury caused by the parent to the child's person (e.g., negligence, assault, battery).
4. Some states will permit any child (emancipated or not) to sue the parent for intentional torts causing injury to the person, but continue to forbid actions for negligence causing injury to the person.
5. A few states allow the child to sue the parent for all intentional torts causing injury to the person, except where a tort arises out of the parent's exercise of discipline over the child.

Other Related Persons

Brothers and sisters, aunts and uncles, grandparents and grandchildren, and other relatives can sue each other in tort. The restrictions imposed on spouse suits and child suits do not apply to tort actions involving other relatives.

ASSIGNMENT 17.1

To answer the following questions, you may have to check both the state code and the opinions of courts sitting in your state. (See General Instructions for the State-Code Assignment and General Instructions for the Court-Opinion Assignment in Appendix A.)

a. Under what circumstances, if any, can one spouse bring a tort action against the other spouse in your state? Is it relevant that liability insurance exists?
b. Can divorced spouses sue each other in tort?
c. Under what circumstances, if any, can a child bring a tort action against its parent in your state?
d. Pick any tort action that one family member *can* bring against another in your state. Draft a complaint in which the cause of action is this tort. (See General Instructions for the Complaint-Drafting Assignment in Appendix A.)

ASSIGNMENT 17.2

A husband in your state intentionally kills his wife and son. Can the estate of the wife bring a tort action against him for wrongful death? Can the estate of the son bring a tort action for wrongful death against his father? (See General Instructions for the State-Code Assignment and General Instructions for the Court-Opinion Assignment in Appendix A.)

ASSIGNMENT 17.3

a. A father shows his minor son pornography and sexually abuses him. Can the son bring a tort action against the father? (See General Instructions for the Legal-Analysis Assignment in Appendix A.)

b. Dave knows that he has contagious genital herpes, but does not tell Alice, who contracts the disease from Dave. Can Alice sue Dave for battery? For intentional infliction of emotional distress? For deceit (misrepresentation) or fraud? Does it make any difference whether the disease was communicated before or after Dave and Alice were married? Does it make any difference that they are now divorced? (See General Instructions for the Legal-Analysis Assignment in Appendix A.)

c. Jim and Helen live together for a year before they are married. They separate two years after the marriage. While preparing to file for divorce, Helen discovers that she has contracted chlamydia trachomatis, a serious venereal disease that attacks the ovaries. Her reproductive system is permanently damaged. Assume that Jim gave her this disease through intercourse during the marriage. Jim carelessly thought that he was not capable of infecting Helen. Can she sue Jim for negligence in your state? (See General Instructions for the Court-Opinion Assignment in Appendix A.)

CASE

Hakkila v. Hakkila

112 N.M. 172, 812 P.2d 1320 (1991)
Court of Appeals of New Mexico

Background: *Arnold Hakkila sued Peggy Hakkila for divorce. Peggy counterclaimed for divorce on the ground of cruel and inhuman treatment and also sought damages for the tort of intentional infliction of emotional distress based upon conduct occurring during the marriage. The district court granted the divorce and awarded Peggy $141,000 in damages for the tort. The case is now on appeal before the Court of Appeals of New Mexico.*

Decision on Appeal: *Reversed. The husband's insults and outbursts during the ten-year marriage were insufficiently outrageous to establish liability for intentional infliction of emotional distress.*

Opinion of the Court:

Justice HARTZ delivered the opinion of the court. . . .

Husband and wife were married on October 29, 1975. Each had been married before. They permanently separated in February 1985. Husband filed his petition for dissolution of marriage the following month. Husband, who holds a Ph.D. in chemistry, had been employed at Los Alamos National Laboratory throughout the marriage. Wife, a high school graduate with credit hours toward a baccalaureate degree in chemistry and a vocational degree as a chemical technician, had been employed at the laboratory as a secretary for seven years and as a chemical technician for about seven and one-half years. She voluntarily terminated her employment in December 1979.

The district court found that "[wife's] emotional and mental health, especially since the parties' separation, has been shown to have been characterized by acute depression and one psychotic episode." The district court's findings noted conflicting testimony concerning wife's past and current mental condition. The district court summarized one psychologist's testimony as diagnosing wife "as subject to a borderline personality disorder pre-dating the parties' marriage," and summarized another's as diagnosing her as "an intellectualizing personality in the early years of her marriage and as suffering from acute depression since approximately 1981." Apparently all the experts agreed that wife was temporarily emotionally disabled at the time of the hearing.

Finding No. 22 summarized husband's intentional misconduct: The manner in which [husband] treated [wife] during the marriage and which resulted in her disability and impairment is as follows. [Husband] on occasions throughout the marriage and continuing until the separation[:] **a.** assaulted and battered [wife,] **b.** insulted [wife] in the presence of

continued

CASE

Hakkila v. Hakkila—*Continued*

guests, friends, relatives, and foreign dignitaries, **c.** screamed at [wife] at home and in the presence of others, **d.** on one occasion locked [wife] out of the residence over night in the dead of winter while she had nothing on but a robe, **e.** made repeated demeaning remarks regarding [wife's] sexuality, **f.** continuously stated to [wife] that she was crazy, insane, and incompetent, **g.** refused to allow [wife] to pursue schooling and hobbies, **h.** refused to participate in normal marital relationship with [wife] which ultimately resulted in only having sexual relations with [wife] on four occasions in the last three years of the marriage, **i.** blamed his sexual inadequacies upon [wife]. Finding No. 26 stated: [Husband's] acts in intentionally inflicting severe emotional distress upon [wife] was so outrageous in character and so extreme in degree as to be beyond all possible bounds of decency and were atrocious and utterly intolerable. . . . With respect to each of the matters listed by the district court in Finding No. 22, the record shows:

> **a.** There was evidence of several incidents of assault and battery. In late 1984 when wife was pushing her finger in husband's chest, he grabbed her wrist and twisted it severely. In 1981 during an argument in their home husband grabbed wife and threw her face down across the room, into a pot full of dirt. In 1978 when wife was putting groceries in the camper, husband slammed part of the camper shell down on her head and the trunk lid on her hands. In 1976 and "sometimes thereafter" during consensual sexual intercourse husband would use excessive force in attempting to stimulate wife with his hands.
>
> **b.** The one incident in which husband insulted wife in the presence of others was at a friend's Christmas party. At about 11:00 p.m. wife approached husband, who was "weaving back and forth with his hands in his pockets," and suggested that they go home. Husband began screaming, "You f_____ bitch, leave me alone." Wife excused herself and walked home alone.
>
> **c.** Wife also testified that when she and husband were home alone he would go into rages and scream at her. There was no evidence of his screaming at her in the presence of others except for the incident described in "b."
>
> **d.** The locking-out incident occurred after husband returned from a trip. Wife had been at a friend's home where she had eaten dinner and had some wine. During an argument that had ensued when he returned, she grabbed his shirt and popped all the buttons off. She went downstairs and stepped outside. He closed and locked the door. She went across the street to a home of neighbors, who let her in. He then threw his clothes into a camper and drove off for the night. When he returned the next morning, they made up and made love.
>
> **e.** On several occasions husband told wife that "you prefer women to men." He did not use the word "lesbian." He testified that he meant only that wife preferred the company of other women to his company. She did not testify that his remarks had sexual connotations.
>
> **f.** Throughout the marriage husband made remarks such as, "You're just plain sick, you're just stupid, you're just insane."
>
> **g.** With respect to the finding that husband "refused to allow [wife] to pursue schooling and hobbies," husband's brief-in-chief contends that no evidence supports the finding. Wife's answer brief does not respond to the contention, so we will not consider that finding as support for the judgment.
>
> **h., i.** With respect to the final two items in the finding, husband acknowledges that their sexual relationship atrophied and that wife testified that (1) it was his decision not to engage in sexual relations more frequently, and (2) he blamed her for their poor sexual relationship.

Should We Recognize the Tort of Intentional Infliction of Emotional Distress in the Marital Context?

Husband argues that as a matter of public policy one spouse should have no cause of action against the other spouse for intentional infliction of emotional distress. . . . We reject, at least for the time being, husband's suggestion. Nevertheless, the policy grounds opposing recognition of the tort in this context counsel caution in permitting lawsuits of this nature. . . .

The tort (also known as the tort of "outrage") is described in *Restatement (Second) of Torts* Section 46 (1965) (the *Restatement*): Outrageous Conduct Causing Severe Emotional Distress. (1) One who by extreme and outrageous conduct intentionally or recklessly causes severe emotional distress to another is subject to liability for such emotional distress, and if bodily harm to the other results from it, for such bodily harm. . . .

Wife contends that we must recognize the tort when committed by one spouse against the other because New Mexico has abandoned immunity for interspousal torts. . . . Yet the abolition of immunity does not mean that the existence of the marriage must be ignored in determining the scope of liability. After explaining the reasons for abolition of interspousal immunity, the commentary to *Restatement* Section 895F points out: The intimacy of the family relationship may . . . involve some relaxation in the application of the concept of reasonable care, particularly in the confines of the home. Thus, if one spouse in undressing leaves shoes out where the other stumbles over them in the dark, or if one spouse spills coffee on the other while they are both still sleepy, this may well be treated as not negligence. Id., comment h. The comment refers to Section 895G comment k, which explains that despite abolition of parental immunity: The intimacies of family life also involve intended physical contacts that would be actionable between strangers but may be commonplace and expected within the family. Family romping, even roughhouse play and momentary flares of temper not producing serious hurt, may be normal in many households, to the point that the privilege arising from consent becomes analogous.

Thus, the family relationship can be an important consideration in analyzing intrafamilial torts, both negligent and intentional. Despite the abolition of interspousal immunity, we must still evaluate wife's claims in light of the marital context in which they arose. . . .

Conduct intentionally or recklessly causing emotional distress to one's spouse is prevalent in our society. This is unfortunate but perhaps not surprising, given the length and intensity of the marital relationship. Yet even when the conduct of feuding spouses is not particularly unusual, high emotions can readily cause an offended spouse to view the other's misconduct as "extreme and outrageous." Thus, if the tort of outrage is construed loosely or broadly, claims of outrage may be tacked on in typical marital disputes, taxing judicial resources.

In addition, a spouse's most distressing conduct is likely to be privileged. Partners who are pledged to live together for a lifetime have a right to criticize each other's behavior. Cf. Cole, *Intentional Infliction of Emotional Distress Among Family Members,* 61 Den. U.L. Rev. 553, 574 (1984) ("Because the family's functioning depends on open and free communication, even negative give and take is necessary."). Even though one may question the utility of such comments, spouses are also free to express negative opinions of one another. "You look awful" or even "I don't love you" can be very wounding, but these statements cannot justify liability. See *Restatement* § 46 illustration 13 (you look "like a hippopotamus").

Not only should intramarital activity ordinarily not be the basis for tort liability, it should also be protected against disclosure in tort litigation. Although the spouse who raises a claim of outrage has no right to complain of the exposure of matters relevant to the claim, courts must be sensitive to the privacy interests of the defending spouse. Any litigation of a claim is certain to require exposure of the intimacies of married life. This feature of the tort distinguishes it from intramarital torts already recognized in New Mexico. For example, a suit by one spouse against another arising out of an automobile accident poses no such risk. Nor does one ordinarily think of exposure of an incident of battery as implicating legitimate privacy interests. In contrast, in this case the judge found that it was extreme and outrageous conduct for husband to refuse sexual relations with wife. Should we really use this tort as a basis for inquiry into a matter of such intimacy? Cf. *Thompson v. Chapman,* 93 N.M. 356, 600 P.2d 302 (Ct. App. 1979) (actions for alienation of affections engender more harm than good.). In determining the scope of the tort of outrage in the marital context, it is necessary to consider the privacy interests of the accused spouse.

Moreover, largely because so much interspousal communication is privileged (not in the evidentiary sense, but in the sense that it cannot be the basis for liability), a reliable determination of causation is difficult if not impossible when outrage is alleged in this context. The connection between the outrageousness of the conduct of one spouse and the severe emotional distress of the other will likely be obscure. Although the victim spouse may well be suffering severe emotional distress, was it caused by the outrageousness of the conduct or by the implied (and privileged) message of antipathy? What could be more devastating to one's spouse than to say, "I don't love you any more"—a statement that could not form the basis for a cause of action? Rejection alone can create severe emotional distress. Suicides by jilted lovers are legion. Every adult knows individuals who have sunk into disabling depression when a spouse seeks divorce. As a result, litigation of an interspousal claim of outrage could easily degenerate into a battle of self-proclaimed experts performing psychological autopsies to "discover" whether the cause of the emotional distress was some particular despicable conduct or simply rejection by a loved one. Of course, no such problem arises in the context of previously recognized intramarital torts. If one spouse

continued

CASE

Hakkila v. Hakkila—*Continued*

commits battery on another or causes an accident by driving negligently, the injuries to the other spouse can readily be tied to the tortious conduct. . . .

A cautious approach to the tort of intramarital outrage also finds support in the public policy of New Mexico to avoid inquiry into what went wrong in a marriage. New Mexico was the first state to provide for no-fault divorce on the ground of incompatibility. See NMSA 1978, § 40–4–1(A) (Repl. Pamp. 1989). New Mexico apportions community property without regard to fault, and grants alimony without consideration of punishment to either spouse.

In addition, although the tort has not been formally abolished, our courts have expressed dissatisfaction with the tort of alienation of affection, which has features similar to the tort of outrage in the marital context. . . .

Consequently, in determining when the tort of outrage should be recognized in the marital setting, the threshold of outrageousness should be set high enough—or the circumstances in which the tort is recognized should be described precisely enough, e.g., child snatching,—that the social good from recognizing the tort will not be outweighed by unseemly and invasive litigation of meritless claims.

Some jurisdictions have apparently set the threshold of outrageousness so high in the marital context as to bar all suits. See *Whittington v. Whittington,* 766 S.W.2d 73 (Ky. Ct. App. 1989) (no tort of outrage for adultery and fraud by spouse); *Pickering v. Pickering,* 434 N.W.2d 758 (S.D. 1989) (barring tort of intentional infliction of emotional distress if predicated on conduct which leads to dissolution of marriage). Cf. *Harris v. McDavid,* 553 So. 2d 567 (Ala. 1989) (no tort of outrage in termination of affair of unmarried couple); *Chiles v. Chiles,* 779 S.W.2d 127 (Tex. Ct. App. 1989) (tort of intentional infliction of emotional distress not recognized in divorce proceeding). But see *Simmons v. Simmons,* 773 P.2d 602 (Colo. Ct. App. 1988) (marriage does not preclude wife's action for damages for outrage). . . .

Thus far, however, New Mexico has not witnessed an onslaught of claims of outrage by one spouse against the other. There is no need at this time to adopt husband's recommendation that all such claims be barred.

We now move to the specifics of the case before us. The merits of wife's claim can be disposed of summarily. Husband's insults and outbursts fail to meet the legal standard of outrageousness. See, e.g., *Sanders v. Lutz,* 109 N.M. 193, 196, 784 P.2d 12, 15 (1989) (to recover, must show conduct was "'beyond all possible bounds of decency . . . and utterly intolerable'"). He was privileged to refrain from intercourse. There was no evidence that the other conduct caused severe emotional distress, as opposed to transient pain or discomfort. See *Restatement* § 46 emotional distress.)

Indeed, this case illustrates the risk of opening the door too wide to claims of this nature. Despite the claim's lack of merit, husband was subjected to a six-day trial, to say nothing of discovery and other preparation, surveying the rights and wrongs of a ten-year marriage. Motions for summary judgment should be viewed sympathetically in similar cases. If the potential harms from this kind of litigation are too frequently realized, it may be necessary to reconsider husband's suggestion that the tort of outrage be denied in the interspousal context.

We reverse the decision in favor of wife on her claim of intentional infliction of emotional distress.

ASSIGNMENT 17.4

If you were the judge, how would you have decided *Hakkila v. Hakkila?* In the second to last paragraph of the opinion, the court suggests that the *husband* was a victim. Do you think he was?

WRONGFUL LIFE, BIRTH, AND PREGNANCY

Doctors and pharmaceutical companies have been sued for negligence that results in the birth of an unwanted child. When the child is born deformed or otherwise impaired, two categories of suits have been attempted:

Wrongful life: An action by or on behalf of an unwanted child who is impaired; the child seeks its own damages in this action.

Wrongful birth: An action by the parents of an unwanted child who is impaired; the parents seek their own damages in this action.

Assume that a woman contracts German measles early in her pregnancy. Her doctor negligently advises her that the disease will not affect the health of the child. In fact, the child is born with severe defects caused by the disease. If the woman had known the risks, she would have had an abortion.

In such cases, a small number of states allow suits for wrongful life to cover the child's damages. The vast majority of states, however, do not. Courts are very reluctant to recognize a right not to be born. Several reasons account for this result. One is the enormous difficulty of calculating damages. According to a New Jersey court, it is literally impossible to measure the difference in value between life in an impaired condition and the "utter void of nonexistence.[3] Some courts also feel that allowing the suit might encourage unwanted children to sue for being born to a poverty-stricken family or to parents with criminal records. Finally, anti-abortion activists have argued that no one should be allowed to sue for missing the opportunity to have been aborted. Recently, the highest court in France (the Cour de Cassation) ruled for the first time that damages for wrongful life could be awarded to a severely handicapped child. The ruling created an uproar and led to a national debate over the implication of the ruling. The head of gynecology at a Paris hospital said, "This is the first time that doctors have been condemned for not having killed." A leading legislator in the country told the press, "This sends a message to handicapped people that their life is worth less than their death."[4]

Wrongful birth cases, on the other hand, are far less controversial and have been more successful. Here the parents sue for their own damages to cover their emotional distress, the cost of prenatal care and delivery, and other expenses attributed to the child's impaired condition.

Finally, we examine negligence that leads to the birth of an unwanted *healthy* child:

> **Wrongful pregnancy:** An action by the parents of an unwanted child who is healthy; the parents seek their own damages in this action.

Cases of wrongful pregnancy (also called *wrongful conception*) are allowed in most states. The most common example is a suit against a doctor for negligently performing a vasectomy or against a pharmaceutical company for producing defective birth control pills. Damages are limited to the expenses of prenatal care and delivery; they rarely extend to the costs of raising a healthy child. Furthermore, the unwanted healthy child is usually not allowed to bring the same kind of action in his or her own right.

ASSIGNMENT 17.5

A pregnant woman in your state has a genetic disease that could lead to the birth of a deformed child. Her doctor negligently fails to diagnose this disease and inform the woman. The child is born deformed with this disease. If she had known of the disease, she would have aborted the pregnancy. Who can bring an action in your state against the doctor for negligence and for what damages? (See General Instructions for the Court-Opinion Assignment in Appendix A.)

WRONGFUL ADOPTION

Suppose that an adoption agency misrepresents the physical or mental health of a child or misrepresents the medical history of the child's birth family.

> *Alice and Stan Patterson want to adopt a child. They go to the Riverside Adoption Agency (RAA), which introduces them to Irene, an infant available for adoption. The Pattersons adopt Irene. Before the adoption,*

---

[3] *Berman v. Allen,* 404 A.2d 8, 12 (N.J. 1979).

[4] Marlise Simons, *French Uproar Over Right to Death for Unborn,* N.Y. Times, Oct. 12, 2001, at A3.

RAA tells the Pattersons that Irene does not have any genetic disorders. This turns out to be false. Also, RAA knows that Irene had been sexually abused, but they do not inform the Pattersons of this. After Irene has been living with the Pattersons for a while, they discover that she has severe medical and psychological problems.

Can the Pattersons sue RAA for damages covering the increased cost of child rearing? The period for challenging the adoption itself may have passed. Furthermore, the adoptive parents may have bonded with the child and do not want to "send" the child back even if it were possible to annul or abrogate the adoption. In such cases, some states have allowed the adoptive parents to sue, particularly when they made clear to the agency that they did not want to adopt a problem child. Their argument is that they would not have adopted the child if they had been presented with all the facts. They cannot expect a guarantee that the child will be perfect. But they are entitled to available information that might indicate a significant likelihood of future medical or psychological problems. The failure to provide such information may constitute the tort of **wrongful adoption.** In an action for this tort, the adoptive parents seek damages from the adoption agency for wrongfully stating or failing to disclose available facts on the health or other condition of the child (the adoptee) that would have been relevant to their decision of whether to adopt.

wrongful adoption
A tort seeking damages for wrongfully stating or failing to disclose to prospective adoptive parents available facts on the health or other condition of the adoptee that would be relevant to the decision of whether to adopt.

CONSORTIUM AND SERVICES

Loss of Consortium

Consortium is the companionship, love, affection, sexual relationship, and services (e.g., cooking, making repairs around the house) that one spouse provides another. There can be a recovery for a tortious injury to consortium. At one time, only the husband could recover for such a **loss of consortium.** In every state, this view has been changed by statute or has been ruled unconstitutional as a denial of the equal protection of the law. Either spouse can now recover for loss of consortium.

loss of consortium
A tort action for the loss of or the interference with the companionship, love, affection, sexual relationship, and services that the plaintiff enjoyed with his or her spouse before the latter was wrongfully injured by the defendant.

Have to be married

The loss-of-consortium action works as follows:

- Rich and Ann are married.
- Paul, a stranger, injures Ann by negligently hitting her with his car.
- Ann sues Paul for negligence. She receives damages to cover her medical bills; lost wages, if any; pain and suffering; and punitive damages, if any.
- Rich then brings a *separate* suit against Paul for loss of his wife's consortium. He receives damages to compensate him for loss or impairment he can prove to the companionship he had with Ann before the accident—to the love, affection, sexual intercourse, and services that she gave him as his wife before the accident.

In his action against Paul, Rich cannot recover for injuries sustained by Ann. Ann must recover for such injuries in her own action against Paul. Paul's liability to Rich is limited to the specific injuries sustained by Rich—loss or impairment of his wife's consortium. If Ann loses her suit against Paul (e.g., because she was contributorily negligent), Rich will *not* be able to bring his consortium suit. To recover for loss of consortium, there must be an underlying successfully litigated tort.

Most states deny recovery for loss of consortium to individuals who are not married.

- *Jim and Rachel are engaged to be married. The defendant negligently incapacitates Rachel the day before the wedding. Rachel sues the defendant to recover for her injuries.*

- *Mary and John have lived together for forty years. They have never married and do not live in a state that recognizes common law marriage. The defendant negligently incapacitates John, who sues the defendant to recover for his injuries.*
- *George and Bob are homosexuals who have lived together as a couple for ten years. The defendant negligently incapacitates Bob, who sues the defendant to recover for his injuries.*

Clearly, Jim, Mary, and George have experienced a loss of consortium. They arguably have suffered in the same manner as Rich, whose wife, Ann, was negligently hit by Paul. The difference, however, is that Jim, Mary, and George (unlike Rich) were not married at the time their consortium was damaged. Most states deny an unmarried person the right to sue for loss of consortium. This may seem unfair, particularly to a couple who is hours away from being married. The law, however, must draw a line somewhere. A court would have a difficult time distinguishing between Jim and Rachel (a day away from their wedding) and an engaged couple whose wedding is one or two years away. What about someone six months or six weeks away? The practical problem of drawing the line plus the bias of the law in favor of marriage have led courts to limit the action for loss of consortium to married individuals.

The word *consortium* sometimes also refers to the normal companionship and affection that exists between a parent and a child. The right of a child to the companionship and affection of a parent is referred to as **parental consortium.** The right of a parent to the companionship and affection of a child is referred to as *filial consortium.*

parental consortium
The right of a child to the normal companionship and affection of a parent.

- *Bill is the father of Sam.*
- *The defendant negligently incapacitates Bill, who sues the defendant to recover for Bill's injuries.*
- *The defendant negligently incapacitates Sam, who sues the defendant to recover for Sam's injuries.*

In the first case, Sam has also suffered a loss—a loss of parental consortium. Yet many states do *not* allow suits for damage to this kind of consortium. Suppose, however, that the parent (Bill) dies from the defendant's negligence. There are some states whose wrongful death statute gives children the right to damages for the loss of companionship and affection they had with their parent (in addition to the financial losses caused by the death). But most states would *not* allow a suit for loss of parental consortium when the injured parent is still alive.

In the second case, Bill has also suffered a loss—a loss of filial consortium. As we will see in a moment, parents can sue someone who interferes with their right to receive the services of their children such as doing household chores. States differ, however, on the parent's right to recover for interference with the companionship and affection the parent has with a child—filial consortium. Many states deny such recovery. There are, however, a fair number of states that take a different position and allow recovery for interference with filial consortium.

Loss of Services

A parent has the right to the services of his or her unemancipated child. This would include tasks such as cutting the grass and running errands for the household.

Mary is the twelve-year-old child of Victor and Helen. The defendant negligently injures Mary in a car accident. In a negligence action against the defendant, Mary can recover damages for her injuries.

loss of services
A tort action for the loss of or the interference with the right of a parent to the services and earnings of his or her unemancipated child because of the wrongful injury inflicted on the child by the defendant.

Victor and Helen can also recover damages from the defendant for causing a **loss of services** by Mary to them. As a twelve-year-old who is dependent on her parents, Mary is unemancipated. She probably helps around the house.

The parents can recover for any interference with these services that are wrongfully caused. As with an action for the loss of consortium, an action for the loss of services requires an underlying successfully litigated tort.

ASSIGNMENT 17.6

a. Describe the loss of consortium action that can be brought in your state by a person whose spouse has been negligently injured.
b. Can a child sue a third party for loss of parental consortium in your state?
c. Can a parent bring an action for loss of child services and earnings in your state?

(See General Instructions for the State-Code Assignment and General Instructions for the Court-Opinion Assignment in Appendix A.)

OTHER TORTS

In some states, special torts can be used by one family member because of what the defendant did with or to another family member. These actions consist of the following torts:

- Alienation of affections
- Criminal conversation
- Enticement of spouse
- Abduction or enticement of a child
- Seduction

To establish any of these causes of action, there is no need to prove an underlying tort; they are torts in their own right.

heart-balm statute
A statute that abolishes heart-balm actions.

A number of states have passed statutes (sometimes called **heart-balm statutes**) that have abolished some or all of the above tort actions. The actions are not looked upon with favor and are seldom used today even where they have not been abolished.

Alienation of Affections

Elements of Alienation of Affections

1. Defendant (e.g., a lover, an in-law) intended to diminish the marital relationship between the plaintiff and the latter's spouse.
2. Affirmative conduct of the defendant carried out this intent.
3. Affections between the plaintiff and his or her spouse were in fact alienated.
4. Defendant caused the alienation.

Criminal Conversation

Element of Criminal Conversation

Defendant had sexual relations with the plaintiff's spouse (adultery).

Enticement of Spouse

Elements of Enticement of Spouse

1. Defendant intended to diminish the marital relationship between the plaintiff and the latter's spouse.
2. Affirmative conduct by defendant:
   a. enticed or encouraged the spouse to leave the plaintiff's home, *or*

   b. harbored the spouse and encouraged the latter to stay away from the plaintiff's home.

3. Plaintiff's spouse left home.
4. Defendant caused the plaintiff to leave home or to stay away.

Abduction or Enticement of a Child

Elements of Abduction or Enticement of Child

1. Defendant intended to interfere with the parent's custody of the child.
2. Affirmative conduct by the defendant:

   a. abducted or forced the child from the parent's custody, *or*
   b. enticed or encouraged the child to leave the parent, *or*
   c. harbored the child and encouraged the latter to stay away from the parent's custody.

3. The child left the custody of the parent.
4. Defendant caused the child to leave or to stay away.

Some states have created special statutory torts to replace this abduction/enticement tort. For example, an Ohio statute establishes a civil action to recover damages for interference with a "parental or guardianship interest." Recovery can include:

> Full compensatory damages, including, but not limited to, damages for the mental suffering and anguish incurred by the plaintiffs, damages for the loss of society of the minor, and, if applicable, damages for the loss of the minor's services and damages for expenses incurred by the plaintiffs in locating or recovering the minor.[5]

An example of a violation of this statute would be a grandparent who wrongfully hides a grandchild from its parents. This statute does not apply to parent-against-parent custody interference. Many states are reluctant to add tort suits to the arsenal of weapons that one parent can lodge against another in bitter custody and visitation battles. Nevertheless, there are some states in which such torts are allowed, particularly when a parent has violated court custody orders.

Seduction

Element of Seduction

The defendant has sex with the plaintiff's minor daughter by force or with the consent of the daughter.

ASSIGNMENT 17.7

a. Can any of the above five causes of actions be brought in your state? Check your state code and opinions written by courts in your state. If you find older cases that have permitted any of these actions, shepardize these cases to be sure that they still represent good law in your state. (See General Instructions for the State-Code Assignment and General Instructions for the Court-Opinion Assignment in Appendix A.)

b. Olivia is the mother of Irene, who is married to George. Olivia had begged Irene not to marry George—to no avail. After the marriage and the birth of a son, Olivia warns Irene that George has a violent disposition. Irene and George separate. Has Olivia committed any torts? (See General Instructions for the Legal-Analysis Assignment in Appendix A.)

---

[5]Ohio Revised Code § 2307.50(1).

VICARIOUS LIABILITY OF FAMILY MEMBERS

vicarious liability
Being liable because of what someone else has done. Standing in the place of someone else who is the one who actually committed the wrong.

Vicarious liability means that one person is liable solely because of what someone else does. For example, if a trucker negligently hits a pedestrian while making a delivery, the trucker's boss, the *employer,* is liable. The liability is vicarious, since it is based on what someone else—the employee—has done.

The person injured could also sue the employee who is directly responsible for the injury. We are all personally liable for our own torts even if someone else is vicariously liable. Often, however, the one directly responsible has minimal resources out of which to satisfy a judgment. The person who is vicariously liable is usually the **deep pocket,** who does have such resources.

deep pocket
The person or organization that probably has sufficient resources to pay damages if a judgment is awarded by the court.

In general, vicarious liability cannot exist among family members. While there are exceptions, the basic principle is that one family member is not liable for the torts of another family member. Thus, a spouse is not liable for the torts committed by the other spouse. Children are not liable for the torts of their parents, and vice versa. For example:

> *Mary is the ten-year-old daughter of Diane. Mary throws a brick through the window of Jim's hardware store.*

Jim must sue *Mary* for the damage done to the store. Her mother is *not* vicariously liable for the tort of her daughter.

parental responsibility law
A statute that imposes vicarious liability (up to a limited dollar amount) on parents for the torts committed by their children.

The first exception to this rule is fairly limited. A number of states have passed statutes (called **parental responsibility laws** or *parental liability laws*) that make parents vicariously liable for the torts of their children, but only up to a relatively modest amount (e.g., $1,000).

In the above example involving Diane and her daughter, note that there was no indication that Diane did anything wrong or improper herself. Suppose, however, that Diane knew that her daughter, Mary, had a habit of throwing bricks into windows. Or assume that Diane was with Mary when she threw the brick at Jim's window. If Diane failed to use reasonable care to control Mary in these circumstances, Diane *would* be liable to Jim. But this would not be a case of vicarious liability. When parents act unreasonably in failing to use available opportunities to control their children, the parents are *independently* liable for negligence in a suit brought by the person injured by the child. Since, however, parents are rarely with their children when the latter act mischievously, and rarely know when their children are about to commit specific acts of mischief, it is usually very difficult to prove that the parents negligently failed to control and supervise their children.

ASSIGNMENT 17.8

Jim is the thirteen-year-old son of Harry. Jim takes Harry's car on a joy ride and negligently injures George. Whom can George sue? (See General Instructions for the State-Code Assignment and General Instructions for the Court-Opinion Assignment in Appendix A.)

family-purpose doctrine
The owner of a car who makes it available for family use will be liable for injuries that result from an accident that is wrongfully caused by a member of the owner's immediate family while using the car with the owner's consent for a family purpose.

The second exception to the rule of no intrafamily vicarious liability is the **family-purpose doctrine,** according to which a defendant will be liable for torts committed by a driver of the defendant's car who is a member of the defendant's family. Not all states have the doctrine, and those that have it do not all agree on its elements. Generally, the elements of the doctrine are as follows:

Elements of Family-Purpose Doctrine

1. Defendant must own the car, or have an ownership interest in it (e.g., co-owner), or control the use of the car.

2. Defendant must make the car available for family use rather than for the defendant's business (in some states, the defendant must make it available for general family use rather than for a particular occasion only).
3. The driver must be a member of the defendant's immediate household.
4. The driver must be using the car for a family purpose at the time of the accident.
5. The driver must have had the defendant's express or implied consent to be using the car at the time of the accident.

The defendant does not have to be the traditional head of the household and does not have to be in the car at the time of the accident. Again, individual states, by case law or by statute, may impose different elements to the doctrine or may reject it entirely.

ASSIGNMENT 17.9

a. Is there a family-purpose doctrine in your state? If so, what are its components or elements? (See General Instructions for the State-Code Assignment and General Instructions for the Court-Opinion Assignment in Appendix A.)

b. Fred has just bought a used car, but it will not be ready for a week. During the week he is waiting, he rents a car, paying a per-mile charge on it. He tells his family that the car is to be used only to drive to work. One day while the car is at home and Fred is at the supermarket, his child becomes sick. Fred's mother, who is staying with Fred until an opening comes up in a local nursing home, drives the child to the hospital. On the way, she has an accident, injuring the plaintiff. The plaintiff sues Fred for negligence. Apply the five elements of the family-purpose doctrine to determine whether it would apply. (See General Instructions for the Legal-Analysis Assignment in Appendix A.) How would this case be handled in your state? (Refer to your answer to part [a] above.)

SUMMARY

An award received by a spouse for a personal injury tort may be subject to property division to the extent that the award covers economic damages such as loss of income that would have helped support both spouses. There is an immunity for some intrafamily torts, which means that the injured party cannot sue. Courts traditionally have been reluctant to allow suits for intrafamily torts, since the courtroom is hardly the best place to resolve family conflicts. But immunity is not the rule in every case. It depends on who the parties are and on what tort has been committed.

Intrafamily torts that damage property (e.g., trespass) are treated differently from torts that injure the person (e.g., battery). Generally, spouses can sue each other for negligent or intentional damage to property. The same is true for such damage caused by the parent to a child's property. There is no immunity for property torts. For torts against the person, in many states, one spouse cannot sue another, and a child cannot sue a parent; immunity does apply to these torts in such states. There are some exceptions to these rules. For example, many states grant immunity only for negligent injury to the person; thus, any family member can sue another for intentional injury to the person in such states.

If a defendant such as a doctor makes a negligent mistake that results in the birth of a deformed child, the parents can bring a wrongful-birth action. If the child is born healthy, the parents may be able to bring an action for wrongful pregnancy or for wrongful conception, but the damages are limited. The courts, however, usually do not allow the child to bring his or her own separate wrongful-life action. The failure of an adoption agency to give prospective adoptive parents available information about the health or other condition of the prospective adoptee may constitute the tort of wrongful adoption.

Loss of consortium covers injury to the companionship, love, affection, sexual relationship, and services that one spouse provides another. Loss of services covers an interference with the right of parents to the services of their unemancipated child. States differ on whether parents and children can sue for tortious interference with parental or filial consortium. Other family torts include alienation of affections, criminal conversation, enticement of a spouse, abduction or enticement of a child, and seduction.

Vicarious liability exists when one person is liable for someone else's tort. Vicarious liability cannot exist among family members, with two major exceptions. First, some states have statutes that impose limited vicarious liability on parents for the torts committed by their children. Second, under the family-purpose doctrine, the owner of a car can be liable for a tort committed by a family member driving the car for a "family purpose."

KEY CHAPTER TERMINOLOGY

tort
intrafamily tort
immunity
unemancipated
emancipated
liability insurance
wrongful life
wrongful birth
wrongful pregnancy
wrongful adoption
loss of consortium
parental consortium
loss of services
heart-balm statute
vicarious liability
deep pocket
parental responsibility law
family-purpose doctrine

ETHICS IN PRACTICE

You are a paralegal working at the law office of Francis Reardon, Esq. Reardon represents David Richardson, who is suing his ex-wife, Mary Richardson, to attempt to stop Mary from aborting the child conceived months before the divorce. You are an ardent abortion rights advocate. Any ethical problems?

ON THE NET: MORE ON INTRAFAMILY TORTS

Domestic Violence, Domestic Torts, and Divorce
http://www.nesl.edu/lawrev/vol31/vol31-2/DALTON.htm

Family Law Today: Can You Sue for Emotional Distress?
http://jprlawcorp.com/pages/canyousue.htm

Domestic Torts in New Jersey
http://www.gourvitz.com/dom_tort.htm

Interspousal Tort Claims (Texas)
http://www.divorcesource.com/research/edj/torts/98jul80.shtml

Alienation of Affections
http://www.students.washington.edu/kwood/familylaw/terms.htm

GENERAL INSTRUCTIONS FOR THE ASSIGNMENTS IN THE BOOK

Throughout the chapters of this book, there are eleven major kinds of skill assignments:

- State-Code Assignment
- Legal-Analysis Assignment
- Complaint-Drafting Assignment
- Agreement-Drafting Assignment
- Court-Opinion Assignment
- Checklist-Formulation Assignment
- Investigation-Strategy Assignment
- Interview Assignment
- Interrogatory Assignment
- Flowchart Assignment
- Systems Assignment

On the pages where these assignments are found, you will be given *specific instructions.* In addition, a set of *general instructions* is available for each of the eleven categories of assignments. These general instructions are provided here in Appendix A. Throughout the chapters of the book, you are referred to Appendix A for *general instructions* for most of the assignments.

THE CARTWHEEL

Several of the assignments, particularly the state code and court opinion assignments, ask you to check basic law books such as the statutory code (containing the full text of the statutes of the legislature) and the digest (containing summaries of the court opinions printed in full in reporters). The **CARTWHEEL** will help you find materials in the code and digest. The CARTWHEEL is an index technique. Its objective can be simply stated: to help you develop the habit of phrasing every word involved in the client's problem *fifteen to twenty different ways!* When you go to the index of a law book, you naturally begin looking up the words and phrases that you think should lead you to the relevant material in the book. If you do not find anything on point, two conclusions are possible:

cartwheel
A research technique that helps you identify a large variety of word or phrase substitutes to check in an index.

- There is nothing on point in the law book.
- You checked the wrong words in the index.

Too often we make the mistake of thinking that the first conclusion is accurate. Nine times out of ten, the second conclusion is more accurate. The solution is to be able to phrase a word in as many different ways and in as many different contexts as possible—hence the CARTWHEEL.

Suppose the problem of the client involved, among other things, a wedding. The structure of the CARTWHEEL for this example is illustrated in Exhibit A.1.

Exhibit A.1 The CARTWHEEL: Using the Index of Law Books

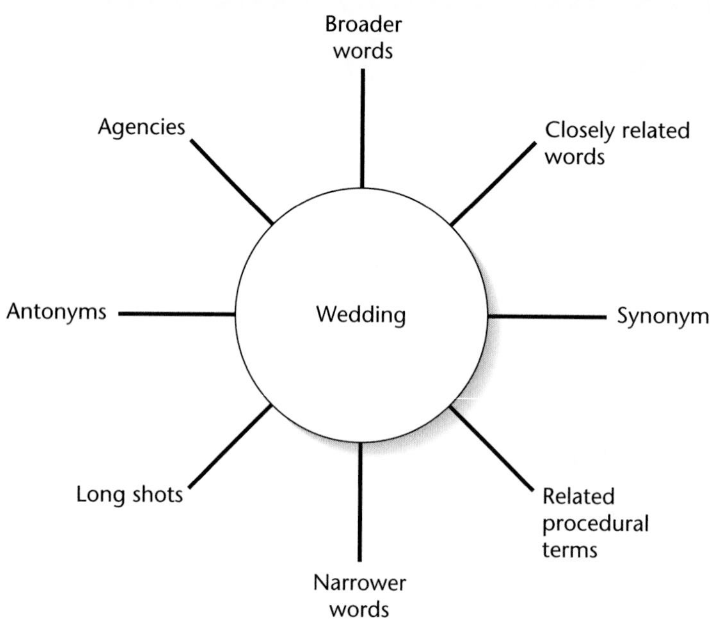

1. Identify all the *major words* from the facts of the client's problem (e.g., wedding); most of these facts can be obtained from the intake memorandum written following the initial interview with the client. Place each word or small set of words in the center of CARTWHEEL.
2. In the index, look up all of these words.
3. Identify the *broader categories* of the major words.
4. In the index, look up all of these broader categories.
5. Identify the *narrower* categories of the major words.
6. In the index, look up all of these narrower categories.
7. Identify all of the *synonyms* of the major words.
8. In the index, look up all of these synonyms.
9. Identify all of the *antonyms* of the major words.
10. In the index, look up all of these antonyms.
11. Identify all words that are *closely related* to the major words.
12. In the index, look up all of these closely related words.
13. Identify all *procedural* terms related to the major words.
14. In the index, look up all of these procedural terms.
15. Identify all *agencies,* if any, that might have some connection to the major words.
16. In the index, look up all of these agencies.
17. Identify all *long shots.*
18. In the index, look up all of these long shots.

Note: The above categories are not mutually exclusive.

The first step would be to look up the word "wedding" in the index of any law book. Assume that you are not successful with this word (either because the word is not in the index or because the page or section references after the word in the index do not lead you to relevant material in the body of the book). The next step is to think of as many different phrasings and contexts of the word "wedding" as possible. This is where the eighteen steps of the CARTWHEEL can be useful.

If you applied the steps of the CARTWHEEL to the word *wedding,* here are some of the words and phrases that you would check:

1. *Broader words:* celebration, ceremony, rite, ritual, formality, festivity.
2. *Narrower words:* civil wedding, church wedding, golden wedding, proxy wedding, sham wedding, shotgun marriage.
3. *Synonyms:* marriage ceremony, nuptial.
4. *Antonyms:* alienation, annulment, divorce, separation, legal separation, judicial separation.
5. *Closely related words:* matrimony, marital, conjugal, domestic, husband, wife, bride, license, anniversary, custom, children, blood test, premarital, spouse, relationship, family, home, consummation, cohabitation, sexual relations, betrothal, minister, wedlock, path, contract, community property, name change, domicile, residence.
6. *Procedural terms:* action, suit, statute of limitations, complaint, discovery, defense, petition, jurisdiction, court, superior court, county court.
7. *Agencies:* Bureau of Vital Statistics, County Clerk, Department of Social Services, License Bureau, Secretary of State, Justice of the Peace.
8. *Long shots:* dowry, common law, single, blood relationship, fraud, religion, illegitimate, remarriage, antenuptial, alimony, bigamy, pregnancy, gifts, chastity, impotence, incest, virginity, support, custody, consent, paternity, etc.

If the CARTWHEEL can generate this many words and phrases from a starting point of just one word (wedding), potentially thousands more can be generated when you subject all of the important words from the client's case to the CARTWHEEL. Do you check them all in the index volume of every code, digest, encyclopedia, practice manual, and treatise? No. You can't spend your entire legal career in the law library working on one case! Common sense will tell you when you are on the right track and when you are needlessly duplicating your efforts. You may get lucky and find what you are after in a few minutes. For important tasks in any line of work (or play), however, being comprehensive is usually time-consuming.

A legal thesaurus or a general thesaurus can often be helpful in generating word alternatives when using the CARTWHEEL technique. See, for example, West's *Legal Thesaurus/Dictionary* or *Roget's International Thesaurus.*

As indicated in the chart, the categories may overlap; they are not mutually exclusive. Also, it is not significant whether you place a word in one category or another as long as the word comes to your mind as you comb through the index. The CARTWHEEL is, in effect, a *word association game* that should become second nature to you with practice. Perhaps some of the word selections in the above categories seem a bit far-fetched. You will not know for sure, however, whether a word will be fruitful until you try it. Be imaginative, and take some risks.

ASSIGNMENT A.1

Cartwheel the following words:

a. cruelty
b. support
c. paternity
d. sex

ASSIGNMENT A.2

a. The statutory code of your state probably has a number of different statutes that deal with "children." Use its indexes to help you find as many of these statutes as you can (up to a maximum of ten). Use the CARTWHEEL to help you think of many different phrasings and contexts for the word *children.* Give a brief summary of what each statute says about children.
b. Repeat the above assignment for the word *woman.*

STATE-CODE ASSIGNMENT

A great deal of family law grows out of the state statutory law written by your state legislature. This law will be found within a multivolume state statutory code.

It is important that you become acquainted with the family law sections of your statutory code. Many of the assignments in this book ask you to examine this code on a particular family law topic.

The general instructions for all statutory code assignments follow.

General Instructions for the State-Code Assignment

1. The first step is to make sure you know the name and location of the statutory code for your state. Some states have more than one code—each from a different publisher.
2. Be sure you are using the latest edition of the state code.
3. Use the CARTWHEEL technique to help you use the various indexes in the code. (There is often a general index at the end of the code volumes as well as smaller indexes after each volume or set of volumes covering the same topic area.)
4. Statutes can be changed or repealed, and new statutes can be added. Be sure that you are aware of such modifications by:

   - Checking the pocket part, if any, of every volume you use
   - Checking replacement volumes, if any
   - Checking supplement volumes or pamphlets, if any
   - Shepardizing the statute. To Shepardize something means to use the volumes of *Shepard's Citations* to obtain specific information about a document. When you shepardize a statute, you go to the set of *Shepard's Citations* covering your state code and examine all of the references provided on your statute (e.g., amendments, repeals, opinions interpreting the statute). Find the citation of your statute in black bold print within each *Shepard's* pamphlet and bound volume. The references, if any, will be found in columns immediately beneath the citation of your statute.

5. It is possible to find statutes online. If you have access to WESTLAW, LEXIS-NEXIS, and LOISLAW, you can locate the statutes of every state online. To look for statutes on a family law topic, you go to the database that contains the statutes of your state legislature and formulate a "query," which is simply a question. The CARTWHEEL can help you decide what words or phrases to use in your query.
6. Many state statutes are also available online through the Internet. Check the laws of your state on a general legal search engine (*examples:* www.findlaw.com; www.lawsonline.com; www.hg.org/usstates.html; and http://www.law.cornell.edu/states/listing.html). Also go to the home page of your state government: www.state.xx.us (insert your state's postal abbreviation in place of xx). On this page, look for links to the legislature of your state. You will probably be told what statutes are available. On the dangers of relying on law found on the Internet, see "Family Law Online" at the end of chapter 1.
7. Give a complete citation to every statute that you think covers the assignment. (A citation is a reference to any material printed on paper or stored in a computer database. It is the "address" where you can locate and read the material.) Ask your teacher to explain the standard citation format used in your state. It will often include components such as:

   - The title or chapter number of the statute
   - The abbreviated name of the code
   - The section number of the statute
   - The date of the code. (Use the date you find on the spine of the volume, or the date you find on the title page, or the latest copyright year—in this order of preference.)

8. When you quote from a statute, use quotation marks around the language you are quoting.
9. If the assignment asks you to apply the statute to the facts of a problem in the assignment, follow the General Instructions for the Legal-Analysis Assignment, page 533.
10. When you need help in understanding a statute, use the following approaches:

    - See if there are definition statutes that define some of the words in the statute you are examining. (If such definition statutes exist, they will usually precede the statute you are examining at the beginning of the cluster of statutes on that topic.)

- Examine cases that have interpreted the statute. You can obtain leads to these cases, if any exist, by checking the Notes to Decisions which are summaries of cases and are found immediately after the text of the statute in annotated editions of the code. (Annotated simply means organized by subject matter with research references such as Notes to Decisions or other commentary.) You can also find cases interpreting the statute by Shepardizing the statute.

11. If you cannot find what you are looking for in the statutory code, proceed as follows:
    - Repeat step 3 above. Frequently, the difficulty is the failure to use the indexes creatively. Do the CARTWHEEL exercise again to try to come up with more words and phrases to be checked in the indexes of the statutory code.
    - Check the court rules of your state courts to determine whether they treat the topic you are pursuing.
    - Check the constitution of your state to determine whether it treats the topic you are pursuing.
    - Find out if any court opinions have been written by your state courts on the topic you are pursuing. For techniques to find court opinions, see the General Instructions for the Court-Opinion Assignment, page 537.

ASSIGNMENT A.3

a. What is the name of the statutory code of your state? (If more than one exists, list each one.)
b. Who publishes it?
c. How is it updated? By pocket parts? By supplemental pamphlets? Both?
d. Give the address of any two Internet sites that give the text of some or all of the statutes in your state.
e. In this question, you will locate the same statute (i) in the code volumes and (ii) on the Internet. Go to your code and pick any statute on divorce or on any other area of family law. Quote the first line of the statute you select. Give the citation of the quote in the code. Now go on the Internet and try to find the same statute. Quote the first line. Give the citation of the quote on the Internet. If you cannot find the same code statute on the Internet, pick a different code statute.

LEGAL-ANALYSIS ASSIGNMENT

Before we examine the general instructions for the legal-analysis assignment, here is a brief introductory refresher on legal reasoning or **legal analysis**. The process of legal analysis can be diagrammed as follows:

legal analysis
The application of rules to facts for the purpose of resolving a legal dispute or preventing one from arising.

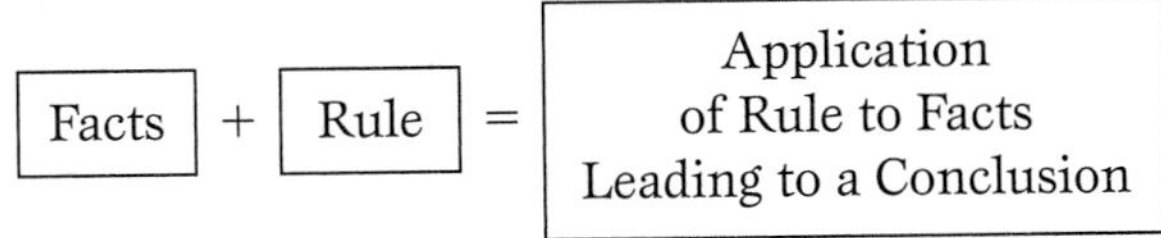

Let's look at an example.

Facts: George and Helen are married. One day, after a big argument, George walks out of the house and says, "Good-by. Find someone else to take care of you." As he walks out, he resolves to stay away forever.
Rule: One spouse abandons another by leaving without any intention of returning.
Application of rule to facts: When George walked out of the house resolving to stay away forever, he left "without any intention of returning." This is abandonment.

Most legal analysis, however, is not this simple. This can be due to a number of reasons, including the following:

- A word or phrase in the rule is ambiguous.
- You feel that you need more facts than you are given.

Ambiguity in the Rule

Facts: George and Helen are married. One day, after a big argument, George walks out of the apartment and says, "Good-by. Find someone else to take care of you." As he walks out, he resolves to stay away forever. He moves downstairs to a vacant, never-used room in the same building he and his wife jointly own. The room has its own exit to the street.

Rule: One spouse abandons another by leaving without any intention of returning.

There is ambiguity in the rule. What does "leaving" mean? At least two interpretations are possible:

- Moving out of the entire dwelling.
- Moving out of the part of the dwelling in which both spouses normally live together.

Which is the correct definition of "leaving"? The difference in the definitions is critical. Depending on which definition is adopted, a different result is reached:

- According to the first definition, George did not abandon Helen because he did not move out of the entire dwelling.
- According to the second definition, George did abandon Helen, since he moved out of the rooms where they both normally lived. Under this definition, he can commit abandonment without moving out of the entire building.

Your task in legal analysis is to be sensitive to such ambiguity in the rules that you are trying to apply to facts. Unfortunately, most students are not. They do not like to search for ambiguity; they accept language at face value. To combat this tendency, you should look at every word in the rule you are applying and ask yourself: What is the definition of this word? Is more than one definition possible? If my initial answer is no, I need to think harder! Am I sure that both sides of the controversy would agree on the definition of the word I am examining?

When you are using legal analysis in an interoffice memorandum or in a school examination, one of the biggest mistakes you can make is to hit the reader over the head with one conclusion. Don't overlook ambiguity. When it exists, find it and write about it. Good legal analysis articulates both sides of the controversy. If you personally favor one side over the other, you may state your opinion, but only after you have placed yourself in the shoes of both sides and presented the best argument for each.

Once you have identified ambiguity in the rule being applied from the perspective of both sides, what do you do next? How do you *resolve* the ambiguity? You have to do legal research (e.g., find out whether any courts have interpreted any of the ambiguous words/phrases). Has a court ever defined the word *leaving* in our rule? If so, you need to find the opinion containing the definition. (For purposes of the legal-analysis assignments in this book, however, you will not do any legal research unless the instructions in the assignment, or your instructor, tell you otherwise.)

The Need for More Facts

In the process of trying to connect rules to facts, you may sometimes feel that you need more facts to assess whether the rule applies. If so, state what additional facts you would like to have and *state why they may be helpful to your analysis.*

In the example involving George and Helen, suppose we are told that George said to Helen, "Good-by. Find someone else to take care of you," but we are not told whether he walked out. In your analysis, you would have to point out that the facts do not state what George did immediately after he made this statement to Helen. You need additional facts. You need to know whether he left the building or any part of the building after he made the statement. The rule refers to "leaving," and you do not know whether or how he left.

Also, if the facts do not clearly show that George left with the intent of never returning, you would need additional facts to help resolve the intent issue. For example:

- Did he take all of his clothes with him?
- Did he speak to anyone else after he left about what he was doing?
- How far away did he go when he left?
- Did he change his address officially (e.g., at the post office)?
- Did he open any new bank accounts or change old ones?
- Did he call Helen or otherwise contact her after he left? If so, how long after he left, how often, and about what?

State why you need the additional facts. For example, if George took all of his clothes with him when he left, it would be some indication that his departure was permanent (i.e., that he had no intention of returning when he left). This should be stated as such in your legal analysis.

Analysis of Elements

One of the most important skills of legal analysis is the ability to break down any rule into its **elements.** An element of a rule is defined as follows:

element
A portion of a rule that can be conveniently discussed separately from the rest and is a precondition to the applicability of the entire rule.

Element

1. A *portion* of a rule that can be conveniently discussed separately from the other elements, and
2. A *precondition* to the applicability of the entire rule (if one of the elements of the rule does not apply, the entire rule does not apply).

To a very large extent, legal analysis proceeds by element analysis, as we shall see. In addition, we use element analysis as an aid in performing other tasks. For example:

- When drafting a complaint, the drafter often tries to allege enough facts to establish each element of the cause of action. (A cause of action is a legally acceptable reason for suing; it is simply a theory of recovery.)
- When a trial judge gives instructions (the charge) to a jury, he or she must cover all of the elements of the cause of action and of the defenses. When counsel submits proposed instructions to the judge, the elements must likewise be covered.
- When an attorney is conducting a deposition, he or she will frequently organize the questions around the elements of the causes of action and defenses in the case.
- The organization of a memorandum of law will often follow the list of elements of the rules being discussed.

A major characteristic of *sloppy* legal analysis is that it does not clearly take the reader through the elements of a rule. Good analysis discusses every element, with an emphasis on the element(s) in contention. No element is passed over.

Suppose you are analyzing the following rule found in a statute:

§ 25–403 A pharmacist must not sell prescription drugs to a minor.

Note that the rule is not broken down into elements. You must identify the elements on your own:

Elements of § 25–403

1. Pharmacist
2. Must not sell
3. Prescription drugs
4. To a minor

No violation exists unless all four elements of this statute are established. If a pharmacist sells simple aspirin (a nonprescription drug), he or she is not liable under the statute. The third element cannot be established. Hence no violation, since one of the elements (preconditions) cannot be met.

For a number of reasons, rules such as statutes and regulations can be difficult to break into elements. For example, the rule may be long or may contain:

- Lists
- Alternatives
- Exceptions or provisos

Nevertheless, the same process is used. You must take the time to dissect the rule into its component elements. Examine the following rule and its elements:

> **§ 5** While representing a client in connection with contemplated or pending litigation, a lawyer shall not advance or guarantee financial assistance to his client, except that a lawyer may advance or guarantee court costs, expenses of investigation, expenses of medical examination, and costs of obtaining and presenting evidence provided the client remains ultimately liable for such expenses.

Elements of § 5

1. A lawyer
2. Representing a client in connection with contemplated litigation or in connection with pending litigation
3. Shall not advance financial assistance to his client or guarantee financial assistance to his client, except that the following is proper:
   a. lawyer advances or guarantees court costs, or
   b. lawyer advances or guarantees expenses of investigation, or
   c. lawyer advances or guarantees expenses of medical examination, or
   d. lawyer advances or guarantees costs of obtaining and presenting evidence
   provided the client remains ultimately liable for all expenses ("a"–"d").

When an element is stated in the alternative, list all the alternatives within the same element. Alternatives related to one element should be kept within the phrasing of that element. The same is true of exception or proviso clauses. State them within the relevant element, since they are intimately related to the applicability of that element.

In the above example, the most complicated element of § 5 is element 3. Within it there are a list, alternatives, an exception, and a proviso. But they all relate to the same point of the propriety of financial assistance. None of the subdivisions of the third element should be stated as a separate element. You sometimes must do some unraveling of a rule in order to identify its elements. This certainly had to be done with the third element of § 5. Do not be afraid to pick the rule apart in order to cluster its thoughts around unified themes that should stand alone as elements. Diagram the rule for yourself as you examine it.

If more than one rule is involved in a statute, regulation, constitutional provision, charter, ordinance, etc., treat one rule at a time. (Often each sentence can be treated as a separate rule.) Every rule should have its own elements, and, when appropriate, each element should be subdivided into its separate components, such as alternatives, exceptions, etc.

Once you have broken the rule into its elements, you have the structure of the analysis in front of you. Each element becomes a separate section of your analysis. You discuss one element at a time, concentrating on those that pose the greatest difficulties.

ASSIGNMENT A.4

Break the following rules into their elements:

a. § 800. The parties can by mutual agreement elect to terminate their separation agreement.

b. § 52. A court of this State shall not exercise its jurisdiction under this Act if at the time of filing the petition a proceeding concerning the custody of the child was pending in a court of another state exercising jurisdiction substantially in conformity with this Act, unless the proceeding is stayed by the court of the other state because this State is a more appropriate forum or for other reasons.

c. § 10.2. With respect to a child who has no presumed father under Section 4, an action may be brought by the child, the mother or personal representative of the child, the appropriate state agency, the personal representative or a parent of the mother if the mother has died, a man alleged or alleging himself to be the father, or the personal representative or a parent of the alleged father if the alleged father has died or is a minor.

d. § 107(b). When the mental or physical condition (including the blood group) of a party, or a person in the custody or under the legal control of a party, is in controversy, the court in which the action is pending may order the party to submit to a physical or mental examination by a physician or to produce for examination the person in his custody or legal control. The order may be made only on motion for good cause shown and upon the notice to the person to be examined and to all parties and shall specify time, place, manner, conditions, and scope of the examination and the person or persons by whom it is to be made.

To do legal analysis, you must identify the **legal issue.** To fail to identify the issue would be like trying to steer a ship without a rudder or to drive a car without the steering wheel: your legal analysis would drift aimlessly.

legal issue
A legal question; a question of whether a particular rule of law applies to a particular set of facts.

A legal issue has two components:

- A brief quote from the element of the rule in contention
- The major facts to which you are applying that element

In formal legal analysis, both components should be present in your statement of the legal issue.

Every element of a rule is potentially the basis of a separate issue. A rule with five elements, for example, could lead to five separate issues, each structured around whether one of the elements applies. In practice, however, it is rare for every element to lead to a separate issue. This is because every element of a rule will probably not be an **element in contention.** To have such an element, you must be able to make a reasonable prediction that the parties to the dispute will probably disagree on whether the element applies. If it is clear that both parties will agree on the applicability or nonapplicability of a particular element, it would be a waste of time to construct an issue around that element and to spend time analyzing it.

element in contention
The portion of a rule (i.e., the element) that forms the basis of a legal issue because the parties disagree on the interpretation or application of that element to the facts of the case.

At the time you write your memorandum, you may not know for certain what the other side will eventually say about the applicability of a rule. You must do your best to anticipate what your opponent *might* argue about the rule and any element within it.

There are two main kinds of disagreements that the parties can have about an element:

1. *Disagreement about the facts.* If you anticipate that the other side will disagree over whether the facts fit within an element, you should construct an issue around that element. In a child-custody case, for example, each parent may present numerous conflicting facts on whether it would be in the "best interests" of the child to be placed with one parent or the other. An issue clearly exists on the element of "best interests."

   Sometimes fact gaps will interfere with your ability to identify issues. (See the earlier discussion on the need for more facts.) If, for example, a tax deduction can be taken for alimony payments, but we are not told in the problem whether the alimony was in fact paid by the ex-husband, we have a fact gap. We will not know whether there is an alimony-tax issue until we close this gap by finding out.
2. *Disagreement about definitions.* If you anticipate that the other side will disagree over the definition of an element, you should construct an issue around that element. We saw an example of this earlier when we asked whether "leaving" in the abandonment rule meant moving out of the entire dwelling or moving out of that part of the dwelling in which both spouses normally live together.

Let's return to the pharmacy example:

§ 25–403 A pharmacist must not sell prescription drugs to a minor.

Suppose the following facts are involved:

Facts: Fred Jones owns a drugstore and is a licensed pharmacist. One day he sells tetracycline to Phil, a nineteen-year-old male.

Has Fred violated § 25–403? Step one in answering this question is to break § 25–403 into its elements:

Elements of § 25–403

1. Pharmacist
2. Must not sell
3. Prescription drugs
4. To a minor

These elements become a checklist from which we begin to explore the presence of legal issues.

Elements 1 and 2 are not realistic candidates for legal issues. There is no reasonable doubt over whether Fred is a pharmacist and over whether he engaged in selling. The facts clearly tell us that he is a pharmacist who did make a sale.

What about element 3? Should it become the basis of a legal issue? Did Fred sell a "prescription drug"? Is tetracycline such a drug? There is a *factual* gap that hinders our ability to answer the question at this point. The facts do not tell us whether tetracycline is sold over the counter or whether Phil purchased it by prescription. Further interviewing or investigation is needed on this factual question. This is a "next step" that should be listed at the end of the memo.

Element 4 clearly poses some ambiguity. What is a minor? Is a nineteen-year-old a minor? It is not clear. This ambiguity should prompt the preliminary draft of a legal issue:

Is a nineteen-year-old a "minor" within the meaning of § 25–403?

An alternate (more formal) phrasing of the issue would be as follows:

When a pharmacist sells tetracycline to a nineteen-year-old, has the pharmacist violated § 25–403, which prohibits sales of "prescription drugs" to "a minor"?

Every element is part of a checklist that must be examined in the above manner. If one element is glossed over, a potential legal issue may be missed. Recall the components of a legal issue:

- A brief quote from the element in contention
- The major facts to which you are applying that element

We have just explored how you go about determining whether an element is in contention. The next question is, How do you know which facts are major? Fortunately, the process of determining when an element is in contention will also tell you which facts are major. A fact is major, and therefore should be included in the phrasing of a legal issue, when that fact raises some doubt or ambiguity in your mind on whether the element is in contention. The fact that Phil is a nineteen-year-old is a major fact because this is the fact that prompted us to ask the question, What is a minor? Hence the reason for the first phrasing of the above issue:

> Is a nineteen-year-old a "minor" within the meaning of § 25–403?

Note that the fact that Phil is a male is left out of the statement of the issue. It does not appear to be relevant to the applicability of § 25–403 that the buyer is a male or female. Gender is not major, but age is.

Note also that we have used more facts in the alternative (more formal) phrasing of the same issue (e.g., pharmacist, selling, tetracycline). We phrased the issue in this way for two reasons. First, this phrasing raises the question of the applicability of the entire rule rather than simply one of the elements of the rule. Second, this phrasing contains facts that provide a context to an understanding of the issue even if all of the facts are not major to the element primarily in contention. Both reasons can justify a longer statement of a legal issue, provided the issue does not become so lengthy that it is too awkward to read, and provided the added facts will not detract from the focus on the element primarily in contention. Neither of these difficulties exists in the alternative (more formal) phrasing of our issue.

Examine the following statements of legal issues:

- Does § 504 apply?
- The issue is the admissibility of the confession.
- Does he have the burden of proof?

In general, you should avoid phrasing issues in this way. They are weak and incomplete because of the absence of facts. Legal disputes do not arise in the abstract. There must be a set of facts in order for a legal dispute to exist. You cannot comprehend the issue until you know the facts that give rise to that issue. This does not mean that the statement of the issue must contain a statement of all the facts; again, only the major ones need to be stated, along with perhaps a limited number of additional facts that help give context to the issue. Another reason these three statements of issues are incomplete is that they do not quote the pertinent language in the element of the rule that is in dispute (e.g., that is ambiguous) when applied to the major facts.

To summarize, the two guidelines that should govern the phrasing of issues are as follows:

1. The legal issue should contain a statement of the major facts from the problem that raise the ambiguity in the language of an element. A limited number of context facts may also be added.
2. The legal issue should also contain a brief quotation from the language of the element that is ambiguous in view of the major facts of the problem.

The components of the legal issue do not have to be stated in the above order—as long as both components are present in the legal issue.

ASSIGNMENT A.5

In each of the following situations, you are given a fact situation plus a rule in the form of a statute. Phrase the legal issue involved in each situation.

a. *Facts:* Len is divorced from Mary, who is now deceased. His twenty-year-old son, Sam, has just graduated from Benton College. Len paid all of Sam's expenses at Benton. Sam has been accepted by the Benton College of Law to study to become an attorney. Len can afford to pay Sam's law school expenses but refuses to do so. Sam says that his father is obligated to pay these expenses.

Statute: § 49(g). Child support shall include payment of college expenses if the child has the ability to attend and the parent has the ability to pay.

b. *Facts:* Jane and her two children by a former marriage receive public assistance. Jane's friend Jack, who is a traveling salesman, stays at Jane's apartment during his monthly business trips. This allows him to stay in town five to ten days at a time. He does not give Jane any money while he is with her.

Statute: § 11351. Whenever an unrelated adult male resides with a family applying for or receiving public assistance, he shall be required to make a financial contribution to the family which shall not be less than it would cost him to provide himself with an independent living arrangement.

One format in which you present your legal analysis to your supervisor is the **interoffice memorandum.** Exhibit A.2 presents an example.

interoffice memorandum
A written report addressed to someone in the office where you work, usually a supervisor. If the report explains how the law applies to a given set of facts, it is a memorandum of law.

Exhibit A.2 Interoffice Memorandum

INTEROFFICE MEMORANDUM

TO:	Mary Adams
FROM:	George Wilson
DATE:	March 26, 2001
NAME OF CASE:	Hagerty v. Hagerty
OFFICE FILE NO.:	01-49
COURT DOCKET NO.:	B-408-01
RE:	"Serious marital discord" and the refusal to seek alcoholism treatment under § 402(b)

Statement of Assignment

You have asked me to determine whether our client Linda Hagerty can prevent her husband from dissolving the marriage on the ground of "irretrievable breakdown" under § 402(b).

Issue

Is there "serious marital discord" constituting an "irretrievable breakdown" of a marriage under § 402(b) when one party believes that the marriage can be saved if the other party seeks treatment for alcoholism, which the latter refuses to seek?

Facts

Paul Hagerty has filed for dissolution of the marriage on the ground of "irretrievable breakdown of the marriage." Linda and Paul Hagerty have been married for four years. They have two children. Paul has a serious drinking problem according to our client. While intoxicated, he breaks furniture and is abusive to the children and his wife. She has repeatedly asked him to seek rehabilitation treatment through AA or some other counseling service. Two months ago she told him that he must leave unless he seeks treatment. He did leave but has refused treatment. She now insists that he return and undergo treatment. He has filed for a dissolution of the marriage on the ground of an "irretrievable breakdown of the marriage." He feels that their marriage is hopeless. Our client wants to defend the action and prevent the dissolution.

Analysis

Section 402(b) provides as follows:

> A court may make a finding that there has been an irretrievable breakdown of the marriage relationship if the finding is supported by evidence of serious marital discord adversely affecting the attitude of the parties toward the marriage.

Two elements must be present before a court will declare the existence of an "irretrievable breakdown of the marriage":

(1) serious marital discord;
(2) adversely affecting the attitude of the parties toward the marriage.

Section 402(b) has been in existence for less than a year. No case law exists defining the terms of § 402(b), and no other statutes exist providing these definitions.

(1) Serious Marital Discord

Two definitions of the phrase are possible. Mr. Hagerty will argue that "serous marital discord" exists if either party to the marriage feels that there is no likelihood of reconciliation. Our client, on the other hand, should argue that both parties must agree that reconciliation is unlikely, or at least that evidence of marital collapse must exist in addition to the views of only one of the spouses. Under Mr. Hagerty's definition, there is "serious marital discord" because one party (himself in this case) feels that there is no likelihood of reconciliation. Our client feels that a reconciliation is likely if her husband will seek treatment for his alcoholism.

Our client can argue that "marital discord" was meant to refer to the opinions of two people—the partners to the marriage. The agreement of both sides on the likelihood of reconciliation is critical to a determination of whether the marriage can survive. The lack of such a likelihood in the minds of both spouses amounts to an "irretrievable breakdown."

But our client is convinced that the marriage is retrievable. A court should not rule otherwise when one of the parties takes this position. In her view, Mr. Hagerty is sick and is in no position to judge whether a reconciliation is possible. His refusal to seek help for the treatable illness or sickness of alcoholism should disqualify him from making meaningful assessments as to whether the marriage can survive. The legislature could not have intended that a marriage would end simply at the whim of one of the parties, particularly when the party who wants out is too ill to make a considered judgment on the likelihood of reconciliation.

She can further argue that § 402(b) does not state that either party can obtain a dissolution of the marriage simply because one of the spouses says he or she wants it. The statute calls for "evidence" of "serious marital discord." There must be a showing of irreconcilability. This must mean that a court is required to look at the underlying evidence of whether there is hope. A mere statement by one of the parties that there is no hope is not enough "evidence." More is required. The court should examine Mr. Hagerty's condition and listen to whatever expert witnesses she may be able to call. She will want an opportunity to prove through such witnesses that hope does exist because of treatment. This opportunity is destroyed if

continued

Exhibit A.2 Interoffice Memorandum—*Continued*

the court accepts Mr. Hagerty's statement at face value that the marriage cannot be saved. Section 402(b) calls for a more thorough probe by a court.

Mr. Hagerty, on the other hand, will argue that our client is using the wrong definition of "serious marital discord" for purpose of establishing an "irretrievable breakdown." If <u>either</u> side feels that there is no likelihood of reconciliation, a court should find evidence of "serious marital discord" for purposes of establishing an "irretrievable breakdown." Otherwise, one of the parties could force a dead marriage to continue out of stubbornness, unreasonableness, or malice. The legislature could not have intended such a result.

Mr. Hagerty will argue that our client told him to leave and to enter treatment. We can probably assume from the facts that Mr. Hagerty does not want to enter treatment or that he thinks treatment will not be effective. In either event, Mrs. Hagerty has laid down a condition that Mr. Hagerty says cannot be met. He will argue that to force him into treatment would be as unproductive as to force him to continue his marriage.

He will further try to argue that our client's actions demonstrate that even <u>she</u> feels that "serious marital discord" exists. <u>She</u> threw him out, and <u>she</u> insisted on an unacceptable condition. She may say that she thinks the marriage is salvageable, but her actions point to the opposite conclusion.

(2) <u>Adversely Affecting the Attitude of the Parties toward the Marriage</u>

It is unlikely that this element will be in contention. Both parties will probably argue that the difficulties have adversely affected their views of the marriage. The phrase "adversely affecting" is not defined in the statute or in any court opinions. An "attitude" that has been "adversely" affected means no more than negative feelings toward something—the marriage. Even Mrs. Hagerty cannot deny that she has negative feelings about the marriage as a result of the controversy surrounding alcoholism. She may not think the marriage is hopeless, but her feelings are certainly negative, as evidenced by the fact that she told him to leave the house.

It might be significant to note that the second element refers to "parties"—in the plural. The statute does not say "attitude of one of the parties." This point might bolster Mrs. Hagerty's argument on the first element that the legislature intended <u>both</u> parties to feel that reconciliation was not possible.

<u>Conclusion</u>

The only element in contention will be the first. I think that Mr. Hagerty has the stronger argument. If Mr. Hagerty feels that the treatment for his alcoholism will not help the marriage and if he refuses to undergo this treatment, it is difficult to avoid the conclusion that the parties to the marriage cannot be reconciled. The main argument favoring our client is that the legislature may not have intended a marriage to be terminated this easily.

NEXT STEPS

There are two things that I have not yet done on this case. Let me know if you want me to do either of them:

(1) I have not yet checked the legislative history of § 402(b) to determine whether it will provide any guidance on the meaning of § 402(b).

(2) I have not yet checked the statutes of other states to see if they have the same language as our § 402(b). If such statutes exist, then I need to check cases interpreting these statutes as potential persuasive authority for our case.

ASSIGNMENT A.6

Bill and Pat were married in State A on March 13, 1973, where they continue to live. They have one child, Brenda, age fifteen. Since 1990, Bill and Pat have been having marital difficulties. Bill is a traveling salesman who spends a good deal of time away from State A. From 1991 to 1994, he did not see his family at all. He returned on February 4, 1995. He and Pat attended marital counseling sessions for about three months. By the summer of 1995, problems again arose. Bill left home. On the day he left, he said to Pat, "If you can straighten yourself out, I'll consider coming back." He packed all of his clothes and books but left behind the high school trophy he received for swimming. Although the departure was bitter, both sides agreed to maintain their joint checking account. Bill made deposits in the account. Pat wrote checks on the account to cover house expenses. In September of 1995, Bill contacted a real estate broker in State B about renting an apartment for six months in that state. The broker suggested tax advantages of buying a condominium in State B as opposed to renting. Bill was persuaded. He had been in State B only once or twice for his job, but wanted to explore the possibility of more extensive business opportunities there. On October 1, 1995, the broker called to inform Bill of a good condominium prospect in State B. On October 5, 1995, Bill was killed in an automobile accident on a highway in State B while on the way to examine the condominium for the first time.

State B wants Bill's estate to pay a state inheritance tax on the theory that at the time of death, Bill was domiciled in State B. The representative of Bill's estate disagrees and claims that Bill was domiciled in State A at the time of death.

In State B, the following statute exists, which is the basis of State B's claim:

> **§ 14.** Inheritance taxes are owed by persons who die domiciled in this state, which exists when the decedent had a physical presence in the state with the intent of making the state a permanent home.

Prepare an interoffice memorandum of law on the question of State B's right to inheritance taxes. Do not do any legal research on the problem. Do the memo solely on the basis of the information provided above.

The office file number is 95-421. There is no court docket number, since no court action has yet been initiated. The Tax Department of State B has taken the position that inheritance taxes are due under § 14.

The law office where you work has been retained by the representative of Bill's estate, who does not want to pay the inheritance tax to State B. Since the inheritance tax rate for State A is lower than for State B, it would be to the advantage of the estate to obtain a ruling that at the time of death, Bill was domiciled in State A.

For purposes of this assignment, you can assume the following definitions apply:

- *Physical presence:* actually being in a place
- *Intent of making the state a permanent home:* the desire to live in the state indefinitely; the place to which one intends to return when away (a person can have only one permanent home)

General Instructions for the Legal-Analysis Assignment

1. The starting point in the legal-analysis exercise is a set of facts in the assignment. It is to this set of facts that you must apply the rule or rules.
2. How do you find the rule or rules to apply to the facts?
   - By examining the text of the chapter immediately preceding the assignment, or
   - By examining the state code of your state—if you are told to do so in the assignment.

continued

General Instructions for the Legal-Analysis Assignments—*Continued*

3. Carefully examine each word/phrase in the rule being applied. Break the rule into its elements, and concentrate on those elements in contention.
4. Define each important word/phrase in each element.
5. Determine whether more than one definition exists for each important word/phrase.
6. If more than one definition is possible, state each definition and show what effect the different definitions would have on the result of the analysis. How would each side use the definition that is favorable to itself?
7. State the legal issue(s).
8. Carefully examine each of the facts given to you in the assignment.
9. Note any differences between the fact situation given in the assignment and comparable fact situations discussed in the text of the chapter immediately preceding the assignment. Assess whether such fact differences are significant.
10. If you determine that you need more facts to provide the analysis, state what facts you need and why you would like to have the additional facts. Specifically, how will the additional facts assist in completing the analysis?
11. Analyze the facts from the perspective of both sides. Do not be dogmatic in your analysis. Whenever possible, show how the facts might be interpreted differently by both sides.
12. If requested by your instructor, give your answers in the format of an interoffice memorandum of law, as presented in Exhibit A.2.
13. Do not do any legal research on the assignment unless you are specifically instructed to do so.

COMPLAINT-DRAFTING ASSIGNMENT

complaint
A pretrial document filed in court by one party against another that states a grievance, called a cause of action.

pleading
A formal document that contains allegations and responses of the parties in litigation.

cause of action
An allegation of facts that, if proved, would give a party a right to judicial relief; a theory of recovery.

standard form
A frequently used format for a document such as a contract, complaint, or tax return.

Court litigation begins when one party files a **complaint** against another party. This is the **pleading** that must state a **cause of action** such as negligence, breach of contract, or divorce on the ground of irretrievable breakdown. (A cause of action is a theory of recovery—a legally acceptable reason for suing.) See Exhibit 7.4 for a sample divorce complaint.

Before you begin drafting the complaint (or any document) from scratch, find out if someone has already prepared a **standard form** that you can use. These are printed in a number of places, including formbooks, manuals, practice texts, some statutory codes, and some court rules. Many legal stationery stores print and sell them. Most are written by private attorneys. Occasionally, however, a standard form will be written by the legislature or by the court as the suggested or required format to be used.

Considerable care must be exercised in the use of standard forms. They can be very deceptive in that they appear to require little more than a filling in of the blanks. Intelligent use of the forms, however, usually requires much more. The guidelines in the following list should be kept in mind.

How to Avoid Abusing a Standard Form

1. The cardinal rule is to *adapt* the form to the particulars of the client's case on which you are working.
2. Do not be afraid of changing the preprinted language of the form if you have a good reason for doing so. Whenever you make such a change, bring it to the attention of your supervisor for approval.
3. Never use a standard form unless and until you have satisfied yourself that you know the meaning of every word and phrase on it, especially **boilerplate.** The great temptation of most form users is to ignore what they do not understand because the form has been used so often in the past with no apparent difficulty. Do not give in to this temptation. Find out what everything means by:

boilerplate
Language that is commonly used in a document; it is repetitive language that is often nonessential.

- Asking your supervisor
- Asking more experienced paralegals or other knowledgeable people
- Doing other legal research
- Using a legal dictionary

4. You need to know whether the entire form or any part of it has ever been litigated in court. To find out, you must do legal research in the area of the law relevant to the form.
5. Once you have found a form that appears useful, look around for another form that covers the same topic. Analyze the different forms available. Which one is preferable? Why? The important point is to keep questioning the validity of the form. Be very skeptical about the utilization of any form.
6. Do not leave any blank spaces on the form. If a question does not apply to your case, write NA (not applicable) in the space for that question.
7. If the form was written for another state, be sure it can be adapted and is adapted to the law of your state. Very often out-of-state forms are unadaptable.
8. Occasionally you may go to an old case file to find a document in that file that might be used as a model for a similar document that you need to draft for a current case. All of the above cautions apply equally to the adaptation of documents from closed case files.

General Instructions for the Complaint-Drafting Assignment

1. Your objective is to draft a complaint that would be acceptable to a trial court in your state. For an example of the general structure of many divorce complaints, which you need to adapt to the law of your state, see Exhibit 7.4 in chapter 7.
2. Go to your state statutory code and read everything you can about complaints in general and about complaints involving divorce and other domestic relations matters in particular. To help you find material in the statutory code, use the CARTWHEEL technique.
3. Go to the court rules of the courts of your state and read everything you can about complaints in general and about complaints involving divorce and other domestic relations matters in particular. To help you find material in the court rules, use the CARTWHEEL technique.
4. Find out if your state has any standard form complaints written by the court or other official entity. Your state code or court rules will tell you if such forms exist and whether they are optional or required. Caution must be exercised in using standard forms, however. See How to Avoid Abusing a Standard Form.
5. Many states have practice manuals, formbooks, or other practice materials written by attorneys. These materials often contain standard form complaints that may be helpful. See How to Avoid Abusing a Standard Form.
6. In the complaint-drafting assignments of this book, you will often need additional facts in order to write the complaint (e.g., the names of the parties, their addresses, the docket number of the case, some of the basic facts that prompted the plaintiff to file the complaint). You can make up the facts that you need so long as your facts are consistent with the limited facts that are provided in the assignment.
7. The heading or beginning of the complaint is called the *caption.* Normally, it contains:
   - The name of the court
   - The parties' names and their litigation status (plaintiff, defendant, etc.)
   - The docket number assigned by the court
   - The title of the pleading (Complaint for . . .)
8. Each paragraph is usually numbered separately. The content of each paragraph should be limited to a single allegation or to a small number of allegations that are closely related.
9. The *commencement* goes after the caption. Find out what your state requires in the commencement of a complaint (see instructions 1–5 above). Some states require a citation to the statute that gives the court its subject matter jurisdiction (its power to hear this kind of case—see Exhibit 7.4) and a statement of basic facts that covers the residence of the plaintiff, the existence of a marriage, etc.

continued

General Instructions for the Complaint-Drafting Assignment—*Continued*

10. The *body* of the complaint contains a statement of the plaintiff's cause of action. In a divorce action, for example, this would consist of the facts constituting the grounds for the divorce.
11. The cause of action should be stated briefly and concisely. Avoid long recitations of the facts.
12. You cannot draft a complaint unless you know every component or element of the cause of action. For a divorce on the ground of separation, for example, there must be a voluntary living apart for a designated period of time, and the time apart must be consecutive. In most states, there should be allegations of fact in the complaint that cover each of these elements of the ground.
13. With the exception of the citation to the statute on subject matter jurisdiction referred to above in instruction 9, you do not give citations to statutes, court rules, or opinions in the complaint. Limit yourself to the statement of facts—the essential facts.
14. If you are not sure of a fact, you can state it "on information and belief."
15. If the plaintiff has more than one cause of action or theory of recovery, you should state all of them. Each should be stated separately and numbered, I, II, III, etc. Each separate theory or cause of action is called a *count.*
16. The *prayer for relief* should contain everything the plaintiff is asking the court to do.
17. The *verification* is a sworn statement that the contents of the document are true.

AGREEMENT-DRAFTING ASSIGNMENT

Several times in this book you are asked to draft an agreement (e.g., a separation agreement). Here are the general instructions for this assignment. You should keep a *documents file* that contains copies of agreements, complaints, and all the other documents you prepare for this and other courses. Such a file can be enormously beneficial in your job search later on. Prospective employers are often impressed by well-drafted documents, particularly from job applicants who have not had prior legal experience.

General Instructions for the Agreement-Drafting Assignment

1. You will need additional facts in order to draft the agreement (e.g., you may need the names of the parties, their addresses, the property they own, how they own it, other economic facts). You can obtain these facts in two ways:

   - Conduct a mock legal interview of fellow students according to the guidelines in the General Instructions for the Interview Assignment.
   - Make up any of these facts that you need, provided they are reasonable in the context of the circumstances of the assignment.

   Your instructor will let you know which option to take.
2. It is often useful to obtain copies of similar agreements that were written in the past for other clients and/or to obtain copies of model agreements commonly found in formbooks, manuals, practice books, etc. Such material may provide effective starting points for your own drafting. Proceed with caution, however. See How to Avoid Abusing a Standard Form.
3. It is critical that you know the law of the area covered by the agreement. What can and cannot be accomplished by the agreement? What legal pitfalls must be avoided? Research in the area of the law, therefore, is an essential precondition of drafting.
4. For purposes of the agreement-drafting assignments in this book, however, you do not have to do any legal research unless your instructor tells you to do so. You will find all the law you need by reading the chapter text immediately preceding the drafting assignment you are doing.
5. When tax considerations are relevant, take them into account in drafting the agreement.
6. Know what the client wants to accomplish by the agreement. Know the *specific* client objectives. (If you don't know what they are, see instruction 1 above.) It is too general, for example,

to say that the client wants to divide the property of the spouses in an equitable manner. A more specific and acceptable example of an objective would be to have the other spouse use the vacation home for ten years or until she remarries, whichever occurs earlier. Have all the specific objectives in mind when you draft. Each clause in the agreement should relate to one or more of the objectives. Your drafting guide is your statement of objectives.

7. At the beginning of the agreement, label the kind of agreement that it is (e.g., *Separation Agreement*). Also at the beginning, state the names and addresses of the parties entering the agreement.
8. Number each paragraph consecutively (1, 2, 3, etc.). Limit the subject matter of each paragraph to a single topic or to closely related topics. Be as narrow as possible in selecting the topic of a paragraph. For example, in a separation agreement dealing with the disposition of the property that the spouses accumulated during the marriage, each paragraph should cover a separate category of property. Similarly, there should be separately numbered paragraphs covering custody of the children, visitation rights, alimony, etc.
9. A mistake made by many drafters is to assume that everyone will be using the same definition of words. Major words should always be defined. A *major word* is any important word that could have more than one meaning. The word "property," for example, has several meanings (e.g., real property, personal property, property in one's possession now, property to be received in the future, etc.). What meaning did the parties intend for the word *property?* Such words should be carefully defined in the agreement.
10. One sign of an effective agreement is fairness. Avoid trying to take unfair advantage of the other side in drafting the agreement. The result may be an unworkable agreement leading to considerable delay, animosity, and litigation expense. The cooperation of both sides is necessary to make the agreement work. An important incentive to such cooperation is a feeling by both parties that the agreement is fair.

COURT-OPINION ASSIGNMENT

You need to know how to locate court opinions on family law topics for two reasons:

- To help you find opinions that have interpreted statutes on family law topics.
- To help you find the **common law.** A considerable amount of family law is part of the common law, which is judge-made law in the absence of controlling statutory law. If the legislature passes a statute that covers a controversy in litigation, the statute controls even if there is also common law that covers the controversy. Suppose, however, there are no statutes governing the dispute. In such a case, the court is free to create new law to resolve the litigation. If it does so, the new law becomes part of the common law.

common law
judge-made law in the absence of controlling statutory law.

General Instructions for the Court-Opinion Assignment

1. The objective of the assignment is to find opinions on a family law issue. The law library has a number of resources that can provide you with leads to such opinions. The major leads are:

   - Notes to Decisions found within most annotated statutory codes
   - The state digest or the regional digest covering opinions of your state, or the American Digest System
   - *American Law Reports*
   - Footnote references in formbooks, hornbooks, manuals, legal encyclopedias, legal periodical literature, etc.
   - *Words and Phrases*
   - WESTLAW, LEXIS–NEXIS, and LOISLAW
   - Internet
   - Attorneys and paralegals experienced in family law

continued

General Instructions for the Court-Opinion Assignment—*Continued*

2. You may not be familiar with all the legal resources mentioned above. If that is the case, do not wait for a course in legal research before starting to learn how to use them. Start *now* by asking questions. Ask librarians, fellow students, teachers, practicing attorneys and paralegals, etc. Above all, browse through these resources on your own as often as you can. With a little practice and determination, you will soon be able to obtain basic information from them.
3. Notes to Decisions. To know how to use Notes to Decisions, you must first know how to use an annotated statutory code. (Review the General Instructions for the State-Code Assignment.) The notes contain summaries of opinions that have interpreted statutes. Hence, in order to find these notes, you must first find a statute that covers the topic under examination. If opinions exist interpreting this statute, they will be summarized in the Notes to Decisions following the statute. Be sure to check for more recent notes in the pocket parts of the code.
4. Digests. Digests are volumes containing thousands of small paragraph summaries of court opinions. A digest is, in effect, a massive index to court opinions and consequently is often called a "case finder." There are three kinds of digests—all of which contain the same basic material and format:

   - State Digest. Most states have their own digest (i.e., volumes of small paragraph summaries of all the opinions written by courts in a particular state).
   - Regional Digest. There are a number of regional digests covering the opinions written by the state courts of several neighboring states.
   - American Digest System. This is the most comprehensive digest of all, covering the opinions of almost every court in the country.

   The main index in each of these digests is in separate volumes called the *Descriptive Word Index.* To use these indexes effectively, apply the CARTWHEEL technique.
5. *American Law Reports.* These volumes contain the full text of selected court opinions plus extensive research material on issues in the opinions. This material is called an *annotation.* The annotations often include a state-by-state breakdown of the legal issues treated in the annotation. Hence, when you find an annotation on a family law topic, you can look for court opinions from your state on that topic. There are six units of the *American Law Reports* volumes: ALR, ALR2d, ALR3d, ALR4th, ALR5th, and ALR Fed. The main index to these volumes is called the *Index to Annotations.* The CARTWHEEL technique will help you use this index.
6. Footnote references in other books. Often the footnotes are the most valuable part of formbooks, hornbooks, manuals, legal encyclopedias, and legal periodical literature. These footnotes usually give citations to court opinions on the topics being discussed in the body of the text. In a set of books that has extensive footnotes, such as either of the major legal encyclopedias (*Corpus Juris Secundum* and *American Jurisprudence 2d*), the references to court opinions in the footnotes may be organized alphabetically by state, which will make it easier for you to determine if opinions of your state are provided.
7. *Words and Phrases.* This is a multivolume set of books containing thousands of definitions of legal terms. The definitions are quotations from court opinions. Try to find definitions of words from court opinions of your state on the family law topic under examination.
8. WESTLAW, LEXIS-NEXIS, and LOISLAW. It is also possible to find cases online. If you have access to WESTLAW, LEXIS-NEXIS, and LOISLAW, you can locate the court opinions of every state online. To look for cases on a family law topic, you go to the database that contains the opinions of your state courts and formulate a "query," which is simply a question. The CARTWHEEL technique can help you decide what words or phrases to use in your query.
9. Many state court opinions are also available online through the Internet. Check the laws of your state on a general legal search engine (*examples:* www.findlaw.com; www.lawsonline.com; www.hg.org/usstates.html; www.multistate.com; http://www.law.cornell.edu/states/listing.html). Also go to the home page of your state government (www.state.xx.us) (insert your state's abbreviation in place of xx). On this page, look for links to the courts of your state. You will probably be told what opinions are available. On the dangers of relying on law found on the Internet, see "Family Law Online" at the end of chapter 1.
10. Experienced attorneys and paralegals. Never be reluctant to go to attorneys and paralegals in the field of family law to ask them for a lead to a court opinion of your state on a particular topic or to ask them for suggestions on how you might go about finding such an opinion. (For purposes of the assignments in this book, do not seek such suggestions until after you follow instructions 3–9 above on your own.)

ASSIGNMENT A.7

Answer the following questions by going to the nearest large law library to which you have access.

a. Give the name of every reporter in the library that will contain the full text of court opinions written by state courts of your state. Who publishes each reporter? What courts are covered in each?
b. Give the name of every digest that will provide small paragraph summaries of the court opinions of your state.
c. Go to one of the digests you mentioned in part (b) above. Use the index features of this digest to locate a key topic and number for *any* five family law subjects. (Select five different family law subject areas.) What are the key topics and numbers? Give the cite of the first opinion summarized under each key topic and number you have selected.

CHECKLIST-FORMULATION ASSIGNMENT

It is important that you learn how to write checklists that could become part of a manual. Every rule that you are told about or that you read about can be "translated" into a checklist. Checklist formulation should eventually become second nature to you. The sooner you start thinking about and creating lists of do's, don'ts, tasks, etc., the better.

Suppose that you have before you the following statute of your state:

> **§ 1742** No marriage shall be solemnized without a license issued by the county clerk of any county of this state not more than thirty days prior to the date of the solemnization of the marriage.

One way to handle this statute is to create a checklist of questions that you would ask a client in order to determine whether the statute has been complied with or violated. Some of the questions would be:

1. Did you have a marriage license?
2. Where did you get the license? Did you obtain it from a county clerk in this state?
3. On what date did you obtain the license?
4. On what date did you go through the marriage ceremony ("solemnization")? (You want to determine if there were more than thirty days between the date the county issued the license and the date of the ceremony.)

These are some of the questions that must be asked as part of a large number of questions concerning the validity of a particular marriage. If you were creating a manual, the above four questions in your checklist for § 1742 could go under the manual topic of "Marriage Formation" or "Marriage License." Most laws can be translated into checklists in this way.

General Instructions for the Checklist Formulation Assignment

1. The starting point in all the checklist-formulation assignments will be a rule. The rule usually will be found within a statute or a court opinion to which you will be referred.
2. Your objective is to make a list of questions that you would ask yourself, a client, or a witness for the purpose of determining whether the rule might apply.
3. Make sure you understand the rule. Closely analyze it. Make inquiries about what you do not understand in the rule. Consult a legal dictionary. Read closely related rules in order to see the

continued

General Instructions for the Checklist Formulation Assignment—*Continued*

rule you are examining in context. Read the rule again.

4. Break the rule down into elements, as discussed earlier.
5. For each element of the rule, design a question or a series of questions.
6. Every time the rule says that something must be done or that something must not be done, create a question or a series of questions designed to determine whether it was done.
7. Every time the rule imposes a precondition (i.e., *if* such and such occurs, *then* . . .), create a question or a series of questions designed to determine whether the precondition occurred.
8. Be alert to the word *and* in a rule. It usually refers to additional requirements. Create questions designed to determine whether all the additional requirements were met.
9. Be alert to the word *or* in a rule. It usually refers to alternative requirements. Create questions designed to determine which, if any, of the alternatives were met.
10. If you have been diligent in creating checklists, you will be taking major steps toward the creation of your own manual. Even if you do not create manuals, checklist creation is still valuable as a practical way of thinking about any law. (For other components of such a manual, see the General Instructions for the Systems Assignment, page 546.)

THE FACT-GATHERING ASSIGNMENTS

fact particularization
A fact-gathering technique designed to help you identify a large variety of questions you can try to answer through interviewing and investigation.

The next three categories of assignments cover various facets of the fact-gathering process in the area of family law. A cardinal principle in this process is the necessity of obtaining relevant factual detail. This is achieved through a technique called **fact particularization.** Once you identify the facts collected in the case thus far, you assume that these facts are woefully incomplete. For example, they fail to give more than one version of what happened. Then you identify a large number of basic who, what, where, why, when, and how questions that, if answered, will provide as complete a picture of what happened as is possible at this particular time.

Suppose you are working on a child-custody case. To particularize this case, you ask a series of questions centered on the following interrelated and over-lapping clusters: participant details, place details, time details, incident details, and verification details.

1. *Participant details.* Who is involved in the case? Obtain the names of children, parents, grandparents, other relatives, neighbors, government agency workers connected with the case, friends of the children and of the parents, teachers and ministers who know the family, employers of the parents, medical personnel who have treated the children, witnesses to specific events, etc. What does each participant know about current and past family living conditions? How do you know? What have they said? What is the age and the educational background of each participant? Etc.
2. *Place details.* Where do the children live? Where else have they lived? Where do they go for school, religious services, recreational activities, medical care, cultural events, etc? For each place, give the address, how far away from home it is, how the children get there, what costs are involved, who pays them, what happens there, what the feelings of the children are about the place, what they have said about it, what other participants think about the place, etc.
3. *Time details.* In an average day, how much time do the children spend on their normal activities? When did any of the important events occur (e.g., abuse)? How long did it last? Has it occurred more than once in the past? When?

4. *Incident details.* What happened? What events are relevant to the well-being of the children and the fitness of the parents to be guardians? Explain ordinary and extraordinary occurrences in their day-to-day lives.
5. *Verification details.* Every fact you have obtained has a source (e.g., the client, a record). Assume that you wanted to obtain an additional source to verify the original source of every important fact. Where would you go? Whom would you ask? What additional records would you try to obtain? How would you try to obtain them? Assess the believability of each source. Etc.

These categories of questions are interrelated. You will be simultaneously probing for details on people, incidents, dates, etc. There may be considerable overlap in your questions. This is not significant so long as you achieve comprehensiveness in factual detail (i.e., so long as you achieve factual particularity). Also, the above list of questions is just the tip of the iceberg. Scores and scores of additional questions in the same mold must be pursued. Given the complexity of human events and of human relationships, a great deal of factual detail is needed before you are able to achieve factual comprehensiveness. The objective of fact particularization is to get you into the habit of going beneath the surface in order to look at people and events from a variety of perspectives. Nothing is taken at face value.

INVESTIGATION-STRATEGY ASSIGNMENT

In many cases, an enormous number of facts must be gathered and verified. To keep from becoming overwhelmed, a plan of action must be developed. The investigation-strategy assignment is designed to help you construct such a plan in order to give the investigation some direction. The instructions for this assignment follow.

General Instructions for the Investigation-Strategy Assignment

1. The starting point in this assignment is a set of facts you are given in the assignment. Assume you have entered the case after these facts have been collected by someone else.
2. Assume further that these facts are inadequate because *many* more facts are needed, Review the material on *fact particularization* discussed earlier.
3. Closely examine the facts you have. Are they arranged chronologically? If not, rearrange them chronologically so that the facts tell a story with a beginning, middle, and end. Of course, there will be many gaps in the story. Your task will be to identify these gaps and to raise the questions that the investigator would need to ask to try to fill or close the gaps. These questions will become the investigator's strategy or plan for further investigation.
4. The focus of the questions will be on what you *don't* know about the facts you have.
5. Isolate the facts you have into small clusters of facts (e.g., the child is unhappy, the husband left the house in a rage). For each small set of facts that you identify or isolate in this way, make a *large* list of questions that fall into two interrelated categories:
   - Questions designed to obtain additional facts that will help you compile a much more detailed picture of what happened. To aid you in this list, ask the basic who, what, where, why, when, and how questions about every fact. (See the material on fact particularization.)
   - Questions designed to obtain facts that will help substantiate (or prove) the facts that you already have.

   There is no rigid formula to follow in making these lists of questions. The goal is a comprehensive list of questions that, if answered, would provide a comprehensive picture of what happened.
6. Consider structuring questions to elicit details on participants, places, times, and incidents.

continued

Interviewing and Investigation Checklist—Continued

7. Be particularly scrupulous about dates. Ask questions about the dates that you have and also about the dates that are missing.
8. In your questions on participants, try to identify a diversity of *versions.* Make a list of every person who is involved or who could be involved in the facts. Assume that each person potentially has a different version of a critical incident or series of incidents. Structure questions that will elicit these different versions.
9. Preceding most of the assignments will be a discussion of some legal principles or rules of law governing family law topics. Include questions on the elements of any relevant rules of law. (On breaking rules into their elements, see the earlier discussion; see also General Instructions for the Checklist-Formulation Assignment.)
10. The list of questions in this assignment does not have to be written in any particular order. Select any format that is readable.
11. In some of the chapters, you will find lists of interviewing questions and investigation tasks. If these lists are relevant to the area of the assignment, expand on them. Use the lists as points of departure for further fact particularization.

INTERVIEW ASSIGNMENT

The interview assignment relies on some of the skills covered earlier, especially fact particularization and checklist formulation. The instructions for most of the interview assignments follow.

General Instructions for the Interview Assignment

1. In this assignment, you are asked to interview another person (e.g., a fellow student, someone at home).
2. Review the material on *fact particularization.* One of your objectives is to obtain substantial factual specificity. As the interviewer, you should strive for a comprehensive picture of the people and events involved in the assignment.
3. In some of the chapters, you will find lists of interviewing questions. If the lists are relevant to the area of the assignment, expand on them. Use the lists as points of departure for further fact particularization.
4. After you complete the interview, prepare a report from your notes. For the heading of your report, see Exhibit A.2, Interoffice Memorandum. (If you are interviewing a new client, label your report "Intake Memorandum.") Indicate who wrote the report or memo (you), who will receive it (your instructor or supervisor), the name of the person interviewed (the interviewee), the date of the interview, and the date you turned in the report or memo. The first paragraph should state the assignment (e.g., "You have asked me to interview [*name of the interviewee*] in order to [*state the purpose of the interview assignment*].
5. In preparation for your interview, identify every rule of law that might be relevant to the fact situation (see the discussion in the text preceding the interview assignment). Break down each rule into its elements. Be sure to ask questions that are relevant to the applicability of every element. (See also the General Instructions for the Checklist-Formulation Assignment.)
6. Try to arrange the facts in your intake memorandum in roughly chronological order so that the facts unfold as a story with a beginning, middle, and end.
7. *Instructions to Interviewee:* You can make up facts as you go along so long as the facts are reasonably consistent with the facts initially provided. Do not volunteer any information. Simply answer the questions asked.
8. Your instructor may decide to role-play the interview in front of the class. If so, the class may be asked to comment on how the interview was conducted (e.g., did the interview follow the assignment, was there adequate fact particularization, did the interview ramble, was the interviewee placed at ease, how could the interview have been improved?).

INTERROGATORY ASSIGNMENT

The purpose of **interrogatories** is to obtain factual information about the other party's case in order to prepare for trial. The instructions for the interrogatory assignment follow.

interrogatories
A written set of factual questions sent by one party to another before the trial begins.

General Instructions for the Interrogatories Assignment

1. Your objective in writing the questions (i.e., the interrogatories) is to obtain as much information as possible from the other side in order to assist you in preparing a case. See the material on *fact particularization*. The material on preparing investigation strategies should also be helpful in drafting interrogatories.
2. The interrogatories you draft should be acceptable in your state, which means that you should know whatever restrictions exist in statutes and in court rules of your state on the scope and format of interrogatories in family law cases. For example, is there a limited number of questions that can be sent?
3. The scope of questions you can ask is usually quite broad. The test is whether the question is reasonably calculated to lead to evidence that will be admissible in court. This is a much broader standard than whether the answer itself would constitute admissible evidence.
4. Avoid unduly long or oppressive interrogatories.
5. Avoid questions that improperly seek privileged information. For example:

   a. Questions that violate the privilege against self-incrimination (e.g., "Did you burn your house on purpose?").
   b. Questions that violate the attorney-client privilege (e.g., "What did you tell your attorney about the child?").
   c. Questions that violate the doctor-patient privilege (e.g., "What did you tell your doctor about the pain?").
   d. Questions that violate the husband-wife privilege (e.g., "What did you tell your wife about the pain?"). This privilege does not apply when spouses are suing each other.
   e. Questions that violate the attorney work-product rule (e.g., "Does your attorney think my client has a valid claim?").

6. In many states, it is permissible to ask a question that would involve the application of law to fact—some times called "contention interrogatories." For example, "Do you contend that Mr. ______ had no intent to marry you at the time of the wedding ceremony?" or "Is it your position that Ms. ______ took the child out of the state in order to avoid complying with the custody decree?" If you ask such a question, be sure to follow it with a series of detailed questions that seek the factual reasons for the possible answers that could be given.
7. Be careful about the verb tense used in questions. Present tense (e.g., "is") is used to determine facts that are still current. Past tense (e.g., "was") is used to determine events that are over. If a question relates to past and present tense, break the question down into several questions.
8. It can be useful to try to find sample interrogatories in manuals, formbooks, and other practice materials. Such interrogatories, of course, would have to be adapted to the particular needs of the client's case on which you are currently working. On the dangers of using such forms, see How to Avoid Abusing a Standard Form. For a sample set of interrogatories designed to uncover the financial assets of a spouse, see Exhibit 8.2. (As indicated earlier, a copy of all documents you prepare—such as interrogatories—should be placed in a personal documents file for possible later use as writing samples in your employment search.)
9. It can also be useful to go to the closed case file of another case that contains interrogatories in order to try to adapt them. Again, the use of such materials is only a point of departure. Great care must be used in determining what, if anything, can be borrowed from other interrogatories.
10. Before you draft your interrogatories, know the case (on which you are working) inside and out. Read all pleadings filed to date (e.g., complaint, answer, correspondences in the file, intake memorandum, etc.). Many ideas for questions will come from this knowledge. For purposes of the assignments in this book, however, you will not have access to such data, since the assignments will be based on hypothetical cases.
11. Litigation involves causes of action and defenses. Each of these causes of action and defenses can

continued

General Instructions for the Interrogatories Assignment—*Continued*

be broken down into elements. Each of these elements should become the basis of a checklist. Ask questions that seek facts that could potentially be used to support each of the elements. (See also the General Instructions for the Checklist-Formulation Assignment.)

12. Consider phrasing your questions in such a way that the "story" of the facts unfolds chronologically.
13. Be constantly concerned about dates, full names, addresses, exact amounts, etc.
14. Always ask what witnesses the other side intends to rely on to support its version of the facts at the trial. Ask for the names and addresses of such witnesses.
15. Ask what documentation, physical things, or exhibits the other side will rely on to support its version of the facts. You may want to ask that such items be sent along with the answers to the interrogatories (or that such items be brought to a later deposition).
16. Avoid questions that call for simple "yes" or "no" answers unless you immediately follow up such questions with other questions that ask for details.
17. Include a definition section at the beginning of the interrogatories to avoid confusion and undue repetition in the later questions. This section will define words and phrases you intend to use in more than one question. For example: "A 'medical practitioner' as used in these interrogatories is meant to include any medical doctor, osteopathic physician, podiatrist, doctor of chiropractic, naturopathic physician, nurse, or other person who performs any form of healing art."
18. Phrase the questions so that the person answering will have to indicate whether he or she is talking from first-hand knowledge, second-hand knowledge (hearsay), etc.
19. As to each fact, ask questions calculated to elicit the respondent's ability to comment on the fact (e.g., how far away was he or she, does he or she wear glasses, how long has he or she known the party, in what capacity?).
20. Avoid complicated and difficult-to-read questions. Be direct and concise.

FLOWCHART ASSIGNMENT

A flowchart is a step-by-step account of how something is done (e.g., a divorce or a particular kind of administrative proceeding such as a workers' compensation hearing). A number of assignments in this book ask you to prepare a flowchart on the legal process under discussion. The instructions for this assignment follow.

General Instructions for the Flowchart Assignment

1. Design the flowchart based upon the law of your state. The chart will give an overview of how something is done in your state (e.g., how to adopt a child, how to change your name).
2. The two primary sources of information for the flowchart are your state statutory code and the court rules for the courts in your state. See General Instructions for the State-Code Assignment. See also the CARTWHEEL technique for using the index of statutory codes, court rules, or any reference materials.
3. You may be able to obtain information for the flowchart from manuals, formbooks, and other practice material. It is recommended, however, that you try to obtain the information directly from the statutory code and the court rules. The practice materials may be out of date. Furthermore, to use practice materials intelligently, you must know how to check the accuracy and timeliness of such materials by going to the primary sources, namely, the statutory code and the court rules (and occasionally the state constitution).
4. The flowchart must be chronological, moving from the first step of the process to the last step.
5. The structure and graphics that present the steps in the flowchart can be varied:
   - Use a series of boxes (one step per box) with all the boxes connected by arrows to show the progression of the process.
   - Use a list of brief, numbered paragraphs with each paragraph stating one step.

- Use an outline with the major headings being the key phrases of the process (e.g., agency contact, pretrial, etc.).

Use your imagination in designing the sequence of events outlined in the flowchart.

6. The information in the chart should pertain to **procedural law** rather than **substantive law.** Procedural law consists of the technical steps for bringing or defending actions in litigation before a court or an administrative agency. An example would be the number of days within which a party can request an extension of time to file an answer after the complaint has been filed. Substantive law consists of rights and obligations other than purely procedural matters. An example would be the right to a divorce on the ground of irreconcilable differences.
7. For each item of information in the flowchart, state your source (e.g., the citation to the statute or court rule that provided you with the procedural information you used in the flowchart).
8. Statutory codes and court rules may have sections that deal with litigation in general. Such sections are often listed in the index and table of contents of the codes and court rules under broad topics such as "Civil Procedure," "Actions," "Court Procedures," "Courts," etc. You should check these sections to see what, if anything, they say about the topic of your flowchart.
9. In addition, your state statutory code and court rules may have special sections that cover the procedural steps that are peculiar to the topic of your flowchart. Check these as well.
10. If you are flowcharting litigation of any kind, numerous steps are often involved at the pretrial, trial, appeal, and enforcement stages. These steps need to be incorporated into your flowchart. Here are some examples of questions you should ask yourself about most litigation. The answers to such questions must be outlined in your flowchart if they are relevant to whatever you are flowcharting.

- What agency, if any, has jurisdiction over the case?
- What is the application process at the agency?
- What court(s) have jurisdiction?
- How is service of process made?
- How is venue determined?
- Do you need to use any special format for the complaint?
- How is the complaint served and filed?
- Do you need to use any special format for the answer?
- How is the answer served and filed?
- Are there special rules for raising counterclaims?
- Are there any special motions that can be made (e.g., motion to dismiss)?
- What rules govern pretrial discovery: depositions, interrogatories, requests for production of documents and things, requests for admissions, and court-ordered examinations (physical and mental)?
- What sanctions can be imposed for violation of the pretrial discovery rules?
- What preliminary orders can be requested, and how must the request be made?
- What rules govern the issuing of the final judgment?
- How many days does a party have to appeal?
- What court has jurisdiction to hear the appeal?
- How can a judgment be enforced?

The above list is not exhaustive. If there are other steps or more detailed steps that apply to the process you are flowcharting for your state, include them.

SYSTEMS ASSIGNMENT

A system is a method of organizing people and resources to accomplish a task. Great skill is required to design and implement an effective system. A good way to start learning this skill is to identify and describe a system (or lack of a system) in the work lives of others. The systems assignment is designed to help you make such a start. The instructions for this assignment follow.

General Instructions for the Systems Assignment

1. Your goal is to interview practicing attorneys, paralegals, law office administrators, and legal secretaries who handle family law cases in order to identify their system for providing legal services on a certain kind of case.
2. You are seeking the following kinds of information about the system for handling the kind of case involved in this assignment:
   - Who does what on the case? What does the attorney do? The paralegal? The secretary?
   - In what sequence is it all done?
   - How long does the process take from beginning to end? Does the time involved differ from case to case? If so, what are the main factors causing the differences?
   - What equipment is used (e.g., fax machines, computers)?
   - What computer software, if any, is used (e.g., word processing, spreadsheet)?
   - What Internet sites, if any, are sometimes useful?
   - Are any standard forms used?
   - Are any manuals particularly helpful? If so, were they written by the office or by someone else?
   - Has the office changed its system for handling this kind of case? If so, what were the changes and why were they made?
   - Does anyone have any problems with how the present system now works? If so, what are they and what recommended improvements are contemplated?
3. If possible, try to interview someone from another firm that handles the same kind of case so that you can compare the systems used.
4. How do you find practicing attorneys, paralegals, legal administrators, and secretaries in the field of family law?
   - You may have fellow classmates who are secretaries or paralegals.
   - Check with your paralegal association.
   - Check with the local association of legal secretaries or legal administrators.
   - Ask your instructor for leads.
5. Another person who would have valuable information for this assignment is the law office manager or legal administrator of a larger firm.
6. Everyone is busy, particularly those working in a law office. You must not give the impression that you are going to take up a lot of the time of the people you interview. Have a checklist of questions ready. Be prepared. Guard against giving the impression that you are not sure what you want.
7. People you interview should never reveal any information about any particular clients in their offices, including the identity of the clients. This information is confidential. You are seeking generic information on systems for handling categories of cases. If by mistake you learn information about particular clients, be sure that you keep it confidential.

APPENDIX B

UNIFORM CHILD CUSTODY JURISDICTION AND ENFORCEMENT ACT

Where Found in State Codes:

Alabama	Ala. Code § 30-3B-101.
Alaska	Alaska Stat. § 25.30.300.
Arizona	Ariz. Rev. Stat. Ann. § 25-431.
Arkansas	Ark. Code Ann. § 9-19-101.
California	Cal. Family Code § 3400 (West).
Colorado	Colo. Rev. Stat. Ann. § 14-13-101.
Connecticut	Conn. Gen. Stat. § 46b-115.
Delaware	Del. Code Ann. tit. 13, § 1901.
District of Columbia	D. C. Code Ann. § 16-4501.
Florida	Fla. Stat. Ann. § 61, 1302 (West).
Georgia	Ga. Code Ann. § 19-9-40.
Hawaii	Haw. Rev. Stat. § 583-1.
Idaho	Idaho Code § 32-1101.
Illinois	750 Ill. Comp. Stat. Ann. § 35/1 (West).
Indiana	Ind. Code Ann. § 31-17-3-1 (West).
Iowa	Iowa Code Ann. § 598B.101 (West).
Kansas	Kan. Stat. Ann. § 38-1301.
Kentucky	Ky. Rev. Stat. Ann. § 403.400.
Louisiana	La. Rev. Stat. Ann. § 13:1700.
Maine	Me. Rev. Stat. Ann. tit. 19, § 1731.
Maryland	Md. Code Ann., Family Law § 9-201.
Massachusetts	Mass. Gen. Laws Ann. ch. 209B, § 1.
Michigan	Mich. Comp. Laws Ann. § 600.651.
Minnesota	Minn. Stat. Ann. § 518D.101.
Mississippi	Miss. Code Ann. § 93-23-1.
Missouri	Mo. Ann. Stat. § 452.440.
Montana	Mont. Code Ann. § 40-7-101.
Nebraska	Neb. Rev. Stat. § 43-1201.
Nevada	Nev. Rev. Stat. § 125A.010.
New Hampshire	N.H. Rev. Stat. Ann. § 458-A:1.
New Jersey	N.J. Stat. Ann. § 2A:34-28.
New Mexico	N.M. Stat. Ann. § 40-10-1.
New York	N.Y. Dom. Rel. Law § 75-aa (McKinney).
North Carolina	N.C. Gen. Stat. § 50A-101.
North Dakota	N.D. Cent. Code § 14-14.1-01.
Ohio	Ohio Rev. Code Ann. § 3109.21.
Oklahoma	Okla. Stat. Ann. tit. 43, § 551-1012.
Oregon	Or. Rev. Stat. § 109.701.
Pennsylvania	23 Pa. Cons. Stat. Ann. § 5341.
Rhode Island	R.I. Gen. Laws § 15-14-1.
South Carolina	S.C. Code Ann. § 20-7-782.
South Dakota	S.D. Codified Laws Ann. § 26-5A-1.
Tennessee	Tenn. Code Ann. § 36-6-201.
Texas	Tex. Fam. Code Ann. § 152.001.
Utah	Utah Code Ann. § 78-45c-1.
Vermont	Vt. Stat. Ann. tit. 15, § 1031.
Virgin Islands	V.I. Code Ann. tit. 16, § 115.

Virginia	Va. Code Ann. § 20-125.
Washington	Wash. Rev. Code Ann. § 26.27.010.
West Virginia	W. Va. Code § 48-10-1.
Wisconsin	Wis. Stat. Ann. § 822.01.
Wyoming	Wyo. Stat. § 20-5-101.

§ 102. Definitions.

In this [Act]:

(1) "Abandoned" means left without provision for reasonable and necessary care or supervision.

(2) "Child" means an individual who has not attained 18 years of age.

(3) "Child-custody determination" means a judgment, decree, or other order of a court providing for the legal custody, physical custody, or visitation with respect to a child. The term includes a permanent, temporary, initial, and modification order. The term does not include an order relating to child support or other monetary obligation of an individual.

(4) "Child-custody proceeding" means a proceeding in which legal custody, physical custody, or visitation with respect to a child is an issue. The term includes a proceeding for divorce, separation, neglect, abuse, dependency, guardianship, paternity, termination of parental rights, and protection from domestic violence, in which the issue may appear. The term does not include a proceeding involving juvenile delinquency, contractual emancipation, or enforcement under [Article] 3.

(5) "Commencement" means the filing of the first pleading in a proceeding.

(6) "Court" means an entity authorized under the law of a State to establish, enforce, or modify a child-custody determination.

(7) "Home State" means the State in which a child lived with a parent or a person acting as a parent for at least six consecutive months immediately before the commencement of a child-custody proceeding. In the case of a child less than six months of age, the term means the State in which the child lived from birth with any of the persons mentioned. A period of temporary absence of any of the mentioned persons is part of the period.

(8) "Initial determination" means the first child-custody determination concerning a particular child.

(9) "Issuing court" means the court that makes a child-custody determination for which enforcement is sought under this [Act].

(10) "Issuing State" means the State in which a child-custody determination is made.

(11) "Modification" means a child-custody determination that changes, replaces, supersedes, or is otherwise made after a previous determination concerning the same child, whether or not it is made by the court that made the previous determination.

(12) "Person" means an individual, corporation, business trust, estate, trust, partnership, limited liability company, association, joint venture, government; governmental subdivision, agency, or instrumentality; public corporation; or any other legal or commercial entity.

(13) "Person acting as a parent" means a person, other than a parent, who:

(A) has physical custody of the child or has had physical custody for a period of six consecutive months, including any temporary absence, within one year immediately before the commencement of a child-custody proceeding; and

(B) has been awarded legal custody by a court or claims a right to legal custody under the law of this State.

(14) "Physical custody" means the physical care and supervision of a child.

(15) "State" means a State of the United States, the District of Columbia, Puerto Rico, the United States Virgin Islands, or any territory or insular possession subject to the jurisdiction of the United States.

[(16) "Tribe" means an Indian tribe or band, or Alaskan Native village, which is recognized by federal law or formally acknowledged by a State.]

(17) "Warrant" means an order issued by a court authorizing law enforcement officers to take physical custody of a child.

§ 103. Proceedings Governed by Other Law.

This [Act] does not govern an adoption proceeding or a proceeding pertaining to the authorization of emergency medical care for a child.

§ 104. Application to Indian Tribes.

(a) A child-custody proceeding that pertains to an Indian child as defined in the Indian Child Welfare Act, 25 U.S.C. § 1901 et seq., is not subject to this [Act] to the extent that it is governed by the Indian Child Welfare Act.

[(b) A court of this State shall treat a tribe as if it were a State of the United States for the purpose of applying [Articles] 1 and 2.]

[(c) A child-custody determination made by a tribe under factual circumstances in substantial conformity with the jurisdictional standards of this [Act] must be recognized and enforced under [Article] 3.]

§ 105. International Application of [Act].

(a) A court of this State shall treat a foreign country as if it were a State of the United States for the purpose of applying [Articles] 1 and 2.

(b) Except as otherwise provided in subsection (c), a child-custody determination made in a foreign country under factual circumstances in substantial conformity with the jurisdictional standards of this [Act] must be recognized and enforced under [Article] 3.

(c) A court of this State need not apply this [Act] if the child custody law of a foreign country violates fundamental principles of human rights.

§ 106. Effect of Child-Custody Determination.

A child-custody determination made by a court of this State that had jurisdiction under this [Act] binds all persons who have been served in accordance with the laws of this State or notified in accordance with Section 108 or who have submitted to the jurisdiction of the court, and who have been given an opportunity to be heard. As to those persons, the determination is conclusive as to all decided issues of law and fact except to the extent the determination is modified.

§ 107. Priority.

If a question of existence or exercise of jurisdiction under this [Act] is raised in a child-custody proceeding, the question, upon request of a party, must be given priority on the calendar and handled expeditiously.

§ 108. Notice to Persons Outside State.

(a) Notice required for the exercise of jurisdiction when a person is outside this State may be given in a manner prescribed by the law of this State for service of process or by the law of the State in which the service is made. Notice must be given in a manner reasonably calculated to give actual notice but may be by publication if other means are not effective.

(b) Proof of service may be made in the manner prescribed by the law of this state or by the law of the state in which the service is made.

(c) Notice is not required for the exercise of jurisdiction with respect to a person who submits to the jurisdiction of the court.

§ 109. Appearance and Limited Immunity.

(a) A party to a child-custody proceeding, including a modification proceeding, or a petitioner or respondent in a proceeding to enforce or register a child-custody determination, is not subject to personal jurisdiction in this State for another proceeding or purpose solely by reason of having participated, or of having been physically present for the purpose of participating, in the proceeding.

(b) A person who is subject to personal jurisdiction in this State on a basis other than physical presence is not immune from service of process in this State. A party present in this State who is subject to the jurisdiction of another State is not immune from service of process allowable under the laws of that State.

(c) The immunity granted by subsection (a) does not extend to civil litigation based on acts unrelated to the participation in a proceeding under this [Act] committed by an individual while present in this State.

§ 110. Communication Between Courts.

(a) A court of this State may communicate with a court in another State concerning a proceeding arising under this [Act].

(b) The court may allow the parties to participate in the communication. If the parties are not able to participate in the communication, they must be given the opportunity to present facts and legal arguments before a decision on jurisdiction is made.

(c) Communication between courts on schedules, calendars, court records, and similar matters may occur without informing the parties. A record need not be made of the communication.

(d) Except as otherwise provided in subsection (c), a record must be made of a communication under this section. The parties must be informed promptly of the communication and granted access to the record.

(e) For the purposes of this section, "record" means information that is inscribed on a tangible medium or that is stored in an electronic or other medium and is retrievable in perceivable form.

§ 111. Taking Testimony in Another State.

(a) In addition to other procedures available to a party, a party to a child-custody proceeding may offer testimony of witnesses who are located in another State, including testimony of the parties and the child, by deposition or other means allowable in this State for testimony taken in another State. The court on its own motion may order that the testimony of a person be taken in another State and may prescribe the manner in which and the terms upon which the testimony is taken.

(b) A court of this State may permit an individual residing in another State to be deposed or to testify by telephone, audiovisual means, or other electronic means before a designated court or at another location in that State. A court of this State shall cooperate with courts of other States in designating an appropriate location for the deposition or testimony.

(c) Documentary evidence transmitted from another State to a court of this State by technological means that do not produce an original writing may not be excluded from evidence on an objection based on the means of transmission.

§ 112. Cooperation Between Courts; Preservation of Records.

(a) A court of this State may request the appropriate court of another State to:

(1) hold an evidentiary hearing;

(2) order a person to produce or give evidence pursuant to procedures of that State;

(3) order that an evaluation be made with respect to the custody of a child involved in a pending proceeding;

(4) forward to the court of this State a certified copy of the transcript of the record of the hearing, the evidence otherwise presented, and any evaluation prepared in compliance with the request; and

(5) order a party to a child-custody proceeding or any person having physical custody of the child to appear in the proceeding with or without the child.

(b) Upon request of a court of another State, a court of this State may hold a hearing or enter an order described in subsection (a).

(c) Travel and other necessary and reasonable expenses incurred under subsections (a) and (b) may be assessed against the parties according to the law of this State.

(d) A court of this State shall preserve the pleadings, orders, decrees, records of hearings, evaluations, and other pertinent records with respect to a child-custody proceeding until the child attains 18 years of age. Upon appropriate request by a court or law enforcement official of another State, the court shall forward a certified copy of those records.

§ 201. Initial Child-Custody Jurisdiction.

(a) Except as otherwise provided in Section 204, a court of this State has jurisdiction to make an initial child-custody determination only if:

(1) this State is the home State of the child on the date of the commencement of the proceeding, or was the home State of the child within six months before the commencement of the proceeding and the child is absent from this State but a parent or person acting as a parent continues to live in this State;

(2) a court of another State does not have jurisdiction under paragraph (1), or a court of the home State of the child has declined to exercise jurisdiction on the ground that this State is the more appropriate forum under Section 207 or 208, and:

(A) the child and the child's parents, or the child and at least one parent or a person acting as a parent, have a significant connection with this State other than mere physical presence; and

(B) substantial evidence is available in this State concerning the child's care, protection, training, and personal relationships;

(3) all courts having jurisdiction under paragraph (1) or (2) have declined to exercise jurisdiction on the ground that a court of this State is the more appropriate forum to determine the custody of the child under Section 207 or 208; or

(4) no court of any other State would have jurisdiction under the criteria specified in paragraph (1), (2), or (3).

(b) Subsection (a) is the exclusive jurisdictional basis for making a child-custody determination by a court of this State.

(c) Physical presence of, or personal jurisdiction over, a party or a child is not necessary or sufficient to make a child-custody determination.

§ 202. Exclusive, Continuing Jurisdiction.

(a) Except as otherwise provided in Section 204, a court of this State which has made a child-custody determination consistent with Section 201 or 203 has exclusive, continuing jurisdiction over the determination until:

(1) a court of this State determines that the child, the child's parents, and any person acting as a parent do not have a significant connection with this State and that substantial evidence is no longer available in this State concerning the child's care, protection, training, and personal relationships; or

(2) a court of this State or a court of another State determines that the child, the child's parents, and any person acting as a parent do not presently reside in this State.

(b) A court of this State which has made a child-custody determination and does not have exclusive, continuing jurisdiction under this section may modify that determination only if it has jurisdiction to make an initial determination under Section 201.

§ 203. Jurisdiction to Modify Determination.

Except as otherwise provided in Section 204, a court of this State may not modify a child-custody determination made by a court of another State unless a court of this State has jurisdiction to make an initial determination under Section 201(a)(1) or (2) and:

(1) the court of the other State determines it no longer has exclusive, continuing jurisdiction under Section 202 or that a court of this State would be a more convenient forum under Section 207; or

(2) a court of this State or a court of the other State determines that the child, the child's parents, and any person acting as a parent do not presently reside in the other State.

§ 204. Temporary Emergency Jurisdiction.

(a) A court of this State has temporary emergency jurisdiction if the child is present in this State and the child has been abandoned or it is necessary in an emergency to protect the child because the child, or a sibling or parent of the child, is subjected to or threatened with mistreatment or abuse.

(b) If there is no previous child-custody determination that is entitled to be enforced under this [Act] and a child-custody proceeding has not been commenced in a court of a State having jurisdiction under Sections 201 through 203, a child-custody determination made under this section remains in effect until an order is obtained from a court of a State having jurisdiction under Sections 201 through 203. If a child-custody proceeding has not been or is not commenced in a court of a State having jurisdiction under Sections 201 through 203, a child-custody determination made under this section becomes a final determination, if it so provides and this State becomes the home State of the child.

(c) If there is a previous child-custody determination that is entitled to be enforced under this [Act], or a child-custody proceeding has been commenced in a court of a State having jurisdiction under Sections 201 through 203, any order issued by a court of this State under this section must specify in the order a period that the court considers adequate to allow the person seeking an order to obtain an order from the State having jurisdiction under Sections 201 through 203. The order issued in this State remains in effect until an order is obtained from the other State within the period specified or the period expires.

(d) A court of this State which has been asked to make a child-custody determination under this section, upon being informed that a child-custody proceeding has been commenced in, or a child-custody determination has been made by, a court of a State having jurisdiction under Sections 201 through 203, shall immediately communicate with the other court. A court of this State which is exercising jurisdiction pursuant to Sections 201 through 203, upon being informed that a child-custody proceeding has been commenced in, or a child-custody determination has been made by, a court of another State under a statute similar to this section shall immediately communicate with the court of that State to resolve the emergency, protect the safety of the parties and the child, and determine a period for the duration of the temporary order.

§ 205. Notice; Opportunity to Be Heard; Joinder.

(a) Before a child-custody determination is made under this [Act], notice and an opportunity to be heard in accordance with the standards of Section 108 must be given to all persons entitled to notice under the law of this State as in child-custody proceedings between residents of this State, any parent whose parental rights have not been previously terminated, and any person having physical custody of the child.

(b) This [Act] does not govern the enforceability of a child-custody determination made without notice or an opportunity to be heard.

(c) The obligation to join a party and the right to intervene as a party in a child-custody proceeding under this [Act] are governed by the law of this State as in child-custody proceedings between residents of this State.

§ 206. Simultaneous Proceedings.

(a) Except as otherwise provided in Section 204, a court of this State may not exercise its jurisdiction under this [article] if, at the time of the commencement of the proceeding, a proceeding concerning the custody of the child has been commenced in a court of another State having jurisdiction substantially in conformity with this [Act], unless the proceeding has been terminated or is stayed by the court of the other State because a court of this State is a more convenient forum under Section 207.

(b) Except as otherwise provided in Section 204, a court of this State, before hearing a child-custody proceeding, shall examine the court documents and other information supplied by the parties pursuant to Section 209. If the court determines that a child-custody proceeding has been commenced in a court in another State having jurisdiction substantially in accordance with this [Act], the court of this State shall stay its proceeding and communicate with the court of the other State. If the court of the State having jurisdiction substantially in accordance with this [Act] does not determine that the court of this State is a more appropriate forum, the court of this State shall dismiss the proceeding.

(c) In a proceeding to modify a child-custody determination, a court of this State shall determine whether a proceeding to enforce the determination has been commenced in another State. If a proceeding to enforce a child-custody determination has been commenced in another State, the court may:

(1) stay the proceeding for modification pending the entry of an order of a court of the other State enforcing, staying, denying, or dismissing the proceeding for enforcement;

(2) enjoin the parties from continuing with the proceeding for enforcement; or

(3) proceed with the modification under conditions it considers appropriate.

§ 207. Inconvenient Forum.

(a) A court of this State which has jurisdiction under this [Act] to make a child-custody determination may decline to exercise its jurisdiction at any time if it determines that it is an inconvenient forum under the circumstances and that a court of another State is a more appropriate forum. The issue of inconvenient forum may be raised upon motion of a party, the court's own motion, or request of another court.

(b) Before determining whether it is an inconvenient forum, a court of this State shall consider whether it is appropriate for a court of another State to exercise jurisdiction. For this purpose, the court shall allow the parties to submit information and shall consider all relevant factors, including:

(1) whether domestic violence has occurred and is likely to continue in the future and which State could best protect the parties and the child;

(2) the length of time the child has resided outside this State;

(3) the distance between the court in this State and the court in the State that would assume jurisdiction;

(4) the relative financial circumstances of the parties;

(5) any agreement of the parties as to which State should assume jurisdiction;

(6) the nature and location of the evidence required to resolve the pending litigation, including testimony of the child;

(7) the ability of the court of each State to decide the issue expeditiously and the procedures necessary to present the evidence; and

(8) the familiarity of the court of each State with the facts and issues in the pending litigation.

(c) If a court of this State determines that it is an inconvenient forum and that a court of another State is a more appropriate forum, it shall stay the proceedings upon condition that a child-custody proceeding be promptly commenced in another designated State and may impose any other condition the court considers just and proper.

(d) A court of this State may decline to exercise its jurisdiction under this [Act] if a child-custody determination is incidental to an action for divorce or another proceeding while still retaining jurisdiction over the divorce or other proceeding.

§ 208. Jurisdiction Declined by Reason of Conduct.

(a) Except as otherwise provided in Section 204 [or by other law of this State], if a court of this State has jurisdiction under this [Act] because a person seeking to invoke its jurisdiction has engaged in unjustifiable conduct, the court shall decline to exercise its jurisdiction unless:

(1) the parents and all persons acting as parents have acquiesced in the exercise of jurisdiction;

(2) a court of the State otherwise having jurisdiction under Sections 201 through 203 determines that this State is a more appropriate forum under Section 207; or

(3) no court of any other State would have jurisdiction under the criteria specified in Sections 201 through 203.

(b) If a court of this State declines to exercise its jurisdiction pursuant to subsection (a), it may fashion an appropriate remedy to ensure the safety of the child and prevent a repetition of the unjustifiable conduct, including staying the proceeding until a child-custody proceeding is commenced in a court having jurisdiction under Sections 201 through 203.

(c) If a court dismisses a petition or stays a proceeding because it declines to exercise its jurisdiction pursuant to subsection (a), it shall assess against the party seeking to invoke its jurisdiction necessary and reasonable expenses including costs, communication expenses, attorney's fees, investigative fees, expenses for witnesses, travel expenses, and child care during the course of the proceedings, unless the party from whom fees are sought establishes that the assessment would be clearly inappropriate. The court may not assess fees, costs, or expenses against this State unless authorized by law other than this [Act].

§ 209. Information to Be Submitted to Court.

(a) [Subject to [local law providing for the confidentiality of procedures, addresses, and other identifying information], in] [In] a child-custody proceeding, each party, in its first pleading or in an attached affidavit, shall give information, if reasonably ascertainable, under oath as to the child's present address or whereabouts, the places where the child has lived during the last five years, and the names and present addresses of the persons with whom the child has lived during that period. The pleading or affidavit must state whether the party:

(1) has participated, as a party or witness or in any other capacity, in any other proceeding concerning the custody of or visitation with the child and, if so, identify the court, the case number, and the date of the child-custody determination, if any;

(2) knows of any proceeding that could affect the current proceeding, including proceedings for enforcement and proceedings relating to domestic violence, protective orders, termination of parental rights, and adoptions and, if so, identify the court, the case number, and the nature of the proceeding; and

(3) knows the names and addresses of any person not a party to the proceeding who has physical custody of the child or claims rights of legal custody or physical custody of, or visitation with, the child and, if so, the names and addresses of those persons.

(b) If the information required by subsection (a) is not furnished, the court, upon motion of a party or its own motion, may stay the proceeding until the information is furnished.

(c) If the declaration as to any of the items described in subsection (a) (1) through (3) is in the affirmative, the declarant shall give additional information under oath as required by the court. The court may examine the parties under oath as to details of the information furnished and other matters pertinent to the court's jurisdiction and the disposition of the case.

(d) Each party has a continuing duty to inform the court of any proceeding in this or any other State that could affect the current proceeding.

[(e) If a party alleges in an affidavit or a pleading under oath that the health, safety, or liberty of a party or child would be jeopardized by disclosure of identifying information, the information must be sealed and may not be disclosed to the other party or the public unless the court orders the disclosure to be made after a hearing in which the court takes into consideration the health, safety, or liberty of the party or child and determines that the disclosure is in the interest of justice.]

§ 210. Appearance of Parties and Child.

(a) In a child-custody proceeding in this State, the court may order a party to the proceeding who is in this State to appear before the court in person with or without the child. The court may order any person who is in this State and who has physical custody or control of the child to appear in person with the child.

(b) If a party to a child-custody proceeding whose presence is desired by the court is outside this State, the court may order that a notice given pursuant to Section 108 include a statement directing the party to appear in person with or without the child and informing the party that failure to appear may result in a decision adverse to the party.

(c) The court may enter any orders necessary to ensure the safety of the child and of any person ordered to appear under this section.

(d) If a party to a child-custody proceeding who is outside this State is directed to appear under subsection (b) or desires to appear personally before the court with or without the child, the court may require another party to pay reasonable and necessary travel and other expenses of the party so appearing and of the child.

§ 301. Definitions.

In this [article]:

(1) "Petitioner" means a person who seeks enforcement of an order for return of a child under the Hague Convention on the Civil Aspects of International Child Abduction or enforcement of a child-custody determination.

(2) "Respondent" means a person against whom a proceeding has been commenced for enforcement of an order for return of a child under the Hague Convention on the Civil Aspects of International Child Abduction or enforcement of a child-custody determination.

§ 302. Enforcement Under Hague Convention.

Under this [article] a court of this State may enforce an order for the return of the child made under the Hague Convention on the Civil Aspects of International Child Abduction as if it were a child-custody determination.

§ 303. Duty to Enforce.

(a) A court of this State shall recognize and enforce a child-custody determination of a court of another State if the latter court exercised jurisdiction in substantial conformity with this [Act] or the determination was made under factual circumstances meeting the jurisdictional standards of this [Act] and the determination has not been modified in accordance with this [Act].

(b) A court of this State may utilize any remedy available under other law of this State to enforce a child-custody determination made by a court of another State. The remedies provided in this [article] are cumulative and do not affect the availability of other remedies to enforce a child-custody determination.

§ 304. Temporary Visitation.

(a) A court of this State which does not have jurisdiction to modify a child-custody determination, may issue a temporary order enforcing.

(1) a visitation schedule made by a court of another State; or

(2) the visitation provisions of a child-custody determination of another State that does not provide for a specific visitation schedule.

(b) If a court of this State makes an order under subsection (a) (2), it shall specify in the order a period that it considers adequate to allow the petitioner to obtain an order from a court having jurisdiction under the criteria specified in [Article] 2. The order remains in effect until an order is obtained from the other court or the period expires.

§ 305. Registration of Child-Custody Determination.

(a) A child-custody determination issued by a court of another State may be registered in this State, with or without a simultaneous request for enforcement, by sending to [the appropriate court] in this State:

(1) a letter or other document requesting registration;

(2) two copies, including one certified copy, of the determination sought to be registered, and a statement under penalty of perjury that to the best of the knowledge and belief of the person seeking registration the order has not been modified; and

(3) except as otherwise provided in Section 209, the name and address of the person seeking registration and any parent or person acting as a parent who has been awarded custody or visitation in the child-custody determination sought to be registered.

(b) On receipt of the documents required by subsection (a), the registering court shall:

(1) cause the determination to be filed as a foreign judgment, together with one copy of any accompanying documents and information, regardless of their form; and

(2) serve notice upon the persons named pursuant to subsection (a) (3) and provide them with an opportunity to contest the registration in accordance with this section.

(c) The notice required by subsection (b) (2) must state that:

(1) a registered determination is enforceable as of the date of the registration in the same manner as a determination issued by a court of this State;

(2) a hearing to contest the validity of the registered determination must be requested within 20 days after service of notice; and

(3) failure to contest the registration will result in confirmation of the child-custody determination and preclude further contest of that determination with respect to any matter that could have been asserted.

(d) A person seeking to contest the validity of a registered order must request a hearing within 20 days after service of the notice. At that hearing, the court shall confirm the registered order unless the person contesting registration establishes that:

(1) the issuing court did not have jurisdiction under [Article] 2;

(2) the child-custody determination sought to be registered has been vacated, stayed, or modified by a court having jurisdiction to do so under [Article] 2; or

(3) the person contesting registration was entitled to notice, but notice was not given in accordance with the standards of Section 108, in the proceedings before the court that issued the order for which registration is sought.

(e) If a timely request for a hearing to contest the validity of the registration is not made, the registration is confirmed as a matter of law and the person requesting registration and all persons served must be notified of the confirmation.

(f) Confirmation of a registered order, whether by operation of law or after notice and hearing, precludes further contest of the order with respect to any matter that could have been asserted at the time of registration.

§ 306. Enforcement of Registered Determination.

(a) A court of this State may grant any relief normally available under the law of this State to enforce a registered child-custody determination made by a court of another State.

(b) A court of this State shall recognize and enforce, but may not modify, except in accordance with [Article] 2, a registered child-custody determination of a court of another State.

§ 307. Simultaneous Proceedings.

If a proceeding for enforcement under this [article] is commenced in a court of this State and the court determines that a proceeding to modify the determination is pending in a court of another State having jurisdiction to modify the determination under [Article] 2, the enforcing court shall immediately communicate with the modifying court. The proceeding for enforcement continues unless the enforcing court, after consultation with the modifying court, stays or dismisses the proceeding.

§ 308. Expedited Enforcement of Child-Custody Determination.

(a) A petition under this [article] must be verified. Certified copies of all orders sought to be enforced and of any order confirming registration must be attached to the petition. A copy of a certified copy of an order may be attached instead of the original.

(b) A petition for enforcement of a child-custody determination must state:

(1) whether the court that issued the determination identified the jurisdictional basis it relied upon in exercising jurisdiction and, if so, what the basis was;

(2) whether the determination for which enforcement is sought has been vacated, stayed, or modified by a court whose decision must be enforced under this [Act] and, if so, identify the court, the case number, and the nature of the proceeding;

(3) whether any proceeding has been commenced that could affect the current proceeding, including proceedings relating to domestic violence, protective orders, termination of parental rights, and adoptions and, if so, identify the court, the case number, and the nature of the proceeding;

(4) the present physical address of the child and the respondent, if known;

(5) whether relief in addition to the immediate physical custody of the child and attorney's fees is sought, including a request for assistance from [law enforcement officials] and, if so, the relief sought; and

(6) if the child-custody determination has been registered and confirmed under Section 305, the date and place of registration.

(c) Upon the filing of a petition, the court shall issue an order directing the respondent to appear in person with or without the child at a hearing and may enter any order necessary to ensure the safety of the parties and the child. The hearing must be held on the next judicial day after service of the order unless that date is impossible. In that event, the court shall hold the hearing on the first judicial day possible. The court may extend the date of hearing at the request of the petitioner.

(d) An order issued under subsection (c) must state the time and place of the hearing and advise the respondent that at the hearing the court will order that the petitioner may take immediate physical custody of the child and the payment of fees, costs, and expenses under Section 312, and may schedule a hearing to determine whether further relief is appropriate, unless the respondent appears and establishes that:

(1) the child-custody determination has not been registered and confirmed under Section 305 and that:

(A) the issuing court did not have jurisdiction under [Article] 2;

(B) the child-custody determination for which enforcement is sought has been vacated, stayed, or modified by a court having jurisdiction to do so under [Article] 2;

(C) the respondent was entitled to notice, but notice was not given in accordance with the standards of Section 108, in the proceedings before the court that issued the order for which enforcement is sought; or

(2) the child-custody determination for which enforcement is sought was registered and confirmed under Section 304, but has been vacated, stayed, or modified by a court of a State having jurisdiction to do so under [Article] 2.

§ 309. Service of Petition and Order.

Except as otherwise provided in Section 311, the petition and order must be served, by any method authorized [by the law of this State], upon respondent and any person who has physical custody of the child.

§ 310. Hearing and Order.

(a) Unless the court issues a temporary emergency order pursuant to Section 204, upon a finding that a petitioner is entitled to immediate physical custody of the child, the court shall order that the petitioner may take immediate physical custody of the child unless the respondent establishes that:

(1) the child-custody determination has not been registered and confirmed under Section 305 and that:

(A) the issuing court did not have jurisdiction under [Article] 2;

(B) the child-custody determination for which enforcement is sought has been vacated, stayed, or modified by a court of a State having jurisdiction to do so under [Article] 2; or

(C) the respondent was entitled to notice, but notice was not given in accordance with the standards of Section 108, in the proceedings before the court that issued the order for which enforcement is sought; or

(2) the child-custody determination for which enforcement is sought was registered and confirmed under Section 305 but has been vacated, stayed, or modified by a court of a State having jurisdiction to do so under [Article] 2.

(b) The court shall award the fees, costs, and expenses authorized under Section 312 and may grant additional relief, including a request for the assistance of [law enforcement officials], and set a further hearing to determine whether additional relief is appropriate.

(c) If a party called to testify refuses to answer on the ground that the testimony may be self-incriminating, the court may draw an adverse inference from the refusal.

(d) A privilege against disclosure of communications between spouses and a defense of immunity based on the relationship of husband and wife or parent and child may not be invoked in a proceeding under this [article].

§ 311. Warrant to Take Physical Custody of Child.

(a) Upon the filing of a petition seeking enforcement of a child-custody determination, the petitioner may file a verified application for the issuance of a warrant to take physical custody of the child if the child is immediately likely to suffer serious physical harm or be removed from this State.

(b) If the court, upon the testimony of the petitioner or other witness, finds that the child is imminently likely to suffer serious physical harm or be removed from this State, it may issue a warrant to take physical custody of the child. The petition must be heard on the next judicial day after the warrant is executed unless that date is impossible. In that event, the court shall hold the hearing on the first judicial day possible. The application for the warrant must include the statements required by Section 308 (b).

(c) A warrant to take physical custody of a child must:

(1) recite the facts upon which a conclusion of imminent serious physical harm or removal from the jurisdiction is based;

(2) direct law enforcement officers to take physical custody of the child immediately; and

(3) provide for the placement of the child pending final relief.

(d) The respondent must be served with the petition, warrant, and order immediately after the child is taken into physical custody.

(e) A warrant to take physical custody of a child is enforceable throughout this State. If the court finds on the basis of the testimony of the petitioner or other witness that a less intrusive remedy is not effective, it may authorize law enforcement officers to enter private property to take physical custody of the child. If required by exigent circumstances of the case, the court may authorize law enforcement officers to make a forcible entry at any hour.

(f) The court may impose conditions upon placement of a child to ensure the appearance of the child and the child's custodian.

§ 312. Costs, Fees, and Expenses.

(a) The court shall award the prevailing party, including a State, necessary and reasonable expenses incurred by or on behalf of the party, including costs, communication expenses, attorney's fees, investigative fees, expenses for witnesses, travel expenses, and child care during the course of the proceedings, unless the party from whom fees or expenses are sought establishes that the award would be clearly inappropriate.

(b) The court may not assess fees, costs, or expenses against a State unless authorized by law other than this [Act].

§ 313. Recognition and Enforcement.

A court of this State shall accord full faith and credit to an order issued by another State and consistent with this [Act] which enforces a child-custody determination by a court of another State unless the order has been vacated, stayed, or modified by a court having jurisdiction to do so under [Article] 2.

§ 314. Appeals.

An appeal may be taken from a final order in a proceeding under this [article] in accordance with [expedited appellate procedures in other civil cases]. Unless the court enters a temporary emergency order under Section 204, the enforcing court may not stay an order enforcing a child-custody determination pending appeal.

§ 315. Role of [Prosecutor or Public Official].

(a) In a case arising under this [Act] or involving the Hague Convention on the Civil Aspects of International Child Abduction, the [prosecutor or other appropriate public official] may take any lawful action, including resort to a proceeding under this [article] or any other available civil proceeding to locate a child, obtain the return of a child, or enforce a child-custody determination if there is:

(1) an existing child-custody determination;

(2) a request to do so from a court in a pending child-custody proceeding;

(3) a reasonable belief that a criminal statute has been violated; or

(4) a reasonable belief that the child has been wrongfully removed or retained in violation of the Hague Convention on the Civil Aspects of International Child Abduction.

(b) A [prosecutor or appropriate public official] acting under this section acts on behalf of the court and may not represent any party.

§ 316. Role of [Law Enforcement].

At the request of a [prosecutor or other appropriate public official] acting under Section 315, a [law enforcement officer] may take any lawful action reasonably necessary to locate a child or a party and assist [a prosecutor or appropriate public official] with responsibilities under Section 315.

§ 317. Costs and Expenses.

If the respondent is not the prevailing party, the court may assess against the respondent all direct expenses and costs incurred by the [prosecutor or other appropriate public official] and [law enforcement officers] under Section 315 or 316.

§ 401. Application and Construction.

In applying and construing this Uniform Act, consideration must be given to the need to promote uniformity of the law with respect to its subject matter among States that enact it.

§ 402. Severability Clause.

If any provision of this [Act] or its application to any person or circumstance is held invalid, the invalidity does not affect other provisions or applications of this [Act] which can be given effect without the invalid provision or application, and to this end the provisions of this [Act] are severable.

§ 403. Effective Date.

This [Act] takes effect. . . .

§ 404. Repeals.

The following [act is] hereby repealed:

The Uniform Child Custody Jurisdiction Act. . . .

§ 405. Transitional Provision.

A motion or other request for relief made in a child-custody proceeding or to enforce a child-custody determination which was commenced before the effective date of this [Act] is governed by the law in effect at the time the motion or other request was made.

C

PARENTAL KIDNAPING PREVENTION ACT OF 1980

(28 U.S.C.A. §1738A)

§ 1738A. Full faith and credit given to child custody determinations

(a) The appropriate authorities of every State shall enforce according to its terms, and shall not modify except as provided in subsection (f) of this section, any child custody determination made consistently with the provisions of this section by a court of another State.

(b) As used in this section, the term—

(1) "child" means a person under the age of eighteen;

(2) "contestant" means a person, including a parent, who claims a right to custody or visitation of a child;

(3) "custody determination" means a judgment, decree, or other order of a court providing for the custody or visitation of a child, and includes permanent and temporary orders, and initial orders and modifications;

(4) "home State" means the State in which, immediately preceding the time involved, the child lived with his parents, a parent, or a person acting as parent, for at least six consecutive months, and in the case of a child less than six months old, the State in which the child lived from birth with any of such persons. Periods of temporary absence of any such person are counted as part of the six-month or other period;

(5) "modification" and "modify" refer to a custody determination which modifies, replaces, supersedes, or otherwise is made subsequent to, a prior custody determination concerning the same child, whether made by the same court or not;

(6) "person acting as a parent" means a person, other than a parent, who has physical custody of a child and who has either been awarded custody by a court or claims a right to custody;

(7) "physical custody" means actual possession and control of a child; and

(8) "State" means a State of the United States, the District of Columbia, the Commonwealth of Puerto Rico, or a territory or possession of the United States.

(c) A child custody determination made by a court of a state is consistent with the provisions of this section only if

(1) such court has jurisdiction under the law of such State; and

(2) one of the following conditions is met:

(A) such State (i) is the home State of the child on the date of the commencement of the proceeding, or (ii) had been the child's home State within six months before the date of the commencement of the proceeding and the child is absent from such State because of his removal or retention by a contestant or for other reasons, and a contestant continues to live in such State;

(B)(i) it appears that no other State would have jurisdiction under subparagraph (A), and (ii) it is in the best interest of the child that a court of such State assume jurisdiction because (I) the child and his parents, or the child and at least one contestant, have a significant connection with such State other than mere physical presence in such State, and (II) there is available in such State substantial evidence concerning the child's present or future care, protection, training, and personal relationships;

(C) the child is physically present in such State and (i) the child has been abandoned, or (ii) it is necessary in an emergency to protect the child because he has been subjected to or threatened with mistreatment or abuse;

(D)(i) it appears that no other State would have jurisdiction under subparagraph (A), (B), (C), or (E), or another State has declined to exercise jurisdiction on the ground that the State whose jurisdiction is in issue is the more appropriate forum to determine the custody of the child, and (ii) it is in the best interest of the child that such court assume jurisdiction; or

(E) the court has continuing jurisdiction pursuant to subsection (d) of this section.

(d) The jurisdiction of a court of a State which has made a child custody determination consistently with the provisions of this section continues as long as the requirement of subsection (c)(1) of this section continues to be met and such State remains the residence of the child or of any contestant.

(e) Before a child custody determination is made, reasonable notice and opportunity to be heard shall be given to the contestants, any parent whose parental rights have not been previously terminated and any person who has physical custody of a child.

(f) A court of a State may modify a determination of the custody of the same child made by a court of another State, if—

(1) it has jurisdiction to make such a child custody determination; and

(2) the court of the other State no longer has jurisdiction, or it has declined to exercise such jurisdiction to modify such determination.

(g) A court of a State shall not exercise jurisdiction in any proceeding for a custody determination commenced during the pendency of a proceeding in a court of another State where such court of that other State is exercising jurisdiction consistently with the provisions of this section to make a custody determination.

UNIFORM INTERSTATE FAMILY SUPPORT ACT

Where Found in State Codes:

Alabama	Ala. Code § 30-3A-101.
Alaska	Alaska Stat. § 25.25.101.
Arizona	Ariz. Rev. Stat. § 25-621.
Arkansas	Ark. Code Ann. § 9-17-101.
California	Cal. Fam. Code § 4900 (West).
Colorado	Colo. Rev. Stat. Ann. § 14-5-101.
Connecticut	Conn. Gen. Stat. Ann. § 46b-212.
Delaware	Del. Code Ann. tit. 13, § 601.
District of Columbia	D.C. Code Ann. § 30-341.1.
Florida	Fla. Stat. Ann. § 88.0011 (West).
Georgia	Ga. Code Ann. § 19-11-100.
Hawaii	Haw. Rev. Stat. § 576B-101.
Idaho	Idaho Code § 7-1001.
Illinois	750 Ill. Comp. Stat. Ann. § 22/100 (West).
Indiana	Ind. Code Ann. § 31-18-1-1 (West).
Iowa	Iowa Code Ann. § 252K.101 (West).
Kansas	Kan. Stat. Ann. § 23-9, 101.
Kentucky	Ky. Rev. Stat. Ann. § 407.5101.
Louisiana	L.S.A., Children's Code arts. 1301.1.
Maine	Me. Rev. Stat. Ann. tit. 19, § 2801.
Maryland	Md. Code Ann. Family Law § 10-301.
Massachusetts	Mass. Gen. Laws Ann. ch. 209D, § 1-101.
Michigan	Mich. Comp. Laws Ann. § 552.1101.
Minnesota	Minn. Stat. Ann. § 518C.101.
Mississippi	Miss. Code Ann. § 93-25-1.
Missouri	Mo. Ann. Stat. § 454.850.
Montana	Mont. Code Ann. § 40-5-101.
Nebraska	Neb. Rev. Stat. § 42-701.
Nevada	Nev. Rev. Stat. § 130.0902.
New Hampshire	N.H. Rev. Stat. Ann. § 546-B:1.
New Jersey	N.J. Stat. Ann. § 2A: 4-30.65.
New Mexico	N.M. Stat. Ann. § 40-6A-101.
New York	N.Y. Family Ct. Act, 580-101.
North Carolina	N.C. Gen. Stat. § 52C-1-100.
North Dakota	N.D. Cent. Code § 14-12.2-01.
Ohio	Ohio Rev. Code Ann. § 3115.01.
Oklahoma	Okla. Stat. Ann. tit. 43, § 601-100.
Oregon	Or. Rev. Stat. § 110.303.
Pennsylvania	23 Pa. Cons. Stat. Ann. § 7101.
Rhode Island	R.I. Gen. Laws § 15-23-1.
South Carolina	S.C. Code Ann. § 20-7-960.
South Dakota	S.D. Codified Laws § 25-9B-101.
Tennessee	Tenn. Code Ann. § 36-5-2001.
Texas	Tex. Fam. Code Ann. § 159.001.
Utah	Utah Code Ann. § 78-45f-100.
Vermont	Vt. Stat. Ann. tit. 15B, § 101.
Virgin Islands	V.I. Code Ann. tit. 16, § 391.

Virginia	Va. Code Ann. § 20-88.32.
Washington	Wash. Rev. Code Ann. § 26.21.005.
West Virginia	W. Va. Code § 48B-1-101.
Wisconsin	Wis. Stat. Ann. § 769.101.
Wyoming	Wyo. Stat. Ann. § 20-4-139.

§ 101. Definitions.

In this[Act]:

(1) "Child" means an individual, whether over or under the age of majority, who is or is alleged to be owed a duty of support by the individual's parent or who is or is alleged to be the beneficiary of a support order directed to the parent.

(2) "Child-support order" means a support order for a child, including a child who has attained the age of majority under the law of the issuing state.

(3) "Duty of support" means an obligation imposed or imposable by law to provide support for a child, spouse, or former spouse, including an unsatisfied obligation to provide support.

(4) "Home state" means the state in which a child lived with a parent or a person acting as parent for at least six consecutive months immediately preceding the time of filing of a [petition] or comparable pleading for support and, if a child is less than six months old, the state in which the child lived from birth with any of them. A period of temporary absence of any of them is counted as part of the six-month or other period.

(5) "Income" includes earnings or other periodic entitlements to money from any source and any other property subject to withholding for support under the law of this State.

(6) "Income-withholding order" means an order or other legal process directed to an obligor's employer [or other debtor], as defined by [the income-withholding law of this State], to withhold support from the income of the obligor.

(7) "Initiating state" means a state from which a proceeding is forwarded or in which a proceeding is filed for forwarding to a responding state under this [Act] or the Uniform Reciprocal Enforcement of Support Act, or the Revised Uniform Reciprocal Enforcement of Support Act.

(8)"Initiating tribunal" means the authorized tribunal in an initiating state.

(9) "Issuing state" means the state in which a tribunal issues a support order or renders a judgment determining parentage.

(10) "Issuing tribunal" means the tribunal that issues a support order or renders a judgment determining parentage.

(11) "Law" includes decisional and statutory law and rules and regulations having the force of law.

(12) "Obligee" means:

(i) an individual to whom a duty of support is or is alleged to be owed or in whose favor a support order has been issued or a judgment determining parentage has been rendered;

(ii) a state or political subdivision to which the rights under a duty of support or support order have been assigned or which has independent claims based on financial assistance provided to an individual obligee; or

(iii) an individual seeking a judgment determining parentage of the individual's child.

(13) "Obligor" means an individual, or the estate of a decedent:

(i) who owes or is alleged to owe a duty of support;

(ii) who is alleged but has not been adjudicated to be a parent of a child; or

(iii) who is liable under a support order.

(14) "Register" means to [record; file] a support order or judgment determining parentage in the [appropriate location for the recording or filing of foreign judgments generally or foreign support orders specifically].

(15) "Registering tribunal" means a tribunal in which a support order is registered.

(16) "Responding state" means a state in which a proceeding is filed or to which a proceeding is forwarded for filing from an initiating state under this [Act] or a law or procedure substantially similar to this [Act], the Uniform Reciprocal Enforcement of Support Act, or the Revised Uniform Reciprocal Enforcement of Support Act.

(17) "Responding tribunal" means the authorized tribunal in a responding state.

(18) "Spousal-support order" means a support order for a spouse or former spouse of the obligor.

(19) "State" means a state of the United States, the District of Columbia, Puerto Rico, the United States Virgin Islands, or any territory or insular possession subject to the jurisdiction of the United States. The term "state" includes:

(i) an Indian tribe; and

(ii) a foreign jurisdiction that has enacted a law or established procedures for issuance and enforcement of support orders which are substantially similar to the procedures under this [Act], the Uniform Reciprocal Enforcement of Support Act, or the Revised Uniform Reciprocal Enforcement of Support Act.

(20) "Support enforcement agency" means a public official or agency authorized to seek:

(i) enforcement of support orders or laws relating to the duty of support;

(ii) establishment or modification of child support;

(iii) determination of parentage; or

(iv) to locate obligors or their assets.

(21) "Support order" means a judgment, decree, or order, whether temporary, final, or subject to modification, for the benefit of a child, a spouse, or a former spouse, which provides for monetary support, health care, arrearages, or reimbursement, and may include related costs and fees, interest, income withholding, attorney's fees, and other relief.

(22) "Tribunal" means a court, administrative agency, or quasi-judicial entity authorized to establish, enforce, or modify support orders or to determine parentage.

§ 102. Tribunal of State.

The [court, administrative agency, quasi-judicial entity, or combination] [is the tribunal] [are the tribunals] of this State.

§ 103. Remedies Cumulative.

Remedies provided by this [Act] are cumulative and do not affect the availability of remedies under other law.

§ 201. Bases for Jurisdiction over Nonresident.

In a proceeding to establish, enforce, or modify a support order or to determine parentage, a tribunal of this State may exercise personal jurisdiction over a nonresident individual [or the individual's guardian or conservator] if:

(1) the individual is personally served with [citation, summons, notice] within this State;

(2) the individual submits to the jurisdiction of this State by consent, by entering a general appearance, or by filing a responsive document having the effect of waiving any contest to personal jurisdiction;

(3) the individual resided with the child in this State;

(4) the individual resided in this State and provided prenatal expenses or support for the child;

(5) the child resides in this State as a result of the acts or directives of the individual;

(6) the individual engaged in sexual intercourse in this State and the child may have been conceived by that act of intercourse;

(7) the individual asserted parentage in the [putative father registry] maintained in this State by the [appropriate agency]; or

(8) there is any other basis consistent with the constitutions of this State and the United States for the exercise of personal jurisdiction.

§ 202. Procedure When Exercising Jurisdiction over Nonresident.

A tribunal of this State exercising personal jurisdiction over a nonresident under Section 201 may apply Section 316 (Special Rules of Evidence and Procedure) to receive evidence from another state, and Section 318 (Assistance with Discovery) to obtain discovery through a tribunal of another state. In all other respects, Articles 3 through 7 do not apply and the tribunal shall apply the procedural and substantive law of this State, including the rules on choice of law other than those established by this [Act].

§ 203. Initiating and Responding Tribunal of State.

Under this [Act], a tribunal of this State may serve as an initiating tribunal to forward proceedings to another state and as a responding tribunal for proceedings initiated in another state.

§ 204. Simultaneous Proceedings in Another State.

(a) A tribunal of this State may exercise jurisdiction to establish a support order if the [petition] or comparable pleading is filed after a pleading is filed in another state only if:

(1) the [petition] or comparable pleading in this State is filed before the expiration of the time allowed in the other state for filing a responsive pleading challenging the exercise of jurisdiction by the other state;

(2) the contesting party timely challenges the exercise of jurisdiction in the other state; and

(3) if relevant, this State is the home state of the child.

(b) A tribunal of this State may not exercise jurisdiction to establish a support order if the [petition] or comparable pleading is filed before a [petition] or comparable pleading is filed in another state if:

(1) the [petition] or comparable pleading in the other state is filed before the expiration of the time allowed in this State for filing a responsive pleading challenging the exercise of jurisdiction by this State;

(2) the contesting party timely challenges the exercise of jurisdiction in this State; and

(3) if relevant, the other state is the home state of the child.

§ 205. Continuing, Exclusive Jurisdiction.

(a) A tribunal of this State issuing a support order consistent with the law of this State has continuing, exclusive jurisdiction over a child-support order:

(1) as long as this State remains the residence of the obligor, the individual obligee, or the child for whose benefit the support order is issued; or

(2) until all of the parties who are individuals have [each individual party has] filed written consent with the tribunal of this State for a tribunal of another state to modify the order and assume continuing, exclusive jurisdiction.

(b) A tribunal of this State issuing a child-support order consistent with the law of this State may not exercise its continuing jurisdiction to modify the order if the order has been modified by a tribunal of another state pursuant to this [Act] or a law substantially similar to this [Act].

(c) If a child-support order of this State is modified by a tribunal of another state pursuant to this [Act] or a law substantially similar to this [Act], a tribunal of this State loses its continuing, exclusive jurisdiction with regard to prospective enforcement of the order issued in this State, and may only:

(1) enforce the order that was modified as to amounts accruing before the modification;

(2) enforce nonmodifiable aspects of that order; and

(3) provide other appropriate relief for violations of that order which occurred before the effective date of the modification.

(d) A tribunal of this State shall recognize the continuing, exclusive jurisdiction of a tribunal of another state which has issued a child-support order pursuant to this [Act] or a law substantially similar to this [Act].

(e) A temporary support order issued ex parte or pending resolution of a jurisdictional conflict does not create continuing, exclusive jurisdiction in the issuing tribunal.

(f) A tribunal of this State issuing a support order consistent with the law of this State has continuing, exclusive jurisdiction over a spousal support order throughout the existence of the support obligation. A tribunal of this State may not modify a spousal support order issued by a tribunal of another state having continuing, exclusive jurisdiction over that order under the law of that state.

§ 206. Enforcement and Modification of Support Order by Tribunal Having Continuing Jurisdiction.

(a) A tribunal of this State may serve as an initiating tribunal to request a tribunal of another state to enforce or modify a support order issued in that state.

(b) A tribunal of this State having continuing, exclusive jurisdiction over a support order may act as a responding tribunal to enforce or modify the order. If a party subject to the continuing, exclusive jurisdiction of the tribunal no longer resides in the issuing state, in subsequent proceedings the tribunal may apply Section 316 (Special Rules of Evidence and Procedure) to receive evidence from another state and Section 318 (Assistance with Discovery) to obtain discovery through a tribunal of another state.

(c) A tribunal of this State which lacks continuing, exclusive jurisdiction over a spousal-support order may not serve as a responding tribunal to modify a spousal-support order of another state.

§ 207. Recognition of Controlling Child Support Order.

(a) If a proceeding is brought under this [Act] and only one tribunal has issued a child-support order, the order of that tribunal controls and must be so recognized.

(b) If a proceeding is brought under this [Act], and two or more child-support orders have been issued by tribunals of this State or another state with regard to the same obligor and child, a tribunal of this State shall apply the following rules in determining which order to recognize for purpose of continuing, exclusive jurisdiction:

(1) If only one of the tribunals would have continuing, exclusive jurisdiction under this [Act], the order of that tribunal controls and must be so recognized.

(2) If more than one of the tribunals would have continuing, exclusive jurisdiction under this [Act], an order issued by a tribunal in the current home state of the child controls and must be so recognized, but if an order has not been issued in the current home state of the child, the order most recently issued controls and must be so recognized.

(3) If none of the tribunals would have continuing, exclusive jurisdiction under this [Act], the tribunal of this State having jurisdiction over the parties shall issue a child-support order, which controls and must be so recognized.

(c) If two or more child-support orders have been issued for the same obligor and child and if the obligor or the individual obligee resides in this State, a party may request a tribunal of this State to determine which order controls and must be so recognized under subsection (b). The request must be accompanied by a certified copy of every support order in effect. The requesting party shall give notice of the request to each party whose rights may be affected by the determination.

(d) The tribunal that issued the controlling order under subsection (a), (b), or (c) is the tribunal that has continuing, exclusive jurisdiction under Section 205.

(e) A tribunal of this State which determines by order the identity of the controlling order under subsection (b) (1) or (2) or which issues a new controlling order under subsection (b) (3) shall state in that order the basis upon which the tribunal made its determination.

(f) Within [30] days after issuance of an order determining the identity of the controlling order, the party obtaining the order shall file a certified copy of it with each tribunal that issued or registered an earlier order of child support. A party who obtains the order and fails to file a certified copy is subject to appropriate sanctions by a tribunal in which the issue of failure to file arises. The failure to file does not affect the validity or enforceability of the controlling order.

§ 208. Multiple Child Support Orders for Two or More Obligees.

In responding to multiple registrations or [petitions] for enforcement of two or more child-support orders in effect at the same time with regard to the same obligor and different individual obligees, at least one of which was issued by a tribunal of another state, a tribunal of this State shall enforce those orders in the same manner as if the multiple orders had been issued by a tribunal of this State.

§ 209. Credit for Payments.

Amounts collected and credited for a particular period pursuant to a support order issued by a tribunal of another state must be credited against the amounts accruing or accrued for the same period under a support order issued by the tribunal of this State.

§ 301. Proceedings Under [Act].

(a) Except as otherwise provided in this [Act], this article applies to all proceedings under this [Act].

(b) This [Act] provides for the following proceedings:

(1) establishment of an order for spousal support or child support pursuant to Article 4;

(2) enforcement of a support order and income-withholding order of another state without registration pursuant to Article 5;

(3) registration of an order for spousal support or child support of another state for enforcement pursuant to Article 6;

(4) modification of an order for child support or spousal support issued by a tribunal of this State pursuant to Article 2, Part 2;

(5) registration of an order for child support of another state for modification pursuant to Article 6;

(6) determination of parentage pursuant to Article 7; and

(7) assertion of jurisdiction over nonresidents pursuant to Article 2, Part [A].

(c) An individual [petitioner] or a support enforcement agency may commence a proceeding authorized under this [Act] by filling a [petition] in an initiating tribunal for forwarding to a responding tribunal or by filling a [petition] or a comparable pleading directly in a tribunal of another state which has or can obtain personal jurisdiction over the [respondent].

§ 302. Action by Minor Parent.

A minor parent, or a guardian or other legal representative of a minor parent, may maintain a proceeding on behalf of or for the benefit of the minor's child.

§ 303. Application of Law of State.

Except as otherwise provided by this [Act], a responding tribunal of this State:

(1) shall apply the procedural and substantive law, including the rules on choice of law, generally applicable to similar proceedings originating in this State and may exercise all powers and provide all remedies available in those proceedings; and

(2) shall determine the duty of support and the amount payable in accordance with the law and support guidelines of this State.

§ 304. Duties of Initiating Tribunal.

(a) Upon the filing of a [petition] authorized by this [Act], an initiating tribunal of this State shall forward three copies of the [petition] and its accompanying documents:

(1) to the responding tribunal or appropriate support enforcement agency in the responding state; or

(2) if the identity of the responding tribunal is unknown, to the state information agency of the responding state with a request that they be forwarded to the appropriate tribunal and that receipt be acknowledged.

(b) If a responding State has not enacted this [Act] or a law or procedure substantially similar to this [Act], a tribunal of this State may issue a certificate or other document and make findings required by the law of the responding State. If the responding State is a foreign jurisdiction, the tribunal may specify the amount of support sought and provide other documents necessary to satisfy the requirements of the responding State.

§ 305. Duties and Powers of Responding Tribunal.

(a) When a responding tribunal of this State receives a [petition] or comparable pleading from an initiating tribunal or directly pursuant to Section 301 (c) (Proceedings Under [Act]), it shall cause the [petition] or pleading to be filed and notify the [petitioner] where and when it was filed.

(b) A responding tribunal of this State, to the extent otherwise authorized by law, may do one or more of the following:

(1) issue or enforce a support order, modify a child-support order, or render a judgment to determine parentage;

(2) order an obligor to comply with a support order, specifying the amount and the manner of compliance;

(3) order income withholding;

(4) determine the amount of any arrearages, and specify a method of payment;

(5) enforce orders by civil or criminal contempt, or both;

(6) set aside property for satisfaction of the support order;

(7) place liens and order execution on the obligor's property;

(8) order an obligor to keep the tribunal informed of the obligor's current residential address, telephone number, employer, address of employment, and telephone number at the place of employment;

(9) issue a [bench warrant; capias] for an obligor who has failed after proper notice to appear at a hearing ordered by the tribunal and enter the [bench warrant; capias] in any local and state computer systems for criminal warrants;

(10) order the obligor to seek appropriate employment by specified methods;

(11) award reasonable attorney's fees and other fees and costs; and

(12) grant any other available remedy.

(c) A responding tribunal of this State shall include in a support order issued under this [Act], or in the documents accompanying the order, the calculations on which the support order is based.

(d) A responding tribunal of this State may not condition the payment of a support order issued under this [Act] upon compliance by a party with provisions for visitation.

(e) If a responding tribunal of this State issues an order under this [Act], the tribunal shall send a copy of the order to the [petitioner] and the [respondent] and to the initiating tribunal, if any.

§ 306. Inappropriate Tribunal.

If a [petitioner] or comparable pleading is received by an inappropriate tribunal of this State, it shall forward the pleading and accompanying documents to an appropriate tribunal in this State or another state and notify the [petitioner] where and when the pleading was sent.

§ 307. Duties of Support Enforcement Agency.

(a) A support enforcement agency of this State, upon request, shall provide services to a [petitioner] in a proceeding under this [Act].

(b) A support enforcement agency that is providing services to the [petitioner] as appropriate shall:

(1) take all steps necessary to enable an appropriate tribunal in this State or another state to obtain jurisdiction over the [respondent];

(2) request an appropriate tribunal to set a date, time, and place for a hearing;

(3) make a reasonable effort to obtain all relevant information, including information as to income and property of the parties;

(4) within [two] days, exclusive of Saturdays, Sundays, and legal holidays, after receipt of a written notice from an initiating, responding, or registering tribunal, send a copy of the notice to the [petitioner];

(5) within [two] days, exclusive of Saturdays, Sundays, and legal holidays, after receipt of a written communication from the [respondent] or the [respondent's] attorney, send a copy of the communication to the [petitioner]; and

(6) notify the [petitioner] if jurisdiction over the [respondent] cannot be obtained.

(c) This [Act] does not create or negate a relationship of attorney and client or other fiduciary relationship between a support enforcement agency or the attorney for the agency and the individual being assisted by the agency.

§ 308. Duty of [Attorney General].

If the [Attorney General] determines that the support enforcement agency is neglecting or refusing to provide services to an individual, the [Attorney General] may order the agency to perform its duties under this [Act] or may provide those services directly to the individual.

§ 309. Private Counsel.

An individual may employ private counsel to represent the individual in proceedings authorized by this [Act].

§ 310. Duties of [State Information Agency].

(a) The [Attorney General's Office, State Attorney's Office, State Central Registry or other information agency] is the state information agency under this [Act].

(b) The state information agency shall:

(1) compile and maintain a current list, including addresses, of the tribunals in this State which have jurisdiction under this [Act] and any support enforcement agencies in this State and transmit a copy to the state information agency of every other state;

(2) maintain a register of tribunals and support enforcement agencies received from other states;

(3) forward to the appropriate tribunal in the place in this State in which the individual obligee or the obligor resides, or in which the obligor's property is believed to be located, all documents concerning a proceeding under this [Act] received from an initiating tribunal or the state information agency of the initiating state; and

(4) obtain information concerning the location of the obligor and the obligor's property within this State not exempt from execution, by such means as postal verification and federal or state locator services, examination of telephone directories, requests for the obligor's address from employers, and examination of governmental records, including, to the extent not prohibited by other law, those relating to real property, vital statistics, law enforcement, taxation, motor vehicles, driver's licenses, and social security.

§ 311. Pleadings and Accompanying Documents.

(a) A [petitioner] seeking to establish or modify a support order or to determine parentage in a proceeding under this [Act] must verify the [petition]. Unless otherwise ordered under Section 312 (Nondisclosure of Information in Exceptional Circumstances), the [petition] or accompanying documents must provide, so far as known, the name, residential address, and social security numbers of the obligor and the obligee, and the name, sex, residential address, social security number, and date of birth of each child for whom support is sought. The [petition] must be accompanied by a certified copy of any support order in effect. The [petition] may include any other information that may assist in locating or identifying the [respondent].

(b) The [petition] must specify the relief sought. The [petition] and accompanying documents must conform substantially with the requirements imposed by the forms mandated by federal law for use in cases filed by a support enforcement agency.

§ 312. Nondisclosure of Information in Exceptional Circumstances.

Upon a finding, which may be made ex parte, that the health, safety, or liberty of a party or child would be unreasonably put at risk by the disclosure of identifying information, or if an existing order so provides, a tribunal shall order that the address of the child or party or other identifying information not be disclosed in a pleading or other document filed in a proceeding under this [Act].

§ 313. Costs and Fees.

(a) The [petitioner] may not be required to pay a filing fee or other costs.

(b) If an obligee prevails, a responding tribunal may assess against an obligor filing fees, reasonable attorney's fees, other costs, and necessary travel and other reasonable expenses incurred by the obligee and the obligee's witnesses. The tribunal may not assess fees, costs, or expenses against the obligee or the support enforcement agency of either the initiating or the responding state, except as provided by other law. Attorney's fees may be taxed as costs, and may be ordered paid directly to the attorney, who may enforce the order in the attorney's own name. Payment of support owed to the obligee has priority over fees, costs and expenses.

(c) The tribunal shall order the payment of costs and reasonable attorney's fees if it determines that a hearing was requested primarily for delay. In a proceeding under Article 6 (Enforcement and Modification of Support Order After Registration), a hearing is presumed to have been requested primarily for delay if a registered support order is confirmed or enforced without change.

§ 314. Limited Immunity of [Petitioner].

(a) Participation by a [petitioner] in a proceeding before a responding tribunal, whether in person, by private attorney, or through services provided by the support enforcement agency, does not confer personal jurisdiction over the [petitioner] in another proceeding.

(b) A [petitioner] is not amenable to service of civil process while physically present in this State to participate in a proceeding under this [Act].

(c) The immunity granted by this section does not extend to civil litigation based on acts unrelated to a proceeding under this [Act] committed by a party while present in this State to participate in the proceeding.

§ 315. Nonparentage as Defense.

A party whose parentage of a child has been previously determined by or pursuant to law may not plead nonparentage as a defense to a proceeding under this [Act].

§ 316. Special Rules of Evidence and Procedure.

(a) The physical presence of the [petitioner] in a responding tribunal of this State is not required for the establishment, enforcement, or modification of a support order or the rendition of a judgment determining parentage.

(b) A verified [petition], affidavit, document substantially complying with federally mandated forms, and a document incorporated by reference in any of them, not excluded under the hearsay rule if given in person, is admissible in evidence if given under oath by a party or witness residing in another state.

(c) A copy of the record of child-support payments certified as a true copy of the original by the custodian of the record may be forwarded to a responding tribunal. The copy is evidence of facts asserted in it, and is admissible to show whether payments were made.

(d) Copies of bills for testing for parentage, and for prenatal and postnatal health care of the mother and child, furnished to the adverse party at least [ten] days before trial, are admissible in evidence to prove the amount of the charges billed and that the charges were reasonable, necessary, and customary.

(e) Documentary evidence transmitted from another state to a tribunal of this State by telephone, telecopier, or other means that do not provide an original writing may not be excluded from evidence on an objection based on the means of transmission.

(f) In a proceeding under this [Act], a tribunal of this State may permit a party or witness residing in another state to be deposed or to testify by telephone, audiovisual means, or other electronic means at a designated tribunal or other location in that state. A tribunal of this State shall cooperate with tribunals of other states in designating an appropriate location for the deposition or testimony.

(g) If a party called to testify at a civil hearing refuses to answer on the ground that the testimony may be self-incriminating, the trier of fact may draw an adverse inference from the refusal.

(h) A privilege against disclosure of communications between spouses does not apply in a proceeding under this [Act].

(i) The defense of immunity based on the relationship of husband and wife or parent and child does not apply in a proceeding under this [Act].

§ 317. Communications Between Tribunals.

A tribunal of this State may communicate with a tribunal of another state in writing, or by telephone or other means, to obtain information concerning the laws of that state, the legal effect of a judgment, decree, or order of that tribunal, and the status of a proceeding in the other state. A tribunal of this State may furnish similar information by similar means to a tribunal of another state.

§ 318. Assistance with Discovery.

A tribunal of this State may:

(1) request a tribunal of another state to assist in obtaining discovery; and

(2) upon request, compel a person over whom it has jurisdiction to respond to a discovery order issued by a tribunal of another state.

§ 319. Receipt and Disbursement of Payments.

A support enforcement agency or tribunal of this State shall disburse promptly any amounts received pursuant to a support order, as directed by the order. The agency or tribunal shall furnish to a requesting party or tribunal of another state a certified statement by the custodian of the record of the amounts and dates of all payments received.

§ 401. [Petition] to Establish Support Order.

(a) If a support order entitled to recognition under this [Act] has not been issued, a responding tribunal of this State may issue a support order if:

(1) the individual seeking the order resides in another state; or

(2) the support enforcement agency seeking the order is located in another state.

(b) The tribunal may issue a temporary child-support order if:

(1) the [respondent] has signed a verified statement acknowledging parentage;

(2) the [respondent] has been determined by or pursuant to law to be the parent; or

(3) there is other clear and convincing evidence that the [respondent] is the child's parent.

(c) Upon finding, after notice and opportunity to be heard, that an obligor owes a duty of support, the tribunal shall issue a support order directed to the obligor and may issue other orders pursuant to Section 305 (Duties and Powers of Responding Tribunal).

§ 501. Employer's Receipt of Income-Withholding Order of Another State.

An income-withholding order issued in another state may be sent to the person or entity defined as the obligor's employer under [the income-withholding law of this State] without first filing a [petition] or comparable pleading or registering the order with a tribunal of this State.

§ 502. Employer's Compliance with Income-Withholding Order of Another State.

(a) Upon receipt of an income-withholding order, the obligor's employer shall immediately provide a copy of the order to the obligor.

(b) The employer shall treat an income-withholding order issued in another state which appears regular on its face as if it had been issued by a tribunal of this State.

(c) Except as otherwise provided in subsection (d) and Section 503, the employer shall withhold and distribute the funds as directed in the withholding order by complying with terms of the order which specify:

(1) the duration and amount of periodic payments of current child-support, stated as a sum certain;

(2) the person or agency designated to receive payments and the address to which the payments are to be forwarded;

(3) medical support, whether in the form of periodic cash payment, stated as a sum certain, or ordering the obligor to provide health insurance coverage for the child under a policy available through the obligor's employment;

(4) the amount of periodic payments of fees and costs for a support enforcement agency, the issuing tribunal, and the obligee's attorney, stated as sums certain; and

(5) the amount of periodic payments of arrearages and interest on arrearages, stated as sums certain.

(d) An employer shall comply with the law of the state of the obligor's principal place of employment for withholding from income with respect to:

(1) the employer's fee for processing an income-withholding order;

(2) the maximum amount permitted to be withheld from the obligor's income; and

(3) the times within which the employer must implement the withholding order and forward the child support payment.

§ 503. Compliance with Multiple Income-Withholding Orders.

If an obligor's employer receives multiple income-withholding orders with respect to the earnings of the same obligor, the employer satisfies the terms of the multiple orders if the employer complies with the law of the state of the obligor's principal place of employment to establish the priorities for withholding and allocating income withheld for multiple child support obligees.

§ 504. Immunity from Civil Liability.

An employer who complies with an income-withholding order issued in another state in accordance with this article is not subject to civil liability to an individual or agency with regard to the employer's withholding of child support from the obligor's income.

§ 505. Penalties for Noncompliance.

An employer who willfully fails to comply with an income-withholding order issued by another state and received for enforcement is subject to the same penalties that may be imposed for noncompliance with an order issued by a tribunal of this State.

§ 506. Contest by Obligor.

(a) An obligor may contest the validity or enforcement of an income-withholding order issued in another state and received directly by an employer in this State in the same manner as if the order had been issued by a tribunal of this State. Section 604 (Choice of Law) applies to the contest.

(b) The obligor shall give notice of the contest to:

(1) a support enforcement agency providing services to the obligee;

(2) each employer that has directly received an income-withholding order; and

(3) the person or agency designated to receive payments in the income-withholding order or if no person or agency is designated, to the obligee.

§ 507. Administrative Enforcement of Orders.

(a) A party seeking to enforce a support order or an income-withholding order, or both, issued by a tribunal of another state may send the documents required for registering the order to a support enforcement agency of this State.

(b) Upon receipt of the documents, the support enforcement agency, without initially seeking to register the order, shall consider and, if appropriate, use any administrative procedure authorized by the law of this State to enforce a support order or an income-withholding order, or both. If the obligor does not contest administrative enforcement, the order need not be registered. If the obligor contests the validity or administrative enforcement of the order, the support enforcement agency shall register the order pursuant to this [Act].

§ 601. Registration of Order for Enforcement.

A support order or an income-withholding order issued by a tribunal of another state may be registered in this State for enforcement.

§ 602. Procedure to Register Order for Enforcement.

(a) A support order or income-withholding order of another state may be registered in this State by sending the following documents and information to the [appropriate tribunal] in this State:

(1) a letter of transmittal to the tribunal requesting registration and enforcement;

(2) two copies, including one certified copy, of all orders to be registered, including any modification of an order;

(3) a sworn statement by the party seeking registration or a certified statement by the custodian of the records showing the amount of any arrearage;

(4) the name of the obligor and, if known:

(i) the obligor's address and social security number;

(ii) the name and address of the obligor's employer and any other source of income of the obligor; and

(iii) a description and the location of property of the obligor in this State not exempt from execution; and

(5) the name and address of the obligee and, if applicable, the agency or person to whom support payments are to be remitted.

(b) On receipt of a request for registration, the registering tribunal shall cause the order to be filed as a foreign judgment, together with one copy of the documents and information, regardless of their form.

(c) A [petition] or comparable pleading seeking a remedy that must be affirmatively sought under other law of this State may be filed at the same time as the request for registration or later. The pleading must specify the grounds for the remedy sought.

§ 603. Effect of Registration for Enforcement.

(a) A support order or income-withholding order issued in another state is registered when the order is filed in the registering tribunal of this State.

(b) A registered order issued in another state is enforceable in the same manner and is subject to the same procedures as an order issued by a tribunal of this State.

(c) Except as otherwise provided in this article, a tribunal of this State shall recognize and enforce, but may not modify, a registered order if the issuing tribunal had jurisdiction.

§ 604. Choice of Law.

(a) The law of the issuing state governs the nature, extent, amount, and duration of current payments and other obligations of support and the payment of arrearages under the order.

(b) In a proceeding for arrearages, the statute of limitation under the laws of this State or of the issuing state, whichever is longer, applies.

§ 605. Notice of Registration of Order.

(a) When a support order or income-withholding order issued in another state is registered, the registering tribunal shall notify the nonregistering party. The notice must be accompanied by a copy of the registered order and the documents and relevant information accompanying the order.

(b) The notice must inform the nonregistering party:

(1) that a registered order is enforceable as of the date of registration in the same manner as an order issued by a tribunal of this State;

(2) that a hearing to contest the validity or enforcement of the registered order must be requested within [20] days after notice;

(3) that failure to contest the validity or enforcement of the registered order in a timely manner will result in confirmation of the order and enforcement of the order and the alleged arrearages and precludes further contest of that order with respect to any matter that could have been asserted; and

(4) of the amount of any alleged arrearages.

(c) Upon registration of an income-withholding order for enforcement, the registering tribunal shall notify the obligor's employer pursuant to [the income-withholding law of this State].

§ 606. Procedure to Contest Validity or Enforcement of Registered Order.

(a) A nonregistering party seeking to contest the validity or enforcement of a registered order in this State shall request a hearing within [20] days after notice of the registration. The nonregistering party may seek to vacate the registration, to assert any defense to an allegation of noncompliance with the registered order, or to contest the remedies being sought or the amount of any alleged arrearages pursuant to Section 607 (Contest of Registration or Enforcement).

(b) If the nonregistering party fails to contest the validity or enforcement of the registered order in a timely manner, the order is confirmed by operation of law.

(c) If a nonregistering party requests a hearing to contest the validity or enforcement of the registered order, the registering tribunal shall schedule the matter for hearing and give notice to the parties of the date, time, and place of the hearing.

§ 607. Contest of Registration or Enforcement.

(a) A party contesting the validity or enforcement of a registered order or seeking to vacate the registration has the burden of proving one or more of the following defenses:

(1) the issuing tribunal lacked personal jurisdiction over the contesting party;

(2) the order was obtained by fraud;

(3) the order has been vacated, suspended, or modified by a later order;

(4) the issuing tribunal has stayed the order pending appeal;

(5) there is a defense under the law of this State to the remedy sought;

(6) full or partial payment has been made; or

(7) the statute of limitation under Section 604 (Choice of Law) precludes enforcement of some or all of the arrearages.

(b) If a party presents evidence establishing a full or partial defense under subsection (a), a tribunal may stay enforcement of the registered order, continue the proceeding to permit production of additional relevant evidence, and issue other appropriate orders. An uncontested portion of the registered order may be enforced by all remedies available under the law of this State.

(c) If the contesting party does not establish a defense under subsection (a) to the validity or enforcement of the order, the registering tribunal shall issue an order confirming the order.

§ 608. Confirmed Order.

Confirmation of a registered order, whether by operation of law or after notice and hearing, precludes further contest of the order with respect to any matter that could have been asserted at the time of registration.

§ 609. Procedure to Register Child-Support Order of Another State for Modification.

A party or support enforcement agency seeking to modify, or to modify and enforce, a child-support order issued in another state shall register that order in this State in the same manner provided in Part 1 if the order has not been registered. A [petition] for modification may be filed at the same time as a request for registration, or later. The pleading must specify the grounds for modification.

§ 610. Effect of Registration for Modification.

A tribunal of this State may enforce a child-support order of another state registered for purposes of modification, in the same manner as if the order had been issued by a tribunal of this State, but the registered order may be modified only if the requirements of Section 611 (Modification of Child-Support Order of Another State) have been met.

§ 611. Modification of Child-Support Order of Another State.

(a) After a child-support order issued in another state has been registered in this State, the responding tribunal of this State may modify that order only if, after notice and hearing, it finds that:

(1) the following requirements are met:

(i) the child, the individual obligee, and the obligor do not reside in the issuing state;

(ii) a [petitioner] who is a nonresident of this State seeks modification; and

(iii) the [respondent] is subject to the personal jurisdiction of the tribunal of this State; or

(2) the child, or a party who is an individual, is subject to the personal jurisdiction of the tribunal of this State and all of the parties who are individuals have filed written consents in the issuing tribunal for a tribunal of this State to modify the support order and assume continuing, exclusive jurisdiction over the order. However, if the issuing state is a foreign jurisdiction that has not enacted a law or established procedures substantially similar to the procedures under this [Act], the consent otherwise required of an individual residing in this State is not required for the tribunal to assume jurisdiction to modify the child-support order.

(b) Modification of a registered child-support order is subject to the same requirements, procedures, and defenses that apply to the modification of an order issued by a tribunal of this State and the order may be enforced and satisfied in the same manner.

(c) A tribunal of this State may not modify any aspect of a child-support order that may not be modified under the law of the issuing state. If two or more tribunals have issued child-support orders for the same obligor and child, the order that controls and must be so recognized under Section 207 establishes the aspects of the support order which are nonmodifiable.

(d) On issuance of an order modifying a child-support order issued in another state, a tribunal of this State becomes the tribunal having continuing, exclusive jurisdiction.

§ 612. Recognition of Order Modified in Another State.

A tribunal of this State shall recognize a modification of its earlier child-support order by a tribunal of another state which assumed jurisdiction pursuant to this [Act] or a law substantially similar to this [Act] and, upon request, except as otherwise provided in this [Act], shall:

(1) enforce the order that was modified only as to amounts accruing before the modification;

(2) enforce only nonmodifiable aspects of that order;

(3) provide other appropriate relief only for violations of that order which occurred before the effective date of the modification; and

(4) recognize the modifying order of the other state, upon registration, for the purpose of enforcement.

§613. Jurisdiction to Modify Child-Support Order of Another State When Individual Parties Reside in this State.

(a) If all of the parties who are individuals reside in this State and the child does not reside in the issuing state, a tribunal of this State has jurisdiction to enforce and to modify the issuing state's child-support order in a proceeding to register that order.

(b) A tribunal of this State exercising jurisdiction under this section shall apply the provisions of Articles 1 and 2, this article, and the procedural and substantive law of this State to the proceeding for enforcement or modification. Articles 3, 4, 5, 7, and 8 do not apply.

§ 614. Notice to Issuing Tribunal of Modification.

Within [30] days after issuance of a modified child-support order, the party obtaining the modification shall file a certified copy of the order with the issuing tribunal that had continuing, exclusive jurisdiction over the earlier order, and in each tribunal in which the party knows the earlier order has been registered. A party who obtains the order and fails to file a certified copy is subject to appropriate sanctions by a tribunal in which the issue of failure to file arises. The failure to file does not affect the validity or enforceability of the modified order of the new tribunal having continuing, exclusive jurisdiction.

§ 701. Proceeding to Determine Parentage.

(a) A tribunal of this State may serve as an initiating or responding tribunal in a proceeding brought under this [Act] or a law or procedure substantially similar to this [Act], the Uniform Reciprocal Enforcement of Support Act, or the Revised Uniform Reciprocal Enforcement of Support Act to determine that the [petitioner] is a parent of a particular child or to determine that a [respondent] is a parent of that child.

(b) In a proceeding to determine parentage, a responding tribunal of this State shall apply the [Uniform Parentage Act; procedural and substantive law of this State,] and the rules of this State on choice of law.

§ 801. Grounds for Rendition.

(a) For purposes of this article, "governor" includes an individual performing the functions of governor or the executive authority of a state covered by this [Act].

(b) The governor of this State may:

(1) demand that the governor of another state surrender an individual found in the other state who is charged criminally in this State with having failed to provide for the support of an obligee; or

(2) on the demand by the governor of another state, surrender an individual found in this State who is charged criminally in the other state with having failed to provide for the support of an obligee.

(c) A provision for extradition of individuals not inconsistent with this [Act] applies to the demand even if the individual whose surrender is demanded was not in the demanding state when the crime was allegedly committed and has not fled therefrom.

§ 802. Conditions of Rendition.

(a) Before making demand that the governor of another state surrender an individual charged criminally in this State with having failed to provide for the support of an obligee, the governor of this State may require a prosecutor of this State to demonstrate that at least [60] days previously the obligee had initiated proceedings for support pursuant to this [Act] or that the proceeding would be of no avail.

(b) If, under this [Act] or a law substantially similar to this [Act], the Uniform Reciprocal Enforcement of Support Act, or the Revised Uniform Reciprocal Enforcement of Support Act, the governor of another state makes a demand that the governor of this State surrender an individual charged criminally in that state with having failed to provide for the support of a child or other individual to whom a duty of support is owed, the governor may require a prosecutor to investigate the demand and report whether a proceeding for support has been initiated or would be effective. If it appears that a proceeding would be effective but has not been initiated, the governor may delay honoring the demand for a reasonable time to permit the initiation of a proceeding.

(c) If a proceeding for support has been initiated and the individual whose rendition is demanded prevails, the governor may decline to honor the demand. If the [petitioner] prevails and the individual whose rendition is demanded is subject to a support order, the governor may decline to honor the demand if the individual is complying with the support order.

§ 901. Uniformity of Application and Construction.

This [Act] shall be applied and construed to effectuate its general purpose to make uniform the law with respect to the subject of this [Act] among states enacting it.

State Child-Support Enforcement Agencies

In general, see
http://www.acf.dhhs.gov/programs/cse/extinf.htm#exta.

ALABAMA
Child Support Enforcement Division
50 North Ripley Street
P.O. Box 304000
Montgomery, AL 36130
800-284-4347
334-242-0210
334-242-0300
http://www.dhr.state.al.us/csed/default.asp

ALASKA
Child Support Enforcement Division
550 West 7th Avenue, Suite 310
Anchorage, AK 99501
800-478-3300
800-269-6900
907-269-6800
http://www.csed.state.ak.us

ARIZONA
Department of Economic Security
3443 North Central, 021A
P.O. Box 40458
Phoenix, AZ 85012
800-882-4151
602-252-4045
http://www.de.state.az.us/links/dcse/index.html
http://www.supreme.state.az.us/dr/default.htm

ARKANSAS
Office of Child Support Enforcement
P.O. Box 3278
Little Rock, AR 72203
800-264-2445
501-682-8398
501-682-2242
http://www.state.ar.us/dfa/childsupport/index.html

CALIFORNIA
Department of Child Support Services
744 P. Street MS 17-29
Sacramento, CA 95814
800-952-5253
916-654-1532
http://www.childsup.cahwnet.gov/Default.htm
Los Angeles
213-889-2991
http://da.co.la.ca.us/childsupport/service.htm

COLORADO
Division of Child Support Enforcement
1575 Sherman Street, 2d Floor
Denver, CO 80203
303-866-5994
http://www.childsupport.state.co.us

CONNECTICUT
State of Connecticut
Child Support Enforcement Bureau
25 Sigourney Street
Hartford, CT 06105
800-842-1508
800-842-2159
860-424-4926
http://www.dss.state.ct.us/svcs/csupp.htm

DELAWARE
Division of Child Support Enforcement
1901 North DuPont Highway
P.O. Box 904
New Castle, DE 19720
302-577-7171
302-577-4863
http://www.state.de.us/dhss/dcse/index.html
dcseinfo@state.de.us

DISTRICT OF COLUMBIA
Child Support Enforcement
441 4th Street, NW
Washington, DC 20001
888-689-6088
202-724-1444
202-645-7500
http://www.csed.dcgov.org

FLORIDA
Department of Revenue
P.O. Box 8030
Tallahassee, FL 32314
800-622-KIDS
850-922-9590
http://www.sun6.dms.state.fl.us/dor/childsupport

GEORGIA
Division of Family and Children Services
P.O. Box 38450
Atlanta, GA 30334
800-227-7993
404-657-2780
http://www.acf.dhhs.gov/programs/cse/extinf.htm#exta

HAWAII
Child Support Enforcement Agency
601 Kamokila Boulevard, Suite 251
Kapolei, HI 96707
888-317-9081
808-587-3698
http://kumu.icsd.hawaii.gov/csea/csea.htm

IDAHO
Department of Health and Welfare
450 West State Street
Boise, ID 83720
800-356-9868
208-334-5710
http://www.idahochild.org
http://www2.state.id.us/dhw/childsupport/index.htm

ILLINOIS
Department of Public Aid
201 South Grand Avenue East
Springfield, IL 62763
800-447-4278
217-524-4602
217-782-1200
http://www.state.il.us/dpa/html/cs_child_support_news.htm

INDIANA
Bureau of Child Support
IGC-South, Room W360
402 West Washington
P.O. Box 7083
Indianapolis, IN 46207
800-622-4932
317-233-5437
http://www.state.in.us/fssa/children/support/index.html
Marion County
http://www.marioncounty.org

IOWA
Child Support Enforcement
1305 East Walnut
Des Moines, IA 50319
515-281-5767
515-281-5580
http://www.dhs.state.ia.us/HomePages/DHS/csrunit.htm

KANSAS
Child Support Enforcement
415 SW 8th
Topeka, KS 66603
888-219-7801
913-296-3237
http://www.srskansas.org/srslegalservice.html

KENTUCKY
Division of Child Support Enforcement
275 East Main Street
Frankfort, KY 40621
800-248-1163
502-564-2285 x466
502-696-KIDS
http://www.law.state.ky.us/childsupport/Default.htm

LOUISIANA
Department of Social Services
P.O. Box 3776
Baton Rouge, LA 70821
800-256-4650
504-342-4780
http://www.dss.state.la.us

MAINE
Bureau of Family Independence
11 State House Station
Whitten Road
Augusta, ME 04333
800-371-3101
207-287-2826
http://www.state.me.us/dhs/main/bfi.htm

MARYLAND
Child Support Enforcement Administration
200 North Howard Street
Baltimore, MD 21201
800-332-6347
410-767-7619
http://www.dhr.state.md.us/csea/index.htm

MASSACHUSETTS
Department of Revenue
Child Support Enforcement
51 Sleeper Street
P.O. Box 9492
Boston, MA 02205
800-332-2733
617-577-7200 x30488
617-626-4000
http://www.state.ma.us/cse/cse.htm

MICHIGAN
State Court Administrator
309 North Washington Square
P.O. Box 30048
Lansing, MI 48909
800-524-9846
517-373-7570
517-373-0130
http://www.mfia.state.mi.us/CHLDSUPP/CS-INDEX.htm

MINNESOTA
Child Support Enforcement Division
121 7th Plaza
St. Paul, MN 55155
800-672-3954
651-296-2542
http://www.dhs.state.mn.us/ecs/Program/csed.htm

MISSISSIPPI
Division of Child Support Enforcement
750 North State Street
Jackson, MS 39205
800-948-4010
800-434-5437
601-359-4861
http://www.mdhs.state.ms.us/cse.html

MISSOURI
Division of Child Support Enforcement
3418 Knipp Drive, Suite F
P.O. Box 2320
Jefferson City, MO 65102
800-585-9234
800-859-7999
573-751-4301
http://www.dss.state.mo.us/cse/cse.htm

MONTANA
Child Support Enforcement Division
3075 North Montana Avenue
Helena, MT 59601
800-346-KIDS
406-442-7278
http://www.dphhs.state.mt.us/divisions/cse/csed.htm

NEBRASKA
Child Support Enforcement
P.O. Box 94728
Lincoln, NE 68509
800-831-4573
402-471-5555
http://www.hhs.state.ne.us/cse/cseindex.htm

NEVADA
Child Support Enforcement
2527 North Carson Street
Carson City, NV 89706
800-992-0900
702-687-4744
775-687-4128
http://www.state.nv.us/ag/agpub/chldsupp.htm

NEW HAMPSHIRE
Office of Program Support
6 Hazen Drive
Concord, NH 03301
800-852-3345 x4427
800-371-8844
603-271-4427

NEW JERSEY
Division of Family Development
P.O. Box 716
Trenton, NJ 08625
800-621-5437
609-588-2915
609-292-2400
http://www.njchildsupport.org

NEW MEXICO
Child Support Enforcement Division
P.O. Box 2348
Santa Fe, NM 87504
800-288-7207
800-585-7631
505-827-7200
505-476-7040
http://www.state.nm.us/hsd/csed.html
http://childsupport.hsd.state.mn.us

NEW YORK
Division of Child Support Enforcement
1 Commerce Plaza
P.O. Box 14
Albany, NY 12260
800-343-8859
518-474-9081
518-474-1078
http://www.dfa.state.ny.us/csms

NORTH CAROLINA
Office of Child Support Enforcement
Social Services Division
325 North Salisbury Street
Raleigh, NC 27603
800-992-9457
919-571-4114
http://www.dhhs.state.nc.us/dss/cse/cse_mission.htm

NORTH DAKOTA
Child Support Enforcement
1929 North Washington Street
Bismarck, ND 58501
800-755-8530
701-328-3582
http://lnotes.state.nd.us/dhs/dhsweb.nsf/ServicePages/ChildSupportEnforcement

OHIO
Office of Child Support
50 West Broad Street
Columbus, OH 43206
800-686-1556
614-752-6561
http://www.state.oh.us/odhs/ocs

OKLAHOMA
Child Support Enforcement Division
2400 North Lincoln Boulevard
P.O. Box 25352
Oklahoma City, OK 73125
800-522-2922
405-522-5871
http://www.okdhs.org/childsupport

OREGON
Division of Child Support
1162 Court Street, NE
Salem, OR 97310
800-850-0228
503-378-5567
http://www.afs.hr.state.or.us/rss/childsupp.html

PENNSYLVANIA
Child Support Enforcement Bureau
P.O. Box 8018
Harrisburg, PA 17105
800-932-0211
717-787-3672
http://www.pachildsupport.com

RHODE ISLAND
Child Support Enforcement
77 Dorrance St.
Providence, RI 02903
800-638-5437
401-222-2847
http://www.childsupportliens.com/RI/index.html

SOUTH CAROLINA
Department of Social Services
1535 Confederate Avenue
P.O. Box 1015
Columbia, SC 29202
800-768-5858
803-737-5875
http://www.state.sc.us/dss/csed

SOUTH DAKOTA
Division of Child Support Enforcement
700 Governors Drive
Pierre, SD 57501
800-827-6078
605-773-3641
http://www.state.sd.us/social/CSE/index.htm

TENNESSEE
Child Support Enforcement
400 Deaderick Street
Nashville, TN 37248
800-838-6911
800-446-0814
615-253-4394
http://www.state.tn.us/humanserv

TEXAS
Child Support Enforcement Division
P.O. Box 12548
Austin, TX 78711
800-252-8014
512-460-6000
http://www.oag.state.tx.us/child/mainchil.htm

UTAH
Office of Recovery Services
515 East 100 South
Salt Lake City, UT 84102
800-257-9156
801-536-8500
http://www.ors.state.ut.us

VERMONT
Office of Child Support
103 South Main Street
Waterbury, VT 05671
800-786-3214
802-241-2319
http://www.ocs.state.vt.us

VIRGIN ISLANDS
Paternity and Child Support
7 Charlotte Amalie
St. Thomas, VI 00802
809-775-3070

VIRGINIA
Division of Child Support Enforcement
730 East Broad Street
Richmond, VA 23219
800-468-8894
804-692-2458
http://www.dss.state.va.us/division/childsupp

WASHINGTON
Division of Child Support
P.O. Box 45860
Olympia, WA 98504
800-457-6202
360-586-3162
http://www.wa.gov/dshs/dcs/index.html

WEST VIRGINIA
Bureau of Child Support Enforcement
1900 Kanawha Blvd., East
Charleston, WV 25305
800-249-3778
304-558-3780
http://www.wvdhhr.org/bcse

WISCONSIN
Bureau of Child Support
1 West Wilson Street
Madison, WI 53707
888-300-4473
608-266-9909
http://www.dwd.state.wi.us/bcs

WYOMING
Child Support Enforcement
2300 Capitol Avenue
Cheyenne, WY 82002
800-970-9258
307-777-6948
http://dfsweb.state.wy.us/csehome/cs.htm

Appendix F

State Child Welfare Agencies

Alabama Department of Human Resources
Adult, Child & Family Services Division
http://www.dhr.state.al.us

Alaska Department of Health and Social Services
Division of Family and Youth Services
http://www.hss.state.ak.us/dfys

Arizona Department of Economic Security
http://www.de.state.az.us

Arkansas Department of Human Services
http://www.state.ar.us/dhs

California Department of Social Services
http://www.dss.cahwnet.gov

Colorado Department of Human Services
http://www.cdhs.state.co.us/cyf/cwelfare/cwweb.html

Connecticut Department of Children and Families
http://www.state.ct.us/dcf

Delaware Department of Services for Children, Youth and Their Families
http://www.state.de.us/kids/index.htm

District of Columbia Child and Family Services Agency
http://www.dc.gov/agencies/detail.asp?id=6

Florida Department of Children and Families
http://sun6.dms.state.fl.us/cf_web

Georgia Department of Human Resources
http://www.dhr.state.ga.us

Hawaii Department of Human Services
http://www.state.hi.us/icsd/dhs/dhs.html

Idaho Department of Health and Welfare
http://www.state.id.us/dhw/hwgd_wwwhome.html

Illinois Department of Children and Family Services
http://www.state.il.us/dcfs/default.htm

Indiana Family and Social Services Administration
Division of Family and Children
http://www.state.in.us/fssa/HTML/PROGRAMS/2a.html

Iowa Department of Human Services
http://www.dhs.state.ia.us

Kansas Department of Social and Rehabilitation Services
http://www.ink.org/public/srs/main.html

Kentucky Cabinet for Families and Children
http://cfc-chs.chr.state.ky.us

Louisiana Department of Social Services
http://www.dss.state.la.us

Maine Department of Human Services
http://janus.state.me.us/dhs/welcome.htm

Maryland Department of Human Resources
http://www.dhr.state.md.us/dhr

Massachusetts Department of Social Services
http://www.state.ma.us/dss

Michigan Family Independence Agency
http://www.mfia.state.mi.us

Minnesota Department of Human Services
http://www.dhs.state.mn.us

Mississippi Department of Human Services
http://www.mdhs.state.ms.us

Missouri Department of Social Services
http://www.dss.state.mo.us/index.htm

Montana Department of Public Health and Human Services
http://www.dphhs.state.mt.us

Nebraska Health and Human Services
http://www.hhs.state.ne.us

Nevada Division of Child and Family Services
http://www.state.nv.us/hr/dcfs

New Hampshire Department of Health and Human Services
http://www.dhhs.state.nh.us

New Jersey Division of Youth and Family Services
http://www.state.nj.us/humanservices

New Mexico Children, Youth and Families Department
http://cyf_abq.state.nm.us
ALBUQUERQUE_300SM.CLGARCIA@cyf02

New York Department of Family Assistance
http://www.dfa.state.ny.us

North Carolina Department of Health and Human Services
http://www.dhhs.state.nc.us

North Dakota Department of Human Services
http://207.108.104.74/dhs/dhsweb.nsf

Ohio Department of Human Services
http://www.state.oh.us/odhs

Oklahoma Department of Human Services
http://www.okdhs.org

Oregon Department of Human Resources
Office for Services to Children and Families
http://www.scf.hr.state.or.us

Pennsylvania Department of Public Welfare
http://www.state.pa.us/PA_Exec/Public_Welfare/overview.html

Rhode Island Children, Youth and Families
http://www.state.ri.us/manual/data/queries/stdept_.idc?id=20

South Carolina Department of Social Services
http://www.state.sc.us/dss

South Dakota Department of Social Services
http://www.state.sd.us/social/social.html

Tennessee Department of Children's Services
http://www.state.tn.us/youth/children/index.htm

Texas Department of Protective and Regulatory Services
http://www.tdprs.state.tx.us

Utah Department of Human Services
Children and Family Services
http://www.hsdcfs.state.ut.us

Vermont Department of Social and Rehabilitation Services
http://www.state.vt.us/srs

Virginia Department of Social Services
http://www.vip-view.net

Washington Department of Social and Health Services
http://www.wa.gov/dshs

West Virginia Department of Health and Human Resources
http://www.wvdhhr.org

Wisconsin Department of Health and Family Services
http://www.dhfs.state.wi.us

Wyoming Department of Family Services
http://dfsweb.state.wy.us

See also National Adoption Information Clearinghouse
http://www.CALIB.COM.NAIC

Appendix G

Marriage Laws

(As of April 1, 1991)

State	Age with Parental Consent		Age without Consent		Physical Exam & Blood Test for Male and Female		Waiting Period	
	Male	Female	Male	Female	Maximum Period between Exam and License	Scope of Medical Exam	Before License	After License
Alabama*	14a	14a	18	18	—	b	—	s
Alaska	16z	16z	18	18	—	b	3 da., w	—
Arizona	16z	16z	18	18	—	—	—	—
Arkansas	17c	16c	18	18	—	—	v	—
California	aa	aa	18	18	30 da., w	bb	—	h
Colorado*	16z	16z	18	18	—	—	—	s
Connecticut	16z	16z	18	18	—	bb	4 da., w	ttt
Delaware	18c	16c	18	18	—	—	—	e, s
Florida	16a, c	16a, c	18	18	—	b	3 da.	s
Georgia*	aa	aa	16	16	—	b	3 da., g	s*
Hawaii	16d	16d	18	18	—	b	—	—
Idaho*	16z	16z	18	18	—	bb	—	—
Illinois	16	16	18	18	30 da.	b, n	—	ee
Indiana	17c	17c	18	18	—	bb	72 hrs.	t
Iowa*	18z	18z	18	18	—	—	3 da., v	tt
Kansas*[y]	18z	18z	18	18	—	—	3 da., w	—
Kentucky	18c, z	18c, z	18	18	—	—	—	—
Louisiana	18z	18z	18	18	10 da.	b	72 hrs., w	—
Maine	16z	16z	18	18	—	—	3 da., v, w	h
Maryland	16c, f	16c, f	18	18	—	—	48 hrs., w	ff
Massachusetts	16d	16	18	18	60 da.	bb	3 da., v	—
Michigan	16c, d	16c	18	18	30 da.	b	3 da., w	—
Minnesota	16z	16z	18	18	—	—	5 da., w	—
Mississippi	aa	aa	17gg	15gg	30 da.	b	3 da., w	—
Missouri	15d, 18z.	15d, 18z	18	18	—	—	—	—
Montana*[yy]	16	16	18	18	—	b	—	ff
Nebraska*[yy]	17	17	18	18	—	bb	—	—
Nevada	16z	16z	18	18	—	—	—	—
New Hampshire	14j	13j	18	18	30 da.	b, l	3 da., v	h
New Jersey	16z, c	16z, c	18	18	30 da.	b	72 hrs., w	s
New Mexico[y]	16d	16d	18	18	30 da.	b	—	—
New York	14j	14j	18	18	—	nn	—	24 hrs., w, t
North Carolina	16c, g	16c, g	18	18	—	m	v	—
North Dakota	16	16	18	18	—	—	—	t
Ohio*	18c, z	16c, z	18	18	30 da.	b	5 da.	t, w
Oklahoma*	16c	16c	18	18	30 da., w	b	—	s
Oregon	17	17	18	18	—	—	3 da., w	—
Pennsylvania*	16d	16d	18	18	30 da.	b	3 da., w	t
Puerto Rico[y]	18c, d, z	16c, d, z	21	21	—	b	—	—
Rhode Island*	18d	16d	18	18	—	bb	—	—
South Carolina*	16c	14c	18	18	—	—	1 da.	—

continued

State	Age with Parental Consent		Age without Consent		Physical Exam & Blood Test for Male and Female		Waiting Period	
	Male	Female	Male	Female	Maximum Period between Exam and License	Scope of Medical Exam	Before License	After License
South Dakota	16c	16c	18	18	—	—	—	tt
Tennessee	16d	16d	18	18	—	—	3 da., cc	s
Texas*y	14j, k	14j, k	18	18	—	—	—	s
Utah	14	14	18x	18x	30 da.	b	—	s
Vermont	16z	16z	18	18	30 da.	b	3 da., w	—
Virginia	16a, c	16a, c	18	18	—	b	—	t
Washington	17d	17d	18	18	—	bbb	3 da.	t
West Virginia	18c	18c	18	18	—	b	3 da., w	—
Wisconsin	16	16	18	18	—	b	5 da., w	s
Wyoming	16d	16d	18	18	—	bb	—	—
Dist. of Columbia*	16a	16a	18	18	30 da., w	b	3 da., w	—

*Indicates 1987 common-law marriage recognized; in many states, such marriages are only recognized if entered into many years before. (a) Parental consent not required if minor was previously married. (aa) No age limits. (b) Venereal diseases. (bb) Venereal diseases and Rubella (for female). In Colorado, Rubella for female under 45 and Rh type. (bbb) No medical exam required; however, applicants must file affidavit showing non-affliction of contagious venereal disease. (c) Younger parties may obtain license in case of pregnancy or birth of child. (cc) Unless parties are over 18 years of age. (d) Younger parties may obtain license in special circumstances. (e) Residents before expiration of 24-hour waiting period; non-residents formerly residents, before expiration of 96-hour waiting period; others 96 hours. (ee) License effective 1 day after issuance, unless court orders otherwise, valid for 60 days only. (f) If parties are under 16 years of age, proof of age and the consent of parents in person are required. If a parent is ill, an affidavit by the incapacitated parent and a physician's affidavit to that effect required. (ff) License valid for 180 days only. (g) Unless parties are 18 years of age or more, or female is pregnant, or applicants are the parents of a living child born out of wedlock. (gg) Notice to parents necessary if parties are under 21. (h) License valid for 90 days only. (j) Parental consent and/or permission of judge required. (k) Below age of consent parties need parental consent and permission of judge. (l) With each certificate issued to couples, a list of family planning agencies and services available to them is provided. (m) Mental incompetence, infectious tuberculosis, venereal diseases and Rubella (certain counties only). (n) Venereal diseases; test for sickle cell anemia given at request of examining physician. (nn) Tests for sickle cell anemia may be required for certain applicants. Marriage prohibited unless it is established that procreation is not possible. (p) If one or both parties are below the age for marriage without parental consent (3 day waiting period). (s) License valid for 30 days only. (t) License valid for 60 days only. (tt) License valid for 20 days only. (ttt) License valid for 65 days. (v) Parties must file notice of intention to marry with local clerk. (w) Waiting period may be avoided. (x) Authorizes counties to provide for premarital counseling as a requisite to issuance of license to persons under 19 and persons previously divorced. (y) Marriages by proxy are valid. (yy) Proxy marriages are valid under certain conditions. (z) Younger parties may marry with parental consent and/or permission of judge. In Connecticut, judicial approval. (zz) With consent of court.

Source: Gary N. Skoloff, Skoloff & Wolfe, Livingston, NJ. Reprinted by permission.

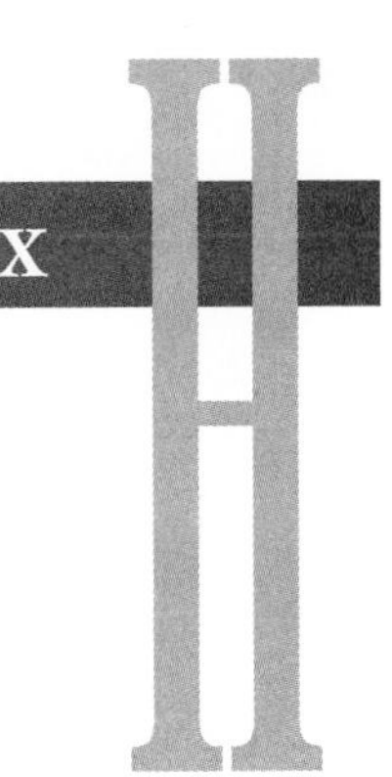

APPENDIX

DIVORCE, MARRIAGE, BIRTH, AND DEATH RECORDS

WHERE TO WRITE FOR VITAL RECORDS

An official certificate of every birth, death, marriage, and divorce should be on file in the locality where the event occurred. The federal government does not maintain files or indexes of these records. These records are filed permanently either in a state vital statistics office or in a city, county, or other local office.

To obtain a certified copy of any of the certificates, write or go to the vital statistics office in the state or area where the event occurred. Addresses and fees for your state are given at http://www.cdc.gov/nchs/howto/w2w/w2welcom.htm (see the home page of this site on the following page).

To ensure that you receive an accurate record for your requests and that your request is filled with all due speed, follow the steps outlined below for the information in which you are interested:

- Write to the appropriate office to have your request filled.
- Under the appropriate office, information has been included for birth and death records concerning whether the state will accept checks or money orders and to whom they should be made payable. This same information would apply when marriage and divorce records are available from the state office.
- For all certified copies requested, make your check or money order payable for the correct amount for the number of copies you wish to obtain. Cash is not recommended because the office cannot refund cash lost in transit.
- Type or print all names and addresses in the letter.
- Give the following facts when writing for **birth or death records:**
  1. Full name of person whose record is being requested.
  2. Sex.
  3. Parents' names, including maiden name of mother.
  4. Month, day, and year of birth or death.
  5. Place of birth or death (city or town, county, and state; and name of hospital, if known).
  6. Purpose for which copy is needed.
  7. Relationship to person whose record is being requested.
- Give the following facts when writing for **marriage records:**
  1. Full names of bride and groom.
  2. Month, day, and year of marriage.
  3. Place of marriage (city or town, county, and state).
  4. Purpose for which copy is needed.
  5. Relationship to persons whose record is being requested.
- Give the following facts when writing for **divorce records:**
  1. Full names of husband and wife.
  2. Month, day, and year of divorce or annulment.

3. Place of divorce or annulment.
4. Type of final decree.
5. Purpose for which copy is needed.
6. Relationship to persons whose record is being requested.

The state addresses are contained at the following site.

ORGANIZATIONS AND RESOURCES

American Academy for Adoption Attorneys
P.O. Box 33053
Washington, DC 20033
202-832-2222
http://www.adoptionattorneys.org

American Academy of Family Mediators
5 Militia Drive
Lexington, MA 02421
800-292-4AFM
781-674-2663

American Academy of Family Physicians
http://www.aafp.org

American Academy of Matrimonial Lawyers
150 North Michigan Avenue
Chicago, IL 60601
312-263-7682
http://www.aaml.org

American Association for Marital and Family Therapy
1717 K Street, NW
Washington, DC 20006
202-429-1825
http://www.aamft.org

American Bar Association Center on Children and the Law
http://www.abanet.org/child/home.html

American Bar Association Juvenile Justice Center
http://www.abanet.org/crimjust/juvjus/home.html

American Bar Association Section of Family Law
http://www.abanet.org/family/home.html

American Coalition for Fathers and Children
1718 M Street, NW
Washington, DC 20036
800-978-DADS
http://www.acfc.org

American College of Family Trial Lawyers
http://www.acftl.com

American Society for Reproductive Medicine
1209 Montgomery Highway
Birmingham, AL 35216
205-978-5000
http://www.asrm.com

Association of Family and Conciliation Courts
6515 Grand Teton Plaza, Suite 210
Madison, WI 53719
608-664-3750
http://www.afccnet.org
afcc@afccnet.org

Association of Reproductive Health Professionals
http://www.arhp.org

Centers for Disease Control
http://cdc.gov

Child Find of America
P.O. Box 277
New Paltz, NY 12561
914-255-1848
800-I-AM-LOST

Children's Defense Fund
25 E Street, NW
Washington, DC 20001
202-628-8787
http://www.childrensdefense.org

Children's Rights Council
3000 I Street, NW
Washington, DC 20002
202-547-6227
http://www.gocrc.com

Child Welfare League of America
http://www.cwla.org

Equal Employment Opportunity Commission
800-669-4000
www.eeoc.gov

Federal Office of Child Support Enforcement
http://www.acf.dhhs.gov/programs/cse

Feminist Majority: Women's Issue Links
http://www.feminist.org

Hotlines
AIDS
800-342-AIDS
Domestic Violence
800-799-SAFE
Missing Children
800-THE-LOST

International Academy of Matrimonial Lawyers
http://www.abanet.org/child/home.html

Men's Issues
http://www.vix.com/pub/men
http://menstuff.org
http://www.mensdefense.org
http://www.tnom.com

National Adoption Information Clearinghouse
http://www.calib.com/naic

National Association of Counsel for Children
1205 Oneida Street
Denver, CO 80220
800-525-0246

National Association of Social Workers
750 First Street, NE
Washington, DC 20002
800-638-8799
202-406-8600

National Center for Lesbian Rights
870 Market Street, Suite 570
San Francisco, CA 94102
415-392-6483

National Center for Missing and Exploited Children
2101 Wilson Boulevard, Suite 550
Arlington, VA 22201
800-843-5678
http://www.ncmec.org
http://www.missingkids.org

National Center for Youth Law
114 Sansome Street
San Francisco, CA 94014
415-543-9024

National Child Support Enforcement Association
400 North Capitol Street, Suite 414
Washington, DC 20001
202-624-8180
http://www.ncsea.org

National Clearinghouse for Child Abuse and Neglect Information
http://www.calib.com/nccanch

National Coalition Against Domestic Violence
1201 East Colfax 385
P.O. Box 18749
Denver, CO 80218

National Council for Adoption
1930 17th Street, NW
Washington, DC 20009
202-328-1200

National Council of Juvenile and Family Court Judges
1041 North Virginia Street
Reno, NV 89557
775-784-6012
http://www.ncjfcj.unr.edu

National Domestic Violence Hotline
800-799-SAFE
http://www.ndvh.org

National Gay and Lesbian Task Force
2320 17th Street, NW
Washington, DC 20009
202-332-6483

National Organization for Men
11 Park Place
New York, NY 10007
212-686-MALE
http://www.tnom.com

National Organization for Women
1000 16th Street, NW
Washington, DC 20036
202-331-0066
http://www.now.org

National Right to Life Committee
419 17th Street, NW
Washington, DC 20004
202-626-8800

Parents Without Partners
8807 Colesville Road
Silver Spring, MD 20910
800-737-7974

Partners Task Force for Gay and Lesbian Couples
http://www.buddybuddy.com

Rape Treatment Center
http://www.911rape.org

Single Parents by Choice
1642 Gracie Square Station
New York, NY 10028
212-988-0993

Stepfamily Association of America
650 J. Street, Suite 205
Lincoln, NE 68508
800-735-0329

Stepfamily Foundation
333 West End Avenue
New York, NY 10023
http://www.stepfamily.org

Victims of Child Abuse Legislation
800-745-8778

GLOSSARY

abandonment See *desertion.*

abduction The unlawful taking away of another.

absolute divorce See *divorce.*

abuse Physically harming a person.

abuse of process A tort with the following elements: (1) a use of civil or criminal proceedings, (2) for an improper or ulterior purpose, (3) resulting in actual damage. For example, you have someone arrested in order to pressure him to marry your daughter, whom he impregnated. Encouraging marriage is not the purpose of the criminal law.

acceptance An assent or acquiescence to an offer.

accounting A statement or report on the financial condition or status of a person, company, estate, transaction, enterprise, etc.

account receivable A regular business debt not yet collected.

acknowledgment A formal recognition or affirmation that something is genuine.

active registry A reunion registry that does not require both the adoptee and the biological parent to register their consent to release information. Once one of them registers, an agency employee will contact the other to determine his or her wishes for the release of information.

actuarial Pertaining to the calculation of statistical risks, premiums, estate values, etc.

actuary A statistician. A person skilled in mathematical calculations to determine insurance risks.

adjudicate To decide by judicial process; to judge.

adjusted basis See *tax basis.*

adjusted gross income The total amount received after making allowed deductions.

administration The management and settlement of the estate of a decedent.

administrative agency A part of the executive branch of government whose function is to execute or carry out the law.

administrator A person appointed by a court to manage or administer the estate of a deceased, often when no valid will exists. See also *personal representative.*

adoption The legal process by which an adoptive parent assumes the rights and duties of the natural (i.e., biological) parent. The latter's parental rights are terminated.

adoption by estoppel See *equitable adoption, estopped.*

adoption exchange An organization that seeks to find adoptive parents for foster care or special care children.

adultery Sexual relations between a married person and someone other than his or her spouse.

adversarial proceeding A proceeding in court or at an agency where both parties to a dispute can appear and argue their opposing positions.

adversary (1) Involving a dispute between opposing sides who argue their case before a neutral official such as a judge; (2) an opponent.

AFDC Aid to Families with Dependent Children, a public assistance program.

affidavit A written statement of facts given under oath or affirmation.

affinity Relationship by marriage rather than by blood.

affirmative defense A defense that raises new facts not in the plaintiff's complaint.

agency A relationship in which one person acts for another or represents another by the latter's express or implied authority. See also *administrative agency.*

agency adoption An adoption in which a child is placed for adoption by a public agency responsible for adoptions or by an approved private adoption agency.

aggravated damages Money paid to cover special circumstances that justify an increase in the amount paid (e.g., the presence of malice).

aggrieved (1) Injured or wronged; (2) the person injured or wronged.

alienation The act of transferring property or title to property.

alienation of affections A tort that is committed when the defendant diminishes the marital relationship between the plaintiff and the latter's spouse.

alimony Money or other property paid in fulfillment of a duty to support one's spouse after a separation or divorce. Note, however, that the Internal Revenue Service uses a broader definition of alimony for purposes of determining whether it is *deductible.* See also *rehabilitative alimony.*

alimony in gross Lump-sum alimony.

allele One member of a pair or series of genes.

alternate payee A nonemployee entitled to receive pension benefits of an employee or former employee pursuant to a qualified domestic relations order.

a mensa et thoro See *legal separation.*

American Bar Association A voluntary, national organization of attorneys.

American Digest System See *digest.* The American Digest System is the most comprehensive digest in existence. It covers almost every court in the country.

American Jurisprudence, 2d A national legal encyclopedia.

American Law Reports A set of reporters that contain selected opinions from many different courts. In addition, the ALR volumes contain research papers—called *annotations*—that give surveys of the law on particular issues found in the opinions.

amicus curiae Friend of the court; a nonparty to litigation who gives advice or suggestions to a court on resolving a dispute before it.

amnesty Forgiveness; a general pardon from the state.

ancillary Subordinate; auxiliary, aiding.

annotated Organized by subject matter with research references or other commentary.

annotation A set of notes or commentaries on something. The most widely used annotations are those printed in American Law Reports.

annuity A fixed sum payable to an individual at specified intervals for a limited period of time or for life.

annulment A declaration by a court that a valid marriage never existed.

answer The pleading filed by the defendant that responds to the complaint of the plaintiff.

antenuptial agreement See *premarital agreement.*

appearance Formally going before a court.

appellant The party bringing an appeal because of disagreement with the decision of a lower tribunal.

appellee The party against whom an appeal is brought.

appreciation An increase in the value of property.

arbitration The process of submitting a dispute to a third party outside the judicial system who will resolve the dispute for the parties.

arm's length, at As between two strangers who are looking out for their own self-interests; at a distance; without trusting the other's fairness; free of personal bias or control.

arraignment Bringing the accused before a court to hear the criminal charges and to enter a plea thereto.

arrears, arrearages Payments that are due but have not been made.

artificial insemination The impregnation of a woman by a method other than sexual intercourse.

assign To transfer rights or property to someone. The noun is *assignment.* The person who makes the transfer is called the *assignor.* The person who receives the transfer is called the *assignee* or one of the *assigns.*

assignee The person to whom ownership or rights are transferred. See also *assign.*

assignment The transfer of ownership or other rights.

assignor The person who transfers ownership or rights to another.

assisted conception A pregnancy resulting from (1) fertilizing an egg of a woman with sperm of a man by means other than sexual intercourse or (2) implanting an embryo.

assisted reproductive technologies (ART) Treatments or procedures in which eggs are surgically removed from a woman's ovaries and combined with sperm to help a woman become pregnant.

at arm's length See *arm's length, at.*

attachment A court authorization of the seizure of the defendant's property so that it can be used to satisfy a judgment against him or her.

attorney-client privilege The right of a client to refuse to answer questions that would disclose communications between the client and his or her attorney. The purpose of the communication must be the facilitation of legal services from the attorney to the client. The client can also prevent the attorney from making such disclosures.

attorney work product The following material is protected from discovery: (1) the private memoranda of an attorney and (2) mental impressions or personal recollections prepared or formed by an attorney in anticipation of litigation or for trial.

a vinculo matrimonii See *divorce.*

banns of marriage A public announcement of a proposed marriage.

basis See *tax basis.*

bastardy Pertaining to a child born before his or her parents were married, or born to parents who never married.

battered woman syndrome Psychological helplessness because of a woman's financial dependence, loneliness, guilt, shame, and fear of reprisal from her husband or boyfriend who has repeatedly battered her in the past.

beneficiary The person named in a document such as a will or insurance policy to receive property or other benefit.

bequest A gift of personal property in a will.

best interests of the child A standard of decision based on what would best serve the child's welfare.

betrothal A mutual promise to marry.

BFOQ See *bona fide occupational qualification.*

Bias An inclination or tendency to think and to act in a certain way; a danger of prejudgment.

bifurcated divorce A case in which the dissolution of the marriage—the divorce itself—is tried separately from other issues in the marriage such as the division of property.

bigamy Entering or attempting to enter a marriage when a prior marriage of one or both parties is still valid.

bilateral divorce A divorce granted by a court when both the husband and the wife are present before the court.

bill A proposed statute offered for passage by the legislature.

bill for divorce Petition or complaint for a dissolution of the marriage.

biological parent One's natural parent; a parent by blood.

black market adoption An adoption that involves a payment beyond reasonable expenses in order to facilitate the adoption.

boilerplate Language that is commonly used in a document. It sometimes refers to nonessential language often found in the same kind of document.

bona fide occupational qualification (BFOQ) Sex discrimination that is reasonably necessary for the operation of a particular business or enterprise.

book value The value at which an asset is carried on the balance sheet.

broker An individual who coordinates various service providers needed to accomplish a legal objective such as an adoption.

camera See *in camera.*

canon (1) A rule of behavior; (2) a maxim or guideline.

canon law Church or ecclesiastical law.

canons of ethics Rules that embody standards of conduct. In the legal profession, the canons of ethics are often referred to as a *code of ethics* or as a *code of professional responsibility* that governs attorneys. The current canons of ethics of the American Bar Association are found within the *Model Rules of Professional Responsibility.*

capacity (1) The legal power to do something; (2) the ability to understand the nature and effects of one's actions or inaction.

capital improvements Structural improvements on property, as opposed to ordinary maintenance work.

capitalization The total amount of the various securities issued by a corporation.

caption of complaint The heading or beginning of the complaint that contains the name of the court, the names of the parties, their litigation status, and the name of the document (e.g., Complaint for Divorce).

CARTWHEEL A research technique designed to increase the effectiveness of your use of an index in a reference book. The technique helps you identify a large variety of word or phrase substitutes to check in an index.

case law The body of law found in court opinions. See *court opinion.*

cash surrender value The amount of money that an insurance policy would yield if cashed in with the insurance company; the amount an insurer will pay upon cancellation of the policy before death.

cause of action An allegation of facts that, if proved, would give a party a right to judicial relief. A cause of action is a legally acceptable reason for suing; it is a theory of recovery.

ceremonial marriage A marriage that is entered in compliance with the statutory requirements (e.g., obtaining a marriage license, having the marriage performed [i.e., solemnized] by an authorized person).

challenge for cause The elimination of a prospective juror during voir dire, which is the jury selection process, for a specific reason such as bias.

chambers A judge's private office.

chattel See *personal property.*

child abuse Physically harming a child other than by accident.

child-support guidelines State-mandated calculation of child-support payments that must be paid by parents.

Chinese wall Steps taken in an office to prevent a tainted employee from having any contact with a particular case in order to avoid the disqualification of the office from the case. The employee is tainted because he or she has a conflict of interest in the case.

choice of venue See *venue.*

chose in action The right to recover something through a lawsuit.

citation A reference to any material printed on paper or stored in a computer database. It is the "address" where you can locate and read the material.

civil contempt See *contempt of court.*

civil fraud See *fraud.*

civil procedure The body of law governing the methods and practices of civil litigation.

civil union A same-sex legal relationship in Vermont that grants the same benefits, protections, and responsibilities under Vermont law that are granted to spouses in a marriage.

closed case file The file of a client whose case is no longer being worked on.

code A book or set of books that contain rules or laws organized by subject matter. The state code, also called the *state statutory code,* is a collection of statutes written by the state legislature, organized by subject matter.

code of ethics See *canons of ethics.*

code of regulations Laws written by administrative agencies, organized by subject matter.

cohabit To live together as husband and wife.

cohabitants Two unmarried people living together in the way that husbands and wives live together.

cohabitation Living together as husband and wife.

cohabitation agreement A contract made by two individuals who intend to stay unmarried indefinitely that covers financial and related matters while living together, upon separation, or upon death.

collateral attack A nondirect attack or challenge to the validity of a judgment; an attack brought in a different proceeding.

collusion (1) An agreement to commit fraud; (2) an agreement between a husband and wife in a divorce proceeding that one or both will lie to the court to facilitate the obtaining of the divorce.

comity The court's decision to give effect to the laws and judicial decisions of another state as a matter of deference and mutual respect even if no obligation exists to do so.

commingling Placing funds from different sources into the same account.

common law Judge-made law created in the absence of other controlling law such as statutory law.

common law marriage The marriage of two people who have not gone through a ceremonial marriage. They have agreed to be husband and wife, lived together as husband and wife, and held themselves out to the public as husband and wife. In Texas, the name for a common law marriage is *informal marriage.*

common law property Property acquired during the marriage that can be owned by the spouse who earned it. Upon divorce, marital property is divided equitably, which may or not be an equal division.

common representation See *multiple representation.*

community estate The community property of a husband and wife.

community property Property in which each spouse has a one-half interest because it was acquired during the marriage, regardless of who earned it or who has title to it. (It does not include property acquired by gift or inheritance, which is the separate property of the spouse who receives it.) *Common law property,* on the other hand, is property owned by the spouse who earned it.

compensatory damages Money that will restore the injured party to the position he or she was in before the injury or loss; money that will make the aggrieved party whole.

competent Using the knowledge, skill, thoroughness, and preparation reasonably needed to represent a particular client.

complaint A pretrial document filed in court by one party against another that states a grievance, called a cause of action.

conciliation The resolution or settlement of a dispute in an amicable manner. A *conciliation service* is a court-authorized process whereby a counselor attempts to determine if parties filing for divorce can be reconciled, and if not, whether they can agree on the resolution of support, custody, and property division issues.

concurrent jurisdiction When two or more courts have the power to hear the same kind of case, each court has concurrent jurisdiction over such a case.

condonation An express or implied forgiveness by the innocent spouse of the marital fault committed by the other spouse.

conducive to divorce Tending to encourage or contribute to divorce.

confidence A confidence is any information protected by the attorney-client privilege. A *secret* is any information gained in the professional relationship if the client has requested that it be held secret or if its disclosure would embarrass or be detrimental to the client.

confidentiality The ethical obligation not to disclose information relating to the representation of a client.

confidential relationship A relationship of trust in which one person has a duty to act for the benefit of another.

conflict of interest You have a divided loyalty that actually or potentially places a person at a disadvantage even though you owe that person undivided loyalty.

conflict of law An inconsistency between the laws of different legal systems such as two states or two countries.

conjugal Pertaining to marriage; appropriate for married persons.

connivance A willingness or a consent by one spouse that a marital wrong be done by the other spouse.

consanguinity Relationship by blood.

conservator A person appointed by the court to manage the affairs of an adult who is not competent to do so on his or her own.

consideration Something of value that is exchanged between the parties (e.g., an exchange of money for services); an exchange of promises to do something or to refrain from doing something.

consortium Companionship, love, affection, sexual relationship, and services that a person enjoys with and from his or her spouse. See *loss of consortium.*

constitution The basic legal document of a government that allocates power among the three branches of the government and that may also enumerate fundamental rights of individuals.

constructive desertion The conduct of the spouse who stayed home justified the other spouse's departure; or the spouse who stayed home refuses a sincere offer of reconciliation from the other spouse who initially left without justification.

constructive trust A trust created by operation of law against one who has improperly obtained legal possession of or legal rights to property through fraud, duress, abuse of confidence, or other unconscionable conduct. See also *trust.*

Consumer Price Index A monthly report by the U.S. Bureau of Labor Statistics that tracks the price level of a group of goods and services purchased by the average consumer.

consummation Sexual intercourse for the first time between spouses.

contact veto A denial of consent to have contact between the adoptee and the biological parent, although permission for the release of identifying information might be given.

contempt of court Obstructing or assailing the authority or dignity of the court such as by intentionally violating a court order. The purpose of a *civil* contempt proceeding is to compel future compliance with a court order. The purpose of a *criminal* contempt proceeding is to punish the offender.

contested Disputed; challenged.

contingency An event that may or may not occur.

contingent Conditional; dependent on something that may not happen.

contingent fee A fee is contingent if the amount of the fee is dependent on the outcome of the case. A *fixed fee* is paid regardless of outcome.

continuance The postponement or adjournment of a proceeding to a later date.

continuing, exclusive jurisdiction (cej) Once a court acquires proper jurisdiction to make an order, the case remains open, and only that court can modify the order.

contract An agreement that a court will enforce. The elements of a contract are offer, acceptance, and consideration. The parties must have the legal capacity to enter a contract. Some contracts must be in writing. See also *cohabitation agreement, implied contract, premarital agreement, separation agreement.*

contract cohabitation See *cohabitation agreement.*

conversion (1) The unauthorized exercise of dominion and control over someone's personal property; (2) once a judicial separation has been in place for a designated period of time, the parties can ask a court for a divorce on that basis alone (called a *convertible divorce*).

conveyance The transfer of an interest in land.

co-parenting Two individuals who share the task of raising a child. Usually at least one of the individuals is not a biological parent of the child. Sometimes, however, co-parenting refers to two biological parents who have joint custody of the child.

copulate To engage in sexual intercourse.

co-respondent The person who allegedly had sexual intercourse with a defendant charged with adultery.

corpus The body of something; the aggregate of something.

Corpus Juris Secundum A national legal encyclopedia.

corroboration Additional evidence of a point beyond that offered by the person asserting the point.

count A separate and independent claim or charge in a pleading such as a complaint.

counterclaim A claim made by the defendant against the plaintiff.

court opinion The written explanation by a court of why it reached a certain conclusion or holding.

court rules Rules of procedure that govern the mechanics of litigation before a particular court.

covenant A promise or agreement.

covenant marriage A form of marriage that requires proof of premarital counseling, a promise to seek marital counseling when needed during the marriage, and proof of marital fault to dissolve.

coveture The status of being a married woman.

credit clouding To notify a creditor or credit bureau that a debtor is delinquent on certain debts.

criminal contempt See *contempt of court.*

criminal conversation A tort committed by having sex with the plaintiff's spouse.

criminal fraud See *fraud.*

criminal law The body of law covering acts declared to be crimes by the legislature for statutory crimes or by the courts for common law crimes.

curtesy The right of a husband to the lifetime use of all the land his deceased wife owned during the marriage (if issue were born of the marriage).

custodial parent The parent with whom the child is living; the parent with physical custody of the child.

custody See *joint legal custody, joint physical custody, legal custody, physical custody, sole legal custody, sole physical custody, split custody.*

damages Money paid because of a wrongful injury or loss to person or property. See also *aggravated damages, compensatory damages, mitigation of damages, punitive damages.*

decedent The person who has died; the deceased.

deep pocket The person or organization that probably has sufficient resources to pay damages if a judgment is awarded by the court.

de facto adoption See *equitable adoption.*

default judgment A judgment rendered when the other side failed to appear.

defendant The party against whom a claim is brought at the commencement of litigation.

defense Allegations of fact or legal theories offered to offset or defeat claims or demands.

Defense of Marriage Act (DOMA) A federal statute that says one state is not required to give full faith and credit to a same-sex marriage entered in another state.

defined-benefit plan A pension plan where the amount of the benefit is fixed but the amount of the contribution is not.

defined-contribution plan A pension plan where the amount of the contribution is generally fixed but the amount of the benefit is not.

deposition A pretrial discovery device, usually conducted outside the courtroom, during which one party questions the other party or a witness for the other party.

depository The party or place where something is stored.

depreciation A decrease in value.

descent Acquiring property by inheritance rather than by will; acquiring property from a decedent who died intestate.

desertion One spouse voluntarily but without justification leaves another (who does not consent to the departure) for an uninterrupted period of time with the intent not to return to resume cohabitation. Also called *abandonment.* See *constructive desertion.*

devise Land acquired by will. The person to whom land is given by will is the *devisee.*

digest (1) Set of books containing small paragraph summaries of court opinions; (2) a summary of a document or a series of documents.

direct attack A challenge to the validity of a judgment made in a proceeding brought specifically for that purpose (e.g., an appeal of a judgment brought immediately after it was rendered by the trial court).

direct income withholding A procedure whereby an income withholding order may be mailed directly to the obligor's employer in another state, which triggers withholding unless the obligor contests. No pleadings or registration is required.

dirty hands Wrongdoing or other inappropriate behavior that would make it unfair or inequitable to allow a person to assert a right or a defense he or she would normally have.

disaffirm contracts The right of a minor to repudiate and refuse to perform a contract he or she has entered.

disbursement Payment.

discharged Released; forgiven so that the debt is no longer owed.

discipline Imposing correction or punishment.

discovery Steps that a party can take before trial to obtain information from the other side in order to prepare for settlement or trial.

disinterested Impartial; having no desire or interest in either side winning. See also *bias.*

dissipate Waste, destroy, or squander.

distributable Subject to distribution to the parties; pertaining to property that can be divided and distributed to spouses upon divorce.

distributive share The portion of an estate that a person receives from a person who dies intestate (i.e., without leaving a valid will).

divided custody See *split custody.*

divided loyalty Representing a client when a conflict of interest exists. See *conflict of interest.*

divisible divorce A divorce decree that is enforceable in another state only in part. That part of a divorce decree that dissolves the marriage is enforceable (if the plaintiff was domiciled in the state), but that part of the divorce that ordered custody, alimony, child support, or a property division is not (if the court did not have proper jurisdiction for these orders).

divorce A declaration by a court that a marriage has been dissolved so that the parties are no longer married to each other.

divorce kit A package of do-it-yourself materials containing standard forms and written instructions on how to obtain a divorce without an attorney.

DNA testing Genetic testing on deoxyribonucleic acid removed from cells.

docket number A docket is a list or calendar of cases to be tried or heard at a specific term of the court. Cases on this list are assigned a number.

doctor-patient privilege The right of a patient to refuse to disclose any confidential (private) communications with his or her doctor that relate to medical care. The patient can also prevent the doctor from making such disclosures.

domestic partners Individuals in a same-sex relationship (or in an unmarried opposite-sex relationship) who are emotionally and financially interdependent and also meet the requirements for registering their relationship with the government so that they can receive specified marriage-like benefits.

domestic relations exception Federal courts do not have subject matter jurisdiction over divorce, alimony, or child-custody cases even if there is diversity of citizenship among the parties.

domestic torts Torts committed by one spouse against another. Also called *interspousal torts.*

domicile The place where a person has been physically present with the intent to make that place a permanent home; the place to which one intends to return when away. A residence, on the other hand, is simply the place where you are living at a particular time. A person can have more than one residence, but generally can have only one domicile.

domicile by choice A domicile chosen by a person with the legal capacity to choose.

domicile of origin The place of one's birth.

domiciliary One who is domiciled in a particular state.

donee The person who receives a gift.

donor The person who gives a gift.

dower The right of a widow to the lifetime use of one-third of the land her deceased husband owned during the marriage.

draft (1) As a verb, draft means to write a document (e.g., a letter, contract, or memorandum); (2) as a noun, it means a version of a document that is not yet final or ready for distribution.

dual divorce A divorce granted to both the husband and the wife.

durational maintenance See *rehabilitative alimony.*

duress Coercion; acting under the pressure of an unlawful act or threat.

election against will Obtaining a designated share of a deceased spouse's estate in spite of what the latter provided or failed to provide for the surviving spouse in a will; a forced share of a decedent's estate.

element A portion of a rule that is a precondition to the applicability of the entire rule.

element in contention The portion of a rule (i.e., the element) that forms the basis of a legal issue because the parties disagree on the interpretation or application of that element to the facts of the case.

emancipated Legally independent of one's parent or legal guardian.

emolument Compensation or other gain for services.

encumber To impose a burden, claim, lien, or charge on property.

encumbrance A claim, lien, or other charge against property.

Enoch Arden doctrine The presumption that a spouse is dead after being missing for a designated number of years.

equitable adoption For purposes of inheritance, a child will be considered the adopted child of a person who made a contract to adopt the child but failed to go through the formal adoption procedures. Also called *de facto adoption.*

equitable distribution The fair, but not necessarily equal, division of all marital property in a common law property state. Also called *equitable division* and *distributive award.*

equitable estoppel See *estopped.*

escalation clause A provision in a contract or other document that provides for an increase or decrease in the amount to be paid based upon a factor over which the parties do not have complete control.

escrow Property (e.g., money, stock, deed) delivered by one person (called the *grantor, promisor,* or *obligor*) to another (e.g., a bank, an escrow agent) to be held by the latter until a designated condition or contingency occurs, at which time the property is to be delivered to the person for whose benefit the escrow was established (called the *grantee, promisee, obligee,* or *beneficiary*).

essentials test Did the matter go to the heart or essence of the relationship?

estate (1) All the property left by the deceased. After being used to pay debts, this property is distributed to those entitled under the will or the laws of intestacy; (2) the amount or extent of one's interest in property.

estopped Prevented from asserting a right or a defense because it would be unfair or inequitable to do so.

ethics Standards or rules of behavior to which members of an occupation, profession, or other organization are expected to conform.

et ux And wife.

evidence Anything offered to establish the existence or nonexistence of a fact in dispute.

exclusive, continuing jurisdiction The authority of a court, obtained by compliance with the Uniform Child Custody Jurisdiction and Enforcement Act to make all initial and modifying custody decisions in a case to the exclusion of courts in any other state.

exclusive jurisdiction A court has exclusive jurisdiction when only that court has the power to hear a certain kind of case.

executed Carried out according to its terms.

execution of judgment The process of carrying out or satisfying the judgment of a court. Using a writ of execution, a court officer (e.g., a sheriff) is commanded to seize the property of the losing litigant, sell it, and pay the winning litigant out of the proceeds.

executor A person designated in a will to carry out the terms of the will and handle related matters. If a female, this person is sometimes called an *executrix.* See also *personal representative.*

executory Unperformed as yet.

executrix See *executor.*

exemplary damages See *punitive damages.*

ex parte With only one party (usually the plaintiff or petitioner) present when court action is requested.

ex parte divorce A divorce rendered by a court when only one of the spouses was present in the state. The court did not have personal jurisdiction over the defendant.

extradition The process by which a state or country turns over an individual who has been accused or convicted of a crime to another state or country.

facilitation of divorce That which makes a divorce easier to obtain.

fact particularization A fact-gathering technique designed to help you identify a large variety of questions you can try to answer through interviewing and investigation.

fair market value The amount that a willing buyer would pay a willing seller for property, neither being under any compulsion to buy or sell and both having reasonable knowledge of or access to the relevant facts.

false arrest An arrest of an individual without a privilege to do so.

family law The body of law that defines relationships, rights, and duties in the formation, existence, and dissolution of marriage and other family units.

family-purpose doctrine The owner of a car who makes it available for family use will be liable for injuries that result from an accident that is wrongfully caused by a member of the owner's immediate family while using the car with the owner's consent for a family purpose.

family violence indicator (fvi) A designation placed on a participant in a child-support case indicating that he or she may be a victim of child abuse or domestic violence.

fault grounds Marital wrongs that will justify the granting of a divorce (e.g., adultery).

Federal Case Registry (FCR) A national database of information on individuals in all IV-D cases and non–IV-D orders. The FCR is part of the Federal Parent Locator Service.

Federal Parent Locator Service (FPLS) See *Parent Locator Service.*

fee splitting (1) A single bill to a client covering the fee of two or more lawyers who are not in the same firm; (2) giving a nonlawyer part of the fee of a particular client. The latter is often done as payment for making a referral of the client.

fiduciary (1) Pertaining to the high standard of care that must be exercised on behalf of another; (2) as a noun, a person who owes another good faith, loyalty, trust, and candor; a person who owes another an obligation to protect his or her interest and to provide fair treatment.

filial consortium The right of a parent to the normal companionship and affection of a child.

filiation A judicial determination of paternity. The relation of child to father.

filius nullius The status of an illegitimate child at common law ("the son [or child] of no one").

fixed fee See *contingent fee.*

flowchart An overview of the step-by-step process by which something is done.

forced share See *election against will.*

foreign divorce A divorce obtained in another state or country.

forensic Pertaining to use in courts.

formbook A practical treatise or manual containing standard forms along with checklists, summaries of the law, etc. See also *treatise.*

fornication Sexual relations between unmarried persons or between persons who are not married to each other.

forum (1) The place where the parties are presently litigating their dispute; (2) a court or tribunal hearing a case.

forum non conveniens The discretionary power of a court to decline the exercise of its jurisdiction when it would be more convenient and the ends of justice would be better served if the action were tried in another court.

forum shopping Seeking a court that will be favorable to you; traveling from court to court until you find one that will provide a favorable ruling.

forum state The state in which the parties are now litigating a case.

foster home A temporary home for a child when his or her own family cannot provide care and when adoption either is not possible at the present time or is under consideration.

IV-D agency A state agency that attempts to enforce child-support obligations.

fraud Knowingly making a false statement of present fact with the intention that the plaintiff rely on the statement. The plaintiff's reasonable reliance on the statement harms him or her. See also *statute of frauds.*

fraudulent transfer A transfer made to avoid an obligation to a creditor.

friendly divorce A divorce proceeding in which the husband and wife are not contesting the dissolution of the marriage, or anything related thereto; an uncontested divorce.

front loading Making substantial "alimony" payments shortly after the separation or divorce in an attempt to disguise a property division as deductible alimony.

full faith and credit clause "Full Faith and Credit shall be given in each State to the public Acts, Records, and judicial Proceedings of every other State." Article IV of the United States Constitution.

garnishment A proceeding whereby a debtor's money or other property under the control of another is given to a third person to whom the debtor owes a debt.

genetic testing The analysis of inherited factors of mother, child, and alleged father to help prove or disprove that a particular man fathered a particular child.

gestational surrogacy The sperm and egg of a couple are fertilized in vitro in a laboratory, and the resulting embryo is then implanted in a surrogate mother who gives birth to a child with whom she has no genetic relationship.

get A bill of divorcement in a Jewish divorce.

gift The voluntary delivery of something with the present intent to transfer title and control, for which no payment or consideration is made. Once the item is accepted, the gift is irrevocable. The person making the gift is the *donor.* The person receiving it is the *donee.*

goodwill The reputation of a business that causes it to generate additional customers.

grantor A transferor; a person who makes a grant.

gross income The total amount received or earned before deductions.

grounds (1) Acceptable reasons for seeking a particular result; (2) foundation or basis for one's belief or conduct.

guarantee A warranty or assurance that a particular result will be achieved.

guardian ad litem (GAL) A special guardian appointed by the court to represent the interests of another.

guardianship The legal right to the custody of an individual.

harassment See *hostile environment harassment, quid pro quo harassment.*

harmless Without injury or damage.

headnote A small paragraph summary of a portion of a court opinion that is printed before the opinion begins.

hearsay Testimony in court of a statement made by another out of court when the statement is being offered to assert the truth of the matter in the statement.

heart-balm action An action based on a broken heart (e.g., breach of promise to marry, alienation of affections, and seduction).

heart-balm statute A statute that abolishes heart-balm actions.

heir One who receives property by inheritance rather than by will.

hold harmless In the event of trouble, to relieve someone of responsibility or liability.

holographic Wholly in the handwriting of a person.

holding The court's answer to a legal issue in an opinion.

home state The state where the child has lived with a parent for at least six consecutive months immediately before the custody or support case begins in court or since birth if the child is less than six months old.

homestead One's dwelling house along with adjoining land and buildings.

hornbook A text that summarizes an area of the law, usually with commentary and extensive footnotes. See also *legal treatise.*

hornbook law Elementary principles of law often summarized in law books called *hornbooks.*

hostile environment harassment Pervasive unwelcome sexual conduct or sex-based ridicule that unreasonably interferes with an individual's job performance or that creates an intimidating, hostile, or offensive working environment, even if no tangible or economic consequences result.

hotchpot Mixing or blending all property, however acquired, to achieve greater equality.

husband-wife privilege See *marital communications.*

illegitimate child A child born when his or her parents are not married to each other.

illicit cohabitation Sexual intercourse between unmarried persons who are living together. See also *cohabitation.*

imminent Near at hand; coming soon; about to happen; immediate.

immunity A defense that prevents someone from being sued for what would otherwise be wrongful conduct.

impediment A legal obstacle that prevents the formation of a valid marriage or other contract.

implied contract A contract that is not created by an express agreement between the parties but is inferred as a matter of reason and justice from their conduct and the surrounding circumstances; a contract that is manifested by conduct and circumstances rather than words of agreement; a contract that a reasonable person would infer exists, even though there is no express agreement. Also called an *implied in fact contract.*

impotence The inability to have sexual intercourse.

imputed disqualification Something is imputed when it is forced upon or attributed to someone or something else. If, for example, a lawyer or paralegal causes a law firm to be disqualified, we have an imputed disqualification.

imputed income Income that will be assumed to be available regardless of whether it is actually available.

in camera In the judge's private chambers; not in open court.

incest Sexual intercourse between two people who are too closely related to each other as defined by court cases or statute.

inchoate Partial; not yet complete.

incident to Closely connected to something else.

incompatibility A no-fault ground for divorce that exists when there is such discord between the husband and wife that it is impossible for them to live together in a normal marital relationship.

inconvenient forum The state or jurisdiction where it is not as convenient to litigate a matter as another state or jurisdiction.

incorrigible Habitually disobedient and disruptive.

indemnify To compensate another for any loss or expense incurred.

indemnity The right to have another person pay you the amount you were forced to pay.

independent adoption An adoption in which a child is placed for adoption by its natural parent, often with the help of facilitators.

independent professional judgment Advice given by an attorney who is not subject to a conflict of interest. See *conflict of interest.*

indigent Poor; without means to afford something.

informal marriage The name for a common law marriage in Texas.

in forma pauperis As a poor person. As such, certain court filing fees are waived.

inheritance Property received from someone who dies without leaving a valid will. The state determines who receives such property.

initiating state The state in which a support case is filed in order to forward it to another state (called the *responding state*) for enforcement proceedings under the Uniform Interstate Family Support Act.

injunction A court order requiring a person to do or to refrain from doing a particular thing.

in loco parentis Standing in the place of (and able to exercise some of the rights of) parents.

innocent spouse relief A former spouse will not be liable for taxes and penalties owed on prior joint returns if he or she can prove that at the time he or she signed the return, he or she did not know and had no reason to know that the other spouse understated the taxes due. The IRS must conclude that under all the facts and circumstances of the case it would be unfair to hold the innocent spouse responsible for the understatement of tax on the return.

in personam jurisdiction See *personal jurisdiction.*

in rem jurisdiction The power of the court to make a decision affecting a particular *res,* which is a thing or status.

instrument A formal document such as a will, deed, mortgage, or contract.

intake memorandum A written report that summarizes an interview with a new client of the office. It normally contains basic facts on the client and on his or her legal problems. See also *interoffice Memorandum, memorandum of law.*

intangible Pertaining to that which does not have a physical form.

intentional infliction of emotional distress Intentionally causing severe emotional distress by extreme or outrageous conduct.

intentional torts Torts other than negligence and strict liability (e.g., assault, battery).

inter alia Among other things.

intercept program A procedure by which the government seizes designated benefits owed to a parent in order to cover the latter's delinquent child support payments.

interlocutory Not final; interim.

Internet A self-governing network of networks to which millions of computer users around the world have access.

interoffice memorandum A written report addressed to someone in the office where you work, usually a supervisor.

interrogatories A written set of factual questions sent by one party to another before the trial begins.

interspousal Between or pertaining to a husband and wife.

interspousal torts Torts committed by one spouse against another Also called *domestic torts.*

Interstate Compact on the Placement of Children (ICPC) A statute that governs adoption of a child born or living in one state who will be adopted by someone in another state.

intestate Dying without leaving a valid will.

intestate succession Obtaining property from a deceased who died without leaving a valid will. The persons entitled to this property are identified in the statute on intestate distribution.

intrafamily tort immunity Family members cannot sue each other for designated categories of torts.

intrafamily torts Torts committed by one family member against another.

in vitro fertilization The surgical removal of a woman's eggs and their fertilization with a man's sperm in the laboratory.

irreconcilable differences A no-fault ground for divorce that exists when there is such discord between the husband and wife that there has been an irremediable breakdown of the marriage.

irremediable breakdown See *irreconcilable differences.*

irrevocable That which cannot be revoked or recalled.

issue (1) Everyone who has descended from a common ancestor; (2) a legal question. See also *legal periodical.*

joint and several liability More than one person is legally responsible. They are responsible together and/or individually for the entire amount.

joint custody See *joint legal custody, joint physical custody.*

joint legal custody The right of both parents to make the major child rearing decisions on health, education, religion, discipline, and general welfare.

joint physical custody The right of both parents to have the child reside with both for alternating (but not necessarily equal) periods of time.

joint representation See *multiple representation.*

joint tenancy Property that is owned equally by two or more persons with the right of survivorship.

joint venture An express or implied agreement to participate in a common enterprise in which the parties have a mutual right of control.

judgment debtor/judgment creditor The person who loses and therefore must pay a money judgment is the judgment debtor. The winner is the judgment creditor.

judicial notice Recognition or acceptance of a fact or conclusion by a court without requiring a party to offer evidence or authority on the fact or conclusion.

judicial separation See *legal separation.*

jurisdiction (1) The power of a court to act in a particular case; (2) the geographic area over which a particular court has authority. See also *concurrent jurisdiction, exclusive jurisdiction, in rem jurisdiction, personal jurisdiction, retain jurisdiction, subject matter jurisdiction.*

juvenile delinquent A young person under a designated age whose conduct would constitute a crime if committed by an adult.

latchkey child A child who is at home after school without supervision of adults; a self-care child.

law review/law journal A law review is a legal periodical published by a law school. Also called a *law journal.* See *legal periodical.*

legal advice Telling a specific person how the law applies to the facts of that person's legal problem or concern.

legal analysis The application of rules of law to facts in order to answer a legal question or issue.

legal capacity See *capacity.*

legal custody The right and duty to make decisions about raising a child.

legal encyclopedia A multivolume set of books that summarize almost every major legal topic.

legal issue A question of law. See also *legal analysis.*

legal malpractice See *malpractice.*

legal newspaper A newspaper (published daily, weekly, etc.) devoted to legal news.

legal periodical An ongoing publication (e.g., published quarterly) that contains articles, studies, reports, or other information on legal topics.

legal separation A declaration by a court that parties can live separate and apart even though they are still married to each other. Also called a *judicial separation,* a *limited divorce,* a *divorce a mensa et thoro,* and a *separation from bed and board.*

legal treatise A book written by a private individual (or by a public official writing as a private citizen) that provides an overview, summary, or commentary on a legal topic.

legatee A person to whom property (usually personal property) is given by will.

legitimacy The status or condition of being born in wedlock.

legitimation The steps that enable an illegitimate child to become a legitimate child.

legitimize To formally declare that children born out of wedlock are legitimate.

letter of authorization A letter that tells the recipient that the office represents the client and that the client consents to the release of any information about the client to the office.

letter of nonengagement A letter sent by an attorney to a prospective client explicitly stating that the attorney will not be representing this person.

levy The collection or seizure of property by a marshal or sheriff with a writ of execution.

LEXIS–NEXIS A legal database for computer research.

liabilities That which one owes; debts.

liability insurance Insurance that pays the liability that is incurred by an insured to a third party.

lien A security or encumbrance on property; a claim or charge on property for the payment of a debt. The property cannot be sold until the debt is satisfied.

limited divorce See *legal separation.*

living apart A no-fault ground for divorce that exists when a husband and wife have lived separately for a designated period of consecutive time.

long-arm jurisdiction The personal jurisdiction that a state acquires over a nonresident defendant because of his or her purposeful contact with the state.

loose-leaf service A law book published as a three-ring binder containing pages that can be inserted and removed with relative ease.

Lord Mansfield's rule The testimony of either spouse is inadmissible on the question of whether the husband had access to the wife at the time of conception if such evidence would tend to bastardize (i.e., declare illegitimate) the child.

loss of consortium A tort action for the loss of or the interference with the companionship, love, affection, sexual relationship, and services that the plaintiff enjoyed with his or her spouse before the latter was wrongfully injured by the defendant.

loss of services A tort action for the loss of or the interference with the right of a parent to the services and earnings of his or her unemancipated child because of the wrongful injury inflicted on the child by the defendant.

lucid interval A period of time during which a person has the mental capacity to understand what he or she is doing.

maintenance Food, clothing, shelter, and other necessaries of life.

majority A designated age of legal adulthood in the state, usually eighteen.

malice Animosity; the intent to inflict injury.

malicious prosecution A tort with the following elements: (1) to initiate or procure the initiation of legal proceedings—civil or criminal, (2) without probable cause, (3) with malice, and (4) the proceedings terminate in favor of the person against whom they were brought.

malpractice Professional wrongdoing. Legal malpractice normally refers to negligence by an attorney.

manual A practical treatise often containing standard forms along with checklists, summaries of the law, etc. Sometimes called a *practice manual.* See also *treatise.*

marital communications Those communications between a husband and wife while cohabiting. According to the privilege for marital communications, or the husband-wife privilege, one spouse cannot disclose in court any confidential communications that occurred between the spouses during the marriage.

marital property Nonseparate property acquired by a spouse during the marriage and the appreciation of separate property that occurred during the marriage. See also *separate property.*

market value See *fair market value.*

marriage See *ceremonial marriage, common law marriage.*

marriage penalty If both spouses earn substantially the same income, they pay more taxes when filing a joint return than they would if they could file as single taxpayers.

married women's property acts Statutes removing all or most of the legal disabilities imposed on women as to the disposition of their property.

Martindale-Hubbell The *Martindale-Hubbell Law Directory* contains a listing of the names and addresses of many of the practicing attorneys in the country. It also has a feature called the "Martindale-Hubbell Law Digest," which contains brief summaries of the law of every state.

materiality test If a specific event had not occurred, would the result have been different?

mediation The process of submitting a dispute to a third party (other than a judge) who will help the parties reach their own resolution of the dispute.

memorandum Any writing or notation sent to a person or to a file. It can be a highly formal and lengthy document or a simple one-line note. The plural of memorandum is *memoranda.*

memorandum of law A written explanation of how the law applies to a given set of facts. See also *intake memorandum.*

meretricious Pertaining to unlawful sexual relations; vulgar or tawdry.

meritorious Having merit; having a reasonable basis to believe that a person's claim or defense will succeed.

microfilm Reels or cassettes that contain images or photographs that have been greatly reduced in size. Many law books and periodicals have been placed on microfilm.

migratory divorce A divorce obtained in a state to which one or both of the spouses traveled before returning to their original state.

mini-DOMA A statute of a state declaring that its strong public policy is not to recognize any same-sex marriage that might be validly entered in another state.

minimum fee schedule A list of fees announced by the bar association that an attorney *must* charge, at a minimum, for designated services rendered. Charging lower than the minimum would be unethical. (Today, however, minimum fee schedules are illegal.)

minor Someone under the age of majority in the state, which is usually eighteen.

miscegenation Mixing the races; the marriage or cohabitation of persons of different races.

mitigating circumstances Facts that in fairness justify a reduction in damages because of the conduct of the aggrieved party.

mitigation of damages Steps the aggrieved party could have taken to lessen the amount of injury or harm caused by the wrongdoer.

Model Rules of Professional Responsibility See *canons of ethics.*

mortgage An interest in land that provides security for the performance of a duty or the payment of a debt.

multiple representation Representing more than one side in a legal matter or controversy. Also called *joint representation* and *common representation.*

mutual consent registry See *passive registry.*

National Conference of Commissioner on Uniform State Law See *uniform laws.*

National Directory of New Hires (NDNH) A national database that is part of the Federal Parent Locator Service. It contains new hire and quarterly wage data from every state and federal agency and unemployment insurance data from states.

necessaries The basic items needed by family members to maintain a standard of living. These items can be purchased and charged to the spouse who has failed to provide them.

neglect The failure to provide support, medical care, education, moral example, discipline, and other necessaries.

negligence Unreasonable conduct that causes injury or damage to someone to whom you owe a duty of reasonable care.

nisi Not final; interim.

no-fault grounds Reasons for granting a divorce that do not require proof that either spouse committed marital wrongs.

nonage Below the required minimum age to enter a desired relationship or perform a particular task.

non compos mentis Of unsound mind.

noncustodial parent The parent with whom a child is not living.

nonengagement See *letter of nonengagement.*

nonmolestation clause A clause in an agreement that the parties will not bother each other.

notes to decisions Small paragraph summaries of court opinions that have interpreted a particular statute. These paragraphs are printed after the text of the statute within annotated codes.

nuisance An unreasonable interference with the use and enjoyment of land.

objectivity The state of being dispassionate; the absence of a bias.

obligor/obligee The person who has an obligation is the *obligor.* The person to whom this obligation is owed is the *obligee.*

offer To present something that can be accepted or rejected.

online Being connected to a host computer system or information service—often through a telephone line.

open adoption An adoption in which the natural parent maintains certain kinds of contact with his or her child after the latter is adopted.

operation of law Automatically because of the law. A result occurs by operation of law when it happens because the law mandates the result, not because a party agrees to produce the result.

opinion See *court opinion.*

order to show cause (OSC) An order telling a person to appear in court and explain why a certain order should not be entered.

outstanding Unpaid.

palimony A nonlegal term for payments made by one nonmarried party to another after they cease living together, usually because they entered an express or implied contract to do so while they were living together or cohabiting.

paralegal A person with legal skills who works under the supervision of an attorney or who is otherwise authorized to use those skills.

parens patriae Parent of the country, referring to the state's role in protecting children and those under disability.

parental alienation syndrome A disorder suffered by some children at the center of a custody dispute. They idealize one parent while expressing hatred for the other, even though the relationship with both parents was relatively positive before the dispute.

parental consortium The right of a child to the normal companionship and affection of a parent.

parental liability law See *parental responsibility law.*

parental responsibility law A statute that imposes vicarious liability (up to a limited dollar amount) on parents for the torts committed by their children. Also called *parental liability law.*

Parent Locator Service, State A state government agency that helps locate parents who are delinquent in child-support payments. If the search involves more than one state, the Federal Parent Locator Service (FPLS) can help. The FPLS also helps in parental kidnaping cases.

partition The dividing of land held by joint tenants and tenants in common. The division results in individual ownership.

partnership A voluntary contract between two (or more) persons to use their resources in a business or other venture, with the understanding that they will proportionately share losses and profits.

passim Here and there, throughout.

passive registry A reunion registry that requires both the adoptee and the biological parent to register their consent to release identifying information. When both have registered and a match is made, an agency employee will contact both. Also called a *mutual consent registry.*

paternity The biological fatherhood of a child.

payee One to whom money is paid or is to be paid.

payor One who makes a payment of money or who is obligated to do so.

pecuniary Pertaining to or consisting of money.

pendente lite While the litigation is going on.

per curiam By the court. A court opinion that does not name the particular judge who wrote it.

peremptory challenge The elimination of a prospective juror during voir dire, which is the jury selection process. No reason need be given.

periodic payments The payment of a fixed amount for an indefinite period or the payment of an indefinite amount for a fixed or indefinite period.

personal jurisdiction The power of a court to render a decision that binds the individual defendant. Also called *in personam jurisdiction.*

personal property Movable property; any property other than real property. Also called *chattels.*

personal representative An executor or administrator of the estate of the deceased; someone who formally acts on behalf of the estate of the deceased.

petition A formal request that the court take some action; a complaint.

physical custody (1) The right to decide where the child will reside; (2) the actual residence of the child.

plaintiff The party bringing a claim against another.

pleadings Formal documents that contain allegations and responses of the parties in litigation. The major pleadings are the complaint and answer.

pocket part A pocket in the inside back cover of some bound volumes. In this pocket, you will find a pamphlet that updates the bound volume.

polygamy The practice of having more than one spouse at the same time, usually more than two.

POSSLQ Person of the opposite sex sharing living quarters.

postnuptial After marriage.

postnuptial agreement An agreement between spouses while they are married. If they are separated or contemplating a separation or divorce, the agreement is called a *separation agreement.*

practice manual See *manual.*

practice of law Assisting another to secure his or her legal rights. See *unauthorized practice of law.*

prayer A formal request.

premarital agreement An agreement between prospective spouses made in contemplation of marriage and to be effective upon marriage. It is a contract made by two individuals who are about to be married that covers spousal support, property division, and related matters in the event of the separation of the parties, the death of one of them, or the dissolution of the marriage by divorce or annulment. Also called *antenuptial agreement.*

premises (1) Lands and buildings; (2) the foregoing statements; matters stated earlier (in consideration of the premises).

prenuptial Before marriage. See *premarital agreement.*

preponderance of evidence A standard of proof that is met if the evidence shows it is more likely than not than an alleged fact is true or false as alleged.

presents, these This legal document.

present value The amount of money an individual would have to be given now in order to produce or generate a certain amount of money in a designated period of time.

presumption An assumption of fact that can be drawn when another fact or set of facts is established. The presumption is *rebuttable* if a party can introduce evidence to show that the assumption is false.

presumptive Created or arising out of a presumption; based on inference.

primary authority Any *law* that a court could rely on in reaching its conclusion (e. g., a constitutional provision, statute, regulation, ordinance, other court opinion).

primary caregiver presumption The primary person who has taken care of the child should have custody.

privilege A benefit, advantage, or right enjoyed by an individual.

privilege against self-incrimination The right to refuse to answer questions that directly or indirectly connect the individual to a crime.

privilege for marital communication See *marital communications.*

probate A court proceeding at which a will is proved to be valid or invalid.

probation Restricted and supervised living in the community in lieu of institutionalization.

procedural law Laws that pertain to the technical steps for bringing or defending actions in litigation before a court or an administrative agency. An example would be the number of days within which a party can request a jury trial in a divorce case after the complaint has been filed.

proctor A person appointed for a particular purpose (e.g., protect the interests of a child).

professional responsibility See *canons of ethics.*

pro hac vice For this particular occasion.

proof of service A statement that service of process on the defendant has been made.

property division The distribution of property accumulated by spouses as a result of their joint efforts during the marriage. Sometimes referred to as a *property settlement.*

pro se On one's own behalf; not using an attorney.

prosecute To commence and proceed with a lawsuit.

pro se divorce A divorce obtained when a party represents himself or herself.

protective order A court order directing a person to refrain from harming or harassing another.

provocation The plaintiff incited the acts constituting the marital wrong by the other spouse.

proxy marriage The performance of a valid marriage ceremony through agents because one or both of the prospective spouses are absent.

psychological parent An adult who is not legally responsible for the care of a child, but who has formed a substantial emotional bond with the child.

public assistance Welfare or other forms of financial help from the government to the poor.

public policy The principles inherent in the customs, morals, and notions of justice that prevail in a state; the foundation of public laws; the principles that are naturally and inherently right and just.

punitive damages Money that is paid to punish the wrongdoer and to deter others from similar wrongdoing. Also called *exemplary damages.*

putative Alleged or reputed.

putative father (1) A man who may be the child's father but who was not married to the child's mother and has not established the fact that he is the father in a court proceeding. (2) The person who the child's mother believes to be the father of the child but who has not yet been medically or legally declared to be the father.

putative father registry A place where the father of a child can register so that he can be notified of a proposed adoption of the child.

putative spouse A person who reasonably believed he or she entered a valid marriage even though there was a legal impediment that made the marriage unlawful.

QDRO See *qualified domestic relations order.*

QMCSO See *qualified medical child support order.*

qualified domestic relations order (QDRO) A court order that allows a nonemployee to reach pension benefits of an employee or former employee in order to satisfy a support or other marital obligation to the nonemployee.

qualified medical child support order An order, decree, or judgment issued by a court that orders medical support or health benefits for the child of a parent covered under a group health insurance plan.

quantum meruit "As much as he deserves." Valuable services are rendered or materials are furnished by the plaintiff, and accepted, used, or enjoyed by the defendant under such circumstances that the plaintiff reasonably expected to be paid.

quasi-community property Property acquired during marriage by the spouses when they lived in a non–community property state before moving to a community property state. If they had acquired it in a community property state, it would have been community property.

quasi contract A contract created by the law to avoid unjust enrichment.

quasi-marital property Property that will be treated as having been acquired or improved while the parties were married even though the marriage was never valid.

quid pro quo harassment Submission to or rejection of unwelcome sexual conduct is used as a basis for employment decisions such as promotion or other job-related benefits.

quitclaim A release or giving up of whatever claim or title you have in property. You are turning over whatever you have, without guaranteeing anything.

ratification Approval retroactively by agreement, conduct, or any inaction that can reasonably be interpreted as an approval. The verb is *ratify.*

rational basis test Discrimination in a law is constitutional if the law rationally furthers a legitimate state interest. See also *strict scrutiny test.*

realize To obtain something actually, rather than on paper only.

real property/real estate Land and anything permanently attached to the land.

reasonable See *unreasonable.*

rebuttable presumption See *presumption.*

recapture rule The recalculation of a tax liability when the parties have improperly attempted to disguise a property division as alimony through front loading. See *front loading.*

receivership The court appointment of someone to control and manage the defendant's property in order to ensure compliance with a court order.

reciprocal beneficiaries relationship A form of domestic partnership in Vermont for parties related by blood who are ineligible to form a civil union or marriage with each other. Hawaii also has a reciprocal beneficiary law.

reconciliation The full resumption of the marital relationship.

recrimination The party seeking the divorce (the plaintiff) has also committed a serious marital wrong.

regional digest See *digest.* A regional digest contains summaries of opinions written by courts in a designated cluster of states. The full text of the opinions is found in the corresponding regional reporter for the digest.

regional reporter The volumes that contain the full text of opinions from courts within a designated cluster of states.

regulation A law enacted by an administrative agency.

rehabilitative alimony Support payments to a spouse for a limited time to allow him or her to return to financial self-sufficiency through employment or job training. (Also called *durational maintenance.*)

remand To send back for further proceedings.

remedy The method or means by which a court or other body will enforce a right or compensate someone for a violation of a right.

remise To give up or release.

reporter The volumes that contain the full text of court opinions.

reprimand A form of public discipline by which an attorney's conduct is declared to have been improper but his or her right to practice law is not limited.

request for admissions A request from one party to another that it agree that a certain fact is true or that a specified document is genuine so that there will be no need to present proof on such matters during the trial.

res A thing or object; a status.

rescission The cancellation of something.

residence The place where someone is living at a particular time. See also *domicile.*

res judicata When a judgment on its merits has been rendered, the parties cannot relitigate the same dispute.

respondeat superior An employer is responsible for the conduct of employees while they are acting within the scope of employment.

respondent The party responding to a position or claim of another party; the defendant. See also *appellee.*

responding state The state to which a support case was forwarded from an initiating state for enforcement proceedings under the Uniform Interstate Family Support Act.

Restatement of Torts A treatise written by the American Law Institute that articulates or restates the law of torts. The second edition is Restatement (Second) of Torts.

restitution An equitable remedy in which a person is restored to his or her original position prior to the loss or injury; restoring to the plaintiff the value of what he or she parted with.

restraining order A form of injunction, initially issued ex parte, to restrain the defendant from doing a threatened act.

resulting trust A trust implied in law from the intention of the parties; a trust that arises when a person transfers property under circumstances that raise the inference that he or she did not intend the transferee to actually receive any interest in the property. See also *trust.*

retainer (1) The contract of employment between attorney and client; (2) money paid by a client to ensure that an attorney will be available to work for the client; (3) prepayment or deposit against future fees and costs of representation.

retain jurisdiction To keep the case open so that the court can more easily modify a prior order or take other appropriate action.

reunion registry A central adoption file that could be used to release identifying information about, and allow contact between, adult adoptees and biological parents. See also *active registry, passive registry.*

right of survivorship When one owner dies, his or her share goes to the other owners; it does not go through the estate of the deceased owner.

rules of professional responsibility See *canons of ethics.*

sanctions Penalties or punishments of some kind. (The word *sanction* can also mean approval or authorization.)

secondary authority Any *nonlaw* that a court could rely on in reaching its conclusion (e. g., article in a legal periodical, a treatise).

second-parent adoption The adoption of a child by a partner (or cohabitant) of a natural parent who does not give up his or her own parental rights.

secret See *confidence.*

security interest An interest in property that provides that the property may be sold on default in order to satisfy a debt for which the security interest was given.

self-incrimination See *privilege against self-incrimination.*

separate maintenance Court-ordered spousal support while the spouses are separated.

separate property Property one spouse acquired before the marriage by any means and property he or she acquired during the marriage by gift, will, or intestate succession. In community property states, separate property also includes community property the parties have agreed to treat as separate property.

separation See *legal separation, separation agreement.*

separation agreement A contract between spouses who have separated or who are about to separate in which the terms of their separation are spelled out (e.g, support obligations, child custody, division of property accumulated during the marriage). The agreement may or may not be later incorporated and merged in a divorce decree. Contracts (such as separation agreements) made during a marriage are also called *postnuptial contracts.*

sequester To remove or hold until legal proceedings or legal claims are resolved. The noun is *sequestration.*

service of process Providing a formal notice to the defendant that orders him or her to appear in court in order to answer the allegations in the claims made by the plaintiff.

settlor See *trust.*

severable Removable without destroying what remains. Something is severable when what remains after it is taken away can survive without it. The opposite of severable is essential or indispensable.

severally Individually, separately.

sham Pretended, false, empty.

shepardize To use the set of law books called *Shepard's Citations* to obtain specific information about a document (e.g., whether an opinion has been overruled or whether a statute has been repealed).

sole custody See sole *legal custody, sole physical custody.*

sole legal custody Only one parent has the right to make the major child rearing decisions on health, education, religion, discipline, and general welfare.

solemnization The performance of a formal ceremony in public.

solemnize The verb for solemnization.

sole physical custody Only one parent has the right to decide where the child resides.

sole proprietorship A form of business in which one person owns all the assets.

solicitation Asking or urging someone to do something.

specialization The development of experience and expertise in a particular area of practice.

specific performance A remedy for breach of contract that forces the wrongdoing party to complete the contract as promised.

split custody Siblings are in the physical custody of different parents.

standard form A frequently used format for a document such as contract, complaint, or tax return. The form is designed to be used by many individuals, often by filling in blanks that call for specific information commonly needed for such documents.

standing The right to bring a case and seek relief from a court.

State Case Registry (SCR) A database, maintained as part of the statewide automated child-support system, which contains information on individuals in all IV-D cases and non–IV-D orders.

State Directory of New Hires (SDNH) A child-support database, maintained by each state, which contains information regarding newly hired employees for the respective state.

State Parent Locator Service (SPLS) See *Parent Locator Service.*

statute An act of the legislature declaring, commanding, or prohibiting something.

statute of frauds The requirement that certain kinds of contracts be in writing in order to be enforceable (e.g., a contract for the sale of land, a contact that by its terms cannot be performed within a year).

statute of limitations The time within which a suit must be brought. If it is brought after this time, it is barred.

statutory code See *code.*

stepparent A person who marries the natural mother or father of child, but who is not one of the child's natural parents.

sterility Inability to have children; infertile.

stipulation An agreement between the parties on a matter so that evidence on the matter does not have to be introduced at the trial.

strict scrutiny test Discrimination in a law is presumed to be unconstitutional unless the state shows compelling state interests that justify the discrimination and also shows that the law is narrowly drawn to avoid unnecessary abridgments of constitutional rights.

sua sponte On its own motion.

subject matter jurisdiction The power of the court to hear a particular category or kind of case; its authority to make rulings on certain subject matters.

subpoena A command to appear in court.

subpoena duces tecum A command that specific documents or other items be produced.

subscribe To sign at the end of the document.

substantive law Laws that pertain to rights and obligations other than purely procedural matters. An example would be the right to a divorce on the ground of irreconcilable differences.

substituted service Service of process other than by handing the process documents to the defendant in person (e.g., service by mail).

succession Obtaining property of the deceased, usually when there is no will.

summary dissolution A divorce obtained in an expedited manner because of the lack of controversy between the husband and wife.

summons A formal notice from the court served on the defendant ordering him or her to appear and answer the allegations of the plaintiff.

supervised visitation Visitation by a parent with his or her child while another adult (other than the custodial parent) is present.

surety bond The obligation of a guarantor to pay a second party upon default by a third party in the performance the third party owes the second party.

surrogate mother A woman who is artificially inseminated with the semen of a man who is not her husband, with the understanding that she will surrender the baby at birth to the father and his wife.

survivorship See *right of survivorship.*

syllabus A one-paragraph summary of an opinion found at the beginning of the opinion.

system An organized method of accomplishing a task that seeks to be more effective or efficient than alternative methods.

tainted Having a conflict of interest in a case.

Talak "I divorce you." Words spoken by a husband to his wife in a Muslim divorce.

tangible Having a physical form; able to make contact with through touch or other senses.

tax basis One's initial capital investment in property. An adjusted basis is calculated after making allowed adjustments and deductions to the initial capital investment (e.g., an increase in the basis because of a capital improvement).

tax effect (1) To determine the tax consequences of something (v.); (2) the tax consequences of something (n.).

Temporary Assistance for Needy Families (TANF) The welfare system that replaced Aid to Families with Dependent Children (AFDC).

tenancy by the entirety A joint tenancy held by a married couple and, in Vermont, by a same-sex couple in a civil union. See *civil union, joint tenancy.*

tenancy in common Property owned by two or more persons in shares that may or may not be equal, with no right of survivorship. Each tenant in common has a right to possession of the property. See also *right of survivorship.*

tender years presumption Mothers should be awarded custody of their young children, since they are more likely to be better off raised by their mothers than by their fathers.

termination of parental rights A judicial declaration that ends the legal relationship between parent and child. The parent no longer has any right to participate in decisions affecting the welfare of the child and no longer has any duties toward the child.

testament A will.

testate Dying with a valid will.

testator The person who has died leaving a valid will.

tort A civil wrong that has caused harm to a person or property for which a court will provide a remedy. Conduct that consists of a breach of contract or a crime may also constitute a tort.

tort immunity One who enjoys a tort immunity cannot be sued for what would otherwise be a tort.

transferor/transferee The person who transfers property is the transferor; the person to whom property transferred is the transferee.

transitory divorce A divorce granted in a state where neither spouse was domiciled at the time.

transmutation The voluntary change of separate property into community property or community property into separate property.

treatise Any book written by a private individual (or by a public official writing in a nonofficial capacity) that provides an overview of and commentary on an area of the law. Hornbooks, manuals, and formbooks are treatises.

trespass Wrongfully intruding on land in possession of another.

trimester Three months.

trust When property is in trust, its legal title is held by one party (the trustee) for the benefit of another (the beneficiary). The creator of the trust is called the *settlor.*

UIFSA See *Uniform Interstate Family Support Act.*

unauthorized practice of law Performing functions that only attorneys are allowed to perform; violating the state statute on who can practice law; engaging in legal tasks without attorney supervision and/or without special authorization to engage in such tasks.

unconscionable Shocking to the conscience; substantially unfair.

uncontested Not disputed; not challenged. See also *friendly divorce.*

undertaking A promise, engagement, or enterprise.

unemancipated Legally dependent on one's parent or legal guardian.

unethical conduct See *canons of ethics, ethics.*

unfit Demonstrating abuse or neglect that is substantially detrimental to a child.

Uniform Interstate Family Support Act (UIFSA) A state law on establishing and enforcing support obligations against someone who does not live in the same state as the person to whom the support is owed.

uniform laws Proposed statutes written by the National Conference of Commissioners on Uniform State Law. The proposals are submitted to state legislatures for consideration.

unjust enrichment Receiving property or benefit from another when in fairness and equity the recipient should make restitution of the property or provide compensation for the benefit even though there was no express or implied promise to do so.

unreasonable That which is contrary to the behavior of an ordinary, prudent person under the same circumstances.

venue The place of the trial. When more than one court has subject matter jurisdiction to hear a particular kind of case, the selection of the court is called *choice of venue.*

verification of complaint A sworn statement that the contents of the complaint are true.

vested Fixed so that it cannot be taken away by future events or conditions; accrued so that you now have a right to present or future possession or enjoyment.

viable Able to live outside the womb indefinitely; able to live outside the womb indefinitely by natural or artificial means.

vicariously liable Being liable because of what someone else has done; standing in the place of someone else who is the one who actually committed the wrong.

visitation The right of a noncustodial parent to visit and spend time with his or her children.

void Invalid whether or not a court declares it so.

void ab initio Invalid from the time it started.

voidable That which can be invalidated if a person chooses to do so; valid unless and until canceled.

voir dire Jury selection.

waiver The relinquishment or giving up of a right or privilege because of an explicit rejection of it or because of a failure to take appropriate steps to claim it at the proper time.

ward An individual, often a minor, under the care of a court-appointed guardian.

welfare See *public assistance.*

WESTLAW® A legal database for computer research.

will A document that specifies the disposition of one's property and provides related instructions upon death.

Words and Phrases A multivolume legal dictionary published by West Group. Most of its definitions come from court opinions.

work product, attorney See *attorney work product.*

World Wide Web A tool that allows you to navigate locations on the Internet that are often linked by hypertext.

writ of execution See *execution of judgment.*

wrongful adoption A tort seeking damages for wrongfully stating or failing to disclose to prospective adoptive parents available facts on the health or other condition of the adoptee that would be relevant to the decision on whether to adopt.

wrongful birth An action by parents of an unwanted deformed child for their own damages. The defendant wrongfully caused the birth.

wrongful life An action by or on behalf of an unwanted deformed child for its own damages. The defendant wrongfully caused the birth.

wrongful pregnancy An action by parents of a healthy child that they did not want. The defendant wrongfully caused the birth. Also called *wrongful conception.*

zygote A cell produced by the union of a male sex cell and a female sex cell.

INDEX

E

N

O

P

T

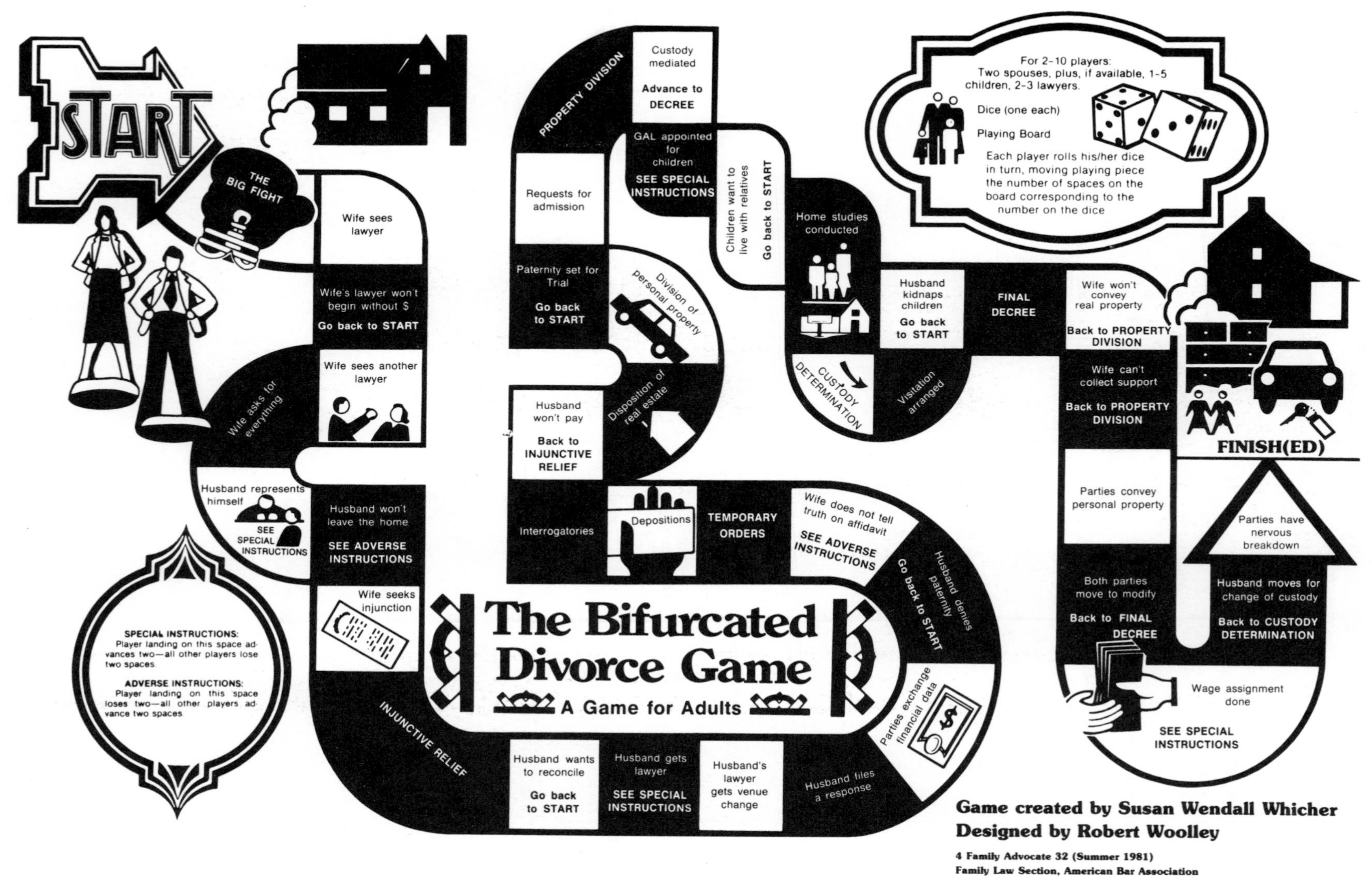

Game created by Susan Wendall Whicher
Designed by Robert Woolley

4 Family Advocate 32 (Summer 1981)
Family Law Section, American Bar Association